INLAND TRANSPORTATION

INLAND TRANSPORTATION

Principles and Policies

A REVISION AND EXTENSION OF
"RAILWAY TRANSPORTATION"

BY
SIDNEY L. MILLER, Ph. D.
*Professor of Transportation,
University of Iowa*

SECOND EDITION
SECOND IMPRESSION

McGRAW-HILL BOOK COMPANY, INC.
NEW YORK AND LONDON
1933

PRINTED IN THE UNITED STATES OF AMERICA

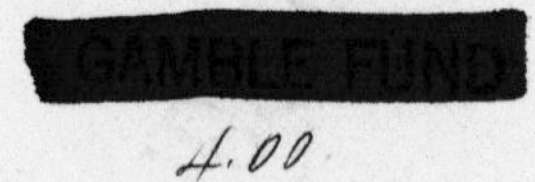

THE MAPLE PRESS COMPANY, YORK, PA.

To my stanch, mettlesome three,

MARGARET, SIDNEY

AND

GEORGE

PREFACE

AN ORDERED progress, characteristic of inland transportation in the United States since the appearance of the railway a century ago, has given place within a brief span of years to change that is fundamental in nature and disconcerting in rapidity. Through unnumbered generations overland transportation was slow, costly, and laborious; the railway represented man's first significant advance after the development of the wheel. But this instrumentality, which has contributed greatly to effective transportation, compelled public consideration of other problems of a challenging character and a variable aspect. In the preface to a volume dealing with railway transportation which appeared less than a decade ago the author said, in speaking of the problem of inland transportation, a railway problem still, "The railway problem . . . is now no less important than it was in the days of the railway pioneer, nor is it less complex." To the study of this problem in its various aspects much thought was given, for its solution a great diversity of courses of action advised. With the growth of economic understanding there came readjustments in both public and corporate policies that bade fair to effect a reasonable harmony between public service and private gain. It was at this point, with a solution of the *railway* problem seemingly close at hand, that the *transportation* problem emerged to plague a people already beset.

For, as compared with the transportation problem that now faces modern nations, the railway problem of the recent past was simple. A decade ago there were few who sensed, even remotely, the serious threat of those agencies, now recognized as effective competitors of the railway, to the financial stability of the established agency, perhaps to the continuance of service upon many lines. Yet today there are great numbers, particularly among those who have failed to analyze closely modern transportation needs and the capacity of each agency to serve those needs, who believe that the railway is an outmoded form of transport moving rapidly toward that oblivion into which the oxcart, the stagecoach, and the freighter's wagon have disappeared. Sharply beset by the motor vehicle in its various forms operating upon highways increasingly adapted to speedy and economical movement, challenged by the airplane moving upon steadily improved schedules and offering comparative safety, deprived both directly and indirectly of tonnage by the extension of improved pipe lines, and pressed in particular areas by a revitalized and aggressive barge service, the railway has a less certain future than the holders of billions of dollars of railway securities might wish; less certain, too, than is requisite to the peace of mind of those who have other billions of dollars invested in land, structures, and established business enterprises, the values of which are in considerable measure contingent upon the maintenance by the railway of an important place in the field of transport. The heavy inroads upon railway traffic made by competitive forms of transport during the past decade, coupled with the striking decline in the demand for transportation service during the years since 1929, make the railway outlook dark. Is the future of this agency to be regarded with foreboding, or does there remain for it a broad field of social usefulness? And what are the appropriate limits within which the motor vehicle, the airplane, the pipe line, the barge, shall serve? It is this that is fundamental in the transportation problem of today, a problem of which the future of the railway is but a single aspect.

In the solution of the railway problem economic intelligence and statesmanship are increasingly needed. To the solution of the broader, more difficult problem that has superseded it, clear understanding and effective leadership are essential if a staggering social waste is to be avoided, if the evils of unrestrained competition are to be escaped—with those wastes and those evils already in striking evidence in consequence of inadequate control, of public confusion. Today, for perhaps the first time in history, a surplus of transportation service of high character exists; furthermore, the scope of regulatory authority is so broad under successive decisions from the time of *Munn v. Illinois* to *Stephenson v. Binford* that public policy, not constitutionality, is the major problem to be faced. In short, the transportation problem today demands, as a first step toward its solution, the formulation of a transportation plan under which each agency now capable of rendering a satisfactory public service is assigned its proper place and within reasonable limits restricted thereto.

In the formulation of such a plan it is commonly assumed by those who discuss bases of determination that the place of train, truck, plane, or other instrumentality will be fixed by the relative costs of comparable services and that cost will be given important weight in all cases where no comparability of service exists. To such an assumption the writer takes positive exception; the problem is not so simple. At a particular time the public has a given total need for transportation service—and a proper transportation plan should make such use of the various agencies as will meet that total need at minimum cost. To the formulation of this proper plan, then, unrestrained competition will be of no service; rather, its formulation must proceed from the careful study of all pertinent facts, painstakingly gathered and effectively organized. No satisfactory transportation plan will "jes' grow," therefore; the social cost of "muddling through" in dealing with the existing transportation problem, as was done so largely with its immediate predecessor, the railway problem, will be such as to give pause to the most ardent advocate of *laissez faire.*

The organization and presentation of material in this volume have as their prime purpose aid to those who seek an understanding of the existing transportation situation; it is the author's hope that it may furnish helpful guidance to thought and to constructive action. Part I states briefly the scope of this volume and indicates the general character of transportation prior to the appearance of the railway a century ago. Part II sketches the spectacular development of the American railway net and traces the growth of public regulation; in its final chapters the recent status of this agency, which the Interstate Commerce Commission declares will remain the backbone of a national transportation system, is presented in some detail. In Part III the services of the railway are described briefly, that those unfamiliar with the more important phases of the carrier-shipper relationship may be informed. Appropriate reference is made in the course of this discussion to competitive agencies and to their relation to railway service. Because the economic characteristics of the transportation business are so generally misunderstood or ignored, Part IV is given largely to an analysis which will, the author hopes, indicate what is sound and what is inadvisable in public policies, actual and proposed. In this section emphasis is placed upon the railway, since it alone has developed sufficiently to permit of the certain statement of characteristics and principles; yet, to the extent that facts justify, reference is made to the newer forms of transport. In Part V these newer forms of transport are discussed at considerable length: a factual presentation concerning each is followed by an analysis of the problems pressing for solution, and a statement is made of what the author believes to be an appropriate public policy with respect to each. In closing, proposed "solutions" of the transportation problem are outlined, and the author offers what he believes to be a comprehensive and defensible program of action calculated to bring some measure of order from the confusion that now characterizes the field.

To those who contributed in inspiration, counsel, and direct assistance to the volume of which this is a successor the author wants to express again his appreciation and gratitude. To this list he desires to add the names of those individuals and agencies whose services have contributed much to the completion of this volume. To his colleague, Dr. Floyd B. Haworth, the author is deeply indebted for assistance in gathering material, for suggestions, and for graphical aid. To others of his colleagues, notably Professors H. H. McCarty and R. W. Nelson, he is indebted for counsel and material assistance. Miss Gladys Hamilton has rendered an invaluable service in editing the manuscript, and to Miss Hazel Coutts he is heavily indebted for long hours of faithful, effective effort in gathering needed data and putting the manuscript into final form. To Mr. George M. Cummins, Traffic Commissioner, Chamber of Commerce, Davenport,

Iowa, he is also deeply obligated for helpful suggestions, counsel, and direct aid upon certain chapters. Then to numerous organizations, notably the Bureau of Railway Economics, the National Automobile Chamber of Commerce, the St. Lawrence-Tidewater Association, and the National Association of Motor Bus Operators, he is indebted for unfailing courtesy and aid in furnishing material. By the Interstate Commerce Commission, too, every courtesy was shown and needed facts supplied.

In gathering, sifting, and organizing for presentation the material offered upon the succeeding pages, important facts have perhaps been overlooked; the field of inland transport has broadened tremendously within a brief time. Furthermore, of all details of the program suggested for the solution of the transportation problem as it now exists the author is not certain; as the field of transport has broadened, its complexity has increased. Yet diligent search has been made for pertinent data and the author firmly believes that a defensible plan has been offered for future action, albeit one in which modifications may be necessary as experience broadens and as available data increase. The facts here offered will give the reader a basis upon which to rest judgments, and the conclusions stated will do no less than to provoke critical thought upon the problem that now confronts the American public in the field of transport and that demands immediate, intelligent action. To the degree that the material here offered assists in the formulation of sound judgments, to the extent that it stimulates constructive action, the joy that the author has found in the preparation of this volume will be increased.

SIDNEY L. MILLER.

IOWA CITY, IOWA,
June, 1933.

CONTENTS

PAGE

PREFACE vii

PART I
INTRODUCTION

CHAPTER I

NATURE, SCOPE, AND SIGNIFICANCE OF TRANSPORTATION 3

The meaning and scope of transportation. Problems of management. The transportation service. Types of transportation agencies. Influence of transportation upon the division of labor. Utilization of natural resources. Relationship to population and progress. Political importance of transportation. Relation to production, consumption, and exchange. Distribution modified by efficient transportation. Transportation burdened with a public interest. Scope and purpose of this volume.

CHAPTER II

EARLY HISTORY OF TRANSPORTATION 14

Obstacles to development of trade and transportation. Periods in the development of transportation. Early man's primitive methods. The wheel. Progress in transportation by water. The costs of primitive transportation. Social and economic influences of high rates. Historic trade routes in Eurasia. Important European water and land routes.

CHAPTER III

THE EARLY DEVELOPMENT OF TRANSPORTATION IN THE UNITED STATES 25

Natural water routes used by the colonists. Important overland routes. Early canal projects in the East. The Great Lakes-Mississippi system. Primitive character of early overland routes. The development of toll projects. Transportation costs by land and water. Charges upon overland movements. The costs of canal movement. Economic burden of transportation costs. Important routes of trade and travel: water; trails. Need of improved transportation facilities.

PART II
RAILWAY HISTORY OF THE UNITED STATES

CHAPTER IV

BEGINNINGS OF THE AMERICAN RAILWAY NET 45

Development of the track. Evolution of the car. Importance of the locomotive. Early use of steam. The work of Trevithick. The interest and work of Evans. Further progress—the Rain Hill trial. American interest in the railway. Initial locomotive operation. The railway as an effective transportation agency. Early engineering problems: the roadway; the problem of power; diversity in track gage; difficulties of train operation. Public opposition to the railway. Inadequate supply of capital. Railway construction at the close of the first period. Forces behind railway building. Summary.

CHAPTER V

ACCEPTANCE OF THE RAILWAY: EXPANSION OF NET 63

Important factors in railway development. Extent of railway expansion. Causes

PAGE

of rapid mileage growth. Public aid an important cause. Land grants in aid of railway construction. Development of our land-grant policy. The appearance of large railway systems. Public interest and consolidation. Early proposals to establish transcontinental service. The Union Pacific-Central Pacific project. Other Pacific railways.

CHAPTER VI

ACCEPTANCE OF THE RAILWAY: REGULATION AND GENERAL POLICIES. 77

Early Commission activities. Public complaints against rate levels. Other complaints against the railways. The appearance of positive control. Validity of regulatory acts. Recession of movement toward positive control. The appearance of competition. Efforts to control competition. Financial aspects of construction and operation. Progress toward plant efficiency. Consequences of decline in railway charges. Extent of the railway net.

CHAPTER VII

GENESIS OF THE RAILWAY PROBLEM: MILEAGE EXTENSION AND FINANCE. 91

Influence of extraneous events. The increase in railway mileage. Mileage growth and public aid. Foreign support of American railway construction. The western movement of population. Extension of transcontinental service. Policy of public aid abandoned. Investment in railways. Overcapitalization and its causes. Changes in financial policy.

CHAPTER VIII

GENESIS OF THE RAILWAY PROBLEM: COMPETITION AND ADVANCE IN REGULATION. . 105

Continuance of intense competition. Influence of competition on rates. Lowered rate levels. Discrimination becomes a major problem. Decline of water traffic. Increase in efficiency of railway operations. Further development of railway cooperation. Southern Railway and Steamship Association. Reappearance of the demand for regulation. The Interstate Commerce Act of 1887. The Interstate Commerce Act and legal procedure. Emasculation of the Act of 1887. Results of federal legislation. Importance of the third period in railway history.

CHAPTER IX

DEVELOPMENT OF THE RAILWAY PROBLEM: MILEAGE GROWTH AND CREDIT. 121

Factors influencing development. Mileage increase, 1894–1919. Extensive growth prior to 1908. Mileage development after 1907. The problem of railway credit. The need for railway expansion. Progressive decline in railway growth. Decline reflected by railway capitalization. Reasons for the weakness of railway credit. Decline in net operating income. Uncertainty of governmental policy. A summary. Appearance of large ownership groupings. Methods and gains of federation. Railway mechanical progress, 1893–1919.

CHAPTER X

DEVELOPMENT OF THE RAILWAY PROBLEM: THE PERFECTION OF REGULATION. . . . 136

Demand for effective regulation. Upward movement of freight rates. Growing importance of rebates. The Elkins Act. Railway regulation a paramount issue. Important powers given the Interstate Commerce Commission. Prohibitions in the Act. Work of the Commission. Application of the Commodities Clause. Further restrictive legislation. Operation of the Mann-Elkins Act. The valuation of railways. Other legislative enactments affecting the railways. Extent and scope of state regulation. A judgment upon our regulatory policy.

CHAPTER XI PAGE

DEVELOPMENT OF THE RAILWAY PROBLEM: FEDERAL OPERATION. 154

Organization of the Railroad's War Board. Work of the War Board. Federal operation of railways. Reorganization of the railways. The standard contract. Compensation paid the railways. Work of the Federal Railroad Administration: rates; wages and labor disputes; capital expenditures; miscellaneous undertakings; results of federal operation; classification and rates; the labor policy; financial results and conclusion. Final comments.

CHAPTER XII

THE TRANSPORTATION ACT OF 1920—HISTORY AND PROVISIONS 170

Dual character of the problem. Senate and House take action. Points of agreement and differences, House and Senate bills. Transfer to private operation. Railway interrelations. Control of construction and abandonment. Regulation of security issues. Settlement of labor disputes. Provisions dealing with rates and surplus. State and federal jurisdiction. Miscellaneous rate provisions. Control over routing and service. Changes in Commission organization.

CHAPTER XIII

RECENT RAILWAY HISTORY: ECONOMIC CONDITIONS AND INTERCORPORATE RELATIONS 185

Situation of the railways at termination of federal operation. The postwar boom and depression. Renewed business activity: the peak and the great trough. Price relations in postwar years. A period of stress. Consolidation: the tentative plan; the final plan; modifications of the final plan; summary and conclusion. Acquisition of control: extent of acquisition of control; principles governing. Interlocking directorates. Pooling. The holding company.

CHAPTER XIV

RECENT RAILWAY HISTORY: LABOR, SERVICE, RECAPTURE, AND MISCELLANEOUS RATE POWERS. 208

The wage increase of 1920. Abrogation of the national agreements. Decreases in wages. The shopmen's strike. Important problems faced by the Labor Board. Abolition of the Board. The Railroad Labor Act of 1926. Operation of the Labor Act. The regulation of service. Construction and abandonment. Regulation of security issues. The Recapture clause. The division of joint rates. Miscellaneous rate powers.

CHAPTER XV

RECENT RAILWAY HISTORY: RATES, RATE OF RETURN, AND EVALUATION OF POLICY. 230

Railway rates: increases in rates authorized; intrastate rates; demand for decreased rates; reductions made by Commission and railways; proposed general increases in rates. The Fifteen per Cent Emergency Rate Increase application. The Hoch-Smith Resolution: provisions, influence, and final adjudication. Financial results under the Act. A critical situation. Variations in earnings. The financial outlook. Valuation. A judgment upon federal regulatory policy; uninformed criticisms of regulatory policy; considered criticisms.

PART III

THE RAILWAY SERVICE

CHAPTER XVI

THE RAILWAY ENTERPRISE. 261

Nature and advantages of the corporation. Types of corporations. Regulation

PAGE

of quasi-public corporations. The problem of jurisdiction. The railway charter. Contractual nature of railway charters. Magnitude of the railway corporation. Financial interest of public in railways. The problem of management. The function of the stockholder. The directors and executive committee. The corporate officers. The president. The secretary and treasurer. The legal department. Organization and work of the accounting department. The traffic department. Importance of the operating department. Staff and line officers. Divisional v. departmental organization. Railway purchasing. The real-estate agent. The efficiency of railway organization.

CHAPTER XVII

TERRITORIAL GROUPINGS 281

Major territorial groupings. Minor territorial groupings: New England; Trunk Line; Southern; Granger; Southwestern; Transcontinental. Permanence of existing territorial groupings. Dominant position of Class I railways. Relation of mileage to population and area, America and Europe. Vital importance of the railway.

CHAPTER XVIII

THE RAILWAY NET: ROUTES AND TERMINALS 295

Major traffic routes: Trunk Line; Piedmont; Northwest-Atlanta; Mississippi Valley; Midwest-Gulf; Granger; Transcontinental. Terminals: importance and problems of locations. The passenger terminal. The freight terminal. Services beyond the rail terminal. Regulatory control of terminal properties and operations. The future.

CHAPTER XIX

FREIGHT SERVICE 316

Freight papers: the bill of lading of major public concern; the live-stock contract. The nature of carrier liability. Important legal problems: beginning and termination of carrier liability; other legal problems. The waybill. Other papers: forms used at destination. Handling freight at terminals. The movement of traffic. Demurrage, reciprocal demurrage, and track storage. Evolution of railway interline practice. Compensation for use of "foreign" cars. Private cars in railway service: advantages and disadvantages. The future of private-car development.

CHAPTER XX

FREIGHT CHARGES 331

Importance of the freight service. Nature and value of freight tonnage. Increase in demand for service. Steps in determining the rate. Development of classification practice. Present classification territories. Classification committees. The consolidated freight classification. Determinants of classification. Commodity rates. Designation of classes. Items listed and number of ratings. Fundamental considerations in rate making. Types and scope of tariffs. Determination of the total charge. Uniformity of classification. Uniformity of rate relations. Development of freight traffic.

CHAPTER XXI

PASSENGER SERVICE AND CHARGES 348

Differences in freight and passenger traffic. Types of trains in service. Character of through service. Classification of tickets. Ticket accounting. Privileges accorded to travelers. Classification of passenger service. Class service in the United States. The growth of the Pullman service. Advantages of Pullman service. The Pullman contract. Determination of the Pullman charge. Comparative passenger-service

PAGE

statistics. Service and efficiency. Development of additional traffic. Elimination of abuses. The problem of competition. The future of railway passenger traffic.

CHAPTER XXII

THE MINOR SERVICES—MAIL AND EXPRESS. 370

The mail service. The railway and the mail service. Development of the railway post office. Closed-pouch service. Volume of railway mail. The terminal post office. The parcel-post service: its establishment; the determination of parcel-post rates; regulations and privileges; volume and financial results. Problem of railway mail pay: present basis of compensation. The express service: a general statement. Brief history of the business. Railway Express Agency, Incorporated: organization and administration. The railway-express contract: the early adjustment; a modified railway-express agreement; disposition of "net income for division"; modifications of the new contract. Demand for regulation. Classification and rates prescribed. Rates made upon a distance basis. Determination of the charge. Express traffic declines. The future.

CHAPTER XXIII

RAILWAY ACCOUNTING AND STATISTICS. 396

Organization of the accounting department: the expenditures division; freight-revenue records; the passenger-revenues division; work of the car accountant's staff. Freight claims a legal problem. Divisional v. centralized accounting. Regulation of railway accounting demanded. Investment and operating accounts. Income and profit and loss accounts. The general balance sheet. Specimen statements. Evaluation of prescribed system. Railway statistics: basis; scope; further development; sources of data.

PART IV

SOME ECONOMIC ASPECTS OF TRANSPORT

CHAPTER XXIV

COMPETITION 413

Early belief in efficacy of competition. Competition varied and far-reaching. Traffic competition. Market competition. Industrial competition. Competition assumes two forms. Reasons for intensity of competition: continuous operation; nontransferability of railway capital; railway business one of increasing returns. Immediate and ultimate results of competition.

CHAPTER XXV

COMBINATION. 426

Appearance of pooling agreements. Division of territory. Movement toward closer unification and consolidation. Factors promoting unification and consolidation. Need for unity of action. Progress by voluntary action or compulsion. Past monopolistic character of railways. Monopolistic position of the single carrier. Analysis of the traffic of a railway. Modification of types by extraneous influences. The business problem: competition and monopoly. Tendency toward larger corporate units. Tendency toward concentration of control.

CHAPTER XXVI

RAILWAY UNIFICATION. 442

Recession of consolidation movement. The formation of systems: Vanderbilt system; the Pennsylvania Lines; the Baltimore and Ohio system; the Van Swer-

PAGE

ingen system; the Morgan group; the Hill system; the Union Pacific system; Missouri Pacific Lines; minor ownership groupings. The Canadian systems. Important independent properties. Distribution of railway shares. Tendency in distribution of railway shares. A growing problem.

CHAPTER XXVII

CAPITALIZATION AND CAPITAL VALUE 459

Gross and net capitalization of the American railway net. Increase in the bond ratio. Capitalization per mile of line, railways as a whole and individual lines. Types of railway stocks. Borrowed capital in the railway field. Overlapping of claims. Capitalization and true worth. The problem of valuation: earning capacity as a basis of valuation; nature and validity of historical cost; cost of reproduction. Valuation practice.

CHAPTER XXVIII

SECURITY REGULATION 474

Watered stock: meaning and tests. Reasons for stock-watering. Overcapitalization: causes and conditions promoting. Morality of stock-watering. Demand for security regulation. Control by the states. Movement toward federal regulation. Section 20*a* of the Transportation Act. The application for authority. The problem of jurisdiction. Items capitalizable and capitalization. Stock dividends. Type of security issued. Sale and purchase of securities. Reorganization. Miscellaneous problems. Attitudes toward security regulation. General conclusion.

CHAPTER XXIX

AN ANALYSIS OF RAILWAY FINANCIAL DATA 492

Sources of railway revenue. Revenue variations among railways. Nonoperating income: importance and sources. Operating expenses. Deductions from gross income. Disposition of net income. Movement of operating revenues and expenses. The operating ratio. Evaluation and trend of the operating ratio. Interest on railway bonds. Dividends on stock. Market status of railway securities. Needed changes to effect credit rehabilitation.

CHAPTER XXX

THEORIES OF RATE MAKING 509

Need of sound and definite principles. Theories of rate determination. Ability theories: "value of the service"; "keep everybody in business"; the developmental principle; "value of the commodity"; "what the traffic will bear." Cost of service. Types of cost of service. The ascertainment and application of cost. The strength of cost of service. Conclusions concerning cost as a rate base. Social need. Concluding statement. Position of regulatory bodies. A reasonable theoretical basis for railway rates.

CHAPTER XXXI

RATE-MAKING PRACTICE 527

Variations in economic conditions among traffic areas. The distance principle in rate making: background and nature of the percentage plan; adjustments in the percentage plan. The basing-point system: analysis of the basing-point system; public policy. The equalization principle: early Western Trunk Line adjustments; other relations established; summary statement. The "blanket" rate: Texas Common Point territory; "blanketing" in Transcontinental rates. The graded-and-maximum plan: nature of the adjustment; modification of the Texas intra-

PAGE

state structure. Recent major rate revisions: early Commission action; more recent action. Trends in rate making. Passenger rates.

CHAPTER XXXII

COMPARATIVE RAILWAY CHARGES 554

Freight and passenger traffic units. Computation of unit costs. Railway costs and charges: influence of construction differences and efficiency upon costs; effect of wage and price levels; traffic factors; quantity of shipment. Nominal v. real costs: length of haul; type of traffic; character of service; purchasing power of money. Evaluation of rate comparisons. Express charges. American freight rates. American and European charges. American passenger rates; comparison with foreign charges. Conclusion.

PART V

MODERN TRANSPORT

CHAPTER XXXIII

MOTOR TRANSPORTATION: ITS DEVELOPMENT 571

The highway. The Roman roads. French and English highways. Early highways in America. Federal aid. State and local mileage. The vehicle. The modern motor vehicle. Development in the United States. Data on bus and truck. Traffic. The individual passenger car. The bus: advantages of the bus; financial results of bus-line operations. The motor truck: types of trucks in use; truck ownership; nature of truck traffic. Movements by truck of live stock, fruit and vegetables, cotton, cement, coal, automobiles, and other tonnage. Truck traffic: length of haul; volume. Advantages of the truck. Loss of traffic by railways. The motor-vehicle problem.

CHAPTER XXXIV

MOTOR TRANSPORTATION: SOME MAJOR PROBLEMS. 602

Highway finance. The old highways. Financing the new highways. Increased costs and the motor vehicle. A summary statement. Fundamentals of tax apportionment. Motor-vehicle charges: the license; the gasoline tax; other taxes. Apportionment of the tax burden: a suggested motor-vehicle tax program. Power to regulate: a general statement; regulation under the police power; regulation under the proprietary power; the regulation of common carriage. The jurisdictional problem. Public policy: the motor vehicle and a transportation plan; present state regulation of the common carrier by highway; evils in the existing situation. Demand for effective regulation: a program of state action; a program of federal action. A concluding statement.

CHAPTER XXXV

INLAND WATERWAYS: REVIVAL AND PROGRAM. 637

Early interest in waterways, natural and artificial. Decline of American waterway traffic. Revival of interest in inland waterways: causes of revived interest numerous and varied. Major inland waterway projects: Lakes-to-Gulf waterway; Upper Mississippi River project; Ohio Valley projects; Missouri River development; Lower Mississippi Valley projects; Intracoastal system; New York State Barge Canals—history of canal systems and present status of properties; St. Lawrence Deep Waterway; other projects.

CHAPTER XXXVI PAGE

INLAND WATERWAYS: ECONOMIC ANALYSIS 661

Federal expenditures on waterways. Types of channels: natural; semi-artificial; artificial. Disadvantages of waterways: inherent and artificial. The problem of individual as against social cost. Judgment upon a proposed waterway. Observations concerning the Barge Canals: Intracoastal system; Ohio River system; Lower Mississippi; Upper Mississippi; Missouri River; Lakes-to-Gulf waterway; St. Lawrence waterway. Basis of river rates. The problem of public policy.

CHAPTER XXXVII

AIR TRANSPORTATION 693

Man's persistent interest in flying. The lighter-than-air ship: the balloon; the airship. The airplane: the first flight; a decade of development; the immediate postwar period. Physical prerequisites to successful airt ransport: airplane, airway, airport. Air traffic: mail; passenger; goods. Financial aspects of air transport. Regulation of air transport.

CHAPTER XXXVIII

PROGRESSIVE TRANSPORT. 717

Railway progress: the locomotive; the car; track and terminal; railway policy. Progress of other transport agencies: motor, air, water. Coordinated transport: rail-motor; rail-water; air-rail; water-highway. The pipe line: oil; gasoline; natural gas; summary and outlook.

CHAPTER XXXIX

THE TRANSPORTATION PROBLEM. 747

Transportation problem old. Earlier solutions offered. The problem becomes acute. Emergency action taken. Consideration of matters of policy: Joint Committee of Railroads and Highway Users; National Transportation Committee, majority and minority reports. Other general proposals. Commission recommendations, official and individual.

CHAPTER XL

A NATIONAL TRANSPORTATION POLICY 765

Elements of a national transportation policy. Appropriate emergency action. Needed changes in railway legislation. Public policy relative to newer agencies of transport. The responsibilities of management: waste, increased efficiency; labor; competitive policy; finance; The coordination of agencies of transport. Some basic needs of successful regulation. Government ownership of railways as a solution. The goal of a transportation plan.

APPENDIX. 789

INDEX 801

PART I

INTRODUCTION

Chapter I

NATURE, SCOPE, AND SIGNIFICANCE OF TRANSPORTATION

THROUGHOUT the entire period of human development the problem of transportation has been of outstanding importance. From the time of his earliest appearance upon the earth man has earnestly and persistently sought means of moving himself and his possessions more easily and more quickly from place to place, and, with progress in other fields, there has been a parallel forward movement in the efficiency of his transportation agencies. That forward movement in transportation has been so great during the past century, however, that the facts pertinent to the existent problem are to be gathered largely from a study of this recent period. Indeed, the two agencies which now render most effective service in the transportation of goods and persons were both unknown at the beginning of the nineteenth century—the railway serving those located inland and the steam-driven craft those with ready access to water. And the newer agencies, the motor vehicle and the airplane, have developed to their present high point as factors in the transportation situation since the twentieth century opened.

Of the older agencies the railway, because of its peculiar economic character and because of the large numbers dependent immediately upon it for service, has given rise to the more varied and difficult problems. However, because the services rendered by the railway and the water craft were essentially supplementary, it has been only with the development of the motor vehicle and the airplane that the transportation situation has become so complicated that the minds of statesman and economist alike are taxed to devise a policy that is logically sound and socially defensible. But to devise such a policy is not enough: it must obtain sufficient support to assure its application from a public that often lacks both a factual basis for judgment and an appreciation of the significance of data at hand. Involved as the transportation problem increasingly becomes, intertwined as it is with others of an economic and social character, it is only through a clear appreciation of fundamentals that an understanding can be gained of the situation in the United States today. Without that understanding any solution urged must depend for its success upon chance rather than upon a foundation laid by intelligent and purposive action.

The Meaning and Scope of Transportation.—The word transportation, like many another of our English words, is of Latin origin. Derived from *trans*, across, and *portare*, to carry, transportation is concerned with the carrying across or transferal of all things capable of movement. Outstanding among the things desired by man and transportable by him are material commodities of infinite number and variety. With the production and distribution of these he has always been concerned and to facilitate their movement he has sought earnestly to increase the efficiency of carriage by land and sea. The movement of persons has also been a matter of fundamental concern and much of the effort expended in the improvement of transportation facilities has been put forth that man might move himself from place to place with greater rapidity and ease. A more recent transportation function, one which increases in importance to the peoples of the world with the growth of intelligence, is that concerned with the movement of ideas. The expeditious movement of the written or printed word and the transmission of ideas by wire or wireless have gained a place of supreme importance in modern society. Another and still later phase of transportation is concerned with the transfer of power between distant points. This has greatly facilitated the development and utilization of electrical energy during the past quarter of a century, and even more important and more rapid progress is probable in the near future.

Just as the field of transportation is of great significance, so is the scope of that field exceedingly broad—so broad, indeed, that it would be impossible even to sketch all phases of it within the confines of a single volume. Nevertheless, before indicating the phases with which this treatment is concerned, the various points of view from which a study of transportation may be made merit note. The mechanism rendering the service is, in itself, deserving of attention. That mechanism may be considered from the standpoint of construction; if so regarded, the problem becomes essentially an engineering one. To it must be given the attention of civil engineers, of mechanical and electrical engineers, and of those concerned with problems of propulsion by steam or gas. These technicians find themselves faced with two major problems, to construct the roadway and to design the varied types of equipment utilized upon it in the actual carriage of goods, persons, and other material objects from place to place. Incident to the one problem arise questions of railway roadbed and location, of highway construction, of airports, and of harbor and waterway plans; incident to the other, matters of ship design, locomotive and gas-engine construction, and the development of the various kinds of cars and other conveyances necessary to handle efficiently widely diverse types of traffic.

Problems of Management.—The mechanism rendering the service may also be studied from the standpoint of management. The control of any transportation agency, large or small, presents two basic problems. Of these the more varied is that of administration. Numerous forms of organization variously suited to different conditions have been developed through long years of experience. Among these forms responsible administrative officers must choose with a view to achieving maximum results. A choice once made, to keep that organization functioning continuously in such manner as to render an adequate service at a reasonable rate with at least a fair profit to the business unit challenges the administrator as he is challenged in few other fields. The second problem of management is that of securing the business, and to this end efforts are made not only to lure existing business from competitors, but also to develop new industries and new wants which must, perforce, add to the volume of traffic.

The Transportation Service.—But, instead of considering transportation from the point of view of the mechanism that renders the service, it may be regarded from the point of view of the service rendered. When so regarded, the field offers quite different problems for the consideration of the student. Here emphasis may be placed upon the various *types* of service, such as freight, passenger, and express; or, on the other hand, attention may center upon those questions and problems arising out of the contact of the transportation agency with its patron. And, again, emphasis upon the service rendered may direct study toward that interesting relation between carrier and government which has developed in the United States during the past half century.

Types of Transportation Agencies.—The types of transportation agencies developed by man throughout his existence have been numerous and varied. Upon land he has evolved methods of movement peculiar to certain geographic and climatic conditions, such as the caravan and the sledge. Even yet, in primitive sections, the pack train and the wagon train function importantly in the movement of goods, while throughout great areas the runner and the mounted messenger continue to serve peoples in the transmission of ideas. In modern nations, however, the railway and the motor vehicle play an almost exclusive part in the overland movement of goods and persons, though the pipe line occupies an important place in its specialized field. In the movement of ideas modern man need no longer rely solely upon even the locomotive and the motor car, but is able to call upon such marvelous agencies as the telephone, the telegraph, and the radio to assist him. In the field of power, transmission-line development has made striking progress during recent years not only in extent but also in efficiency. Upon water, where the variety of agencies is far less than upon land, three significant types have been developed for the movement of goods or persons: the man-propelled raft or boat, the sailing vessel, and the steamship. These, together with cable lines, long served exclusively in the transmission of ideas between land areas. Development in the air is much more recent than upon either land or water;

it is only within the last few years that man has succeeded in navigating the air at will. What the future may hold for the Zeppelin type of airship, for the airplane, or for other such craft, as effective instruments for the transportation of goods, persons, or ideas, as well as what it may hold for the wireless, it is impossible to predict. It is probable, however, that the great development of the future will lie in the air rather than upon land or water, for it appears that a degree of perfection has been attained here which will permit of no further growth comparable with that expected in the newer and more fascinating field of open space.

Influence upon the Division of Labor.—A realization of the importance of transportation has been the major driving force which has induced man to devote so much thought and energy to increasing its efficiency. Through long ages he has earnestly sought to increase his productivity that he might better satisfy his expanding wants. To this increase in productivity perhaps no other factor has contributed so generously as has the division of labor. Occupational division of labor appeared within the group early in man's history, even before exchange between groups had shown itself to be highly advantageous. This type, however, was limited by the extent of the market as was technical division of labor—with its advantages of increased skill, economy of time, more effective use of labor and of capital, stimulation of invention, and substitution of machinery for human effort—to an even greater degree. Except as exchange had developed among groups—indeed, except as it arose among considerable numbers of groups—neither type of division of labor could be utilized extensively. And the great obstacle to such exchange was slow and costly transportation. Therefore, upon the increased efficiency of transportation facilities depended, in large measure, the extended utilization of both occupational and technical division of labor. But wholly upon that efficiency depended the third type, the territorial division of labor, with its outstanding advantages in the production of goods: such division can progress only in so far as man is able to move goods effectively from one area to another. During the earlier periods this territorial division of labor existed only in nonperishable goods of high unit value, such as teas, spices, silks, and jewels; but, as the efficiency of transport increased, the market for perishables and commodities of low unit value has broadened until today fresh fruits, vegetables, meats, sea food, and grain, lumber, coal, and numerous other items are consumed regularly hundreds, even thousands, of miles from the point of production.

Utilization of Natural Resources.—Efficient transportation is also of supreme importance in the utilization of natural resources. It matters little that a nation possess rich coal deposits and great quantities of metallic ores if those two resources cannot be brought together at low cost; without the former the latter is of little service. Tremendous possibilities of water-power development have no significance unless the energy available can be effectively distributed and utilized to drive the wheels of industry. The existence of vast resources of potash and of nitrates means nothing to exhausted soil if those restoratives cannot be efficiently transported to the farms where they are needed. To the thousands and hundreds of thousands, indeed, to the millions throughout the world who find themselves huddled together in small spaces, inadequately housed and fed, it matters little that nature has provided vast forests and fertile empires capable of producing enough to meet the millions' every need except as the product of forest and farm can be moved at a sufficiently low cost to permit the amelioration of their condition.

Related closely to the division of labor and the utilization of natural resources, and with them dependent upon the nature of existing transportation facilities, is the development of important production and market centers. Throughout man's entire history the great centers of population have been at the crossing of trade or transportation routes. This was especially true prior to the appearance of industrialism, though, with its coming, centers of production in which occupational and particularly technical division of labor has been carried far have gained increasing prominence. To these centers come vast quantities of raw material and from them go out in every direction and to all parts of the world an infinite variety of finished products. With the ever-increasing efficiency of transportation agencies, the economic future may be said to belong to those places which, for various reasons, have become centers of production or of trade and particularly to those which are so fortunate as to enjoy advantages both in the fabrication of goods and in commerce. Yet, however great the power of a manufacturing area may become, a temporary cessation of the inward flow of raw materials or the outward flow of finished products—even an adverse change in transportation charges—must convince the most arrogant of centers that upon the maintenance of adequate transportation at low cost depends its entire success, present and future. To the greatest of the world's markets any serious impairment of the means of transportation brings paralysis, immediate and complete.

Relation to Population and Progress.—The character of transportation facilities available has a direct relation to certain problems of population. With an increase in the efficiency of transportation a foundation is laid for the development of great population centers. Without railway and steamship it is impossible to conceive of such centers of population as London, New York, and Chicago expanding further, even continuing to exist as they are: there would be neither the economic basis for profitable employment nor the means of supplying the millions with the bare necessities of life. Yet improved transportation not only makes possible this more frequent appearance and striking growth of populous places, but it also makes more feasible the antithesis of such a movement. Through the opening of new territories and the possibility of developing new industries in old, added and important opportunities are presented which tend to draw people from the older and more densely populated areas into the newer sections and industries. Thus is counteracted measurably the gregarious instinct that has contributed so importantly to the development of the city; the physical barriers that inadequate transportation facilities present to *extensive* growth are minimized or removed.

The growth of culture and intelligence is another consideration intimately associated with the degree of advancement of transportation. Primitive peoples find themselves compelled to engage with nature in a struggle so keen that present needs are satisfied only with difficulty: the accumulation that enables man to expend effort and thought upon matters other than the satisfaction of immediate and pressing wants is lacking. In consequence, intellectual and cultural development proceeds at little more than a snail's pace, if at all. Because more efficient transportation has increased man's productivity, to it must be ascribed in large measure the gradual accumulation of that surplus which has permitted him to devote an increasing portion of his efforts to aesthetic and intellectual interests in life.

But not alone has transportation functioned thus in the development of those things which we term civilization. As it has increased in efficiency there were offered "new worlds to conquer" and the stimulus of this challenge has always made for progress. Furthermore, greater efficiency of transportation has increased contacts between peoples and between cultures, and the establishment and maintenance of such contacts are essential not only if progress is to be furthered, but even if heights already gained are not to be lost. History is replete with illustrations of peoples who, because of an isolation imposed by nature or by social will, have progressed rapidly for a time but, through lack of stimulus, have lost their early impetus and have even retrograded with the passage of time. Indeed, forward movement has been stimulated by contact rather than by lack of contact, and nothing has promoted such contacts more than participation in trade and commerce, the extent of which, in turn, depends almost wholly upon the character of transportation facilities available.

Political Importance of Transportation.—The influence of transportation has been no less important upon the political unit, however, than it has been upon the economic and cultural life of the world. The city state of ancient Greece would be as ill adapted to modern conditions as a United States, Russia, or an Australia would have been impossible during that earlier period. The stability of the state varies directly with the cultural and intellectual unity of its peoples, and no single element contributes more strikingly to the development of homogeneity than these numerous contacts that result from the existence and generous utilization of efficient agencies for the movement of goods, person, and ideas. That this fact is clearly recognized in the modern state was shown more than a half century ago by the readiness of the United States to pay whatever price seemed necessary for the early construction of a railway from the Middle West to the Pacific coast, the avowed purpose of which was to bind the newly developed Far West more closely to the older East than was possible when the pony express, the wagon train, and the steamship offered the most effective means of communication. The East sought thus to forestall a movement toward disunion which must otherwise have appeared. More recently, the same purpose was evidenced in the construction by the Australian Commonwealth of hundreds of miles of railway through a desert area, that the rapidly developing southwestern region might be more closely knit to the developed eastern section.

Efficient transportation serves a political purpose aside from the solidification and stabilization of the political unit; it greatly strengthens the hand of that unit in armed conflict. The easy and rapid transportation of troops employed in Indian warfare, with the consequent better protection of frontier settlements from raids, was one of the important reasons for government aid to railway construction in the American West. The Trans-Siberian railway was intended to serve a military as well as an economic end, and its failure to function adequately in the movement of troops and war materials was one of the important reasons for the defeat of Russia at the hands of Japan. The "Cape to Cairo" and "Berlin to Bagdad" projects won ready support from Great Britain and Germany, respectively, because of their immediate offensive and defensive military values as well as the ultimate economic benefits which they promised to confer. All students of the recent World War realize that one of the most important elements of Germany's strength was a system of railways adapted to her military needs and adequate to that end, and realize also that, perhaps even more than internal corruption and treachery, the inadequacy and final collapse of the Russian railways explain the fearful debacle of 1917–1918 in that country. If the political structure is to be solidified, if protection against internal foes and external aggression is to be enjoyed, if successful offensive warfare is to be waged, then painstaking effort must be made to develop an adequate and efficient transportation machine.

Relation to Production, Consumption, and Exchange.—It is difficult to overemphasize the significance of transportation from an economic standpoint. Any change in the efficiency of that agency influences production profoundly. Productive itself in that it created place utility, it is an important factor in the rendition of form and time utility as well as of personal service; lacking adequate transportation, the performance of society must be tremendously less. Productive capacity and efficiency advance with improvements in transportation. If, however, facilities for handling traffic fail to keep pace with industrial and commercial advancement because of neglect, of technical stagnation, or of lack of credit, then business and trade must inevitably suffer the binding and crippling effects of this failure. Since the efficiency of transportation service determines largely the range of goods available upon the market, and since, as that range increases, man's wants themselves become more varied, it is evident that consumption as well as production is peculiarly dependent upon the stage of carrier development. Furthermore, because of the higher productive efficiency that follows in the wake of improved transportation, goods are cheapened and the consumer's real income is increased. Improved methods of movement, then, both widen the range of man's consumption and make possible the enjoyment of a greater quantity of goods.

Distribution Modified by Efficient Transportation.—Yet the distribution of wealth among the productive factors is affected more markedly and perhaps in a more interesting manner. Rent is characteristically defined as the difference between the value of the product and the expense of obtaining that product upon marginal land, or at the intensive margin when land is cultivated most advantageously. But the value of that product depends not only upon its quantity but also upon the expense of placing it in the market—depends, in short, upon both the quality and location of the land. Therefore, variations in the efficiency of transportation must inevitably influence directly the amount of the rent. This is especially true to the degree that location is important because, after all, location is not an absolute, physical thing, but rather a matter of relationship—it is not miles but, rather, time and cost that are the fundamental elements in location. The development of more efficient transportation agencies or the extension of those agencies into new areas may lower or may raise rents, depending upon the market situation resulting; the rapid expansion of the railway net in the Mississippi Valley increased rents in that area and, in consequence, increased land values; but it lowered them in the older sections, unable to compete upon even terms with the fertile western lands thus made available for cultivation. Yet even quality of land is influenced somewhat by transportation. As efficiency of movement increases, it becomes easier to secure for application to the land those elements of fertility, such as nitrates and potash, that are needed to adapt it to a particular purpose and are lacking or have been exhausted through long or unwise use.

Interest, that share of the social product assignable to capital chiefly for services rendered by it in the productive process, is also influenced by the character of transportation facilities available. Improved transportation facilities tend both to increase and to equalize interest rates. The former tendency is due to two facts. As the efficiency of transportation increases, the productive capacity of particular units of capital as well as of society as a whole rises, and total productive capacity is always a limiting factor in determining the extent of the reward. Furthermore, the widening of opportunities consequent upon improved transportation augments the demand for capital, and this demand forces the loan rate upward and compels it to approximate more nearly the actual worth of capital to the entrepreneur. The equalization of rates results from improved communication and increased contacts: it is thus that surplus accumulations of funds in certain sections are made more available for other areas in which demand is intense.

Wages, both nominal and real, are also dependent in considerable measure upon the efficiency of existing transportation facilities. As productivity increases, the worker shares with capital in that gain and enjoys the added advantages that result from a decline in prices and an increase in the demand for labor resulting from industrial expansion. Greater ease of movement permits the worker to take advantage more readily of high wage levels at other points and thereby assists in increasing the rate of wages which must be paid him by the entrepreneur. Did the worker but realize, no factor of production has more to gain through technical advancement and through increased efficiency in the operation of the various agencies of transportation than that portion of society which is dependent upon its daily wage for livelihood.

Another who profits through any improvements in the methods or mechanism of transportation is the entrepreneur, who, as the residual claimant in the productive process, benefits from any increase in opportunity. The improvement of transportation makes immediately possible the intensive development of industry and commerce in older areas and offers an infinite variety of new opportunities in the recently opened fields. Until the ultimate adjustment to new conditions is made, therefore, the entrepreneur shares with the owners of land and capital and with the seller of labor power in the social gains or losses resulting from progress or deterioration in the instruments of transportation.

Transportation Burdened with a Public Interest.—Because of the close relation that has existed from the very beginning between his agencies of transportation and his social, economic, and political status, man has long regarded these agencies in a manner quite different from others. They have fallen within that group of enterprises which is regarded as "burdened with a public interest" and, to the degree that the public has suffered unfair treatment from these agencies or that dissatisfaction has developed because of policies pursued under a competitive régime, a widespread and insistent demand has been made for their regulation in the interests of society. For many years in the United States there appeared no clear evidence that the railway was functioning in a manner prejudicial to public interest; the railway had been in operation in America for more than a generation before it threatened, because of certain economic characteristics which will be discussed fully elsewhere, to do serious injury to society. No sooner was that threat apparent, however, than the public acted to protect its interests. Government regulation in behalf of that public was upheld by the highest state courts and their position was confirmed by the United States Supreme Court in the famous case of *Munn v. Illinois*,[1] with scarcely an intimation as to the existence of limits upon the scope of public control. That this power had remained unused for so long a period did not serve at all to estop the public from utilizing it when the need arose: it was clearly recognized that the old common-law principles governing common carriers still controlled, even though the agency involved was new. Since the transportation function is, economically and historically, thus heavily freighted with public interest, regulation followed not only naturally but legitimately in the wake of serious abuses.

Scope and Purpose of This Volume.—The vast extent of the transportation field, and the complexity of the problems that have arisen therein, make it necessary to limit the scope of any single volume sharply. This treatise will discuss transportation in the United States with particular reference to the railway, which is and bids fair to continue as the basic element in America's transportation system, with appropriate recognition given to such other agencies as have won an undisputed place in our economic life. It is hoped that this discussion will give to all who read a sufficient grasp of fundamentals that more intelligent judgments may be passed upon the many transportation questions of business and citizenship import that now face us and that will arise in increasing numbers as the economic and social structure becomes more complex.

At no time in transportation history have sound judgment and clear understanding of fundamentals by the public been more needed than today. There is no type of business enterprise that is not profoundly affected, directly and/or indirectly, by transportation. Furthermore, as citizens the American people face a heavy responsibility. For a half century one or another of our governmental agencies has sought to control the railway, and today we find engaged in that "great national pastime" 48 state legislatures and Congress, together with an almost equal number of state regulatory commissions and the Interstate Commerce Commission. In addition to these, any court of record, state or federal, may be asked to function as a supplementary regulatory agency. It seems clear that our railways are regulated well, rather than wisely—and this, despite the need of wisdom in so important a field. In contrast to the situation of the railway, other more recent agencies that both supplement and compete with the railway are regulated neither wisely nor well—with these gaps in the regulatory structure threatening disaster to the public quite as much as to those more directly involved. No more important internal problem faces the American people today than the sound solution of the relation of the various transportation agencies, the one to another,

[1] 94 U. S. 113.

and the relation of those agencies to government. What place is assignable to the railway, to the motor vehicle, to the inland waterway, and to the airplane in a national transportation plan? Is a general policy of regulation sound in the light of existing conditions? Or should regulation be continued, modified greatly to meet the current situation? Or, indeed, must we admit the inadequacy of regulation in dealing with an agency so intimately related to public well-being and, therefore, abandon that policy in favor of some form of government ownership and operation of all or of certain transportation facilities?

To these problems the present generation of American citizens should give a definite answer; no longer should we muddle through. A wise answer can be made only by those who have examined the facts with an open and unprejudiced mind. To each reader, then, as a student of affairs, as an active participant in industrial and commercial life, as a stockholder in government, this treatment of the American transportation situation is commended in the hope that it will give a better basis of understanding for positive conclusions and constructive action.

REFERENCES

Beale, J. H., and Bruce Wyman: *Railroad Rate Regulation,* W. J. Nagel, 1906.

Johnson, E. R., and T. W. Van Meter: *Principles of Railroad Transportation,* D. Appleton & Company, 1921.

Meyer, B. H.: *Railway Legislation in the United States,* The Macmillan Company, 1903.

Walker, Guy M.: *The Measures of Civilization,* pp. 119–135, Guy M. Walker, 1917.

Weyl, Walter E.: *The Passenger Traffic of Railways,* in Publications of University of Pennsylvania, 1901.

Chapter II

EARLY HISTORY OF TRANSPORTATION

TRANSPORTATION and trade are but two sides of a single problem. Without trade, transportation would have but little economic basis, and the development of trade is limited by the nature of available transportation facilities. When transportation facilities are inadequate, the market for bulky commodities of low value and for perishables must be narrow, with exchange between even relatively adjacent areas confined to goods such as the precious metals, jewels, silks, spices, and like items which dominated trade in both ancient and medieval times. Step by step with improvements in transportation, the movement of commodities of low value has been extended, and perishable goods which formerly were consumed locally have come to enjoy a national, even a world market. This is evidenced by our enormous low-grade tonnage of today and by the movements of fresh meats, fruits, and vegetables through the aid of the cold room and the refrigerator car. Not only the quantity but also the variety of goods interchanged increases with each improvement in transportation.

Obstacles to Development of Trade and Transportation.—This intimate relation between transportation and trade causes such obstacles to the development of the latter as may exist from time to time to delay improvements in the mechanism of the former also. It may be added that, though the one interacts with the other, transportation is the more dynamic factor of the two. These obstacles to the development of trade, which tended to delay the appearance of an interdependent economic organization in the past and which still function in varying degree among different peoples, are of a diverse character. Professor Clive Day has classified them into four groups. The first group includes those that may be termed personal obstacles. Through years or even generations of living in an accustomed way, certain wants and certain methods of satisfying those wants become characteristic of individuals and groups; in consequence, custom bars the introduction of new goods and new methods. Then, too, the suspicion of primitive man has been another important subjective barrier to change. Not only does primitive man suspect the stranger, as shown by the identity of "enemy" and "stranger" in the language of many peoples, but he also suspects the nature and integrity of the goods that the stranger offers. Ignorance of goods other than those common to his experience and the lack of trading machinery that would bring the individual and the new goods into contact constitute a final personal barrier to progress.

A second significant obstacle to the development of interchange among peoples lies in the risk of loss which threatens from various quarters. It is only within recent centuries that brigandage has been stamped out in Western Europe, and so recent has piracy been that the American sailor played an active part in driving the black flag from the Mediterranean Sea, about which Western civilization developed. In less advanced sections of the world plundering bands infest the highways even today, and the pirate still plies his trade in many waters of the Orient. Yet the trader suffers at the hands of others than plunderers alone. The almost constant warrings of early peoples made him too often the legitimate prey of public enemies. In addition to these dangers resulting from man's dissensions, nature's many and varied perils have ever been present and important. Many a caravan and wagon train have strayed during a storm, leaving behind them only the story told by bleaching bones upon desert or prairie. Upon the sea dangers have been more numerous and more grave. Scylla and Charybdis represent merely a personification of the dangers faced by the early mariner. To an unusual degree the seafarer of old must have been a man of dauntless courage and of great hardihood.

A third barrier to the growth of trade appears in the numerous political restrictions placed upon commerce. These rest in part upon the mercantilistic theory that the individual is incapable of acting intelligently in his own interest; in part upon the desire to use the movement of goods as a source of revenue. The early belief in the incapacity of citizen and merchant, unguided by the state, to serve his highest interest caused the movement of goods into or out of a political unit, often in both directions, to be taxed for the public good. It is, however, as a source of income that restrictions have operated most significantly. It is said that in the seventeenth century 15 tolls and national export taxes were levied between Paris and the mouth of the Seine and that upon the river Oise, within a distance approximating that from Albany to New York City, there were 18 tolls to be paid. On the river Loire tolls were collected at 74 different points within a distance of about 175 miles, though not all articles were taxed by each gatherer of toll; yet it is said that, even though the tolls were paid, there was no assurance that the toll gatherer's agents might not plunder the cargo a few miles beyond. These tolls imposed a double burden: an increase in the cost of goods resulted, with a consequent diminution in the volume of trade, and the considerable time consumed in the collection of toll in money or, particularly, in kind, often caused the partial or complete loss of perishable commodities.

A final obstacle to the development of trade, but a spur to the discovery of more effective modes of transportation, appears in the many physical barriers that nature has thrown across man's pathway. Impassable ranges of mountains have separated peoples for centuries almost as effectively as though they dwelt on opposite sides of the earth. Oceans and even inland seas have blocked commercial and social intercourse. Rivers, which were later destined to become channels of trade, proved, for primitive peoples, barriers of no little importance, as indicated by the fact that even today they form the boundaries between many nations. Wide expanse of desert area also has been an insulating factor in man's history. At times these natural barriers effectively prevented all trade; more often they have made the movement of all but goods of high value unprofitable because of the consequent heavy cost of transportation.

Advancement in the field of transportation minimizes each of these obstacles. Improved facilities increase the number of personal contacts greatly and so serve to break down the power of custom as well as to destroy that instinctive suspicion of things new. There is also a multiplication of those desires upon which the development of trade must rest. Risk of loss, too, diminishes as efficiency of transportation increases; with that increase come the elimination of brigandage, the diminution of warring, and the reduction of losses by the elements. Since the modern political state is largely an outgrowth of more efficient transportation, it is inevitable that political restrictions should vary inversely with improvement in that field: the enlargement of the political unit by merging principalities into nations has steadily lessened the number of national boundaries to be crossed. And, finally, it is evident that any betterment in methods of movement must lessen the importance of physical obstacles—indeed, such improvement is, in essence, a victory over mountain and stream, over desert and ocean, over distance itself.

Periods in the Development of Transportation.—Although the development of transportation has been essentially continuous throughout man's existence, certain distinct stages may be discerned. Herrick distinguishes among periods upon the basis of the power used. During the first of these periods man was dependent upon human effort for movement: upon land he dragged or carried his burden, and upon water his muscles likewise served as the source of power. During the second period he came to rely upon power other than his own—upon the animal for movement by land, upon the wind by water. Man probably domesticated animals first for other purposes but they soon served him most helpfully during his wanderings. Upon the water nature was harnessed to the performance of man's will and the movement of the wind-driven craft was directed by the rudder. The third period is characterized by the use of mechanical power, a period so brief as yet that it may rightly be said to have begun but yesterday in man's development. Steam was first to be utilized, but within the memory of millions now living electricity and the internal-combustion engine have been employed to do the work of the modern world, on both land and water. This period interests us especially because it is both so recent and so significant. Herrick but states the conclusion of all students when, in commenting upon developments in transportation, he declares that "man has made greater advance during the past 125 years than in all preceding history."

Another interesting division of periods has been made by Carver upon the basis of the area covered by man. During the first of these periods, the potamic, man traversed land and rivers freely but crept timidly along the shores of inland seas. Gaining courage with experience, and aided by the development of his craft, man navigated the inland seas during the second, or thalassic, period as freely as he had the rivers before, and even explored in hesitating fashion the great unknown—the seemingly illimitable expanse of ocean. However, with the perfection of instruments and further improvements in boat construction, the entire water area of the world became man's field. The first conspicuous figure during this third, or oceanic, period was the great Portuguese prince, Henry the Navigator, though perhaps the most world-famed of these early sailors was Christopher Columbus. In the field of exploration we find man's progress painfully slow during the two earlier periods, but, in the comparatively short time that has elapsed since the fifteenth century, man has almost wiped out the unknown and has permitted few portions of the world to remain unexplored.

Early Man's Primitive Methods.—It is impossible to give within the confines of a single chapter a full description of the development of transportation, but it is, nevertheless, of value to sketch briefly the course of that development. According to geologist and anthropologist the beginning of the Pleistocene era, which dates back about 200,000 years, witnessed the separation of man into the four great groups known today—the European, the Asiatic, the African, and the Australian. Perhaps 200,000 years previous to this differentiation, during the Pliocene period, the so-called Neanderthal man separated from the common stem. Yet, long as man has been in the course of development, it is doubtful if aught but dragging as a means of transport was known to him earlier than 400,000 years ago. In short, only in the period since the appearance of the Neanderthal type has any but the most primitive method of movement been employed.

Progress in land transportation was marked by the employment of the "pack-a-back" method as a first step, and it is probable that, because of the highly developed muscular organization of primitive man, the burdens which he so carried were astonishingly large. The second step in advance appeared in the substitution of animal for man power. Man had domesticated animals for religious and food purposes, also as pets, early in his history, and he learned gradually to employ those types adapted to his purpose as packers and draggers of burdens. This marked a tremendous forward step, since it increased both the quantity of the load and the distance which it could be transported. The third step in the development of land transportation came with the discovery and evolution of the wheel.

The Wheel.—Where or how the principle of the wheel chanced to be discovered will perhaps remain forever unknown, but the most reasonable explanation offered is this: primitive man, using a rounded pole as a lever, accidentally permitted that pole to fall beneath the load and discovered that the load moved far easier than it had before. There is nothing in the history of man's development to justify crediting him with the conscious and purposive application of the principle of the wheel to the movement of heavy objects. Once discovered, however, man did seek consciously to develop the wheel. His first step in advance appears in the long roller with axle protruding at either end: upon this axle rested the load. This was later modified by cutting away all but the end sections of the roller, and then came, in the course of time, the idea of the wheel revolving upon a fixed axle. Finally those wheels, instead of taking the awkward form of sections of a tree trunk, were modeled and shaped to give us the modern spoked type. The utilization of animals for land movement was an important forward step, but the advance which resulted from the discovery and later development of the wheel was epochal. Indeed, next to fire it is perhaps man's greatest single discovery.

The wheeled vehicle was of profound importance itself, but its indirect results were of almost equal significance, since it compelled a development of road and bridge building which previously had been merely a matter of convenience and therefore but little regarded. To permit the easy movement of wheeled carriages the path was broadened and smoothed into a road, and to facilitate the movement of wheeled vehicles over roads much used, or of great military importance, the constructed highway, which the Romans built so efficiently, appeared. The single log thrown across the stream became two logs, and eventually a floored structure, while the rude ferry that had sufficed for wider streams no longer served effectively and was displaced among some peoples by crude suspension bridges, among others more advanced by the arch bridge, which was perfected and widely used during the Roman period.

The final step in the development of land transportation came with the application of mechanical power to the wheeled carriage. Steam, the most common and simplest source of mechanical power, was first utilized. It was applied initially by means of the stationary engine and cable-wrapped drum, later through the steam-driven carriage, of which the locomotive is a common type. More recently, electricity and the internal-combustion engine have been utilized, and future development seems to lie largely in the mastery and further utilization of these sources of power.

Progress in Transportation by Water.—No less interesting than the history of the development of transportation by land is the record of progress by water. As "pack-a-back" represented man's first forward step on land, so man astride the single log, using hands and feet for propulsion, marked his first advance by water. Experience, however, convinced him of the heavy risks incident to this mode of movement; so, when he discovered by chance the added security of the raft, he was quick to adapt it to his needs. Having discovered the raft, man then constructed it purposively by lashing sticks together with vines and grasses. But a second development of the single log followed a somewhat different line and resulted in the canoe. Appearing first as merely a hollowed log, the dugout, this type of craft was later constructed by the use of bark or skin. Typical of this development is the birch canoe of the American Indian and the skin canoes of peoples widely scattered in time and place—in Babylon, Greenland, and the Mississippi Valley. From the raft developed the Chinese junk and the European vessel of the type in which Columbus sailed to America, a type of craft which has been properly called a "glorified raft." From the canoe developed types of greater significance in navigation. To secure a vessel more capable of withstanding the sea, man devised the constructed boat. Soon appeared vessels of plank of the type made famous by the Norsemen, first with framework inserted and later built about a framework. From this vessel developed slowly the frigate, which differs but little, fundamentally, from modern craft.

As important as the evolution of the form of the vessel has been the development in propulsion. Undoubtedly man early found hands and feet less satisfactory in making progress than the use of a stick held in the hands. This stick, probably used originally as nature gave it, in time became a paddle, and the paddle a fixed oar. But man's desire to escape muscular effort soon led him to utilize the wind as a source of power. At first, perhaps, nothing but a leafy bough or even a standing figure on boat or raft offered a surface to the wind, but an actual sail was later employed and tied between two fixed masts. This double mast became a single one with cross arms, and in time there developed the boat of many masts, full rigged, as at the opening of the nineteenth century when mechanical power was first employed. This application of power to water movement, first to a wheel, side or stern, later to a screw propeller, was the third and last great forward step in water transportation.

In even a brief chronicle of the development of water transportation mention must be made of certain seemingly incidental features which are of fundamental significance. The paddle early employed to guide the boat driven by human or wind power soon became a fixed oar and this, in turn, a rudder. However, to take full advantage of the wind, it was necessary to move against as well as with that force. To accomplish this man was compelled to tack, which necessitated the application of a center board, a development credited to the Chinese. Yet another item of tremendous importance in navigation was the discovery and utilization of the compass. The early mariner stood in terror of the open sea, not so much because of its obvious dangers but because, out of sight of land during cloudy or foggy periods, he could determine neither location nor direction. This difficulty was met by the Arabs who mounted the magnetic needle, also of Chinese origin, upon a point, thus enabling the mariner upon an open expanse of water to determine the direction of his course.

The Costs of Primitive Transportation.—As might be expected, the cost of transportation by primitive means is high. In China where wages are approximately 10 cents a day, it is said that a single man with a pole and basket will move about 80 pounds 25 miles a day at a cost of 10 cents per ton-mile, while two men with wheelbarrows will move 350 to 400 pounds from 18 to 20 miles per day at a cost of about 6 cents per ton-mile. An interesting comparison of costs by primitive and by modern transportation is found in the statement that the movement of a bale of rugs 90 miles by camel cost $4.70, while the movement of that same bale 17,000 miles by steamer cost $4.30. But it is not necessary to go as far afield as China to secure contrasts between movement costs under modern and under more primitive conditions. Prior to the building of railways westward from the Missouri, charges which now seem almost prohibitive were levied upon shipments. By ox train, freight moved from Atchison to Denver at a cost of about $100 per ton while similar movements by mule team were said to have averaged approximately 50 cents per ton-mile, or about $250 per ton. The first Colorado gold ores to go out moved by mule team to Atchison and thence by the Missouri and Mississippi rivers to New Orleans for trans-shipment to Wales; the price charged to Atchison was but $40 a ton since a back haul over a down grade was involved. Upon a wagon train of merchandise moving from Atchison to Virginia City a total charge of more than $40,000 was assessed. By pack train rates were even higher, a common charge being $1 per pound per hundred miles or $20 per ton-mile. Early transportation costs were comparably high, also, for the movement of persons. The stage fare from Atchison to Denver was $175 and the regular charge from Atchison to Placerville, Calif., was $225. The transportation of mail by pony express cut the time between Independence, Mo., and San Francisco to 11 days or less, but the cost was $5 per half ounce.

Social and Economic Influences of High Rates.—The effect of such high costs upon the social and economic life of a people has been so great that man has made positive and persistent efforts to lessen their restrictive influence by improving the means of transportation. To this end the early Babylonians built many canals and the Egyptians constructed a waterway between the Nile and the Red Sea. China is estimated to have had at one time 200,000 miles of usable canals, and reliance has been placed upon canal construction as a means of reducing transportation costs in Western Europe from a very early day. Invariably these canals were built to supplement river systems which were already intensively used. But the desire to secure more efficient transportation not only furthered canal building; it also stimulated the construction of roads. Aside from serving a distinct trade function, such highways proved of inestimable value in the rapid movement of troops. Like canals, highways were built initially to supplement the waterways, first the rivers and later the canals. The early history of America is replete with instances of road building, the greatest project undertaken being the Cumberland Road, which was never completed because the highway was superseded by the railway as the most efficient means of transportation. The tremendous advantage enjoyed by those cities and peoples which were so situated as to benefit from the cheap and relatively rapid movement that waterways, first the rivers and later the canals, afforded, enabled them to attain first that high place which results from improved social and economic conditions. With the passage of centuries, the center of economic and social gravity moved from the river people to those located upon the inland seas and, still later, the center of power and influence swung to the nations that faced the open waters. To these nations, "scouring the seven seas" in the frail craft of an earlier time or in the leviathan of today, the world is indebted in great measure for that spectacular material progress which characterizes modern times.

Historic Trade Routes of Eurasia.—No story contains more of human interest, a record of greater success or of deeper tragedy, than that of great trade routes. The Phoenicians, first in time among the great commercial nations of history, traded over well-marked routes with Memphis, with the cities of Armenia and of the valley of the Euphrates, with Gerrha on the Persian Gulf, and with the peoples of southern Arabia. In addition to using these land routes, the Phoenicians not only braved the terrors of the Mediterranean but are supposed to have traveled as far north as the British Isles, from which tin was secured. During the Middle Ages three well-defined routes were used in trade between Europe and the Orient. The northern or overland route struck toward the Orient from Novgorod and Tana on the north and Trebizond on the south, to Bokhara, thence eastward to a point where the caravan chose between an onward journey to "Cathay" and the southward trail into India. A central route was also much used, goods moving over this route across the Indian Ocean and up through the Persian Gulf, thence to Bagdad by river and overland from there to Antioch or to Alexandria. The southern route was essentially a water route, traffic moving from India by boat to Berenice on the Red Sea, thence overland to Cairo and down the Nile to Alexandria. With the development of more efficient transportation many of these earlier routes have fallen into disuse, though others still occupy an important place, as is shown by the fact that the Red Sea remains a highway of commerce between the East and the West and that caravans still journey between Bokhara and Peiping.

Important European Water Routes.—Even prior to the extensive utilization of the various routes just noted over which commerce moved between Europe and the East, certain pathways of trade within Europe had come into use generally. Of these, perhaps the more important were

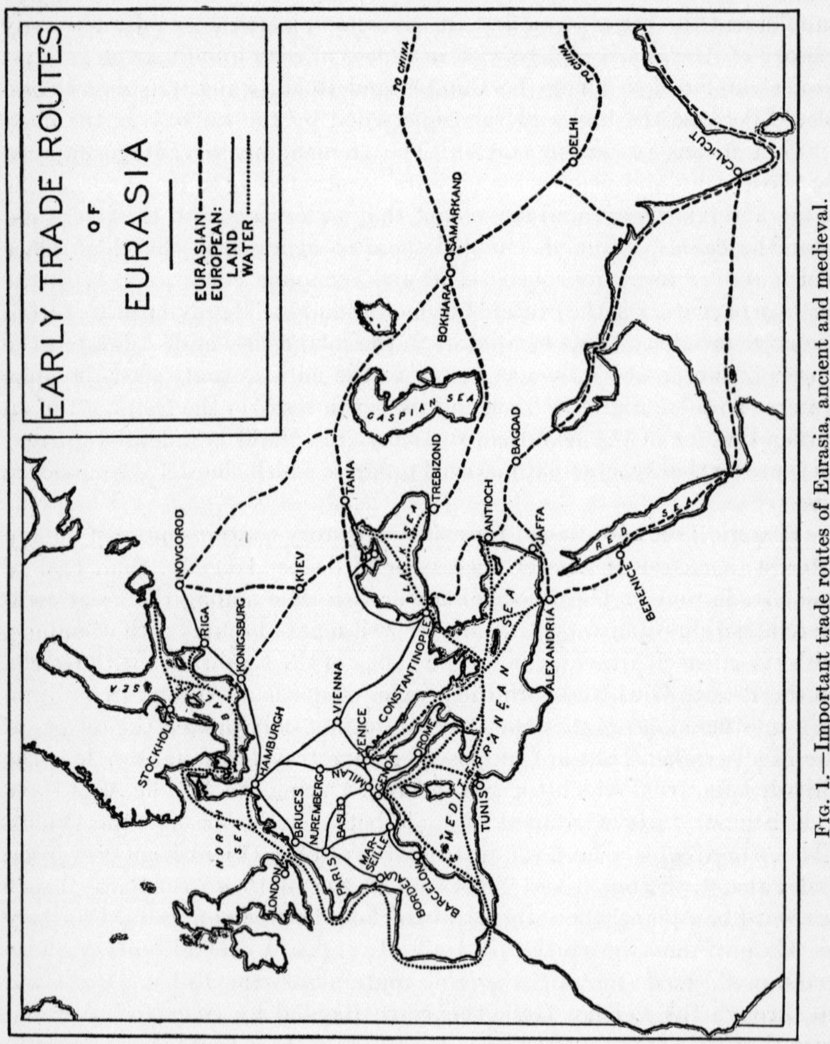

Fig. 1.—Important trade routes of Eurasia, ancient and medieval.

by water: the dangers of the sea and at the hands of the lawless who sailed the sea were little greater than the risks of land movement. Furthermore, political chaos added greatly to the already higher costs of overland movement. Too, it was possible to serve Western Europe well by water, river and sea being so accessible that long overland journeys were rarely essential.

During medieval times, vessels carrying the flags of the Italian maritime cities sailed the Mediterranean from Jaffa to Gibraltar and from Tunis and Alexandria to Constantinople. Northward these fleets sailed through the Bosporus into the Black Sea and as far as Trebizond and the mouth of the Don. From Gibraltar the route of the old Phoenician galleys was followed to Britain and into Bruges. Sailing the North Sea were the ships of the Hanseatic League, these striking as far north and west upon open waters as Iceland; as far north and east upon the Baltic as Stockholm, Riga, and the later site of Leningrad.

Though ignorance and lack of adequate equipment bound sailors of the medieval period close to the shore and held them within the narrow limits of the then known world, increased knowledge and improved instruments made it possible for the hardier to venture more widely. The Portuguese continued to reach southward along the west coast of Africa until in 1487 the Cape of Good Hope was reached and in 1498 Vasco da Gama reached India—as Columbus had sought to do when, sailing westward, he had found America in 1492. With these voyages made and other worlds opened, new and far-flung routes of trade were opened. Each country, all of the maritime peoples of Western Europe, sought lands and traded over established routes with colonies of their own nationals or with those peoples located within a "sphere of influence." Certain routes were used by many—as that round Good Hope, while others—as those to the Americas—were followed almost exclusively by the ships of one flag except as one fleet might offer a deliberate challenge to another by sailing in unaccustomed waters. The modern steamship now follows routes that vary little from those over which the small wind-driven vessel labored during preceding centuries, except as such engineering feats as the Suez and Panama canals permit of an unbroken water movement where formerly transfer of cargo had been required as an alternative to a much longer route.

Important Land Routes in Europe.—Because a greater diversity of routes was possible upon land, the course of trade was less definite than by water. However, there were certain general routes over which commerce moved in considerable volume—routes determined in part by the configuration of the country but more largely by the location and variety of products of cities. One of the major courses over which movements were regular followed roughly the North and Baltic sea coasts from Paris as far as Novgorod, while another extended from Barcelona through Marseille and Milan. Between north and south, traffic moved from Paris to Bordeaux, also to Marseille along the Rhone Valley. At Basle converged movements from Paris and Hamburg, these going over St. Gotthard Pass to Milan; while from Hamburg another road struck south through Nuremberg and over Brenner Pass to Venice. From Hamburg, too, a route led southeasterly through Leipzig and Vienna to Constantinople. Kiev was the point of convergence of routes from Königsberg and Novgorod—and from Kiev the line of movement was to the Sea of Azov where a junction was formed with an overland route from Constantinople that followed the western shores of the Black Sea. Of interconnecting routes there were many, of course, but over those broadly sketched here a large part of Europe's overland commerce moved in medieval times.

Indeed, these routes were but little modified in the main through the several centuries preceding the railway; perhaps the interconnecting network became more minute with the rise of new cities but it was over the old routes that major movements were made. And an examination of the location of railway lines in modern Europe suggests that this improved agency has continued to serve, though far more expeditiously and at lower cost, the territories that were once traversed only by highways over which goods moved in slow-drawn cart or upon pack animal. Established channels of trade, coupled with certain physical determinants, fixed the location of railways in the Old World to a greater degree than in America, where conditions were such as to give greater freedom to the builders of this revolutionizing agency of transport.

REFERENCES

CARVER, T. N.: *Principles of Political Economy,* Ginn & Co., 1919.
DAY, CLIVE: *A History of Commerce,* Longmans, Green & Co., 1919.
HERRICK, C. A.: *History of Commerce and Industry,* The Macmillan Company, 1917.
KEITH, ARTHUR: *Antiquity of Man,* J. B. Lippincott Company, 1915.
MASON, O. T.: *The Origins of Inventions,* Charles Scribner's Sons, 1895.
MORRISON, A. J.: *East by West,* Sherman, French and Co., 1917.
PARKER, JOHN: *Roads and Railroads,* John W. Parker, 1839.
STARR, FREDERICK: *Some First Steps in Human Progress,* The Chautauqua Press, 1895.
WALKER, GUY M.: *The Measure of Civilization,* Guy M. Walker, 1917.
WEBSTER, W. C.: *A General History of Commerce,* Ginn & Co., 1903.
WILSON, DANIEL: *Prehistoric Man,* The Macmillan Company, 1876.

CHAPTER III

THE EARLY DEVELOPMENT OF TRANSPORTATION IN THE UNITED STATES

THE natural routes of transportation that a country enjoys are of fundamental economic and social significance in determining the course of its development. But however vital such routes may be, they are of primary concern to the student of railway transportation only as their inadequacy, due to service capacity or location, serves as an added spur to the development of more convenient and efficient agencies for the movement of goods, persons, and ideas. Since no small part of the energies of those who built the economic foundations of this country was absorbed in the effort to overcome certain physical obstacles to the development of trade and commerce by supplementing such avenues as nature had provided, a brief statement concerning the more important routes of travel used by the colonists is desirable as a background for the story of the development of the American railway net.

Natural Water Routes Used by the Colonists.—Movement by water enjoys the double advantage of lower cost and fewer obstacles as compared with movement by land. It is not strange, then, that, just as in other undeveloped parts of the world, a large part of the early traffic in America moved by water. Two types of water traffic were of importance during the colonial period. Operating between the principal seaports from Maine to Georgia were numerous sailing craft engaged in coastwise trade. Yet more important, perhaps, was the river traffic, because numerous streams gave access to the great inland areas which produced the principal items of colonial commerce—grains, cotton, tobacco, etc. Although a few streams of minor importance tapped that portion of the New England coast lying north of Cape Cod, the important waterway giving access inland in this northeastern portion was the Connecticut River. To the westward of the Connecticut lay the Hudson and its tributaries, most important of which was the Mohawk; together, these provided cheap transportation for a wide and productive area. The territory to the south and west of that served by the Hudson utilized the Delaware River and its tributaries, of which the Schuylkill and the Susquehanna were the most important, in the movement of agricultural products and of coal. This last-named stream, through the Juniata and the West and East Branches, served much of the state of Pennsylvania as well as a portion of southwestern New York. To the southward lay the Potomac and the James, both of which aided materially in the development of that portion of the country. Farther south and flowing into the Atlantic lay the Santee, the Roanoke, the Savannah, and the Altamaha. Tributary to the Gulf were several important streams east of the Mississippi, but, because of the slow development of that section, they played only a small part in the early commerce of the colonies.

Fig. 2.—Rivers and trails used in the development of Eastern United States.

Beyond the Allegheny Mountains and giving access to a considerable portion of the Northwest Territory, an area of unusual promise and great extent, was the Ohio River with its many tributaries. These reached far eastward, southward, and northward into the undeveloped area. Important among those reaching eastward and southward and generally utilized in the movements of goods and of persons into this new section were the Allegheny and Monongahela converging at Pittsburgh, and the

Kanawha, the Kentucky, the Cumberland, and the Tennessee, which entered the Ohio in turn. However, since development west of the Allegheny Mountains had progressed little as compared with that on the east, the waterways that exerted a primary influence upon colonial life were those flowing into the Atlantic.

The location of these natural waterways influenced the course of economic development and the distribution of population of the early colonies in a definite way. The large commercial centers were, on the whole, those enjoying the advantages of a trade with inland areas, which was made possible by the existence of water routes; the order of the development of inland areas was determined essentially by the courses of these rivers. Furthermore, the location of these streams had an important bearing upon colonial unity. In general, each of the important water routes from tidewater into the hinterland lay within a single state or formed at least a portion of the boundary line between states. In consequence, river traffic exerted no unifying influence, economically or socially. Boston and New York, New York and Baltimore, Baltimore and Norfolk, Norfolk and Savannah, were more closely united commercially with England than with each other. Certainly it would seem that nature did little to build an economic foundation for colonial unity in America.

Important Overland Routes.—Although water routes were used in so far as possible, they were early supplemented by land routes. At first such roadway development was merely an adjunct to a water course, but, with the passage of time, land movement played an increasing part in the economic and social life of the colonists. Yet the development of land routes into the West was distinctly circumscribed by nature: the Appalachian Barrier long served as an effective bar to westward movement. However, it might be added that this bar was perhaps advantageous to the early colonists since otherwise the few millions of adventurous peoples which comprised the population of the 13 colonies at the time of the birth of the United States would have been scattered so widely over the eastern half of the continent that the establishment of political unity and the maintenance of successful resistance to the British would have been impossible.

The many thousands who sought entry into the West moved largely over three rather well-defined routes. The first of these, the Northern Route, led up the Mohawk by water or by road, thence westward to Lake Erie, the southern shore of which was followed in the movement to the West. The Central Route led to Pittsburgh, but three different avenues of approach were used. From Philadelphia traffic might proceed westward to the Susquehanna, thence along the West Branch to the Allegheny, and down it to Pittsburgh. Another route from Philadelphia was that afforded by the Juniata River, traffic moving from a point near its source to an east-lying branch of the Allegheny, thence by the Allegheny to

Pittsburgh. The third avenue of entry followed the Potomac westward, striking from that river to the Youghiogheny or Monongahela, thence descending to Pittsburgh. The Southern Route led westward from the upper reaches of the James River, through Cumberland Gap, and thence west and north to the Falls of the Ohio, the present site of Louisville. This route was used by the tens of thousands who went into Kentucky and Tennessee, as well as by many whose destination lay to the north of the Ohio. Several routes were used to reach Cumberland Gap from the east and beyond the barrier various roads diverged, but the trail most used became famed in story as the Wilderness Road and carries with it many memories of the work of that great frontiersman, Daniel Boone. Beyond the Ohio, certain trails were much used but, to quote Meyer:[1]

> In general, the development of roads across the mountains and in the Ohio Region followed the lines of the old Indian trails. Although the Indian often preferred a water route, for most purposes he used a land route. The more important of these trails ran north and south, following, in a general way, the river courses, but there were several important east-and-west trails. Probably these trails were originally made by animals, but they became, through a process of adaptation, first Indian trails, then roads of the early settlers, and later the commercial highways of the state. . . . These trails followed the water divides, and their origin at those points on the Ohio River which communicated with the settled portions of Kentucky, Maryland, Virginia, and Pennsylvania afforded a convenient and ready route to the Northwest Territory. . . . Incidentally, it is interesting and significant that the routes of all the main trails are today occupied by important railway lines. The New York Central and the Lake Shore follow the old Lake Shore Trail; the Pennsylvania follows the old Mahoning Trail; the Toledo and Ohio Central follows the Monongahela Trail; the Baltimore and Ohio follows the Great or Big Trail; another Pennsylvania line follows the Moravia-Scioto-Beaver Trail; the Hocking Valley, the Sandusky-Richmond Trail; the Norfolk and Western follows the Scioto Trail; the Cincinnati, Hamilton and Dayton follows the Miami Trail; the Wheeling and Lake Erie, the Muskingum Trail. It is also worthy of note that these were among the first railways constructed and were suited, as the trails were, to form the basis of our modern railway system, since these locations have been topographically, economically, and socially justified in a continuous development of commercial service for a rapidly increasing population and volume of traffic.

Early Canal Projects in the East.—The inadequacy of natural routes of transportation by water and by land served to restrict both the utilization of natural resources and industrial development. It is not strange, therefore, that the attention of the colonists was early directed toward obtaining more adequate facilities. To this end numerous canal projects were urged. Indeed, even prior to the Revolution attention had been given to certain undertakings, one of which, the Potomac project, enjoyed the active interest of George Washington. These various projects, purposed to

[1] MEYER, B. H., *History of Transportation in the United States before* 1860, p. 6.

establish cheaper communication, may be divided with reasonable accuracy into five groups. These are the coastal, the Atlantic-Ohio, the Atlantic-Great Lakes, the Great Lakes-Mississippi, and a miscellaneous group of local projects. The first group is properly termed the coastal system. A series of artificial waterways was suggested which was to make possible the movement of traffic from Boston to Wilmington, N. C., without entry into the open seas except for short distances. In the north it was proposed that a canal be cut from Boston to Providence, and another across the narrowest portion of Cape Cod. The second link in this system was the Raritan project, which was dug from Brunswick on the Raritan River to Trenton on the Delaware. The third link was to be a canal from the Delaware to the upper end of Chesapeake Bay, while the final project involved cutting through the Dismal Swamp from a point near Norfolk to Albemarle Sound. This coastal system commanded active interest but had not progressed far toward completion when interest in railway building caused the canal to lose favor.

To facilitate movement into the West, two groups of canals were proposed; the one to connect with western rivers, the other, directly or indirectly, with the Great Lakes. In the former system the clearing of rivers and necessary canalization about falls and other obstructions that could not be removed played a considerable part. These opened streams constituted, in each case, the major part of the route. The northernmost one of the river projects was the so-called Pennsylvania Portage System which utilized the Juniata River and an eastern branch of the Allegheny, with a portage running across the divide. Farther south the earlier Potomac project was revived, the plan being to move traffic by water as far up the Potomac as Cumberland, Md., thence by a constructed highway to the nearest tributary of the Ohio, the Monongahela. To the southward a third project was undertaken with the expectation of making possible an unbroken water movement between east and west. This plan involved the use of the James River on the east and the Kanawha River on the west, with the construction of a canal between the two. So attractive did this route appear that even as late as the early seventies it received the approval of certain western interests and of the Federal Board of Engineers as providing a cheaper means of movement between the two sections than the railways then afforded. A fourth river project far south was designed to connect the headwaters of the Tombigbee River with the Tennessee. Work upon all of these projects was begun and upon the first three considerable progress was made, though the only one that was completed sufficiently to render any considerable service was the Pennsylvania Portage System.

Two canal projects were urged to establish water communication with the Great Lakes and both of these were completed. The more important was to make possible the movement of goods up the Hudson and the Mohawk valleys into west central New York, thence to Lake Erie and to Lake Ontario. The purpose of canal construction in western New York was fundamentally economic, a response in part to the desire of the port of New York to gain major control of trade not only of the western portions of the state, but also of business originating along Lake Erie and upon its tributaries; in part to the desire of those dwelling in western New York to secure cheaper and more adequate transportation for their products eastward. Work was begun seriously upon this project as early as 1793, but through traffic from Buffalo to Troy was not possible until 1825.

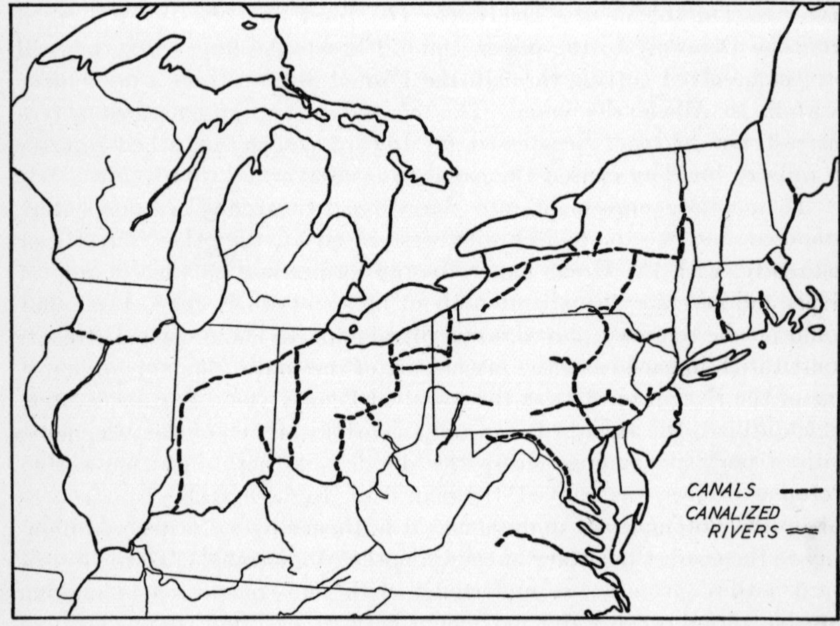

Fig. 3.—Canals and canalized rivers serving prior to the railway.

The magnitude of the undertaking may be better appreciated when it is realized that the completed canal was 363 miles long with a width of 40 feet at the top and 28 feet at the bottom, and a minimum depth of 4 feet. The final project was wholly an artificial waterway with the exception of a few miles near the western end, and 83 locks, excluding the double locks at Lockport, were necessary to raise and lower the boats throughout its length. The second of these projects, the Champlain Canal, was constructed from Whitehall at the head of sloop navigation on Lake Champlain to Troy, where it joined the Erie Canal. Of the 64 miles covered, almost three-fourths represented artificial construction, the remainder the utilization of creek and river. Because of its location, however, it never proved comparable in importance with its sister project which opened the West.

The Great Lakes-Mississippi System.—A fourth system of canals was purposed to connect the Great Lakes and tributaries of the Mississippi. Moving westward, the first two were designed to join Lake Erie with the headwaters of the Allegheny—the one proceeding from Erie, Pennsylvania, the other from Cleveland, Ohio. Another proposal involved the connection of Lake Erie with the Ohio by a canal from Cleveland through Columbus to Portsmouth. Yet a third Lake Erie-Ohio waterway was proposed from Toledo to Cincinnati. Water communication between Lake Michigan and tributaries of the Mississippi was also planned; one canal was to join the Fox and Wisconsin rivers and a second, the more important, Lake Michigan and the Illinois River. All of these projects were carried to completion and at least three still render some service.

Other waterways which commanded interest and which were undertaken on a considerable scale were those that might be classed under the general head of internal improvements. These canals had no single purpose as did the other systems mentioned: each was designed to accomplish some particular purpose. Most of these projects were small and of minor significance from a national standpoint, though invariably regarded as vital to the community served. Certain ones were undertaken and carried to completion, the more important being in southern New York and central and eastern Pennsylvania, where the major purpose was to provide cheap transportation to tidewater for coal. Other proposals of a more general character were discussed, however, such as a canal from Boston to Albany which was to enable New England to share in western trade. But this project, as well as others of an ambitious character, was permitted to lapse with the development of the railway. Except for the appearance of this new agency of transportation, canal building in the United States would have moved forward with rapid strides during the second quarter of the nineteenth century, since the need of better transportation facilities was urgent.

Primitive Character of Early Overland Routes.—Important as the development of waterways was to the early settler, it was even more essential that he obtain efficient land transportation because of the great areas which had no immediate access to water. Early highways followed the old Indian trails rather closely, but, unfortunately, these highways in many cases represented no advance over the primitive trail except as they had been broadened slightly to accommodate wagon traffic. Comments of early travelers are replete with statements which indicate a wholly unsatisfactory condition. One traveler, in speaking of the Albany-Schenectady road, declared it to be "in shameful condition," while another, in speaking of the road between Baltimore and Washington, stated that it was "in a very rude state, the driver being obliged to wind as well as he could between the remaining stumps." Another writer, in describing this same highway, says, "The roads are so exceedingly bad that a carriage will sometimes sink so deep as to defy the utmost exertions of the strongest horse to draw it forward; and in some parts that would otherwise be totally impassable, causeways, constructed of trees, are thrown across the road; but these frequently break asunder and constantly expose a traveler to the most imminent danger. The bridges built across creeks are equally perilous, being formed of a few loose boards that totter while a carriage passes over them. Such is the highroad to the federal city of Washington."

Numerous other comments concerning the condition of roads in the colonies might be given, but perhaps no statement indicates the primitive character of land transportation during this and earlier periods better than the description given of the mail route from Athens, Ga., to New Orleans. Meyer says, in summarizing this report:[1]

> In some places the road had never been cleared or was greatly obstructed by fallen trees. There were numbers of streams to be crossed, over which there were neither bridges nor ferries, and over the narrowest of which trees were felled, which enabled the post rider to creep across, holding the mail on his back, and swimming his horse. Over the wider streams dependence was had upon canoes furnished by families living near the crossings.

The utter inadequacy of such roads was brought out most forcibly in the course of the War of 1812. Armies operating inland had to hew and build their own highways with a resultant decrease in efficiency and an increased cost in money and in life. Describing a journey from Wheeling to Maysville, through Ohio, a traveler declares the roads are "altogether in a state of nature, the trees only just chopped off about a foot from the ground, and the rocks and stones and gullies left to be gotten over as we can." He describes the successful movement of immigrant wagons and families over the mountains as being "a little less than a continuance of miracles." Another writer states that merchants of Cincinnati who purchased their stocks in Philadelphia required three months for the round trip, while the delivery of the goods required an average of 50 days. Meyer states, "In some sections the roads were so bad that the fact found expression in local terminology and even in names of towns. A New Jersey village enjoyed the suggestive name of 'Long-a-coming,' while a town in Indiana was, in a more realistic way, called 'Mudholes.' "[2]

Not only were the roads often in execrable condition, but bridges were unsatisfactory as well as few in number. The larger streams were seldom bridged, so it was necessary to ford where ferries were not available. Usually such bridges as existed were of none too safe a character; a poet in speaking of early Virginia bridges characterized them as being

[1] MEYER, B. H., *History of Transportation in the United States before* 1860, p. 58.
[2] *Ibid.*, p. 62.

Made of a few uneasy planks
In open ranks
Over rivers of mud.

Of the eight streams that Jefferson found it necessary to cross in his journey from Monticello to Washington for his presidential inauguration, but three could be crossed by bridge.

The type of construction of these early bridges varied widely. Across the narrower streams logs were thrown and planks laid from one log to another, while upon the wider streams bridges were supported by boards, rafts, or piles. So little attention, however, was given to either the construction or maintenance of these important adjuncts to roadway transportation that in any but the highly developed sections Meyer's quotation from Earl fairly characterizes the situation: "The early bridges of provincial days were but insecure makeshifts in many cases, miserable floating bridges being common across the wide rivers."

The Development of Toll Projects.—The wretched condition of roads and bridges made land transportation both slow and expensive. Realizing the need of more efficient transportation and the inadequacy of waterways throughout great areas, the desirability—indeed, the necessity—of improving the conditions of land movement impressed people generally. As a result of this demand for improved land transportation, the last decade or more of the eighteenth century, as well as that portion of the nineteenth century which preceded the acceptance of the railway, was marked by rapid progress in the improvement of both roads and bridges. The development of toll projects represents the first step in this direction. These were built by private corporations with the expectation that the charges collected would be sufficient not only to cover the cost of maintenance but to provide at least an adequate return upon the capital invested. In Pennsylvania alone it is said that 102 companies constructed 2,380 miles of road at a cost of approximately $8,500,000. Similar activity was in evidence in other states, particularly throughout New England and the Middle Atlantic area. Bridge building was also extensively undertaken by private interests as indicated by the fact that prior to 1813 charters for 36 toll bridges had been granted in New York and stock to the amount of $509,000 authorized. The first two bridges across the Hudson were toll bridges and many of the important early projects in Pennsylvania were likewise built by private capital. Within six years preceding 1815 Pennsylvania authorized the construction of some 20 toll bridges.

The characteristic failure of toll projects to yield a reasonable return upon the investment, however, caused a gradual loss of interest in these enterprises on the part of private capital. Furthermore, the amount of such capital available in a new territory for undertakings of this character was inadequate to meet the need. It became necessary, therefore, for the government to extend aid. To meet this very general demand for improved transportation facilities, city, township, county, and state all became involved in road- and bridge-building projects. Public aid was extended particularly in the newer and less developed areas of the West and South, since it was highly essential to the rapid development of those areas that satisfactory land transportation be provided between rivers and between rivers and lakes. Indeed, during this period the federal government itself was persuaded to give assistance. Such aid was justified by the politically dominant strict constructionists upon the ground that it would both provide more adequate military protection and assist materially in the transmission of intelligence from one section of the country to another. It was further recognized that such projects would serve a distinct economic purpose in the development of new areas. The most famous of the turnpikes constructed through federal aid was the Cumberland Road, which was planned to run from Cumberland, Md., to Jefferson City, Mo. Though provision was made for its construction as early as 1806, it was not until 1811 that work was actually begun. Seven years later it reached the Ohio River and, before work was stopped by the panic of 1837, it had been driven westward to Vandalia, Ill. This point proved the western terminus of the road since by that time the railway had proved its supremacy in the movement of traffic over long distances.

Transportation Costs by Land and Water.—That transportation charges should be heavy under conditions as described was inevitable and a relatively high money charge was materially increased by the long period of time consumed in the movement of traffic. The charge made for moving goods overland varied generally from 15 to 20 cents per ton-mile, 20 cents being perhaps the characteristic figure. The heavy burden of such charges may perhaps be appreciated more fully when we know that the cost of moving goods from Albany to Buffalo by land was $90 per ton, a similar charge being made for movement from New York to Pittsburgh, partially by water but principally by land. Water movement was, of course, much cheaper, traffic moving down the Hudson from Albany to New York at 15 cents per hundredweight and from Albany to Buffalo through the Erie Canal at a rate of $8.53 per ton, of which $5 was assignable to tolls. From Louisville to New Orleans a charge of $1 per hundredweight was made, but for the trip up river the rate was $5. A usual charge for the movement of passengers by land was 6 cents per mile. However, the charge rarely dropped lower and often was greater, the movement from Boston to Albany averaging 9 cents and from Charleston to Columbia as high as 30 cents. Travel by water was somewhat less expensive than by land, though 5 to 6 cents was a common charge, and this type of movement normally consumed much greater time than did overland stage. In the West the down-river movement from Louisville to New Orleans cost $75, while the return movement cost $125, the one-way distance being approximately 1,600 miles.

Charges upon Overland Movements.—In addition to road costs there were toll and ferry charges to be considered. According to Gallatin's report on internal improvements, ferry charges across the Catawba River from 1788 to 1808 were as follows:

For every man and horse	4 d
For every foot passenger	2 d
For every wagon and team	3 to 6 d
For every rolling hogshead	1 to 6 d
For every two-wheeled carriage	2 to 4 d
For every head of cattle ferried or swum	3 d
For every head of sheep, hogs, or goats	2 d

Upon Zane's Trace the following tolls were recorded as the charges across the Scioto and Ohio rivers:

	Scioto	Ohio
Man and horse	$0.12½	$0.18½
Man alone	0.06½	0.09¼
Wagon and team	0.75	1.15
Horned cattle	0.06¼	0.09¼

Few records seem to remain of charges made for the use of toll bridges, but, again quoting Meyer,[1] "They seem to have ranged from 2 cents for foot passengers, 15 cents for carriages drawn by one horse, 15 cents for two horses, and 25 cents for four horses, up to $1 per carriage. There seems to have been great variation."

Charges made for turnpike movements varied rather widely throughout the country but the following, which appears in the act of incorporation of the Philadelphia and Lancaster Turnpike, is reasonably representative and, in addition, shows the detail with which charges were worked out:

For every score of sheep, ⅛ dollar; for every score of hogs, ⅛ dollar; for every score of cattle, ¼ dollar; for every horse and his rider, or led horse, 1⁄16 dollar; for every chariot, coach, stage, wagon phaeton, or chaise with two horses and four wheels, ¼ dollar; for either of the carriages last mentioned with four horses, ⅜ dollar; for every other carriage of pleasure under whatever name it may go, the like sums according to the number of wheels and horses drawing the same; for every cart or wagon whose wheels do not exceed the breadth of four inches, ⅛ dollar for each horse drawing the same; for every cart or wagon whose wheels shall exceed in breadth four inches and not exceed seven inches, 1⁄16 of a dollar for every horse drawing the same; for every cart or wagon the breadth of whose wheels shall be more than seven inches and not more than ten inches or being a breadth of seven inches shall roll more than ten inches, five cents for each horse drawing the same; for every cart or wagon the breadth of whose wheel shall be more than ten inches and not exceed twelve inches, or being ten inches shall roll more than fifteen inches, three cents for every horse drawing

[1] *Ibid.*, p. 47.

the same; for every cart or wagon the breadth of whose wheel shall be more than twelve, two cents for every horse drawing the same.

This practice of charging lesser sums for broader wheeled vehicles appears to be typical of early tolls; indeed, during the winter and spring seasons there is evidence that the use of certain turnpikes was wholly denied to narrow-wheeled vehicles because of the injury done to the road while in soft condition.

The Costs of Canal Movement.—As indicative of the charge made for canal movement, the amounts assessed for canal passage along the Potomac River in 1808 upon the following articles will perhaps suffice:

Per bushel of wheat, peas, beans, or flaxseed	$0.02
Per barrel of pork	0.23
Per barrel of flour	0.11
Per ton of hemp, flax, potash, bar or manufacturing iron	1.12
Per ton of pig iron or castings	0.38
Per ton of copper, lead, or other than iron ore	0.89
Per ton of stone or iron ore	0.19
Per hundred cubic feet of planks or scantling	0.38
Per gross hundredweight of all other commodities and packages	0.06

Tolls upon the Susquehanna Canal were practically identical with those above quoted. A maximum toll was set by New York for movements between the Hudson River and Lake Ontario of $25 per ton, though in 1820 the rate upon merchandise moving through the Erie Canal, so far as it had been completed, was about 2 cents per ton per mile, a rate of 1 cent applying on commodities such as flour, meal, and grains.

Economic Burden of Transportation Costs.—Any accurate statement of the total cost of transportation to the people of any particular section during this early period is impossible, but sufficient figures are available to allow an estimate. During 1818, it was estimated that not less than $18,250,000 worth of merchandise moved from Philadelphia to Pittsburgh by wagon at a cost of approximately $750,000. For the three years 1817–1819 the total transportation cost for all goods moved to Pittsburgh has been estimated at about $1,560,000 per year. Since the cost of wagon movement from Philadelphia and Baltimore seems to have varied from $7 to $10 per hundredweight, the result was that only articles of high value were capable of bearing this heavy cost burden. Such high charges necessarily restricted industrial development of both new and old areas. Though this situation led to that diversification of industry characteristic of the independent community, Meyer declares that "any incidental advantages were certainly inconsiderable in comparison with the economic disadvantages consequent upon isolation and remoteness from markets for agricultural products." Not only did this high cost of movement prejudice the interests of the East in the newer territory, but it also handicapped Western producers in the Atlantic coast market. In speaking of the effect of inadequate transportation facilities upon home industry, the following statement[1] is made:

> A ton of goods by weight or measurement (of 40 cubic feet) was frequently brought from Europe, a distance of 2,000 miles, for 40 shillings or about $9; this rate admitted salt, coal, stone, lumber, and most bulky articles which were imported from beyond the seas cheaper than they could be conveyed for a short distance by land, since a ton of goods could not be carried on good roads, for the same price, more than 30 miles. . . . A coal mine might, therefore, exist in the United States not more than 10 miles from valuable ores of iron and other materials and both of them be useless until a canal were established between them as the price of land carriage was too great to be borne by either.

Even the cost of water movement by canal or river boat, and by coastwise vessels, was such that:[2]

> Goods were frequently brought from Europe at nearly as low a cost as they could be conveyed by sea from Baltimore to Philadelphia, cities which by land are not more than 100 miles from each other. This was remarkably the case with respect to coal, which was brought into most of our maritime cities from Liverpool and sold as cheap as it could be brought to them from James River, not one-sixth of the distance.

Important Routes of Trade and Travel.—*Water.*—Upon earlier pages the efforts of the American pioneer to improve transportation facilities by land and water have been described briefly. However, no discussion of early transportation facilities would be complete without further emphasis upon the significant contribution of natural watercourses to trade and travel during more than the first half century of America's national life, or without mention of certain famous trails that featured in the development of newer areas.

The importance of the rivers flowing into the Atlantic upon colonial development has already been suggested. Certain of these streams made notable contributions to the prosperity of extended areas, among them being the Hudson, the Delaware, the Potomac, the James, the Roanoke, and the Savannah, together with their tributaries. Lacking the cheap and unhindered transportation afforded by these watercourses, colonization would have proceeded far more slowly and the utilization of natural resources would have been long delayed. However, if such natural and easy routes be regarded as important in the early growth of that narrow territory east of the Allegheny Mountains, then the rivers west of that barrier were vital to the early settlement of that great expanse which constitutes the Mississippi Valley.

Though those who settled Kentucky and pioneered in the Northwest Territory came westward by trail and trace, it was upon the Ohio River

[1] "Observations Respecting the Chesapeake and Delaware Canal," as quoted by B. H. Meyer in *History of Transportation in the United States before* 1860.

[2] *Ibid.*

and its important tributaries that they soon depended—and especially was this true after the Louisiana Purchase had made the lower Mississippi an American river and New Orleans a center of American, instead of French, activity. Navigation was begun with small, crudely constructed vessels, the flatboat still being an important factor during the young manhood of Lincoln. Later, small steamers plied the Ohio from Pittsburgh to Cairo and ventured upon many tributaries—especially the Kanawha, the Cumberland, and the Tennessee reaching southward, and the Beaver, the Muskingum, the Scioto, and the Wabash serving the area toward the Great Lakes. From the many tributaries of the Ohio came great quantities of agricultural products and animals, some of which found a market in rapidly growing centers such as Cincinnati and Louisville, the remainder moving down river toward New Orleans. As early as 1823 Congress passed the first river and harbor bill, and federal funds were soon being used to prepare the Western rivers for steam navigation. In 1840 some 4,600 vessels passed Cairo, Ill., in the course of the year, and in 1848 about 1,200 steamboats were in service upon the Western rivers. Indeed, it is declared that by 1856 the steam tonnage of the Mississippi River system equaled the total steam tonnage of Great Britain.

Following in due course the effective utilization of the Ohio and its tributaries, together with the Lower Mississippi, came the extended use of the Upper Mississippi and the Missouri. Trade from Minneapolis-St. Paul to St. Louis assumed large proportions and the Illinois River, supplemented by a canal, permitted the movement of tonnage to and from Chicago by water. Up the Missouri moved a considerable traffic to such points of departure for the Western hinterland as Independence and Kansas City, Leavenworth, St. Joseph, Atchison, and, farther north, Omaha and Sioux City. It is impossible to overstress the part played by these streams and other portions of the Mississippi system in furthering the early growth of this tremendous inland empire.

Rivers tributary to the Gulf of Mexico were important factors in the early settlement of the Gulf states. These streams and their many tributaries, from the Apalachicola on the east to the Rio Grande on the west, contributed immeasurably to the agricultural growth of this area. And upon the west coast the San Joaquin, the Sacramento, the Columbia, and other lesser streams speeded settlement and aided in the utilization of natural resources.

Important Trails.—Contributing much to the development of areas to which no natural watercourses gave access and in which the construction of canals was not feasible were the early overland routes or trails. Of those rendering conspicuous service in the Eastern portion of the United States, certain ones have been mentioned. But more famous than any of the Eastern routes, unless it be the Wilderness and Cumberland Roads, were certain ones followed in opening the great West. Earliest entry into southwestern United States was over the Spanish Trail from Vera Cruz to Santa Fe but, as contacts between the Santa Fe region and the northern peoples became more frequents, it was overshadowed by the Santa Fe Trail. This trail, running in a general westerly direction from the Missouri River to the early capital of the Southwest, has been of particular

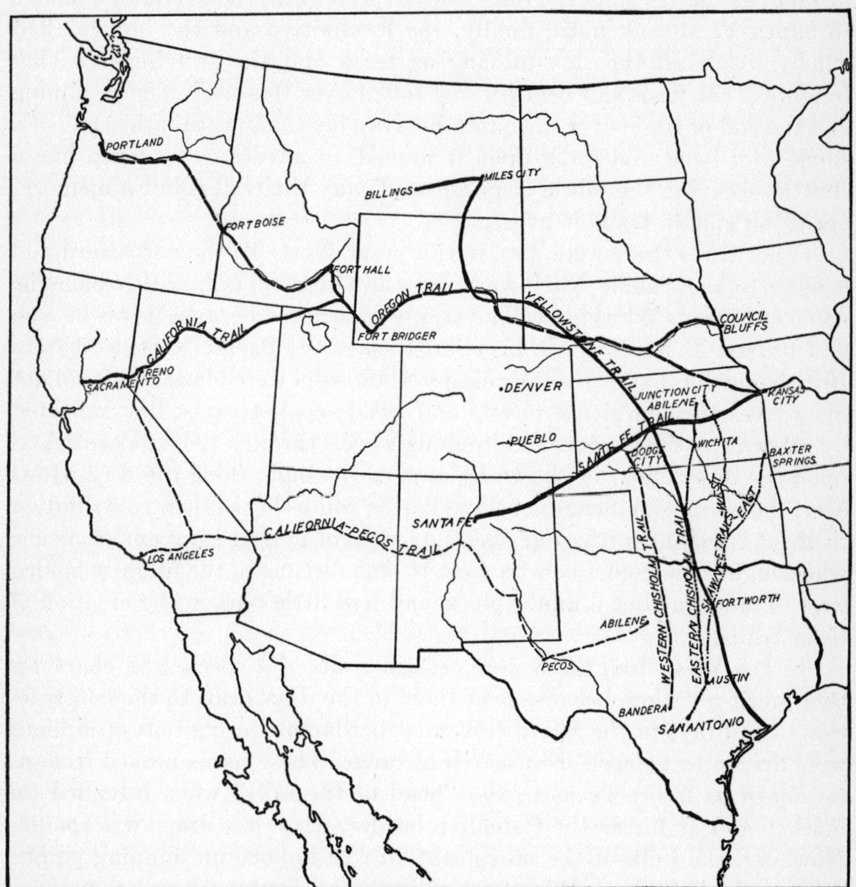

FIG. 4.—Important Western trails.

interest to the author because of a boyhood spent beside the old roadway over which caravans, great and small, moved through a barren country occupied by wandering, warring Indians and ranging bison herds.

The route from the Missouri into the Southwest was traversed by a trading expedition first, it appears, in 1812—an expedition that accomplished only imprisonment for its personnel. However, in 1821 a successful journey was made, and from that time onward trade grew in volume. Occasionally protected by an escort of United States troops, these wagon trains generally had to provide for their own defense against Indian and pirate of the plains. Manufactured goods moved from St. Louis by steamer to Franklin, then Independence, and finally Westport (Kansas City), Mo., from which an 800-mile overland journey was begun. The more important items carried by the returning caravans were furs, precious metals, and wool. The last wagon train from Westport Landing departed in 1866; as the "head of the rails" moved westward, the overland distance to Santa Fe shrank until, finally, the locomotive and the box car had wholly displaced the slow-moving ox team and the swaying, creaking freighter that for a half century had toiled over this trail. The beginning and the end of trade over the Santa Fe Trail lay easily within the span of a single life; back and forth upon it moved an adventurous group like a shuttle, weaving the fabric of progress. Today the trail is but a memory, yet as an epic in trade it lives.

Other trails there were, too, in this great West. To the northward and leading to the Pacific Northwest was the Oregon Trail, with which the name of Marcus Whitman will always be associated because it was he who first braved its hardships in his effort to save the Pacific Northwest from British control. Later, trails leading to California were blazed—blazed not upon trees through dense forests and beside cool streams, but indicated by ruts cut by sharp hoofs and lurching wheels through the sage brush and upon the desert floor or shown by rock cairns built along the way. However, the major significance of these Pacific routes lay in their contribution to the settlement of the Far West: over them moved caravans of people who sought new homes or who went to woo fortune in the literally golden west. Trade was but a minor phase and had little part in the creation of these trails.

In the West, too, there were certain trails of a specialized character that merit mention, because over them in the days prior to the construction of railways in the Southwest great herds numbering tens of millions were driven to market or in search of range. These herds moved from as far south as lower Texas to the "head of the rails" when intended for market and as far as the Canadian border, when pasturage was sought. However, the bulk of the movement was to important shipping points, among which Abilene, Wichita, Caldwell, and Dodge City were perhaps outstanding. From 1867 to 1895 it is estimated that almost a hundred million head of cattle, as well as perhaps ten million horses, moved northward over various trails. Surely there was a material basis for the fame in song and story of the old cattle trails which, with others that traversed the West, have now passed into history.

The part played by the various highways of commerce—river, lake, and trail—in the early economic and social development of North America is difficult for us of the twentieth century to realize, even vaguely, and almost impossible to overestimate. And, had not the railway appeared, ocean and lake, river and road, must have been for a long period the channels through which commerce—driven by the wind and drawn by horse or oxen—must have flowed.

Need of Improved Transportation Facilities.—Inasmuch as distance is fundamentally a matter of time and cost rather than of miles, it may rightly be said that the United States was a country of "magnificent distances" even at the close of the eighteenth century and before its great territorial expansion. A comparatively small portion of the total area of the United States is accessible by natural waterways. Canal construction was incapable of serving more than a relatively small additional area with even partial adequacy except as prohibitive building and operating costs were assumed. The United States was, therefore, peculiarly in need of a more efficient system of land transportation than any known as late as 1825. The almost unlimited natural resources scattered over a broad expanse of territory gave unusual opportunity for service to improved transportation agencies. Of this, convincing evidence is given by the ready acceptance of the railway once its success was assured, and by the tremendously rapid expansion of mileage in the face of adverse conditions during the first half century of development.

REFERENCES

Armour's Livestock Bureau: *Cattle Trails in Livestock Market Development, Monthly Letter to Animal Husbandmen,* vol. 7, No. 1.

Bogart, E. L.: *The Economic History of the United States,* Longmans, Green & Co., 1915.

Callender, G. S.: *Selections from the Economic History of the United States* 1765–1860, Ginn & Company, 1909.

Carter, C. F.: *When Railroads Were New,* Henry Holt & Company, 1909.

Cleveland, F. A., and F. W. Powell: *Railroad Promotion and Capitalization,* Longmans, Green & Co., 1909.

Duffus, R. L.: *The Santa Fe Trail,* Longmans, Green & Co., 1930.

Haney, Lewis: A Congressional History of Railways in the United States to 1850, *University of Wisconsin Bulletin* 211.

Inman, Henry: *The Santa Fe Trail,* The Macmillan Company, 1897.

Johnson, E. R., and others: *History of Commerce of the United States,* Carnegie Institute of Washington, 1915.

Meyer, B. H.: *History of Transportation in the United States before* 1860, Carnegie Institute of Washington, 1917.

Pangborn, J. C.: *The World's Railway,* Winchell Printing Co., 1894.

Parker, John: *Roads and Railroads,* John Parker, 1839.

Parkman, Francis: *The Oregon Trail,* Little, Brown & Company, 1919.

Peyton, John: *The American Transportation Problem,* Courier Journal Job Printing Co., 1909.

Phillips, U. B.: *The History of Transportation in the Eastern Cotton Belt,* Columbia University Press, 1908.

Ringwalt, J. L.: *Development of Transportation Systems in the United States,* J. L. Ringwalt, 1888.

Ripley, W. Z.: *Railroads: Rates and Regulation,* Longmans, Green & Co., 1912.

Webster, W. C.: *A General History of Commerce,* Ginn & Company, 1903.

PART II

RAILWAY HISTORY OF THE UNITED STATES

CHAPTER IV

BEGINNINGS OF THE AMERICAN RAILWAY NET

AMERICAN railway history has been divided into periods variously by those seeking to present its important features in an orderly way. By some mileage growth has been used as a measure, by others the nature of interrailway relations, and by yet others the extent and character of public regulation. However, the use of any single yard-stick fails to give proper place and emphasis to the others. Therefore, in the division of the railway era, now just beyond its centenary, it has seemed desirable to combine as nearly as possible several bases, with primary emphasis upon the growth of the railway net and upon the relations existing between the railway and public. Using this composite measure, railway history seems to fall into five periods. The first of these closes in 1850 and the second in 1873. The third, and one of the most important because within it are to be found the beginnings of some of the important railway problems of today, ended in 1893, and the fourth period terminated in 1920 with the close of federal operation of railways.

Practical railway development, both here and abroad, dates from 1830. No agency such as the railway, however, springs into being fully developed: behind it lie long years of patient effort marked by almost imperceptible progress. Behind it, too, will always be found the deep interest and the life work of many men. Indeed, before the railway was accepted by the public, it had become the grave of the highest hopes and of the life endeavors of more than one pioneer. But this development was essentially mechanical in character, so its detailed history lies beyond the scope of this treatise. Nevertheless, it will not be amiss to describe briefly the evolution of the railway before presenting the story of American progress.

Development of the Track.—Of the three major elements constituting the railway as we know it today—the track, the car, and the locomotive—the track first approximated its modern form, perhaps because it is the simplest of them all. The earliest track consisted of parallel planks laid end to end; later, the ends were joined to maintain alignment, and, to prevent variations from the gage adopted, crosspieces were used at intervals. These were known as ties or sleepers. Although durable woods were used, the planks deteriorated so rapidly that soon they were faced with strips of iron, usually about ½ inch thick and from 2 to 3 inches wide. The development of iron working made easy and natural the transition from plated wooden rails to rails of cast iron, a distinct step forward in roadway construction.

When first introduced, about 1767, the cast-iron rail carried a flange on the outer edge to prevent the carriage from slipping from the track. Subsequently this flange was transferred to the inner edge of the rail, and in 1789 to the wheel, where it remained. Under heavier loading, the brittle cast-iron rail proved unsatisfactory and was replaced by the long wrought-iron rail.

There is no clear record of the earliest use of the track. It seems certain, however, that it developed in English collieries about 1600. The first definite record of such use is in 1630, when a Mr. Beaumont laid down wooden rails from his coal pits near Newcastle to the river side. In speaking of this early track Stretton states that it consisted of

> . . . cross sleepers placed about two feet apart upon which were nailed wooden planks or rails six feet long and about four inches wide. This pioneer of progress also introduced four-wheeled wagons to run on the wooden ways instead of the ordinary two-wheeled carts. Like most men, however, who sought to make innovations upon English methods, Beaumont lost his fortune in the attempt and emerged from his reforming schemes reduced to poverty.

As early as 1671, the track was used in manufacturing establishments, and from that time its use broadened until by 1750 the track was employed widely and for a diversity of purposes throughout England.

In America, however, it appears that the first railway was not constructed until 1807—a short line ascending Beacon Hill, Boston. In 1809, 1810, 1818, and 1825 other short stretches of track were built in Delaware, Virginia, Pennsylvania, and New Hampshire, but it was not until 1826 and 1827, with the building of the Quincy and Mauch Chunk lines, upon which stationary engines were used to handle loads on inclined planes, and the Delaware and Hudson project between Carbondale and Honesdale, that this new means of transporting goods was put to practical use. This last-named railway was 16 miles in length and, like the Mauch Chunk undertaking, was designed to facilitate the movement of coal.

Evolution of the Car.—The second essential element of the railway to receive consideration was the car. Upon the early plank tracks single, heavily loaded wagons or cars were operated. Because of the frequent replacement of track made necessary by this concentration of burden, the load was distributed later among several smaller cars and these, linked or chained together, were operated as a train. This plan had the further advantage of increasing tractive capacity. The development of the car was slower, however, than of the track; at the time that track, car, and locomotive first functioned together, this element was still in primitive form. However, the tardy development resulted, in part, from the peculiar conception entertained for many years as to the nature of railways: it was thought that, as common carriers, they must be open at will to all upon the payment of a reasonable toll; also that individual users should furnish their own cars. In fact, when cars were still horse drawn, the patron was often expected to furnish even his own motive power.

Importance of the Locomotive.—As long as the railway was compelled to rely upon animal power for traction or, indeed, upon aught but the locomotive (at least two of the early railways in the United States experimented with the sail and many with the stationary engine and drum), the railway could be regarded only as supplementary to the canal and canalized river. Its future as a dominant factor in the movement of goods and persons depended upon the building of a successful locomotive, a goal attained by 1830, from which year railway development dates. The evolution of this final and all-important factor in the success of the railway justifies a somewhat detailed description. To indicate the steps in its development is, therefore, our next problem.

Early Use of Steam.—The evolution of the locomotive, unlike that of the track and the car, has definitely associated with it the names and the accomplishments of certain outstanding figures. The machine that proved its supremacy in the great test at Rain Hill, by which the place of the locomotive was made secure, was the product of the brains of many men, the culmination of the hopes and efforts of many earnest workers. In 1695 Papin perfected a stationary engine which produced a vacuum by the condensation of steam. Power was thus derived alternately from steam and air pressure. In 1713 the natural boyish preference of the lad Potter for play rather than for the task of opening and closing valves by alternately pulling certain cords led him to attach those cords to the mechanism in such manner as to make the operation automatic. In 1720, Leupold further improved the engine by employing high-pressure steam, using "two single-acting cylinders placed upon the boiler, each with a steam pipe piston moved alternately by steam admitted through a four-way cock."

The first serious effort to utilize steam for the propulsion of land carriages was made by a French artillery officer, Nicolas Cugnot. Desiring a more effective source of power for the movement of artillery than that furnished by animals, Cugnot constructed without guidance a mechanism which was, despite all defects, little short of remarkable. Although the machine traveled at a speed of but 2½ miles per hour and labored under the additional handicap of a steam supply that was inadequate for more than 15 minutes' continuous operation, yet to Cugnot, because of results thus attained in 1769, belongs the honor of moving the first land carriage under steam power.

To Oliver Evans, of Philadelphia, goes the honor of making the next important step in the development of the steam locomotive. In 1779, he perfected the high-pressure noncondensing steam engine and introduced the multitubular boiler so that both heating area and fuel efficiency were increased. But Murdoch, an assistant to James Watt, was the next man to make serious effort to apply steam power to the driving of vehicles. Watt had obtained a patent for a carriage to be operated by high-pressure steam as early as 1769, but at this point he stopped. Henceforth he opposed bitterly any proposal to proceed further in the use of this "dangerous force" or in its application to land movement. However, the assistant, who sensed possibilities as the arrogant master did not, continued to interest himself in the matter until, in 1784, his machine was ready for trial. With this contrivance its builder was able to attain a speed of from 6 to 8 miles an hour—but the price of continued work was to be the loss of his position with Watt. Inasmuch as his place meant more to Murdoch than further work in this field, it remained to others to carry on.

The Work of Trevithick.—The next important figure in the development of the locomotive was Richard Trevithick, a Cornishman. After constructing a successful model as early as 1796, he built engines of working size after the expiration of certain of Watt's restrictive patents in 1800. His first creation appeared in 1801 and proved a success. It attained a speed of 4 to 5 miles per hour and made moderate grades without difficulty. This locomotive was operated by high-pressure steam and utilized Evans' idea of the multitubular boiler. The two main difficulties lay in maintaining steam pressure and in obtaining adhesion adequate to give tractive power. Despite the promise his work gave, Trevithick encountered bitter opposition, particularly at the hands of Watt, who insisted that, for his persistence in the use of high-pressure steam, Trevithick "ought to be hanged." Yet this pioneer's work was such as to keep alive a discussion of the relative merits of high- and low-pressure steam and of the possibility of utilizing steam for the propulsion of land carriages. As a result of this controversy a wager was made, to win which Trevithick constructed his second engine. To succeed, it was necessary that the locomotive should draw, by its own power, wagons containing 10 tons of iron upon a tramway in South Wales.

Operating with an elevation of 1 foot in 50 and in the face of other obstacles, the locomotive built by this Cornish genius met every requirement and hauled the specified load at a rate of about 5 miles per hour: the first movement by steam upon rails was an accomplished fact. In 1805 Trevithick built another and simpler machine, and in 1808 his last and most effective locomotive was built. Determined that London should know of progress made, he exhibited this last product there upon a circular track built especially for it. The weight was about 10 tons and a speed of from 12 to 15 miles per hour was attained. Finally, after some weeks of operation, a rail broke and the locomotive was overturned. Trevithick, out of money and with no influential friends to aid him, hopeless of success and utterly discouraged after a battle of almost 10 years, gave up. He was later laid to rest in a pauper's grave.

The Interest and Work of Evans.—In the meantime, Oliver Evans, the American, had again interested himself in the application of steam to the movement of wheeled vehicles. In 1786, his application to the legislature of Pennsylvania for permission to introduce the new idea was refused, but in Maryland he was more fortunate. Full of enthusiasm, he predicted that "the time will come when carriages propelled by steam will be in general use for the transportation of passengers as well as goods and will travel at the rate of 15 miles an hour or 300 miles a day." Not until 1804, however, did Evans apply his idea of land movement by steam in a practical way. In that year he moved a 20-ton dredge, which he had built for the city of Philadelphia, some distance from the point of construction to the Schuylkill River, employing steam as motive power. Then, utilizing that same power to turn a paddle wheel, Evans steamed down the Schuylkill and up the Delaware some miles to the point of delivery specified! Despite the faith of the inventor and despite this demonstration, support was not forthcoming and opposition was strong. Indeed, as late as 1812, he declared in a discouraged tone,

> When we reflect upon the obstinate opposition that has been made by a great majority to every step toward improvement, from bad roads to turnpikes, from turnpikes to canal, from canal to railways for horse carriages, it is too much to expect the monstrous leap from bad roads to railways for steam carriages at once. One step in a generation is all we can hope for. If the present shall adopt canals, the next may try the railways with horses, and the third generation use the steam carriage.

Further Progress—The Rain Hill Trial.—Evans' pessimism proved unwarranted, however, for, from about this time onward, interest in the new idea quickened and many men concerned themselves in the development of the steam locomotive. Most prominent among these was George Stephenson who, fortunate in his support and in the positions which he occupied, continued undiscouraged in his efforts with the locomotive until his final triumph in the Rain Hill trial. Of equal importance in making possible this sweeping triumph, however, was the building of railways during the period of Stephenson's development of the locomotive. In England, the Stockton and Darlington, with a length of 37 miles, was projected in 1817, and in 1822 the building of the Liverpool and Manchester was proposed; in the United States, Pennsylvania had authorized the construction of a railway from Philadelphia to the Susquehanna in 1823. Many locomotives of widely varying type were built in England and several in America, while in England the Stockton and Darlington utilized the locomotive as a source of power. Yet this English experiment was proving not wholly satisfactory and only the excellent work of Hackworth, a former pupil of Stephenson, prevented the abandonment of steam in favor of horse power.

By common consent, the Liverpool and Manchester project came to be regarded as the test of the practicability of the locomotive and upon its acceptance of steam power depended the immediate future of that mechanism. Although Stephenson was chief engineer of the property, the directors were undecided as to the type of power to be used—steam or horse. Finally, despite doubts as to success, the board decided upon a public trial, prescribing conditions. The trial was held upon a level stretch of track at Rain Hill, over a distance of 1½ miles with an additional ⅛ mile at each end to gain speed and to stop. Conforming sufficiently to specifications to permit participation were three locomotives, the "Rocket," constructed by Stephenson, the "Sans Pareil," by Hackworth, and the "Novelty," by Erickson.

The results of the trial were most gratifying to the champions of this new source of power. Because of mechanical difficulties the "Novelty" was early compelled to withdraw, though not before attaining a speed of almost 40 miles per hour. The "Sans Pareil" was unable to complete the test because of minor troubles, but it made a highly creditable showing, averaging approximately 15 miles per hour and attaining a maximum speed of almost 23 miles per hour. The "Rocket" succeeded beyond the expectations of all but its most enthusiastic champions, completing the trial at an average of about 15 miles per hour and attaining a maximum speed of slightly more than 29 miles per hour.

The unqualified success of the Rain Hill trial put the stamp of engineering and public approval upon the steam locomotive. The period of struggle for recognition was ended; there now remained but the task of adapting and perfecting this instrument of progress. To Stephenson has been given almost entire credit for the development of the first successful locomotive. Undoubtedly great credit is due him, for it was he who so combined ideas as to make hope a reality, whose execution made possible the earlier attainment of the goal. Yet none of the essential principles involved in the construction of the "Rocket" was original with him. He was indebted to Evans and his successors for the multitubular boiler and for the high-pressure noncondensing engine; to Hackworth, a competitor in the trial, for the idea of utilizing exhaust steam to hasten combustion by means of a forced draft; to Trevithick and others for the lessons which could grow out of practical experience alone. Almost beside him—and, certainly in the case of Evans, the disappointed American, and Trevithick, the persistent Cornishman, entitled to equal credit with him—stand a group of men who remain unsung but who contributed generously in effort and in enthusiasm toward the attainment of final success.

American Interest in the Railway.—In America, just as in England, interest in the railway as a supplementary, even a rival, agency to the canal developed rapidly during the decade prior to 1830. As early as 1824 there was formed in Philadelphia the Pennsylvania Society for the Promotion of Internal Improvements in the Commonwealth, with a primary interest in railway construction. In 1825, this society sent an engineer to Europe to study work done and experiments under way there, particularly with reference to grade, roadway construction, and locomotive machinery. Further evidence of growing interest and of an increased realization of the possibilities of the railway, even without the locomotive, appears in the chartering of the Baltimore and Ohio as early as 1827 and of the Charleston and Hamburg, later the South Carolina Railroad, in the same year. A suggestion was also made in 1825 by the Governor of Massachusetts in his legislative message of the possibility of joining Boston with Albany by railway and this suggestion was approved by a committee of that body in an exhaustive report made 4 years later.

Initial Locomotive Operation.—Despite the important early work of Evans in America, the mechanical ingenuity of his contemporaries and successors seems to have been absorbed largely in fields other than that of locomotive development. For this situation the unwillingness of capital to furnish necessary funds for experimentation was responsible in great measure. Reed in 1790 and Stevens at a later period, as well as Evans, received no support whatever. It is not strange, therefore, that the first locomotive operated in America, the "Stourbridge Lion" in 1829, was one of English manufacture, though it might be added that as early as 1825 Stevens constructed a model that made 2 miles per hour upon a small experimental railway. This English locomotive was ordered for the Delaware and Hudson by Horatio Allen and, with Allen at the throttle, the first locomotive run in America was made. Brief trial indicated clearly, however, that the "Lion" was so ill adapted to the light roadway and the sharp curves of the road as to make its operation dangerous; it forthwith went to the shed. Americans now became interested in locomotive construction, and in 1830 the first American-built locomotive was ready for service.

This locomotive was the "Tom Thumb," so-called because of its diminutive size, its total weight being about a ton. It was essentially the product of the mechanical genius and the persistence of Peter Cooper, a New York merchant. During an early test this diminutive locomotive drew a load of approximately 4½ tons over a poorly constructed roadway and around sharp curves at an average speed of more than 12 miles per hour. In commenting upon this accomplishment Winans, an engineer on the road, declared that, when due regard is given to the conditions of operation controlling the tests of the "Rocket" and this American product, "the superiority of 'Tom Thumb' is very strongly apparent." Yet the first railway definitely to abandon all thought of the use of horses was the Charleston line, which put into service this same year the second American-built locomotive, the "Best Friend." However, the Baltimore and Ohio has the distinction of being the first railway in the world to hold forth as a common carrier, its service dating from May 22, 1830.

The Railway as an Effective Transportation Agency.—Although American railway development may properly be said to have begun prior to 1830, that year represents the beginning of effective railway construction. This initial period of development, continuing to 1850, was characterized particularly by experimentation and by the building of short lines. Despite the assured position the railway seemed to occupy at the beginning of this period, certain important and difficult problems remained.

Early Engineering Problems.—*The Roadway.*—Conspicuous among these were problems of construction and operation. One of these was concerned with the roadbed itself. Engineers first sought to construct a solid and relatively indestructible base. To this end the Boston and Lowell, and later the Baltimore and Ohio, laid rails upon granite supports. Such a roadway proved so unyielding, however, that equipment suffered seriously. Therefore, within a few years, the desirability of a more elastic roadbed was recognized. But it was only after extensive experimentation that a satisfactory type was developed. Indeed, it is said that in the construction of the early portion of the Baltimore and Ohio every known mode of track construction was tested, including, "the iron on the granite sill; the wood and iron on stone blocks; the wood and iron on wooden sleepers, supported by broken stone; the same supported by longitudinal ground sills; the log sill formed of the trunks of trees worked to a surface on one side to receive the iron and supported by wooden sleepers crosswise; together with wrought iron rails"[1] of English make. Yet another type of track construction tried upon an extended scale was that of building upon piles. This error is estimated to have cost the New York and Erie Railroad more than a million dollars. Finally the modern type of roadbed was evolved and proved so satisfactory that it gained universal acceptance.

A second important construction problem, which affected equipment rather than roadway, nevertheless grew out of the physical character of that roadway. In England gradients were low and curves were of sufficient radius to offer slight difficulty to the locomotive builder. In America, on the other hand, gradients were heavy and curves sharp. Several facts explain this difference. The inadequate supply of capital compelled the early railway corporation to economize sharply and, as a result, the road often ran up hill and down dale when cuts and fills were needed. Then, too, it was quite natural that this improved agency of transportation should follow the old trails. Often certain areas were accessible only by the winding trails long traveled by Indian and pioneer, and often, too, to depart far from these trails would have deprived the railways during the early years of operation, years destined to be lean at best, of

[1] Pangborn, J. C., *The World's Railway*, pp. 85–86.

considerable traffic which the more settled sections were able to furnish. Finally, the lack of capital not only during this period but even later made the railway highly responsive to local offers of aid, and the highest bids rarely came from localities that constituted a direct route. To enable the locomotive to take the numerous and sharp curves with less likelihood of injury to track or mechanism, various plans were suggested. Among the strangest of these were devices which might be characterized as props, extending at an angle from the sides of equipment in use and reaching groundward almost to the roadway—their purpose being, in case of threatened derailment, to maintain the equipment in an upright position. Far more practical were the development of the swivel truck, which gave greater flexibility, and the use upon the locomotive of the pony or guiding truck, which reduced the likelihood of derailment when rounding curves at considerable speed.

The Problem of Power.—Another important construction problem had to do with power. There was an almost universal absence of faith on the part of even locomotive enthusiasts in adhesion as a basis of tractive power. To meet this presumed difficulty, which was greater in America because of heavier gradients, many and peculiar devices were suggested. By some it was proposed that the locomotive be equipped with extra wheels fitted with knobs and claws, while others felt that the solution of the problem lay in operation by means of a third or rack rail. Possibly the strangest device proposed was the so-called "mechanical traveler," a contrivance difficult to describe but with a striking resemblance to the hind legs of a great grasshopper and intended to operate in such manner as to push the locomotive forward by the alternate movement of the two "travelers" with which it was to be equipped. Finally, however, engineers realized that reliance might be placed upon the friction between rail and driver. Thus another basic problem was solved.

A second power problem arose through the difficulty that the early American railways had in securing satisfactory locomotives. Those of English construction, of which the "Stourbridge Lion" was typical, proved too heavy for the light track and bridges in America and were ill adapted to sharp curves. To meet this situation Americans from varied walks of life—engineers, watchmakers, and business men—interested themselves in locomotive construction. Naturally, the locomotives built varied widely, but soon certain of the characteristic lines of the modern locomotive were generally accepted. Though the construction of locomotives was at no time limited to a few plants, a small number of builders soon occupied a commanding position in the field. Among these was the West Point Foundry Works, which put the "Best Friend" into service in 1830 and the ' DeWitt Clinton" in 1831. Another company which early occupied an important position—a position still retained—in the field of locomotive construction was that headed by Mathias Baldwin of

Philadelphia, whose first engine, "Old Ironsides," was put into service in 1832.

Early efforts to adapt the locomotive to American conditions resulted in the adoption of the swivel truck already mentioned. Two additional problems of major importance remained: the one of keeping all drivers upon the rail at all times, despite inequalities in the light and cheaply constructed roadway, the other of giving the drivers a small measure of lateral flexibility to facilitate taking sharp curves. As a solution of the first difficulty there appeared the equalizing beam, a combination of levers which keeps each wheel of a set of drivers in contact with the rail at all times. This device lessened the likelihood of breakage through overburdening a portion of the drivers and materially increased tractive capacity. To meet the second difficulty the flexible beam truck was developed with a sufficient lateral movement of each pair of drivers to make possible an adjustment to all but the sharpest curves.

Diversity in Track Gage.—Another construction problem, one with interesting economic consequences, was that of the gage of the track. English gage was that of the wheel base of the early English road cart which measured 4 feet 8½ inches from inside rim to inside rim. In America, however, except on roadways built to conform to English standards of locomotive construction, the gage varied greatly. English standard gage was the usual minimum, indeed, with gages up to 6 feet upon certain of the earlier lines. In New England and the Middle West standard gage, as the 4 feet 8½ inches came to be termed, was generally adopted by railway builders; in the South the gage was typically 5 feet; while in New York, Pennsylvania, and other adjoining states, gage varied from as low as 4 to as high as 6 feet. In Pennsylvania and Ohio alone there were seven different gages, six of which approximated standard. These variations increased the cost of movement both because of the expense of transferring interline shipments and because of the delays resulting from these transfers. Another unfortunate result, though perhaps less immediate and obvious, was the stimulation of carrier individualism, with a consequent failure to attain earlier that cooperation which is essential to successful railway operation and to the equitable treatment of shippers under competitive conditions. The universal adoption of standard gage by all except avowedly narrow-gage properties was almost a half century in coming.

Difficulties of Train Operation.—Difficulties incident to train movement proved most troublesome during the early years of railway development. Two conditions occasioned difficulty: the lack of any rapid communication such as the telegraph and telephone, and the conception of the railway as a specialized turnpike—a common road available for use to all. Until telegraphic communication was established on the railways about 1850, the expeditious movement of trains presented serious obstacles. Various methods were used, though none proved more than a stop-gap. Schedules were carefully drawn and points of meeting were definitely fixed; as long as all went well and no efforts were made to insert extra trains, operation proceeded smoothly. However, during these early years when railways were least able to deal with the unusual, the unusual was particularly likely to occur—roadway, car, and locomotive were all but little beyond the experimental stage. On some lines, if one train failed to meet another at the appointed place or did not reach its terminal within a reasonable period, a voyage of discovery was undertaken by rail or even by horse to determine location and difficulty with a view to performing rescue service. Some lines established primitive signaling. Of the system employed by the New Castle and Frenchtown as early as 1837 the following statement is made:

> The poles were of cedar . . . and had cleats fastened on them, forming a sort of Jacob's ladder. The signaling was done thus: the operator would go to the top of the pole forming his station, and with his spyglass sight the next station in the direction of the approaching train. If the train was coming and the signal showed a flag, it meant all is well. If a big ball was shown, and no train in sight, it signified an accident. . . . These signals were methodically exchanged until an understanding was had from one end of the road to another.

In the absence of whistles, warnings and signals were given from the locomotive by raising the valve stem on the steam dome by hand, which permitted the steam to escape with a hissing sound, and the conductor had either to run the length of the train or use agreed signs to communicate with the engineer. Advanced practice in communication was illustrated by the engineer's running up a flag on the tender when he wished the brakemen to set the brakes. Stopping a train was essentially a matter of physical strength on the part of the trainmen and resulted in serious discomfort to passenger and in scrambled freight; the jolting was often "tantamount to a shock scarcely less severe than would be caused on a superior modern train by a collision."

But the peculiar conception early entertained as to the nature of the railway complicated a difficult matter still further.

> It was not the intention of early legislators that railroad companies should have any preferential or exclusive use of the means of transportation upon their tracks. With the exception of the Baltimore and Ohio, few railroad companies of this period were granted charters which did not expressly provide that the road might be used by any person who would comply with necessary rules as to form of wheels, style of cars, and weight of loads. The idea was distinctly in mind that the railroad was to be operated precisely like a turnpike, with gates at intervals along the route for the collection of tolls.

The railroad being regarded as a public highway upon which all who wished might place at will their own cars for movement by power supplied by themselves, complications were inevitable. Disputes as to right of way often delayed and sometimes blocked traffic, and the use of the railways by the general public on a toll basis interfered with any orderly operation by the railway officials themselves. With the proved superiority of the locomotive, however, the railway soon gained exclusive control of its roadway, and it was not long before it was recognized that even the right of the individual to furnish cars must be exercised in accordance with appropriate regulations.

Public Opposition to the Railway.—But the difficulties faced by the railway pioneer extended far beyond mere problems of plant construction and operation: positive opposition had to be overcome and the support of capital enlisted. By some this new means of transportation was received as an invention of the devil and a herald of social catastrophe, an agency calculated to overturn an ordered state and to erect, in its stead, an organization as menacing as was the railway to all natural laws respecting speed of movement. "Illustrating this opposition: in Connecticut, we are told, an eloquent divine went about lecturing in opposition to railroads, declaring that their introduction would necessitate the building of a great many insane asylums, as people would be driven mad with terror at the sight of locomotives rushing across the country with nothing to draw them. And the townspeople of Newington, in the same state, having learned that a line of railroad was projected through their neighborhood, are said to have presented to the directors a remonstrance which represented that they were a peaceable, orderly people, and begged that their quiet might not be interrupted by steam cars and the influx of strangers."[1]

By considerable numbers the railway was regarded, rightly or wrongly, as inimical to their own economic welfare and was fought with that bitterness which characterizes only a man's defense of his bread-and-butter interests. Large sums of money had been invested in canal projects by individuals and by government; hence active effort was immediately made to protect these undertakings. In New York, the Utica and Schenectady was prohibited in its charter of 1833 from carrying any property other than the baggage of passengers and not until 1844 was it permitted to handle freight—then only during the period of suspension of navigation and upon payment to the state of a sum equal to the canal tolls leviable had the movement been through the Erie Canal. As late as 1848 the General Incorporation Act required canal tolls of lines parallel to and within 30 miles of canals and not all restrictions were removed until 1851. In Pennsylvania the charter of the Pennsylvania Railroad required the payment of a tonnage tax of 5 mills during about 9 months of the year, a tax not wholly lifted until 1861, while in New Jersey the Camden and Amboy was forced to agree, as the price of its charter, that it would complete the Raritan Canal project, which constituted a rival route.

[1] Cleveland, F. A., and F. W. Powell, *Railroad Promotion and Capitalization*, p. 76.

Turnpike companies and the proprietors of stage lines also bitterly opposed the introduction of the railway. The Utica and Schenectady was forced to buy up the shares of an established turnpike company at an agreed price, and railway charter grants were frequently delayed by such rival interests. Allied with those whose financial interests were directly identified with canal, turnpike, and stage line as investors were a large group whose incidental relation was such as to make their interests one with the investors. This group included innkeepers and coach drivers, even the farmers who feared that their market for horses and, in consequence, for hay and grain would be ruined. Such was the general attitude displayed in many quarters that Josiah Quincy declared "the believer in railroads was not only to do the work and pay the bills for the advantage of his short-sighted neighbor, but, as Shakespeare happily phrases it, 'Cringe and sue for leave to do him good.' " Rivalry even among railway promoters delayed development; where no competition for traffic threatened, prospective competition for financial support often caused promoters to block one another's plans.

Inadequate Supply of Capital.—The difficulty of securing capital for early railway construction was assignable in part to the scarcity of capital in the United States, in part to the natural hesitancy of capital to support a relatively unproved enterprise. As is true of any new country with large areas of undeveloped territory and with great natural resources, the demand for capital greatly exceeded the supply: funds were at a premium. Relief during the early years of development was not to be anticipated from the more highly developed sections of Western Europe because at this time the rapid movement toward industrialization offered opportunities for profitable investment there. In consequence, early railway construction in the United States had to be financed locally. But access to these funds was difficult: capital is essentially conservative, venturing timidly into new fields when investment opportunities of proved character are offered. Certainly, the first 10 years of railway building and operation were so characterized by experimentation that only enthusiasts felt that financial success could be immediate.

But when, in addition to a reasonable doubt as to the success of this new agency, there existed public apathy in some quarters and bitter opposition in others, it is in no wise strange that investors were hesitant. When a leading paper in Boston declared, in 1827, concerning a proposed railway from Boston to the Hudson instead of the canal which had been suggested earlier, that it was "a proposal which everyone knows, who knows the simplest rule of arithmetic, to be impracticable, but at an expense little less than the market value of the whole territory of Massachusetts; and which, if practicable, every person of common sense knows would be as useless as a railroad from Boston to the moon," it would have been odd had capital rallied immediately to the support of the enterprise.

Because it was difficult to secure financial support, many projects were undertaken during this period with wholly inadequate funds. In consequence, numerous roads were but partially completed, which, in turn, was highly conducive to financial disaster. Or, perchance, those financially interested in the project decided to throw good money after bad in the hope of retrieving the original sums invested. Yet, even with the project complete, difficulties were not ended. Inadequate working capital and slender revenues during early years often resulted in a serious situation. In this connection Ringwalt says,

> An early employee of the Philadelphia, Germantown, and Norristown, which subsequently became one of the most profitable short lines in the country, reports that he was obliged to buy oil to grease the axles with his own money. An old engineer on a New England road "relates how men were sometimes put on the tender with a sawhorse and saw, to cut the wood to make steam for the trip, because there was no supply on hand, and no money to buy any. It is said that an official once gave up his gold watch as security when a train was seized for debt while en route."

The financial way of the railway builder was truly a hard one during early years: it was more difficult to secure the support of capital during this period for sound projects than it was later, during the speculative era, for the most impossible of promoters' schemes.

Table I.—Total Mileage Construction of 18 Railroads, 1850

Road	Date begun	Mileage 1849
Boston and Albany	1834	241
Boston and Maine	1836	74
New York, New Haven and Hartford	1839	123
Old Colony	1845	126
Rutland	1849	120
Baltimore and Ohio	1830	182
Cincinnati, Sandusky and Cleveland	1848	169
Michigan Central	1838	218
New York Central and Hudson River	1831	452
New York, Lake Erie and Western	1841	259
Pennsylvania	1832	155
Philadelphia and Reading	1832	122
United New Jersey Railroad and Canal Company	1832	132
Georgia Railroad and Banking Company	1838	215
South Carolina	1830	243
Western of Alabama	1841	111
Wilmington and Weldon	1840	164
Chicago and North Western	1848	43

Railway Construction at the Close of the First Period.—That construction prior to 1850 reached the proportions which it did stands as splendid testimony to the enthusiasm and perseverance of the railway pioneer. With but little more than a score of miles in operation in 1830, that decade witnessed the completion of 2,265 miles of line and the following decade an additional mileage sufficient to show a total of 7,310 at the close of the 20-year period. The mileage of some of the more important lines at the end of this period, together with the date of their beginning, is indicated in Table I.

An interesting fact not shown by the foregoing table is that the South Carolina Railroad Company, with 137 miles in operation at the close of 1833, was for a time the longest railway in the world under a single management. But not alone are mileage facts respecting particular lines of interest: the territorial distribution of mileage is also significant. Of the total indicated at the close of the fifth decade, the distribution was as shown in Table II following. When relative areas are considered, it is evident that construction had progressed at a comparatively rapid rate in the more populous sections but had moved forward slowly in the agricultural South and the undeveloped West.

Table II.—Sectional Mileage Distribution in the United States, 1850

Area	Miles
New England States	2,256
Middle Atlantic States, Ohio, Michigan, and Indiana	3,204
Southern States	1,706
Midwestern States	97
Southwestern States	47

Yet practically all important centers of population in the United States had been linked by railways at the close of this period. In the South, Charleston and Savannah reached westward to Chattanooga, via Atlanta; and Wilmington was connected, through Richmond and Washington, with Baltimore. Baltimore, in turn, had access to western Maryland and was joined with Wilmington, Delaware, and Philadelphia. Philadelphia enjoyed rail connections with both Pittsburgh and New York. New York was linked with Albany and Buffalo, also with all important centers in southern New England, including Boston; and Boston had direct access to Albany, also to Portland, Concord, Burlington, and other cities of importance in New England. In the West, Cleveland and Cincinnati were joined and Detroit was connected with Lake Michigan. In many cases, adjacent points were connected by the line of a single corporate organization, but more often, and this was especially true of more distant centers, connection lay over the lines of several carriers. The early lines were typically local in character, largely because of the need of arousing local interest to make the project possible.

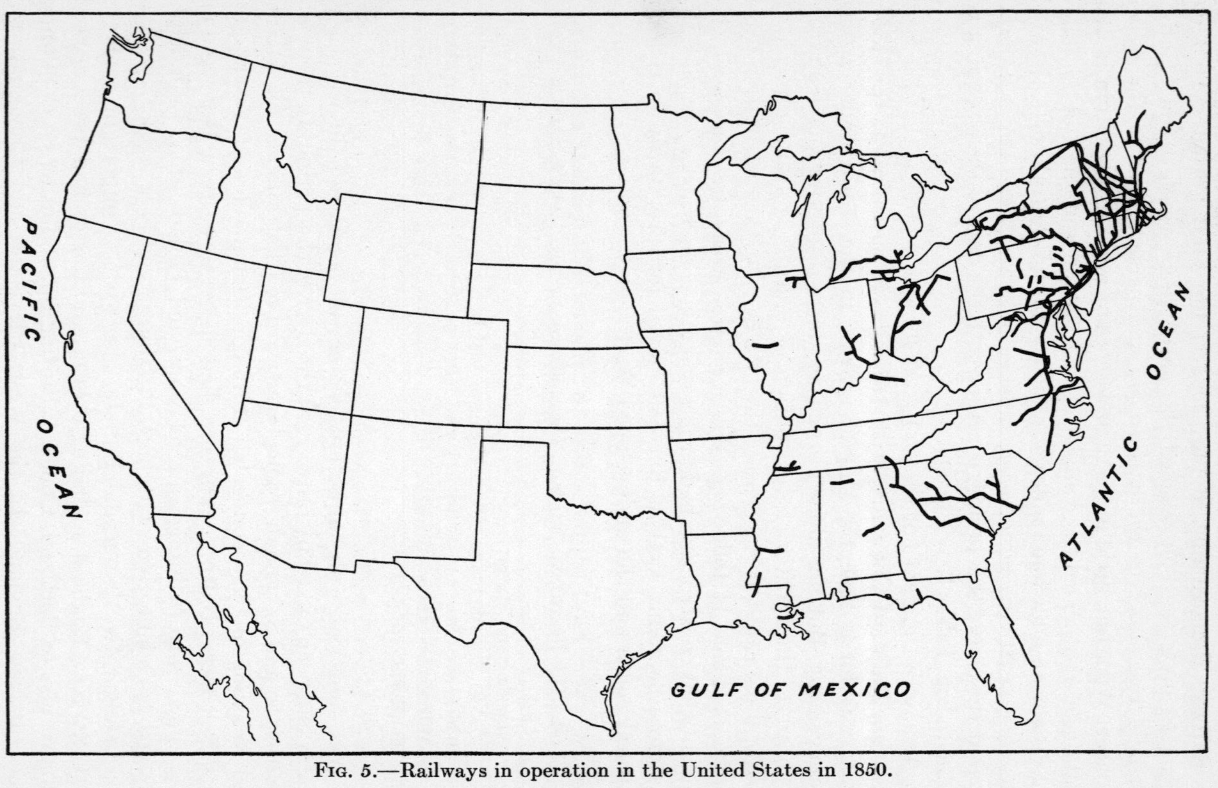

Fig. 5.—Railways in operation in the United States in 1850.

Forces behind Railway Building.—Behind railway construction during this period there lay, roughly, four impelling motives. Of these perhaps the most significant was the desire of important market centers on the Atlantic coast to participate upon a favorable basis in the business of that great area beyond the Appalachians. To the rivalry among Boston, New York, Philadelphia, Baltimore, and Charleston was due the early construction of the Boston and Albany, the lines westward from New York to Lake Erie, the Pennsylvania, the Baltimore and Ohio, and the South Carolina, each of these projects enjoying primary support from those who hoped to profit from the resulting trade. Similar in its general nature was a second motive, that of building from market centers into contiguous territory that the tributary area might be extended. This was the purpose that actuated the construction of the many short lines which characterized the early years of development. As a supplementary motive, if it might be so termed, to the two already mentioned, there was the intense desire of isolated sections to secure rail connections with market centers and more highly developed territories, to speed the economic development of the newer section. It was because of this desire that, throughout the entire history of railway construction in the United States, it has been relatively easy to enlist local capital under the banner of a pioneer enterprise. A fourth factor promoting railway construction during this period was the desire of the promoter to reap a generous harvest. Although not coming into full flower until a later time, the influence of this wily citizen was clearly apparent even before the railway had emerged from the experimental stage.

Summary.—To summarize, it may be said that this first period in railway development was characterized outstandingly by experimentation, with heavy resultant losses compensated by rapid technical progress. It was also an era of short-line construction, since the railway was early regarded as supplementary to natural and artificial waterways and of service in opening areas where waterway construction was not economically feasible. Responsible in part for short-line building, too, were lack of capital and the failure of early leaders to visualize the railway system as we know it today. A third feature of this period was the comparative absence of construction in all but the more populous sections of the United States. It was here that the railway gave greatest promise of immediate success and here it was, likewise, that capital was to be had. Finally, though complete victory by the railway over canal and turnpike did not come until later, the performance of the newer agency was such, and its future promised so well, that a definite check was given both types of rival enterprise after the panic of 1837.

REFERENCES

Bogart, E. L.: *Economic History of the United States*, Longmans, Green & Co., 1915.

Callender, G. S.: *Selections from the Economic History of the United States*, 1765–1860, Ginn & Company, 1909.

Carter, C. F.: *When Railroads Were New*, Henry Holt & Company, 1909.

Cleveland, F. A., and F. W. Powell: *Railroad Promotion and Capitalization*, Longmans, Green & Co., 1909.

Gephart, W. F.: Transportation and Industrial Development in the Middle West, *Columbia University Studies*, vol. XXIV, No. 1.

Haney, Lewis: *A Congressional History of Railways in the United States*, Carnegie Institute of Washington, 1915.

Hungerford, Edward: *The Modern Railroad*, A. C. McClurg & Co., 1911.

Johnson, E. R., and others: *History of Commerce in the United States*, Carnegie Institute of Washington, 1915.

Meyer, B. H.: *History of Transportation in the United States before* 1860, Carnegie Institute of Washington, 1917.

Pangborn, J. C.: *The World's Railway*, Winchell Printing Co., 1894.

Phillips, U. B.: *History of Transportation in the Eastern Cotton Belt*, Columbia University Press, 1908.

Ringwalt, J. L.: *Development of Transportation Systems in the United States*, J. L. Ringwalt, 1888.

Ripley, W. Z.: *Railroads: Rates and Regulation*, Longmans, Green & Co., 1912.

Thompson, Slason: *A Short History of American Railways*, D. Appleton & Co., 1925.

Van Metre, T. W.: *Trains, Tracks and Travel*, Simmons-Boardman Publishing Co., 1926.

Chapter V

ACCEPTANCE OF THE RAILWAY: EXPANSION OF NET

WITH the close of the fifth decade of the nineteenth century terminated the experimental period in American railway history. In 1850 the railway, tried and found adequate, entered the second stage of its development, which continued through 1873. Various facts mark the opening of the sixth decade as the beginning of a new era. The discovery of gold in California in 1849 compelled a new interest in the West and gave a tremendous stimulus to business activity. Then, too, the vast territory that the victorious conclusion of the Mexican War added to the United States opened a great area for development. Finally, the initiation in 1850 of the federal land-grant policy, the significance of which will be indicated later in the chapter, further served to separate this from the preceding period.

As 1850 marks the beginning of the second period in the growth of the American railway net, so do the early seventies mark its close. The year 1871 witnessed the enactment of the last of a series of land-grant acts designed to stimulate the building of mileage throughout the undeveloped West and Southwest. Immediately following the Civil War, too, there came a change in public attitude toward the railway, a change partly attributable to resentment against abuses, but more largely, perhaps, to failure to understand the essential nature of the railway business. This reaction found expression in various regulatory acts, some of which were not passed until 1874, but all of which resulted, nevertheless, from the agitation of an earlier date. But perhaps the fact that marks 1873 definitely as the close of this period is the sharp drop in railway construction immediately following that disastrous year.

Important Factors in Railway Development.—Before beginning a discussion of the outstanding features of this period in railway history, it is desirable to mention certain important factors that modified the course of railway activity. Prior to the panic of 1837, the railway was an unproved agency but one of which much was hoped. During the years between recovery from the results of financial excesses and the close of this first period such rapid progress was made in the solution of engineering difficulties that doubt no longer existed as to the ability of the railway to meet the most exacting demands of shippers. Increased reliance upon the railway by the shipping public resulted in a tremendously greater volume of traffic, and this, in turn, inspired confidence in the enterprise and justified financial support. Second, the discovery of gold in California, with its resultant effect upon business, quickened railway expansion. This stimulus was both direct and indirect. The addition of large amounts of gold to the circulating medium tended to increase prices, which, in turn, augmented business activity. Indirectly it exerted a psychological influence, both at home and abroad, upon those interested in business enterprise, comparable to that of a powerful stimulant upon the physical organism. Though the upward trend of business was sharply interrupted by the panic of 1857, only the outbreak of the Civil War prevented rapid recovery and further expansion. During and after the war, however, excesses of such magnitude again appeared that the panic of 1873 seemed necessary to restore normal conditions.

The Civil War also exerted a deep influence upon enterprise, no less upon the railway than upon industry and commerce. For a decade preceding its outbreak, the jealousies and antagonisms of North and South limited railway expansion. Furthermore, during the war years and the period immediately following there was little construction: the energies of both North and South were largely absorbed in the conflict and little capital was available for any but war purposes. Indeed, in the active war zone a considerable destruction of railway property accompanied each change in control. Though the war resulted temporarily in restricted building, the railway ultimately profited. The hostility between the two sections which finally culminated in war had long blocked all efforts to transform the Pacific railway projects into reality. Withdrawal of the representatives of the seceding states from Congress and the consequent protracted control of Congress by the North offered the desired opportunity. Also, the restlessness of the men who returned from the front and their desire to seek fortune in the undeveloped West did much to furnish an economic basis for railway expansion there. Then, too, the active part played by the railway in military campaigns gave clear proof, if such were needed, of its great utility. And, finally, the inadequacy of waterways in meeting war needs, together with the increased use of the railways in certain sections due to war interruptions of water traffic, greatly strengthened the railway.

Extent of Railway Expansion.—One of the most important as well as most striking characteristics of the development of the American railway net from 1850 to 1873 was the sharp increase in mileage. The number of miles of railway in the United States at the close of 1873 was 68,215, an increase, in less than a quarter of a century and in the face of heavy obstacles, of more than 60,000 miles. The distribution of mileage at the close of this period as among the various sections of the country, an index of the varying force of expansionist tendencies, is indicated in Table III.

TABLE III.—SECTIONAL DISTRIBUTION OF MILEAGE IN THE UNITED STATES, 1873

Area	Mileage	Increase over 1849
New England States	5,374	3,118
Middle Atlantic States, Ohio, Michigan, and Indiana	23,442	20,238
Southern States	12,472	11,036
Midwestern States	17,959	17,862
Louisiana, Arkansas, Indian Territory	636	589
Dakota, Nebraska, Kansas, Texas, and West	8,332	8,332
Total	68,215	61,175

As interesting as the distribution of mileage by sections is its distribution among the various years of the period. By the close of 1859 mileage had grown from 7,310 to 27,420, but during the following decade total mileage added was only 16,091. Construction dropped to 574 miles in 1863 and stood at less than 1,000 miles per year during the years 1862 to 1865, inclusive, with more than half of the total contribution added during the last few years of the decade. The striking rally from subnormal construction during the war years appears in 1869–1873, inclusive, when about 25,000 miles of line were laid. In 1872 alone almost 7,500 miles were built.

Causes of Rapid Mileage Growth.—Several facts explain this rapid extension of mileage. During the early years of railway growth the lack of capital for such development had been an important restrictive element. The supply of funds in the United States, a new country with unusually rich natural resources awaiting utilization, was inadequate to meet the needs of railway construction even when freely offered. But when uncertainty as to the future of the railway discouraged the investment of even these limited funds, it was inevitable that construction should proceed slowly. By the close of the first period, however, the future of the railway appeared certain and the success of many of the earlier projects had been such as to rouse the interest of investor and speculator alike. During the second period, therefore, railway enterprise not only enjoyed the complete confidence of local capital but gained strong foreign support. In speaking of this increased interest, Ripley says, "Enthusiasm grew abroad until as little discrimination came to be applied in supporting all kinds of enterprises as had characterized their (European) condemnation 10 years earlier. Until the panic of 1873 European investors bought our railway securities eagerly." Indeed, many important railway properties in this country which date from that period have enjoyed the continued interest of foreign capital, among these being the Illinois Central and Chicago and North Western. Railway development proceeded rapidly when supported thus by the possessors of funds both at home and abroad.

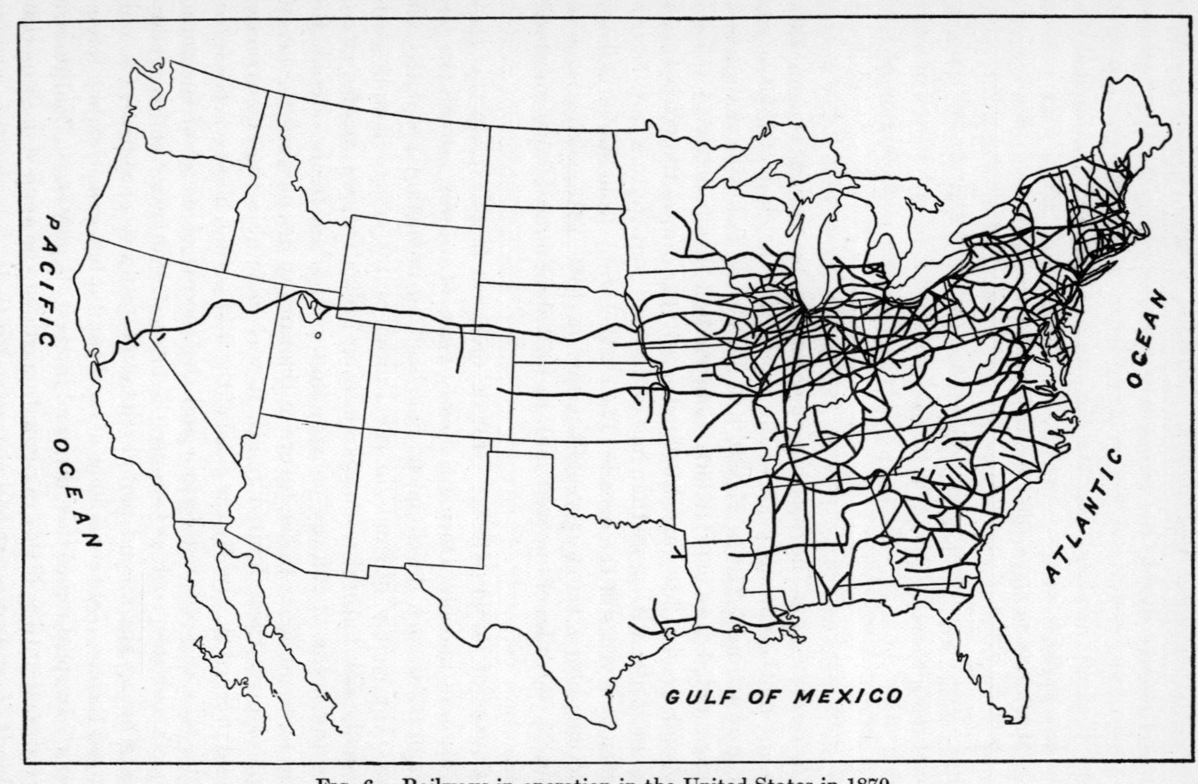

Fig. 6.—Railways in operation in the United States in 1870.

It was but natural that the railway situation should appear encouraging, particularly during the immediate postwar years. To the westward lay a broad and fertile area which promised to become the granary of the world. Beyond the prairies lay the mountains which imagination endowed with unparalleled mineral wealth. Into these new areas were pressing thousands upon thousands of restless Americans and into them was also flowing a constant stream of thrifty and hard-working European immigrants. The opportunity seemed indeed golden, and sharp struggles ensued in many of the newer sections between groups interested in establishing prior claim to a territory through the early construction of lines. Thousands of miles of railway were built in the Middle West and Southwest during this period to make accessible to market those richer sections which labored under the handicap of distance. By 1873 Michigan, Ohio, Indiana, Wisconsin, Illinois, Iowa, and southern Minnesota were gridironed by the railway beyond the dreams of even the most optimistic in 1850, while farther west the building of the transcontinentals occupied an important place. In the Southwest, also, striking progress had been made, particularly in eastern and southern Texas.

Public Aid an Important Cause.—The rapid increase in mileage, which featured not only this period but also the one following, resulted primarily, however, from the extensive public aid enjoyed by the railways during those years. Though such assistance was not unknown prior to 1850, it was during the 40 years following that it played a striking rôle in railway development. America, with vast areas and tremendous undeveloped resources which could be served efficiently during this period only by the railway, found itself facing that always difficult problem of securing an extension of mileage into new sections which were unable, as yet, to furnish adequate economic support for such enterprises. The essentially individualistic character of early economic life in America, as well as the influence exerted by a *laissez-faire* philosophy, caused government construction and operation of new lines to receive but scant consideration. So positive was the sentiment against the entrance of government into the railway field as an active participant that even an alternative policy, that of government construction followed by transferal of title to private corporations for operation upon such terms as were reasonable in view of the immediate prospects of the property, was given equally scant consideration. But it was obvious that pioneer mileage would increase slowly if compelled to rely for support solely upon private funds in search of investment opportunity. A third method of assuring early and rapid expansion of the railway net remained, namely, that of private construction and operation with such aid toward building from private and governmental sources as the situation demanded. This plan long enjoyed enthusiastic and widespread support.

The reasons underlying this generous aid to railway construction were several. Individuals gave freely in effort and in money because of an expected pecuniary gain. Indeed, the enthusiasm of those along a projected pioneer line was often so great that farms were mortgaged and the mortgages either exchanged for stock (which all too often proved worthless) or, in extreme cases, donated to aid in building the property. This individual interest in railway construction was primarily economic in character; its major purpose was to obtain increased prices for grain, live stock, and other farm products or an increased volume of trade. The desire of frontier communities which hungered for intellectual and social contact with other sections and which regarded the railway as an instrument capable of greatly increasing those contacts served as a further justification for heavy individual sacrifice when sacrifice was essential to secure immediate construction.

Aside from self-interest, which underlay largely individual and local —county, township, and municipal—public aid, there was a larger governmental purpose that prompted state and federal assistance to railways. The utilization of great areas of vacant but fertile land and of exceptional mineral and timber resources awaited only the coming of the railway. To further the prosperity and well-being of the state, or of the nation as a whole, appeared a sound justification of grants of aid; to populate that vast expanse of territory, ranged by Indian and by bison, with tens of thousands of industrious citizens seemed indeed a worthy goal. Then, too, behind state and federal aid lay a political purpose: constant friction with the Indians necessitated adequate and rapid transportation of troops and, further, it could be said of the United States and even the larger states that unity could not be developed except as contacts were increased by improved transportation facilities. It is interesting to note, also, that in the case of federal aid, particularly with respect to grants of land, subventions were justified upon the ground of pecuniary gain to the government. It was freely urged by many that the alternate sections which, under the terms of various grants, remained to the government would be of greater value to it than the entire area without the railway. In the words of Henry Clay, speaking in support of the Illinois grant, such a policy was destined to "bring millions of acres of land immediately into the market which will otherwise remain for years and years entirely unsalable."

As indicated previously, public aid prior to 1850 had played a part in the development of the railway net. Such aid came largely from the states themselves and generally took two forms, of which the more important was the loan. Massachusetts early extended its credit to aid railway construction, as did New York. Virginia followed a definite policy of subscribing for two-fifths of the stock of Virginia projects when the remaining three-fifths of the sum necessary to complete construction had been secured. Pennsylvania and Georgia, as well as Indiana and Michigan in the West, actively embarked upon a program of railway construction. These early grants were of comparatively little importance, however; especially so since construction during early years was confined largely to the more populous and developed portions of the country in which the need of aid was slight. Furthermore, the venture of certain states into the field of construction and operation proved so thoroughly unsatisfactory that the few properties held were soon sold to private corporations, and thought of further expansion by that method was abandoned. Both types of assistance, in fact, resulted in loss to the states involved. One interesting feature of the charters of many of these early state-aided properties was that, after a lapse of a fixed number of years, the state should have the right to take over the property upon fairly compensating stockholders and creditors interested therein. To those who know American railway history it is needless to say that this option was in no instance exercised.

Land Grants in Aid of Railway Construction.—In the years following 1850 railway building was pushed largely in the newer and less developed sections of the United States. This fact, together with a growing enthusiasm for railway construction, led to demands for aid of a far more extended character than during preceding years. Financial aid by the states continued, particularly in the South, and large sums were received from the various local governmental units also. The outstanding feature of public aid, however, and that which was characteristic of the period 1850–1873, was the federal land-grant policy. This was initiated in 1850 by a grant to aid in building the Illinois Central and closed in 1871 with a large grant in behalf of the Texas and Pacific. During this time, too, state grants of land to aid in railway construction were made in the Western area where alone title to public lands remained in the individual state.

That federal land grants had not been made prior to 1850 is explained, perhaps, by the doubt of Congress as to its constitutional power to take such action rather than by its unwillingness to assist. An increasing readiness to construe the Constitution broadly in such matters, coupled with political strategy of high order on the part of Stephen A. Douglas, made possible the Illinois Central grant; but, to minimize legal difficulties, title to the lands that were to assist in financing this line was transferred to the state of Illinois with the understanding that the land be regranted by the state to the railway. With the Illinois Central grant was passed also an act extending aid to the Mobile and Ohio; these properties were to provide railway service between Chicago and the Gulf. Later, under a more liberal construction of the Constitution, it was held that grants might be made directly to the corporation instead of through the states. In consequence, this was done after 1862 for the building of mileage through territories and, beginning with 1866, the same policy was followed with respect to construction through the various states.

In general, the Illinois Central grant was the model for all later acts. Under these acts, the railway received a strip of land 200 feet wide for right-of-way purposes through all public lands traversed and received alternate sections, the even numbered, of land on each side of the line for a distance which varied widely in different grants, with the right of substitution of other public lands within a certain distance of the line for such areas as had previously passed from the hands of the government. In certain of the acts it was provided that the land retained by the government was not to be sold at less than a stipulated figure, perhaps $2.50 an acre. These acts invariably fixed a time limit within which the work must be finished and stated the conditions that should govern the transfer of title to the land, the usual provision here being that, upon the completion of each 20 miles of line, title to the lands along that stretch subject to the grant should pass to the railway. One other provision quite generally overlooked, but one which has proved to be no small burden to the railways, declared that over land-grant roads property and persons moving at the cost of the government shall be transported at reduced rates, that reduction varying among the different roads from 15 per cent less than the regular tariff to free movement. Indeed, by the railways it is claimed that this provision has resulted through the years in an actual net gain to the government despite the apparent liberality of the grants in aid of construction.[1]

Development of Our Land-grant Policy.—The various federal grants made directly or indirectly in aid of railway construction differed most with respect to the amount of land to be transferred per mile of line built. As might be expected, the first grant, to a mid-west project, gave a minimum amount—alternate sections for a distance of 6 miles on each side of the railway; but, as additional grants were made, this distance was increased to a maximum of 40 miles through territories for some of the Western undertakings. This growing generosity on the part of Congress is to be explained upon at least three grounds. As the policy of granting public land to aid in railway construction became more definitely accepted and established, fewer questions were raised concerning the amount of land offered. Furthermore, and perhaps of greater importance, it is obvious that later grants involved areas of little value as compared with the prairie lands of Illinois. And, finally, these later grants were made in behalf of a much more difficult type of construction, the building of the Pacific lines.

[1] "Figures given by the railroads for the 5-year period 1924–1928 show that the benefit accruing to the government through rates lower than commercial rates on account of land grants, in connection with the movement of mail, government materials, and troops, amounted to $21,328,940, or $4,265,788 per year." *Coordination of Motor Transportation*, p. 89.

Although accurate figures showing the exact extent of grants made in aid of railway construction are difficult to secure, it appears that perhaps some 160,000,000 acres passed to the railways during this period under the various federal and state grants.[1] Texas, of the states, was the only primary contributor of importance. The acreage made available in particular years during the land-grant period, 1850–1871, varied widely. The first grants of considerable magnitude were made in 1856, when more than 12,000,000 acres were placed at the disposal of the railways, but the acreage made available in 1862 totaled almost 15,500,000. The banner years, however, were those of 1864 and 1866, when approximately 51,000,000 and 65,000,000 acres, respectively, were offered as an incentive to early construction. These large areas went almost wholly to aid the various Pacific projects, as did the last grants of more than 24,000,000 acres in 1871.

The refusal of Congress, after 1871, to extend further aid to the railways through grants of public lands was due to several causes. Throughout the entire land-grant period there had been strong opposition to the policy, particularly in the Eastern and more populous areas, but noticeable even in the West. Various factors combined to swell this protesting minority into a controlling majority. It was felt that adequate provision had been made for railway mileage through the West by the grants of the sixties and that further aid would represent unquestionably an extravagant use of public lands. Then, too, the position of those who had long championed the husbanding of our land resources for homestead use was greatly strengthened by the tremendous demand for free land that arose with the westward movement of population after the Civil War. A third factor weighing against the extension of further aid was that growing hostility toward the railways which was evidenced so clearly and so positively by the so-called Granger legislation of the early seventies.

The Appearance of Large Railway Systems.—A second important feature of American railway development between 1850 and 1873 was the linear consolidation of short lines and the construction of through lines. As a result of this movement there appeared, during these years, the first of the railway systems which are characteristic of our mileage today. Even in the forties it became evident that the railway was destined to serve in a more significant way than merely to connect water routes or to tap near-lying areas which were inaccessible by water. As intersectional exchange developed, the serious inconvenience entailed by the shipment of goods, even by the movement of persons, over successive short lines appeared. To lessen this handicap to the speedy handling of goods, the

[1] The total area made available to the railways as an incentive to construction is estimated to have exceeded 215,000,000 acres. Of the land granted by the federal government title to some 128,000,000 actually passed to the railways; to this must be added, to obtain the grand total, some 32,150,000 acres received under Texas grants.

fast freight line was established and, as a long step in the same direction, there developed a demand for, and a definite movement toward the adoption of, a standard gage. The coordination and eventual consolidation of many short connecting lines were given further impetus by the dawn of the idea of great railway systems in the minds of such leaders as Vanderbilt and those directing the Pennsylvania and the Baltimore and Ohio. Another reason for the consolidation of short lines, and one of great force, was the westward construction of through lines such as the Erie and the Baltimore and Ohio. To compete successfully with such roads it was absolutely essential that connecting short lines should operate as a unit. Then, too, the enforced cooperation of railways for military purposes during the Civil War emphasized the advantages of unified operation. Finally, during this period certain legal obstacles to the unification of operations disappeared; Pennsylvania, for example, repealed all legislation designed to compel a transfer from one road to another, at or near Erie, of all freight moving between west and east through that portion of the state, thus furthering railway consolidation and the rapid handling of traffic.

The extent to which the consolidation of connecting lines was carried during this period may perhaps be best indicated by example. The New York Central Railroad, operating between New York and Buffalo by way of Albany, represented a consolidation of no less than 12 companies, and Chicago was reached by the absorption of Western lines. The Pennsylvania Railroad from Philadelphia to Pittsburgh was the product of a series of consolidations also; the modern property includes mileage formerly owned by more than 200 separate corporations. Even in the West consolidation was an important factor in the creation of large railway systems: the Chicago and Rock Island, the Chicago and North Western, the Chicago, Burlington, and Quincy, and the Milwaukee and St. Paul all grew rapidly in mileage by this method as well as by construction.

Public Interest and Consolidation.—That public interest was promoted by consolidation is undoubted. It served to make through movements both cheaper and speedier, and aided shippers by making recovery more certain for losses or damages suffered. In speaking before the Windom Committee in 1873, Mr. Worcester, secretary of the New York Central, said in part, "All the permanent and progressive reduction of rates that I have spoken of, and the whole practical efficiency of the entire railroad system, have been due entirely to consolidation or to the concentration of lines originally distinct." Indeed, the riper judgment of students of the railway problem with respect to consolidation might be summed up in the words of the Massachusetts Railroad Commissioners in their 1873 report in which they commented upon British experience with consolidation:

> The evidence seems almost conclusive that positive benefit rather than injury has there resulted from amalgamation so far as it has gone. Not only have the evils anticipated not resulted, but it would seem that the public has invariably been better and more economically served by the consolidated than by the independent companies. . . . The time and attention of the officers are not mainly absorbed in questions of corporate hostility and the money of the companies is wasted in a somewhat less degree in warfare with each other. There is, in fact, far less friction in the work of transportation and far more system.

Despite the manifest advantages flowing from consolidation there were certain aspects of it that gave rise to strong public opposition. In part this opposition was mistaken, as at Erie, Pa., where those whose livelihood depended upon the transfer of goods and persons from one road to another rioted and destroyed property in their efforts to block the development of through movement. However, opposition was better grounded in its protest against the greatly increased powers which combined properties possessed over community life as compared with the individual component lines. Consolidation seemed to threaten the continuance of active competition also, and this, during a period throughout which such implicit reliance was placed in competition as a protector of public weal, might well have been expected to arouse intense antagonism. A further cause for complaint against the policy of consolidation appeared in the increased capitalization which so frequently accompanied the combination of properties. Seldom, indeed, was it that a unified property did not show a capitalization distinctly in excess of the total capitalization of its constituent units, and this was especially true during the intense speculative activity of the closing years of this period. It is probable that popular opposition to the railway, which culminated in the Granger laws, resulted in no small measure from widespread hostility to the consolidation of properties.

Early Proposals to Establish Transcontinental Service.—A third important feature of the period which closed with 1873 was the establishment of transcontinental service over the Union Pacific-Central Pacific line. The first proposal to establish service between the settled East and the Pacific coast was made anonymously in 1819—for this purpose it was suggested that the Bactrian camel be used as a means of communication between water routes. In the next year, and almost a decade before the Rain Hill trial, Robert Mills of Baltimore urged the construction of a portage railway for such distance as might be necessary to connect the upper reaches of the Missouri with the Columbia. During the next 20 years numerous plans were offered. Perhaps the first to suggest the construction of a steam railway was the writer of an editorial in *The Emigrant* of Ann Arbor in 1832, who introduced his proposal with an apology for suggesting a plan which might appear exceedingly visionary. The first advocate of a transcontinental, or Pacific, railroad to gain recognition, however, was Asa Whitney. In 1844 he offered to build a railroad from Lake Superior or the upper Mississippi to the Pacific Northwest, the cost of this line to be defrayed by the sale of lands from a grant which he proposed Congress should give him at a nominal price along the entire route. Throughout the period during which Whitney's plan received consideration, other proposals also took more or less definite form, but without exception these possessed one important common feature—governmental participation. Most of the projects called for private construction and operation with government aid through land grants or loans, though others urged, both because of the expense involved and because of the social and political importance of such a line, that the government itself construct and operate the property.

After the territorial adjustment at the close of the Mexican War, the problem of selecting a route was added to the confusion which resulted from the proposal of many widely divergent methods of financing construction. Prior to that time but a single route was available, one which would reach the Pacific coast near the mouth of the Columbia or at some point on Puget Sound. Following the Mexican cession, however, additional routes were opened, which may be grouped under the heads of central and southern. By 1853 interest in the development of transcontinental service had become so great that Congress authorized an exploration of the possible routes with a view to determining the most feasible. The report was made in 1865 but, in the intervening years, political changes occurred that made action possible without the aid of support such as an unbiased finding might give. Withdrawal of Southern representatives from Congress in 1861 broke the deadlock that had existed respecting routes and made it possible for that body to act with little delay upon proposals to link the East and the Far West.

The Union Pacific-Central Pacific Project.—In 1862 a bill providing for the building of the Union Pacific-Central Pacific line became a law. No work was done upon the project, however, until 1864, when construction eastward was started by the Central Pacific, the Union Pacific beginning its movement westward the following year. Because this project was the first to join the East with the Pacific coast and probably the most difficult to carry through, certain details with respect to it will be noted. Council Bluffs was made the eastern terminus of the line, which assured a satisfactory bridging of the Missouri River, while the Central Pacific built eastward from Sacramento, which had water connections with San Francisco. The two major obstacles faced by those in charge of the Union Pacific, aside from finances which were equally troublesome to both corporations, were the crossing of the continental divide and difficul-[illegible]f building through an area over which warlike and hostile Indian [illegible]ned almost at will. Search for a satisfactory pass occasioned [illegible]y and it is stated that the ultimate discovery of South Pass was made by General Dodge, in charge of the undertaking, by mere chance during a running fight with Indians. Although no record remains of the number of lives lost through Indian raids, it is certain that hundreds of men were killed before the property was completed.

In driving the Central Pacific to the Great Salt Lake, Chief Engineer Judah found his first and perhaps most difficult problem to be that of discovering a pass through the Sierra Nevadas, an even more serious obstacle to railway construction than the continental divide. It is said that Judah located his route by chance also. Noting the flight of an eagle which disappeared into what he had thought to be a solid wall of granite, he investigated the area and found that wall cleft by the only feasible pass for a direct line from Sacramento to the Great Plateau. Besides surmounting the Nevada range, the western line faced two additional problems of great difficulty. Every pound of iron and steel used in the construction of the Central Pacific and every piece of equipment employed in its service had to come from the East and most of it was moved around Cape Horn in clipper ships. Yet even with the material at hand, the management was faced with the seemingly insurmountable difficulty of securing labor. This essential factor was scarce even in the newer sections of the East, but upon the Pacific coast men could not be hired. It was obvious, therefore, that workers must be imported in great numbers. The problem was solved by bringing shipload after shipload of Chinese from the Orient to perform the major part of the work incident to construction. Indeed, had it not been for the service of the Chinese coolie, railway construction in the West would have been long delayed in time and the cost of building would have been greatly increased.

In addition to the two men already named who participated actively in planning and building this first transcontinental railway, others deserve mention. Judah, by great effort, interested in the western section a group of Sacramento merchants, of whom Collis P. Huntington and Leland Stanford later became national figures because of their railway and political activities, and it was by these men that the project was pushed to completion after the early death of Judah himself. Prominent among those interested in the Union Pacific were the Ames brothers, Durant, and Dillon, all of whom devoted great energy to the completion of the project but all of whom were besmirched through their relation with the Crédit Mobilier, which played so active a part in financing the eastern portion of this pioneer Pacific project. But, however much these men and their lieutenants might have exerted themselves, the fact remains that except for unusual government assistance this first transcontinental line must have remained a paper railway for many years: aid was given it in the form not only of lands but also of loans of government credit to the approximate amount of $55,000,000.

Upon the completion of the project an impressive ceremony was held. As the last tie, California laurel, highly polished and bearing an appropriately inscribed silver plate, was slipped into position, four spikes, two of silver and two of gold, were passed to Governor Stanford and Durant who put them in place. When the silver hammer fell a signal indicating the completion of the line was flashed over the wires, and throughout the entire country was celebrated the establishment of railway communication between the East and the West.

Other Pacific Railways.—Although a railway over the central route was the only one of those undertaken which was completed during this second period, others of importance were begun. The Northern Pacific, for which plans were made as early as 1864, began construction in 1870 and at the close of 1873 had built 530 miles of line. Ground was broken for the Atchison, Topeka and Santa Fe a year earlier and at the end of the period it was operating almost 450 miles; the Texas and Pacific, actually begun in 1864, had completed at the close of this period 283 miles of line to the westward. The Southern Pacific, originally intended to join the Texas and Pacific at the Colorado River, had built 102 miles of line by 1869, to which were added from 1871 to 1873 an additional 172 miles. During the following years of railway development all of the projects mentioned, together with others, were pushed forward to completion, thus making available to the public prior to 1893 numerous routes from the Middle West to thc Pacific coast.

(See close of Chap. VI for references.)

CHAPTER VI

ACCEPTANCE OF THE RAILWAY: REGULATIONS AND GENERAL POLICIES

ANOTHER distinguishing and significant feature of the second period in the development of the American railway net was the demand for regulation that crystallized in the so-called Granger laws. Despite the eagerness with which the railway had been accepted, the "coming of the rails" sought and celebrated, some semblance of regulation had been attempted by the several states from the beginning. The basis of such control had been, in general, the charter. Early charters followed closely in form those of American turnpike and canal companies, also the English railway charters of that period. Though it was generally declared that the company might charge "such rates per mile as may be agreed upon and established from time to time by the board of directors of said corporation," maximum rates for the movement of both freight and passengers were often set and occasionally it was provided that the legislature might reduce rates if a return were earned in excess of a stipulated percentage. Some charters required publicity of rates and a few sought to bar discrimination, though this difficulty was quite unforeseen by most legislatures. It was generally assumed that charter provisions would be self-executory or enforceable through ordinary legal channels, but occasional provision was made for administrative control.

Early Commission Activities.—That public interest might be safeguarded more effectively, Rhode Island created in 1836 a commission with the power,

> . . . upon complaint or otherwise, whenever a majority of them shall deem it expedient, personally to examine into any or all of the transactions or proceedings of any railroad corporation that now is, or hereafter may be, authorized and established in this state, in order to secure to all the citizens and inhabitants of the same the full and equal privileges of the transportation of passengers and property at all times that may be granted, either directly or indirectly, by such corporation to the citizens of another state or states.

In 1845 New Hampshire made provision for a commissioner who possessed broad powers of inquiry and was required to collect railway data. And prior to 1860 Connecticut, Vermont, New York, and Maine had acted along similar lines. However, none of these commissions was permitted to exercise positive control, which was equally true of the Massachusetts commission created in 1869.

None the less, the creation of the Massachusetts commission represented a long forward step in the direction of control in public interest of the railways of that state. The powers and duties of this body were (1) to determine whether railway corporations were complying with charter and statutory requirements; (2) to advise the railways concerning "the security and accommodation of the public"; (3) to investigate the railways upon complaint or upon its own motion and to summon witnesses and compel testimony under oath from them; (4) to prescribe a uniform system of railway accounts and inspect corporate records; (5) to arbitrate disputes between railways and public; (6) to submit an annual report to the legislature setting forth "the actual working of the system of railroad transportation in its bearing upon the business and prosperity of the commonwealth," and suggest such legislation as seemed needful for the adequate protection of public interest. This commission, functioning in a conservative community in which construction was largely completed and dealing with properties locally owned as well as managed to the general satisfaction of the people served, succeeded from the first.

Public Complaints against Rate Levels.—Ineffective as was the charter in the older sections of the United States, it was of even less worth in the newer areas. So eager were the areas for additional mileage and so little care was given to charter provisions that where corporate grants were not fragmentary in character they were valueless as instruments of control. For a period complaints against the railway were sporadic and local but, because of certain abuses, real and imagined, which appeared incident to the construction and operation of pioneer properties, criticism later became general and continued. The grounds for criticism were varied, but perhaps the rate level was subject to greatest attack. A higher level of rates than prevailed in the East was possible in many sections of the West because of the monopolistic position that the railway occupied; but such higher level was often necessary because Western traffic was less in volume and generally of relatively low-grade commodities. While the prices of agricultural products had declined sharply following the close of the Civil War, railway rates had remained almost stationary. This increased the burden of rates markedly and the public was in a mood to follow any leadership that promised a reduction of that burden, whether the reduction was justified by railway costs or not: monopolistic oppression was urged as the sole explanation, and relief through regulation was demanded.

Other Complaints against the Railways.—In addition to the complaint against the rate level the appearance of discrimination had inflamed the public. This discrimination was both personal and place in character but, more conspicuously the latter—and it was this place discrimination which peculiarly inflamed those located at noncompetitive points. Actual sacrifices in aid of railway building had been made more often by community and individuals alike at such points than at the favored competitive points. To the locality that had bonded itself heavily to aid construction, to the farmer who had contributed in money and time, perhaps mortgaged his farm to secure the contribution asked, nothing could be more offensive than preference shown to points where such sacrifices had not been made. To argue the economic necessities of competition was worse than useless. When to high rates and discrimination was joined a railway policy well expressed by the words ascribed to Commodore Vanderbilt, "The public be damned," it is not strange that the independent and aggressive pioneer did a bit of damning himself. No more unpromising ground for the arrogance of railway management existed than the West, where arrogance was substituted all too often for diplomacy.

Public opinion at this time was affected unfavorably, also, by the numerous financial scandals incident to railway construction and control. The construction company, of which the Crédit Mobilier of the Union Pacific was a current and odorous example, was employed generally and so utilized by insiders as to rouse a strongly adverse public criticism. Sharp, even fraudulent financial practices, so well illustrated by the manipulation of Erie securities by the Gould-Drew-Fisk interests, which resulted in burdening properties with excessive capitalization upon which it was hoped that the public might be mulcted for a return, further estranged public confidence and support. Then, too, financial reorganization and readjustment frequently resulted in squeezing out smaller interests, often the general public, to the advantage of controlling groups, a practice that deeply stirred those injured. Yet, before this background of manipulation and fraud, in the face of heavy financial losses suffered in the West through railway investments and through adverse general conditions, the officials of these corporations, owned largely in the East and in Europe, appeared in hamlet and city alike with silk hat, frock coat, white gloves, and patent boots; they typified prosperity to the hard-pressed Western farmer whose very home, often clouded with a mortgage, was jeopardized during many of the hard years. Here appears another explanation of Granger legislation—the apparent prosperity of foreign corporations which, in the face of local poverty, continued rates adjusted to a higher level of prices for farm products.

The Appearance of Positive Control.—This change in attitude toward the railway in the years following the war resulted in action by certain states. The battle, first fought out at the polls, was transferred to legislative halls, and from there to the highest courts, state and federal. While an older state, Massachusetts, was content to meet the situation with an advisory commission, the demand for positive control was overwhelming in the West. Mandatory action first took the form of prescriptive legislation. Illinois in 1871 enacted laws that fixed maximum fares, prohibited extortionate and discriminatory freight rates, and established a commission without extended powers. Minnesota in the same year fixed by law a schedule of maximum rates and fares and provided for a railway commissioner to gather data and administer the regulatory act. In 1874 Wisconsin placed upon the statute books the Potter law, which not only fixed maximum charges for both freight and passenger service but also established a commission of the mandatory type. And in 1874 Iowa, after a bitter political campaign, passed the maximum rate law, which was intended to accomplish the equalization of rates and the elimination of unreasonable discrimination. This last-named statute is of particular interest because by it railways were classified upon the basis of gross earnings per mile of line and those with lower gross earnings were permitted a higher level of rates. Though it was the action of these states that largely gave title to the so-called Granger legislation, other states also acted in response to the wave of popular protest against the railways and railway policies. Federal interest in the problem did not at this time go beyond authorization by Congress of the Windom Committee, which reported in 1874.

This committee, headed by Senator Windom of Minnesota, declared the significant need of the period to be lower rates. Clinging to the belief that competition constituted the major defense of the shipping public, the committee made two recommendations. First, it was urged that natural waterways be improved and certain canals be constructed to provide competition along the main channels of traffic movement. As a further means of forcing rates downward it was suggested that, under the power possessed by Congress to establish postroads, a railway should be built from the Mississippi River to the Atlantic seaboard. This railway was to be owned and operated by the government and was to render freight service upon such terms as would insure a reasonable level of rates between the Middle West and the East over lines privately owned and operated. Another and a more fundamentally sound recommendation made by this committee was for the establishment of governmental control over railway capitalization and financial policies. Even at this early date the practices of railway promoter and manipulator had become malodorous.

Validity of Regulatory Acts.—Defeated after a bitter struggle in their opposition to the enactment of positive regulatory measures, the railways had immediate resort to the courts. Regulatory acts which imposed serious limitations and acts which transferred to administrative bodies broad powers were attacked, in general, upon three grounds. (1) It was urged that the railway business was private in nature. Throughout almost a half century of development its public obligation had not been emphasized and, in consequence, management was loath to accept the principle that the enterprise was henceforth to be regarded as "burdened with the public interest." (2) It was contended that the typical charter provision, bestowing upon directors and officers the right to collect such rates and fares as they, in their judgment, saw fit, debarred the legislature from regulating charges: the interpretation of the charter as set forth in the Dartmouth College case was urged as guaranteeing protection against public interference. (3) Numerous of these early laws were contested upon the ground that their provisions were repugnant to the federal Constitution; it was asserted that they amounted to a regulation of interstate commerce, which power had been expressly delegated to Congress.

These major propositions and others of lesser importance were urged upon the lower courts and upon the United States Supreme Court with great force in the Granger cases, but, despite the appeal that the carriers made to Constitution, statute, and charter, the final decision was adverse to them upon every point. After giving its approval to the common-law principle that "when private property is devoted to public use, it is subject to public regulation" and declaring that "a power of government which actually exists is not lost by non-user," the United States Supreme Court accepted without question the principle that carrier property is burdened with a public interest and therefore subject to governmental control.[1] That general charter provisions recognizing the right of the corporation to fix a scale of charges for services rendered by it did not constitute an exemption from public control was also upheld by the courts.[2]

> It was within the power of the company to call upon the legislature to fix permanently this limit and make it a part of the charter; and, if it was refused, to abstain from building the road and establishing the contemplated business. If that had been done the charter might have presented a contract against future legislative interference. But it was not; and the company invested its capital relying upon the good faith of the people and the wisdom and impartiality of legislators for protection against wrong under the form of legislative regulation.

And again, the Court quotes with approval from counsel,[3]

> The privilege, then, of charging whatever rates it may deem proper is a franchise which may be taken away under the reserve power[4] but the right to charge a reasonable compensation would remain as a right under the general law governing natural persons and not as a special franchise of privilege.

In answer to the contention that state regulation represented an infringement upon federal rights the Court declared, in the Munn case, while speaking of grain elevators,[5]

[1] *Munn v. Illinois,* 94 U. S. 113.

[2] *Chicago, Burlington and Quincy Railroad Company v. Cutts,* 94 U. S. 155.

[3] *Peik v. Chicago and North Western Railway Company,* 94 U. S. 164.

[4] This charter was secured from Wisconsin, the constitution of which allows amendment at will by the legislature.

[5] *Munn v. Illinois,* 94 U. S. 113.

Incidentally they may become connected with interstate commerce but not necessarily so. Their regulation is a thing of domestic concern and certainly until Congress acts in reference to their interstate relations, the state may exercise all the powers of government over them, even though in so doing it may indirectly operate upon commerce outside its new jurisdiction.

And again, in the Cutts case, which dealt with the regulation of railways, it said,[1]

This road, like the warehouse in that case [Munn], is situated within the limits of a single state, its business is carried on there and its regulation is a matter of domestic concern. It is employed in state as well as in interstate commerce and, until Congress acts, the state must be permitted to adopt such rules and regulation as may be necessary for the promotion of the general welfare of the people within its own jurisdiction, even though in so doing those without may be indirectly affected.

In the Peik case the Supreme Court went still further and approved limited state regulation of interstate commerce until such time as Congress had acted. At every point, then, the public scored a sweeping legal victory over the railways.

Recession of Movement toward Positive Control.—This legal victory was far more sweeping, however, than the economic success of railway regulation by statute and commission during this period. Even before the Supreme Court had handed down its decisions in the Granger cases early in 1877, many of the states that had imposed restrictions upon the carriers had either repealed such restrictions or so modified them as largely to remove carrier opposition. The causes for this reversal in policy were several. Railway supporters urged strongly the partial responsibility of such control for the sorry financial plight of the carriers following the panic of 1873 and urged, too, the necessity of a change in public policy if financial rehabilitation were to be effected and further construction undertaken. Furthermore, in many jurisdictions mandatory action had failed to secure the desired results. This failure was due to three factors, mainly. Certain of the laws were not drawn with sufficient care to accomplish the purposes actuating their enactment and few of them made adequate provision for enforcement, with the result that in some cases the law was practically a dead letter. Furthermore, carrier opposition was at all times strong and relatively skillful. Then, too, the seeming success of the advisory commission, notably that of Massachusetts, encouraged those states in which mandatory control had succeeded badly, for one or several reasons, to modify their policy. This method of dealing with the carriers was not only urged by many upon impartial grounds but enjoyed the enthusiastic support of the carriers. And here appears a final reason for a change in policy by many states: the railways had accepted the

[1] *Ibid.*

political challenge that was offered by regulation. Interested only incidentally and spasmodically in politics prior to this time, the carriers now set about with consummate skill molding public opinion, reaching out for the control not only of the legislative and executive departments of government but also of the judiciary. Thus regulation, or the determination to ward off regulation, drew the railways into a field in which they played an active and not particularly savory part from 1870 onward for almost 40 years. During those years it was commonly recognized that certain railways exerted a continued and controlling influence in particular states. Only by persistent and tremendous effort were public leaders able to crowd this undesirable rider from the political saddle in the early years of the new century.

In consequence of these various influences, positive control was abandoned by Minnesota in 1875, by Wisconsin in 1876, and by Iowa in 1878. The example of these states was followed somewhat later by other states, among them being Tennessee, South Carolina, and Kentucky. Illinois alone, among the states that acted during this initial period, held fast, retaining its Railroad and Warehouse Commission, to which had been given power to fix reasonable rates. Thus ended a movement that represented a striking change in public attitude toward the railway. In speaking of this change Ringwalt makes this interesting comment,

> It seemed to be considered a prominent part of the duty of legislatures and Congress to devise methods for regulating railways and modes of conducting railway operations after 1870, whereas previous to that time the chief concern of the national and state law makers was to devise measures for facilitating the construction of new lines. It is to be regretted that the amount of wisdom brought to both of these tasks fell considerably below the desired quantity.

Perhaps it is not amiss to add that legislatures and Congress continued for many years to act with less than needed wisdom upon railway questions.

The Appearance of Competition.—The conditions surrounding early construction and operation were such as to prevent the appearance of active railway competition throughout the first period of development. During this second period, however, competition developed rapidly and became a seriously disturbing factor by the late sixties. The reasons for this change were several. In the first place, the consolidation of connecting lines and the construction of through lines, mentioned earlier, brought properties into direct conflict in their struggle for business. This was true not only of the business of particular centers, but also of the business of large areas; with the completion of the New York Central and the Erie to points on Lake Erie, and the Pennsylvania and the Baltimore and Ohio to points on the Ohio River, sharp competition developed for control of the heavy tonnage moving into and out of Western territory.

This type of competition was fostered by keen rivalry between important market centers such as Baltimore, Philadelphia, New York, and Boston in the East, and St. Louis and Chicago in the Middle West. Another factor that stimulated railway rivalry during this period was the construction of mileage greatly in excess of the economic needs of the territory served. Yet it is only fair to add that, even though this situation had not existed, the very nature of the railway business would have encouraged outbreaks of rate cutting such as occurred during the latter part of this period and the early years of the one succeeding. Subject to the operation of the law of increasing returns, even a group of uniformly prosperous carriers become involved finally in a struggle to obtain additional traffic except as some method of cooperation serves to check such action.

Although rate fluctuations had been experienced earlier, the full force of competition did not appear until about 1868, but from that time forward cutthroat, rather than normal, competition was characteristic until effective methods of cooperation were developed. Perhaps nowhere was the intensity of the struggle greater than in that portion of the country now known as Trunk Line territory. Illustrative of the wide and rapid movement in rates the following data serve excellently:

TABLE IV.—NEW YORK-CHICAGO RATES, FIRST CLASS
In cents per hundredweight

Date	Rate	Date	Rate
1869:		1869:	
Feb. 4	188	Oct. 13	125
Feb. 24	40	Nov 1	140
Mar. 15	160	Nov. 29	150
July 1	188	1870:	
July 31	70	June 13	112
Aug. 4	40	July 12	80
Aug. 5	30	July 25	65
Aug. 7	25	July 28	50
Aug. 30	43	Aug. 22	100
Sept. 30	30	Sept. 8	125
Oct. 4	50	Nov. 28	160
Oct. 9	75	Dec. 26	180

This fluctuation continued in 1871, when rates dropped as low as \$0.30 per hundredweight, first class, and rose to \$1.25; also, in 1872 and 1873, when maximum and minimum figures were \$0.75 and \$0.27, \$1.25 and \$1, respectively. That the struggle for particular commodities was equally keen, perhaps keener, is shown by the brief quotation of a rate of \$1 per car for live stock from Buffalo to New York City by the two carriers serving between those points. Passenger business was also affected by the competitive activities of rival carriers, but ridiculously low rates did not appear prominently in this field until the following period, except for a short time during the late fifties.

Efforts to Control Competition.—So disturbing and so destructive did competition become that definite and positive efforts to establish control were inevitable. As early as 1854 agreements among the New York Central, Erie, Pennsylvania, and Baltimore and Ohio were reached which led President J. E. Thomson of the Pennsylvania to say in his annual report covering that year,

> With a view of agreeing upon general principles which should govern railroad companies in competing for the same trade, and preventing *ruinous competition*, a free interchange of opinions took place during the past year between the officers of the four leading east-and-west lines, and also with those of their western connections. The influence of these conferences, it is believed, will be felt in reducing expenses, correcting abuses, and adding to the net revenue of the several companies, while the public will be served with equal efficiency and greater safety.

The failure of this agreement to hold competition in leash led to a second attempt in 1858, when the presidents of each of the four trunk lines named above conferred, to quote President Thomson again, "for the purpose of agreeing upon remunerative rates, abolishing injudicious practices, and effecting a harmony of purpose conducive to the mutual advantage of the railway and the public." The resulting agreement covered not merely passenger business, but also certain classes of freight traffic, especially east-bound livestock movements and west-bound merchandise tonnage. It provided, further, for a referee with authority to render a binding decision should those party to the agreement be unable to arrange a mutually satisfactory settlement of controversies arising thereunder.

Efforts on the part of carriers operating in competitive areas during this period to maintain peace through agreement upon rates were both widespread and open. Failing to accomplish this purpose through the simple agreement, Commodore Vanderbilt, of the New York Central, sought to perfect the machinery at the Saratoga Conference, called after the disastrous rate wars of the years from 1868 to 1873, by giving to a central board the power to fix rates and prescribe rules. That this plan should rouse intense public opposition because of its apparent monopolistic character was but natural; that certain of the competing carriers rejected it seems strange, however, until it is realized that rejectors were weaker lines striving to secure a larger proportion of the competitive tonnage, a goal that could be attained only through competitive activity, with financial shipwreck as the price of failure. Experience showed clearly that the simple agreement, as an agency of control, gave no assurance of the curtailment of destructive warfare. In the hope of gaining increased assurance of financial stability for all properties, the pool was substituted for the less formal arrangement. This form of agreement was early employed in New England, but its first important application was to all competitive traffic handled by the railways between Omaha and Chicago. Since the pool is more characteristic of the succeeding period, however, it will be described in the next chapter.

Financial Aspects of Construction and Operation.—During this period the financial aspects of railway construction and operation became significant for the first time. Although building before 1850 was comparatively active, railway mileage had absorbed, prior to that year, an amount of capital somewhat less than $300,000,000. During the ensuing decade, however, expansion was rapid, with the result that at its close the investment figure was slightly in excess of $1,150,000,000, a tremendously large sum, both absolutely and relatively, to be devoted to a single type of enterprise in America at that time. Yet, however large looms railway investment prior to 1860, the astounding fact appears in the approximate doubling of that investment during the decade following. Despite the Civil War, railway projects had appealed so strongly to domestic and foreign capital that in 1870 railway properties represented an actual outlay in excess of $2,200,000,000, and this figure must have been increased to little less than $3,000,000,000 as the result of rapid construction in the closing years of the period. That heavy investment in railway enterprises, many of which seemed to lack any immediate economic justification, should have an important influence upon the general financial situation of the country was inevitable. This influence was evidenced most strikingly in the panics of the period, particularly those of 1857 and 1873, though the minor "flurry" of 1854 first indicated a causal connection to those interested.

In an effort to explain the financial difficulties faced in 1854 the annual report of the Pennsylvania Railroad for the following year suggested various factors: hostilities in Eastern Europe with a resultant tightening up of investment funds abroad, excessive credit expansion, fraudulent activities on the part of railway management, and injudicious construction. In closing, this statement appears:

> Although to some extent sufferers from the difficulties attending this condition of the money market, we cannot but feel satisfied that the general good will, in the end, be advanced by the timely check placed upon many of the schemes of improvement that had been commenced and were maturing throughout the west, as well as in our own state. It is hoped that the lessons of the past will be a warning to capitalists to use greater discrimination in the future in the investment of the means with which fortune has favored them.

Late in 1854, President Pierce, in his annual message to Congress, seriously questioned the wisdom of stimulating railway construction through grants of public lands, saying that, "if constructed by private capital, the stimulant and the check go together, and furnish a salutary restraint against speculative schemes and extravagance." Commenting upon the situation in 1857 the *American Engineer* of Aug. 29, 1857, declared: "There are one thousand million dollars invested in railroads in the United States, and where it has been believed that this property could pay $70,000,000 yearly, it does not pay $40,000,000—a yearly deficit of more than $30,000,000." This last statement indicates that experience early brought out the essential nature of that explanation of crises now rather generally known as the overcapitalization theory.

However, if railway construction and finance were closely related to financial collapse in the fifties, these two factors were inextricably interwoven in the severe crash of September, 1873, a crash that weighed heavily not only upon railways but also upon industry, agriculture, and commerce, for some years to follow. During the years preceding the panic of 1873, railway building had gone forward by leaps and bounds. Much of the new mileage was situated in undeveloped areas and owed its existence to generous public aid, particularly to grants of land. Early in 1873 the results of overreaching were in evidence: a decline of prices, a "superabundance of railway securities." The first definite blow to public confidence was struck by the collapse of a small Eastern property, and this was immediately followed by a second failure which left the financial structure a mass of ruins. This second was the failure of Jay Cooke and Company and the collapse of closely affiliated financial houses. Fundamentally responsible for the bankruptcy of this firm of international repute was an agreement under the terms of which the Northern Pacific project was underwritten. By this agreement the banking house contracted to dispose of a sufficient amount of bonds from time to time to meet construction costs, a task beyond its power both because of the general overextension of railway mileage and credit and the dubious prospect of this project in particular. The general collapse of 1873 forced the thorough reorganization of weaker railway properties, seriously embarrassed even the strongest, and reduced construction to a minimum for several years. Time was needed to insert an economic substructure beneath many of the projects begun or completed during the latter part of this period—railways lured into being far in advance of public need by the attractive bait of public aid and the glowing promises of glib-tongued promoters.

Progress toward Plant Efficiency.—Among other matters of interest during this period was a distinct forward movement in the mechanics of railway construction and operation. American roadway standards were steadily improved and to this end nothing contributed more than did a beginning in the substitution of the steel rail for the iron. This was made possible by the development of the Bessemer process and occurred during the latter part of the period. The general substitution of iron and masonry for the old type of covered wooden structure greatly improved bridge construction. Numerous large and important streams were bridged for the first time by the railway, among them being the Mississippi, the Ohio, and the Monongahela. Advancement in types of both locomotives and locomotive construction was in evidence: the consolidation and mogul types of greatly increased size and tractive power appeared, and in locomotive construction the steel tire and the use of steel in fire box and boiler represented long forward strides. It was early during this period, too, that the first successful coal-burning locomotives were put into service after long experimentation and numerous failures. Car construction progressed, in the freight field as to both capacity and mechanical perfection; in the passenger, primarily as to comfort. Of the many improvements in the passenger car none was more important than those made by George Pullman, who constructed, in 1864, the first satisfactory sleeping car operated upon American railways.

In the operation of trains two forward steps of fundamental significance were made: the utilization of the telegraph and the development and application of the Westinghouse air brake. Telegraphic communication removed the major obstacle to certainty and speed of train movement, thereby increasing traffic capacity greatly, and the air brake gave the engineer such a degree of control over his train that it gained immediate acceptance even in an undeveloped form. First employed in the late sixties, this improvement quickly displaced hand braking on passenger trains and ultimately supplanted it in every field of operation.

Consequences of Decline in Railway Charges.—The general decline in the level of railway charges during this period as compared with the one preceding also deserves comment. In a summary made by Ringwalt for the year 1848, it appears that the average charge per passenger-mile for first- and second-class passenger service, covering more than 6,700 miles of line, was 3.6 and 3.21 cents, respectively, the state averages varying from a minimum of 2.43, first class, in Massachusetts, and 1.50, second class, in New York, to 5.35 for both classes in Mississippi. For first- and second-class freight the average rates per ton-mile for the entire country were 8.97 and 6.16 cents, the extreme figures being 4 cents, first class, in Vermont, and 3.12 cents, second class, in Maryland, and 24.3 and 17.3 cents, respectively, for Mississippi. Although wholly comparable figures are not available for a later period, a marked change in the general level of freight charges is indicated by the fact that in 1870 average ton-mile earnings for the New York Central, the Erie, and the Pennsylvania were 1.853, 1.333, and 1.549 cents, respectively. The decline in passenger charges was comparatively less, however, an improved service being offered instead.

During this period also the railways first gave clear evidence of the great part that they were to play in the commerce of the country. Perhaps this growth in traffic importance can be shown no better than by comparing the tonnage statistics of the Erie Canal and the essentially parallel rail lines, the New York Central and the Erie. In 1856 those three agencies moved 2,107,678, 776,112, and 943,215 tons, respectively, and in 1872 the figures stood 3,662,560, 4,393,965, and 5,564,274 tons. Canal tonnage increased, but that increase was negligible as compared with that of the competing rail lines. Gains were registered by the railways at the expense of lake traffic also in the movement of wheat and flour, particularly the latter, with respect to which a sharp decline occurred in lake shipments in favor of rail. Another indication of the preponderant part played by railways toward the close of this period appears in the statement of internal-revenue collections from the various agencies upon the basis of a 2½ per cent tax on gross receipts; the railways contributed, in 1867, a total of $4,128,255.24, more than ten times the sum received from all other sources, the largest single figure other than railway receipts being less than $250,000 from stage coaches!

Extent of the Railway Net.—At the close of this period, there were practically no centers of importance that were not linked by rail with the older and more highly developed areas. Chicago was reached in the early fifties from the East, and shortly thereafter St. Louis and other points on the Mississippi were gained, from which lines were soon extended to the Missouri at several points. St. Paul and Duluth were joined by rail with the East and the completion of the first transcontinental linked the Pacific coast with country east of the Missouri. Numerous lines had also been constructed in the South serving the more important areas as well as all the larger centers, among them being Memphis, Nashville, New Orleans, Mobile, and Norfolk. By the close of this era the framework of the railway structure east of the Missouri and Mississippi had been constructed and needed, in the main, only filling in. But to the west lay a great empire awaiting the coming of the rails.

REFERENCES

Bogart, E. L.: *Economic History of the United States*, Longmans Green & Co., 1915.

Callender, G. S.: *Selections from the Economic History of the United States*, 1765–1860, Ginn & Company, 1909.

Carter, C. F.: *When Railroads Were New*, Henry Holt & Company, 1909.

Cleveland, F. A., and F. W. Powell: *Railroad Promotion and Capitalization*, Longmans, Green & Co., 1909.

Davis, J. P.: *The Union Pacific Railway*, S. C. Griggs and Co., 1894.

Dodge, G. M.: *How We Built the Union Pacific Railway*, Government Printing Office. Printed as Senate Document 447, 61st Congress, 1st Session.

Gephart, W. F.: Transportation and Industrial Development in the Middle West, *Columbia University Studies*, vol. 34, No. 1.

HANEY, LEWIS: A Congressional History of Railways in the United States, 1850–1885, *University of Wisconsin Bulletin* 342.

JOHNSON, E. R., and others: *History of Commerce in the United States*, Carnegie Institute of Washington, 1915.

MARTIN, GEORGE W.: Reasons for Railway Land Grants, *Railway Age*, vol. 92, p. 214.

MEYER, B. H.: *History of Transportation in the United States before* 1860, Carnegie Institute of Washington, 1917.

PHILLIPS, U. B.: *History of Transportation in the Eastern Cotton Belt*, Columbia University Press, 1908.

RIEGEL, R. E.: *The Story of the Western Railroads*, The Macmillan Company, 1926.

RINGWALT, J. L.: *Development of Transportation Systems in the United States*, J. L. Ringwalt, 1888.

RIPLEY, W. Z.: *Railroads: Finance and Organization*, Longmans, Green & Co., 1915.

———: *Railway Problems*, Ginn & Company, 1913.

THOMPSON, SLASON: *A Short History of American Railways*, D. Appleton & Company, 1925.

United States Senate, Document 43, 72d Congress, 1st Session, *Coordination of Motor Transportation*, pp. 89–90, United States Government Printing Office.

VAN METRE, T. W.: *Trains, Tracks, and Travel*, Simmons-Boardman Publishing Co., 1926.

WARMAN, CY.: *The Story of the Railroad.* D. Appleton & Company, 1898.

WHITE, H. K.: *History of the Union Pacific Railway*, University of Chicago Press, 1895.

Ninth Census of the United States.

Chapter VII

GENESIS OF THE RAILWAY PROBLEM: MILEAGE EXTENSION AND FINANCE

IF, AS one writer has suggested, the first period in the development of American railways be regarded as the infancy of that great enterprise and the second as the age of youth, then it may be truly said that during this, the third period, maturity was attained both in size and in capacity for effective public service. Indeed, at the close of this period, the railways stood ready to serve beyond the economic capacity of the country to support such service adequately—a fact that has had in the years since an important bearing upon their status.

Marking off this third period from the one preceding is the panic of 1873 with its consequences, direct and incidental—the decline in construction of new lines and the financial reorganization of many properties already wholly or partially completed, together with the disappearance for a time, especially in the West, of the insistent demand for the stringent regulation of railways. During the depression which followed this sharp collapse, funds would have been difficult to secure for the most promising of enterprises, but after the unbounded confidence of American and foreign investor alike had been well-nigh destroyed by the thoroughness of the financial disaster which overtook many promising projects, it is not strange that construction declined sharply for a time. And the anomaly of regulating railways because of excessive rates, when much of the mileage in those sections where patrons demanded regulation most insistently was in the hands of receivers, become apparent to legislatures in the Granger states upon which the burden of the depression rested perhaps most heavily. It might be added, however, that the possibilities of intelligent and constructive regulation were never greater for railway and public alike. At the close of the period there developed a situation somewhat comparable to that faced at its beginning—the panic of 1893, with its resultant cessation in construction and general financial overhauling and reorganization of railway properties. The panic of 1873 caused a temporary cessation in spectacular extensive development; the panic of 1893 marked its end.

Influence of Extraneous Events.—During this third period, railway development was influenced materially by three extraneous occurrences. Although each of these operated as a causative factor upon the railway, in reality an interaction existed which makes it difficult even now for students to distinguish cause and effect unerringly. The first of these occurrences was the rapid westward movement of population which featured this period as it has perhaps none other in American history since the first great trek across the Appalachian Barrier. The magnitude of this movement is clearly seen in the population figures for 1870 and 1890. The census of the former year showed 10,471,630 people, a little more than a fourth of the national total, in Illinois, Wisconsin, and the states west of the Mississippi. In the next 20 years the population of this western area more than doubled while that of the remainder of the United States increased but slightly more than 40 per cent. During this period Kansas and Nebraska alone showed a growth in population of 2,000,000—four times the combined population for 1870. Many of the newer states in the Mountain territory enjoyed an even more striking development; the state of Washington in 1890 had more than fifteen times the number of inhabitants that it had in 1870.

A second development clearly apparent during this third period and particularly from the late seventies down to about 1891 was the movement toward industrialization. The extent of this movement is best shown, perhaps, by the following figures:

Year	Number of establishments	Number of employees	Amount of capital	Value of products
1870	252,148	2,053,996	$2,118,208,769	$4,232,325,442
1880	253,852	2,732,595	2,790,272,606	5,369,579,191
1890	355,415	4,251,613	6,525,156,486	9,372,437,238

The influence of the panic of 1873 is clearly apparent in the slower rate of progress made in the decade prior to 1880 as compared with the following 10 years. Industrial progress was both intensive and extensive: additional plants were established in older areas and in new industrial districts, and new enterprises were developed. Extensive progress was probably the more important, however, and served as a basis for the further expansion of the railway net, just as the other necessitated a minor intensive growth.

A third factor was the series of financial crises which occurred throughout the period. Of these the most serious marked its close—the panic of 1893, of which more is said later. Nevertheless, the brief disturbance of 1884, often called the railroad panic because of the important part which too rapid building played in precipitating the crisis, also left its mark, as did the less important hesitation in 1891 that followed the Baring collapse. Had any one of these three important factors been lacking, the course of railway development would have been materially modified in the score of years here under discussion.

The Increase in Railway Mileage.—Without doubt the most striking feature of the two decades embraced within the third period is the increase of mileage, an increase which was nothing short of spectacular. With but 68,215 miles of railway in operation at the close of 1873, official records show 176,461 miles completed by midyear in 1893, with a probable total of approximately 177,500 miles at the close of the year—an addition of about 109,000 miles within a score of years, an average of nearly 5,500 miles per year. Never in history has there appeared another such long-sustained orgy of railway building and it is doubtful that the world will ever again witness such a mad forward drive of "the end of the rails" as characterized this era in America. But not the total figure alone is of interest; the distribution of this construction by years reflects strikingly the financial and speculative temper of the period. As might be expected, the years immediately following the panic of 1873 were ones of recuperation; indeed, it was not until 1879 that mileage construction exceeded normal. In that year completed mileage exceeded 5,000—more than double that of the one preceding. Dropping but little the following year, the annual increment reached 8,125 in 1881 and in 1882 reached the enormous total of 11,116. In 1883 the total dropped slightly, though 9,751 miles were added even that year; in 1884 and in 1885 the financial difficulties of 1884 caused a sharp slump in construction. In 1886 the upward trend was again resumed and in 1887 the amazing total mileage of 12,041 was added, an amount practically equal to the 10-year construction of the decade 1911–1920. That such a pace could be continued was impossible, yet the impetus of operations during that year resulted in the addition of 9,320 miles in the succeeding year. Following 1888 activity diminished, the annual average for the remaining 5 years of the period being approximately 5,000 miles. That construction was particularly rapid during the eighties is established clearly by the fact that the decade beginning with 1880, despite several years of scant construction, must be credited with the addition of 71,073 miles to the railway net, a total which exceeds that of the first 45 years of railway building in the United States and which falls but little below that of the past 40 years. Truly a phenomenal record! In the face of the complexity of business and financial relations which necessarily arose as a result of this great and rapid expansion, it is not strange that the combination of public inaction and of unwise or ineffective action should fail completely to protect either public or corporate interests.

As might be expected, the bulk of the increase in mileage which featured this period was in the West. To the total railway construction of this period the New England states contributed less than 2 per cent, while the rest of what constitutes the Eastern District and the Southern District each contributed 16 per cent. To the Western District is assignable, therefore, over 66 per cent of the total mileage, of which a third was built in Illinois, Wisconsin, Minnesota, Iowa, and Missouri. The predominant position of Western construction during the two peak years also is shown in the fact that in 1882 more than 2,000 miles of railway were laid down in the states just named and almost 5,500 in the remainder of Western Territory, while in 1887 the figures for these two portions stood at 1,651 and 8,105 respectively. As building progressed, the saturation point was approached in the older sections and the railway pioneer moved west and southwest with the economic and social frontier.

Mileage Growth and Public Aid.—This unparalleled expansion of the railway is to be explained by no single factor, but perhaps most important during this, as the preceding period, was public aid. This aid took many forms, but the land grant probably contributed more to pioneer mileage than did any several other factors combined. As early as 1880 more than 15 per cent of the total mileage of the country was land-grant mileage, and this despite the fact that comparatively little progress had been made as yet by many corporations operating under the more recent grants. That the land grant was bound to influence construction markedly during the remainder of the period is indicated by railway ownership as late as 1880 of some 78,000,000 acres received from federal and state sources. It is only fair, however, to point out that land-grant aid was not so significant as acreage would indicate. The Grand Rapids and Indiana received the highest average price obtained by land-grant railways for acreage sold up to 1880—$12.50 an acre for about 250,000 acres. This figure was much in excess of that generally received, however. A large part of the land granted lay in the West, and there few figures in excess of $2 are shown; indeed, more than 2,000,000 acres had been marketed prior to 1880 at prices varying from 14 cents to as low as 6 cents per acre. It is said that the holdings of the Texas and Pacific averaged that corporation approximately 13 cents per acre, sold as they were at an early date, though later sales of even Western prairie lands undoubtedly brought a higher average price.[1] The railways which were able to finance construction without the immediate sale of granted lands fared better, but few of the early projects were so strongly situated financially as to permit of the adoption of such a conservative policy.

Grants of land represented but one form of public aid. State aid had been given almost universally during an earlier period: commonwealths north, south, east, and west extended an enthusiastic material support to railway projects in the form of donations, stock subscriptions, or loans secured by railway bonds. Yet it might be added that, whatever

[1] "Sales of public lands for cash in the states in which lands were granted in aid of railway construction over a period extending from July 1, 1850, to July 30, 1870, showed receipts of about 94 cents per acre. Upon this basis the value of the total acreage (federal grants) patented to the railways up to 1930 would have equaled $120,320,000." *Coordination of Motor Transportation*, pp. 90–91.

the original form, such aid was generally the equivalent of a donation in the end. Even the federal government lent its credit to the construction of early transcontinentals to an amount approaching $65,000,000. During the period, however, state aid had been eliminated largely by constitutional prohibitions, except in the South where considerable sums were given to encourage railway construction during the reconstruction era. But, though state aid had largely passed, minor political units—county, township, even city and village—fell easy prey to the wiles of the promoter. Each section, each locality, pictured itself upon the threshold of a glorious future—and too frequently the enthusiasms of the moment caused the voters to forget that bonds must ultimately be paid; indeed, even to forget the need of so circumscribing issues as to make certain of the construction of the railways for which bonds were voted. Many localities voted themselves into poverty to secure a railway of doubtful value—and some failed even to secure the railway. In Nebraska alone 43 counties voted railway aid to the extent of $4,918,000 between 1869 and 1892, and this was typical of the generosity of the West during this, a period of feverish development. When to governmental aid in land and moneys are added the large sums contributed by individuals, the important *direct* part played by the public in railway construction is evident.

Estimating the total of financial aid alone received by the railways at $700,000,000, Ripley says,

> Wisconsin in 1874 had officially subsidized its roads to the amount of over $21,000,000, including lands at three dollars per acre. This sum was sufficient to have met half the legitimate cost of construction then existent. Reliable evidence tends to show that the state and national governments, up to 1870, had pledged themselves one way or another for a sum equivalent to one-fifth of the cost of construction of the 47,000 miles of line then in the United States. And approximately another fifth, at the very least, must have been contributed from local and municipal sources.

Yet during early years that aid was, from a railway standpoint, offset all too often by the losses resulting from premature and excessive construction; where not thus offset, the almost criminal failure of the public to control financial practices resulted in the enrichment of speculator and promoter at the expense of those who later came into possession of the properties and were charged with their administration.

Foreign Support of American Railway Construction.—Although public aid in the form of loans and grants of land served as the immediate basis of railway development, the ready market which Europe furnished for governmental securities and for the large volume of land-grant bonds made it possible, in considerable degree, to obtain the actual funds necessary for the construction of the property. Even during the second period in the development of America's railway mileage the overseas contribution was large, as is shown by the fact that $150,000,000 of railway securities, largely land-grant bonds, in default in 1873–1874 were held in England, Holland, and Germany; also by the fact that, as late as 1876, 86 per cent of the outstanding Illinois Central stock was held abroad. And Dutch investment in the Chicago and North Western was long sufficient to justify a representation of two on the board of directors. Discouraged by the losses of the early seventies, due to financial malpractice and to the collapse of many properties during the panic of 1873, foreign investments were sparingly made for a brief time. However, American railway securities appeared so attractive that they again drew the attention of European investors, and it seems that not less than two billion dollars' worth of American railway paper was sold abroad during this period. Table V, below, shows that foreign stockholdings in American railways were large, and it is certain that bonds found an even readier market abroad than did stocks. These, as well as other facts, such as the close relationship of the failure of the Atchison, Topeka and Santa Fe to the collapse of the English house of Baring, indicate that foreign interests supplied in no small degree the sinews of construction for that phenomenal expansion which began in the late seventies and closed with the panic of 1893.

Table V.—Stockholdings of Foreign Investors in American Railways, 1890–1896*

Railroads	Percentage
Illinois Central	65
Pennsylvania	52
Louisville and Nashville	75
New York, Ontario, and Western	58
New York Central and Hudson River	37
Reading	52
Great Northern	33
Baltimore and Ohio	21
Chicago, Milwaukee, and St. Paul	21

* Ripley, W. Z., *Railroads: Finance and Organization*, p. 5.

The Westward Movement of Population.—Yet a third factor which did much to promote railway building during this period was the tremendous westward sweep of population before noted. True, in many cases the railway arrived first, blazed the trail, but had there not been reasonable assurance that, with the railway in the field, settlers in considerable numbers would quickly follow, even much of the land-grant mileage could not have been financed. Quite naturally the enthusiasm of those who hoped to reap a financial harvest from the construction of these pioneer roads led them to paint an altogether too rosy picture for that time; the financial disillusionment following exerted a depressing influence in later years upon the position of railway securities in the investment market.

Indeed, the operations of the speculative fraternity, with the oily-tongued promoter in the van, may well be regarded as a fourth significant factor in the spectacular increase in mileage during this third period. In the main, such operations were most successful in sections inadequately supplied with railway mileage. In such areas properties were built which lacked a sound economic basis for more than a quarter of a century, serving in the meantime only to discredit the railway with investor and patron alike; others, which proved to be wholly without justification, were soon chronicled only in tables of "Mileage Abandoned." But, even in older sections, speculative construction made its appearance, and here in that inexcusable form of parallel building. Typical of such operations were the building of the West Shore to compete with the New York Central and the New York, Chicago, and St. Louis (the "Nickel Plate") to compete with the Lake Shore and Michigan Southern, with the expectation in each instance of forcing the older properties to take over the newer at a profit—to the promoter—to avoid disastrous competition. This latter field of operation was opened to the speculator by the general abandonment of the policy of chartering each railway corporation by special legislative act, with an accompanying inquiry "into the necessity and usefulness of the line proposed, or the financial ability and integrity of the parties who propose to construct it." Certain it is if the modern requirement of a certificate of convenience and necessity had been applied during the period of rapid construction, it would have been of inestimable service to railway, investor, and public.

Extension of Transcontinental Service.—Closely associated with the increase of mileage just described and an integral part of it, yet sufficiently important to warrant separate consideration, is a second major feature of the period, the development of transcontinental service. Although practically all of the lines which had reached the coast by 1893 had been begun under one name or another prior to 1873, but one had been completed prior to the panic of that year. During the third period no less than four major routes were opened and a fifth combination of routes appeared. Of these new routes, the first to bridge the gap from East to West was the Southern Pacific. Though it was the original plan to meet the Texas and Pacific at the Colorado River, construction was pushed forward so rapidly under the direction of the experienced builders of the earlier Central Pacific that the connection was made east of El Paso instead. The route, essentially that advocated by the South prior to the Civil War, follows closely the southern boundary of the United States, crossing the Colorado River near the Mexican border. Thence the line runs to Los Angeles and through the valley of the San Joaquin to San Francisco. This property, completed in 1881, was supplemented at an early date by boat lines operating from Gulf ports to New York and other Atlantic ports, thus providing the only transcontinental movement of traffic, by a single management, in the United States.

In this southern section a second line appeared during this period, the Atchison, Topeka, and Santa Fe. The project was born in the midst of a famine period in the Southwest, and there is little wonder that its prophet, Colonel Cyrus Holliday, was greeted with wild laughter when he painted, at a celebration held in honor of the completion of the first few miles of track, a glorious picture of its future progress to the Gulf of Mexico on the south and the Golden Gate in the West. Yet within a quarter century the prophet's dream was an accomplished fact. With the support of Boston capitalists and, through them, of foreign investors, the project was pushed vigorously. Building through New Mexico and Arizona to Barstow, Calif., upon the basis of the old Atlantic and Pacific grant, a junction was formed with the Southern Pacific property at that place in 1885; from that point San Francisco was reached by a series of leases, the needed properties being later purchased. In the meantime construction had been carried to the eastward with the result that the Santa Fe was for many years the only one of the transcontinental lines to operate over its own rails from Chicago to the west coast. It may well be added, however, that the tremendous expansion of the property during this period resulted in failure in 1891 and again in 1893 when a drastic reorganization was forced upon its security holders in the interest of future strength.

Nor was transcontinental construction progressing in the Southwest only; rapid headway was being made also in the Northwest. The Northern Pacific, well under way at the close of 1873, had been brought to an absolute halt by the collapse of Jay Cooke in that year, and important construction work was not resumed until 1880. But in 1881 a new leader, Henry Villard, appeared; under his direction and in response to his leadership the property was completed to the Pacific Coast before the close of 1883. Incidentally it is worthy of note that this railway enjoyed perhaps the heaviest aid, through its land grants, of any of the transcontinentals, much of the acreage received being covered by valuable timber. In this northern section there was completed during the period a second railway from the Twin Cities to the Pacific coast. This project is of special interest because land-grant aid was of minor importance in its construction; also because it was the development of this property, with its beginnings in an earlier bankrupt project taken over by James J. Hill in 1879, that signalized the rise of another strong leader in the railway field. A bankrupt railway, reorganized as the St. Paul, Minneapolis, and Manitoba, was extended and later leased, together with other connecting roads, to the Great Northern, which completed its line into Seattle in 1893. Under the masterful guidance of Hill odd scraps of railway and financially decrepit properties were welded together into a transcontinental carrier which was soon to form the nucleus of one of the great ownership groupings of American railways and, as such, to dominate a rival which even yet has not wholly forgotten its early contempt for the plebeian origin of its neighbor.

Because of the character of the country through which another central route must be built, the Union Pacific-Central Pacific route was confronted with little that might be regarded as competitive construction during this period. True, under the leadership of General William J. Palmer, the Denver and Rio Grande had been driven westward from Pueblo and thence northward to Salt Lake City by 1883, and another line from Ogden to the coast had appeared in 1884 with the junction of the Oregon Short Line, the Utah Northern, and the Oregon Railway and Navigation Company, Portland being the terminus of this route. However, these lines, even though operated in conjunction, were in no position to compete with the older route because of location and higher operating costs. And today there exists no effective competition in this section, though competition is keen among the railways both to the north and the south.

Policy of Public Aid Abandoned.—The almost complete abandonment of the policy of public aid to railway construction is a third outstanding characteristic of the 20 years following 1873. Perhaps the major factor explaining this reversal of policy was a gradual realization that the gains were not worth the cost, yet it is undoubted that certain evils incident to the policy had tended to prejudice the public against its continuance. Then too, after the amazing extension of mileage during the eighties, the feeling was widespread that it was time to begin "catching up" economically to the mileage already in existence. The reaction against the artificial stimulation of construction first appeared in declining state and local aid, but because each section and each locality seemed to have to learn the painful lesson from its own experience, aid from these sources has been the last to disappear. Against the entire policy of public aid Cleveland and Powell summarize the case well in saying that it

> . . . was not only unnecessary and productive of extravagance and fraud, but also that it was of questionable value to the companies themselves. It has been urged by some that the corporations as a whole would have been better capitalized and better managed if they had been left entirely to private investment interests. If some lines were built earlier than could have been possible without public aid, many others were constructed over routes which could not furnish enough traffic to support them. This not only involved a great loss of public money, but it was in large part responsible for much of the subsequent controversy over the matter of rates.

Excessive and ill-placed mileage, corruption of the legislature or of the electorate as the case might demand, fraudulent operations under legislative acts, and plain evasions of the law developed in connection with state and local aid. That restrictive measures, intended to end practices which had resulted in much harm and comparatively little good, should be placed upon the statute books and even in state constitutions themselves, was inevitable. In few commonwealths can the minor units now contribute at all and even fewer commonwealths themselves are permitted to aid in financing such an enterprise as a railway, either by donation or by the extension of credit. Indeed, so closely are both state and local governments bound that it is often exceedingly difficult for the public to aid in the case of carefully considered and meritorious projects such as the Moffatt Tunnel in Colorado for the Denver and Salt Lake Railroad.

The states and local units were not alone in harvesting tares from grants of aid in behalf of railways. Aside from the fact that much of the mileage constructed under land grants was built years too soon and that, where an economic basis existed, lines would have been built with but little delay without such aid, other objections and evils appeared. Grants were invariably interpreted in a liberal manner from a corporate standpoint, with the result that indemnity lands were withdrawn from settlement and reserved, oftentimes for years—in 1887 an adjustment of grants restored 20,000,000 acres to settlement; and in cases where grants had expired the courts held that no forfeiture worked except as positive action to that end was taken by Congress. Furthermore, the policy of certain railways of reserving lands instead of opening them for development proved inimical to public interest. Then too, outright fraud was often charged and too frequently present. But apart from the opposition aroused by evils incident to the system and the general feeling that construction had surpassed needs, the desire to reserve remaining lands for settlement under the homestead and other land-settlement acts served to strengthen the hand of those demanding a discontinuance of that policy.

The opposition to giving further lands took definite form first in the refusal to assist additional projects after the large grant to the Texas and Pacific in 1871. As opposition increased, a few specific forfeiture acts were passed, but it was not until 1890 that a general act could be placed upon the statute books providing for the forfeiture of all lands along projected routes which were not at that time completed and in operation. Title to considerable areas of land, particularly in California, has been in dispute even within recent years and, because of certain minor legal and administrative obstacles that have delayed action, patents have not yet been issued to all lands to which title is claimed by the railways in other portions of the West. There is every reason to believe that a century will have elapsed from the time of the first grant until "finis" can be written to the chapter on federal aid. Yet, whatever criticism may rightly be made of federal assistance to railway construction, it is evident that, when results are judged from a political and social standpoint as well as from the standpoint of economic gains, a happier balance appears. To such aid is attributable in considerable measure the early gridironing of the new West; and this, in turn, made possible rapid settlement and development.

Investment in Railways.—No discussion of this third period in railway development is complete without at least a brief presentation of significant characteristics and policies of carrier finance, both because of the immediate influence exerted upon general financial conditions and because of its relation to railway development during the succeeding period. That the tremendous expansion of the railway net during these two decades should result in a marked increase in the total capitalization of the enterprise was natural. From a figure somewhat in excess of $3,000,000,000 in 1873, it had mounted to more than three times that sum in 1893, so it can be said, roughly, that, while mileage was increasing about 160 per cent, the total of securities based upon that mileage increased about 200 per cent. Since considerable sums were undoubtedly spent in improving older properties, this difference would not necessarily be of particular significance were it not that a considerable portion of the mileage added during the period was laid in a territory where construction costs were relatively low—the plains country—and also were it not for the added fact that a large portion of this mileage was laid to the tune of governmental and private aid. These facts make it appear that not only was the generosity of a public hoping to benefit immediately or ultimately from the construction of mileage capitalized liberally by the builders of these projects, but that perhaps those individuals went even beyond that point in their generosity to themselves—for it was characteristic of early railway construction that those within the "charmed circle" were the gainers at the expense of even fellow stockholders who were not so fortunately placed.

Overcapitalization and Its Causes.—Without doubt the excessive capitalization of many properties built during this period is explained by the highly speculative character of the projects themselves. So great was the risk that those in financial control were compelled to sell even bonds at a heavy discount and it is in no wise strange that large amounts of stock were issued with little basis except the hoped-for success of the enterprise. Indeed, it was not unusual for stock to be given as a bonus to aid in the promotion of bond sales, and the promoters of early enterprises in the West were never parsimonious in compensating themselves in stocks for the various services performed.

But the significance of the general upward movement of capitalization during this period and the high capitalization of particular properties as compared with actual investment is perhaps not to be explained always upon so natural and so innocent a basis. For this was a period characterized as no other in the history of railway construction and operation by fraudulent financial practices. The construction company, a relatively unknown instrument prior to this time for the tapping of railway treasuries, the Crédit Mobilier being the first outstanding instance of its use, might almost be said to have become a characteristic feature of building operations during the era of great expansion. These "inside organizations" were capable of contributing in a material and effective manner to the prosecution of the various projects with which they were connected, but too often they were created and utilized merely as vehicles for plundering those who actually contributed funds to make the proposed lines possible; their whole record—even the phrase—has become, from a public standpoint, an odious one.

But fraudulent practice played a part in the movement toward excessive capitalization beyond, in point of time, the construction of the property. The complete absence of control over the issuance of corporate securities throughout this entire period made it invitingly easy for those of speculative tendencies who chanced to be in control of a railway to utilize that control to issue securities which enriched the controlling interest at the expense of the corporation thus burdened. And it may well be said further that the readiness with which the market, at home and abroad, absorbed railway issues during this period, and the unconcern with which the fundamental worth of such issues was regarded, presented a situation which not only tempted those in control to benefit themselves but served as an incentive to the Goulds, the Sages, and others deliberately to seek control of properties for quite other reasons than those associated with public service. And woe betide such properties in future years as fell into the manipulator's grasp: more than one railway is today wearily bearing a burden of funded debt and of stocks that is explained on grounds varying from the capitalization of false and ungrounded hopes to the payment of current operating expenses from the proceeds of bond sales that railway operating income might thereby appear greater.

Yet it is only fair to say that, however much student and public may reprobate the actions of certain manipulators who came into control of railway properties almost half a century ago, it must be remembered that in retrospect it is never difficult to outline a sound program. The then dominant *laissez-faire* philosophy supported a policy of noninterference. And furthermore, the public itself was party to the speculative activities to this period, both actively and by passive consent. Indeed, to quote,[1]

> . . . it was only after the division of the spoils had been made, when each individual citizen had capitalized whatever advantage he had gained, when a large majority of persons residing within a given territory was required to produce in order to prosper . . . when he no longer felt that he was being benefited by the practices which we now condemn, that there began to be a moral uprising against the corporation, the officer, or the corporate trustee who, under the contracts which represented his share in the division of the spoils of territorial

[1] Cleveland, F. A., and F. W. Powell, *Railroad Promotion and Capitalization*, pp. 147–148.

conquest, continued to profit under the system. . . . The new morality of today is the product of new economic and social conditions, which requires that the government become the effective agency representing general welfare, and that this agency be vigorously employed to guard the public against the exercises of the special privileges and private monopolies created under a regime of private spoliation of a new continent, the title to which rested in the general government. The promoter of the railroad of yesterday was the enterprising citizen; he was the man, who, accepting conditions as they were, made the most of them; and whatever conclusion may be drawn with reference to his morality when measured by new standards, it must be said that he did much to organize the forces which have given to America the best equipped transportation service in the world.

It may be further said that the worst of financial practices in the railway field during the "golden age" for speculator and manipulator in no wise surpass similar practices of recent years in the industrial field, and the latter is now regarded as competitive and private in character not a whit less than was the railway field until relatively recent years.

Changes in Financial Policy.—But beyond the difficulties to which this period gave rise because of the part speculation and fraud played in railway finance, it is of interest and importance because of a change in financial policy which took place. Early railway construction had been financed largely through the sale of stock, but the railways of the third period—indeed, even of the latter part of the second—were located largely in undeveloped territory, and had to be financed, therefore, by outside capital. This capital demanded security and when the investor displaced, as a source of funds, the man who hoped to profit directly from the service of the railway, bonds gained a position of increasing prominence. Ripley states that in 1855 the capital stock of American railways exceeded bonded indebtedness by 42 per cent; even in 1868 the railways of Ohio had capital stock outstanding considerably in excess of the total of bonds. However, in the years immediately preceding the panic of 1873 a change came, due to the greater ease of marketing bonds, to the pioneer character of projects involved, and to the increased interest of the promoter in the railway enterprises, as well as to the endeavors of land-grant roads to secure funds upon the basis of the grants received. This change contributed measurably to the panic mentioned; yet, despite a temporary change in policy during the next few years that had as its purpose a reduction in fixed charges, increasing resort was had to bonds as the years passed. This gradual rise in the bond ratio during the years prior to the panic of 1893 had more than a casual relation to the widespread failure of railways which was one of the significant features of that general collapse. Indeed, the failure of certain projects to meet expectations played so large a part in the minor collapse of 1884 that it has been called "the railroad panic," and the temporary halt in business in 1891 was largely due to railway financial difficulties. Just as it would be difficult to magnify the importance of the collapses in general business in 1873, 1884, 1893, with their following years of depression, particularly the first and last named, so would it be difficult to magnify the part played by the building of excessive mileage and by unwise or fraudulent railway financial practices in precipitating such general failures.

(See reference list at the close of Chap. VIII.)

Chapter VIII

GENESIS OF THE RAILWAY PROBLEM: COMPETITION AND ADVANCE IN REGULATION

THE expansion of railway mileage that took place in the United States in the years between 1873 and 1893 has never been equaled in the history of our own or another country, nor even closely approached. And it must be said to our shame that railway expansion was never attended with more dubious financial methods than characterized the activities of many of the promotors and speculators of this period. In most cases construction represented a hazard later justified by economic and social gains, but too often it was prompted by a desire to mulct the investor, the public, or railways already in the field. Indeed, not infrequently profits were harvested at the expense of all three. In most cases financial policies were dictated by necessity and were in harmony with the *laissez-faire* spirit of the times, but in others they were wholly fraudulent in purpose and execution. From such rapid, unregulated construction and uncontrolled financial operations important consequences were certain to flow. Of these perhaps the most significant were the intensification of competition with its many results and the reappearance of the demand for effective regulation.

Continuance of Intense Competition.—An early noted and persisting feature of the third period in railway development was a continuance and an intensification of competitive action which had first proved disturbing late in the preceding period. During this further development of competition all of the influences which operated in the years prior to 1874 continued to exert undiminished force and, in certain instances, greater force because of the further extension of the railway net. Market competition among the Atlantic ports, each with its representative railway, continued with increased vigor, and the struggle among the market centers of the Middle West was sharpened by the addition of other lines. To these phases of market competition were added the struggle of the Gulf ports to share with the Atlantic gateways in the grain traffic of the West, and the appearance of market rivalries in the Rocky Mountain and Pacific regions. Excessive construction also continued as a disturbing factor, entering even into the older regions in the form of "hold-up," or parallel, construction which appeared upon a large scale during this period. But in addition to these factors and the very nature of the railway business itself, two new causes for competition appeared. Of these, one was temporary in character but the other has become more important with the passage of years. The first was the pressure which the depression following the severe panic of 1873 exerted upon the railways to secure business and to secure it with but little regard to source or method. This pressure was felt keenly not only in areas of light traffic but in older and more developed sections as well. The second and the more significant was the appearance of industrial competition. With the rapid industrialization of that area lying between Buffalo and Pittsburgh on the east and Chicago and St. Louis on the west, the dominance of the eastern industrial section was challenged not only in the Middle West and the South, but even in the Far West, with fundamental effects upon competitive conditions which were reflected in rate adjustments and railway relationships, individual and group. These various forces operating together compelled competition of an extreme type, the keenest and most ruthless in American railway history. Its results were definite and striking.

Influence of Competition on Rates.—The immediate consequence of this struggle for business appeared in sudden and wide fluctuations of rates. Competitive carriers indulged in open warfare over freight traffic

Table VI.—New York-Chicago Rates, First Class, in Cents per Hundredweight, 1874–1888

1874—January	100	1881—August	45
August	75	November	60
1875—January	100	1882—January	45
May	40	November	75
1876—January	75	1885—January	50
July	15	November	75
1877—March	75	1888—November	50
October	100	December	75
1878—February	75		

more often than over passenger business, yet both were involved. As illustrative of the extremes of competition for live stock shipments it is declared "that at one time cattle were hauled from Chicago to Pittsburgh without charge, and that in certain instances they were hauled from Chicago to the seaboard for $5 per carload"—and this in the face of a normal rate for the latter service of $110 per car. Grain was hauled from Chicago to the Atlantic ports for as little as 7½ cents per hundredweight, and a Boston merchant is reputed to have found that he could make a profit by shipping lemons, grown in California and forwarded to him in the East, back to California for resale on the basis of current rates. This wide fluctuation of freight rates is illustrated also by a brief record of the charge from New York to Chicago on first-class shipments, as shown in Table VI above.

But cutthroat activity was not confined to the freight business. Immigrants were carried from New York to Chicago for as little as $1 a head and at one time, as a result of a rate war for Pacific coast passenger business, a like rate from Chicago to San Francisco, including meals, is reputed to have been made. Other instances comparable to these might be cited, in both the freight and passenger fields, but the facts already given permit of no doubt as to the startling and destructive character of the struggle. And this struggle injured shipper as well as railway, for even high rates are less disturbing and less hurtful to the patron than rapidly and widely changing rates.

Lower Rate Levels.—Though both parties lost through sharp fluctuations of rates when competition got beyond control, competition must be credited with a decline in the general rate level during these years, particularly with respect to freight traffic. This decline was great in certain areas, and apparent for the railways of the entire country. Although the downward movement was essentially continuous throughout the period, the major decline appeared in the years preceding 1886. During those years the average earnings per ton-mile upon the New York Central dropped from 1.573 cents to less than 0.9 cent, while the decrease on the Pennsylvania, a rival line, was from 1.416 cents to less than 0.75 cent. Upon the Pittsburgh, Fort Wayne, and Chicago, the average declined from 1.40 cents in 1873 to slightly less than half that in 1884, and the charges for all important lines radiating from Chicago in an eastern, southern, and western direction dropped from 1.813 cents to 1.071 cents during the same period. For the country as a whole, the average ton-mile rate fell from approximately 1.6 cents in 1873 to slightly above 1.1 cents in 1884 and less than 0.9 cent in 1893. And a corrected index, based upon averages of effective published rates, shows for the entire country an equally striking decline; the average for 1878, the first year for which it has been computed, was 1.30 cents per ton-mile, while in 1893 it had fallen to less than 0.8 cent.

Discrimination Becomes a Major Problem.—Another result largely attributable to the intense competition of this period was the appearance of discrimination as a major problem. Although railways had long given preference to communities in which they were particularly interested and had shown certain favoritism even as among shippers, it was not until the mad competitive scramble of the seventies and eighties that these discriminations became general and pronounced. Place discrimination developed at both monopolistic and competitive points, yet against the former alone could discrimination be economically justified even from the standpoint of the railway; personal discrimination had no economic justification, resulting essentially from official favoritism or from unwise, vicious competition. The higher level of rates at noncompetitive points normally resulted from a decline of rates between competitive centers rather than from any increase in rates at the expense of those complaining of prejudice. This policy with respect to the competitive centers was forced upon the railways by their inability, for legal or business reasons, to maintain a schedule of rates between such points that would be reasonably compensatory. But, however necessary such concessions may have been from a carrier standpoint, they occasioned loud and bitter complaints from those sections in which competition did not exist, and especially so since often those noncompetitive areas had given more generously to the construction of the property than competitive centers already supplied with mileage. The reasonableness of hauling goods a greater distance to a competitive point for a lesser sum than that assessed against like shipments to a nearer monopolistic point was not evident to the farmer and tradesman little versed in the economics of railway operation, and, it might be added, could be explained in no logical manner by those learned in such matters. Even the rate which did not run directly counter to the distance principle, but was in no wise proportionate to distance and always to the advantage of the competitive center, was seriously questioned. Discrimination between competitive and noncompetitive areas became increasingly unreasonable as competition developed and as means of cooperation proved inadequate. Discrimination was rightly stressed by the Cullom Committee in 1886 as one of the outstanding evils of this period.

To discrimination against noncompetitive points during this period was added preferential treatment at competitive points. Here place discrimination was a minor factor, though railway policy often decreed that an advantage should be given to one competitive point over another. But at competitive points personal discrimination was the outstanding evil. Although upon first thought there appears no possible excuse for offering one of several business competitors at a given point a better rate than is accorded to his fellows, the railways actually found that such a policy, if judiciously followed, might result in increased tonnage. An open rate, known to competitive lines and equaled or undercut by them, made no inroads upon the competitor's tonnage; but, if a secret rate were accorded an enterprising shipper, he would be enabled to overreach his rivals and, as his volume of business increased, the tonnage of the cooperating carrier would increase proportionately. It was not long, however, until the value of the secret rate was realized by all competing carriers and, with that, it lost its value to all and became a menace not only to enterprises not favored but also to the carriers. Indeed, so serious a financial menace did it become to the carriers and so firm a grip did it obtain that the railways later were forced to invoke governmental assistance to enable them to "let go": they found it impossible to deal unaided with the powerful industrial units toward whose semi-monopolistic position they had earlier and unwittingly contributed so much.

Public protest during the early seventies had been against a rate level which seemed abnormally high in proportion to the value of goods, particularly farm products; during this period it was against discrimination. Prejudiced communities and prejudiced individuals felt justified in complaining against the highly discriminatory charges and, however much the exigencies of competition may have compelled certain departures from a normal standard of equitable treatment, it is evident that discrimination often went much farther than the competitive situation demanded and partook of gross personal favoritism. The public was in error in its efforts to curb attempts made by the carriers to bring competition under control: discriminatory practices, which persisted *because* of inadequate control, were largely responsible for the rising tide of popular opposition that culminated in demands for further regulation during this and the succeeding period.

Decline of Water Traffic.—Yet another consequence of sharp competition and the resultant decline of the general rate level was the realization by the railways that they could carry profitably, as additional business, even low-grade traffic. As they thus extended their traffic field an actual decline in water traffic followed. This decline was noticeable not only in canal and river traffic but even in coastwise movements, particularly the Pacific-Atlantic tonnage. Few canals had rendered more than a minor service following the Civil War, the Erie Canal alone retaining a position of importance. This waterway in 1855 carried twice the tonnage handled by all the trunk lines and during the late sixties practically all grain shipped to New York moved by canal; in the early sixties, however, the railways attained a general tonnage parity and in 1873 the canal handled little more than a quarter of the tonnage destined into New York alone. During this period the decline had been relative, however, rather than absolute, but after 1873 it tended to become absolute as well. Indeed, at the close of 1883 the Erie Canal was carrying not only a smaller total tonnage but its proportion of the tonnage entering New York had declined to little more than a tenth; during the later seventies control of the grain traffic passed largely to the railways.

This same movement of traffic from rivers and even from coastwise trade toward the railways was evident. An estimate of the value of Ohio River traffic in 1869 and in 1886 indicated that in the latter year it had dropped to less than half of the total shown for 1869; in explanation, this comment appears:[1]

> The apparent decline of river traffic at various points is not indicative of commercial decay of such communities. The almost omnipresent rail competition is an element in the count that brings up commercial footings to several times more than the totals of water transportation for all points where the two run counter to each other.

[1] Report to Secretary of the Treasury by Chief of Bureau of Statistics, Jan. 30, 1888.

In the commercial year of 1872–1873 New Orleans received more than 75 per cent of the total value of all receipts by water, while in 1886–1887 that percentage had been reduced to little more than a third, with a decline in actual values received by water for the latter year to approximately two-fifths of the figure for the former. Even at St. Louis, which was already a railway center in the early seventies, the percentage of total tonnage received and shipped by water dropped from about 34 in 1871 to little more than 10 in 1887, with an absolute decrease also shown. After 1880 the great Western rivers became steadily of less significance, and traffic upon all but the most important and easily navigable streams had "gone down Salt Creek" a decade or more previously. That the railways had succeeded in wresting the control of tonnage which might move by rail or by coastwise vessels from the hands of the water carriers by the close of this period is attested by a decline in coastwise shipping, despite the sharp increase in the amount of competitive tonnage available. This was true not only of traffic which might move between North Atlantic ports and South Atlantic or Gulf ports but also between the Pacific coast and the eastern portion of the United States. Indeed, statistics for the latter movement show that as late as 1878 the railways moved but about 25 per cent of the Pacific-Eastern business, while in 1890, following several years of open warfare, it was estimated that from 90 to 95 per cent of the business was handled by rail. Tonnage moving by canal, river, and in coastwise trade had, by the close of this period, been reduced to negligible proportions.

Increase in Efficiency of Railway Operations.—A final result ascribable in considerable degree to the severity of competition was the distinct impetus given to the efficiency of railway operation during this period. This efficiency resulted in part from a better understanding of the nature of the railway business and the improvement in organization and management which followed, though perhaps more largely from that mechanical advancement which characterized the entire field of American industry during the last third of the nineteenth century. This better understanding came largely through the spur of necessity. Revenues were being sharply depleted by rate cutting; if financial disaster were to be avoided there must be a comparable reduction in the cost of handling traffic. Illustrative of the more effective use of the plant which resulted was a change in locomotive practice. The traditional policy of assigning a locomotive to a particular crew, thus limiting its use by the capacity of the one crew to serve, was abandoned in favor of the "first in, first out" rule. Another illustration is found in increased emphasis upon heavier car loading and heavier train loading, with a consequent demand for larger cars and greater locomotive tractive capacity. In response to this influence the 10-ton load capacity of the seventies had increased to 20 tons in the later eighties, with a distinct increase in the proportion of the paying load to gross weight; the average train load was increased, too, through the more effective use of motive power as well as by improvements in that field, the increase being from approximately 100 tons to perhaps two and a half times that figure. With this more efficient handling of traffic came corresponding improvements in the roadway itself. At the beginning of the period roadway construction was comparatively primitive —cinders and coarse sand were used on such mileage as was ballasted, and the steel rail was just coming into use. By its close, marked advances had been scored: the roadbed itself had been greatly improved by the use of crushed rock, slag, and other durable material which gave good drainage, and the iron rail was rapidly disappearing. By 1880 the percentage of total mileage laid with steel had reached 29.1 and in 1893 the figure stood at 83.7, advancing to 96 within another decade. During this period, too, switching and signaling were greatly improved; the interlocking system made for greater efficiency and increased safety at important junctions and terminals, while the development of an elementary block system aided in moving traffic "out on the line" more expeditiously and with less likelihood of collision. An advance in knowledge and the use of steel further improved bridge construction and during the period several important structures were completed; the Hudson was bridged at Poughkeepsie, the Ohio at Cairo, and the Niagara a short distance below the falls, while structures across the Mississippi as far south as Memphis and Vicksburg were authorized. Growing traffic and a better realization of the importance of that portion of the railway plant led to greater attention to way, terminal, and shop facilities. Passenger stations were improved, freight terminals expanded and bettered, and shops for the maintenance and construction of equipment were enlarged and modernized. Not only did locomotives almost double in number during this period but, more important from the standpoint of efficiency, they also increased tremendously in size and capacity. The consolidation and mogul types, introduced in the sixties, were enlarged and gradually substituted for less efficient motive power in the freight service, and the speed of passenger locomotives was increased until in 1886 the New York Central made the 149 miles between Syracuse and Buffalo in 136 minutes running time, averaging, therefore, 65.6 miles per hour. For one stretch of 12.8 miles an average speed of 74.93 miles was attained. The development of standard types with interchangeable parts reduced costs, and the use of higher steam pressure with a better mechanism improved results. In addition to the increased capacity of freight cars already mentioned, a greater diversity of types to suit the needs of different industries appeared and the work of the Master Car Builders' Association, begun in 1865, resulted in improved and much more uniform construction of such equipment. Another important mechanical advance came in the development and gradual adoption of the Westinghouse automatic air brake, first upon passenger equipment, later upon all. The early air brake depended for action upon the application of pressure but it sometimes failed to operate properly and, in the case of a break in the train, was quite useless. The improved mechanism acted in the *absence* of pressure; in consequence, any closing of pipes, leakage, or "breaking" resulted in an immediate application of brakes. This improvement not only promoted safety but made possible much greater speed of movement without an undue increase in risk.

Further Development of Railway Cooperation.—Try as they would, however, many railways were unable to counterbalance the decrease in rates either by more efficient operation or by a volume of business increased by rate wars and the rapid industrial development of the country. As a result, each indulgence in cutthroat competition crowded the weaker lines involved just a little closer to the edge of the financial precipice; yet it was generally those weaker properties which were least willing to accept the *status quo*, and first to take steps which would bring about a collapse of the rate structure for a greater or lesser period. It was in an effort to escape the financial disaster threatened by such warfare that the movement to establish more effective control over competitive activities originated. This movement is yet another feature of this third period.

In the previous chapter it was noted that the first step toward the control of competition was the rate agreement. These agreements had uniformly collapsed, violation sometimes becoming evident almost before the ink was dry; the incentive to undercut secretly was stronger than the deterrent forces, even though the secret violation must ultimately, or perhaps immediately, precipitate a renewal of hostilities. As indicated elsewhere, the initial forward step was represented by the pool. The pooling agreement embodied two fundamental provisions, the maintenance of rates upon an agreed basis and the apportionment of competitive business. This apportionment was typically upon the basis of operations during the preceding year under the pooling agreement, though perhaps upon the basis of a somewhat longer period at the inception of the organization. Pools were of two basic types, the traffic pool and the money pool; the former divided competitive *tonnage* upon an agreed basis, thus practically necessitating the use of "eveners," but the latter divided the *gains* from competitive business upon a prescribed basis while permitting tonnage to move as it would. Of these two, the latter was the more common, since it avoided the preferential treatment accorded to large shippers who served as "eveners" and placed in the hands of the pooling organization certain sums which might be declared forfeited to those faithful to the pooling arrangement in case of recalcitrance on the part of one or more of the carriers party to the agreement. And this feature was of vital importance to the maintenance of the terms of the agreement, extra-legal as the pool was. Perhaps one of the best illustrations of this form of control which was used widely during the seventies and early eighties was the Chicago-Omaha pool. This pool was organized in 1870 and controlled interrailway competition in its particular territory until superseded by a more highly developed type of organization. It was of the money type, and called for the equal division among the parties to the agreement—the Rock Island, the Burlington, and the North Western—of 55 per cent of the revenues from competitive passenger operations and 50 per cent of similar freight revenues. Only for a few months during its entire history did it fail to hold competition under complete control. Many other pools were organized throughout the country during this period which were attended with a considerable degree of success, but in the middle eighties they gave way to a broader type of organization, the traffic association.

Southern Railway and Steamship Association.—The scope of these association agreements varied somewhat but prior to 1887 the pooling of earnings or tonnage on competitive business was common to practically all, as was an accompanying provision covering the rates which were to govern the movement of such business. In addition, these agreements generally laid down rules to govern the solicitation of traffic; centered in the association the control of service in such manner as to minimize the severity of that form of competition; permitted the organization to determine the extent to which various privileges should be accorded shippers; and even prescribed the types of tickets that might be issued. Of the various associations which sprang into being during this period none is of greater interest than the Southern Railway and Steamship Association, organized in 1875 and operating in the section south of the Potomac and Ohio rivers and east of the Mississippi. Made essential because of the active and therefore dangerous character of competition in this section, rail, river, and coastwise rivalry being abetted by both market and industrial competition, this organization was able to secure that high degree of centralization of power so necessary to the success of such an undertaking. The legislative function was exercised by a body of men which met annually, this body consisting of one representative of each carrier member. Administrative functions were largely exercised by the general commissioner, whose powers were broad, and the success of the association was due largely to the unusual capacity of the first man who served as general commissioner, Albert Fink. Certain administrative functions, together with those of a judicial character, were vested in an executive committee which considered matters that the commissioner was unable to handle, these matters being further referred to a board of arbitrators for adjudication unless a unanimous decision could be had from the committee. Under the operations of this association order soon was brought from chaos in the territory concerned and, although members sought to withdraw and thereby threatened the reestablishment of earlier conditions, disciplinary action was such that it invariably brought the wanderer back in a chastened mood and tended to discourage further rebellion Percentage allotments were made annually and, in the effort to increase the controlling percentage, competition persisted among the parties to the agreement as well as among member and nonmember carriers within the area covered, and between the carriers of this territory and of others in the form of market and industrial competition. The result, therefore, seemed to be the elimination of excessive competition rather than such competition as might be advantageous to both railway and public. And this conclusion would seem to be justified with respect to the operation of similar associations and organizations designed to control competition in other sections, and throughout the United States as a whole.

Reappearance of the Demand for Regulation.—A further movement toward regulation became evident comparatively early during this period. Of the various causes accounting for the initial demands for positive control of railways at the close of the preceding era, only one was of less significance during this. However, the very force of that competition which lessened complaints against the high level of rates greatly magnified discrimination, both personal and place, and tended to abet the continuance of financial abuses rather than lessen or remove them. Furthermore, the continued and obstinate refusal of railway management to recognize any justification for public interference, together with the means employed to block action, incensed the public increasingly as time passed.

But in addition to these older influences certain new ones became operative. The fear of monopoly was thoroughly ingrained in American political consciousness, and the increasing effectiveness of railway cooperation seemed to bode ill for an economic system resting upon the competitive ideal. Anti-monopoly organizations were formed in various states, the attitude of which was well put by a western governor who declared that from consolidation arose an antagonism between railway and public which had increased until a situation existed that was deeply inimical to the business and commercial interests of the people. In New York state the Hepburn Committee was created by the legislature to investigate the effect of railway cooperation upon the business interests of that commonwealth. Other evidences of public displeasure were apparent. However erroneous popular adherence to a competitive policy was, and however exaggerated by the public were the injuries suffered as a result of railway cooperation, it was sufficient that the public believed in, and political leaders vehemently urged, the need of the rigid enforcement of a competitive policy.

In response to popular insistence, regulation of a positive character was not long in making its reappearance. Georgia established in 1879 a commission with power to fix rates and in the same year California made constitutional provision for a body with like powers. In 1885 Minnesota again resorted to positive control and in 1888 Iowa, after ten years of experience with an advisory commission, gave to its commission mandatory powers. In 1891 the Texas Railroad Commission was organized with wide powers and, prior to the panic of 1893, other states took positive action. But popular insistence upon railway regulation was now making itself felt beyond state legislatures. In 1874 a measure providing for the regulation of rates passed the national House of Representatives and in 1877 the Reagan Bill was approved by the House by a yet larger majority, though neither could be brought to a vote in the Senate. In 1884, however, measures were passed by both houses of Congress but it was impossible to effect a compromise between the rather conservative Senate measure and the more radical House program. A further spur was needed to compel the enactment of needed legislation.

A double spur to such action came in 1886. In that year the Cullom Committee made a significant report to the Senate. In the years following the Windom report railway rivalry had so lowered the general level of rates upon class and commodity traffic that, by the middle eighties, this burden was not oppressive. However, such rivalry had resulted in widespread and rank discrimination: the prime need now appeared to be a requirement that *all* persons, *all* places, and *all* types of traffic receive equal treatment. Beyond condemnation of discrimination, the report took notice of financial practices and, for the second time, regulation was recommended. Though it is probable that public hostility to the railways, reenforced by the vigorous protest of the Cullom report, would have impelled Congressional action, further impetus was furnished in the same year by the decision of the Supreme Court in the Wabash[1] case. By its decision in the Peik[2] case the Court had recognized the right of the state to regulate interstate traffic in which it had a direct interest, Congress having taken no action. But in this later holding the state was denied all powers with respect to interstate movements. Thus a major portion of the total traffic lost all governmental protection. The reestablishment of control became an immediate issue.

The Interstate Commerce Act of 1887.—Within a brief time after the Wabash decision had been rendered, the House and Senate had composed their differences and a conference bill was passed overwhelmingly by both early in 1887. Positive control, based upon the interstate commerce powers of the federal government and enjoying judicial sanction in the Granger cases, had an indubitably sound constitutional basis. This Act to Regulate Commerce consisted of 24 sections and covered all interstate movements of passengers and freight by railway as well as continuous rail-and-water movements. It declared that all charges should be just and reasonable; it specifically prohibited personal, place, and commodity discrimination; it banned a greater charge for a shorter than for a longer

[1] *Wabash, St. Louis and Pacific Railway Company v. Illinois,* 118 U. S. 557 (1886).

[2] *Peik v. Chicago and North Western Railway Company,* 94 U. S. 164 (1877).

haul "over the same line and in the same direction . . . under substantially similar circumstances and conditions"; and it prohibited pooling. Rates and fares must be printed and posted, and no advance in charges might be made except on 10 days' notice. A commission was established with power to compel testimony, to require reports, and to enlist the aid of the federal courts in the enforcement of its orders.

Though bitterly opposing the passage of the Act of 1887, the railways conformed to its provisions for several years with good spirit. As a consequence of such cooperation on the part of the carriers definite progress was made toward uniformity of classifications, toward the elimination of commodity discrimination, and toward the elimination of long-and-short-haul violations not only in Trunk Line territory but also in Southern territory where a complex competitive situation had made the violations both numerous and glaring. Pooling was abandoned and a beginning was made in the collection of valuable data. But such happy relations between the railways and the Commission were not to continue: in 1890 the Act was subjected to test and attacks continued upon it until its effectiveness was largely destroyed.

The Interstate Commerce Act and Legal Procedure.—To eliminate personal discrimination which had persisted despite the prohibitions of the Act, the primary need of the Commission was adequate evidence. But such evidence could rarely be secured except from the benefited shipper or the carrier's agent. In attempting to compel one Counselman, suspected of enjoying a lower than published rate upon grain, to testify, the Commission met defeat. The shipper based his refusal upon the constitutional provision that "no person . . . shall be compelled in a criminal case to be a witness against himself," and, though the Act granted immunity from criminal prosecution upon the basis of forced testimony, the Supreme Court held that "a statutory enactment to be valid must afford absolute immunity for the offense to which the question relates."[1] To meet this decision Congress amended the Act without delay, giving both civil and criminal immunity. However, the amended Act was challenged in due course and it was not until 1896 in the Brown case[2] that the power of the Commission to compel testimony was effective. In the meanwhile, immeasurable injury had resulted from inability to secure, during the critical period of 1890–1896, much-needed evidence.

A second embarrassment of the Commission arose from the fact that its orders became binding only after an affirmative order of a federal court. To carry a case through to conclusion before the Commission took time; to appeal to the courts took additional time; and to carry cases through successive courts to the United States Supreme Court took yet further time until, in certain instances, years elapsed ere a final judgment was

[1] *Counselman v. Hitchcock*, 142 U. S. 547 (1892).

[2] *Brown v. Walker*, 161 U. S. 591 (1896).

had. And, though this judgment be favorable to the Commission, the intolerable delay reacted disadvantageously to the Commission and favorably to the carriers. But this handicap was greatly increased by the refusal of the courts to accept findings of fact made by the Commission as final. Considering cases upon appeal *de novo*, the courts made trial before the Commission but a preliminary skirmish, with the result that that body was compelled to make many decisions upon the basis of an incomplete statement of facts—decisions properly reversed by the courts later upon the basis of all the evidence. At length, in the Social Circle case,[1] the Supreme Court recognized the unwisdom of handling appeals in such manner—but again, in the interim, the Commission had suffered serious harm in a public mind that failed to appreciate the difficulties of the situation.

Emasculation of the Act of 1887.—The first serious reversal of the Commission in its attempt to apply the Act arose from its endeavor to eliminate discrimination against domestic and favorable to import or export tonnage. Upon the latter the carriers made rates far below those charged for similar movements of domestic traffic, to the disadvantage of the domestic producer. The railways justified the disparity upon the basis of conditions beyond their control—of competition they must meet if they shared in the traffic at all, but the Commission held such discrimination unreasonable: it interpreted its powers as limited to the consideration of domestic conditions only. Upon appeal, the Supreme Court reversed the Commission, declaring that body must give weight to *all* facts and conditions influencing, whether operating within or without national boundaries.[2]

A second and far more serious blow to the Act was suffered when the Supreme Court in the Maximum Freight Rate case[3] denied the Commission the right to prescribe maximum freight rates. For almost 10 years that body had assumed itself possessed of the right to fix reasonable rates and orders fixing such rates had been observed by the carriers without question. However, after the Supreme Court intimated in its Social Circle decision that there seemed to be no legal basis for rate prescription by the Commission, the railways lost no time in challenging the right of that body to act. And in 1897, in the Cincinnati Freight Bureau case—otherwise known as the Maximum Freight Rate case, the Supreme Court categorically denied the Commission's power to fix reasonable rates. Declaring that bestowal of such an important power is "not to be presumed or implied from any doubtful and uncertain language," the Court

[1] *Cincinnati, New Orleans and Texas Pacific Railway Company v. Interstate Commerce Commission*, 162 U. S. 184 (1896).

[2] *Texas and Pacific Railway Co. v. Interstate Commerce Commission*, 162 U. S. 197 (1896).

[3] *Interstate Commerce Commission v. Cincinnati, New Orleans and Texas Pacific Railway Company*, 167 U. S. 479 (1897).

insisted that, since "the words and phrases efficacious to make such a delegation of power are well understood," such language would have been used "if Congress had intended to grant such a power to the Interstate Commerce Commission." No longer able to prescribe rates effective for the future, the Commission was able to do no more than the courts—to judge the reasonableness of a rate *after* the fact and to award damages upon the difference between the rate charged and a rate regarded by the Commission as reasonable. However, it could take this further almost futile action—it could ban as unreasonable the specific rate found to be unreasonable, almost futile because it left the carrier free to charge legally *any* rate less than the one prescribed quite without regard to the reasonable rate upon the basis of which reparation had been given. Furthermore, the excessive rate will long since have been paid by the consumer in increased prices, so no protection of public interest exists under any reparation scheme.

But if denial of the power to fix maximum rates seriously crippled the work of the Commission, the final blow was delivered by the Supreme Court in the Alabama Midland case,[1] in which the regulatory body had sought to apply the Long-and-Short-Haul clause of the Act. Though difficulty had been experienced earlier as a consequence of the Osborne case,[2] the Court in the Social Circle case so interpreted the word "line" as to give the Commission clear control over shipments moving interline. However, in its interpretation of the phrase, "under substantially similar circumstances and conditions," the Supreme Court so acted as to make Sec. 4 a dead letter. The Commission held that dissimilarity of circumstances might result from the competition of rail carriers not subject to the Act, from the competition of water carriers, and from "rare and peculiar circumstances" of which the Commission itself would judge. The carriers, on the other hand, urged that other elements, such as carrier and market competition, must be recognized as making for dissimilarity—factors which had largely occasioned the abuse with which Congress sought to deal by the inclusion of Sec. 4 in the Act. In 1897, in the case named, the Supreme Court upheld the contention of the railways, but the Commission, hoping to salvage something from Sec. 4, sought to inject the element of reasonableness into a later case involving place discrimination. However, when the case came before the Supreme Court, that body held adversely to the Commission,[3] thus stripping away its last hope of power to act positively in behalf of public interest. In successive decisions the Supreme Court gave proof of the contention that no man knows what

[1] *Interstate Commerce Commission v. Alabama Midland Railway Company,* 168 U. S. 144 (1897).

[2] *Chicago and North Western Railway Company v. Osborne,* 52 Fed. Rep. 912 (1892).

[3] *East Tennessee, Virginia and Georgia Railway Company v. Interstate Commerce Commission,* 181 U. S. 1 (1901).

the law is until the courts, in their wisdom, have indicated what they believe the legislature meant or should have said.

Results of Federal Legislation.—As a consequence of the successive denials of power to the Commission, it found itself without cases for consideration: it had become merely a fact-finding body, marking time until its inevitable restoration to power. But certain positive benefits had resulted from the Act: discrimination had been lessened, particularly in Trunk Line territory; freight classifications had been greatly improved; and the statistical data accumulated in the years following 1887 and prior to 1906 have great value. Furthermore, experience under the Act showed, as nothing else could have done, how effective legislation should *not* be phrased if it were to be interpreted by the courts as intended by Congress and in a manner favorable to the public. And, finally, the federal experiment in regulation had encouraged a more careful study of railway matters and thereby assisted in the development of a more comprehensive grasp of the problems in that field by both the general public and its leaders.

Importance of the Third Period in Railway History.—On the whole, this third period is perhaps the most striking of all in its individual characteristics and the most significant, since it clearly gave rise to evils that influenced development during the later period in a more profound way than did any other in American railway history. The addition of mileage and the development of transcontinental service were phenomenal, and the reversal of a policy of generous aid to railway construction was striking. Unwise building and improper financing during these years lie at the bottom of much of the difficulty of the succeeding period, and the issue which was clearly joined between railway and public during the 20 years was destined to bring in its wake a complete system of regulation. This, conceived in antagonism and born of an ignorance of railway fundamentals, was bound to give punitive rather than constructive control of our railways. Indeed, an understanding can be gained of the great majority of the problems and difficulties which arise in the next period only through a careful study of this, the crucial period in the growth of a vital transportation agency.

REFERENCES

BOGART, E. L.: *Economic History of the United States*, Longmans, Green & Co., 1915.

CARTER, C. F.: *When Railroads Were New*, Henry Holt & Company, 1909.

CLEVELAND, F. A. and F. W. POWELL: *Railroad Promotion and Capitalization*, Longmans, Green & Co., 1909.

GEPHART, W. F.: Transportation and Industrial Development in the Middle West, *Columbia University Studies*, vol. 34, No. 1.

HANEY, LEWIS: A Congressional History of Railways in the United States, 1850–1885, *University of Wisconsin Bulletin* 342.

HUDSON, J. F.: *The Railways and the Republic*, Harper and Brothers, 1886.

Oberholtzer, E. P.: *Jay Cooke* (Deals with Northern Pacific), G. W. Jacobs and Co., 1907.

Paxson, F. L.: *The Pacific Railroads and the Disappearance of the American Frontier*, American Historical Association, Annual Report, 1907.

Pyle, Joseph G.: *Life of James J. Hill*, Doubleday, Doran & Company, Inc., 1917.

Report of the Industrial Commission, vol. 19, pp. 259–304.

Riegel, R. E.: *The Story of the Western Railroads*, The Macmillan Company, 1926.

Ringwalt, J. L.: *Development of Transportation Systems in the United States*, J. L. Ringwalt, 1888.

Ripley, W. Z.: *Railroads: Finance and Organization*, Longmans, Green & Co., 1915.

———: *Railroads: Rates and Regulation*, Longmans, Green & Co., 1912.

———: *Railway Problems*, Ginn and Company, 1913.

Thompson, Slason: *A Short History of American Railways*, D. Appleton & Company, 1925.

United States Census, 1880 and 1890.

United States Senate Document 43, 72d Congress, 1st session, *Coordination of Motor Transportation*, a report by L. J. Flynn, United States Government Printing Office.

Villard, Henry: *Memoirs* (Deals with Northern Pacific), Houghton Mifflin Company, 1904.

Warman, Cy: *The Story of the Railroads*, D. Appleton & Company, 1898.

Chapter IX

DEVELOPMENT OF THE RAILWAY PROBLEM: MILEAGE GROWTH AND CREDIT

THE fourth period in the progress of the American railway net is marked in a peculiar degree by events which were essentially the results of conditions that developed during preceding periods. The panic of 1893 closed one period and introduced another period. This event left a definite impress upon the course of railway growth and organization, particularly in the years immediately following. The rapid construction of mileage which featured the decade and a half prior to this financial debacle gave place to meager building and building never again reached its former magnitude. The panic also caused the financial collapse of a considerable fraction of our railway mileage and compelled numerous and drastic reorganizations from 1894 to about 1897. These reorganizations, as well as the need of continued support from important financial interests, gave splendid opportunity for the formation of the large ownership groupings of railways so characteristic of the period. Another feature of this period which exerted a strong influence upon railway development was the rapid industrialization which began in the later nineties. And as 1894 begins this final period, so does 1919 mark its close. Two years of federal operation ended early in 1920 with the return of all properties to private management. But of no less importance than this change to private control was the fact that the railways were returned subject to legislation which constituted a distinct departure from past regulatory policy, both state and federal. The year 1920 opened a new era in the relationship of carrier and public.

Factors Influencing Development.—During this period several factors exerted marked influence upon railway development. Among these perhaps none was more important, directly or indirectly, than the tremendous industrial growth in the years following recovery from the panic of 1893. Although industrial development had been noteworthy during the previous period it now became as spectacular as had been that of the railways during the score of years preceding 1893. The direct result of this industrial development was a tremendously increased demand for service; not only was the quantity of tonnage offered greater but need for a higher character of service appeared. This growing demand for service early taxed the capacity of the carriers in more highly developed territory, and, in consequence, certain of the more important—particularly those in the

Eastern District—faced the necessity of increasing facilities if the principle of increasing costs were not to apply. That railways in need of increasing plant capacity found difficulty in financing such expansion is ascribable in part to this very industrial development which threw upon them the greater burden. Such development, with its promise of a more generous reward to the investor than the railways could offer, absorbed large amounts of capital that would otherwise have been available for railway use.

A second important influence which operated throughout the major portion of this period was a rising price level. The upward movement began with recovery from the depression of the middle nineties and continued, with but minor recessions, until the peak was reached early in 1920. This increase in prices affected the railways perhaps more adversely than any other type of enterprise because, in the face of rising costs of operation, rates remained almost stationary under regulation until the financial needs of the carriers became so urgent that rectification could be postponed no longer. This relaxation in the parsimonious policies of regulatory bodies, particularly state commissions, came too late, however, to prove of material assistance in remedying during this period the ills which were so largely the result of long years of error.

A third feature that influenced the railways during these years was the general movement toward "big business" which was particularly pronounced in the decade closing with 1907. The advantages accruing from combination loomed large in the public eye and belief that certain of these advantages might be enjoyed in the railway field is indicated by public approval, or acceptance, of the large ownership groupings as well as the consolidation of lesser properties into large systems. Had not this movement encountered legal barriers there is little doubt but that, at the close of the period, the railways of the country would have been consolidated into a relatively small number of great systems, each occupying a semi-monopolistic or monopolistic position in the territory served by it.

A fourth factor of great significance during the later years of this period was the European war. Even before the United States entered the conflict the influence of that great struggle upon finances and upon operations had made itself felt. Not alone did America find it impossible to enlist the aid of European capital in either intensive or extensive programs of expansion; the American investor was forced to absorb enormous quantities of railway paper which had previously been held abroad. Railway operation was also affected. The large tonnage resulting from war orders by European combatants increased the demand for service upon the railways and a peculiar traffic situation developed: the dominant eastward movement of loaded cars, together with the congestion resulting from the dislocation of ocean commerce, cast a burden upon the carriers that was increasingly difficult to carry prior to the time of America's entry into the struggle. The further demand for service resulting from active participation in the war created a situation to which the most logical answer was federal operation. This temporary but radical departure from past policy came as the immediate result, therefore, of the war. However, as will be indicated later, other factors contributed in important degree to the condition which brought forth the presidential proclamation late in 1917 authorizing government operation as a war measure.

Mileage Development, 1894–1919.—The period ending in 1893 was marked by a spectacular increase in mileage, peak construction being reached in the late eighties; construction in the period beginning in 1894 reached its peak in 1906, about the middle of the period, only to decline progressively until, during the last few years, an actual shrinkage in total mileage occurred. From approximately 177,500 miles of railways at the close of 1893, the mileage of the United States increased to 253,152 at the close of 1919, an addition of more than 75,500 miles. The maximum mileage shown, however, is that of June 30, 1916, which stood at 254,251. The year-by-year distribution of this total mileage increase, which averages about 2,900 miles per year for the entire period, is interesting. As might be expected, development was slow immediately following the panic of 1893, the average for the first 5 years being somewhat less than 2,000 miles annually. Beginning in 1899, however, construction went forward more rapidly, the number of miles gradually increasing until the high point of the period was reached in 1906. In that year 6,262 miles of line were added. In the decade following 1906 a progressive decline characterized building, until, in 1917, for the first time in American railway history, more miles of railway were abandoned than constructed, the net decrease for that year being 625 miles. A decrease also marked each of the 2 succeeding years which closed the period, the approximate net loss for 3 years being 1,100 miles. The gradual decline in construction during the later years of this period is perhaps best indicated by certain summary figures. During the first 10 years following 1893 there were built, despite adverse financial conditions, about 34,000 miles of line, while in 10 years closing with 1919 but 17,000 miles were added; of the total mileage increase of more than 75,500 for the entire period, about 57,000 were laid during the first 15 years. That a large part of this extensive development should lie in the West was but natural since that section was less adequately served by railways than others, and offered greatest immediate opportunities for development. Development in the South, however, was much more pronounced than in the East, but here again the explanation lies in the less extensive railway development there during earlier years.

Extensive Growth Prior to 1908.—Mileage development justifies breaking this period into two parts, the years closing with 1907 and those following that date. Prior to 1908, building progressed in a normal manner; projects that had been undertaken during the course of the preceding period were carried to completion, and many older properties discovered the value of certain extensions—building, in consequence, mileage not contemplated originally. Although certain new projects appeared, these were of a minor character, their existence often due to encouragement given their promoters by older and well-established lines. Among the forces which lay back of construction at this stage, one of the more important was the desire to round out existing properties and to establish claim to new areas by the construction of branch mileage into it or by construction which tended to envelop certain areas and thus discourage competitive building. Another influence was the rapid industrial progress of this era, with its consequent demand for additional mileage in new areas and old. Too, the westward movement of population, so conspicuous during the previous period, continued through the early part of this. And that movement, despite overconstruction in the less developed sections prior to 1893, called for the addition of certain mileage.

On the whole, the first half of the fourth period in the growth of our railways may be regarded from a construction standpoint as normal, with a complete absence of the phenomenally extensive development that so featured the score of years ending in 1893. However, this decline in construction from unusual to normal was inevitable; indeed, it was to be welcomed. Extensive growth had progressed to the point of near-saturation and, with the stabilization of the industry, those speculative opportunities offered the promoter by pioneer enterprises had largely disappeared.

Mileage Development after 1907.—Mileage development in the United States after 1907 was, compared with that during any equal time for 40 years preceding, of negligible importance, and the actual mileage deficit finally experienced was in startling contrast to the steady increase during the more than three-quarters of a century preceding. The minor construction of these years was mainly of two types, the expansion of larger properties in less developed areas, West and South, and the closer gridironing of certain older sections in the interest of intensive development. No new systems of any consequence appeared; nominally independent lines, such as the Western Pacific, represented merely an effort on the part of older properties to accomplish through subsidiary corporations certain strategic ends. Railway stagnation in a relatively new and rapidly developing industrial nation, with no effective alternative transportation agencies then available, threatened disastrous results to carriers and to public alike.

The mileage deficit which appeared during the closing years of the period is not difficult to explain and the explanation introduces no dangerous factor. Indeed, one phrase, the war, both explains and justifies a policy of curtailing new projects, while the abnormal situation arising out of war conditions might reasonably be expected to plunge weaker properties into financial difficulties so serious as to force the cessation of operation, even the complete abandonment of mileage. Emphasis upon winning the war and the marshaling of all resources to that end left but little capital free for railway expansion not essential to war purposes. Then, too, during the period of federal control no railway executive associated with either operating or corporate interests had reason to plan or urge extensions.

The abandonment of mileage justifies somewhat more careful scrutiny, however. Analysis has shown that many of the abandoned properties had been built for a special purpose—the removal of some natural resource such as lumber or ore, and, that removal completed, there remained little economic basis for continued operation. The change in the economic situation during the war period was such as to loosen the grip of these properties upon economic solvency as well as to make them of greater value when scrapped than they were likely to be at any later time. Other properties built to serve a general purpose also found that the disturbance of long-standing relationships of revenues and expenses was so great that solvency, maintained for many years with the greatest difficulty, could not be protected longer: the tremendous upward movement of operating expenses in the face of slowly advancing or even stationary rate levels, ground these properties as between the upper and the nether millstones. That greater mileage was not abandoned was due to the courageous work of the sponsors of many of these weaker properties, together with a belated recognition of the needs of these enterprises by regulatory bodies and the shipping public. But despite all efforts, an excess of abandonment over construction has characterized the years since 1920 also—abandonment due initially, perhaps, to maladjustments growing out of the war but chargeable to more fundamental and permanent causes during recent years.

The Problem of Railway Credit.—Nevertheless, it is clear that the European war influenced the extensive development of our railway net even prior to our entry into the struggle. Indeed, had it not been for certain consequences of the European struggle from 1914 onward, it is doubtful if a mileage deficit would have been experienced so soon. With financial conditions in the United States none too sound when the war first opened, the situation abroad not only made it impracticable to secure further funds for expansion there, but the desire of Europeans to obtain gold forced American investors to absorb enormous security holdings which normally would have remained abroad. The necessity of absorbing these foreign holdings and unusual industrial opportunities that soon developed at home made the flotation of additional railway securities upon reasonable terms well-nigh impossible; the tremendous stimulation of industrial activities occasioned by war demands and a consequent "sellers' market" meant huge earnings in many fields, handsome gains in practically all. Such spectacular gains, when compared with the investment return in the railway field, inevitably crowded carrier securities, already weak, quite into the background.

The explanation of the readiness with which railway securities, known to the financial public for years, gave way to industrials, many of which were new and untried, involves an analysis of the status of railway securities at the outbreak of hostilities and during the early war years. Such an analysis calls for a complete examination of the credit situation of the railway; the once popular "railways" could not have occupied a position such as they did at this time except through a gradual but certain weakening of their credit fiber. The fundamental explanation of the cessation in railway development seems to lie, therefore, in the gradual failure of credit rather than in any peculiar and unusual situation such as war conditions.

To gain an understanding of the extent to which railway credit failed, particularly during the latter part of this period, railway financial needs must be determined and realizations compared therewith.

The Need for Railway Expansion.—In the years since 1920 the motor vehicle and the airplane have greatly changed the transportation situation. Prior to that time, however, to say that continuous expansion of transportation facilities was essential was tantamount to saying further development of the railway net must occur. That such continuous expansion is vital in a progressive country is patent: without it the public cannot be adequately served and without it railways could not avoid overtaxed facilities and operation under conditions of increasing cost. To the railways it was also essential if they were to escape condemnation and punitive action from a public hampered by a service inadequate to meet growing needs. Since the best index of the rate at which expansion should proceed is the actual rate at which the demand for service has grown, a study of traffic history is pertinent. Experience covering a score of years prior to 1910 indicated that freight tonnage tended to double every 12 years, while the volume of passenger traffic doubled in approximately 15 years. And in the next decade this rate of growth was maintained. To assume that the capacity of the railway plant, considered both extensively and intensively, must double within each such period or prove inadequate was an error, since many lines in the South and West had not yet reached the maximum efficient capacity of the plant to serve. Nevertheless, if railway expansion were to fall short of an approximate 8 per cent per annum for an extended period, during years when the railway was the sole effective agency of inland transport, industry and commerce must feel the crippling effects of progressively inadequate facilities.

The most obvious type of expansion, though one of diminishing significance, has been that of line mileage. So thoroughly were the more productive areas gridironed during the period of linear growth that the saturation point was reached in many large sections. A second type of expansion, however, which may be termed intensive, increased in importance as the other declined. Intensive development takes various forms. It involves, in part, the construction of multiple trackage; in part, an increase in switching facilities, both yards and sidings; in part, added equipment—locomotives and cars, both passenger and freight. That the actual rate of expansion of the railways, both intensively and extensively, fell far short of the indicated traffic needs of the country for a considerable time prior to 1920 is shown clearly by a statistical analysis of pertinent data.

Progressive Decline in Railway Growth.—Attention has already been directed to the declining rate of expansion in railway mileage, but perhaps that condition may be better realized when the percentage rate of increase from period to period is given. In the 5½ years prior to the close of the fourth period in 1919, the total increase in line mileage was but 0.07 per cent; during the preceding 5-year period the percentage of expansion was 10.4, with a percentage of 11.6 for the period from 1905 to 1909, inclusive. From these figures it is clearly evident that the extensive development of the railway plant had in no sense kept pace with traffic growth. However, it was of greater significance that the railway plant failed to keep pace with industrial needs by intensive development. This failure is evident in every phase of intensive growth. Although from 1905 to 1909 multiple trackage increased by something less than 7 per cent per year and from 1910 to 1914 by almost 6.5 per cent, even those figures fell short of traffic needs and a total increase of less than 13 per cent for the last 5½ years of the period, an average of less than 2.5 per cent a year, gives clear proof of inadequacy. The same conclusion holds true for the construction of yards and sidings. During the first 5-year period this mileage increased at the rate of about 5 per cent a year; during the second period at the rate of approximately 4 per cent per year; but during the last period mentioned it grew by less than 1 per cent per year. And if increase at any point is essential to the avoidance of congestion and consequent delays, it is in switching facilities: yards and sidings, particularly in terminal areas and important centers, represent the "neck of the bottle" in the handling of business.

In the provision of additional equipment the railways of the United States failed to meet growing traffic demands as signally, on the whole, as in the case of mileage and trackage. From 1905 to 1909 inclusive, the number of locomotives in service increased by less than 4.5 per cent annually, while during the succeeding 5 years the annual increase dropped to less than 3 per cent. For the remaining 5½ years, closing with 1919, the annual rate of increase was but little more than 1 per cent. This same decline is evident, though not to the same degree, happily, when measured in terms of locomotive tractive capacity, the annual averages for the three periods mentioned being 8.5, 5.6, and 4 per cent, approximately. In the matter of freight cars in service, the percentages run closely parallel to those of the number of locomotives, though the increase in tonnage capacity of all freight equipment diminished more rapidly, those figures being, for the three periods discussed, approximately 9, 5, and 1.4 per cent. An examination of the rate of increase in passenger equipment shows an even less favorable situation when stated in percentages, though perhaps this condition was not serious because the railways had not attained maximum utilization of passenger equipment generally. In the 5 years beginning with 1905, the annual rate of increase of such equipment in service averaged less than 3 per cent, for the next 5-year period approximately 3.5 per cent, while for the period closing with 1919 the annual rate of growth was less than 1 per cent.

Decline Reflected by Railway Capitalization.—From the foregoing facts it is clear that, even though considerable "slack" in the capacity of American railways to serve had existed as a result of overexpansion during earlier years, the railway plant began to lag seriously some years prior to 1920. As further evidence of this failure to meet the growing traffic needs of the United States, the increase of railway capitalization may be cited. It is impossible to discover the net amount of railway securities outstanding and not held by railway companies prior to 1910, but a comparison of the total amounts outstanding at the beginning and at the close of the 5-year periods 1905–1909 and 1910–1914, together with a comparison of the net amount outstanding at the beginning and at the close of the period 1915–1919, is significant. During the first 5-year period in question, total outstanding securities increased by almost $4,275,000,000, an average of almost 6.5 per cent per annum, but during the next 5-year period the increase was little more than $2,760,000,000, or slightly above 3 per cent, showing thus a decline in the rate of increase to slightly less than one-half for the second period. And the third period shows an increase in the net outstanding of slightly less than $316,000,000, an almost negligible 0.3 per cent annually. An analysis of the comparatively satisfactory situation during the first 5-year period for which data are given shows that bonds increased at almost double the rate of stock. This fact is doubly significant: it indicates the growing difficulty experienced by the carriers in marketing stock with its secondary claim upon inadequate revenues, and shows a willingness to market bonds when existing issues were already pressing the margin of safety all too closely. Although during the last 5-year period the bond total diminished slightly and outstanding stock increased by 4 per cent, practically the entire increase in the latter came during the first 2 years of the period; after that time there was no market for railway stock. These facts alone show the precarious condition of railway credit, for no enterprise can long remain upon a sound basis when forced to depend wholly or even largely upon the issuance of bonds for the funds requisite to expansion.

Reasons for Decline in Railway Credit.—The reasons for this decline in railway credit are too numerous and too involved to permit of a complete portrayal here. A brief sketch, however, of some of the more important causes is desirable. Among them was the loss of confidence in railway securities by the investment public because of numerous past failures, as well as the threat so generally made to "squeeze the water" out of railway issues. Two outstanding causes for the failure of American railways appear, of which the more significant is overconstruction. One of the penalties which the American public has paid for the early appearance of railway mileage in sections not yet justifying such construction economically has been the financial collapse and reorganization of practically all properties so built. Another cause of failure and one which, because of its nature, has been advertised beyond its actual importance in the field, is fraudulent financial management. Such management brought disaster not only because it often plunged the property into immediate bankruptcy, but also because it weakened the financial structure and thus made the property susceptible to financial ills to which it otherwise might have been immune. But despite the influence which failure and reorganization had upon the standing of railway securities in years past, perhaps the constantly and emphatically voiced insistence upon lowering capitalization was even more disquieting. This, with no valuation data to reassure prospective investors, inevitably deflected capital from the railway to other and less scrutinized fields.

A second cause for the decline of railways securities in the market and one applying more particularly to stocks of a somewhat speculative character was the substantial disappearance of speculative opportunities in the railway field after about 1905. Both because of rising standards of financial morality and because of legal restrictions imposed, gains through financial operations incident to construction or to consolidation had been minimized or eliminated. The regulation of rates and services had, in similar manner, removed practically all opportunity of speculative gains accruing from the operation of the more favorably situated properties. Then, too, with the aging and solidification of the railway industry, the opportunities for unusual gains gradually disappeared.

A third factor which tended to weaken progressively the position of railway securities in the financial market was the rise of rival investments. These were of two types, the more important being the "industrials," which first attained prominence in the early years of recovery from the depression of the middle nineties. Prior to that time rails had occupied an almost exclusive position in the large security markets but, as time passed, industrials gained increasing attention until, by 1906, they had overshadowed rails in the eyes of the investor. This rapid rise was due essentially to the absence of regulation; the legal position of such enterprises was such that a closer correlation of risk and profit existed than it was possible to secure under a parsimonious policy of control in a field "burdened with public interest" as is railway enterprise. But not only did railway securities have to compete with industrial issues which offered to those of speculative leanings a high return and to those desiring investment paper a comparative degree of safety, but also with great quantities of tax-exempt bonds issued by minor government units—township, city, village, and even school district. These governmental issues offered a degree of safety comparable in most cases to that of the best railway bonds, yet paid a rate often distinctly above that offered by railways upon equally sound issues. Caught thus between industrials which offered high returns with measurable safety and governmentals which offered safety with a relatively high return, the plight of railway issues became increasingly serious.

Decline in Net Operating Income.—Intimately related to this growing disfavor with which railway securities were regarded in financial markets —in fact, underlying that situation as a major causative factor, was the decline in net operating income of the railways. This decline was due in part to a rapid increase in expenses, in part to a rate level which remained stationary during a long upward price movement. Beginning in the late nineties, the railways found themselves obliged to pay progressively higher prices for everything they used—capital, materials, and labor— and this upward movement was quickened during the latter part of the period by war conditions. Another explanation of the increase in expenses appears in the situation of certain properties in more highly developed areas; the plant was asked to render service beyond maximum efficient capacity. Indeed, as early as 1906 it appears that the law of increasing cost had begun to operate in portions of the Eastern District and by 1919 this condition was the rule rather than the exception among the more important properties in that territory. Then, finally, expenses had been augmented gradually but surely as the result of growing public requirements. Not only did taxes assessed against railway properties increase out of all proportion to the change in the ability of the railways to pay, but demands and restrictions imposed upon the railways with respect to the physical plant and its operations involved considerable expense also. Certain of these demands and requirements were often entirely sound in character and justified—the separation of grade crossings, the installation of safety devices, and even more adequate terminal facilities. But, on the other hand, the requirement of stations beyond the need of particular communities and interference with operations through such statutes as "full-crew" and maximum train-length laws accomplished little more than a needless increase in railway expenses.

In the face of this increase in expense, rates failed to advance in proportion, if at all. The explanation of this stationary rate level is somewhat involved but without doubt it resulted largely from the popular hostility of the period to the railways and the influence of that hostility upon commissions, state and federal. This situation was aggravated by the almost complete lack of authentic data upon the true value of properties devoted to the public service, which fact made it impossible to determine whether or not a reasonable return was being earned. Even as to the nature of this reasonable return there was distinct uncertainty: both commissions and courts often confused it with that minimum which just escapes the constitutional prohibition against confiscation. In consequence, rates were too frequently adjusted to yield a return barely sufficient to maintain the existing plant, rather than one sufficient to draw into the railway field from time to time those sums necessary for expansion. And last, but by no means least as an explanation of stationary rates throughout this period, was the transfer of the burden of proof to the railways in rate-increase cases. Because of the inadequacy of their data covering property values and operating costs, the railways found it impossible to establish clearly a case for higher rates and their situation became increasingly more difficult.

In consequence of this diminution in net operating income, the amount available for payment of interest and dividends, instead of increasing with considerable regularity as it had from the middle nineties until 1910–1914, dropped off after that time. This downward trend of income lessened the margin of safety upon bonds and caused the average rate of dividends declared upon all stocks, which reached its maximum in 1911, to decline from that time to the close of the period.

Uncertainty of Governmental Policy.—Perhaps a final factor contributing to the decline of railway credit was the growing uncertainty as to the probable future relation between railways and government. Among certain groups there appeared a growing sense of the failure of regulation, as it had existed, to accomplish satisfactorily its public purpose and, with this sense of failure, there soon developed an attitude which might be termed fatalistic or perhaps even helpless. Neither among those high in public service nor among those who shaped railway policy had there been the insight or the vision to devise a constructive solution of the problem. Added to doubt as to the ultimate success of regulation on the part of some who had favored it in the past was the growing demand on the part of certain radical groups for government ownership and operation of the railways of the United States. With so much uncertainty with respect to the ultimate relation of railway and government best suited to serve public interest, it is not strange that private capital should hesitate to enter the field.

A Summary.—The failure of the railways to expand extensively and intensively during these years to meet increasing traffic demands was not due to the unwillingness of those carriers to enlarge the plant. Rather, it was the consequence of weakened credit, a result in part of certain unusual conditions but in greater measure of unsound policies on the part of both railways and public, many of which date back to the last quarter of the nineteenth century. But whatever the explanation, the necessity of the situation seemed obvious: either needed expansion of the railway net must be made possible under private ownership and operation through the adoption of a constructive policy, or the failure of that plant to expand would so restrict commerce and industry as to make government ownership and operation inevitable. The public will be content with nothing less than adequate service.

Appearance of Large Ownership Groupings.—A third conspicuous characteristic of this fourth period in American railway history was the further expansion of large systems and particularly the appearance of large ownership groupings. Although linear consolidation had created certain large properties prior to 1873, and although construction into new areas had given birth to certain other large properties during the succeeding period, it was not until after 1893 that "big business," familiar to the public in the field of industry and commerce, appeared in the railway field. This consolidation of carriers was but a phase of the general movement toward consolidation which characterized business enterprise in those years following recovery from the depression of the middle nineties and prior to the panic of 1907. It was felt that the economies of large-scale production might be realized in the field of transportation as well as in others and the movement was furthered by the desire of the railways to escape legal restrictions imposed upon cooperative action. Not only had states forbidden pooling and other forms of association regarded by the railways as necessary to the elimination of injurious competition, but the anti-pooling clause of the federal Act of 1887 banned the pooling of interstate business, and the application of the Sherman Act to the railways in the Trans-Missouri Freight Association case of 1897 illegalized rate agreements. In view of these facts it is not strange that the railways sought to strengthen their position by the federation of properties to such an extent as was possible within the law.

Methods and Gains of Federation.—This federation of properties took two major forms of which the simpler and more effective was the actual unification of railways through amalgamation or merger. But this method could be employed on a broad scale only by noncompetitive lines, as in the case of the Southern Railway, which is the result of the consolidation of lines serving important points in the South. The federation of properties more often took a somewhat less final form and represented more or less intimate cooperation rather than actual unification.

In some instances cooperation was attempted through a holding company, the control of both competitive and noncompetitive properties being vested in that agency. The decision in the Northern Securities case in 1904, however, eliminated the holding company as a means of securing cooperation among competitive properties, though it was often used to link connecting properties together, conspicuous instances being the Rock Island System and the Atlantic Coast Line. Another means of bringing about effective cooperation was through stock ownership. This method was employed to "harmonize" both competitive and noncompetitive lines throughout the major part of the entire period, control sometimes arising out of the ownership by one railway of stock in another, sometimes out of the common ownership by individuals of large security holdings in those lines which it was desired to coordinate. Here again legal difficulties were finally encountered by railways which sought to exercise control over competitive lines, as shown by the Union Pacific-Southern Pacific decision.[1] Yet the coordination of properties through individual holdings, which characterized the Great Northern-Northern Pacific system, seemed to escape the ban. A third means of coordinating properties appears in that relation which has been variously termed community of interest and the interlocking directorate. This plan, although representing an exceedingly loose type of cooperation, proved not only effective with competitive properties but useful in the case of supplementary lines as well. It also enjoyed the important advantage of escaping, in the case of competitive properties, the legal prohibitions which lay upon unification or coordination through either the holding company or railway stock ownership. This plan was widely used by the railways of the United States but was peculiarly serviceable in Eastern territory where the threat of competition always hung heavy.

That definite gains to the railways resulted from the formation of large ownership groupings during this period is undoubted, although they are impossible of measurement. Certain it is that in no section of the United States throughout this entire fourth period was there an outbreak of such rate or service wars as characterized the period preceding. True, other stabilizing factors must be credited in part for this situation, but centralization of control contributed largely to the desired end. Economies of operation resulted also from this movement toward consolidation, such savings increasing in direct proportion to the degree to which properties were unified in a physical as well as an ownership sense. Although competition is still regarded by the American public as a desirable feature of railway policy, it is undoubtedly true that, within certain limits, unified control is advantageous. A final gain resulting from this movement toward consolidation lay in the stronger financial support which large and well-articulated properties were able to obtain. Indeed,

[1] *United States v. Union Pacific Railroad Company*, 226 U. S. 61 (1912).

many of the groupings which took place were made possible by the support of certain large banking interests and later received from those groups such financial assistance as enabled them to bridge over, without collapse, otherwise almost inevitable periods of distress during the years from the late nineties to the inception of federal control. Had it not been for the legal barriers erected by state and federal governments, it is quite probable that the movement toward consolidation, particularly in the years from the late nineties to the outbreak of the European war in 1914, would have witnessed the grouping of the railways of the United States into that relatively small number of systems which the Transportation Act contemplates, though it is not certain that these systems would have developed in consonance with public interest except as constructive cooperation might have been offered by state and federal regulatory bodies.

Railway Mechanical Progress 1893–1919.—The fourth period in railway growth witnessed rapid improvement of the physical plant, and this contributed much to the efficiency of railway operations which characterized this period. To meet the demands made upon the roadway by larger locomotives and heavier car loading, lines of high traffic density were more heavily ballasted and the old 65- to 75-pound rail was replaced by steel weighing from 85 to 100 pounds, with the 120-pound rail appearing. Bridges were correspondingly strengthened and the cost of maintenance of roadway and structure was markedly reduced by many railways through scientific timber treatment. During this period, also, important gains were scored in the field of motive power. The average tractive capacity of locomotives in service increased by more than half, and certain improvements made the locomotive a more efficient mechanism. Perhaps most significant of these improvements was the superheater, just coming into general use, which largely eliminates the inefficiency resulting from the use of wet steam in the cylinders, and the compound locomotive which, first attaining prominence during this period, is designed to use to the maximum the power resident in steam developed. The mechanical stoker, made necessary by the introduction of mammoth locomotives, also represented a distinct advance.

Great progress was made in car construction, that other factor so intimately related to railway efficiency. This held true not only as to type of construction and capacity but also as to diversification in types. In the modern passenger coach wood construction gave way wholly to steel and in the building of freight equipment the steel underframe was universally adopted. In fact, increasing numbers of cars, particularly of the gondola type, were constructed entirely of steel or with steel framework. Though figures relative to the capacity of passenger coaches are not available, a casual comparison of coaches built in the years just prior to 1920 with such survivors of the eighties as were yet in service on branch or suburban lines made it evident that passenger capacity had increased sharply. This increase resulted in no reduction in the dead weight per passenger, however; on the contrary, due to steel construction, this weight increased. Average freight-car capacity, like tractive power, increased during the period by more than 50 per cent and with that increase in capacity came a wide diversification in types of equipment to meet the needs of a rapidly developing and diversified industrial life. But diversification was not peculiar to freight equipment; in the passenger field, during the quarter of a century embraced within this period, many new types of equipment were brought out better to satisfy the needs and desires of the traveler, both for him who is willing to pay an additional sum for special service and for the "forgotten man," who must ride in such equipment as is placed at the disposal of the ordinary passenger.

(See reference list at the close of Chap. X.)

Chapter X

DEVELOPMENT OF THE RAILWAY PROBLEM: THE PERFECTION OF REGULATION

THE years that lay between the panic of 1873 and the sharp collapse of 1893 were turbulent, marked not only by bitter struggles among the railways themselves but by contests no less bitter between the railways and the public. These contests between carrier and shipper were waged upon a broad front—in the open forum, in legislative halls, and in the chambers of lesser and superior courts. An economic depression, astute leadership, and corruption, together with faulty regulatory technique, enabled the railways to repel the first general assault upon their legal status with success during the early seventies. In the succeeding period, benefiting by previous experience, the public returned to the attack upon both the state and federal fronts. States that had earlier abandoned their attempts to exercise positive control were joined by others in the establishment of mandatory commissions and the enactment of other legislation purposed to curb railway action. The Interstate Commerce Act was passed and for a time gave promise of giving over interstate movements the control exercised by certain of the states over intrastate movements. But in a previous chapter the emasculation of that Act was outlined: by successive interpretations the federal courts stripped from the Commission functioning thereunder all effective power.

Demand for Effective Regulation.—In the years immediately following 1893 the American people as a whole were so deeply concerned with returning prosperity, with a war and its resulting problems, with "trusts," and with other lesser matters, that comparatively little thought was given to the development of a comprehensive scheme of regulation. Beginning about 1897, however, certain positive influences began to operate and these, supplemented by continuing causes for complaint, resulted within a decade in positive and effective action. One of the more important of these factors was the movement toward railway consolidation which had its beginnings in the general financial collapse of the railways during the depression period. This movement accomplished, in a brief time, the grouping of much of the railway mileage of the country into a comparatively small number of ownership systems, dominated by powerful individuals or banking groups and centering largely in New York. Public protest against consolidation rested upon two principal grounds. It was urged that such unification of properties threatened the commercial interests of important centers: these, formerly important termini and perhaps the pride of some particular carrier, feared that they might become but way stations upon a consolidated property and the object of a widely divided affection. Furthermore, it was contended that the consolidation of properties represented a clear and positive movement toward monopoly. And this tendency was the object of attack not only because it was felt that such control would result in direct exploitation of the public through higher rates and poorer service, but also because the intimate relations between certain important railway interests and great industrial combinations gave basis for the fear that the public would suffer indirectly from railway consolidation at the hands of these industrial giants.

Upward Movement of Freight Rates.—A second impelling force operating during these years to hasten effective regulation was the upward movement of freight rates. Prior to the close of the nineteenth century, the movement of charges had been steadily downward and even the railways themselves expected that trend to continue. A reversal appeared, however, to the great concern of the public. For this change one cause was the lessening of competition that resulted from consolidation and integration of railways, as well as from the establishment of some measure of control over competitive action as business improved. A more important cause, however, lay in the upward swing of prices that began in the late nineties and continued, with only certain minor and temporary recessions, for almost a quarter of a century. With an increase in both labor and material costs, the carriers regarded an increase in rates as clearly equitable. Then, too, certain of the railways operating in heavy traffic areas found that, as they neared the maximum efficient capacity of the plant, the operation of the law of increasing returns was correspondingly less in evidence: indeed, not only did costs tend to increase in almost direct proportion to traffic but in certain instances the law of increasing costs became operative.

Growing Importance of Rebates.—A third factor, and significant in arousing public opinion, was the rapidly growing importance—and deep threat—of personal discrimination. Though such discrimination was prohibited by the Act of 1887, the statutory provisions were such that effective control had been impossible: indeed, during the 16 years following its passage, convictions under the Act had scarcely exceeded that figure, despite an almost universal prevalence of "concessions." A section inadequate to control personal discrimination even prior to the period of "big business" failed miserably in the face of demands for favors by great industrial units. Because of their magnitude, when these units were not *offered* concessions by traffic representatives seeking to increase tonnage, concessions were *forced* from unwilling carriers in the form of lower rates and better service than were accorded to independent competitors.

Among the outstanding recipients of favors from the railways during this period were the beef and sugar interests, the Standard Oil Company, and the International Harvester Company. Inadequate though existing legislation was to eliminate favoritism, it caused the railways to substitute for the *obvious* rebate or lower-than-published rate a most ingenious array of devious, yet equally effective, methods. Of the more important and "contriving" of these brief mention will be made. For those concerns owning railway equipment, such as refrigerator and tank cars, excessive compensation for use by the railways offered an excellent method of giving concessions. Corporations owning industrial, spur, and tap lines were generously compensated for "important services rendered." Shippers were encouraged to lodge excessive damage claims with the assurance that these would be handled by a sympathetic adjuster. Some concerns that paid standard rates received higher than market prices for material sold the railways. "Midnight tariffs" were employed, favored shippers being informed in advance so that they might avail themselves of the temporary rate to maximum advantage. Certain shippers were favored in the distribution of equipment during periods of car shortage; others were relieved of demurrage charges. But perhaps no more ingenious method was employed than one well illustrated by rates upon oil into the South. Because of its knowledge of a special tariff, publicly filed, from a point near its Whiting, Indiana, refinery to an important point in the South, the Standard Oil Company was able for a considerable period to dominate largely the oil traffic of that section. Thus, in innumerable ways and in a countless number of cases, the spirit of the law prohibiting personal discrimination was violated, yet the consequences of that violation were avoided.

The diminution in carrier revenues as a result of concessions made to shippers cannot be estimated accurately because even a painstaking examination of records would fail to reveal all the facts. An investigation begun by the state of Wisconsin in 1903 disclosed that one railway had allowed direct rebates amounting to $7,000,000 within a period of 6 years prior to that date, while other important lines were shown to have lost upwards of $500,000 in a single year. If to these sums be added the losses by concealed rebates, and figures were available for all railway lines, an enormous total results. To this evil consequence must be added the part played by such special favors in the upbuilding of certain large industrial units that came to dominate in their particular fields. This threat of industrial monopoly, added to the uncertainty of the small shipper as to what handicap the morrow might impose upon him in comparison with his greater competitor, finally so aroused public opinion that remedial legislative action was inevitable. And the carriers, unable because of competitive influences to bring this Frankenstein under control, gladly supported amendments designed to make the provisions of the Act against personal discrimination more effective.

The Elkins Act.—As a consequence of united action on the part of two normally antagonistic groups, the Elkins Act was passed by Congress in 1903 almost without opposition. This measure modified the Act of 1887 in certain significant particulars. The carrier—the actual beneficiary—as well as its agent was made punishable; the published tariff was made binding and any departure therefrom constituted a violation; the recipient of the rebate was made equally liable with the giver; and, in the hope of making conviction easier, punishment was to be by fine only—imprisonment was eliminated as an alternative penalty. Furthermore, the issuance of injunctions by any federal court against departures from published tariffs or against any other type of prohibited discrimination was authorized.

Until 1905 the amended Act was invoked little but, beginning then and extending through several years, many prosecutions were undertaken with highly satisfactory results. Among the concerns penalized were many of the old-time offenders—Standard Oil, the "Beef Trust," and the "Sugar Trust" being among the more conspicuous. From the first-named the government collected almost $600,000 within 18 months, while from the last about half that sum was collected. In the 5 years immediately following the passage of the Act, the evil of personal discrimination was reduced to small proportions, though such discrimination, disguised more carefully, persisted for many years and has even yet not been wholly eliminated. However, federal action in this field has proved as effective as legislation is likely to be.

Railway Regulation a Paramount Issue.—The Elkins Act accomplished much toward the elimination of a particular abuse, but it was only an opening skirmish in the battle for that effective control of the railways which Congress had seemingly intended to establish in 1887. As early as 1894 attempts were made to strengthen the Act but another decade was to pass before public sentiment crystallized and action was demanded of Congress. In 1904 President Roosevelt, in his message to Congress, characterized the enactment of railway legislation as "a paramount issue." Under the spur of popular demand and executive pressure, the House of Representatives passed the Esch-Townsend Bill by an overwhelming majority, but the Senate, where the railways were strongly intrenched, delayed action pending an investigation. The facts disclosed by this investigation only added fuel to the fire of public indignation, however, and this fire was fanned to a white heat by the exposure of a thoroughgoing and detailed plan to influence public opinion by every means from bogus conventions to "controlled" editorials and garbled news. The House again acted, passing the Hepburn Bill almost unanimously, and circumstances so developed as to force action by the Senate. For, "at the psychological moment came the general breakdown and congestion of railroad service all over the country; the insurance investigation in New York; the Pennsylvania Railroad coal scandal; the Atchison rebate disclosures, with 'barefaced disregard for law,' besmirching a member of the President's cabinet."[1] With slight modifications made in conference, the Hepburn Bill became law and effective federal regulation became an accomplished fact.

Important Powers Given the Commission.—In the Hepburn Act the losses suffered by the Commission through interpretations of the Act of 1887, as well as later experience, were capitalized. In the first place, the scope of the Act was broadened to include private car lines, express companies, sleeping-car companies, pipe lines, and all terminal and switching properties: the first and the last because of the part they had played in personal discrimination, express and sleeping-car companies because of exorbitant and oftentimes discriminatory rates, and pipe lines in an effort to strike at the monopolistic position of the Standard Oil Company. But more important than the broadened scope of the Act were new powers granted. Of these, the outstanding was the power to prescribe just and reasonable maximum rates. Such rates were to become effective after 30 days and were to remain in force for a period of 2 years except as suspended, modified, or set aside by a court of competent jurisdiction. And the Commission was empowered to apportion joint rates when carriers were unable to agree upon their division; to establish through routes; and to fix reasonable charges for services or property provided by shippers.

A second important provision was that empowering the Commission to prescribe a uniform system of accounts for all agencies subject to the Act. Though progress had been made under the Act of 1887, the Commission had been compelled to rely upon voluntary cooperation rather than being in a position to compel railway conformance to suggestions. For various reasons a uniform system of accounts for railways is desirable. To the railway it assures more honest and often more efficient operation; to the investor a far more accurate record of financial operations, particularly with reference to capital expenditures and maintenance; to the public greater equality of treatment and a sounder factual basis for the determination of rates; and to labor a more detailed and accurate knowledge of the industry upon which to base, in part, its demands relative to wages and working conditions.

Prohibitions in the Act.—In addition to the powers noted, the Hepburn Act contained certain prohibitions and restrictions affecting the railways. Of these perhaps the most important was the so-called Commodities clause. Designed to eliminate active participation by the "hard-coal roads" in the mining and marketing of anthracite coal, a menace to the independent operator, it provided that

> After May 1, 1908, it shall be unlawful for any railroad company to transport from any state . . . to any other state . . . any article or commodity other

[1] Ripley, W. Z., *Railroads: Rates and Regulation*, p. 499.

than timber produced by it or under its authority or which it may own in whole or in part or in which it may have any interest, direct or indirect, except such articles or commodities as may be necessary and intended for its use in the conduct of its business as a common carrier.

A second prohibition, if such a general statement might be so termed, was intended to narrow the scope of judicial review to questions of law when appeals were taken from the Commission, also to protect the Commission against surprise action before the courts and to secure to it the benefit of the judgment of three judges when an injunction was sought against its orders. However, fearful that the courts would not recognize a strong statement of the desire of Congress, the provisions were not positive and it was not until the decision of the Supreme Court in the Illinois Central Coal Car Distribution case that the problem of review was settled to public advantage. A third prohibition dealt with the issuance of free transportation, or "passes," to persons moving in interstate commerce, except to named groups. Since most of the states had already acted to eliminate this evil intrastate, the use of free transportation was now quite effectively eliminated as a corrupting factor. And to these prohibitions may be added certain other provisions: imprisonment was restored as an alternative penalty for rebating and forfeiture to the government of triple the sums rebated during a 6-year period prior to prosecution provided; the Carmack Amendment gave the shipper of goods moving over two or more roads the legal right to recover for loss or damage from the initial carrier which might, in turn, recover from the other carriers involved to the extent that facts justified. And, to enable it to meet its increased responsibilities, Commission membership was enlarged to seven, the term of office was made seven years, and salary fixed at $10,000.

Work of the Commission.—After the brief time necessary to acquaint the shippers with the possibilities of this new legislation, the increase in the work of the Commission was striking. From 1905 to 1907 the total of formal and informal complaints increased almost tenfold; great activity was shown in the handling of loss and damage claims; the Commission secured a reduction in the number of tariffs filed to less than half within 5 years, thus simplifying the determination of rates; misrouting of shipments was greatly reduced; and progress was made in the elimination of personal discrimination. Furthermore, the Commission immediately devised a partial set of accounts for the railways, effective in 1907, which was completed and applied in 1914. And at later dates the Commission prescribed systems of accounts for other agencies subject to its jurisdiction. Although deliberate violation and varied interpretation have lessened the effectiveness of the prescribed systems in the past, the former has almost disappeared and the latter has been reduced to a minimum by Commission inspection and cooperation. In consequence, this phase of the Commission's work has proved most helpful and, though not spectacular, highly important in regulation.

The effectiveness of the Commission was advanced markedly by a cooperative attitude on the part of the Supreme Court in the matter of the scope of judicial review of Commission decisions. In the Social Circle case the evils of broad review were recognized and in the Hepburn Act a curb upon such review was suggested by Congress. In 1906, shortly after the passage of the Act, the Supreme Court confirmed the attitude taken some years earlier, but it was not until 1910 that the finality of the Commission's findings of fact was unmistakably declared. In commenting upon the general function of the judiciary with respect to statutory enactments, the Court said,[1]

> Plain as it is that the powers just stated are of the essence of judicial authority and . . . may not be curtailed . . . it is equally plain that such perennial powers lend no support whatever to the proposition that we may . . . usurp merely administrative functions by setting aside a lawful administrative order upon our conception as to whether the administrative power has been wisely exercised. . . . Power to make the order, and not the mere expediency or wisdom of having made it, is the question.

This position, with but slight modifications, has been maintained by the courts in succeeding years, with the result that Commission findings of fact are seldom challenged upon appeal.

Application of the Commodities Clause.—Only with respect to one feature of the Hepburn Act did difficulty of enforcement arise. The purpose of the Commodities clause was clear, but the situation with which it dealt was complex. In certain instances the railways owned and operated mines directly, in others they owned the stock of operating coal companies. The first case to reach the Supreme Court dealt with the latter situation and, though the constitutionality of the clause was upheld, its effectiveness was destroyed: the Court, in conformance with previous holdings to the effect that ownership of stock in a corporation did not constitute ownership of the property of the corporation, declared that the Delaware and Hudson Railroad, through possession of the stock of the coal company, had no interest in the coal shipped by its subsidiary which would make it subject to the Commodities clause.[2] Indeed, the Court went further and suggested that, though the railway were the legal owner of coal at the mouth of the mine, it might escape the application of the Act by selling the coal at that point. This decision, with its helpful counsel to those railways which owned mining properties directly, soon led to an organization of the business that presumptively put the carriers beyond the reach of the law.

[1] *Illinois Central Railroad Company v. Interstate Commerce Commission,* 215 U. S. 452 (1910).

[2] *United States v. Delaware and Hudson Company,* 213 U. S. 366 (1909).

However, the Supreme Court somewhat later in the Lehigh Valley[1] and Lackawanna[2] cases gave greater weight to the spirit of the law, stating that the drawing of mere corporate lines could not be permitted to obscure the real identity of interest: a separation *in fact* was ordered in each case. And in 1920 the Court took in the Reading case[3] a yet more advanced position. The Reading Company, a holding company, owned the Philadelphia and Reading Railway Company on the one hand and the Reading Coal and Iron Company on the other, with no interlocking between railway and coal companies; but the Reading Company was ordered to dispose of either its carrier or coal interests. Whether such separations as were compelled were advantageous to the public is problematical, but the Court's emphasis upon realities rather than upon the letter of the law was in itself beneficial.

Further Restrictive Legislation.—Shortly after the passage of the Hepburn Act certain influences became operative that led to further legislation. The railways contested the findings of the Commission at every point, the courts by certain decisions inflamed an already aroused public, a general rate increase was impending, and before the Commission for consideration was a group of cases involving the violation of the long-and-short-haul principle in Transcontinental territory. Finally, the political situation was favorable—a combination of "insurgents" and Democrats controlling Congress. However, the administration initiated action in accord with party pledges and an administration bill was presented to both houses of Congress. This bill suggested the authorization of pooling, subject to Commission approval; the creation of a Commerce Court to handle all cases upon appeal from the Commission; and bestowal upon the Commission of the power to suspend proposed increases in rates pending investigation. The anti-railway groups in Congress immediately declared war upon the authorization of pools and upon a Commerce Court with members thereof designated by the President. They also demanded certain other provisions and, in consequence, the Mann-Elkins Act of 1910 represented the further development of a restrictive policy of regulation.

Under the Act of 1906 the Commission could, after investigation, order rates to be lowered but it could not act to protect against such a general advance as was in prospect in 1910: the increased rates might later be reduced but that gave no protection to the public meanwhile. To afford this protection the Commission was given the power to suspend any proposed increase for a period of 120 days beyond the otherwise effective date, with the privilege of extending this period of suspension for not to

[1] *United States v. Lehigh Valley Railroad Company,* 220 U. S. 257 (1911).

[2] *United States v. Delaware, Lackawanna and Western Railroad Company,* 238 U. S. 516 (1915).

[3] *United States v. Reading Company,* 253 U. S. 26 (1920).

exceed an additional 6 months if its investigation had not been completed. And it was further provided that, in the case of all advances of rates after Jan. 1, 1910, the burden of proof should rest upon the carriers as to the justice and reasonableness of the proposed increase.

A second important provision represented a rehabilitation of Sec. 4, giving to the Commission effective control of long-and-short-haul violations. To meet the situation not only in the South but also in the West where railway rate-making policy had been highly inimical to the Intermountain territory, the wording of the Act of 1887 was changed in important particulars. To the phrase "over the same line" was added "or route," and the phrase "under substantially similar circumstances and conditions" was stricken out, thus removing the basis of judicial emasculation in the Alabama Midland and Chattanooga cases: henceforth only with the specific approval of the Commission might a greater charge be made for a shorter haul over the same line and in the same direction, and then only after an appropriate investigation. It was also provided that no through rate be more "than the aggregate of the intermediate rates subject to the provisions of this Act," and that, "whenever a carrier by railroad shall, in competition with a water route or routes, reduce the rates . . . of freight to and from competitive points, it shall not be permitted to increase such rates unless, after hearing by the Interstate Commerce Commission, it shall be found that the proposed increase rests upon changed conditions other than the elimination of water competition."

Despite considerable opposition, a Commerce Court was created, with the selection of judges and their rotation such as to insure presumably against corporate control. Its purpose was twofold: (1) to expedite the handling of appeals from the Commission, (2) to make sure that those appeals were heard by a body familiar with regulatory problems. To give statutory basis for existing Commission practice, that body was given the power to institute inquiries upon its own motion and to establish and enforce the reasonable classification of freight. The scope of Commission authority was extended to cover telegraph, telephone, and cable companies. And power was given to establish joint through rates and classifications, maximum joint rates, and to prescribe the division of such rates and the conditions under which such routes should be operated. Other provisions of minor importance were included, and passed with the Act was an authorization for the appointment of a committee to investigate the need of federal regulation of railway securities. Regulation had been pledged in 1908 by the Republican party platform, but requisite action was to be yet longer delayed.

Operation of the Mann-Elkins Act.—The first important use of its new powers by the Commission came in connection with the so-called Ten Per Cent Rate case, in which the carriers in Trunk Line and Western territories sought such an increase. The advanced rates, filed in 1910, were at once suspended and early in 1911, after an extended investigation, the increase was denied. The railways introduced a great mass of evidence, not particularly well handled, but the diversity of conditions among the carriers proved the stumbling-block, together with the burden of proof now resting upon them. This power of suspension was again invoked upon a broad scale in the Five Per Cent case in 1913, the Western Rate Advance case in 1915, and the Fifteen Per Cent case in 1917. In each instance the railways were largely the losers; in retrospect it appears that the Commission might to advantage have followed a less parsimonious policy. The concept of a regulatory body as a protector of the public against rapacious railways still controlled, and, though there is evidence of the dawning of the judicial concept in Commission attitudes during these years, public opposition, together with a strict constructionist attitude on the part of the Commission and lack of an authoritative valuation as basis for a fair return blocked constructive action. But the Act of 1910 accomplished its purpose: advances were made difficult to secure.

With its renewed control over departures from the long-and-short-haul principle, the Commission was able to make rapid progress in reducing the number of departures through the elimination of the least justifiable. In general, four justifications for relief were given recognition: industrial competition, with slight recognition of market competition; the existence of active water competition; the need of circuitous routes seeking to meet competition—with comparatively few applications granted; and violations resulting from differences in intra- and interstate rates. In the South, where the basing-point system had prevailed for many years, the Commission moved slowly—first eliminating the less defensible exceptions and later establishing a new rate structure that rested primarily upon the distance principle. In the Intermountain territory relief was also given, action first being taken in 1911 with changes made thereafter as conditions justified. Recognizing the equity of lower charges to coast than to inland points when water competition was an actual factor, the Commission divided the country into five zones for purposes of rate relations and declared that rates to inland cities might vary from equality to 25 per cent above those charged on similar traffic to the Pacific ports. In other portions of the United States departures from the long-and-short-haul principle were carefully scrutinized and today such departures as exist throughout the country may be assumed to have a clear justification in existing facts.

In contrast to rate suspension and a rehabilitated Sec. 4, the Commerce Court was a conspicuous failure. With an apparently satisfactory personnel, the Court soon showed that it was destined to impede and obstruct: in matters of law it was conservative and in matters of fact it insisted upon that broad review that had long been the despair of commission and public. In the case of practically every appeal, the Commerce

Court reversed the Commission—and, in turn, was as often reversed by the Supreme Court. Saved for a time by administration support, the Commerce Court was abolished during the first year of the Wilson regime. And thus ended an experiment that had contained much of promise, but had worked badly.

To study the problem of federal security regulation, President Taft appointed, in conformance with the provisions of the Act, an eminent group of men. Curiously, however, this group was dominated by a belief in the efficacy of *laissez-faire* in the entire field of industry. So, though the Securities Commission studied the problem with care, it brought in a report of which certain portions justified little confidence or support. The declaration that no basis for public interest in capitalization existed, because there was no relation between outstanding security issues and either rates or service was, at best, but partially true. The suggestion of no-par stock in the face of the fact that there is no *absolutely* reasonable rate, the Cotting case[1] notwithstanding, and of the further fact that no definite valuation of railway properties was available, seemed peculiar. And the recommendation of full publicity for financial abuses, while promising some improvement, was wholly inadequate. The one valuable and constructive feature of the report was that advising a valuation of all the railway properties of the United States. For this the progressives, led by Senator R. M. LaFollette, had sought earnestly and the support of the Securities Commission—so eminently "safe and sane"—proved of invaluable assistance.

The Valuation of Railways.—In response to continued demands on the part of the proponents of strict regulation and with the belated support of railway leaders who realized the necessity of having available authentic valuations if the need of rate increases were to be established, the Valuation Act was passed early in 1913. By it the Interstate Commerce Commission is required to do the following important things: to make a physical inventory of all "used and useful" carrier property; to ascertain for each piece of property the original cost to date, the cost of reproduction new and less depreciation, together with "other values and elements of value, if any"; to determine the original cost and present value of all lands devoted to public service; to investigate the history of each property, reporting particularly concerning security issues and financial results of operation; and to ascertain the amounts and value of all grants and donations received by the carriers from all sources and the sums derived from the sale of all land grants from governmental units. Tentative valuations were to be published and, after a hearing if protest were made, final valuations were to be issued which were to serve as *prima facie* evidence of carrier value in proceedings under the Act to Regulate Commerce.

[1] *Cotting, v. Kansas City Stock Yards Company,* 183 U. S. 79 (1901).

To execute the provisions of the Valuation Act, the Commission organized the Bureau of Valuation. In it were three sections: the first inventoried the physical property of the carriers; the second assumed charge of accounting and statistical work; while the third was to ascertain land values. And parallel to the Commission organization each railway set up a similar organization to cooperate with and check the work of Commission employees. Before work had progressed far the carriers and the Commission were in controversy with respect to three questions. The carriers contended that any property operating at 100 per cent efficiency should not be depreciated; that in valuing land the multiple principle should be recognized; and that many intangibles should be included. Against the first two the Commission took a firm stand and intangibles received but scant consideration—though at this point the courts may be more generous.

The magnitude of the task, obstacles to its rapid prosecution resulting from the World War, and legal uncertainties delayed the completion of the work far beyond the expected period. None the less, in the Rate Advance case of 1920, sufficient progress had been made to justify the Commission in estimating the value of all railway properties as of Dec. 31, 1919, at $18,900,000,000, a figure some $2,000,000,000 in excess of the total amount of railway securities then in public hands and only slightly below book value as shown upon the carriers' records. And in 1931, in connection with the Fifteen Per Cent Rate case, the Commission offered a final value figure for the railways of the United States of approximately $22,250,000,000. This figure, based upon complete valuation data, is more than $3,000,000,000 in excess of net capitalization of the railways as shown at that time—and the Commission's findings are generally regarded as representing minimum estimates. True, many properties have been shown to be overcapitalized, some grossly, but these are largely smaller properties and properties serving relatively undeveloped areas. On the other hand, the major and more prosperous railways early gave evidence of valuations greatly in excess of outstanding securities.

In making the valuations under the Act of 1913, the Commission has gathered an enormous volume of information but it has been unable generally to meet the order of Congress to determine historical cost because of the lack of cost data. The valuations issued have been based upon reproduction less depreciation, largely as of prewar dates, with prewar prices applied to all inventory items, to which have been added actual expenditures since the date of valuation of the particular properties. That this method is not satisfactory as a means of determining value for purposes of the Recapture clause, at least, was declared by the United States Supreme Court in the so-called O'Fallon case,[1] the Court holding that present price levels must be given weight in determining fair value—

[1] *St. Louis and O'Fallon Railroad Co. v. United States,* 279 U. S. 461 (1929).

the Commission having made the serious error of joining issue with the courts by seeming to give in its decision an unappreciated lesson in valuation economics. Unquestionably, then, the final value of the railways as judicially approved will be something in excess of Commission figures—which, as indicated, are well in excess of net capitalization. This represents a rather unhappy termination of the valuation question for those who have gained and held place in public life upon the basis, in part, of bitter denunciation of "watered stock" and extortionate rates based thereon in the railway field. To be sure, these champions of public interest have already taken steps to justify themselves in challenging the basis of valuation, both by questioning land values fixed and by demanding the exclusion of all donated properties as well as the proceeds therefrom. Yet with respect to no one of these points does opposition seem to be well taken: the Commission has at every point given careful regard to public interest and there is no indication that the courts will be overgenerous with the carriers.

Other Legislative Enactments Affecting the Railways.—In the Mann-Elkins Act incidental effort was made to protect water carriers from cut-throat railway competition. In the Panama Canal Act of 1912 Congress endeavored to protect the independent water carrier from the railway-owned boat line—and to that end it prohibited the operation of water carriers in which a railway subject to the Interstate Commerce Act had an interest through the Panama Canal or elsewhere, where such common carrier by railway competes or may compete. With respect to operations elsewhere the Commission might, if continuance of carrier ownership appeared in public interest and competition was not reduced, approve continued railway ownership; however, this exception proved of no benefit to the carriers in the face of strict construction of the Act by the Commission. Provisions were also included in the Act intended to break port and dock monopolies and to eliminate exclusive agreements between particular rail and water carriers. To this end the Commission was given power to order suitable physical connections between rail and water lines, to establish through routes and maximum joint rates over the carriers so connected; to establish maximum proportional rail rates to and from ports on joint rail-and-water traffic; and to require any railway to make like terms for handling through tonnage with all water carriers. Though much was expected of this Act, it is doubtful if its benefits have been great: certainly the separation of rail and water carriers generally has seemed to operate as often to public disadvantage as to public gain.

In the development of federal regulation prior to 1920, major emphasis was placed upon rate control. However, the passage in 1916, in response to serious congestion of traffic at that time, of the Esch Car Service Act represented a first important step in the direction of service regulation. Under this law the Commission was given power to establish, after hearing, rules governing the movement, distribution, exchange, interchange, and return of cars, and also payment for their use. In an emergency such rules might be suspended or modified without hearing and the Commission might require carriers to file car-service rules as a part of their tariffs. Though these new powers were not exercised by the Commission, their possession made for greater willingness to cooperate with other railways by certain carriers formerly loath to do so, thus justifying the law.

Although legislation affecting the railways has dealt largely with carrier-shipper relations, certain legislation has been purposed to stabilize relations between the carriers and their employees—its justification being the continuous operation of the railway plant. The first of these laws was passed in 1888 after a serious clash between certain railways and particular classes of workers, but this measure was a dead letter. In 1898, however, the Erdman Act was passed and under it many important cases were handled. It provided for mediation by the Commissioner of Labor and the chairman of the Interstate Commerce Commission, with voluntary arbitration by a board of three as an alternative, for all disputes between the railways and the train-service employees. To strengthen this Act against rising labor antagonism, Congress passed the Newlands Act in 1913. This law provided for a permanent Board of Mediation with power to act upon its own initiative, as well as boards of arbitration of either three or six who might by majority vote make a binding award and to whom all disputed questions arising from the award must be referred. However, this improved machinery proved inadequate to meet the emergency that arose in 1916: pressed by rapidly increasing living costs and conscious of their power, the train-service workers, functioning through the "Big Four," demanded the basic 8-hour day and time and a half for overtime. No arbitration could be effected and, in the face of the threat of a nation-wide strike, Congress acted with unseemly celerity in passing the Adamson Act. This measure provided for the basic 8-hour day but without punitive overtime and, though challenged in the courts, was upheld. Having met the emergency, however, Congress did nothing of a constructive character as suggested by President Wilson: basic labor legislation remained unchanged until 1920.

In addition to the legislation already discussed, many laws were passed dealing with safety and health incident to railway operations and other laws, aimed primarily at other fields of endeavor, affected the railways. Important among the latter have been the Sherman Anti-trust Act and the Clayton Act. Under the former all rate agreements, without regard to reasonableness, were declared illegal in the Trans-Missouri Freight Association case in 1897, and the use of the holding company to unite competing carriers was outlawed in the Northern Securities case in 1904. The Clayton Act had a section aimed at railway stock holdings in other railways where the effect was to lessen competition substantially and another purposed to eliminate evils arising from the interlocking of railway directorates and official rosters with railway-supply concerns, by which means "insiders" were alleged to have profited at the expense of both general stockholder and public.

Extent and Scope of State Regulation.—Before effective federal action had been taken to regulate carriers engaged in interstate commerce, many of the states had developed a system of positive and comprehensive control. The demand for regulation that had first appeared in the early seventies and had reappeared in the eighties, swept forward with a force not to be denied as economic conditions improved after the depression of the middle nineties. In consequence, there appeared rapidly upon the statute books of the various states legislation of a diverse character, but designed in each instance to meet, in what seemed to be the most effective manner, outstanding abuses. In general, such legislation created the so-called mandatory commissions in contrast to the advisory commissions which had existed earlier. These mandatory commissions, as the name would indicate, were vested with prescriptive powers; by 1914 such a commission functioned in every state within the United States except Delaware.

Although the powers exercised by these state regulatory bodies varied widely, the legislation under which they acted almost without exception permitted positive control of freight rates and of service, passenger rates having been fixed in many jurisdictions by definite legislative act. The power to control accounting practices was also generally given, as well as all powers necessary to the elimination of discrimination, personal, place, or commodity. Certain of the states exercised control in public interest over both the construction and abandonment of mileage; some gave to their respective regulatory bodies broad powers over the issuance of securities and over certain other financial practices. Operating policies were also affected in many states but, aside from giving to commissions the power to order physical connections, to establish joint stations, and regulate car service, such control was exerted generally through prescriptive legislation such as maximum train-length laws, "full-crew" laws, laws designed to secure a minimum average daily movement of shipments, and statutes fixing types of equipment to be used—these last enacted in the interest of the safety of worker and public. From these statements it appears that state regulation in certain instances was more comprehensive and was, at times, of a more constructive type than federal prior to 1920. Yet, to say that state control evidenced a better understanding of the nature and needs of the railway industry, on the whole, than federal control—indeed, was even equal to it—is an exaggeration. Nevertheless, the work of certain of the more progressive states, such as Wisconsin, New York, Massachusetts, Texas, and California, formed a splendid experimental background for the development of a sound, more constructive type of federal control as well as of state control in other jurisdictions. Once again the state was the laboratory in which various theories and principles were tested, to the ultimate benefit of the lesser as well as the greater unit.

A Judgment upon Our Regulatory Policy.—Beginning in 1887 with the Act to Regulate Commerce, the first phase of federal control terminated with the effective date of the Transportation Act, Mar. 1, 1920. During this period the public was engaged primarily in establishing its mastery of a great industry that had been peculiarly individualistic and, therefore, keenly resentful of interference. Recognition of public supremacy came slowly and only after a bitter, long-drawn-out struggle at the polls, in the halls of Congress, and before the courts; but by the close of the period the carriers had accepted the inevitable and were evidencing a fine spirit of cooperation generally. The Commission possessed broad powers over rates; it was able to suspend tariffs and fix maximum charges, both absolute and relative. A large degree of control was exercised over service and, though discrimination persisted, the Commission had reduced all types to a minimum. Control over accounting practices was complete and a large element of publicity had been attained. Furthermore, intercorporate relations regarded as inimical to public interest had been sharply restricted by the anti-pooling clause, the Sherman Act, the Panama Canal Act, and the Clayton Act.

As the result of regulation prior to 1920, certain definite gains had accrued. The public had benefited from comparatively low rates and had been largely relieved of the evils of discrimination with respect to both rates and service. Public control, together with a rising standard of business morality, served to give more adequate protection to the investor, particularly to the owner of stocks. The railways, too, had benefited: they had been largely relieved of pressure from important patrons for special privileges and consideration; greater corporate honesty followed from "letting in the light" through publicity; and railway management was brought to a better understanding of underlying principles governing the business of transportation. Finally, the railways profited from regulation because of the greater unity of action developed, as typified by the work of various sections of the American Railway Association and of different executive groups.

There are, however, certain important criticisms of regulation as it functioned prior to 1920. Most deserving of criticism, perhaps, was the spirit that largely actuated regulatory measures: rather than constructive, it was restrictive and punitive. Though this was natural in view of the bitter struggle necessary to establish public supremacy, the persistence of that spirit was unfortunate. Furthermore, while often overzealous in the control of rates and intercorporate relations, legislative bodies too frequently failed completely to provide adequate control in other fields, conspicuously labor and finance. Legislative acts, too, were designed to meet immediate situations; rarely did regulatory measures result from a careful study of the long-time needs of railway and public. And commissions, in the administration of laws that proceeded from a hostile attitude toward the railways, commonly exercised their powers with a view to immediate public advantage rather than in such a manner as to suggest a realization of the long-time mutuality of interest of the contending parties. In short, regulation was political rather than statesmanlike in character. Assignable in no small measure to the restrictive and parsimonious character of regulation, state and federal, during these years were the growing inadequacy of the plant and the progressive weakening of the railway financial structure that became so apparent shortly before the period of federal operation. And assignable to it in considerable degree, also, was the diminishing attractiveness of the railway field to the able and trained mind. A field in which the opportunity for individual initiative and for the employment of constructive imagination was lessening rapidly was in poor position to attract and hold a considerable number of men as capable as those who directed railway operations during formative years; yet increasingly, as the situation became difficult and problems complex, the railways have had need of administrative talent of high order. It has been the misfortune of both the public and the railways that, as the need for strong leadership in this field has grown, the attractiveness of the field has diminished.

Regulation accomplished much of good during the years prior to 1920, yet its character was such that it carried serious threat to both corporate and public interests. There was sore need of a detailed, analytical study of the transportation situation with a view to devising a constructive plan of regulatory action, a plan calculated to serve ultimate public interest by the adequate protection of the railways. However much certain groups may emphasize divergences of interest between railway and public, the interests of the two are and seem destined to remain so close that action which prejudices the one must injure the other. The period of federal operation offered opportunity for such careful study and consideration, though thoughtful interest had been shown in the problem by public leaders as early as 1915. After a brief discussion of this interim period of federal operation, the results of a judgment based upon experience and analysis will be presented as they took form in the Transportation Act of 1920, the first broadly constructive federal enactment dealing with the railways.

REFERENCES

Bogart, E. L.: *Economic History of the United States*, Longmans Green & Co., 1915. Bureau of Railway Economics.

Dixon, F. H.: *Railroads and Government*, Charles Scribner's Sons, 1922.

Dunn, S. O.: *The Regulation of Railways*, D. Appleton & Company, 1918.

Gephart, W. F.: Transportation and Industrial Development in the Middle West. *Columbia University Studies*, vol. 34, No. 1.
Haines, H. S.: *Efficient Railway Operation*, The Macmillan Company, 1919.
———: *Problems of Railway Regulation*, The Macmillan Company, 1911.
Hearings before Joint Committee on Interstate and Foreign Commerce, 64th Congress, 1st Session, Nov. 20, 1916, to Dec. 19, 1917.
Hungerford, Edward, *The Modern Railroad*, A. C. McClurg & Company, 1911.
Interstate Commerce Commission: *Annual Reports; Reports; Statistics of Railways.*
Johnson, E. R., and T. W. Van Metre: *Principles of Railroad Transportation*, D. Appleton & Company, 1921.
Jones, Eliot: *Principles of Railway Transportation*, The Macmillan Company, 1924.
Kennan, George: *Biography of Edward H. Harriman*, Houghton Mifflin Company, 1922.
McPherson, Logan: *The Working of the Railroads*, Henry Holt & Company, 1906.
Pyle, Joseph G.: *Life of James J. Hill*, Doubleday, Doran & Company, Inc., 1917.
Railway Age.
Railway Age Gazette.
Report of the Industrial Commission, vol. 19, pp. 259–304.
Riegel, R. E.: *The Story of the Western Railroads*, The Macmillan Company, 1926.
Ripley, W. Z.: *Railroads: Finance and Organization*, Longmans, Green & Co., 1915.
———: *Railroads: Rates and Regulation*, Longmans Green & Co., 1912.
———: *Railway Problems*, Ginn & Company, 1913.
United States Supreme Court Reports.

Chapter XI

DEVELOPMENT OF THE RAILWAY PROBLEM: FEDERAL OPERATION

YET another conspicuous feature of the period which closed with 1919 was federal control of the railroads; or, to speak with greater exactitude, government operation of those carriers. This unusual combination of private ownership and government operation of railways developed out of war conditions. Though due immediately to our own entry into the struggle, its causes reach back very clearly into the transportation situation as it developed during the latter part of 1916 and through the year 1917. Traffic during the last half of the year 1916 was unusually heavy and an important element of that tonnage was export business. This fact, because of the difficulty of properly coordinating railway and port facilities and because of the disturbance of ocean shipping consequent upon the German submarine campaign, made it increasingly difficult to secure the release of cars and their return to the owning roads. The terminals of eastern carriers became badly congested and the accumulation of loaded cars began to reach westward, filling all available yards and sidings. In consequence it was increasingly impossible to handle shipments expeditiously. Carriers in the West and South were embarrassed because of the situation confronting the carriers which served Atlantic ports; it was almost impossible to secure the return of empty cars belonging to them even when those cars had been unloaded—the Eastern carriers retained them to replace equipment of their own which was so generally serving a warehouse function. To meet this condition there was established by the American Railway Association at Washington, in December, 1916, a so-called Car Service Commission. This commission was authorized to obtain necessary information concerning the need for equipment and to issue orders for its return. The magnitude of the problem and the failure of certain of the carriers to observe the orders of this commission made it impossible to improve the situation greatly. Due to the activity of the Interstate Commerce Commission, however, the railways were stimulated to accomplish a reorganization of the Car Service Commission, the carriers agreeing to be governed by such rules as it might prescribe. Trusting that the situation would now be handled satisfactorily without positive action on its part, the legality of which was in doubt, the Interstate Commerce Commission confined itself to cooperation with the carriers. In May, however, through the passage of the Esch Act, the Interstate Commerce Commission was clearly empowered to deal with the situation. In the meantime, however, the United States had declared war upon the Central Powers. The problem immediately became a broader and more difficult one than that of securing relative equality among shippers in various sections of the country; the goal of a nation at war was maximum service from the railways as an aid in winning the war.

Organization of the Railroads' War Board.—Prior to the declaration of war, steps had been taken by the carriers to provide for such an emergency. At the suggestion of Mr. Daniel Willard, president of the Baltimore and Ohio Railroad and associated in an advisory capacity with the Council of National Defense, for which provision had been made in the Army Appropriation Act of August, 1916, the American Railway Association had provided a special Committee on National Defense, composed of 18 railway officials from various parts of the United States. This committee met with the Secretary of War and others early in March, and at this meeting general plans were developed for the effective cooperation of railways and government in case of war. Immediately following America's declaration of war, at a general conference of railway executives in Washington attended by about 700 railway presidents representing practically the entire mileage of the United States, the Committee on National Defense was enlarged and from it was selected a committee of five which was to function as the Railroad's War Board. This Board, with headquarters in Washington, endeavored, with the assistance of various subcommittees, to accomplish that "continental railway system" which the general meeting of the executives had indicated as the railways' goal.

Work of the War Board.—This War Board immediately set about increasing the efficiency of the railway plant. In its efforts it enjoyed splendid cooperation from both the Council of National Defense and the Interstate Commerce Commission and, in the face of difficulties arising both from war conditions and from its complete dependence upon the voluntary cooperation of individual carriers, accomplished much in the better adaptation of service to war needs. The Board issued orders governing the transfer and use of special types of equipment; pooling of coal shipments was ordered; box cars were pooled; passenger service was curtailed that freight movements might be increased; and a drive for the more intensive loading of both cars and locomotives was made which, through the cooperation of shippers and the efforts of the carriers themselves, resulted in distinct gains. But despite its best efforts, the War Board realized late in 1917 that coordination of the railways under a voluntary scheme must fail to give maximum results. The average load per car had shown an almost steady increase in response to the demand for heavier loading; the average number of car miles per day had been increased also by a campaign among the carriers to that end, but this improvement steadily declined from the maximum attained in May. In December, because of peculiarly difficult operating conditions, the figures had dropped to less than 75 per cent of that of 8 months previous. Serious difficulties were encountered in securing that complete cooperation which was essential to the maximum utilization of the railway plant, and yet there was serious doubt in many quarters as to the legality of the transfer of broad powers by competitive carriers to any central body. Nevertheless, late in November it became so apparent no other plan would succeed that the railways in the Eastern District took measures to pool "all available facilities on all railroads east of Chicago . . . to the extent necessary to furnish maximum freight movement." The operating committee supervising this undertaking established headquarters at Pittsburgh and took immediate and drastic steps to accomplish the end in view; traffic was rerouted; unnecessary passenger and fast freight service was suspended; and rules looking toward the maximum use of equipment adopted. Effective results were obtained but the combination of circumstances facing the carriers at this time made the problem almost impossible of private solution.

Federal Operation of Railways.—In the meantime, the Interstate Commerce Commission had been investigating the railway situation and early in December recommended in a special report to Congress one of two alternatives—that the President take over the railways and operate them for the duration of the war, or that all legal obstacles to the complete unification of the railways for that period be removed and that the government give the railways such financial assistance as might prove necessary. Although the Commission as a body offered these two alternatives, Commissioner McChord was emphatic in his own separate statement that voluntary cooperation among the carriers was insufficient to solve the problem even though all barriers be removed, declaring that "the strong arm of government authority is essential if the transportation situation is to be radically improved." Experience during the month of December seemed to offer support to this latter position. Although the entire difficulty lay in the territory between Chicago and St. Louis on the west and the Atlantic ports on the east, the situation in this strategic area became so bad that on Dec. 26, 1917, President Wilson issued a proclamation under which he took possession, in the name of the United States, of all railways and waterways of the country in accordance with the war powers granted in 1916 by Congress.

The President was influenced to take this radical step by at least three major considerations. (1) The situation demanded the essential unification of transportation facilities, yet two obstacles to this unification existed: the legal barriers to close cooperation and those barriers inherent in the nature of private competitive enterprise—the fear of financial loss through cooperative action and the psychological unpreparedness of men trained in competitive struggle to surrender independence of action. (2) Adequate provision for the expansion of the railway plant, to meet both normal needs and the exigencies of war traffic, had to be made. Private operation faced two important difficulties here. Railway credit was weak and this situation was certain to be aggravated by competition for funds with a government actively engaged in Liberty Loan drives. But even with funds available, it would be more difficult for the railways than for the government to secure needed materials under the priority system in force. (3) Finally, it seemed that government operation would give added assurance of that continuity of service so utterly essential during a critical period. The railways had lost, at the close of 1917, large numbers of employees through the operation of the draft and to war industries which attracted workers by a high level of wages, and it was certain that those employees remaining in the service must receive a sharp increase in wages immediately to compensate for rapidly rising living costs, else the country would face the possibility of a strike. And such a prospect was disturbing, since the position of railway labor was perhaps stronger at this time than it had been at any time before and its sense of injustice had been thoroughly stirred by the relative inadequacy of railway wages. Such, then, were the principal reasons for the advent of government operation of railways in 1918 and, although there may remain always a doubt in the minds of some as to the necessity for this step, a careful study of the situation at the close of 1917 indicates that President Wilson, not knowing how long the war might continue, acted wisely.

Reorganization of the Railways.—Under the original order issued, the entire railway system of the United States was taken over by the government, but during the first 6 months of 1918 a large number of minor properties were turned back under the reservation made in the original proclamation. About 560 properties were retained and operated by the government until the close of the period of federal control. Included among these were practically all Class I railways and a large number of facilities such as union-station companies, terminal companies, and switching companies, here being included belt-line railways. For purposes of administration the properties retained by the government were divided territorially, first into three districts, Eastern, Southern, and Western, later into seven. This division had for its prime purpose more efficient management. In so far as possible the boundaries of the various districts were so fixed as to make them correspond to natural traffic areas and to include entire railway properties within a single district. Of the seven districts four lay to the east of the Mississippi and three to the west.

At the head of this great national system was placed William G. McAdoo, Secretary of the Treasury, who was designated as Director-

General of Railroads. Cooperating with him in Washington was the so-called Central Administration with the following major sections:

Division of Law
Division of Operation
Division of Public Service and Accounts (later separated)
Division of Labor
Division of Capital Expenditures
Division of Traffic
Division of Finance and Purchases
Division of Inland and Coastwise Waterways
Board of Wages and Working Conditions

At the head of each of these sections was placed a man of broad experience in the railway field and, although changes in personnel were made from time to time, at no time were other than practical railway men in charge of important work. That men of such standing as C. A. Prouty, Carl R. Gray, Judge R. S. Lovett, W. S. Carter, Edward Chambers, and others of like caliber though perhaps lesser reputation, served upon the central administration staff, is clear evidence both of the desire of the Director-General to establish an effective organization and of his success in enlisting, through patriotic appeal, the services of the best men available.

At the head of each regional organization was placed an official designated as regional director. To these posts able railway executives were appointed, among them being A. H. Smith, president of the New York Central; C. H. Markham, president of the Illinois Central; Hale Holden, president of the Chicago, Burlington and Quincy; R. H. Aishton, president of the Chicago and North Western; and others of equal capacity. In general, the man selected to serve in a particular region was an executive of long experience in that territory, a policy which made for a peculiar effectiveness of service. At each of the regional headquarters a staff organization was developed and, by way of illustration, a sketch of that organization for the Eastern Region will be given. Among the various divisions were a budget committee, a purchasing committee, a freight-traffic committee, a committee supervising North Atlantic ports freight traffic, a passenger-traffic committee, a coal and coke rate committee, and a marine department. Functioning at the head and as members of these committees were men of practical railway experience, possessed of familiarity with the field in which they worked. Subordinate and reporting directly to the regional director were the executives of the individual railways within the region as the mileage was organized for operation. In general, these units were coextensive with the old corporate properties, each unit being directed by an individual designated as "federal manager." During the early months of federal operation, the president of the property had remained in executive control, no distinction being made between the corporate and federal organizations. Later, because of an

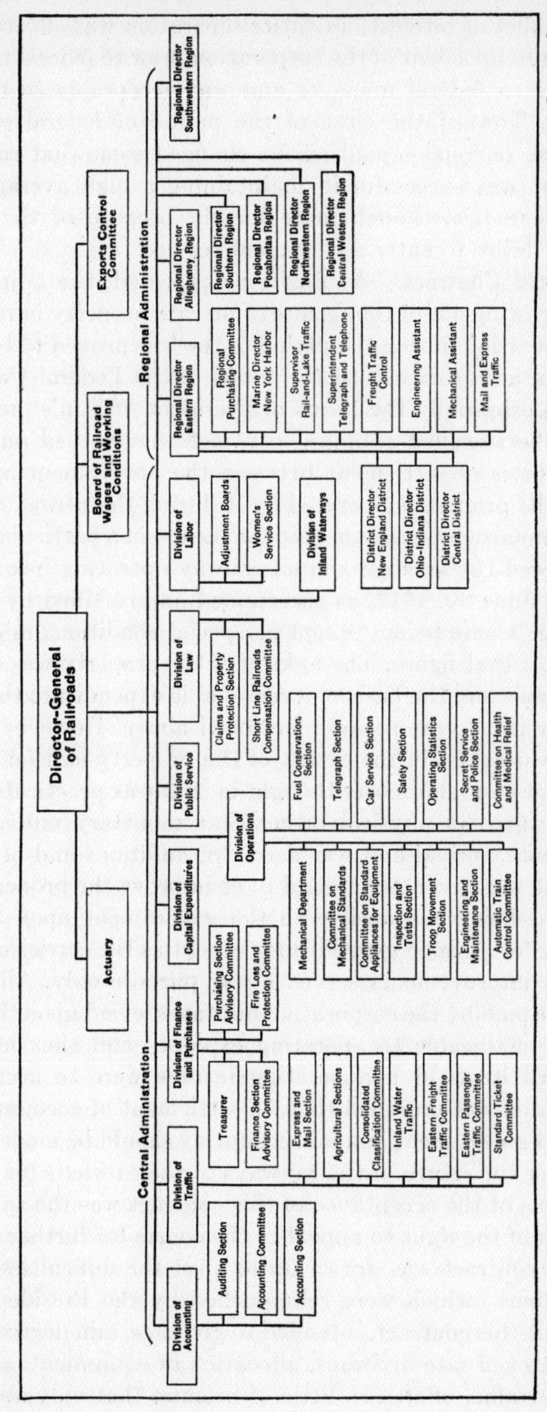

FIG. 8.—Diagram showing main features of the organization of the Federal Railroad Administration. (Other regional organizations similar to that shown for Eastern region.)

inescapable conflict of interest, an entire separation was effected though, in most cases, the president of the corporation prior to federal control was willing to serve as federal manager and was acceptable to the federal administration. Toward the close of the period of federal control the personnel of the regional organizations changed somewhat rapidly, yet the government was successful in maintaining a high average of both ability and experience, though more largely because of the country's need than of a desire to enter government service.

The Standard Contract.—As might be expected, the adjustment of relationships growing out of the seizure of private property in railways for government operation during the period of the war proved to be involved and difficult. In accordance with the terms of the Federal Control Act, which followed essentially the terms of President Wilson's proclamation late in 1917, the so-called standard contract was worked out and this served as the basis of settlement between the government and a large proportion of the properties operated by it during the period. Under this contract the annual compensation paid for the use of a particular property was not to exceed the average annual railway operating income for the 3 years ending June 30, 1917, as ascertained and certified by the Interstate Commerce Commission, except as special conditions might justify a modification of that figure. The upkeep of the property was chargeable to the government and the basis of a reasonable expenditure therefor was the average for the 3-year period mentioned above. However, provision was made for variations in the extent of the property and for variations in both material and labor costs though, in so far as practicable, upkeep was to be measured in physical rather than monetary units. To make provision for both normal and war needs for additions and betterments, the government was permitted to add to or improve the property at will, the corporation being responsible to the government upon the return of the property for all such expenditures except as the carrier might show that particular improvements served a war purpose only. All corporate taxes were to be paid by the corporation but taxes levied upon the physical property were chargeable to operating expenses and thus met by the government. All items of nonoperating income were to accrue to the corporation and it was provided that, in settlement of accounts between the railway and government, a final accounting should be made as soon as practicable after the return of the railways to their owners for operation. One of the terms of the acceptance of this contract was the surrender by the corporation of the right to appeal to the courts for further compensation. A special contract was drawn up to meet the difficulties of the so-called "short lines" which were relinquished by the President prior to July 1, 1918, but this contract, intended to give a certain degree of protection in the matter of rate divisions, allocation of equipment, and routing of competitive traffic, offered so little of promise that only about 15 per cent of the lines accepted it. These small, and, by combination of circumstances, unfortunate properties were indemnified later for war losses, under the Transportation Act.

Compensation Paid the Railways.—Although complaint had been voiced in certain quarters as to the terms of the contract from a public standpoint, the railways were little better satisfied with it than were railway-baiting politicians. It provided no compensation for the diversion of business which must inevitably modify shipping habits later and in no wise indemnified the railway for the disruption of organizations built up with great care and effort. Furthermore, the terms of the contract failed to make provision for the exceptional property, the one for which returns during the "test period" were not typical because of unusual conditions or of policies which reduced operating income, such as generous maintenance. Furthermore, no limit was placed upon additions and betterments, but this objection proved to be almost unfortunately theoretical, since properties remained essentially at a standstill during federal operation. Yet recourse to the courts or to Congress promised the carriers little. In consequence, all but a relatively small number of properties, which regarded themselves as particularly aggrieved under the agreement outlined, signed the contract. This contract obligated the government to pay annually to the railways approximately $945,000,000, a figure which was variously characterized by friends and foes of the railways as reasonable and as criminally excessive. Yet this sum fell perhaps $10,000,000 to $15,000,000 per year short of a 6 per cent return upon the closest approximation available of the fair value of those railway properties operated by the government during this period.[1] Not only does this fact indicate that the compensation was not excessive, but an examination of the individual years covered by the test period leads to the same conclusion. The year 1915 was unusually lean but 1916 was the best in railway history, while 1917 might properly be characterized as good. Using yet another basis of comparison, the British plan under which the single year preceding government operation was used, it appears that the sum paid to the railways of the United States would have been practically the same as it was upon the basis of the 3-year average.

Work of the Federal Railroad Administration.—To describe the work of the Federal Railroad Administration in the brief way possible here is

[1] As of Dec. 31, 1919, the Interstate Commerce Commission in 1920 estimated the value of all railways at $18,900,000,000. Upon the basis of complete valuation data an estimate for 1919 of some $17,000,000,000 was later made by that body. The 92 per cent of total mileage operated by the government represented at least 95 per cent of the value of American railways. Applying this percentage of value to the smaller total figure given above, it appears the value of the properties in the hands of the government in 1919 was in excess of $16,000,000,000. And certainly a rate of return of 6 per cent was not excessive during 1918–1920. Compensation under the standard contract would seem, then, to have been equitable to both railways and government.

difficult. However, attention should be called to certain of the major tasks accomplished or undertaken. Effort was made to secure certain economies in service, in part as a war measure, in part as a general movement. To this end passenger service was reduced sharply until well after the Armistice, when a gradual restoration became evident. The elimination of competitive activities was also sought. The abolition of numerous off-line and downtown ticket offices was a step in that direction, as was the almost complete cessation, for a time, of all activities looking toward the acquisition of traffic, including not only personal solicitation but also advertising. As a further economy measure, steps were taken to reduce both the number of railway officials receiving $5,000 or more, and the salaries paid those officials. As a result of this campaign the number of such officials was reduced by 11 per cent and salaries were also pared down, the maximum sums paid being $50,000 to certain of the regional directors.

A number of changes were made to increase the efficiency of the plant. Whenever such action promised to promote the effective movement of traffic, terminal facilities were unified and all efforts to retain cars upon the owning road, or to return to it cars transferred under load to another line, were abandoned. In fact, not only was freight equipment pooled but, in emergencies, passenger equipment and motive power were also moved freely from one line to another. To increase the efficiency of freight handling, various steps were taken. Among these were the short routing of carload shipments, the routing of all less-than-carload shipments to a given point over a particular line, and the establishment of "sailing days" and store-door delivery. Special effort was also made to concentrate tonnage and move it in train-load lots. To cut down or eliminate, if possible, the use of freight cars for warehouse purposes, demurrage rates were sharply increased; store-door delivery assisted in lessening storage demands at terminals. Efforts were also made to lessen idle time by appeal to the patriotism of the shipper.

Another measure adopted, in part to secure increased efficiency, was the standardization of equipment. Although certain objections were made by the railways at the time and later to this step, it was sound, certainly, as an emergency measure and has much to recommend it as a permanent policy. As a war measure, standardization made possible the more rapid delivery of equipment orders and considerable economies resulted from the abandonment of that excessive individualism characteristic of American cars and locomotives. To accomplish more effective results in the express field the four great companies, Adams, American, Wells Fargo, and Southern, were encouraged to consolidate into the American Railway Express Company. This organization was, after a period of private operation, taken over by the Federal Railroad Administration and operated by it until the close of the period of federal control. To reduce cross hauling and other wastes resulting from the indiscriminate movement of coal, a zoning plan was adopted under which particular sections of country could be supplied only from certain mining districts. A permit system, first used to control the movement of traffic essential for war but later employed more widely, was adopted, under which it was impossible for a shipper to secure service without a permit from the Car Service Bureau and this permit was given only upon evidence of ability to load and unload the equipment requested without delay. Yet another important innovation was that of zoning the United States for export movements. This scheme had for its prime purpose the relief of the tremendous congestion of the principal North Atlantic ports from Boston to Norfolk. Finally, the separation of corporate and federal staff had, as a partial purpose, increased efficiency. The elimination, in so far as possible, of dual allegiance, secured more effective support for the work of the Federal Railroad Administration.

Rates during Federal Operation.—One of the most interesting and at the same time difficult questions which the Federal Railroad Administration had to face was that of the control and adjustment of rates. It was obvious early in 1918 that, if the federal government wished to avoid a heavy deficit, a sharp increase in rates was essential. To this end the Administration announced, on May 25, 1918, a 25 per cent increase in freight rates effective a month later, with an increase in passenger rates to not less than 3 cents per mile, effective June 10. Certain other changes affecting both freight and passenger service were also made which further increased the cost of movement to patrons. Under the Federal Control Act it was unnecessary to secure the approval of either state or federal regulatory bodies for changes in rates, although it was clearly understood that the Interstate Commerce Commission might later, upon hearing, order a readjustment to secure justice for particular shippers or localities. The Federal Railroad Administration also initiated a movement designed to accomplish greater uniformity in the classification of commodities. Out of this developed the present consolidated classification, to be later described, in accordance with the order of the Interstate Commerce Commission in 1919. Due to unexpected changes in the volume of traffic, however, as well as to the hesitation of the Railroad Administration further to advance rates to keep pace with the rising costs of operation, large deficits were incurred by the government. These tended to increase as time passed, but the Administration refused to make further advances, holding that such responsibility should be assumed by the proper regulatory bodies after the return of the railways to private management.

Wages and Labor Disputes.—One of the most important chapters in the work of the Railroad Administration deals with wages and working conditions. When the railroads were taken over by the government it was patent that an increase in wages, particularly for the lower paid groups, was essential. To obtain a factual basis for action the Railroad Wage Commission was appointed at once by the Director-General. While awaiting its report, the Administration stabilized conditions by the promise to make all increases retroactive to Jan. 1. The recommendations of this board resulted in the issuance of General Order No. 27. Under it increases varying from 43 per cent for lower paid workers to none whatever for those receiving $250 or upward per month, were granted, the compensation paid for each particular position in December, 1915, serving as the base. Certain resulting inequalities were corrected by later supplementary orders. For the hearing of cases relating to inequalities in pay and regulations, also affecting general labor policies, a Board of Wages and Working Conditions was organized. To handle all other labor questions four bipartisan boards of adjustment were created with equal representation from the Administration and the employees, each board having jurisdiction over disputes arising between the carriers and certain groups of employees. Though provision was made for dealing with unorganized workers, the organization of all railway employees was encouraged with the result that, at the close of the period of federal operation, the railways faced not merely the strongly intrenched operating brotherhoods but a considerable number of greatly strengthened or new organizations which comprised practically all types of employment and included practically all workers in the service. General Order No. 27 and its supplements, together with other changes in wages and working conditions, resulted in an increase in the annual wage bill of American railways which was estimated by the Administration itself to be approximately $965,000,000. Yet, because of the continued upward movement in living costs, labor made further demands in 1919 to which the government refused to accede. Thus federal operation left to private control a second troublesome heritage in the form of an insistent demand by greatly strengthened labor organizations for additional pay.

Capital Expenditures.—Since one of the purposes of taking over the railways was to provide adequately for additions and betterments, brief mention should be made of results here. At the head of the Capital Expenditures Division in Washington was placed Judge R. S. Lovett, and expenditures were authorized to the total amount of $1,279,000,000 during 1918, of which $659,000,000 was to be spent for equipment, $573,000,000 for additions and betterments, and $47,000,000 for extensions. In 1919, the Armistice having been signed, the Administration took the position that no further expenditures for capital purposes should be made unless absolutely necessary, since the desire of the public for an early return of the properties to private control was clear. In consequence, only minor additional contracts were let during that year and such undertakings completed as had been begun during the year preceding. Total expenditures for the 26-month period of federal control as shown by Director-

General Davis early in 1921 totaled $1,144,000,000, an average of less than $500,000,000 per year, a figure far below the needs of the period and the more so when translated into physical materials and labor at inflated prices.

In addition to these major undertakings and problems of administration, there are other miscellaneous matters worthy of mention. The Pullman Company service was taken over; steps were made toward harmonizing accounting practices among the various railways; a uniform interline waybill was adopted; and federal operation was utilized to eliminate, or at least to greatly simplify, interrailway settlements. The government assumed all property risks, dropping insurance with outside companies wholly for both fire and theft.

Results of Federal Operation.—It is impossible to appraise accurately the results of federal operation, yet certain general conclusions can be drawn. In the field of operation there were certain clear-cut gains. Principal among these were the benefits resulting from the elimination of competitive activities, which varied from closing "off-line" offices to minimizing competitive passenger service and unifying terminals. Noteworthy savings were claimed by the Railroad Administration from these and other policies, such as reductions in the official payroll, but it is doubtful if these gains were entirely free of offset during the war period, and certainly from the signing of the Armistice forward to the close of the period the gains were slight. Coal-zoning, "sailing-day," short-routing, minimized passenger service, and even the elimination of advertising expense soon went by the board. However, the government undoubtedly operated the railways during the entire period in question as effectively as could those private corporations from whose control they were taken and, had the duration of the war been greater, the comparative gain from federal operation would have been correspondingly increased.

Classification and Rates.—In the field of classification and rate control the Federal Railroad Administration is to be credited with one distinct forward step, the adoption of the consolidated classification: though work upon this had been in progress for some years, the Administration undoubtedly hurried matters to a conclusion. And, furthermore, the Director-General showed good strategy in securing the approval of the Interstate Commerce Commission for the change, thus reassuring shippers and giving it a more permanent basis. The handling of rates by the Administration is scarcely to be commended, however. Despite the continuous and sharp increase in the costs of operation during the period, but one increase in rates was made, that effective June, 1918. By this order freight, passenger, and Pullman rates were advanced materially upon all governmentally operated railways, yet it soon became evident that even the new rates were inadequate. Nevertheless, throughout the year of 1919 and the early months of 1920, the Administration steadfastly refused to accept responsibility for a further iucrease, despite the absolute power possessed of initiating both interstate and intrastate rates. Perhaps it was reasonable to decline further responsibility; perhaps it was just to pay deficits from the general treasury, thus regarding them as war costs; but certainly the financial results of government operation would have been quite different had rates advanced with costs, and the financial situation of the railways upon the resumption of private operation would have been vastly improved.

The Labor Policy.—In no field did greater changes occur during the 26 months of federal operation than in that of labor. For a period prior to America's entry into the war, railways in manufacturing districts found it well-nigh impossible to hold skilled workmen in competition with industry and this handicap was increased by the feverish activities following our entry into the conflict. A wage advance was made even more urgent by the demand of those remaining in the service for compensation commensurate with the increased and still rising cost of living, particularly since that demand came in part from the operating brotherhoods which had shown their coercive power a year previously in compelling Congress to pass the Adamson Act. Persuaded to remain faithful to their employment by the promise that all increases awarded would be made retroactive to Jan. 1, 1918, the great army of employees awaited eagerly the findings of the Railroad Wage Commission. Upon the basis of those findings was issued General Order No. 27, as previously mentioned. For the first time workers of slight bargaining power received a wage commensurate with their worth to the carrier rather than one based upon a lack of compulsion. A second demand by the employees for a general increase the Administration refused to meet, postponing settlement first on the ground that the cost of living would drop and later on the ground that the matter should be handled upon the return of the railways to their owners early in 1920. This procrastination and failure to meet the issue squarely contributed largely to the labor unrest of 1920; indeed, the "outlaw" switchmen's strike was a direct consequence of procrastination.

Other important matters relating to labor policy must be mentioned before dismissing the subject. The introduction of the bipartisan boards of adjustment is noteworthy, both because its use was new in this field and because of the unusual success of these boards. Then, too, central control of matters affecting labor made almost inevitable the standardization of wages, rules, and working conditions throughout the United States, with its eventuation in the so-called national agreements, while the friendly attitude of the Administration toward labor organizations so stimulated unionism in the railway field that membership increased from 551,500 in 1914 to 1,538,519 at the close of the period of federal operation. The basic 8-hour day was established for all railway labor and steps were made toward such a shorter day in actuality.

In summarizing results with respect to labor, one writer says "It is no exaggeration to say that the gains made by railroad labor . . . in the power of collective bargaining, in the development of union organization, in the standardization and nationalization of practices and policies, were greater than in the entire previous period of their existence."[1] Yet these gains were necessarily made at the expense of some group, the railways or the public, perhaps both, and may not have been wholly justified.

Financial Results and Conclusion.—Judged from an absolute standpoint, the financial results of federal operation were disastrous. Deficits accruing from the operation of Class I railways during the period of federal control totaled more than $667,500,000, to which was added approximately $75,000,000 accruing from the operation of other transportation agencies, land and water, and further sums that bring the total for the 26 months to about $900,000,000. To this must further be added an estimated $200,000,000 for undermaintenance, outstanding claims, and additions and betterments serving only a war purpose. But this enormous sum of $1,100,000,000 does not represent the total cost: the 6-month guarantee following the period of federal operation, which was designed to ease the "return to normalcy" for the railways, cost approximately $550,000,000 more. Thus it appears that the total direct cost to the government of federal operation of railways approximated $1,650,000,000. To this must be added as a temporary outlay, since the government found it necessary to fund railway indebtedness for capital outlays in most instances, a "forced loan" approximating $1,000,000,000.

To regard even the former figure as a total loss is an error, however: it merely represents that amount below a fair total cost which the consumers of railway service paid during the period in question, a sum to be regarded as a war expense. In commenting upon the financial results of government operation, Director-General Hines declared, in his final report,

> It not only did not cost more than private control would have cost during the same period, but cost considerably less on account of the economies growing out of unifications, and the total burden put upon the public (through rates and taxes) on account of railroad costs was substantially less than would have been necessary if the railroads had remained in private control and rates had been raised enough to preserve their credit; it protected the investment in railroad properties, whereas without federal control those investments would have been endangered.

And it would seem, upon careful appraisal, that this contention would be hard to disprove.

In conclusion, it may be said that the period of federal operation will never be one to which advocates of governmental entry into the transportation field can "point with pride"; but it is equally true that the bitterest opponents of the policy adopted to meet better a war emergency

[1] DIXON, F. H.: *Railroads and Government*, p. 189.

will be as troubled to establish their right to exhibit it as a "horrible example." Mistakes were undoubtedly made and these are particularly visible to those who judge after the fact, yet it is difficult to understand how the railways of the country could have been operated with maximum efficiency and with minimum injury for the future except as they were. In short, federal operation may not have been an entire success, but, when judged upon the basis of its accomplishments and failures, the obvious defense is that results might easily have been less satisfactory under any other plan.

Concluding Comments.—To make a summary statement concerning the period that began with the panic of 1893 and closed with the termination of federal operation is difficult, primarily because those years are so recent that it is impossible to consider them in a wholly objective manner and to discern results clearly and surely. Certain it is that many of the features of this period, particularly the difficulties faced, had their roots in that score of years which ended in the disaster of 1893, and certain it is, too, that many of the features of this period—the experience of state and federal governments with regulation, the gradual failure of the railway plant to meet traffic needs because of credit and other conditions, and even the experience of federal operation with its nondescript results—were to exert a marked influence upon railway policy during the years which lay immediately ahead. If expectations for those years were to be judged in the light of the situation of the railway industry at the close of the period here discussed, pessimism would have been clearly justified. But that both the railways and the public would profit by and capitalize the experience which lay behind was only reasonable to expect. Such expectations tinted the picture with brighter colors. Indeed, the law which marked the close of this period, the Transportation Act of 1920, suggests clearly a change from public antagonism, with its resultant punitive and restrictive regulation, to public understanding and consequent constructive action. The American public has been persistently unfortunate in its failure to foresee and to meet constructively the great problems arising in the railway field; instead, under the leadership too often of politicians rather than statesmen, it has, in a spirit of righteous indignation, many times "locked the door after the horse was stolen." Yet in 1920 there appeared to be greater justification than at any earlier time for optimism; better reason to believe that, despite its failure to act as "hindsight" might demand, or as a statesmanlike understanding might prompt, the American public would, with the railway problem just as with many others, do something more than merely muddle through. That this hope for the years following 1920 did not fructify is the consequence of changes in the transportation situation during those years that were little short of kaleidoscopic, and with which public opinion was not able to remain abreast.

REFERENCES

Bureau of Railway Economics.

CUNNINGHAM, W. J.: *American Railroads*, McGraw-Hill Book Company, Inc., 1922.

DAGGETT, STUART: *Principles of Inland Transportation*, Harper & Brothers, 1928.

Director-General of Railroads: *Annual Reports* and other documents.

DIXON, F. H.: *Railroads and Government*, Charles Scribner's Sons, 1922.

———, and J. H. PARMELEE: *War Administration of the Railways in the United States and Great Britain*, Oxford University Press, 1918.

Hearings before Senate Committee on Interstate Commerce, 65th Congress, 3d Session, on *Extension of Tenure of Government Control*, Jan. 3 to Feb. 21, 1919.

Hearings before House Committee on Interstate and Foreign Commerce, 66th Congress, 1st Session, July 15 to Aug. 19, 1919.

Hearings before Senate Committee on Interstate Commerce, 67th Congress, 1st Session, on *Railroad Revenues and Expenses*, May 10, 1921, to June 1, 1922.

HINES, WALKER D.: *War History of American Railroads*, Yale University Press, 1928.

Interstate Commerce Commission, *Special Report*, Dec. 1, 1917 (47 I.C.C. 757): *Statistics of Railways in the United States.*

JOHNSON, E. R., and T. W. VAN METRE: *Principles of Railroad Transportation*, D. Appleton & Company, 1921.

JONES, ELIOT: *Principles of Railway Transportation*, The Macmillan Company, 1924.

Railway Age, particularly vols. 62–69, inclusive.

SHARFMAN, I. LEO: *The American Railroad Problem*, Century Company, 1921.

War Adjustments in Railroad Regulation, *The Annals of the American Academy of Political and Social Science*, vol. 76, No. 165.

See also Readers' Guide for numerous magazine articles dealing with the period of federal operation.

Chapter XII

THE TRANSPORTATION ACT OF 1920—HISTORY AND PROVISIONS

WHILE the war endured, the American people voiced no protest against government operation of the railways. With the signing of the Armistice in November, 1918, however, the railway problem was again forced upon public attention. The determination to center all energies upon the successful prosecution of the war gave place, almost overnight, to a strong desire to revert quickly to a prewar status. As early as December, 1918, President Wilson urged upon Congress in his annual message the early and constructive consideration of the railway problem. Such consideration was given during the following year not only by Congress but by individuals and by groups. Indeed, it seems indisputable that more intelligent interest was evidenced in the railway problem during this period and that more constructive thought was expended upon its solution than in any previous year in the history of American railway development. At last it appeared that public, railway, and government had come to a realization of the necessity of abandoning the old restrictive policy in behalf of a more constructive one.

Numerous plans were offered, some representing relatively slight modifications of past policy and others advocating striking departures therefrom. Space forbids the discussion of these plans in detail here but it is desirable, perhaps, to indicate certain differences among them. All solutions offered called for the abandonment of federal operation at the earliest practicable date, except that presented by the Federal Railroad Administration itself: proposed extension of such operation was urged both that the government might meet certain problems in leisurely fashion and that the public might have an opportunity to study and evaluate government operation under normal conditions. All other plans but one called for the continuance of private ownership and operation: this one, offered in behalf of the railway workers, provided for government ownership and for operation by a directorate composed of representatives of the public, the railway officials, and the classified employees. Practically all proposals provided for the retention of competition. None ignored the desirability of the regulation of security issues or the necessity of adequate revenues if railway credit were to be restored. As an answer to the railway labor problem suggestions varied from compulsory arbitration through mere voluntary measures to the extreme of ignoring the matter altogether. To strengthen and maintain railway credit adequately provisions ran the gamut from a guaranteed minimum return upon fair value to failure to note need of change in policy. From among the elements of the solutions proposed, it was both the privilege and the obligation of Congress to choose such features as it felt should characterize the future relationship between government and railways. However, return to private operation by the railway corporations seemed to be the one clear public wish.

Dual Character of the Problem.—The problem faced by Congress following the Armistice was of a dual character: it was essential that a sound permanent policy be outlined and that certain temporary provisions should be made to ease the difficulties incident to the return of control to the owners. During the period of federal operation the Administration made no effort to protect the individual character of the numerous properties or to preserve either their traffic or personnel. Then, too, during the period of federal operation many additions and betterments were made by the government, and much equipment purchased and assigned to particular carriers. A demand by the government for the immediate payment of such indebtedness would have caused serious embarrassment, even to many of the stronger roads, in the face of the railway credit situation in 1920. Finally, the government was morally obligated to render financial assistance until revenues could be increased to cover expenses: failure to advance rates as costs mounted in 1918 and 1919 had made deficit operation a certainty until the rate level was raised. In short, it was quite as essential that Congress prescribe conditions making possible the return of the patient to normal, as that it establish a régime reasonably assuring the maintenance of good health, once attained.

Senate and House Take Action.—Attention was early given by the Committee on Interstate Commerce of the Senate to the railway problem. Hearings were held from Jan. 3 to Feb. 21, 1919, and, as a result of these hearings and further investigations by a subcommittee, there was introduced into the Senate the first Cummins bill. Further consideration resulted in the introduction of a substitute measure by Senator Cummins, chairman of the committee. This committee bill, for such it was since it represented the position of the entire committee with the exception of Senator La Follette, was offered to the Senate Nov. 10, and was considered at length upon the floor of the Senate from Dec. 2 to Dec. 20. Upon this latter date the bill was passed and, with the House measure which had been submitted previously to the Senate for consideration, was referred to a joint conference committee.

The railway problem was first presented to the House of Representatives through the introduction of the so-called Esch-Pomerene bill on June 2, 1919. This bill, embodying essentially the views of a considerable majority of the members of the Interstate Commerce Commission, was introduced into the House by Chairman Esch of the Committee on Interstate and Foreign Commerce, and into the Senate by Senator Pomerene. Upon this bill hearings were held by the House committee from July 15 to Oct. 4 and, as a result, a new bill was reported to the House on Nov. 10. During the entire week following the bill was debated upon the floor, passing on Nov. 17. It was then submitted to the Senate for consideration as the Esch bill.

Agreement and Differences between the Two Bills.—In certain particulars the bills passed by the House and Senate were quite similar. Especially was this true of the provisions designed to ease the transfer from federal to private operation. Little difficulty was experienced, therefore, in formulating this portion of the conference report. Agreement was also striking with respect to many matters of permanent policy—among these being regulation of security issues, control of construction and abandonment, broad control over rates and service, permissive pooling, and joint use of facilities. But interesting as were the points of similarity between the two measures, the differences were more striking. Grounded solidly as it was upon experience and conservative in outlook, the House bill was eminently sound in that it ventured at no point upon uncharted waters. But such a policy has elements of weakness in the face of new problems that arise from time to time. The Senate measure, on the other hand, though also grounded in part upon experience, took cognizance of new problems and sought to meet them in a positive and constructive manner. Where the Esch bill would solve problems by agreement, the Cummins bill would apply compulsion through channels specifically provided. Compulsory consolidation, compulsory arbitration of labor disputes, more definite statutory provisions calculated to secure to the railways a fair return, and a drastic reorganization of federal regulatory machinery were among the challenging provisions of the Senate measure.

The impossibility of harmonizing certain important features of the two bills led to compromise. In this compromise the untried features of the Cummins measure were greatly modified or eliminated, though its influence is clearly discernible in the text of the conference report. This report was submitted to the House and the Senate after almost 2 months of committee effort, was passed by both without amendment within a brief time, and signed by President Wilson on Feb. 28, 1920. And on Mar. 1 the railways were returned to their owners for operation under the Presidential proclamation of Dec. 24, 1919. Known officially as the Transportation Act of 1920, this epoch-making measure has been more widely termed the Esch-Cummins Act—and as such has featured prominently in political controversies during later years.

Transfer to Private Operation.—Since the immediate problem facing Congress was the transfer to private control of the railway mileage operated by the government under the Federal Control Act, the Transportation Act concerned itself first with the two phases of that problem. It declared that, at 12:01 A. M. Mar. 1, 1920, the President should relinquish possession and control of all railways and other systems of transportation then operated subject to his powers. Next, provision was made for a final settlement with the various carriers concerned. To this end certain additional sums were placed at the disposal of the Federal Railroad Administration and access to all necessary records, together with such other powers as were needful to protect governmental interests, was given. To carriers with whom no contract had been signed, the President was authorized to pay sums needed to meet certain expenses enumerated in the standard contract, such as interest on funded debt; final adjudication was left until a later date. All legal proceedings arising out of federal control were to be brought against an agent designated by the President.

The first important feature of the Act provided for the funding of carrier obligations to the United States. Though the right of a set-off of the carriers' indebtedness to the government for capital expenditures against any federal obligation arising out of the standard contract was recognized, no set-off was to be made that would deprive the carrier of sums necessary for the payment of interest, taxes, corporate charges, and expenses accruing during federal operation, or of sums requisite to the payment of dividends. Further, no set-off should be made except as the government had paid the carrier as much as one twenty-fourth of its operating expenses for the calendar year 1919, to provide the carrier with working capital. Upon request by the carrier, obligations to the United States for additions and betterments were to be funded for a period of 10 years or less at the option of the carrier, with interest at 6 per cent, the carrier to give security as the President should prescribe. Such necessary evidences of indebtedness as were given by the carrier under this provision might issue "without the authorization or approval of any authority, state or federal, and without compliance with any requirement, state or federal, as to notification."

For reasons previously given, the guarantee under which the carriers had operated during federal operation was extended for an additional 6 months at the option of the carriers and applied not only to railways operated by the government under the Federal Control Act, but also to the many other carriers—largely the less important lines not so operated. Indeed, with respect to the latter, the guarantee was made retroactive for the entire period of federal operation, thus compensating them for heavy financial losses and remedying a grievous injustice suffered during the period throughout which practically all larger and stronger properties had been protected. To obviate controversy with respect to the continuance of charges authorized by the Railroad Administration, all rates, classifications, regulations, and practices in effect on Feb. 29, 1920, upon carriers subject to the Interstate Commerce Act continued in force until changed by federal or state authority. To safeguard the federal government against adverse state action prior to Sept. 1, 1920, no rate was to be reduced and no classification, regulation, or practice so modified as to result in a reduction of the charge, except as approved by the Interstate Commerce Commission. All sums in excess of the guarantee collected by individual carriers electing to accept the same were to be paid into the treasury of the United States, except as it might be necessary for any carrier to retain sums to meet fixed charges accruing during the guarantee period. The certification of deficits under the guarantee was to be made by the Interstate Commerce Commission to the Secretary of the Treasury with the provision that, during the period, advances not to exceed the estimated guarantee might be made to enable the carrier to meet fixed charges and operating expenses. The guarantee was also extended to the American Railway Express Company, subject to election by that corporation.

That the carriers might be better enabled "properly to serve the public during the transition period immediately following the termination of federal control," a revolving fund of $300,000,000 was created, out of which loans were to be made to them. Such loans were to be made upon the approval of the Interstate Commerce Commission, in accordance with applications made by the carriers and upon the basis of information furnished by them. If the facts disclosed in hearing or by investigation indicated the need of such loan and gave reasonable assurance of the carrier's ability to meet all financial obligations incident to the loan, the Interstate Commerce Commission "may certify to the Secretary of the Treasury its findings of fact and its recommendations as to: the amount of the loan which is to be made; the time, not exceeding 5 years from the making thereof, within which it is to be repaid; the character of the security which is to be offered therefor; and the terms and conditions of the loan." Upon the basis of this certificate the Secretary of the Treasury, at any time within 36 months from Mar. 1, 1920, was authorized to make a loan not exceeding the maximum amount recommended by the Commission, such loan to bear interest at 6 per cent. Here again it was provided that evidences of indebtedness issued were not subject to the authorization or approval of any authority or to any requirements as to notification. With the aid of this revolving fund it was hoped that, despite the then doubtful credit position of the bulk of the carriers and despite the unpromising financial market, sufficient funds might be made available to meet the pressing needs of the railways.

Railway Interrelations.—After making provision for the transition period, the Act deals with changes in permanent regulatory policy. One of the more important of these changes concerns the problem of intercarrier relations. For more than 30 years pooling had been strictly prohibited. Believing that such a policy no longer represented maximum public advantage, Congress legalized such pooling arrangements as may, from time to time, receive the approval of the Interstate Commerce Commission after a hearing to determine whether the proposed pooling agreement "will be in the interest of better service to the public, or economy of operation, and will not unduly restrain competition." Further, the Commission is authorized, upon application by any carrier or carriers and after hearing, to approve "the acquisition . . . by one of such carriers of the control of any other such carrier or carriers, either under a lease or by the purchase of stock or in any other manner not involving the consolidation of such carriers into a single system for ownership and operation," upon such a basis as may be found by that body to be just and reasonable. However, public interest is at all times protected by reserving to the Commission the right to issue necessary supplementary orders incident to pooling and unification agreements.

But more striking in its nature and more important in its effect upon interrailway relations is the provision relative to "the consolidation of the railway properties of the continental United States into a limited number of systems." The Interstate Commerce Commission is instructed to prepare a tentative plan and, after hearings upon it, to "adopt a plan for such consolidation and publish the same." This plan is subject to modification at any time if change seems desirable in the public interest. In the division of the railways into systems under the plan adopted, "competition shall be preserved as fully as possible and wherever practicable the existing routes and channels of trade and commerce shall be maintained. Subject to the foregoing requirement, the several systems shall be so arranged that the cost of transportation as between the competitive systems and as related to the values of the properties through which the service is rendered shall be the same, so far as practicable, so that these systems can employ uniform rates in the movement of competitive traffic and, under efficient management, earn substantially the same rate of return upon the value of their respective railway properties." Thus Congress hoped to solve the strong- and weak-line problem which has been so troublesome a factor in the past.

Progress toward consolidation, however, is dependent upon the extent to which the plans adopted parallel railway self-interest, since all consolidations are to be voluntary. If the proposed consolidations are approved by the particular carriers involved, then their corporate interests and properties may be merged in accordance with the terms of the Act. One feature of particular interest in this connection is the requirement that the outstanding securities at par value of the corporation which assumes the consolidated properties "shall not exceed the value of the consolidated properties as determined by the Commission." All consolidations effected in pursuance of this Act are relieved from the operation of all restraints or prohibitions by law, state or federal, designed to protect the public against agreements in restraint of trade or monopolistic control. The Act also made provision for the unified control of the express business of the country by the American Railway Express Company, subject to the approval and authorization of the Interstate Commerce Commission.

Yet another portion of the Act affecting interrailway relations was that dealing with the interlocking directorate. After Dec. 31, 1921, it was declared unlawful for any person to hold the position of officer or director of more than one carrier "unless such holding shall have been authorized by order of the Commission upon due showing . . . that neither public nor private interests will be adversely affected thereby." The effective date of that provision of the Clayton Act governing the interlocking of railway and supply company directorates was extended to Jan. 1, 1921, except for such corporations as were organized after Jan. 12, 1918. These two provisions gave the Commission further control over corporate interrelations—preventing a community of interest inimical to public service in the one case, and an interlocking prejudicial to the financial success of the railway as well as ultimately burdensome to the shipper in the other.

Control of Construction and Abandonment.—The American people have long realized the folly of competitive construction. To prevent such waste many states had acted, but it was not until 1920 that a corporation proposing the construction of a new line or of additional mileage was required to secure federal approval in the form of a certificate of convenience and necessity from the Interstate Commerce Commission. Such a certificate is also required of any carrier proposing to acquire or operate any line of railroad or extension thereof. Furthermore, "no carrier . . . shall abandon all or any portion of a line of railroad or the operation thereof unless and until there shall first have been obtained from the Commission a certificate that the present or future public convenience and necessity permit of such abandonment." However, it is provided that such a certificate need not issue incident to the construction and abandonment of switching and similar tracks situated wholly within one state or of electric railways not operated as a part of a general steam-railway system of transportation. That public interest may be adequately protected, the Act provides in a detailed manner an opportunity for a full presentation of facts.

Regulation of Security Issues.—Closely related to the control of construction and abandonment of lines is the broad power given the Commission over the issuance of railway securities. For almost 50 years such federal control had been urged and for many years certain states regulated with varying success. To facilitate federal regulation and to eliminate the confusion resulting from diverse control, the federal government under this statute assumed exclusive jurisdiction. After 120 days following the effective date of the Act no securities might be issued legally by any carrier subject to regulation except upon Commission approval. Such approval is to be given only if the issue or assumption of responsibility "(1) is for some lawful object . . . and compatible with the public interest . . . and (2) is reasonably necessary and appropriate for such purpose." Here again, the Act provides for a hearing of various parties at interest and reserves to state regulatory bodies the right to make such representations "as they may deem just and proper." It is further declared that such validation of issues shall in no sense "imply any guarantee or obligation as to securities on the part of the United States." The only securities issuable without approval are notes maturing not more than 2 years from date, "aggregating (together with all other then outstanding notes of maturity of 2 years or less) not more than 5 per cent of the par value of the securities of the carrier then outstanding." "In the case of securities having no par value, the par value for the purposes of this paragraph shall be the fair market value as of the date of issuance."

Settlement of Labor Disputes.—Another provision of peculiar interest relates to the settlement of the carriers' labor disputes. Declaring that "it shall be the duty of all carriers . . . to exert every reasonable effort and adopt every available means to avoid any interruption of the operation of any carrier, growing out of any dispute between the carrier and the employees and subordinate officials thereof," the law provided that railroad boards of labor adjustment "may be established by an agreement between any carrier, group of carriers, officials of carriers, or organization or group of organizations thereof." These boards were to judge disputes involving grievances, rules, or working conditions not settled through conference. The Act also established a Railroad Labor Board of nine members, selected by the President by and with the advice and consent of the Senate; three were to be chosen from a list of nominees offered by and representing the employees, three from a list submitted by and representative of the railways, and the remaining three, chosen without restriction, were to represent the public. The members of the Board served for a period of 5 years at an annual compensation of $10,000 and all members were required to sever active relationship with labor organization or carrier. Nor might Board members have a pecuniary interest in any railway.

The Labor Board was a body of original jurisdiction in all disputes involving grievances, rules, or working conditions in the absence of the appropriate adjustment board and an appeal board upon matters concerning which any adjustment board certified that it "has failed or will fail to reach a decision within reasonable time or in respect to which the Labor Board determines that any adjustment board has so failed or is not using due diligence in its consideration thereof." Under the Act, the Labor Board took original jurisdiction also in all cases involving disputes with respect to wages or salaries of employees or subordinate officials, "if it is of the opinion that the dispute is likely substantially to interrupt commerce." No decision by this Board could be rendered except by a majority of its membership, with the further provision that in any case involving wages or salaries at least one public member must concur in the majority decision to validate it. That the Labor Board might function effectively, wide powers were given it to compel testimony, force the production of papers and other evidence needed, and require access to all pertinent records. A peculiar feature of the labor provisions of the Act was that neither strike nor lockout was prohibited during the period of investigation and that the findings of the Board were enforceable in no legal manner; such findings were observed at the option of the interested parties, with only public opinion available to compel conformance thereto.

To guide the Labor Board and such adjustment boards as might be created in the determination of wages or working conditions, the law declared that

> . . . the Board shall, so far as applicable, take into consideration among other relevant circumstances:
>
> 1. The scale of wages paid for similar kinds of work in other industries.
> 2. The relation between wages and the cost of living.
> 3. The training and skill required.
> 4. The hazards of the employment.
> 5. The degree of responsibility.
> 6. The character and regularity of the employment.
> 7. Inequalities of increase in wages or of treatment, as the result of previous wage orders or adjustments.

Any violations of a decision of the Labor Board or an adjustment board, by either carrier or employee, or organization thereof, might be advertised in such manner as that body determined, after due notice and hearing.

Provisions Dealing with Rates and Surplus.—Though the labor sections of the Transportation Act occupied an important place in public attention for a period, attention had been directed more persistently toward provisions concerning rates and surplus. Against these features of the Act the weight of the House members of the conference committee was thrown, but the Senate members clung tenaciously to them, sacrificing other provisions that these might be retained. The first important provision instructs the Commission so to fix rates that the:

> . . . carriers as a whole (or as a whole in each of such rate groups or territories as the Commission may from time to time designate) will, under honest, efficient, and economical management . . . earn an aggregate annual net railway operating income equal, as nearly as may be, to a fair return upon the aggregate value of the railway property of such carriers, held for and used in the service of transportation.

The determination of what percentage of the aggregate property value shall constitute a fair return thereon rests with the Commission, the sole permanent limitation being that the percentage shall be uniform for all rate groups. In fixing such percentage "it shall give due consideration, among other things, to the transportation needs of the country and the necessity (under honest, efficient, and economical management of existing transportation facilities) of enlarging such facilities in order to provide the people of the United States with adequate transportation." A temporary limitation was imposed upon Commission action, however: a fair return for the 2 years beginning Mar. 1, 1920, was declared to be a sum equal to 5½ per cent of the aggregate value of railway properties, except as the Commission might add an additional one-half of 1 per cent to make provision for improvements, betterments, or equipment chargeable to capital account. The "aggregate value" to which reference is made is to be determined by the Commission under the Valuation Act of 1913, and the Act declares that this body "shall give to the property investment account of the carriers only that consideration to which, under such law, it is entitled in establishing values for rate-making purposes."

Although Congress hoped for the establishment ultimately of railway systems of relatively equal financial strength under the consolidation provisions of the Act, until strong and weak properties were grouped many strong carriers would earn at a rate in excess of that fixed by the Commission for the carriers as a whole. To meet this situation, the Act provides that any carrier receiving during any year "a net railway operating income in excess of 6 per cent of the value of the railway property held for and used by it in the service of transportation, one-half of such excess shall be placed in a reserve fund established and maintained by such carrier, and the remaining one-half thereof shall . . . be recoverable by and paid to the Commission for the purpose of establishing and maintaining a general railway contingent fund." If, during any later year, the net railway operating income of a property falls below 6 per cent of the value of its property, a carrier may draw from its individual reserve fund to make up the difference. However, the accumulation of this individual reserve fund need not extend beyond a sum equal to 5 per cent of the value of its railway property, "and when such fund is so accumulated and maintained, the portion of its excess income which the carrier is permitted to retain . . . may be used by it for any lawful purpose." As the one exception to the operation of this recapture provision the Commission may permit any new project "to retain for a period not to exceed 10 years all or any part of its earnings derived from such new construction."

The general railroad contingent fund to be built up from the government's share of earnings beyond 6 per cent is to serve as a revolving fund, administered by the Commission "in furtherance of public interest in railway transportation." This may be "either by making loans to carriers to meet expenditures for capital account or to refund maturing securities originally issued for capital account or by purchasing transportation equipment and facilities and leasing the same to carriers." In making application for a loan from this fund or for the lease of equipment purchased by moneys appropriated from it, the carrier must indicate, among other things, the purpose of the loan, the character of security offered, and the public need to be served.

State and Federal Jurisdiction.—Because of the close relation existing between it and those provisions of the Act designed to secure a fair return for the carriers as a whole, the enactment of the Shreveport principle into law may well be mentioned next.[1] Though the Interstate Commerce Commission is authorized to confer with the state regulatory bodies "on any matter wherein the Commission is empowered to act and where the rate-making authority of the state is or may be affected by the action taken by the Commission," federal supremacy is clearly asserted. "Whenever . . . the Commission finds that any such rate, fare, charge, classification, regulation, or practice" as is imposed by the authority of any state "causes any undue or unreasonable advantage, preference, or prejudice, as between persons or localities in intrastate commerce on the one hand and interstate or foreign commerce on the other hand, it shall prescribe . . . in such manner as, in its judgment, will remove such advantage, preference, prejudice, or discrimination." Such prescription of rates, fares, etc., shall be observed by the carriers affected, "the law of any state or the decision or order of any state authority to the contrary notwithstanding."

Miscellaneous Rate Provisions.—Certain important modifications in our regulatory policy with respect to rates appear in the Act. The broad power of the Commission to suspend proposed changes in rates, fares, classifications, etc., pending investigation was modified so that, beyond an initial suspension of 120 days, a further delay of not more than 30 days was possible. However, if the Commission has not completed its investigation at the end of this maximum period, it possesses the power to require "the interested carrier or carriers to keep accurate account in detail of all amounts received by reason of such increase" as the basis of a refund if the final decision of the Commission is adverse. The Act also gives the Commission the power to prescribe minimum as well as maximum rates,

[1] From 1886 onward for a quarter century sharp differentiation between the state and federal fields of regulatory action was accepted without challenge: the state's authority over intrastate commerce was regarded as complete and as exclusive as federal jurisdiction over interstate movements. In 1913, however, the United States Supreme Court in the Minnesota Rate Cases (230 U. S. 352) intimated that state regulation prejudicial to interstate commerce could not be maintained—and in 1914, in the Shreveport Case (234 U. S. 342), the Court nullified the order of a state commission fixing intrastate rates when that order was shown to be prejudicial to interstate commerce. This decision is one of major importance in regulation.

fares, and charges, except in the case of joint rates where one of the carriers is a water line. In such case the maximum rate alone can be set.

Another interesting extension of Commission authority over rates is found in its control, under the Act, of the divisions of joint fares, rates, and charges. Acting upon complaint or upon its own initiative, the Commission may, if it finds existing divisions "unjust, unreasonable, inequitable, or unduly preferential or prejudicial, as between the carriers which are parties thereto . . . prescribe the just, reasonable, and equitable divisions thereof to be received by the several carriers." In prescribing such division, the "Commission shall give due consideration, among other things, to the efficiency with which the carriers concerned are operated, the amount of revenue required to pay their respective operating expenses,

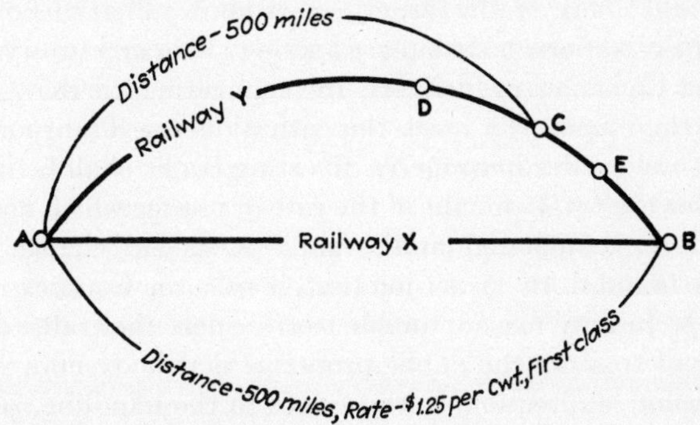

In accordance with the Transportation Act the rate from *A* to *C*, via Railway *Y*, may not exceed that charged by Railway *X* upon a like shipment from *A* to *B*, if Railway *Y* has been granted Fourth Section relief upon movements from *A* to *B*. To *D*, any point intermediate to *A* and *C*, the maximum charge will be that from *A* to *C*; to *E*, however, the charge may at the discretion of the Interstate Commerce Commission exceed the limit fixed by statute to *C*. But if Railway *Y* does not seek Fourth Section relief to permit it to compete for traffic moving from *A* to *B*, then rates to all points on its line (such as *D* and *C* and *E*) may be fixed without reference to the charge from *A* to *B* via Railway *X*.

FIG. 9.—The 1920 amendment of Sec. 4. illustrated.

taxes, and a fair return on their railway property . . . and the importance to the public of the transportation services of such carriers," together with such other facts as would ordinarily "entitle one carrier to a greater or less proportion than another carrier" of the joint charge. The purpose of this control over rate divisions is twofold—it gives the weaker line which is a party to joint tariffs adequate protection against its stronger connection and also enables the Commission to deal effectively and directly with those abnormal divisions to plant facilities which represent indirect rebating.

A final change affecting rates gave legal sanction to a policy of the Commission with respect to Sec. 4, as amended, in 1910. In granting exceptions to the long-and-short-haul principle, "the Commission shall not permit the establishment of any charge to or from the more distant points that is not reasonably compensatory for the service performed." And, if a circuitous route be permitted, because of its circuity, to meet the charges of a more direct route between competitive points, intermediate points on the circuitous route shall not be charged a higher rate than is charged by the direct route between such competitive points except as the distance over which traffic is moved on the circuitous route shall be greater than the length of the direct route (see Fig. 9). A further restriction was added which declares that no authorization for exceptions "shall be granted on account of merely potential water competition, not actually in existence."

Control over Routing and Service.—The new legislation broadened greatly the control of the Interstate Commerce Commission over the routing of traffic. Many railways, either without affiliations or "at outs" with connecting carriers, have suffered serious financial injury because of the improper diversion or delivery by connecting carriers of tonnage routed over their lines. To meet this situation the Transportation Act declares that the carrier improperly diverting traffic shall be liable to the injured line for the total amount of the rate or charge which it would have received had it participated in the haul. A second change in routing regulations is found in the provision that, in case the Commission believes any railway is, for any reason, unable to transport the traffic offered it in such manner as to serve the public properly, that body may "make such just and reasonable directions with respect to the handling, routing, and movement of the traffic of such carrier and its distribution over other lines or roads, as in the opinion of the Commission will best promote the service in the interest of the public and the commerce of the people." This adjustment shall be made upon such terms as the carriers may fix by agreement or, in case of disagreement, as the Commission shall determine to be just and reasonable. When traffic has not been routed by the shipper, "the Commission may, whenever public interest and a fair distribution of the traffic require, direct the route such traffic shall take after it arrives at the terminus of one carrier or at a junction point with another carrier, and is to be there delivered to another carrier." Furthermore, in time of war or threatened war the Commission may, upon certification by the President that certain traffic should enjoy preference or priority in transportation in the interest of public safety, direct that such preference or priority be afforded.

The power of the Interstate Commerce Commission over matters of car service and joint use of facilities was also greatly extended. Following the declaration that it shall be the duty of every carrier "to furnish safe and adequate car service and to establish, observe, and enforce just and reasonable rules, regulations, and practices with respect to car service," certain specific requirements are made concerning the distribution of cars for the transportation of coal among the coal mines served by any railway. The maintenance of just and reasonable ratings during periods of car shortage is required and the Act states that "each and every car furnished to or used by any such mine for transportation of coal" shall be counted against that mine. It is further provided that the Commission may, whenever it "is of the opinion that shortage of equipment, congestion of traffic, or other emergency requiring immediate action exists in any section of the country," order, with or without hearing, a suspension of all regulations then established with respect to car service for such time as the Commission may determine. Further, it may "make such just and reasonable directions with respect to car service, without regard to the ownership as between carriers of locomotives, cars, and other vehicles, during such emergency, as in its opinion will best promote the service in the interest of the public and the commerce of the people," compensation to be fixed by agreement between or among the carriers or, if dispute arises, by the Commission. Indeed, "if the Commission finds it to be in the public interest and to be practicable, without substantially impairing the ability of a carrier owning or entitled to the enjoyment of terminal facilities," it shall have the power to require the joint or common use of terminals, including main-line track or tracks for a reasonable distance outside of those terminals, on such terms and for such compensation as may be fixed by mutual agreement between the carriers or, in event of their failure to agree, by the Commission.

Changes in Commission's Organization.—The Transportation Act of 1920 placed heavier burdens upon the Interstate Commerce Commission in fields formerly occupied by regulation and, in addition, added heavily to its work in the form of new duties and responsibilities. To enable that body to discharge these added functions the membership of the Commission was increased from 9 to 11 and, at the same time, the compensation was increased to $12,000 per year. No restriction is imposed upon the President in the appointment of these Commissioners, "by and with the advice and consent of the Senate," except that not more than 6 shall be appointed from any one political party. That the Commission might have statutory authorization for a change in its method of procedure which is intended to increase efficiency, it is empowered by its order to divide the members into such divisions of not less than 3 as it may deem necessary. To afford greater elasticity, specific authorization is given for such changes in organization from time to time as the judgment of the Commission dictates.

Such, then, are the major provisions of the Transportation Act of 1920 which has so largely determined the relation between railways and government since Mar. 1, 1920. In the next chapters the operation of the Act will be described, further legislation summarized, and a brief analysis of our regulatory policy made.

REFERENCES

CUNNINGHAM, W. J.: *American Railroads*, McGraw-Hill Book Company, Inc., 1922.

DAGGETT, STUART: *Principles of Inland Transportation*, Harper & Brothers, 1928.

DIXON, F. H.: *Railroads and Government*, Charles Scribners' Sons, 1922.

Hearings before Committee on Interstate Commerce, United States Senate, 65th Congress, 2d session, on *Extension of Tenure of Government Control of Roads.*

Hearings before House Committee on Interstate and Foreign Commerce, 66th Congress, 1st session, on H.R. 4378, *Return of the Railroads to Private Ownership.*

JONES, ELIOT: *Principles of Railway Transportation*, The Macmillan Company, 1924.

LOCKLIN, D. P.: *Railroad Regulation Since* 1920, McGraw-Hill Book Company, Inc., 1928 and 1931 (Supplement).

MCVEAGH, ROGERS: *The Transportation Act of* 1920—*Sources, History and Text*, Henry Holt & Company, 1923.

Monthly Labor Review, vol. 10, pp. 880–887, April, 1920.

Railway Age, Feb. 20, 1920, pp. 555–572.

RICH, EDGAR L.: The Transportation Act of 1920, *American Economic Review*, vol. 10, p. 507.

SHARFMAN, I. L.: *The American Railroad Problem*, Century Company, 1921.

Transportation Act of 1920.

CHAPTER XIII

RECENT RAILWAY HISTORY: ECONOMIC CONDITIONS AND INTERCORPORATE RELATIONS

THE years since 1920 have been for the railways years of sharp contrasts; within them have fallen periods of heavy traffic with consequent satisfactory net earnings and within them, too, have fallen periods with traffic so light as to imperil the solvency of much of the nation's mileage. These years have been critical ones for the railway as a major factor in the field of transport, also: perhaps at no time since operation of the first railway in the United States about a hundred years ago has the future of the railway been questioned as during the past decade. Yet these years marked by wide fluctuations in earnings and shadowed by a growing uncertainty concerning the railway outlook were begun under legislation that was rightly heralded as constructive rather than restrictive in character, representing a "new deal" in federal regulation. Has it been, then, that hopes of accomplishment were too high or that the unexpected has made impossible the realization of those hopes? Both, undoubtedly, have a place in explaining the gap between expectations and actuality, though it is certain that extraneous circumstances and conditions account to greater degree for the existing situation than do errors in legislation or in Commission policy. Of these extraneous factors none other has been so significant as changes in the general economic situation. To assist the reader in understanding more clearly developments in the railway field in the years of stress and almost kaleidoscopic change since the termination of federal operation, the record of those years will be traced briefly.

Situation of the Railways at Termination of Federal Operation.— Before indicating the course of events following federal operation, however, it is important that certain facts be presented relative to the railways as they resumed operation under corporate direction. An exceedingly difficult situation was faced during the period immediately following federal operation: a period of deflation, marked by sharp maladjustments, widespread social unrest, and disturbed conditions abroad, offered serious obstacles to normal railway operations. But this situation was further aggravated by other factors. The railways were returned to their owners in poor condition to meet the demands of ordinary traffic, yet the volume of traffic in 1920 surpassed that of all previous years in railway history. Furthermore, the railways were returned in an unsatisfactory physical condition: though the actual amounts expended during the period of federal operation indicate a liberal maintenance policy, an examination of detailed facts seemed to justify the carriers' contention of deficit maintenance of roadway and structure, and even of certain types of equipment. And contributing in an important degree to the railway's incapacity to render maximum service, too, was the human factor. Traffic departments had been largely wiped out, many operating staffs had been riddled, and, more hurtful than either, the morale of the rank and file had been seriously impaired. Employee loyalty, which had been characteristic of the workers on every line in prewar years, had suffered seriously as a consequence of lesser interest in the job and greater interest in the wage rate, and seriously also from what seemed to be a deliberate campaign to destroy worker *esprit de corps* to further the so-called Plumb plan for government ownership and employee operation of the railways. Indeed, it is possible that the half-truths and falsehoods broadcast in the interest of that visionary plan were more responsible than unsatisfactory physical condition for certain postwar defects in railway service—and far more persistent.

A second heritage from federal operation was a wholly inadequate rate level. Shortly after the government had taken over the railways, freight rates were increased by 25 per cent and passenger rates to a minimum of 3 cents a mile. The Railroad Administration hoped this increase would be sufficient and, despite the deficit of 1918, Mr. McAdoo continued to show an "amazing optimism." The growing deficits of the early months of 1919, due to diminished traffic, indicated that even worse showings were yet to follow. Serious consideration was then given to a further increase of rates, but Director-General Hines, after careful consideration of the problem and consultation with the President, declined to act: the Administration desired to avoid giving any excuse for additional increases in the rapidly ascending cost of living; furthermore, it contended that, in view of the approaching return to private operation, the question of an additional increase in rates was properly one for the Interstate Commerce Commission. Yet it is doubtful if an adequate increase in rates would have raised prices materially and certain it is that the Administration showed inconsistency with respect to its second justification for inaction in negotiating the national agreements with railway labor within a few months of the close of the period of federal operation.

A third problem which the railways faced upon the termination of federal operation lay in the field of labor. Large increases in wages had been granted in 1918 and these were followed by readjustments, generally upward. However, the wage level was still unsatisfactory to labor: with the increase in the cost of living in 1919, insistent demands were made for additional increases. These demands were refused by the Railroad Administration, President Wilson himself urging labor to delay until the general attack upon profiteering had been made. When the futility of this method of reducing prices became apparent, the President and the Director-General urged further delay: as in the matter of rates, they contended that the readjustment of wages should be made under private operation by such tribunal as might be set up by pending legislation. To this second plea railway labor leaders also acceded, though the workers were demanding immediate action: they felt the pinch of increased prices and, in the face of delays, had become restless and resentful. This fact tended to weaken further the morale of railway labor during the first months of private operation.

Yet, in the face of the handicaps of undermaintenance of the physical property, of disruption of staff and weakening of morale, of inadequate rates and a labor force demanding an immediate upward revision of the wage scale, private management was compelled to handle immediately and during months of readjustment a hitherto unequaled traffic. That the task was creditably performed was the good fortune of the public and a basis for congratulation to the railways.

The Postwar Boom and Depression.—When the Armistice was signed in November, 1918, American business enterprise was at flood tide. Immediately a decline in activity appeared, that decline being reflected in reduced car loadings by February—and loadings continued low until the usual heavy seasonal movements began in the autumn. In the late spring of 1919, however, business had begun to revive and the price level, which had dropped following the Armistice, moved upward in an almost unbroken course from February, 1919, to May, 1920, when it stood at 246.7.[1] In July, 1919, car loadings began to reflect the increase in business activity; from that month forward, despite the coal and steel strikes during the autumn months, tonnage increased steadily as compared with the previous year. Perhaps no fact more clearly shows the changed situation early in 1920, as compared with that of the preceding year, than a car shortage of about 85,000 then in contrast to a surplus of 450,000 in 1919. The railways were returned to their owners when the wave of prosperity was sweeping forward irresistibly, with business activity at the crest. The public was buying freely, even extravagantly, and the major complaint of the producer was inability to keep pace with orders. Labor shortages existed in every field and the volume of traffic exceeded the capacity of the railways to serve—with the result that a car shortage, appearing in January, became steadily greater until in August it had mounted to 130,000. But by August prices had begun to break, and from that time forward business activity dropped precipitously, also: the turn had obviously come.

[1] All price index numbers used are those compiled by the United States Bureau of Labor, 1913 base.

In the months from May, 1920, until June, 1921, prices declined rapidly and uninterruptedly—from 246.7 to 141.6. Business activity, too, receded during this period by almost 30 per cent. While the price

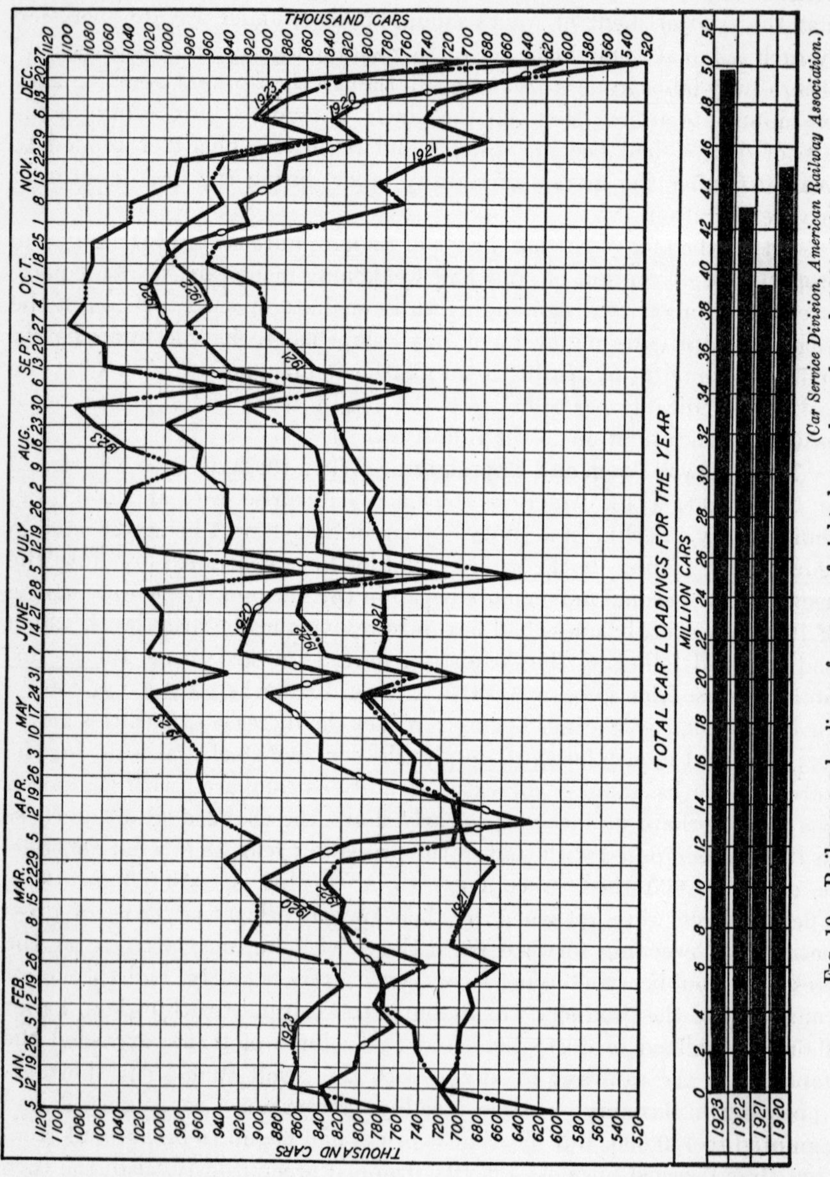

FIG. 10.—Railway car loadings of revenue freight, by weeks and total, 1920–1923.
(Car Service Division, American Railway Association.)

level fluctuated but little during 1921, business activity was increasing irregularly—and during 1922 that increase became pronounced. The price level tended to keep pace with the upward swing of business, both reaching a high in the late spring of 1923. That the sharp decline in business activity late in 1920 should leave its impress upon railway traffic was inevitable: mines were closed, furnaces shut down, manufacturing operations curtailed or stopped, and retail distribution reduced to low levels. In consequence, car loadings in December, 1920, were markedly below those of the preceding year and from that time forward until February, 1922, no month showed a reasonable parity with 1920. Throughout 1921 monthly loadings were far below the figures for the corresponding months of the preceding year, the total for 1921 standing more than 13 per cent below the more than 45,000,000 cars loaded in 1920. Ton-miles show this

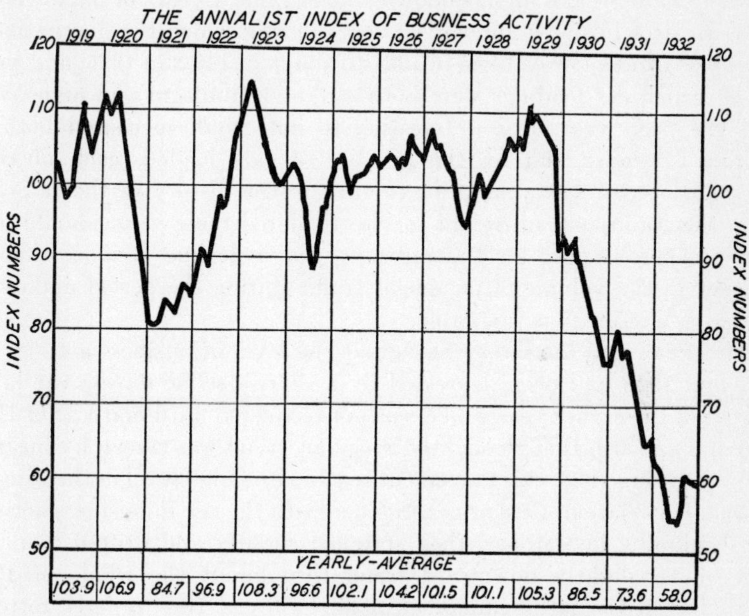

Reproduced by permission of the Annalist.

FIG. 11.—Fluctuations in business in the United States, 1919–1932.

decline in traffic even more clearly, a decrease of 25 per cent appearing in that figure. Because of this slump a car surplus of considerable proportions developed late in 1920, continuing until midyear, 1922; its peak was reached in April, 1921, when a surplus of 493,000 cars, almost 20 per cent of the total railway equipment in service, was shown. And at no time prior to September, 1922, did the surplus fall below 100,000.

Renewed Business Activity.—With the increase in prices and the upward sweep of business activity that became more pronounced as the year 1922 progressed, railway car loadings continued to gain; indeed, by the close of the year total loadings had fallen short of the high figure of 1920 by less than 2,000,000 cars. So great became the pressure for equipment that late in 1922 a major car shortage developed, but this shortage was gradually reduced by increased efficiency on the part of the carriers until, in September, 1923, a car surplus of some 50,000 cars was shown, despite loadings far in excess of any previous period in railway history. The year 1923 showed a high average level of business activity; the level of wholesale prices had advanced to 153.7—some five points above the previous year—and loadings for that year exceeded the previous high by almost 5,000,000 cars, revenue ton-miles being some 1½ per cent in excess of 1920.

In 1924 prices receded moderately, business activity dropping back to the levels of 1922; car loadings, however, fell but some 6 per cent short of the previous year's high. Following 1924 came 4 years of high activity in the field of business enterprise, years during which the fluctuation in prices was from a low of 136.5 in 1927 to a high of 148.3 in 1925, and years during which car loadings were both strikingly uniform and high—with 1926 the peak year. It is interesting to note that, measured both by revenue ton-miles and by the number of cars loaded, each of these 4 years exceeded any year prior to 1925 in the history of the railways. From the standpoint of freight service rendered these years should have been prosperous ones for the railways, but a decline of more than 10 per cent in the volume of passenger traffic during the period makes the composite picture less favorable.

The Peak and the Great Trough.—The level of business activity for 1927 and 1928 had been depressed by a sharp decline during the latter months of the earlier year which was not recovered until midyear of 1928. A strong upward, though slightly irregular, trend was shown by business activity during 1928, this movement reaching its high level in the summer of 1929. Until late in 1928 prices stiffened with the rise in business activity but, beginning in October, they softened slightly and drifted aimlessly with but a slightly downward trend throughout the whole of 1929. Beginning in the late summer of 1929, however, the "orderly retreat" of business became a rout—and, with but two brief stays in its downward course, business activity plunged steadily toward lower and lower levels. By midsummer, 1932, the decline from the high point of 1929 was double that of the decline of 1920–1921, a low level being attained that has been equaled by few of the business depressions which America has experienced. That the activity of business in 1929 should be reflected in traffic offerings to the railways was but natural: as measured in ton-miles the volume of freight traffic exceeded even 1926 by a narrow margin. It was but natural, too, that the steady recession of business activity through a period of almost 3 years should be reflected in the volume of railway traffic—and the unparalleled decline in traffic volume bears evidence to the havoc that the depression has played with the railways. In 1930 car loadings dropped below 1924 levels and in 1931 total loadings were some 2,000,000 below the depression year of 1921. Loadings for 1932 achieved a new low level,

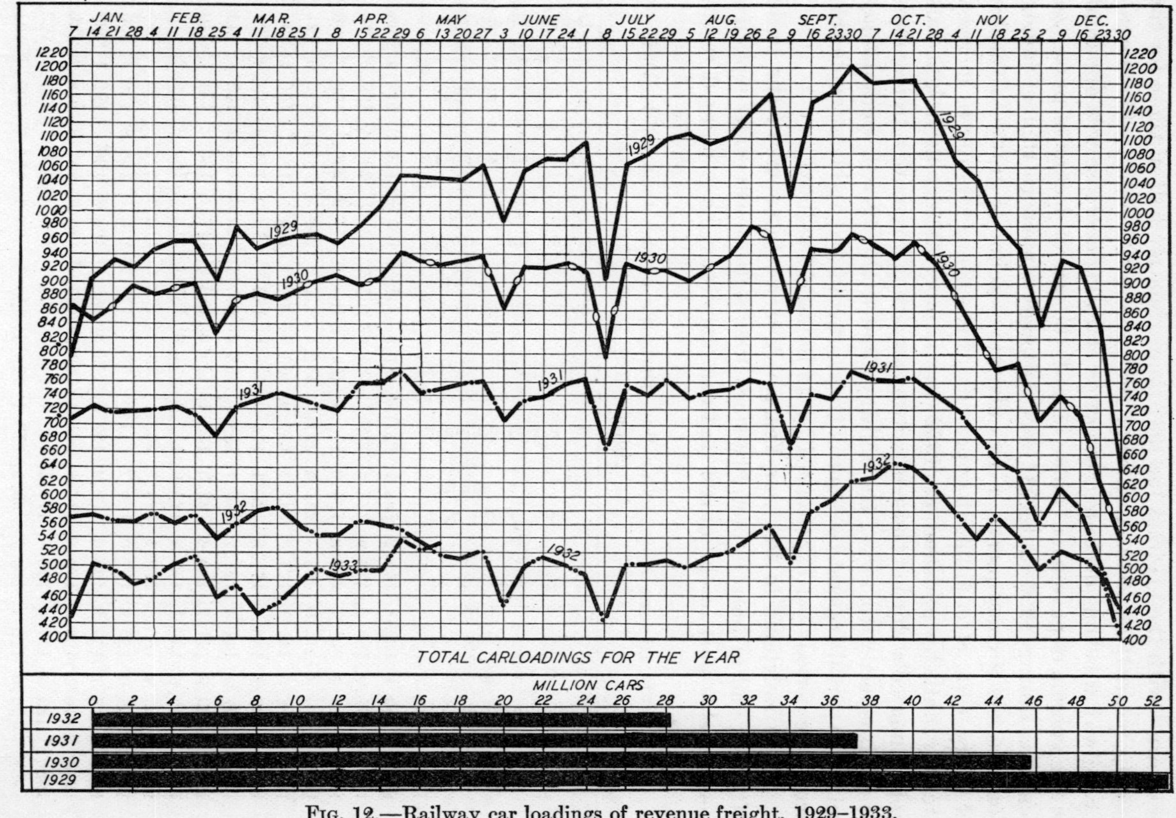

FIG. 12.—Railway car loadings of revenue freight, 1929–1933.

with the result that a decline from the previous year of about 30 per cent is shown—with the loadings for 1932 approximately half of those for the average year, 1925–1929. And, while the volume of freight traffic moving by railway was thus declining, the same alarming decrease was apparent in the volume of passenger traffic; indeed, the rate of decline of passenger business during 1930 and 1931 was strikingly similar to that of freight tonnage. As a consequence of this alarming decline in traffic, a surplus of every type of equipment appeared—this surplus tending to increase steadily until by midsummer, 1932, the number of surplus freight cars approximated a third of those in railway service. Thus, with a tremendous unused capacity to serve, the railways ended the 12-year period since return to private operation—one of the most confused and least explicable economic periods yet experienced by an industrial society.

Price Relations in Postwar Years.—A mere statement of the trend of prices and of business activity since 1920 fails, however, to explain a considerable part of the unrest and complaint that have marked recent

TABLE VII.—INDEX NUMBERS OF WHOLESALE PRICES, BY YEARS, 1917–1932
(1913 = 100)

Year	Farm products	Foods	Building materials	Chemicals and drugs	Fuel and lighting	Hides and leather	House-furnishing goods	Metal and metal products	Textile products	Miscellaneous	All commodities
1917	180.4	162.8	155.6	205.7	171.9	181.8	131.8	165.9	172.3	174.9	168.3
1918	207.0	185.5	173.9	227.3	178.1	184.6	165.7	150.3	239.4	192.6	188.1
1919	220.4	201.7	203.9	195.8	170.1	255.7	188.1	144.2	236.1	199.3	198.6
1920	210.8	214.0	264.7	205.4	267.0	251.5	251.9	164.5	287.6	240.0	221.2
1921	123.6	141.1	171.8	143.4	157.9	160.4	200.7	129.4	164.9	156.4	139.8
1922	131.2	136.4	171.6	125.1	175.0	153.6	183.8	113.3	174.9	133.0	138.5
1923	137.9	144.4	191.7	126.1	158.7	153.0	193.4	120.4	194.2	142.8	144.1
1924	139.9	141.7	180.4	123.3	150.1	149.0	186.3	117.1	186.2	134.1	140.5
1925	153.6	156.1	179.4	126.9	157.4	154.6	183.1	113.7	189.0	156.2	148.3
1926	139.9	155.8	176.4	124.7	163.1	146.8	177.6	110.1	174.5	143.3	143.3
1927	139.0	150.6	167.0	120.7	144.0	158.1	173.2	106.1	166.8	130.4	136.7
1928	148.1	157.3	166.0	119.2	137.5	178.3	168.9	106.8	166.7	129.1	138.5
1929	146.7	155.6	168.3	117.5	135.4	160.2	167.5	110.7	157.8	118.3	136.5
1930	123.5	141.0	158.6	111.1	128.1	146.8	164.7	101.4	140.1	111.3	123.8
1931	90.6	116.2	139.7	98.9	110.1	126.4	150.8	93.1	115.7	100.0	104.6
1932	67.4	95.0	125.9	91.6	114.7	107.0	133.4	88.3	95.8	92.3	92.8

years. That prices should decline sharply from their highs of the war and immediate postwar period was inevitable; that the downward movement should be regular as among the various commodity groups was highly desirable. Yet the lesser resistance of certain groups made the readjustment clumsy and halting, acute distress being induced by inequalities that appeared. The extent of the maladjustments that developed and the persistence of those maladjustments become increasingly apparent as closer attention is given to Table VII.

Among the groups that have suffered particularly because of an adverse price relationship, agriculture is of outstanding importance. What was for many others an orderly decline soon assumed the aspect for the farmer of a collapse; but, assisted by extraneous factors and his own efforts, his position was later improved until an advantage was gained upon the basis of the price level as a whole—only to have that advantage swept away and an increasing disparity develop as the depression extended beyond 1929. This recurring disadvantage of the farmer has been little greater than that of certain other groups but, because of the numerical importance of the farmer and his political power, his plight has attracted general attention and persistent legislative interest. This interest has shown itself in many tangible ways, only two of which have direct interest for the student of transportation, the Hoch-Smith Resolution and the furtherance of the program of inland waterway development.[1]

A Period of Stress.—It is obvious from the brief statement of facts preceding that the years since the termination of federal operation of the railways have been years of maladjustment and strain in the economic structure and years of particular difficulty for the railways, affected as they are not only by business activity but also by competitive conditions. The "return to normalcy" in the United States proved a hard journey and, as the public made this backward "trek," the air was filled with the recriminations of the various groups, each of which believed—rightly or wrongly—that his was the roughest path. But, when the railways had begun to share in the improvement in economic conditions, the small cloud of competition upon the horizon of their prosperity grew rapidly to assume a threatening aspect. None the less, so long as general well-being ruled, disaster in no wise impended. With the collapse of industry and trade that began in 1929 and its suggestion that normalcy was perhaps but a mirage, however, the railways entered upon a period that has brought even the strong to the brink of receivership. Indeed, except for governmental support through the Reconstruction Finance Corporation, bankrupt mileage at the close of 1932 would have been greater, both absolutely and relatively, than at any previous time in our national experience. From heights to depths industrial activity swung twice before the final peak was reached in 1929—and from that peak activity has declined to hitherto unexplored low ground. It is under such abnormal conditions that the railways have been compelled to serve the public, that regulation has been compelled to function, that important

[1] For a discussion of the Hoch-Smith Resolution see p. 237, and for a statement of the inland waterway program Chap. XXXV.

changes in regulatory policy have received their test. If, during such troubled years, moderately satisfactory results have been attained, then a favorable presumption is justified as to the effectiveness of our railways and the basic soundness of governmental policies.

Consolidation.—No portion of the Transportation Act represents a sharper break with past policy or has stimulated greater discussion than that which looked toward the consolidation of the railways of the United States into a limited number of competitive systems. To the end that it might comply with the procedure set forth in the Act, the Interstate Commerce Commission moved immediately toward the formulation of the prescribed tentative plan. This plan,[1] modeled upon a suggested grouping of railways submitted to the Commission at its request by

[1] In 63 I.C.C. 455, certain systems and alternatives were suggested. These follow, the name of the system appearing in italics, with the names of other major properties in the grouping appended.

1. *New York Central*—Western Maryland; Boston and Maine; also lines then controlled by the New York Central.
2. *Pennsylvania*—Toledo, Peoria, and Western, with important properties then a part of the Pennsylvania system.
3. *Baltimore and Ohio*—Reading; New Haven; Monon; Lehigh and New England.
4. *Erie*—Delaware and Hudson; Lackawanna; Wabash (east of Mississippi River).
5. *Nickel Plate-Lehigh Valley*—Wheeling and Lake Erie; Pittsburgh and West Virginia.
6. *Père Marquette*—Ann Arbor; Detroit, Toledo, and Ironton.
7. *New England*—New Haven; Boston and Maine; Maine Central; Lehigh and New England; New York, Ontario, and Western.

7a. *New England-Great Lakes*—Same as No. 7, adding Delaware and Hudson; Lackawanna; Buffalo, Rochester, and Pittsburgh.

8. *Chesapeake and Ohio*—Virginian.
9. *Norfolk and Western*—Toledo and Ohio Central, with subsidiaries.
10. *Southern*—Alabama and Vicksburg; also all properties controlled by the Southern, including Mobile and Ohio.
11. *Atlantic Coast Line-Louisville and Nashville*—Atlanta, Birmingham, and Atlantic; Richmond, Fredericksburg, and Potomac; Florida East Coast; Clinchfield; Gulf, Mobile and Northern.
12. *Illinois Central-Seaboard*—Gulf and Ship Island; Clinchfield; Tennessee Central.
13. *Union Pacific–North Western*—Lake Superior and Ishpeming; Wabash (west of the Mississippi River); all properties controlled by both the Union Pacific and North Western.
14. *Burlington-Northern Pacific*—Chicago Great Western; Minneapolis and St. Louis; Spokane, Portland, and Seattle.
15. *Milwaukee-Great Northern*—Terre Haute; Duluth, Missabe, and Northern; Green Bay and Western; Spokane, Portland, and Seattle.
16. *Santa Fe*—Colorado and Southern; Denver and Rio Grande; Western Pacific; Northwestern Pacific.
17. *Southern Pacific-Rock Island*—El Paso and Southwestern; Midland Valley; Chicago, Peoria, and St. Louis.
18. *Frisco-Katy-Cotton Belt*—Chicago and Alton; Louisiana Railway and Navigation Company.

Professor W. Z. Ripley, whose earlier work had won him merited recognition, was published in the late summer of 1921.

The Tentative Plan.—Carrier groupings were made in accord with certain principles. Systems were confined as largely as possible to a single one of the traditional territorial divisions; lines in the Eastern District centered upon New York and upon Chicago and St. Louis; Western lines centered in Chicago; and Southern properties were pivoted upon Atlanta. Efforts were made to group lines in such way as to give to each system, in so far as possible, the benefit of profitable long-haul traffic. And, because of the vital importance of free access to large centers, provision was made for the independent operation of certain major terminal and "bridge" lines. Volume of traffic, rather than mileage, was the accepted index of size, and a proper balance between trunk and feeder lines was sought.

Hearings were instituted upon the tentative plan in accord with statutory requirements, these extending over a period of more than 18 months and producing a tremendous mass of testimony and data: testimony alone totaled almost 12,000 pages, and exhibits, most of them voluminous, approximated 650 in number. During the early hearings carrier activities were directed largely toward criticism of the plan and the principles upon which it rested; later, at the suggestion of the Commission, the carriers contributed a great volume of basic data relative to traffic movements and traffic interchange that was of fundamental value. While the plan was supported in many quarters and by diverse interests, opposition was also voiced by railways as well as by public groups. In some instances railway opposition arose from the assignment of a weak property to a stronger line, as the Seaboard Air Line to the Illinois Central, and in others from failure to benefit from the assignment of a desirable line, as the assignment of the Reading to the Baltimore and Ohio instead of to the New York Central. Complaint was offered, too, against proposed disruptions of long-standing alliances, as illustrated by the Hill system and Pennsylvania-Norfolk and Western relations. Public opposition seems to have proceeded largely from fear of local disadvantage rather than from antagonism to the principle of consolidation, despite past insistence upon enforced competition. Various ports protested certain groupings that to them seemed to threaten volume of tonnage; New England interests were

19. *Chicago-Missouri Pacific*—Chicago and Eastern Illinois; Kansas City Southern; Orient; Gulf Coast Lines; Texas and Pacific; International and Great Northern; Fort Smith and Western.

The tentative plan, as published, took no note of the many short lines in the areas served by the systems suggested. Too, certain properties were included in more than one system, these representing alternative placement. Other properties, controlled by the Canadian Pacific and the Canadian National Railways, were not covered by the tentative plan, the more important among these being the Central Vermont and the Soo.

generally opposed to the inclusion of New England lines in Trunk Line systems, fearing that their interests would be subordinated to those of areas to the westward; inland centers, terminals of important railways, objected to any consolidation of lines that might make of them mere way stations on a through route; and yet other communities and areas protested against such a consolidation of lines as would deprive them of the benefits of competition.

In the course of the extended hearings the diversity of judgments concerning various aspects of consolidation became clearly evident. The railways, on the whole, favored voluntary consolidation—with that consolidation proceeding in accordance with no fixed plan; rather, they indicated a preference for consolidation along lines of their own choosing, subject only to the approval of the Commission. During the period of the hearings, public enthusiasm for consolidation as a species of panacea, coupled with fear of groupings that would be prejudicial to public interest, led to the advocacy by many public leaders of grouping according to a set plan as provided by the Act and to the application of compulsion if satisfactory progress were not made upon a voluntary basis. Upon these diverse and often conflicting judgments, as well upon the great mass of factual material adduced, the Commission had good reason—and a long period—to ponder.

The Final Plan.—Arguments upon the tentative plan were completed early in 1924. Then, after the lapse of a year during which no final plan had been published, the Commission recommended to Congress that the law be so modified as to relieve it of the duty of publishing such plan. This recommendation was made to Congress upon later occasions, also, but legislative action was not had. Pending action by Congress, however, the final plan was withheld until at length, appearing to lose hope of Congressional action, the Commission published such plan in December, 1929.[1] While there is a general comparability between the groupings of railways under the tentative plan and under the final plan,[2] there are

[1] 159 I.C.C. 522.

[2] While the tentative plan dealt, in general, only with the major railways of the United States, the final plan was complete in that it made provision for the lesser properties as well as the greater. Indeed, the assignment of short lines was so extensive that the plan itself is of considerable length: attached to many single major systems were upwards of 60 lesser properties and to some the assignments ran even higher. In the outline of the final plan that follows it is obvious, then, that only the major and key properties of each system can be given.

1. *Boston and Maine*—Delaware and Hudson; Bangor and Aroostook; Maine Central; Rutland (Ontario branch).

2. *New Haven*—New York, Ontario, and Western; Lehigh and Hudson River; Lehigh and New England.

3. *New York Central*—Boston and Albany; Michigan Central; Big Four; Pittsburgh and Lake Erie; Virginian; Rutland (except as noted); numerous fractional interests in minor properties.

some striking differences—and a certain few of these are such as to confound those who do not have access to the record upon the basis of which, presumptively, groupings under the final plan were made. Unquestionably some of the changes that appear are the consequence of facts developed in the course of the hearing, theory giving way to realities; others represent an effort to make the final plan conform to existing railway interrelations more closely than did the tentative plan; and yet others are evidence of the acceptance of new principles as a basis for grouping.

---

4. *Pennsylvania*—Long Island; West Jersey and Seashore; numerous fractional interests in minor properties.

5. *Baltimore and Ohio*—Chicago and Alton; Reading-Jersey Central; Buffalo, Rochester, and Pittsburgh; half interest in Monon and in Detroit, Toledo, and Ironton; numerous fractional interests in minor properties.

6. *Chesapeake and Ohio-Nickel Plate*—Hocking Valley; Père Marquette; Erie; Lackawanna; Bessemer and Lake Erie; certain fractional interests and important trackage rights. Chesapeake and Ohio of Indiana assigned to System 7.

7. *Wabash-Seaboard*—Lehigh Valley; Wheeling and Lake Erie; Pittsburgh and West Virginia; Western Maryland; Ann Arbor; Akron, Canton, and Youngstown; Chesapeake and Ohio of Indiana; Seaboard Air Line; Norfolk and Western; half interest in Detroit, Toledo, and Ironton; important trackage rights; fractional interests in minor properties.

8. *Atlantic Coast Line*—Louisville and Nashville; Nashville, Chattanooga, and St. Louis; Clinchfield; Atlanta, Birmingham, and Coast; Gulf, Mobile and Northern; New Orleans Great Northern; one-fourth interest in Monon.

9. *Southern*—Tennessee Central; Florida East Coast; Norfolk Southern; Georgia and Florida; one-fourth interest in Monon. Mobile and Ohio excluded from Southern system.

10. *Illinois Central*—Gulf and Ship Island; Central of Georgia; Yazoo and Mississippi Valley; Minneapolis and St. Louis; St. Louis Southwestern.

11. *Chicago and North Western*—Chicago, Minneapolis, St. Paul, and Omaha; Chicago and Eastern Illinois; Mobile and Ohio.

12. *Great Northern-Northern Pacific*—Minnesota and International; Spokane, Portland, and Seattle; Oregon Trunk and Oregon Electric.

13. *Milwaukee*—Duluth, Missabe, and Northern; Duluth and Iron Range; trackage rights.

14. *Burlington*—Colorado and Southern; Fort Worth and Denver City; Missouri-Kansas-Texas; Green Bay and Western; half interest in Trinity and Brazos Valley.

15. *Union Pacific*—Los Angeles and Salt Lake; Oregon Short Line; Oregon-Washington Railroad and Navigation; St. Joseph and Grand Island; Kansas City Southern.

16. *Southern Pacific*—Northwestern Pacific; Texas and New Orleans; San Diego and Arizona.

17. *Santa Fe*—Gulf, Colorado, and Santa Fe; Panhandle and Santa Fe; Orient; Chicago Great Western; Missouri and North Arkansas; Midland Valley.

18. *Missouri Pacific*—Gulf Coast Lines; Texas and Pacific; Denver and Rio Grande Western; Western Pacific; Denver and Salt Lake.

19. *Rock Island-Frisco*—Louisiana and Arkansas; half interest in Trinity and Brazos Valley; Alabama, Tennessee, and Northern.

20. *Canadian National*—Grand Trunk Western; Duluth, Winnipeg, and Pacific; Central Vermont; National lines in Maine.

21. *Canadian Pacific*—Soo; Duluth, South Shore, and Atlantic; Spokane International; Mineral Range; Canadian Pacific lines in New England.

While space forbids extensive comment, certain major features of the final plan will be called to the attention of the reader. In response to the demand of New England interests for autonomy, two systems were created in that area—each having access to the anthracite district and to Lake Ontario. In Trunk Line territory five systems remained, the fifth—the Wabash-Seaboard—being one of the "inexplicables": its justification from any point of view constituted a challenge to casual and careful student alike. Alignments were not changed markedly in Southern territory except that the Mobile and Ohio was assigned to the Chicago and North Western: this property, with the Chicago and Eastern Illinois, was to carry the Granger line from Chicago to the Gulf—another of the changes from the tentative plan that is difficult to explain. In Granger and Southwestern territories numerous shifts in grouping were made. No two of the major lines of System 18 of the tentative plan remained together under the final plan: combined with the Frisco was the Rock Island, and with the Katy the Burlington, while the Alton was assigned to the Baltimore and Ohio and the St. Louis Southwestern to the Illinois Central. Some significant changes were also made in Transcontinental groupings. The Great Northern and Northern Pacific were grouped together, the Milwaukee being reenforced by certain ore properties in the Lake Superior area. But the Great Northern-Northern Pacific lost its Chicago connection as did the Union Pacific, the latter being carried to the Gulf by the Kansas City Southern—which is a third change that puzzles. The Missouri Pacific, in addition to receiving extensive mileage in Southwestern territory, was to become a "transcontinental" through control of the Denver and Rio Grande Western and the Western Pacific. The Santa Fe lost the properties last named and acquired but one important line, the Chicago Great Western—this carrying it, as would the Minneapolis and St. Louis the Illinois Central, to the Twin Cities. On the whole, the final plan gave recognition to existing railway alliances, though sufficient disruptions of such alliances were proposed to arouse considerable protest.

Modifications of the Final Plan.—Sharpest protest against the final plan was stirred by the Commission's allocation of properties in the area served by the Trunk Line railways: even to important lines included in the Wabash-Seaboard system was this fifth grouping objectionable and by the key properties of the four other systems it was regarded not only as wholly unsound but also as inimical to cherished hopes. After extended discussion, numerous conferences, and much "horse-trading," there was submitted on behalf of the New York Central, the Pennsylvania, the Baltimore and Ohio, and the Chesapeake and Ohio to the Interstate Commerce Commission the so-called Four System Plan. This proposal, offered in October, 1931, provided for the allocation of all major railway properties between the Atlantic seaboard and the Middle West among the four lines submitting the plan in such manner as to eliminate from consideration the objectionable fifth system. On the whole, the allocation of lines as suggested by the carriers followed the final plan except as to the distribution of the component parts of the fifth system among the four—together with such necessary modifications as might follow that distribution. After extended hearings and careful consideration, the Four System Plan was, with certain modifications that were only incidental to its purpose, approved by the Commission in July, 1932.[1] Thus, in the early modification of its "final plan" by approval of sweeping readjustments, the Commission gave support to the statement issued when the final plan was published: that the final plan, published in compliance with the statute, was not *final* in the sense that changes would be refused. Its willingness to modify the final plan has been in evidence in other cases, too—perhaps most notably that of the St. Louis Southwestern. This property, allocated to the Illinois Central, has since been permitted to pass into the control of Southern Pacific interests, despite the sharp opposition of other Southwestern lines that fear loss of interchange traffic from the Southern Pacific destined to points in the Middle West. Thus, while the

[1] The Four System Plan, as approved in 185 I.C.C. 403, assigned to one or another of the groupings approved all major and minor properties operating in the territory involved except such as were reserved for future decision or were designated as terminal properties and therefore kept independent. The more important properties allocated to each system follow:

3. *New York Central*—Boston and Albany; Big Four; Lackawanna; Michigan Central; Pittsburgh and Lake Erie; Rutland (except Ontario Division); Virginian; West Shore.

4. *Pennsylvania*—Detroit, Toledo, and Ironton; Long Island; Norfolk and Western; Toledo, Peoria, and Western; Wabash.

5. *Baltimore and Ohio*—Ann Arbor; Alton; Lehigh and Hudson River; Reading-Jersey Central; Buffalo, Rochester, and Pittsburgh; Western Maryland.

6. *Chesapeake and Ohio-Nickel Plate*—Bessemer and Lake Erie; Chicago and Eastern Illinois; Erie; Hocking Valley; Lehigh Valley; Père Marquette; Wheeling and Lake Erie; Pittsburgh and West Virginia (west of Gould's Tunnel).

In addition to the exclusive assignment of many properties to a single system, joint ownership is provided for numerous railways whose location is such that they are of value to two, three, or all of the four systems. Typical here are the Akron, Canton and Youngstown; the Lehigh and New England; the Montour; the Monongahela; the New York Connecting; and the Pittsburgh and West Virginia (east of Gould's Tunnel). Further, and it was with respect to this that much negotiation was necessary among the four major systems, a most interesting maze of trackage rights has been provided, these filling gaps in such a way as to obviate construction and as to give access to strategic points.

As a consequence of the groupings approved under the Four System application, the Seaboard Air Line is cut adrift and the North Western system of the final plan loses the Chicago and Eastern Illinois. The Monon, in which the Baltimore and Ohio was given a dominant interest by the final plan, remains as the Chicago connection of the two major systems of Southern territory. It is important to note, too, that the Commission indicated clearly its unwillingness to approve applications looking toward the consolidation of properties allocated to the Pennsylvania unless and until Pennsylvania interests have retired from the control of New England properties.

Commission has in no wise laid itself open to the charge of inadequately safeguarding public interest, it gives clear evidence of willingness to approve such relationships as give promise of realization and do not run counter to public advantage.

Summary and Conclusion.—Much was expected of the consolidation provisions of the Transportation Act at the time of its passage and for several years after 1920, yet the expectations of many were far in excess of the gains that could accrue from a grouping of railways: the likely savings were greatly exaggerated and variations in economic conditions will make it impossible to maintain exactly balanced transportation systems even though, at a particular moment, balance might be attained. To characterize the consolidation provisions a "failure," however, because not a single consolidation has been authorized[1] in the years since 1920, is to ignore the possibilities that may lie in the near future. Preliminary to any consolidation were the publication of the final plan and at least an approximate valuation of railway properties so that the Commission could enforce the prohibition against the capitalization of the consolidated properties at a figure in excess of their value. The final plan is now available and the Commission has at hand needed valuation data, with final figures within easy ascertainment. No activity is likely during the period of depression but, upon the approach of normal conditions and with the willingness of the Commission to consider favorably modifications in the final plan that accord with carrier interest but do not run counter to public benefit, activity is likely. Indeed, as is shown in a later chapter,[2] progress toward consolidation has been made by many carriers through the acquisition of control with Commission approval of units of particular systems outlined in the final plan.

Yet it is interesting to note that at least one outspoken opponent of consolidation has appeared in the several years past, the Association of Railway Labor Executives. This group, the official voice of organized labor in the railway field, has emphasized upon every occasion its unwillingness

[1] In February, 1930, the Interstate Commerce Commission approved a unification plan submitted in July, 1927, by the Great Northern and Northern Pacific (162 I.C.C. 37). This plan provided for the operation under lease of the properties of those two corporations by the Great Northern Pacific, a new corporation. Such conditions were attached by the Commission to its approval, however, that no steps were taken to make the plan effective—the primary obstacle being the requirement that "the Burlington shall be divorced from control by the Northern Companies within a reasonable period of time, such period to be stated as nearly as may be practicable." Even though the Commission suggested the possibility of retention by the Northerns of the Burlington line between the Twin Cities and Chicago, the major companies were unwilling to proceed.

It is interesting to note that the Great Northern Pacific would have been a combination quite comparable to that proposed in the Northern Securities Company, declared illegal in 1904 (193 U. S. 197). Strong opposition to the Commission's decision developed among the state commissions of the Northwest, perhaps in part a survival of the earlier antagonism.

[2] See Chap. XXVI.

to approve consolidations, taking the position that such savings as will result from the grouping of railways will be largely at the cost of railway labor; therefore, in the interest of maintaining jobs and not because of any broad public concern, unification is fought. However much the position of this group may influence the decision of the Commission when a specific case is before it, it is improbable that such a make-work policy will succeed in the long run in benefiting even the single group in whose behalf it is urged. It is upon maximum service at minimum cost that the railways must depend for success in the competitive struggle ahead and any obstacle placed in the way of the attainment of those ends cannot promote the interests of railway labor any more than of capital invested in railway enterprise.

Acquisition of Control.—It is perhaps without point to speculate upon the place that a legislative body expected a particular provision of a law to play in progress toward a desired end, yet it is quite certain that those responsible for the inclusion of a provision in the Transportation Act permitting the Interstate Commerce Commission to approve the acquisition of control of one carrier by another in a manner "not involving the consolidation of such carriers into a single system for ownership and operation" had little realization that it was to contribute in an important degree to railway unification since 1920. But, in the face of administrative obstacles blocking utilization of the consolidation provisions of the Act, resort has been had thus far to acquisition of control upon a broad scale in the development of railway systems.

Extent of Acquisition of Control.—In the period prior to Oct. 31, 1932, some 436 applications for permission to acquire control had been lodged with the Commission, of which 385 had been approved and but 20 denied; the remainder have been dismissed, withdrawn, or are still pending. In approving applications that were shown to be consonant with public interest, the acquisition of control of some 65,500 miles of line has been recognized—control varying in degree from mere acquisition of a majority of the outstanding stock to the execution of 999-year leases. The mileage figure given, however, represents certain duplications—the consequence of the acquisition of control of one property by another and then of the combined property by a third or of acquisition of control by stock purchase first and later by lease. Yet such duplications are minor as compared with the total. By means of this procedure certain systems have been greatly extended, notable among them being the Baltimore and Ohio, the Atlantic Coast Line, and the Missouri Pacific, and by it certain other systems have been more closely unified for purposes of efficient operation, conspicuous among these being the New York Central, the Pennsylvania, the Santa Fe, and the Southern Pacific.

Principles Governing.—While no statement of principles in accord with which applications for permission to acquire control must be drawn has been offered by the Commission, it has become increasingly clear that proposals must comply with certain requirements to win approval.[1] Fundamental among these requirements is "a clear and strong showing of public gain," declared the Commission in *Control of Virginian Railway.*[2] And continuing, in this decision that denied the Norfolk and Western permission to acquire control of the Virginian, the Commission said, "Real and substantial advantages of railroad grouping are capable of reasonable proof. So are the disadvantages. There must be of record a substantial preponderance of evidence in favor of an application before we are warranted in giving it favorable consideration." As bearing upon this question of public gain the effects of the proposed unification upon competition, upon service, and upon costs of operation will be given weight. Another requirement is that the financial plan for the grouping must be satisfactory, from the standpoint of both public policy and minority interests. One of the primary grounds for the rejection of a proposal to permit the Kansas City Southern to acquire control of the Missouri-Kansas-Texas and the St. Louis Southwestern was the fact that, in addition to the smallest property of the group occupying the dominant place, the financial plan would have made it possible to control properties worth approximately $600,000,000 by an investment of some $11,000,000 in the common stock of the Kansas City Southern at the then market price: this was "too small a base upon which to build such a financial pyramid."[3] And it was the failure of the plan under which the Van Sweringen interests proposed a unification of the Nickel Plate, the Chesapeake and Ohio, the Hocking Valley, the Père Marquette, and the Erie, to provide fairly for minority interests that was the major obstacle to Commission approval.[4]

A third feature essential to a plan that is to meet with approval, and this is likely to be emphasized increasingly, is provision for the short lines in the territory occupied by the carrier of which control is sought. The attitude of the Commission on this point was clearly stated in the Nickel Plate decision to which reference has been made:

[1] An examination of certain decisions suggests that upon occasion expediency plays a part, too. It must have given the Commission great joy to find the Santa Fe willing to take the perennially needy Orient to its prosperous arms, and undoubtedly the same joy was felt when the Atlantic Coast Line assumed responsibility for the derelict Atlanta, Birmingham, and Atlantic. Acceptance of responsibility by major railways for short lines built to exploit natural resources has also been regarded kindly by the Commission, with such offers scrutinized perhaps less closely than others that contribute little to the solution of a problem. And in the recent approval of the acquisition of control by the Southern Pacific of the St. Louis Southwestern, the Commission confessed it was influenced in reaching its decision by the fact that the latter property was in immediate need of such financial support as the Southern Pacific was in a position to give. For a discussion of this last case see 183 I.C.C. 663.

[2] 117 I.C.C. 67.

[3] 124 I.C.C. 401.

[4] 105 I.C.C. 425.

One of the chief criticisms of the unifications which have been proposed or suggested has been that certain of them do not embrace related weak lines, although the union of the weak with the strong lines is one of the ends which Congress apparently had most definitely in mind. . . . Every applicant should assume the burden of making reasonable provision in its plan for the possible incorporation of every connecting short line now in operation in the territory covered or to be covered by the proposed grouping or unification.

And in later decisions short lines have uniformly been given consideration, reasonable effort to acquire them being made in certain cases a condition of final approval by the Commission. Yet another matter that has been given weight by the Commission in passing upon applications has been the relation of the proposed grouping to the probable final plan, prior to its issuance, and, since that time, to that plan as published. While approval has been given to proposals that run counter to Commission plan, such approvals have been accorded only after that body has been convinced by the evidence that the facts adduced justify a change in that plan. In short, the Commission has naturally sought to escape doing that with its left hand which it might have to undo with its right.

It is upon this point of policy that certain sharp divisions have arisen within the Commission. Though many approvals have been given without sharp dissent, if any, these have involved largely the establishment of closer relations within established systems. In other cases, however, where control was sought over independent properties, a strong minority decision has characteristically been forthcoming—with Commissioner J. B. Eastman a moving minority spirit. Taking the position that many acquisitions of control are tantamount to consolidation, Commissioner Eastman held consistently that decision should be delayed until publication of the final plan. This plan issued, he has been highly exacting in his judgment of proposals offered—and opposed the approval of the Four System Plan on the ground that it seriously disrupted the final plan as issued, as it did. The extent to which acquisition of control will be utilized in the future, now that the final plan has been published, is problematical. Yet it seems likely that it may be employed often as a first step toward complete consolidation: control by purchase of stock, operation under lease, and actual incorporation within the system may well be characteristically successive steps.

Interlocking Directorates.—While the interlocking of railway directorates and officers[1] did not, subsequent to the passage of the Transportation Act, carry the threat of oppression that such interrelations may have

[1] For purposes of administration the Commission has defined "officer" to include "president, vice-president, secretary, treasurer, general counsel, general solicitor, general attorney, comptroller, general auditor, general manager, freight-traffic manager, passenger-traffic manager, chief engineer, general superintendent, general land and tax agent, or chief purchasing agent."

done prior to the establishment of effective federal regulatory control, this provision of the Act has none the less been administered with great care by the Commission. Though the Commission has formulated no definite rules to govern its decisions in applications for permission to serve two or more carriers, certain general principles have been observed. If the application is for the privilege of serving upon the board or as an officer of an affiliated or subsidiary property—for the privilege of service within the system, so to speak—the likelihood of approval is strong. If the application is for permission to serve properties whose interests are in conflict, refusal is probable. If, prior to late in 1931, the privilege was sought of serving complementary or even disassociated lines, the Commission's decision was governed by the facts brought forward at the hearing—the point of primary interest being whether such interlocking tended to restrict competition or to interfere with the free flow of traffic. In a decision in October, 1931, however, the Commission set forth a new policy relative to this third class of applications. A request for permission to continue to serve as director of the Cleveland, Cincinnati, Chicago and St. Louis and also to serve as a director of the Frisco was refused, with the declaration[1]

> Actual independence of the systems concerned will not be subserved by permitting the same persons to serve upon the boards of directors of two major carriers, each of which is an important member of a different independent system. . . . The Act specifically requires that carriers establish and maintain nondiscriminatory facilities in the matter of traffic interchange with their connections, and it seems the performance of this obligation will be best insured by the independence of each system.

Requests to serve various of the properties within a system are prompted by a desire to increase efficiency and to provide for a certain uniformity of policy, while requests to serve disassociated or complementary lines—characteristically as members of the boards of directors—have resulted largely from either the diverse financial interests of an individual or a desire to improve traffic relations.[2] Though some few applications to

[1] *Application of Frank C. Rand, etc.*, 172 I.C.C. 584.

[2] A wealth of factual data relative to railway directorates is to be found in *Regulation of Stock Ownership in Railroads*, House Report 2789, 71st Congress, 3d Session, particularly pp. 1412–1660. From these pages a great number of illustrations as of the approximate period of the investigation (1930) might be drawn, but only a few are offered. The president of a major property in Western territory serves as an officer or director of 6 controlled lines, of 2 lines in which a partial control is held, and of 1 connecting line. Another man serves as director of the Northern Pacific and of 2 of its subsidiary properties, of the Nevada Northern, and of the Erie. An automobile manufacturer serves the Ann Arbor, the Erie, and the Milwaukee. Another man whose interests are wholly financial serves upon the boards of the Milwaukee, the Cincinnati, Indianapolis, and Western, the Denver and Rio Grande Western, the St. Louis and San Francisco, the Western Pacific, and the Wheeling and Lake Erie. The president of one of the anthracite lines in Eastern territory serves also in various capacities the Erie, the Kansas City Southern, the New York, Ontario, and

serve another railway have been refused as contrary to public interest, the Commission has approved some 4,660 such applications. For the year ending Oct. 31, 1932, 354 individual and 5 carrier applications were granted; one individual application was denied, and 6 individual applications and 1 carrier application were withdrawn. However, as the principles of Commission action become clearer, fewer applications that might be challenged are filed. There seems to be little doubt but that such perils as might lie in the interlocking of interests through directors or officers have been effectually overcome by Commission regulation.

Pooling.—The prohibition against pooling came as the aftermath of the formation, during the seventies and early eighties, of a number of successful pools that covered important competitive routes. While the railways stood opposed to the prohibition, no significant public voice was raised in favor of a relaxation of policy until 1910, when President Taft recommended the change finally effected in 1920. Yet, despite the numerous opportunities to pool traffic that have existed during the years since pooling agreements have been conditionally legalized, the struggle for advantage among carriers has been so keen that a surprisingly small number of such agreements have been submitted to the Commission. The first arrangement to be approved was between the Gulf Coast Lines and the Santa Fe, covering traffic originating upon the Gulf and Northern.[1] The second agreement covered passenger traffic between Seattle-Tacoma and Portland, the parties to it being the Northern Pacific, the Great Northern, and the Oregon-Washington.[2] The Northern Pacific, the Soo, and the Great Northern later negotiated a pooling agreement covering passenger traffic between Minneapolis-St. Paul and Superior-Duluth.[3] The Northern Pacific and the Soo still later pooled ore traffic from the Cuyuna district to the head of the lakes, as well as certain coal tonnage.[4] The last agreement negotiated calls for the operation of joint passenger-train service between St. Louis and Dallas-Fort Worth, as well as other Texas points, and between Tulsa and Dallas-Fort Worth. This agreement, to which the Missouri-Kansas-Texas and Frisco are parties and by which provision is made for the use of portions of the line of each company, shortens mileage and also reduces the cost of rendering the service.

The present need for economy, as well as for convenient rather than competitive service, suggests that pooling might be used advantageously

Western, the Wheeling and Lake Erie, the Wharton Valley, and the National Railways of Mexico. And it is interesting to note that the late George F. Baker served not only as a director of the New York Central and 4 controlled properties but also of the Lackawanna and of the Erie—services that, while offering possibilities of conflict, had the approval of the Commission as being in public interest.

[1] 74 I.C.C. 444.

[2] 96 I.C.C. 116; 167 I.C.C. 308; 169 I.C.C. 244.

[3] 107 I.C.C. 493; 112 I.C.C. 402; 132 I.C.C. 413.

[4] 154 I.C.C. 279.

by the carriers in many situations. That Commission policy is unlikely to block agreements which bear the stamp of reasonableness is apparent from the fact that the Commission has itself suggested to the carriers a curtailment of competitive passenger activities, thus accomplishing in certain areas a reduction in the number of trains as well as a schedule of train departures more satisfactory to the traveling public. The important and almost insuperable obstacle to such action by the railways, however, lies in the fact that between competitive points lines serve quite different areas—and local service must also be considered.

The Holding Company.—The holding company has long been utilized in the railway field: it was through the Northern Securities Company that James J. Hill sought to unify his control of the Great Northern and the Northern Pacific in 1901; it was by means of the holding company that the Ried-Moore group, with a comparatively small outlay, was able to dominate the Rock Island-Frisco combination for more than a decade prior to 1914; it was a holding company, the Reading Company, that controlled the Philadelphia and Reading Railway Company and the Philadelphia and Reading Coal Company at the time the Commodities clause was applied with unexpected success in 1920. The holding company had not so functioned in the railway field until recent years, however, as to suggest that it might become an obstacle to the development of Commission regulatory policies. Yet, in its annual report for 1929, the Commission indicated that it had become an obstacle: indeed, a threat. This change in the status of the holding company has come almost wholly as a result of the operation in recent years of numerous railway holding companies in behalf of the Van Sweringen and Pennsylvania interests. Among the more important of the Van Sweringen units have been the Vaness Company, the General Securities Corporation, the Allegheny Corporation, the Chesapeake Corporation, and the Virginia Transportation Corporation; conspicuous among those operating in behalf of the Pennsylvania have been the Pennroad Corporation and the Pennsylvania Company. Through the agency of these corporate units, wholly free of Commission regulation, a bitter struggle has been waged for the control of strategic properties in Eastern territory—control being extended and maintained over lines for which Commission approval could not be obtained.

In response to a suggestion made by the Commission, a comprehensive investigation of the situation was sponsored by the House Committee on Interstate and Foreign Commerce and the findings of fact made available.[1] This report shows that, in addition to properties controlled by Pennsylvania interests through the Pennsylvania Railroad Company, the holdings of the Pennroad Corporation and the Pennsylvania Company gave those interests control of the Detroit, Toledo, and Ironton, the

[1] *Regulation of Stock Ownership in Railroads,* House Report 2789, 71st Congress, 3d Session.

Canton Railroad, the Pittsburgh and West Virginia, the Raritan River, the Wabash, the Ann Arbor, the Lehigh Valley, and the Norfolk and Western—with perhaps a dominant voice in the Boston and Maine, the New Haven, and the Seaboard Air Line. And through various holding companies the Van Sweringen interests dominate the Chesapeake and Ohio, the Erie, the Nickel Plate, the Père Marquette, the Wheeling and Lake Erie, and the Missouri Pacific; in addition, they have an important interest in the Kansas City Southern and obtained an option upon a controlling interest in the Chicago and Eastern Illinois. Though there are other holding companies operating, it has been the sweeping and defiant advance of these two groups that prompted the Commission to recommend in 1931 to Congress that railway holding-company operations be subjected to regulatory control and that holding companies, upon entering the railway field, be subject thereafter to regulation of accounts and capitalization, also that the Commission be given power to order the divestment by any noncarrier company of a controlling interest in a railway if such control had not had Commission approval and should be found prejudicial in any respect to the plan of consolidation adopted by the Commission. Because there was no sound reason for failure to embody the recommendation into law and no constitutional obstacle to enforcement, with certain obvious and definite gains to result therefrom, the Emergency Transportation Act of 1933 provided the desired control.[1]

(See reference list at close of Chap. XV.)

[1] See Appendix, p. 794.

CHAPTER XIV

RECENT RAILWAY HISTORY: LABOR, SERVICE, RECAPTURE, AND MISCELLANEOUS RATE POWERS

ONE of the novel and significant features of the Transportation Act was the plan for the settlement of labor disputes. Though a detailed history of the operation of the plan and of that policy which superseded it in 1926 cannot be given, the principal developments will be indicated.

The Wage Increase of 1920.—Scarcely had federal operation terminated when the outbreak of numerous local and outlaw strikes evidenced the extent of labor unrest. Of these outbreaks the most important was the "outlaw" switchmen's strike in April, 1920, that spread rapidly from Chicago and seriously embarrassed the railways for a considerable time. Urged by the impatience of all railway workers, the Railroad Labor Board immediately upon its organization in April instituted an investigation of the wage situation. To minimize the restlessness of labor during the course of this investigation, a necessary preliminary to a wage decision, the Board declared that all increases granted should be retroactive to May 1. With the investigation under way, however, the wage issue was clouded by a demand from the carriers for the abrogation of the national agreements negotiated toward the close of federal operation. Yet, because the question of wages seemed to be the dominant one, the Board postponed consideration of the agreements for the time being and directed its whole efforts to determining what increases were to be given.

In its effort to arrive at some formula by which a just and reasonable wage might be determined, the Labor Board was no more successful than many other agencies have been. Giving weight to the elements enumerated in the Act, among which hazard, skill, and responsibility were stressed, primary emphasis was accorded the cost of living. Wage comparisons were made as far as possible with industry, and other measures of a proper wage were sought. But, all in all, the increase seems to have been demanded largely upon the basis of higher living costs and approved by the Board upon proof of such increase, though it is clear that the reasonableness of an existing wage cannot be settled thus: changes alone can be predicated upon price movements. The increase granted by the Board in its decision of July 20, 1920, approximated 22 per cent and increased the labor cost of rendering transportation service by approximately $600,000,-

000 according to Board estimates. This large increase, effective throughout 4 months of the 6-month guarantee period while increased rates were effective for but a few days of that time, accounts in no small measure for the heavy deficits incurred by the government under that guarantee.

Abrogation of the National Agreements.—The promise given by the Board that it would examine the national agreements when wage rates had been adjusted was redeemed by the institution of hearings early in 1921. In mid-April of that year a decision was published decreeing that all such agreements should terminate July 1, following, and that, in the meantime, conferences should be held between the carriers and their employees for the negotiation of new and reasonable systems of rules. Should the employees occasion undue delay, these agreements were to terminate for the guilty groups on July 1; if the carriers offended, the agreements might be continued until such date as fixed by the Board; and, in the case of disagreement, the Board indicated its purpose to formulate rules to control after July 1. To govern the negotiation of these new rules the Board stated certain principles, the whole often designated as a labor code. These principles were equitable and comprehensive: had they been observed in letter and spirit by carrier and workers, much of the conflict in succeeding years would have been avoided.

Decreases in Wages.—When traffic and revenues dwindled late in 1920, the railways lost no time in seeking wage reductions—first, unsuccessfully, by negotiation with their employees and later with the Labor Board. The demand was made that the entire increase of 1920 be canceled, the financial inability of the carriers to pay the higher scale and the decline in the cost of living being urged in justification of the decrease sought. After extended hearings, a reduction of approximately 12 per cent was ordered. The railways, disappointed, indicated that efforts would be made to secure further reductions by negotiation and, failing that, by appeal to the Board.

Worker resentment against the reduction in wages was keen: many of the railway-labor organizations took "strike votes" upon the cut ordered and in each instance the vote was overwhelmingly in favor of resistance. With the support of this vote, the leaders of the train-service brotherhoods ordered a strike for Sept. 30, 1921. The strike order was canceled, however; the pressure of an adverse public opinion, the failure of other railway-labor groups to join the movement, the declaration by the national Administration that the whole weight of governmental authority would be forthcoming in support of the Board decision, as well as Board diplomacy, secured compliance. The withdrawal of this strike order was a notable victory for the law in its efforts to control the performance of railway labor without the use of legal compulsion.

Impelled by the continued poor earnings of 1921, the railways again sought reductions in the wages of particular groups early in 1922, justifying their demands upon two grounds: the payment of lower wages to workers of like skills in competitive industry, and a further decline in living costs. Despite bitter opposition on the part of the workers and over the vehement protest of its labor members, the Board ordered, late in May and early in June, further reductions in pay for a considerable group of employees—among whom were maintenance-of-way and shop laborers, skilled shopmen, and clerical and station workers. Yet it was the judgment of the majority of the Board that the purchasing power of wages, as reduced, was still greater than after the sharp increase in 1920.

It was the vitriolic arraignment of the majority of the Board by the labor minority in this case that first brought clearly to the fore the unsound basis upon which the Board was constituted: partisan representation was all too partisan. And in this case, too, the divergence between the demands of labor and the point of view of management, as well as of the public, as to the proper basis of wage fixation became apparent: labor's demand for a "living wage" as defined by the United States Bureau of Labor Statistics for governmental employees in Washington—an income sufficient for the "hypothetical family of five with three dependents below sixteen years of age," supported by one wage-earner—was impossible of attainment upon the basis of the existing national income and lacked justification in the light of the actual average number of dependents per adult male worker. There was in labor's attitude strong evidence of failure to take a broad public point of view, even to realize the long-run identity of interest of worker and carrier.

The Shopmen's Strike.—This failure was further emphasized by the determined fight made against the decision just noted. Strike votes were taken immediately by most of the organizations affected and almost unanimous approval given to aggressive action. Realizing the threat to the success of a strike of a large number of unemployed, brotherhood leaders hesitated. The membership of the shopmen's organization, however, was determined upon action and a strike was called as of July 1. Four points were given as justifying the strike order: the decrease in wages, the modification by the Labor Board of restrictive rules beneficial to the workers, the policy of "contracting out" shop work by certain roads, and the failure of the railways to accede to the establishment of adjustment boards upon a national basis.

Upon the date set, shop work was brought to a halt throughout the United States. Though early victory was expected by both the railways and the workers, it soon became apparent that the struggle was to be bitter. The railways set a final date for the return of the shopmen if they desired to protect their seniority and pension rights, so failure to return made a workers' victory more essential. President Harding then proposed two compromises, one of which was rejected by the carriers and the other by labor. By this time violence had appeared upon a considerable scale and, on Sept. 1, a temporary injunction was granted upon the demand of Attorney-General Daugherty, the basis urged being interference with interstate commerce. As a consequence of this injunction, as well as of the ability of the railways to replace the striking shopmen from among the unemployed, the strike was so largely broken that making the temporary injunction permanent in July, 1923, was of little importance. As early as September, 1922, separate agreements were negotiated by the shopmen with certain roads upon the basis of the Willard-Jewell treaty, this calling for the reemployment within 30 days at the Board wage scale of all men not guilty of violence and the determination of seniority matters by negotiation later. Other roads took the strikers back as individuals, but refused to recognize the union, organizing company unions. And still others closed the door to all striking workers. In short, the shopmen lost their strike and, on the whole, saved little more than the wreckage of their organization. Perhaps the only gain to come from an experience so costly to worker, carrier, and public was the experiment in cooperation between the Baltimore and Ohio and its shopmen—an experiment in which the workers undertook with a considerable degree of success to lower shop costs and increase output.

Important Problems Faced by the Board.—In the performance of its work the Labor Board faced several difficult questions, of which jurisdiction was one. To find relief from the alleged higher cost of work done by shopmen working under carrier supervision and subject to Board jurisdiction, perhaps for other reasons, several railways adopted the practice of "contracting out" their work—this practice extending, in extreme instances, to maintenance of way. The Labor Board upheld the protests of railway labor against this policy as a studied evasion of the law and, after a struggle, the carriers were induced to abandon the policy, but not until deep resentment had been stirred among workers.

A second jurisdictional problem arose in a controversy between the Board and the Pennsylvania Railroad in consequence of the refusal of that carrier to deal with designated representatives of certain labor groups. Upon investigation, the Board condemned the Pennsylvania policy—and the Pennsylvania secured an injunction against the publication of the adverse statement by the Board. Upon appeal to the Supreme Court[1] the Board was the victor but, despite Board censure, the Pennsylvania persisted in its defiance. The workers then sought an injunction to compel observance by the carrier of the Board's pronouncements concerning employee rights, but this effort failed; the Supreme Court, hearing the case upon appeal, condemned the carrier's willful flouting of the statute but declared that no power of enforcement other than by pressure of public opinion resided in the law.[2]

[1] *Pennsylvania Railroad v. Labor Board*, 261 U. S. 72 (1923).

[2] *Pennsylvania Federation v. Pennsylvania Railroad Company*, 267 U. S. 203 (1925).

The question of jurisdiction again arose in a wage controversy in July, 1924. An increase in wages was demanded for all enginemen in Western territory—and the carriers, acting collectively through the Managers' Committee, countered by asking for the revision of certain rules. A deadlock resulted and, when the Board took jurisdiction, the representatives of labor refused to appear: they held that, as the *individual carriers* had not failed to effect adjustments with the national organization, the Board had no jurisdiction. Seemingly labor hoped to force by strike threat acceptance from a few key properties, as they had done in Eastern territory and as they succeeded in doing later in the Western District, then compel conformance by all others in turn. Judge J. H. Wilkerson, of the District Court of Northern Illinois, held in two test cases brought before him that the Board was within its powers in ordering both a resident of that judicial district and a resident of another judicial district[1] to appear before it as witnesses. Both cases were appealed, but only the case of the nonresident was pressed: here the decision of the lower court was reversed and the Board was held to have no power to summon witnesses from without the judicial district in which it was situated.[2] Yet such power was essential to a determination of the facts in any controversy before the Board for adjudication. Had the entire plan of settling labor disputes between railways and employees as set up by the Transportation Act not been abandoned shortly, it would have been necessary to extend the jurisdiction of the Board by statutory change to prevent its becoming impotent.

Abolition of the Labor Board.—The Railroad Labor Board was compelled to function during a difficult economic period. It was further handicapped by certain weaknesses in the law governing the settlement of labor disputes. Perhaps the most important weakness lay in the tripartite character of the Board itself: with six of its members partisan, the three labor representatives proving aggressively so, it was impossible for the Board to function with the impartiality expected of it. The failure of the law to specify the basis upon which adjustment boards were to be organized made possible a deadlock between carriers and workers—with the consequent overloading of the Labor Board. Then, too, certain railways that had been disciplined became bitter opponents of the Board and railway labor was quite unanimous in its opposition. Labor objected on principle to such a plan of settlement: it limited collective action. Labor held the public representatives on the Board unsympathetic with the worker and condemned sharply the actions of one such member in particular. Labor was bitter because of the refusal of the Board to set up a high standard for the "living wage," and condemned the consideration of carrier ability to pay in fixing substandard wages upon certain weak

[1] *Railroad Labor Board v. McGuire and Robertson*, 3 Fed. (N.S.) 488 (1925).

[2] *Robertson v. Railroad Labor Board*, 268 U.S. 619 (1925).

railways. And, finally, it was felt that the decisions of the Board were far more effective against labor than against the carrier: the Pennsylvania victory was contrasted with the failure of the shopmen's strike.

As a consequence of labor opposition, a determined effort was made to pass the Howell-Barkley bill, sponsored by all the brotherhood groups in 1924. This measure would have abolished the Board and have set up a group of bipartisan boards upon a national basis, each with jurisdiction over particular classes of workers. This measure was defeated as a result of strong opposition by the railways and a lingering public support. But, prior to the next sitting of Congress a small, though aggressive, group of men—among whom President Atterbury of the Pennsylvania was conspicuous—had prevailed upon the Association of Railway Executives to abandon the Labor Board; the Watson-Parker bill was passed with little opposition and a quite different plan for the settlement of railway-labor disputes appeared—a plan that effectively eliminated the public from any part in settlements, despite the fact that the public must ultimately "pay the bill." It is a plan, too, that is strongly reminiscent of those which worked poorly prior to federal operation because of railway labor's uncooperative and defiant attitude. The appearance of an Atterbury and of railway-labor leaders with shoulders pressed against the same yoke was novel, yet surely no more novel than effective: their united efforts brought the abandonment of a plan for the settlement of railway-labor disputes that, modified and strengthened, would have given vastly greater promise of equitable treatment to all through a period of years than the plan which displaced it.

The Railroad Labor Act of 1926.—Declaring that "it shall be the duty of all carriers, their officers, agents, and employees to exert every reasonable effort to make and maintain agreements concerning pay, rules, and working conditions . . . to avoid any interruption of commerce," the Railroad Labor Act of 1926 provides for a permanent Board of Mediation of five members. This Board shall intervene upon the request of either party, or upon its own motion, in any unsettled dispute with a view to effecting an amicable settlement. Failing this, its obligation is to urge an agreement to submit the dispute to arbitration by a special board, consisting of three or six members—one or two being chosen by each interested party, these choosing the neutral arbitrator or arbitrators. While submission to arbitration is voluntary, the findings of an arbitration board are binding at law. Should either or both of the parties to the dispute refuse to arbitrate and if, in the judgment of the Board of Mediation, the dispute threatens to interrupt commerce, the President of the United States is notified. He then appoints an emergency board to investigate and report to him; but, for a period of 30 days after the emergency board has reported, no change in conditions shall be made by the contending parties. During this brief period it is hoped that public opinion will compel conformance to the judgment given. And, in addition to this machinery, the Act declares that adjustment boards *shall* be organized to consider matters other than wages, rules, and working conditions, these boards to be bipartite in character and possessed of the power to make a binding award.

The Operation of the Labor Act.—Even prior to the abolition of the Labor Board the upward trend in railway earnings and prices was sufficient to justify wage increases, such being awarded by the Board to certain low-paid groups as early as October, 1922, and to clerical and station forces the following year. Agreements were also negotiated between the carriers and train-service, shop, and other workers that provided for higher rates of pay. But upon the inauguration of the new plan of handling railway-labor disputes there came a multitude of major demands from railway workers: during the first fiscal year, closing June 30, 1927, the Board of Mediation had before it for adjustment 265 cases involving changes in rates of pay, rules, or working conditions and 62 cases of a minor character involving grievances or the interpretation or application of existing agreements. The number of major cases has mounted steadily during succeeding years until at the close of the fiscal year of 1931 the total for the 6 years had reached 728—and during the same period the number of lesser cases had grown to 878, with almost one-third of that total submitted in the last fiscal year. Of the 1,317 cases of which disposition had been made by the close of the 1932 fiscal year 515 had been settled by mediation, 229 by arbitration, 426 by withdrawal through mediation, and 147 in other ways. Only a small number of emergency boards have been required and the judgments of these boards have been accepted by the contending parties with but one exception; and while in a period of 6 years strike ballots have been spread to the number of 28, the disputes which led to the submission and receipt of such strike ballots were finally settled otherwise in an orderly way. Thus it appears that railway-labor disputes have been handled successfully under the new law, the more since no serious interruption of service, or threat of it, has occurred. And, though during the first few years of the life of the Act few adjustment boards were created because of differences between carriers and employees as to the basis upon which they should be organized, the situation has improved steadily; 272 such boards were functioning at the end of 5 years.

Yet, granting that splendid work has been accomplished under the law, and that the Board of Mediation has a record of high performance, success is more apparent than real. In short, the law has not been subjected to any severe test. During more than 3 years of the operation of the Act, the financial situation of the carriers was such that they were able to bear the drain of steadily increasing wages—of wages that, through negotiation and arbitration, advanced for certain important groups to levels above those of 1920, despite the materially lower level of prices. Labor, naturally, was content under the operation of a plan that improved its status in practically every controversy that arose; indeed, in the few instances in which objectives were not reasonably attained, railway labor protested vehemently. Throughout 1930 and 1931 railway workers stood steadfastly against any decrease in wages and it was only in the face of clear determination on the part of management that a temporary 10 per cent cut in wage rates was accepted early in 1932; this cut was initially limited to a period of 1 year, but early in 1933 it was extended by agreement until October, 1933. When it becomes necessary for the Board of Mediation to press for reductions in wage rates, when arbitration boards act adversely to the immediate interests of powerful railway brotherhoods, there is no reason to believe that labor will accept defeat more gracefully under this Act than it did under previous legislation—to the breakdown of which the Adamson Act stands as a grim memorial.

The Regulation of Service.—The service powers of the Interstate Commerce Commission under the Transportation Act are extensive and varied, sufficiently broad in both respects to give to the public all privileges and protection that regulation might be expected to accomplish. Yet it is interesting to note that the mere *possession* of power by the Commission has served to meet the needs of ordinary circumstance, such possession making the occasional railway of selfish and individualistic bent ready to cooperate effectively in improving service. Therefore the extension of broad powers over service has had the ideal result of removing largely the need of the exercise of those powers.

In the interests of safety the Commission early acted under the power given it to require the installation of automatic train-control devices. After appropriate investigation in cooperation with the American Railway Association, installations were ordered upon a number of railways and supplementary orders were issued requiring further installations until late in 1928. Since that time further demands upon the carriers have ceased and more recently the Commission has waived operation on certain divisions where control had been provided under its order, this relaxation in policy being predicated upon light traffic and an excellent general safety record on the part of those benefiting.

The power of the Commission over car service has given rise to many cases of minor significance but only one of major import, this involving the distribution of equipment among shippers, particularly mines, during periods of car shortage. Because certain cars were "assigned" to particular mines and those mines shared pro rata in the distribution of equipment generally available, a preference early existed. This preference had been minimized by the Commission prior to 1910, when it was held that "assigned" cars set out at any mine should be counted against its distributive share. Yet, until 1923, when further action was taken upon the basis of increased powers, any number of "assigned" cars might be placed at a particular mine for service: the distributive share in such case constituted no limitation. But the Commission, in 1923, over the protest of powerful consuming interests and of railways concerned over the continuous flow of fuel supplies from off-line mines, declared that the principle of assignment should no longer be recognized: that all available equipment must be pooled and distribution made upon a pro rata basis, This order was attacked vigorously but was upheld by the Supreme Court,[1] with the result that all preference has been eliminated. And, while dire predictions were made as to the consequences of this change to particular types of enterprise, these seem not to have been realized.

Upon but a few occasions has the Commission felt it necessary to exercise the emergency powers given it. Heavy traffic and carrier unreadiness to function effectively following the termination of federal operation occasioned the issuance of certain emergency orders in the spring of 1920. A second emergency arose in the autumn of 1922, precipitated immediately by a coal strike but fundamentally chargeable in large measure to the condition of equipment resulting from the shopmen's strike. In addition to ordering the movement of traffic by the most direct routes and making special provisions to hasten the movement of coal, as had been done in 1920, preference was accorded a variety of items; among these were foodstuffs, live stock and live-stock feeds, medicines, and newsprint. Again, as a consequence of the congestion of traffic that accompanied the later stages of the Florida "boom" in 1925, the railways were compelled to resort to embargoes and Commission action was necessary: for a period of months all Southern railways were under orders to forward shipments by the most available routes without regard to routing instructions. This infrequent exercise of public authority has been due largely, however, to the effective work done by the railways through the Car Service Division of the American Railway Association: the work of the Division directly and its accomplishments through the so-called shippers' advisory boards, organized upon a regional basis, have contributed much to the astonishing freedom of general shipping from delays since the autumn of 1922.

While the Transportation Act gives the Commission power to require joint use of railway terminals and of facilities incident thereto, this power has been utilized charily that orders may not be successfully challenged upon the basis of certain constitutional guarantees enjoyed by owners of property. In every case that has come before it involving joint use the Commission has proved a jealous guardian of the interests of the railway that has expended large sums in developing adequate terminal facilities and that has by its efforts established valuable traffic connections, as against another railway seeking to reap where it has not sowed. And in

[1] *United States and Interstate Commerce Commission v. Akron, Canton, and Youngstown Railway Company et al.*, 274 U. S. 564 (1927).

few cases has the insistence upon joint use been urged in public behalf so much as in the interest of a rival carrier. Yet the existence of Commission power over terminal use has made negotiation easier with the favorably situated carrier by a railway seeking privileges and, too, it has effectively destroyed the "closed" terminal in situations where cloture is unjustified by the facts.

Construction and Abandonment.—The power to require a showing of public convenience and necessity before the construction of a railway line is undertaken would have been of tremendous social consequence during years of rapid development. It has been of secondary importance, however, during more recent years. None the less, the Interstate Commerce Commission has by its denials, in certain cases where justification was not clear, rendered an important public service. In acting upon applications the Commission has often been compelled to serve as arbiter among rival interests in rapidly developing areas, with its decisions of major local significance. Since the power to control construction was designed to prevent the unnecessary duplication of existing lines as well as the building of lines that have no prospect of profitable operation, it is logical that each application should be scrutinized carefully upon these points. Where it appears that the major source of tonnage will be diversions from existing lines, denial has been almost invariable—with perhaps the best illustration of this the proposed New York, Pittsburgh, and Chicago. Though the Commission recognized the operating superiority of the proposed line to existing routes between New York and Pittsburgh, failure to show important sources of tonnage other than that which could be wrested from carriers now in the field served as a bar to approval: the loss by existing lines of tonnage now carried by them would be of serious public consequence. While the Commission is not bound by law to reject all applications which are financially doubtful, proposals that are definitely visionary have been given short shrift—the more if the application is vague or inaccurate as to construction costs, uncertain as to traffic prospects, and indefinite as to means of financing the project.

In the exercise of its powers over construction, the Commission has had to face the problem of conflict of jurisdiction. Exclusive control as to interstate construction lies clearly with the federal body, but it seems that an intrastate railway might be built without regard to federal law. Yet the Interstate Commerce Commission has made it clear that, such property having been built, no argument in its behalf based upon the investment of capital in the enterprise will be given weight: as to participation in interstate commerce, the line is nonexistent.[1] And, as a consequence of this positive stand, recourse for approval has regularly been had to the federal body. A second problem has arisen incident to temporary exemption of the projected line from the operation of the recapture provisions.

[1] 86 I.C.C. 796.

Because of the speculative character of new lines, exemption has been granted commonly to independent undertakings, though not to lines built directly or indirectly by strong railways or to lines constructed in the interest of some industry.

One of the most interesting and perhaps significant cases to come before the Commission involving construction arose in Oregon. Upon investigation, prompted by action on the part of the Oregon Public Service Commission at the behest of Oregon interests, the Interstate Commerce Commission ordered the Oregon-Washington Railroad and Navigation Company to construct an east-west line through central Oregon at an estimated cost of $9,000,000. While admitting that the extension would not show sufficient revenues to yield a profit, the federal Commission held that traffic furnished by it to the Union Pacific system would be sufficient to make the new line valuable to the system as a whole. This exercise of power was rested by the Commission upon a broad construction of a phrase appearing in the Transportation Act, which states that the Commission may "authorize or require . . . any carrier by railroad subject to this Act . . . to extend its line or lines"—a phrase which Union Pacific interests asserted was applicable to the construction of short and perhaps connecting lines but not to the building of a 181-mile railway through unproductive territory. Defeated in the Federal District Court, the Interstate Commerce Commission appealed to the United States Supreme Court, which affirmed early in 1933 the judgment of the lower court, thereby annulling the construction order.[1] After an examination of all facts, the Supreme Court declared that this extension ordered would lie outside of territory that the Oregon-Washington served or professed to serve; and therefore that either the statute under which the Commission acted is invalid or the order of the Commission is not supported by the law. And, following the usual policy of the courts in upholding if possible the constitutionality of a statute, the Commission was held to have exceeded its powers in issuing the order. It is interesting to note, however, that three judges dissented.

Since the effective date of the Act, certificates have been issued authorizing the construction of 9,659 miles of line. Of the mileage authorized, some 6,495 miles have been laid, this construction lying largely in rapidly developing agricultural areas—with building in Southwestern territory occupying an important place.

Because of economic conditions and the rise of rival agencies of transport during the years since 1920, control by the federal Commission of railway abandonments has been important throughout the period. Not only has a heavy responsibility been placed upon the Commission in the determination of policy in particular instances, but that body has

[1] *Interstate Commerce Commission v. Oregon-Washington Railroad and Navigation Company*, 53 Sup. Ct. Rep. 226.

also found arising from abandonment proceedings some troublesome legal questions. In a relatively early case arising under the Act, the Supreme Court held that the Interstate Commerce Commission might authorize abandonment as to interstate but not intrastate commerce in the case of an independent intrastate railway,[1] control of intrastate commerce remaining with the state. In a later case, however, involving the abandonment of an intrastate branch of an interstate property, exclusive jurisdiction was held to lie with the federal Commission on the ground that the continued operation of nonremunerative branch lines in intrastate commerce might impose an undue financial burden upon interstate operations.[2] But, despite these evidences of conflict between federal and state authority, cooperation between the federal and state commissions upon abandonment cases has generally been close. Hearings are often held by the state body for the federal Commission and every effort has been made to harmonize interests.

While it is impossible to indicate invariable justifications for abandonment, certain conditions seem to obtain approval of applications to terminate operations. If the public will not be seriously inconvenienced, either because of light traffic or because of the existence of alternative means of transport, or if operations have shown a loss over a period of years and there is no promise of improvement in the future, approval of applications is probable. Often the application is temporarily denied, to give those protesting abandonment an opportunity to increase the traffic of the line; but, in the event no material improvement is shown during a test period, final disposition is made by approval of abandonment. Yet the mere fact of continued loss by a branch line is not clear justification for abandonment: the business of the company must be considered in its entirety, the carrier having no right to "earn a net profit from every section into which its road might be divided."[3]

Since control over abandonments has been exercised by the Interstate Commerce Commission, applications for the termination of operations have been approved for some 10,483 miles of line. These abandoned properties are largely short lines, independently operated, few being more than 50 miles in length.[4] The causes for such abandonments are

[1] *State of Texas v. Eastern Texas Railway Company*, 258 U.S. 204 (1922).

[2] *State of Colorado v. United States, Interstate Commerce Commission et al.*, 271 U. S. 153 (1926).

[3] *Abandonment of White Cloud Branch by Père Marquette Railway Company*, 72 I.C.C. 303.

[4] In the calendar years of 1930, 1931, and 1932, the Interstate Commerce Commission authorized the abandonment of 1,807, 1,127, and 1,657 miles of line, respectively. In those years the mileage of new lines approved was 1,596, 133, and 41. Therefore, had all mileage approved been constructed, the net decline in railway mileage for the 3 years would have been 2,821—with 2,610 miles of that decline chargeable to 1931 and 1932 (*United States Daily*, Jan. 12, 1933, p. 1).

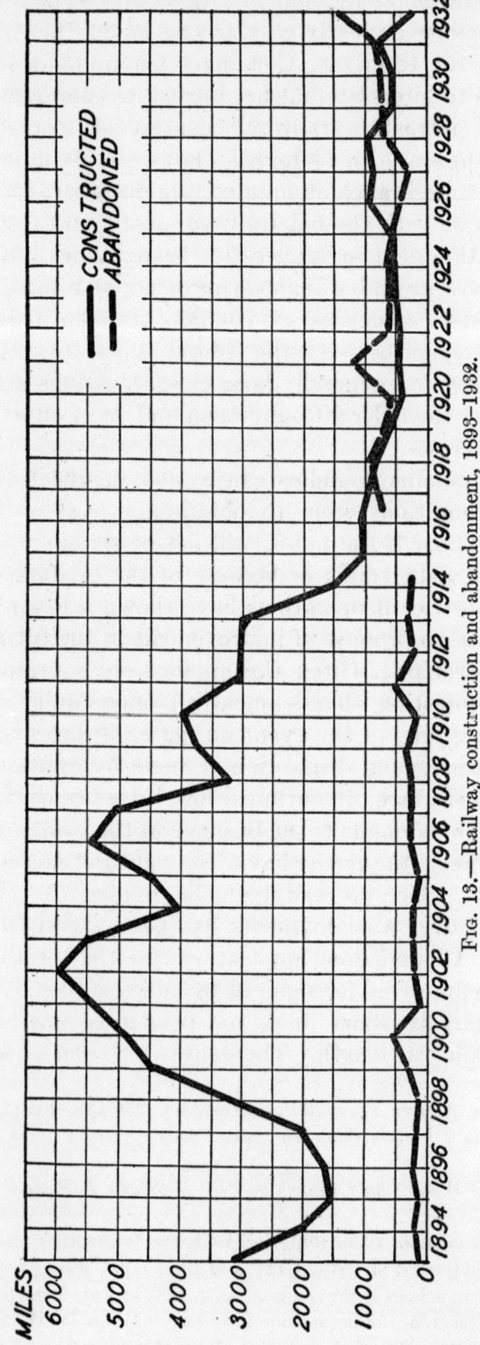

Fig. 13.—Railway construction and abandonment, 1893–1932.

many. Among the more important are exhaustion of the natural resources that prompted the construction of the line, the competition of other railways, and highway competition. The first cause is a natural and inevitable one, a cause that has been operative throughout the history of railway development. The second is largely a consequence of uncontrolled construction. Highway competition, however, is a new and increasingly significant factor; while the often inadequate service of branch and short lines justifies resort to highway transport, this latter type may not meet the full needs of the area and may likewise enjoy certain unfair competitive advantages. The transport problem is a major one to each community and one of continuing significance; careful thought is essential to the determination of a policy that will protect all shipping interests as fully as possible.

While the construction and abandonment provisions of the Transportation Act have been administered with a minimum of public criticism, some agitation has resulted from conflict between state and federal authority with respect to the building of new lines and the scrapping of old. Authorization to abandon has given rise to local resentment, often, but more vocal have been complaints against the federal Commission because of refusal to permit construction. Bills have been introduced into Congress from time to time to deprive the Interstate Commerce Commission of power to control construction, much of this agitation centering in western Texas where rivalry to build has been keen since 1920—with the federal body attempting to limit construction to the demonstrably reasonable needs of the area. It is unlikely, however, that federal control will be relaxed: coming though it did at a late date, it is none the less of such value as to justify retention as a part of our regulatory policy.

Regulation and Security Issues.[1]—Financial abuses that had cried for correction during a period of 75 years, abuses that ran the gamut from barefaced fraud on the part of promoter and moneyed buccaneer to managerial ineptitude, served to effect that interesting unanimity of opinion which made certain the inclusion in the Transportation Act of a clause providing for federal regulation of railway security issues. Because of general support of the principle, it has been possible for the Commission to administer this portion of the Act with little friction and with the full cooperation of railways and banking houses. While the Commission and financial houses have differed, naturally, with respect to certain questions of policy, perhaps the controversy over marketing securities through regular banking channels or upon the basis of competitive bids occasioning greatest controversy, it is an accepted fact that Commission supervision has given strength in the financial markets to railway issues during a difficult period. In the years 1921–1932 the records of the Commission

[1] For a more detailed discussion of security regulation under the Transportation Act, see Chap. XXVIII.

show the approval of more than $14,500,000,000 of securities, new and refunding issues; and during that period, in spite of a rapidity of economic change that might well have constituted the background for extensive manipulation and fraud, no railway has disturbed public confidence by its financial maneuvers, much less shocked public conscience by gross abuse. So successful has been the regulation of railway security issues by the federal Commission that the abandonment of the policy has been suggested in no quarter, nor has any basic change been urged. This statute, with its provisions rested upon state experience in the field, is one of the definitely approved portions of federal regulatory legislation.

The Recapture Clause.—One of the distinctive and novel features of the Transportation Act is the Recapture clause. Embodied in the law to aid in meeting the strong-and-weak-line problem, pending the consolidation of railways, tardiness in effecting such consolidation has given it a more important rôle than was originally planned. Though not difficult to justify in principle, the Recapture clause has encountered serious administrative obstacles in the years since its adoption. Of these obstacles the important continuing one has been the lack of accepted valuation data upon the basis of which excess earnings might be computed. As a temporary basis for such computation, pending final value determination, the Commission asked each carrier to fix a value upon its property and to pay into the general contingent fund one-half of any sums earned during any year in excess of 6 per cent on that estimated value—with corrections to be made when the Commission's final value figure should be issued and become binding. Upon this basis various railways have paid into the fund some $9,900,000 which now, with interest received, amounts to almost $12,900,000; yet, because the bulk of the payments have been made subject to protest or reservation, these moneys have not been available for the purposes intended. However, the Commission has estimated the amount due from all railways showing an excess income[1] for the period

[1] In its *Forty-sixth Annual Report* the Commission says on pp. 96–97: "According to our best estimates, 448 carriers (a system composed of two or more carriers being included as one carrier) earned net railway operating income in excess of 6 per cent of their fair value during one or more years in the period 1920–1930, inclusive. Of these 448 carriers, 90 are Class I roads, 137 are Class II roads, 137 are Class III roads, and 84 are Class IV roads. Earnings of Class I roads account for 92.96 per cent, Class II roads account for 4.43 per cent, Class III roads account for 0.71 per cent, and Class IV roads account for 1.90 per cent of the total estimated recapture liability.

"One-half of the excess income, under the law, accrues in and is to be collected for each separate year. It is interesting to find that if the period of excess income were 10 years instead of 1, our estimates would still show considerable accruals of excess income. Estimated recapture liability computed over the period of 11 years from 1920 to 1930, inclusive, decreases the number of carriers from 448 to 163, classified as follows: 45 Class I carriers, 54 Class II carriers, 35 Class III carriers, and 29 Class IV carriers; the percentage of recapture liability being 93.52 per cent, 4.06 per cent, 0.63 per cent, and 1.79 per cent, respectively. Should the years 1931 and 1932 be added to the 11-year period a further decrease

1920–1930 to be more than \$360,000,000[1] and to this total the obligations of eight railways, presumed to owe in excess of \$10,000,000 each, contributed more than half.[2] Yet, because the valuation base employed in arriving at excess income for each of the various properties was fixed in accord with the O'Fallon method, definitely rejected by the Supreme Court, that grand total is overstated in some measure. None the less, the obligation is large and it is interesting that considerable sums are estimated as due from some railways now tottering upon the brink of, or actually in, receivership.

The first important challenge to the application of the Recapture clause came from a small intrastate carrier in Texas, deriving its revenues mainly from intrastate business. This carrier, the Dayton-Goose Creek Railway, sought to enjoin the Commission from ordering payment under the clause in question; and, defeated in the lower court, the railway appealed to the United States Supreme Court. The Supreme Court, too, upheld the constitutionality of the recapture provision:[3] it declared that no common carrier can maintain title against the public to more than a reasonable return and, if an excess is received, the seizure of a portion thereof does not constitute the taking of property without due process of law. Furthermore, it held that the application of the Act to both inter- and intrastate commerce constituted no invasion of state rights. In general, the Court regarded the clause as an essential part of a comprehensive plan to provide adequate transport facilities for the United States and, as such, sound. The principle of recapture of excess earnings, therefore, has been given solid footing.

The computation of sums due the general contingent fund, however, necessitates an exact final value figure—and, for the collection of those sums, it is essential that such final value be acceptable to the carrier or have judicial approval. Since the divergence between public and private interest in the matter of valuation is likely to be so great as to preclude

---

would be noted but it is highly probable that there would still be some "recapture roads."

"Analyses of these computations disclose that those carriers falling in the recapture class are not confined to any particular section of the country. They are located in all the recognized rate groups. It is interesting to note, however, that the consistent excess earners are in the majority of instances eastern coal-carrying roads and so-called industrial roads (owned or controlled by an industry), particularly those owned or controlled by the steel corporations."

[1] For the estimated indebtedness of individual railways to the general contingent fund, see *Hearings* on House Resolution 7116 and 7117, pp. 359–373, before Committee on Interstate and Foreign Commerce, House of Representatives, 72d Congress, 1st session. Also for a brief statement see *Traffic World*, vol. 49, p. 342.

[2] These railways, with the estimated obligation of each, are: Chesapeake and Ohio, \$47,779,611; Norfolk and Western, \$42,106,462; Duluth, Missabe, and Northern, \$25,462,836; St. Louis-San Francisco, \$19,556,512; Southern, \$15,838,881; Reading, \$13,749,555; Bessemer and Lake Erie, \$11,370,624; and Atchison, Topeka and Santa Fe, \$11,015,315.

[3] *Dayton-Goose Creek Railway v. United States*, 263 U. S. 456 (1924).

correspondence of judgment, even compromise, it is apparent that each "base" for the determination of excess earnings must be a matter for judicial decision—at least until valuation principles and procedure have been further clarified. Thus it was that an important valuation case came before the United States Supreme Court in consequence of the efforts of the Interstate Commerce Commission to compel payment of sums allegedly due the fund. In the Court's decision in the so-called O'Fallon case,[1] the entire denial of weight to *present value* by the Commission in arriving at final value was disapproved. Though it is possible that, had the Commission not gone to extreme lengths in its decision in emphasizing adherence to the investment standard in the face of a long series of judicial holdings that give place to the element of present value, reversal might not have been suffered.

This reversal has been important in that it has greatly delayed the effective application of the Recapture clause, for all valuations issued by the Commission prior to it had then to be increased. With a view to determining the extent to which weight must be given to present value, for upon that point the Court made no definite pronouncement, the final value figure of the Richmond, Fredericksburg, and Potomac Railroad Company was revised and a recapture order issued upon the basis of the increased valuation. This order will shortly be before the Court for review and, by the decision given, the Commission will be guided in its subsequent action. But it may be noted in passing that the sharp decline of prices since 1929 promises to obviate the need of any radical upward revisions of final value figures to take account of current *present value;* indeed, it is conceivable that even lowered figures may be justified for recent years.

Yet it is possible that the Recapture clause as a compelling influence in valuation activity may be removed. The clause was opposed from the beginning by most financial and corporate interests as an invasion of private rights; its friends have recognized the inequity of the computation of excess earnings upon the basis of single-year operations and have come increasingly to an appreciation of the difficulties of its successful application—primarily because of valuation controversies. Then, too, quite aside from the fact that moneys now in the fund cannot be loaned because payments thus far have been made under protest, the legislative requirement that all loans be adequately secured and bear interest at the rate of 6 per cent gives little opportunity to aid the weaker railways—and such was the purpose of the general contingent fund. In consequence of all these factors, a strong movement for the repeal—even retroactively[2]—of the Recapture

[1] *St. Louis and O'Fallon Railway Company v. United States*, 279 U. S. 461 (1929).

[2] Retroactive repeal has won widespread support as a means of strengthening railway credit; it has also been urged to avoid numberless battles that otherwise must be fought before commission and courts to determine *actual net income* and to *fix final value* upon which sums due under the Recapture clause are to be computed. While the latter justifica-

clause has developed in Congress, with such repeal supported by the Interstate Commerce Commission. This body, after giving consideration to amendments designed to liberalize and improve the clause, declares, "in our considered opinion the practical objections outweighed the theoretical advantages of recapture, so that the wiser course to pursue would be to repeal the recapture provisions in their entirety."[1] Thus it appears that an element of the Transportation Act regarded as significant and one that was assuredly well grounded in its purpose may soon disappear.[2]

The Division of Joint Rates.—The provision of the new Act empowering the Interstate Commerce Commission to determine the division among railways of joint rates in accordance with, among other things, "the amount of revenue required to pay their respective operating expenses . . . and the importance to the public of the transportations services of such carriers," was first invoked by that body to assist the New England lines. The 40 per cent rate increase in August, 1920, was inadequate for them and proceedings were instituted immediately to secure increased divisions from the Trunk Line railways on interline traffic. When the carriers failed to accomplish results through negotiations opened at its suggestion, the Commission ordered that, upon all joint class rates and upon all joint commodity rates divided upon the same basis as the class rates, the proportion of the New England lines should be increased by 15 per cent.[3] This order was attacked by connecting lines but it was upheld by both the lower court and the Supreme Court, in each case without a dissenting opinion. In its decision supporting the order of the Commission, the Supreme Court viewed the Act in its broad aspects and declared there could be no question of the right of the Commission to deal with the problem in the manner in which it had,

tion has force, the more widely accepted reason does not bear critical analysis: doubtless relief from recapture obligations would benefit the credit of the debtors to the extent of the sums waived, but of those owing the larger sums the great proportion are railways whose credit even during a depression remained comparatively high. Of the 15 railways estimated to owe in excess of $5,000,000 each, only 1 can be termed weak and only 3 are not strong. It will be somewhat difficult to strengthen greatly the credit of the weak lines by waiving heavy obligations due the government from the strong.

[1] *Forty-fifth Annual Report of the Interstate Commerce Commission*, p. 93. And in the *Fifteen Per Cent Rate* case the Commission said, "The present recapture provisions impose in their enforcement a vast expenditure of time and money upon both the government and the railroads, they provoke litigation over complicated questions of valuation and accounting, they encourage extravagant expenditures by the more prosperous companies when times are good, they hang like a cloud over the credit of many companies when times are bad, and under the present law there is no effective way of using the funds to public advantage if they are recaptured. The problem presented by the varying earnings of different railroads can better be met in other ways, such as consolidations, pooling arrangements, and the adjustment of divisions." 178 I.C.C. 539.

[2] The Recapture Clause was repealed retroactively by the Emergency Transportation Act of 1933. See Appendix, p. 796.

[3] 66 I.C.C. 196.

in the absence of allegations that the divisions ordered resulted in confiscation.[1]

> What the Commission did was to raise the additional revenues needed by the New England lines, in part directly, through the increase of all rates 40 per cent and in part indirectly, through increasing their divisions on joint rates. . . . It is not true, as argued, that the order compels the strong roads to support the weak. No part of the revenues needed by the New England lines is paid by the western carriers. All is paid by the community. . . . The special needs of the New England lines were at all times before the Commission. That these needs were met by two orders, instead of one, is not of legal significance.

The power of the Commission to prescribe the division of joint rates has also been utilized by that body to assist individual properties in sore financial straits. In 1922 connecting lines were ordered to pay to the hard-pressed Kansas City, Mexico and Orient Railway increased divisions upon all interline traffic.[2] This order was at once challenged and, because of the Commission's failure to observe certain technical requirements concerning evidence, was reversed by the United States Supreme Court.[3] The case was again docketed by the Commission, however, and all technical requirements met to such degree that the second order increasing Orient divisions was accepted without challenge—for so clearly had the Court indicated the legal soundness of the principle when reversing upon technical grounds that opposition seemed pointless.

Thus it appears the Interstate Commerce Commission possesses a noteworthy power that, in its judgment, may be invoked for the benefit of individual railways or groups of railways in situations where such needy properties interchange traffic upon a considerable scale with prosperous lines. The exercise of this power will contribute to the solution of the problem of the weak line in a generally prosperous area and will also make unnecessary the establishment of a multitude of small rate groups intended to meet the needs of carriers serving a limited territory. Yet it is clear that, in increasing divisions for the benefit of the impecunious, no order that reduces the portion of the stronger carriers to a confiscatory level will stand.

Miscellaneous Rate Powers.—One of the important extensions of Commission power over rates by the Transportation Act appears in the right to fix minimum rates. Responsibility is placed upon the Commission by the Act for fixing rates in such manner as to provide for the railways an adequate return; to permit one or more railways, acting in self-interest, to undermine a structure designed to accomplish that purpose would be

[1] *Akron, Canton, and Youngstown Railway Co. v. Interstate Commerce Commission*, 261 U. S. 184 (1923).

[2] *Kansas City, Mexico and Orient Divisions*, 73 I. C. C. 319 (1922).

[3] *United States v. Abilene and Southern*, 265 U. S. 274 (1924).

contrary to public policy and subversive of the intent of the law. Power to fix minimum rates also makes it possible to prevent the establishment of noncompensatory or inadequate rates upon certain commodities or between particular points, with a consequent increase of the burden upon other traffic. Then, too, possession of this power enables the Commission to check rate wars between railways when the struggle for traffic becomes so keen as to destroy that carrier cooperation which is essential to a sound rate structure. And, finally, discrimination may result quite as well from the disparity of reasonable and unreasonably *low* rates as from the disparity of reasonable and unreasonably *high* rates.

This power to protect the rate structure and to block unsound slashing of rates has been used by the Commission in a number of instances, of which three will be mentioned as illustrative. Competition among the producers of salt in New York, Michigan, Louisiana, and Kansas and, in turn, among the railways serving those areas, for a dominant place in the market finally led the Commission to prescribe a minimum rate from the south into Chicago.

At a later time, because of its affiliation with the extensive Ford industries, the Detroit, Toledo, and Ironton Railroad was able to show such improvement in earnings that it asked the Interstate Commerce Commission to approve a lower schedule of rates. Not only was there a suggestion that this was a "handsome gesture" on the part of the Ford interests but there was also clear evidence that such a decrease in rates by this railway would force the readjustment downward of all rates in Central Freight Association territory—and it was shown that the properties in that area were not then earning the statutory return. The application of the Ironton was denied.

And yet more recently the Minneapolis and St. Louis, in receivership, asked permission to lower the rate on grain between Minneapolis and Chicago, via Peoria: because of its circuity it contended that it was necessary to make this lower rate to obtain a reasonable portion of the tonnage. At the time the new rate was filed the Western Trunk Line carriers were before the Commission with a proposal to increase rates sufficiently to provide adequate revenues and, in opposing the lowered grain rate, the competing lines asserted that if it went into effect they would have to make similar reductions—when their need was increased revenue. Again the proposed decrease was denied. Yet it should be noted that the Commission has used this power to fix minimum rates sparingly: except as it can be shown clearly that the interests of the carriers as a whole will be unduly prejudiced by a proposed reduction, it is permitted to become effective.

Results under the minimum rate power have justified it, though in the past few years agitation in behalf of its modification or repeal has developed. This agitation has been a consequence, largely, of the inability of the railways to adjust rates at will to meet the exigencies of motor-vehicle and water competition; some even urge that the statutory requirement of 30 days' notice of a change in rates be lightened or removed as a further aid to the railways in meeting unregulated competition. But, when one reviews the situation which notice and minimum rates were designed to eliminate, a situation marked by discrimination and abuses, it would seem that the more logical solution is the imposition of like requirements upon agencies competing with the railway. Until such action is taken to establish equitable conditions, a continuation of the Commission's recent policy of permitting competitive rates to go into effect upon less than statutory notice, and of holding to minimum rates only when such action is necessary, will be helpful.

A second significant power over rates, bestowed in 1910 but modified in 1920, is that of suspension. The extent to which this power is invoked is indicated in the successive annual reports of the Commission. In its forty sixth (1932) report the Commission states that during the preceding year suspensions were asked in 626 instances; of this number 253 represented reductions, 278 represented increases, 73 represented both increases and decreases, and 22 no change. In disposing of these protests 198 adjustments were suspended, 266 were permitted to become effective, and in the case of the remainder the schedules were rejected or there was a withdrawal of schedule or protest. Of 174 cases of which disposition was made during the year, 120 involved formal hearing and report, while 54 were settled by informal hearing.

Because the Interstate Commerce Commission found the shortened time limit for suspensions as fixed by the Transportation Act unsatisfactory, the statute was modified in 1927: as 120 days, with an additional 6 months, was burdensomely long for the railways, so was 120 days, with an additional 30 days, too short to permit the Commission to function properly. The present provision in accord with which suspension runs for 120 days, with an additional 3 months permitted, represents a reasonable compromise between the two extremes. Under the law as it now stands cases have been handled with little complaint from any interested party.

Another important power of the Commission over rates that was also modified slightly in 1920 is that which appears in Sec. 4, the Long-and-Short-Haul clause. As indicated in an earlier chapter, immediately upon the rehabilitation of Sec. 4 in 1910 the Commission became active in its efforts to eliminate unjustifiable departures. Prior to 1920 much had been accomplished, and following that year greater aggressiveness was shown. With the thorough revision of rates in Southern territory in accord with orders issued in 1925 and later, Fourth Section departures were largely eliminated: rates were, except as *actual* water competition existed, put upon a "dry-land basis." By this action the Commission dealt effectively with one of the areas in which long-and-short-haul departures had occasioned sharp controversy. By following a rigid policy of denying Fourth Section relief to the transcontinental railways for some years the Commission met in a positive way the situation in the other difficult area. While this refusal of relief to transcontinental railways placed a handicap upon them and upon Middle West interests, there is little doubt but that the strict interpretation and application of Sec. 4 after 1920 reflected the sentiment of Congress during the period. There is a strong reason to believe, had the Commission permitted the railways to make lower rates between points east of the Rocky Mountains and points on the Pacific coast than from the east to the Intermountain cities, that one of the several "Gooding Bills" would have been passed, thus depriving the Commission largely of its power to grant departures. Thus, in the face of economic justification for rates that would permit them to hold certain traffic against canal competition, the railways were handicapped by Commission rulings that conformed to an unsound political set-up rather than to need or even equity. More recently, because of the sore need of the rail carriers and perhaps because of a modification in public attitude upon the matter as a consequence of competitive changes, the Commission has relaxed its policy in some degree: limited Fourth Section relief has been accorded in a few instances. It is to be hoped that this presages an administration of Sec. 4 in accord with the facts of competition.

That the Fourth Section work of the Commission is comparatively heavy appears from its annual reports. Again summarizing from the report for 1932: in that year applications numbered 362, in response to which 271 orders were issued. Of these orders 182 were denials or approvals of permanent relief, 89 authorized temporary relief. In addition to the work involved in handling these cases, there were some 193 petitions for modification of orders, of which 145 were granted and 25 denied, as well as further work done on the disposition of applications for relief filed after the passage of the Mann-Elkins Act in 1910; at that time more than 5,000 applications were presented, upon which final judgment had not yet been passed with respect to 107 at the close of 1932—though it is interesting to note that during 1931 and 1932 the number of these old applications in the files had been reduced by 645, a splendid showing in the face of the heavy burden of work resulting from a multiplicity of duties and an acute transportation situation. But it is well that the files will soon be clear, for, with the rehabilitation of inland water transport, *actual* water competition will give rise to an increasing volume of applications by railways for Fourth Section relief.

(References follow at the close of Chap. XV.)

CHAPTER XV

RECENT RAILWAY HISTORY: RATES, RATE OF RETURN, AND EVALUATION OF POLICY

THE weakening of railway credit had been progressive for almost a decade prior to federal operation. This deterioration for a time was perceptible only to the more careful students of railway finance, but by 1915 it had become sufficiently apparent to command Congressional interest. Because public attention was soon centered upon problems relating to the World War, the report of the Newlands Committee,[1] so-called, did not receive wide attention, yet it furnished valuable data for those who were devising "solutions" for the railway problem during the period of federal operation. These "solutions," with few exceptions, made provision for strengthening railway credit; one important plan even urged that the government guarantee a minimum return upon capital invested in the railway industry. And an important purpose of the Act of 1920 was to secure to the carriers revenues necessary to the maintenance of an adequate national system of railway transport.

Railway Rates.—Recognizing that the level of rates was entirely inadequate when the transfer to private operation was made, the railways acted immediately to secure the needed increase. As a property basis for this increase the carriers urged upon the Interstate Commerce Commission the recognition of the book cost of road and equipment, a figure slightly in excess of 20 billion dollars. While the railways and the Commission were wrestling with the problem of the amount of the increase, the Railroad Labor Board advanced wages at an estimated cost to the railways of $600,000,000: a further upward revision of operating revenues was therefore necessary. Late in July, 1920, the Interstate Commerce Commission announced its decision. Instead of using book value as suggested by the railways, the Interstate Commerce Commission used the figure of $18,900,000,000, reducing the book account of Eastern carriers by about 2½ per cent and of the Southern and Western roads by more than 8 per cent. This figure, according to a statement by Mr. E. E. Clarke, then chairman of the Commission, was fixed primarily upon two bases, the valuation data at its disposal and the actual investment of more than $6,000,000,000 in the railway plant after the establishment of the prescribed system of property accounts in 1907; book cost influenced the final figure little.

[1] *Hearings*, Joint Committee on Interstate and Foreign Commerce, 64th Congress, 1st Session, Nov. 20, 1916, to Dec. 19, 1917.

Increases in Rates Authorized.—For purposes of rate increases, the Commission divided the United States into four districts: of these the Eastern and Southern coincided with those districts as defined by the Commission for statistical purposes, the Western lay to the west of these and east of the Colorado Common Points, and the Mountain-Pacific extended westward to the coast. To secure to the railways the 6 per cent return which the Commission believed should be provided upon the "aggregate value" by districts, one-half of 1 per cent to be applied to capital account, percentage increases in the rates then in force were allowed as follows: Eastern—40; Southern—25; Mountain-Pacific—25; Western—35; and upon interterritorial movements 33⅓. An increase of 20 per cent in passenger rates was authorized, making a minimum of 3.6 cents per mile, and 20 per cent was added to the rates on milk and cream. A surcharge, equal to one-half the Pullman fare and payable to the railway, was authorized upon Pullman movements, the justice of this surcharge resting upon the obviously greater cost to the railway of moving passengers in Pullman equipment than in ordinary coaches. These increases were effective Aug. 26, 1920, and were applicable to all interstate traffic;[1] it was the expectation that, by state action, they should apply also to intrastate movements. It was estimated that operating income would be augmented by these higher rates about 20 per cent over that of the test period as defined by the standard contract. The adequacy of resultant revenues depended, however, upon variables of which the volume of traffic was the most important. That the adjustment failed to accomplish its purpose indicates the fruitlessness of prophesy in the railway field, rather than the fallibility of Commission judgment.

Intrastate Rates.—Although there was some general public protest against the sharp increases in rates at this time, primary protest came from certain states which had looked forward expectantly to returning, at the close of the guarantee period, to the old practice of enforcing upon the carriers scales of charges which barely escaped confiscation. Despite the fact that representatives of the National Association of Railway Commissioners had sat through the entire rate case with the Interstate Commerce Commission and had concurred in its decision, more than a score of states failed in whole or in part to approve the new scale of rates. Some state commissions approved the increases in freight rates without hesitancy but refused to order the application of the 3.6-cent passenger rate, being barred from so doing by 2-cent fare laws. Such refusal was logical, but the failure of certain other state bodies to approve the freight increases authorized by the federal Commission is difficult to explain: it was, perhaps, a consequence of parsimoniousness, of provincialism, or of antagonism toward the railways—or possibly of all of these. Faced by the refusals of numerous state bodies, the railways appealed to the Interstate

[1] For this important decision see *Ex Parte* 74, 58 I.C.C. 220.

Commerce Commission for aid. In the meantime, many carriers were collecting the advanced rates under the protection of injunctions which blocked state interference, pending final determination of the question. The Commission upheld the application of the increased rates to intrastate business and, upon appeal by certain states from the order of the Commission, its right thus to act was upheld in 1922 by the United States Supreme Court in the Wisconsin Passenger Fare case.[1] Not only did the recalcitrant states meet defeat in their efforts to hold intrastate rates at an unreasonably low level, but they precipitated by their opposition to needed increases a judgment by the Court that approved heavy inroads by federal authority upon the power of the state to regulate intrastate commerce.

Demand for Decreased Rates.—Even prior to the application of the increased rates the "buyers' strike" had begun and price declines were in evidence. For several months car loadings remained high but by December they were dropping sharply. Because price declines were heavy, certain producers of raw materials found the rate burden serious, particularly since the scheme of percentage advances employed had increased the load more sharply upon low-grade than upon high-grade commodities in proportion to their ability to pay. Though few had protested the increased level of rates in August, the comparatively greater weight of railway charges resulting from the downward sweep of prices soon gave rise to widespread and bitter complaint. Immediate reduction of rates now charged to be extortionate was demanded—though it is interesting to note that only the farmer, of several groups which suffered seriously, was able to enlist the deep interest of political leaders.

A reduction of rates was urged upon two grounds. It was contended that a lower schedule of rates would tend to decrease commodity prices to the consumer and, by stimulating purchases, increase industrial activity. It was also urged, and this reason was more widely offered, that rates were in excess of the ability of traffic to bear them and that, without regard to any influence upon railway revenues, those rates should be lower: the railway had no right to ask exemption from the burden of deflation. Though there is no evidence that the 1920 increase in rates was responsible either for the business collapse or for the continued depression, the Interstate Commerce Commission declaring that it was not convinced that the high level of freight rates had been "more than a minor

[1] *Railroad Commission of Wisconsin v. Chicago, Burlington, and Quincy Railroad Company*, 257 U. S. 563 (1922). In this decision the Court upheld the application to intrastate traffic of the rates prescribed for interstate movements, both upon the basis of direct discrimination against interstate traffic (Shreveport case, 234 U.S. 342) and upon the ground that lowered revenues from intrastate business would necessitate burdening interstate business unduly if rates were to be adjusted to yield a fair return upon a fair value of the railways of a particular district.

factor in bringing about distress," the farmer was determined. Aided by his political power and by widespread sympathy, he pressed for action: even the President exerted pressure upon the Commission in the farmer's behalf.

Reductions Made by Commission and Railways.—Three cases were presented to the Commission for consideration, two of which affected important farm products. In its decision late in 1921 upon the first of these the Commission suggested, despite its assertion that "the right of a railroad to charge a certain sum does not depend at all upon the fact of whether its customers are making or losing by their business," a reduction of 20 per cent upon long hauls of live stock where the rate exceeded 50 cents per hundredweight.[1] With this suggestion the carriers complied. In the second case the Commission ordered the Western carriers to reduce the charges upon wheat and hay approximately 13 per cent and upon coarse grains by 21 per cent, declaring that, though current railway earnings gave no ground for a decrease, the result reflected its "best judgment as to the basis which may reasonably be expected for the future to yield a prescribed return."[2] These two decisions are estimated by the carriers to have reduced revenues in the Western District alone by more than $40,000,000, yet in the third case, involving rates upon Southern lumber, further reductions were made.[3]

The carriers then voluntarily reduced rates by 10 per cent upon all such agricultural products as had not already enjoyed a reduction. But other interests demanded concessions, too; so, following an investigation, the Commission ordered in May, 1922, a reduction of 10 per cent upon all commodities upon which an equal or greater reduction had not been previously made.[4] This reduction was justified by the Commission upon the ground that it would result in increased tonnage and that this, with the decline in expenses, would enable the carriers to earn a return of 5¾ per cent upon the aggregate fair value of their property. Although the Commission erred in its estimate with respect to return, its decision in this case is of especial importance because in it responsibility was acknowledged for fixing a general rate level sufficiently high to provide adequately for the transportation needs of the public, present and future.

In addition to these general changes in rates, many modifications were ordered from time to time in the charges upon individual items. Rate relations were also modified in an attempt to restore those that had previously governed. Almost without exception these modifications and changes were downward. Numerous important commodities benefited from voluntary reductions by the carriers, too. The percentage decreases

[1] 63 I.C.C. 107.
[2] 64 I.C.C. 85.
[3] 66 I.C.C. 68.
[4] 68 I.C.C. 676.

of 1921 and 1922 represent, therefore, but a major portion of the benefits accruing to various shipping groups.[1] To the extent that the carriers felt concessions did not threaten their financial integrity, they showed a genuine willingness to ease any unusual burden.

Proposed General Increases in Rates.—In the several years following the 10 per cent reduction in rates ordered by the Interstate Commerce Commission in 1922, there were numerous cases before that body involving particular rates and some few that were concerned with the readjustment of rates in considerable areas. Yet cases of this latter type were intended to accomplish the simplification of rate structures and the elimination of unreasonable discrimination: they were in no sense revenue cases, intended to diminish or augment the earnings of carriers serving the areas concerned. Because, however, of the unsatisfactory showing of the carriers in the Western District as a whole and particularly those serving other than Southwestern territory, the Commission was asked in 1925 to approve a 5 per cent increase in all rates. This increase, estimated to yield $80,000,000, was to be supplemented by increased charges upon express and mail, upward revision of particular rates, and a later advance of class rates in Western Trunk Line territory. In the course of the hearings upon the proposed 5 per cent increase, holders of the securities of Western railways asked for an additional advance of 15 per cent, declaring that this sharp upward revision was necessary to secure to the railways of the Western District a fair return. After extended hearings, the application of the carriers for this small horizontal increase was denied in July, 1926, in the face of the Commission's admission that the railways as a whole in that area were earning far less than was purposed by the Transportation Act.[2] This denial seemingly followed from the Hoch-Smith Resolution: an increase upon agricultural products was inconsistent with its purpose and a horizontal increase is likely to result in a shift in the burden of rates as among commodities. The sole consolation that the railways could wring from the decision lay in the refusal to lower rates upon agricultural products, as demanded by agricultural interests, and the expressed willingness of the Commission to entertain a plan for the upward revision of class rates in Western Trunk Line territory.

Following shortly the Commission's adverse action upon the 5 per cent proposal, hearings were instituted upon a plan submitted by the railways

[1] In a letter, written by Chairman Henry C. Hall of the Interstate Commerce Commission to Senator E. D. Smith, chairman of the Senate Committee on Interstate Commerce, and printed in the *Congressional Record* of June 3, 1924, appears the following statement: "It has been estimated that from July 1, 1922, to the end of 1923 the shippers and consumers of the country have paid nearly $800,000,000 less in charges for transportation of property than would have accrued if no reductions had been made below the basis established on Aug. 26, 1920."

[2] *Revenues in Western District*, 113 I.C.C. 3.

for the upward revision of Western Trunk Line class rates. In 1930 an order was issued providing not only for an improved basis for making rates in the territory involved but also for the establishment of a level of rates that was expected to yield to the carriers an increase of some $11,000,000, providing intrastate rates—particularly burdensome to the railways in this area—were similarly advanced.[1] The effective date of this order was long delayed, however, because of carrier difficulty in constructing tariffs that met the approval of the Commission and because of a steady stream of demands from shipping interests for adjustments to eliminate some particular discrimination or to lessen some resultant disadvantage, real or alleged. And, long before the minor benefits of this increase were available, the sharp decline in traffic consequent upon the depression compelled the railways of this area to join with all others of the United States in an application to the Commission for a general upward revision of rates—to the end that carrier solvency might be protected in so far as possible.

The Fifteen Per Cent Rate Advance Application.—This application, made in June, 1931, was for a 15 per cent increase in all rates, the same to be applicable without delay. Within a brief time the Commission heard 658 witnesses, took almost 12,000 pages of testimony, and received more than 1,000 exhibits. Rigidly applied, it was thought by the carriers that the yield would be about a half billion dollars, which would bring the rate of return to 4 per cent on book value; yet it was recognized that many individual rates would have to be held at old levels and others increased but little because of the competitive situation. The application of the carriers was strongly supported by witnesses representing the holders of railway securities: of some $7,500,000,000 railway bonds that then qualified under New York laws for savings-bank and trustee purchase, some three-fourths were declared to be "in grave danger of being stricken from the list." Opposed to the application, however, was a powerful and numerous group representative of the shipping public—with state regulatory bodies and other spokesmen for the general populace of doubtful mind or actively against the carrier proposal. Opposition was based in part upon the general financial distress of industry and commerce, the situation in many fields being even worse than that faced by the railways, it was asserted: agriculture, especially, was represented as being "in a state of unprecedented collapse and prostration." But it was also declared that to increase rates at such a juncture would be "more likely to harm than to help the general situation." It was urged that the railways should not expect to escape from the rigors of the period, and it was also asserted that there were "unusual opportunities for reducing transportation expenses."

Believing that the situation called for some measure of administrative relief, yet unwilling to authorize an increase that would put railway rates

[1] 164 I.C.C. 1.

at "a pinnacle in railway history," the Commission devised a plan[1] for particular increases, from which live stock, major agricultural products, and certain other named items were specifically exempted. Upon coal, coke, ores, sand and gravel, certain timber products, and other named items an increase of $3 per car was authorized; upon phosphate rock, sulphur, pig and scrap iron, crude petroleum, and certain stones an increase of $6 per car was approved. Upon certain agricultural products, largely fresh vegetables and nondeciduous fruits, refined petroleum products, brick, and other named items an increase of 1 cent per hundredweight was permitted; while upon all other commodities, including less-than-carload freight, an advance of 2 cents per hundredweight was authorized. Attached to this complex adjustment, however, were certain limitations upon the advances to be made—prominent among these being the establishment of 10 per cent as the maximum increase in carload charges. Switching and lighterage charges might also be increased under the decision by not to exceed 10 per cent.

Yet to this authorization of rate increases was attached a most interesting condition. Declaring that the situation was such as to require the benefits of increased revenues to accrue to the carriers whose solvency was threatened, the Commission instructed the railways to work out a plan for pooling revenues from these increases and to allocate the funds in such manner as to accomplish the end in view—this, as a condition to the rates becoming effective. After careful consideration of the whole problem, including the Commission's novel proposal that the strong railways give from their earnings to aid the weak, the railway executives drew up a plan under which additional earnings would be earmarked as suggested; but, instead of transferring them as a gift to the needy lines, loans would be made through a corporation set up to administer the plan. This modification of the Commission's original purpose was accepted by that body and the advanced rates became effective, to continue until Mar. 31, 1933.[2]

This decision of the Commission in *Ex Parte* 103 is of interest also because of a discussion of the future of the railways with which it closes. The Commission makes certain suggestions, significant among which are changes in the law: the repeal of the section (15*a*) intended to secure to the carriers a fair return, and the substitution of "a better section designed to accomplish the same purpose," is urged; the repeal of the Recapture clause is recommended; the insertion of a section stressing the importance of an *average income*, through good years and lean, is advocated; the regulation of motor and waterway transport agencies upon an equitable basis

[1] 178 I.C.C. 539.

[2] This date was advanced in March, 1933, after extended hearings, to Oct. 1, 1933, though the railways refused to continue the loaning of emergency rate earnings to weaker lines through the Railroad Credit Corporation for the period of this extension. Slight modifications were made in the emergency rates for the period of the extension.

is suggested, as is control of the so-called car-forwarding companies; and assumption by the public of a greater part of railway expenditures for essentially nonproductive properties, as illustrated by the separation of grade crossings, is offered for consideration. To these points are added others that concern management directly: the retention of a greater part of surplus in liquid form to meet emergencies; the solution of the passenger problem—consideration of pooling, with perhaps complete retirement from the field by certain railways suffering heavy losses; more effective cooperation among carriers to reduce competitive waste; greater alertness of traffic officers to opportunities in competition with other agencies of transport and of operating officers to opportunities for improvements in service and reductions in cost. Perhaps the one important omission from this list was the acceptance by the Commission itself of a greater measure of responsibility for the financial stability of the railway industry, now subject to its control in such considerable degree: recognition of the principle that the Commission's primary function is to establish *an equitable relation between carrier and public*, rather than "to regulate the railways." Until such a change occurs in Commission policy, statutory provisions calculated to insure to the carriers a fair return are certain in operation to fall short of their purpose.

The Hoch-Smith Resolution.—Perhaps one of the most interesting incidental facts which appeared in connection with the widespread demand for lower rates, particularly on behalf of agricultural products, was the advocacy of such lessened charges because of the inability of those products to bear existing rates. During the many years preceding, when railway costs were low, the representatives of agriculture before regulatory bodies had insisted that charges rest upon "cost of service." During the period of postwar adjustments, when railway costs were exceptionally high, these representatives experienced a remarkable change of heart:[1] they then demanded that the level of rates take account of the inability of agricultural products to bear a high level of charges. But, despite its readiness to "temper the wind to the shorn lamb," decisions of the Commission continued to evidence its unwillingness, merely to satisfy a group of public opportunists, to reverse a long-standing and fundamental policy of basing rates upon cost of service. In this the Commission was wholly right: if cost is a sound basis when it reacts to the advantage of the shipper, it does not become unsound only because, later, the carrier is the gainer. None the less, Congressional action was had in 1925 by those who were determined to secure lower rates for agricultural products, such action taking the form of the Hoch-Smith Resolution.

[1] This change of heart with respect to rate theories by shippers was paralleled by as great a change of heart by the railways: where prime emphasis had been placed by the railways during years of low cost upon *ability to pay* as a basis of rates, *high costs* were now urged as a justification for maintaining existing rate levels.

Its Nature.—This Resolution states, "It is hereby declared to be the true policy in rate making to be pursued by the Interstate Commerce Commission in adjusting freight rates, that the conditions which at any given time prevail in our several industries should be considered in so far as it is legally possible to do so, to the end that commodities may freely move." The Resolution instructed the Commission to institute a comprehensive investigation of freight rates with a view to eliminating unreasonable or unjustly discriminatory rates, giving weight in readjustments to "the general and comparative levels in market value of various classes and kinds of commodities as indicated over a reasonable period." But the driving power behind Congressional action appears in the specific direction that the Commission, because of the plight of agriculture, "effect with the least practicable delay such lawful changes in the rate structure of the country as will promote the freedom of movement by common carriers of the products of agriculture affected by that depression, including live stock, at the lowest possible lawful rates compatible with the maintenance of adequate transportation service." And, that the Resolution might confer immediate benefits, it was made applicable to cases before the Commission at the time of its passage.

The Resolution in Action.—By many it was contended that this Resolution was no more than a political gesture by a Congress seeking to appease the demand of agriculture for more favorable treatment, but by others it was taken as an important declaration of policy. Among these latter was the Interstate Commerce Commission which, in pursuance of instructions given, instituted a number of separate investigations under the head of No. 17,000, *Rate Structure Investigation.* Among these perhaps the more significant have been *Revenues in Western District, Iron and Steel, Grain and Grain Products*, and *Live Stock.* In each of these and some 10 other cases the Commission took extensive testimony, *Grain and Grain Products* alone being productive of more than 50,000 pages of testimony and 12,000 pages of briefs. And, while decisions were reached as rapidly as possible, the burden imposed upon the Commission by the Resolution was so great that more than 5 years were required to complete this study.

The first case decided in which the Resolution played an important part was *Revenues in Western District.* While holding that the carriers had not shown clearly the need of relief at that time, the real justification urged by the Commission in behalf of its adverse action seemed to be the declaration of the Hoch-Smith Resolution favorable to rates upon agricultural products: by a general percentage increase those rates would be lifted with others, and this was not to be countenanced except in an emergency. Of the several decisions ordering reduced rates upon agricultural products, perhaps the most famous is that rendered in the so-called *California Fruit Growers'* case[1] by which the rates on fresh

[1] *California Fruit Growers' and Shippers' Protective Association v. Southern Pacific,* 129 I.C.C. 25.

deciduous fruits from California to the Middle West and the East were lowered. This decision was specifically rested upon the Hoch-Smith Resolution: it represented the reversal of a previous decision in which the rates here lowered had been held reasonable.

Judgment of the Supreme Court.—Because of its vital importance to the carriers, the order in *California Fruit Growers* was attacked by them in the courts without delay. Defeated in the lower court, appeal was taken to the United States Supreme Court, which reversed the Commission and, in its decision, placed such an interpretation upon the troublesome Resolution as to make its statement of rate-making policy a mere bit of advice rather than a binding rule.[1] Asserting that rates had always been made "to the end that commodities may freely move," the Court declared that the Resolution effected no change. And the Court further declared that the instruction to the Commission to effect "with the least practicable delay such lawful changes in the rate structure of the country as will promote the freedom of movement . . . of the products of agriculture affected by . . . depression . . . at the lowest possible lawful rates compatible with the maintenance of adequate transportation service" was but "a hopeful characterization of an object deemed desirable if, and in so far as, it may be attainable." The Court's intimation was clear that if the Resolution were to be taken more seriously, it would be in violation of certain constitutional principles.

With this decision the Hoch-Smith resolution disappeared as a disturbing element in rate making, except as it seemed to have influenced the Commission in its decision in *Grain and Grain Products within Western District.*[2] This decision was issued after the emasculation of the Resolution by the Supreme Court, yet there seems to be some justification for the carriers' charge that it was "a Hoch-Smith decision with references to the Resolution stricken out, following its final adjudication by the Supreme Court." Because compliance with the orders of the Commission in this case would have lowered revenues by an estimated $15,000,000 at a critical time, this decision was also challenged in the courts. Before resorting to the courts, however, the railways asked for a rehearing before the Commission upon various grounds; among these was the obvious fact that economic conditions had changed sharply since the evidence had been taken upon which the decision was predicated. Though the carriers were defeated in the lower court, the United States Supreme Court upheld the protest, declaring,[3]

> It is plain that a record which was closed in September, 1928 . . . cannot be regarded as representative of the conditions existing in 1931. That record

[1] *Ann Arbor Railroad Company et al. v. United States,* 281 U.S. 658 (1930).

[2] 164 I.C.C. 619.

[3] *Atchison, Topeka and Santa Fe Railway Company v. United States,* 284 U.S. 248 (1932).

pertains to a different economic era and furnishes no adequate criterion of present requirements . . . This is not the usual case of possible fluctuating conditions, but of a changed economic level. And the prospect that a hearing may be long does not justify its denial if it is required by the essential demands of justice.

Financial Results under the Act.—Conspicuous among the purposes of the Transportation Act was that of securing to the carriers adequate revenues. Financial results under the Act are, therefore, of particular interest. In 1920 railway revenues were protected for 8 months: for 2 months the carriers were operated by the government and for the next 6 months they enjoyed a governmental guarantee. In consequence the railway *corporations* showed, for the year, satisfactory earnings. Railway net operating income was, on the other hand, pathetically meager. Materials prices were high, wage rates were sharply increased, and operating efficiency was subnormal. Furthermore, operating expenses were greatly increased by expenditures made to counterbalance inadequate maintenance during federal operation, while operating revenues suffered because of wholly inadequate rates until the very close of the guarantee period. In consequence of all these adverse factors, the railways earned but 0.006 per cent upon the Commission's tentative valuation, perhaps the most unsatisfactory showing in railway history.

TABLE VIII.*—EARNINGS AND RATE OF RETURN, CLASS I RAILWAYS, INCLUDING SWITCHING AND TERMINAL COMPANIES, 1921–1932

Year	Net operating income	Investment road and equipment,‡ millions	I.C.C. primary value, millions	Rate of return	
				Investment, per cent	Primary value, per cent
1921	$ 615,945,614	$19,965	$17,905	3.09	3.44
1922	776,880,593	20,096	18,036	3.87	4.31
1923	983,736,225	21,041	18,981	4.68	5.18
1924	986,717,759	21,745	19,685	4.54	5.01
1925	1,138,632,320	22,222	20,162	5.12	5.65
1926	1,233,003,087	22,753	20,693	5.42	5.96
1927	1,085,141,596	23,170	21,110	4.68	5.14
1928	1,194,487,806	23,503	21,443	5.08	5.57
1929	1,274,595,403	24,025	21,965	5.31	5.80
1930	885,011,325	24,311	22,251	3.64	3.98
1931§	525,628,000	24,439	22,379	2.16	2.31
1932†§	334,325,000	24,500	22,440	1.36	1.49

* House Committee *Hearings*, H. R. 7116 and 7117, *work cited* p. 357.

† Data for this year only approximate.

‡ Includes accounts 701 and 702, materials, supplies, and cash.

§ Earnings shown for Class I railways only, excluding switching and terminal companies.

The income data presented in Table VIII indicate, however, that the record of the next 3 years was one of steady improvement. The sharp decline in traffic of 1921 was more than offset by diminished costs, this latter resulting largely from increased efficiency—with this greater efficiency attained largely through the more effective use of labor: the proportion of operating revenues paid for services declined from 55.4 for 1920 to 46.9, thus again approaching normal conditions. Earnings of 3.44 per cent for 1921 (Commission valuation) were further increased to 4.31 per cent in 1922, this favorable result again being a major consequence of increases in efficiency: though revenues increased but slightly, operating expenses were diminished by 3.4 per cent. The continued improvement to 5.18 per cent in 1923, however, resulted from a greater proportionate increase in revenues (13.1 per cent) than in expenses (10.9 per cent) for the carriers: the higher level of business activity had stimulated loadings sharply. Quite naturally, the steady financial gain made by the railways during these years did much to restore public confidence and to make capital available.

As a consequence of the markedly lower level of business activity during 1924 as compared with the preceding year, the volume of railway traffic diminished and revenues declined almost 6 per cent. With a decrease of 7.8 per cent in expenses, however, the carriers were able to show a larger net for this leaner year. Yet, because of the increase in value of plant during 1923, the rate of return for 1924 dropped slightly—to 5.01 per cent. But the following year, with its higher level of business activity and a consequent upturn in car loadings, showed improvement: while revenues advanced 3.3 per cent, the advance of costs was a mere 0.5 per cent—and, for the first time, the railways approached the "fair return" of 5.75 per cent as defined by the Commission in 1922 with 5.65 per cent. Results for 1926 were still better: business activity was well sustained at high levels, the volume of railway freight traffic increased further, and a firm hand upon expenses held that advance to 2.9 per cent as compared with a revenue advance of 4.2 per cent. Thus was completed a second 3-year cycle of improvement, the carriers earning at the rate of 5.96 per cent in 1926 and exceeding for the first time the prescribed "fair return."

The year 1927 begins another 3-year cycle in railway financial results. Though it was a year of declining business activity, the volume of traffic did not drop sharply. None the less, the diminution in tonnage was sufficient to cause a decrease of 4 per cent in revenues, while expenses declined but 2.1 per cent. This resulted in a reduction of the rate of return to 5.14 per cent, which was increased to 5.57 per cent in 1928. This increase was attained in the face of a 0.5 per cent decline in revenues: a reduction of 3.4 per cent in expenses made possible the improved showing. It is interesting to note that in 1928 the drop in revenues is chargeable to a striking decline in passenger revenues that more than offset freight revenue gains. The improved average level of business activity in 1929 was reflected in the volume of railway freight traffic, this being the best freight year in railway history. As a consequence, and in consequence also of the car-

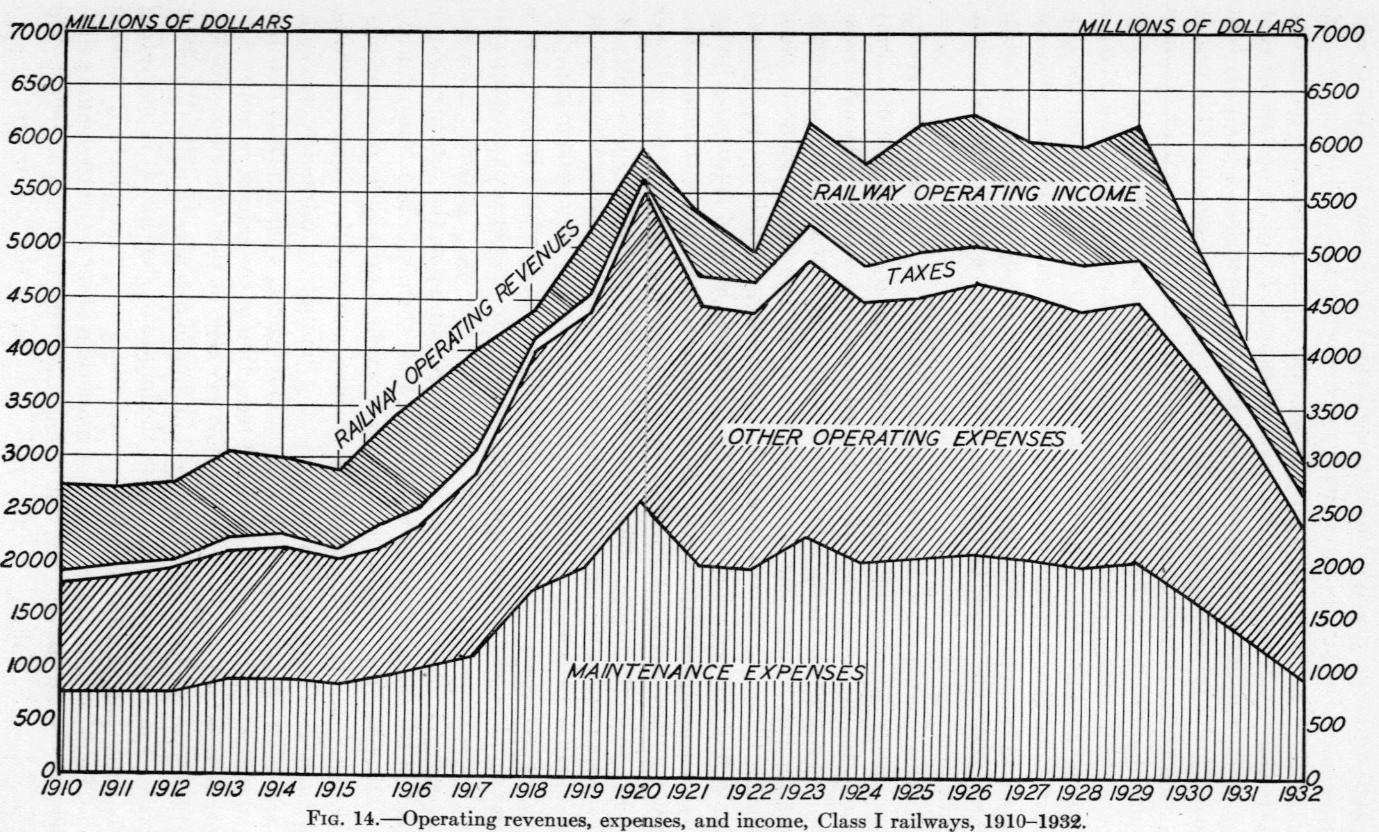

FIG. 14.—Operating revenues, expenses, and income, Class I railways, 1910–1932.

riers' ability to restrain increases in expenses, the rate of return was advanced to 5.80 per cent—this despite a continuance of the decline in passenger revenues. This return, except for that shown for 1926, was the best that the railways had earned during the first decade under the Transportation Act; except for the greater than seasonal decline in traffic late in 1929 there was nothing to suggest that a period lay ahead during which net earnings and rate of return were to decline steadily to astonishingly low levels.

A Critical Situation.—The year 1930 began with car loadings comparable in number to 1928, but a divergence soon appeared that became steadily greater; for the 12 months freight tonnage showed a decline of about 14 per cent and total revenues of 16 per cent. Since expenses were reduced but 12.8 per cent, a decline in the rate of return to 3.98 per cent was to be expected. During the year 1931 loadings closely paralleled those of the preceding year, with the important difference that the level was some 20 per cent lower; total operating revenue for the 12 months dropped 20.7 per cent below 1930. Despite a 17.9 per cent reduction in expenses, the rate of return declined to 2.31 per cent—a figure so low as to occasion grave concern both to those interested directly and to those with a collateral interest, such as insurance companies and banking institutions, in the financial stability of the railways. To lessen the likelihood of an epidemic of railway receiverships, with their attendant losses and serious disturbance of the financial structure, both the carriers and the government acted: the carriers asked for an increase in rates and a decrease in wage rates, each objective being attained in part, while the small credit that the Railroad Credit Corporation was able to offer[1] was heavily reenforced by aid from the Reconstruction Finance Corporation. The law permits this latter agency, with access to government funds, to loan to any railway upon the basis of adequate security, if such loan has been approved as to purpose and amount by the Interstate Commerce Commission. Funds obtained from the Reconstruction Finance Corporation have been used in a diversity of ways—to meet maturing obligations, to pay interest upon bonds or notes, to meet current costs, to undertake construction or deferred maintenance projects—and have become increasingly the bulwark of many properties against financial collapse.[2] For not

[1] The sums made available for needy carriers through the Railroad Credit Corporation, these sums representing the proceeds of the emergency rate increases authorized late in 1931, totaled approximately $57,000,000 for the full year ending Feb. 28, 1933. For a detailed description of this Corporation see *Forty-sixth Annual Report of the Interstate Commerce Commission*, pp. 11–12.

[2] The Act creating the Reconstruction Finance Corporation and under which it functions became effective Jan. 22, 1932. Prior to Nov. 1, 1932, the Interstate Commerce Commission had certified to the Corporation loans to 69 carriers aggregating $346,829,179. The principal purposes for which loans have been approved and the amount for each purpose appears in the Interstate Commerce Commission's *Forty-sixth Annual Report*, p. 13:

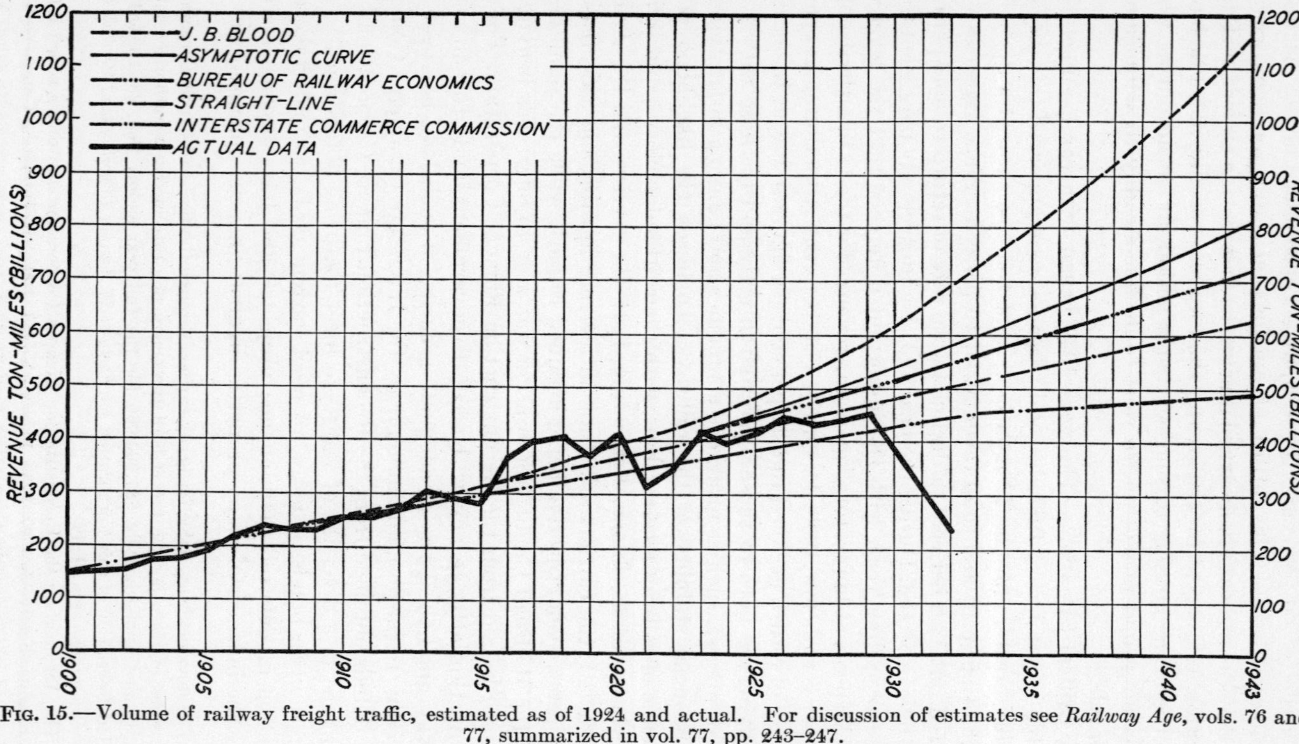

FIG. 15.—Volume of railway freight traffic, estimated as of 1924 and actual. For discussion of estimates see *Railway Age*, vols. 76 and 77, summarized in vol. 77, pp. 243–247.

only did car loadings begin the year 1932 at a level more than 20 per cent below that of the preceding year of light traffic, but a steady decline in loadings widened the gap until past midyear when loadings surged upward in a manner reminiscent of periods of normal traffic; for 1932 car loadings dropped approximately 25 per cent below 1931 and freight revenues declined comparably, while the decrease in passenger revenues was almost one-third. In 1932 the volume of freight traffic declined to levels of 20 years earlier and passenger traffic yet lower. Under conditions of abnormally light traffic, despite a decrease in operating expenses of approximately one-fourth below the perilously low level of the preceding year, the rate of return for 1932 fell to little more than 1.35 per cent. Since the ratio of bonds to total railway capitalization approaches 60 per cent and the average rate of interest upon bonds is little less than 5 per cent, it is obvious that in the third year of the depression the railway net of the United States failed, as a whole, to earn fixed charges; in fact, approximately 75 per cent of the Class I carriers and 75 per cent of the total mileage operated by such carriers showed an operating income insufficient to meet bond interest by about $150,000,000. It is obvious, then, that except as governmental funds were available to the railways many, even of those properties that have been regarded as strong under normal economic conditions, must have accepted receivership.

Variations in Earnings.—In preceding paragraphs the wide variations in earnings, year by year, for the entire railway net have been described. Yet, in lean years and in fat, the differences in earnings among districts have been striking—with these differences small, in turn, as compared to

Bond interest	$68,815,734
Bond maturities	54,144,460
Additions and betterments	53,964,007
Short-term maturities	40,702,413
Bank loans	39,803,100
Equipment-trust maturities	21,829,181
Taxes	20,467,204
Audited vouchers	14,080,492
Equipment-trust interest	5,115,054
Preferential claims	6,986,742
Rentals	7,050,059

In addition, some $7,200,000 was approved as "work loans," to be expended upon the construction or repair and rehabilitation of roadway and equipment. The purpose of these loans, made in accord with federal make-work policies, has been solely to aid employment, directly and indirectly.

At the close of business Dec. 31, 1932, the Reconstruction Finance Corporation had authorized loans to 62 railways, aggregating $337,435,093. Of this sum the major part bears 6 per cent interest; only the loan to the Denver and Rio Grande Western to build Dotsero Cut-off and the make-work loans have been made at a lower rate, 5 per cent. Private borrowings of the railways during 1932, from banks and the Railroad Credit Corporation, totaled more than $350,000,000 additional.

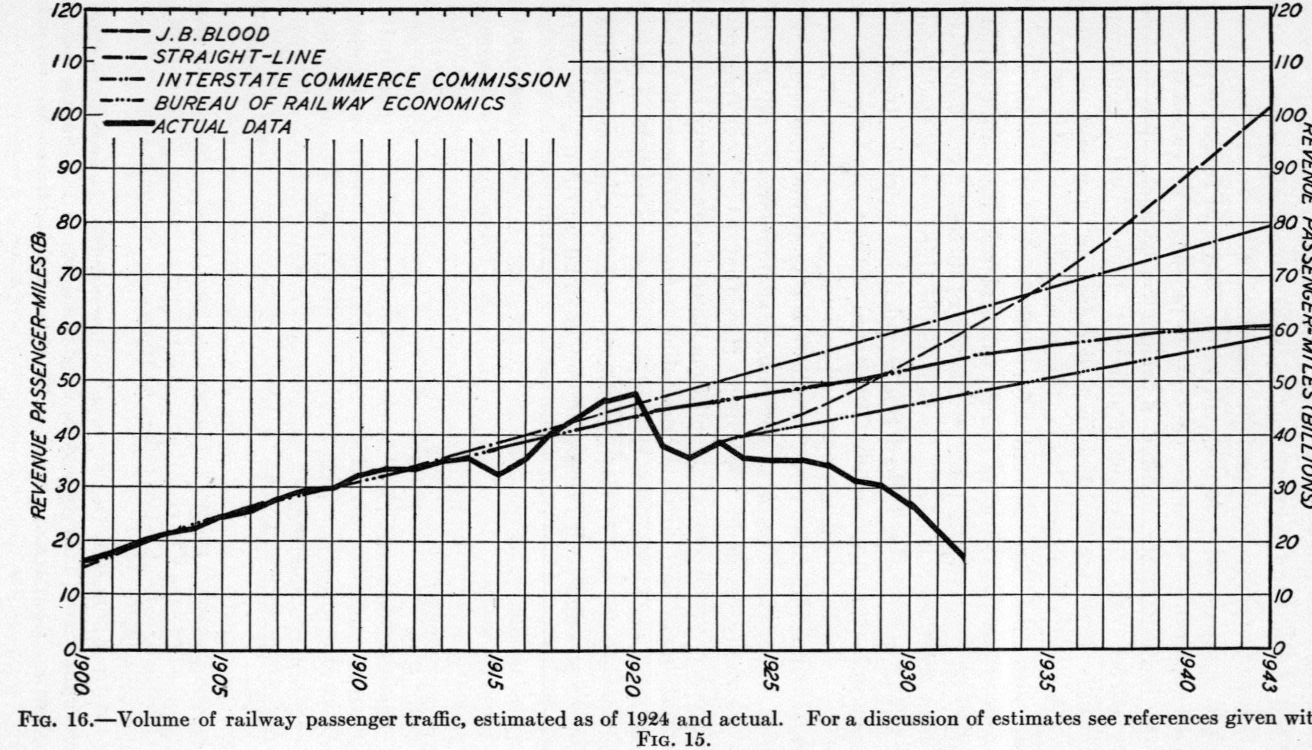

FIG. 16.—Volume of railway passenger traffic, estimated as of 1924 and actual. For a discussion of estimates see references given with FIG. 15.

the results obtained by individual railways operating in the same district upon the basis of comparable rates. Differences as among districts are well shown in Table IX, the years for which data are given portraying condi-

TABLE IX.—RATE OF RETURN BY DISTRICTS IN SELECTED YEARS*
(In percentage)

District	1921§	1926	1929	1931	1932
Eastern†	3.26	5.68	5.57	2.26	1.78
Southern‡	2.67	5.48	4.04	1.34	0.79
Western	3.59	4.45	4.56	1.86	0.79
United States	3.33	5.13	4.95	1.98	1.25‖

* Bureau of Railway Economics, rate of return based on property investment of the carriers except as noted.
† Including Pocahontas District.
‡ Excluding Pocahontas District.
§ Rate of return, 1921, based on tentative valuation.
‖ Difference in rate of return here and as noted in Table VIII due to differences in property investment figure used.

tions at their best and worst. The relative well-being of districts varies, though only once has the Western District made the best showing (1921) and in but three years has Southern led (1922–1924, inclusive). Of recent years Southern has had the unenviable distinction of the poorest record, despite highly unsatisfactory results in Western. That the differences are wide as between particular carriers, also, is attested by the high earnings of some that serve the same general areas occupied by others that barely escape receivership—or, upon occasion, fail so to do. And that variations from year to year are great for a single property is evidenced clearly by the fact that the St. Louis-San Francisco, thrown into receivership in 1932, was estimated by the Interstate Commerce Commission to owe to the recapture fund almost $20,000,000 because of excess earnings in the years prior to 1930—with the Orient's estimated recapture obligation of almost $1,775,000 even more at variance with its characteristically impecunious state. As and if economic conditions tend to stabilize, as less developed areas approach maturity, as progress is made in linking strong properties and weak as illustrated by the fortunate absorption of the Orient by the Santa Fe, and as competition among the various agencies of transport is stabilized also, such variations as now exist should be greatly reduced. If to this can be coupled the determination of regulatory agencies to adjust the rate level so as to give through a period of years to all types of property rendering a common-carrier service the "fair return upon fair value" to which the common carrier is entitled under the common law, an approach to a transport millennium will seem to have been attained.

The Financial Outlook.—What the immediate future may hold for individual railways and for the entire railway net is problematical, but the *sine qua non* of the attainment once more of financial independence is an increase in the volume of traffic—with costs held to a minimum. Such an increase in traffic may come in some small measure as a result of restrictions placed upon competitive agencies, particularly the commercial motor vehicle, in the interest of highway conservation and in accordance with some definite transportation policy; yet it is only a quickening in the tempo of business activity that can make available the tonnage needed to reestablish railway earning power. And what, too, may be the ultimate consequence upon the relation between railway and government of large loans through the Reconstruction Finance Corporation is even more uncertain than the immediate future. Many of the borrowing railways will be able to repay when and as economic conditions improve, but some to whom aid has been extended must face drastic financial reorganization—with perhaps the abandonment of a considerable mileage that, because of changed transportation conditions, no longer justifies operation. Can final accounts be settled without heavy loss to the government or, as another alternative, the enforced entry of government into the field of railway ownership and operation? The answer to this and other questions of a like nature depends upon a number of important factors, concerning none of which certainty exists. Among the more significant of these are the further duration of the extreme depression, the formulation of a transportation policy in accord with which each instrument of transport is accorded its place and that place is assured, and the patience with which investors and public deal with a complex and difficult situation. It is the misfortune, not only of the people of the United States but also of all other modern peoples, that it has become necessary to meet the problems arising from little less than a revolution in inland transport during a period when the economic machine is so strained and wracked. The keenest intelligence, the highest statesmanship, and the greatest forbearance during the period of readjustment may well be evidenced; if the prejudices, the antagonisms, the predilections, the blind self-interest, and the demagoguery that so tangled the threads of the "railway problem" are to have as free play when approach is made to the more difficult "transportation problem," the wise may well be troubled concerning the outcome.

Valuation.—One of the major continuing duties of the Interstate Commerce Commission has been that of the completion of the task imposed upon it by the Valuation Act of 1913. Each annual report of that body has indicated progress: in 1931 the Commission declared that all hearings on protests against tentative valuation reports were concluded, that final valuation reports had been adopted in 947 cases covering 181,948 miles of line, and that rapid progress was being made in acquiring the basic data necessary to the determination of the value of some 198 properties owning 5,843 miles of line which have come into being since the passage of the Act; it was stated in 1932 that the last of the primary valuations had been completed, that satisfactory progress was being made with the properties built subsequent to 1913, and that major efforts were then being directed toward bringing all records to date. Upon the basis of reports filed with the Commission since 1914 by the various carriers, adjustments will be made in the physical inventory record of each to correspond to changes in the plant; these changes, involving additions, betterments, and retirements, have aggregated for the railway net since 1920 an average increase in the investment account of about half a billion dollars annually. More than 60 per cent of this work of bringing individual carrier records to date is now complete and it is expected that all physical inventory records will be current by June 30, 1934. As a further step toward bringing records to date studies are being made continuously of changes in the price level so that it will be possible, upon short notice, to issue valuations that conform to the judicial requirement that *present value* be given weight in the determination of a final value figure. Such progress had been made with both aspects of making valuations current that the Commission was able within a period of 6 weeks to submit, in the *Fifteen Per Cent Rate Advance* case late in 1931, an exhibit as of July, 1931, presenting all facts necessary to conclusions as to the value of the railways as a whole and by recognized rate-making groups.[1]

When the Valuation Act was passed, it was declared by its supporters that the data sought would be available within a few years. The surprising magnitude of the task and unexpected obstacles delayed completion; among the obstacles the World War and the necessity of diverting the efforts of the Bureau of Valuation to recapture studies have been perhaps outstanding. It appears that the goal set by the statute some 20 years ago is now attained; yet, with this progress made, strong demand has appeared in many quarters for the abandonment of all valuation work for the future. This is urged upon the grounds of public economy and the small importance of Commission valuations, once they are fixed; supporting this demand for abandonment are important business interests and certain railway influences. It must be admitted that the cost of valuation to the railways and the government, when complete, will approximate $200,000,000. But the major necessary expenditures have been made; and, furthermore, this cost represents an outlay of less than 1 per cent of the value found for the railway plant—and the valuation of a commercial property rarely costs so little. Then, too, with no authoritative statement of worth available, the bogey of "watered stock" will be dragged forth

[1] Among the data submitted relative to the railway plant were reproduction value as of Dec. 31, 1930, using 1930 period prices and 1931 spot prices; estimated historical cost of all property except land as of Dec. 31, 1929; present value and estimated value of rights and lands as of dates of primary valuation and Dec. 31, 1930, respectively; and summaries of aids, gifts, grants of right of way, and donations—both used, and owned but not used, in railway service—as of the dates of primary valuations and as of Dec. 31, 1930.

by a certain group from the grave to which valuation results consigned it and used again to inflame public opinion against the railways during a period when thoughts of the future rather than resentments of the past should control action. And, with no official figure upon the basis of which rate of return may be computed, the railways can well anticipate even greater difficulty in obtaining rates that are sufficient to provide a fair return upon the property devoted to public service. It would seem that, at least so long as private ownership and operation of railways are retained, a continuation of the work under the Valuation Act—modified from time to time as occasion may suggest—will be advantageous to all interests; economies attained through abandonment might well be regarded as falling into that category of actions denominated as "penny wise and pound foolish."

An Evaluation of Federal Regulatory Policy.—No discussion of the years since 1920 is complete without a statement and an evaluation of criticisms that have been directed toward certain features of our regulatory plan, particularly toward provisions of the Transportation Act. Such criticisms fall, roughly, into two groups: those that rest upon a misrepresentation or misapprehension of statutory provisions, and those that proceed from a divergence of judgment as to what constitutes a sound regulatory policy. The demand of those who condemn some phase of regulatory policy is characteristically for repeal, the demand of those who have constructive suggestions is commonly for modification—or, perchance, for additional legislation. In the interval since the termination of federal operation of railways the "railway problem" and, more recently, the "transportation problem" have loomed large; the character of the criticisms and suggestions that are summarized upon succeeding pages is indicative of the intellectual level upon which destructive and constructive discussion has operated.

Uninformed Criticisms of Regulatory Policy.—Of the criticisms that rest upon misapprehension or misrepresentation of statutory provisions, the one most often heard, yet with least foundation of fact, is that "the Esch-Cummins Act guarantees the railways a fixed return." This criticism had, perhaps, a tenuous though brief justification in the continuance of the guarantee for 6 months and the statement of the Act that the Commission should so fix rates for the first 2 years of its operation as to yield a 5½ or 6 per cent return. However, the 6 months' guarantee soon passed and even the statutory obligation of the Commission has long since expired, though during its life it constituted nothing more than a legislative definition of the common law "reasonable return." Since Mar. 1, 1922, however, there has been not even a crutch upon which the guarantee allegation may lean. But still in the public statements of "bitter-end" opponents of the railways and of farm agitators—even members of Congress—this misrepresentation appears. Its continued assertion must be ascribed to inexcusable ignorance of fact or to malicious purpose: in either case those who make it show themselves unworthy of public confidence.

A second unsound criticism declares that by this Act "billions of dollars of watered stocks have been validated." The inaccuracy of this statement is clearly evident when attention is directed to the Act itself which states that the valuation upon which rates shall be based shall be that fixed in accordance with the Valuation Act of 1914. In rate cases, beginning in 1920, the Interstate Commerce Commission has constantly utilized all available valuation data. That Commission valuations were fixed upon too low rather than too high a level was made evident in the O'Fallon decision;[1] therefore, rather than *less* it is quite certain that the final and judicially approved "aggregate value" will be *more* than that used in fixing rates. And to complain against a valuation because it gives weight to cost of reproduction less depreciation is quixotic, to say the least, since that principle has been almost universally recognized by regulatory bodies and invariably upheld by the courts; by even such a progressive body as the Wisconsin Railroad Commission it has been accorded weight for more than a score of years. Yet, were the valuation of the railways reduced by half, as the "opposition" contend it should be, rates could be lowered by no more than 10 per cent; operating costs, which constitute the major expense of railway service, are in no wise affected by property value.

Another unwarranted criticism of the Act, though one that points to its administration, is that it enabled the railways to escape their share of the postwar deflation. Even though such an escape had been the lot of the carriers, its inequity would not be so clear: if rates be lowered during prosperous years to prevent the carriers from earning more than a reasonable return, then charges must be maintained or even advanced during bad years if an *average* fair return is to be enjoyed. And such is the common-law right of a regulated enterprise. However, the facts show that the railways actually have borne a heavy burden. From Sept. 1, 1920, the close of the guarantee period, to Dec. 31, 1932, the railways failed by more than $3,200,000,000 to receive that amount which would have constituted, upon the basis of the Commission's value, a fair return.[2] And it is probable that this figure will prove to be less than fair value, when recognition has been given to all elements of value approved by the courts In short, during those years the railways received little more than 75 per cent of the total earnings to which they were reasonably entitled. Thus it becomes apparent that the carriers have suffered, as have other groups, during the postwar period. It has been considered inadvisable to

[1] *St. Louis and O'Fallon Railroad Company v. United States*, 279 U. S. 461 (1929).

[2] The actual earnings of the railways, 1921–1932, "fair return" based upon the Interstate Commerce Commission's primary values, and the yearly deficits appear

advance rates during lean years except as an emergency measure, and increases have been blocked during years of business activity. Yet, if an average fair return is to be earned by capital invested in the railways, it seems that they must be permitted to earn in excess of a reasonable return during prosperous years so that rates need not be advanced when business suffers a collapse. Indeed, by higher earnings during good years an equitable basis might be established for actually lowering rates during a period of depression, thus assisting somewhat in business recovery.

A final charge wrongly made against federal regulatory policy, and directed particularly toward the Transportation Act, is one that relates closely to the criticism just considered: the public has been forced to accept the burden of extortionate rates. While various groups have given voice to this charge, it has emanated largely from the spokesmen for agriculture: the "embattled farmer," among others, has suffered seriously during all periods of economic maladjustment and he, more than any other sufferer, has had the political power to command at least lip service from aspiring leaders. But before the reader examines this charge of extortionate rates, the data given in Table X merit thoughtful consideration; for, though this is an oft-neglected fact, the rate is high or low—even justified or unjustified—as it relates to the value of the product offered for shipment or to the costs upon which it rests, rather than upon any absolute scale.

These data in Table X show that, while during the postwar period the level of railway rates as measured by the ton-mile charge has averaged some

below. For 1921 "fair return" was computed at 6 per cent, for later years at 5¾ per cent.

Year	Actual earnings	Fair return (000 omitted)	Deficit (000 omitted)
1921	$ 615,945,614	$ 1,074,300	$ 458,354
1922	776,880,593	1,037,070	260,189
1923	983,736,225	1,091,407	107,671
1924	986,717,759	1,133,856	147,138
1925	1,138,632,320	1,159,315	20,683
1926	1,233,003,087	1,189,847	43,156 (Cr.)
1927	1,085,141,596	1,215,936	130,794
1928	1,194,487,806	1,235,117	40,629
1929	1,274,595,403	1,262,987	11,608 (Cr.)
1930	885,011,325	1,279,433	394,422
1931	525,628,000	1,289,030	763,402
1932	334,325,000	1,290,300	955,975
Total...........	$11,034,104,728	$14,258,598	$ 3,279,257

Average earnings for years shown, 4.46 per cent.

points above that of farm products, the index of rates continued steadily until 1931 upon a definitely lower level than the cost of living. That railway rates could be maintained upon so low a level in view of the trend of railway wages as shown is surprising—and the more, in view of the fact that labor costs constitute approximately 45 per cent of total railway costs under normal conditions. And it is interesting to note that the average annual income of railway workers had, by 1916, advanced 9 per cent from 1914, the base year for all items except wages in Table X. Also it is interesting to note that the 1914 ton-mile rate stood about 14 per cent *below* the 1890–1899 average, while the price index of farm products in 1914 stood more than 55 per cent *above* the average for the period named. Upon the basis of long-time relations, then, railway rates do not appear to have been excessive during the decade past; rather, railway management is to be commended for its ability, in the face of abnormal increases in labor costs and a constantly mounting tax burden, to move tonnage at the rates effective and yet escape financial disaster. The basis for that identity of interest between producer and wage-earner, often stressed by political leaders who seek to make allies of farmer and railway worker, is not clearly apparent in the figures here given.

TABLE X.—MOVEMENT OF RELATIVE PRICES
(1914 = 100 per cent)*

Year	Cost of living†	Farm products‡	Railway rates§	Hourly wages railway labor§
1920	198	217	144	238
1922	162	132	161	217
1924	169	140	152	220
1926	172	140	147	223
1928	167	149	147	231
1930	160	124	145	240
1931	144	91	142	240‖
1932	129	68	141¶	216‖

* Hourly wages of railway labor based upon 1916, first year for which comparable data are available.
† Data compiled by the National Industrial Conference Board.
‡ United States Department of Labor, Bureau of Labor Statistics.
§ Interstate Commerce Commission, Statistics of Railways of the United States.
‖ Estimated, with the 10 per cent reduction accepted by railway labor for a limited period applied to 1932.
¶ Estimated, upon the basis of a preliminary figure issued by the Bureau of Railway Economics.

Considered Criticisms of Regulatory Policy.—There have been levied against our federal regulatory policies as they affect the railways certain criticisms that merit thoughtful consideration, however. Some of the weaknesses in our present plan have already been mentioned; among the more important of these are defects in the consolidation, labor, and recapture provisions. There is little doubt but that the statutory requirement of a "final plan" as a guide to consolidation served to block progress during a period when the economic and financial situation was ripe for action. There seems to be little promise in existing railway-labor legislation for troubled economic times; like the Erdman and Newlands Acts, the Watson-Parker Act seems likely to be but a fair-weather craft—with slight chance of remaining afloat when it is necessary to sail in the teeth of, rather than with, the demands of railway-labor organizations. The repeal of the Recapture clause has been asked by the Commission, primarily upon administrative grounds; perhaps such action is desirable, despite the fundamental soundness in principle of the scheme of rate making of which it is an integral part. If recapture is retained, then certainly recapturable income should be computed upon the basis of earnings over a period of years, rather than single-year earnings. And, too, if it is to be retained, justice demands that the Commission accept a greater measure of responsibility for providing a "fair return" in accordance with the statute.

It is upon this matter of "fair return" that the intent of the Transportation Act has failed of realization perhaps most conspicuously. As noted upon a previous page, in only 2 years since 1920 have the railways of the United States equaled or exceeded the return fixed as "fair," and for the period since that date a considerable "deficit" has accumulated.

True, during certain of those years—such as 1921, 1931, and 1932—the volume of traffic fell so low that it is likely no schedule of rates that a regulatory body might reasonably impose would have provided the needed sums; yet such was not true at least of the typical year since 1920. Responsibility for this situation rests, in part, upon the Commission; yet it is probable that its reluctance to authorize increased rates was due largely to the attitude of Congress as evidenced by the consideration of many and the enactment of a few such measures as the Hoch-Smith Resolution. But responsibility goes also to the railways, which often failed to cooperate in action necessary to stabilize rates and thus protect revenue. And, finally, the increasing force of motor competition has been felt. With all these forces working in conjunction, it is not strange that railway earnings fared badly.

Another matter that troubles some of the students of regulation is the increasing tendency to center authority in the Interstate Commerce Commission—and one of the points that disturbs most is how such a tendency can be reversed, with transportation becoming increasingly inter- rather than intrastate in its character. The federal body has made sincere efforts to establish a basis for cooperation with state commissions and, upon certain matters, works consistently with and even through them; yet, where responsibility rests, authority must lie. If, as will undoubtedly eventuate within a few years, the powers of the federal Commission are extended to interstate commercial motor transport, it is quite probable that provision will be made for initial jurisdiction over many matters by state bodies; these commissions will be, in short, the local representatives of federal authority. Perhaps through such cooperation a breadth of vision can be developed on the part of state regulatory agencies that will make it possible safely to intrust to them original jurisdiction upon many matters of railway regulation, thus obtaining the benefit of local point of view and local knowledge and at the same time lightening the burden of the federal Commission. In this matter of the distribution of power between state and federal bodies lies an important problem for those who are concerned with and troubled by certain tendencies in government.

But there are, in our policy of railway regulation, errors of omission as well as of commission. The operations of the holding company in the railway field in recent years have led to a demand that it be made subject in some degree to Commission regulation. The same demand has been made with respect to refrigerator and other types of special car lines; while the rates that the railway may charge for transportation in such special equipment lie within the jurisdiction of the Commission, the purposes of regulation would be furthered if the companies owning the equipment were subject in all their relationships to regulation.[1] Demand for the regulation of the forwarding company, which has gained prominence during the past several years, has also appeared. These consolidators and shippers of freight serve as an intermediary between railway and public to an increasing degree in the movement of small-lot shipments; there seems to be no reason why they, with opportunities to discriminate and otherwise burden the public, should not be brought within the scope of regulation.

But undoubtedly the most important omissions in regulatory policy are those that affect the railways in another way, the failure to establish for competing agencies regulation of a type comparable to that now resting upon the railways. The alternative to the extension of regulation of those agencies is, if equitable conditions are to exist and solvency to be assured to even a major portion of the railway net, the repeal of much of the legislation under which the commissions, state and federal, function to restrict railway action. And, while there are those who propose a reversion to *laissez-faire*, there are few students of the transportation problem who believe that public benefit lies in that direction; in truth, it is difficult for the advocate of such a course to justify, from a public point of view, any single major "retreat" in regulatory policy. The

[1] There has been evident recently a tendency on the part of large shippers who are, at the same time, owners directly or through subsidiary companies of private cars, to dispose of that equipment to non-shipper owners. This change, if it persists, would remove certain objections to the nonregulation of special-equipment companies; none the less, there seems to be ground for extending regulation to companies that maintain, in essence, a private "car pool" upon which the railways may draw in case of need.

final chapters of this volume are devoted to an analysis of the relation of the railways to other inland-transport agencies and to extensions or modifications in regulatory policy. Until that discussion is reached perhaps it will be sufficient to say that, despite the fact that much of our regulatory legislation has been the consequence of public antagonism toward the railways and that administrative agencies have too often fallen short of those high standards of understanding and statesmanship so essential to the proper exercise of important powers, regulation has justified itself as a public policy. Through it the public has obtained lower rates and improved service, by it the antisocial policies and practices of a few in the railway industry have been sufficiently curbed to permit of the continuance of private ownership and operation in a field peculiarly fraught with importance to the millions for whom the railway is an essential instrument. The lessons taught by more than half a century of regulation should not be lightly thrust aside, nor should a sharp change in railway policy to "right" or "left" be made until every effort has been made to benefit from past regulatory experience and until every aspect of the existing problem has been examined with care and in detail.

REFERENCES

American Railway Association, Car Service Division.

Association of Railway Executives: miscellaneous material published and distributed to the public.

Bureau of Railway Economics.

Cunningham, W. J.: *American Railroads*, McGraw-Hill Book Company, Inc., 1922.

Daggett, Stuart R.: *Principles of Inland Transportation*, Harper & Brothers, 1928.

Dixon, F. H : *Railroads and Government*, Charles Scribner's Sons, 1922.

Ellingwood, A. R., and Whitney Coombs: *The Government and Railroad Transportation*, Ginn & Company, 1930.

Grodinsky, Julius, and Emory R. Johnson: *Railroad Consolidation*, D. Appleton & Company, 1930.

Hearings before Subcommittee on Interstate Commerce, United States Senate, 68th Congress, 1st Session, on Senate Bill 2646. *Arbitration between Carriers and Employees* (Howell-Barkley bill).

Hearings before the Committee on Interstate Commerce, United States Senate, 67th Congress, 1st Session, pursuant to Senate Resolution 23, *Railroad Revenues and Expenses*.

Hearings before Committee on Interstate and Foreign Commerce, United States House of Representatives, 69th Congress, 1st Session, on H. R. 11212, *Railroad Consolidation*.

Hearings before Committee on Interstate and Foreign Commerce, United States House of Representatives, 72d Congress, 1st Session, on H. R. 7116 and 7117, *Railroad Legislation*.

Hearings before Committee on Interstate Commerce, United States Senate, 68th Congress, 2nd Session, on S. 2327, *Long-and-Short-Haul Charges*.

House Report 2789, United States House of Representatives, 71st Congress, 3d Session, *Regulation of Stock Ownership in Railroads*.

Interstate Commerce Commission: *Annual Reports; Reports; Statistics of Railways*.

Investment Bankers Association, Committee on Railroad Securities· *The Federal Valuation of Railroads*, 1922.

JOHNSON, E. R., GROVER G. HUEBNER, and G. L. WILSON: *Principles of Transportation*, D. Appleton & Company, 1928.

Joint New England Railroad Committee: Rehabilitation by Cooperation: A Railroad Policy for New England, *Report to the Governors of the New England States.*

JONES, ELIOT: *Principles of Railway Transportation*, The Macmillan Company, 1924.

Labor, vols. 1–14 (weekly newspaper published by the Railway Brotherhoods, Washington, D. C.).

LOCKLIN, D. PHILIP: *Railroad Regulation Since 1920*, McGraw-Hill Book Company, Inc., 1928 (Supplement, 1931).

OLDHAM, J. E.: *A Plan of Railroad Consolidations*, Investment Bankers Association, 1921.

PLUMB, G. E., and W. G. ROYLANCE: *Industrial Democracy*, B. W. Huebsch, Inc., 1923.

Railroad Legislation, *Proceedings of the Academy of Political and Social Science*, vol. 8, No. 4.

Railroad Telegrapher, vols. 37–50.

Railroad Trainman, vols. 37–50.

Railway Age, vols. 68–94.

Railway Conductor, vols. 37–50.

Report of Joint Committee of Agricultural Inquiry, vol. 3, Transportation.

SHARFMAN, I. L.: *The American Railroad Problem*, Century Company, 1921.

SNYDER, CARL: *Business Cycles and Business Measurements*, The Macmillan Company 1927.

SPLAWN, WALTER M. W.: *Consolidation of Railroads*, The Macmillan Company, 1925.

The Annalist, vols. 12–41.

The Traffic World, vols. 25–51.

THOMPSON, SLASON: *A Short History of American Railways*, D. Appleton & Company, 1925.

United States Bureau of Labor Statistics.

United States Department of Commerce: *Commerce Yearbook*, 1930, vol. 1, United States Government Printing Office.

United States Supreme Court Reports.

VANDERBLUE, H. B., and K. F. BURGESS: *Railroads*, The Macmillan Company, 1923.

WOLF, HARRY D.: *The Railroad Labor Board*, University of Chicago Press, 1927.

In addition to the above general and specific references, the *Reader's Guide* and other compilations of magazine articles will give innumerable references to valuable material dealing with certain phases of the railway situation since 1920. Discussions found in the *American Economic Review*, the *Quarterly Journal of Economics*, *Annals of the American Academy of Political and Social Science*, the *Journal of Political Economy*, and others of similar type are especially meritorious.

PART III

THE RAILWAY SERVICE

Chapter XVI

THE RAILWAY ENTERPRISE

IN THE preceding chapters the development of the American railway net has been described with primary emphasis upon physical growth and governmental control. In the chapters immediately following a study will be made of railway service. As an introduction to that study, a brief description will be given of the nature of the business unit through which management functions in the railway field and of the administrative organization of that unit.

Nature and Advantages of the Corporation.—The unit of management in railway enterprise is, almost without exception, the corporation. Indeed, in no other field is the corporation so characteristic as in this, the field of railway operations. The corporation is variously defined. Perhaps the most widely known definition is that given by Chief Justice Marshall in the Dartmouth College case:[1] a corporation is "an artificial being, invisible, intangible, and existing only in contemplation of law." A somewhat more explicit definition appears in Clark and Marshall:[2] "A corporation is a body, or artificial person, consisting of one or more individuals, or sometimes an individual and other corporations, created by law and invested by the law with certain legal capacities as the capacity of succession; the capacity to sue and be sued; to make contracts; to take, hold, and convey property; to commit torts and crimes; and to do other acts, however numerous its members may be, like a single individual."

In the railway field, to an even greater degree than in the industrial, the corporation has rendered an invaluable service to both investor and society. During the first half century of railway development in the United States one of the outstanding characteristics of this enterprise was its speculative nature. Because of that fact it would have been exceedingly difficult to attract capital under any plan of organization except one which limited, as does the corporation, the liability of the investor to the amount initially put into the business. A second distinct advantage which the corporation enjoys in the railway field is that of continuity: because of the large investment and because of the very nature of the enterprise it is essential that the railway business unit have an uninterrupted life. Then, too, the nature of the investment in railways

[1] *The Trustees of Dartmouth College v. Woodward,* 4 Wheaton 518 (1819).

[2] *Corporation Law,* p. 1.

is of such character that easy transferability of interests is a factor of importance. The large enterprise can be more efficiently managed, also, when organized as a corporation than under any plan of management that necessitates the direct participation of a considerable number of interested parties in the current affairs of the business. And, finally, the corporation has proved its worth to railway undertakings in a peculiar degree because this form of organization has made available vast sums of capital which otherwise would not have been placed at the disposal of the railways: instead of participating as partners in an enterprise possessors of funds may purchase any of a number of different types of securities, depending upon the relative importance attached by them to safety and to high return. So striking have been the advantages resulting from the use of the corporate form of organization that it is difficult to conceive of adequate railway development in the United States under private direction had this or a similar type of business unit not been available.

Types of Corporations.—Corporations are, in general, classified under three heads—private, public, and quasi-public. The status of the private corporation is essentially that of the individual: with few exceptions the same duties and obligations rest upon it, while its rights and privileges are likewise comparable within the limits imposed by charter. The management of such a corporation lies exclusively with the owners except as it may be subject to public control under the police power, and its purpose is normally private gain. The life of the private corporation is determined by the law under which the charter issued and may not be terminated short of that period except as some act works forfeiture of the charter.

The public corporation, on the other hand, is created by public authority and may be dissolved at any time. It is organized for purposes of government; it exercises, within established limits, governmental functions; and it enjoys privileges peculiar to government, as exemption from taxation. Among corporations clearly public are the various municipal corporations, any banking or industrial enterprise wholly owned and managed by some governmental unit, and educational institutions exclusively controlled by the state. However, many corporations which are commonly regarded as public because of public participation therein do not enjoy such legal status—and here might be mentioned many agricultural societies, hospitals established by private funds, and controlled boards of trustees not publicly chosen, and even such organizations as the Federal Reserve and the Federal Land Banks.

The third type of corporation, of particular interest to the student of railways, is that commonly termed quasi-public. Quoting Clark and Marshall again,[1]

[1] *Corporation Law*, p. 49.

Some private corporations are organized for a purpose which is of a public nature or, rather, for a purpose which renders them particularly beneficial, if not necessary, to the public and are, for this reason, called quasi-public corporations; and, because of their quasi-public nature, they are sometimes given rights and privileges that are not granted to other corporations, as the right of eminent domain. For example, railroad companies engaged in the common carriage of passengers and goods are quasi-public corporations in this sense. . . . These corporations, though because of their objects they are called quasi-public, are created for private gain and are mere private corporations just as a banking company or insurance company is a mere private corporation.

In ownership, then, this third or mixed type of corporation is clearly private, but in its responsibility to its patrons it is public.

Upon this quasi-public character of the railway industry rests the entire structure of regulation that has developed gradually until today the management of railway properties, even to many minor details, must be shared by its staff with public agencies. Out of this regulation, it may be added, have grown many complicated problems of an administrative and financial nature, and also many exceedingly nice problems of law and of jurisdiction. Public control has also made the "railway problem" loom large in American political life. On the one hand, the fear of such control often resulted during years past in the shameful perversion of public government to private ends—in the control from time to time by purchase or guile of legislature, court, and executive. This perversion, in turn, caused the accumulation of a tremendous and righteous public wrath that wreaked havoc upon both the just and the unjust, once that public overcame the obstructions to its will. On the other hand, the "soulless railroad corporation" served splendidly during long years as an object of indiscriminate attack for self-confessed statesmen and demagogues, in their struggles to gain political preferment and power. And, it might be added, all delineations of evil in the railway field have not even yet an altruistic purpose or, when judged from the standpoint of sound public policy, a constructive goal.

Regulation of Quasi-public Corporations.—During the first 40 years of railway development in the United States the private character of the railway business was not questioned. The American public was still dominated by the *laissez-faire* philosophy and, beyond this, the need for additional transportation service was so much more evident than were the abuses of existing agencies that emphasis was placed wholly upon additional facilities. The struggle, in legislative halls and in the courts, to establish public control has already been described: not until the decision of the United States Supreme Court in *Munn v. Illinois*,[1] rendered in 1877, and in other cases following, was the constitutional right of the government to regulate certain agencies, including railway

[1] *Munn, v. Illinois*, 94 U. S. 113 (1877).

corporations, fully recognized. The basis of such regulation rests, of course, upon the protection of public interest and, though efforts have been made to limit this power and to circumscribe its use since that noteworthy decision, no attack has succeeded in challenging successfully the inherent power of the public thus to act. Rather, as economic relations have become more complex, the scope of public control has been broadened.

In the regulation of all quasi-public corporations it is now recognized that certain powers inhere in the legislature as directly representing public will, but that such legislative power must be exercised within the limits fixed by the Constitution as interpreted by the courts. The legislative function is essentially that of the prescription of services and the determination of rates—in short, that of positive regulation. This branch of government may function in either of two ways: it may by specific legislation prescribe rates, fares, classifications, and even service, or it may enact general laws requiring that all rates, fares, etc., be reasonable and provide for an administrative body or commission *to determine what is reasonable* in a particular case. Of these two methods, the latter has proved the more efficient, with the result that railway regulation seldom proceeds today from specific legislative enactment.

In the absence of legislation the courts may exercise control over the railway upon the basis of the common law, which requires that common carriers render an adequate service at reasonable rates without undue discrimination. Such control is negative in character, however, and has therefore proved inadequate to protect public interest. A specific rate, service, or practice of an objectionable character may be eliminated by judicial action, but it is impossible thus to initiate and enforce any rate, service, or practice found reasonable by the court. If positive regulations have been laid down by legislative action the judicial function is twofold: the court examines such regulations in the light of constitutional guarantees and, if not in violation of one or another of those safeguards, it interprets those regulations in their application.

The Problem of Jurisdiction.—Railway regulation, because of the dual character of our government, state and federal, gives rise to difficult jurisdictional problems. Under the federal Constitution the state retained jurisdiction over intrastate movements while to the federal government has been delegated the control of all interstate and foreign commerce. The question as to what was to be regarded as intrastate and what as interstate commerce was settled with little difficulty, but the determination of the boundary line between the fields of state and of federal control has been one of the most difficult legal problems facing legislative bodies and courts during the past half century. Though a detailed delineation of the struggle between state and federal governments during that period cannot be given here, it is well to note that the scope of state authority has swung from almost one extreme to another—from the power to control interstate commerce in the absence of federal action[1] to the denial of exclusive control over purely intrastate traffic if, in the exercise of such control, interstate commerce is prejudiced.[2]

The Railway Charter.—As has been indicated, the corporation is the usual type of business unit found in the railway field. This corporation lives because of the charter granted to it and possesses only such privileges and powers as are enumerated in that charter. As defined by Cleveland and Powell,[3] the charter "is a formal grant by the state to persons associated for the purposes of exercising powers and enjoying privileges which they could not otherwise enjoy." In this country, with a dual system of government, charters have been granted by both the states and the federal government. However, so few charters have been granted to railways by the latter that, for practical purposes, we may regard the state as the source of the railway charter. These instruments were granted to railway corporations in early years by specific act of the legislature, just as they were to other corporate undertakings, but this method proved quite unsatisfactory. The consideration of charter applications consumed the time of legislative bodies which was needed for other matters, and the launching of a corporate enterprise was necessarily delayed if the legislature was not in session. Even more objectionable was this policy of granting special charters because of the corruption which accompanied the promotion of many projects. To escape the difficulties growing out of incorporation under specific act, a movement toward the enactment of general statutes governing incorporation gained such great headway that, during the past half century, few charters have been granted except under such statutes. This policy of incorporation under general statutes has also made for uniformity in contrast to the almost infinite variety of charter provisions under special legislation.

The early railway charter is of interest today primarily because it gives evidence of a peculiar conception of the nature of railway enterprise. These instruments were patterned closely after the older turnpike charters and therefore contained many provisions which now seem very strange. Cleveland and Powell in *Railroad Promotion and Capitalization*[4] declare:

> As the first railroads were regarded as improved highways, their charters in many cases conferred the right to collect toll for the use of the road and an additional charge for conducting transportation when the equipment of the company was used. Thus the charter of the Boston and Providence gave the right

[1] *Peik v. Chicago and North Western Railway Company*, 94 U. S. 164 (1877).

[2] *Houston, East and West Texas Railway Company v. United States*, 234 U. S. 342 (1914).

[3] *Railroad Promotion and Capitalization in the United States*, p. 155.

[4] P. 160.

to build railroads which might be used by any persons who would comply with the necessary regulations and authorized the directors "to erect toll houses, establish gates, appoint toll gatherers, and demand toll upon the road."

Characteristic of early charter limitations were three provisions: a prescription of maximum tolls, a limitation upon profits, and a prohibition upon discrimination in favor of citizens of another state served by the railway. Among various powers extended by the early charter, the grant of the right of eminent domain always appeared. Sometimes, too, assurance of protection against competition and exemption from taxation were given, usually for a specified number of years.

Contractual Nature of Railway Charters.—During the early years of railway development many special charters were granted containing provisions inimical to public interest. This was particularly apparent after the decision of the United States Supreme Court in the Dartmouth College case,[1] in which it was held that even a charter granted by the English monarch during colonial days was a definite contract and not to be altered by public act except with the consent of the grantee. However, failure to fulfill the terms of the grant in many cases worked a forfeiture of too-generous charters and bankruptcy canceled others. That unduly liberal terms be not accorded in the future, state constitutions were so amended after the Dartmouth decision to limit the power of the legislature to grant privileges or exemptions. Where powers inimical to public interest were actually being exercised under existing charters, two avenues of escape were found—by bargaining with the corporation for the surrender of objectionable provisions in return for certain added privileges later sought, and by recourse to the police power as in the Stanislaus case.[2] In this decision it was held that a certain burdensome provision included in the charter granted a water company under an early general incorporation law passed by the California legislature could no longer be enforced against the public, the Court applying the principle stated by Bentham and quoted with approval in an earlier case:[3]

> All laws may be said to be framed with a view to perpetuity; but perpetual is not synonymous with irrevocable and the principle on which all laws ought to be and the greater part of them have been established, is that of defeasible perpetuity—a perpetuity defeasible by an alteration of circumstances and reasons on which the law is founded.

The typical charter of today under which railway operations are conducted has been granted by the state under general laws providing for incorporation and is comparable to the charters granted other cor-

[1] *The Trustees of Dartmouth College v. Woodward*, 4 Wheaton 518 (1819).

[2] *Stanislaus County v. San Joaquin and King's River Canal and Irrigation Company*, 192 U. S. 201 (1904).

[3] *Christ Church Hospital v. Philadelphia County*, 24 Howard 300, 16 Law Ed. 602 (1861).

porate organizations. The only charter problem remaining arises from the divergence of various general incorporation laws. Essential uniformity in the future can be secured in two ways—adoption of uniform incorporation laws by the 48 states, or compulsory federal incorporation of all railways doing an interstate business. Since this latter plan would eliminate divergent provisions from existing state charters, it seems superior if uniformity be important.

Magnitude of the Railway Corporation.—Beginning as small organizations in the early years, many railway corporations have become large and powerful entities. The Pennsylvania Railroad, including leased lines, with an investment account of about $2,000,000,000, has shown annual revenues of $700,000,000, while the New York Central and leased lines have an indicated investment of about $1,700,000,000 and normal annual revenues in excess of $475,000,000. In the South the Southern Railway has an investment exceeding $500,000,000 and typical revenues of about $150,000,000, while the Illinois Central, with an investment of $700,000,000, enjoys annual revenues of about $160,000,000. In the Southwest, the Southern Pacific and Atchison, Topeka and Santa Fe represent an investment of more than a billion dollars each, and each has shown annual revenues of approximately $225,000,000; to the north lie the Union Pacific, the Northern Pacific, and the Great Northern, each with an investment that exceeds three-quarters of a billion and normal annual revenues of approximately $120,000,000.

TABLE XI.—GROWTH IN NUMBER OF STOCKHOLDERS IN TWELVE IMPORTANT AMERICAN RAILWAYS, 1904 TO 1930

Railway	1904, June 30	1917, Dec. 31	1930, Dec. 31
Pennsylvania Railroad	44,175	100,038	233,414
Atchison, Topeka and Santa Fe	17,823	44,561	58,202
New York Central and Hudson River	11,781	27,062	56,635
Southern Pacific	2,424	37,853	54,942
Union Pacific	14,256	33,875	46,450
Baltimore and Ohio	7,132	29,360	44,598
Great Northern	383	26,716	42,258
Northern Pacific	368	25,780	36,394
New York, New Haven and Hartford	10,842	25,545	29,581
Illinois Central	9,123	10,788	20,320
Chicago and North Western	4,109	12,770	16,577
Chicago, Milwaukee, St. Paul, and Pacific	5,832	20,549	10,728
Total	128,248	394,897	650,099

Financial Interest of Public in Railways.—The financial interest of the public in railways is clearly shown by the extent of both individual holdings and the holdings of investment institutions of a semi-public character. Data furnished the Interstate Commerce Commission indicate that in 1931 the total number of stockholders of Class I railways was 876,056, having increased from 762,923 since 1928. And the present holdings in certain important railways, as well as the trend, are shown in Table XI. Naturally, duplications appear in data showing the number of railway stockholders but nevertheless it is evident that increasing numbers are investing their savings in the stocks of American railway corporations.

Not only have great numbers of individuals placed their funds in railway securities directly but heavy investments have also been made by banks and insurance companies in this field, particularly in bonds. These investments have been variously estimated, but there is reason to believe that commercial and savings banks hold some $2,700,000,000 and life insurance companies some $2,600,000,000 of railway bonds—while other public and semipublic institutions, such as hospitals, libraries, and endowments, have not less than $1,000,000,000 in railway paper, largely bonds.[1] What becomes of the railways concerns, therefore, perhaps 50,000,000 policyholders, 12,500,000 depositors,[2] and great numbers of others whose interest is indirect: both investment and earnings are entitled to every protection consonant with the public's right to receive a *complete and adequate* transportation service at minimum cost.

The Problem of Management.—The railway corporation has attained an important place in our present economic structure. Upon the financial soundness of these corporations depends not only the well-being of hundreds of thousands of security holders and employees with direct interests, but also the well-being and prosperity of many millions of others with a *service* interest—millions who are dependent upon these properties in considerable or entire measure for transportation upon such terms as will further economic and social development. Since this successful conduct of railway enterprise is dependent to an unusual degree upon efficiency of organization and administration, a brief presentation of that phase of the carrier business is well suited to serve as an introduction to the study of the major services rendered.

To render maximum service to the public at minimum cost to the railway, to insure the regular operation of an intricate machine in which the major factor is the human element, often variable and undependable, has been a problem which has taxed the ingenuity and capacity of masters of organization. That different types of organization should develop is only natural; to expect methods and policies successful in one situation to

[1] THORPE, MERLE, What Has Happened to the Railroads, *Nation's Business*, vol. 20, No. 11, p. 28.

[2] The Railroads Explain Their Plight, *Nation's Business*, vol. 20, No. 3, p. 34.

be equally successful in another quite different is unreasonable. However, the general lines of development in railway administration have been sufficiently uniform to justify the presentation of what might be termed the typical organization for the conduct of the transportation business.

The Function of the Stockholder.—As with other corporations, primary control of the affairs of the railway resides in the stockholders. This control is normally exercised at the annual meeting of stockholders through the expressions of opinion and through participation in the election of directors. Expression of opinion, however, carries little weight except as it comes from important stockholders: too often the annual meeting is only a formality—protests and suggestions voiced by minority interests are heard patiently, then buried by the controlling group with an avalanche of votes. Minority representation upon the board of directors is often wholly lacking. Indeed, the absence of any system of voting devised to secure the representation of even strong minority interests upon boards of directors is a major weakness and danger of corporate procedure in the United States. Nevertheless, without regard to the weaknesses of the present plan, the fact remains that through his vote at the annual meeting the stockholder must exercise such influence as he possesses upon the management and policies of the corporation. To this statement there is but one exception—the existence of a situation which justifies judicial interference with the policies of management. Yet, because such interference can rarely be justified, the stockholder's protection lies in the honesty and integrity of controlling interests, or in the identity of his interests with those of the dominant group.

The Directors and Executive Committee.—At this annual meeting certain of the stockholders are chosen to serve upon the board of directors. Railway boards are composed of from 9 to 21 men, representing large stockholders, supporting banking institutions, interested railways, and occasionally important commercial enterprises. To effect greater continuity in policy, directors are so selected as to make impossible a complete change in personnel, even though desired, in less than 3 to 5 years. The major functions of the board of directors, acting as a body, are three: it determines general policies, it chooses the executive committee, and it is responsible for the selection of the major officers of the corporation. To the executive committee extensive powers are delegated. Operation, finance, competition, and administration give rise to an infinite variety of difficult problems demanding consideration at the hands of others than appointive officers. Yet the entire board of directors, composed of men with scattered residence and important individual business interests, cannot meet frequently to consider vital matters.

This executive committee is composed of from three to seven men, though typically three. To serve upon this committee the board selects from its own members those most familiar with railway operations and best situated by location and business interests to deal with problems as they arise. The chairman of the board of directors normally serves, *ex officio*, as chairman of this active body and, if the president of the property is a member of the board of directors he, too, is usually designated as a member of the "inner circle." Since the primary responsibility and the greater burden of the work performed by the executive committee usually fall upon the shoulders of the chairman of the board and the committee, this individual must be a man of broad training and experience in the railway field, possessed of exceptional judgment—a diplomat, statesman, financier, administrator, and railway expert all in one; otherwise both the immediate and long-time interests of the property will be prejudiced. The three outstanding matters with which the committee is concerned are the supervision of administrative policies, the planning and administration of financial matters, and the direction of the legal interests and policies of the corporation.

The Corporate Officers.—The selection of corporate officers often represents little more than the approval of recommendations made by the executive committee or by the president of the railway. Although there are variations among railways as to the officers so chosen, the selection of the president, as well as of those immediately subordinate to him and directly responsible for operations, traffic, accounting, finance, and law, normally requires the formal approval of the entire board. The men thus chosen serve until they are superseded by definite action, or until resignation removes them from the service. The number of such officers subordinate to the president and reporting directly to him varies greatly among the different roads and is determined largely by the organization of the property for operation. Upon the major officers rests a dual burden, the responsibility of building up an effective organization through employee loyalty and efficient management, and the obligation of so conducting the business in relation to the public and to the opportunities of the areas served that the long-time interest of the property will be served.

The President.—Among the various railway officials the president is first in responsibility and outstanding in the public mind. He is chosen by the directors with the greatest care, for upon his capacity and efficiency depends very largely the success of the property. To him report both the staff officers, who function in an advisory capacity, and the line officers, who direct active operations. Although invariably possessed of specialized training in some phase of railway work, it is impossible for the president to have a detailed knowledge of all matters subject to his control. His success, therefore, depends upon his soundness of judgment in the choice of lieutenants. Chosen in early days largely because of his financial or general prestige, the president was in many cases little more than a figurehead.

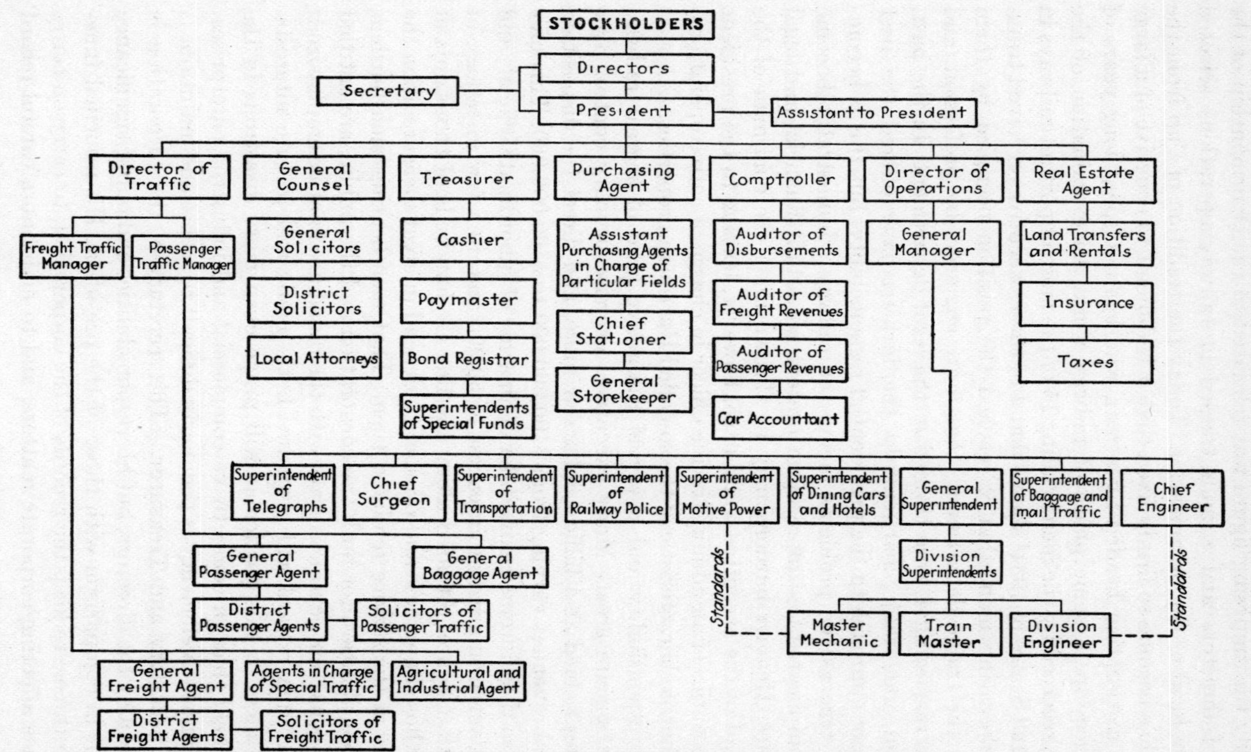

FIG. 17.—Outline plan of typical American railway organization.

Gradually this imposing figure was relegated to the chairmanship of the board of directors and a man trained in railway operations selected as active head of the organization. Today the tradition of "up from the ranks" has become so firmly fixed that it is difficult to conceive of a large railway corporation headed by a man who has not spent long years of apprenticeship in some phase of railway work. An examination of the training received by the men heading 15 of the more important railways in the United States in 1931[1] shows that 4 of these executives received training as operating men, that 2 reached the position occupied by them through the traffic department, that 5 are engineers by profession, and that the remaining 4 were trained in the legal department. In the past, operation and traffic, particularly the former, have offered the best avenues of approach to the presidential responsibility, but this is becoming less true as the problems facing the railway administrator become more complicated and more often present important financial and legal difficulties. Heavier burdens may be thrown upon the chairman of the board and of the executive committee, however, leaving to the president only the duties of an administrative officer in charge of active operations. This policy is characteristic of the so-called Harriman properties.

The responsibility and power of the active head of a great railway organization are great. Many executives exercise primary control over properties valued at a billion dollars or more, and direct the disposition of annual revenues varying from $100,000,000 to $400,000,000. This official is also the supreme commander of an army of subordinate officials and workers, often numbering in excess of 50,000 and, in a few instances, of double that figure. Situated along the line are hundreds of thousands of people whose happiness and prosperity depend in great measure upon the character of the service rendered them. That men bearing such burdens and responsibilities, for both the corporation and the public, are entitled to a compensation commensurate with their load need not be emphasized; to refuse such reward will prejudice both public and private interests. Niggardliness in this particular will prove even more disastrous in the railway field than in competitive commercial and industrial enterprises: it is one in which efficiency is peculiarly difficult to secure and maintain.

The Secretary and Treasurer.—The secretary of the corporation is also chosen by the directors, but his responsibilities and public significance are slight in comparison with those of the president. His principal functions are three—to keep the records of the corporation, to carry on correspondence affecting corporate matters, and to maintain a careful record

[1] The New York Central, Pennsylvania, Baltimore and Ohio, the Erie, the Southern, the Illinois Central, the Southern Pacific, the Atchison, Topeka and Santa Fe, the Chicago, Rock Island and Pacific, the Union Pacific, the Chicago and North Western, the Chicago, Milwaukee, St. Paul, and Pacific, the Chicago, Burlington, and Quincy, the Great Northern, and the Northern Pacific.

of the ownership of all outstanding shares of the corporation. A second official whose work is also confined mainly to matters within the corporate organization is the treasurer. This official, like the secretary, is generally chosen by the board of directors, and sometimes bears the title of vice-president. In his department will be found a subordinate organization of some extent, headed by one or more assistant treasurers. Subordinate to an assistant treasurer will be a cashier in active charge of all moneys, a bond registrar upon whom rests the obligation of meeting payments of both interest and principal upon all bonded indebtedness, and a paymaster whose problem it is to care for the monthly or semimonthly payroll of the corporation. Among the subordinates of the treasurer may also be the superintendents of various special funds, such as pension and relief.

The General Counsel and His Staff.—The typical legal department of the railway is headed by a general counsel. This individual is usually a lawyer of high skill and long experience in the railway field, an important servant to the railway though but little known to the public. Upon him the president depends largely for advice with respect to important proposals. The major functions of the legal department are four: it renders legal advice to the various officials seeking counsel, directs all litigation to which the railway is a party, makes and executes all contracts in which railway interests are involved, and directs rate cases before public bodies. To assist him in this work the general counsel often has several assistant general counsels, together with general solicitors in charge of large districts, perhaps entire states, and assistant general solicitors whose function it is to aid their principals. The organization is further localized by the selection of district solicitors and by the appointment in practically every county seat of consequence along the line of a particularly able attorney whose aid might prove helpful either as a lawyer or as an influential citizen. Responsible also to the general counsel or to one of his subordinates is often the chief claim agent.

Organization and Work of the Accounting Department.—Another department within the railway organization that is concerned primarily with internal operations and has little contact with the public is the accounting department. This department is headed by a man who usually bears the title of comptroller, and in some organizations also that of vice-president. Upon this officer rests the obligation of maintaining an efficient and adequate staff to handle the tremendous mass of details incident to railway operations. The duties of the accounting department vary widely, the extent of this variation depending upon the precise character of the work assigned to it. As a basis for the enumeration of duties, therefore, it may be well to give the organization of the typical department. Immediately subordinate to the comptroller in the typical accounting department is an assistant comptroller, or general auditor, who is generally in active charge of the administrative work of the department. Reporting to him are the auditor of expenditures or disbursements, the auditor of freight revenues, the auditor of passenger revenues, and usually the car accountant. Reporting to him also may be the auditor of freight claims, though this section, once wrested from the traffic department, tends to rest finally under the jurisdiction of the legal department. The obligations of this typical accounting department—fully discussed in a later chapter—are fivefold: to maintain a complete record of all transactions incident to handling traffic and to commercial activities; to compare regularly the accounts of this department with those kept by the treasurer, and to inspect as frequently as possible the books of all officers and agents handling corporate funds; to verify and secure the necessary approvals for all vouchers; to keep an accurate record of all car movements upon the line; and to compile statistical data for the use of the railway as well as for various commissions and other public bodies.

The Traffic Department; Organization and Functions.—Coming into closer contact with the public than divisions thus far mentioned is the traffic department. The responsible head, chosen by the directors, has the rank of vice-president and immediately subordinate to him are two officials, one in active charge of freight traffic, the other of passenger traffic. Reporting to the freight-traffic manager, who serves as chief adviser to the vice-president in all matters pertaining to freight movements, is the general freight agent who in turn directs the work of certain assistant general freight agents and division freight agents. To the division agents report the active solicitors of traffic. General agents in charge of special traffic, such as coal, also report to the freight-traffic manager. The organization of the passenger department is similar to that of the freight department just described; a general passenger agent reports to the passenger-traffic manager, and to him in turn report the assistant general passenger agents and the district passenger agents with their subordinates, the solicitors of passenger traffic. Reporting also to the passenger-traffic manager is the general baggage agent, with jurisdiction over all matters pertaining to baggage and, often, to the railway mail and express service.

In this department are also found the agricultural and industrial agents, whose function is the creation of new traffic in areas tributary to the particular carrier. Working in conjunction with state colonization bureaus, cooperating closely with agricultural colleges, associations of commerce, and farmer organizations, many railways serve a splendid public purpose, though concerned immediately with nothing more than the development of additional traffic.

The major functions of the traffic department are four: to solicit traffic—that sharp struggle of one road with another and of the railway with other agencies for the privilege of handling the large quantities of competitive business; to fix rates and, over the signatures of the general freight and passenger agents, to issue the various tariffs governing the movement of goods and persons; to study the service and to recommend improvements to the operating department; and to create, through study and leadership, new business for the company.

Importance of the Operating Department.—Second only to the president in importance among railway officials is usually the vice-president in charge of operation. This man, selected by the board of directors with great care and with special emphasis upon his capacity to accomplish results quickly and efficiently, is a graduate of the school of experience in the operating field where, perhaps, he began his railway career at menial tasks. Reporting directly to the operating vice-president may be both line and staff officers, though generally only the one or more general managers report directly to him. To the general manager, in such case, both staff and line officers are immediately responsible. Three functions vital to financial success and to adequate public service are discharged by the operating department: it is charged with the maintenance of all properties, supplies additional equipment, and supervises expansion activities; it operates the trains; and furnishes service at stations and elsewhere in connection with freight and passenger business.

The Staff Officers.—In the typical organization there report to the general manager a number of officials in charge of sections whose work is relatively inconspicuous, though nevertheless indispensable to successful operation. Among the less conspicuous subordinate organizations are those headed by the chief surgeon, by the superintendents of railway police, of dining cars and hotels, of telegraphic service, and sometimes of relief and insurance. More important, comparatively, than these are the chief engineer and superintendent of motive power. These two officers may exercise direct supervision over line operations but are generally staff officers. The former, in the typical American organization, fixes engineering standards for maintenance and minor construction work and rarely, except in the case of important construction, is on a parity with the general manager. Immediately subordinate to the chief engineer are assistant engineers, a supervisor of tests, and the chief signal engineer. The superintendent of motive power, whose duty it is to fix standards for all equipment-repair work and to advise concerning the standards to be required in the purchase of new equipment, has immediate supervision of certain mechanical engineers, an engineer in charge of tests, and the foremen of any general shops upon the system.

The Line Officers.—Responsible for the actual operation of the largest groupings of railway mileage are the general superintendents who report to the general manager. The mileage over which each of these officials has jurisdiction varies with traffic conditions and with the problems of operation, but a general superintendent may reasonably be expected to supervise the operation of from 1,000 to 1,500 miles of line. He must be a master administrator, familiar with the problems of operation and intimately acquainted at all times with conditions over his division, and his work is the harder because it consists largely of solving the knottiest problems of his immediate subordinates. This official is held responsible by his superior for results, yet those results must be obtained by him through subordinates with whom he cannot maintain more than a semblance of personal contact. He is given, therefore, a relatively free hand in the selection of men for responsible positions under him, and upon his skill in selecting those subordinates largely depends his success.

Reporting to the general superintendent are several division superintendents, the number varying in general from two to five. In speaking of the work of such officers, Morris declares,[1]

> Division superintendents are expected to know everything, and they are not supposed to need any sleep; they must be ready at any hour of day or night to go to any part of their district where there is trouble and to go there quickly, and they will almost invariably have to take the first executive action in the case of fire, or flood, or strike, or train wreck, although they will keep headquarters fully advised, by wire, of what they are doing.

Not only is the proper selection of a division superintendent essential from the point of operating results, but, since he is the first official possessing authority with whom the public has contact, his success in dealing with that public is of greater importance than railway management has often realized. Upon the typical American railway, the division superintendent is, to an unusual degree, monarch of all he surveys, and upon his ability to handle men, to deal with the public, and to cope successfully with technical problems, depends the success or failure of operations over his particular portion of the line.

Responsible to the division superintendent directly are three men, the division engineer, the master mechanic, and the trainmaster. To the first of these fall all matters relative to roadway and structures, to the second the maintenance of equipment, while the third is responsible for the movement of trains. Subordinate to the division engineer are the general foreman of the bridge and building "gang," the signal supervisor, and the roadmaster. The staff of the master mechanic is less extensive: his immediate subordinates are the traveling engineers concerned with problems of motive-power efficiency and the foremen of division shops. To the trainmaster report a variety of groups. Under his jurisdiction are the enginemen and trainmen, as well as those in charge of various yards on the division. The station agents with their various subordinates and oftentimes the chief dispatcher are also responsible to him. To an even greater degree than the division engineer or the master mechanic must the trainmaster be an "outside man"; the scope of his authority

[1] Morris, Ray, *Railroad Administration*, p. 102, D. Appleton & Company, 1919.

is so broad that only by constant movement over the line can he maintain adequate touch.

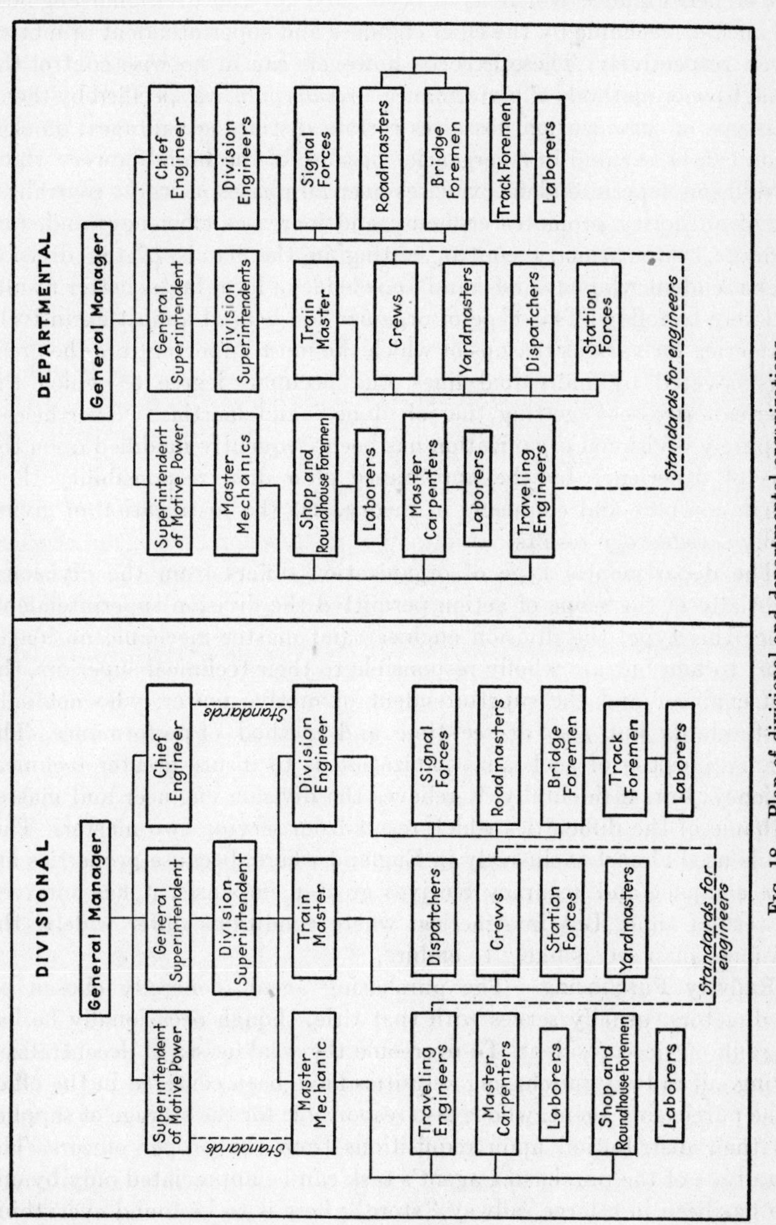

FIG. 18.—Plan of divisional and departmental organizations.

Divisional v. Departmental Organization.—The type of organization just described, typical of American operations, is the so-called divisional.

Here complete authority over all phases of work on the division is vested in the division superintendent; his power is limited only by those standards of performance which have been fixed for the divisional engineer and master mechanic by the chief engineer and superintendent of motive power, respectively. These experts, however, can in no wise control the actual time or methods of performance—*results only* are specified by them. This type of organization possesses certain distinct advantages: quicker action can be secured in emergencies because of the broad powers which the division superintendent exercises over all phases of work; centralization of authority promotes economy and increases efficiency; and, furthermore, with primary control resting in the hands of the division superintendent who has first-hand knowledge of local facts, better results are likely to follow. This type of organization is used almost exclusively in America for various reasons of which the most important are the great areas covered by individual lines, the peculiar degree to which the American stresses "getting the job done," and inertia. Nevertheless, the purely divisional organization has been frequently modified upon the basis of experience by the appearance of a dual responsibility that, though complex and confusing in theory, has the justification of giving wholly satisfactory results.

The departmental type of organization differs from the divisional essentially in the scope of action permitted the division superintendent. Under this type, the division engineer and master mechanic no longer report to him but are wholly responsible to their technical superiors, the chief engineer and the superintendent of motive power, who not only fix standards but also decree time and method of performance. The primary purpose of such an organization is to insure greater technical efficiency; but, incidentally, it relieves the division engineer and master mechanic of the difficulties which result from serving two masters. This plan is used almost exclusively in England where, because properties are more compact and accuracy receives greater emphasis, it has survived the test of time. But in America, where conditions differ widely, the divisional plan seems likely to endure.

Railway Purchasing.—The purchasing agent, generally chosen by the directors, usually serves with that title, though occasionally he has the rank of vice-president. To overcome the weaknesses of decentralized buying, all railway purchasing activities have been centered in the office of the purchasing agent, who is also responsible for the storage of supplies and their distribution upon requisitions from the proper officers. The magnitude of the purchasing agent's task can be appreciated only by one who has been in a large railway "store"; here is to be found everything from pins and paper clips to great castings, the variety of items included being almost comparable to the listings of a mail-order catalogue. Immediately subordinate to the purchasing agent may be certain assistant purchasing agents, some of whom are often in charge of single important items such as coal, lumber, and steel, while others have more general scope. Reporting also to the purchasing agent is the chief stationer in charge of office supplies, and the one or more general storekeepers. To them report in turn the storekeepers, who act as custodians of local stores of material. Large railway systems maintain from one to three "general stores," with smaller stores at practically every division point.

The Real-Estate Agent.—The final official whose work justifies consideration here is the real-estate agent, who may be designated as vice-president in charge of real estate. This official, generally chosen by the board of directors, performs, with the assistance of any assistant real-estate agents he may have and such local agents as may be needed, four functions. He directs the purchase and sale of all real estate by the corporation; he executes all rental contracts between the railway and private individuals—contracts concerning the lease of ground for elevators, warehouses, coal sheds, or the rental of building space; he handles all tax matters, including tax adjustments and payments; and manages all matters of insurance. Railway policy with respect to insurance varies rather widely: certain railways insure wholly with outside corporations, while others meet all losses from a special insurance fund set aside by them. Some roads carry their own risk except on large structures, while others follow yet different plans. Whatever the plan may be, however, its execution rests in the hands of this department.

The Efficiency of Railway Organization.—With the organization just outlined the American railway endeavors to accomplish its dual purpose, to serve the interests of its stockholders and to render effective transportation service to the public. On the whole, both groups have been served faithfully and well: that many carriers have failed in one or the other purpose, or in both, is to be regretted, of course, but such failure has rarely been chargeable to the plan of organization or to the conduct of the faithful thousands of major and minor employees who man the great railway net of America; rather, it lies at the door of men higher up, or is attributable to circumstances over which man has little control. However, a marked improvement in the soundness of the railway financial structure, the greater efficiency of organization, and a higher sense of public obligation on the part of officers and employees alike, should make future failures even fewer and less serious than those of earlier years.

With this preliminary survey of the organization of the railway for service, an examination will be made in successive chapters of the services performed in the transportation of freight, passengers, mail, and express. But, because of its basic significance, attention will first be given to the railway net rendering such services.

REFERENCES

CLARK, WILLIAM L., and WILLIAM L. MARSHALL: *Corporation Law*, Keefe-Davidson Co., 1901.

CLEVELAND, F. A., and F. W. POWELL: *Railroad Finance*, D. Appleton & Company, 1912.

———: *Railroad Promotion and Capitalization*, Longmans, Green & Co., 1909.

Dartmouth College Case, 4 Wheaton 518 (1819).

HAINES, H. S.: *American Railway Management*, John Wiley & Sons, 1897.

———: *Efficient Railway Operation*, The Macmillan Company, 1919.

HINE, CHARLES D.: *Modern Organization*, The Engineering Magazine Company, 1912.

———: *Letters from an Old Railway Official*, 2 vols., Simmons-Boardman Publishing Company, 1912.

HUNGERFORD, EDWARD: *The Modern Railroad*, A. C. McClurg and Co., 1912.

JOHNSON, E. R. and G. G. HUEBNER: *Railroad Traffic and Rates*, vols. 1 and 2, D. Appleton & Company, 1911.

——— and T. W. VAN METRE: *Principles of Railroad Transportation*, D. Appleton & Company, 1921.

KRUTTSCHNITT, J.: Operating Organization of the Union Pacific and Southern Pacific System, *Railway Age*, vol. 46, p. 1113.

LOREE, L. F.: *Railroad Freight Transportation*, D. Appleton & Company, 1922.

MCPHERSON, LOGAN: *The Working of the Railroads*, Henry Holt & Company, 1906.

MEYER, B. H.: *Railway Legislation in the United States*, pp. 53–107 (good treatment of railway charters), The Macmillan Company, 1903.

MORRIS, R., and W. E. HOOPER: *Railroad Administration*, D. Appleton & Company, 1930.

Munn v. Illinois, 94 U. S. 113.

Official Guide of the Railways and Steam Navigation Lines of the United States. Published monthly by the National Railway Publication Company, New York City (contains lists of higher officers of all departments of various railroad companies).

RINGWALT, J. L.: *Development of Transportation Systems of the United States*, J. L. Ringwalt, 1888.

RIPLEY, W. Z.: *Railroads: Rates and Regulation*, Longmans, Green & Co., 1912.

Chapter XVII

TERRITORIAL GROUPINGS

IN PRECEDING chapters the development of the American railway net has been considered as a whole: only incidental mention has been made of particular properties or of mileage serving certain areas. Preliminary to a consideration of the services rendered, however, a discussion of such facts is pertinent. For such detailed study of the entire railway net, a grouping of the various properties is helpful, if not essential. Not only will its magnitude be more clearly appreciated if attention be fixed successively upon certain portions of it, but an identity of interest which rests both upon traffic and upon ownership can be more clearly indicated also. Furthermore, it is desirable for statistical purposes to group comparable properties according to some plan; so doing facilitates the compilation of data and gives a basis for comparison and analysis. These groupings are generally made along two lines, territorial and ownership, and, although it is impossible to avoid certain overlappings, reasonably clear lines are discernible in each case.

Major Territorial Groupings.—Two territorial groupings of the railways of the United States are recognized generally. In accordance with the one, the major (which is the more important from a statistical standpoint), continental United States is, like ancient Gaul, divided into three parts. These districts are known as Eastern, Southern, and Western. The first of these lies east of Lake Michigan and a line drawn from Chicago through Peoria, to St. Louis and east of the Mississippi to the junction of that river with the Ohio, and is bounded on the south by the Ohio and Potomac rivers. The Southern District lies south of the Eastern and east of the Mississippi, while the Western includes that great area to the west of the two already defined. Although inconsistencies are discernible, this division is justified to the extent that there is justification for the definition of any such large areas. Production conditions differ widely among the three sections. Traffic and the conditions under which that traffic is handled are so diverse as to have resulted in the development of a separate classification of goods for each. Striking differences exist also in the density and the employment of the population. Furthermore, the actual location of railway lines makes it relatively simple so to divide the United States; in fact, it is improbable that any boundaries, other than those named, could be chosen which would result in less overlapping of lines. Few properties operate more than a small mileage in a second district and those operating in three are of negligible importance. This major grouping serves two important practical purposes: statistical data are compiled by the Interstate Commerce Commission for each district, and often within recent years the carriers in each of these districts have acted in concert upon important matters such as the rate level and wage rates.

For statistical purposes the Interstate Commerce Commission has broken the three major districts into smaller units. The boundaries of these are indicated by the map that accompanies this discussion and the

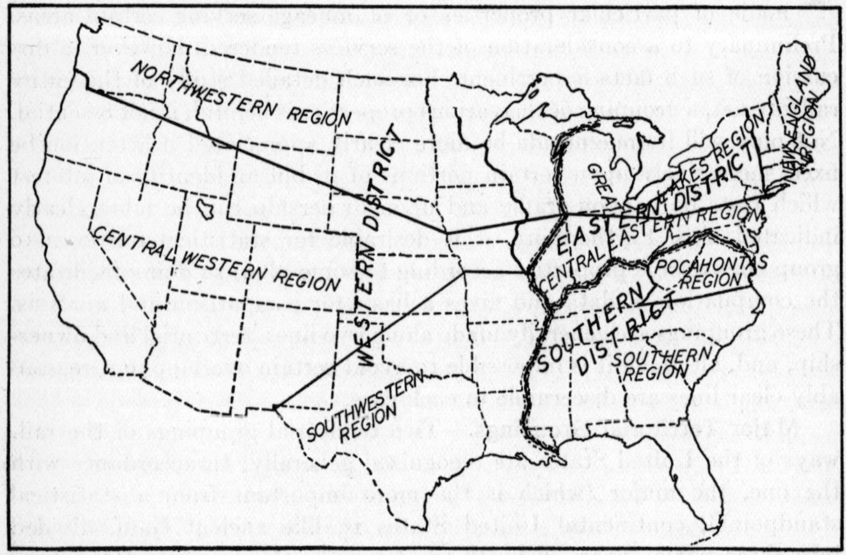

Fig. 19.—Major territories and subdivisions recognized by the Interstate Commerce Commission in compiling statistics.

reasons underlying such division as well as boundary locations may be clearly realized from a study of the railway map of the United States.

Minor Territorial Groupings. *New England.*—These major groupings are so large, however, that wide differences exist within a single district—traffic varies greatly, physical conditions governing operations are quite divergent, and certain lines seem to form a local unit rather than to constitute an integral part of the mileage of the large area. Further differentiation, using traditional though somewhat unofficial boundaries, is, therefore, both helpful and needful to an accurate understanding. Of the minor territorial groups at least six may be clearly distinguished. The first of these, New England territory, has a threefold basis for separate consideration. Traffic in the area is largely local and its lines operate almost without exception exclusively in the New England states. Furthermore, these properties have been largely owned and controlled by New

England capital from their beginning and have long been identified primarily with the industrial and commercial development of that restricted district. Geographically, two distinct groupings of lines exist within the New England territory; the northern, which serves northern Massachusetts and the three states to the north and northeast; and the southern, which serves the remainder of the area. Among the more important properties operating in the northern area are the Boston and Maine, Central Vermont, Rutland, Maine Central, and Bangor and Aroostook—these serving, among others, the following major centers: Boston, Lowell, Nashua, Manchester, Concord, Portland, Lewiston, Augusta, Bangor, Rutland, Montpelier, Burlington, Troy, and Albany. In the south the most important properties are the New York, New Haven and Hartford and the Boston and Albany—with the Central New England and Central Vermont playing a minor rôle. These railways serve, among others, Boston, Worcester, Springfield, Albany, Fall River, Providence, Hartford, New Haven, Bridgeport, and New York.

As a group, the New England railways carry a comparatively large tonnage of manufactured goods and a relatively small tonnage of mineral products. Passenger business is also an important item. The significance of manufactured goods and of passenger traffic is greater in the southern portion than in the northern, however; in the latter, agricultural and certain animal products are more important traffic elements. The struggle for traffic among rail lines, motor carriers, and coastwise vessels is keen in New England, though only a small degree of rail competition exists. Market competition, more particularly between New England coast points and New York centers, also appears as a factor.

Trunk Line Territory.—A second area which is set apart both by tradition and by fact is the so-called Trunk Line territory, an area identical with the Eastern District mentioned before except for the exclusion of New England. Here again the physical location of lines, both historical and present, serves to give unity to the area. Its railways center in Chicago and St. Louis on the west and in New York, Philadelphia, and Baltimore on the east, Buffalo and Pittsburgh being the principal intermediate centers. Furthermore, Trunk Line territory evolved and long maintained a separate and distinctive rate structure which constituted an added basis for its differentiation. In this territory there are, by virtue of differing interests, really two groups of lines; the one comprises those properties interested primarily in the movement of general tonnage and this largely in an east-and-west direction, the other the so-called anthracite roads, which are concerned principally in the movement of hard coal. Among the more important of the so-called through lines are the New York Central, the Erie, the Pennsylvania, the Baltimore and Ohio, the Nickel Plate, the Grand Trunk, and the Michigan Central, these roads serving generally not only the important eastern and western termini already mentioned, but innumerable intermediate centers among which Indianapolis, Cincinnati, Detroit, Cleveland, Toledo, and Columbus are perhaps outstanding. The principal anthracite roads are the Delaware, Lackawanna and Western, the Philadelphia and Reading, the Lehigh Valley, and the Delaware and Hudson, all of which radiate from the anthracite district to Buffalo, Philadelphia, New York, and Albany.

The tonnage of the railways operating in the Trunk Line area shows a heavy movement of minerals and mineral products, also of manufactured goods. A comparatively heavy passenger business is likewise handled. Although the tonnage of other types of traffic is relatively light, certain individual items such as grain and grain products, fruits and

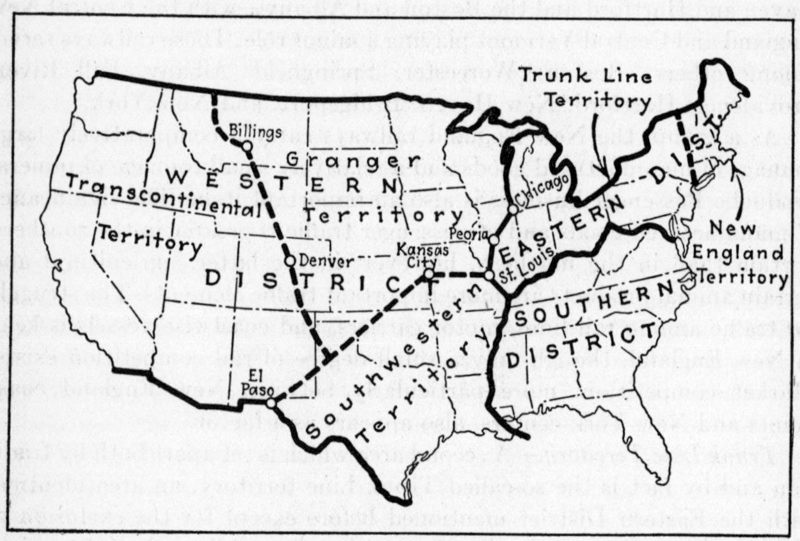

FIG. 20.—Major and minor territorial groupings.

vegetables, and packing-house products, are proportionately heavy. A large part of our import and export business moves through this territory, also. From a competitive standpoint rivalry has been and continues keen in this territory, both among the rail lines themselves and between the rail lines and the various water routes: boat lines that operate upon the Great Lakes and barges moving through the Erie Canal and, increasingly during recent years, upon certain of the rivers. And in the short-haul field the motor truck plays an increasingly important rôle. Competition is also keen among certain of the large market centers, particularly New York, Philadelphia, and Baltimore in the east and Chicago and St. Louis in the west. However, market rivalry is in no sense confined to the points named, but is active among the lesser centers throughout intervening territory; it is today, with rail and water competition under control, the most potent factor in the area making for a modification of rates.

Southern Territory.—The third of the so-called minor groupings corresponds precisely to the Southern District as defined by the Interstate Commerce Commission and is known as Southern territory. The separate consideration of this area rests upon three grounds. From an historical standpoint the railways serving the area developed quite apart from the mileage of adjacent sections, the two rivers which form its principal boundaries on the north and west remaining unspanned for many years; even yet only one Southern property operates more than a small mileage in adjacent territories. A second reason for separate consideration lies in the fact that the railways of this area serve, and are almost exclusively interested in, one or another of the important ports of this section—Norfolk, Charleston, and Savannah on the Atlantic; Pensacola, Mobile, and New Orleans on the Gulf; and Memphis and Louisville on the rivers—or in outstanding interior points such as Atlanta, Birmingham, Chattanooga, and Nashville. There developed in this area also a rate structure quite distinct from that found in any other considerable portion of the United States.

Though commonly the roads operating in Southern territory are grouped as a whole, a somewhat more accurate picture of conditions may be had if the larger area be divided, upon the basis of traffic and geographical location, into three lesser ones. The first of these, the Pocahontas district, is served by the so-called soft-coal carriers, conspicuous among which are the Norfolk and Western, the Chesapeake and Ohio, and the Virginian. These lines also extend eastward to tidewater. The Louisville and Nashville, although its principal mileage is located to the westward, might also be grouped with these from a tonnage standpoint. Among the important centers served by these properties are Norfolk, Portsmouth, Richmond, Roanoke, Charleston, and Huntington.

From the Potomac southward on the eastern slope of the Appalachian Mountains lies the Atlantic or Piedmont area which includes Virginia, the Carolinas, and a major portion of both Georgia and Florida. Prominent among the properties which operate in this section are the At antic Coast Line, the Southern, the Seaboard Air Line, the Central of Georgia, and the Florida East Coast. In addition to the Atlantic ports from Norfolk to Tampa, these properties serve Washington, Richmond, Wilmington, Charlotte, Asheville, Charleston, Columbia, Macon, Augusta, Columbus, and Atlanta. West of the Appalachian Mountains and of Georgia lie the Mississippi Valley lines, which include, among others, the Louisville and Nashville, the Southern, the Illinois Central, the St. Louis-San Francisco, and their subsidiaries. These properties serve, besides the Gulf and river ports from Pensacola to Covington, Ky., such important inland points as Lexington, Knoxville, Nashville, Chattanooga, Birmingham, Montgomery, Meridian, and Jackson. The last two roads named above are the only properties operating in the South upon a large scale with an important interest in another territory.

Naturally, the tonnage of the soft-coal lines consists largely of the commodity which gives its name to the group. Coal also forms an important part of the tonnage of the Louisville and Nashville. An unusually large proportion of the tonnage of other roads operating in Southern territory, however, both in the Piedmont section and in the Mississippi Valley, consists of the products of agriculture, among which grains, cotton, and fruits and vegetables are most important. The forests of the South also contribute a relatively large tonnage, and passenger traffic furnishes only a slightly lesser proportion of total operating revenues in this section of comparatively low income than for the United States as a whole. Competitively, no section of the United States is more interesting than Southern territory; even today, despite the stabilization resulting from interrailway agreements and from the development of large ownership groupings, it is active. Although rivalry between rail lines has been minimized and river traffic was long quiescent, the possibility of coastwise movement has long exerted an important influence upon rates. This influence has been direct upon tariffs from the North Atlantic states to points in the Piedmont and Gulf sections; indirect upon rates west of the Appalachian mountains through the operation of market and industrial competition. It is competition of this latter character, however, that is particularly sharp here; the struggle between the industrialized New England and North Atlantic states and the newer area, lying between Chicago and St. Louis on the west and Buffalo and Pittsburgh on the east, is exceedingly keen and difficult to control, and market competition has always been a peculiarly disturbing factor in Southern territory. Indeed, it may be said truly that these two types of competition, industrial and market, were largely responsible for the persistence of the basing-point system of rate making in the South which was highly provocative of public protest.

Granger Territory.—The great area included within the Western District comprises three minor territories. One of these lesser sections, known as Granger territory, lies between Chicago and St. Louis on the east and the Rocky Mountains on the west, thus embracing western Illinois, northern Missouri, a major part of Kansas, eastern Colorado, and all that country northward to the Canadian border. Here, again, essentially the same three bases for differentiation exist as for Trunk Line and Southern territories. The early properties of importance operating in this territory were built westward from Chicago, St. Louis, Kansas City, and Minneapolis-St. Paul, and confined their operations largely if not wholly to the Granger section. Among these were the Chicago and North

Western; the Chicago, Milwaukee, St. Paul, and Pacific; the Chicago, Rock Island, and Pacific; the Chicago, Burlington, and Quincy; the Atchison, Topeka, and Santa Fe; the Great Northern; the Northern Pacific; the Minneapolis, St. Paul, and Sault Ste. Marie; and the Chicago Great Western. In later years many of these properties were extended until today only four of the great railways named remain primarily Granger in interest—the Burlington, the Great Western, the North Western, and the Soo. A second reason for differentiating this area lies in the fact that the interests of properties operating therein, at least to the extent that they are Granger in character, are identified with important midwestern points such as Duluth-Superior, Milwaukee, and Chicago on the lakes; Minneapolis-St. Paul and St. Louis on the Mississippi; Kansas City and Omaha on the Missouri; and Denver farther west. Then, too, a separate rate structure governs in this area, with commodity rates still the outgrowth largely of market competition. Though certain of the railways which were originally Granger are now much interested elsewhere, it can be safely said that even these depend largely for their prosperity upon the traffic of this section.

In this territory agricultural and animal products contribute an unusual proportion of the total tonnage; the percentage in Granger territory for both groups is almost double that of the nation as a whole. Among agricultural products the most important items are grain and grain products, hay, and fruit and vegetables; live stock and packing-house products form the bulk of the tonnage of the other group. Manufactured products contribute a slightly larger proportion of the tonnage than for the country as a whole, and passenger business is approximately normal, but the tonnage contribution of minerals and mineral products falls especially low. During early days competition among railways was exceedingly active in this section, but interrailway agreements have reduced that type of rivalry to a minimum. In consequence, market competition alone remains an active and important factor. However, it has been so powerful a force throughout the entire history of the development of this area that an unusual rate adjustment resulted. The struggle between Chicago and St. Louis and Chicago and the Twin Cities on the one hand, and between Kansas City and Omaha, as well as numerous minor centers, on the other, for advantage in buying raw materials as well as manufactured articles and in the distribution of finished products, constantly threatened the stability of compromise adjustments and continues to do so except as rates and rate relations are fixed by public authority. In addition to the important points already named, there are in this area many others, among them being Rockford, Moline-Rock Island-Davenport, Cedar Rapids, Des Moines, St. Joseph, Topeka, Pueblo, Cheyenne, Lincoln, Sioux City, Sioux Falls, Butte, Great Falls, Winona, Fargo, Kenosha, Racine, and Madison. In this area motor-vehicle competition, truck and bus, is rapidly becoming more important though, as in the South, such competition did not become serious as early as in the Eastern District.

Southwestern Territory.—A second minor division of the great Western District is commonly known as Southwestern territory and lies west of the Mississippi and, roughly, south of a line from St. Louis through Kansas City to El Paso. Originally served almost wholly by lines built from St. Louis and Kansas City on the north and from the Gulf ports on the south, and even yet served chiefly by properties whose major interest is Southwestern, this area has been entered by many other lines, particularly Granger and Transcontinental. For those lines operating almost exclusively in this territory, even for those others which are but partially interested here, the principal outlying centers of interest are St. Louis, Memphis, and New Orleans on the Mississippi; Port Arthur, Houston, and Galveston on the Gulf; and El Paso, Wichita, and Kansas City on the west and north. Within this area lie other important points such as Oklahoma City, Tulsa, Fort Worth, Dallas, Wichita Falls, Waco, San Antonio, Beaumont, Shreveport, Little Rock, and Fort Smith. Here again, a rate structure peculiar to the territory developed, and in its determination the quite unusual tariff governing movements throughout the state of Texas played an interesting and important part.

Among the more important properties operating almost wholly in this section are the Missouri-Kansas-Texas, the St. Louis-San Francisco, the Missouri Pacific, the St. Louis Southwestern, and the Kansas City Southern, all of which radiate from St. Louis and Kansas City, together with the Texas and Pacific, the International and Great Northern, and the Gulf Coast lines. The Southern Pacific has a large mileage in this section, as have the Santa Fe and the Rock Island. Agricultural products furnish a relatively heavy proportion of the traffic of the Southwestern lines, grains and grain products, cotton, and fruits and vegetables being the important items. Manufactured goods also contribute a comparatively large tonnage, petroleum and other oils being an outstanding item. Beyond this, wide variation exists in the character of traffic; the railways operating in the southeastern portion of the territory show a heavy tonnage of forest products; those in the northeast of mineral products, among which bituminous coal is important, while those in the western portion have a relatively large movement of live stock.

Competition among individual railways has never been especially keen in this area but, as instruments in the struggle between industrial areas and among market centers, the carriers have played an important and active rôle. The rivalry between the New England-Middle Atlantic industrial area and that of the Middle West, between the market centers of Kansas City and St. Louis, between those northern gateways and the Gulf ports on the one hand and river ports such as Memphis on the other, between the Louisiana jobbing centers and those of Texas, and among the almost innumerable distributing points, large and small, throughout Texas, offers to the carriers a difficult problem indeed. With time, the situation has become increasingly complex, and doubtless both industrial and market competition will remain a disturbing factor in this section for many years to come. Recently the competitive situation has become threatening: the rapid development of highway service, particularly freight service, has brought to the fore many interesting and difficult problems that call for early solution.

Transcontinental Territory.—The third lesser area within the Western District is known as Transcontinental territory and includes that great expanse of country to the west of the Granger and Southwestern districts. The mileage in this territory is largely of a transcontinental character, as the term has come to be used, interest centering primarily in Los Angeles, San Francisco, Portland, and Seattle in the west and the western Gulf ports, Kansas City, Omaha, Chicago, Duluth, and Minneapolis-St. Paul in the east. In this territory, also, a peculiar rate adjustment developed from the exigencies of water competition via Cape Horn and Panama, and from railway self-interest. In Transcontinental territory there are three groupings of lines based upon geographical location. In the north are the Great Northern, the Northern Pacific, and the Chicago, Milwaukee, St. Paul, and Pacific, which serve Portland and Puget Sound in the west, and Duluth, Minneapolis-St. Paul, and Chicago in the east. Spokane, Butte, and Helena are major intermediate points. In the central group fall the Union Pacific-Central Pacific and the Denver and Rio Grande Western-Western Pacific, both combinations serving San Francisco on the west, and Ogden, Salt Lake City, and Denver in the intermediate section. The eastern terminus of the Denver and Rio Grande Western on transcontinental movements is Denver or Pueblo, but for the Union Pacific it is Council Bluffs. In the southern section lie two important routes also, the Santa Fe and the Southern Pacific. These, like the northern properties, are through lines under single ownership. These two carriers, as transcontinentals, serve San Francisco, Los Angeles, and San Diego on the west, Phoenix and El Paso in the intermediate area. In the east, however, the Southern Pacific has its prime interest in Texas and the Gulf ports while the Santa Fe, despite a considerable Texas and Oklahoma mileage, is concerned more particularly with points between Denver and Kansas City and with business originating, or received by it from others, between Kansas City and Chicago. As will be noted from this discussion, there is considerable overlapping of the Granger and northern transcontinental lines as well as of the southern transcontinentals and the Granger and Southwestern properties. Yet this overlapping is not so serious as to justify the neglect of clear lines of demarcation with respect to both physical location and traffic.

To describe traffic as a whole in Transcontinental territory is exceedingly difficult because of wide differences among the three groups of carriers. In the case of all, however, the products of agriculture as well as of animals and animal products contribute a much greater proportion of the total tonnage than they do for the entire United States. Lumber and lumber products also contribute heavily except for the central lines, while manufactures run slightly above normal except for the northern group. The tonnage of minerals and mineral products is comparatively small throughout the entire area and passenger business is light except for the two southern properties. Among the individual items which loom large on all roads are grain and grain products, also fruits and vegetables. Live-stock tonnage is conspicuous in the case of the central and northern groups as is oil in the south. Import and export traffic moving through this territory is another important, though declining, source of revenue.

In discussing the competitive situation two facts deserve especial note. The struggle among railways which played an important rôle during earlier years has been brought under effective control and market competition in the intermediate territory has also been reduced, though it is active among coast points and also between those points and intermediate centers. Competition between the railways and water carriers has developed rapidly in recent years, however, with the separation of the Southern Pacific from its boat lines and with the advantages offered by the Panama Canal. This competition has been sharpened by the fact that it is largely a vehicle for industrial competition: the struggle for control of the intermediate and Pacific coast business is exceedingly keen between those two rivals, the New England-Middle Atlantic section and the Middle West. Indeed, were it not for rigid control of rates by the Interstate Commerce Commission, competition would soon become cutthroat here.

Permanence of Existing Territorial Groupings.—Changes in economic conditions and in railway alliances, the construction of new mileage, and other factors may result in certain modifications of the territories just described. It is unlikely that such changes will shift materially the boundaries of the New England, Trunk Line, and Southern territories; extensive consolidation alone could change points of major interest and modify rate structures that are suited to particular sections. Boundaries in the West, however, are less definite and final and the identity of particular carriers with certain areas less fixed, as is clearly attested by the westward extension of the Santa Fe and, later, the Milwaukee; by the entry of the Rock Island and the Santa Fe into Southwestern territory; and by the expansion of the Burlington into a semi-transcontinental. Traffic conditions will change greatly as time passes, particularly in the West and South; the steady shift from frontier to live stock and agriculture and from these to industry will be accurately chronicled in the tonnage of the railways.

Competitive conditions will be modified by many factors. The development of motor-truck transportation in the more populous areas will be rapid and to this new agency will go much of the short-haul tonnage. Future policy concerning waterway development and plans for the more extensive utilization of existing routes will greatly concern the railways, too, and will alter competitive adjustments. These will be changed, also, by the development of new industrial areas and by modification in the relations of railways, both competitive and supplementary. And, finally, to the extent that regulatory bodies exercise active control over matters of detail and of policy, competition will assume new aspects.

Railway Mileage of the United States.—The magnitude of the railway system of the United States has already been suggested to the reader. That a more definite appreciation may be had of the extent and significance of this great field of enterprise, however, certain data portraying various phases will be presented. The total railway mileage of the United States at the close of 1930 was 249,052, of which 240,675 was operated by Class I companies. The total trackage exceeds that figure, however, by perhaps as much as 165,000 miles. These properties in 1930 were owned, it would appear, by 1,497 separate corporations, but of these only 697 were engaged actively in operation. The concentration of mileage control is greater, however, than the number of proprietary or operating corporations would indicate. In fact, 156 Class I railways own 69 per cent and operate more than 92 per cent of the total mileage of the country and 30 of the largest of this group, less than 5 per cent of the total number of active companies, operate almost 70 per cent of that mileage. Indeed, 97 per cent of the mileage of the United States is operated by the Class I and Class II roads, which constitute but 55 per cent of the total number of operating properties.

Relation of Mileage to Population and Area.—Absolute mileage figures give a less accurate representation of facts and have less of true meaning, however, than a figure which indicates the extent of mileage development in proportion to those two significant factors, population and area. In the determination of such relative figures, population per mile of line and miles of line per 100 square miles of territory have been widely used: upon that basis Table XII has been constructed to show the position in 1930 of certain of the states.

Complete figures indicate clearly that the number of miles of railway per unit of population is tremendously greater in the less densely settled areas, South, Southwest, and Transcontinental, while the mileage per unit of area tends to vary directly with population density. To say what should be regarded as a satisfactory relation is exceedingly difficult, though certainly it would appear that something nearer an equality than is shown by the extremes in the table is desirable. On such basis it would appear that the area lying between Chicago and St. Louis in the west, and New York and Baltimore on the Atlantic seaboard, is perhaps better supplied with mileage from both standpoints than any other considerable section of the United States. Ranking next are the New England states, and following in turn are the Southern, Granger, Southwestern, and Transcontinental territories. For the United States as a whole, 1930 shows 8.4 miles of line per 100 square miles of territory and 493 people per mile of line.

TABLE XII.—POPULATION PER MILE OF LINE AND MILES OF LINE PER 100 SQUARE MILES OF AREA FOR SELECTED STATES, 1930*

State	Population per mile of line	Rank in United States	Miles per 100 square miles	Rank in United States
Western				
Nevada	42	48	1.93	48
Montana	102	47	3.58	42
Wyoming	109	46	2.09	47
North Dakota	129	45	7.51	35
New Mexico	150	44	2.31	45
Eastern				
New York	1,517	5	17.43	10
Connecticut	1,657	4	20.17	6
New Jersey	1,753	3	30.63	1
Massachusetts	2,109	2	25.20	2
Rhode Island	3,506	1	17.82	8

* *Railway Statistics of the United States*, 1930, p. 22.

TABLE XIII.—POPULATION PER MILE OF LINE AND MILES OF LINE PER 100 SQUARE MILES OF AREA—SELECTED COUNTRIES OF EUROPE*

Country	Population per mile of line	Miles per 100 square miles
Europe (as a whole)	2,026	5.6
Germany	1,723	19.9
France	1,227	15.6
Italy	2,983	10.9
Belgium	1,153	58.8
Great Britain and Ireland	1,991	20.0
Spain	2,208	5.0
Denmark	1,080	19.2
Sweden	603	5.8
Norway	1,172	1.9
Russia (European)	3,239	1.6

* *Railway Statistics of the United States*, 1930, p. 32.

That an accurate basis of comparison may be had between the United States and the European countries where railway development has been carried farthest beyond our own boundaries, the figures for certain of the more important of those European countries, with respect to both population and area are given in Table XIII, the same units being employed as in the case of the United States.

Vital Importance of the Railway.—The importance of the railway, the history of which has been told in preceding chapters and the economic significance of which has been indicated by the facts immediately preceding, cannot easily be exaggerated in a consideration of the development of our material resources, past and future. A Russian economist has attributed America's phenomenal economic progress to the rapid construction of railway mileage into new areas awaiting development, and has argued that this forward movement has been, and may be expected to continue to be, directly proportionate to railway expansion.[1] It is easy to confuse cause and effect, to explain economic progress in terms of railway building when that building was the consequence of development, yet it is a truism that, without satisfactory transportation, both economic and social progress are almost imperceptible. Until Russia, Siberia, China, and, indeed, the numberless newer and less known areas in South America and Africa are pierced and gridironed by the railway or served by some equally effective agency of transportation, notable progress will be impossible. In America, thousands of miles of railway were built into undeveloped areas and these lines constituted the highway which the strong-hearted and the adventurous traveled as they went out to seek victory upon the frontier. That others followed in great numbers and to an effective purpose is attested by the striking utilization of our natural resources and by the appearance, within the span of a few decades, of great states and populous cities in the now almost conquered West. The railways have been of inestimable value in the past; upon their effective service, or upon the service of a successor which has not yet appeared, rests largely the continuance of that economic progress which has distinguished the century of railway development now barely closed. The improvement and extension of agencies of transportation are vital to future progress, economic, social, political, and even intellectual; essential, as one of those agencies, is the railway.

REFERENCES

Bureau of Railway Economics: *Statistical Reports.*

Bureau of Railway News and Statistics: *Railway Statistics of the United States.*

Daggett, Stuart: *Principles of Inland Transportation*, Harper & Brothers, 1928.

Goldstein, J. M.: America's Wealth and Railway Expansion, *Railway Age*, vol. 71, p. 875.

[1] Goldstein, J. M., in the *Railway Age*, vol. 71, p. 875.

Haney, Lewis H.: *The Business of Railway Transportation*, Ronald Press Company, 1924.
Interstate Commerce Commission: *Statistics of Railways in the United States* (annual).
Johnson, E. R., and T. W. Van Metre: *Principles of Railroad Transportation*, D. Appleton & Company, 1921.
Raper, C. L.: *Railway Transportation*, G. P. Putnam's Sons, 1912.
Sakolski, A. M.: *American Railroad Economics*, The Macmillan Company, 1916.

CHAPTER XVIII

THE RAILWAY NET: ROUTES AND TERMINALS

THE recognized territorial groupings of American railways, with mention of the major lines serving each group, have been discussed in the chapter preceding. Before undertaking a presentation of the significant features of the various services rendered by the railways, it is desirable to give certain facts relative to flow of traffic as well as to the facilities utilized by the railways in important centers in handling both freight and passengers. A presentation of essential facts relative to traffic routes will first be made and that followed by some observations concerning terminals designed to give the reader a better understanding of the problem there presented.

TRAFFIC ROUTES

Major Traffic Routes.—In a country possessed of such a network of railways as is the United States there are inevitably almost numberless combinations of lines over which traffic regularly flows, channels through which persons and goods move from one area to another. To indicate all these and to set forth the character of traffic movements over each would be both a monumental and bootless task; it is, however, important that the major of these routes be indicated broadly and basic facts given as to the present situation as well as to the probable future of each.

Yet before so doing it will be well, perhaps, to suggest the explanation for the existence and the continuance through long periods of rather definite routes. Agencies of transport are but instrumentalities in the exchange of goods and the transfer of persons. Conditions that tend to promote trade or movement between two areas also tend, therefore, to bring into being needed instrumentalities and to stimulate the rendition of requisite services. Exchange of goods is most likely as between areas unlike in character: between the area that produces raw materials and that which offers finished products; between the territory that is climatically fitted to produce the hardier cereals and that which Nature designed to provide items grown only in the warmer climes. Important routes may come into being and persist, too, because they represent channels through which traffic moves to more distant points—in import or export trade. Analysis will show that in practically each instance differences in the character of production, because of industrial or climatic differences, explain the existence of a particular route; and, *pari passu*, as such variance becomes greater or less, the importance of routes will be correspondingly modified.

The significant rail traffic routes of the United States are seven in number. These are,

1. Trunk Line route.
2. Piedmont route.
3. Northwest-Atlanta route.
4. Mississippi Valley route.
5. Midwest-Gulf route.
6. Granger route.
7. Transcontinental route.

Of these some are more deeply etched in our national economic life than are others because of greater economic importance, because of age, or

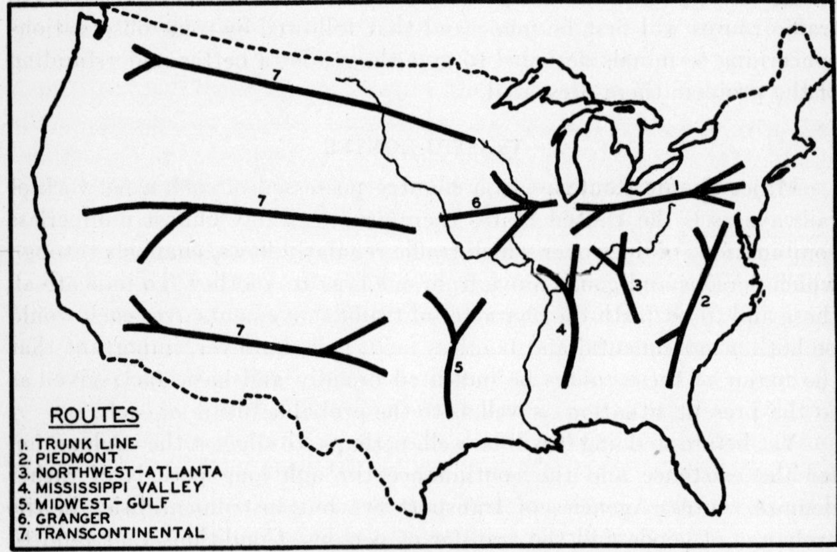

FIG. 21.—Major railway traffic routes in the United States.

because of the conjunction of both factors. To these major routes might be added others of a specialized character, such as from the Pocahontas district, or those of lesser general significance, such as the Pacific coast route. However, the essential purpose of this presentation will be accomplished by the consideration of the seven listed above.

The Trunk Line Route.—This route had its inception in the dreams of the pioneers who looked across the Appalachian Barrier and saw the Northwest Territory as a hinterland for the industries of the older states and for Atlantic ports. The first step toward the realization of these dreams came in the construction of the Erie Canal and the Pennsylvania

Portage Railway—and the second, a long stride forward, with proof that the railway was a practicable agency of transport. When the railways from the North Atlantic ports had advanced to Chicago and to St. Louis in the Middle West, they occupied at once an important place in the economic scheme. As other railways were pushed westward into Granger territory and as the "transcontinentals" were constructed, the Trunk Line channel increased in significance: it early became and has continued to be the most important of all rail traffic routes in the country, for both tonnage and passengers.

This preeminence is the consequence of a number of causes. The Middle Atlantic and New England states became industrialized early: they desired a market for finished products and had need of the agricultural products which the great Mississippi Valley was able to furnish cheaply. The Trunk Lines also furnished the cheapest and most accessible route for the movement of the agricultural surplus of the West into export trade: cheapest because natural conditions were favorable to railway operation and accessible because European steamship lines did not serve Gulf ports nor did north-and-south railway service equal that to the east. For these and other reasons not only a great volume of domestic traffic moved over this route but it was also able to dominate the import and export trade—serving a hinterland that comprised the whole of the United States beyond the Allegheny Mountains except for that area contiguous to the Gulf. With the passage of time and the change in conditions, this dominance has lessened—yet not sufficiently to imperil the first rank of the Trunk Line route: its losses have been divided among too many other routes, rail and water.

Prior to the industrialization of the East North Central states the Trunk Line route carried finished products westward for use in that area and beyond the Mississippi, such products originating in the New England and Middle Atlantic states. Westward also moved imports in considerable volume. Eastward were transported agricultural products and certain other raw materials produced in the Lake and Valley states. With the gradual industrialization of those states, the westward flow of finished products lessened but the eastward movement of agricultural and other raw materials continued in even greater volume as railway construction opened great areas to the westward of Chicago and St. Louis. This eastbound movement was in part for domestic consumption, in part for export. And, as industrialization in the Western area progressed, a considerable eastbound tonnage of manufactured goods was offered for use along the Atlantic seaboard and for export. As a consequence of the different character of the west- and eastbound tonnage, the volume of the latter much exceeded that of the former.

The significance of the Trunk Line route is indicated by freight statistics: in 1930 the railways of the Eastern District, constituting but 24 per cent of our mileage, carried more than half of the revenue tons moved by the railways of the United States in that year and are credited with more than 43 per cent of the revenue ton-miles. And it may not be amiss to add that these same railways carried 65 per cent of the passengers and rendered 57 per cent of our passenger business as measured in passenger-miles. To this predominance in both passenger and freight business the Pennsylvania and the New York Central contribute well-nigh half, subsidiary properties ignored. However, there are at work influences that will tend to deflect traffic from this area and over other routes. Of these discussion will appear in proper course. Yet it is unlikely that the dominant position of this route, serving an area of dense population and constituting a principal avenue from east to west, will be imperiled within the predictable future.

The Piedmont Route.—In the period prior to the railway, exchange of goods between the industrial North and the agricultural South was important. As the railway net was extended, however, this new instrumentality was utilized in the place of coastwise vessels, first driven by wind and later by steam. Natural conditions are favorable to railway operation through the Piedmont territory and, as the major properties serving in this area enter the heart of the old South, they spread in such manner as to serve from the Atlantic seaboard westward to Alabama. Northward over this route have long moved cotton, deciduous and citrus fruits, lumber, and vegetables, while the return traffic has been largely finished goods seeking a market. A number of important cities are served by the railways between Richmond and Washington, the northern termini of these lines, and Atlanta, which is the objective of every railway entering the southeastern portion of the United States.

Operative in the district served by the lines that constitute the Piedmont route are forces that suggest impending change. Almost exclusively agricultural in the past, the Southern grower depended for his finished goods upon other areas, giving cotton and items of lesser importance in exchange therefor. In more recent years, however, an increase in industrial activity has been apparent in the South, with a suggestion of a quickening in the trend. Should this movement continue, the southeastern section will become increasingly capable of satisfying its own needs for finished goods, though the outbound movement of such items as cotton, fruit, vegetables, and other specialized products will show little diminution.

Of the railways serving in Southern territory, only three appear as important carriers in this district: the Southern, the Atlantic Coast Line, and the Seaboard Air Line. Other railways here, with the exception of the Florida East Coast, participate but incidentally in the commercial and industrial life of the Piedmont area.

Northwest-Atlanta Route.—Early in the period of railway development business interests in the "Old South" evidenced a keen interest in establishing satisfactory contact with the Ohio River territory and such markets upon the Ohio as Cincinnati and Louisville were equally eager to distribute in the South. To serve this reciprocal interest railways were early constructed and the service thus rendered has been augmented through the years to meet a growing interest of the rapidly industrializing Lake states area in Southern markets. The active entry of the industrial district developing west of the Allegheny Mountains into these Southern markets precipitated sharp competition between the carriers constituting the Piedmont route and those from the northwest serving the area for which Atlanta is the distributing center. This resulting railway competition became cutthroat at times and was always difficult to keep in hand: sometimes, indeed, it broadened so far as to involve Trunk Line carriers in its follies—tonnage moving into the South from the Chicago district via eastern seaboard points and from those points via Cincinnati and Cairo. At all times the rivalry between the industrial interests of the East and the Lower Lakes area exerted a strong influence upon the adjustment of rates from those sections into the South, an attempt being made to maintain an agreed relationship between the Baltimore-Atlanta and the Ohio River-Atlanta rates. In the earlier years this adjustment was definitely favorable to the East but as time has passed various forces have operated to effect the establishment of a more equitable relation. Yet always in the background was the presence of water competition between the North and South Atlantic ports as a rate-determining force.

The character of the traffic moving between the southeastern states and the northwest differs not greatly from that between the former and the northeast. Into the North move fruit, vegetables, lumber, and cotton; to the South move manufactured goods, with this southbound movement supplemented by a considerable volume of grain and grain products, and meats. North of the Ohio interchange traffic has the choice of many railway lines to and from the Ohio River Crossings; from those Crossings southward, however, service is largely in the hands of the Louisville and Nashville, the Southern, and Illinois Central systems. Of these, the two first named are able to dominate because they offer more direct routes, with the Louisville and Nashville the more aggressive because of its exclusive interest in this route as against the Piedmont. Essentially the same modifying factors are operative upon this route as upon that occupying the Atlantic coastal plain; over the Northwest-Atlanta route, however, there seems to be in grains and meats and in the agricultural products of the South a permanent basis of exchange.

Mississippi Valley Route.—The advantage enjoyed by movement upon navigable streams over movement by highway made the Mississippi an artery of commerce early in the development of the West. With the acceptance of the railway, it is not strange that interest was evidenced early in the construction of a line between Chicago and the Gulf. Indeed, it was to make such a line a reality that the first federal land grants in aid of railway construction were made. From this beginning in the middle of the past century, construction moved forward until by the close of that century a great network of lines was available to those using this route—a network that converges upon Chicago in the North and upon New Orleans in the South, but that is in the lower Valley of considerable width.

This route is one that depends for its volume of traffic upon production differences between the North and South in part, in part upon import and export business. Moving southbound are grains and grain products, meat products, manufactured articles for domestic and export trade, and other lesser items. Northbound are sent the agricultural products of the South—cotton, lumber, fruits and vegetables, and sugar—as well as a great volume of import business: coffee, sugar, fertilizers, tropical fruits, and a great variety of other goods for which a demand exists in the upper Mississippi Valley. For this import and export traffic the competition is keen—and has been from early days: there is sharp rivalry not only among the divergent railways that constitute this route but, in more recent years, between them and the revivified river routes. And competition between the carriers of the Trunk Line route and those operating between Lake Michigan and the Gulf has been, and continues to be in an even increasing measure, a factor in the determination of rates.

The number of railways over which traffic may move between Chicago and points on the Ohio and Mississippi between Louisville and St. Louis is large: among the more important of these are the Monon, the Chicago and Eastern Illinois, the Alton, the Wabash, the Big Four, and the Illinois Central. Beyond the river Crossings but one of these properties, the last named, continues into the South; however, an effective system of interchange enables the Louisville and Nashville, the Mobile and Ohio, the Missouri Pacific system, and other combinations of properties to render a service that is competitive with the one through line. Because of sharp differences in the character of the territory served by northern and southern sections of the Valley route, and because there is but a comparatively slight movement toward industrialization in the lower Valley area, it is likely that the volume of interchange will increase rather than decline with the years. This route is also certain to occupy an important place in import and export trade, a place that will doubtless become significant in time. Except, therefore, as the river cuts sharply into the volume of traffic handled by the railways, it is probable that tonnage upon the lines in this area should be at least constant—except as local traffic is diverted to the highways.

Midwest-Gulf Route.—Another route from the North Central states into the South lies to the west of the Mississippi River and constitutes a channel through which flows a wide variety of traffic moving in domestic and foreign commerce. Because the trans-Mississippi area was settled later than the territory to the east, the development of this route has been comparatively recent in point of time: indeed, because of certain shifts in production and trade, it has undergone striking changes within the past score of years and is likely to experience further change in the immediate future.

The first area west of the Mississippi to give promise of tonnage sufficient to justify railway construction was Texas. Initially served from the Gulf ports by wagon and later by short railway lines, it proved a lodestone for railways projected from the North and Northeast: to gain a place in this market construction was pushed from St. Louis and Kansas City. This construction brought many railways into the territory—some having an almost exclusive interest in it and others representing extensions from adjacent areas. Among the former the more important are the Missouri-Kansas-Texas, the St. Louis-San Francisco, the Missouri Pacific, the Kansas City Southern, and the St. Louis Southwestern, while among the latter are the Chicago, Rock Island, and Pacific and the Atchison, Topeka, and Santa Fe.

For a considerable period the southbound tonnage over these lines consisted largely of manufactured goods and food products for domestic consumption, while the northbound movement was dominantly live stock, lumber, fresh fruits and vegetables, and certain other products of the territory. An excess of mileage and the relatively small volume of tonnage long made the financial way of these carriers hard as compared with others in Western territory; however, with the discovery of petroleum throughout the Southwest and the development of a considerable volume of export movement of grains via the western Gulf ports, the situation changed sharply and the status of the railways serving this area improved. This improvement has been checked measurably, however, by the appearance of the motor vehicle in large numbers upon the highways: in no section is the struggle between the railway and its more recent competitor more keen than in the Southwest.

Granger Route.—The railways had hardly entered Chicago from the east before, in response to public demand for better transportation service to the westward, lines were projected into that great agricultural hinterland toward and beyond the Mississippi River. These projected lines rapidly became an actuality and into Chicago there poured as into the mouth of a funnel a volume of agricultural products that increased steadily with the years. By construction and by the acquisition of short, independent properties the territory that has come to be identified by the term Granger was soon gridironed by those major carriers named in the chapter preceding. For many years almost the entire surplus of grains, live stock, and other farm products moved over the rails of these carriers into Chicago. From this point these foodstuffs were moved eastward in great volume in domestic and export trade, with a lesser diversion into Southern territory. Time has effected considerable modifications in channels in the case of this outbound movement, however, particularly with respect to grain and grain products. From Duluth and Superior grain tonnage is moving in increasing volume to eastern lake ports; the growing importance of the western Gulf ports in the export grain trade has trenched upon the eastward flow from southern Granger territory; and the determined efforts to reestablish service upon the Mississippi may cause an important further diversion from Chicago and the lines carrying eastward from that center. Because of the peculiar needs of the traffic, animals and animal products still continue to move eastward over old routes—with dairy products of increasing significance.

Westbound into Granger territory has moved from early days a wide variety of manufactured goods. Initially these moved from the eastern industrial district over the trunk lines and through Chicago into the agricultural areas; later traffic originated largely in the East North Central states; and, in due course, the Chicago district itself became the important source of supply. More recently, with the development of industry in Wisconsin, western Illinois, Missouri, Iowa, Minnesota, and even in states beyond, local supply has become more significant. Yet inbound traffic is largely of this type, supplemented by lumber, fruits, fresh vegetables, and other consumption items. However, these lines which constitute the Granger route serve yet another function: they act as "bridge lines" for tonnage interchanged between carriers to the east and the so-called transcontinental railways, except in the few instances where those transcontinentals reach Chicago over their own rails. The "Granger roads" have played a great part in the upbuilding of the upper Mississippi Valley and remain essential to its prosperity, yet the volume of traffic moving by rail in recent years has not been such as to give promise of a particularly bright future for them.

Transcontinental Routes.—It has been common experience that a railway is constructed from a given point to some definite objective, perhaps widely removed, with the expectation that the intervening territory will develop sufficiently to provide for the enterprise an adequate economic substructure. Yet it is improbable that even the most optimistic among those whose energy and vision made possible the building of the early transcontinental railways envisioned an intermediate territory contributing heavily in the form of traffic to the financial success of those projects. Rather, these lines represented largely an attempt to bridge that great stretch of mountain and desert that lay between the rapidly developing Mississippi Valley and the Pacific coast. Such was clearly the purpose that lay back of the initial undertaking, the Union Pacific-Central Pacific, likewise the Northern Pacific, the Southern Pacific, and the Santa Fe. However, expectations of the intermediate area were higher on the part of those who drove to completion the Great Northern and the Denver and Rio Grande Western, as well as, in later years, the western extension of the Milwaukee.

The railways that serve Transcontinental territory fall into three groups, as noted in the chapter preceding. The effective eastern terminus of the northern lines is Chicago, and until recently these lines have been interested in the West only in Portland and the Puget Sound ports. But by recent construction, and through cooperation with the Western Pacific, the Great Northern now becomes an active competitor in the San Francisco area. The central transcontinentals have a fundamental western interest in the San Francisco district, with an eastern interest that is less definite: the Union Pacific terminates as to traffic in Chicago, while the Missouri Pacific-Denver and Rio Grande Western-Western Pacific base primarily upon St. Louis and Kansas City, with Chicago as a secondary traffic point. However, through the Oregon Short Line and the Oregon-Washington Railroad and Navigation Company the Union Pacific reaches the Pacific Northwest, and southern California is reached by the Los Angeles and Salt Lake. Similarly, in the case of the southern transcontinentals, overlapping is clearly evident. Both the Southern Pacific and the Santa Fe serve the San Francisco area and the former reaches north to Portland. In the Mississippi Valley both of these southern lines serve the Gulf, and the Santa Fe has long been an active factor in the Chicago district—competing there with both the northern and central lines. More recently the Southern Pacific has, through its acquisition of control of the St. Louis Southwestern, reached northward to St. Louis, thus coming into more active competition with the central route. It is clearly evident that there is no lack of rivalry for the long haul, both west- and eastbound, between the Middle West and the Pacific coast. And the more is this true with an increasing volume of traffic moving through the Panama Canal in recent years—a volume that will increase if the expectations of those urging internal waterway development are realized in any major degree.

In the chapter preceding a brief statement has been made concerning the character of the traffic of the transcontinental lines. Suffice it here to say that, because of the increasing use of the Panama route, the participation of the railways in traffic between the Eastern as well as the Midwestern states and the Orient has declined, as has the railway portion of traffic originating at and destined to Pacific coast points. The greater the extent to which a particular "transcontinental" must rely for its financial success upon miscellaneous through business, the more serious its problem in recent years. Nor does it seem that the intermediate territory, long the victim of an unreasonably discriminatory rate structure, is likely to profit in the long run because of the Interstate Commerce Commission's refusals during recent years to give the railways Fourth Section relief that they may withstand more successfully the inroads of water competition. Tonnage into and out of the Intermountain states these railways will hold and traffic with respect to which speedy service is of greater importance than the rate, such as vegetables and fruits, will also tend to remain with the rails. As to other business, however, the future is uncertain.

TERMINALS

At such times as the railway occupies place in our thinking, it is probable that with few exceptions it is visualized as a grade occupying the center of a right of way and extending from horizon to horizon, this grade surmounted by parallel lines of steel upon which a powerful locomotive draws cars laden with passengers or with freight. Some few might picture the railway as a great and dynamic organization concerned with the handling of traffic, but the individual is rare who includes as a part of his concept those portions of the property of the railway known as the terminals. And, if such is done, it will be some metropolitan passenger station, palatial in its stone and marble and glass, that comes into mind—or possibly some freight station to which deliveries have been made or from which shipments have been moved. But that intricate and elaborate network of trackage utilized in the rendition of diverse services through the passenger and freight station, over the shipping platforms of industrial concerns, and from extensive public teaming tracks, is known to few and by as few is its importance realized. Yet here it is that success or failure is largely determined: equipment is so largely standardized, methods of operation so closely comparable, and time between terminals fixed within such narrow limits by physical conditions and competitive considerations, that differences have come to lie largely in the terminal.

Importance of Terminals.—In general, the two fundamental factors in determining whether traffic will move over one rather than another of competitive lines are accessibility and speed. Just as the shipper will move his tonnage over the line to which goods can be delivered at least cost, speed of movement being equal, so will the traveler utilize the service of that property that necessitates least preliminary and consequent movement—for it is not enough that the terminal situation be satisfactory at the point of origin: the situation at destination is quite as significant. Vital elements, then, in the terminal problem are *location* and *organization*—with the former perhaps to be stressed because standard layouts and standard practice have tended to produce a degree of uniformity in organization that has minimized its importance except as certain physical limitations have served to make it impossible to operate particular terminal properties as effectively as others not suffering such limitations. And, because terminal location is a matter of great significance to the city as a whole, exerting certain determining influences upon city growth, it might be added that municipalities are concerning themselves increasingly with this aspect of railway operations—even to the extent of compelling changes, presumptively in public interest, that impose heavy burdens upon the carrier or carriers affected.

The superiority of the early railway over all other means of transport was so great and the problems of line operation so difficult that attention tended to concentrate upon such operating problems. Only as competition developed and as preference might be shown did the need of adequate terminal facilities appear prominently. For railways built from or into important centers of population such terminals were difficult to acquire: costs were in general such as to prohibit the acquisition of sufficient areas centrally located to meet immediate needs. Characteristically, therefore, less valuable property was acquired not far from the center of manufacture and trade—about which development was rapid in the growing cities of the United States. Today, in consequence, terminals that were initially outlying now frequently occupy areas of high value in the heart of the business district. And railways so intrenched have occupied a position of advantage from which newer entrants into that field have found it impossible to dislodge them: the older enjoy a species of competitive advantage that is so marked as to constitute partial monopoly.

At centers that grew up along the railway in new territory, adequate terminals for the pioneer property were merely a matter of foresight in reserving for railway use sufficient areas to meet future needs. Where this was done, the early entrants again found themselves possessed of exceptional advantages over later arrivals. True, such advantages in our cities have not been an unmixed blessing: while a central site is more accessible to shipper and traveler, its possession makes expansion difficult; entails heavy expenses in complying with growing social requirements; imposes upon the carrier a heavy tax burden; and increases sharply the value of the property upon which a fair return must be earned. None the less, the losses due to an unfavorable location have been such that no price seemed too great to pay for access to the heart of the city if that price be within the credit limitations of the carrier suffering handicap. The Pennsylvania Railroad made outlays in excess of $100,000,000 to gain entry to Manhattan Island over its own rails, while the New York Central spent upon its new station in New York City little less than $200,000,000. Upon such magnificent structures to serve passenger traffic the railways of the United States have spent huge sums: no great city considers itself treated with proper respect by the railways serving it unless untold millions have been expended to add thus to the architectural wonders of the place. And too often it is the number of such grand structures that stirs the pride of the citizenry, rather than development in accordance with a plan that will provide maximum public service at minimum cost to the railways concerned. Of vital significance to the railway, yet at the same time often an almost intolerable burden, adequate terminals that are suitably located to permit the carrier to share in competitive traffic have presented a problem exceedingly difficult of solution—though a problem that becomes, because of the decline in passenger traffic and the possibilities of the motor vehicle, increasingly less acute.

The Passenger Terminal.—While the traveler performs for himself, in the main, the loading and unloading for which the carrier must assume responsibility at freight stations, the carrier finds that to appeal effectively for passenger traffic it must give weight to certain considerations that are of little consequence in the case of freight. Large sums have been expended for facilities promoting the more effective handling of freight, yet these are in no sense comparable to the fortunes that have been expended to provide the ultimate in convenience in major cities for the passenger. For the passenger, too, many services are required that impose an additional burden. And it is vital that the passenger station be centrally located with respect to urban transportation lines: a difference of but a few blocks in the distances of the stations of rival properties from surface line, subway, or elevated has often been the difference between success and failure in the competitive struggle.

In monumental passenger stations cities have taken great pride and to secure them have often exerted great pressure. Upon such stations the railways have expended not only huge sums but also most careful thought—for these structures, built largely in the days when passenger traffic was expected to increase steadily with the years, were expected to care not only for all present needs but also to make it possible to handle an increased volume of business by minor additions and modifications to the plant. A sufficient area for the construction of a station having been acquired and effective access to that area gained, the primary problems remaining were those of track layout and station arrangement. The problem of financing such a huge undertaking must not be ignored, however, for few such represent an outlay of less than ten to twenty million dollars—and from that point the figure mounts until the costs of the Grand Central and Pennsylvania terminals in New York City are reached.

Because the minimum cost of a large passenger terminal is so great and because accommodations in excess of the needs of a single railway can be provided without a proportionate increase in total expenditure, coupled with the fact that traveler convenience is often served by the joint terminal, it has been quite common for railways to cooperate in the construction and operation of expensive passenger terminals. This cooperation extends from provision for related lines, as in the case of the Long Island's use of the Pennsylvania's terminal upon Manhattan, to the use of a common terminal by all important properties entering a city, as illustrated by the situation in Denver, Kansas City, St. Louis, Washington, and a few other important centers—with occasional instances of adjacent stations such as have been developed in Omaha. A more common situation, however, is that illustrated by Chicago, where a few stations serve all but a small number of lines—a tendency evidencing itself for those lines to use a common terminal that serve diverse areas. Illustrative of this is the grouping of the Pennsylvania, the Alton, the Milwaukee, and the Burlington in the Union Station.

As railway terminals interfere increasingly with city growth and city planning, however, there appears a definite tendency to attempt to force further unification of terminals and the acceptance of locations consonant with city needs. It is such a problem that the railways and the city of Chicago have faced and for the solution of which a plan had been devised before passenger traffic began to decline so sharply as to make doubtful the wisdom of large expenditures for passenger accommodation. Because of this drop it is possible that financial expediency will compel a modification of previous plans. But in any relocation of passenger terminals, high importance must continue to be attached to ease of accessibility to urban transportation agencies if the carrier's competitive position is to be maintained: this, despite the fact that heavy costs—indeed, the financial burden of stations now in use—can ill be borne by the dwindling volume of traffic.[1] Many railways are today facing the necessity of deciding whether economic justification longer exists for the continuance of such costly service and more will face that same necessity except as passenger-traffic trends are reversed. What the solution may be is uncertain, but it is possible that the success of the plan evolved by the Baltimore and Ohio for handling Manhattan passengers to and from its Jersey terminals by bus is suggestive of changes that can be made to the railways' great financial advantage. And perhaps palatial structures devoted to commerce and trade will suffice for those whose civic pride led them in another economic era to demand magnificence in stations upon a parity with or superior to all urban rivals.

The Freight Terminal.—While the location and organization of the passenger terminal will vary within certain limits because of differences in conditions in the cities under consideration, such limits of variance will be narrow as compared with those that govern in the location of freight terminals and that determine the character of such terminals. Indeed, the freight-terminal problem is an individual one for each area

[1] One type of passenger traffic using the great urban passenger terminals that is unlikely to decline so long as city growth continues is the suburban or "commuter" traffic. To the extent that this type of business is significant at any particular point, extensive use will continue to be made of a terminal. Yet it is highly improbable that the carrier can afford to construct—or perhaps even to maintain—great structures for this traffic unless rates are increased sharply over present low levels. An important volume of commuter use of a railway complicates its problem greatly. Could some plan be devised under which the commuter might be brought in speedily by the steam lines and transferred directly to urban transport lines for delivery to destination? Or is there some other possible solution that offers promise?

in which freight originates: no plan, devised to meet the needs of one such area, and capable of so doing in a satisfactory manner, can be superimposed upon another without modification. But to make such a statement clear it is well to indicate of what stuff a freight terminal is made. In general, it consists of three features, the various freight houses, the industrial siding, and the public teaming track. In smaller cities served by but one line, a single freight house handles both inbound and outbound package freight and no transfer problem exists except as such cities are junction points at which an interchange of freight becomes essential. Industrial, or "private," sidings in such a community will be relatively few in number and team tracks will appear merely as portions of the carrier's sidings. As soon as such a city is served by two or more carriers, however, complexities develop. While the handling of package freight need not necessarily be changed greatly, it is possible that carrier agreements may call for the interchange there of small-lot interline shipments, which will necessitate a transfer house or the performance of that function at some other designated point. Demands will be made, too, for physical connection to facilitate the interchange of carload freight. To the extent that freight is interchanged incident to a continuous line-haul movement, no troublesome problem arises but a railway is often asked to perform a terminal service when no line-haul revenue accrues to it. The operation of all trackage within an area as a unit is highly advantageous to the patron of the railway, yet such unit operation is characteristically accepted only under the pressure of law or necessity by particular carriers that are favorably situated with respect to the control of originating traffic.

Unification so far as package shipments are involved may be attained by the maintenance of "universal" freight stations at reasonable intervals throughout a large city. Such stations, to serve most effectively, should handle both inbound and outbound lot shipments. They are generally located upon the rails of one or another of the carriers serving in the area and operated by that carrier, though they may be at off-line points—freight being trucked to and from rail points. Or, indeed, such service may be rendered by another agency of the character of the Chicago Tunnel railway. The larger the city, the greater the problem of package interchange becomes, yet the more important does a service of this character become to the shipper whose place of business may be many miles by busy city streets from the nearest freight station of the railway that must handle a particular consignment. Certainly one of the steps that can be made to further shipping by rail is to unify great terminals for the small-lot shipper as they have been unified for the user of railway service in car-lot units.

Terminal unification for the carload shipper may result from the establishment of reciprocal switching. In accordance with such an agreement, each carrier serving within the terminal area accepts cars for "spotting" upon designated teaming tracks or industrial sidings from all other railways in the area, in return for which final delivery is had of carload freight upon which this line has enjoyed the line haul. To facilitate such reciprocal switching the belt line is almost essential—and nowhere, perhaps, has the belt line been used to better advantage than in the Chicago district where, among others, the Belt Railway, the Baltimore and Ohio Chicago Terminal, the Elgin, Joliet, and Eastern, the Chicago Junction, the Chicago and Western Indiana, the Manufacturers' Junction, and the Indiana Harbor Belt cooperate to give users in that district a splendid service. Of these and other belt lines serving, some have their trackage wholly within the metropolitan area and place the car for loading and unloading; others, as inner or as outer belt lines, perform more largely an interchange function. And it is of interest to note that all belt and switching lines in the Chicago area, with the exception of the Elgin, Joliet, and Eastern—an outer belt line controlled by the United States Steel Corporation—are owned individually or jointly by the major railways serving that area.

A second method of "opening" a terminal is exemplified by St. Louis and New Orleans. In the latter the terminal properties are owned by the municipality, while in the former title to all terminal facilities—including a great union passenger station—lies in the Terminal Railroad Association of St. Louis. This unified property is owned and managed by the major railways serving the St. Louis district and such a private monopoly of facilities vital to the city seems to have legal sanction so long as certain policies are observed—among the more important of these being the admission of other railways to joint ownership and control upon reasonable terms, also the privilege of use of any terminal facilities by a railway refusing to become a joint owner upon the payment of a fair rental for such use. This plan for the unification of terminal operations is superior, perhaps, to that resting upon reciprocal switching among line-haul roads through belt lines variously owned—and especially would it seem superior if adopted early and developed in accordance with a comprehensive plan. However, where individual development has gone far and where a semi-fanatical adherence to competition is dominant among shippers, it is probable that reciprocal switching represents the more practical and more politic approach to terminal unification.

The magnitude of the task performed by the railways within a great terminal is well shown by a study made of operations in the Chicago area and published in 1927. In this area of 1,750 square miles served by 7,726 miles of trackage were moved during the test period an average of 34,791 cars daily—307 trains inbound and 302 trains outbound. These cars divided as follows:

Local traffic	Cars	Per cent
Inbound	10,409	30
Outbound	10,409	30
Intra-terminal	9,414	27
Total	30,232	87
Through traffic	4,559	13
Grand total	34,791	100

Of the inbound cars, 7,893 were loaded, and divided according to destination:

Destination	Cars	Per cent
Freight houses	1,108	14
Team tracks	760	10
Industries	6,025	76

Of the outbound local cars, 4,811 were loaded, and divided according to origin:

Origin	Cars	Per cent
Freight houses	2,118	44
Team tracks	264	5½
Industries	2,429	50½

Intra-terminal loaded-car movements totaled 3,634, and were handled thus:

Service facility	Originated		Destined	
	Cars	Per cent	Cars	Per cent
Freight houses	890	24	1,133	31
Team tracks	129	3	192	5
Industries	2,615	72	2,309	64

Of these loaded cars rendering an intra-terminal service 60 per cent originate and terminate on the same railway, 62 per cent originate and 51 per cent terminate on belt or switching railways, and 32½ per cent move in less-than-carload service. Outbound package-freight volume was double that of inbound and such outbound tonnage moved largely in home or home-route cars. In so far as possible, through traffic is interchanged (85½ per cent in this study had to be interchanged for delivery to destination) as far from the congested area as possible. Eighteen per cent was dropped off at the Elgin, Joliet, and Eastern or points equally distant, and an additional 43 per cent before the Indiana Harbor Belt had been reached—some 19 miles from the downtown area; a further 32 per cent had been dropped by the time the Belt Railway was reached some 10 miles out, another 6½ per cent interchanged before coming within 5 miles of the congested district, and only 19 cars (one-half of 1 per cent) were handled through the downtown zone—these being loaded largely with perishables, requiring special service.

Services beyond the Rail Terminal.—A very considerable volume of railway freight (97.5 per cent in 1930 upon Class I railways) moves in carload lots, being loaded by the consignor upon his own tracks characteristically and unloaded by the receiver under similarly advantageous conditions. In handling such traffic no problem of an *entire* transportation service arises because such a service is rendered. Other carload traffic is loaded on team tracks or unloaded at such point, perhaps both. Here only a *railway* transportation service is rendered and the same is true with respect to all small-lot shipments except as there be departure from standard practice. This partial performance of the transportation function by the railway compels the shipper and/or consignee to turn to others for completion. In the period that knew only the horse-drawn truck, recourse must be had to that tedious and somewhat costly means—and city streets were congested by these aids to service. Such was the nature of this agency, however, that hauls had of necessity to be short. With the widespread use of the motor truck the situation has changed strikingly: by this more effective agency both the consignor and consignee have benefited greatly, though the same cannot be said of the railways or the noncommercial user of the highways and streets.

But before considering the problem now confronting the railways in terminals as a consequence of the rise of motor-truck transport, it will be well to note what the steam carriers have done to meet the need of patrons for a more complete service. One of the early steps was to provide trap-car, sometimes called ferry-car, service. The trap car is placed upon the private tracks of an industrial or commercial concern, and into it are loaded all outbound small-lot shipments; when the loading is complete, the car is moved to a freight house where the shipments are unloaded, classified, and forwarded to destination. Similarly, into the trap car are loaded a miscellany of package shipments at the freight house, consigned to a particular concern with a private siding, the car being moved to that siding for unloading. The trap car thus reduced greatly the amount of drayage. For those enterprises lacking private sidings "universal" stations have been established in certain cities: to these, as indicated previously, shipments destined to points on any railway may be delivered. This again serves to hold drayage at a minimum.

Yet another method used by the railways to improve service within the terminal has been the off-track station. Such stations may be maintained by a single carrier, or cooperatively—in the latter case being in effect inland "universal" stations. To them less-than-carload shipments may be delivered and from them like shipments received, the railways assuming responsibility as at on-line points. Perhaps the most widely known use of such off-track stations is found in St. Louis, where the Columbia Transfer Company has long functioned as agent for the carriers in the operation of this unusual service. Closely akin to the off-line station in principle but rather different in fact is the so-called constructive station. At these latter none of the facilities for handling and storing shipments exists: rather, the constructive station is a point off the rails of the carrier and named in the tariff to which the carrier transports goods as a part of a continuous movement from or to the place of business of the consignor or consignee—liability between the railway and the constructive station resting upon the carrier and beyond such station upon the truck operator. In short, the actual operation of the constructive station plan places it in an intermediary position between the off-track station and store-door delivery.

Store-door delivery of package freight has long been an accepted feature of English freight service but, while it had been considered carefully by American railways from time to time, the record indicates its use by them until recent years was confined to Baltimore and Washington. Store-door delivery may represent an optional service for which an additional payment is made, as is true of the English and Canadian systems; it may rest upon compulsion, a single augmented rate covering the entire transportation service; or it may be optional, but with the cost of the additional service absorbed by the carrier under the rate formerly covering the rail movement alone. Certain advantages of store-door delivery are urged, among the more important of which are: inbound freight houses can be cleared expeditiously; lower trucking costs will result for most users from more efficient loading, more continuous operation, and reduction of duplicate services to a minimum; railways lacking centrally located terminals can compete more effectively for package movements—and, by the same sign, costly terminal expansion can be avoided and even expensive facilities replaced by less expensive; and, finally, it is urged as offering perhaps the only effective weapon to the railways in their struggle to regain, even hold, any considerable portion of the small-lot shipments that have been shifting so rapidly of late from railway to highway. Among the factors that have deterred the railways from moving in the direction of store-door delivery are the opposition of trucking interests; increased carrier responsibility in extending its service; unwillingness of concerns with trucking equipment to pay the railway for performance of this service; increase in rates necessary to meet added costs; and, perhaps most significant of all, inertia. But it seems that a program, carefully devised and sufficiently flexible to meet varying conditions, might be successfully adopted. Such a program will probably call for an optional service for which the consignor and consignee will be charged an additional sum representing bare cost; for full carrier responsibility for freight from door to door; and for the gradual application of the practice as experience shows the way. And, to lessen local opposition as well as to relieve the carrier of a heavy added responsibility, contracts might well be made with local trucking concerns to handle all small-lot shipments between door and rail. Or, as another alternative, the railway-owned Railway Express Agency might perform such collection and delivery of freight as it now does of express under a proper contractual arrangement. Either would seem preferable to direct operation of delivery equipment by the carrier—at least in all except the larger cities, and even here direct operation would seem to be of dubious wisdom, because of the added administrative burdens imposed. Experience indicates, however, that store-door delivery can be furnished at less cost by a railway through a controlled motor transport company than through contracts with private truckers—and yet direct administrative responsibility avoided.

Regulatory Control of Terminals.—The vital significance of terminal operations both to the railways and to the shipper, together with the opportunities for conflict of interest that are afforded, makes it inevitable that public authority be invoked to compel a proper service and to eliminate unreasonable discrimination. To this end certain specific legislation has been enacted by the states and state regulatory commissions have also functioned under general laws. Statutes and commission orders thereunder have dealt most often, perhaps, with the problem of physical connections between railways at points served by two or more railways and with construction of industrial spurs and sidings. The adequacy of facilities for handling freight has also been regarded and certain commissions have had the power to order the construction and operation of union passenger stations. Other matters, such as adequacy of service within the terminal and the determination of the boundary of a free switching district, have also often lain within the scope of state commission action. Yet, while a great number of cases affecting terminals have been handled by the states, their concern has been more largely with matters of detail than with broad and fundamental problems.

Under a system of regulation giving broad scope to state action, the intervention of federal authority did not seem essential; until 1920 the Interstate Commerce Commission had no authority over terminals except that conferred by the original Act which declared, "every common carrier . . . shall . . . afford all reasonable, proper, and equal facilities for the interchange of traffic between their respective lines. . . . " Yet it is stated, "but this shall not be construed as requiring any such common carrier to give the use of its tracks or terminal facilities to another carrier engaged in like business." True, the Commission might require physical connection between a railway and "any lateral branch line of railroad," but this proviso the courts interpreted strictly, with the result that the scope of regulatory action was slight. Under the preceding clause, however, the Commission was able to compel uniformity of railway policy with respect to the opening of a terminal: if a particular terminal were opened to one railway, to hold it closed to others was held to constitute unreasonable discrimination. Then, too, in the Panama Canal Act a step was taken by Congress to open rail-and-water terminals by breaking port and dock monopolies, also to eliminate exclusive agreements between particular rail and boat lines that effectively blocked competition.

It was in 1920 that the Interstate Commerce Act was so modified as to give broad powers over terminal operations. The law as it now stands declares, "If the Commission finds it to be in the public interest and to be practicable, without substantially impairing the ability of a carrier owning or entitled to the enjoyment of terminal facilities to handle its own business, it shall have power to require the use of any such terminal facilities, including main-line track or tracks for a reasonable distance outside such terminal, of any carrier, by another carrier or other carriers, on such terms and for such compensation as the carriers may agree upon"—with further provisions for the determination of the compensation in event of disagreement. Obviously, this provision definitely subordinates private advantage to public interest; and, because a power is conferred that certainly could be successfully challenged, if exercised too broadly, the Commission has proceeded slowly. To this sweeping power the Act as amended in 1920 adds that of emergency jurisdiction over terminals by the Commission: this body now has, in event of a shortage of equipment, traffic congestion, or other emergency situation, the power "to require such joint or common use of terminals, including main-line track or tracks for a reasonable distance outside of such terminals, as, in its opinion, will best meet the emergency and serve public interest." What may be the judgment of the courts concerning these two provisions, the one touching normal conditions and the other an emergency situation, is problematical. Both still stand, however, and undoubtedly their existence upon the statute books, even without extensive application by the Commission, has served to make the railways more willing than they would have been otherwise to cooperate along lines of public interest—even at the cost of some measure of competitive advantage.

The Future.—Perhaps the one statement that can be made with assurance concerning the future of the terminal problem is that its significance will increase with the further concentration of population in urban centers, the further congestion of city streets, and the increasing inability of terminal facilities that have "jes' growed" to meet added strain.

What the place will be in terminal operation of the universal and off-line or constructive stations, of store-door delivery, of such unusual facilities as the Chicago Tunnel railway, is highly problematical. And no less problematical are the relative parts that railway and motor vehicle will play in getting tonnage into and out of our cities. Will individual rail terminals be removed for reasons of economy and public convenience to outlying areas and all rail operations within the city be in the hands of a unified terminal facility, owned by the railways served by it or by the municipality? Will the costs of terminal operation become so great as to compel an increase of rates into and from the larger cities burdened by these costs, thus giving a positive stimulus to the decentralization of population and industry? Answers to these and to many other questions must be had, either through careful study and experimentation or as an aftermath of muddling through. It is to be hoped that the problem will be approached in the former manner, with the solution in each city fitted to the peculiar needs and problems presented. Certainly the next decade will see further departures from past policy in terminal operation—and it is to be hoped that the movement will be toward a more orderly, more effective, and more economical performance of this vital function.

REFERENCES

Committee on Coordination of Chicago Terminals: *The Freight Traffic of the Chicago Terminal District*, 1927.

DAGGETT, STUART: *Principles of Inland Transportation*, Harper & Brothers, 1928.

FAGG, CHARLES J. (Ed.): *The Freight Traffic Red Book*, Traffic Publishing Company, 1932.

HAINES, H. S.: *Efficient Railway Operation*, The Macmillan Company, 1919.

HANEY, L. H.: *The Business of Railway Transportation*, Ronald Press Company, 1924.

HOLMES, FRED L.: *Regulation of Railways and Utilities in Wisconsin*, D. Appleton & Company, 1915.

HUEBNER, G. G., and E. R. JOHNSON: *The Railroad Freight Service*, D. Appleton & Company, 1926.

Interstate Commerce Commission: *Statistics of Railways in the United States* (annual).

JOHNSON, E. R., G. G. HUEBNER, and G. L. WILSON: *Principles of Transportation*, D. Appleton & Company, 1928.

LOREE, L. F.: *Railroad Freight Transportation*, D. Appleton & Company, 1922.

PULVER, L. G.: *Store-door Collection and Delivery* (an unpublished manuscript prepared in the Graduate School at the University of Iowa), 1931.

VANDERBLUE, H. B., and K. F. BURGESS: *Railroads*, The Macmillan Company, 1923.

The *Railway Age* and the *Traffic World*. Consult index of successive volumes upon such topics as are treated in this chapter.

Chapter XIX

FREIGHT SERVICE

IT IS even more true today than it was in earlier years that judgment concerning the financial promise of any railway project hinges upon the production of affirmative evidence that an adequate freight traffic exists or is in reasonable prospect. Without such adequate tonnage the outcome could be nothing short of disastrous. It is not strange, therefore, that the mechanism of existing lines has been developed largely about the freight service, that even the route itself has often been determined more largely by tonnage considerations than by topography, by minimum distance and curvature, or by gradients. To the description of this mechanism, which makes possible the efficient handling of railway freight traffic, and to the discussion of those questions which are incidental thereto, this chapter is addressed.

Freight Papers of Major Public Concern.—That public and railway requirements relative to the movement of freight may be most effectively met, the issuance of certain papers in connection with each shipment is requisite. These papers are available to shipping and receiving agents in standard form. The first document in point of time which may be issued upon less-than-carload shipments is the so-called *receipt for freight.* This is given to the shipper by the local agent upon delivery of the consignment to the carrier and represents no more than a receipt for goods; in fact, it is seldom issued by smaller stations, but at larger ones some record is necessary if the consignor is to receive adequate protection. The second paper issued and the one which is of basic concern to the shipper is the *bill of lading.* This is issued to cover both carload and less-than-carload movements and contains numerous items of information. Among these items are the name of the shipper and the point of origin; the name of the consignee and the point of destination; such routing of the shipment as may be desired by consignor; the number of packages shipped, together with a description of the items, their weight, the rate per hundred pounds, and the total charges due. If it is a carload movement, the number and initials of the car in which the goods have been loaded are also given. This document, signed by both the shipper and the local agent, represents a contract between the carrier and the consignor. Upon the bill of lading there appears, among other matters, an enumeration of conditions under which the railway is relieved of that unusual liability which the law imposes upon common carriers. Among the bases for which exemption from such liability is recognized are an act of God, the act of a public enemy, the administration of quarantine regulations or other legal

(Uniform Domestic Straight Bill of Lading, adopted by Carriers in Official, Southern and Western Classification territories, March 15, 1922, as amended August 1, 1930.)

2

UNIFORM STRAIGHT BILL OF LADING

Original—Not Negotiable

Shipper's No.________
Agent's No.________

THE .... COMPANY

RECEIVED, subject to the classifications and tariffs in effect on the date of the issue of this Bill of Lading,

at________________________, 193___

from________________________

the property described below, in apparent good order, except as noted (contents and condition of contents of packages unknown), marked, consigned, and destined as indicated below, which said company (the word company being understood throughout this contract as meaning any person or corporation in possession of the property under the contract) agrees to carry to its usual place of delivery at said destination, if on its own road or its own water line, otherwise to deliver to another carrier on the route to said destination. It is mutually agreed, as to each carrier of all or any of said property over all or any portion of said route to destination, and as to each party at any time interested in all or any of said property, that every service to be performed hereunder shall be subject to all the conditions not prohibited by law, whether printed or written, herein contained, including the conditions on back hereof, which are hereby agreed to by the shipper and accepted for himself and his assigns.

(Mail or street address of consignee—For purposes of notification only.)

Consigned to________________________

Destination____________ State of____________ County of____________

Route________________________

Delivering Carrier____________ Car Initial____________ Car No.____________

No. Packages	DESCRIPTION OF ARTICLES, SPECIAL MARKS, AND EXCEPTIONS	★WEIGHT (Subject to Correction)	Class or Rate	Check Column

Subject to Section 7 of conditions, if this shipment is to be delivered to the consignee without recourse on the consignor, the consignor shall sign the following statement:

The carrier shall not make delivery of this shipment without payment of freight and all other lawful charges.

....
(Signature of consignor.)

If charges are to be prepaid, write or stamp here, "To be Prepaid."

....

Received $.................... to apply in prepayment of the charges on the property described hereon.

....
(Agent or Cashier)

Per.................................
(The signature here acknowledges only the amount prepaid.)

Charges advanced:

$____________

★ If the shipment moves between two ports by a carrier by water, the law requires that the bill of lading shall state whether it is "carrier's or shipper's weight."

Note—Where the rate is dependent on value, shippers are required to state specifically in writing the agreed or declared value of the property.

The agreed or declared value of the property is hereby specifically stated by the shipper to be not exceeding

____________ per ____________

____________ Shipper. ____________ Agent.

Per____________ Per____________

Permanent post-office address of shipper____________

(All copies in white)

FIG. 22.—Specimen of uniform straight bill of lading.

processes, natural shrinkage, strikes and riots, and an act or default on the part of the shipper or owner.

Of interest to the ordinary shipper are two kinds of bills of lading, the more common of these being the so-called "straight" bill. All copies of this type are made out on white paper, the original and triplicate going to the shipper, while the duplicate is filed by the shipping agent. This "straight" bill represents little more than a receipt for freight with

(Uniform Domestic Order Bill of Lading, adopted by Carriers in Official, Southern and Western Classification territories, March 15, 1922, as amended August 1, 1930.)

1

UNIFORM ORDER BILL OF LADING

ORIGINAL

Shipper's No.________

Agent's No.________

THE .... COMPANY

RECEIVED, subject to the classifications and tariffs in effect on the date of the issue of this Bill of Lading,

At________________________________ 193__

From________________________________

the property described below, in apparent good order, except as noted (contents and condition of contents of packages unknown), marked, consigned, and destined as indicated below, which said company (the word company being understood throughout this contract as meaning any person or corporation in possession of the property under the contract) agrees to carry to its usual place of delivery at said destination, if on its own road or its own water line, otherwise to deliver to another carrier on the route to said destination. It is mutually agreed, as to each carrier of all or any of said property over all or any portion of said route to destination, and as to each party at any time interested in all or any of said property, that every service to be performed hereunder shall be subject to all the conditions not prohibited by law, whether printed or written, herein contained, including the conditions on back hereof, which are hereby agreed to by the shipper and accepted for himself and his assigns.

The surrender of this Original ORDER bill of Lading properly indorsed shall be required before the delivery of the property. Inspection of property covered by this bill of lading will not be permitted unless provided by law or unless permission is indorsed on this original bill of lading or given in writing by the shipper.

Consigned to ORDER of________________________

Destination____________ State of____________ County of____________

Notify________________________

At____________ State of____________ County of____________

Route________________________

Delivering Carrier____________ Car Initial________ Car No.________

No. Packages	DESCRIPTION OF ARTICLES, SPECIAL MARKS, AND EXCEPTIONS	★ WEIGHT (Subject to Correction)	Class or Rate	Check Column

Subject to Section 7 of conditions, if this shipment is to be delivered to the consignee without recourse on the consignor, the consignor shall sign the following statement:

The carrier shall not make delivery of this shipment without payment of freight and all other lawful charges.

....
(Signature of consignor.)

If charges are to be prepaid, write or stamp here, "To be Prepaid."

....

Received $.............................. to apply in prepayment of the charges on the property described hereon.

....
(Agent or Cashier)

Per..
(The signature here acknowledges only the amount prepaid.)

Charges advanced:

$..

★ If the shipment moves between two ports by a carrier by water, the law requires that the bill of lading shall state whether it is "carrier's or shipper's weight."

Note—Where the rate is dependent on value, shippers are required to state specifically in writing the agreed or declared value of the property.

The agreed or declared value of the property is hereby specifically stated by the shipper to be not exceeding

____________ per ____________

__________________ Shipper. __________________ Agent.

Per__________________ Per__________________

Permanent post-office address of shipper__________________

(Original in yellow, others in blue)

FIG. 23.—Specimen of uniform order bill of lading.

certain added information, thereby differing markedly from the second type, the "order" bill. Shipments moving under the straight bill are in almost all instances consigned by the shipper, A, to the consignee B.

Under an order bill they are usually consigned by the shipper, A, to himself or order with instructions to notify B, though A retains a partial control if the shipment is consigned to B or order: in either case the carrier surrenders the shipment only upon presentation of the bill of lading, properly indorsed. The original of the order bill is made out on yellow paper with duplicate and triplicate on blue and this original serves generally as a negotiable instrument. The prime purpose of this type of bill of lading is to eliminate the transaction of business upon a credit basis: it enables the shipper to secure payment before goods pass from his control. Its use, however, erects an extra barrier between carrier and consignee: oftentimes, because of chance slips in business arrangements, the railroad finds itself obliged to deny delivery to a consignee who is anxious to meet the obligation imposed by the order bill and who is seriously inconvenienced because of a temporary inability to complete the transaction and thereby obtain possession of the goods. And invariably the carrier is condemned for refusing delivery. Yet so serviceable has the order bill proved to business concerns that, despite the additional burden placed upon the carrier and the recipient, its use seems likely to increase rather than diminish.

The Live-stock Contract.—Because of the wide divergence between problems arising from the shipment of ordinary freight and those encountered in the handling of live animals, a specialized type of bill of lading has been developed to cover that portion of railway traffic. This Live-stock Contract, so-called, is issued to cover the movement of all live stock and wild animals and is a straight bill, nonnegotiable in character. Several important differences appear in a comparison of this document with the ordinary bill of lading. The shipper is required to state clearly whether the live stock offered for movement is ordinary or other than ordinary. If the latter, the value must be declared and a rate is made which varies with the value set forth. Upon the back of the contract are definite stipulations concerning the liability of the carrier for loss or damage suffered, also provisions relative to the care of stock while en route and their handling under quarantine. Here too, is a separate agreement which must be executed by any caretaker accompanying the shipment. This agreement contains a statement of the carrier's obligations to such caretaker and of the nature of its liability for any injuries suffered by him.

Important Legal Problems.—Until recent years it was a common practice among railways to attempt, through a provision in the bill of lading, to limit their liability for loss or damage by compelling the shipper to agree to a fixed value upon the consignment. To meet this practice, Congress passed the so-called Cummins amendment in 1915, which denied the carrier the right thus to limit its liability by contract. Certain carriers have countered this legislation by the issuance of tariffs under which rates are fixed upon the basis of a definite valuation, with a sliding scale of rates governing the movement of articles upon which a greater than the standard valuation is placed. In event of the failure of the railway so to adjust its tariffs, however, the carrier is liable for the full value of the shipment except as the value given constitutes a misrepresentation of the worth of the consignment so gross as to result in the bestowal by the carrier of lesser care upon shipment than that to which its true nature entitles it. The shipper's valuation is, therefore, just as other statements in the bill of lading, mere evidence rather than proof.

A number of complicated and difficult legal problems arise incident to the shipment of goods. Among these, one of the most important concerns the character of the liability of a carrier. The law has long held the carrier liable, not merely for "reasonable care" or "due diligence" with respect to good intrusted to its care for transportation but, rather, as an *insurer*. The explanation of this unusual liability lies in the fact that, during the period of transportation, the goods are wholly beyond the control of both the consignor and the consignee, a situation which makes fraud upon the part of the carrier peculiarly possible. However, the railway is not liable as an insurer under *all* circumstances when in possession of a shipment—that liability terminates and liability as a *warehouseman* governs if goods are placed in the hands of the railway an undue time before possible shipment or are permitted to remain in its possession beyond a reasonable period after arrival at destination. As warehouseman, the railway is liable merely for ordinary care. Furthermore, as noted on a preceding page, liability as an insurer does not extend to losses which result from contingencies wholly beyond the carrier's control.

Another important legal question which arises is that of title to the shipment. With respect to this the courts have held that, under usual conditions, title lies in the consignee and, in consequence, that the carrier functions as his agent. Immediately upon the delivery of a consignment to the carrier, then, legal title passes to the party to whom the shipment is consigned, a second party under the usual straight bill. In view of this fact the commercial practice of reconsigning goods moving under a straight bill, A to B, gives rise to an interesting problem. Although such orders from shippers for reconsignment are very frequent and are usually executed by the railways, carriers generally recognize their liability to the consignee for any loss suffered through such conversion by compelling the consignor to furnish an indemnity bond to protect them against legal action on the part of an injured consignee. In the case of goods shipped subject to an order bill of lading, a diversion order rarely raises this question since the usual billing is from A to self or order.

Beginning and Termination of Carrier Liability.—Many disputes between carrier and patron have arisen out of yet another problem, the point at which carrier liability begins in handling a shipment and the point at which it ceases. Although the holdings of the courts in various jurisdictions are not the same, the meeting of any one of three conditions seems to have been accepted generally as constituting delivery to the carrier. Delivery is held to have been made if an item for shipment has been deposited in the customary place, even though no notification has been given to the carrier's representative. If deposit has been made in other than a customary place, however, delivery has not been completed until the agent of the carrier has been duly notified. Again, delivery is completed when the carrier's agent has assumed control over the shipment. If, for example, that agent should direct the loading of goods from truck to car and damage should be suffered while making that transfer, the carrier would be held liable upon the basis of completed delivery even though the goods were never placed in the car. This liability as an insurer terminates, unless modified by statutory enactment, after a reasonable period following the arrival of the shipment at the destination—usually after 48 hours. If notice is customarily given, then the meeting of this requirement, or reasonable effort to meet it, must be shown to modify liability to that of warehouseman. If, however, it is not customary to give notice, the mere holding of the goods for a reasonable period terminates the carrier's liability as an insurer.

Other Legal Problems.—Additional important and intricate legal problems arise from the movement of goods, but of even the major ones only passing mention can here be made. If delivery of a shipment cannot be effected, the consignor may be held liable not only for the freight charges due, but also for any storage costs which have accrued. If, in the handling of traffic, it has been necessary to render any extraordinary service, such as the unloading and drying of a shipment which has been wet through no fault of the carrier, consignee or consignor is liable for that added expense. Should damage, which is traceable to improper crating or to the improper loading of carload shipments, be suffered, the loss rests upon the patron rather than upon the carrier. With respect to claims for so-called "hidden losses," the policy of the railways in the past has been to allow such claims upon the declaration of loss. However, because of the heavy financial burden placed upon the carriers by that practice, the tendency has been increasingly in the direction of demanding full proof of the occurrence of such loss while the goods were *actually in possession of the carrier*. This movement was furthered by the policy of the government during the period of federal operation; no "hidden-loss" claims whatever were then allowed except as the claimant clearly established the carrier's liability.

Other Papers.—A second important paper which is issued in connection with the movement of each freight shipment, whether large or small, is the *waybill*. This document is not issued for the shipper but rather for the convenience of the carrier itself and contains, in addition to the items of information appearing in the bill of lading, other facts essential to the expeditious and certain handling of the shipment, such as car initials and number, also junction points. Besides the original, two copies

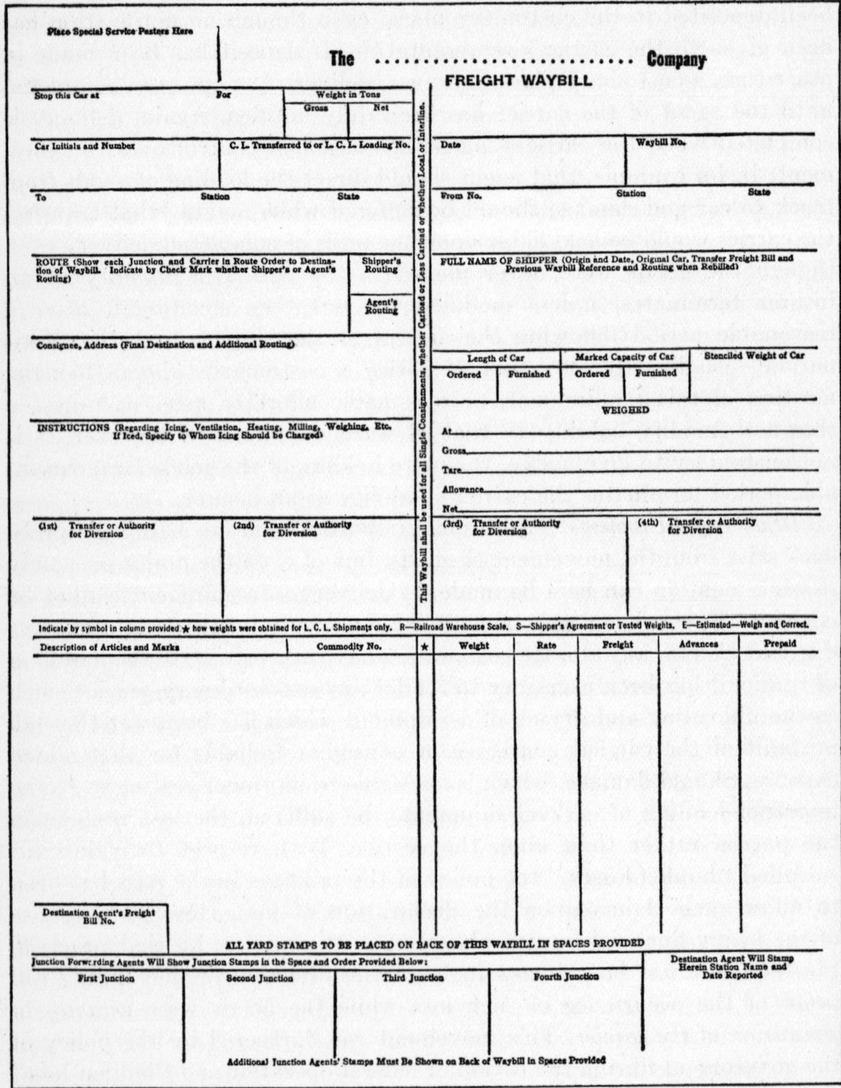

Place Special Service Pasters Here

The .... Company

FREIGHT WAYBILL

Stop this Car at | For | Weight in Tons (Gross, Net)

Car Initials and Number | C. L. Transferred to or L. C. L. Loading No.

Date | Waybill No.

To | Station | State

From No. | Station | State

ROUTE (Show each Junction and Carrier in Route Order to Destination of Waybill. Indicate by Check Mark whether Shipper's or Agent's Routing) | Shipper's Routing | Agent's Routing

FULL NAME OF SHIPPER (Origin and Date, Original Car, Transfer Freight Bill and Previous Waybill Reference and Routing when Rebilled)

Consignee, Address (Final Destination and Additional Routing)

Length of Car (Ordered, Furnished) | Marked Capacity of Car (Ordered, Furnished) | Stenciled Weight of Car

WEIGHED

INSTRUCTIONS (Regarding Icing, Ventilation, Heating, Milling, Weighing, Etc. If Iced, Specify to Whom Icing Should be Charged)

At

Gross

Tare

Allowance

Net

This Waybill shall be used for all Single Consignments, whether Carload or Less Carload or whether Local or Interline.

(1st) Transfer or Authority for Diversion | (2nd) Transfer or Authority for Diversion | (3rd) Transfer or Authority for Diversion | (4th) Transfer or Authority for Diversion

Indicate by symbol in column provided ★ how weights were obtained for L. C. L. Shipments only. R—Railroad Warehouse Scale. S—Shipper's Agreement or Tested Weights. E—Estimated—Weigh and Correct.

Description of Articles and Marks	Commodity No.	★	Weight	Rate	Freight	Advances	Prepaid

Destination Agent's Freight Bill No.

ALL YARD STAMPS TO BE PLACED ON BACK OF THIS WAYBILL IN SPACES PROVIDED

Junction Forwarding Agents Will Show Junction Stamps in the Space and Order Provided Below:

First Junction | Second Junction | Third Junction | Fourth Junction

Destination Agent Will Stamp Herein Station Name and Date Reported

Additional Junction Agents' Stamps Must Be Shown on Back of Waybill in Spaces Provided

FIG. 24.—Specimen of uniform freight waybill.

of the waybill are usually made. The original is forwarded to the point of destination, either by the conductor in charge of the train upon which the shipment moves, or by mail. In the latter case the conductor is furnished a card giving the information necessary to the proper handling of the shipment. One copy of the waybill is filed by the forwarding agent and the other is sent to the auditor of freight receipts. From this last copy most carriers compile their statistics of freight movements and revenues. Sometimes, however, instead of supplying this information to the office of the auditor of freight receipts upon a copy of the waybill, it is furnished upon a so-called "forwarded abstract." In any case, it is the general practice to make this abstract and to transmit it to the auditor's office as an aid in maintaining accurate check upon the delivery of shipments.

Two types of waybill are issued by each carrier, the local for movements wholly upon its own lines, and the interline when the shipment must move over lines of two or more carriers. In the case of the interline shipment an additional copy is issued for each of the carriers participating in the movement; this furnishes them not only a basis for freight accounting, but also a record which will assist them in tracing the shipment. In the past each railway had its own "form" for both interline and local movements but this situation gave rise to such confusion and inconvenience that all railways now issue bills of lading patterned upon a standard form prescribed by the Interstate Commerce Commission.

Forms Used at Destination.—Upon the arrival of a shipment at destination two papers, together with a notification of arrival to the consignee, are made up. The first of these is the so-called *freight bill* upon which such data are given as will indicate to the consignee the nature of the shipment and the charges thereupon. In addition to the freight bill there is also made up a *delivery receipt* which, signed by the consignee when the shipment is placed in his possession, constitutes a record of completion of the contract undertaken in the bill of lading. Should any shortage be discovered or any evidence of "hidden loss" or damage be indicated by the condition of the shipment at the time of delivery, such facts are properly noted upon the delivery receipt as evidence that the shipment has been transferred to the consignee incomplete or in bad order. Such a notation forms a definite basis for a later claim.

Handling of Freight at Terminals.—At each point touched by the railway it is necessary, of course, both to deliver shipments and to receive them. Of those offered, some involve line movements, others interline. That maximum efficiency may be attained in the handling of these shipments, it has been necessary, particularly in cities of any size, to devise a plan to reduce confusion and increase the speed of handling. The first step in the accomplishment of this end has been the separation of incoming and outgoing less-than-carload business, the latter being handled at the so-called outbound freight house, the former at the inbound. After the delivery of small-quantity shipments to the carrier has been made by the shipper at the outbound house, efficient handling necessitates grouping these consignments, first by divisions and then by destination. These two steps taken, the less-than-carload shipments are ready to be stowed into waiting cars. A further problem remains, however: the goods must be so loaded as to minimize or eliminate loss and damage. This involves a careful grouping of shipments according to character and method of packing, and compact stowing. Should precautions not be taken in these particulars, injury and consequent damage claims are certain to result.

When a car loaded with less-than-carload shipments arrives at its destination, it is "spotted" at the inbound freight house and, as unloaded, a "blind check" is made of the contents of the car. This blind check, which indicates accurately the type of all goods unloaded as well as the number of units of each type, is then compared with the waybill or waybills accompanying the particular car-lot shipment. Experience has proved that such a record, made without knowledge of the nature or number of items supposed to be in the car, will show more accurately the actual contents than would a checking of the contents of the car against the waybill itself. With the car unloaded, consignments are then grouped to expedite their delivery. Such grouping may be made according to the nature of the commodity, alphabetically according to consignees, or by an arbitrary grouping of consignees. However, in large stations all three methods are often used; such items as petroleum and petroleum products are grouped by commodity, shipments for the general public are classified alphabetically, and consignments to individuals or concerns receiving considerable quantities of goods are placed according to arbitrary groupings. In any case, the system employed will be essentially that which, with a minimum expenditure of effort upon the part of truckers, will give maximum efficiency in the delivery of the goods.

A third instrumentality employed in the handling of less-than-carload shipments is the transfer house which, because of its character, should be located between the inbound and the outbound houses except, perhaps, at terminals. The first function of the transfer house is to break up miscellaneous less-than-carload shipments received from smaller stations and regroup such shipments by destination. This facilitates the proper placement of interline shipments and often permits the consolidation of less-than-carload shipments into carload groupings. A second function of the transfer house is to break up carload groupings of less-than-carload freight, distributing these shipments according to station for delivery upon the next division. And it is the transfer house, too, that will serve as the center of operations for trap-car service as well as any similar service offered by motor truck.

A final instrumentality utilized in the receipt and delivery of goods is the industry track or the public teaming track. Upon request from a shipper for equipment which will enable him to move his goods in carload lots, an empty car is delivered by the railway upon the spur or industrial track serving that particular shipper or, if he is not so served, upon the public teaming tracks. This car, after being loaded by the shipper, is moved by the railway to destination where it is spotted for unloading according to the consignee's instructions.

The Movement of Traffic.—The work of the carrier, however, is in no sense ended, once the car is loaded at the freight house or by the shipper; indeed, its work has just begun. The whole question of the efficient movement of that car to destination remains. In accordance with the usual method, loaded cars are switched to the so-called "loaded" tracks and the yard service then groups them by type of freight. Fast-freight shipments of perishables or rush orders are grouped together and regular freight likewise. Commodity freight, such as coal, ore, and lumber, forms a third group. Once separated according to type, the cars are further grouped by divisions. The final step in the direction of efficient handling remains, that of so grouping the cars in the train that a minimum of switching is required to accomplish their delivery. To this end cars are grouped, in so far as possible, by stations and are ordered from engine to caboose as the stations lie upon the division.

To facilitate this grouping of cars, two methods of switching are employed, the one the so-called flying switch, the other the gravity or "hump." Where comparatively little switching is necessary, the former method is the less expensive, but at points where the carriers must "make" and "break" large numbers of trains the hump has come into general use. In accordance with this method, cars are pushed, one by one, out upon a sharp down grade and these cars, moving under the force of gravity, follow the main track until diverted to one of the many switch tracks tapping it. Upon each of these switch tracks will be accumulated cars of a certain grouping, division or otherwise. When a particular track is almost filled it is emptied by the yard service and, once manned, this string of cars is on its way as a train. Hump switching is much faster than the flying switch and perhaps results in somewhat less injury to car and contents.[1] Yet the use of either of these methods is at best destructive, and together they account in no small measure for the heavy increase in damage claims during recent years.

One of the particularly interesting features of the freight service appears in the development of a fast or preference freight movement. Such movement has for its purpose the more rapid handling of freight so classified. To facilitate handling, preference freight is consolidated as far as possible into solid preference trains which enjoy rights superior to other types of freight movement and even to certain local passenger service. This more rapid movement of freight tonnage has, from the standpoint of the producer, greatly broadened the area available for the

[1] The injury to car and lading by gravity switching has been greatly lessened during recent years by the development and general use of the "car retarder." By the use of retarders in switching impact is much reduced. These "brakes" are controlled from a central point and electrically operated.

production of perishable items; from the standpoint of the consumer it has increased the supply of goods and has thereby lowered prices. This plan has also proved of advantage because it makes possible the handling of rush shipments at a rate of speed impossible under normal method.

Demurrage, Reciprocal Demurrage, and Track Storage.—Perhaps in connection with this discussion it may be well to note certain additional facts with respect to carload shipments. In case the consignor desires to ship in quantity it is necessary for him to requisition from the railway, through its local agent, the number of cars wanted, indicating the time when they are desired and the point upon industry or public teaming track at which they are to be spotted. If, for any reason, when the cars are delivered according to the shipper's request, he fails to complete loading within a reasonable period, usually 48 hours, or if the consignee fails to unload within a similar period after arrival, a charge in addition to the freight rate is assessed. This additional assessment, called demurrage, is intended to minimize the time that the car is employed in handling a particular shipment. The charge, now $2 per day for the first 4 days after the expiration of free time and $5 per day thereafter, is fixed by the carriers except as modified by state or federal action and, in periods of car shortage such as were experienced during the recent World War, may be increased sharply to serve as a further inducement to the efficient use of equipment. In practice, shippers are allowed under the average agreement a credit on cars released in less than 24 hours which reduces the penalties incurred by them upon other equipment detained beyond the period of free time.

Another type of charge once assessed in certain jurisdictions in connection with the movement of goods was reciprocal demurrage. Such charge was fixed by legislative or commission action and was in the nature of a penalty assessed because of the failure of the carrier to furnish, within a reasonable period, equipment requisitioned by shippers, or for failure to move loaded cars at a prescribed average daily speed. Reciprocal demurrage laws were unsound economically because they tended, especially during periods of car shortage, to discriminate in favor of the shippers of the state assessing such penalty as against those in a state with no reciprocal demurrage provision. And such penalties were held to be illegal also, as the carrier's obligation to serve is not an *absolute* one under all circumstances: rather, a *reasonable* service is due and with it reciprocal demurrage is not in accord.

During periods when the railways experience unusual congestion yet a third charge may be levied, that of track storage. This assesses the consignee or consignor, as the case may be, for the use of track space occupied by the car upon which demurrage is accumulating and is intended to serve as a further spur to the laggard user to place the car, loaded or empty, at the disposal of the carrier at the earliest possible date.

Evolution of Railway Interline Practice.—Although the railways have now perfected a mechanism and developed plans for the efficient handling of interline traffic, a serious problem existed with respect to it during early years. Because of differences in gage and in the construction of equipment, as well as because of the high degree of individualism which characterized early railway enterprise, the interchange of loaded cars destined to points on other lines was unknown; at junction points goods had to be transferred to a car belonging to the next line. As a result of this situation there were organized, to expedite freight movements, many "fast freight lines" which owned their own cars, solicited their own business, fixed their own charges, and paid the railways for moving car and lading from point of origin to point of destination. The gradual consolidation of railway properties, the general adoption of a standard gage, and an increased willingness on the part of railway managements to cooperate, resulted in the gradual displacement of the fast freight lines by the cooperative freight lines or car pools. At the disposal of this cooperative organization each participating carrier placed a certain amount of equipment of a given type, which was administered by a general manager chosen by the member carriers. Profits realized were prorated in conformance to a definite agreement, usually upon the basis of the number of cars furnished. But with the further development of cooperation and an increased readiness of the railways to interchange equipment, the importance of the cooperative freight lines in turn declined.

Compensation for Use of "Foreign" Cars.—During the early years of car interchange, compensation for the use of cars by foreign lines was based upon mileage, the amount varying from ½ cent per car-mile for less valuable equipment, such as stock cars, to as high as 1 cent per car-mile for refrigerator equipment, with certain variations among the different sections of the country. The mileage basis of payment, however, proved unsatisfactory. Mileage accumulated upon a foreign line was often in no measure proportionate to the length of time the home line was deprived of the use of that equipment, particularly in the case of short hauls. Further, it was impossible for the home line to know accurately the mileage made upon foreign lines except as a check was made of the records of those lines, a wasteful policy even though possible. And, finally, if equipment were idle on the foreign line, even under demurrage charge, no revenue accrued to the home line although it was deprived of the use of its equipment.

As a solution of this problem, compensation was put upon a per diem instead of a mileage basis. This new plan was applied only to railway-owned equipment, however, because the private owners of equipment in railway service were unwilling to transfer to the new basis. This per diem plan has two distinct advantages: the carrier can determine from its records the exact number of days that equipment has been absent upon a foreign line and, without regard to the use to which the car is put by that foreign road—or, indeed, its nonuse—compensation accrues to the owning line. The principal difficulty, of course, has been that of fixing a charge which should not yield a too liberal compensation to the home line and yet, at the same time, should penalize the foreign line sufficiently to provide an incentive for the early return of borrowed equipment. Prior to the recent war the per diem payment for ordinary freight cars was 45 cents, but today, due to the increased cost of equipment, it stands at $1, a charge that has been vigorously protested by the small railways which own little or no equipment and depend largely upon connecting lines for cars. Interrailway settlements governing the use of equipment are made monthly, each railway setting off its debit to a particular carrier against its credits with that carrier, the difference being paid in cash. The problem of settlement could be greatly simplified through the establishment of territorial clearing houses but such a movement has gained little headway among the carriers.

Private Cars in Railway Service.—The discussion of equipment must not be concluded without a brief statement of the problem arising from the ownership by private corporations of many cars used in railway service. These cars, though varied in type, are largely tank, refrigerator, and gondola, ranking in number as named. Privately owned equipment made its appearance at an early date, both because of the failure of the railways to meet adequately the needs of new industries as they developed, and because many shippers, especially the larger ones, desired to be independent of the carrier in this particular. Two distinct types of organization which own equipment are found. The *private car line* proper is owned by a corporation unaffiliated with an industry; this corporation leases cars, largely refrigerator and stock, to the railway to be used in varied ways, though this equipment is employed largely in the movement of fruit, dairy products, and live stock. The *shipper's car line*, on the other hand, is owned by or affiliated with some industrial concern which uses the cars primarily for the shipment of its own products but, when a surplus is available, leases them to the railway; such cars are then used by the carriers to meet the general demand for specialized equipment. Conspicuous among the car lines of this type are those that handle meat, oil, and ore. The owners of such equipment are compensated, as noted before, on a mileage basis; though in the case of highly specialized equipment, such as tank cars, any excess of empty mileage over loaded necessitates a payment by the owner of that equipment to the railway of a certain fixed sum per mile for haulage in addition to the refund of the mileage payment for each mile in excess of loaded mileage.

Advantages and Disadvantages.—Certain distinct benefits have resulted from the development of privately owned equipment in the railway field. Besides the fact that specialized equipment has been made available earlier, such lines, except under a policy which is the equivalent of pooling railway-owned equipment, make for a higher degree of mobility and, consequently, for the more efficient use of existing equipment: privately owned cars are shifted from line to line with entire freedom as traffic demands vary. In addition, a high-class service has very generally been rendered. However, objections of such weight have been urged by shippers and public that the soundness of countenancing the continuation of such a "wheel within a wheel" has been called into question. Mileage allowances made have often been excessive, yielding unreasonably high returns upon the investment. To this objection may be added the fact that such excessive returns to shipper's car lines are the equivalent of rebates upon shipments made by concerns owning cars. Then, too, if the carrier relies upon such an organization for specialized equipment, the small independent shipper who depends upon the railway for specialized service sometimes finds himself unable to secure proper equipment in adequate quantity because his competitor, to meet his own need, has withdrawn it from general carrier use. It is also contended that, when such equipment is placed in general service, inspection—as, for example, of refrigerated shipments at icing stations or elsewhere—by representatives of these lines gives the larger enterprise an opportunity to gain a too intimate knowledge of important facts concerning the lesser rival's business, its customers, and volume of trade.

The Future of Private-car Development.—For some years the railways have not only made efforts to cut the mileage allowances of various types of privately owned equipment to a more reasonable level, but they have also purchased additional specialized equipment. For a time it appeared that, as a result of these two movements, the private car would occupy a relatively less important position in the equipment field with the passage of time.[1] More recently, however, the railways have shown an increased willingness to depend upon outside agencies for needed equipment, due perhaps to the difficulty experienced of late in obtaining funds.

[1] The number of private cars in railway service in 1921 as reported by the Commission of Agricultural Inquiry was 225,724, and as reported for April, 1932, by the *Equipment Quarterly* was 282,522. These cars were grouped as follows:

Type of car	1921	1932
Box cars	766	324
Stock cars	3,878	3,527
Coal cars	28,615	17,497
Flat cars	1,410	1,024
Tank cars	132,465	146,116
Refrigerator cars	56,124	113,293
All other cars	2,466	741
Total	225,724	282,522

In consequence of this tendency and also of the fact that the amount of railway-owned equipment has been practically stationary during the past 10 years, the proportion of privately owned equipment to railway-owned now exceeds 12 per cent. Yet, should the railways find funds more readily available during the next decade, it might well be that efforts will be made to reduce that figure. And upon the basis of all the facts, it seems that this movement would accord with public interest.

REFERENCES

Armour, J. O.: *The Packer, the Private Car Lines, and the People*, Henry Altemus Company, 1906.

Beale, J. H.: *Cases on Carriers*, Harvard University Press, 1909.

Burdick, Charles K.: *Cases on (the Law of) Public Service* (including the Law peculiar to) *Common Carriers and Innkeepers*, 2d ed., Little, Brown & Company, 1924.

Cavanagh, J. R.: The Pooling of Freight Cars, *Annals of the American Academy of Political and Social Science*, vol. 29, pp. 260–265.

Federal Trade Commission: *Report on Private Car Lines.*

Green, Frederick: *The Law of Carriers*, West Publishing Company, 1927.

Haines, H. S.: *Efficient Railway Operation*, The Macmillan Company, 1919.

Huebner, G. G., and E. R. Johnson: *The Railroad Freight Service*, D. Appleton & Company, 1926.

Interstate Commerce Commission: *Annual Reports; Reports.*

Johnson, E. R., and G. G. Huebner: *Railroad Traffic and Rates*, vol. 1, D. Appleton & Company, 1911.

———, and T. W. Van Metre: *Principles of Railroad Transportation*, D. Appleton & Company, 1921.

Loree, L. F.: *Railroad Freight Transportation*, D. Appleton & Company, 1922.

Lust, H. D.: *Loss and Damage Claims*, The Traffic Law Book Company, 1931.

McPherson, Logan: *Railroad Freight Rates*, Henry Holt & Company, 1909.

Report of Joint Commission of Agricultural Inquiry, Part 3, 1921.

Ripley, W. Z.: *Railroads: Rates and Regulation*, Longmans, Green & Co., 1912.

Robinson, G. H.: *Cases (and authorities) on Public Utilities*, Callaghan and Company, 1926.

Smith, Young B., and Noel T. Dowling: *Public Utilities*, West Publishing Company, 1926.

CHAPTER XX

FREIGHT CHARGES

THE elaborate mechanism evolved for handling freight traffic has been described. The consideration of the nature of that traffic, of the general method of determining the charge upon individual services, and of certain problems which arise from freight movements remains. To these points this chapter will be successively directed, with particular emphasis upon classification and the determination of rates.

Importance of the Freight Service.—Though the freight service touches directly the everyday life of the average citizen less than certain others rendered by the railway, that service is, from the standpoint of both railway and public, the most significant of those rendered. Upon its regular and uninterrupted performance depends individual well-being and national prosperity; a temporary cessation of service imperils public comfort and, in industrialized and more densely populated areas, even life itself, while a permanent cessation would force an immediate and complete revolution in our entire productive and social organization. Despite the availability of other means of transport, as a consequence of a permanent cessation of railway service, territorial and technical division of labor would be profoundly modified; the splendid utilization of resources upon which our industrial progress so largely rests would be a thing of the past; great cities would dwindle; indeed, intellectual and cultural progress, as well as political unity, would be endangered.

From the standpoint of the carrier also the freight service is of great importance. Quite naturally, revenues derived from the movement of goods vary widely from road to road: in the more densely populated sections of the country this service occasionally contributes little more than half of the total operating revenues while for certain carriers, particularly those concerned with the movement in great quantities of low-grade traffic, such as coal and ores, the proportion of the total operating revenue derived from freight traffic occasionally runs above 95 per cent. Considering the country as a whole, however, the freight service yielded for many years approximately 70 per cent of all moneys derived from railway operations, though an even larger proportion of the *net* revenue is derived from the freight service. With the steady and rapid decline in railway passenger traffic during the past decade, however, the percentage contribution of freight traffic to total operating revenues has increased until it is now almost 80. And it is probable it will increase further.

Nature and Value of Freight Tonnage.—This service is concerned with the movement of an infinite variety of articles. To gain even an approximate conception of the nature of the tonnage handled by American railways, a rough grouping of the many thousands of items is necessary. Such a grouping of all freight moved has long been made by the carriers and so, for many years past, there is available, in the reports of individual carriers and also in the statistical reports of the Interstate Commerce Commission, the tonnage by classes and by districts, together with the proportion which each particular type forms of the total. From year to year these proportions vary little for the country as a whole, though during the past 20 years the proportions of the total contributed by the products of mines and by manufactures have increased, largely at the expense of the products of forests. As might be expected, there are interesting differences in the relative proportions of various types of traffic between various sections of the country, these differences being merely a reflection of variations in the character of business and industry in the sections. This is true, of course, to an even greater degree as between road and road, the figures for a Granger carrier differing widely from those of a coal road and both varying greatly from those of a carrier operating through an industrialized region. To the total tonnage moved by American railways, the products of agriculture contribute approximately 10 per cent, products of forests about 7 per cent, while manufactures and miscellaneous constitute approximately 26 per cent of the total tonnage. Products of mines regularly form something in excess of 50 per cent of the aggregate tonnage of our railways. That portion of the tonnage remaining is divided between animals and animal products and less-than-carload shipments not included under the general headings given.

For the year closing Dec. 31, 1930, Class I carriers alone reported the movement of 2,063,077,591 tons of freight but, after deducting for duplications due to the handling of certain traffic by two or more roads on interline movements, it appears that shippers delivered 1,153,196,636 tons to the rail carriers for transportation. In the movement of this traffic the railways rendered a revenue ton-mile service of almost 383,500,000,000, the average haul per ton delivered for movement being 316.21 miles. It is impossible to ascertain the value of this tonnage with accuracy, but if values per ton of $60 for products of agriculture, $300 for animals and animal products, $8 for products of mines, $30 for products of forests, $100 for manufactures, and $200 for miscellaneous commodities be assigned, a value of approximately $55,000,000,000 attaches to the freight moved during that one year. In the rendition of this service the railways employed approximately 2,635,000 freight cars and utilized a considerable portion of the 60,000 locomotives in their service, this equipment yielding for the year more than 25,600,000,000 car-miles and in excess of 581,000,000 locomotive-miles in freight service. For this service Class I railways received an aggregate of approximately $4,076,000,000, a sum representing $16,830 per mile of line, $1.97542 per ton of freight handled, and $0.01063 per ton-mile of service rendered.

Increase in Demand for Service.—The demand made upon American railways for service, measured in terms of ton-miles, has increased at a much more rapid rate than our population during the 42 years for which approximately accurate tonnage statistics are available.[1] This demand in 1930 represented an increase of more than 529 per cent over the 61,000,000,000 ton-miles of service performed in 1888. The ability of the railways to meet this tremendously increased demand for service, with a plant which has increased but slightly in comparison, has resulted largely from greater efficiency of operation. During the period indicated above, the revenue tonnage per train increased from 176 to approximately 710 tons, while the average carload increased from 17 to 24 tons in the 20 years ending with 1930. This increase in operating efficiency has been made possible largely by the greater tractive capacity of locomotives, supplemented by an increase in average car capacity: from 1915 to 1930 the total tractive capacity of steam locomotives increased 28 per cent, despite an actual decrease in number of approximately 10 per cent, and the capacity of cars increased 18 per cent with a numerical gain of less than 1 per cent during the same period.

Steps in Determining the Rate.—In the determination of the rate applicable to a given shipment two steps are involved. It is first necessary to determine the classification of the good offered and then to discover the rate applicable to this particular class. To the layman this method of ascertaining the rate to be applied seems to involve an unnecessary step. The impracticability, however, of giving in any tariff single rates to be assessed against individual commodities, moving greater or lesser distances, is evident. To obviate this tremendous extension of tariffs, the principle of classification was early adopted and its application steadily extended and refined.

Development of Classification Practice.—Transportation agencies antedating the railway recognized the desirability of classifying shipments. Wagoners quite generally classified goods offered for carriage as "heavy" and as "light"; the former group consisted of commodities whose weight was considerable as compared with bulk while the latter included those items whose weight was of less consequence than the space occupied. For "heavy" goods charges were assessed upon a poundage basis but for "light" they were levied according to cubical content. Canals carried the system of classification somewhat further, but highly organized and de-

[1] This rate of increase in the demand for railway service has dropped sharply since 1920, the number of revenue ton-miles of service in the peak year of 1929 being only about 9 per cent above the corresponding figure in 1920 and but 6 per cent in excess of the average for the 5-year period preceding 1929.

tailed classifications appeared as a result of the development of the railway. Successive steps in the evolution of these classifications seemingly were not often made a matter of record, though a document issued by the South Carolina Railroad in 1855 indicates that goods were then classified by it into four groups. Among other items, the first group included such a variety of articles as "bonnets, saddles, pianos, and tea"; and the second "dry goods, glass, raisins, turpentine, feathers, certain spices and stoves." In the third class appear numerous items, among which were "butter, lard, tobacco, dry hides, tin, copper, machinery and boxes, guns, wool, crockery, and melons," while the fourth class covered "bacon, sugar, nails, ice, coal, green hides, stone, hay, tanbark, dry fruits, car springs, copper ore," and others. In addition to these classified articles were fowls at so much per dozen, and live stock at so much per head. As late as 1873 it is recorded that the Louisville and Nashville Railroad classified goods under three heads, the first covering bulk goods, the second goods of considerable weight, and the third live stock. In other sections of the country classification was developed little or no further than in the South.

With the rapid development of railway mileage and the concurrent increase in the volume of traffic following the Civil War, there came an equally rapid elaboration of classifications. This elaboration, however, was of an individual character rather than uniform and general in its nature, with the result that, in a short time, well-nigh intolerable conditions developed. Indeed, it is declared that there were, at one time, 138 distinct classifications in Trunk Line territory alone, and this number had been reduced only to about 130 at the time of the adoption of the Interstate Commerce Act of 1887. In the face of a rapid development of through traffic this complication of classifications proved inconvenient to the carriers and highly objectionable to the shipper, both because of the uncertainty which must necessarily result as to the rate applicable to a shipment moving over two or more lines and because of the wide variations in treatment received by competing concerns at the hands of different railways.

Present Classification Territories.—The economic necessity of simplification, together with the passage of the Interstate Commerce Act, led the railways in the Eastern territory to adopt a common classification in 1887 and, within the next 2 years, similar steps were taken in Southern and Western territories. This gave to the United States the three major classification areas which continue to the present time, known as Official, Southern, and Western. The territory governed by the Official classification is, with certain minor exceptions, that portion of the United States lying north of a line from Norfolk through Petersburg, Lynchburg, and Roanoke to Ashland, Ky., and of the Ohio River, and east of Lake Michigan and a line drawn from Chicago, through Peoria, to St. Louis, thence to the mouth of the Ohio River. The Southern classification controls south of Official territory and east of the Mississippi, while the remainder of the United States is governed by the Western classification, again with certain unimportant variations. Generally speaking, these three classifications cover all shipments made within their respective territories, but certain exceptions and overlappings should be noted in passing. An individual railway, to meet conditions existing upon its line, may publish exceptions upon certain items. Intrastate shipments in certain states are governed by state-prescribed classifications which vary in character from the publication of mere exception sheets in some to a broad exercise of power in others. Another problem arises in connection with the movement of goods

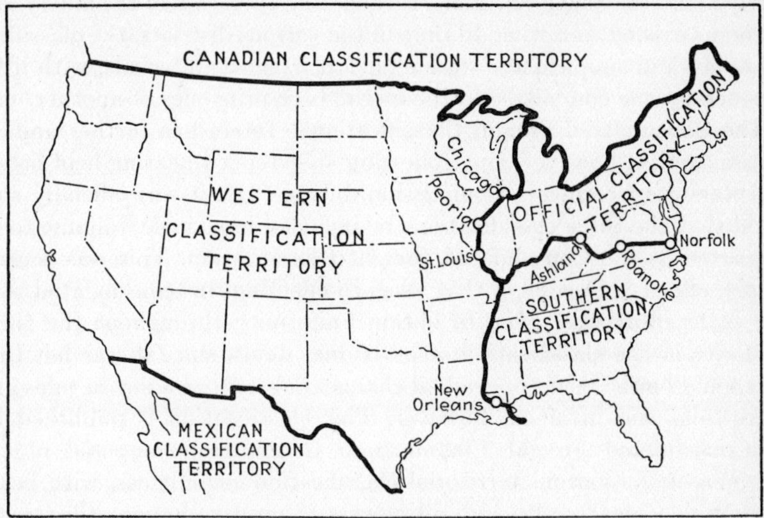

FIG. 25.—Classification territories.

from one classification territory into another. In such a situation the tariff governing the movement indicates what classification controls; commonly the classification applicable at point of origin or at point of destination governs the entire movement on joint through shipments but, in the case of movements upon through rates which represent the aggregate of the several locals, each factor is governed by the classification controlling it.

Classification Committees.—Dating from the establishment of these three classification territories, classification lists were long published separately for each. These lists were not constructed by the railways themselves but rather by committees acting in behalf of the "participating" lines, so called because they were willing to participate in collective action and to accept in the main the rulings of the committee. Until a comparatively recent date these committees were composed of traffic officials of the various lines; they met periodically and possessed merely the power to recommend to the carriers operating in their respective territories certain classifications which should apply. This system, however, proved unsatisfactory for several reasons with the result that in 1914 the Western Classification Committee was so reorganized as to consist of a small number of men not identified with any carrier concerned. This Committee sits constantly for the consideration of classification matters and possesses the power to fix the classification of various items without reference to its respective principals. Each carrier is free, however, to publish an exception sheet in which classifications for that line are prescribed which are at variance with those fixed for the territory. In 1916 the Official Classification Committee was reorganized upon similar lines and, shortly after, the Southern. Thus, through the operation of the machinery which has existed from time to time in the various districts, the classification books and supplements were issued at irregular intervals, with little reference by one committee to the methods or principles of another.

The Consolidated Freight Classification.—Interest in further unification was active, however, and, following an extended hearing held before the Interstate Commerce Commission during 1919, it was officially suggested that the three classifications be included in a single volume, to be designated as the Consolidated Freight Classification. This was accomplished, effective Dec. 30 of that year. In effecting this consolidated issuance little effort was made to obtain uniformity throughout the three territories in the classification of individual items, since it was felt that this should be the result of gradual change. Substantial unity in rules and descriptions was attained, however. This classification is published by the Consolidated Freight Classification Committee, composed of the chairmen of the various territorial classification committees, with headquarters at Chicago, although all powers of positive action still remain with the territorial committees. The only significant change incident to this policy was the bestowal upon the committees in Official and Southern territories of power to determine classifications without reference to the individual railways, similar to that enjoyed by the committee in Western territory. The present Consolidated Freight Classification No. 7 represents the seventh issue of this volume within a period of 13 years and stands as Official Classification No. 51, Southern Classification No. 50, and Western Classification No. 62. During the period controlled by this issue, all freight will move subject to the classifications therein given, except as official supplements are issued from time to time, as individual roads in certain sections modify that classification through the publication of individual exception sheets covering particular items, or as intrastate movements are subject to classification fixed by particular states.[1]

[1] The number of supplements to a given classification frequently becomes large. Before the effective date of Consolidated Classification No. 7, more than 60 supplements had been issued, this within a period of some 27 months. To simplify the use of these supplements an issue appears from time to time summarizing changes made in preceding supplements.

To give a clearer conception of the nature of a classification certain items from the latest consolidated classification, selected to illustrate particular features and differences, are presented in Table XIV.

TABLE XIV.—SPECIMEN ITEMS FROM CONSOLIDATED FREIGHT CLASSIFICATION No. 7

Articles	Ratings		
	Official	Southern	Western
Beet Pulp:			
Dry			
In bags or barrels, L.C.L.	5	*D* or 10	4
In packages or in bulk, C.L., minimum weight 34,000 lb.	6	*D* or 10	*C*
Wet			
In bags or barrels, L.C.L.	5	6	4
In packages or in bulk, C.L., minimum weight 36,000 lb.	6	6	*E*
Bicycle racks (bicycle stands)			
Iron or steel			
S.U., loose or in packages	1½	*D*1	*D*1
K.D., or folded flat, in boxes, bundles, or crates	3	1	1
Wooden			
S.U., loose or in packages	*D*1	*D*1	*D*1
K.D., or folded flat, in boxes, bundles, or crates	1	1	1
Furnaces (assayers)			
In barrels, boxes, or crates, L.C.L.	2	2	3
In packages named, C.L., minimum weight 30,000 lb.	4	4	5
Paper weights			
Glass, in barrels or boxes	*R*25	2	2
Metal, in barrels or boxes	2	2	2
Other than glass or metal, in barrels or boxes	1	1	1
Willowware, N.O.I.B.N.			
In bundles	3*t*1	3*t*1	3*t*1
In crates	3*t*1	*D*1	2½*t*1
In barrels or boxes	3*t*1	*D*1	*D*1

Determinants of Classification.—In the classification of individual items, traffic officials and classification committees are governed by two major considerations, cost and "what the traffic will bear." To the latter of these the greater weight is accorded. This greater weight given the ability principle is undoubtedly due in large measure to the part which it played through years past, prior to effective legislation, and to the force which it has thereby gained through custom and precedent, rather than to any conscious preference given it today. However, because it is the obligation of a traffic official to endeavor so to adjust rates as to secure adequate revenue, he will always give greater consideration to what a particular type of traffic can afford to pay than will the operating official, whose prime guide will tend to be the relative costs of handling different types of traffic.

To say, however, that cost and what the traffic will bear serve as guiding principles in the classification of particular items means little because of the exceedingly general character of the statement. More specifically, the classification of goods is determined by such considerations as space occupied, value, risk, quantity shipped, and competitive conditions governing. That space occupied should be given consideration in classifying articles is wholly reasonable. A car loaded to the roof with hay would not approach the maximum weight capacity of the car; loaded with iron or steel products, or even grains, this same car would afford the railway a far greater paying weight. In view of this consideration, bulky items generally move under a relatively high classification—with the rating of the same article oftentimes considerably lowered, as in the case of compressed cotton, when it is shipped in such form as to materially lessen bulk. Value is a second consideration of importance in determining the classification of goods. The greater the value of a particular article, not only the greater will be the cost of handling, due to a higher degree of care and protection which must be given it en route and heavier loss if the article be damaged in transit, but also the greater is the ability of the item to bear a high charge.

Another basic factor in determining the classification of an individual item is risk. Risk may take various forms: risk of breakage, risk due to the perishable character of the goods, or risk incident to the nature of the commodity—its inflammability or its explosive character, for example. It should be noted, though, that certain of these considerations involve not only the risk incident to the goods themselves but also the danger to other shipments that results from handling them. Still another important consideration is quantity. Like risk, this is essentially a cost factor. If goods are shipped in less-than-carload lots it is the universal custom of American railways to handle the various packages at terminals and transfer stations with their own labor force. Indeed, the railways are moving rapidly toward the general establishment of collection and delivery service for small-lot shipments. If goods be moved in carload quantities, however, all handling costs are borne by shipper and consignee, and the railway is also relieved of much work incident to transfers en route. The justification of a lower rate upon carload movements than upon less-than-carload shipments is therefore clear, though care has always been exercised by regulatory bodies—in accord with what has been regarded as sound public policy—that the difference in rates be not so great as to prejudice unduly the interests of the shipper whose volume of business is insufficient to enable him to take advantage of carload ratings. Finally, competition must be considered in fixing the classification of goods. If keen rivalry exists between different carriers or, as has been increasingly true during the past decade, between different types of carriers, such as rail and highway and water, items suitable for movement by two or all will enjoy the advantage of a lower classification than would govern were this competition absent. This factor, as does value, emphasizes ability considerations rather than cost.

Commodity Rates.—Competition may not only result in giving a particular item a lower classification than would otherwise be enjoyed, but it may even be so keen as to cause the elimination of an article from the classification lists entirely. Other factors may also occasion the substitution of a commodity rating for a standard classification. Among these are the inability of a particular type of traffic, such as sand or gravel, to bear a charge based upon a classification rating; the movement of a particular commodity in large volume; and the desire of a carrier to encourage the development of a particular type of traffic by giving for a period a lower rate than its standard classification would permit. In determining the status of a particular item an examination of the classification book alone is not sufficient, therefore, because the rating there given may have been superseded by an exception or by the extension of a commodity rate, designed to accord the item a degree of preferential treatment impossible under classification control.

Designation of Classes.—Guided by the considerations which have been indicated and by conditions that govern in the various districts, the classification committees endeavor to assign to each article a reasonable rating and to lay down certain general rules governing the handling of those items listed in the classification book. To distinguish among the various classes, letters, numbers, and multiples are generally used, the distinguishing designations differing somewhat among the various classification territories. In Official classification territory articles are divided into eight classes generally, these being known as, 1, 2, Rule 25, 3, Rule 26, 4, 5, and 6, the "rules" given being classifications which accord rates 15 and 20 per cent less, respectively, than the numbered classes preceding. In Southern territory the ordinary classifications number 12, the designations being 1, 2, 3, 4, 5, 6, 7(*B*), 8(*A*), 9(*C*), 10(*D*), 11, 12. In Western territory the designations employed roughly parallel those in Southern, these being 1, 2, 3, 4, 5, *A*, *B*, *C*, *D*, and *E*. In addition to these numbered and lettered groups, there are also certain multiple classifications in each of the three territories, these covering items which, because of bulk, value, risk, or other cause, are listed higher than first class. These multiples run 1¼, 1½, 2, 2½, 3, 3½, and 4 in all three areas and are shown as 1½, *D*1, 2½*t*1, 3*t*1, etc.

Items Listed and Number of Ratings.—Thus far nothing has been said to indicate that the number of items listed in a classification, and the number of ratings therein given, may vary widely. Even a casual examination of a freight classification shows, however, that the number of ratings greatly exceeds the number of different items listed. Indeed, in 1919, with not more than 6,000 different items listed, 15,730 ratings were given, of which 10,790 were for less-than-carload movements, the remainder covering the transportation of goods in carload quantities. Yet contributing in a more important degree to the larger number of ratings than separate listings upon carload shipments is the multiplicity of ratings that results from various methods employed in packing particular goods for shipment. Even such a common article as lard is given five less-than-carload ratings; the particular one applicable depends upon such facts as whether the lard is "in glass or earthenware, packed in barrels or boxes," in pails, in tubs, in fiber cans or cartons, or in bulk, in barrels or boxes. Such differences are explained largely by variations in the risk incident to the movement of the goods. With the development of the sciences and the arts the number of items listed in a classification will increase, yet the number of ratings will increase much more rapidly because of new methods of shipment and because of the increased extent to which it is found desirable to give carload ratings to meet the growing demands of industry and commerce.

Fundamental Considerations in Rate Making.—But, just as one blade of a pair of shears would be useless without the other, so a classification of various items offered for movement by freight would be useless without a tariff or rate book to be used in connection therewith. The discussion therefore remains of the general problems underlying the determination of rates applicable to the various classes and the description of the nature of the tariff sheets so evolved.

In the final determination of its tariffs a railway must give fundamental consideration to the relation that it seeks to maintain between revenues and expenses. This relation will be likely to vary with the form of control exercised. Under government ownership and operation, rate schedules might be so adjusted as to yield a profit upon the business as did the Prussian railways before the World War; or, on the other hand, it might be considered preferable from a social point of view to operate the property on a cost basis, with a consequent lower schedule of charges. Indeed, under such a system of control it is conceivable that it might be held consonant with public good to handle the total business at a loss—for a figure equal to or even less than the operating expenses incurred, the deficit being met by taxation. On the other hand, under a system of private ownership and operation but two conceivable relationships between revenues and expenses can be considered as permanent. If private interest is permitted to work out its policies free of control by public authority or competition, a system of rates would be imposed upon the public which would yield more than a fair return; in fact, monopoly gain. Subject to public control, however, railway rates are usually fixed upon a cost basis, with aggregate revenues sufficient to meet all necessary expenses, operating and capital. And uncontrolled competition may so operate as not only to keep rates upon a cost basis but even to force them below that level which is necessary to meet all legitimate charges against traffic moved. Inasmuch as the American railway system is privately owned and operated, the frequently conflicting desire of the owners to realize a maximum surplus profit and of the public to secure service at minimum cost are the basic considerations in the determination of rates.

In accord with the general policy of regulation in the United States, the carrier initiates and adjusts rates, subject to governmental approval. In the determination of the particular rate the railway traffic official upon whom this responsibility rests is guided by certain general considerations. The *maximum* charge which can be assessed upon the item is, of course, that which the shipper will pay rather than dispense with the service, while the *minimum* long-time rate which can be legitimately fixed is the additional cost of the specific service. Between these extremes the railway official has a wide range of choice, and his conception as to the point at which the charge ought to be fixed will be determined largely by the particular rate theory which he accepts as basic and the weight he attaches thereto.

But regardless of his conception as to what constitutes a "good" rate, before reaching a final decision he must give attention to certain extraneous factors, for the best rate, like the best tax, is the one which works best. Under competitive conditions the charge over other routes and by other types of carriers must be given careful consideration. The revenue needs of the carrier constitute another influence which will, in times of adversity, result in a higher rate and, in times of prosperity, a lower one. Then, too, the carrier must at all times give weight to the long-time interest of railway and shipper—even though certain conditions seem to justify heavy charges at a particular time, it may be an act of wisdom for the carrier to pocket a temporary loss rather than risk "killing the goose that lays the golden egg." Finally, the determination of a rate is influenced by the various public requirements which exist, requirements establishing absolute limits as well as rate relations.

Complexity of Rate Making.—The magnitude of the problem involved in rate making is little appreciated by the lay mind. Perhaps a better realization of its tremendous complexity may be had if we imagine all tariffs destroyed and all knowledge of them wiped out. In the face of such a situation let us assume that a group of men is charged with the construction of freight tariffs covering the movement of innumerable items between an infinite number and combination of points, and under existing industrial and competitive conditions. Even though such a body possessed a knowledge of general principles and procedure in rate making, it would be expecting the impossible to hope that, within any brief period, a workable system of rates could be devised. The magnitude of the problem of determining a rate upon a new item of commerce or modifying an old tariff is greatly lessened by the existence of other tariffs with which comparisons can be made. However, in the determination of a single rate it is necessary, before a definite figure can be fixed, that traffic officials shall agree upon the general policy which shall govern the movement of the particular item in question and that a large fund of information concerning the ability of the traffic to bear, the tonnage immediately and prospectively available, and the competitive situation, be known. But, even with such extensive information at hand, any new rate fixed or old rate modified represents merely the most accurate estimate that can be made as to what the rate should be. The experimental character of original rates is clearly attested by the fluctuations in rate structures preceding stabilization.

Types and Scope of Tariffs.—The traffic official, in the determination of tariffs governing movements with which his railway is concerned, must construct two types of tariffs as to the nature of the goods covered. The first of these is the so-called class tariff, which gives the rate applicable upon each class of goods between various points. The commodity tariff, on the other hand, instead of showing the rate applicable between two points upon that large group of items which constitutes a class, gives the rates between various points or groups of points upon single items which have been removed from the classification and accorded special consideration. Class tariffs and commodity tariffs may be either local or joint as to scope; the former cover movements upon a single line, whether these points be adjoining stations or be as far removed from each other as Chicago and New York or Chicago and San Francisco, while the latter cover the movement of traffic between points situated on different lines. Joint tariffs result from an agreement between, or among, the participating carriers, and are often published by agents who act for several railways. These agents, possessed of power of attorney from each carrier for which they act, issue the tariffs under which a great portion of the long-distance interline and interterritorial traffic moves. And, where the situation demands, agents join with agents in publishing tariffs applicable over a wide area. Since joint tariffs have not been issued to cover many of the possible movements, however, certain interline shipments move at the sum of the local rates.

Determination of the Total Charge.—The method of determining the charge upon any given shipment can now be clearly described. If the shipment moves upon a class rate, the first step in ascertaining the total charge is the determination of the classification of the goods. With the destination known, the agent will turn to that tariff, either local or joint, which gives the schedule of rates applicable between point of origin and point of destination. If the shipment weighs more than 100 pounds, it will move at a total charge secured by multiplying the rate by the number of hundredweight to be transported. If the shipment weighs less than 100 pounds, however, the charge will be that for the full 100 pounds. In the case of carload shipments moving under class rates, the total charge for the movement is determined by multiplying the class rate applicable by the weight of the shipment, the minimum carload weight being the smallest multiplier used. If the shipment moves under a commodity rate, instead of employing the classification book and the rate book the agent will use a commodity tariff, local or joint, and, since commodity rates infrequently apply except to carload shipments, the total charge will be ascertained in the same manner as in the case of carload shipments at class rates.

Uniformity of Classification.—Two problems which touch the determination of the charge have received considerable attention from railways and regulatory bodies alike, uniformity of classification and uniformity of relation in rates among the various classes. Because of their importance a brief discussion of each will be given. The movement toward uniformity of classification throughout the entire United States dates back to the Interstate Commerce Act of 1887. During several years succeeding the passage of that Act the railways, at the behest of the Commission, made efforts to attain a greater degree of uniformity. Such efforts were attended with little success beyond the establishment of the three territorial groups, and it was not until 1907 that the matter was again given consideration. An investigation made by a commission of railway officials resulted in the suggestion that certain preliminary steps be taken looking toward the unification of classification rules, of minimum carload weights, and of the descriptions of items. That the carriers might work more effectively to this end, a committee was organized in 1908 to carry the work forward. In 1910 the Interstate Commerce Commission was given control over freight classifications, and further pressure was exerted in the direction of uniformity.

There are certain obstacles, however, which tend to overshadow the gains resulting from the simplicity of a uniform classification and the greater ease of detecting discriminations that follows therefrom. Of these, differences in economic and commercial conditions and the general readjustment of rates which must necessarily follow any extensive changes in classification are the more important. Early in 1918 the movement toward unification was furthered by an inquiry made of the carriers by the Interstate Commerce Commission as to why a complete unification of rules and description of articles governing in Official, Southern, and Western Classification territories was not possible in the near future. Following extended hearings such a general unification was suggested, and from this movement came the present Consolidated Classification. Although progress was made in the unification of rules and descriptions, there remained a great diversity in the classification of particular articles among the various territories as Table XV, taken from the Commission's 1921 report, indicates:

TABLE XV.—COMPARISON OF CLASSIFICATION RATINGS

Ratings not uniform	L.C.L.	Per cent	C.L.	Per cent
Alike in Official and Southern	1,369	12.69	671	13.58
Alike in Official and Western	2,012	18.65	1,435	29.05
Alike in Southern and Western	1,906	17.66	349	7.07
All different	1,303	12.08	1,531	30.99
Total	6,590	61.08	3,986	80.69
Ratings uniform	4,200	38.92	954	19.31
Total ratings	10,790	100.00	4,940	100.00

However, the Consolidated Classification Committee is under instructions to proceed with the unification of ratings as rapidly as is feasible, and the controlling classification committees are bound by an order that any rating which is now, or shall be, uniform in all territories must not be changed except to a rating which shall also be uniform in all territories. The Interstate Commerce Commission, in its report for 1923, stated that most of the 112 increases and the 675 reductions made in ratings during the preceding year were in the direction of uniformity. Of these reductions, more than 60 per cent represented the establishment of carload ratings, in addition to the any-quantity ratings which alone had been offered previously. And in its 1931 report the Commission declared,[1]

> There has been continuous, although not rapid, progress in the last year in unifying ratings for commodities in the Official, Southern, and Western Classifications, particularly in less-than-carload ratings and carload ratings for commodities rated in the upper end of the scale. Much, however, remains to be done. Further study of the subject of classification uniformity and the experience which we have gained in recent years in fixing class rates make it increasingly apparent that, while complete unification and merger of the Southern and Western Classifications is possible, such unification can not be fully extended to embrace the Official Classification unless and until there is a closer alignment of the basic rate structures, as between Official territory and the other sections of the country, than it has so far been found practicable to accomplish, although revisions heretofore required by us have been in that direction.

Progress has also been made in harmonizing state classifications with those governing the area of which those states seeking to control classification are a part. Thus it appears that the movement toward unification promises success. Constant pressure exerted by the Interstate Commerce

[1] *Forty-fifth Annual Report of the* Interstate Commerce Commission, p. 67.

Commission and the general willingness of the carriers to comply, will accomplish much. The regular publication, side by side, of the classifications of a particular item in the various territories has caused differences to be questioned, and, where without justification, to be eliminated. Finally, with the further development of newer portions of the country, economic and commercial dissimilarity among the various sections will diminish, and this will lessen accordingly the importance of one of the major barriers to uniformity of classification.

Uniformity of Rate Relations.—The problem of securing throughout the entire country a relatively constant relation between rates upon the various classes has received little attention in the past, and the application of a scale of rates in various portions of the United States that should bear a definite relation to all other portions of the United States has received even less. However, in the investigation made relative to the unification of classifications, the Interstate Commerce Commission suggested rather definitely not alone the desirability of adopting a 10-classification system of the entire United States, but went even further—it indicated that the percentage relation among rates upon the various classes should conform closely to the following standard, the Class 1 rate being 100 per cent; 100, 85, 70, 60, 45, 35, 30, 25, 22½, 20. Under this plan it was suggested that all less-than-carload traffic be confined to the first four classes and that many of the articles moving under commodity rates and under exceptions to the classification be assigned ratings upon the basis of such a scale as would not substantially modify the charges applicable.

During the period of federal operation, the Railroad Administration gave serious consideration to an even more radical step toward the standardization of rate relations, the construction and application of a uniform rate scale for the entire United States.[1] Mileage differences in this scale as

[1] The uniform rate scale proposed by the Federal Railroad Administration follows in shortened form:

Percentages	100	85	70	60	47	51	40	30	25	20
Classes	1	2	3	4	5	A	B	C	D	E
Miles	Rate	Rate	Rate	Rate	Rate	Rate	Rate	Rate	Rate	Rate
5	25	21	18	15	12	13	10	8	6	5
10	27	23	19	16	13	14	11	8	7	5
15	29	25	20	17	14	15	12	9	7	6
20	31	26	22	19	15	16	12	9	8	6
25	33	28	23	20	16	17	13	10	8	7
50	43	37	30	26	20	22	17	13	11	9
75	51	43	36	31	24	26	20	15	13	10
100	58	49	41	35	27	30	23	17	15	12
200	88	75	62	53	41	45	35	26	22	18
300	112	95	78	67	53	57	45	34	28	22
400	132	112	92	79	62	67	53	40	33	26
500	150	128	105	90	71	77	60	45	38	30
600	166	141	116	100	78	85	66	50	42	33
700	178	151	125	107	84	91	71	53	45	36
800	190	162	133	114	89	97	76	57	48	38
900	202	172	141	121	95	103	81	61	51	40
1.000	214	182	150	128	101	109	86	64	54	43

offered varied from 5 to 25, as 105, 110, 115, and 900, 925, 950. And, since it was obviously impossible to apply such a scale uniformly throughout the United States, it was proposed that, in areas of high traffic density, the rates should be but 75 per cent of the scale; that, in areas of moderate traffic density, the scale as given should be applied; and that, in areas of low traffic density, rates as high as 125 per cent of the scale should be applied. While it is unlikely that any plan as rigid as this will be considered seriously for years to come, if at all, the fact remains that the Interstate Commerce Commission is making an earnest and proper effort to correlate rates in adjacent areas. As an excellent example of this stands the linking of Western Trunk Line class rates, under a recent decision, with rates in Eastern territory on the one hand and in Southwestern on the other. Except as the competition of new agencies prevents such accomplishment, the railway rate structures of the United States bid fair under Commission direction to become a harmonious whole, instead of a hodgepodge of particular rates.

As the Commission has pressed forward in the revision of class rates in major rate territories the importance of this uniform relationship has been emphasized increasingly. Instead of a 10-class scale, however, a 23-class scale is suggested. The Class 1 rate being 100 per cent, it is suggested that lower classes follow as 92.5, 85, 77.5, 70, 65, 60, 55, 50, 45, 40, 37.5, 35, 32.5, 30, 27.5, 25, 22.5, 20, 17.5, 16, 14.5 and 13. Using such a gradation it is expected that ultimately all commodities will move under a class tariff—for, with the percentage of first class dropping to 13, even such items as sand and gravel could find place.

Development of Freight Traffic.—Another problem in connection with the freight service relates to the development of additional traffic. To the extent that any carrier operates upon the basis of increasing returns, the clear advantage of such added traffic is evident. And, in the case of those roads that are operating at maximum efficient capacity, the possibility of adding further traffic will justify the intensive development of the property at an earlier date. Various methods have been used by the railways to secure such additional tonnage. Advertising has been employed moderately but "copy" has been directed more often toward the solicitation of passenger traffic rather than of freight. Off-line offices have been maintained at strategic points to gain readier access to available traffic. A third method of obtaining a share of available business is that of direct solicitation by freight agents of various rank and degree. Such methods, however, are essentially competitive in character, and represent a struggle among carriers for existing business.

In contrast to such endeavors are carrier efforts that are intended to increase the total tonnage available for movement. Here the work of agricultural and industrial agents is particularly worthy of mention. These representatives of the railways, through experimentation, investigation, and intelligent publicity, independently or in cooperation with public agencies, frequently contribute much to the economic progress and prosperity of the areas served. In this particular many carriers have done significant work, but perhaps the accomplishments of none are more worthy of mention than are those of the Northern Pacific and Great Northern which, under the leadership of the great James J. Hill, played a most active part in the development of that northern and northwestern territory served by them. Another important type of developmental work appears in the rendition of special services, such as the operation of live stock or fruit "specials," and even of the "peddler car" which makes possible the local distribution of perishable products in small quantities. Much has been accomplished by individual railways in winning traffic from competitors and much has been accomplished in the stimulation of agriculture and industry through the developmental activities of the various carriers. Opportunities still remain, however, particularly in the latter field, and closer cooperation between the railways and governmental agencies should make possible important further gains to the advantage of both carrier and public.

REFERENCES

Fyfe, Robert W.: *Freight Classification*, LaSalle Extension University, 1923.

Interstate Commerce Commission: *Annual Reports; Statistics of Railways; Reports.* See particularly *Consolidated Classification Case*, 54 I.C.C. 1.

Johnson, E. R., and G. G. Huebner: *Railroad Traffic and Rates*, vol. 1, D. Appleton & Company, 1911.

———, G. G. Huebner, and G. L. Wilson: *Principles of Transportation*, D. Appleton & Company, 1928.

——— and T. W. Van Metre: *Principles of Railroad Transportation*, D. Appleton & Company, 1921.

Lust, H. C.: *Loss and Damage Claims*, Traffic Law Book Co., 1931.

Principles of Classification and Application of Principles, *Traffic Library*, vols. 2 and 3, American Commerce Association, 1916.

Ripley, W. Z.: *Railroads: Rates and Regulation*, Longmans, Green & Co., 1912.

———: *Railway Problems*, Ginn & Company, 1913.

Stromberg, J. F.: *Freight Classification*, Houghton Mifflin Company, 1912.

Vanderblue, H. B., and K. F. Burgess: *Railroads: Rates, Service, Management*, The Macmillan Company, 1923.

Chapter XXI

PASSENGER SERVICE AND CHARGES

DESPITE the overshadowing economic importance of the freight service to the public and to the carrier, the passenger service looms even larger in the public mind. This high place in the estimation of society is due in part to the direct participation of the passenger in service rendered, in part to the stimulus given by rapid and cheap movement of persons to the development of culture and to intellectual activity. Contacts have been enormously increased by more efficient movement and, in consequence, the human mind has developed the breadth and power which are essential to continued growth. Likewise, the readier transportation of persons has furthered the territorial extension of political units and aided in maintaining those units against disintegrating factors operating from within and hostile forces attacking from without.

To the passenger service the railways also have long attached a significance quite out of proportion to its revenue contribution. The service represents the maximum of speed and comfort attainable under given conditions and is therefore a source of great pride. It offers an opportunity for the artist's touch in a workaday field, a field largely occupied by the commonplace. Then, too, the railways often regard the passenger service as an advertising medium; high-class service is held to be an effective magnet for competitive freight traffic just as poor service is deemed likely to lessen the proportion of such tonnage received. However, in recent years, as railway passenger revenues have steadily declined with the rise of competitive facilities, passenger service has tended to become a financial millstone about the necks of particular carriers whose competitive situation is weak. Such railways, especially, wonder what the future holds for this service.

Differences in Freight and Passenger Traffic.—Passenger and freight service differ widely in many respects. One of the most conspicuous of these differences appears in the movement of traffic. Although a limited quantity of freight moves on definite schedule, tonnage is normally moved as the accumulation of goods justifies; variations from the few fixed freight schedules elicit little protest as compared with that provoked by lesser variations from passenger schedules, because the public does not consider making regular time a typical function of freight movement. Passenger movements, on the other hand, to be of any considerable worth, must follow a definite schedule; regular service must be offered day after day, whether traffic is heavy or light, and slight departures from schedule arouse public criticism. Closely allied to this problem of fixing and maintaining passenger schedules is another, that of regularly meeting connections, which is of prime importance to the traveling public and occasions no little difficulty and expense to the railway. Then, too, the passenger and freight services vary widely with respect to the considerations required of the operating staff. In the case of the former, safety is of fundamental social significance, but in the case of the latter it is only of commercial importance through its influence upon shipper patronage and upon loss and damage payments. For one a high average rate of speed is required while for the other speed was long considered but an incidental factor. In the handling of persons comfort and convenience loom large while quite other considerations rule in the movement of goods.

Another point at which passenger service differs from freight is in the method of handling at terminals. Perhaps the fact that passenger rates vary directly with the distance as freight rates do not, reflects the belief of traffic officials that the movement charge in the case of persons should be "loaded" with no terminal factor because passenger traffic handles itself. Yet this apparent economy is balanced, if not outweighed, by the abnormal expenditure demanded for the accommodation of passengers at stations. Again, passenger traffic is more nearly balanced than freight, if normal passenger traffic alone be considered. Though, if a study be made of special traffic, particularly of excursion movements, it will oftentimes be found that passenger movements are less balanced than freight; in the one case a predominant tonnage movement flows regularly in a certain direction while in the other the number of passengers moving each way is, though equal for the year, seasonally unbalanced. The evils of such unbalanced traffic are no less than if it were unbalanced for the entire year.

Another interesting contrast between the two types of service appears in a comparison of certain trends in these two fields. Though in 1916, just prior to our entry into the World War, both freight and passenger rates averaged approximately the same as they did 25 years earlier, passenger business showed through that period a steadily diminishing margin of profit to the railways generally in comparison with freight. And, in the years since 1916, this margin of profit has diminished further—to the point of disappearance. This difference has been largely due, of course, to the inability of the railways to avail themselves of increased economies in the movement of passengers as they have done in the movement of freight. While the average freight-train load increased approximately threefold from 1891 to 1916 and by a third from 1916 to 1929, the average number of passengers per train increased but 45 per cent in the first period and declined by almost 8 per cent in the second. This striking divergence in trend between the two services has been the consequence of several factors. Significant among these were the slower rate of increase and recent decline in the volume of passenger traffic, and the constant necessity of adding trains to meet public demand or competitive need. Then, too, the movement of passenger traffic on schedule stands as a permanent bar to the rapid increase of efficiency in the passenger field.

The relative importance of the revenues derived from the freight and passenger services has already been indicated, but it is not amiss, perhaps, to restate the fact that freight revenue now contributes about 80 per cent of the total operating revenues of American railways, while the passenger revenue approximates 15 per cent—these figures contrasting with perhaps 70 per cent and 20 per cent within the decade past. Upon individual railways the importance of passenger revenue varies widely as between the conspicuously tonnage lines and passenger roads operating through densely populated sections—percentages varying from less than 1 per cent on the Duluth, Missabe, and Northern, an ore property, to more than 70 per cent upon the Long Island. In general, however, the passenger service rarely contributes less than 10 per cent of the operating revenue and seldom more than 25 per cent, and such disparities would normally tend to diminish as the density of population increases in areas where passenger traffic is light. Until the advent of the motor vehicle it appeared that revenues from the movement of persons would tend to contribute an increasing proportion of the total, also, but the trend has been definitely in the opposite direction during recent years—with the railways' efforts to hold this traffic accomplishing little more, seemingly, than to diminish the rate of loss.

Types of Trains in Service.—In the movement of passenger traffic, various types of trains are operated. In general, trains may be classified as local and through, the former concerned primarily with the movement of passengers for short distances, the latter with the transportation of persons between distant centers. Through movement often involves operation over the entire length of an extended line or combination of lines, as from Chicago to New York, Chicago to New Orleans, Chicago to San Francisco or Seattle. In handling local traffic several types of trains are employed. In the vicinity of large cities certain trains are concerned solely with the movement of the commuter, but the typical local passenger service is rendered by trains stopping at practically all stations and covering, in the course of the daily run, seldom less than 100 miles, and often three times that distance. The local usually carries only day coaches and renders a service in which the railway takes no pride, despite the fact that many patrons are dependent upon it and that local sentiment toward the railway will be shaped by it. Local service is also rendered by the so-called "mixed" train, which combines both the freight and the passenger functions. Service of this kind is seldom offered on the main line, except by the local or "way freight," but it is characteristic of branch-line operations—and upon the poorer branch lines such service alone is offered. During recent years yet a third type of local service has gained prominence—that rendered by the railway motor car. In the years from 1923 to 1929 railway motor-car mileage was trebled, in the latter year aggregating almost 10 per cent of the steam-operated mileage. And it is probable that such service will play an increasingly important rôle upon light-traffic lines—particularly where the motor bus cannot be used by the railway to advantage. Indeed, were it not that railway management has shown undue conservatism in utilizing a mechanism driven by power other than steam, it is probable that the railway motor car would have enjoyed wide acceptance earlier: a single light car, motor driven, enjoys a distinct advantage from an expense standpoint over even the short locomotive-drawn train, however ancient or diminutive and therefore incapable of main-line service that locomotive may be.

Character of Through Service.—Through service on American railways differs from local service in two significant particulars. More powerful locomotives, a superior main-line roadway, and fewer stops make possible a much higher average rate of speed. Indeed, an important feature of through service is speed, and this feature is advertised widely in the solicitation of traffic. The second distinguishing characteristic lies in the character of the service offered. In this field is employed not only the highest grade of standard coach equipment but also a large number of cars built for the purpose of rendering a super-service to the patrons of the road. In fact, many of the important through trains are made up largely or wholly of Pullman equipment. These through trains are usually operated over the tracks of a single railway corporation or its subsidiaries though, in certain instances, they are moved over the lines of independent connecting carriers. Such interline service is invariably of high character, measured in terms of both speed and equipment. Well known among such jointly operated trains have been the Overland Limited between Chicago and San Francisco via the Chicago and North Western, the Union Pacific, and the Central Pacific; the Golden State Limited, between Chicago and Pacific coast points via the Chicago, Rock Island, and Pacific, the El Paso and Southwestern, and the Southern Pacific; and the Dixie Flyer between Chicago and points in the South, via the Chicago and Eastern Illinois and the Louisville and Nashville. With the further development of railway cooperation such trains may well become increasingly characteristic of American long-distance passenger service.

Since passenger traffic is largely self-directed at terminals and junction points, the mechanism necessary to handle it is much simpler than that for the handling of freight. Because of the smaller number of trains and the far smaller number of cars in each, the problem of "making and breaking" trains at terminals and division points is relatively simple.

Indeed, the task of handling equipment in the coach yard, where unused cars are stored, oftentimes involves little more than attaching a switch engine to a train which has just finished its journey and pushing that train into the yard where, after thorough cleaning and reequipment, it is ready for the outbound trip. The station problem is also less difficult than for freight traffic, though the modern policy of constructing immense and almost palatial passenger terminals in large cities has thrown upon the carriers a burden of expense quite out of proportion to the revenue importance of the business involved.

Classification of Tickets.—In handling freight traffic the issuance of a considerable number of papers for each shipment is necessary. However, because of the nature of the passenger business the ticket is the only document employed in connection with the movement of passengers. Tickets vary widely in type and it is rather difficult to classify them under a few heads, though two major groups are distinguishable. The great proportion of the tickets sold authorize movement between points upon the issuing line and are known as local tickets; others, termed interline tickets, cover movements over portions of two or more lines. These local and interline tickets are of varied character. Most common among these is the regular first-class ticket, either one way or round trip. This ticket is available the year round and sells at the standard rate. A second type of ticket of importance is the so-called excursion ticket, which is sold at a reduced rate for round-trip movement between certain dates. Such tickets may have a relatively brief life or, as in the case of summer or winter movements, may be valid for several months. Another type of ticket is that offered at a reduced fare for either one-way or round-trip movement, here being included commutation, immigrant, and harvester travel, as well as tickets sold to the clergy, to indigent persons, and to children. A fourth type of authorization upon which the individual may travel is the mileage book: transportation in certain districts may be purchased in 1,000, 1,500, 2,000, or greater blocks, and used at the buyer's option. Often these books are accepted by any railway in a given area. A final type of travel moves upon miscellaneous authorizations, among these being the drover's ticket, the conductor's memorandum issued as a receipt for cash fare, and the pass, trip or annual.

Ticket Accounting.—The peculiar character of the ticket compels the exercise of great care in distributing and accounting for all tickets issued, and this is true whether they be of the type which authorizes movement between two named points or whether they be forms in blank to be completed by the selling agent. Ticket stocks are distributed through the office of the auditor of passenger revenues, and the sales records and the unsold stocks of the various local agents are checked against the record of tickets charged. The sale of tickets rests primarily with the various local agents along the line, though sales are also made by uptown ticket offices and other agencies established for the convenience of the public.

The responsibility for collecting tickets rests upon the passenger conductor and it is his obligation to see that no person travels on his train without a ticket or other authorization for transportation. To secure a more accurate record of passenger movements and to check against sales indicated, each conductor must forward to the office of the auditor of passenger revenues at the end of every run all tickets, stubs, and other records of movement collected by him, together with a summary of those authorizations in his conductor's report.

Privileges Accorded to Travelers.—Certain privileges incident to the possession of an authorization for transportation should be noted. Perhaps the most significant of these is that of the free transportation of a limited quantity of baggage. In the United States the baggage privilege permits the passenger to have moved, free of charge, personal effects weighing not in excess of 150 pounds for every full ticket possessed by him, half that amount being permitted upon half tickets. This privilege is extended to the passenger with carrier liability attaching to the railway up to a fixed sum, generally $100, such liability beginning and terminating under essentially the same conditions as in the case of freight movements. This baggage privilege seems reasonable, even generous, when compared with the much more limited free-baggage allowance of European railways. Another privilege of some importance accorded the possessor of certain types of tickets is the stop-over. Stop-over privileges are accorded sparingly to the holders of one-way tickets but are extended rather generously to purchasers of round-trip tickets, whether of the regular or excursion type. Stop-overs are permitted most readily at points of great historic or scenic interest or at important commercial centers.

Classification of Passenger Service.—Recognition of the principle of classification in the rendition of passenger service is common throughout the world, though markedly less so in America than elsewhere. In general, three regular services are offered to patrons—first, second, and third class—these often being supplemented by certain other services such as special excursions, workmen's trains, etc., even occasionally by a fourth class. Where classification of passenger traffic is made, the great bulk of travel is third class. For such traffic railways offer characteristically a slow service, with inexpensive or superannuated equipment providing few comforts or conveniences to the passenger. However, the difference between the charges for this and for the higher class service is such that the poorer classes of people gladly avail themselves of the lower. Second-class service generally affords the traveler as fast time as the first, the difference lying primarily in the character of the accommodation and in the social distinction implied. This service, however, is used by a relatively small proportion of travelers except in a few countries where a large middle class exists. First-class service is comparable in speed and general convenience to the regular first-class services in America, though certain differences may give first-class travel abroad a small advantage in comfort and speed, besides a marked social advantage, over service of the same class here.

Class Service in the United States.—The rather sharp contrast between the classes of service offered abroad and the relative absence of such classifications in America is striking. Although lower grade services, such as colonist and immigrant services as well as excursion opportunities, are offered in the United States with a relatively poor type of service, these contribute but an insignificant portion to the total of American passenger traffic. Indeed, little effort has been made by American railways to effect a definite classification of standard traffic; the only evidence of such a movement was the second-class ticket which was sold, particularly in the West, for a number of years at a rate somewhat below that charged for first-class movement. Despite the fact that the actual service enjoyed by such second-class passengers did not differ materially in practice from that afforded first-class traffic, the number of persons availing themselves of this lower rate for second-class service was so small that the railways did not feel justified in continuing the sale of such tickets. Therefore, the only general classification of passengers in the United States appears in the differentiation between those moving first class and those who, by an extra payment, avail themselves of special privileges afforded by Pullman service, or of the unusual advantages of the extra-fare train. This difference in price rests largely upon differences in cost of service; and, it may well be added, the line between first-class and super-first-class patrons cannot be so clearly and finely drawn as it is in European countries upon the basis of the social or financial status of those availing themselves of these two types of service.

The justification of classification in the passenger field has been based on both economic and social grounds. Because the service rendered is enjoyed by the individual paying for it, the principle of "ability to pay" can much more easily and much more justly be invoked here than in the freight service. Then, too, there are those who are able and willing to pay for a higher type of service than can be maintained as standard. On the two grounds, therefore, a differentiation is urged for economic reasons. The social justification for differentiation of service applies strikingly in countries where social classes are sharply marked and, under such conditions, may even be regarded as necessary. Such a justification, however, seems to have little basis of fact in America where, despite wide differences in wealth, class lines are not definitely marked and the antagonism toward anything tending to establish such lines is conspicuous. To think of a workman's wife and family traveling in a first-class carriage in England with some member of the nobility would require a considerable stretch of the imagination, yet many times daily there will be found traveling side by side, in perhaps any except de luxe trains with heavy additional charges, almost equally divergent elements in American social life. If any development of classification comes in the United States, with clear-cut recognition of differences in ability to pay, it will come through emphasis upon the economic justification of price differences and in spite of antagonism toward things smacking of social distinction.

The Growth of the Pullman Service.—Such super-service as is now found on American railways is rendered almost exclusively by the Pullman Company—indeed, so completely identified has this type of service become with the name that it is normally designated as "Pullman service" to distinguish it from coach service. The history and development of this service, together with the peculiar relation which it bears to the railway company, are of both general and transportation interest. Despite even the relatively short lines and local movements which characterized early railway operations in the United States, it was realized within a few years after the beginning of the railway that specialized night service was needed. As early as 1836 an effort was made to provide sleeping quarters for passengers en route, but this early attempt and the endeavors of the next 20 years were crude and unsatisfactory. Indeed, it was not until George Pullman undertook his work for the Chicago and Alton, in 1859, that the development of satisfactory sleeping cars began. Under the leadership of this man progress in the direction of specialized services was rapid, and, since 1867, the Pullman Company has been furnishing American railways with sleeping cars, dining cars, club cars, and other passenger equipment of an increasingly higher type. So successful has the Pullman Company been in establishing itself in the railway field that it now has almost exclusive control of sleeping-car service throughout the United States.

The place of super-service upon American railways has long been recognized by all as important, but its relative magnitude is realized by few—with even fewer realizing how pronounced has been its positive trend during a period when passenger traffic as a whole is diminishing. In 1908, the first year for which the Interstate Commerce Commission gives separate figures for coach mileage and for the mileage of sleeping, parlor, and other special cars, the latter group moved a distance of 537 million miles. In so doing they contributed about 29 per cent of the total passenger-car mileage for that year. Car mileage of special equipment tended upward with but one major drop, for the year of 1918, until in 1920 it reached 881 million—38 per cent of the total. Because of the economic depression ruling during the following year, such mileage dropped slightly for 1921. However, from that year it increased without a break until 1929, when it was approximately 1,257 million—more than 51 per cent of the total passenger-car mileage for that year. In 1930 a slight decline appeared, though the decline in special-car mileage was less than half that shown for coach mileage. Thus, as measured in terms of car mileage, the advantage that went to the special equipment in 1929 for the first time in railway history was slightly increased. This increase and present dominant position of special equipment in the railway passenger-service field are the more striking because the Pullman Company operates over only slightly more than half of the railway mileage of the United States and it is unlikely that the railways offer parlor and other special-car service over any considerable additional mileage. Whether this extensive and increasing use of special equipment has been due essentially to a rising high level of economic well-being in this country or to the fact that for this type of traffic there has not yet developed an effective type of competition is not certain, though the latter explanation seems the more significant. In any event, it will be most interesting to follow the trend of the two types of traffic with a view to reaching judgment.

Advantages of Pullman Service.—The peculiar position occupied by the Pullman Company with respect to the railways has been largely the outgrowth of two factors. The first of these, and by far the more important, is the saving to the individual railways which results from renting or leasing equipment under the terms of the typical Pullman contract as against owning that equipment. From season to season passenger traffic varies widely, this being particularly true of those roads which have a large amount of special traffic, excursion or resort. For individual lines to provide reasonably for the peak load would necessitate a heavy outlay for equipment, much of which would lie idle for many months; but, with the privilege of requisitioning equipment from and returning it to the Pullman organization at will, the railway is more happily situated. Another factor that undoubtedly has operated to further Pullman control of the special-service field has been the desire of the railways to be relieved of many problems and responsibilities which would otherwise devolve upon them.

That the arrangement which has proved advantageous to the railways has been highly profitable to the Pullman Company is attested by that company's remarkable expansion out of earnings, decade by decade, in the face of liberal and regular dividends. Whether the Pullman Company, a "wheel within a wheel," will continue to dominate the field is uncertain; if and as the railways are consolidated into larger systems, with each system operating in territories where traffic demands are supplementary rather than cumulative, it may prove advantageous for such systems to own the special equipment used rather than to pay generously for its use. Or, as the spirit of cooperation among the railways develops, it may be possible for the railways to take over and operate as a joint enterprise the property of the Pullman Company, just as they have done in the case of the express business.

The Pullman Contract.—The contract between the Pullman Company and the railway varies in certain particulars from road to road. Of all contracts, however, it may be said that the railway agrees to carry Pullman employees and officers free of charge while on company business; to furnish adequate ticket quarters; to haul, switch, and inspect cars; and to pay for all running repairs, whether made by the railway or in the Pullman shops. In return, the Pullman Company agrees to provide an adequate supply of cars; to furnish such cars not only with materials needed but also with such servants as are necessary; and to restrict the purchase of space upon the basis of tickets held, requiring a minimum of one ticket for the reservation of a full section, one and one-half tickets for a compartment, and two tickets for a drawing room. Compensation is the point at which Pullman contracts differ widely. In the case of weaker lines which are in no position to purchase and operate their own special equipment, the Pullman Company drives a relatively hard bargain, this section of the contract often calling for what amounts to a guarantee of a certain gross revenue per car per year for all equipment used on that line, with the receipt by the Pullman Company of all moneys in excess of the minimum figure. Stronger lines appear to be able to make better terms and often succeed not only in fixing a lower minimum figure per car-year but even in compelling the Pullman Company, as a price of obtaining the contract, to share with the railway all sums received by it in excess of the minimum assured.[1]

Determination of the Pullman Charge.—The basis of determining Pullman fares is largely the time such service is utilized, though distance is also a factor. Other considerations, such as the density of the traffic, the cost of operation, and even the relation which the passenger fare via a given route bears to the fare charged over another route, also enter. Berth charges are determined primarily by the time during which the accommodations are used, while seat rates vary, in general, with the distance. The Pullman service gives rise to two troublesome problems: the establishment of a proper relation between the charges for upper and lower berths, and the assessment of the Pullman passenger, as compared with the coach passenger, a sum commensurate with the greater cost to the railway of his movement. The first of these problems, and the simpler, was definitely settled by the Interstate Commerce Commission in a decision that fixed the rate for the upper berth, despite all considerations of cost and lesser

[1] In testimony before the Interstate Commerce Commission in the Pullman surcharge hearing, the following division of revenues from the Pullman service between that corporation and the Atchison, Topeka, and Santa Fe Railway Company, effective Jan. 1, 1923, was indicated: to the Pullman Company the first $9,000 per car-year; to the railway the next $1,500; between $10,500 and $14,500, half to the railway; and above $14,500, three-fourths to the railway. Under the previous contract the division point was $7,250 and the Santa Fe received half in excess of $8,750.

use, at not to exceed 80 per cent of the sum charged for the lower. Against this relation there has been little public protest through a period of years, though the 80 per cent basis has not served as a sufficient incentive to encourage general use of upper berths. For the second problem it is not so certain a permanent solution has been found.

It is only within recent years that serious consideration has been given to the problem raised by the greater cost of handling a passenger traveling in Pullman equipment than of handling the same passenger by coach. This greater cost results both from the lower average number of passengers per car-mile carried in Pullman equipment[1] and from the much greater weight of Pullman cars as compared with coach equipment. The first step toward meeting this problem was taken during the period of federal operation when an extra ½ cent per mile was exacted of all passengers who occupied Pullman space. Following the period of federal operation the Interstate Commerce Commission authorized the continuance of an extra charge for the benefit of the railway. This surcharge, however, is assessed upon the basis of the Pullman fare, the figure being 50 per cent additional. Against this surcharge bitter complaint was voiced by many, the attack being led by a strong and determined organization of commercial travelers. When repeated efforts failed to convince the Interstate Commerce Commission that the surcharge should be abandoned, its opponents sought to abolish it by Congressional enactment. Though these attempts were attended by greater support than the cause justified and by far greater recognition than the principle of legislative interference with a considered Commission action merited, the House of Representatives stood as an immovable barrier to the accomplishment of this political effort. For several years past there has been little active protest against the so-called Pullman surcharge and it is only reasonable to expect that the railway will be permitted to continue to demand from the passenger traveling in special equipment a sufficient amount in excess of the regular mileage charge for coach movement to compensate for the extra cost incurred. Indeed, it is anomalous that the Pullman passenger, with an admittedly higher average of ability to pay, has been permitted by regulatory bodies to ride at the partial expense of the coach traveler as long as he has.

Comparative Passenger-service Statistics.—The importance of the passenger business to the average citizen, together with certain tendencies in the passenger field, is well shown by statistics relative to this service. The number of railway journeys taken by the average American compares poorly with the number taken by the typical western European. The

[1] In 1929 the average number of revenue passengers riding in Pullman equipment was 10, while the average for all equipment (including Pullman) was 13, thus indicating an average for coach equipment in excess of 15, since total car mileages were approximately equal.

average number of trips per person in the United States was in 1930 only 5.7, while recent data show that the average of France stands at 18, of the United Kingdom at 38, and of Germany at 31. This apparent lesser patronage is partially offset, however, by the greater average length of journey in the United States. These figures are approximately 13, 15, and 26 miles, for the United Kingdom, Germany, and France, respectively, and 40 for the United States. The trend in the United States with respect to the number of persons carried, total passenger-miles, and the average length of journey, was definitely upward until 1920, as is evidenced by increases of approximately 150 per cent, 295 per cent, and 58 per cent, respectively, for the period 1890–1920. Since 1920, however, the number of passengers and total passenger-miles have steadily declined—largely due to motor-vehicle competition—while average length of journey has increased, the figures for 1929 being 63 per cent, 66 per cent, and 105 per cent of those for 1920.

National figures, however, fail to suggest wide differences among the three territories for which statistics are compiled. Of the total number of passengers carried in 1929, more than 71 per cent were handled in Eastern territory, and about 18 per cent in Western, though the latter contributed more than 32 per cent of the total passenger-miles of service for that year as compared with barely 56 per cent for the Eastern. This divergence in the percentages suggests the wide difference in the average length of journey per passenger which appears in fact: the average for Eastern territory was about 30 miles while that for Western was more than 73, Southern showing an average of almost 50. Such figures explain the considerable difference in the average total revenue per passenger in the various districts, the figures for the year 1929 being $0.82, $1.56, and $2.09 for Eastern, Southern, and Western territories, respectively. The density of passenger traffic per mile of line is, as might be anticipated, much greater in Eastern territory than elsewhere, the average number of passenger-miles per mile of line for that region being 289,772, as compared with 82,222 for Southern, and 74,090 for Western.

Service and Efficiency.—From the inception of the railway, management has sought constantly to increase the efficiency of operations that larger profits might be had or that losses from a particular service—occasionally service as a whole—might be minimized. Striking progress has been made in the past by the railways in the handling of freight, and those gains continue. Such progress has never been evident in the handling of passengers, however, because of certain features of this phase of the business. And during the past decade, despite the efforts of the rail carriers to meet the situation, passenger-mile costs have increased to such point as to threaten disaster to passenger service. From 1890 to 1920 the total number of passenger-miles of service rendered increased 295 per cent as against an increase in the number of passenger train-miles of 97 per cent—in short, the average train load approximately doubled during a period when the average freight-train load had increased by 269 per cent. From 1920 to 1929, while total passenger-miles of service decreased by 34 per cent, passenger train-miles were declining a mere 0.2 per cent, and passenger service as measured in terms of car-miles increased more than 5 per cent—with a resultant decline in the number of passengers per train of more than 30 per cent. Yet during this period the average freight-train load increased by 13 per cent.

This unhappy contrast of passenger with freight efficiency, first relatively but more recently absolutely, is the consequence of several factors. In the first place, the rate of increase in the volume of passenger traffic was less than that of freight even before the former began to decline. But despite the fact that passenger trains already scheduled were operated with lean loads, public demand and railway competition added other trains steadily—though perhaps of these two factors the latter was the more important. Railway traffic officials have long acted upon the belief that men with tonnage to offer "ship as they ride" through competitive territory and, driven by this thought, have vied actively among themselves to provide the speediest, most frequent, and most comfortable—even luxurious—service between competitive points. So long as passenger traffic increased even slowly, there was a semblance of justification in such uncontrolled competition—but in the past decade many actions that have resulted from such rivalry have seemed illogical. And the more so since, a service once established, it is difficult to secure the approval of regulatory bodies for its cancellation. In 1929 the railways were rendering a speedier, more comfortable service than in 1920 at an average revenue per passenger-mile less than for any previous year since the standard fare was advanced to 3.6 cents per mile, and operating as many trains—yet total revenue had declined in that period by 33 per cent. It is obvious that decreases must be made by the railways in the cost of passenger service comparable to declines in revenue; if competitive or other conditions block such action, then governmental pressure must be exerted, for the passenger service should not be materially subsidized by the freight service over a long period, either in equity to shippers or in fairness to the railways.

Development of Additional Traffic.—The only alternative to a sharp cut in railway passenger service lies in the development of added traffic, which is today one of the two pressing problems in this field. For a period of 90 years following the appearance of the railway in the United States, there was no practical alternative to the railway for those who desired to journey. During those years passenger traffic grew normally and steadily: the major efforts of the railway's passenger solicitor were directed to obtaining as large a part of planned movements as possible, in competition with other lines. Such competition persists and keen competition has developed between the railways and the common-carrier bus, but the decline in passenger traffic is largely due to use by the traveler of the private automobile instead of the railway coach. Since no adjustment of schedules and no probable reduction in rates—indeed, no added comforts—are likely to lure any considerable proportion of these travelers back to railway travel and since such highway journeys are likely to become longer as the highway system is improved, it appears that any increase in railway passenger traffic is likely to be the result of travel interest aroused in those who might otherwise give no thought to such journeys or who have no other satisfactory means of making trips. In short, it seems that the principal problem of the railway traffic official is to develop new business. And the incentive to do so is strong, since the volume of passenger travel could be increased markedly with scarcely any increase in costs. Even in 1918–1920, when the average number of passengers per car was 20, a large margin of empty space remained; today, with the average load not in excess of 13, and with an average of more than 4 cars per train, the surplus of space is great.

Efforts to increase the volume of railway passenger traffic have been in the past decade increasingly active and intelligently directed. Wide use has been made of advertising in its many forms: newspaper space has been used generously, intriguing pamphlets have been issued and scattered broadcast, posters have been employed, pictures shown. Indeed, few means of compelling attention have been overlooked by one or another of the railways. By such campaigns tens of thousands have been familiarized with places as diverse as Glacier National Park and Florida's sunny beaches and with events as different as the Mardi Gras and the International Live Stock Exposition. Such advertising has been relatively unimportant in amount, however, and has been directed too often toward the solicitation of business already existent, rather than toward the creation of the "travel urge" in the stay-at-homes. It seems clear that definite possibilities remain for educating the American public to travel more often and farther. To this end well-located ticket offices in the larger cities and the maintenance of a staff of alert traffic agents, whose function it is to convince the public that rail travel is inexpensive and not difficult, will contribute.

The railways are now encouraging excursion traffic of both a special and a seasonal character, and the development of such traffic should be the concern of passenger-traffic officials to an increasing degree in the future. As the American public becomes more "travel-broken," resort traffic should become an important item—such resorts as are advertised being too distant to reach conveniently by automobile. Closely akin to excursion traffic are the "conducted tours," an innovation that has made its appearance upon railways peculiarly well situated to attract sightseers, and these tours have experienced a steady growth. Another type of traffic developed in an extensive way by railways operating into large cities is the suburban traffic. The necessity of dwelling close in so that work may be reasonably accessible has been greatly lessened by the operation of high-class suburban service. The accessible area has been so extended by the railways that it now has a usual radius of from 30 to 40 miles. The one objection to such traffic, however, lies in its too-often unremunerative character; rates must be low, yet a service rendered that has two sharp peaks daily, and terminal costs are high. Unless closely watched, suburban traffic may become a burden.

To stimulate increased passenger movements, American railways have centered their attention primarily upon the betterment of the service. Lessened road time and a higher quality of service have been the lures commonly used to draw traffic, but such means represent the traffic man's competitive weapons and fail to solve the *real* problem in the passenger field—the creation of *more* business for all roads. It is possible that such an end may be attained more readily through the introduction of graduated fares—in short, the application of the class principle. Such a course seems distinctly distasteful to the average passenger-traffic official, who insists that it is "un-American" and therefore must fail. Yet such reductions are characteristic of the efforts of the railways to increase seasonal and resort traffic and definite classifications are recognized in certain territories in the tourist and the standard sleeping car. However, concessions have generally been made sparingly, the reductions often being too slight to accomplish successfully the purpose in mind. No extended use has been made of regular reduced fares for a service somewhat below standard even in an experimental way but, while the opportunities for the development of a class service in the United States are less than in European countries, there certainly is economic justification for experimentation in this direction.[1]

Elimination of Abuses.—A second problem incident to passenger traffic, but one of which both phases have been largely solved, involves abuses which a score of years ago occasioned great outcry by the public and the railways, respectively, the "pass" and ticket "scalping." Of the two, the "pass" constituted the greater public danger, and this problem was first met. In the "good old days" every shipper of significance, every important man in a community, every public official from district attorney and county judge to governor and occupants of the Supreme

[1] To meet highway competition between Chicago territory and the Pacific coast three classes of rail travel, *in fact* though not *in name*, have been established. The highest charge is made to those who wish to avail themselves of standard sleeping-car accommodations; a lesser charge is made to those who are content to use tourist sleeping cars; and a rate almost 30 per cent below the "standard charge" is available to those who make the entire journey by coach, accepting thus accommodations that are comparable to those offered by bus.

bench, were gladly furnished free transportation; indeed, to pay fare was a clear confession of unimportance in the business and social structure. However, this discrimination, as well as the corrupting influence of the practice, brought a veritable avalanche of anti-pass legislation in the early years of the present century. In consequence, the use of passes is now restricted, interstate and intrastate, to those giving essentially full-time service to the railways and to their immediate families, togethei with certain other limited groups. The other evil, that of selling transportation at less than regular prices, still persists, despite strong railway effort to eliminate it and rather general public cooperation. In early days the railways themselves participated in the practice: blocks of tickets, which agreements prevented the railways marketing directly to the public at less than a fixed price, were transferred to brokers at "bargain" prices with the understanding that the broker sell them at less than the standard rates. This practice—"scalping," so-called—was designed, of course, to attract additional business to the particular carrier. Today, however, scalping is largely confined to the merchandising of unused portions of through and round-trip tickets. Not only does this practice lessen the carrier's revenues but it often represents a breach of faith on the part of the original purchaser of the ticket, since many of the tickets purchased and so handled are nontransferable in character. Furthermore, the scalper all too often resorts to dishonest practices, such as altering dates, erasing marks, and plugging holes punched by such agents of the carrier as may have handled the ticket. During the period of federal control the practice was practically stopped, but it has reappeared on a small scale. A few years should see its complete elimination as a commercial enterprise.

The Problem of Competition.—A final problem of increasing difficulty and of growing significance is that of competition. The earliest type of passenger competition of importance to which the steam railway was subjected was that of the electric railway. This agency, initially serving an urban constituency, expanded later into the suburban field where it first became a serious competitive factor. When it entered the interurban field it constituted a still more serious menace to the steam carrier. Enjoying the advantages which result from the use of electric power—the easier adjustment of the unit to the immediate traffic need, greater cleanliness, and ability to coordinate with street railways and thus to reach downtown sections of the cities as well as residential districts—this competitor threatened seriously for a time. Expansion proceeded at a progressive rate until about 1914, by which date a considerable network of interurban electric railways had been built in the more populous areas. Certain steam railways to which the interurban constituted a particular menace sought to meet the situation by acquiring control of these competitors; others endeavored by means of lowered rates and improved service to maintain the normal volume of passenger and freight business against the rival agency. However, because of lower construction and operating costs, the advantage lay with the interurban; in consequence, it continued to gain steadily at the expense of the steam railway for a period. Yet today those properties that operate at a profit are few.

The explanation of this change in the situation lies in the rise of yet another competitor of the steam railway, one even better adapted to handling local business than the interurban and favored quite generally for a period by public subsidy and relative freedom from restrictive regulations. This newer agency is the motor bus. The construction of interurbans was interrupted in 1914 because of a shortage of funds for such undertakings, and it was impossible to resume until after the close of the war. By that time the possibilities of the motor vehicle had been discovered and, ere construction could be resumed upon old electric-railway projects or new ones launched, the motor bus and the motor truck, ably seconded by the private automobile, were threatening existing interurbans with bankruptcy. Nor was it long until bankruptcy overtook numerous projects—bankruptcy terminated sometimes by reorganization and sometimes by abandonment of service. Yet, despite the fact that the interurban electric railway has been generally eliminated as a competitor, this system of transportation has potentialities that might make it an active force in the future if all appropriate costs and close governmental restrictions were imposed upon its highway competitors. To meet this potential danger and also to cope more effectively with bus and truck, steam railways may well continue to give serious thought to electrification in populous areas and in suburban territory, even in other districts where the cost of electrical energy compares favorably with the cost of steam power.

Another competitor of the steam railway in the movement of persons is the airplane. With the first successful flights made during the early years of the present century, the airplane was given little thought as an agency for the regular movement of persons over established routes for almost a score of years. After a brief period of experimentation, however, service expanded rapidly until at the close of 1931 operations were being maintained regularly over more than 50,000 miles of airways. From less than 6,000 passengers carried over regular routes in 1926 the number increased in 1931 to 522,345, a figure more than three times that for 1929, despite the sharp curtailment of general business. And the volume of traffic in 1932 exceeded that of the preceding year. A record of growth such as this for a new type of transport agency that does not yet command full public confidence is striking, and the more so since the average level of charges has been high as compared with those of other agencies. However, it is undoubted that as the public becomes "air-minded" the saving in time is increasingly attractive—and the steady decline in rates for air travel has contributed greatly to continued expansion during 1930 and

1931. It is now possible to ride over many airways at a cost but little in excess of that of the regular rail fare plus Pullman charges, with hours of travel time saved and waits eliminated.

For the strong competitive position of air transport several factors are accountable. The cost of transporting passengers by air is in excess of the low level of charges now effective upon many lines, if no more than the costs borne by line operators are considered: payments for the handling of air mail have occasioned a considerable loss to the government in recent years, and such disguised subsidy is likely to continue. Indirect aids are also provided by federal and minor governmental units that constitute another, though less obvious, subsidy. Then too, the railway is at a disadvantage because its train schedules have not kept pace with the demand for increased speed. When the alternative to railway travel was the horse-drawn vehicle, average train speeds in excess of 35 miles an hour represented high accomplishment, while to traverse long distances at a speed approaching 45 miles an hour was comparable to travel upon the wings of the wind: indeed, upon the wings of a considerable gale. Yet today, with the cruising speed of passenger planes varying from 135 to 185 miles an hour, such speeds by rail are not adequate.

Therefore, if the railway is to retain any considerable portion of its super-traffic, the only traffic that has developed at a normal rate during the past decade, it seems that train speeds must be materially increased and time between terminals sharply reduced. If the steam locomotive is not suited to these higher speeds, then the railways should begin to experiment seriously without delay to discover some superior and suitable instrument. Speed and comfort, rather than reduced travel costs, are of prime interest to a numerically important class of travelers: comfort the railways have provided upon the better trains but adequate speed is lacking; upon the modern transport plane a considerable degree of comfort is accorded and speed greatly in excess of rail movement is offered. It does not require the gift of prophecy to visualize heavy inroads upon the better class of railway passenger traffic within even a decade unless active efforts are made to quicken rail service. And, indeed, it is conceivable that the most effective struggle to keep a considerable part of such traffic upon the rails is fated to fail: to retain control the railways may well find it necessary to supplement service by train with service by plane.

In short, to the end of rendering a more complete and varied service the railways may well give serious consideration to active entry into the field of air transport. Cooperation with established air lines will be helpful and such steps have been taken hesitatingly by a number of railways, but it is probable that more active and direct participation will be advantageous. Of such developments more will be said in a later chapter: suffice it now to indicate the rapid development of air transport and its potential threat to the continued movement of super-service passenger traffic by rail.

With the decline of the interurban electric railway, and in large part responsible for that decline, there arose yet another competitor for the railway in the movement of persons. This competitor, the motor vehicle, first gained serious attention in the several years prior to 1920; since that date its inroads have been increasingly heavy. Those inroads have become so great as not only to prevent the railway from realizing upon its expectations of a normal increase in travel but even to cause an actual decline of serious proportions. In 1929, a prosperous year, the number of passengers carried had dropped 37 per cent from the peak of 1920 and the total number of passenger-miles had declined 32 per cent in the same period. Indeed, not since 1905 had the railways carried so few passengers as they did in 1929 and not since 1909 rendered so small a service as measured in terms of passenger-miles. In 1930 and 1931 there were further sharp declines in the number both of passengers and of passenger-miles; in the former year declines of 10 and 14 per cent, respectively, are shown below 1929, while the 1931 figures stand 17 and 18 per cent, respectively, below the disturbingly low record of performance of 1930.

Experience in the period prior to 1915 indicated that the volume of railway passenger traffic tended to double every 15 years. In 1915 the railways rendered 32.5 billion passenger-miles of service, so 65 billion passenger-miles would have been a reasonable expectation for 1930—yet but 27 billion were rendered. However, in that period the number of registered motor vehicles designed to move persons had increased tenfold—to more than 23 million—and in 1930 common-carrier buses alone moved in intercity service some 504 million passengers as compared with less than 704 million by the railways for that year. And no data are available for the movement of persons in the passenger automobile, privately owned and operated. Additional evidence could easily be adduced from official reports to show that railway passenger traffic is in a "parlous" state, but to do so would be only to add detail to the picture: its essential character is clear.

There are no data available that will make possible a certain answer to many questions the analyst would put concerning developments within the past decade affecting passenger traffic or to indicate probable trends with assurance. Some conclusions seem justified, however. It is certain that the private automobile has accounted for the greater portion of the loss of passenger traffic to the railway and it is unlikely that any significant part of this traffic is recoverable to the railways through either railway rate reductions or reasonable restrictions upon highway operations. It is probable too, that the average length of haul for bus passengers is low as compared with that for railway passengers and it is unlikely that the bus will become a serious competitor of the railway for long-distance movements. However, with the improvement and extension of the highway net, opportunities for movement by bus will increase and time schedules will be shortened; in consequence, the bus will compete with growing success in the intermediate-distance field. Indeed, certain more recent figures suggest that it is already doing so—and the scope of use of the private automobile will also extend as highways are improved. Another conclusion justified by available data, as indicated upon a preceding page, is that the decline in railway passenger traffic has been basically a decline in coach traffic rather than a general decline. Though the number of passengers riding in coaches and the number riding in super-equipment are not readily available for earlier years, car-miles for coach movement and for special equipment have been compiled since 1908. In 1929 coach mileage stood some 10 per cent below that of 1908, while car-miles of service rendered super-travelers showed an increase of 135 per cent: traffic of the so-called Pullman type lacked but little of developing at the old rate of 100 per cent in each 15 years. But this traffic, as mentioned before, will feel the competition of air transport most keenly—a competition that promises to be progressively active and general.

If it be, then, the coach passenger who has shifted from rail to rubber and continues so to shift, what defensive measures may the railways take that give promise of measurable success? Or, to approach the problem positively, what manner of offensive may the railways launch with the hope of recovering traffic? Before either question can be answered intelligently, the reasons for the shift must be known. These reasons are many, varying from an unreasoning antagonism toward the railway or travel by rail on the part of some to the desire to travel at least cost on the part of large numbers. The owner of a car ignores railway service when distances are not excessive because he enjoys the exhilaration of driving; because he can come and go essentially at will; because at destination or at intermediate points he has in his car a serviceable instrument; because he can avoid waits at intermediate stops or actually make better time than do the trains available; because he can travel at less cost by car than by rail—or mistakenly believes that he can; and for numberless other lesser reasons. The bus rider travels by highway because the bus offers a type of transportation somewhat similar to that of the individual car in which the rider finds delight; because of more convenient hours or more direct service; because bus stations are normally in the downtown district; because of a possibly more intimate view of the countryside during the journey; because the smaller unit is more personal than the heavy trains; because the cost of travel by bus is often lower than by rail; and for other causes more individual. To what extent can these actuating factors be met?

None of the mentioned advantages of the individual car can be offset by rail movement unless, perhaps, the driver can be convinced that he errs in his estimate of cost: frequently only immediate outlays for gasoline and oil are reckoned by him as costs. However, the greater safety of travel by rail than by car might be stressed, especially in these days of highway congestion and lax traffic control. Of the advantages of the bus, many can be met in part or in whole by the railway—or counterbalanced by railway or social action. More frequent service can be rendered by the railways at a comparatively low cost by the use of an improved gasoline-motor car. If these units be small, light, and perhaps mounted on rubber tires, operating costs will be low and a more personal vehicle is available. Such lower operating costs would enable the railway to make a rate comparable to that offered by bus lines— a rate even below bus rates may be possible, indeed, when bus traffic bears its total costs and is subjected to the same broad regulation now resting upon the railways. Indeed, there seem to be few of the advantages of the bus that cannot be met largely—and to this the railway can add greater safety as well as materially greater speed, if train schedules be shortened. However, with a view to maintenance of control of passenger traffic to railway advantage and to the ultimate benefit of the public through the better coordination of all transport agencies, it seems desirable that the railway should enter the field of bus service. In this way the railway can utilize the bus at points where it offers an advantage, can employ it effectively as a "feeder," and can serve a hinterland that will be seized by the independents if unoccupied by the railway. That many railways have already become bus operators indicates a realization that this instrument can be used effectively as a substitute for, and a supplement to, service by rail. Of this phase of railway expansion more will be said later but it may well be stated here that such development, too long delayed by many roads, should proceed rapidly within the next few years. And governmental barriers to such integration of service are to be deprecated; more, to be fought vigorously in public interest. The advantages to public and to carriers alike of integration are too great to let the fear of monopoly have great weight at a time when regulation has been so highly developed.

The Future of the Railway Passenger Traffic.—In the face of a continued and striking decline in railway passenger traffic and in view of the fact that competition is likely to become increasingly severe, what is the probable future of this one-time dominant agency in the field of passenger transport? It is difficult to find a sound basis for prediction: there are too many elements of uncertainty in the situation both as to the development of the competing agencies and as to railway policy. Furthermore, the situation of individual railways differs widely: some, by the most intelligent of efforts, will not be able to continue more than a shell of the rail service offered in the past; others will retain a considerable volume of traffic in spite of an inadequate policy. Upon some railways passenger service may ultimately be abandoned because of inability to make it meet even out-of-pocket costs but it seems improbable that the movement of passengers by rail will become a thing of the past in the predictable future. Particularly will this be true if the maximum of intelligence and effort is directed toward the adaptation of railway passenger service to the necessities of present-day competition and if the railways closely coordinate rail with other forms of transport that can be made supplementary and supporting rather than competitive and destructive. Within considerable limits the future of passenger movements by rail is what railway management makes it.

REFERENCES

BERGE, GEORGE W.: *The Free Pass Bribery System* (attack on pass evil in politics), Independent Publishing Company, 1905.

Bureau of the Census: *Street and Electric Railways*, 1912.

FLYNN, LEO J.: *Coordination of Motor Transportation.* Report to Interstate Commerce Commission, published as Senate Document 43, 72nd Congress, 1st Session, Government Printing Office.

HAINES, H. S.: *Efficient Railway Operation*, The Macmillan Company, 1919.

HUNGERFORD, EDWARD: *The Modern Railroad*, A. C. McClurg and Co., 1912.

Interstate Commerce Commission: *Annual Reports; Statistics of Railways in the United States; Reports.* See particularly *Coordination of Motor Transportation*, 182 I.C.C. 263.

JOHNSON, E. R., and G. G. HUEBNER: *Railroad Traffic and Rates*, vol. 2, D. Appleton & Company, 1911.

———, and T. W. VAN METRE: *Principles of Railroad Transportation*, D. Appleton & Company, 1921.

MCPHERSON, LOGAN: *The Working of the Railroads*, Henry Holt & Company, 1909.

Pullman Company, *Annual Reports.*

The Ticket-scalping Fight in Houston, Texas (pamphlet.)

WEYL, W. E.: *The Passenger Traffic of Railways*, in Publications of the University of Pennsylvania, 1901.

See the references at the close of Chaps. X, XXIV and XXXVIII for additional citations relative to the movement of persons by highway and by air.

Chapter XXII

THE MINOR SERVICES—MAIL AND EXPRESS

BESIDES the two major services already discussed, the American railway offers various incidental services. Of these, but two—mail and express—are outstanding, each having a significance to the public quite out of proportion to carrier revenues therefrom. Of the two, the mail service, although yielding less than 2.11 per cent of total railway operating revenue for 1930 as compared with approximately 2.17 per cent for the express business, is the more important to society. For that reason a discussion of its outstanding features will be presented first.

THE MAIL SERVICE

The cultural and business worth of this service to man is impossible of measurement. The regular and cheap movement of freight is of tremendous economic and social importance and the worth of the passenger service is great, but to lose that close intellectual contact which our present mail service affords, to lose the socializing and broadening influence exerted by newspapers and periodicals which circulate cheaply and in enormous numbers among people in all walks of life, would be a social calamity of the first magnitude. Yet an adequate mail service does more than render invaluable assistance in the promotion of public intelligence and the maintenance of closer personal relations; it serves a most important end in business life. Occasional interruptions of mail movements for but short periods indicate to the business man the heavy losses that would follow in the wake of irregularities in service, much less a complete cessation.

Just as the demands of freight and passenger service upon the railways increase more rapidly than population, so does the demand for postal service and facilities. No accurate measure of the volume of mail exists but the increase in postal revenues may be accepted as a rough measure of the growing demands made upon the Post Office Department. Departmental records show that increase from 1890 to 1930 to have been almost 1160 per cent, though population increased during those years but 96 per cent. The increase in the complexities of business relations and the rising level of culture represent, therefore, a more accurate index to the need for additional service than does the growth of population.

The Railway and the Mail Service.—However important the mail service may be, it would concern a student of railway transportation little were it not that a large portion of the mail has long been handled by the railways. Indeed, the Postmaster General has estimated that 90 per cent of the weight of all mails is carried by them. This movement of mail by railways dates back to 1834, almost to the beginning of the railways themselves. For some years serious doubt was entertained by many as to the ability of the railways to compete successfully with the stagecoach, either in average speed or in promptness. In fact, certain early railway lines failed so signally in handling mail that their contracts were not renewed and the service was again performed by the stagecoach. But gradually the stagecoach was compelled to give place and, within a comparatively brief time, it was used only in such areas as were not served by rail. In the discussion of the mail service to follow, an effort has been made to discriminate between those functions and problems which are essentially governmental in character and those which sufficiently concern the railways to justify consideration here.

As indicated, the service of the railway is of fundamental importance in the transportation of mail, though this work is supplemented by other agencies which also perform an indispensable service. Movements are made over electric railways, the mileage so utilized in 1932 being 5,984. Steamboats and other power boats also function, their mileage being, for the same year, 42,546. And air transportation is utilized where there is a sufficient demand for exceptionally fast service to justify its establishment, this mileage at the close of 1931 being 26,745. Another important type of service supplementing the railways is that rendered by the so-called Star Routes, over which much mail moves into the hinterland. In 1932, 12,443 such routes were in operation, covering 239,714 miles. The shortest of these routes is but a few miles in length, while the longest cover distances of many hundreds of miles through the wilds of Alaska.

Development of the Railway Post Office.—When the railway mail service was established there was no thought that it would extend beyond the movement of sacks of mail. As early as 1840, however, consideration was given to the possibility of sorting mail en route. In 1847 the Postmaster General, through a representative, made a study of the English scheme but his conclusion, that such a plan would prove too expensive for the American mail service at that time, killed effectually for a period any positive movement in that direction. In 1862, however, the question was again brought forward, this time by William A. Davis, assistant postmaster at St. Joseph, Missouri. To expedite the departure of mails from St. Joseph to the many points westward which were served by stagecoach and rider, he conceived the idea of equipping cars for mail distribution en route, so that the mail would be ready for immediate dispatch upon its arrival at that frontier post. With the consent of the Post Office Department a trial was made on the Hannibal and St. Joseph; an old baggage coach, crudely fitted with racks and boxes, served as equipment. The experiment proved a success but it was not until 1879 that the railway post-office car was fully recognized by law as a part of our postal system. Since that year the use of this type of car has steadily increased until, in 1932, there were made in these cars almost 16 billion distributions and redistributions of all types of mail, with a distribution accuracy of about 99.99 per cent. Indeed, a large part of all the mail carried by the railways is distributed or handled by the railway mail service en route. In his 1921 report, the Postmaster General said,

> The service is one vast traveling post office functioning simultaneously throughout the entire country and in which the necessary separations, distributions, and dispatches of the mails that would otherwise be made in the post office are made in the swiftly moving railway post-office cars. Thus the mails are advanced in delivery the greatest possible time and the post offices are relieved of a work the magnitude of which they would be unable to handle.

Although preference is given the transmission of letters and daily papers, all other classes of mail matter, including the circular, catalogue, and parcel-post merchandise mails, are handled with due regard to their importance to the public. There were in operation on June 30, 1932, 200,166 miles of railway post-office service, with 250,818,140 miles of annual travel, this being supplemented by 68,888 miles of closed-pouch service with an annual mileage of 107,870,541.

All equipment employed in the railway mail service is owned by the carriers. This equipment consists of two general types: ordinary baggage or express cars which serve adequately for all closed-pouch movements, and cars built to facilitate the sorting of mail en route. Plans and specifications, covering in detail every feature entering into the construction of cars used for the distribution of mail, are worked out by the Post Office Department and the cars are built in accordance with such plans. To make easier the adjustment of such special equipment to the varying space needs of the Department, and to make possible the conversion of such special equipment to ordinary baggage or express service, fixtures in the newer cars are so arranged as to make possible this adaptation at a minimum expense of time and money. For many years railway post-office equipment was built of wood but because of the frequent loss of life of mail messengers in wrecks, due to the location of the car in the train, legislation has compelled a gradual change from wooden to steel equipment, the proportion of mail cars in service in 1931 with steel underframe or entirely of steel being almost 82 per cent. In that year there were employed 4,352 full and apartment mail cars, besides the baggage and express equipment used in connection with closed-pouch movements.

Closed-pouch Service.—In addition to the railway post-office service, which handles a great part of the mail moved by these carriers, there is also rendered a closed-pouch service of two types. Between large centers in various sections of the country it is possible to move mail in quantities and this fact has given rise to the fast mail train. Such trains carry cars loaded to capacity with mail in closed pouches and, at times, render an incidental passenger service, though the more important of these trains handle mail alone. These mail trains have right of way over all other traffic and operate at a high rate of speed. Generally the privilege of handling through mail is one which is eagerly sought by the railways, success or failure in securing the contract for a particular period, as a result of speed tests, being the occasion of joy or regret to railway officials and employees alike. The operation of the "fast mail," like the de luxe train in passenger service, is a source of great pride to the railway man. The second type of closed-pouch service, consisting of mail carried in locked pouches in baggage car and even caboose, is far less conspicuous but nevertheless of great importance. It is usually found on branch lines and is rendered also either by local or by "mixed trains" on main lines, the pouches being unloaded and picked up, station by station, en route.

Volume of Railway Mail.—The importance of the railway in the rendition of adequate mail service cannot be exaggerated. Mail was carried in 1932 over 211,809 miles of line in the United States, a decrease of 4,482 from the preceding year, largely because of elimination of trains, with a total number of miles of regularly authorized space units of 491,852,460. It is difficult to estimate with accuracy the weight of mails moved by the railways since the adoption of the space basis of payment. In 1917 it was estimated that 826,090,715 ton-miles of service were rendered by the railways and in 1931 the Post Office Department indicated that 1,277,996,522 ton-miles of domestic non-local mail service was rendered. Of this huge total, it is certain that the railways performed an overwhelming portion. As compensation for this service the government paid all railways $101,158,361 in 1932 as compared with $57,728,603 paid to all other agencies of transport, the former representing an increase of only 95 per cent over 1916 as compared with 410 per cent for the latter; yet it is probable the proportion of railway ton-miles of service to the total had diminished little.

The Terminal Post Office.—A feature of the general mail service, so intimately connected with the railway function that it cannot be ignored, is the terminal railway post office. Such offices are generally located in or near the large railway passenger terminals and handle an enormous amount of mail. The heavy demand upon them in the rapid movement of mail is indicated by the extensive floor space occupied where such post offices are maintained. Near the Union Station in Chicago a special structure has been erected for use by the Post Office Department and in New York two such terminals are maintained, using floor space in excess of 100,000 square feet. These terminal offices are usually leased from the railways by the government and both supplement the railway post-office service and serve as centers for the dispatching of storage mail.

The Parcel Post Service: *Its Establishment.*—Mail matter has long been classified, this classification resting upon both social considerations and cost. These classes are known in the United States as first, second, third, and fourth, though the consolidation of the latter two has been recommended by the Postmaster General. In addition to the classified revenue matter carried, there is also a large amount of mail handled free of charge for various governmental departments. However, since the problem of classification is one which concerns the Post Office Department, not the railways, no discussion either of its justice or of the bases recognized need here be presented. Indeed, were it not for the peculiar relationship which the fourth-class service, known as parcel post, bears to the express and even, in certain cases, to the freight service, no discussion of postal administration would be germane here. But the growing significance of this parcel-post service requires that a description of the system be given.

Agitation for the establishment of a parcel-post system in the United States dates back many years. Opposition to it came mainly from three groups. The express companies opposed it as a dangerous competitor and offered perhaps the most effective political obstacle to its adoption. Indeed, it was once said facetiously, "There are five reasons for the failure to establish parcel post system in the United States: the Adams Express Company, the American Express Company, the United States Express Company, the Wells, Fargo Express Company, and the Southern Express Company." The second source of opposition was the small retailer who was fearful of mail-order competition. The third group opposing the establishment of this system was small and composed largely of those conservatives who felt that the government should not thus enter the commercial field: they feared that this entry might be but the opening wedge of socialism. However, the continued efforts of proponents of the idea finally secured the passage of a law which authorized the establishment of parcel-post service beginning with Jan. 1, 1913. The law, as originally passed, gave the Postmaster General the power to restate from time to time, with the approval of the Interstate Commerce Commission, classifications, weight limits, rates, zones, or other factors, in order to promote maximum public service. Under this provision many changes have been made, particularly with respect to the weight limit, to rates, and to special features such as insurance and c.o.d. privileges, with a view to improving the service.

The Determination of Parcel-post Rates.—Perhaps the most interesting and certainly the most stable feature of the law is the system of rate making prescribed. Under the law, zones were established, the zone location of any point being determined basically by the direct distance of that point from the point of shipment. These zones are numbered from 1 to 8, the maximum radius of each being 50, 150, 300, 600, 1,000, 1,400, 1,800, and over 1,800 miles, respectively, a local zone also being recognized covering movements through a single office. To determine more easily the zone location of the point of destination and hence facilitate the determination of the rate, the United States has been divided into a series of squares 30 minutes each way. To the northernmost tier, moving westward, have been given the numbers 0, 50, 100, 150, 200, 250, etc., and successive squares south of these have been numbered

POST OFFICES BY STATES—UTAH, VERMONT

No.	P. O. & County	Unit	Zone
48392	°Spring City†, Sanpete	4520	----
48393	Springdale, Washington	4674	----
48394	Springville†, Utah	4518	----
48336	Spry, Garfield	4572	----
48504	Standardville†, Carbon	4419	----
48397	Sterling, Sanpete	4520	----
48308	Stockton, Tooele	4568	----
48104	(Sugarhouse, Sta. Salt Lake City)	4517	----
48305	Sulphurdale, Beaver	4621	----
48401	Summit, Iron	4623	----
48399	Summit Point, San Juan	4272	----
48462	°Sunnyside†, Carbon	4369	----
48403	Sweet Mine, Carbon	4469	----
48404	Tabiona, Duchesne	4418	----
48470	Talmage, Duchesne	4368	----
48406	Teasdale, Wayne	4472	----
48408	Thistle, Utah	4519	----
48409	Thompsons, Grand	4321	----
48411	°Tooele†, Tooele	4567	----
48412	Topliff, Tooele	4568	----
48413	Toquerville, Washington	4674	----
48414	Torrey, Wayne	4472	----
48415	Tremonton†, Box Elder	4565	----
48416	Trenton, Cache	4515	----
48422	Tridell, Uintah	4318	----
48417	Tropic, Garfield	4573	----
48447	Yost, Box Elder	4715	----
48454	Zion National Park§, Washington	4624	----
	VERMONT		
	All post offices in this State are money-order offices		
02001	Adamant, Washington	560	----
02002	Albany†, Orleans	559	----
02003	Alburg†, Grand Isle	659	----
02005	Andover, Windsor	612	----
02006	Arlington†, Bennington	662	----
02007	Ascutney, Windsor	562	----
02008	Averill, Essex	509	----
02009	Bakersfield, Franklin	609	----
02010	Barnard, Windsor	611	----
02011	Barnet†, Caledonia	560	----
02000	Barre†, Washington	610	----
02012	Barton†, Orleans	559	----
02014	Bartonsville, Windham	612	----
02016	Beebe Plain†, Orleans	558	----
02017	Beecher Falls†, Essex	508	----
02500	°Bellows Falls†, Windham	562	----
02036	Bridgewater Corners, Windsor	611	----
02037	Bridport, Addison	661	----
02039	Bristol†, Addison	660	----
02040	Brookfield, Orange	610	----
02042	Brownsville, Windsor	562	----
02043	Burke, Caledonia	509	----
02200	°Burlington†, Chittenden	660	----
	Branch Post Offices		
02203	Fort Ethan Allen† (Ind.).		
02201	Winooski† (Ind.).		
	Stations		
02207	C. O. D.		
02202	No. 1.		
02044	Cabot†, Washington	560	----
02045	Calais, Washington	560	----
02046	Cambridge†, Lamoille	609	----
02047	Cambridge Junction, Lamoille	609	----
02048	Cambridgeport, Windham	612	----
02049	Canaan, Essex	509	----
02050	Castleton†, Rutland	661	----
02051	Cavendish†, Windsor	612	----
02052	Cedar Beach§, Chittenden	660	----
02053	Center Rutland, Rutland	661	----
02055	Charlotte†, Chittenden	660	----

FIG. 26.—Portion of a specimen page, parcel post guide.

1, 2, 3, etc.; 51, 52, 53, etc.; 101, 102, 103, etc. All post offices are supplied with a parcel-post guide which gives the block or unit location of each post office. In addition, all offices are furnished a "zone key," this key being different for each block throughout the United States. Having determined the block number of the office of destination, it is but a moment's work to ascertain from the key the zone in which it is situated. These keys are constructed from maps upon which, with the midpoint of each block as the center, concentric zones have been drawn: all squares lying wholly within a concentric circle, as well as those which lie partially within that circle, take the rate applicable to that zone.[1] Copies of both

[1] This general principle has been modified slightly:

"Parcels subject to the pound rates, mailed for delivery within the first or second zones, are, when the distance by the shortest regular mail route from the office of

the guide and particular unit-number keys may be obtained through the Superintendent of Documents, Washington, and many who use the parcel-post service thus equip themselves that they may have rate information immediately available. A specimen page from a late directory appears on page 375, a zone key is shown below. Charges assessed for the movement of parcel-post material vary from 7 cents for 1 pound to 42 cents for 70 pounds moving locally, and from 15 cents for 1 pound, to

OFFICIAL ZONE KEY TO PARCEL POST GUIDE FOR UNIT NUMBER 2371

POST OFFICE DEPARTMENT

Series 1

By order of the Postmaster General

Unit Nos.	Zone.	Unit Nos.	Zone.	Unit Nos.	Zone.	Unit Nos.	Zone.	Unit Nos.	Zone.	Unit Nos.	Zone.
00- 012	8	1818–1824	3	2217–2225	2	2462–2466	3	2778–2787	4	3476–3789	5
9- 464	6	1825–1836	4	2226–2229	3	2467–2475	2	2788–2804	5	3790–	6
465- 466	5	1837–1839	5	2230–2238	4	2476–2480	3	2805–2814	4	3801–3838	5
508- 510	6	1855–1865	4	2239–2253	5	2481–2488	4	2815–2827	3	3839–	6
511- 516	5	1866–1875	3	2254–2261	4	2489–2503	5	2828–2837	4	3851–3887	5
558–	6	1876–1887	4	2262–2266	3	2504–2511	4	2838–2854	5	3901–	6
559–1264	5	1888–1889	5	2267–2275	2	2512–2516	3	2855–2865	4	3902–3936	5
1265–1275	4	1905–1914	4	2276–2280	3	2517–2525	2	2866–2875	3	3937–3952	6
1276–1283	5	1915–1927	3	2281–2288	4	2526–2529	3	2876–2887	4	3953–3985	5
1314–1327	4	1928–1937	4	2289–2303	5	2530–2538	4	2888–2904	5	3986–4003	6
1328–1333	5	1938–1939	5	2305–2311	4	2539–2553	5	2905–2917	4	4004–4033	5
1364–1379	4	1955–1963	4	2312–2316	3	2554–2562	4	2918–2924	3	4034–4054	6
1380–1395	5	1964–1977	3	2317–2319	2	2563–2567	3	2925–2936	4	4055–4082	5
1396–1398	6	1978–1987	4	2320–2322	1	2568–2574	2	2937–2955	5	4083–4106	6
1415–1430	4	1988–	5	2323–2325	2	2575–2579	3	2956–2986	4	4107–4130	5
1431–1446	5	2005–2011	4	2326–2330	3	2580–2588	4	2987–3005	5	4131–4158	6
1447–1449	6	2014–2028	3	2331–2338	4	2589–2603	5	3006–3035	4	4159–4178	5
1465–1481	4	2029–2060	4	2339–2353	5	2604–2612	4	3036–3056	5	4179–4210	6
1482–1496	5	2065–2069	3	2354–2361	4	2613–2617	3	3057–3084	4	4211–4225	5
1497–1499	6	2070–2072	2	2362–2366	3	2618–2624	2	3085–3106	5	4226–4264	6
1515–1532	4	2073–2079	3	2367–2369	2	2625–2629	3	3107–3134	4	4265–4270	5
1533–1546	5	2080–2112	4	2370–2372	1	2630–2638	4	3135–3157	5	4271–4832	6
1547–1549	6	2113–2117	3	2373–2375	2	2639–2653	5	3158–3183	4	4833–4851	7
1562–1583	4	2118–2124	2	2376–2380	3	2654–2662	4	3184–3208	5	4852–4880	6
1584–1596	5	2125–2129	3	2381–2388	4	2663–2669	3	3209–3232	4	4881–4903	7
1599–	6	2130–2138	4	2389–2403	5	2670–2672	2	3233–3258	5	4904–4927	6
1610–1634	4	2152–	5	2404–2411	4	2673–2679	3	3259–3281	4	4928–4955	7
1635–1644	5	2154–2162	4	2412–2416	3	2680–2688	4	3282–3309	5	4956–4974	6
1649–	6	2163–2167	3	2417–2419	2	2689–2703	5	3310–3330	4	4975–5009	7
1657–1684	4	2168–2174	2	2420–2422	1	2704–2713	4	3331–3361	5	5010–5020	6
1685–1690	5	2175–2179	3	2423–2425	2	2714–2728	3	3362–3379	4	5021–5721	7
1706–1735	4	2180–2188	4	2426–2430	3	2729–2738	4	3380–3412	5	5752–	8
1736–1755	5	2202–2203	5	2431–2438	4	2739–2753	5	3413–3427	4	5753–5769	7
1756–1786	4	2204–2211	4	2439–2453	5	2754–2763	4	3428–3464	5	5802–5803	8
1787–1789	5	2212–2216	3	2454–2461	4	2764–2777	3	3465–3475	4	5813–	7
1805–1817	4										

The following are wholly within the indicated zone:

CONNECTICUT, 5; DELAWARE, 5; DISTRICT OF COLUMBIA, 5; MAINE, 6; NEW JERSEY, 5; Virgin Islands, 8.

The following shall be considered as of the 8th zone:

ALASKA
CANAL ZONE
GUAM
HAWAIIAN IS.
PHILIPPINE IS.
PORTO RICO.
SAMOA IS.

FIG. 27.—Official zone key for unit Number 2371 (St. Louis, Mo.).

$7.74 for 70 pounds to Zone 8. However, there has been made this interesting exception to the standard rates—packages when mailed on rural routes shall be 2 cents and 3 cents per parcel less for local and other than local delivery, respectively, than when mailed elsewhere.

Regulations and Privileges.—In accordance with the regulations now governing, domestic parcel-post mail includes merchandise; farm and factory products; seeds, bulbs, and plants; meats; and a great variety of other items. Parcel-post packages are limited as to both size and weight,

origin to the office of delivery is 300 miles or more, chargeable with a higher rate of postage than the regular second-zone rate, as shown in the exceptions . . . in the Official Postal Guide."

the combined length and girth of a package being limited to 100 inches as compared with 72 inches when the Act first went into force, and to 70 pounds in weight for all distances as compared with the limitation of 11 pounds in the beginning. Careful wrapping of all parcels is prescribed and liquids, fragile articles, and perishables are received subject only to detailed requirements. When desired, the sender of any parcel by post may secure a simple receipt for the same upon payment of 1 cent at the office to which it is delivered.

Two privileges of particular interest are accorded by the government in connection with the parcel-post service. The first of these is that of insurance. This covers all except a few specified types of parcels and protects against loss, rifling, and damage, the fee charged varying from 5 cents for an actual value not exceeding $5 to 35 cents for articles with an actual value not in excess of $200. If loss or damage is suffered and the shipment was packed and indorsed in accordance with postal requirements, recovery may be had for the actual value of the article lost within the limits set by the insurance placed upon it, or for "the actual, usual, direct, and necessary cost of repairing partially damaged articles." All claims for indemnity, if recovery is to be had, must be filed within 6 months of the date of mailing. A second interesting privilege offered is that of collection upon delivery. Parcel-post matter, again excepting certain articles, may be sent c.o.d. from any domestic money-order post office or United States naval vessel to another office or vessel having money-order service, upon the payment of fees varying from 12 cents in addition to the postage when the amount to be remitted does not exceed $10 to 45 cents additional when the amount does not exceed $200. Remittance is made by post-office money-order, the addressee paying the order fee. This c.o.d. fee protects against loss and damage and against nonreceipt of returns. Goods shipped c.o.d. are not subject to examination prior to delivery and indemnity for lost c.o.d. parcels is paid under the same conditions which govern for lost insured parcels.

Volume and Financial Results.—Because of the heavy and increasing losses suffered by the Post Office Department, that organization has made cost analyses of the business done by it. The 1932 analysis shows that to a total weight of mail of 6,375 million pounds, parcel post contributed 3,796 million or almost 60 per cent. In terms of space occupied, parcel post was even more significant—its portion being 70 per cent. For handling this business it was estimated $146,296,605 were expended, with a net loss of $32,716,267. A department analysis indicates losses aggregating $34,431,027 on parcel post moving to Zones 1, 2, 3, and 4, with gains to all others reducing the net loss to the total given. To meet this deficit a new schedule of rates was submitted to the Interstate Commerce Commission for approval. Approved and made effective Oct. 1, 1932, rates for the first pound have been increased to all zones by 1 to

2 cents, but the rate for each additional pound has been decreased from 0.5 to 1 cent except for Zones 1 and 2 (in which losses are heaviest) where an increase of 0.1 cent is made, and for local movement and Zone 3 where the charge remains unchanged. This change was sharply opposed by the Railway Express Agency as an effort, with lower rates on the longer hauls and recent increases in size and weight limits, to secure more of the long-haul traffic. Political opposition appeared to the minor increases proposed: there was a strong demand from Congress that the power to pass upon rate changes be taken from the Interstate Commerce Commission and exercised by Congress itself. Happily, no such change was made in the law: Congressional interference is to be deplored, for the judgment of that body is certain to be rested more largely upon political than upon cost considerations.

Problems of Railway Mail Pay.—One of the most difficult and important problems incident to the relation between the railways and the government in the handling of mail has been the determination of a proper basis of payment to the carrier. In its demands upon the railways the government has always been most exacting, as it might properly be with respect to a service of such fundamental social and economic importance. Not only does the Post Office Department have power to designate any train as a mail train and to demand that all mail trains be given the right of way over other trains but it may also go much farther: it can demand such types of equipment as it desires, designate routes over which mail shall move, control the construction of cars and their placing at terminals, and require the carrier to load and unload mail at stations and terminals. In fact, it has exacted the performance of many other services and compelled the acceptance of many other responsibilities including, until very recently, such extra services as the transportation of mail to and from numerous post offices. Under the law of 1873, which first gave expression in a definite manner to various practices and principles of compensation which had developed through an evolutionary process, compensation was paid essentially upon the basis of the average daily weight carried on each route, with an additional allowance for full railway post-office cars of 40 feet or more in length. It is interesting to note that this Act, which governed, with minor modifications, for many years, permitted the Postmaster General to fix the compensation for service rendered to his department.

In the relation thus established there were three noteworthy features, all of which gave rise to more or less dissatisfaction on the part of railway or government. The first of these and perhaps the least important was the situation of the land-grant road which was compelled to render service at 80 per cent of the sum paid others for a similar service. Whatever hardship this may have worked upon individual roads, no sound basis for complaint upon the ground of unfairness existed in view of the benefits received in the past by such carriers through federal aid; indeed, the terms of the grants provided for service to the government at less than commercial rates. The absence of mutual consent in the determination of the rates to be paid for mail service gave rise to the second problem. Certain services, many of which went beyond the mere transportation of the mails, were demanded of the carrier and compensation was fixed by the head of the department benefiting therefrom. Regardless of how fair the Postmaster General might attempt to be in the determination of rates, there was always the temptation to reduce the oft-recurring postal deficit at the expense of the railways. The third problem was that of obtaining the average daily weight of the mail transported, upon the basis of which payments were made. The determination of this figure represented a constant expense to the government, since the quadrennial weighing was in progress each year in one of the four districts into which the United States was divided. It also gave opportunity for fraudulent practice, both on the part of those interested in increasing the volume of mail during the 90-day weighing period in particular sections and those interested in depleting it in so far as that was possible.

Present Basis of Compensation.—Largely as a result of the method of determining the compensation for service rendered, sharp disagreement existed for many years between the Post-office Department and the railways, the one seeking constantly to justify a reduction in the rate of mail pay, the other alleging gross underpayment. Numerous Congressional committees investigated the problem and, with but one exception, recommended a complete change in the basis of payment. After 43 years of struggle between the railways and the Post Office Department, Congress placed upon the statute books, in 1916, over the protest of the railways, a law which authorized a change in the basis of payment from weight of mail transported to car space requisitioned.

The advantages of this latter system are several. The government pays and the railways receive payment for neither a greater nor a lesser service than is rendered, and the cost and inconvenience of quadrennial weighing, with the temptation to pad or deplete the mails, are eliminated. The new plan encourages efficiency on the part of the Post Office Department in the utilization of space; with the rapid development of the parcel post, a space system is fairer to the railways than a system based upon quadrennial weighing; and the plan is so clear and definite that any citizen can readily understand it. Finally, it is asserted that, after all, the weight of the mail transported is relatively unimportant as compared with the space occupied in all except heavily loaded storage cars, because of the dead weight of the car, or portion of car, utilized.

This law also took from the Postmaster General the power to fix compensation, placing it in the hands of the Interstate Commerce Commission. Under its terms appeal was early made to the Commission for an official determination of the rates to govern the performance of the various services, the railways protesting against the rates tentatively fixed by the Postmaster General. After a careful investigation of the matter the Interstate Commerce Commission, in its decision of Dec. 23, 1919, approved the wide application of the space principle made by the Postmaster General under the permissive feature of the Act and ordered its application extended to cover all railway mail routes.

This decision also prescribed a scale of rates for each mile of service by various types of equipment. That scale of rates has been modified from time to time since, with the last order issued effective Aug. 1, 1928. Under its terms the following rates of pay are generally applicable:[1]

For each mile of service by—	Rate, cents	For each mile of service by—	Rate, cents
60-foot railway post-office car	39.00	15-foot storage space	13.00
30-foot apartment car	21.50	12-foot storage space	11.00
15-foot apartment car	14.50	9-foot storage space	8.75
70-foot storage car	47.00	6-foot storage space	6.25
60-foot storage car	40.50	3-foot storage space	3.50
30-foot storage space	21.50	15-foot closed-pouch space	14.50
27-foot storage space	20.00	12-foot closed-pouch space	12.50
24-foot storage space	18.50	9-foot closed-pouch space	10.25
21-foot storage space	16.75	6-foot closed-pouch space	7.50
18-foot storage space	15.00	3-foot closed-pouch space	4.50

However, it is provided that the minimum payment on any mail route, over any part of which mail is transported not less than 6 days a week, shall be $72.00 per mile per annum.

The rates shown above as generally applicable, however, are increased by approximately one-third for the benefit of the railways operating in New England, the minimum payment there guaranteed being $96.50. For all separately operated railways, not exceeding 100 but more than 50 miles in length, the basic scale was advanced approximately 87.5 per cent, while for all separately operated properties less than 50 miles in length base rates were increased about 135 per cent. The minimum payment on all such short routes was fixed at $112.50 per mile per annum. The original decision and later changes have been accepted by the railways with relatively good grace and, under a postal administration which has not been antagonistic to the carriers but, instead, willing to pay a fair compensation, it seems that "the ghost has been laid" in the railway-mail controversy. However, this settlement has been reached only after many years of acrimonious discussion, fruitless debate, and more or less bootless investigation.

[1] 144 I.C.C. 675.

THE EXPRESS SERVICE

A General Statement.—The second important incidental service rendered by the railways is that concerned with the handling of express. This service, although akin to freight in character, is largely concerned with a certain few types of commodities and shipments. Important among them are perishables, small packages of high value, various articles forwarded in response to "rush" orders, and valuables such as bullion, currency, jewels, and securities of different sorts. Throughout the world generally this service is rendered by the individual railway itself. In the United States, however, the express, or "special fast freight," service was long rendered by a separate organization: only since 1929 have the railways come into control. This was due initially to the early entry of individuals into the field and persisted primarily because the railways were thus able to relieve themselves of certain obligations and often, at the same time, to obtain an even greater profit from the business at the high rates charged by the separate companies than they could have secured through conducting the business themselves. Despite the fact that this service was independent of the railway, no real competition existed between the railway and the express company because railway profits were greater if goods moved by express and because, by agreement, the express rate was at all times a multiple of the freight rate, this multiple being rarely less than two, often more.

Brief History of the Business.—The origin of the express business in the United States dates back to 1839 when one William Harnden established a route between New York and Boston. He was soon followed by Alvin Adams and these two companies in 1854 became the Adams Express Company. The American Express Company was established in 1850 and represented a consolidation, as did the Adams, of several smaller organizations. Wells, Fargo and Company, the third important entrant, was established in 1852, its field being essentially the California business, packages and other items being transported with regularity across that great stretch of territory lying between the Missouri River and the Pacific coast where danger from Indians and outlaws was always great. The fourth major company to enter the field was the United States Express Company, also organized in 1854. In 1886 the Southern Express Company was organized as a subsidiary of existing companies to handle the Southern business. Other smaller concerns have entered the field from time to time, most of these operating, however, over but a single line and existing because of disagreement between that particular railway and one of the existing companies.

The five major companies operated in rather definite sections of the country but, even when territories overlapped, competition was not in evidence. The Wells, Fargo organization served primarily in the West and

Southwest and the Southern wholly in Southern territory. The United States operated along the eastern coast, centering about New York and Philadelphia, while the Adams and the American companies operated mainly in the eastern and north-central portions of the United States. The control which these four corporations exercised over the express business of the United States—the United States Express Company dissolved shortly after the establishment of the parcel post—is indicated by the fact that in 1917 they operated over about 92 per cent of the railway mileage of the country and controlled approximately 95 per cent of the business.

In 1918 the four great express companies of the United States consolidated and the American Railway Express Company was organized to control, during the period of the war, all express business formerly handled by them. The stock of the resultant corporation was taken by the four parent concerns, an inverted holding company thus being formed. This company took over the contracts, organization, and physical properties of its predecessors, though certain financial functions, such as the issuance of money orders and letters of credit are still performed by at least one of the parent corporations, and the handling of foreign shipments has been retained, the American Express Company playing the major rôle here. So satisfactory was the conduct of the express business by the one corporation that the Interstate Commerce Commission, acting under the authority of the Transportation Act of 1920, later held the consolidation to be in public interest and hence legalized its continuance. The American Railway Express Company became a permanent feature, therefore, and controlled during its life the entire express business of the United States with the exception of operations over the lines of the Southern Railway and its subsidiary properties. As the result of a disagreement between the express company and the railway company, the Southeastern Express Company handled all express business over Southern lines and continues to do so.

Railway Express Agency, Incorporated.—The conduct of the express business in the United States by corporate entities quite distinct from the railways themselves was anomalous. However, the first definite step to change that situation was not taken until early in 1928 when the Association of Railway Executives announced that it would canvass the railways to determine their attitude toward the assumption of the express business. Many railway contracts with the express company expired Feb. 28, 1929, so that date would be an opportune one for a change. When an attitude favorable to the change became clear, definite work was undertaken to accomplish the end in view. The plan generally favored involved the purchase of the assets of the American Railway Express Company by a new corporation to be formed, this new corporation to be owned by the railways. The alternative to this plan was the purchase of the stock of the express company. However, willingness of the company to negotiate made it possible to adopt the preferred plan and on Mar. 1, 1929, title to all properties of the old organization passed to the Railway Express Agency, Incorporated, which at the same time took over the conduct of the business.

The properties of its predecessor were taken over by the Agency at cost less depreciation, in accordance with a provision in the old contract, a price of $30,613,117 being fixed subject to revision. The new corporation issued 1,000 shares of no-par stock, these shares being assigned to some 86 railways in proportion to the volume of the express business: to the New York Central and the Pennsylvania went 144 and 126 shares, respectively, while to the Abilene and Southern and to the Lehigh and New England were assigned but 1 each. To some 350 short lines, doing 2 per cent of the business, no shares were assigned but the same privileges and rights are accorded these lines as are enjoyed by shareholders. These shares are nontransferable except to the Agency or to a successor railway corporation. Although planned to operate over the owning railways primarily, the new corporation possesses the legal right to operate in connection with other transport agencies—and is doing so, as will be shown later. To pay for the properties purchased, as well as to provide for certain needed expansion, the new corporation issued $32,000,000 of bonds that were distributed to the public. With all arrangements completed, the Railway Express Agency, Incorporated, took over the express business of the old company on Mar. 1, 1929. With this change came the establishment of a relation so logical that it is strange its consummation was so long delayed.

Organization and Administration.—The internal organization of the Railway Express Agency, Incorporated, is simple. In addition to a staff of major officers such as is characteristic of any large organization, including the heads of the treasury and accounting departments, there is, for each of several large areas, a regional vice-president with a general manager subordinate to him. Reporting to each regional vice-president are division superintendents, and to them, in turn, are responsible the local agents. Certain of these agents are employed on a full-time basis, though others—often railway station agents—situated in smaller places and performing but a part-time service, are paid on the basis of their cash collections, the usual allowance being 10 per cent.

Four papers are employed in the handling of express traffic. The first of these is the receipt issued to the shipper upon delivery of the goods to the express company. This document corresponds to the bill of lading in the case of freight shipments. This receipt contains certain essential data such as the name of the consignor, name and address of the consignee, a description of the goods, their declared value, the charges covering, and a statement of the terms and conditions of the contract between shipper and company. This receipt is signed by the consignor and the company agent and is nonnegotiable. The second paper issued is the label, which is attached to all shipments except those of money. Prepaid shipments have attached to them yellow labels, while upon "collect" and c.o.d. shipments white and green labels are used, respectively. These various colored labels are employed to distinguish the more clearly among the three types of shipments named and thus to avoid double collection of charges or failure to collect on c.o.d. movements. For its own purposes, the express company issues a waybill for each shipment, a copy of which accompanies the shipment, serving in that connection the same function as the freight waybill. The waybill contains essentially the same information as the receipt, together with such shipping instructions as may be necessary. All movements of goods are under the control of an express messenger and at destination shipments are turned over to the local agent who is responsible for delivery to the consignee. Upon delivery the consignee must sign in the delivery book, indicating the receipt of the shipment. Such losses and damages as may occur impose upon the express company the same character of liability which attaches to the railway itself and all claims growing out of such losses or injuries are paid by the express company.

The Railway-Express Contract: *The Early Adjustment.*—Prior to the organization of the American Railway Express Company a separate contract was made between each express company and the individual railways over which it operated. These contracts were essentially uniform in all but one particular: the percentage of gross operating revenue payable to the railway as compensation for services rendered. In this typical contract the railway agreed to furnish all necessary equipment for the transportation of express shipments and to haul the same in conjunction with the movement of passenger or mail traffic or by special train; to provide terminal space for handling such traffic, and to furnish free transportation for company material, as well as for all officers and employees moving in pursuit of duty. The express company, in return, agreed to pay a reasonable compensation for all separate facilities used or constructed for its use, to transport free of charge all moneys and packages moving on railway account, to assume all risk of loss or damage to goods or persons, and to pay to the railway a certain percentage of the annual gross operating revenue. This percentage varied rather widely, however, and was determined primarily by the bargaining power of the carrier in question. The figure ran close to 60 per cent for the stronger roads, and as low as 40 per cent upon those which were, because of financial situation or low density of traffic, in a poor position to render the service themselves and, in consequence, had slight bargaining power.

A Modified Railway-Express Agreement.—During the period of federal operation of railways and prior to the assumption of the express business by the government, the American Railway Express Company executed a single contract with the Director-General of railroads. Following the termination of federal operation of both the railway and the express business on Mar. 1, 1920, it became necessary to work out a new contract to govern the relation between the two parties. This contract, as worked out and approved by the Interstate Commerce Commission, called for an agreement between the express company and the roads serving each of the districts designated by the Commission—under the original order the Eastern, Southern, Western, and Mountain-Pacific, but later only three because of the consolidation of the two last named. The contract was thus made with the roads of each group as a whole. Under the form of contract adopted, the first problem was that of ascertaining the income for division. To obtain this figure it was necessary accurately to determine gross and net operating revenues. In gross operating revenue were included all express-transportation receipts, the rent of buildings and other property, car mileage and per diem income, together with the net income from so-called miscellaneous physical properties. Specifically excluded from gross income, however, were such non-carrier revenues as brokerage fees and revenues from c.o.d., money-order, and other financial operations. To arrive at the net figure desired, there was deducted from gross revenue the sum of all operating expenses, which included depreciation and other like charges, compensation to any railways served by the express company but not parties to the agreement, uncollectible transportation revenue, taxes attributable to transportation, rent for real property used jointly, and rent for rolling-stock equipment not otherwise provided for. Deductible also were interest and discount on funds expended to provide additional property and equipment necessary for the express business at a rate not to exceed 6 per cent per annum, with the provision that, so long as this money remained unpaid, it was not to be considered a part of the average value of the capital employed in the express business.

Disposition of "Net Income for Division."—The sum remaining after proper expense deductions had been made from gross operating revenue represented net operating income and was termed "income for division." After the deduction of 2.5 per cent of that sum for express-company purposes, the balance remaining, designated "net income for division," was distributed among the railroads in the group in the proportion that gross express-transportation revenue for the month earned on the line of each railroad bore to the gross transportation revenue earned on all lines in that group for the particular month in question. If the 2.5 per cent of the income for division retained by the express company exceeded in amount 6 per cent of the value of the entire real property, equipment, and capital employed by the express company in the transaction of its business, such excess was termed "profit" and divided one-half to the railways, to be distributed upon a prescribed basis, and one-half to the express company. The excess assignable to the latter was to be accumulated until it amounted to 10 per cent of the value of the entire property owned by the company and devoted to the express business, after which time all "profit" was to be divided one-fourth to the express company and three-fourths to the railways.

Modifications of the New Contract.—When the Express Agency succeeded to the business of the separately owned corporation that had functioned since the World War, it was inevitable that certain modifications should be made in the adjustment between the individual railways and the new enterprise. However, these changes were surprisingly few and of relatively slight importance. Upon carload shipments of express 85 per cent of the gross revenue for transportation was to be retained by the railway or railways participating. Four territorial groupings of carriers were provided instead of the three recognized under the preceding régime. In addition to these modifications, several other minor changes were included in Sec. 5 of the new contract, but basically the old contract carried over.

Demand for Regulation.—Prior to 1906 no basis for the regulation of interstate express business existed. By that time, however, high rates, unreasonable discrimination, arbitrary treatment of patrons, and other abuses of power had engendered such sharp public hostility that express companies were subjected to the same regulation as were the railways. In compliance with legal requirements tariffs were filed with the Interstate Commerce Commission, but they proved to be of a highly objectionable character. As a result of many complaints lodged with that body alleging exorbitant and discriminatory rates, protesting against certain irritating abuses and practices such as double collection and delays in the settlement of claims, and declaring that rate schedules were so complex as to be incomprehensible to the shipping public, the Interstate Commerce Commission made an extensive study of the problem. Upon the basis of that study the Commission prescribed not only a system of rate making but also a schedule of rates and, though the latter has been changed from time to time, the former still governs essentially as it was laid down by that body in 1913.

Classification and Rates Prescribed.—The first problem to which the Interstate Commerce Commission addressed itself in the effort to straighten the express tangle was that of the reclassification of commodities. Under the order finally issued it was provided that all commodities should be charged the first-class rate except food products and beverages, given a second-class rating, certain specified items listed as third class, valuables moving subject to the money classification, and goods covered by commodity tariffs. Other commodities, such as those of high value or large bulk compared with weight, move under a multiple of first-class rates. The second problem was one of segregating the various types of costs borne by the business as a basis for allocating to the individual shipment an amount sufficient to cover each type. Under the new scheme devised the express rate was a composite of three factors, an allowance for collection and delivery or express-terminal cost, an allowance for rail-terminal cost, and an allowance to cover the haulage or transportation cost. In the matter of the relation between classes, it was held that second-class shipments should take rates not in excess of 75 per cent of the first-class rate, while the third-class rate, applicable to

ILLINOIS

District Bureau No.	Office	Block No. and Sub-Bl. Letter	Scale No.	District Bureau No.	Office	Block No. and Sub-Bl. Letter	Scale No.	District Bureau No.	Office	Block No. and Sub-Bl. Letter	Scale No.
051	Brighton (C. & A.)	1035 Q	....	051	Cambridge	835 Q	....	051	Chestnut	936 Q	....
	(Macoupin Co.)			051	Cameron	935 B	....	010	Chester (d)	1236 A	....
010	Brighton (C., B. & Q.)	1035 Q	....	053	Campbell	938 O	....	059	Chesterfield	1035 M	....
	(Macoupin Co.)				(Vermilion Co.)			059	Chesterville	1037 G	....
051	Brimfield	936 A	....	051	Camp Grove	836 O	....	051	Chicago (d)	838 B	....
051	Bristol, Kendall Co.	837 G	....	....	Campbell Hill...SE.	1236 B	....	059	Chicago Heights (d)	838 K	....
059	Broadlands	1037 D	....	051	Camp Point (d)	934 Q	....	059	Chicago Ridge	838 E	....
051	Broadmoor	836 O	....	059	Campus	837 P	....	051	Chillicothe (d)	936 C	....
051	Broadwell	936 P	....	051	Canton (d)	935 H	....	059	Chrisman	1038 B	....
059	Brocton	1038 E	....	051	Capron	737 K	....	010	Christopher (d)	1236 D	....
051	Brookfield	838 A	....	051	Carbon Cliff	835 L	....	051	Cicero (d)	838 B	....
010	Brookport	1237 O	....	010	Carbondale (d)	1236 H	....	051	Cisco	937 O	....
059	Brothers	938 N	....	059	Cardiff	837 P	....	059	Cisne	1137 G	....
006	Broughton	1237 C	....	051	Carlinville (d)	1036 I	....	059	Cissna Park	93[illegible] E	....
010	[illegible]field	123[illegible]		05[illegible]	[illegible]				[illegible]		
	[illegible]ontgomer[illegible]			059	[illegible]man	10[illegible]			Colmar	[illegible]35 I	....
051	Byron (d)	736 P	....	059	Charleston (d)	1037 H	....	051	Colona	835 L	....
				051	Charlotte	937 C	....	....	Columbia (d)....SE.	1135 M	....
				051	Charter Grove	737 O	....	051	Colusa	934 H	....
	C			051	Chatham	1036 F	....	051	Colvin Park	737 N	....
051	Cabery	937 D	....	051	Chatsworth	937 C	....	051	Compton	836 H	....
010	Cache	1236 P	....	059	Chatton	934 Q	....	010	Conants	1136 P	....
059	Cadwell	1037 F	....	059	Chautauqua (Sn)	1135 C	....	010	Concord	1035 C	....
007	Cairo (d)...REA.SE.	1236 Q	....		(Jersey Co.)			059	Congerville	936 H	....
051	Caledonia, Boone Co.	737 I	....	051	Chebanse	838 N	....	051	Cooksville	937 F	....
051	Calhoun	1137 H	....	051	Chemung	737 K	....	010	Cora City	1236 B	....
	(Richland Co.)			059	Cheneyville	938 K	....	051	Cordova	835 G	....
059	Calvin	1137 Q	....	051	Chenoa (d)	.937 B	....	059	Cornell	937 B	....
059	Camargo	1037 D	....	051	Cherry, Bureau Co.	836 M	....	051	Cornland	1036 C	....
010	Cambria	1236 D	....	051	Cherry Valley	737 N	....	051	Cortland	837 B	....

FIG. 28.—Portion of specimen page from Express Directory.

but very few commodities, was fixed at 1 cent for each 2 ounces or fraction thereof, the minimum charge being 15 cents. Such commodity rates as the express companies desired to make were not to be governed by the terms of this order.

Rates Made upon a Distance Basis.—The method of determining express rates was the third major problem which the Interstate Commerce Commission attacked in its general investigation, and the scheme instituted bears on its face a rough likeness to the parcel-post plan, though it differs widely in detail. For the purposes of rate computation the United States was divided into blocks 1 degree square, these being marked by the intersecting parallels of longitude and latitude. These blocks are numbered from west to east, beginning in the northwest corner of the United States, the numbers in the first tier running 101, 102, 103, etc.; in the second tier 201, 202, 203, etc.; in the third tier 301, 302, 303, etc. Each succeeding tier southward thus constitutes a higher "hundred series." Each individual block is, in turn, divided into 16 sub-blocks, these being lettered from *A* to *Q*, inclusive, omitting the letter *J*. The United States was also divided into five zones, now three, upon the basis of differences in the nature and density of traffic.

Under the plan thus devised the determination of the express class rates, upon which the bulk of traffic moves, is not a matter of judgment or opinion. In arriving at the main-block first-class rate per hundred pounds

RATE TABLE 1. BLOCK 1041.

MAIN BLOCK TARIFF.

100		200		300		400		500		600		700		800	
Block	Scale	Block	Scale	Block	Scale	Block	Scale	Block	Scale	Block	Scale	Block	Scale	Block	Scale
103	203	201	211	302	207	402	211	501	216	601	224	702	229	803	213
104	203	203	199	302½	211	402½	207	502	207	602	216	703	222	804	218
106	190	204	195	303	203	403	203	503	207	603	216	704	222	805	197
107	182	205	190	305	186	404	199	504	203	606	184	705	201	807	176
108	176	206	182	306	182	405	190	507	184	607	180	710	159	810	159
[illegible]	[illegible]	[illegible]	178	[illegible]	[illegible]	[illegible]	[illegible]	[illegible]	[illegible]	608	176	[illegible]	[illegible]	[illegible]	[illegible]
133	76	237	68	333	70	455	84	541	44	637	45	739	32	837	36
		257	90	334	67	455½	78	542	44	638	40	740	32	838	32
		258	90	335	67	456	78	543	44	639	36	741	32	839	28
				336	65	457	81	549	59	640	36	742	32	840	24
				337	65	458	87	550	61	641	40	743	36	841	24
				338	65	458½	87	551	63	642	40	745	40	842	24
				339	62			552	67	643	40	746	40	843	28
				340	58			553	69	646	47	747	44	844	32
				341	58			554	70	647	47	748	50	845	36
				357	87			555	74	648	50	749	53	846	40
				358	87			556	74	649	53	750	56	847	44
								557	81	650	56	751	61	848	47
								558	84	651	59	751½	61	849	53
								559	87	652	63	752	61	850	56
										653	69	753	67	851	61
										654	70	754	69	852	63
										655	70	755	69	853	65
										656	71			854	67
														855	70
														856	71

FIG. 29.—Portion of express main block tariff, Block 1041 (Cincinnati, Ohio).

the Commission, in an order issued early in 1924 that somewhat modified earlier decisions, specified that it be constructed by combining an express-terminal allowance of 35 cents, a rail-terminal allowance of 30 cents and a haulage factor that varies with distance. This haulage factor in Zone 1, roughly Eastern territory, is 25 cents for the first block; this decreases at the rate of 0.5 cent for each block of travel beyond the originating block for a total of 21 blocks, including the originating block, after which the haulage factor per block of travel remains constant. In Zone 2, approximately Southern territory, and in Zone 3, approximately Western, the basic haulage factors are 27.5 cents and 30 cents respectively, with the same principle governing the determination of the rate for additional blocks as stated for Zone 1. In computing the number of blocks, the count is made as of the base and perpendicular of a right-angled triangle. When

RATE TABLE 2. BLOCK 1031.
SUB-BLOCK TARIFF.

To— Blk.	Sub-bl.	From block 1031, sub-block— A	B	C	D	E	F	G	H	I	K	L	M	N	O	P	Q
1030	A	13	13	16	16	13	16	16	22	16	22	22	22	16	22	22	22
1030	B	11	13	13	16	13	13	16	22	13	22	16	22	16	16	22	22
1030	C	10	11	13	13	11	13	13	22	13	16	16	16	13	16	16	22
1030	D	9	10	11	13	10	11	13	16	11	16	13	16	13	13	16	16
1030	E	13	16	16	22	13	13	16	22	13	22	16	22	16	16	22	22
1030	F	13	13	16	16	11	13	13	22	13	16	16	16	13	16	16	22
1030	G	11	13	13	16	10	11	13	16	11	16	13	16	13	13	16	16
1030	H	10	11	13	13	9	10	11	16	10	13	13	13	11	13	13	16
1030	I	16	16	22	22	13	16	16	22	13	16	22	22	13	16	16	22
1030	K	13	16	16	22	13	13	16	22	11	16	16	22	13	13	16	16
1030	L	13	13	16	16	11	13	13	22	10	13	16	16	11	13	13	16
1030	M	11	13	13	16	10	11	13	16	9	13	13	16	10	11	13	13
1030	N	16	22	22	22	16	16	22	22	13	22	22	22	16	16	22	22
1030	O	16	16	22	22	13	16	16	22	13	16	22	22	13	16	16	22
1030	P	16	22	22	22	16	16	22	22	13	16	16	22	13	13	16	16
1030	Q	13	13	16	16	11	13	13	16	10	11	13	13	9	10	11	13

To— Blk.	Sub-bl.	From block 1031, sub-block— A	B	C	D	E	F	G	H	I	K	L	M	N	O	P	Q
1031	A	8	9	10	11	9	10	11	16	10	13	13	13	11	13	13	16
1031	B	9	8	9	10	10	11	13	16	11	16	13	16	13	13	16	16
1031	C	10	9	8	9	11	13	11	16	13	13	13	13	13	16	13	16
1031	D	11	10	9	8	13	11	10	13	13	13	11	13	16	13	13	13
1031	E	9	10	11	13	8	9	10	13	9	13	11	13	10	11	13	13
1031	F	10	11	13	11	9	8	9	13	10	11	10	11	11	13	11	13
1031	G	11	13	11	10	10	9	8	11	11	10	9	10	13	11	10	11
1031	H	16	16	16	13	13	13	11	8	16	13	10	9	13	13	11	10
1031	I	10	11	13	13	9	10	11	16	8	11	13	13	9	10	11	13
1031	K	13	16	13	13	13	11	10	13	11	8	11	13	10	9	10	11
1031	L	13	13	13	11	11	10	9	10	13	11	8	9	11	10	9	10
1031	M	13	16	13	13	13	11	10	9	13	13	9	8	13	11	10	9
1031	N	11	13	13	16	10	11	13	13	9	10	11	13	8	9	10	11
1031	O	13	13	16	13	11	13	11	13	10	9	10	11	9	8	9	10
1031	P	13	16	13	13	13	11	10	11	11	10	9	10	10	9	8	9
1031	Q	16	16	16	13	13	13	11	10	13	11	10	9	11	10	9	8

FIG. 30.—Portion of sub-block tariff, Block 1031 (St. Joseph, Mo.).

the points of origin and destination are in different zones, the haulage or transportation element of each compounded rate is the sum of the allowances for each zone traversed for the number of blocks of travel in that zone, but based upon the number of blocks in the entire distance.

TABLE XVI.—EXPRESS RATES GOVERNING SUB-BLOCK MOVEMENTS

	Zone 1, cents	Zone 2, cents	Zone 3, cents
First block of travel:			
First sub-block	90	80	85
Second sub-block	95	85	90
Third sub-block	100	85	90
Fourth sub-block	105	90	95
Second block of travel:			
First sub-block / Second sub-block	115	105	110
Third sub-block / Fourth sub-block	125	120	125
Third block of travel:			
All sub-blocks	145	145	155

Adjustments are permitted when necessary to avoid incongruous or anomalous results, the purpose being to produce a symmetrical and equitable rate structure. The basis for the determination of the first-class sub-block rates per hundred pounds, applicable to movements within a block or to movements between bordering or cornering blocks, has also been prescribed by the Commission; here a scale is used that is somewhat higher than for main-block rates. Rates from the sub-block of origin to the sub-block of destination appear in Table XVI.

Determination of the Charge.—To enable him to ascertain the rate applicable from one station to another, the local agent is provided with an *Official Directory of Express Stations* in which are given the block and sub-

Schedule of First and Second-Class Express Rates in cents.

	Scale Numbers.																	
	127		128		129		130		131		132		133		134		135	
Pounds.	1st Class	2d Class	1st Class	2d Class	1st Class	2d Class	1st Class	2d Class	1st Class	2d Class	1st Class	2d Class	1st Class	2d Class	1st Class	2d Class	1st Class	2d Class
1	41	41	41	41	42	42	42	42	42	42	42	42	42	42	42	42	42	42
2	48	48	48	48	48	48	48	48	48	48	48	48	48	48	49	49	49	49
3	54	54	54	54	55	55	55	55	55	55	55	55	55	55	55	55	56	56
4	61	61	61	61	61	61	61	61	62	62	62	62	62	62	62	62	62	62
5	67	67	67	67	68	68	68	68	68	68	68	68	69	69	69	69	69	69
6	74	74	74	74	74	74	75	75	75	75	75	75	75	75	76	76	76	76
7	80	74	80	75	81	75	81	76	82	76	82	76	82	76	83	77	83	77
8	87	74	87	75	87	75	88	76	88	76	89	76	89	76	89	77	90	77
9	93	74	93	75	94	75	94	76	95	76	95	76	96	76	96	77	97	77
42	306	229	308	231	310	232	312	234	314	235	316	237	318	238	321	241	323	242
43	312	234	314	235	317	238	319	239	321	241	323	242	325	244	327	245	330	247
44	319	239	321	241	323	242	325	244	328	246	330	247	332	249	334	250	336	252
45	325	244	327	245	330	247	332	249	334	250	336	252	339	254	341	256	343	257
46	332	249	334	250	336	252	339	254	341	256	343	257	345	259	348	261	350	262
47	338	253	340	255	343	257	345	259	348	261	350	262	352	264	355	266	357	268
48	345	259	347	260	349	262	352	264	354	265	357	268	359	269	361	271	364	273
49	351	263	353	265	356	267	358	268	361	271	363	272	366	274	368	276	371	278
50	357	268	360	270	362	271	365	274	367	275	370	277	372	279	375	281	377	283

FIG. 31.—Segment of specimen page of schedule of rates.

block location of each station, a *Block Tariff* and the *Local and Joint Schedule of Rates*. The block tariff gives the number of the schedule or scale of rates applicable between nonadjacent blocks and between sub-blocks of the same or adjacent blocks, the number of this controlling scale increasing with distance. In the schedule are given the 405 scales, each of which gives the rates upon first- and second-class shipments varying in weight from 1 to 100 pounds. These rates, however, are based upon a released value of $50 for each 100 pounds or less, and not exceeding 50 cents per pound in excess of 100 pounds. If a greater value is placed upon the shipment an extra charge of 10 cents per $100 or fraction thereof, in excess of the released value, is made. In handling a shipment of unusual value, special care is exercised and receipt for it must be given by each successive employee in whose charge that shipment is placed in the course of its movement, that a complete record may be available.

With such a scheme of rate making governing, and with the general level of charges determined by the Interstate Commerce Commission, the various grounds of complaint against express rates have been largely eliminated, and arbitrary practices designed to serve solely the financial interest of the corporation have been effectively controlled. Within the last score of years, through regulation by the Interstate Commerce Commission and through competition from various quarters, the "express monopoly"—against which such violent attacks were directed before commissions and legislative bodies in the years past—has taken its place among the other enforcedly domesticated "servants of the public" in the broad field of regulated enterprise.

Express Traffic Declines.—But what of the outlook for this undertaking that has undergone such rapid and striking changes during the past 20 years as those portrayed upon preceding pages? Though a service comparable to our express service is rendered in many countries by the individual railways, it seems more logical that traffic be handled by a single organization operating over all railway lines and controlled by the railways. It is unquestioned that the express business is now efficiently managed: movement costs are not excessive and an excellent service is maintained. Yet, in the face of a sound plan and competent direction, the express business—when measured by gross transportation revenue—has not grown; rather, after remaining almost stationary for a period following 1920, it shows a definite tendency to decline. Express revenue in 1929 was below that of 1921, though the former was a year of unusual business activity and the latter notoriously "lean." In 1930 and in 1931 the decline was accelerated, being 16 and 19 per cent, respectively; yet for the fiscal year of 1931 parcel-post revenue was only 3 per cent below the total for 1929—and for 1932 the decline was 17 per cent as compared with the preceding year.

Since its establishment the parcel-post business has made heavy inroads upon traffic that once moved by express, and, with the gradual increase in size of packages accepted for parcel-post shipment,[1] provision

[1] This increase is shown well in this table, taken from the *Railway Age*, vol. 93, p. 825.

Effective date	Weight limit, pounds	Size limit, length and girth combined, inches	Zones
1901	4	...	Books only
Jan. 1, 1913	11	72	All zones
Aug. 15, 1913	20	...	Zones 1 and 2
Jan. 1, 1914	20	...	All zones
	50	...	Zones 1 and 2
July 10, 1915	...	84	All zones
Mar. 15, 1918	70	...	Zones 1 to 3, inclusive
	50	...	Zones 4 to 8, inclusive
Aug. 1, 1931	70	100	All zones

of satisfactory insurance and c.o.d. privileges, and extensions of the field otherwise, the governmentally operated enterprise promises further growth at the expense of the express service. Then, too, present parcel-post rates provide a cheaper service than does express for small shipments moving relatively short distances, and statistics show that both express and parcel-post business consist largely of such. In districts where rural free delivery exists, the parcel-post system enjoys a further advantage. The primary advantages of the express service follow from the more careful handling of goods; the acceptance of bullion, money, and other valuables at full risk; and the acceptance for movement of any-quantity shipments, from small packages to carload lots. Also, on heavier shipments moving long distances, express costs have generally been less than parcel-post charges, yet this advantage of express has recently been lessened by decreases made in parcel-post rates to the more distant zones. In some measure, also, the express service gains through the operation of a package-collection service in larger centers.

PARCEL-POST REVENUES AND EXPENDITURES, 1932*

Movement	Revenue	Expenditure	Loss	Gain
Local delivery........	1,907,127.76	1,853,259.80	....	53,867.96
Zones 1 and 2.........	37,079,213.49	62,945,656.73	25,866,443.24	
Zone 3..............	24,211,022.80	31,669,372.14	7,458,349.34	
Zone 4..............	22,495,277.33	23,443,531.50	948,254.17	
Zone 5..............	14,286,050.68	13,967,054.14	....	318,996.54
Zone 6..............	5,021,654.02	4,796,423.03	....	225,230.99
Zone 7..............	3,120,636.74	2,862,957.94	....	257,678.80
Zone 8..............	5,004,785.73	4,508,445.73	....	496,340.00
Library books........	91,923.11	249,903.56	157,980.45	
Total.............	113,580,337.21†	146,296,604.57	32,716,267.36	

* Cost-ascertainment Report, 1932, United States Post-office Department, p. 9.

† Includes $362,645.55 revenue from special-handling service.

The fundamental disadvantage under which express labors in competition with parcel post appears in the heavy subsidy enjoyed by the latter. The express company, as a private enterprise, is compelled to provide or to pay an adequate rental upon all property used in the rendition of service; it is compelled to meet its operating expenses; it is required to contribute to the costs of government through the payment of taxes upon its properties. For the parcel post needed floor space is provided by the government without cost, no contribution of taxes is made, and operating deficits are met from the public treasury. The extent of the annual subsidy is impossible of determination, for there is no way of assigning with accuracy to the parcel-post service a sum that represents the cost of providing floor space in government structures, maintenance and depreciation upon such structures, and the tax load of comparable facilities privately owned. Yet it would seem reasonable that such a sum should be no less than $5,000,000. If this be added to the deficit shown by the results of the cost study of the Post-office Department summarized above, it appears that parcel-post revenues for the fiscal year of 1932 represent only 75 per cent of the cost of rendering the service. Were parcel-post rates increased to cover even a major portion of this deficit, the competitive position of the Railway Express Agency would be greatly strengthened. And is such a suggestion economically or socially unsound or unreasonable?

Just as the parcel-post service has tended to take the small-package business from the express company, so has the development of truck transportation tended to take from it heavier shipments moving relatively short distances; in more populous sections of the country the motor truck competes actively for traffic moving distances of several hundred miles. The continued development of this type of service, together with better organization for the solicitation of traffic and the use of improved equipment upon lines well coordinated, will undoubtedly result in further inroads upon the express business. Indeed, in combination with the parcel post, it threatens to destroy the financial basis of an express service functioning as at present. That such a service is highly essential will be disputed by few, yet costs of operation are constant to such an extent that, as a consequence of the decline in the volume of business, unit costs have mounted dangerously. If the express business is to continue upon a self-supporting basis, it becomes increasingly apparent that some drastic changes must be effected, either in the competitive situation or in the scope of the express business. And the need of such readjustment becomes more pressing with the cut in parcel-post rates for the longer movements.

The Future.—What should be the nature of such readjustment is problematical, but the fundamental requirement for a prosperous express enterprise is a larger volume of business over which to distribute constant costs. Various proposals have been made, varying from slight modifications to revolutionary changes. Of the latter, perhaps the most interesting is the suggestion that all less-than-carload freight be handled by the existing Express Agency. Organized to provide a collection-and-delivery service, store-door delivery could then be placed in the hands of an appropriate agency and the carriers relieved of direct responsibility for the service. Under such a plan the regular movement of small-lot freight shipments would be speeded through supervision by an organization that had as one of its major responsibilities the rapid handling of less-than-carload traffic; an expedited freight service could be rendered upon certain shipments at rates somewhat above those normally charged for freight movements; and the standard express service would be continued. It is probable that, in addition to adapting small-lot service to the shippers' needs as the railways have not been able to do, rates could be lowered upon express traffic with a consequent strengthening of the competitive position of the express organization in the field in which it now serves.

But, whatever may be the changes that are made in the character of the express business, drastic or slight, it is unlikely that a service of long standing and of high social value will be permitted to go into the discard. Certainly it will be interesting to watch developments in the near future, with particular attention given to policies dictated by competitive conditions, to efforts to equalize competition by eliminating subsidies, and to the possibilities of a new transportation order.

REFERENCES

Mail Service

Columbian Correspondence College: *History of Railway Mail Service.*

Dunn, John: *History of the Railway Mail Service to 1885*, Government Printing Office.

Haines, H. S.: *Efficient Railway Operation*, The Macmillan Company, 1919.

Haney, Lewis H.: Congressional History of Railways in the United States to 1850, *University of Wisconsin Bulletin* 211.

———: Congressional History of Railways in the United States, 1850–1887, *University of Wisconsin Bulletin*, 342.

History of Railway Mail Service, 48th Congress, 2d Session, Executive Document 40, 1885 (also published under the name of John Dunn as listed above).

Interstate Commerce Commission: *Annual Reports; Reports; Statistics of Railways in the United States.*

Johnson, E. R., and G. G. Huebner: *Railroad Traffic and Rates*, vol. 2, D. Appleton & Company, 1911.

———, G. G. Huebner, and G. T. Wilson: *Principles of Transportation*, D. Appleton & Company, 1928.

———, and T. W. Van Metre: *Principles of Railroad Transportation*, D. Appleton & Company, 1921.

Lander, M. K.: *The Railway Mail Pay Controversy*, thesis prepared at the University of Wisconsin, 1919.

Newcomb, H. T.: *The Postal Deficit*, W. M. Ballantyne and Sons, 1900.

Pamphlets, circulars, etc., issued from 1914 to 1916 by the Committee on Railway Mail Pay concerning the Moon bill.

Postmaster General, Report of (annual).

Reports, Hughes Commission on Second-class Mail Matter, Washington, 1912. Bourne Joint Committee on Postage on Second-Class Mail Matter and Compensation for the Transportation of Mail, 63rd Congress, 2d Session, House Document 89, 1914.

Tunnell, G. G.: *Railway Mail Service, Comparative Study of Railway Rates and Service*, The Lakeside Press, 1901.

Express Service

Bureau of Census: *Express Business in United States*, Special Reports, 1908.

Chandler, W. H.: *Express Service and Rates*, La Salle Extension University, 1927.

Establishment of Railway Express Agency, *Railway Age*, vols, 84–86 (consult index).

Express and Parcel-post Services, *Traffic Library*, American Commerce Association, 1918.
Four Express Companies to be Consolidated, *Railway Age*, vol. 64, p. 1377.
HUNGERFORD, EDWARD: *The Modern Railroad*, A. C. McClurg & Company, 1912.
Interstate Commerce Commission: *Annual Reports; Reports; Statistics of Express Companies.*
JOHNSON, E. R., and G. G. HUEBNER: *Railroad Traffic and Rates*, vol. 2, D. Appleton & Company, 1911.
———, G. G. HUEBNER, and G. L. WILSON: *Principles of Transportation*, D. Appleton & Company, 1928.
——— and T. W. VAN METRE: *Principles of Railroad Transportation*, D. Appleton & Company, 1921.
Revision of Express Rates Prescribed, I.C.C. 13,930, *Railway Age*, vol. 75, p. 1073.

Chapter XXIII

RAILWAY ACCOUNTING AND STATISTICS

An accurate and complete record of the affairs of the railway corporation is important to a degree little appreciated even by many railway executives who have been trained in the operating, traffic, or other active fields of railway endeavor. Not only must careful records of all business dealings be kept, but it is also essential that a detailed record be maintained of all properties owned by the railway; in no other way can a clear picture be had of the financial status of the corporation at any particular time. To elaborate upon the value of adequate financial and property records to the corporation is surely unnecessary, but it is desirable to suggest the worth of such records to the investor and to the public. Without access to the information afforded by proper records, the investor or prospective investor has little upon which to base judgment as to the comparative soundness of the corporation's financial situation; with accurate and detailed records available, however, a clear and sound judgment can be formed. To the public, also, proper records are of great value, because the point beyond which the constant public demand for lower rates and better service may not be justly pressed, is fixed largely by the financial status of the enterprise as disclosed by its accounts.

Organization of the Accounting Department.—The accounting department, by which the financial and property records are kept, constitutes a separate organization on all railways and is under the general direction of an official known upon different railways as vice-president, comptroller, or general auditor. Beyond the fact, however, that each road has a separate accounting department, exact similarities cease; departments differ slightly as to the scope of work and vary widely as to the nature of the internal organization. Nevertheless, though the title and scope of certain major divisions may vary, all such departments handle the property accounts, the records of revenues and expenses incident to freight and passenger operations, and the records of other receipts and disbursements of moneys. To this work is generally added the responsibility for records designed to show the movement of equipment and, not infrequently, freight claims also are handled by a special division of the accounting department.

It is in the matter of internal organization that accounting departments differ most widely from road to road. The typical major divisions are expenditures, freight revenues, passenger revenues, and equipment records. But often, because of peculiar conditions or for less obvious reasons, other divisions may be made. Upon roads which have a large coal tonnage there is sometimes found, in addition to a freight-revenues division which, in such case, accounts only for revenues accruing from miscellaneous freights, a coal-revenues division dealing entirely with that one commodity. Because of the extent and importance of the work incident to station accounting, certain roads handle this work through a separate division, apart from the freight-revenues organization, while yet other roads place all records of the receipt and issuance of materials in the hands of an independent division. Frequently there is also a miscellaneous-accounts division and occasionally all statistical work is concentrated under the direction of a chief statistician instead of being divided among the various departments. However, the organization which may be regarded as typical in the railway accounting field has immediately subordinate to the head of that department four officers, the nature of whose work is indicated in a general way by the title given. These officials are the auditor of expenditures or disbursements, the auditor of freight revenues, the auditor of passenger revenues, and the car accountant. The character of the work performed by each of these divisions will be described briefly in turn.

Work of the Expenditures Division.—In this typical department the expenditures office performs a wide variety of tasks. A stores section maintains a detailed record of the receipt and issuance of materials by the storeskeeping organization, showing not only total quantities and prices, but also minor details such as the cost of specific items, coal or even signal oil, issued to particular locomotives. A second section in the expenditures office handles payrolls. To this section come the payrolls made up by the many officers charged with that duty, its obligation being twofold: first, to audit the rolls and, second, to distribute by accounts the expenditures indicated thereupon. The voucher section is responsible for securing the proper signatures upon vouchers issued, for classifying these vouchers by accounts, and maintaining an accurate record of them. The bill section checks all bills issued by other companies against that corporation and handles the issuance of bills against other corporations to cover sums due from them on commercial transactions. A joint-facility section is provided with copies of all contracts between the particular carrier and other carrier corporations and individuals, governing the joint use of properties. Upon the basis of these contracts, bills are issued against others and bills issued by others are checked as to accuracy. In addition to checking and rendering the bills, these last-named sections keep a careful record of the date of receipt or issuance of every bill or voucher.

Frequently included within the expenditures division is a section variously named by different roads but dealing with essentially the same problem, capital-expenditures records. After estimates have been made by the engineering department for some project, this section makes a careful check of quantities and prices. When the project is completed a comparison of actual with estimated expenditures is made and an explanation is asked of those in charge for any wide divergence between totals or upon single items. In the bookkeeping section are brought together various records and, in addition, certain matters such as dining service, pits and quarries, etc., are here handled. To the statistical section goes a summary statement of all transactions for the period as reported by other sections and by it undistributed items are properly "spread" to the various accounts and accounting divisions. By it are also compiled the final statistics showing the cost of operation by accounts for the entire property. All in all, the accounting work of the expenditures division is more difficult and, if an understanding of the business is to be had, more important than that of other divisions.

Freight-revenue Records.—The auditor of freight revenues heads the largest division within the accounting department. The size of this division is due both to the relative importance of the railway's freight business and to the detailed nature of the records needed. Within this division perhaps the most important section is that which handles station accounts. It is here that each station is debited with all sums properly chargeable to it under the rules which govern, and credited with all moneys remitted as well as with such "reliefs for charges" as may be given upon the basis of peculiar circumstances arising from time to time. The primary function of the waybill transit section is that of maintaining a check upon the movement of freight by means of "forwarded" and "received" abstracts and the waybills. To this section is due the automatic tracing of less-than-carload shipments which follows within a certain prescribed period after the shipment had been forwarded, if an "open record" indicates it has failed to reach destination. The inexpertness of many freight agents in quoting tariffs and the possibility of chance errors have led to the establishment of two sections to check the rates applied, the one dealing with local movements, the other with interline. Often, because of the volume of work, it is impossible to check all bills but, in any case, all bills showing a total charge in excess of a specified sum, both local and interline, are examined. Equal emphasis is placed upon the rectification of errors by which the carrier has profited and errors which have resulted in loss to it. The remaining section in the freight-revenues office deserving of particular note is that charged with the compilation of tonnage and revenue data. It is interesting to know that the detailed work incident to the performance of this obligation is being done increasingly by highly efficient sorting and tabulating machines using cards punched from the waybills.

The Passenger-revenues Division.—Because passenger revenues comprise but a small part of the total earnings of the railway, and because the accounting incident to each individual transaction is less than in the handling of freight, the passenger-revenues division is smaller and less important to the railway than the one just discussed. In this office revenues from both local and interline sales are distributed by accounting divisions, and upon both types of sales the rates, as charged by the selling agents, are checked for accuracy. All tickets and other evidences of transportation rights turned in by the various conductors are checked against his report and also, at intervals, against sales as indicated by various local agents. This division, contrary to the practice in the freight field, handles all claims growing out of the purchase and use of tickets, and here are usually maintained records of the issuance of ticket stock to agents, of supplies for dining cars and hotels, and of other incidental matters which arise from time to time in connection with passenger business. In the passenger-statistics section, passenger revenue and mileage data are compiled for various property units, accounting and operating, and for the road as a whole.

Work of the Car Accountant's Staff.—In the office of the car accountant is performed work of a highly detailed and important character. A complete record is maintained of the daily movement of all cars upon the line, these records showing not only where the car is located but also whether it is loaded or empty. Furthermore, from these records are determined the number of home cars delivered to other roads and of foreign cars received by the recording road, together with date and place of such delivery or receipt. Upon the basis of these car records the bills against other roads are made for the use by them of equipment belonging to the "home" line, and the bills submitted by such other roads for the use of "foreign" cars by the home road are checked. In addition to records of carrier-owned equipment, records are here kept of private-car movements and settlement is made with the owners of such equipment upon the basis of mileage shown. The tracing section also bases its work upon the car records: its function is that of locating carload shipments which have failed to reach destination, and effecting their early delivery.

In the car accountant's office are compiled detailed statistics relative to locomotive performance and car mileage. The mileage of each locomotive and of locomotives as a whole is compiled upon the basis of train service, switching service, work service, etc. An accurate record of time in service and in shop undergoing repairs is often maintained; ratings are given the various classes and types of locomotives upon the different divisions that a ready record of the capacity of a particular locomotive may be available for those charged with the utilization of equipment. In the car-mileage section data are compiled covering train mileage and car mileage by different classes of service—freight, passenger, etc.; and, in the case of carriers which obtain tonnage statistics from the conductor's "wheel report" rather than the waybill, gross and net tonnage by various divisions and for the entire road are also computed here.

Freight Claims a Legal Problem.—Though the division of freight claims is included in many accounting departments, it does not seem properly to be a part of that organization. Rather, its location here seems to represent an intermediate step in the course of transfer from the traffic to the legal department. The claims division was universally a part of the traffic department at one time but the temptation to allow doubtful or even fraudulent claims, when made by valuable patrons, particularly if those patrons were located at competitive points, subjected the railway to serious loss of revenue and the honest shipper to distinct disadvantage. It seemed desirable, therefore, to remove this work from the traffic department and the usual first step was to transfer it to the accounting department. With many carriers it has gone, and with all it should go, to the legal department because, after all, a claim for loss or damage raises not only the question of fact but also the question of liability, which is a legal problem.

Divisional *v.* Centralized Accounting.—The very nature of their work is such that the work of the auditors of freight revenues and passenger revenues and of the car accountant must be concentrated in a single place. The expenditures division, on the other hand, because expenditures are essentially local in character, may be organized upon either a divisional or a centralized basis. If organized upon a divisional basis, all details are handled locally and the central organization at headquarters receives from the various divisional groups summaries which need only be combined to make available a complete record. This type of organization has two distinct advantages which, in addition to the inertia of early usage, have led to its retention by the majority of roads: it is in closer contact with the transactions involved, and those handling the work have a knowledge of railway matters such as is rarely true of clerks in a central office. However, because of the temptation of local offices to yield to local pressure with a resultant distortion of records, and because of the impossibility of maintaining a high degree of uniformity of accounts even under a prescribed system when work is decentralized, there has been a growing movement toward the centralization of expenditures accounting in the general office. This plan avoids the difficulties of the divisional organization, makes possible greater accuracy through closer supervision by responsible officers, and permits of the more effective use by the general administrative organization of the detailed records of all transactions.

Regulation of Railway Accounting Demanded.—Throughout the long period during which the carriers enjoyed complete freedom from public interference, railway accounting was regarded as no more a matter of public concern than the accounting of other private corporations. With the development of regulation, however, divergence in carrier accounting, both as to system and as to detail, constituted a serious obstacle to a ready grasp of the financial status of the railways. Furthermore, the accounting plans of many carriers were so involved and complex as to make a clear understanding possible only after great effort and study. State regulation could result only in "confusion worse confounded"; the solution of the problem lay in federal control. The importance not only of control, but of absolute uniformity in railway accounting, has been urged upon three bases. Such uniformity is of inestimable service to the investor if a proper system be prescribed, and of equal importance to a public interested in effective regulation. For the corporation such uniformity is desirable also; without it, analysis is difficult and the intelligent comparison of results almost impossible. Because of the growing conviction that a standardized system of accounts was essential to intelligent regulation and justified in the interest of the carrier and the investor, Congress in 1906 gave to the Interstate Commerce Commission the power to prescribe a uniform system for all carriers subject to the Act. In 1907 a partial plan was submitted for the guidance of the railways but not until 1914, after careful study and effort, did the Commission promulgate the comprehensive system of accounting now used by all carriers reporting to that body.

Investment and Operating Accounts.—In accordance with the final plan of the Commission, railway accounts are grouped under six main headings, the individual accounts under each heading being numbered. The first of these groups is entitled Investment in Road and Equipment Accounts, and the numbers 1–100 inclusive have been reserved for them. Of these numbered accounts, 1–47, inclusive, cover capital expenditures for roadway and structure; accounts 51–58, inclusive, cover equipment outlays; while expenditures of a general character properly chargeable to investment are grouped under numbers 71–77, here being included such items as organization and legal expenses, interest during construction, etc. The unused numbers are reserved here, as in the groups later mentioned, for future contingencies.

The second major grouping is termed Operating Revenue Accounts and for them the numbers 101–200 are reserved. The group is divided into four sub-groups, Transportation–Rail Line, including accounts 101–116, Transportation–Water Line accounts 121–128, Incidental, accounts 131–143, and Joint Facility, 151–152. To the various accounts of this group are credited, as the group name would indicate, all revenues derived directly from the operation of the line, together with such revenues as are incident to that operation. The most difficult problem involved in handling these accounts arises in determining whether revenues from certain sources, particularly such incidentals as privileges and rentals, are operating or nonoperating in character. However, the Commission has, in various interpretations made by it, indicated in considerable detail the character of the items to be included under each account, thereby facilitating the proper and uniform handling of particular items by all carriers.

Since railway expenditures may be for a great variety of purposes, it is only natural that to the third grouping, Operating Expense Accounts, should be assigned a broad range of numbers, 201–500 inclusive being here reserved. This group of accounts has been divided into eight sub-groups, of which the first is Maintenance of Way and Structures, accounts 201–279. To the individual accounts in this group are charged the expenditures necessary to the proper maintenance of roadbed, fences, buildings, and other structures utilized in the operation of the property. The outstanding feature of the accounts here prescribed, as well as of the following sub-group, is the fact that, in every instance where an initial outlay has been made for physical property, there is provided not only a corresponding maintenance account but also another to care for depreciation. As illustrative, the tie accounts may be used: investment—No. 8; maintenance—No. 212; depreciation—No. 213. The second sub-group, Maintenance of Equipment Expenses, 301–350, inclusive, covers all expenditures for locomotives, freight-train and passenger-train cars, motor and work equipment, etc.

The third sub-group, accounts 351–370, which is characterized as Traffic Expenses, includes all expenditures made in the solicitation or development of business and the determination of the rates thereon. Transportation–Rail Expenses, accounts 371–420, are those which arise from the actual movement of traffic by rail, including such important items as trainmen's wages, fuel, and station expenses. The desire of the Commission to separate rail and water operations not only in the matter of revenues but also expenses, resulted in the designation of a fifth sub-group—Transportation–Water Expenses, accounts 431–440, under which are included all items of expenditure incident to the operation of water equipment used to supplement the transportation service of the railways.

Under Miscellaneous Operations Expenses, accounts 441–450, are grouped outlays which are necessary to the maintenance of dining service, the operation of hotels and restaurants and of grain elevators, stock yards, etc. Under General Expenses, accounts 451–500, fall all items of cost which are not definitely assignable to any particular branch of the service. Here are included the salaries of all general officers, together with clerks and attendants employed by them; the cost of office supplies; law expenses; insurance, relief, and pension outlays; valuation expenses, etc. The eighth sub-group, Transportation for Investment–Credit, represents a bookkeeping operation which is designed to transfer from Operating Expenses to the appropriate Investment in Road and Equipment account all expenditures resulting from the transportation of materials used in additions or betterments. In building an extension, for example, it may be necessary to transport rails, ties, and other materials hundreds of miles; the performance of this work necessitates expenditures which are charged to the various operating expense accounts—maintenance of way and structures, maintenance of equipment, transportation—rail, general, and so forth. Yet such expenditures are *properly* chargeable to rail, tie, or other investment accounts, since the total capital cost of the extension includes the expense of transporting the needed materials to the place where used. As a correction, then, a general credit of an amount equal to the regular tariff charges upon such material is made to operating expenses as Transportation for Investment, and the proper investment account is debited with the same sum.

Income and Profit and Loss Accounts.—The fourth major group of accounts are the Income Accounts, 501–600. Among the credits here included, comprising accounts 501–530, there appear in addition to railway operating revenues a varied group of items often termed nonoperating revenues, such as hire of freight cars, rent from locomotives and passenger-train cars, dividend income, income from funded securities, etc. Among the debits, accounts, 531–556, there are, in addition to railway operating expenses, a considerable group of items oftentimes characterized as nonoperating expenses. Of these latter, the more important are hire of freight cars—debit balance, rent for locomotives and for passenger-train cars, rent for leased roads, interest on funded debts, and dividend appropriation of income.

The Profit and Loss Accounts, Nos. 601–700, are purposed[1]

> . . . to show the change in the corporate surplus or deficit during each fiscal period as affected by the operations and business transactions during that period, by any disposition of net profits made solely at the option of the accounting company, by accounting adjustments of matters not properly attributable to the period, or by miscellaneous gains or losses not provided for elsewhere; and to show also the unappropriated surplus of the carrier at the date of the balance sheet.

Among the credit items, accounts 601–607, there appear, in addition to Credit Balance and Credit Balance Transferred from Income, such items as Delayed Income Credits, Unrefundable Income Charges, and Donations. Among the debit items, accounts 611–621, appear not only Debit Balance and Debit Balance Transferred from Income, but also Dividend Appropriation of Surplus, Stock and Debt Discount Extinguished Through Surplus, and Loss on Retired Road and Equipment.

The General Balance Sheet.—The final major grouping comprises the so-called General Balance Sheet accounts, Nos. 701–800. Among the primary accounts here provided, the debits or assets include Nos. 701–

[1] *Instructions—Profit and Loss Accounts,* Interstate Commerce Commission.

729, and cover items of every character and description which represent a resource to the carrier. These asset accounts are grouped under four heads: Investments, Current Assets, Deferred Assets, and Unadjusted Debits. Among the credits or liabilities, accounts 751–784, appear, on the other hand, all items which represent an obligation of the reporting railway corporation. These accounts are classified under seven heads: Stock, Government Grants, Long-term Debt, Current Liabilities, Deferred Liabilities, Unadjusted Credits, and Corporate Surplus. To aid the carrier in making up the balance sheet, the Interstate Commerce Commission has issued numerous special instructions and the final form in which it shall appear is described.

Specimen Statements.—That the relation of the various groups of accounts may be understood more clearly and that the definite steps essential to the determination of net income, as well as of surplus, may be more readily grasped, the somewhat shortened summary statement follows.

TABLE XVII.—INCOME AND PROFIT AND LOSS ACCOUNTS, CLASS I RAILWAYS, 1931[1]

Income Account	
Railway operating revenues	$4,188,343,244
Railway operating expenses	3,223,574,616
Net revenues from railway operations	$ 964,768,628
Railway tax accruals	303,528,099
Uncollectible railway revenues	891,140
Railway operating income	$ 660,349,389
Revenues from miscellaneous operations	$ 3,148,406
Expenses of miscellaneous operations	2,917,802
Net revenue from miscellaneous operations	$ 230,604
Taxes on miscellaneous operating property	177,934
Miscellaneous operating income	$ 52,670
Total operating income	$ 660,402,059
Net railway operating income	$ 525,627,852
Hire of freight cars—credit balance	10,862,542
Rent from locomotives	10,791,896
Rent from passenger-train cars	14,043,059
Other items of nonoperating income	348,469,619
Total nonoperating income	$ 384,167,116
Gross income	$1,044,569,175
Hire of freight cars—debit balance	$ 107,360,597
Rent for locomotives	10,318,296
Rent for passenger-train cars	18,493,366
Other items deducted	773,635,005
Total deductions from gross income	$ 909,807,264
Net income	$ 134,761,911

TABLE XVII.—INCOME AND PROFIT AND LOSS ACCOUNTS, CLASS I RAILWAYS, 1931.[1]—(*Continued*)

Income applied to sinking and other reserve funds	$ 6,080,576
Dividend appropriations of income	80,036,685
Various other appropriations of net income	1,993,387
Total appropriations of income	$ 88,110,648
Income transferred to profit and loss	$ 46,651,263
Profit and Loss Account	
Credit balance transferred from income	$ 179,505,466
Profit on road and equipment sold	3,567,948
Delayed income credits	1,067,832
Unrefundable overcharges	658,977
Donations	2,798,176
Miscellaneous credits	28,368,831
Total credits during year	$ 215,967,230
Debit balance transferred from income	$ 132,854,203
Surplus applied to sinking and other reserve funds	2,577,314
Dividend appropriations of surplus	250,114,188
Surplus appropriated for investment in physical property	4,171,747
Stock discount extinguished through surplus	1,112
Debt discount extinguished through surplus	13,091,752
Miscellaneous appropriations of surplus	12,547,359
Loss on retired road and equipment	33,624,337
Delayed income debits	65,629,895
Miscellaneous debits	22,888,286
Total debits during year	$ 537,500,193
Net increase during year	$ 321,532,963(d)
Balance at beginning of year	$3,552,054,925
Balance at end of year	$3,230,521,962*

[1] Interstate Commerce Commission, *Preliminary Abstract of Statistics of Common Carriers, 1931.*

(d) Indicates deficit or other reverse item.

* The discrepancy between the profit and loss balance shown is explained by the fact that when a Class I steam railway files an annual report for a period ending prior to Dec. 31, the income and profit and loss account is included in the tabulations, but the balance sheet is not included.

Evaluation of Prescribed System.—As might be expected, complaints have been lodged by many carriers against this uniform and mandatory system of accounting. These complaints tend to be directed against two features, the rigidity of the system and its failure to permit particular matters to be handled in accordance with the desires of individual carriers. However, it seems inevitable that the price of uniformity must be a considerable measure of rigidity, and the failure of the Commission to interpret particular accounts in accordance with a given officer's understanding or desire is scarcely to be regarded as a weighty charge against the system. Most assuredly the present uniform system of railway accounting is infinitely superior to the old individualistic systems from the standpoint of both the investor and the public, and its simplicity is in sharp contrast with the involved methods frequently employed by strictly private enterprise, permitting those so disposed grossly to misrepresent actual conditions and results. Indeed, once the generation of railway accountants, accustomed to an individualistic system capable of modification at pleasure, has been displaced by younger men, carrier protests will largely disappear and the superiority of a system which offers simplicity and greater possibilities of comparison and analysis will be generally acknowledged.

Railway Statistics.—An examination of the detailed records of the operations of all railway corporations or even of a single corporation would give only a confused idea of results. That these results may be more apparent and more readily available, statistical data are compiled. The purpose of such data is to secure summaries which will facilitate comprehensive understanding and accurate comparisons. These comparisons may be made for a particular road between year and year or between division and division or, upon occasion, between specific tasks. They may also be made between or among various roads. Such comparisons are of fundamental value to the corporation, for they show the trend of revenues and expenses, and make it possible to gain quickly a more accurate knowledge of the strong and the weak features of its operations. These comparisons are of vital significance to the investor also, because upon them he must base his judgment of the progress or decline of a particular property. Such data are likewise invaluable to the public and to public bodies, for without them there would be available no sound basis for conclusions upon which action, designed to modify existing relations between carrier and public, might be predicated.

All statistics dealing with railway operations as a whole must rest upon data made available by individual carriers. Such data represent summaries from the carrier's detailed records and may be compiled, as was indicated earlier in the chapter, in either of two ways. Within each major division of the accounting department there may be a statistical section compiling summary figures for each division, such as expenditures, freight operations, and passenger operations, these summary figures then being placed in the hands of an organization whose function it is to assemble and organize the report. On the other hand, a separate statistical division may exist to which the various sections send detailed statistical data. In such case, not only must the data for the report be organized in the central office, but the responsibility for a major part of all underlying compilations and calculations also rests there.

The individual railway compiles its statistical data by units. The large carrier may summarize according to major divisions, by "lines east," and "lines west," or "lines north" and "lines south," but all carriers compile data by operating divisions. Figures for the latter generally represent a summary of data for the several accounting divisions which are coextensive with each operating unit. For specific purposes statistical data are often compiled for still smaller units, covering, for a definite period of time, such restricted scope as the single station or a single type of traffic. But, whatever may be the minor divisions for which figures are compiled, summary statistics are always made up for the entire property and these are the only data available to the public. Compilation by smaller divisions, however, is of distinct value, if not essential, to the carrier in the effective utilization of such data for closer analysis of business results.

Scope of Railway Statistics.—The statistics compiled by the carrier cover a great variety of matters. One important grouping is that of service mileage statistics. Data are prepared, showing revenue and non-revenue mileage by classes of service: freight train; freight locomotive—principal, helper, and light; freight car, empty and loaded. Similar figures are prepared for passenger and switching service, as well as for mileage according to the direction of movement and whether tonnage has moved in carload or less-than-carload lots. Revenue data are compiled according to types of service—freight, passenger, etc.—on the basis of road mileage and even by commodities and by classes of goods. In this connection also are computed average ton-mile and passenger-mile revenues. Expenses are shown according to the Interstate Commerce Commission's classification of accounts and are also computed according to mileage. Very complete data are prepared covering equipment, not only as to the number of units of each of the various types but also as to expenses; the records give the total cost of each item, even to waste, charged to locomotives as a whole and to individual locomotives. Data of a similar character, though less detailed, are prepared for freight cars, passenger cars, and other equipment.

Upon the basis of this information, and upon other facts given in special statements which may be requested by the Interstate Commerce Commission, such as accident reports, that body compiles its annual report, *Statistics of Railways in the United States*. In this volume appear a summary statement of results for the roads of the United States as a whole and the individual statements of all carriers reporting to that body. Among the summary statements are those which present statistics relative to railways in the hands of receivers, to mileage, equipment, railway employees, and capitalization—nominal and actual, as well as selected statements dealing with physical operations. Here, too, are found the income and profit and loss statements, the condensed balance sheet; investment in road and equipment; also miscellaneous items, such as fuel consumption and rail and tie replacements. All in all, the statistical data compiled by the railways and by them reported to the Interstate Commerce Commission are very complete, giving the student an excellent picture not only of the physical but also of the financial operations and status of the property.

Further Development of Statistics.—Despite the completeness of present railway statistical compilations, certain further needs appear. A divergence in method exists in the determination of net tonnage figures, certain railways compiling them from the waybill, others from the conductor's wheel reports. It is also urged by those connected with the compilation of railway statistics that certain practical features are overlooked by the Interstate Commerce Commission in its requirements. A greater defect than these has been the failure of the carriers to develop and apply cost accounting in the field of railway operations; in consequence, there is a striking lack of those data vital to any positive knowledge of the results of particular phases of operation and essential to more effective organization and conduct of the enterprise. Without doubt there will be a steady improvement in the compilation and organization of railway statistics, but marked progress is in large measure contingent upon an improved factual basis for which, in turn, further developments in accounting analysis by the individual carriers are essential.

Sources of Data.—For the individual seeking statistical information relative to railways, the annual report of the particular railway, as well as the data given for it in the annual *Statistics of Railways,* also certain monthly statistical statements and summaries of a varied nature, issued by the Interstate Commerce Commission, are to be recommended. Poor's *Manual of Railways* was long an excellent source, as are now certain volumes of an investment character, such as Moody's *Railroads.* Additional information of value pertaining primarily to railway operations as a whole may be found in the various publications of the Bureau of Railway Economics and of the Bureau of Railway News and Statistics, both of which are supported by the railways of the country. Certain states also, usually through the railway or public-utility commission, publish information of a valuable character and, up to and including 1890, the United States Census contains most important data. Beyond these sources there are also a number of special reports which have been published by government bureaus and by Congressional committees embodying the results of investigations made. Indeed, with the passage of time, the number of reliable sources of information concerning railway operations has multiplied rapidly, with the result that there exists today a great body of material of an impartial nature, as well as a large amount of a partisan character intended to further the interests of labor, of the carriers, and of particular public groups. The plea of lack of access to material dealing with railways can excuse no one today for ignorance of the basic facts in that field, though material from many sources must be carefully scrutinized for propaganda. Many are the axes which designing owners hope the public will grind.

REFERENCES

ADAMS, H. C.: *Railway Accounting*, Henry Holt & Company, 1918.

CLEVELAND, F. A., and F. W. POWELL: *Railroad Finance*, D. Appleton & Company, 1912.

COLE, W. M.: *Accounts: Their Construction and Interpretation*, Houghton Mifflin Company, 1908.

COPELAND, M. T.: *Business Statistics*, Harvard University Press, 1917.

EATON, JAMES SHIRLEY: *Handbook of Railroad Expenses*, McGraw-Hill Book Company, Inc., 1913.

HOOPER, W. E.: *Railroad Accounting*, D. Appleton & Company, 1915.

Interstate Commerce Commission: *Annual Reports; Prescribed System of Uniform Accounts; Reports of Accidents, Classifications of Train Miles, etc.; Statistics of Railways.*

JOHNSON, E. R., and G. G. HUEBNER: *Railroad Traffic and Rates*, vols. 1, 2, D. Appleton & Company, 1911

———, and T. W. VAN METRE: *Principles of Railroad Transportation*, D. Appleton & Company, 1921.

MCPHERSON, LOGAN: *The Working of the Railroads*, Henry Holt & Company, 1906.

MAXEY, EDWARD P., JR.: *Accounting Systems*, vol. 10 of Alexander Hamilton Series (contains samples of large number of forms used in railway accounting procedure), 1911.

SAKOLSKI, A. M.: *American Railroad Economics*, The Macmillan Company, 1916.

WHITE, JOSEPH L.: *Analysis of Railroad Operation*, Simmons-Boardman Publishing Company, 1925.

WOODLOCK, THOMAS F.: *The Anatomy of a Railroad Report and Ten Mile Cost*, Thomas Nelson & Sons, New York, 1900.

WOODSON, E. R.: *Railroad Accounting Procedure*, Railway Accounting Officers Association (published annually).

PART IV

SOME ECONOMIC ASPECTS OF TRANSPORT

Chapter XXIV

COMPETITION

AT THE time of its inception almost 100 years ago the railway business was regarded as competitive in character and by the great mass of the American people is still so considered. The persistence of that popular misconception in the face of long experience may be readily understood, however, if the background of railway development be scrutinized.

Perhaps the most important factor in determining public attitude was the dominant influence of the *laissez-faire* philosophy during the first half of the past century. When the railway first became an assured agency of transport, few even among those who gave careful and serious thought to economic matters had challenged this controlling philosophy, and it was quite natural that the belief in the beneficence of competition in existing fields should carry over into this new one, the field of railway construction and operation. Another major factor in convincing the public of the competitive character of railway business was the accepted relation of those agencies which the railways superseded. The competitive operation of stagecoaches was common in all settled portions of the country; boats owned by rival interests were operated through canals; upon the natural waterways—river, lake, ocean—keen competition was evident. That the same economic force which had served public interest advantageously in connection with these earlier agencies of transportation should function with expedition and efficiency in behalf of that same public in its dealings with this new instrument seemed wholly reasonable.

Two facts clearly indicate that confidence in competition dominated the thought as well as the action of the public concerning railways during many years. In the earliest charters granted this improved agency of transportation, provisions appeared relative to and governing the common use of the constructed roadways by equipment variously owned. But indisputable evidence of the controlling force of this conception of the nature of the railway industry appears in the fact that, for almost half a century following initial construction, the public sought protection from practices and policies which they regarded, rightly or wrongly, as inimical to their interests by encouraging the construction of rival lines rather than by the regulation of existing lines. No small portion of the American railway mileage owed a premature existence to the full determination of the public to regulate existing carriers through the agency of competition.

Competition Varied and Far-reaching.—Competition in the transport field functions between or among various routes. Traffic moving from one point common to two or more transport agencies to another point common to these same or to connecting lines has, from an early period, been affected by active competition. Not alone, however, does competition function between railways—it functions also between and among rail lines, water lines, and, more recently, motor and air lines. Water competition is now most important along our extended coast, upon the Great Lakes, and upon certain navigable streams; motor competition is found widely, being especially keen in populous sections; while air routes become increasingly numerous and significant. Water competition was, for a long period, the important type encountered; it affected not only railways directly concerned but also, in many cases, those operating at a considerable distance. As an example of this may be cited the influence exerted upon railway rates from Chicago territory into the South by the struggle between the railway and water lines which operate from the North Atlantic to the South Atlantic ports. The railways east of the Allegheny Mountains must fix rates with respect to water-movement costs; the Western lines, struggling with the Eastern for participation in Southern business, must conform closely to the scale of charges fixed by the latter or surrender a considerable portion of the traffic which they now enjoy. However, in more recent years, motor competition has gained rapidly in significance. The motor vehicle, bus and truck, has exerted its major influence upon local or short-haul traffic in contrast to boat and barge which bid largely for long-haul movements.

Traffic Competition.—Three distinct types of competition in the transport field are distinguishable. The first and most obvious of these is *traffic competition*. This involves a struggle between or among lines variously situated for tonnage and for passenger movements which may exercise a choice of routes. Such traffic competition shows itself most obviously and most actively in the case of *parallel* routes, the carriers involved operating in essentially the same territory with lines lying perhaps side by side for many miles or diverging but little throughout their entire course. Carriers so situated struggle for the control of business in the same production areas and the same centers of population along the entire route. Parallel building of railways, though characteristic neither of the early period nor of more recent years, was all too common during the years 1850–1880, and represented a heavy economic waste until agricultural and industrial development had absorbed the resultant surplus capacity to serve. With the construction of hard roads, however, railways have been paralleled widely by motor lines, several such lines often rendering service throughout the same areas. Competition of parallel routes is frequently offered also by waterways.

Only a small proportion of our transport lines lie side by side. Rather, while serving adjacent areas, these lines possess in common many important centers. Competition among *diverse* routes is, therefore, perhaps the most common and the most important type of traffic competition, when measured quantitatively. Between Chicago and New York City goods and persons may travel over any one of half a dozen railways that operate in the intervening territory from as far north as Montreal to as far south as Norfolk; between Chicago and Minneapolis-St. Paul lines operate which serve Milwaukee on the east and Grinnell, Iowa, on the west; between Chicago and Omaha lines run through a zone approximately 150 miles in width; between Chicago and St. Louis lines follow closely the Mississippi River on the one hand and the eastern boundary of the state of Illinois on the other. Between St. Louis and Omaha competing routes exist through points as divergent as Kansas City and Freeport, Ill.; from Chicago to Seattle traffic moves by such widely separated routes as the Canadian Pacific system and the Denver and Rio Grande Western. Indeed, from Denver, traffic destined for San Francisco has a choice of routes which would carry it through Ogden, Utah, or points in southern Arizona. And between all centers named a further diversity of routes exists because of the operation of motor-bus and motor-truck lines or connection by navigable water—and sometimes both types of transport are available as alternatives to rail movement. An infinite number of additional instances of divergent railway routes which compete for traffic between two common points might be given, but the general extent and the obvious importance of such competition make further illustration unnecessary.

A third form of traffic competition, and one less familiar to the shipping public but nevertheless of fundamental significance to shipper and carrier, is that often termed *right-angled* competition. It differs from competition of parallel and of diverse routes in that it usually represents a struggle between or among groups of lines rather than individual lines. One of the clearest illustrations of right-angled competition is to be found in the struggle for the control of the grain traffic of the upper Western Mississippi Valley. This battle is waged between the carriers, both rail and water, serving Gulf ports on the one hand and those serving Atlantic ports, particularly the North Atlantic group, on the other. So sharp has been the struggle between these two groups and so nice is the present adjustment of rates upon grain traffic which may move either eastward or southward that the lowering of an intrastate railway rate upon corn in Texas, directly affecting the Gulf carriers alone, finally caused a decrease in the rate upon flour from Minneapolis to New York City. The reduction of the Texas intrastate rate upon corn forced a reduction upon the interstate corn rate from Kansas and Nebraska to points southward. This in turn necessitated a lower rate upon wheat, which compelled a reduction of the rate upon flour, because of certain relations which the railways have found it needful to maintain between the rates upon corn and wheat, and upon wheat and flour. To prevent an advantage in Eastern and foreign markets accruing to the milling industry of the Southwest in consequence of this reduction upon flour moving to Gulf ports, the railways serving the spring-wheat area were forced to make a corresponding cut in charges. And thus the train of causation ends—at least so far as the American producer and carrier are concerned. Another illustration of right-angled competition is found in the struggle for business moving from St. Louis to Atlantic ports and in export trade. Rail and water carriers from St. Louis southward compete among themselves and, as a group, vie with those rail carriers operating to the eastward. Denver is served from the Atlantic coast by all-rail lines, as well as by water to Gulf ports and thence by rail. Another excellent illustration of this form of competition appears in the north with the completion by the Canadian government of the railway from The Pas to Hudson Bay. That railway and connecting boat lines, operating northward to Fort Churchill and through Hudson Bay to Europe, will be in sharp competition with those rail and boat lines which move a heavy grain tonnage eastward and southward to various St. Lawrence and Atlantic ports for export.

Yet another form of traffic competition, and one that seems strange if not well-nigh impossible to those who have given little thought to the problem, is between carriers which normally function as connecting or supplementary lines. This might well be termed *end-to-end* competition. To regard the Pennsylvania, operating from Chicago to the east coast, as a competitor of the Santa Fe, the Union Pacific, or perhaps the Northern Pacific, would seem to call for the exercise of an active imagination. Yet, in the case of tonnage movement from Chicago to the Orient, the Pennsylvania, connecting with steamship lines that operate through the Suez Canal, is an active rival of the Hill system which serves ocean lines that run westward to the Orient. Indeed, even in the case of traffic moving to Pacific coast points, a considerable tonnage originating at inland points as far from the Atlantic coast as Pittsburgh and Cleveland, even Chicago, instead of moving westward by rail moves *eastward* by rail, thence to destination by water via the Panama Canal. Clear recognition of this fact was shown by the Interstate Commerce Commission in a revision of the Transcontinental rate structure in 1911, concerning which comment is made in a later chapter.

Market Competition.—A second type of competition, perhaps not so obvious as competition for traffic but none the less highly important in the determination of transport policy, is that characteristically known as *market competition.* This type of rivalry is found throughout the entire United States and has exerted a tremendous influence not merely upon rate structures but even upon the actual construction of railways. In the early years of American railway construction, the desire to extend the market area tributary to a particular commercial center actuated the building of considerable mileage. The Pennsylvania Railroad made peculiar appeal to the residents of Philadelphia because its construction was designed not only to extend the market territory tributary to that city within the state of Pennsylvania, but also to tap the great reservoir of traffic west of the Ohio River from which a heavy tonnage was expected to flow eastward. The Baltimore and Ohio was similarly a local project, designed to maintain the commercial position of Baltimore, and from Charleston westward the Charleston and Hamburg was built for a like reason. Indeed, the entire history of railway building abounds with illustrations of market competition as a driving force in railway construction.

Market competition has shown itself more widely and more persistently, however, in the adjustment of rates among the various commercial centers. It was early found necessary, as will be shown more fully in connection with the study of railway rate structures, to make certain adjustments on traffic moving from the east through Chicago and through St. Louis which would enable those two distributing centers to compete upon a relatively equal basis in the territory lying to the west and north. At a later time it was found essential that Kansas City and St. Louis be put upon a parity in Southwestern territory. In fact, the various rate territories of the United States abound with areas, some small, some large, which enjoy rates to central markets identical with or comparable to those applicable from other sections, that equality of opportunity may be maintained. Not only has market competition shown itself in the desire to control the distribution of goods, but it has likewise appeared in the struggle among important points to bring about the centralization, each in its own hands, of traffic originating in territory which might, because of its location, be tributary to any one of several such centers. An outstanding instance of this phase of market competition appears in the struggle among Boston, New York, Philadelphia, Baltimore and Norfolk—indeed, the South Atlantic and Gulf ports are evidencing an increasingly active interest in this matter—for an advantage in export trade, each city supported by one or more carriers whose interests are identical with those of the commercial centers named. Similar rivalries appear among other groups of ports—South Atlantic, East Gulf, West Gulf, South Pacific, North Pacific, even Great Lakes—and an infinite number of illustrations of such competition may be found by a study of the relation of inland traffic centers.

Industrial Competition.—Difficult to distinguish from the type of competition just discussed, competition which might be characterized as *of* markets, is another type—or different phase of the type just considered—which may be termed *industrial competition*, or competition *for* markets. This type, as distinguished from market competition, appears in the form of a struggle among producing units and producing areas for a dominant position in important market centers and market areas. Industrial competition is very keen, for example, between the New England and Middle Atlantic states on the one hand and the newly developed industrial area north and west of the Ohio River on the other, and this struggle evidences itself in Southern territory, in Southwestern territory, in the great Inland Empire, and even upon the Pacific coast. Producers of salt in Kansas struggle with Michigan producers of that same commodity for a dominant position in intervening territory. Kansas flour and Minnesota flour are keen rivals for the favor of housewives located to the eastward. Anthracite coal from Pennsylvania and soft coal from the Indiana and Illinois districts "lock horns" throughout many Northern and Northwestern states. The struggle between the growers of citrus fruits in California and in Florida is in evidence throughout the entire territory east of the Mississippi River and at points to the westward. Though numberless additional illustrations might be given, they are unnecessary: the important fact to be noted is that, in the development and maintenance of such rivalries, agencies of transport are always important and active instrumentalities.

So significant have market competition and industrial competition been in years past, and so important do they remain, that a considerable measure of current recognition is justified of the time-worn assertion that railway traffic officials do not *fix* rates; rather, they make an effort to determine what forces have so operated as to *compel the carrier to accept* a certain rate or schedule of rates. The maintenance and the expansion of industries tributary to a particular route are of vital importance to it as well as to the owners of those industries. In consequence, therefore, any action on the part of one carrier, rail or water, which threatens to prejudice producers tributary to another in a certain market, compels the latter to take immediate and retaliatory action if its own future is to be adequately protected. To admit, however, that transport agencies are often forced by market and industrial conditions to act in certain ways by no means justifies all vagaries in rates, individual and group, which carriers have endeavored to explain upon such grounds.

Competition Assumes Two Forms.—Carrier competition has evidenced itself in two forms. The more spectacular and, in years past, the more important of these has been competition in rates. In a struggle for business, rates were very generally pared and, as the contest became keener, were sometimes cut so sharply that the carriers handled competitive business at an out-of-pocket loss. Fluctuations during the period of a rate war were generally both wide and rapid, downward movements being checked by agreements which usually attempted to restore the old rate or one approaching it. These agreements, however, were seldom effective for any extended period and their failure always resulted in renewed warfare.

Another form which carrier rivalry takes is service competition. During the period characterized by railway rate wars, service competition, though existent, occupied an unimportant position. Once rate competition had been brought under relatively effective control, as it was during the latter part of the nineteenth century, competition in service alone remained, and for many years it has played an important part in the efforts of rail carriers to acquire existing business. Beginning about 1900, however, the various railway associations were able except at intervals to fix competitive limits even in the field of service; yet, within those limits, opportunity remained to the individual railway to render a service better suited to the needs of shippers than that offered by competitive lines. This rivalry in service functions almost exclusively in connection with the struggle for traffic, playing generally only a minor part in either market or industrial competition.

With the development of motor competition and the revitalization of inland waterway service in consequence of river improvements as well as of federal support for river operations, competition in the transport field has become much more active. And this is quite as true of competition in rates as in service. Railway tariffs have been modified where motor-vehicle or waterway rivalry is particularly keen, railway service has been speeded in time and broadened in character. Not only have rates been lowered upon shipments made in the ordinary way but so-called container service has been made available to shippers by certain railways within limited areas, this service resulting in both lowered shipping costs and greater convenience. The time of passenger trains in through service has been shortened and the same is true of regularly scheduled freight movements, but perhaps the most striking service change in the history of American railroading is the establishment upon a broad scale of collection and delivery of small-lot shipments. However, in this endeavor of the railways to maintain ascendancy in the field of transport, it is interesting to note, that, when material changes are made in rates or in service, the railways concerned tend to act together, thus presenting upon most occasions a united front.

Reasons for Intensity of Competition.—In so far as competition has functioned in the railway field because of voluntary action on the part of railway management or relations enforced by public authority, it has been peculiarly intense in character and destructive in results. Indeed, so widely does the railway business vary from the typical commercial enterprise that a knowledge of the results of active rivalry in the latter field gives no understanding of the effect of unrestrained competitive action in the transportation of persons and of goods by rail.

Continuous Operation.—The railway differs from other types of enterprise, even other types of transport agencies, in important particulars. In the first place, it is subject to the necessity of continuous operation. Not only is regularity of service a fundamental requirement and demanded without exception by the public, but the railway finds that self-interest also compels the maintenance of essentially continuous service. If such service is not maintained in the competitive portion of its field, business becomes habituated to movement over the rival lines; if no other outlet for traffic exists, the railway must maintain regular service to prevent the complete throttling of industries thus wholly dependent upon it. Furthermore, because much of the expense incident to operation is of a continuous character, a railway corporation oftentimes finds it economically more desirable to continue operations in the face of heavy losses than to cease operations altogether and thus suffer a still heavier loss. Such continuous operation necessitates, whether service be rendered on alternate days or during alternate hours, a certain minimum standard of maintenance, both of roadway and structure and of equipment. In the face of this minimum expenditure, which changes comparatively little with changes in the volume of traffic, the incentive to struggle for additional business is irresistible. Steady loss will cause the ordinary commercial or industrial enterprise to close down its plant partially or wholly, but not so the railway business: its nature is such that, despite financial results, it must maintain a continuous service or withdraw permanently from the field. And not infrequently the law denies recourse to this alternative. The necessity of continuous operation is alone sufficient to explain the unusual severity of railway competition under conditions of inadequate traffic. This factor is of significance in common carrier operations of motor vehicle and barge but of far less weight than with the railways—primarily because the railway is compelled to provide its own right of way, as its rivals are not.

Nontransferability of Railway Capital.—A second factor which operates to make competition in the railway field exceedingly sharp is the peculiar degree to which capital in that enterprise is fixed and, in consequence, incapable of utilization for an alternative purpose, even in an alternative location. When an ordinary enterprise becomes insolvent, creditors usually have the choice of either of two solutions: the plant may be closed and dismantled, with land and buildings devoted to other purposes and equipment transferred elsewhere; or operations may be continued, following reorganization or following the sale of the property and assumption of control by a new management. In the railway field, however, insolvency under normal conditions presents no alternatives—continued operation alone is possible because the sacrifices demanded of creditors in dismantling the property would be heavier, except under most unusual circumstances, than those compelled by reorganization.

This is true because relatively little of the capital invested in roadway or structures can be recovered in dismantling the property: the one exception to this statement which has ever come to the writer's attention was a small property built through a plains country prior to the European war, which was "junked" about the time that prices of steel, lumber, and other items had reached their peak. Terminal sites, right of way, even track materials and structures, normally have comparatively slight value except as component parts of an operating unit. Indeed, instead of an insolvent railway being eliminated from the field as a competitive factor, which is often true in the case of commercial or industrial enterprises, such a property becomes an even more dangerous competitor because, while operated by a receiver, it is relieved of the necessity of meeting fixed charges currently and is therefore in a position to cut more deeply into established rates than before receivership. However precarious, therefore, may be the financial situation of a particular property, two factors tend to force it to remain in the field—the necessity of continuous operation and the peculiar degree of fixity of capital. And so long as that property remains in the field it will compete actively, often fiercely, for traffic.

Nontransferability of capital does not weigh heavily in the case of any of the effective rivals of the railway in the field of transport. Motor carriers for hire have no funds invested in right of way and such terminal properties as are owned can be turned to other uses at comparatively slight loss. Carriers by air likewise have no investment in immovable properties except as moneys may have been expended upon landing fields—and such costs have been borne in the United States largely by interested municipalities or by other financial groups. Barge lines, too, have a free right of way—and to a very considerable degree municipalities are asked to furnish docks and other facilities. A motor truck or a river barge can no more be transformed at the investor's wish into a summer cottage or into copper pigs than can a railway locomotive or a refrigerator car: sums once invested in such particular capital items represent in that sense fixed investments. None the less, these items are *mobile* and can be shifted to areas where the promise of remuneration is greater, as is in no sense true of the investment in railway way and structure. And, since the proportion of railway capital in the latter forms is many times greater than is the case with rival forms of transport, nontransferability of capital will always be a greater spur to competition in the case of the railways than of other transport agencies.

Railway Business One of Increasing Returns.—A third element, which has intensified railway rivalry and which has proved an important stimulant to competitive action upon the part of both prosperous and "weak" carriers, has been the universal operation until recent years of the law of increasing returns in the field of railway operation. This fact is explained by the high proportion of constant to total costs. Expenditure by the typical American railway for maintenance of roadway and structures is made necessary by the action of the elements to an even greater degree than by the use of the property. Outlays for the maintenance of equipment are attributable in part to the action of the elements and to deterioration through age, though such outlays are progressively due, as the volume of traffic increases, to use in service. Expenses incident to the movement of trains are also constant, in part; whether 1 train or 20 be operated over the line each day, it is necessary to maintain essentially the same administrative staff at division points, the same station forces, and other like groups concerned with movement of business. Traffic expenses, miscellaneous expenses, and general expenses will also vary little with the amount of traffic handled, the proportion for these being essentially constant. In addition to such operating expenses there is, of course, that group which might be termed fixed charges; these are almost wholly constant in character. Because the relation of expenses to the extent of operations will be understood more clearly if definite percentages are given, Table XVIII—based on past performance—is presented.

TABLE XVIII.—CONSTANT AND VARIABLE EXPENSES IN RAILWAY OPERATION

Type of expense	Percentage of operating expenses			Percentage of total expense		
	Both	Constant	Variable	Both	Constant	Variable
Maintenance of way and structures...	16	10.5	5.5	12.0	8.0	4.0
Maintenance of equipment..........	28	10.0	18.0	21.0	7.5	13.5
Transportation....................	50	25.0	25.0	37.5	18.75	18.75
General, including traffic, miscellaneous, etc....................	6	6	....	4.5	4.5	
Total....................	100	51.5	48.5			
Capital costs....................	...	....	....	25.0	25.0	
				100.0	63.75	36.25

This table shows that approximately two-thirds of the necessary expenditures of a railway under given conditions are constant in character, while but one-third vary in proportion to the amount of business done. In view of this fact, it is clear that if an individual railway can double its traffic it will increase its expenses only by approximately one-third, enjoying therefore a tremendously increased margin as profit. Indeed, so great is the gain which results from handling additional business that an individual carrier can afford to move such business at distinctly lower rates than those normally charged—therefore the great temptation to indulge in cutthroat tactics in the struggle to secure additional tonnage. And such extreme competitive action may characterize the relation existing between roads that in no wise feel the pinch of financial necessity quite as well as those that are fighting for corporate existence. To the extent, therefore, that a given railway property is able to operate upon a basis of increasing returns, competition will characterize its dealings with other carriers so long as law or custom precludes a mutual understanding among independent properties concerning rates or the grouping of railways under some form of intercorporate relation.

Here, perhaps, it is in place to add that the railways of the United States have operated upon the basis of increasing returns to a peculiar degree throughout almost their entire history. During each successive stage of railway development, facilities remained far in advance of the traffic demands made upon them: speculative interest, promoters' activities, public aid, and other factors all combined to that end. Not until about 1906 did the railways of any extensive portion of the United States have more than a theoretical knowledge of the existence of a law of decreasing returns. For a time, however, it appeared that certain railways operating in the more highly developed areas were the losers through an increase of traffic, unable as they were to increase their facilities because of the weakness of railway credit. However, as a result of increased facilities and the appearance of rival transport service, it is probable that this situation no longer exists. The mileage in Southern and Western territories will now not only benefit from any increase in traffic but also gives promise of continuing to benefit for an indefinite period. And this is the more true because of shifts to competitive agencies of traffic formerly moved by rail.

To the extent that the application of the principle of increasing returns gives place to that of increasing cost, a reduction in competition might seem to be in prospect. Nevertheless, a particular property is slow to realize that conditions have been reversed, so it is probable the struggle for additional business will continue for years after such traffic has become a millstone about the neck of a static property. Then, too, each property hopes for conditions which will permit an expansion of facilities—and in the meantime endeavors to possess itself of all available business. Therefore, even after it has ceased to operate, the law of increasing returns will continue as an active factor in promoting competitive activities—if for no other reasons than those that rest upon inertia and hope.

As a second consequence of freedom from heavy capital and maintenance costs for right of way and specialized structures, those inland transport agencies that compete with the railway feel in far less degree the operation of the principle of increasing returns or of increasing costs. As volume of traffic increases, additional units—be they barge or truck or plane—are added: expenses and revenues will advance together. As the volume of traffic shrinks, withdrawal of units makes possible reductions in total outlay that are comparable to the decline in revenues. It is difficult to visualize a time when increasing costs would appear in the field of air transport, upon inland lakes, or upon most of our inland watercourses; upon the highways this principle may appear, yet, as traffic becomes congested, it is probable that additional facilities will be provided at public cost. Therefore, within broad limits, the principle of increasing returns will not sharpen nor the principle of increasing costs dull, competition for those inland transport agencies that vie with the railways.

During the early years of railway construction and operation in the United States the public encouraged railway management in its competitive activities. However, this management soon learned that competition in the railway field was not the "life of trade" but was, rather, a two-edged sword that injured him who wielded it as well as him who was attacked. Yet, when railway management sought to curb this destructive force, the public endeavored to enforce a relation which experience had shown the carriers to be unsound. Indeed, for more than half a century it has been only as the railways have discovered ways to evade legislation hostile to cooperation that they have succeeded in minimizing the destructiveness of competition.

Immediate and Ultimate Results of Competition.—The results of competition in the field of transport may be designated as immediate and as ultimate from the point of view of both public and the carriers. Historically, the outstanding immediate gain to the public flowing from such rivalry has been a lower level of rates. Offsetting this advantage, however, there has appeared the objectionable fluctuation of rates previously mentioned and a still greater evil, discrimination. Although discrimination might exist under a monopolistic control of the railways, it is unquestionable that competition has served to magnify greatly both the extent and the degree of discrimination and to make its influence felt throughout the entire United States. Not only has *place* discrimination resulted, with abnormally low rates between competitive points and unreasonably high rates, relatively or absolutely, at noncompetitive points, but *personal* discrimination has also developed. At competitive points the railway found that tonnage increased more rapidly if it allied with itself, through especially favorable rates, a conspicuously aggressive and successful man in each field of business enterprise than if it sought instead the favor, upon the basis of regular rates, of *all* shippers who were interested in that particular enterprise. So, without hesitation, the carriers ignored another common-law obligation: competition was a ruthless master.

For the carriers the immediate result of competitive activity has been universally depleted revenues. Though competition usually "broke out" in connection with a particular type of traffic—wheat, cotton, live stock, or immigrant, tourist, etc., it normally broadened until practically all traffic was affected. Frequently it spread from one distinct type of service to another, as from passenger to freight or the reverse. With the depletion of their revenues, all railways indulging in the luxury of active competition inevitably found, within a brief time, that they faced a deterioration of property that definitely lessened their capacity to serve the public effectively. Frequently, indeed, the effect of cutthroat competitive activity was so serious upon weaker carriers involved that it contributed in an important degree to the actual failure of the property. Such failure, the consequence of too heavy a burden of fixed charges, generally resulted in a reorganization accomplishing the reduction of those charges. This reduction so fortified the property that it was able to compete in a yet more vigorous fashion and with less danger of insolvency when the next rate war opened!

From a public standpoint an ultimate result chargeable in considerable degree to competition has been increased hostility to the carriers, based upon the inequitable treatment of persons and places which developed. Perhaps more than from any realization of the ineffective nature of competition as a conservator of public interest, our present-day policy of regulation resulted from this hostility. Upon the railways the ultimate effect of unrestrained competition was so unhappy, for them its menace so great, that management was forced to seek its elimination or, at the least, its control. To this end, successive methods of minimizing or of eliminating competition among rival carriers were evolved. In the following chapter a discussion of those methods appears.

(References to literature dealing with the subject of competition, as well as of combination, will be found at the close of the following chapter.)

CHAPTER XXV

COMBINATION

HAVING experienced the evils of unbridled rivalry, the railways quite naturally sought to bring competition under control through voluntary cooperation. Such cooperation first took the form of interrailway agreements covering matters of rates and services. Almost without exception these agreements called for the maintenance or increase of rates, occasionally adding a stipulation which limited the quality of service to be rendered. The advantage of these agreements lay primarily in their ease of execution and in the readiness with which adjustments could be made to meet changed conditions. Furthermore, such arrangements involved no complexities of contractual relations and no modification in corporate structure: from every standpoint they represented the simplest method of controlling competition. However, certain fundamental weaknesses in the simple agreement soon became evident. A strong temptation always existed for the individual carrier to violate secretly the terms of the arrangement for the purpose of increasing tonnage at the expense of rival lines, a temptation that proved irresistible again and again, especially to the weaker properties. The inducement to break faith was the stronger because of a legal weakness—inability to enforce the agreement against a violator because of the extra-legal character of the understanding. Such contracts were regarded under the common law as agreements in restraint of trade.

Appearance of Pooling Agreements.—After the rate agreement had failed repeatedly to control competition, pooling was attempted. Two types of pools were tried. The traffic pool, the less successful of the two, involved the assignment of a definite percentage of competitive tonnage to each of the rival carriers, and called for the maintenance of that percentage as nearly as possible through the life of the agreement. The money pool represented rather a division of earnings—a contract under which each carrier was permitted to handle all competitive business which it could secure but under which the carrier was required to deposit, for later distribution among the participating lines, a certain portion of all receipts from competitive freight and passenger business. The purpose here was to leave to the handling road merely a sum sufficient to cover the actual outlay incident to the movement of the traffic in question. Periodically the pool fund was divided among the competing carriers in such manner as to secure to those not receiving that portion of the tonnage assigned to them under the agreement, an indemnification for such deficit.

Each type of pool had weaknesses peculiar to itself. Under the traffic-pool agreement, the basic difficulty was the maintenance of assigned percentages. This obligation was frequently undertaken by certain large shippers known as "eveners," who were compensated for shifting a portion or all of their tonnage from one line to another, as conditions necessitated, by a rate somewhat below standard. Such a policy involved favoritism, however, and was, in consequence, objectionable from a public point of view. And, in time, such concessions proved inimical to the carriers; these "eveners," never content with the advantages afforded them, ultimately demanded greater reductions in rates, as compensation for the service rendered, than the railways could afford to grant. Another difficulty faced by the carriers, under both the traffic- and the money-pool agreements, was the readjustment of percentages from year to year. Though percentages were presumably fixed for an indefinite period under the traffic pool, as a new property gained influence in an area a more generous share of the competitive business was demanded and, perhaps, after a brief "war," received—with the revised percentage determined largely by bargaining. Since in the case of the money pool this readjustment was made upon the basis of traffic handled during the previous year, a constant temptation was dangled before every party to the pooling agreement to increase the tonnage handled during a particular year for the sake of an increased participation during the succeeding period, even though the price of that increase might be an immediate out-of-pocket loss to the carrier in question. Still another problem faced by the money pool arose in the determination of what proportion of gross income from competitive business should be retained by the handling carrier and what proportion should be turned over to the pool. In practice, many of the pools were mixed in character: a certain percentage of the competitive traffic was assigned to each carrier participating in the pooling agreement, and the fixed percentage of gross receipts was paid to the pool only on that part of the business in excess of the agreed proportion, the sums so paid being distributed later among those carriers receiving less than the proportion assigned.

Despite the various difficulties encountered under the pooling agreement, the pool, as finally evolved, proved highly successful and resulted in the effective control of competition in many quarters. Indeed, so successful were these arrangements that several pools, organized in the early seventies, continued to operate successfully until eliminated by law in 1887. This success was built largely upon two facts, namely, that the railways had come to a somewhat late, but none the less clear, realization of the necessity of controlling competition, and that the typical pool always had in its possession certain moneys belonging to the carriers that were parties to the agreement. The weaknesses of the pool lay primarily in its extra-legal character, similar thus to the rate agreement, and in the intense degree of public opposition aroused by it. The public believed that such agreements constituted unmistakable evidence of a movement toward monopoly in the railway field and that they were of such nature as to preclude future reductions in rates and improvements in service. That such conclusions were largely erroneous is not significant—intense and universal public opposition was sufficient to bring legal action by both state and federal governments, designed to eliminate this method of minimizing competition.

Division of Territory.—A third type of cooperation which did not appear during the years of early construction, largely because of the implicit belief of even the railways themselves in the essentially competitive character of their business, involved the division of territories. Because of the peculiar degree to which the law of increasing returns applied universally in the railway field until recent years, it would have been highly advantageous if construction had been so planned as to result in the location of pioneer lines in essentially diverse territory. But not until unhappy experiences with competition had awakened railway management to the fundamental fallacy of unrestricted competitive building did such agreements make their appearance. Yet even when made, they proved unenforceable, either in honor or at law, and the negotiation of such arrangements was characteristically followed by a virulent outbreak of competitive building which would result in the construction of mileage many years in advance of the economic ability of the territory served to support it. The agreement made in the seventies between the Santa Fe and the Missouri Pacific, outlining a division of the state of Kansas, may be cited as an illustration of this method of controlling competition. The agreement was soon broken by the management of the former road and the violation caused the Missouri Pacific immediately to punish both itself and the Santa Fe by building hundreds of miles of essentially duplicate trackage throughout central and southeastern Kansas. Though such understandings were regularly violated in early years, hope was not abandoned and with the stabilization of railway relations during the past several decades has come an observance of many tacit agreements between carriers as to the territory which each will occupy and develop in the near future. Tangible evidence of such agreements is, however, and quite naturally, difficult to secure. Or, if such agreements have not been made, the courage of folly is needed by the management of one railway to support it in the "invasion" of the territory of another: rarely, except as driven by stark need, is such invasion now threatened. And where construction is not justified by the facts, legal barriers now block action.

Movement toward Closer Unification and Consolidation.—At times because the law prevented cooperation in an effective manner, at times because it was desirable to unify properties more closely than was possible through mere agreements of the type just discussed, the unification of railway properties was early undertaken. Various methods have been employed to accomplish this end, the particular plan most suitable in a given case being determined by many factors, legal and financial. Of these methods the least tangible and least subjected to early control was that unification attained through a so-called "community of interest." Under this plan there sat upon the board of directors of each of the several competitive lines operating in a considerable area, representatives of the other properties which served that territory. In consequence of this situation, it followed that in the determination of major policies the voices of all interests were heard, a condition which tended to eliminate destructive competition. Such community of interest existed because of a definite need for closer cooperation than the law intended, and rested upon a foundation of negligible security holdings by the interests involved.

In outward form somewhat similar to community of interest, but in underlying character quite different, was stock ownership as a means of unifying the interests and policies of individual lines. The control of a competitive carrier through the ownership of a majority of its stock, or through a sufficient intrenchment to secure an important voice in management, presented two distinct advantages, one financial, the other strategic. It made possible the control of a property through the investment of a comparatively small sum, especially when the stock of the railway was widely distributed. Where it seemed essential to secure and maintain large holdings, the actual outlay was minimized by the use of the collateral-trust mortgage bond. In the second place, control through stock ownership made for a high degree of mobility; if, at any time, a continuance of control seemed undesirable for legal or economic reasons, the property could be surrendered with no resulting corporate difficulties.

A third method of unification employed was that of leasing competitive or supplementary properties. Such leases run for widely varying periods, some for a comparatively brief time such as 5 years, others for as long as 999 years, a term which is tantamount to ownership. The lease presents two distinct advantages: it makes possible the unified control and physical identity of properties without the issuance of additional securities and, furthermore, it can be so drawn as to provide for a readjustment of financial relations as economic and social conditions justify. The lease, however, burdens the operating corporation with charges of an essentially fixed character. In consequence, unless sound judgment has been exercised in the acquisition of control by this method, the lessee corporation often finds itself seriously embarrassed during periods of depression because of its obligation to operate these supplementary properties.

The fourth method employed in the consolidation of railway properties has been the outright sale of one road to another, with the merging of the properties involved. The financial tendency of such consolidation has been to increase capitalization, though often this increase is in the form of stock which saddles the property with no fixed charges. Two distinct advantages, of sufficient importance to justify its extensive use, must be credited to this method. Absolute control for the future rests with the purchasing corporation and the acquired property can be so developed as to meet expected needs without thought of future intercorporate adjustments. In addition, the railways thus joined through sale can be completely unified and operated as a single property, thereby enjoying the financial benefit that results from any increases in efficiency.

Factors Promoting Unification and Consolidation.—As has been stated, this movement toward the unification and close coordination of railway properties, which became conspicuous after the seventies, found its first impetus in the obstacles to effective cooperation erected by the public. Another force, however, which contributed significantly to the furtherance of consolidation during the period 1897–1903, a brief span which witnessed a great many important consolidations and coordinations, might be said to be the general movement toward "big business." This movement found expression in the industrial realm during those few years in the organization of numerous trusts and holding companies designed to secure monopolistic control, partial or complete, in their respective fields. Although railway consolidations have taken place during other periods, the most extensive movement in that direction, by all odds, followed closely our recovery from the business depression of 1893, with its numerous railway receiverships, and terminated with the depression of 1907. Indeed, the temporary cessation in the expansion of business that occurred in 1903 marked the peak of the movement, though it was of importance for several years more.

Need for Unity of Action.—Despite the strong emphasis placed upon the maintenance of competition by the public, the importance of unity of action among various carriers in the interest of most effective service has been clearly recognized since the first few years of railway development. True, the earliest properties were built during a period that magnified the desirability of unlimited competition and frowned upon any efforts looking toward cooperation, and under economic conditions that tended to emphasize further the competitive phase of railway relations. Because of the slow service that resulted from inability or failure to cooperate, there arose in the freight field the so-called "fast freight lines," purposed to overcome, in so far as possible, delay in the movement of traffic. As years passed, however, the fundamental necessity, from the standpoint of both the public and the railway, for cooperative action on the part of competitive as well as supplementary lines received increasing recognition. Indeed, the increased rapidity of movement of goods and persons over long distances has been the result of the more rapid transfer of traffic from one carrier to another as well as the consequence of actual increases in speed.

Unity of action is also essential to convenience in the movement of traffic, freight and passengers. Much, too, has been accomplished in this direction by the railways. Little can the shipper of today who loads a car for a distance movement with fruit, vegetables, or other perishables, with live stock, or even with another type of commodity which demands less attention than these mentioned, visualize the problem of shipping similar commodities during the early decades of railway growth: consignments had to be transferred not merely from car to car but from station to station every few hundred miles that they might continue on their way over connecting lines. This superiority of through movements, apparent from long years of experience in the field of freight traffic, has gradually been recognized in the passenger field; in consequence, it is little more than an ordinary matter today for a passenger to ride from one important railway terminus to another, covering perhaps considerable distances, without finding it necessary to transfer from the coach in which the journey was begun. Indeed, of late years cooperation among railways has developed to such a point that a passenger in Chicago, for example, finds it possible to settle himself comfortably in one car which will carry him without transfer to Atlanta, in another which will place him in Seattle and in a third which moves to San Francisco, these cars operating over the lines of two railways in two instances and of three in the third. The equipment so operated, however, is largely Pullman in character. To the ordinary traveler the satisfaction growing out of through service over portions of several lines is still too generally denied.

From observation and from statements already made, it is clear that many opportunities remain for better coordination and for a greater cooperation, to the distinct advantage of public and of carrier alike. Most conspicuous among these opportunities is the better coordination by connecting carriers of both freight and passenger schedules. All too often does an irate and impatient passenger insist that schedules are carefully and painstakingly constructed in such fashion as to compel the passenger to miss as many connections as possible and consume a maximum period of time upon his journey. However, this absence of coordination in passenger schedules is no more marked than in freight, though more conspicuous because of personal knowledge of the former. Greater cooperation might easily be had among the railways, too, in the establishment of through passenger service over several lines, to the advantage of both railway and passenger. Another type of cooperation that would result happily in the long run for the carriers, and immediately for passengers and shippers, would be the joint use of terminals—both passenger and freight. Here again the need of cooperation is more evident in the passenger field—rare is the person who has not had the experience of missing a train because of the time consumed in transferring across town to another station. Convenience in securing freight from and delivering it to the carriers might also be greatly increased were some plan evolved which would accomplish the districting of the large cities and provide for the acceptance and delivery of freight at certain points for all roads.[1] A like gain would be enjoyed by shippers at small stations were it possible, through joint use of terminals, to eliminate much of the extra haulage arising from the usually scattered locations of freight stations. From a railway point of view, yet another type of cooperation may well be developed further—that of the joint use of certain facilities, such as tracks and bridges; this would generally increase speed and augment plant capacity, yet make possible an actual reduction in costs. A splendid illustration of such action is found in an agreement negotiated between the Southern Pacific and the Western Pacific for the joint use of a considerable parallel trackage in Nevada.

Progress by Voluntary Action or Compulsion.—Of these and the many other steps that may be taken by the railways in the direction of more effective cooperation and coordination, too few have been accorded even serious thought. The patron of a common carrier is reasonably entitled to maximum speed of movement of person or goods and maximum convenience at a minimum cost. The failure of the railways to cooperate in such a way as to accomplish these ends in a thoroughgoing manner can be assigned to various causes, but outstanding among them is the extreme emphasis placed by the public upon the maintenance of a maximum of competitive activity in spirit and in letter. The fear which always exists among competitors that in any cooperative action the rival will secure an advantage, and the inertia resulting from long years of noncooperation, are also important barriers. To serve public interest, therefore, it would seem that existing prohibitions against cooperative action on the part of competitive carriers might well be removed. In their stead, adequate power should be given to regulatory bodies to compel the railways to effect better coordination of schedules, to accomplish an increased unification of terminal facilities, and even to arrange for the joint use of trackage, bridges, and equipment where such joint use would serve public convenience. Indeed, it would seem that one of the outstanding developments which may be reasonably expected in the railway field during the next decade under the spur of the "new competition" is a further extension of cooperative action, voluntary or enforced: otherwise the railways

[1] As a consequence of keener appreciation of their opportunities and under the spur of motor-vehicle competition, the railways are making progress in this particular that promises to gain momentum rapidly. Store-door collection and delivery will, where adopted, however, measurably obviate the need of such joint on- or off-line stations.

will be able neither to defend their position against the further encroachments of competitors nor to wage aggressive warfare in the interest of recovering lost ground. To the degree that adherence to competition appears to be a barrier to needed cooperation, the concept of competition as a ruling force in the field of railway transportation must give way.

Monopolistic Character of Railroads.—In the discussion of the railway industry thus far, the competitive phase of the enterprise has been stressed. Discussion from that angle, however, unquestionably overemphasizes the significance of competition in the field; for, to an increasing degree, the railway industry has come to be regarded by student and public alike as monopolistic in nature. Upon analysis it appears that certain economic characteristics are discernible which justify this change in point of view. As defined by Ely, "Monopoly means that substantial unity of action on the part of one or more persons engaged in some kind of business which gives exclusive control, more particularly although not solely with respect to price." Since a railway produces certain services and sells those services to the users, the railway represents the production-selling type of control. If monopoly exists, it must be able, barring interference on the part of public authority or the operation of some price-determining force other than competition, to fix the charge for its service at the point of highest net returns, adjusting the service offered to the demand at a given price.

A careful examination of the railway business indicates that there are factors which, in the absence of alternative transportation facilities, make for monopoly with respect to the *entire* railway net. The first and perhaps the most significant of these is the law of increasing returns. The operation of this principle, which makes the handling of additional business more remunerative for an existing carrier up to the point of maximum efficiency than for an additional line, and even the cost of constructing and operating a multiple track line much less proportionately than that of several single-track lines handling the same amount of business, tends to concentrate business rather than to scatter it, if the operation of economic laws be undisturbed. Another factor furthering unification in the railway field is that management must ultimately recognize the basic advantages to the public and the carriers of a close articulation of railways in matters of both service and property used. The need and advantages of more closely integrating our railway properties become increasingly evident and, barring public interference, this movement will gather force as years pass.

Monopolistic Position of the Single Carrier.—There are also certain influences which, railway facilities alone considered, make for monopoly in a given area by a particular line. The outstanding cause here operating is the actual scarcity of suitable sites. In a plains region, where an almost indefinite number of lines might parallel each other mile after mile, this limiting factor is not brought home to the casual observer. Yet, if the problem of securing a suitable location in a mountainous territory or contiguous to many important streams is given even brief consideration, the physical impossibility of constructing other lines able to compete effectively with the carrier already in possession of the only natural ground suitable for the purpose can readily be seen. Indeed, no matter how enthusiastically the public might support a competitive régime, it is impossible to conceive of certain properties which, through early construction, have secured possession of the only existing advantageous locations, ever being subjected to a sufficient degree of competition to be worthy the name. Still another phase of this limitation of suitable sites, and one that grew steadily in importance through a long period, is that of satisfactory terminal areas. However fortunately a railway may be located throughout its hundreds or thousands of miles of wanderings, if it begins nowhere and ends "up a tree," that property can never become strong. Nor is it sufficient that a railway enter important cities: its facilities must be so situated and of such character as to enable it to share in the flow of traffic that is the life-blood of all instrumentalities of transport. Only through ready and cheap access to the great gateways of trade can a railway prosper and not only is the actual limitation of space available for terminal facilities readily recognizable but the truly prohibitive cost of securing entry into metropolitan areas by a "parvenu" in the railway field is also apparent. Already older properties have been able to stifle the competition of carriers which might otherwise have become keen rivals through the stranglehold possessed by them upon the terminal situation; and this is particularly true with respect to the freight service, for here voluntary cooperation in the use of terminal facilities is of rare occurrence. It is important to note, however, that the position of those railways disadvantageously situated as to terminal sites has been strengthened in recent years by two developments. The belt-line railway gives the handicapped carrier equal access with more fortunate competitors to most industries to and from which carload freight moves. And, with the development of store-door delivery for small-lot shipments, it is possible that the railway with outlying terminals will be able to render as satisfactory service as others with expensive terminals centrally located—rendering such service at a lesser total cost.

Yet, even though suitable sites may be available for line construction and for entry into important terminal cities, the extent of the development of the territory served may be such that but one carrier is economically justified in occupying the field and perhaps even that carrier is compelled by circumstances to serve without adequate return for a considerable period. A situation of this character will give to the carrier already in the field a monopolistic grip for many years upon the area occupied. This grip is often further strengthened by agreements with other carriers most likely to build into the section, accomplishing thereby a division of territory among roads. In short, there appear to be operating strong forces which make for monopoly of railway service not only in the United States as a whole but also in particular areas. That marked progress has not been made in this direction is largely assignable to two major causes. The legal barriers against combination which have been erected by the various states and by the federal government explain in great measure the persistence of competitive systems. Yet this persistence is also attributable in part to inertia which makes more or less difficult the transformation of an industry that has long been regarded as competitive in character into one so organized as to be more nearly consonant with its monopolistic nature.

Analysis of the Traffic of a Railway.—To emphasize merely the *potentially* monopolistic character of the railway business fails, however, to give an adequate picture of facts as they existed throughout the long

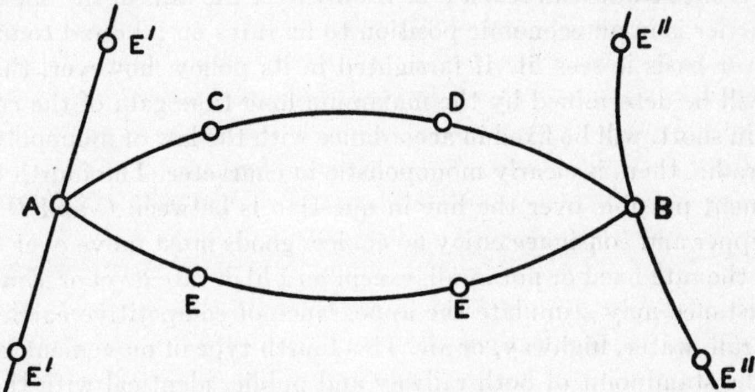

FIG. 32.—A traffic layout.

period prior to the advent of the motor vehicle as an effective instrumentality of transport; a considerable degree of *actual* monopolistic power has been exercised by the railways over certain traffic and such power still exists in certain areas and with respect to certain types of tonnage or movements. That we may the more clearly analyze the various types of traffic movement and determine their economic character the more accurately, let a concrete example be used (see Fig. 32). Suppose that two lines compete for business between the termini, *A* and *B*: upon the one line are situated the intermediate stations *C* and *D*, upon the other intermediate stations which may be designated as *E*. Let it be assumed, further, that into *A* there operates a third carrier with stations *E*′, and into *B* a fourth carrier with stations *E*″ along its line. Between *A* and *B*, over the road upon which *C* and *D* are located, various types of movements can take place. Of these, movements from *A* or *B* to *B* or *A*, respectively, are clearly competitive in character because of the existence of a second carrier operating through *E* between those two points. Movements from

C or *D*, intermediate points between *A* and *B*, to either of the termini are of a somewhat different character. Although no competitive carrier operates through *C* or *D*, the power of the one carrier in the field with respect to outbound traffic is more or less modified: if rates upon outbound movements from these intermediate points are made too high, similar goods from *E*, *E′*, or *E″*, as the case may be, will tend to eliminate goods produced at *C* or *D* from the market, to the detriment both of producers located there and of the railway serving those intermediate points, since it thereby loses tonnage. Only within limits may the carrier fix its outbound charge upon a monopolistic basis, those limits being broad or narrow depending upon the character of market or industrial competition faced in the market at *A* or *B*. Such traffic might be regarded as semi-competitive or semi-monopolistic in character.

A third type of movement over the carrier operating from *A* to *B* through *C* and *D* is that from terminal to local point—from *A* or *B* to *C* or *D*. Since traffic can reach *C* or *D* only over the rails of the one carrier, this carrier is in an economic position to fix rates on inbound tonnage on whatever basis it sees fit. If farsighted in its policy, however, that rate level will be determined by the maximum long-time gain of the corporation—in short, will be fixed in accordance with the law of monopoly price. This traffic, then, is clearly monopolistic in character. The fourth type of movement possible over the line in question is between *C* and *D*. Again the shipper and consignee enjoy no choice: goods must move over the one line at the rate fixed or not at all, except as a high rate level or some other circumstance may stimulate the appearance of competitive carrier service by rail, water, highway, or air. This fourth type of movement is, then, from the standpoint of both railway and public, identical with the third in its economic nature—completely monopolistic.

From the discussion preceding it is clear that the traffic of a railway is in part competitive, in part monopolistic, and in part it is a composite of both. Only a careful and detailed investigation could show what proportion of the total traffic moved by the American railways is of one type and what proportion is of another, but no such investigation has been made. Suffice it to say here that, without doubt, the competitive proportion was long much smaller than popularly thought and that the monopolistic elements were correspondingly more significant. Indeed, were accurate and complete data available, it might well appear that until the last decade the contention sometimes urged—that competition benefited only a small portion of the tonnage movement and the burden of such benefits rested upon the monopolistic portion of the traffic—was measurably sound.

Modification of Types by Extraneous Influences.—The fundamental economic character of the various types of traffic movements which have just been discussed may be modified, however, by extraneous influences.

Through interrailway agreements competition for traffic between *A* and *B* may be brought so effectively under control that such movements might better be characterized as monopolistic than as competitive, though, as has been indicated previously, the difficulty of maintaining these agreements for any length of time is always present. An equally marked influence may be exerted for a time over charges made for inbound movements from terminals, and movements between local points, normally monopolistic in character, by the desire of the railway to stimulate economic development in that section. Such stimulus will, however, be temporary in character because of its very purpose.

Another and more important modification of the essential economic nature of various types of traffic may arise out of public regulation. Regulation has had, in general, a twofold purpose—the preservation of competition where competition exists and can be maintained, and the modification of monopolistic power where it is found to govern. This modification has been sought through various channels. By positive legislation the railways have been prohibited from charging a through rate in excess of the sum of the local rates effective between intermediate points. As a further control a long-and-short-haul clause—prohibiting a higher rate for a shorter than for a longer movement over the same line and in the same direction, except as some reason more cogent than railway policy could be adduced—has been added to the regulatory statutes of state and nation. But the final and most effective effort made by the public to control the railway in its exercise of monopoly power has been through the fixation of maximum rates. This power is now possessed by all railway commissions, state and federal, and has been exercised extensively in public interest, as indicated in preceding chapters. Through such positive regulation major relief from monopolistic control had been gained by 1917, yet need of frequent interference by commissions during the years preceding suggests the strength of the tendency toward monopoly in the railway business and the failure of competition through almost a century to render adequate protection.

A third extraneous influence that has operated powerfully during recent years to change the economic status of particular types of rail movements is the appearance of effective competition. Inland waterways have been rehabilitated and extended; the mileage of air lines has increased with astonishing rapidity; and, most significantly, there has developed upon the highways a competition so keen that the one-time monopolistic position of the railway with respect to a great volume of traffic has wholly collapsed. The railway now has a monopoly of no type of passenger movement; its complete control of carload traffic moving considerable distances is broken; and it finds itself unable to compete upon even terms for much tonnage over which its dominance was once complete. This monopolistic power of the railway net as a whole and of the individual railway in the field of transportation has dwindled steadily and rapidly, standing today as a mere shadow in comparison with even a decade past.

The Business Problem: Competition and Monopoly.—In this and the preceding chapter, the railway has been discussed from a competitive and from a monopolistic point of view. One additional matter of concern alone remains—to contrast the business problem faced by the railway under a competitive and under a monopolistic régime. When operating under competitive conditions the first and most urgent problem confronting the carrier is that of getting the business. The business once obtained, the railway becomes interested in such a coordination of facilities as will enable that particular carrier to render maximum service—a fact that explains in part the suspicion entertained by one carrier of the motives of another when a greater coordination of facilities is urged. With the business obtained and such coordination of facilities accomplished as will make possible its handling with reasonable efficiency, the railway is then free to devote its efforts to the development of additional traffic. But under a competitive régime this last consideration has been and must always remain an afterthought, rather than be a matter of first consideration.

It is at this point, therefore, that under a monopolistic régime the great difference appears. A monopoly, under no necessity of expending its efforts to secure a portion of existing traffic will tend, because of self-interest, to give greater consideration to the creation of new business than competitive railways, driven to seek an easy and immediate increase in traffic, can afford to give to long-time efforts that may benefit rival carriers even more than themselves. So closely will a carrier monopoly follow the effective coordination of facilities needed to render maximum service at minimum cost to itself with a careful and detailed study of the possibilities of the development of more business, that these two considerations will oftentimes seem to be coordinate in the mind of the management. To be sure, under monopolistic control of the carriers, publicly recognized and confirmed, public interest demands comprehensive and effective regulation unless that monopoly be governmental. For, with monopoly accomplished, no portion of the traffic would benefit from the protection of potential competition.

Tendency toward Larger Corporate Units.—Perhaps one of the outstanding tendencies evident throughout the course of railway development in America has been that toward larger corporate units. In the early years of railway building short lines, connecting adjacent points and owned by unrelated corporations, were typical: mention has been made of a southern railway, the Charleston and Hamburg, that by virtue of its 137 miles of line was once the longest railroad under a single management in the world. After a brief time, however, the movement toward unification began and, had it not been for the interference of public authority, the United States would undoubtedly have today a relatively small number of large railway systems. The following facts, in part a repetition from a preceding chapter, indicate the extent to which the larger carriers now predominate, despite the obstacles erected by the government. In 1930, Class I railways numbered but 156 of the 697 active carriers of all classes, yet they operated 242,391 of the total 260,499[1] miles of railway in the United States, and, during that year, originated 1,153,-196,636 tons of the total of 1,220,133,630 for all roads. In short, 22.4 per cent of the operating railway corporations controlled 93.1 per cent of the total mileage and originated 94.5 per cent of the total tonnage. Table XIX further indicates the importance of the Class I carriers, almost 48 per cent of which have incomes running above $10,000,000.

TABLE XIX.—CLASSIFICATION OF CLASS I RAILWAYS BY DISTRICTS, ACCORDING TO OPERATING REVENUES, FOR THE YEAR 1930

Operating revenue	Total	Eastern District	Southern District	Western District
Below 10 million	82	27	19	36
10–25 million	32	11	7	14
25–50 million	13	6	1	6
50–100 million	11	7	1	3
100–200 million	15	1	5	9
Over 200 million	3	3	0	0
Total number roads	156	55	33	68

Evidence of concentration also appears in this: of the 156 Class I carriers tabulated above, the 29 highest "earners," constituting but 18.6 per cent of the total number, received in 1930 some $3,981,615,000, or more than 75 per cent of the total operating revenues.

Tendency toward Concentration of Control.—Not only has the tendency toward larger individual properties been conspicuous, but the movement toward concentration of active control has also been marked, and this has been true even of periods during which the legal consolidation of competitive properties was barred. This movement has been facilitated by several developments. First, a wider distribution of stock has made possible the control of a given property through the possession of a smaller proportion of the outstanding shares. The small holder rarely takes an active interest in corporate management, his participation usually being limited to the contribution of his proxy to those already "in the saddle" to aid in perpetuating the existing management—unless, perchance, that

[1] Represents a duplication of mileage above 249,052.

management has committed the *faux pas* of failing to pay dividends either because of mismanagement or because of conservative direction of the property. Second, the increasing bond ratio has facilitated concentration of control. The causes and dangers of this movement, from a corporate point of view, will be discussed more fully later; here it is of concern merely because the larger the proportion of bonds to the total outstanding securities, the easier does it become to control large and important properties by a relatively small outlay. The development of the holding company has assisted in the attainment of this same end: the inverted pyramid has made possible the control of enormous interests with a very modest investment, as is well illustrated in the case of the old Rock Island Company and the present Atlantic Coast Line Company. Then, too, it may be added that, although legal restrictions have been successful in preventing the *physical identification* of properties, such legal restrictions have not been uniformly effective in preventing an *identity of interest.* Where the sale or lease of a property is forbidden, a common group of stockholders has frequently made essential unity of action possible. Stockholdings of one railway in another may effect the desired identity of interest also and, in cases where such holdings run counter to the law, the interlocking directorate has been widely employed as a means of harmonizing the interests of large competitive properties. Finally, the type of stockholder has so changed in the years since 1900 as to promote this movement toward concentration of control. Railway shares have become less speculative in character and have therefore been acquired by individuals and groups with other financial interests.

The determination of public policy with respect to railways is of fundamental importance. Shall it be enforced competition, which appears to be the goal of anti-pooling and anti-trust acts? Shall it be modified competition among a relatively small number of competing systems of balanced strength, subject to the control and direction of regulatory bodies? Or, shall it be monopoly, with that complete and thoroughgoing control through public agencies which must necessarily accompany private monopoly if public interest is to be protected? And, if monopoly, should it be privately or publicly owned and operated? Experience has seemed to justify a negative answer to the first major question but the problem involved in choosing between the remaining two is no less important and no less pressing. The answer is freighted with tremendous importance to the public and to business enterprise alike. Yet, because of lack of knowledge of the problem on the part of a great portion of our citizenry, because of demagogic and self-seeking leadership, and because of deep-rooted public antagonism, that answer is in danger of being rested largely upon prejudice rather than upon a clear understanding of the fundamental economic principles and social considerations involved.

REFERENCES

Brown, H. G.: *Transportation Rates and Their Regulation*, The Macmillan Company, 1916.

Clarke, J. M.: Standards of Reasonableness in Local Freight Discrimination, *Columbia University in Political Science*, vol. 37, No. 1.

———: *The Economics of Overhead Costs*, University of Chicago Press, 1923.

Daggett, Stuart: *Principles of Inland Transportation*, Harper & Brothers, 1928.

Ely, R. T.: *Monopolies and Trusts*, The Macmillan Company, 1900.

Hadley, A. T.: *Railroad Transportation*, G. P. Putnam's Sons, 1885.

Interstate Commerce Commission: *Intercorporate Relations of Railways in the United States as of June* 30, 1906.

———: *Statistics of Railways in the United States*, 1930.

Johnson, E. R., and G. G. Huebner: *Railroad Traffic and Rates*, vol. 1, D. Appleton & Company, 1911.

———, and T. W. Van Metre: *Principles of Railroad Transportation*, D. Appleton & Company, 1921.

Jones, Eliot: *Principles of Railway Transportation*, The Macmillan Company, 1924.

Langstroth, C. S., and Wilson Stilz: Railway Cooperation, *University of Pennsylvania Bulletin* 15.

McFall, R. J.: Railway Monopoly and Rate Regulation, *Columbia University Studies in Political Science*, vol. 49, No. 1.

Meyer, B. H.: Northern Securities case, *University of Wisconsin Bulletin* 142.

Noyes, W. C.: *American Railroad Rates*, Little, Brown & Company, 1905.

Raper, C. L.: *Railway Transportation*, G. P. Putnam's Sons, 1912.

Ripley, W. Z.: *Railroads: Finance and Organization*, Longmans, Green & Co., 1915.

———: *Railroads: Rates and Regulation*, Longmans, Green & Co., 1912.

———: *Railway Problems*, Ginn & Company, 1913.

CHAPTER XXVI
RAILWAY UNIFICATION

THE most definite expression of the tendency to establish an identity of interest among railways, competitive or supplementary, has been the formation of ownership groupings. The development of these groupings extends over more than three-quarters of a century, the first movement appearing during the late forties and early fifties in the linear consolidation of numerous short and independent properties. As a result of this linear consolidation and of the extension of other railway lines, competition developed to the point where it threatened the financial stability of even the stronger roads. This story of cutthroat competitive activity that reached its worst, perhaps, during the seventies, has been told in preceding chapters; there, too, has been told the story of railway efforts to bring competition under control, thus stabilizing the industry. The failure of the informal agreement has been chronicled, the evolution and ultimate success of the pool noted, and the legal attack upon all types of agreements to restrain competition discussed. In the last chapter the methods employed by the railways to accomplish unification, primarily with a view to circumventing the so-called "anti-monopoly laws," have been presented: elimination or reduction of competition by lease, by stock ownership, by interlocking directorate, and occasionally by actual merger of lines was accomplished upon a broad scale. This movement toward the federation of properties was a consequence, too, of the desire to effect economies through the closer coordination of properties and of the eagerness of promoters as well as banking interests to reap that financial harvest which unification movements often ripen.

This movement toward consolidation or identity of interest on the part of both competitive and supplementary properties, discernible for many years prior to the nineties, flowered during those years of reorganization and reconstruction which intervened between the panic of 1893 and the minor depression of 1903. During this period a very close integration of all major properties in Trunk Line territory was accomplished, stock ownership and the interlocking directorate being the means generally employed. In the South a similar situation resulted from the dominant position gained by the Morgan group in three of the major properties operating in that section and of the formation of a working alliance between the Morgan and other important interests. In the West four important groupings appeared, dominated by Hill,

Harriman, the Goulds, and the Reid-Moore-Yoakum interests, and these groupings largely controlled the mileage of that district; railways not definitely included in these great systems cooperated closely.

Recession of Consolidation Movement.—Between 1903 and the panic of 1907 it became clearly evident, however, that such grouping of properties had reached flood tide and, for a period at least, was destined to recede. This recession was due primarily to two facts: the financial instability of certain of the systems and the illegality, under the interpretation of existing statutes, of certain others. The almost inconceivable financial recklessness of the New Haven management, overreaching by the Goulds, and the combination of plundering by insiders with the inherent economic weakness of the Rock Island combination, soon drove these groups upon the rocks of financial disaster. It was legal action, however, that broke up the Northern Securities Company under the shelter of which Hill and Harriman undoubtedly would have come to control a great part of the mileage of the Western District. It was legal action, also, that compelled the dissolution of the Southern Pacific-Union Pacific organization and the fear of such interference played an important part in "unscrambling" interests in Trunk Line territory. Even yet, proposals to consolidate competitive lines are generally opposed by both public opinion and legal authority, but the unification of supplementary and feeder lines has more widespread support from the former and a measure of acquiescence from the latter. Indeed, not only is there a growing tendency to extend control over supplementary properties but dominant railways are also endeavoring to simplify corporate organization by merging controlled lines with the parent organization, or by unifying them under long-term leases. This is exemplified by the gradual simplification of the corporate structure of such mature properties as the Pennsylvania and the New York Central, as well as by a recent movement to weld by lease into a single operating unit the closely held properties of the Union Pacific system.

The Formation of Systems.—In the years since railway systems or groupings first began to occasion fear to those whose *bête noir* was monopoly, many properties have been linked, some to continue associations thus established for a long period and others to be wrenched apart within a briefer time because of inept or fraudulent management, of legal interference, or of the lack of an adequate economic justification for such union. Certain of these groupings have been achieved and have continued through an important family or banking interest in particular properties, certain others through the dominant rôle assumed by an important railway. Illustrative of the former are the so-called Hill and Vanderbilt groups, the one created by the genius of "the Empire Builder" and the other by that dynamic and far-visioned pioneer of the middle years of the nineteenth century, Cornelius Vanderbilt. Of the latter the Pennsylvania and the Union Pacific are illustrative, though in the development of the Union Pacific the aggressive E. H. Harriman looms larger than does any single man in the development of the former. Some systems, once created, have moved forward in unbroken course; others, because of adverse circumstance, have disintegrated only to rise, Phoenix-like, from the wreckage because of some sound basis for existence—of this the Missouri Pacific grouping is the most conspicuous instance. Because of popular opposition or of legal bars, many properties under common control remained for many years loosely linked. In the years since the Transportation Act made provision for acquisition of control and for consolidation, however, numerous steps have been taken to knit units more closely—and, undoubtedly, as headway is gained in making effective the consolidation of railways into a limited number of systems, greater unity will be attained by existing groups and new systems will appear.

Vanderbilt System.—One of the first important ownership groupings to appear and one whose history has been continuous since its inception is that which had its origin in the constructive imagination of the man whose family now occupies an important place in its councils. This system, operating approximately 21,934 miles of line, is composed of the New York Central and the Chicago and North Western, together with their subsidiaries. Of the many important operating subsidiaries of the former but a single one remains, the Pittsburgh and Lake Erie; the others, among which such properties as the Michigan Central, the Cleveland, Cincinnati, Chicago, and St. Louis, and the Boston and Albany, the West Shore, the Toledo and Ohio Central, and the Cincinnati Northern are most significant, are now operated by the New York Central under long-time leases. The Chicago and North Western has but one important subsidiary and that an operating property, the Chicago, St. Paul, Minneapolis, and Omaha. In addition to clear control of numerous properties the New York Central has had, with the New Haven, a dominant place in the Rutland and with the Baltimore and Ohio in the Reading, as well as a minor interest in both the Lackawanna and the Lehigh Valley. The Reading interest, it appears, has now passed to the Baltimore and Ohio, while the Lackawanna interest has increased sharply in consonance with the proposed System 3 of the final consolidation plan.

This system serves the populous and highly industrialized area westward from New York to Chicago and perhaps the most highly developed and prosperous portion of Granger territory. An important voice in the control of these properties rests with the Vanderbilt interests, though they are far from being in a position to dictate policies. The growth of the system has been normal in every sense and at no time has an ambitious program imperiled the soundness of the structure. Throughout its long history this group of carriers has been among the soundest financially and, so far as territory served and character of management are determinative, has a promising future. There are developments in the field of transport, however, that make the future less assured—and the problem of the North Western, with its short average length of haul on freight and its other handicaps, is perhaps even more difficult than that of the New York Central.

The Pennsylvania Lines.—A second important ownership grouping is that known as the Pennsylvania and dominated by that railway. This system, defined strictly, lies in Trunk Line territory and operates some 17,273 miles of line—though to that figure might be added 10,997 miles of properties in which the Pennsylvania interest is sufficient to control policies, though the Pennsylvania contends that it does not exercise this control. The Pennsylvania Railroad has also used the lease freely during recent years to consolidate its operations, with the result that it now has but one important operating subsidiary, the Long Island. Among the properties operated under lease are those of the Grand Rapids and Indiana, the Pennsylvania, Ohio and Detroit, the Pittsburgh, Cincinnati, Chicago, and St. Louis, the Western New York and Pennsylvania, and the West Jersey and Seashore. Of the independently operated properties which have been or now are to be regarded as an integral part of the Pennsylvania group the Norfolk and Western, the Detroit, Toledo, and Ironton, and the Wabash are most important. In addition, however, the Pennsylvania Railroad and its allied Pennroad Corporation control sufficiently large blocks of stock to permit the domination of each of the following: Pittsburgh and West Virginia, Lehigh Valley, New Haven, Boston and Maine, and Seaboard Air Line—with control of the Ann Arbor following from domination of the Wabash.

The striking fact concerning the Pennsylvania system from the standpoint of control is that its stock is more widely distributed by far than that of any other American railway. Not only does the number of holders approximate a quarter of a million but a recent study shows that the percentage held by some 5,100 of the largest stockholders is but 8.53. The Pennsylvania system is financially strong, it serves a rich territory, and it has been fortunate in the capacity of its leadership through the years, some of America's greatest railway executives serving it. As the railways comprising this group are further unified and as the Pennsylvania approximates revised System 4 as approved by the Interstate Commerce Commission, even greater strength should be assured except as profound changes in the field of transport sap the foundations of railway prosperity.

The Baltimore and Ohio System.—For a long period the property that gives name to this grouping was one of the lesser of the Trunk Line railways, yet its record was good. Later, in an effort to stabilize competition, the Pennsylvania obtained control over it and its opportunities for growth were circumscribed. Under the threat of legal action, rested upon the Sherman Act, the Pennsylvania disposed of its interest and in succeeding years, under wise and aggressive leadership, the Baltimore and Ohio moved forward steadily to an important position in the area served by it. The system now comprises some 10,845 miles of line, all located in Trunk Line territory. The Baltimore and Ohio has no important operating subsidiaries, but among its leased lines are the Buffalo and Susquehanna and the Buffalo, Rochester, and Pittsburgh. Now controlled by the Baltimore and Ohio and assigned to it by the Commission's decision in the Four-system application are the Alton, the Western Maryland, and the Reading—with the two operating subsidiaries of the last named, the Central of New Jersey and the Atlantic City Railroad. The possession of the leased lines named, with the acquisition of the Reading, brings close to realization a long-cherished plan for a direct route from Chicago to New York—the completion of which will greatly strengthen the competitive position of the Baltimore and Ohio.

Careful scrutiny of available data fails to indicate any stock control that gives to any interest or group a clearly dominant voice in the management of this system. The Union Pacific Railroad owns common and preferred stock aggregating 2.56 per cent of the total voting power, but some 2,000 of the largest holders control among them less than a fourth of the stock outstanding. While the Baltimore and Ohio has shown financial weakness upon occasion and faces aggressive competition in its movement of merchandise traffic as well as low-grade tonnage, the character of its leadership and the nature of its territory are such that it should gain steadily in strength if it weathers the current depression and meets successfully the readjustments in transport during the decade just ahead.

The Van Sweringen System.—The most recent of the great ownership groupings to be created in Eastern territory, and one the growth of which has been spectacular, is that given name by the brothers whose leadership has brought it into being. This system had as its beginning the purchase of the New York, Chicago, and St. Louis, or Nickel Plate, from the New York Central in 1916: again the danger of prosecution under the Sherman Act explains the sale of a competitive line. The Lake Erie and Western and the Toledo, St. Louis, and Western were also acquired soon thereafter from the New York Central, and the three railways consolidated under state laws under the name of the parent property. Operating from that point forward through a maze of holding companies, among which the Allegheny Corporation has been most important in the transportation field, the Van Sweringen brothers have extended the scope of their activities rapidly in many directions—of which the significant one here is the railways. Control of the Chesapeake and Ohio was first acquired and, following rapidly, a dominant position was attained in the Erie and the

Père Marquette. The Wheeling and Lake Erie, too, when legal compulsion forced the withdrawal of the New York Central and Baltimore and Ohio from joint participation, came under Van Sweringen direction. Refused approval to unify the Nickel Plate, the Erie, the Père Marquette, and the Chesapeake and Ohio, the Van Sweringens later secured Interstate Commerce Commission approval for control by the last named of the Père Marquette. Still active, the brothers purchased a controlling interest in the Missouri Pacific, an option upon the controlling interest in the Chicago and Eastern Illinois, and a holding sufficient to dominate policy in the Kansas City Southern. If the mileage of the two properties in Southwestern territory be excluded, the mileage of the Van Sweringen lines approximates 11,324, while if these be added an extensive and far-flung railway empire is indeed presented—an empire totaling 26,505 miles.

The railways over which the Van Sweringens have extended their control are possessed, largely, of an unhappy financial past; indeed, in some few instances that past has been unsavory. Neither is their financial present bright nor their future alluring. Of the entire group only the Chesapeake and Ohio can be regarded as a strong property, though all other lines except perhaps the Chicago and Eastern Illinois had attained a measure of prosperity before the depression that began in 1929. It is more than possible that, under the aggressive and effective leadership of the brothers the properties in Trunk Line territory, supplemented by certain others, can be welded into a strong unit to compete upon relatively equal terms with other major systems in that area. Certainly none of the other existing major ownership groupings has had the meteoric rise of this one and no other will be watched with greater interest. Its present constitution presents not only serious problems of management but also difficult problems of regulation, these arising particularly from the extension of Van Sweringen control westward across the Mississippi and the extensive use of the as yet unregulated holding company to gain desired ends.

The Morgan Group.—Another important ownership grouping, with approximately 22,511 miles of railway, is that dominated by the Morgan banking interests and designated accordingly. This system comprises a great network of lines in Southern territory which totals approximately half of the entire mileage of that section. The two parent properties in this system are the Atlantic Coast Line and the Southern, each of which has important operating and nonoperating subsidiaries—though it is apparent that unification of properties under common control by means of the lease has not proceeded far in this territory. The Atlantic Coast Line group includes, among other operating subsidiaries, the Georgia Railroad, the Clinchfield, the Charleston and Western Carolina, the Atlanta, Birmingham and Coast, and the Louisville and Nashville. The Louisville and Nashville, in turn, controls the Nashville, Chattanooga, and St. Louis and, with the Southern, the Chicago, Indianapolis and Louisville (Monon). The mileage of the Atlantic Coast line group aggregates 13,235, exclusive of the Monon. Important among the numerous operating subsidiaries of the Southern are the Alabama Great Southern, the Georgia Southern and Florida, and Cincinnati, New Orleans and Texas Pacific, and the interest in the Monon previously mentioned. Included here, too, until recently was the Mobile and Ohio, of which the Southern has been ordered to divest itself because continued control has been held to represent undue restriction upon competition.

Control, as represented by security holdings, of the Atlantic Coast Line and the Southern contrast rather sharply. The Atlantic Coast Line Railroad Company is dominated by the Atlantic Coast Line Company, a holding company, through the ownership of some 27 per cent of the former's stock. This ownership is reenforced by personal ownership of railroad-company stock by certain financiers who control the holding company by ownership of a majority of its stock. Speaking generally, the stock of the Atlantic Coast Line Railroad is closely held; more than 61 per cent is in the hands of some 350 of the largest holders. In sharp contrast to this is the concentration of less than 32 per cent of the voting power of the Southern in the hands of some 1,150 corporations and individuals, with no allied holdings sufficiently large to dominate. Morgan influence over these properties rests in part upon the service of a great banking house, in part upon a demonstrated capacity successfully to direct extensive railway properties. In contrast with the Vanderbilt and Pennsylvania systems, this group is in no sense the result of gradual and natural growth. Rather, financially weak properties were "picked up" at opportune times and to them were added a few strong lines; these, welded into effective operating units and benefited by the rapid development of the South since 1900, give excellent promise for the future. Although sharp protests are often voiced against "banker management" of railways, it must be admitted that Morgan control in the South has been sane and constructive in character.

The Hill System.—An important ownership grouping in Western territory is that which was developed by James J. Hill and continues, extended and fortified, under the direction of other interests. This group comprises some 27,869 miles of line and rests upon the control of the Great Northern and the Northern Pacific by the dominant group through large stockholdings. The first-named property has no important operating subsidiary and the second but one, the Minnesota and International, and neither has an important nonoperating subsidiary. Jointly, however, the Great Northern and the Northern Pacific control in the Northwest the Spokane, Portland, and Seattle which, in turn, owns the Oregon Trunk. They also dominate jointly a major property, the Chicago, Burlington, and Quincy. The Burlington has but one major operating subsidiary, the Quincy, Omaha, and Kansas City, but it owns a controlling interest in the Colorado and Southern. This property dominates two operating lines, the Fort Worth and Denver City and the Wichita Valley, and controls jointly with the Rock Island the Burlington-Rock Island. Cooperating so closely with the "Hill lines" as to make it almost an integral part of them is the Western Pacific, under the direction of A. C. James, whose holdings in the Great Northern and Northern Pacific are also large: it is this cooperation that now makes the Hill system an effective competitor in San Francisco, a realization of another of the dreams of its founder, and satisfies in part a long-nourished desire of the Burlington for an outlet westward to the Pacific coast. This outlet lies over the indirectly associated Denver and Rio Grande Western and Western Pacific, but the competitive position of this route has been weak; however, with the control by the former line of the Denver and Salt Lake and the construction by it of the Dotsero cut-off, the competitive possibilities of the route will be greatly strengthened.

The growth of this system is of especial interest to the student of transportation because it illustrates so well the development and realization of a great plan, step by step. "Jim" Hill became interested in railway development in the Northwest while working as a stevedore and clerk on the St. Paul docks. His first success was with the then unpromising land-grant project, the St. Paul and Pacific Railroad—and from this time his reach so successfully followed his vision that another northern transcontinental, the Great Northern, was soon ready for service. The bankruptcy of the Northern Pacific in 1893 gave an awaited opportunity to extend control over a rival property, and within a few years the Chicago, Burlington, and Quincy was acquired to give entry into Chicago over a friendly line. In consequence of this step came the titanic struggle for control of the Northern Pacific between the Hill and Harriman forces, with the former emerging victorious. Defeat was suffered, however, at the hands of the government in an attempt to unify control of the two Northerns through the Northern Securities Company—but this defeat still left Hill and associated interests in a dominant position with both properties. Acquisition of the Colorado and Southern by the Burlington gave the Hill lines direct access to the South and particularly to the cotton traffic, in which Hill was interested as an important item in the development of trade with the Orient. It is said that control of the Illinois Central was desired but, losing to Harriman at that point, he obtained control of the Colorado and Southern—and, interestingly, it is Texas that is today the great source of cotton.

The recognized head of this great system was, during his life, James J. Hill. At all times, however, he had the active support of the Morgan interests and these interests came to dominate in the years following the death of the pioneer leader. Today, though there is relatively wide distribution of the stocks of both the Great Northern and Northern Pacific, it seems probable that policies are determined largely by the Morgan banking group and by A. C. James, who has become the largest stockholder in both properties. However, there is no indication that the change in management will operate to the disadvantage of the system; indeed, within the past few years clear evidences of aggressive leadership have been apparent, particularly in central Western territory. The developmental and constructive work that won for Hill the deserved title of "Empire Builder" has given to the two Northerns a relatively stable economic foundation. The Burlington has always been a well-managed property with high earnings that were further augmented by its affiliation with the Hill interests, while the Colorado and Southern, weak and unpromising when acquired, has, through gains resulting from Hill control and from the development of the territory served by it, strengthened greatly. Directed conservatively but with an eye always to future opportunities, this system gives promise for any future in which railway transportation is permitted to occupy its normal place.

The Union Pacific System.—A second major ownership grouping that centers in Western territory, a creation of the genius of E. H. Harriman during those years when Hill was also active, is that headed by the Union Pacific. This unit has a mileage of some 19,281 and includes as major nonoperating subsidiaries the Oregon Short Line, the Los Angeles and Salt Lake, the Oregon-Washington Railroad and Navigation, and the St. Joseph and Grand Island. It may be of interest to note, however, that control of the Oregon-Washington lies in the Oregon Short Line and that the latter property is joint owner with the Union Pacific of the Salt Lake. Union Pacific interests are also dominant in the Illinois Central and have an important voice in the councils of the New York Central, the Baltimore and Ohio, and the Chicago and North Western: Oregon Short Line holdings in the Central exceed even those of the Vanderbilt family; Union Pacific holdings in the Baltimore and Ohio exceed those of any other single group; and the voting power of the Union Pacific in the North Western is exceeded only by that of the Vanderbilt family, both being small in terms of percentage. However, of these lines in which the Union Pacific is powerful only one can be termed a controlled property, the Illinois Central. This railway has as its major operating subsidiaries the Central of Georgia, the Yazoo and Mississippi Valley, and the Gulf and Ship Island.

The story of the development of the Union Pacific System is almost as interesting as and even more spectacular than that of the Hill group. Taking over the Union Pacific after the panic of 1893, when it was aptly characterized as a "right of way and a streak of rust," Harriman, best known to the financial world as a successful broker, extended his control within a decade over approximately 30,000 miles of railway. But the most interesting fact is not that Harriman, through strong banking support and the liberal use of the collateral-trust mortgage bond, was able to establish a railway empire so quickly but that, once in control of a property, he so directed its affairs as to infuse new strength immediately. The goal toward which Harriman appeared to labor in the Southwest, the scene of his major activities, was a monopoly of transportation facilities in that section—and only governmental interference prevented the addition of the Santa Fe to the Southern Pacific and Union Pacific, which were already under his control. Later, governmental authority compelled the separation of these two great properties, action resting upon the Sherman Act. Yet, among the properties with which Harriman was actively associated, all have continued strong and all of them give promise for the future. Indeed, it might seem that it is not essential to success in directing railway properties that an executive shall have entered service in his early years as messenger, section hand, or water boy, certain railway traditions notwithstanding. It is of interest to note that the unification of all Union Pacific subsidiaries under lease with the parent property received Commission sanction in 1932,[1] and that recently succeeding to the leadership of this system has come the son of its builder.

Missouri Pacific Lines.—Yet another major ownership grouping in Western territory is that which has been built about the Missouri Pacific, a grouping that represents the reassembling in considerable degree of the one-time Gould properties[2] in this district. The mileage of this system

[1] A condition attached by the Interstate Commerce Commission to this unification may lead to refusal by the Union Pacific interests to proceed: it appears that the cost of absorbing certain short lines in the area, as prescribed by the Commission, makes the net gain of unification slight.

[2] Interesting not only from an historical standpoint but also because of the light thrown upon the causes of railway failures is an examination of the record of certain of the important ownership groupings that have disintegrated during the past quarter of a century. Among these, none offers more of interest than the Gould system which in 1906 comprised approximately 19,000 miles of line. Important among the properties included in this group were the Missouri Pacific, the Wabash, the Texas and Pacific, the International and Great Northern, the St. Louis Southwestern, the Denver and Rio Grande and, later, the Wheeling and Lake Erie, the Western Maryland, and the Western Pacific. Control of these properties lay in the estate of Jay Gould and was exercised west of the Mississippi through the Missouri Pacific and the estate itself, east of the Mississippi through the Wabash. This system had its inception with the entry of Jay Gould into the railway field many years previously, but it was the heirs who assumed control of these properties following his death who developed what has oftentimes been characterized as the "Gould Dream," the ownership and operation by a single interest of a property extending from coast to coast. To make this dream an actuality, however, it was necessary to bridge the gap between Salt Lake City and the Pacific coast and between the eastern terminus of the Wabash and the Atlantic. To accomplish the former the Western Pacific was constructed, resting heavily upon the Denver and Rio Grande for financial support; to effect the latter, control of the Wheeling and Lake Erie and of the Western Maryland was secured, the gap between these two to be bridged by the so-called Wabash-Pittsburgh Terminal project. When upon the very threshold of realizing the goal set, a transcontinental railway in the fullest sense, the Gould system

aggregates about 14,242 and included in it are, in addition to the Missouri Pacific, two important subsidiaries, the Texas and Pacific and the New Orleans, Texas, and Mexico. Among the important operating subsidiaries of the latter are the International and Great Northern, the St. Louis, Brownsville, and Mexico, and the San Antonio, Uvalde and Gulf. In addition, as was noted previously, the Missouri Pacific controls the Denver and Rio Grande Western jointly with the Western Pacific; thus, while not united, the western and eastern portions of the old "Gould system" from St. Louis to San Francisco cooperate effectively in handling through tonnage.

Control of the Missouri Pacific system in the years following the elimination of Gould influence was not definitely fixed: it is probable that Kuhn, Loeb, and Company had an important voice in the determination of policies. With the purchase of a clear majority of the outstanding stock of the property by the Allegheny Corporation, however, definite control went to the Van Sweringen interests where it now lies. Under Gould direction the old Missouri Pacific system was weak, both because of poor management and because of the economic status of the territory served. In the years since their "deliverance from bondage," these lines have made a better record: management has improved and the territory has developed. Competition in the territory served by the Missouri Pacific is keen and the capital structure of that property is none too favorable. What may be the future of the system under a management helpful to lines that have been under Van Sweringen control for some years is as yet uncertain—as is, indeed, the future of much of the mileage competitive with the Missouri Pacific properties. But at least definite progress has been made toward grouping lines that have a common economic interest—and in so doing definite progress has been made, too, toward the realization of the Interstate Commerce Commission's System 18 of the final consolidation plan.

Minor Ownership Groupings.—In addition to the major systems just described there are several minor groupings of which mention should be made. The oldest of these in point of time is that dominated by the New York, New Haven and Hartford. This group lies wholly within New England territory except for the New York, Ontario, and Western, and includes, in addition to that property, the Boston and Maine, and a half interest, with the New York Central, in the Rutland. At one time the

suffered a general collapse. The old properties had never been conservatively managed and, in the face of panic conditions in 1907, were unable to bear the strain thrown upon them by heavy construction costs and light traffic. One after another of the properties, beginning with the Wabash and the Western Pacific, went into the hands of receivers until finally the control of all but the St. Louis and Southwestern, a minor line, had been lost. A clearer illustration of the financial depletion of properties through failure to follow a conservative maintenance policy and of final wreckage due to overextension cannot be found in American railway history.

New Haven was under judicial order to dispose of its Boston and Maine holdings, held to constitute restraint of trade under the Sherman Act. This group, comprising something less than 5,800 miles of line, came into being as a result of the effort of the New Haven to monopolize the transportation facilities of southern and central New England, control being exercised through stock ownership. As a result of overreaching, a property which once was conspicuously strong was wrecked financially. During the decade past, however, its situation has improved steadily and there is promise that it may once again become as stable and prosperous as the nature of the territory served by it justifies.

Another minor grouping of present as well as historical interest is that of the St. Louis-San Francisco and the Chicago, Rock Island and Pacific. While, during the period of an earlier association of these properties, the former was controlled by the latter,[1] the relation is now reversed: by the ownership of stock giving a voting power of less than 15 per cent the Frisco now dominates this system of some 14,290 miles. Neither property has any major operating subsidiaries except those that exist because of Texas incorporation requirements, though the Rock Island does own jointly with the Burlington a half interest in the Burlington-Rock Island. Both the Frisco and the Rock Island were left seriously weakened by the financial manipulations of Reid-Moore days but both made a greatly improved showing in the years following 1920. Since 1929, however, both roads have

[1] Until a financial group, headed by Reid and Moore, newly rich from the tin-plate field, became interested in it, the Rock Island had been a conservatively managed, prosperous property, operating almost wholly in the richer portions of Granger territory. In 1901–1902, however, the "Tin-plate Crowd" acquired a dominant interest in the property and, under their control, a policy of rapid expansion was instituted. By purchase the Rock Island was extended into Southwestern territory; control of the St. Louis-San Francisco, and, through it, of the Chicago and Eastern Illinois was obtained by the use of the collateral-trust mortgage bond. Control was also secured of the Evansville and Terre Haute, later of the Chicago and Alton, and finally a fourth interest was purchased in the Lehigh Valley, perhaps with the idea of ultimately extending a line to the Atlantic seaboard. The most interesting feature of the Rock Island structure, however, was not the actual control over particular properties, but rather the peculiar financial structure evolved to enable the controlling group to dominate completely a large property without a commensurate investment in it. To this end the Chicago, Rock Island and Pacific *Railroad* Company was created to hold the stock of the Chicago, Rock Island and Pacific *Railway* Company and of other carrier properties. Control of the *Railroad* Company rested, in turn, with the Rock Island Company. Voting power was so restricted in the last-named corporation that the dominant group was able to dictate policies through the ownership of a majority of a relatively small block of preferred shares. Within a comparatively short time the unsound and topheavy financial structure collapsed; the securities of both holding companies became practically worthless and the railway properties controlled through them were plunged into receiverships. This collapse was due to several factors, prominent among which were overcapitalization and the speculative and plundering activities of "insiders." "High finance," as it appeared in Rock Island operations and in the gutting of the New Haven, played no small part in convincing honest railway management and the public alike of the mutual advantage of public regulation of carrier financial operations.

evidenced weakness, the Frisco suffering particularly because of a highly unsatisfactory capital structure. What the future may hold for these lines, individually or as a group, is problematical: certain it is that a combination of skillful management and favorable economic conditions will be needed to restore them to a position comparable even to that recently occupied.

A third minor grouping, one to which reference has been made, is that of the Western Pacific-Denver and Rio Grande Western. This is another grouping of historical interest and another in which a previous relation stands reversed.[1] While the mileage of this unit is relatively small, its importance to the fulfillment of certain plans for the Hill system and to the Missouri Pacific lines is great, and it is likely to be used as an effective instrument under existing management. Yet prosperity, as measured in terms of dividends, appears to lie in the indefinite future for this group: neither the Western Pacific nor the Denver can hope to live except upon through traffic—for which competition is exceedingly keen, not only among the rail lines but also between the rail and water routes.

The Canadian Systems.—In addition to the ownership groups which are essentially our own, there exist two others, both Canadian in affiliation. The first of these, representing properties subsidiary to the Canadian Pacific Railroad, includes the Canadian Pacific lines in Maine, the Duluth, South Shore, and Atlantic, the Minneapolis, St. Paul, and Sault Sainte Marie, and the Spokane and International. These properties, with a total mileage of approximately 5,480, lie in the far eastern, far western, and central portions of northern United States. They represent, in the first case, construction to the Atlantic seaboard; in the second, an effort to share in the tonnage of eastern Washington; and in the third, a desire to participate in the Minnesota-Dakota grain traffic and to secure entry into Chicago. Although a portion of this mileage is poorly situated, affiliation with the Canadian Pacific gives something of promise for even the weakest—the Duluth, South Shore, and Atlantic.

The Canadian National Railways, with a mileage of almost 1,900, comprise properties formerly controlled by the Grand Trunk in Trunk Line and New England territories and by the Canadian Northern in the Northwest. Important among the subsidiaries of the Canadian National in the east are the Central Vermont and the Grand Trunk Western, while the Duluth, Winnipeg, and Pacific is the only important western property. Control is exercised by the Canadian National through stock ownership just as by the Canadian Pacific, but the nature of these properties, to-

[1] The construction of the Western Pacific was financed largely upon the basis of the guarantee of its bonds by the Denver and Rio Grande, but the unprofitable character of the new property forced it into receivership, and this, in turn, precipitated a receivership for the guarantor property. In the reorganization of the Western Pacific an eastern outlet was considered essential, and, in consequence, control of the original parent company was obtained, thus completely reversing the early relation.

gether with the lesser strength of the lines with which they are affiliated, gives less hope of profitable operation in the near future.

Important Independent Properties.—Although thus far discussion of ownership has been confined to more or less important groupings of lines, there are certain independent systems which are quite as significant to the public as some of the major ownership groups. One of these is the Atchison, Topeka and Santa Fe. This railway controls almost 13,400 miles of line and is one of the most important properties in southern Granger territory, in Southwestern territory, and in the Transcontinental field. Its development has come mainly through the construction of mileage, though this has been supplemented by the purchase of minor properties. From its inception in 1870 the property developed rapidly until, in the late eighties, it became overextended. This, together with certain minor frauds, resulted in receivership in 1889 and again in 1891. Since the later nineties, however, the property has steadily strengthened financially while further extending its mileage; in consequence, it stands today as one of the most stable roads in the United States, a splendid monument to the managerial skill of E. P. Ripley, who directed its course for more than a score of years, and of those under whose discerning guidance it has prospered since 1920. The future of the Santa Fe is as promising as its recent past.

A second major independent property is another of the southern transcontinentals, the Southern Pacific. This property operates directly and through subsidiaries some 16,200 miles of line, extending from Portland, Ore., southward to Los Angeles and thence eastward to New Orleans, with a line eastward to Ogden from San Francisco and other lines that gridiron eastern Texas. And recently, through acquisition of control of the St. Louis Southwestern, it reached Memphis and St. Louis. In addition to its rail operations, it controls a steamship line that plies from Gulf ports to New York City and Baltimore. Dominated for many years by that group of men who first built the Central Pacific and later directed the construction and operation of the Southern Pacific system, the property then came under the control of E. H. Harriman. Since the separation of this group of lines from the Union Pacific, no single individual or interest seems to have determined policies: though there are a number of large holders of stock, among them being A. C. James, the stock is widely held—some 15 of the largest holders, individual and corporate, owning less than 12 per cent of the issue outstanding. This system has been the beneficiary of keen, aggressive management throughout its history; its lines are strategically located; and the territory served by it has a promising future. It is more than a matter of passing interest that two of America's major independent lines should develop in the same general territory and should be active competitors, yet that both should rank high upon the basis of past record and of promise for the future.

A third important independent property is the Chicago, Milwaukee, St. Paul, and Pacific, with a mileage of almost 11,350. This property, in its development, has a history somewhat similar to that of the Santa Fe; begun in 1850, construction, supplemented by the purchase of short lines, has accounted for its growth. The early financial record of the St. Paul is an excellent one; but, when it abandoned its position as solely a Granger property through the construction of the Puget Sound extension, it became so burdened that receivership was inevitable—and, as a consequence of a reorganization not sufficiently drastic it has been only through skillful management that a second receivership has been avoided. At present the prospect is uncertain, but, at best, the journey back to prosperity will be both a long and difficult one.

Distribution of Railway Shares.—Following the discussion of control of railways in the United States that appears upon preceding pages, certain facts with respect to the distribution of railway shares will be of interest. In 1918 there appeared a listing of the 20 largest stockholders of the 50 largest railways in the United States as of 1917.[1] This showed that half or more of the stock of 26 of such railways was controlled by the 20 holders named in each case, while 25 per cent or more of the stock was so controlled in the case of 36 railways. Yet among that group of 36 for which concentration was apparent, the realities of the situation were different: of this 36 fully half were controlled by other railways whose stock distribution was wide—3 were subsidiaries of the Union Pacific with a concentration of but 20 per cent and 3 of the Pennsylvania with a concentration of only 11 per cent, while 4 were New York Central subsidiaries, and it had a wide distribution except for a large Union Pacific interest. True, the names of such men as Henry Frick, William Rockefeller, George F. Baker, J. P. Hoes, members of the Harriman and Harkness families, large American brokerage houses, and important investment groups with headquarters in London, Amsterdam, and Berlin, as well as American insurance companies, appeared upon the lists of more than one railway. Yet there was never any evidence that such community of interest reacted in the least to public disadvantage; rather, it is probable that the public gained through the curtailment of harmful competitive activities—for stabilization is important to shipper as well as to carrier.

Though there is no comparable list of railway stockholders for a recent period, the study submitted to the Committee on Interstate and Foreign Commerce, House of Representatives, early in 1931 gives valuable information and indicates that the diffusion of railway control is even greater now than it was in 1917. It is true, of course, that ownership groupings are more numerous than as of that date, yet in general, with the exception of the Van Sweringen properties, extensions of control have been by those properties that have a relatively wide distribution of voting power. Some

[1] *The Annalist*, Apr. 15 and 22, 1918, pp. 306, 421.

15 holders of 10,000 or more shares each control about 18 per cent of the stock of the New York Central; some 19 holders of Pennsylvania stock with like blocks exercise but about 2.5 per cent control over that property; some 10 such holders possess approximately 7.5 per cent of the voting power of the Baltimore and Ohio; some 12 holders about 12 per cent in the Union Pacific; some 15 holders less than 11 per cent in the Southern Pacific; and some 9 holders no more than 6.5 per cent in the Great Northern. Such illustrations could be greatly multiplied, though it must not be forgotten that certain properties show a rather high degree of concentration: 6 large holders in the Atlantic Coast Line possess some 42 per cent of the voting power—and the one large holder, the Atlantic Coast Line Company, is also dominated by a small group; and certain railways of lesser importance show a considerable concentration of voting power—the 18 largest holders of Delaware, Lackawanna and Western stock control almost 35 per cent of the stock, while in the Chicago Great Western the 6 largest holders control more than 30 per cent of the total. Yet it is generally true that, where a comparatively high degree of concentration of voting power is found, such concentration is the result of interrailway stockholding—with an ultimate wide distribution. However, as a consequence of the maze of holding companies through which the Van Swerringens have acted, it is probable that dictatorial powers rest in the hands of those brothers over a very considerable mileage and an enormous investment. And it would seem that the operations of the Pennroad Corporation point in the same direction.

Tendency in Distribution of Railway Shares.—An examination of statistics relative to the ownership of railway securities confirms the thesis stated above that there is a wide diffusion of holdings. And that diffusion

NUMBER OF SHAREHOLDERS IN SELECTED YEARS

Railway	1904	1917	1930
Santa Fe	17,823	27,062	58,202
Southern Pacific	2,424	37,853	54,942
Great Northern	383	26,716	42,258
Union Pacific	14,256	33,875	46,450
Total	34,886	125,506	201,852

has steadily become greater. In 1904, 1,182 railways had 327,851 stockholders and in 1917 Class I and II properties alone showed a total of 647,689. In 1925 Class I railways carried the names of 755,162 holders and in 1931 that figure had risen to 878,056. A study of the distribution of the stocks of particular properties indicates that, as securities gain financial strength and attain investment status, wider distribution develops. In 1904, before the Santa Fe, the Southern Pacific, the Union Pacific, and the Great Northern had proved their stability, the number of stockholders was small; but, as they became more firmly established, public interest grew.

Even in the case of the Pennsylvania, which in 1904 enjoyed investment standing, the increase has been striking, a growth from 44,175 in that year to 233,414 at the close of 1930. Certain it is that, in the face of increased competition for funds and the rise of rival agencies during the two decades past, public interest in railway shares has seemed to broaden.

A Growing Problem.—Yet this very diffusion, while weakening the foundation for charges of monopoly in particular areas, presents a problem; where holdings are scattered widely, a relatively small interest may be able to dominate because of the inertia and disorganization of a great number of small holders—and, by such domination, exercise over a great economic unit a measure of control that is wholly disproportionate to the financial risks accepted. That protection which has long been given the public at large under general regulation may have to be extended to the small investor from time to time because his very numbers make his position weak. This power to interfere with corporate government may well be withheld until clearly needed, but when and if it proves essential the scope of action of the Interstate Commerce Commission may well be so broadened as to permit it to accord such protection as public interest and the then prevailing theory of economic behavior, shall seem to justify.

REFERENCES

Annalist, Apr. 15 and 22, 1918, pp. 306, 421.

Bureau of Railway Economics: *Statistical Reports*.

Bureau of Railway News and Statistics: *Railway Statistics of the United States*.

Interstate Commerce Commission: *Annual Reports; Reports; Intercorporate Relationship of Railways in the United States as of June* 30, 1906; *Statistics of Railways in the United States* (annual).

Johnson, E. R., and T. W. Van Metre: *Principles of Railroad Transportation*, D. Appleton & Company, 1921.

Keenan, George: *Biography of Edward H. Harriman*, Houghton Mifflin Company, 1922.

Meade, E. S.: The Great American Railway Systems—series of articles in *Railway World*, 1903–1906, vols. 47–49. See Cleveland, F. A., and F. W. Powell, *Railroad Finance*, p. 308, for exact references.

Newcomb, H. T.: The Recent Great Railway Combinations, *Review of Reviews*, vol. 24, July, 1901.

Pyle, Joseph G.: *Life of James J. Hill*, Doubleday, Doran & Company, Inc., 1917.

Regulation of Stock Ownership in Railroads, House Report 2789 submitted under House Resolution 114, 71st Congress, 3d Session, by Committee on Interstate and Foreign Commerce, House of Representatives.

Report of Industrial Commission, vol. 19, pp. 304–322.

Ripley, W. Z.: *Railroads: Finance and Organization*, Longmans Green & Co., 1915.

Sakolski, A. M.: *American Railroad Economics*, The Macmillan Co., 1916.

Snyder, C.: *American Railways as Investments*, The Moody Corporation, 1907.

Spearman, Frank H.: *The Strategy of Great Railroads*, Charles Scribner's Sons, 1904.

Van Oss, S. F.: *American Railroads as Investments* (contains outline histories of principal systems), G. P. Putnam's Sons, 1893.

Chapter XXVII

CAPITALIZATION AND CAPITAL VALUE

IN PRECEDING chapters the nature of the corporation and the organization of the railway enterprise for operation were discussed. The portrayal of the financial policies and practices of that corporation remains, also a consideration of the problem which arises from the relation between the amount of financial obligations outstanding and the worth of the property. These matters are important, not only to the business unit and the investor but also to the public, and have commanded increasing attention with the development of regulation. A thorough understanding of both the financial structure of the railway corporation and the relation which capitalization bears to true property value, is fundamental to an appreciation of past conditions and future development.

Capitalization is conceived variously by different groups. To the accountant capitalization is a figure representing the sum total of the permanent liabilities of a corporation. To the financier, concerned only with earnings, capitalization is essentially synonymous with the property account and therefore is regarded as an asset instead of a liability. The economist conceives capitalization to be the declared value of the business, the sum total of the amounts of the various classifications of paper issued by the corporation and to which value has been assigned by it. It is, in short, the representation made by the business as to its worth.

Gross and Net Capitalization of American Railway Net.—In the determination of the capitalization of the American railway net, an analysis must be made if an accurate figure is to be had. On Dec. 31, 1930, the Interstate Commerce Commission reported outstanding $24,331,492,-400 of various types of paper. Included in this figure were $5,265,866,315 of railway securities that were then owned by railway corporations themselves. Instead of the gross capitalization mentioned above, therefore, the figure $19,065,626,085 represents more accurately the capitalization of the American railways since it eliminates a considerable duplication of securities. If, however, a *true* net capitalization of our railways were to be had, it would be necessary to deduct from this latter figure the worth of extensive properties of a non-railway nature held by the American carriers, such as mines, timber lands, industrial enterprises, and grain elevators, as well as of certain properties not yet employed in the rendition of service to the public. Just what the sum is which would fairly represent the worth of railway-owned properties not now "used and useful" in the rendition of carrier service can only be estimated, but it would not fall far short of $2,000,000,000. As illustrative of these "outside investments" it is declared that a major part of the nation's anthracite coal acreage is controlled by but a small number of roads. True net capitalization of the American railways, therefore, probably approximates $17,000,000,000.

Increase in the Bond Ratio.—Of the gross capitalization as of Dec. 31,1930, $10,082,731,671 was outstanding in form of stock while the remainder represented unmatured funded debt. This percentage of 58.6 which the funded debt bears to the total capitalization is in itself a matter of no little importance and represents a gradual increase, since about 1900, from practical equality with outstanding stocks. This increase has resulted from several factors. During that period there has been a considerable concentration of ownership of railway mileage. To secure funds for the purchase of other lines, bonds of either the mortgage or collateral-trust type have often been issued. The appearance of the holding company in the railway field has also tended to increase the bond ratio, since the increase of bonds rather than stocks makes possible the control of large properties with a minimum investment. A third factor which has given a strong impetus to this movement is the preference of the investor in railway securities to participate in the enterprise as a creditor rather than an entrepreneur. This preference rests primarily, it would seem, upon the greater safety of the bond as an investment and the disappearance of speculative opportunities in railway shares. The regulation of railways in such fashion as to limit the return upon stock to a figure below that available to the investor in the industrial field has made it difficult to market stock in a highly competitive market, and has thus compelled an increase in the proportion of bonds to total capitalization. Then, too, the prosperous road is often tempted to issue bonds instead of stock, just as its "poor relation" is compelled to do: the larger the proportion of bonds bearing a low interest rate to the total of securities outstanding, the greater is the stockholder's advantage during prosperous years.

This movement toward bonds has not been without its evils. Railway fixed charges have increased step by step with the increase in interest-bearing paper outstanding and with that increase has come a lessened ability to withstand the financial strain imposed by recurring periods of depression. A second important objection, primarily from a public standpoint, against this movement toward bonds is that it promotes the centralization of control of increasing amounts of capital in the hands of those who have, by comparison with the magnitude of the property dominated, an altogether too small stake in the enterprise. This results in the exercise of power quite out of proportion to the risk involved, a situation without social or economic justification. Still a third objection to the movement toward bonds lies in the fact that, as the bond ratio increases, the margin which should provide against future necessity diminishes. Indeed, it

Table XX.—Capitalization, Book Cost, and Fair Value of American Railways*

Year ended	Total railway capital issued†	Net capitalization §	Cost of road and equipment	Fair value**
June 30, 1890	$ 8,984,234,616	$ 7,577,327,615	$ 8,133,665,432‖	
June 30, 1891	9,290,915,439	8,007,989,723	8,444,856,144‖	
June 30, 1892	9,686,146,813	8,294,689,760	8,690,082,843‖	
June 30, 1893	9,894,625,239	8,331,603,006	8,937,545,760	
June 30, 1894	10,190,658,678	8,646,600,008	9,073,470,532	
June 30, 1895	10,346,754,229	8,899,572,695	9,203,490,619	
June 30, 1896	10,566,865,771	9,065,518,857	9,500,327,733	
June 30, 1897	10,635,008,074	9,168,071,898	9,709,329,228	
June 30, 1898	10,818,554,031	9,297,167,776	9,760,581,424	
June 30, 1899	11,033,954,898	9,432,041,731	9,961,840,805	
June 30, 1900	11,491,034,960	9,547,984,611	10,263,313,400	
June 30, 1901	11,688,147,091	9,482,649,182	10,405,095,085	
June 30, 1902	12,134,182,964	9,925,664,171	10,658,321,376	
June 30, 1903	12,599,990,258	10,281,598,305	10,973,504,903	
June 30, 1904	13,213,124,679	10,711,794,078	11,511,537,131	
June 30, 1905	13,805,258,121	11,167,105,992	11,951,348,949	
June 30, 1906	14,570,421,478	11,671,940,649	12,420,287,938	
June 30, 1907	16,082,146,683	....	13,030,344,328	
June 30, 1908	16,767,544,827	12,833,591,510	13,213,766,540	
June 30, 1909	17,487,868,935	13,914,302,363	13,609,183,515	
June 30, 1910	18,417,132,238	14,375,529,748	14,557,816,099¶	
June 30, 1911	19,208,935,081	15,044,484,894	15,612,378,845	
June 30, 1912	19,752,536,264	15,125,533,485	16,004,744,966	
June 30, 1913	19,796,125,712‡	15,366,472,253‡	16,588,603,109	
June 30, 1914	20,247,301,257‡	15,759,093,913‡	17,153,785,568	
June 30, 1915	21,127,959,078	16,307,502,580	17,441,420,382	
June 30, 1916	21,092,072,245	16,336,000,429	17,689,425,438	
Dec. 31, 1916	21,049,308,582	16,332,578,328	17,842,770,008	
Dec. 31, 1917	21,249,357,241	16,401,780,017	18,574,297,873	
Dec. 31, 1918	20,784,832,841	16,454,339,035	18,984,756,478	
Dec. 31, 1919	20,950,175,145	16,550,310,683	19,300,120,717	$16,903,000,000
Dec. 31, 1920	21,891,450,785	16,993,930,263	19,849,319,946	17,447,000,000
Dec. 31, 1921	22,291,635,792	17,082,875,993	20,329,223,603	17,905,000,000
Dec. 31, 1922	22,290,101,185	17,279,726,169	20,580,168,269	18,036,000,000
Dec. 31, 1923	22,838,607,339	17,810,262,262	21,372,858,161	18,981,000,000
Dec. 31, 1924	23,636,484,234	18,201,897,712	22,182,267,385	19,685,000,000
Dec. 31, 1925	23,644,224,072	18,190,513,329	23,230,915,985††	20,162,000,000
Dec. 31, 1926	23,676,996,957	18,234,311,637	23,880,740,146††	20,693,000,000
Dec. 31, 1927	23,614,325,858	18,136,691,445	24,453,870,938††	21,110,000,000
Dec. 31, 1928	23,747,272,066	18,510,582,609	24,875,983,930††	21,443,000,000
Dec. 31, 1929	23,982,664,091	18,679,706,928	25,465,036,427	21,965,000,000
Dec. 31, 1930	24,331,492,400	19,065,626,085	26,051,000,223	22,251,000,000
Dec. 31, 1931	....	....	....	22,379,000,000

* First three columns compiled from *Statistics of Railways in the United States*, Interstate Commerce Commission; data for fourth column from *Hearings* on H.R. 7116 and 7117, 1932.

† The figures for 1915 to 1921, inclusive, include actually outstanding, nominally issued, and nominally outstanding securities, that they may be comparable to previous years.

‡ Class I and II roads and nonoperating subsidiaries.

§ This figure represents total railway capital issued less railway-owned securities of other railways.

‖ 1893 investment less increases each year on account of change in classification in 1893.

¶ Investment for 1910 originally published is increased by $170,000,000 estimated reserve for accrued depreciation, to make figures comparable with those for other years.

†† Includes investments in proprietary companies increasing from $493,922,931 in 1925 to $1,095,630,527 in 1930.

** As fixed by the Interstate Commerce Commission in 1930 upon the basis of final values, plus or minus investment year by year. Fair value, as here used, corresponds to final value for purposes of rate making.

might be said that the inability of a railway corporation which needs funds to issue any paper but bonds except upon onerous terms points the way clearly to early and serious financial difficulty, if not to receivership. If American railways are to maintain a strong financial position the present proportion of bonds must not be increased and to this end every effort should be made, during more prosperous periods, to finance additions and betterments through the issuance of securities with only a contingent claim upon earnings.

Capitalization per Mile of Line.—A statement of even the net capitalization of American railways in terms of billions of dollars means little: the magnitude of such sums is too great, and an aggregate figure ignores mileage. A more valuable figure, because comprehensible, therefore, would appear to be the capitalization per mile of line, which was in 1930, eliminating railway-owned securities, $77,343 for the entire railway mileage of the United States. This per mile of line figure has been increasing steadily since statistics were first compiled by the Interstate Commerce Commission, the figure for 1930 being almost 78 per cent greater than the figure of $43,562 for 1890. This upward movement has been due in some slight measure to improper financial practices, but the increase is essentially a consequence of an intensive development of the plant. Trackage has increased much more rapidly than mileage, older properties have been improved, and the more recently built lines have, in general, been compelled to bear greater construction costs, due to more difficult topography and higher prices of land, labor, and materials. In fact, the capitalization per mile of line of American railways may properly advance with the years. The necessity of an intensive development, the mounting costs of elements entering into construction, and provision more generally for capital expenditures through the sale of securities rather than out of earnings, as has been the practice of prosperous lines so often in the past, will gradually increase the capitalization figure even under a most conservative financial policy.

As might be expected in a country with such diverse conditions and with properties so variously managed as those in the United States, there exists a wide variation in capitalization per mile among individual companies. An investigation undertaken in 1906, which made available true net capitalization per mile of line of American railways, showed that, although the average for the United States was $58,050 for the railways considered, this figure varied, for properties operated through essentially the same territory, from as low as $31,000 for the Chicago and North Western to as high as $90,000 for the Chicago Great Western; from $84,500 upon the New York Central to $169,000 for the Erie; from $86,400 on the Pennsylvania, a splendid road with expensive terminals, to $92,500 for the Wabash, long a financial derelict. This wide range of capitalization, little less marked today, is due to various factors. Among the more significant are the relation existing between miles of line and miles of track, the cost of terminals in large cities, the structure of the system—whether largely main line or possessing a considerable branch mileage, the financial organization of the company, and, last, but by no means least, the general financial policy which has governed throughout its entire corporate history. Not infrequently will a single factor cause a striking change in the capitalization of a property—an extension of mileage, the construction of expensive terminals, and even the declaration of a stock dividend. As illustrative of the first may be cited the influence of the Puget Sound extension, together with certain minor factors, upon the capitalization of the Chicago, Milwaukee, St. Paul, and Pacific: in 1916 its figure per mile of line was more than double that of a decade earlier. Evidence of the second appeared in the Chicago terminal electrification program of the Illinois Central and of the third in the case of the Lackawanna in 1921.

Capitalization per mile of line for the United States might be greatly increased, however, and yet fall far below the capitalization figures shown for many foreign railway systems which are hardly the equal of our own. Table XXI shows the capitalization per mile of line of the railways in certain of the more important countries in Europe and elsewhere, for the most recent date available.

TABLE XXI.—CAPITALIZATION PER MILE OF LINE OF FOREIGN RAILWAY SYSTEMS*

Country	Year	Capitalization
United Kingdom	1930	$295,057
Canada	1930	95,785
Germany	1930	186,696
Holland	1929	118,404
Italy (state roads only)	1929–1930	205,555
Norway†	1928–1929	95,610
India†	1929–1930	74,894
Japan	1928–1929	184,875
China	1927	150,187
New Zealand†	1929–1930	85,750
Argentine‡	1927	72,952

* Bureau of Railway News and Statistics, *Railway Statistics*, 1930.
† Much narrow-gage mileage.
‡ Various gages.

However, these figures have meaning only as examined with an understanding of certain facts. In certain of the older and more highly developed countries which show a very high capitalization per mile of line, a policy of fully capitalizing reinvestments has long been followed. Then, too, construction costs have been greater in those territories: differences in the nature of the plant—duplicate trackage, permanent roadbed, and terminals—explain in great measure the wide gap between foreign and American figures. On the other hand, the low capitalization shown for certain countries is to be explained by a marked predominance of narrow-gage mileage, the inadequate equipment of the property, and the absence of permanent roadway development. In a general way, the conclusion seems thoroughly justified that American railways are capitalized at the lowest figure per mile of line of any of the railways in the world, type of construction considered, unless, perchance, Canada should be able to show substantial equality with us.

Types of Railway Stocks.—As has already been indicated, railway capitalization consists, in common parlance, of stocks and bonds; or, as sometimes classified by writers in the field of finance, of owned and borrowed capital. Owned capital in the railway field consists largely of common stock which represents a residual claim upon the earnings of the property. Preferred stock is another type which has often been issued. Such stock may have preference as to dividends, assets, or dividends and assets, usually the last. Three types of preferred stock with respect to claim upon earnings are found in the railway field. Of these the most common is what might be termed ordinary preferred, giving to the possessor merely a prior claim upon the earnings to be distributed by the management. Another type of preferred stock is participating preferred. This confers not merely the right to preferential treatment in the payment of dividends up to the percentage fixed as a maximum, but also permits participation in excess earnings during periods of railway prosperity. Chicago and North Western preferred is a stock of this type. The third type of preferred stock found in the railway field is cumulative preferred which, in addition to giving to the possessor first claim upon any earnings distributed, permits the accumulation of unsatisfied claims from year to year until met.

Preferred stock has usually been issued for a specific and definite purpose. In the general corporate field it has frequently been used in cases of consolidation to cover items of real value contributed, common stock representing a speculative interest in future earnings. In the railway field, however, preferred stock generally has been issued for one of three purposes. Perhaps the corporation has desired additional funds when common stock could not be sold advantageously and conservative financing discountenanced an additional issue of bonds. Or a management, needing additional funds and yet desiring to restrict voting power, has issued non-voting preferred stock; its double purpose is thus attained without an increase in fixed charges. A third use, which explains particularly the issuance of cumulative preferred stock by railway corporations, has been in the reorganization of financially decrepit properties, to reduce fixed charges. If the property is to be rehabilitated such charges must be cut down, yet the holders of junior liens upon the property demand some degree of protection. To accomplish both ends in so far as possible, reorganization plans sometimes provide for the issuance of even cumulative preferred stock. This accomplishes, if a seemingly contradictory phrase may be used, the substitution of contingent fixed charges for charges of a definitely fixed character which accrued upon the superseded bond issue or issues.

Borrowed Capital in the Railway Field.—Two types of borrowed capital must be considered, though it is the second which is of fundamental significance. The usual purpose of short-term borrowing, generally in the form of notes, is to furnish needed funds until the money market permits the issuance of long-time securities upon reasonable terms. Advantageous though such financing may be in theory, practice has frequently shown it dangerous. When it becomes necessary to satisfy these short-time obligations the financial situation may be in no wise improved and therefore long-time financing may be just as objectionable as before; yet refinancing on a short-time basis, even though possible, involves heavy expense. Short-term loans are inconsiderable in total as compared with the long-term issues which have been marketed by the railways, though, as years have passed, the importance of issues running for only a few years has grown.

Long-time issues may perhaps well be classified as to the security offered the investor—though experience shows that no railway bond is more secure, whatever may be the protection offered, than the capacity of the specific underlying property to earn. In general, the investor may be protected by a specific and direct lien upon property or by the general credit of the corporation. The so-called secured issues may be protected by claims upon realty, upon personalty, or upon realty and personalty. Of those secured by a claim upon real property, real-estate bonds, land-grant bonds, divisional bonds, and terminal bonds are the more common. Those secured by mortgage upon personal property are, in general, of two types, the collateral-trust mortgage bond and the equipment bond. The former, protected by collateral deposited in trust, has frequently been employed to establish a degree of control over other railways which often approaches ownership: securities which give a controlling interest in one corporation are mortgaged for the purpose of securing funds to extend that control over another. The rather extensive use which has been made of this type of bond explains in considerable degree the difference between gross and net capitalization in the railway field. Equipment bonds have been used by many railroads, even by those which are financially strong. Equipment so mortgaged is used by the railway and paid for, in a sense, upon the installment basis. The equipment-trust certificate, which must be regarded as only indirectly a railway obligation, has practically displaced the equipment bond, however; its greater security has won the investor's favor. Most important among the issues secured by a claim upon both realty and personalty are those variously known as general or "blanket" mortgage bonds, possessing a senior or junior lien, perhaps a mixed lien, upon the entire property of the corporation.

A second type of bond which occupies an intermediate position between those issues which are secured by a direct lien and those resting upon the general credit standing of the corporation, is the income bond. This bond, like cumulative preferred stock, has commonly been issued in connection with reorganizations, the holders of junior liens with a definite annual claim upon earnings accepting, in lieu of their previous holdings, bonds which are secured as to principal by a specific lien upon property, but upon which the interest is contingent upon earnings. A third type of long-term issue which lacks all specific security is known to the American investor as the debenture bond. This bond is merely a promise to pay, protected both as to principal and as to interest by the general credit and earnings of the property. Interest is payable only if earned, and, even in case of default upon the principal, no specific property may be attached: general action against the corporation is the only course open. Such bonds have been but little used by American railways because of the unwillingness of investors to purchase them; when issued, they have been marketed largely in European countries where the debenture bonds of local corporations enjoy high standing because of stable earnings.

Overlapping of Claims.—When discussing the capitalization of a given railway property, it is necessary to realize that a single railway corporation may have outstanding several types of stock and many classes of bonds. This can readily be seen by a casual examination of the stock-exchange listings. The existence of numerous overlapping bond issues gives rise to an involved and difficult situation if inadequate earnings force a reorganization. In the event of such a readjustment, the possessor of a junior lien upon a specific fraction of the property may find himself in a better position than the owner of a bond secured by a lien, yet further removed, upon the entire property of the corporation; on the other hand, the owner of a senior lien upon certain of the property may find his position far less favorable than is the position of the owner of a junior lien upon another portion of the property which is most essential to the successful financial operation of the business.

Capitalization and True Worth.—In the discussion thus far attention has been given exclusively to the problem of capitalization, its nature and amount. The problem of the relation between capitalization and capital value remains. Capitalization constitutes a statement of worth by the issuing corporation. It purports to represent the value of the property and, as the balance sheet will evidence, is offset by asset entries of equal amount. The desirability of a reasonable correspondence between the value placed upon the assets of the enterprise and actual value of those assets becomes more apparent as time passes.

This is true in the field of corporate finance in general, but particularly true in the field of quasi-public corporations. With such reasonable correspondence a more intelligent and readier grasp of the actual situation may be had by investor, shareholder, shipper, and regulatory body alike. The maintenance of such reasonable correspondence between nominal and real values permits all concerned to know whether assets remain stationary, increase, or decrease in net worth as a result of a specific policy. Further, it gives at a glance the figure upon which this business, "burdened with public interest," is entitled to a reasonable return. The determination of the correspondence between capitalization and capital, or, stated otherwise, paper and actual worth, involves the ascertainment not only of the total of outstanding securities but also of the value of the property. The determination of the former is a relatively simple task but the ascertainment of the latter involves the entire problem of valuation.

The Problem of Valuation.—This problem of valuation is an exceedingly difficult and complicated one but, because of its importance in the entire public-utility field, an effort will be made to set forth certain fundamentals, an understanding of which is essential to an evaluation of the many and diverse statements made in economic and political circles. In *Smyth v. Ames*,[1] Justice Brewer enumerated a variety of elements which must be considered in the ascertainment of the worth of a public-utility property, but, fearing that in this lengthy enumeration some considerations may have been inadvertently overlooked, he closed his statement by declaring that not only must the elements named be given consideration but that due weight should also be given to "all other elements of value." That such a general pronouncement is of little value in determining the worth of a particular property is obvious. However, in his catalogue of elements were named the three bases which have been urged most strongly upon commissions and courts as fundamental in the ascertainment of true property value—earning capacity, historical cost, and cost of reproduction.

Earning Capacity as a Basis of Valuation.—Because of its almost universal acceptance in the industrial and commercial field, earning capacity has received generous support from private interests as a method of determining the value of railway properties. The mechanical determination of worth upon this basis is simple: true value is the quotient resulting from the simple process of dividing normal earnings by that rate of return which has been fixed as reasonable in the given field. The ascertainment of earnings and the fixation of the rate of return present the only difficulties and these are not serious. Yet, however applicable such a principle may be in a field where earnings are determined by the free play of competition, it certainly cannot serve as basic in a field in which not only partial monopoly exists, but where earnings are largely the result of positive

[1] 169 U. S. 466(1898).

action by a regulatory body. For regulated enterprises the use of earning capacity as a major factor in determining the rate base would tend to result in an inflexible rate structure. But a more important objection lies against this method: the whole soundness of its use is challenged by the circular reasoning involved. For, in essence, its use in the field of regulated enterprise would base earnings upon earnings, capitalization upon capitalization. Still further, it may be added, any method of determining property values which would cause those values to vary from time to time with the parsimony or generosity of a regulatory body, cannot be accepted as satisfactory or just. In only one situation has earning capacity been recognized as basically sound in the determination of plant value in the public-utility field—that of the so-called misplaced or obsolete plant. Typical instances of such use may be found in the valuation of lumber or logging roads after the lumber traffic has disappeared, or of properties which have been built far beyond immediate public need. As a fundamental factor in the determination of the worth of a railway property, then, earning capacity must be rejected.[1]

Nature and Validity of Historical Cost.—A second basis of valuation is historical cost. Such cost is ascertained by determining the actual total outlay for elements of permanent value from the beginning to date, deducting therefrom the cost of any withdrawals which may have occurred during the life of the enterprise. Historical cost includes not only tangible items such as buildings, machinery, roadway, and equipment, but also any intangibles for which actual, legitimate expenditures have been made—organization expenses, interest and taxes during construction, engineering and administration costs, as well as going value being those most commonly recognized. From this final figure no deductions are made for depreciation except as the property has been poorly maintained and its condition is below normal for the enterprise in question. Of historical cost two interesting variations have been urged with particular insistence during recent years—in part with a view to meeting certain weaknesses in historical cost as such and in part with a view to reducing the valuation upon which a return is to be paid to an absolute minimum. The first of these, estimated historical cost, would fill gaps in the records by the use of comparative data; the second, actual prudent investment, would challenge all records and call for the scrutiny of all acts, all decisions, perhaps many years after they had been made and in the light of greater skill and knowledge. Both these variations introduce the element of judgment, the degree of uncertainty in the latter being particularly significant.

[1] As and to the degree that competition forces upon the railways a schedule of rates that is inadequate to provide a "fair return" upon values fixed otherwise, recognition must be given to earning capacity as a factor in railway valuation. As the situation in the field of transport more nearly approximates that in industry and commerce, the principle determining plant worth under competitive conditions must be given greater weight.

In behalf of historical cost as a basis of determining value certain definite advantages are urged. In general, cost is considered as an index of worth. A figure determined in accord with this principle would seem to have, therefore, a certain natural basis in popular psychology. Furthermore, historical cost is definite in nature and, if data are available, can be ascertained with a high degree of accuracy: only a careful audit of the records and a detailed inventory would be essential to its determination if proper accounts have been kept. In the third place, it is declared that historical cost tends to reward the investor in proportion to his actual sacrifice: it protects him against a value decline on the one hand and denies him unearned increments on the other. And, finally, the administrative merit of this method is urged: the worth of a property as of a particular date may be determined quickly, accurately, and at slight cost.

The criticisms lodged against historical cost as a fundamental basis for the determination of fair value emphasize certain theoretical objections and practical difficulties. In the case of older railway properties, and particularly in the case of railways that represent the consolidation of many smaller properties in times long past, there are numerous and wide gaps in cost records which are difficult, if not impossible, to bridge. And if an attempt is made to fill these gaps by estimates, then historical cost loses in some measure one of its primary virtues—its accuracy and freedom from any element of judgment. Then, too, historical cost as determined under the system of accounting now followed, a system that requires replacements to be made upon the basis of first cost rather than present cost, tends to prejudice the interests of those who poured their money freely into railway enterprises during a period when costs were relatively low but the speculative character of the enterprise was pronounced. Another objection to this method, particularly as a sole basis of value determination, lies in the fact that historical-cost figures as obtained from the records may represent most efficient and careful construction on the one hand, or careless construction and excessive costs, even carefully concealed fraud on the other; in consequence, there is failure to reward efficiency and honesty, to penalize inefficiency and graft. Yet half a century, even a score of years later, it is often most difficult to determine whether costs have been abnormally low or abnormally high—and, if the latter, whether the cause was beyond the builder's control or such as to justify paring sharply the investment accounts. And, again, if such accounts are to be pared in accordance with the principle of actual, prudent investment an element of uncertainty is introduced that occasions criticism and complaint. Finally, if historical cost serves as a sole, even the primary, basis of determining railway values, to avoid a clear injustice to the investor the rate of return must be sharply increased during years of inflation if the property was constructed during a period of low or normal prices and correspondingly decreased during an era of deflation if built when the level of costs was high. For, after all, a "fair return" is definitely related to the purchasing power of funds.

Cost of Reproduction.—A third basis of value determination is that commonly known as cost of reproduction. Cost of reproduction is essentially a theoretical basis, and may be figured as cost of reproduction new or as cost of reproduction new less depreciation. Further, cost of reproduction may mean the reproduction of an identical plant in all essentials or it may mean the cost of building a substitute plant capable of performing the same service, a quite different matter in any field in which rapid technical progress features. And again, cost of reproduction may be estimated either upon the basis of physical conditions as they existed when the plant was originally constructed or as they would be at the present time did the plant not exist. In general, it may be said that cost of reproduction new less depreciation of the identical plant under original conditions is the basis of the estimate made, though the inadaptability of the plant to its use or some peculiar situation may justify a modification of this general policy. In arriving at cost of production not only must all physical property, "used and useful" in the rendition of service, be included in the inventory, but also, as in the case of historical cost, all nonmaterial or intangible items for which a cost can be established and which have legitimate place in "fair value."

Certain evident advantages flow from the adoption of this principle. It gives a value which, at a particular time, represents the present economic cost of property necessary to the rendition of a particular service, and its use avoids the inequities which result when historical cost is applied to competing properties constructed during different periods: the cost of the one property, due to wide differences in the price level or to changed conditions, may diverge sharply from that of another and in consequence a scale of rates that yields a fair return to the less costly may be quite inadequate for the more costly. Cost of reproduction recognizes value increments and value decrements in the field of regulated enterprise, just as the popular mind is accustomed to their recognition in the general field of property. And, finally, the employment of this principle places the burden of excessive cost upon the shoulders of inefficient or dishonest management and fully rewards the efficient and honest builder. As an offset to these advantages, however, there are certain definite objections which have been urged against all types of cost of reproduction as a basis of valuation. The acceptance of such a principle will, in any progressive society, result in a steadily increasing "fair value" to the extent that land forms a part of the property "used and useful"; though it is conceivable that commodity costs might decline with progress in the arts. Such steady increase contributes, of course, to rising service costs. In the second place, cost of reproduction is a matter of estimate, and actual experience shows that the estimates placed upon a given property by different valuation experts have often varied so widely as to arouse serious doubt as to the fundamental soundness of the principle. The acceptance of this principle may also, unless great care is exercised by regulatory bodies, result in giving the holder of an interest in a railway or utility a double return: he may receive not merely a reasonable return upon his holdings in the form of dividends but also an additional return through an increase in capital value. A final criticism of the method rests upon the wide fluctuation of cost figures from time to time and the administrative difficulties resulting: a valuation as of June 30, 1913, during a period of low commodity prices would compare strangely with the valuation of the same property with no additions and betterments, as of June 30, 1920—and almost as strange would the comparison be between the latter date and June 30, 1932. This problem has been partially met, however, by the use of the "unit price," the average cost of the particular item over a period of years sufficient to give what might be regarded as a "normal," or typical, price. Yet even here difficulty arises, since the length of the period covered in computing the average will, during a period of shifting prices, be highly significant in determining results.

One other difficulty, or matter of dispute, relative to the application of cost of reproduction to railway properties has arisen in the type of such cost that may be properly applied. Railway management has insisted that, if the property has been maintained in such condition as to make possible its operation at 100 per cent efficiency, depreciation should not be deducted. Although this matter has not been finally determined by the courts, it is highly improbable that they will hold an old property capable of rendering to the public the same number of units of service as a new one —and such, in essence, is the basis for the demand for the recognition of depreciation. However, since the average depreciation of railway properties will not vary far from 20 per cent, this matter is of such great importance that it will be contested by the carriers and defeat admitted by them only when the highest court has spoken.

Valuation Practice.—During the past 20 years commissions and courts have been forced to deal with the problem of valuation frequently and under widely varying conditions. Yet, as a result of those years of experience, no definite and explicit principles to govern the determination of the worth of a property can be set forth, greatly to the sorrow or exasperation of those whose minds demand invariable rules and those who are convinced that such rules may be applied in all instances and under all circumstances with equity to all parties concerned. Only in general terms have the pronouncements of commissions and courts been phrased. Yet a survey of the ruling decisions indicates that, as a working basis in the determination of capital value, administrative bodies and the judiciary have used cost of reproduction as the cornerstone. This figure seems to be strongly influenced by historical-cost considerations, however, and even by earning capacity to the extent that earnings reflect efficiency of management or intelligent choice of location where several routes were available.

To say that such is the present fundamental basis of determining the value of the property of a regulated enterprise is one thing; to contend that such basis will be permanently accepted is another. Indeed, it appears that, as conditions become more certain and methods of regulation, as well as the principles upon which such regulation rests, become more definite, historical cost will gain increasing acceptance. This acceptance will be hastened, too, by the more extensive and accurate cost records that are being accumulated under a policy of controlled accounting. And attempts to determine "fair value" for rate purposes, both of local and national utilities, during the past score of years have brought to the fore and emphasized the administrative difficulties involved in the use of cost of reproduction in the face of comparatively rapid and wide price changes. None the less, the more theoretical basis must be regarded today as fundamental and, in the determination of the figure to which paper worth ought measurably to correspond, this principle is likely to serve for many years as a guide to commissions and courts. In fact, it requires a considerable degree of assurance to insist that reproduction cost—or "present value," as the term is sometimes used—can ever be properly ignored under all circumstances and conditions. But, recognized as basic though it now is, no precise weight has been given it in the determination of a final valuation figure by a single body or individual, and much less has any general agreement developed. And such agreement is unlikely, it may be added, both because too many elements of judgment are involved to justify an expectation of even approximate unanimity and because of the varying degrees in which prejudice, sympathy, predispositions of mind, influence judgment.

REFERENCES

BONBRIGHT, JAMES C.: *Railroad Capitalization*, Columbia University, 1920.

Bureau of Railway Economics: Miscellaneous studies and reports.

Bureau of Railway News and Statistics: *Railway Statistics of the United States* (annual).

CLARK, WILLIAM L., and WILLIAM L. MARSHALL: *Corporation Law*, Keefe-Davidson Company, 1901.

CLEVELAND, F. A., and F. W. POWELL: *Railroad Finance*, D. Appleton & Company, 1912.

DAGGETT, STUART: *Principles of Inland Transportation*, Harper & Brothers, 1928.

DEWING, ARTHUR S.: *Corporation Finance*, Ronald Press Company, 1931.

DIXON, F. H.: *Railroads and Government*, Charles Scribner's Sons, 1922.

GLAESER, MARTIN: *Outlines of Public Utility Economics*, The Macmillan Company, 1927.

Hearings before the Committee on Interstate and Foreign Commerce, House of Representatives, 72d Congress, 1st Session, on H.R. 7116 and 7117, *Railroad Legislation*, Jan. 19 to Feb. 12, 1932.

Interstate Commerce Commission: *Annual Reports; Reports; Valuation Reports; Texas, Midland, etc.; Statistics of Railways in the United States* (annual).

JOHNSON, E. R., and T. W. VAN METRE: *Principles of Railroad Transportation*, D. Appleton & Company, 1921.

JONES, ELIOT, and T. C. BIGHAM: *Principles of Public Utilities*, The Macmillan Company, 1932.

KIRSHMAN, JOHN EMMETT: *Principles of Investment*, 2d ed., McGraw-Hill Book Company, Inc., 1933.

LOCKLIN, DAVID P.: *Railroad Regulation Since* 1920, McGraw-Hill Book Company, Inc., 1928, Supplement, 1931.

LOUGH, W. H.: *Corporation Finance*, Ronald Press Company, 1917.

LYON, HASTINGS: *Corporation Finance*, Houghton Mifflin Company, 1916.

———: *Investments*, Houghton Mifflin Company, 1926.

MCPHERSON, LOGAN: *Railroad Freight Rates*, Henry Holt & Company, 1909.

MEAD, E. S.: *Corporation Finance*, D. Appleton & Company, 1930.

Report of Industrial Commission, vol. 19, pp. 397–419 (1902).

Report of Railroad Securities Commission to Congress (1911).

RIPLEY, W. Z.: *Railroads: Finance and Organization*, Longmans, Green & Co., 1915.

THOMPSON, SLASON: *A Short History of American Railways*, D. Appleton & Company, 1925.

———: *Service Rendered Value of American Railways*, Bureau of Railway News and Statistics, 1927.

United States Supreme Court Reports.

VANDERBLUE, HOMER, and KENNETH BURGESS: *Railroads: Rates, Service, Management*, The Macmillan Company, 1923.

———: *Railroad Valuation*. Houghton Mifflin Company, 1917.

WHITTEN, R. H., and D. F. WILCOX: *Valuation of Public Service Corporations*, The Banks Law Publishing Company, 1928.

WYMOND, MARK: *Railroad Valuation and Rates*, Wymond and Clarke, 1916.

Much interesting material on valuation can be found in the reports of the various state commissions and state courts. Among the states in which noteworthy work has been done are Massachusetts, New York, California, and Wisconsin.

CHAPTER XXVIII

SECURITY REGULATION

THE demand for the determination of the worth of railway properties has received impetus from two directions. Legislative bodies and commissions have been desirous of having a sum fixed upon which a reasonable return should be paid, as an aid in the determination of rates; without such figure it is difficult to chart a safe course between confiscation and extortion. The second purpose which a valuation of railway properties should serve and one which was perhaps first to appear as a motivating factor is the protection of the investor. For many successive decades railway securities afforded the American people their one great investment and speculative opportunity, but, because of the unregulated issuance of securities and the involved systems of accounting, it was difficult for the possessor of capital to know at a particular time the true status of the security, bond or stock, in which he was interested as an investor, or to be assured of its position even in the immediate future. In consequence of this complete absence of control, the deceits and frauds perpetrated by promoter and by corporate organization upon the investing public during more than half a century of railway history were many and gross; indeed, the overcapitalization of certain railway properties became so notorious that the situation acquired political as well as economic significance. No small measure of the active public antagonism toward the railway during the past 60 years has been the outgrowth of these very excesses.

Watered Stock: Meaning and Tests.—The term "watered stock" has been used so widely in connection with the overcapitalization of the railways that perhaps it may be well to discuss the problem of overcapitalization in terms of watered stock. By this term is meant merely an excess of capitalization or paper obligations outstanding over the value of the property upon which that paper is based. This excess may result from a shrinkage in the value of the assets of the corporation through undermaintenance or retirements in excess of replacements, but normally it has been the consequence of an early issuance of stocks or bonds, or perhaps both, beyond the capacity of the property to give them financial support. Since cost-of-reproduction-new-less-depreciation has, in general, been accepted as fundamental, we might define overcapitalization, or watered stock, as an excess of outstanding securities over and above the present worth of the property as determined in accordance with the principle named. Other indexes of the presence of watered stock have been proposed, particularly the so-called "dividend test" and the "market test." Both of these, however, are unsound. In the railway field, as in all others, dividends must ultimately be determined by earnings and it has already been shown that earning capacity is not a sound basis for value determination except in the competitive field. The market test is in turn equally valueless, since the market value of a security is, in the long run, determined by the earning capacity of the property underlying it. The only test of the presence of watered stock which is of fundamental worth, therefore, is the valuation test.

Before entering upon a discussion of certain facts incident to over-capitalization in the railway field, it will be helpful to comment briefly upon the conditions underlying the issuance of railway securities during the developmental period. Built as they were in the most populous and wealthiest sections of our country in response to a definite traffic need, it was possible to finance the earliest of our railway properties through the sale of stock in the communities served. As the railway extended farther into the West and Southwest, however, covering stretches of territory not yet able to furnish economic support for operations, much less provide funds for their construction, it became impossible to finance such building except through the issuance of bonds. Indeed, so speculative was the character of many of these pioneer enterprises that it was not an uncommon practice to offer with each bond one or more shares of stock at a nominal price, sometimes even as a gift, in the hope that so "baiting the hook" with possible speculative gains would assist in the sale of bonds.

Reasons for Stock Watering.—Although it is impossible to classify completely and explicitly the various reasons lying back of stock-watering operations, or, to put it more fully, the issuance of excessive amounts of securities, certain reasons stand out with sufficient clarity to justify statement. One of the earliest reasons underlying such excessive issuance of securities has already been mentioned—the need of "baiting the hook" sufficiently in the case of pioneer undertakings to interest the prospective purchaser of bonds. A second reason of importance in the railway field, as in the field of industrial operations, has been the desire of the promoter to capitalize for his own benefit any future growth in value of the property. To do this sufficient bonds would be issued to meet a major part of the cost of completing the project, the promoter receiving at a nominal price, or for "services rendered," a considerable issue of common stock upon which he hoped the prosperity of the project would enable him to realize at some future date. Yet another explanation of the issuance of abnormal amounts of securities can perhaps be summarized by the simple word "plunder." All too often in the history of American railways, security issues have been foisted upon a public that has been carefully kept in ignorance of underlying facts, with the result that certain insiders have been able to reap richly in a field in which they have sowed only deceit.

A still further reason for stock watering, but one applying only to bonds, appears in the greater immediate financial advantage to be gained through the sale, at a heavy discount, of a large issue of bonds bearing a low rate of interest rather than through the issuance of bonds at par, carrying the market rate. To make this statement clear: suppose that a corporation is seeking additional funds and that the pressure of immediate needs is such as to justify ignoring largely any future consequences. This corporation, assuming itself able to support an additional interest burden of $500,000, might issue $10,000,000 of bonds bearing 5 per cent, or $20,000,000 at 2½ per cent, the annual burden in either case being the same. But, because of the fact that at the end of the life of the bond the par value must be paid, the railway would be able to realize immediately a larger sum upon the $20,000,000 issue bearing half the market rate than upon the other. Such a policy is shortsighted and, if followed, will prove ruinous, but immediate necessity upon occasion compels a course of action which, from the long-time point of view, is unsound; then, too, those in control may be actuated by personal motives of such character as to make the future of slight concern.

Another factor operating in the railway field to promote stock watering is the desire of the corporation to disguise returns. In the industrial or commercial field the organization that is reaping a rich harvest has no desire to stimulate competition by advertising unusual opportunities through the payment of abnormal dividends. In the railway field those corporations that occupy a peculiarly favorable position are just as eager to conceal from the public and from regulatory bodies a profit which exceeds that regarded as reasonable. And, too, certain corporations have sought to forestall regulatory activity by an excessive issue of securities, particularly bonds, upon which charges must be paid regularly if receivership is to be avoided. In this way they hope to justify the continuance of a level of rates which yields a high return upon fair value of the property.

Overcapitalization and Manipulation.—The existence of certain conditions in the railway field has led, almost invariably, to excessive capitalization. Manipulation of the market by a group controlling a railway has often been accompanied by excess issues of securities. The malodorous and notorious performance of that trio of financial freebooters —Gould, Fiske, and Drew—in their struggle with Vanderbilt for the control of the Erie, is a classic in manipulation and shows clearly how a railway property may be burdened heavily in after years as a result of such operations. A similar situation, in that the work was done by "insiders," is found in the overcapitalization of the Chicago and Alton while under the control of Harriman, a performance which saddled a fine property so heavily with debt that no hope remained of a prosperous future until reorganization should lighten the load. The purpose of stock watering here alone distinguished it from the Erie situation: it was the investing public rather than a rival railway leader that was to be mulcted. Incidentally, the purpose was accomplished with equal thoroughness and success.

Another condition most favorable to capital inflation has been the utilization, in connection with the building of many properties, of the so-called "construction company." Such a company, directed by "insiders" who, acting in dual capacity, offer bids in the name of the construction company and as officials of the railway company vote the acceptance thereof, has succeeded in greatly increasing the capitalization of many railway properties. Significant among such operations have been the work of the Crédit Mobilier on the Union Pacific, which almost doubled the cost of the property; of various companies which operated in connection with the Southern Pacific, increasing tremendously the cost of that road; and, in more recent years, the extension of the now St. Louis-San Francisco into new territory under the shadow of this convenient instrumentality for exploitation.

Other Conditions Promoting Overcapitalization.—The declaration of a stock dividend is still another practice often resulting in overcapitalization. This stock dividend may be declared by the corporation during a period of poor business in lieu of a cash dividend. On the other hand, profitable operations through a series of years may have resulted in an accumulation of a surplus which the management desires to distribute. The distribution of this surplus upon the basis of stock issues outstanding at the particular time might necessitate a sharp increase in the dividend rate. To avoid this and thus escape public notice and condemnation, the railway corporation will issue sufficient stock, prior to "cutting the melon," to make distribution possible without in any way exciting suspicion on the part of the casual observer. Closely akin to the declaration of a stock dividend is the increase of capitalization attended by the exercise of "rights." If the right to subscribe for additional stock is given to the present stockholder at a price below par, an increased gap between capitalization and worth is inevitable. However, even when the right to subscribe is given at par or above par an objectionable dilution of the old stockholders' equity will result if the subscription figure is materially below the market quotation of the stock.

The existence of a considerable sum of unpaid current liabilities presents another situation which strongly tempts the corporation to seek a way out of its difficulty through an increase in capitalization. Unable to meet such current demands from earnings, many corporations have weakly yielded to pressure and have paid off such liabilities with sums secured from the sale of stock or even of bonds. Quite similar in nature to this objectionable policy is another—that of capitalizing replacements. This may result innocently—from a failure to differentiate properly between replacements and betterments, or it may be the consequence of a desire to exploit the property. This tendency to confuse capital and replacement costs has been particularly noticeable in the case of financially weak lines and of roads expending considerable sums upon relocation projects, important bridge replacements, or betterments.

The change of financial plan incident to reorganization has, almost without exception, resulted in an increase in the total of outstanding securities. Greater issues of bonds with a contingent claim upon earnings replace bonds with a fixed claim. Preferred stock, even common, is also issued, generally in amounts much in excess of the par value of the bonds retired, and given to the holders of those junior liens whose claims compel a measure of consideration, yet who find it essential to make certain sacrifices. It is this situation that has given rise to the issue of a considerable portion of the outstanding income bonds and also to no small amount of preferred stock, particularly that with cumulative claims upon earnings. Yet another fruitful source of railway overcapitalization has been the consolidation of properties. It is assumed that such consolidation will result in increased earnings. In an effort to capitalize such earnings at the time of the merger of the properties, securities are issued in amounts beyond the ability of the corporation to support them upon the basis of previous aggregate earnings. If the expected increase in earnings fails to materialize, the consolidated property finds itself, in the normal course of events, burdered excessively for perhaps many years in the future.

Morality of Stock Watering.—In public discussions of railway overcapitalization or stock watering, it is generally assumed that such a practice is and always has been essentially wrong; more, that it is without exception reprehensible as an endeavor to exploit the investing public on the one hand and the rate-paying public on the other. To arrive at a reasonable and sound conclusion relative to the morality of stock watering, however, it is necessary to distinguish between the overcapitalization of pioneer properties during years of rapid development and of speculative building, and the overcapitalization at a later time of developed properties. In early years, when the railway was regarded as a competitive enterprise, such overcapitalization as took place can justly be termed immoral to no greater degree than can the excess capitalization of an industrial corporation today be so regarded, unless fraudulent practices can be shown to have accompanied such excessive issues. Then, too, during this earlier period, railway enterprises were of a highly speculative character and the issuance of amounts of securities greatly in excess of the actual cost of the property can be explained and, in part, justified upon the basis of the heavy risks accepted. In brief, it seems that whatever may be the burden resting upon an individual railway, or upon the railways of the country as a whole, because of excess capitalization, *honestly issued*, during early years, no stigma should attach to the practice. It is unfortunate, of course, but such added public burden is a part of the price which the public must pay for progress. It is in part the price, too, which the present generation must pay for long adherence to an erroneous conception of the essential nature of the railway business, and for dilatory governmental action, once the policy of *laissez-faire* proved to be unsound as applied to the field.

Judgments cannot properly be so charitable with respect to most instances of stock watering during comparatively late years, however, if one believes at all in the maintenance of a reasonable correspondence between capitalization and worth. Indeed, even though one did not believe in such a correspondence, he could not condone practices that have appeared in connection with conspicuous instances of excessive capitalization since about 1900. Practically all of these outstanding illustrations of overcapitalization have been intimately connected with dishonest or grossly unsound management, as, for example, the wrecking of the Rock Island, the collapse of the New Haven, and the plundering of the Frisco. For present and future it would seem that slight justification can be offered by corporate management for burdening a property with excess capitalization, either bonds or stocks.

Demand for Security Regulation.—Indulgence in objectionable capitalization practices, associated as they have often been with unsound management, early led to public demand for the regulation of railway security issues—a demand that became more insistent as the years passed and abuses continued. Such regulation is justified in the interest of the investor. Though a uniform system of accounting has been of great assistance to the investor in portraying the status and trend of a property, it did little to assure him of protection against changes in capitalization which might greatly lessen his equity, perhaps imperil it. Such a situation was inimical, both to the attraction of additional investment interest and to the retention of old. From the standpoint of the patron, overcapitalization is likewise objectionable. The pressure of necessity resulting from a heavy burden of fixed charges, or the desire to maintain dividend payments upon excessive stock issues, may well result, even under a system of regulation, in the adoption by a carrier of the shortsighted policy which calls for the heaviest possible exactions in rates from, and the rendition of minimum service to, the shipper.

The patron is particularly likely to suffer from overcapitalization, however, because of its influence upon service. The need for funds to meet interest and dividend payments will almost invariably result in inadequate maintenance. Furthermore, such demands will make the improvement of service slow and the expansion of the property to meet the growing needs of the community equally tardy. Concrete instances of the influence of an overheavy capitalization upon service, especially if the proportion of bonds be high, are to be found in the history of the Chicago and Alton, of the New Haven, of the Missouri Pacific, and, more recently, of properties too numerous to mention.

Control by the States.—The demand for regulation of security issues was first heeded by certain of the states. Of these New York, Massachusetts, and Texas were among the earliest to act in an effective way, each doing particularly interesting work. In general, state regulation of railway security issues concerned itself with three matters. It was required that the purpose of issue be clearly stated and that a strict accounting be made for all sums received from the sale of that issue. Another feature had to do with the control of the price of sale: regulatory acts often decreed that stocks should not be sold below par, though permitting a certain maximum discount upon bonds at the discretion of the state commission. The third feature of the typical regulatory act was a clear prohibition upon the issuance of securities for certain named purposes, such as replacements, franchises, and leases. Little criticism can properly be made of these regulations except that one which prescribes a definite price of sale; its effect was often to handicap unnecessarily a corporation in meeting a particular situation. Indeed, in connection with the reorganization of the New Haven, the Massachusetts commission, though denying the New Haven the right to issue certain securities because of legal restrictions which hedged that body about, confessed its willingness to do so, were there no intervening legal barriers: the desirability from a public point of view of the issue was clearly admitted. Then, too, nothing could be better calculated to increase the bond ratio during periods of weak railway credit than a "sale at par" provision covering the flotation of stock.

Movement toward Federal Regulation.—Dissatisfaction with state control as it existed, together with the inability of state control alone to meet all problems, led to increasing public insistence upon federal regulation of security issues. This insistence was based upon several facts: that state regulations often conflicted, that many states failed entirely to regulate, and that others regulated well rather than wisely. So insistent became the demand for federal action that, in 1908, the Republican party platform pledged that organization to the enactment of restrictive regulations by Congress. Instead of fulfilling this pledge, however, Congress provided for a commission to investigate the entire problem of the control of security issues. At the head of this commission was placed President Hadley, of Yale University. In its report to Congress, this body contended that capitalization in no way influences rates and services and that regulation of the price of issuance was of no advantage. It recommended, however, that a physical valuation of the railways be undertaken and also suggested the abolition of par value of all railway stocks.

Congress, acting on the basis of this report, refused to provide for the control of railway securities. Yet it did, in the Valuation Act of 1913, provide for a determination of the true value of railway properties of the

United States—and such value was requisite not only to the fixation of rates but also to any intelligent regulation of security issues as well as to all efforts to secure and preserve a reasonable correspondence between capitalization and property worth.

The report of this commission, however, was not given great weight by the public at large and particularly not by those with a deep interest in the solution of the railway problem: the conclusion that there is no relation between capitalization and rates or service was clearly grounded upon a confidence in the time-honored policy of *laissez-faire* as applied to the railways which actual experience had long since shown to be undeserved. Warned by the financial mismanagement and exploitation of certain railway properties during the two decades preceding, it is not strange that practically every proposed solution of the railway problem presented to Congress in 1919 embodied, as one of its main provisions, the complete regulation of security issues by some federal agency. The unanimity of judgment was further evidenced by the inclusion, almost without dissent, of a section in the Transportation Act of 1920 giving to the Interstate Commerce Commission a power that had been suggested almost 50 years earlier by the Windom Committee and again a decade later by the Cullom Committee, but which had been refused or ignored through many years.

Section 20*a* of the Transportation Act.—In a preceding chapter (Chap. XII) certain of the more significant provisions relative to the power of the Interstate Commerce Commission over the issuance of securities by the railways are given. Before turning to a consideration of the exercise of this power, however, further provisions that are of administrative importance will be indicated. That the Commission may fit its action to a situation as it develops under inquiry, it is given the power to grant or deny a carrier application in whole or in part as well as to grant with such modifications and upon such terms as are deemed necessary. To make its control continuous, the Commission has the right to modify subsequently any order issued by it as to the purposes for which securities previously authorized may be used.

All applications for authority under this section must be presented to the Commission in such form as it prescribes and the accuracy of the statements made attested by a responsible officer of the applicant. The law commands that the regulatory body require such reports from each carrier issuing any type of security under its provisions as will indicate "the disposition made of such securities and the application of the proceeds thereof." Any securities issued without authorization for which authorization is requisite are void and provision is made both for the punishment of any officer or agent who "knowingly assents to or concurs" in such action, and for the protection of the innocent investor. Hearings may be held, if the Commission sees fit, but in any event state regulatory bodies and "other appropriate State authorities . . . shall have the right to make before the Commission such representations as they may deem just and proper for preserving and conserving the rights and interests of other people and the states, respectively." And, that there should be no ambiguity in the law leading to confusion in the matter of exclusive control, it is declared that "a carrier may issue securities and assume obligations or liabilities in accordance with the provisions of this section without securing approval other than as specified herein."

The Application for Authority.—Any carrier subject to the Act that seeks nominally, conditionally, or actually to issue securities or to assume obligations with respect to the obligations of others must make application to the Commission in accordance with the rules of that body a sufficient time in advance of the date of the proposed issue or assumption to give not less than 30 days to meet statutory requirements. The application must be made on forms prescribed by the Commission and in the completion of these forms all pertinent facts must be adduced that will aid Division 4 (Finance) in the formulation of a judgment. Among the facts required are the name of the state or states where chartered; the name of each state in which the applicant carrier proposes to operate; the nature of the authority sought, with the purposes and uses of the proposed issue and the proceeds thereof, or of the proposed assumption of obligation or liability; the terms and conditions of the proposed issue; and by whom or through whom the securities are to be issued, with copies of all contracts, underwritings, and other arrangements made or to be made. Entered upon the application, too, must be the facts upon which the petitioner relies to show that the proposed issue is, (1) for some lawful purpose within its corporate purposes and compatible with public interest, and (2) reasonably necessary and appropriate to such purpose. And with the application must be filed certain exhibits, important among which are a copy of charter and by-laws as amended to date; copies of resolutions by directors authorizing the action for which approval is sought; opinion of counsel that the action proposed meets all legal requirements; a map of the carrier's existing lines as well as a profile map of any proposed line or lines to be built from the proceeds of the proposed issue; and a copy of the applicant's general balance sheet as of the latest practicable date. Other pertinent data must be presented, also, depending on whether the application is with respect to construction, the acquisition of equipment, the acquisition of property other than equipment, the discharge or refunding of existing obligations, or reimbursement for income or other moneys expended upon capital items.

Though required by law to notify only the governor of each state in which the applicant operates, the Interstate Commerce Commission has made it a practice to notify also the regulatory body of each state and to inquire of both as to whether there is a desire to be heard. The Commission need make only such investigations as it sees fit, hearings being formal or informal at its discretion. After investigation, generally by an examiner, a proposed report is made, embodying such recommendations as seem appropriate in view of the facts. To this report all parties at interest have the right to file exceptions and to be heard orally before Division 4, the judgment of which is final unless it be modified upon appeal to the Commission sitting *en banc*. The extent of the work done by the Finance Bureau of the Commission in the years since Sec. 20*a* became effective has been prodigious, measured both in the number of applications considered and in the volume of securities authorized: the total of the former to the close of 1932 exceeded 2,500 without the inclusion of supplements and rehearings, and the aggregate of the latter exceeded $14 billion—to which must be added more than 8 million shares of no par stock. Yet some of the most difficult cases before the Commission have resulted in refusals to authorize, thus indicating that even heavier than statistics show is the burden placed upon that body to the end that railway finance may stand upon a higher level in public judgment and that the shipper may be protected.

The Problem of Jurisdiction.—Despite the clarity of the law concerning the exclusive and plenary jurisdiction of the Interstate Commerce Commission over the issuance of railway securities, once Sec. 20*a* became effective, this was one of the first points to be challenged. Because a railway corporation is organized and exists under state laws, it was contended in one situation that such corporation was not answerable to the federal government in the matter of security issues. In another situation it was argued that the jurisdiction of the state commission was primary and that the federal commission might approve only after favorable action had been taken by the state body acting under state statutes. To both these contentions the Interstate Commerce Commission gave a firm negative answer and in its position has been upheld in the lower court.[1] From that decision no appeal was taken, but, while the Supreme Court has not given a direct answer upon this phase of federal regulation, its position has been so positive in all cases where exclusive federal control has been challenged that it may well be the failure to appeal rested upon the obvious hopelessness of state opposition.[2] Where the applicant seeks to do that which is prohibited by state laws under which it is incorporated, the Commission has refused to give its approval,[3] and in all matters the federal body gives a sympathetic hearing to representations by state commissions; however, its judgment appears to be conclusive and is now so accepted generally.

[1] *Pittsburgh and West Virginia Railway Company et al. v. Interstate Commerce Commission et al.*, 293 Fed. 1001.

[2] Among the more important of these have been the Dayton-Goose Creek and the Wisconsin Passenger Fare cases, cited earlier.

[3] Capital Stock of Pittsburgh and West Virginia Railway Company, 82 I.C.C. 704.

A second problem of jurisdiction has arisen in the case of electric railways that handle freight. Section 20*a* excepts from Commission control, among other carriers named, any "interurban electric railway not operated as a part of a general steam-railroad system of transportation." Realizing the difficulty of making such a distinction, the Commission has none the less sought to draw a line between interurban electric railways in the older sense, engaged largely or wholly in the movement of passengers, and the railway electrically operated which differs from the steam lines in little more than power employed. In this endeavor the Commission received the support of the Supreme Court in its assertion of jurisdiction over the Piedmont and Northern;[1] yet, so uncertain is the line of demarcation between properties subject to Commission control under the existing law and properties exempt that final decision must come in each case from the courts. After Commission control of the Piedmont line had been recognized, an attempt was made to take jurisdiction over the issuance of securities by the Chicago, North Shore, and Milwaukee. A lower court held adversely to the Commission but, that there might be no question as to the validity of securities subsequently issued should the federal government obtain a reversal upon appeal to the United States Supreme Court, the North Shore—while not admitting federal jurisdiction—asked, and received, Commission approval "because of the expediency involved in the situation." The finding of the Supreme Court was in accord with that of the lower court, however: because of its important passenger business the North Shore was held to be free of control under the Act.[2] It would seem that Congress might well act to eliminate uncertainty and extend, in line with Commission recommendations, the scope of the Act to cover independently operated electric railways that are engaged in the general transportation of freight in interstate commerce as well as the transportation of passengers. In this way only can the situation be cleared.

Items Capitalizable and Capitalization.—In its administration of Sec. 20*a* the Interstate Commerce Commission was early confronted with the question of what type of assets and expenditures formed a proper basis for the issuance of securities by a particular carrier. Regulatory policy has taken form with the passage of time and today it is quite clear that certain items may, and others may not, be capitalized. Among the former are investments in road and equipment; improvements made in leased property that is virtually owned; realty holdings intended for use in transportation; a reasonable amount of working capital; a portion of surplus; and investments in union stations or in affiliated companies. Coming under the ban of the Commission are operating expenses; earning

[1] *Piedmont and Northern Railway v. Interstate Commerce Commission* 286 U.S. 299 (1932).

[2] *United States v. Chicago, North Shore, and Milwaukee Railroad Company,* 53 Sup. Ct. Rep. 245.

capacity; interest on bonds; the cost of issue and sale of securities; noncarrier securities or properties held; excessive reorganization expenses; and entire surplus. In general, it has been the policy of the Commission to "authorize capitalization of those assets only which have been provided and which are intended for continuing productive use in service of transportation."[1]

Inasmuch as one of the purposes actuating the extension of regulatory power over security issues was to deal with overcapitalization, it was to be expected that all proposals to issue stock or bonds would be scrutinized carefully with a view to determining effects in this particular. Though no effort has been made to correct errors of the past, every effort has been made to avoid discrepancies between capitalization and worth for the future. Applications were denied where excessive issues were proposed, "fair value" being used as a yardstick. Carriers have met with refusal too, when seeking to capitalize properties upon the basis of the Commission's valuation when a lesser sum was paid for those properties. A request to issue bonds at a heavy discount to provide funds for capital expenditures was refused because of the resultant overcapitalization. Yet in a few cases issues were approved that resulted in slight overcapitalization because such action seemed to be in public interest: in one case the only alternative seemed to be receivership for the property.

Stock Dividends.—An early and highly controversial question to come before the Commission had to do with the declaration of stock dividends by the more prosperous carriers, such increase in capitalization being rested upon surplus. This use of surplus was sharply opposed by many on the ground that surplus represents a "public equity," since it is an accumulation beyond a fair return. Logic and equity joined to support the Commission in its recognition of clear title to such surplus in the carrier. In line with this position, the Commission has approved consistently the capitalization of a reasonable portion of surplus—though insisting with equal regularity that "a substantial surplus should remain uncapitalized as a support for the applicant's credit, providing for emergency needs, offsetting obsolescence and necessary investments in nonrevenue producing property, and serving as a general balance wheel."[2]

In only one case has the Commission been asked to approve the issuance of bonds as a dividend, this to be supplemental to a stock dividend, but permission was not granted—this, despite the fact that the surplus was adequate to permit both.[3] The Commission looked with disfavor upon the resulting increase in fixed charges, as well as upon an undue reduction in surplus prior to the determination of final property value. In every instance where approval has been sought for the issuance of a stock

[1] Securities of Louisville and Nashville Railroad Company, 76 I.C.C. 718.

[2] Stock of Delaware, Lackawanna and Western, 67 I.C.C. 426.

[3] Stock of Chicago, Burlington, and Quincy Railroad Company, 67 I.C.C. 156.

dividend the Commission has insisted that such issuance be "compatible with public interest" as well as that a surplus exist adequate to support the increase in capitalization and provide a margin of safety for the applicant.

Type of Security Issued.—Under a régime of regulation of private enterprise in public behalf certain matters must remain as functions of management, else the enterprise becomes private in name only. One of these functions would seem to be the determination of the nature of securities to be issued from time to time. In general, the Interstate Commerce Commission has acquiesced in the judgment of the carrier's board of directors, but in certain instances has felt that public interest justified interference. Because of the high bond ratio of the railway net as a whole and of particular properties, the Commission has looked with favor upon the issuance of stock rather than of bonds, when the credit of the company and the general situation permit. In one important case an application to issue bonds was denied but the issuance of stock instead given approval.[1] The issuance of prior-preferred stock has also received Commission support as against the issuance of bonds, and the use of such stock to retire bonds and thereby reduce fixed charges has been approved. Definite unwillingness to approve the issuance of stock without voting power or with voting power unduly restricted has been evidenced, even though that stock be preferred in type.

Closely allied to this matter of the regulation of the type of issue has been the problem of no-par stock in the railway field. Many who profess to speak in behalf of the public have opposed the use of no-par stock in the field of regulated enterprise and this influence has been sufficiently strong on the Commission itself to discourage its extensive adoption. None the less, the issuance of such stock has been approved in numerous cases—sometimes to be employed in the acquisition of a property but more often in connection with the reorganization of a railway following receivership. In one case that early came before the Commission the exchange of no-par stock for par value was approved, though not without the customary protest from Commissioner J. B. Eastman.[2] On the whole, however, the ruling view of the Commission upon the matter of dictation by that body has perhaps been well expressed by Commissioner Woodlock, "Unless a course of action proposed by managers of a railroad corporation definitely threatens the public welfare, it is, I think, our duty to refrain from interfering with managerial judgment, even though the law, literally construed, gives us power to do so."[3]

Sale and Purchase of Securities.—Power to fix the manner and price of sale of securities to be issued was conferred upon the Interstate Com-

[1] Bonds of Chesapeake and Ohio Railroad Company, 105 I.C.C. 746.

[2] Stock of El Paso and Southwestern Railroad Company, 70 I.C.C. 208.

[3] Bonds of Chesapeake and Ohio Railway Company, 105 I.C.C. 748.

merce Commission by inference rather than by explicit statement. So clear has that inference appeared, however, that no serious effort has been made by any parties at interest to challenge this assumption of power. While it may be reasonably assumed that railway management is interested in marketing securities in such manner as to obtain for the carrier the highest net price, and while this is undoubtedly true except in isolated cases, the Commission but reflected a certain public misgiving when it began as early as 1921 to scrutinize arrangements for the sale of securities through "customary channels." For it has long been known that a large part or all of the financing of particular railways is handled by certain important banking houses, among which J. P. Morgan and Company and Kuhn, Loeb, and Company are conspicuous. At first it seemed that the Commission was considering the imposition of a requirement that all securities be sold under competitive bids, but, after a public hearing and study, it has required that only securities of a uniform type be so sold—equipment-trust certificates being the conspicuous example, though union-station bonds seem to fall into the same general class.

But the Commission has gone further: in certain instances it has fixed the minimum price at which issues may be offered or acquired. In a comparatively early case a minimum of 90 was prescribed for a proposed issue of bonds that the applicant had asked to offer at not less than 80,[1] the lower figure being disapproved because of the excessive cost of capital in case of its acceptance. And in similar manner the Commission has, in numerous cases involving the acquisition of control of one carrier by another, set a maximum figure that may be paid for the stock of the property over which control is to be extended. Determination of price by public authority in such cases represents clearly an invasion of the field of management, yet again its justification seems to lie in public policy: every effort should be made to protect the user of railway service from even occasional errors of judgment on the part of those who are charged with direction of carrier policy.

Reorganization.—One of the difficult problems facing the Interstate Commerce Commission in the administration of Sec. 20*a* has arisen in connection with the termination of railway receiverships and the authorization of security issues for successor companies. Lacking any right to participate in the final settlement of the affairs of the predecessor corporation or in the formulation of the reorganization plan, the Commission is confronted by that plan in final form—a plan to which the old security holders have perhaps been won only after months of delay and through great effort, a plan that received court approval only after further delay, and yet a plan that because of the operation of various influences may contain many elements of weakness. So confronted, the Commission has

[1] Alabama, Florida, and Gulf Railroad Company, 70 I.C.C. 238.

approved reluctantly, holding that less of public injury will follow the approval of a plan that is objectionable in part than will result from a continuation of the receivership. Such a situation is highly unsatisfactory, and, while the Commission has urged earlier cooperation by reorganization committees, the only effective remedy seems to be to make statutory provision for Commission participation in an advisory capacity, at least, in the formulation of plans. Such participation would tend, in the long run, to benefit all interests, for recurrent receiverships resulting from the proposal and enforced acceptance of unsound reorganization plans are as prejudicial to investor as to shipping public.

A second problem incident to reorganization has to do with handling the costs of reorganization. Though believing that the capitalization of such costs by the new company is of questionable wisdom, the Commission has none the less approved such action where the costs have been shown to be "necessary and reasonable." Its belief, however, is that "costs incurred on account of creditors' and protective committees should be borne by the parties concerned." And a third problem raised by reorganization has to do with the compensation of reorganization managers and counsel. Such compensation has been traditionally generous and too often so generous as to raise questions of good faith. Yet it seems clear that, as the law stands, the Commission can do no more than to voice a protest: power to protect those with an immediate financial interest, as well as the shipper, is lacking.[1]

Miscellaneous Problems.—In addition to the major problems that have been mentioned and the questions that have arisen collateral thereto, certain other matters of such interest as to merit brief comment have demanded settlement. The issuance of short-time notes in excess of 5 per cent of the outstanding capitalization is deprecated by the Commission except in the face of unusual circumstances: such high-cost issues should give place to obligations of longer term. While the law makes specific provision for representation by interested states upon applications for the issuance of securities, it appears that a hearing may be demanded by no others. In a case involving this point, the court declared, "under the terms of the Act only authorities of the states through which the carrier passes can object to the issuance of new securities."[2]

General or blanket authority to pledge securities in its possession as collateral for the issuance of short-time notes as and when needed has been denied, the Commission asserting the law requires that each proposal

[1] In the Missouri, Kansas, and Texas reorganization the Commission, by consent, was permitted to fix appropriate reorganization fees, cutting the asked total of $2,364,249.79 to $1,500,000 (76 I.C.C. 84). However, in an effort to cut the fees of the reorganization managers in the Chicago, Milwaukee and St. Paul case (131 I.C.C. 698; 138 I.C.C. 291), the Commission met defeat upon appeal by the managers to the United States Supreme Court (282 U. S. 311).

[2] *Miller v. United States*, 277 Fed. 95.

be investigated—with the decision to rest upon the facts. Strict compliance with the provision that all securities issued, except as provided in the Act, be approved by it has been demanded by the Commission: an issue of bonds was voided in one instance and in another the cancellation of seven shares of stock, issued as qualifying shares to directors chosen, was ordered. And it has become accepted practice for those in charge of properties in receivership to apply for approval for the issuance of receiver's certificates.

Attitudes toward Security Regulation.—There was a striking unanimity among the plans urged for the "solution of the railway problem" prior to the passage of the Transportation Act upon the matter of security regulation. Nevertheless, there was opposition by some to this extension of governmental authority and serious doubts entertained by others. Perhaps the adverse arguments that were given greatest weight were three: that approval of an issue by a governmental body would give to the investor an unwarranted confidence in it; that such regulation would result in intrusion by the Commission into the field of management; and that governmental control would impede the issuance of securities at the particular time when they could be marketed to best advantage. This last-stated argument has proved to be ungrounded, however, and there is no evidence that authorization by the Commission has caused the investor to become more unwary than he has been in the past. The only point at which significant criticism has appeared is where Commission policy has come into conflict with management. Dictation of the price of issue as well as of the type of security to be offered has stirred the resentment of many railway leaders as well as of certain banking interests. The criticism of these same groups has also been directed against the Commission's emphasis upon "competitive bidding" and that body's close scrutiny of banker-railway relations. Yet those relations in the past have not been so free of abuses and so marked by altruistic service of the one to the other that undisturbed continuance merits entire public confidence. Nor has management been so free of errors in judgment or so scrupulously concerned with the protection of all interests that sharp criticism can be levied against the Commission for alleged trespasses in that field. True it is that, under unwise or grasping leadership, the Commission might err seriously; but, until it has and the need arises therefrom for the establishment of statutory limitations upon its activities, the law may well remain unchanged—providing, as it does, greater assurance to both the investor and the rate-paying public.

General Conclusion.—Among the more important criticisms and charges that led to the inclusion of security regulation in the Transportation Act were the overcapitalization of railway properties, the exploitation of the investor by those in control of a property, and such a lack of uniformity among state statutes and policies as to make other than federal control little more than a farce. Exclusive jurisdiction over all issues by the Interstate Commerce Commission has met the one situation effectively and its administration of the law gives every evidence that the future holds slight danger from the others named. While the Commission has in no sense become a crusader, seeking within a brief span to remedy abuses that developed through scores of years, that body has exercised great care to prevent further overcapitalization; yet, in its admonition to certain railways that capital structure be improved if further aid from the Reconstruction Finance Corporation were desired, there is indication of a purpose to deal with the past as well as with the future. Furthermore, there is no suggestion of Commission approval of any financial adjustment or arrangement that involves the unfair treatment by management of minority interests or of majority interests not actively in control; indeed, there are on record several instances of refusal to approve certain managerial policies because prejudice was likely to result.

Considered by and large, the regulation of security issues by the Interstate Commerce Commission under Sec. 20*a* justifies approval: in no other aspect of its work, perhaps, have the interests of all been more effectively furthered and conserved. The shipping public begins to think less of "rates fixed to provide dividends upon watered stock"; the prospective investor has greater confidence in the issues that lie before him; and those in possession of railway securities are reasonably assured that the value of those issues will not be destroyed by manipulation and fraud engineered by insiders, however much such issues may be endangered by a changing transportation world. And the railway, during a period when carrier credit has been in need of every possible support, has benefited from this increased investor confidence and diminished public hostility. Federal regulation of railway security issues has accomplished even more, rather than less, than was expected of it by its proponents.

REFERENCES

Bonbright, James C.: *Railroad Capitalization*, Columbia University, 1920.

Baumgartner, A. C.: *Railway Security Regulation by the Interstate Commerce Commission Since* 1920, unpublished thesis, University of Iowa, 1932.

Cleveland, F. A., and F. W. Powell: *Railroad Finance*, D. Appleton & Company, 1912.

———: *Railroad Promotion and Capitalization*, Longmans, Green & Co., 1909.

Daggett, Stuart: *Railroad Reorganization*, Harvard University Press, 1908.

———: *Principles of Inland Transportation*, Harper & Brothers, 1928.

Dixon, F. H.: *Railroads and Government*, Charles Scribner's Sons, 1922.

Frederick, J. H.: *Federal Regulation of Railway Securities under the Transportation Act of* 1920, University of Pennsylvania, 1927.

Interstate Commerce Commission: *Annual Reports; Reports.*

Johnson, E. R., and T. W. Van Metre: *Principles of Railroad Transportation*, D. Appleton & Company, 1921.

Jones, Eliot: *Principles of Railway Transportation*, The Macmillan Company, 1924.

KENNEDY, RALPH D.: *The Regulation of Railroad Securities by the Interstate Commerce Commission*, unpublished paper, University of Iowa.

Report of Industrial Commission, vol. 19, pp. 397–419 (1902).

Report of Railroad Securities Commission to Congress (1911).

RIPLEY, W. Z.: *Railroads: Finance and Organization*, Longmans, Green & Co., 1915.

———: *Railway Problems*, Ginn & Company, 1913.

———: *Trusts, Pools, and Corporations*, Ginn & Company, 1905.

SAKOLSKI, A. M.: *American Railroad Economics*, The Macmillan Company, 1916.

VANDERBLUE, HOMER, and KENNETH BURGESS: *Railroads*, The Macmillan Company, 1923.

Interesting material dealing with the regulation of railway security issues prior to 1920 will be found in the records of certain state commissions—Massachusetts, New York, Wisconsin, Texas, California, and Washington being noteworthy. Since 1920 the *Annual Reports* and the *Reports* of the Interstate Commerce Commission contain the record of such regulation.

Chapter XXIX

AN ANALYSIS OF RAILWAY FINANCIAL DATA

THE financial importance of the railway business is evidenced by the enormous investment in plants devoted to public service. It is also shown by the large sums of money received and disbursed annually by those carriers. These sums were relatively great in years past, but they have increased in an almost phenomenal manner in the course of the last 20 years, due both to an increase in the volume of traffic and to the sharp upward movement of the general rate level from 1917 to 1920. In the discussion of railway revenues and expenditures following, attention is first directed toward the sources and amounts of revenue, then to the channels through which outlays flow. Finally, the distribution is indicated of those sums remaining to the railway after operating costs have been met and the effect noted of that distribution upon the market position of railway securities.

Sources of Railway Revenue.—Railway revenues are derived primarily from carrier operations—from the movement of traffic and from activities immediately incident thereto. The classification of operating revenues prescribed by the Interstate Commerce Commission for steam railways divides these operating revenues into four groups of which the first and most important is rail-line transportation revenue, which constitutes approximately 97.5 per cent of the total operating revenue. The second grouping, which comprises all water-line transportation revenue accounts, is quite unimportant, yielding little more than 0.5 per cent. From the third group, incidental operating revenue, is derived slightly in excess of 2 per cent of gross operating revenue. Joint-facility operating revenue constitutes the fourth and a negligible group. A statement of operating revenues for Class I carriers for the years ending Dec. 31, 1930 and 1922, also June 30, 1914, appears in Table XXII accompanying.[1]

Revenue Variations between Individual Roads.—A consolidated revenue statement for Class I railways of the United States, such as that accompanying, does not reflect, however, the sometimes wide variations in particular types of traffic which exist between different sections of the

[1] The years of 1930, 1922, and 1914 have been chosen for reasons that seem adequate. Railway financial and traffic data for 1931 are so out of line with preceding years as to make them misrepresentative of any normal situation, while 1929 was abnormal as a peak year. The year 1914 was quite typical of the prewar period and 1922, the midpoint of the extremes chosen, is fairly comparable to 1930 and 1914 from the standpoint of general economic activity.

country and between individual roads. Among Eastern, Southern, and Western Districts the proportion of the total operating revenue derived from freight varied rather widely from the 1930 percentage of 77 for all Class I roads—from 73.5 per cent in Eastern to 82.5 per cent in Southern. The proportion which passenger revenue contributed to the total in each of the several districts also varied widely—from 10.5 per cent in Southern to 17 per cent in Eastern, compared with an average of 14 per cent for all Class I railways of the United States. The proportions contributed by mail and express also vary markedly as among districts, and the same is true of incidental revenues. The great variations are found among the more specialized areas and among the individual roads, however, the data in Table XXIII indicating the wide differences in the proportion of freight and passenger revenues to total operating revenue for selected properties in 1930.

TABLE XXII.—OPERATING REVENUES, CLASS I RAILWAYS*

Sources of revenue	1930		1922		1914	
	Amount	Percentage of total	Amount	Percentage of total	Amount	Percentage of total
Freight	$4,075,698,241	77.17	$3,992,441,331	71.82	$2,059,891,935	69.36
Passenger	728,487,762	13.79	1,074,108,060	19.32	683,748,602	23.02
Excess baggage	4,195,940	0.08	8,407,251	0.15	7,340,859	0.25
Sleeping car	853,742	0.02	2,567,865	0.05	663,204	0.02
Parlor and chair car	1,019,099	0.02	1,304,844	0.02		
Mail	111,449,602	2.11	90,963,715	1.63	53,965,955	1.82
Express	114,664,168	2.17	143,265,115	2.58	74,416,658	2.50
Other passenger train	12,983,194	0.25	11,327,762	0.20	6,201,406	0.21
Milk	32,236,075	0.61	32,647,401	0.59	9,371,952	0.32
Switching	57,591,037	1.09	54,970,539	0.99	31,702,701	1.07
All other rail line	10,066,030	0.19	12,714,584	0.23	8,588,425	0.29
Total rail-line transportation revenue	5,149,244,890	97.50	5,424,718,467	97.58	2,935,891,697	98.86
Total water line	8,958,996	0.17	15,721,366	0.28	†	†
Total incidental	113,036,517	2.14	110,380,455	1.99	31,602,437	1.06
Total joint facility	9,956,467	0.19	8,272,150	0.15	2,404,704	0.08
Total operating revenue	$5,281,196,870	100.00	$5,559,092,708	100.00	$2,969,898,838	100.00

* This table and all others in Chapter XXIX, except as otherwise noted, based upon Interstate Commerce Commission, *Statistics of Railways in the United States.*

† Included with rail-line revenues. No differentiation made.

Nonoperating Income.—In addition, however, to the large revenues received from operation, the railways of the United States have an important nonoperating income. This income accrues largely from the ownership of the securities of other railways and of noncarrier properties. Other important sources of nonoperating income are rent of equipment in the use of other lines and payments made by one railway to another

Table XXIII.—Amounts Received by Selected Railways from Freight and from Passenger Revenues and Total Operating Revenues, 1930*

Name of railway	Freight	Passenger	Total, including miscellaneous	Ratio, freight to passenger
Detroit, Toledo, and Ironton	$ 9,934,468	$ 19,423	$ 10,163,777	511.00
Bessemer and Lake Erie	14,458,741	55,554	14,712,458	260.00
Duluth, Missabe, and Northern	18,450,908	74,878	21,007,438	246.00
Western Maryland	16,599,264	171,606	17,792,694	97.00
Virginian	16,210,622	246,277	17,455,269	66.00
Norfolk and Western	93,168,819	3,869,012	100,530,458	24.00
New York, Chicago, and St. Louis	42,730,002	1,985,385	46,533,185	22.00
Baltimore and Ohio	173,706,337	18,567,622	206,660,435	9.36
Lehigh Valley	50,287,945	5,512,486	60,664,188	9.12
Northern Pacific	65,135,270	7,727,955	80,642,412	8.43
Union Pacific	86,621,720	12,305,458	108,345,285	7.03
Illinois Central	117,232,122	19,385,264	148,455,905	6.05
Atchison, Topeka, and Sante Fe	139,884,059	28,539,138	185,261,863	4.90
Pennsylvania	401,514,573	115,372,527	574,446,955	3.48
New York Central	307,177,576	111,184,744	478,918,350	2.76
Boston and Maine	45,241,697	14,399,500	69,278,336	3.14
Richmond, Fredericksburg, and Potomac	5,173,679	3,161,889	10,343,439	1.64
New York, New Haven, and Hartford	62,857,804	42,274,947	118,885,515	1.49
Atlantic City	1,301,733	1,515,895	3,046,203	0.86
Long Island	10,487,667	27,070,147	39,596,434	0.387

* *Railway Age*, vol. 90, pp. 340–345.

Table XXIV.—Nonoperating Income, Class I Railways

Item	1930	1922	1914
Hire of freight cars—credit balance; Rent from locomotives; Rent from other equipment	$ 48,070,475	$ 50,512,020	$ 5,743,464
Joint-facility rent income	40,807,390	32,386,390	10,109,696
Income from lease of road	5,572,342	6,010,528	623,219
Miscellaneous rent income	25,200,905	15,763,857	4,548,252
Miscellaneous nonoperating property	7,520,397	4,880,328	4,810,446
Separately owned property—profit	12,925,711	1,431,933	1,654,025
Dividend income	181,927,599	133,559,828	57,403,395
Income from funded securities	77,309,081	64,185,435	8,124,535
Unfunded securities and accounts	34,188,287	28,426,196	10,885,032
Sinking and other reserve funds	4,840,019	3,961,540	1,772,024
Release of premium on funded debt	68,850	110,440	35,011
Contribution from other companies	4,396,009	5,864,312	4,962,022
Miscellaneous income	4,937,037	535,855	1,740,606
Total	$447,764,102	$347,628,662	$112,381,727

for the joint use of certain facilities. That a better conception of the nature and magnitude of nonoperating income may be had, in Table XXIV a statement is given of nonoperating receipts of Class I railways for selected years.

Even a casual examination of the record of nonoperating income suggests its importance. And a comparison of the sums derived from various sources is suggestive of the integration of railway properties that proceeded steadily in the years between 1914 and 1930. It should be noted, however, that the item of dividend income is somewhat exaggerated throughout because of certain duplications. The table gives for each year the total figures for all roads; thus dividends received upon stock owned by one road, which are paid in turn to another, will appear twice. No net dividend-income figure is made available.

Importance and Sources of Nonoperating Income.—The proportion which nonoperating income forms of total operating revenues varies among the different districts quite as widely as do the important sources of operating revenue. In 1930 nonoperating income was equal to 8.48 per cent of total railway operating revenues for the United States; for Southern territory the percentage was 6.70, for Eastern 8.25, and for Western 9.54; the amounts were $60,407,829, $194,608,660, and $192,747,613, respectively. That nonoperating income is highly important in many instances is clearly shown by its comparison for particular roads with operating income—the amount remaining from operating revenues after operating expenses, tax accruals, and certain minor items have been deducted. For 1930, a lean operating year, nonoperating income constituted almost 31 per cent of gross. In Table XXV are given figures for certain roads which contributed generously toward this large proportion, together with the most important source of such nonoperating income.

Railway Costs.—The outlays of American railway corporations are of two types: expenses directly incident to the rendition of transportation service, and deductions to cover certain nonoperating costs and fixed charges. Just as revenues are entered by the railways according to classifications prescribed by the Interstate Commerce Commission, so expenses are grouped. The nature of each of various prescribed groups of operating expenses has been explained in a previous chapter, therefore in Table XXVI on page 497 are presented without explanation, for 1914, 1922, and 1930, the sums expended by Class I railways for various purposes and the proportion which the outlay for each group constituted of total operating expenses.

From the percentages given for these years it is evident that, though each item constitutes a relatively constant proportion of total operating expenses, there are, nevertheless, variations in particular groups of expenses. The explanations of such differences, however, are too numerous to receive discussion here—volume of traffic, financial conditions, strikes, even weather, all playing a part.

Greater than in the case of revenue derived from different types of traffic in the three districts are the variations in the proportion which operating expenses bear to operating revenue. In 1930 Class I railways spent 74.43 per cent of their total operating revenues in rendering carrier

TABLE XXV.—OPERATING, NONOPERATING, AND GROSS INCOME OF VARIOUS RAILWAYS WITH MOST IMPORTANT ITEM OF NONOPERATING INCOME, 1930

Name of road	Most important item of nonoperating income	Nonoperating income	Operating income	Gross income
Grand Trunk Western	dividend income	$ 2,571,168	$ 1,703,874	$ 4,275,042
Northern Pacific	dividend income	22,882,104	10,408,818	33,290,922
Erie	dividend income	8,001,882	14,738,818	22,740,700
Great Northern	dividend income	16,945,463	23,707,755	40,653,218
New Orleans, Texas, and Mexico	funded securities	2,849,080	597,034	3,446,114
New York, New Haven, and Hartford	dividend income	9,809,147	32,190,312	41,999,459
Southern Pacific	dividend income	43,949,481	40,173,274	84,122,755
Atlantic Coast Line	dividend income	7,478,871	7,779,646	15,258,517
Pennsylvania	dividend income	60,716,370	107,473,167	168,189,537
Union Pacific	dividend income	26,256,294	29,573,254	55,829,548
New York Central	dividend income	50,047,851	68,090,281	118,138,132
Pittsburgh and Lake Erie	hire of freight cars—credit balance	4,943,392	4,116,422	9,059,814
Colorado and Southern	dividend income	3,486,411	1,647,536	5,133,947
Atchison, Topeka, and Santa Fe.	income from funded securities	15,809,201	38,831,969	54,641,170
International-Great Northern.	rent from locomotives	1,141,897	1,687,042	2,828,939
Duluth, Winnipeg, and Pacific.	contribution from other companies	1,804,877	43,466 (deficit)	1,761,411

service, the range for major districts being from 73.04 per cent for Western to 75.99 per cent for Eastern. In 1922, however, the operating ratio of Class I railways in the Eastern district was 81.85 per cent, in the Southern 74.43 per cent, and in the Western 77.38 per cent. This variation between districts is notable in other years as well: in 1920 the gap was yet wider, the percentages being 99.37, 99.44, and 89.16 respectively. Still more striking differences are to be found among individual roads, the ratio of operating expenses to operating revenues for 1930 being as high as 105–115 per cent for a few unfortunate lines and as low, on the other hand, as 60–65 per cent for the more happily situated and more efficiently operated properties.

Table XXVI.—Operating Expenses, Class I Railways

Items	1930	Per-cent-age	1922	Per-cent-age	1914	Per-cent-age
Maintenance of way and structure	$ 705,470,940	17.95	$ 728,663,534	16.506	$ 403,682,593	18.866
Maintenance of equipment	1,019,265,278	25.93	1,252,517,250	28.373	520,200,274	24.311
Traffic	127,833,478	3.25	86,506,907	1.959	62,366,351	2.914
Transportation—rail line	1,841,728,165	46.85	2,140,149,596	48.480	1,073,981,380	50.192
Transportation—water line	6,455,275	0.16	9,614,227	0.218		
Miscellaneous	52,140,923	1.33	47,653,795	1.079		
General	191,237,312	4.86	156,705,481	3.550	79,525,390	3.717
Transportation for investment—credit	13,202,684	0.33	7,288,456	0.165		
Total operating expense	$3,930,928,687	100.00	$4,414,522,334	100.000	$2,139,755,988	100.000
Operating ratio	....	74.43	....	79.41	....	72.048

Net Income.—To arrive at net income it is necessary to deduct certain items from the sum of operating and nonoperating income, or gross, as it is termed. The most important of these, as shown in Table XXVII, is interest on funded debt; rent for leased roads constitutes the second most important item, this "use cost" being approximately one-third the amount of the interest charges. Incidentally, the material increase in the outlay for lease of lines shows the extent to which the lease has been employed during late years to effect the consolidation of properties. Other important deductions cover joint-facility rents and the rental cost of equipment used but not owned. Of the latter, hire of freight and passenger cars are the important items, a significant portion of this outlay representing payments to private-car lines. The total deductions made from gross income for selected years, together with the amounts of the more important items, appear in Table XXVII below.

Table XXVII.—Deductions from Gross Income, Class I Railways; Important Subheadings and Totals

Account	1930	1922	1914
Hire of freight cars—debit balance	$113,659,907	$ 77,785,533	$ 36,084,056 (both items)
Rent for passenger-train cars	20,155,587	17,587,971	
Joint-facility rents	72,837,038	54,728,699	4,577,012
Rent for leased roads	170,657,043	144,640,039	123,179,765
Interest on funded debt	496,264,358	457,893,803	385,690,578
Interest on unfunded debt	12,467,383	24,424,277	40,749,516
Total (including items not listed)	$924,528,827	$820,418,262	$645,312,783

Deductions from gross income vary widely among individual properties, due largely to differences in financial structure. Heavily bonded properties, or properties which operate a considerable mileage of leased lines, must set aside large sums annually to meet the resulting obligations. On the other hand, properties owned almost wholly by the operating company and but lightly burdened with funded debt find it necessary to deduct a relatively small sum from gross income to arrive at net. And it is net income which is of peculiar concern to management: it is net income that is available for distribution at will. Not only do the total deductions from gross income vary among individual roads but the proportions which individual items form of the total also differ widely. This variation is particularly marked among roads with respect to the items of hire of freight cars—debit balance, rent for leased roads, and interest on unfunded debt. Individual items vary greatly between the major territories, too, and there is a wide difference between them in the percentage of total operating income which total deductions form; in 1930 this percentage for Southern territory was about 76, for Western 95, and for Eastern 97. Had it not been for large nonoperating incomes in the two districts last named, the situation of the carriers operating therein would have been precarious.

Disposition of Net Income.—With various expenses met and deductions made, railway management is free to distribute the remainder, termed net income, in whatever manner it sees fit. Conservative policy often dictates the retention by the enterprise of an important part of this net income, but the claims of stockholders for a return upon their holdings cannot be long ignored when adequate funds are available. Disposition of net income for Class I railways of the United States for different years is indicated in Table XXVIII below.

TABLE XXVIII.—DISPOSITION OF NET INCOME, CLASS I RAILWAYS

Accounts	1930	1922	1914
Income applied to sinking and other reserve funds	$ 7,906,592	$ 9,759,485	$ 10,620,520
Dividend appropriations of income	172,238,375	176,858,099	215,455,542
Stock discount extinguished through income			
Miscellaneous appropriations of income	1,068,859	9,729,684	1,988,859
Income appropriations for investment in physical property	479,138	6,397,024	28,798,194
Total appropriations of income	$181,692,964	$202,744,292	$256,863,115
Income balance transferred to profit and loss	$342,214,508	$166,829,140	$ 93,858,503

The disposition of railway net income measures with considerable accuracy the character of the management: liberal appropriations for physical property and to surplus always indicate a conservatism which promises well for the investor, present and prospective, and for those dependent upon the particular carrier for service, while a contrary policy bodes ill for the future.

Movement of Total Revenues and Expenses.—The trend of total railway revenues and expenses in total and per mile of line for the United States has long been distinctly upward, though a study of the data following indicates that expenses have risen more rapidly than have revenues: the former increased from 1905 to 1931 by approximately 105 per cent, the latter by only 80 per cent. This shift is clearly shown by the ratio which operating expenses have borne, year by year, to operating revenue, that percentage rising from 60–70 prior to 1913 to 94 in 1920. During the past decade the operating ratio declined rather steadily but, with the marked decrease in revenues beginning in 1930 it has again

TABLE XXIX.—MOVEMENT OF REVENUES AND EXPENSES OF THE RAILWAYS OF THE UNITED STATES, 1905–1931

Year	Total		Ratio	Per mile of road	
	Operating revenues	Operating expense		Operating revenue	Operating expense
1931*	$4,188,343,244	$3,223,574,616	76.97	$17,295	$13,311
1930*	5,281,196,870	3,930,928,670	74.38	21,809	16,191
1929*	6,279,520,544	4,506,056,262	71.70	25,993	18,596
1928*	6,111,735,511	4,427,995,036	72.40	25,450	18,380
1927*	6,136,300,270	4,574,177,821	74.50	25,783	19,159
1926*	6,382,939,546	4,669,336,736	73.12	26,975	19,673
1925*	6,122,509,856	4,536,880,291	74.04	25,879	19,115
1924*	5,921,496,325	4,507,885,037	76.08	25,144	19,079
1923*	6,289,580,027	4,895,166,819	77.79	26,743	20,814
1922*	5,559,092,708	4,414,522,334	79.41	23,657	18,786
1921*	5,516,556,455	4,562,668,302	82.71	23,533	19,464
1920*	6,178,438,459	5,827,591,146	94.38	26,327	24,846
1919*	5,143,589,998	4,398,408,414	85.51	22,022	18,732
1918*	4,880,953,470	3,982,068,197	81.35	20,872	16,980
1917	4,178,784,652	2,956,770,809	70.44	17,234	12,140
1916	3,691,065,217	2,426,250,521	65.73	14,344	9,429
1915	2,956,193,202	2,088,682,956	70.66	11,827	8,341
1914†	3,047,019,908	2,200,313,159	72.22	12,387	8,944
1913†	3,125,135,798	2,169,968,924	69.44	12,859	8,929
1912	2,842,695,382	1,972,415,776	69.31	11,849	8,212
1911	2,789,761,669	1,915,054,005	68.59	11,833	8,116
1910	2,750,667,538	1,822,630,433	66.29	11,553	7,658
1909	2,418,677,538	1,599,443,410	66.16	10,356	6,851
1908	2,393,805,989	1,669,547,846	69.75	10,491	7,320
1907	2,580,105,578	1,748,515,814	67.53	11,383	7,687
1906	2,325,765,167	1,536,877,271	66.08	10,460	6,922
1905	2,082,492,406	1,390,602,152	66.78	9,598	6,489

* Class I only.

† Class I and II only.

risen sharply. It might be expected to stabilize between 72 and 75 per cent, but of this there can be no assurance. This movement of operating revenues and expenses since 1905 for the railways of the United States, aggregate and per mile of line, also of the operating ratio, is shown in Table XXIX on the preceding page.

The much more rapid increase of expenses than of revenues is due to various factors, most important of which are the increased cost of labor and material and the mounting tax burden. Had it not been for tremendous advances in railway efficiency, particularly in the heavier loading of both trains and cars, the gain shown by expenses upon revenues would have been even more marked. To give an idea of the increase in the relative cost to the railways during recent years of each of the various groups of expense items, the data in Table XXX are presented.

TABLE XXX.—DISTRIBUTION OF RAILWAY OPERATING REVENUES EXPRESSED IN CENTS PER DOLLAR OF OPERATING REVENUE, CLASS I CARRIERS*

Item	1912†	1916†	1920	1924	1928	1931
Labor (salaries and wages)	40.1	41.0	55.4	44.3	43.0	46.4
Fuel	8.0	7.8	10.9	7.4	5.8	5.3
Material	16.8	18.2	22.1	19.1	18.1	25.3 (Material, loss and damage, depreciation combined)
Loss and damage, injuries to persons and insurance	2.4	2.7	3.6	1.8	1.6	
Depreciation and retirements	2.5	3.0	2.3	3.5	3.9	
Taxes	3.0	4.5	4.4	5.8	6.4	7.2
Hire of equipment, joint-facility net rentals	1.0	1.0	1.0	1.7	2.0	3.2
Total expenses and taxes	74.7	78.2	99.7	83.6	80.9	87.4
Net railway operating profit	25.3	21.8	0.3	16.4	19.2	12.6

* Bureau of Railway Economics.
† Fiscal year ending June 30.

Importance Assigned the Operating Ratio.—In the discussion preceding, attention has been called to the importance, as a measure of the efficiency of railway operations, of the relation of operating expenses to operating revenues. This relation, expressed in the form of a percentage, is known as the operating ratio, and, because of the importance attached to it by students of the railway as an index both of efficiency of operation and of the desirability of railway securities from the investor's point of view, a critical analysis of its worth may well be made. Assuredly, a dependable index of efficiency of operation and of financial soundness would possess high value, both to officials charged with the management of the property and to holders of securities, be they actual or prospective. The operating ratio has long been regarded by many as such an index; to it has been accorded a deference due only to things infallible. This ratio, as computed for various operating divisions and for the property as a whole, has been used by the officers of that property to measure the relative efficiency of the administration of various portions of the property during a particular period, and of the property as a whole for one period as compared with another; investors have ordered their buying and selling of railway securities upon its downward or upward movement. Yet a careful analysis of the situation makes necessary the acceptance of this ratio even by operating officials with certain reservations, and the investor seems justified in placing but slight confidence in a figure which expresses a mere mathematical relation.

Evaluation of Operating Ratio.—An evaluation of the operating ratio as an index shows that three distinct limitations must be recognized. The first and perhaps the most important of these develops from variations in standards of maintenance. Maintenance expenditures normally constitute about two-fifths of total operating expenses, but for a period of time it is possible deliberately to skimp maintenance without depreciation of the physical property being apparent to the casual investigator or reflected in the service rendered. Indeed, it is difficult for those closely associated with the property to follow an absolutely constant maintenance policy from year to year, even though such a policy might be desired. So, though operating officials will be cognizant of any definite change in the maintenance policy and measurably certain of the actual condition of the property at a given time, those beyond the inner circle not only fail to discern slight variations but often fail to discover that a property is being "skinned" until it has depreciated to a point of danger. Because of the maintenance factor, therefore, even the operating official, familiar with the maintenance policy of a property, and knowing of definite changes in it from time to time, must accept the operating ratio with reservations; the investor, acquainted with neither the policy nor the physical property, can place but little reliance upon it.

A second important limitation in the use of the operating ratio as an index of comparative financial soundness lies in the variations among roads in net returns from outside investments. One road, with a high operating ratio, may enjoy a large income from outside investments, thus making the property superior as an investment to another which has a lower operating ratio but enjoys practically no income from other sources. A third limitation arises from wide variations in the capitalization burden borne by various properties. If two properties be assumed to have relatively the same revenue per mile of line from operations and be assumed also to have relatively equal operating ratios, it is clear that, if one property has a low capitalization as compared with the other, there is a proportionate difference in the investment soundness of the two. Particularly is this true if a large portion of this higher capitalization is in the form of bonds, imposing a heavy burden of fixed charges.

In brief, it may be said of the operating ratio that, although it possesses some value as an index of efficiency and of financial situation, its major worth is to those closely associated with the property. To use it as an investment guide is quite without justification. Its upward movement cannot be welcomed by the railways, yet as long as the absolute amount remaining to them tends to increase, serious alarm should not be felt. Reduction of this ratio to the minimum figure consistent with the efficient longtime operation of a property should and will remain the goal of wise operating officials, and any property which finds itself showing an abnormal ratio through a series of years may well search out causes carefully, even though that ratio might not, because of large outside investments or low capitalization, imperil the financial soundness of the corporation.

Trend of the Operating Ratio.—An examination of the trend of the operating ratio for American railways as a whole during years past shows a gradual but nevertheless noticeable increase up to the period of the recent war. During that period the operating ratio increased sharply, due to various causes, chief among which were a rapidly rising price level, a lessened efficiency occasioned by the psychology of the period, and the congestion of traffic. With the return of properties to private operation and the general movement toward "normalcy," this ratio has tended downward. To expect it to drop back, however, to the characteristic figure of 60 to 70 per cent which governed from 1900 to 1913 is scarcely reasonable. The individual road that attains and maintains a normal operating ratio of 65 per cent in the future will be as outstanding in its position as were those properties which, during an earlier period, attained ratios approximating 55 per cent. In fact, the only way in which the older level can be approximately regained is not only through the maximum efficient use of the existing plant but also by the expenditure of billions of dollars for additions and betterments that railway operations may be put upon an even higher level of efficiency in areas where traffic demands press upon transportation facilities. Yet this will cause a heavy increase in fixed charges, perhaps sufficient to offset the gain.

Interest on Railway Bonds.—As has already been indicated, interest payments made by railways upon funded and unfunded obligations are deducted from gross income in the process of ascertaining net. Unfortunately, gross income is not always sufficiently large in the case of all carriers to meet such interest payments, though that situation happily became less common with the economic development of the country. When such payments are not met, the normal consequence is receivership. However, because such defaulted credit obligations are sometimes held by friendly interests, or are held by interests which feel such confidence in the management that they believe their position already protected as adequately as possible under existing traffic conditions, a railway property may continue to operate through its corporate organization, even though failing to meet interest payments.

The rate of interest upon bonds varies widely. Few such issues draw less than 3 per cent and relatively few excepting those floated during periods of "tight money" bear in excess of 6 per cent; if a property is so situated as to make it difficult to float at par an issue bearing 6 per cent, a discount will often be accepted rather than exceed that figure greatly. Only upon bonds bearing a contingent return, such as income and debenture issues, does the usual rate exceed 5 per cent, the rate upon such paper being from 6 to 7 per cent. The total outstanding issue of American railway bonds bears an average interest rate of approximately 4.8 per cent, the individual rate depending upon the security back of the bonds, the general credit of the corporation, the condition of the market, the price at which offered, and other factors of lesser importance.

Dividends on Stock.—Dividends paid upon the stocks of American railway corporations must come out of the net income for the year, from accumulated surplus, or, in part, from both. Because of conditions surrounding and governing the issuance of railway stock during almost the first 75 years of railway development, it is not strange that dividends upon certain issues were infrequent and modest in amount. Table XXXI on page 504 shows for the entire period for which definite statistics are available a gradual improvement of the situation, an improvement evidenced not only in the amount of stock upon which dividends were paid but also an increase in both the average rate on dividend-yielding stock and the ratio of dividends declared to all stock outstanding. This improvement, however, has progressed irregularly: from an abnormally low point in the years 1895–1897 there is evident an almost unbroken advance until the depression of 1907 was reflected in railway earnings; then, following several good years, the record is mixed until the immediate postwar period. In 1923 an advance began which continued steadily until, in 1930, the railway net made perhaps the best showing in its history in percentage of stock yielding dividends (76.93), in amount of stock yielding dividends ($7,702,020,553), and in the ratio of dividends declared to all stock (6.02). This excellent showing was the consequence of a series of years of heavy traffic and increasing efficiency, but the reserves accumulated during these years were wholly inadequate to permit the maintenance of dividends in 1931 by carriers possessing even moderate financial strength, while at the close of 1932 the number of railways paying dividends had been reduced to a point not approached since the middle nineties and perhaps not then equaled.

Such a situation is most disturbing, and even more to those who appreciate the vital part that the railway must continue to have in the transportation of goods in the United States than to others who have thus far failed to analyze the nation's transportation problem. None the less, it is easy to look through the glass darkly during a period of distress, forgetting that the sharp increase in tonnage, which even a modest revival

Table XXXI.—Amount and Percentage of Capital Stock upon Which Dividends Were Declared and Average Rate of Dividends Declared, 1888–1931

Year ended	Percentage of stock yielding dividends	Amount of stock yielding dividends	Average rate on dividend-yielding stock	Ratio of dividends declared to all stock
Dec. 31, 1931	73.20	$7,325,664,369	5.48	4.01
Dec. 31, 1930	76.93	7,702,020,553	7.83	6.02
Dec. 31, 1929	76.23	7,506,264,973	7.47	5.70
Dec. 31, 1928	73.65	7,159,988,649	7.12	5.25
Dec. 31, 1927	70.25	6,701,427,315	8.47	5.95
Dec. 31, 1926	69.12	6,473,279,913	7.32	5.06
Dec. 31, 1925	66.70	6,278,531,563	6.52	4.35
Dec. 31, 1924	64.97	6,042,267,916	6.37	4.14
Dec. 31, 1923	62.09	5,646,076,157	7.30	4.53
Dec. 31, 1922	59.38	5,321,347,138	6.37	3.78
Dec. 31, 1921	56.92	5,059,843,975	9.02†	5.13
Dec. 31, 1920	57.30	5,075,039,642	6.52	3.74
Dec. 31, 1919	59.64	5,298,320,617	6.33	3.77
Dec. 31, 1918	58.09	5,138,851,230	6.60	3.83
Dec. 31, 1917	62.32	5,610,774,033	6.81	4.24
Dec. 31, 1916	62.02	5,430,123,235	6.75	4.19
June 30, 1916	60.38	5,279,427,954	6.48	3.91
June 30, 1915	60.45	5,219,846,562	6.29	3.80
June 30, 1914	64.39	5,667,072,956	7.97	5.13
June 30, 1913	66.14	5,780,982,416	6.37	4.22
June 30, 1912	64.73	5,581,289,249	7.17	4.64
June 30, 1911	67.65	5,730,250,326	8.03	5.42
June 30, 1910	66.71	5,412,578,457	7.50	5.00
June 30, 1909	64.01	4,920,174,118	6.53	4.18
June 30, 1908	65.69	4,843,370,740	8.07	5.30
June 30, 1907*	67.27	4,948,756,203	6.23	4.19
June 30, 1906	66.54	4,526,958,760	6.03	4.01
June 30, 1905	62.84	4,119,086,714	5.78	3.63
June 30, 1904	57.47	3,643,427,319	6.09	3.50
June 30, 1903	56.06	3,450,737,869	5.70	3.20
June 30, 1902	55.40	3,337,644,681	5.55	3.08
June 30, 1901	51.27	2,977,575,179	5.26	2.70
June 30, 1900	45.66	2,668,969,895	5.23	2.39
June 30, 1899	40.61	2,239,502,545	4.96	2.01
June 30, 1898	33.74	1,818,113,082	5.29	1.78
June 30, 1897	29.90	1,603,549,978	5.43	1.62
June 30, 1896	29.83	1,559,024,075	5.62	1.68
June 30, 1895	29.94	1,485,618,453	5.74	1.72
June 30, 1894	36.57	1,767,925,565	5.40	1.97
June 30, 1893	38.76	1,809,600,846	5.58	2.16
June 30, 1892	39.40	1,825,705,437	5.35	2.11
June 30, 1891	40.36	1,796,390,636	5.07	2.05
June 30, 1890	36.24	1,598,131,933	5.45	1.97
June 30, 1889	38.33	1,629,750,927	5.04	1.93
June 30, 1888	38.56	1,490,267,149	5.38	2.08

* Through this date, returns from switching and terminal companies were included.

† This percentage is high, despite many reductions in dividends in 1921, because of large stock dividends that year by the Delaware, Lackawanna, and Western and the Chicago, Burlington, and Quincy railway companies.

of business activity brings, will make an astonishing change in net operating income. Yet optimism must be tempered with a realization that the railways, with the revival of industry and commerce, will be facing such competition as they have never before known when emerging from like depressions: competition which, unless controlled and directed in public interest, may have unexpected and unwanted social consequences as well as political repercussions.

Individual variations among railways, even those paying dividends regularly, have been wide; certain issues, particularly preferred, have received a return as low as 4 per cent, while a few roads have maintained rates of 8–10 per cent throughout a considerable period of years. In general, however, the rate upon the stock of regular "dividend payers" has been from 6 to 7 per cent, though a few of the stronger roads have restricted payments to as low as 5 per cent while others have paid double that figure. Certain properties have been intermittent dividend payers, though during recent years a property has rarely been added to the dividend-paying class until prospects were reasonably good for the maintenance of such payments, and dividends have rarely been passed entirely except as the property finds itself in imminent danger of financial collapse—as many did in 1931 and 1932 when numerous dividend records of long years' standing were clouded by termination of payments.

Market Status of Railway Securities.—In the paragraphs just preceding and in earlier discussion the general situation of railway securities in the investment market has been indicated and certain weaknesses of those issues suggested. True, stock was often issued during early years at but a fraction of its par value, even offered as a gift to purchasers of bonds to make those issues more attractive by the addition of a speculative opportunity. As the years passed, the increase in the value of railway properties, due to the reinvestment of earnings and to social growth, filled in with solid worth a space once given largely to water. Yet certain factors have persisted that have weakened railway stock in competition with other offerings in the market. With the close regulation of rates the opportunity for large speculative gains in the railway field has disappeared largely and with regulation has come a measure of inflexibility in rates that makes it almost impossible to raise the level of charges promptly to meet emergency needs. These conditions are in sharp contrast to the situation of industrial issues, to the heavy disadvantage of railway stocks. And, in addition to the persistence of certain old disadvantages, new elements of weakness have appeared. The failure of an exceptionally well-organized body of workers to realize effectively their peril and to cooperate fully to the end that railway haulage costs be reduced or that competitive agencies be placed upon a parity with the railways, is as puzzling as it is disturbing to those who believe a modestly prosperous railway net is better suited to serve public interest than are impecunious properties. The rise of other agencies of transport—the motor vehicle, the inland waterway, the pipe line, the airplane, and even the transmission line—has undermined the foundation upon which the prosperity of the railway rests: a heavy and continuing volume of traffic. And this undermining has proceeded so rapidly and so far that public fear of the railway future is perhaps more inimical to the sale of railway stocks than are facts, either present or predictable.

The position of railway bonds in the investment market has been characteristically stronger than that of stocks: the greater security of this type of issue, as to both principal and return, has given it a preference that also has the support of investment traditions. This stronger position of railway bonds has contributed, however, to a high bond ratio and this in turn, as indicated in a previous chapter, has lowered the margin of safety for individual railways. It has also absorbed in a large measure such "slack" as might well have been kept by them for use during more critical periods than were faced generally from 1900 through 1917. The rate of interest upon railway bonds was forced upward during the years of rapid industrial expansion by competition of issues from that source, yet the dominant position of railway bonds in the investment market remained unchallenged until recently. Even before the sharp break in security prices late in 1929, junior issues of the stronger lines and even the underlying issues of certain properties whose promise seemed to grow dim were being eliminated from investment portfolios; since that time the standing of railway bonds has weakened sharply and it now seems indubitable that, even with industrial and financial recovery, those issues will occupy a far less important place in the investment market than in the past except as positive and intelligent steps are taken to strengthen railway enterprise.

Needed Changes to Effect Credit Rehabilitation.—The future position of railway securities in the investment market will depend primarily upon two factors: (1) the rate of return that regulatory bodies are willing to allow upon property devoted to the rendition of railway service, and (2) the effectiveness with which the railways can meet the competition of other transport agencies that now beset it. If the billions of dollars now invested in the physical properties of the railways fail to obtain an adequate return, not only will securities now outstanding depreciate but it will become increasingly difficult to market advantageously new issues that must be sold to keep the railway plant abreast of economic and commercial needs. And, should this latter contingency develop, it is conceivable that government ownership and operation of railways might be forced upon an unwilling public as the only means of continuing an essential service. For this reason, then, it becomes essential that regulatory bodies at all times give consideration not alone to the immediate desires and needs of shippers but also to the fundamental financial requirements of the railway industry. Regulatory commissions have shown an increasing tendency to give weight to these requirements as public understanding of the railway situation has increased and public antagonism toward the railway has declined, yet full justice has not yet been done.

Since, in later chapters, more will be said of the new competition now facing the railways and constituting an increasing threat, only a few brief comments will be offered here. The effectiveness of the railways in dealing with a situation that contrasts sharply with that which existed even a score of years ago will hinge largely upon a certain few matters. Can the railways so modify and adapt their service as to meet the demands of the present period? Can the railways accomplish a reduction of costs that will put rates in line with a materially lower price level and make possible the rendition of high-class service at a lesser price? Will the public become sufficiently alert to the inequalities in competitive opportunity between the railway and certain rival agencies soon enough so that disaster to the older system of transport can be escaped? True, there are many other questions to which satisfactory answers must be given if railway enterprise is to know a future comparable to its past; yet, if favorable answers can be had to the three here propounded, a firm foundation will have been laid for further years of effective public service. And, despite the many physical obstacles and personnel barriers in the way of modernization of service and reduction of costs, there is good reason to believe that railway management will accomplish both. Too, there are indications that public apathy with respect to the inequalities of competition as it now exists is disappearing and in its place is developing a determination that each agency shall "carry its own load" in the struggle. The continuance of subsidies in any form to particular competitors is contrary to our sense of fair play and, in the long run, subversive of broad public interest.

The people seem to be coming slowly yet surely to a realization of the need of acting positively in their own behalf and in behalf of the railways upon the service of which dependence is now and promises to continue great. This progress must continue if the interests of both are not to be imperiled: no effort should be spared by understanding minds to impress upon those who shape public policy the fact that differences between railway and public are less real than their mutuality of interest. Dependent in considerable measure upon public opinion is the attainment of a fair return and an equalization of opportunity in the competitive field. Public opinion, too, can do much to assist railway management in eliminating managerial practices and policies, characteristic of the few rather than the many, which are inimical to the financial success—even good name—of the railways as a whole. And railway management can do much, also, to eliminate bases of public criticism and to engender public support. It is to be hoped that the intelligence and the zeal of each group will be equal to the task in prospect; if not, the integrity of railway capital cannot be maintained and neither can adequate service be offered for an extended period into the future.

REFERENCES

Annual reports of individual railroads.

Bureau of Railway Economics: Miscellaneous studies and reports.

Bureau of Railway News and Statistics: *Railway Statistics of the United States* (annual).

CHAMBERLAIN, L., and G. W. EDWARDS: *The Principles of Bond Investment,* Henry Holt & Company, 1927.

HOOPER, W. E.: *Railroad Accounting,* D. Appleton & Company, 1915.

Interstate Commerce Commission: *Statistics in Railways in the United States.*

KIRSHMAN, JOHN EMMETT: *Principles of Investment,* McGraw-Hill Book Company, Inc., 1933.

LYON, HASTINGS: *Investments,* Houghton, Mifflin Company, 1926.

MOODY, JOHN: *Analyses of Railroad Investments,* Analyses Publishing Company and Moody's Investors Service (annual).

———: *How to Analyze Railroad Reports,* Analyses Publishing Company, 1912.

MUNDY, F. W.: *Earning Power of the Railroads,* James H. Oliphant and Company (annual).

Report of the Industrial Commission, vol. 19, pp. 267–274.

RIPLEY, W. Z.: *Railroads: Finance and Organization,* Longmans, Green & Co., 1915.

SNYDER, C.: *American Railroads as Investments,* The Moody Corporation, 1907.

VAN OSS, S. F.: *American Railroads as Investments,* G. P. Putnam's Sons, 1893.

WOODLOCK, T. F.: *The Anatomy of a Railroad Report and Ton-mile Cost,* Effingham, Wilson and Company, 1895.

Current material on railroad stocks and bonds concerning prices, issues, etc., is to be found in *Annalist; Magazine of Wall Street; Wall Street Journal; Commercial and Financial Chronicle;* and others.

CHAPTER XXX

THEORIES OF RATE MAKING

IN AN earlier chapter dealing with the freight service mention was made of certain theories or governing principles of rate determination which exercise more or less influence upon the actual tariff charge for a particular service. As introductory to a brief comment upon certain rate structures, past and present, and to their evaluation, it is necessary that these theories or principles be further elaborated and analyzed. To this end the nature of each of the various principles will be indicated and an examination made of each to determine the degree to which a rate based upon it conforms to the legal requirement that "all rates be just and reasonable." This legal requirement is itself of a somewhat indefinite character, however: though in theory there is *a* reasonable rate, in reality there seems to exist *a zone of reasonableness* of some width, below which rates must be judged confiscatory and above extortionate.

Need of Sound and Definite Principles.—Sound and definite principles of rate making are desirable from the standpoint of the railway. Without the guidance thus given, a rate structure tends to become but a hodge-podge of individual rates fixed upon the basis of particular conditions rather than a *system* of rates, harmonious and orderly. Without such principles it is difficult to initiate or to modify individual rates because of the absence of any yardstick of justice or reasonableness, and it is equally difficult to satisfy the public as to the fairness of particular rates or of rates as a whole. This need of a definite basis for the determination of rates has become even greater with the development of public control. Regulatory bodies, under obligation to deal justly with individuals and places on the one hand, and with the carriers on the other, must act in accord with some definite principle or policy. While it is conceivable that rate making upon private initiative might follow no definite policy, it is improbable that the public would tolerate an absence of such policy on the part of a body designed to protect its interests. For such a body to navigate the seas of regulation without chart or compass might easily aggravate, rather than lessen, conflict between public and private interests. From the standpoint of the business and of the public it is essential, therefore, that a certain definite principle or principles, subject to such modifications as peculiar conditions may necessitate, be accepted as basic in rate making.

Theories of Rate Determination.—Rate making in the past has been in large measure opportunistic, a result primarily of that gradual development of rate structures which followed the extension of the railway net and the diversification of traffic. It is therefore difficult to discover in rate practice, and to isolate, all governing principles which have operated in the determination of particular rates. Certain definite theories are discernible, nevertheless, which are of sufficient importance in rate-making practice to justify individual treatment. These fall under three main heads, *ability to pay*, *cost*, and *social need*. Of these the ability and the cost principles, the one stressing revenue and the other expense as the basic element in rate determination, are, in every sense, most significant. Either group must take into consideration the other element, however, for maximum revenue does not always yield maximum net return and neither the carrier nor the public can emphasize cost to the exclusion of other considerations.

ABILITY THEORIES

"Value of the Service."—Various rate policies or principles, widely divergent in character and purpose, seem to be included properly under the general head of *ability to pay*. One of these is the so-called value-of-the-service principle. By value of the service is meant, fundamentally, *that amount which the public will pay rather than dispense with the service*, a basis which calls for the absorption by the railway of the entire difference between the value of the goods, independently determined, where they are produced and the value in the distant market. Since, in the long run and under competitive conditions, the value of the product in the market will tend to conform to the expense of producing the marginal portion needed, it may be said that this value of the service to the shipper is the difference between the local expense of production and the value of the product upon the central market. In the short run, however, a yet greater sum may be exacted by the carrier, since the subjective value placed upon goods by a producer for the market may be much less than the expense of production, when those goods are considered solely from the standpoint of their own use. At a particular time, therefore, it would appear that the value of the service may greatly exceed the difference as set forth above. In this connection care must be taken to avoid a fallacy which grows out of the relation of the transportation charge to the value of the product in the market or at the point of production. To say that, because the price of wheat in Chicago is $1 a bushel and at a certain Dakota point is 80 cents a bushel, the value of the service is 20 cents, is to forget entirely that the value of wheat in the Dakotas is based upon the Chicago price—that *the difference is fundamentally the cost of transportation itself*. A higher rate for that particular movement would tend immediately to compel a lower price in the Dakotas while a lower rate under like circumstances would tend to increase the price there. The difference between the price paid in the central market and that paid the producer at a particular time is, in no sense, a certain measure of the value of the service; rather, it represents basically and normally the cost of transportation between the two points at that moment.

In the discussion of the value-of-the-service principle it is generally assumed that the expense of production is uniform. Such is not the case, however, either as among individuals or as among producing areas. For the carrier to prescribe a uniform charge based upon the difference in the value of the product in the central market and the local expense of production—if such a difference could be discovered independently—means, therefore, that a particular producer or a particular locality must be designated as marginal, and rates so fixed as to permit that one to enjoy only necessary profits. This, of course, results in the determination of the location of the margin not by natural competitive action but, rather, in accordance with the self-interest of the carrier; or, if uniform charges are not made, the principle involves the development of discriminatory tariffs, so adjusted as among individuals and as among places as to exact from each enterprise and each locality the maximum which can be taken without driving it from the field, *these exactions being in direct ratio to efficiency of production or advantage of location.* That this principle has actually been used in the determination of rates is attested by many experiences that shippers have had with freight tariffs which have increased as prices rose and have declined with recessions in price.

From the standpoint of the carrier such a system of rate making, though yielding to the carrier the maximum revenue obtainable at a particular time, is unsatisfactory. The rate so based is both difficult to determine and unstable in character, the former because of the varying degrees to which transportation enters into the expense of production, the latter because rates made in accordance with such a principle must vary from year to year and from season to season. Its observance also tends to "kill the goose that lays the golden egg." From the standpoint of the public such a basis is indefensible because of its fluctuating character, because of the degree to which individual judgment enters into its determination, and, particularly, because rates so fixed are extortionate and unjust in character: they take all gains due to superior efficiency and advantageous location. Individual incentive to produce is lessened and society's right to be served by those producers who can place their goods upon the market at the lowest cost is thwarted. As a principle of rate making, "value of the service" is wholly unsound from a public point of view and is justifiable from the standpoint of the railway only in the face of extreme need.

"Keep Everybody in Business."—A second principle or policy of rate making, which recognizes ability to pay as basic, is that which has sometimes been characterized by the phrase "keep everybody in business." This policy calls for "just meeting competition" and results in fixing rates by carriers serving the less efficient producers—in fact, by carriers serving entire productive areas which are disadvantageously situated—upon such a basis as to permit the submarginal producer or community to enter a particular market upon an equality with others that are marginal or supramarginal because of either superior efficiency or locational advantage. This policy has been, in some cases, the result of a deliberate determination on the part of a particular carrier or group of carriers to increase tonnage by placing individuals or areas tributary to them into markets that economically belong to others. In certain instances, however, it has been but a by-product of another policy: a railway, in an effort to build up a back-haul traffic that will relieve it of the necessity of returning large numbers of empty cars, offers a rate upon tonnage which opens up, to certain additional producers and areas, markets previously closed to them.

From the standpoint of the railway such a rate policy has the advantage of creating additional business for that carrier and, since the railway business in the United States has been so preeminently one of increasing returns in the past, this additional business has often been carried with profit at rates which were ridiculously low as compared with standard charges. The policy of "keep everybody in business" is likewise advantageous to those individuals or localities favored. On the other hand, the more favorably situated carrier which, because of its location, may rightly expect to control a particular market, is the loser through the adoption by "interlopers" of such a principle. Furthermore, as roads, seeking to recoup such losses, invade the territory naturally tributary to the carrier which first forced entry into the markets of others, the major advantage enjoyed by the aggressor, and flowing from this policy of invasion, is lost. The net long-time result tends to be, therefore, that *no* carrier handles a materially increased tonnage; instead, all handle certain competitive tonnage at abnormally low rates which lessen revenue and, in consequence, increase the burdens that must be borne by other traffic. Then, too, the shipper who is more favorably situated with respect to a particular market, because either of superior efficiency or of more advantageous location, has just ground for complaint against a policy which places all producers in a particular market upon an equal footing, without regard to merit. Such a policy, unless accepted universally, results in the confiscation of a portion of that advantage to which this more favorably situated producer is entitled, and for which he has often paid.

From an economic standpoint the policy of "keep everybody in business" is objectionable. It encourages the premature development of natural resources, perhaps to the advantage of the present generation but certainly to the detriment of the future. Further, it fosters discrimination among commodities, among places, and among individuals, and results in the confiscation at will by the carrier, and to such degree as it sees fit, of surplus gains which flow from superior natural opportunities or exceptional management, rather than from the service of transportation. From a social standpoint such a principle of rate making is objectionable also, because it places the individual and the community completely at the mercy of the carrier and thus presents a strong temptation for favoritism. Indeed, under a competitive system it is only when subject to regulation that such a principle would be in any sense tolerable, but even then rates based upon it would conform in no sense to the legal requirements of justice and reasonableness. "Keep everybody in business" is unsound in theory, unsafe in practice and, in its ultimate results, objectionable from the standpoint of producer, carrier, and public alike. As a theoretical cornerstone for the building of a rate structure it is impossible; the maximum service which it can legitimately render is to modify rates otherwise determined.

The Developmental Principle.—Yet another of those principles which properly seem to fall under the head of ability to pay is that generally termed "developmental." As the name would indicate, the purpose of a rate made in accordance with this principle is to promote the establishment or growth of a new industry. In consequence, the tariff fixed is characteristically much below the general level of rates. Indeed, as the value-of-the-service rate stands at the one extreme, the developmental rate stands at the other. This principle occupies a position in the field of transportation somewhat analogous to that of the bounty sometimes offered by the public to stimulate the development of a particular industry, or its converse, a protective duty levied to the same end. In this, just as in the industrial field, clear justification exists for such a policy if, by its adoption, the public may be reasonably assured of a lesser expense of production after a period of years. Indeed, a carrier may justify, from both its own and a social standpoint, the offering of such a rate when *equality* of cost is the maximum result to be anticipated. There is, however, no justification from the standpoint of the carrier for offering developmental rates upon traffic which gives little or no promise of becoming self-supporting; such a permanent subsidy can be met only by levying higher rates upon other traffic. Society has no more place for parasitic industries than for parasitic individuals.

The developmental principle has been widely employed by American railways in the stimulation of new areas and of new industries. In fact, the tremendously rapid industrial and commercial growth of the United States has been due in great measure to the farsighted policy of the railways, to their willingness to take chances with the producer in the development of new business. The developmental rate, however, is one which the shipper can neither demand as a right and secure, even through public bodies, nor retain, once given, beyond a period which seems desirable to the carrier. This, of course, places a heavy responsibility upon the railway in the selection of industries to be encouraged and the degree to which that encouragement should be carried.

Place of Developmental Principle.—The use of the development rate is attended by certain dangers and difficulties. Many instances may be cited of the excessive stimulation of enterprise: when the time came for the undertaking to assume its proper rate burden, many normally submarginal producers, lured into the field by unusually favorable rates, suffered heavy losses. Then, too, such rates may be mistakenly accorded industries or localities which can never become self-supporting, or they may occasion the overextension of tributary market areas with a consequent overlapping and cross-hauling which cause social loss. Furthermore, the developmental rate has been subject at times to improper use, serving merely as a cloak for favoritism and unjust discrimination. A difficult problem incident to its employment arises when the rate is increased to a normal level. Both the time at which increases should be made and the rate of increase are delicate problems, with error penalizing carrier and producer alike. Nevertheless, this principle appears to be fundamentally sound, both from a railway and from a public point of view, and other traffic, temporarily burdened because of a low rate upon favored items, has no ground for complaint if the future gives reasonable promise of a tonnage which will lessen the expense burden of existing business. However, the wisdom of vesting such extensive power in corporate enterprise conducted for private gain, the cost of whose errors must be paid largely by producers lured into the field, may properly be questioned, except as that power is subject to a greater degree of public control than it now is. Yet such control is, in no sense, a positive guarantee against error in the utilization of the developmental rate: the honest intent of governmental agencies gives no assurance of infallible judgment.

"Value of the Commodity."—Another principle of rate making properly assignable to the ability group is that which is termed "value of the commodity." This principle as an ability index must be differentiated clearly in the beginning, however, from "value of the commodity" as a cost factor. It is evident that the expense of handling traffic varies somewhat with the value of the commodity: goods of high value occasion greater risk, for example, than do goods of low value, and therefore necessitate greater care. Yet quite beyond the cost element, the value of the commodity may be taken as an index of the ability of the good to bear a charge, and rates may therefore be fixed roughly in proportion to the value of the shipment. Such a scheme is akin to the principle of equality of sacrifice in the field of taxation, except that here the particular good rather than the individual is regarded as the unit. That the value-of-the-commodity principle is actually given recognition in rate making is evident from an examination of freight classifications, as indicated in an earlier chapter; on the whole, goods of low value receive a low classification, while goods of high value are given higher ratings. However, it should be recalled that, in the determination of classification, not only are cost considerations intermingled with the estimate of ability to pay but other modifying factors, such as competition, enter to such a degree that no exact relation appears between the value of the good and the classification which it enjoys.

Under any system of rate making, even the most rigid cost-of-service plan conceivably workable, the value of the commodity must enter as a factor. Yet it appears from the decisions of regulatory bodies that its recognition as an ability factor is legitimate only within certain narrow limits, where no appreciable difference in the nature of the products appears. Despite the fact that logs intended for pulp-wood use might bear a higher rate than those intended for lumber, differentiation in rates has been forbidden and, although differences in value among fire, building, and paving bricks exist, it has been held that there is no justification for rate differentiation. On the other hand, it has also been held that cheap china, shipped in the same manner as fine china, is entitled to lower classification than the latter. It seems probable that, as regulatory policy takes more definite form, the justification of a lower classification upon less valuable commodities will be recognized, since it will become increasingly clear with experience that no cost basis of rate making can succeed which attempts to tax rough castings, for example, on even measurably the same basis as other manufactured metal products of higher value per unit of bulk.

"What the Traffic Will Bear."—From the standpoint of actual use the most important of the so-called ability theories is that which is widely known as "what the traffic will bear." Under this principle rates are fixed to yield to the railway the maximum amount consistent with the further development of industry and trade throughout its territory. In fact, it represents essentially the application in the railway field of the principle of monopoly price. Although frequently the term "value of the service" is used in describing a policy of rate making based upon the monopoly principle, it has seemed worth while to the writer to distinguish between the short-time and the long-time point of view. Rates levied in accordance with the former principle are extortionate, equal to "that amount which the shipper will pay rather than dispense with the service," while rates levied in accordance with the latter show an enlightened self-interest on the part of the carriers.

Rates based upon the principle of "what the traffic will bear" will vary somewhat between communities and between commodities; they will offer, to use the words of Acworth, an "equitable concession to the weaker members of the community." These variations, under a system of private ownership and operation, must be determined by private individuals or bodies interested essentially in profits, and hence will rest primarily upon the ability of the particular commodity, locality, or individual to pay. This ability is dependent, in turn, upon natural advantage or superior efficiency. The extent of this ability to pay must be found experimentally, since no definite standard exists, and from time to time it will be modified by the appearance of alternative transportation agencies as well as by changes in the present condition and future prospects of the business in question. It is needful, however, to differentiate clearly between rates fixed upon the principle of "what the traffic will bear" and those designed to "keep everybody in business." The latter principle, fully developed, is essentially an extreme application or extension of the former, the substitution of the individual bargain for the group rate. "Keep everybody in business" represents, in short, merely a high development of class price as opposed to a single monopoly price.

"What the traffic will bear" has been extensively used by railway officials. Indeed, so exclusively has it controlled railway rate making and so active a part in railway development has it played, that it has quite properly been characterized as the "great dynamic force" in American railway development. Various reasons account for its ready acceptance by railway officials; most important of these is, perhaps, that it has given to the American rate structure that elasticity peculiarly essential in a rapidly developing country with changing needs and with new traffic conditions constantly appearing. This principle has also been wholly consonant with the private aspect of railway enterprise since, under it, rates could be adjusted from time to time and in such manner as to yield the highest net profit—the goal of individual business endeavor. Then too, rate making in accordance with this principle gives to railway managers a degree of personal power and a scope for the exercise of individual discretion which has been in no sense displeasing to them. Perhaps other factors have also strengthened railway allegiance to "what the traffic will bear" as a basis of rate determination; at least railway management insists strenuously upon its retention and is sharply opposed to any development which promises to curtail the power long exercised by it.

Evaluation of "What the Traffic Will Bear."—Certain features of the policy of "what the traffic will bear" are difficult to evaluate. Under its influence the American rate structure has assuredly shown itself to be highly elastic and capable of rapid and complete adaptation to changing needs. Yet, in view of conditions which now exist, it appears that the two outstanding needs of the American rate structure are stability and uniformity among sections, even though these may be had only at the expense of a degree of elasticity. Though certain beneficial results have come from its adaptable character in the past, that very elasticity has made for uncertainty and instability of rates and has served the railways as an offensive weapon in the struggle for existing business as often as it has served helpfully in the development of new. Moreover, because of the numerous special rates that are characteristic of an elastic rate structure, our tariffs have become voluminous and complex and the charges borne by standard traffic have been increased. Although not giving rise to discrimination among commodities, places, and persons to the degree that is characteristic of the principle of "keep everybody in business," "what the traffic will bear" must, by its very nature, prove discriminatory; concessions in rates to one individual, to one locality, or to one commodity must necessarily weaken the position enjoyed by another.

Furthermore, this principle of rate making runs counter to public interest in several particulars. The basis of the charge is essentially monopolistic in character, failing thereby to conform to the requirement that rates be just and reasonable to the shipper. To quote Clarke, there may be "between railroad self-interest and truly 'equitable concessions' as wide a difference as between ancient systems of taxation aiming only at the largest obtainable revenue and the modern system intelligently based on the taxpayer's ability to pay." Furthermore, the railway's immediate and dominant interest in traffic is financial, and only in so far as the economic and social effects of railway policies *influence revenue through traffic*, does the carrier give weight to matters of public concern. Under such conditions Clark's observation is well put, that "a skeptical mind would hardly be persuaded that the roads could be wholly trusted to carry out a satisfactory social policy." Indeed, so divergent are public and private purposes that there is no reasonable assurance that, even *in the main*, rates based upon the principle of "what the traffic will bear" result in the market being served by those producers who can "satisfy its wants at the lowest social expense."

To summarize our evaluation of "what the traffic will bear" as a basic principle of rate making: because a schedule of rates rested upon this principle will yield to the railway the highest net return, the theory merits and receives strong support from railway management; because a monopolistic principle cannot be approved as sound from a public point of view, recognition of that aspect of "what the traffic will bear" by legislature or commission is impossible. Railway history requires the student to grant that the fixation of rates in accordance with this principle has been of fundamental significance in furthering the rapid development of industry and trade in the United States, as elsewhere. Yet, while the officer of a private corporation may legitimately construct rates in accordance with his judgment of the relative abilities of goods to bear, this cannot be done by a public body charged with impartial administration of the law: the line between reasonable and unreasonable discrimination is too ill-defined to permit of extended departures from the nearest approach attainable to the goal of regulation, equality of treatment to all. It requires unusual optimism to envision a future for "what the traffic may bear" in its monopolistic sense that is more than a shadow of its past: the very existence of regulatory bodies and frequent appeals to them for assistance have been, and continue to be, occasioned largely by charges that are alleged to be high and discriminatory—manifestations of monopoly in rate making. Furthermore, the monopolistic power of the railway has been largely destroyed by the rise during recent years of competitive agencies, primarily the motor vehicle. For "what the traffic may bear" in a quite different sense, that charge which may be imposed without forcing traffic to some competitive agency, the future may be said to be too rosy: within recent years the problem has changed rapidly from "what *can* the railway charge without crippling those dependent upon it for service" to "what *must* the railway charge that it may share in the available traffic." In short, "what the traffic will bear" is concerned increasingly with *minimum* rates rather than *maximum* rates—and to the determination of the point beyond which the carrier cannot profitably go in paring its tariffs a knowledge of costs becomes vital. Even to the intelligent use by the railway of this ability principle, then, cost becomes important under existing conditions.

COST OF SERVICE

The second important principle that has been given general recognition as a basis for the determination of railway rates is that commonly known by the term "cost of service." Various meanings or interpretations have been given it: if total revenues coincide with total expenses, necessary profits being included in the latter, it has been contended that the railway is rendering service at cost; similarly, though using the term in a somewhat more refined sense, it has been declared that, if the revenues from each particular *type* of service and the expenses incident thereto are approximately equal, service is upon a cost basis. To attempt, however, to justify the charge for a specific service in behalf of a particular patron upon the ground that revenues and expense as a whole, or even revenues and expenses flowing from the particular *type* of service—passenger, freight, and other—are equal, must fail; such reasoning in no wise convinces that shipper of the justness of the individual rate applied. To have any meaning whatever to the shipper, cost of service must imply *a measure of equality between the revenue derived from a particular service and the expenses incident to the rendition of that service.* However fair rates may be as a whole, to shippers as a whole, the test of justice and reasonableness is the burden of particular rates.

Types of Cost of Service.—In the ascertainment of cost of service two major expense elements must be considered. Of these the first in point of appearance, though the lesser in amount, is capital cost, under this head being included all amounts paid for the use of capital employed in the rendition of service. The second cost element, which now constitutes almost 80 per cent of the total expense of rendering railway service, is operating cost. The two important groups of operating costs are expenditures for the maintenance of the various properties and expenditures incident to the actual movement of traffic. The need of distinguishing between these major cost elements appears when a study is made of the various types of cost of service of which three are often differentiated, each shading off gradually into the other.

Considered as a going concern, the railway must meet regularly and in full both operating and capital costs. The sum of these two, representing the total cost of service, may be prorated among the various types of traffic in such manner that each shipment bears its fair proportion of both types of costs. To this interpretation of cost of service is sometimes given the name "average total cost." On the other hand, it may be that existing traffic already bears a burden sufficient to meet capital costs, or, indeed, it is possible that, under conditions of government ownership and operation or of operation by a receiver, effort is made, permanently or temporarily, to meet *only operating cost.* Under such conditions it will be necessary to burden additional traffic, or perhaps all traffic, only by such a rate as will enable it to meet its proper proportion of operating expenses. To this type may be applied the term "average operating cost." Still further, it is not only conceivable, but often true, that existing traffic is sufficiently burdened to meet all expenses, both capital and operating, incident to the rendition of service. What, then, is the minimum charge that the railway can make, without actual loss to itself, for the movement of additional tonnage which will be offered only upon the basis of an unusually low rate? To answer this question it becomes necessary for the railway official to determine with reasonable accuracy the actual increase in outlay attributable to this additional tonnage. To this figure has often been applied the term "additional cost of the specific service."

To make clearer not only the type of cost of service last described, but the other two as well, let an extremely simple situation be assumed—a railway operating from station *A* to station *B*, 50 miles distant, with no intermediate stops. Let us assume further that this railway handles but one type of traffic which moves in standard carload quantities and in trains of uniform tonnage. If, in the course of a year, this carrier moves 1,000,000 tons of freight at a cost of $1,000,000 then the *average total cost of service* for the movement between the termini named would be $1 per ton, or 2 cents per ton-mile. If it be further assumed that, of the total expenses, 80 per cent are attributable to operation, then *average operating cost of service* would be found by dividing $800,000 by the total tonnage, giving a cost per ton of 80 cents and per ton-mile of $0.016. If it be presumed, however, that additional tonnage may be obtained at a rate still below average operating cost, it becomes incumbent upon the railway to discover what rate must be applied in order that the added cost might be covered. If traffic has been moving in train lots averaging

1,000 tons and it is found that an additional 50 tons per train can be handled at a total train cost of $1,010 then, since the average total cost of service for a 1,000-ton train equals $1,000, the *additional cost* attributable to the added car is but $10, an average of 20 cents per ton and $0.004 per ton-mile. Any charge in excess of that figure, all constant costs being met by other traffic, would net a surplus to the carrier and would permit the carrier to lower somewhat the charge against the original traffic without trenching upon necessary profits.

The Ascertainment and Application of Costs.—Because of its simplicity and its definite character, cost of service has long been urged as a basis for the determination of railway rates. Yet certain difficulties inherent in the principle, together with the reluctance of railway management to abandon the use of "what the traffic will bear" as fundamental, has made progress toward a cost basis necessarily slow. Two major difficulties have been encountered in its application. In the first place, cost of service of any type is difficult to ascertain. This is true in part because of the significance of the principle of joint costs in the railway field. The same roadbed is used in the rendition of freight, passenger, express, and mail service, and in many instances the same station buildings and other structures are also jointly used. A single freight train will be made up of carloads of various types of commodities and, in the case of less-than-carload movements, within the same car are found perhaps a hundred different items. Therefore, even though expenses might be properly and accurately allocated among the various types of service, it becomes increasingly difficult as we move from freight as a whole to an individual shipment of a particular commodity, to fix with exactitude that portion of the total cost which is properly attributable to each individual service. This difficulty, growing out of the joint-cost problem, is accentuated by the almost complete absence in the railway field of cost-accounting data. Due largely to the fact that railway officials have not yet awakened to the possible service of cost accounting to that industry, data showing individual costs are fewer in the railway field than in any other of like importance. Once the carriers awake to the need of accurate cost accounting and make sincere efforts to arrive at specific costs, it is probable that the joint-cost obstacle will be found to be far less formidable than it has been pictured by opponents of cost and by theorists.

But the *ascertainment* of costs is only one of the difficulties encountered in utilizing cost of service as a basis of rate making; the *application* of the consequent rates constitutes a troublesome problem in itself. Were the cost of service incident to the movement of each type of traffic capable of most exact ascertainment it would be found that a considerable portion of the tonnage now handled upon low rates would be so heavily burdened by the application of average cost figures as to impede, even prohibit, movement. Then, too, were goods assessed upon a purely cost basis, the rate structure would assume a rigidity ill-adapted to changing conditions and to the development of new traffic.

The Strength of Cost of Service.—Despite difficulties in the ascertainment and in the use of cost of service as a basis of rate making, its virtues recommend it strongly to all impartial students of the problem of rate determination and give it an increasing importance in the decisions of regulatory bodies whose obligation it is to secure for the public just and reasonable rates. The public has become accustomed under a competitive régime to cost as a price basis and, although partially realizing that certain fields are not competitive in character, the only basis of charge which is accepted by that public as *prima facie* reasonable is that which rests squarely upon cost. Then, too, cost of service furnishes a standard much more definite and exact, much less influenced by individual judgment, far less prone to use as a vehicle for favoritism, than any other basis of rate making which has been suggested. Cost of service also, if employed as the fundamental basis in rate determination, would wholly eliminate personal discrimination—an abuse characteristic of our rate system in the past and the basis of complaint against the railways at all times. Furthermore, its application would eliminate very largely those instances of place and commodity discrimination which have been so important in arousing public antagonism against railway management. Then, too, if cost were used as a basis, business uncertainty, due to fluctuations in the rate level, would be minimized: the entire rate structure would assume an aspect of solidity and permanency which has been wanting in the past. And, finally, the more general use of cost would eliminate much cross-hauling of freight, an important present phase of social waste.

Conclusions Concerning Cost as a Rate Base.—Although it is difficult to summarize opposition to cost of service as a basis of rate making, it may safely be said that opposition to it rests largely upon three considerations: it curtails the scope of action of railway management, it presents certain difficulties of ascertainment and application that many regard as insuperable, and it makes for inelasticity of rates. Assuredly no justification exists for delaying the acceptance of cost as basic upon the first score; indeed, it is highly probable that, had railway management had at hand cost data and had appreciated its significance more fully, cutthroat competition would have appeared less often, and the railways would have carried less tonnage at unremunerative rates as a consequence of overzealous efforts to increase volume of traffic. It appears, furthermore, that the difficulties incident to the use of cost can be met in large measure through careful analysis and a reasonable application. The collection of a body of cost-accounting data for the railway industry will lessen materially the significance of joint costs as a barrier and the residuum which is incapable of accurate distribution on an actual cost basis can be so assigned that the resultant figures will represent, on the whole, a much fairer basis for the determination of rates than the judgment of any single railway rate expert or any group of such men with but a fragmentary knowledge of costs and an inevitable tendency to do homage to mere tons and carloads—fairer not only to the public but also to the railway investor who is entitled to a reasonable return. A policy of charging against bulky goods of low value something less than average total cost, and recouping sums lost thereby from higher grade traffic, will meet one problem of application, while the modification of the cost principle upon occasion by certain others will minimize further criticisms.

The retention of some degree of elasticity in the rate structure governing in even a developed territory is important, yet all too often those who insist upon a considerable elasticity do so because they are interested in elasticity as a competitive weapon rather than as an agency for the benefit of shippers as a whole—and this is no less true of the railway traffic official than it is of the patron or group of patrons seeking a concession. Need for changes in governing rates may arise out of changes within the industry itself that justify carrier recognition or the need may arise from a shift in the competitive situation—the disappearance of old forces and the appearance of new. Within recent years the railways have faced loss of traffic to the barge and to the commercial motor carrier, both enjoying a significant indirect subsidy, and to meet this difficulty greater freedom in rate making has been urged—complaint being directed particularly toward governmentally prescribed minimum rates built upon a distance basis. That there is occasion for variations of rates to take account of changed conditions cannot be denied, yet never did the railway traffic official need a clear concept of costs as a guide more than in the face of the present competitive problem; otherwise there is no assurance but that tonnage may be retained at an actual loss to the railway. However, acceptance of cost of service as basic in no sense precludes recognition of the need of adapting the rate structure to new conditions: indeed, to that adaptation it will serve as a most helpful guide and aid. And certainly the acceptance of cost as basic, modified in accordance with need, will avoid the uncertainties and fluctuations of past schedules and yet retain that adaptability essential to the successful conduct of business. Cost, therefore, would seem to form not only a sound theoretical cornerstone for the determination of rates, but also enjoys that peculiar advantage in the public mind of conforming to accepted standards of justice and reasonableness.

SOCIAL NEED

A third general principle of rate making meriting recognition is that which would base rates upon social need. This scheme is sometimes termed the "postal" theory because of the tendency of rates fixed in accordance with it to give little regard to distance. Under a system of private ownership and operation of railways it is unlikely that such a principle of rate making will gain wide acceptance, both because of certain discriminatory aspects thereof and because of the problem of adequate railway revenues under a schedule of rates based upon this concept. However, under any form of government ownership and operation it is entirely conceivable that the prospect of social gain might lead to the application of this principle to particular types of traffic or, possibly, to traffic as a whole. Indeed, the student of railway rate structures is cognizant of limited recognition of the principle in many instances, sometimes by prescription and at others by carrier choice. The State Railroad Commission of Texas, to accomplish certain economic and social ends, adopted and continued in force for many years an intrastate rate structure known as a "graded and maximum" plan under which locational advantage was minimized in great measure—while the railways, for competitive reasons, maintained into Texas territory for many years tariffs that "blanketed" a large portion of that great state upon shipments from beyond certain points. Social purpose in Texas was accomplished by the application of a flat rate to all shipments moving more than a prescribed minimum distance. Rate "blanketing" has not been the consequence of any desire on the part of the carriers to serve a social purpose, however, when adopted of their own volition, as has frequently been the case; rather, it has represented compromise among competing lines and among competing markets. The Hoch-Smith Resolution represented an effort on the part of Congress to inject social considerations into the determination of the *level* of rates to a greater degree but, in general, regulation tends to move toward the recognition and protection of natural advantage rather than contrariwise—both because of the need of avoiding any semblance of discrimination and the necessity of providing for the carriers a fair return upon private property devoted to public service.

CONCLUDING STATEMENT

Position of Regulatory Bodies.—In the era which preceded effective public regulation of railway rates, dominance of the ability principle in one or another of its aspects cannot be questioned. Nor does there seem to be doubt that early regulatory bodies accorded ability major consideration. However, as these bodies gained experience and as they realized increasingly the fallibility of even the experienced traffic official's judgment, also the broad opportunities for discrimination in the recognition of ability uncontrolled by considerations of cost, not only the state commissions but also the Interstate Commerce Commission tended increasingly to minimize the importance of the former and to stress the latter as time passed. This tendency was encouraged by the fact that regulatory policy took definite form during a period when rates made upon a cost basis were more favorable to the shipping public than rates emphasizing ability to pay. As a consequence of various forces a somewhat illogical but workable policy of giving weight to many principles came to govern, but with a trend toward the emphasis of cost evident. Because of the lack of detailed and accurate cost data, it has been quite natural that regulatory bodies should judge the reasonableness of a particular rate that has been called into question by comparing it with other rates governing comparable movements. But, as the powers of commissions increased and more accurate as well as more adequate cost data became available, these bodies gave unmistakable evidence of their purpose to shift from a *relative* to an *absolute* cost basis—with actual costs, ascertained by careful study, constituting the yardstick of reasonableness. Increasingly did shippers demand that the carriers justify each application for an increase in rates by something more specific than a traffic official's "estimate" of revenue need or ability to bear, and increasingly did state and federal commissions insist upon such evidence. In consequence, cost studies became common and cost data of varying worth were introduced, sometimes in great volume, in rate cases. Indeed, many cost studies were conducted under the direction of the Interstate Commerce Commission or in accordance with detailed plans set forth by it.

In the period immediately following 1920 came an interesting and, it might be said, amusing change of front on the part of carrier and shipper—a change comparable to that of public and private interests with respect to valuation theories in the early years of the present century. In the period of readjustment following 1920 the general price level dropped much more sharply than did railway costs—and the prices of agricultural products fell still below the general price level. To support their contention that the level of rates be not unduly lowered, the railways became ardent advocates of cost—endeavoring to justify by cost data that they had before contended were not available or were without value, the maintenance of rates and even certain advances. Public advocates on the other hand, who had anathematized the recognition of the ability principle during an earlier period insisted, now that the lamb had been shorn, upon rates fixed solely in accord with that concept. These advocates succeeded in having that idea embodied into the law in the Hoch-Smith Resolution which, as indicated in an earlier chapter, declares it "to be the true policy in rate making to be pursued by the Interstate Commerce Commission in adjusting freight rates, that the conditions which at any time prevail in our several industries should be considered in so far as it is legally possible to do so, to the end that commodities may freely move"—with the Senegambian in this particular woodpile appearing in a later section in which the Commission was directed to adjust rates particularly in the interest of the "freedom of movement . . . of the products of agriculture." It is to be deemed a happy circumstance that the decision of the United States Supreme Court upon this Resolution was of such nature as to null the obvious intent of the law to create a favored class in the determination of rates.

But however unsound in theory and unworkable in practice its opponents may assert cost of service to be as a principle of rate making, that principle will receive increasing recognition under a system of regulation. While, as suggested, railway managers may make rates in accord with any or no principle—or all principles—and while they have little need to give thought to the avoidance of discrimination when not bound by legislation, a regulatory body must be guided by definite principles capable of explanation and justification. And cost provides the only positive yardstick that has been offered. Therefore, faced by necessity and finding in cost a measure which is actually sound in many, if perhaps not all, particulars, it is not strange that this principle has found increasing acceptance. Willy-nilly, it seems that regulation, to such extent as rates are fixed by authority rather than by competition, must bring in its wake a schedule of freight charges rested fundamentally upon cost of service.

A Reasonable Theoretical Basis for Railway Rates.—From the foregoing discussion it is clear that cost of service finds justification in theory and support in practice: both reason and necessity give basis for the recognition of cost of service as fundamental in the determination of rates. If freight rates so determined be modified by the recognition of such of the ability principles as are legitimate to a particular situation, also by the recognition of social need, it appears that not only a reasonable but also an essentially workable rate structure can be developed. Certainly it would eliminate discrimination largely, it would give to each community and each producing area its legitimate place, it would provide more adequately for the revenue needs of the carriers, and yet would not be so rigid as to preclude those adjustments properly sought by industrial and trade interests. In the passenger field, however, it might be well to give less weight to cost and more to social need as well as to "what the traffic will bear." The former merits recognition because the maximum intermingling of peoples in a country as broad as the United States is desirable for the promotion of cultural unity, while weight to the latter is justified because, in the rendition of passenger service, it is possible to differentiate upon the basis of ability to pay much more surely and definitely than in the field of freight service where the particular commodity or shipment may be used by either rich or poor. A change, gradually and carefully made, of present diverse rate structures built in accord with other principles or in accord with none to a structure conforming roughly to the plan suggested above, might well be undertaken. It must not be forgotten that rate structures devised by the

Interstate Commerce Commission and applied to considerable areas represent a definite movement in this direction. Such a structure would give to the railways a higher degree of financial protection, to the patron a rate not only equitable but one which bears evidence of its reasonableness upon its face. That goal is deserving of the highest efforts of both carriers and public.

REFERENCES

Brown, H. G.: *Transportation Rates and their Regulation*, The Macmillan Company, 1916.

Clarke, J. M.: Standards of Reasonableness in Local Freight Discrimination, *Columbia University Studies in Political Science*, vol. 37, No. 1.

———: *The Economics of Overhead Costs*, University of Chicago Press, 1923.

Daggett, Stuart R.: *Principles of Inland Transportation*, Harper & Brothers, 1928.

Hammond, M. B.: *Rate Theories of the Interstate Commerce Commission*, Harvard University Press, 1911.

Haney, Lewis H.: *The Business of Railway Transportation*, Ronald Press Company, 1924.

Holmes, F. L.: *Regulation of Railroads and Public Utilities in Wisconsin*, D. Appleton & Company, 1915.

Jackman, W. T.: *Economics of Transportation*, McGraw-Hill Book Company, Inc., 1926.

Johnson, E. R., and G. G. Huebner: *Railroad Traffic and Rates.* vol. 1, D. Appleton & Company, 1911.

——— and T. W. Van Metre: *Principles of Railroad Transportation*, D. Appleton & Company, 1921.

Jones, Eliot: *Principles of Railway Transportation*, The Macmillan Company, 1924.

McFall, R. J.: Railway Monopoly and Rate Regulation, *Columbia University Studies*, vol. 19, No. 1.

McPherson, Logan: *Railroad Freight Rates*, Henry Holt & Company, 1909.

Ripley, W. Z.: *Railroads: Rates and Regulations*, Longmans, Green & Co., 1912.

———: *Railway Problems*, Ginn & Company, 1913.

Robinson, M. H.: Railway Passenger Rates, *Yale Review*, vol. 16, pp. 355–399.

———: Railroad Freight Rates, *Yale Review*, vol. 18, pp. 121–153.

Vanderblue, H. B., and K. F. Burgess: *Railroads: Rates, Service, Management*, The Macmillan Company, 1923.

Chapter XXXI

RATE-MAKING PRACTICE

IN NO other country in the world do railways face more varied conditions than in the United States. Wide variations in the competitive situation, wide variations in economic conditions, wide variations in physiographic and climatic conditions and even in opportunities for physical development and growth, together with a gradual evolution both of the transportation system and of industrial life, have combined to compel the railways in various sections of the country to adjust themselves to divergent needs. Out of this there have developed, naturally and inevitably, divergent types of rate structures in the various traffic areas instead of a uniform structure applying throughout the United States. With the extension of the railway net new problems arose and, as each new section was added to the areas already developed, modifications in old practices had to be made and certain new policies of rate making evolved, to meet the necessities arising from the appearance of competitive conditions and economic needs quite different from those previously faced. Within certain natural boundaries or barriers such structures developed, therefore, as seemed best designed to meet the peculiar conditions there found.

The limitations imposed by space preclude a detailed presentation of the evolution of the separate rates structures and of the plan now governing in each of the major rate territories.[1] None the less, a description of the nature of certain of the more significant structures as they illustrate basic principles of rate making is appropriate to the purposes

[1] Of the major rate territories there are seven—of which three lie within the confines of the Eastern District and three of the Western. New England territory corresponds closely to the New England states while in Trunk Line territory is included that area between New England and a line from Buffalo through Pittsburgh and thence following the Ohio River to Kenova, W. Va., its southern boundary being a line from that point through Roanoke and Lynchburg to Norfolk, Va. Central Freight Association territory comprises the remainder of the Eastern District, with the addition of the west shore of Lake Michigan and an added portion of Illinois. Southern Freight Association territory is coextensive with the Southern District. In Southwestern territory lie the states of Texas, Oklahoma, Arkansas, Louisiana (west of the Mississippi), and that portion of Missouri south of the line of the Missouri Pacific Railroad from St. Louis to Kansas City. Western Trunk Line territory is to the northward of the section just defined and covers that portion of the Western District to the east of a line north from Trinidad through Denver, Colo., to Cheyenne and thence to the Canadian border along the western boundaries of Nebraska and the Dakotas. The great area to the westward of the two territories just defined is known as Transcontinental territory.

of this volume. Such a description will, therefore, be undertaken. Yet before a beginning is made upon this, it may be well to stress the lack of any close conformance of rate practice to definite theory or plan: rate making has been essentially pragmatic in character, that rate and that structure of rates being "best"—and therefore made operative—which works "best." And this standard of superiority was a highly elastic one, particular rates being determined by competition, by official predilection, and by fallible judgments upon available facts, rather than by exact computations—and involving the assignment of values to such intangibles and unknowns as public opinion and possible tonnages. It is safe to say, however, that rates were generally made upon the basis of the ability of the traffic to pay in the years prior to the establishment of effective regulation: where no competition was faced, the rate was typically made to *move* the business; where rivalry for traffic was keen, it was the function of the rate to *get* the business. While the estimated out-of-pocket cost of handling particular business was used upon occasion as a yardstick in determining the minimum rate that might be made to attract that business, the inevitable tendency under a régime that put no emphasis upon cost was to press for an increased volume of traffic, with a too incidental interest in the effect of that increase upon net operating income, rather than to seek to attract or to create such traffic as would augment that net.

As suggested, a brief description of the major features of certain characteristic rate structures will be presented. The distinctive features of all the older structures resulted from the interplay of carrier and shipper interests, competition being a vital factor—with public authority exerting little or no influence except in the one instance where public authority imposed a definite plan of rate making upon unwilling railways to the end that a particular conception of social interest be served. Without exception modern rate structures show, however, the impress of the hand of public authority.

The Distance Principle in Rate Making.—While cost was accorded recognition by most railway rate structures that developed prior to the establishment of regulatory control of the railways to the extent that rates tended to increase with distance, this increase was rarely an orderly one and variations were more often a consequence of the operation of competitive forces or of carrier self-interest than of the dictates of cost. Yet, during the years when the railways were subject only to self-imposed restrictions, there was developed one rate structure that has been preeminent because of its conformance to logic and its comparative freedom from attack by shippers. This structure governed interterritorial movements in the Eastern District; or, to be more specific, movements between points in Trunk Line and Central Freight Association territories—with rates between New England and Central Freight Association points correlated thereto by means of arbitraries. The establishment of this orderly system represented an intelligent adjustment by the carriers serving the territory of a problem that threatened disaster to all; its continuance was a testimonial both to the equity of the system and to the ability of its sponsors to maintain that cooperation essential to the life of any comprehensive plan.

Background of the Percentage Plan.—As indicated in an earlier chapter, railway building during the first period was confined to the more populous sections; construction beyond the Ohio was regarded as highly speculative until the later forties and early fifties. Among lines that were essentially local in character competition was slight but, with the consolidation of such local lines into extensive systems and the construction of through lines, competition at many points in the states to the north and west of the Ohio became cutthroat in nature. Particularly was this true at such an important terminal as Chicago where, by 1874, there were four major "Trunk Lines" struggling for tonnage—and to this group must be added active waterway rivalry and the Grand Trunk, a circuitous route. Agreements designed to minimize or to eliminate competition had been attended with but little success and the scarcity of traffic during the depression years of the seventies made competition particularly bitter and difficult to control.

There were, in 1874, four major disturbing elements in the situation. The first, and perhaps the most important, was the rivalry of all-water and all-rail routes. Traffic might move between West and East by lake and canal as well as by rail, and the grain traffic, which contributed heavily to the total of through tonnage, was well adapted to water carriage. Intensifying this struggle was the fact that, if Baltimore and Philadelphia were to hold even a minor position in export trade, movements *must* be by rail instead of by water, and the firm determination of carriers serving those ports to remain "in the market" compelled conformance to certain policies by rival lines. A second disturbing condition grew out of the extension of the grain-growing district to the westward and the efforts of the Western lines serving Chicago and Milwaukee to obtain the lowest possible rates on tonnage moving to the Eastern seaboard; these Western lines were competing sharply, too. A third difficulty arose from the dependence of the Trunk Lines upon the cross-line railways between Pittsburgh and Chicago for a considerable portion of the traffic originating in this territory, a dependence the greater because of the lack of branch mileage at that time. These cross lines had been built largely by local capital and were in many instances extended to lake ports for the express purpose of forcing from Trunk Line connections lower rates on long-haul traffic originated by such cross lines, under threat of delivery to lake carriers. Finally, unhappy conflicts and maladjustments developed between local rates and rates upon highly competitive through tonnage: some method of coordinating local and distance charges was increasingly needed as time passed.

The Percentage Plan.—To insure peace in the area to the eastward of Chicago and St. Louis two important steps were essential, the one an adjustment among various routes and combinations of routes to minimize the danger of future competitive outbreaks, the other a correlation of through and intermediate rates in this extended territory. Since the adjustment as among carriers and routes is not of prime concern here, it will be sufficient to say that certain differentials were applied as between all-water and all-rail, as well as between all possible combinations of standard and differential rail movements, and that the plan proved so satisfactory that it still remains the basis of the competitive adjustment in this territory. The correlation of through and intermediate rates was accomplished by the application of the MacGraham scale, so called because devised by a Pennsylvania rate clerk of that name, in 1876. True, it appears that as early as 1870 certain points intermediate to Chicago and New York had been given rates constituting a definite proportion of the Chicago-New York rate, but the wide application of this principle had to wait the pressure of greater need. The original scale made the rates vary directly with distance but it was soon apparent that the plan was deficient to the extent that it failed to recognize the constant terminal factor. Under the modified plan a charge of 25 cents was assumed and upon this basis governing percentages were computed. Of the assumed 25-cent charge 6 cents was set aside to cover terminal costs, thus leaving 19 cents to be prorated upon the basis of distance. If a point be distant 60 per cent of the distance from Chicago to New York, therefore, the portion of the movement charge applicable to this point from Chicago would be found by taking 60 per cent of the 19 cents. This 11.4 cents would be added to the 6-cent terminal portion, giving a total of 17.4 cents. This figure, translated into terms of a percentage of 25, is 69.6 per cent. So, to determine the class rates to the intermediate point in question this percentage would be applied to the class rates in effect at a particular time between Chicago and New York. If the base rates were changed from time to time, the constant percentage would continue to be used. Governing eastbound movements only when first employed, this plan proved so successful that it was later made applicable to westbound tonnage also.

Adjustments in the Percentage Plan.—Had the distance-percentage principle been applied rigorously, there would have been for each competitive point rates either slightly above or slightly below those applicable to adjacent competitive points. To avoid this confusion, as well as to accomplish certain other ends, one of which was the elimination of all long-and-short-haul violations, the carriers joined in the establishment of *group* or *zone*, in place of *point*, rates. Yet an examination of the boundaries of the existing percentage zones for both eastward and westward movements shows that those boundaries have been influenced by other

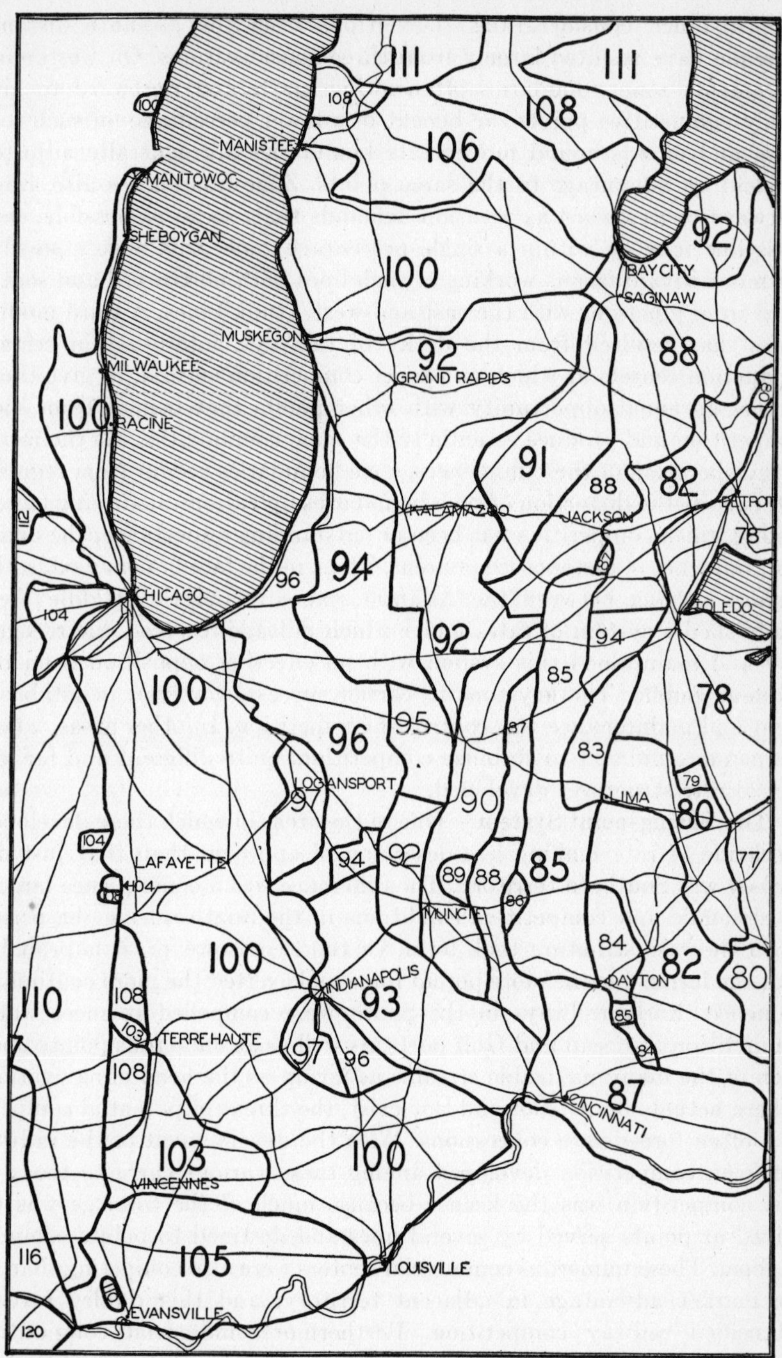

FIG. 33.—Percentage groups, Central Freight Association territory—eastbound.

than distance considerations. Deviations from the absolute distance principle have resulted largely from three considerations. On westbound movements zone boundaries often swing far to the westward to give highly competitive points the benefit of a lower percentage on such tonnage, and on eastbound movements boundaries are generally adjusted to yield an advantage to the same points. Zone boundaries also swing eastward or westward as occasion demands that, so far as possible, each cross line may lie within a single percentage zone; this makes possible the more advantageous working of such lines both northward and southward from junctions with the east-and-west Trunk Lines. A third modification has resulted from the desire of railways, interested in certain production centers at which no carrier competition existed, to give those centers an equal opportunity with other points that benefit from such competition and produce essentially the same commodities. As the result of the operation of these influences, zone boundaries are far from regular; yet, despite the distortion of such boundaries by various modifying forces, among which competition has been of outstanding importance, the dominant influence of distance is apparent. Thus, in the face of heavy odds, the carriers serving between the Atlantic seaboard and the Middle West established a system of rates under which mileage received due recognition and maintained this system with no effective opposition from the shipping public. The keystone to carrier success, however, in establishment and maintenance was control of competition. In other areas, where it was more difficult to stabilize competition, quite different and far less logical rate structures developed.

The Basing-point System.—One of the areas in which there developed a scheme of rate making less deserving of approval than that just described was Southern territory. The difference was a consequence largely of economic and competitive conditions in the South during the period when the rate structure took form. Of the two, however, it is probable that the latter was the more potent force and exerted the more continuing influence. Early railways in the South were compelled to meet water competition at ocean and Gulf ports, as well as at numerous points upon each of the many navigable streams as far up as the head of navigation. Where actual competition did not exist, the threat of potential competition often forced rate concessions. With the development of the railway net keen competition developed among these various carriers, too, and this competition was the keener because much of the tonnage was received at points served by several lines and destined to points common to them. These numerous commercial centers were also competing sharply for market advantage in adjacent territory, and this rivalry further intensified railway competition. Furthermore, industrial competition became a potent force with the rise of industry to the westward of Buffalo and Pittsburgh, this newer area vying with the New England-Middle

Atlantic district for an outlet in the South. Indeed, the importance of this struggle is difficult to exaggerate as a factor in shaping Southern inbound rates, and the struggle has been intensified with the rapid industrialization of the Western area. Shaped by such influences and forces, the system of rate making that evolved persisted until recent years in the face of marked changes in the industrial and commercial life of the South. Even then it was displaced by public authority rather than by cooperative action on the part of carriers and shippers.

Analysis of the Basing-point System.—The physical possibility of goods moving into and from the South through its various sea and river ports compelled the railways to accord those ports lower rates than otherwise would have been given. And, because of the extended coastline and the many rivers reaching inland from the Atlantic and Gulf as well as from the Ohio, such ports were numerous. In addition to the points at which water competition forced rate concessions, there were others that had attained commercial importance prior to the construction of railways in Southern territory, points that held a dominant place in their respective sections because of the characteristic manner of handling the cotton crop. To these "gateway cities" also the railways felt obliged to make concessions in rates. There was yet a third group of points that benefited from preferential rates because of railway policy. Centers of greater or less import that were served by two or more carriers were able to play one against another, thus forcing concessions. To yet other centers where no competition was faced, because from these all "in" and "out" tonnage would be controlled by and increase the revenues of the single line, the same advantage was extended in numerous instances.

It is clear that competition of any type, functioning freely, may force rates at competitive points below a normal level. It is equally obvious that proportionate rates cannot be applied to all points on the line if carrier solvency is to be maintained. Such intermediate points, although handicapped in their competition with localities favored by lower rates, have little basis for complaint against the extension of preferential rates by the railways so long as the forces operative are *genuinely* competitive in nature and *beyond the control of the carriers:* rather, protest must be lodged against the inequalities of Nature. Cause for complaint exists only when the cloak of competition is employed as a disguise for railway self-interest, as an excuse for a policy that is helpful to the carrier but prejudicial to public well-being. To accord, then, lower rates to Southern cities at which actual or definitely potential water competition was faced, than to nearby noncompetitive points, was justifiable. Preferential treatment of the "gateway" cities during early years, perhaps long after economic conditions had changed, was defensible. But the third group of basing points, a consequence of the operation of railway self-interest or of uncontrolled competition, ought never to have come into being and much less have persisted for an extended period: their favorable position as compared with other points made tributary to them represented a species of favoritism that violated every canon of reasonableness and justice in rate making.

To make clear the nature of the basing-point system a more detailed statement will be made, with illustrations drawn from its application in the South. Characteristic of the system is a low rate upon distance traffic into and out of the various basing points. As traffic moved, for example, from Baltimore to New Orleans by rail, it passed successively through a considerable number of favored centers. Yet there was no assurance that, as distance increased, basing-point rates would increase—in fact, basing points located some distance inland took higher rates than those located nearer the Gulf and subject, therefore, to a greater measure of water competition. Thus there long existed in the South not only discrimination between the basing point and the points made tributary to it, but also among basing points themselves, a situation sometimes due to ineradicable conditions, sometimes chargeable to "railway policy."

Surrounding each favored Southern center was an area, rates to points lying within which were "based" upon that center; indeed, it is this fact that has given name to the system. Upon distance movements the rate to a station lacking basing-point privileges was determined by adding to the rate to the basing point the local rate from the basing point to point of destination. To a comparatively low through rate was added, then, a characteristically high local rate—with the lowest combination governing. And this practice was followed whether the point of destination lay beyond the basing point or was located on the transporting line *between the point of origin and the basing point in question.* In the former case there was a violation of the principle that the rate per ton-mile should diminish as the length of haul increases, but it is in the latter case that the peculiar unfairness of the basing-point system of rate making appears: intermediate local points are compelled to pay a rate equal to that charged for a longer movement, *plus an abnormally high local rate for a back haul that is never made.*

Public Policy.—The railways have sought to justify such a system upon the ground that, did no basing point exist, a rate equally high or even higher would govern to the local point in question; although there is an element of discrimination, the carriers contended that the local point suffered, because of extension of a "base" rate to a near-by center, no greater total charge than would otherwise apply. The general truth or falsity of this claim had to be determined in each specific instance; no general conclusion could be adequate. But certain it was that the basing-point scheme is beneficial to the few points and disadvantageous to the many. And certain is it also that, if rates to the basing points be fixed upon a higher level, a lower scale of local rates might apply at noncompetitive points without threat to the financial stability of the carriers.

It was largely as a protest against the discriminations of the Southern basing-point system that the Long-and-Short-Haul clause was included in the Interstate Commerce Act of 1887. It was incident to the application of the clause to the Southern situation that the courts so weakened it by interpretation that relief to prejudiced points was made impossible until the long-delayed amendment of Sec. 4 in 1910. With adequate power to act under the amended section, the Interstate Commerce Commission moved slowly but surely toward the elimination of all but justifiable departures from the long-and-short-haul principle. As a consequence of particular adjustments made and of changes ordered upon the basis of a searching investigation of the whole Southern rate situation, the Commission has put rates in the whole area essentially upon a "dry-land" basis: the distance principle has been accorded general recognition and departures from the long-and-short-haul principle have received Commission approval only where competition of a type beyond regulatory control functions actively. Thus has gone by the board under a régime of regulation the general application of a system of rate making that violated in many situations certain fundamentals of equity, a disappearance that contrasts interestingly with the survival of the percentage plan of adjusting rates previously described.

The Equalization Principle.—A fundamental force in the determination of rates in all areas and during all periods has been the insistence of certain agricultural, industrial, and commercial interests on equality of opportunity with certain other interests competitive with them. No rate structure applicable to a limited or an extensive area has developed that has not borne the marks of adjustments designed to secure such parity—and this is the more true because railway self-interest is at one with the needs of those served by it. Insistence upon equality of opportunity has had its part in fixing zone boundaries under the percentage plan and in the adjustment as among the North Atlantic ports whereby Baltimore and Philadelphia have been accorded differentials below New York upon export traffic from the West; it has had its part in the determination of the relation between the Baltimore-Atlanta and the Ohio River Crossings-Atlanta rates as well as of the relation of rates to Baltimore and to the Crossings from the rival industrial areas to the northeast and the northwest. Such illustrations might be extended, drawing upon major adjustments that have existed in each of the rate areas; but, rather than do this, a brief description will be given of a single rate structure in which the equalization principle was long accorded particular weight and in which it remained significant until recently, despite many changes made by regulatory authority. Indeed, such authority did little until 1931 but give recognition to the irrepressible and continuing competitive forces that compelled the original adjustments.

Western Trunk Line territory has been one of the most prosperous of the United States, with diversified farming and a rapidly developing industrial life. Rivalry among markets has been, perhaps, the principal force in shaping the rate structure; but coupled with it has been sharp traffic competition among the carriers serving the area. As a consequence of the operation of these influences it can scarcely be said that any true *system* of rate making evolved; rather, rates were the result largely of a series of adjustments among competitive points and competitive railways, with the equalization of markets in particular sections as the ultimate goal.

Early Western Trunk Line Adjustments.—The earliest and most difficult problem of adjustment in this area arose as between Chicago and St. Louis. Rates from the East, the source during early years of a large proportion of the goods marketed in the Western Trunk Line territory, gave Chicago a distinct advantage over its rival. To enable St. Louis to participate in the business of this section upon relatively equal terms with Chicago it was necessary that the former city be accorded a compensating differential below Chicago upon traffic to points north and west. Furthermore, because the business of the so-called Missouri River Crossings, lying between Kansas City and Omaha, was of considerable significance, a further adjustment was made that goods moving westward to one or another of these Crossings might pass through either Chicago or St. Louis upon substantially the same rate.

Another interesting feature of the Western Trunk Line structure appears in the construction of rates between the Mississippi and the Missouri rivers. During early years lines operating westward to the Mississippi terminated there; shipments beyond were made over connecting lines. Furthermore, to the Mississippi River Crossings the classification applicable upon tonnage originating east of Chicago was Official, while beyond the Crossings the Western Classification governed—and between these two the differences were much greater in early days than now. The custom of constructing rates, therefore, upon the basis of the rate to, plus the rate beyond, the Mississippi River arose. Traffic moving to the Missouri River might cross the Mississippi at a number of points between St. Louis and Dubuque. But, since St. Louis early enjoyed a lower percentage on westbound traffic than did other Mississippi River crossings, carriers reaching the Missouri River by way of other points than Chicago and St. Louis found themselves handicapped in competition with the carriers serving through those centers. To protect the interest of these roads, the same rates that governed traffic moving through Chicago and St. Louis were made applicable via the lesser Crossings upon traffic moving from the east to Missouri River points. To avoid another struggle, otherwise inevitable, among the carriers operating between the two rivers, a further compromise was reached. In accordance with this agreement rates were made the same on inter-river shipments between all Mississippi River Crossings, St. Louis to Dubuque inclusive, and all Missouri River Crossings, Kansas City to Omaha inclusive, this principle applying to both westbound and eastbound traffic. In making this adjustment of inter-river rates, the 60-cent charge for the 196 miles from Hannibal to St. Joseph, the short-line mileage between the rivers, was used as a base. The divergence of distances included under this uniform rate may perhaps be more fully appreciated when some of the principal mileages are given: the shortest mileage between St. Louis and Kansas City is 277, between St. Louis and Omaha 302, while the distance from St. Louis to Omaha via the Missouri Pacific is 488 and via the Illinois Central through Freeport and Dubuque, 703 miles.[1]

The Twin City Adjustments.—A third important competitive center in Western Trunk Line territory at which and in behalf of which additional adjustments in rates were compelled was Minneapolis-St. Paul. This center is accessible from the east by way of the lakes through Duluth; it is also served by Canadian rail lines and by competitive rail routes which lie wholly within the United States. Traffic from eastern points to the Twin Cities over the all-American rail lines may, furthermore, move through either Chicago or St. Louis. In adjusting the rate to Minneapolis-St. Paul through Chicago it was necessary to make a lower rate upon through traffic from the east than upon local business from Chicago, to take care of lake and Canadian rail competition. The local rate between these two centers was fixed at 75 per cent of the Chicago-Omaha rate while the through rate, via Chicago, was obtained by adding 40 cents and lesser amounts upon first and lower class traffic. Then, too, upon traffic originating at points east of Chicago the classification governing to Minneapolis-St. Paul was Official: these cities constituted a basing point for tonnage moving beyond and, as such, were accorded a rate below that applied on Chicago-Twin Cities local shipments. Since the Twin Cities might also be served via St. Louis over rail lines which did not reach Chicago, it was necessary to make an adjustment between Chicago and St. Louis to these northern cities, the rate from St. Louis to Minneapolis-St. Paul being fixed 5 per cent above the Chicago-Twin City rate. Then, of course, there appeared an insistent demand upon the part of Twin City interests for participation in the trade of the upper Mississippi Valley. Through further compromises this demand was reasonably met.

[1] As a consequence of the prescription of mileage scales in the Western Trunk Line Class case, this conspicuous instance of grouping has wholly disappeared. In this recent decision only such groups were recognized as were justified by industrial unity and these groups were specifically named, as Davenport-Rock Island-Moline, Kansas City, Missouri-Kansas, St. Louis-East St. Louis, and Duluth-Superior.

The final adjustment among these three large centers to the Missouri River gave the Twin Cities an advantage over Chicago upon local traffic as far south as Omaha, where the two were upon a parity. St. Louis, on the other hand, was accorded an advantage over Chicago and the Twin Cities from Kansas City to Omaha, and given equality with Chicago as far north as Sioux City. In brief, then, as among these three centers, it might be said the adjustment reached gave the advantage upon direct shipments to the Twin Cities in certain areas, and to St. Louis in others, while in certain sections Chicago entered the market upon a rate parity with one or the other of the two principal competing points. This statement, however, minimizes unduly the position of Chicago, the apparent disadvantage suffered because of higher rates into particular sections being offset largely by the lower rate applicable to Chicago from points east. Therefore it is perhaps more accurate to say that certain small areas were given into the control of the Twin Cities and of St. Louis while in the major portion of the territory lying between the western rivers and in the cities upon the Missouri, Chicago was accorded equality with one or another or both of its major competitors.

Other Relations Established.—With the further development of trade in Western Trunk Line territory, other adjustments were made. Westbound, Peoria was accorded a differential under the Chicago rate, while to Memphis was given the same rate into Kansas City as applied from Chicago, with a fixed differential above Chicago to other Missouri River crossings. From Cairo the rates to Missouri River crossings lying between Kansas City and St. Joseph were made on a parity with Chicago, while from Nebraska City north to Omaha another fixed differential was applied. Milwaukee, enjoying the same rates from the east as Chicago, was placed upon the same basis in western traffic. Duluth participated in Minnesota and Wisconsin trade upon the basis of agreed arbitraries under and above St. Paul. Interstate rates into Iowa were built essentially upon the Des Moines rate, this Des Moines rate in turn growing out of a series of relations. In its determination the basic factor was the rate governing between St. Louis and St. Paul, the St. Louis-Des Moines charge bearing a definite relation thereto, while the Chicago-Des Moines rate was fixed in relation to the St. Louis-Des Moines charge.

Summary Statement.—To summarize the situation in Western Trunk Line territory, it may well be said that the entire structure developed, not in accord with any governing principle but, rather, in such manner as to equalize market opportunities among important centers and to meet the exigencies of railway competition. Distance was given recognition to such degree as it did not hamper this equalization and departures from the long-and-short-haul rule were comparatively few. As a consequence of these facts and the absence of particular abuses to inflame the shipping public, this scheme of rate making persisted through a long period with little complaint against the principle upon which it rested—the structure giving proof, during its life, of the tremendous significance of competition in the determination of rate relations throughout an important area. It was only as the powerful hand of public authority swept away adjustments and compromises forced by traffic, market, and industrial competition and substituted therefor an orderly plan that a rate structure became effective in the area which conforms to the essential canons of reasonableness and equity.[1]

The "Blanket" Rate.—A great variety of considerations have led to the grouping of points of origin and points of destination for purposes of rate making. Grouping, or "blanketing," serves to equalize opportunity; it constitutes an avenue of escape from violations of the long-and-short-haul rule, while obviating the need of rates graded rigidly according to distance; it gives a measure of recognition to the principle of distance, that measure varying inversely with the extent of the "blanket"; and, too, it is an effective aid to the abbreviation of tariffs in the same manner as is the classification of commodities. The utility of this device was early recognized by the railways and it has been accorded wide use, hardly a rate structure developing that did not give it recognition to greater or lesser degree. In the application of the percentage plan the desirability of percentage zones was early recognized and continued; with the establishment of rates in Southern territory upon a "dry-land" basis the carriers have, quite generally, carried the rate to successive important centers back for considerable distances. In Western Trunk Line territory, too, grouping has been employed widely, but it is incident to Southwestern and Transcontinental rates that the device has flowered. That a clear understanding may be had of the extent to which "blanketing" sometimes proceeds and of the forces impelling resort to it a brief statement concerning several important groupings is justified.

Texas Common Point Territory.—The settlement of Texas long antedated the construction of the first railways in that state; indeed, prior to the appearance of the railway that state had won its independence from Mexico and had become one of the United States. Early settlements lay largely, however, within a narrow strip of country bordering the Gulf: the burden of overland transport was too great to permit of any extensive development of the great "hinterland" to the north and west. But, with the coming of the railway, the situation changed strikingly. The earliest of these carriers were pushed inland from the Gulf; yet, by the early nineties, railways had been built into Texas from the east, from the northeast, from the north, and from the northwest. The Texas market was open to all.

[1] Western Trunk Line Class Rates, 164 I.C.C. 1; 173 I.C.C. 637.

This market immediately became an object of great interest to the rapidly developing Mid-western industrial area and to the carriers over which finished products might flow from it into a territory that had, hitherto, been supplied almost wholly from the northeastern part of the United States: goods had moved by water to the Gulf ports and thence inland by wagon or by rail. Immediately sharp competition developed between carrier groups interested in supplying the market from the rival

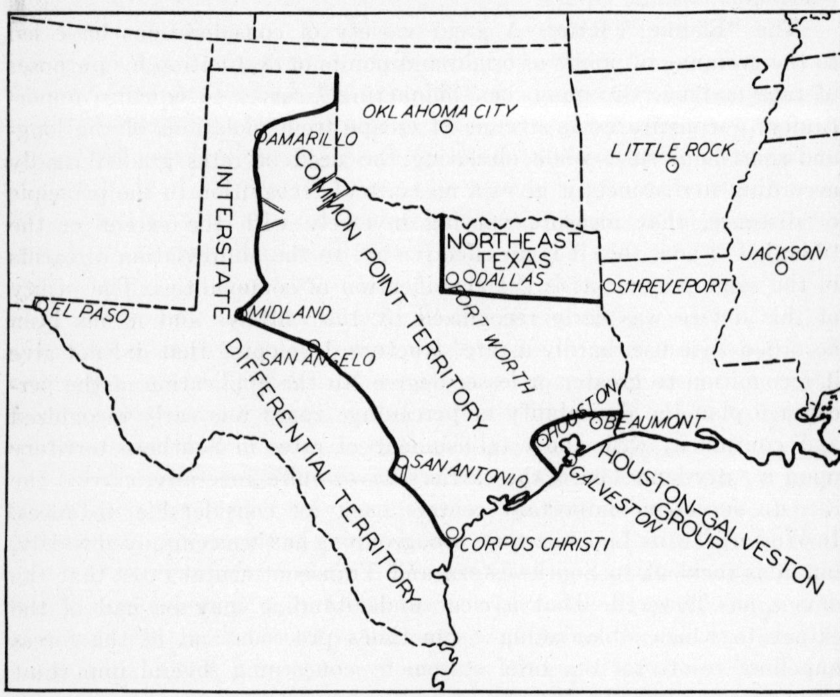

FIG. 34.—Rate areas in Texas, with railways in Common Point territory over which differential rates govern shown.

industrial districts. This competition of carriers was finally composed by the "blanketing" of a major portion of Texas upon shipments originating upon or beyond the Mississippi and Missouri rivers: into a territory with maximum distances of about 500 miles from north to south and 450 miles from east to west the same rate applied—whether the movement was to Denison, just beyond the northern border of the state, or to Corpus Christi, in the far south. And, because of the most unusual intrastate rate structure imposed upon the railways,[1] the opportunity afforded for the distribution of eastern industrial products entering through the Gulf ports was also unusual. Thus was accomplished in an important market area the equalization of the two great industrial regions and of the

[1] See pp. 542 and following for a brief description of this structure.

carriers whose interests were identified with each. And this system long remained effective with but infrequent challenge.

With the passage of time, however, Texas points to the westward of the boundary of Common Point territory gained sufficient strength to compel recognition. Yet against the insistence of such points for the extension of the territory was the desire of the railways to shrink it: already it was so wide as to make it apparent that a rate to northern Texas points must be too high or that same rate to points far beyond must be too low. Then, too, as industry developed in Kansas City and as the volume of movements into Texas increased through the lower Mississippi River Crossings, such as Memphis and New Orleans, certain demands were made for preference as against St. Louis on the basis of distance. In consequence of the operation of these and other influences, certain minor adjustments have been made: the western boundary of Common Point territory has been moved to include more of Differential territory, a Northeast Texas group has been established to which Kansas City enjoys a measure of preference over St. Louis on shipments originating at those points and to which rates on certain commodities have been prescribed from the Defined Territories beyond slightly below the Texas Common Point rate; concessions have been made to the lower Crossings; and a Houston-Galveston group has been recognized, to which lower rates than those to Common Point territory have been accorded from the north to meet competition from the Atlantic seaboard.

In the determination of the rate into the Southwest from points beyond the Mississippi and Missouri rivers the principle of grouping again appears. For many years rates into Texas Common Point territory were quoted from the so-called Defined Territories. These, varying widely in area and in contour, embraced a large part of the United States to the north and east of Southwestern territory, with boundaries determined fundamentally by competitive conditions but fixed so cleverly as to escape change or even major attack until recently. However, in the Consolidated Southwestern cases[1] the Interstate Commerce Commission has ordered an increase in the number of groups which, by decreasing size, gives greater recognition to the advantage of geographical location. Among these older groups were the Omaha-Davenport, the Chicago-Cincinnati, the Louisville, the Nashville, the Carolina, and the Raleigh. From any point in a particular Defined Territory the rate into the Texas Common Point area was found by adding to the St. Louis-Common Point rate the differential applicable, these differentials increasing with distance. Under the plan more recently prescribed the same general scheme of rate making has been preserved, though certain changes of major significance have been made: rates between points in the new Defined Territories and points in the Southwest are based not only

[1] 123 I.C.C. 203.

upon St. Louis but also such other "gateways" as New Orleans, Vicksburg, Memphis, and Kansas City; and groupings have been established in Southwestern territory for movements through each of the "gateways" named. This entire readjustment affecting Southwestern traffic represents an increasing recognition of the distance principle, an abandonment of the extensive "blanketing" so characteristic of Southwestern rates in the past.

"Blanketing" in Transcontinental Rates.—In rate making between the great area to the east of the Rocky Mountains and the Pacific coast the principle of grouping has long been recognized, with respect to both east- and westbound movements. Though space forbids a complete statement of the development of this structure, than which no other is more interesting, certain basic facts justify presentation. Perhaps the most conspicuous use of the "blanket" in the history of American rate making appeared in the westbound structure prior to interference by the Interstate Commerce Commission in 1911 and the establishment then of a more equitable relation not only between Intermountain and Pacific coast points but also between areas of origin in the east. As a result of competitive activity a structure of rates that had given due recognition to distance prior to 1887 had, within a period of 10 years, come to neglect distance to such an extent that the rates from Chicago and from a point such as Portland, Maine, to the Pacific coast were the same—and this "blanket" was later extended westward until the whole of the United States eastward of Denver stood upon the same basis on the west coast. And the rate from Denver to Reno, Nev., was identical with that from the eastern seaboard to Reno. But while this situation existed with respect to westbound movements, eastbound tonnage moved upon rates that varied measurably with distance—with destinations grouped in a reasonably equitable manner.

The unreasonable "blanket" applicable to movements to the West coast could not be expected to stand in the face of effective regulation, nor has it. Instead, westbound tonnage now moves upon rates that grade upward with distance but, again, rates apply from groupings rather than from individual points. These groupings for westbound movement are not the same, however, as those for eastbound: competitive forces do not operate in the same manner.

Thus it appears that, as time has passed, grouping for rate purposes has persisted in Transcontinental territory, though the more unreasonable groupings have been eliminated. Such is true with respect to class traffic but it is much less true of tonnage that moves subject to commodity rates—and much of the long-haul business, both east- and westbound, so moves. For this traffic competition is exceedingly keen both among the railways and between the railways and the boat lines operating through the Panama Canal,—with rivalry no less keen in Eastern markets between certain major products of the Pacific coast area and of other portions of the United States. As a consequence, commodity rates on traffic moving to the West coast tend to neglect even the groupings that normally govern class shipments and rates from the West are often "blanketed" beyond the Mississippi or even the Missouri River. While it is improbable that any long forward step can be taken to eliminate the use of excessive "blankets" so long as water rates through the Canal remain unregulated, it does seem that regulatory action might be taken to limit measurably the scope of interrailway competition and to secure to certain producing areas a greater measure of their natural advantage. Such progress is made slowly, however, and recognition must be given for a great advance beyond the Transcontinental rate structure in 1911 when the Commission first acted upon the basis of adequate powers.

The Graded-and-maximum Rate Plan.—One of the most interesting rate structures applied by American railways to freight traffic is that which applied for a long period to movements within the state of Texas. To an understanding of it a knowledge of its historical background is essential. As indicated before, Texas was settled from the Gulf; beyond was a hinterland of tremendous area and of almost infinite possibilities. At the head of the Texas Railroad Commission, one of the pioneer regulatory bodies of the United States, was Judge Reagan, a strong man possessed of social vision. To promote the more even development of the state, and to make less likely the growth of one or two great centers which would dominate the commercial and industrial life of Texas, he utilized, as the basis of a novel rate structure, a system of rate adjustments that had already developed out of competitive conditions within the state. This unusual structure long controlled all movements of traffic wholly within the state.

Nature of the Adjustment.—The outstanding peculiarity of this scheme was that, beyond a certain distance, traffic moved upon a uniform rate within Texas intrastate Common Point territory, this maximum distance varying with the character of the tonnage. On flour, hay, and grain, rates increased with distance up to 200 miles; on cotton to 210 miles; on first-class shipments, to 245 miles; and on coal, to 790 miles. Beyond these distances, rates did not vary in the eastern portion of the state. However, to the westward of the intrastate Common Point territory, which extended generally somewhat farther west than the interstate Common Point territory, lay a considerable area known as "Differential territory." In that area rates gradually increased with distance beyond the maxima just mentioned, to a maximum charge of $1.05 per hundredweight, first class, except on shipments between points on the Texas and Pacific, Sherman or Dallas and west, or between points on the Southern Pacific, San Antonio, and west, to which a maximum of $1 applied. For the operation of this graded-and-maximum-rate system any point in Texas might be taken as a center, with a result that, despite widely divergent distances from central markets and ports, agricultural and industrial development was measurably uniform throughout the state and the population is served by a large number of distributing centers of relatively equal importance, scattered widely throughout Common Point territory. Indeed, the interstate and intrastate rate structures have so operated in conjunction as to favor, in a peculiar degree, this distribution of trade among markets; by virtue of their joint operation widely separated points, such as San Antonio and Denison, enjoyed the same rate from the Mid-western industrial area, though the former lies approximately 300 miles beyond the state line; and these two centers competed, in territory lying midway between, on relatively equal terms even though such business involved a back haul from San Antonio.

Modification of the Texas Intrastate Structure.—The system of rate making prescribed and maintained by the Texas commission was wholly unsatisfactory to the carriers from a revenue standpoint, yet efforts to secure important modifications availed little: the regulatory body was firm in its determination to make no changes in rate policy that would disturb long-standing adjustments, agricultural and commercial and trade. Material modification of the graded-and-maximum structure resulted, however, from federal action growing out of and following the Shreveport controversy. After successive examinations of the situation, the Interstate Commerce Commission prescribed in 1916 a scale of class rates to govern movements from Shreveport to all points in Texas east of interstate Differential territory, also a scale of differentials to be added to cover movements into that area. Commodity rate scales were also prescribed for a number of important items. These rate scales, class and commodity, were made the yardstick of reasonableness in that section and were, in consequence, imposed upon Texas intrastate movements despite the vigorous protests of Texas shipping interests and the Texas Railroad Commission. The scales have been modified from time to time in the successive Southwestern cases but no change has served to lessen the importance of distance under the new plan or to restore an old structure which ignored distance wholly beyond a prescribed mileage.

Recent Major Rate Revisions.—From the preceding pages the reader must gather a clear realization not only of the wide divergence among rate structures that developed during that period prior to effective federal regulation but also of the various forces that, operating differently as among the numerous districts, accomplished such contrasting results. But it was not reasonable to expect the continuance of structures so widely divergent, once positive control had been established over interstate movements: though many states had acted to eliminate major bases of public complaint against the carriers, those states were helpless in dealing with the structures that were dominant. As a consequence of the interpretations of the Interstate Commerce Act of 1887, the Interstate Commerce Commission found itself unable to deal effectively with any of the outstanding abuses that had inflamed the public mind to the point where federal legislation was demanded. While the Hepburn Act of 1906 gave to the Commission certain needed powers to deal with rates, it was not until 1910 that this body found itself possessed of sufficient power to deal fundamentally and constructively with *rate structures* rather than with *individual rates*. This power once conferred, opportunity for its exercise was not long delayed; indeed, at the time such power was conferred there was before the Commission again for consideration one of its knottiest problems, the relation of rates on traffic from the east to Intermountain and to Pacific coast points.

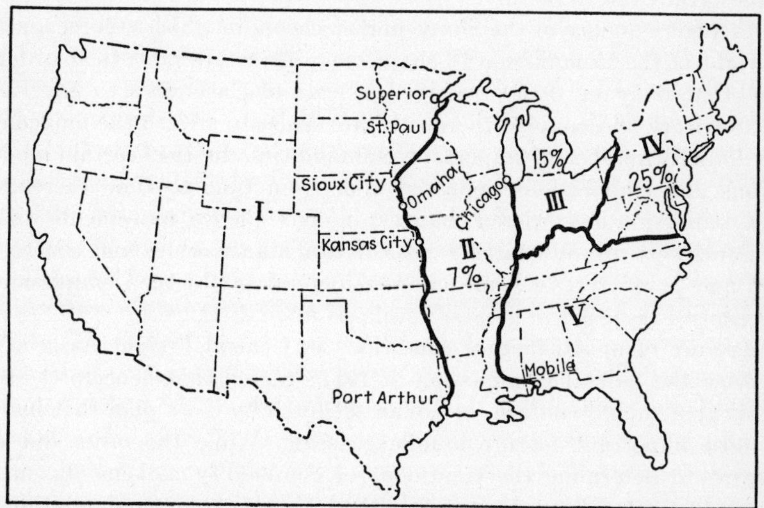

FIG. 35.—Zone boundaries fixed in 1911 by the Interstate Commerce Commission—westbound traffic to Intermountain and Pacific coast points.

Early Commission Action.—After studying carefully the problem presented and giving due weight to the insistence of the carriers that competition made necessary lower rates to coast points than to points in the Intermountain area and the bitter complaint of Intermountain centers against the discrimination to which they had long been subjected, the Commission ordered a modification in carrier policy. The United States was divided into zones, numbered from I to V—Zone I including that area, roughly, westward of a line from Duluth through the Twin Cities, Omaha, Kansas City, and thence south to Port Arthur on the gulf, with other zones lying successively eastward. While no rates were set upon westbound movements to coast and to inland cities, the Commission did prescribe the relation to be maintained between any rates made applicable. Since water competition was a negligible factor from points in Zone I to the West coast, no rate from a Zone I point might be higher to Intermountain territory than to the Western ports; but, as such competition might be a factor in the case of movements from Zone II, the rate to an Intermountain point might be made 7 per cent above that to the coast. From Zone III a differential of 15 per cent was permitted and from Zone IV the rate to an inland center might be 25 per cent greater—increasing percentages being allowed because of the increasing likelihood of active water competition for westbound tonnage. From Zone V, probably because of the small volume of tonnage moving from the South to the Far West, no differential was fixed. Thus, to reduce discrimination from unreasonable to reasonable proportions the Interstate Commerce Commission took its first action in reshaping an important rate structure.[1]

As a consequence of the Shreveport decision, in which was recognized the right of the Commission to shape even intrastate rates to an ordered plan, that body in 1916 prescribed a scale of class rates to govern in that territory and coupled therewith rate scales to govern the movement of a limited number of important commodities. In 1919 certain modifications and elaborations appeared and, from time to time thereafter, the Commission has ordered changes; in consequence, movements within the Southwest are now largely subject to distance scales and control of "in" and "out" rates is being assumed increasingly by the Commission—this control resulting in greater emphasis upon distance.

Because of unsatisfactory conditions in Central Freight Association territory the federal Commission in 1917 ordered that henceforth rates in this area should conform to a plan set forth by it—a plan that had as its most important feature a mileage scale. While the order did not attempt to determine the treatment of commodity movements, many commodity rates have been established that bear a fixed relation to class rates and change with class rates. And in New England, again because of the impossibility of coordinating an existing hodgepodge of rates into a system, the Commission applied in 1918 essentially the same scheme of class rates that had been made effective the previous year in Central Freight Association territory. Here the mileage scale could be applied upon a point-to-point basis, largely because of the small number of stations involved in contrast to the plan of publishing group

[1] Permission to the railways to make lower rates to Pacific coast ports than to cities in the Intermountain area was suspended in 1917 because of the disappearance during the war period of water competition through the Panama Canal. With the reappearance of such competition, however, the Commission refused to approve the publication of rates upon the previous percentage basis. Because of continued refusal of Fourth Section relief to the railways on west-bound tonnage to the coast, both the railways and the Middle West have suffered economically—with the gains of the Intermountain cities doubtful.

rates in the western area. Commodity rates were again left untouched and have continued to correlate little with class rates.

Later Commission Action.—The attention of the Interstate Commerce Commission seems to have been largely directed for a time to matters other than an attempt to bring order from chaos in other rate areas. In 1922, however, the Commission initiated an investigation of rates in Southern territory. After a thorough study of the situation a sweeping order was issued in 1925, this order being supplemented and modified at later dates. The prime purposes of Commission action in this area have been to reduce discrimination to a reasonable basis and to make a harmonious whole of Southern class and commodity rates, intrastate and interstate, as well as of class rates between the South and other territories. To this end rate scales that are based fundamentally upon distance have been imposed, though competition has been given weight in the application of such scales and "blanketing" for considerable distances has displaced the basing-point principle with its definite violation of distance. Again commodity rates have remained essentially untouched, though an increase in the number of classifications in Southern territory was made in the hope of reducing the number of exceptions and of commodity rates, carload and less-than-carload. Among other matters with which the Commission dealt was the situation of the so-called "weak lines," these being accorded rates in excess of the rates applicable over standard railways.

In 1924 an investigation of rates in Trunk Line territory was instituted upon the motion of the federal Commission. This investigation was later broadened at the insistence of the railways—their interest being increased revenues—to cover the whole of the Eastern District and the Commission's report, with supplemental orders, indicates a purpose to harmonize and unify rate structures in that highly important traffic area.[1] First-class rates were prescribed to govern interstate class movements between key points in the Eastern District, with variations to meet the needs of light-traffic areas and individual lines, and the carriers were ordered to establish 22 classes below first class but related thereto upon a prescribed percentage basis. The lowest percentage indicated is 13, with 8 below 30, it being again the expectation that the carriers will progressively relate commodity rates to the first-class rate and thereby simplify tariff publication. Mileage scales were also prescribed to apply to specified movements of certain named commodities; among the more important items for which such scales were set forth are iron and steel, stone and sand and gravel, cement, lumber, live stock, and grain—though the rates prescribed for the movement of some commodities have territorially a rather limited application.

[1] Eastern Class Rate Investigation, 164 I.C.C. 314; 171 I.C.C. 481; and 177 I.C.C. 156.

The rate situation in Western Trunk Line territory had long been recognized as chaotic. Competition—market, industrial, and carrier—had played a large part in fixing certain relations but the complexities resulting therefrom had been increased further by a sharp diversity in intrastate policies among the states. From time to time the Interstate Commerce Commission had acted to eliminate abuses and to reduce discrimination and the carriers had acted similarly. Such piecemeal

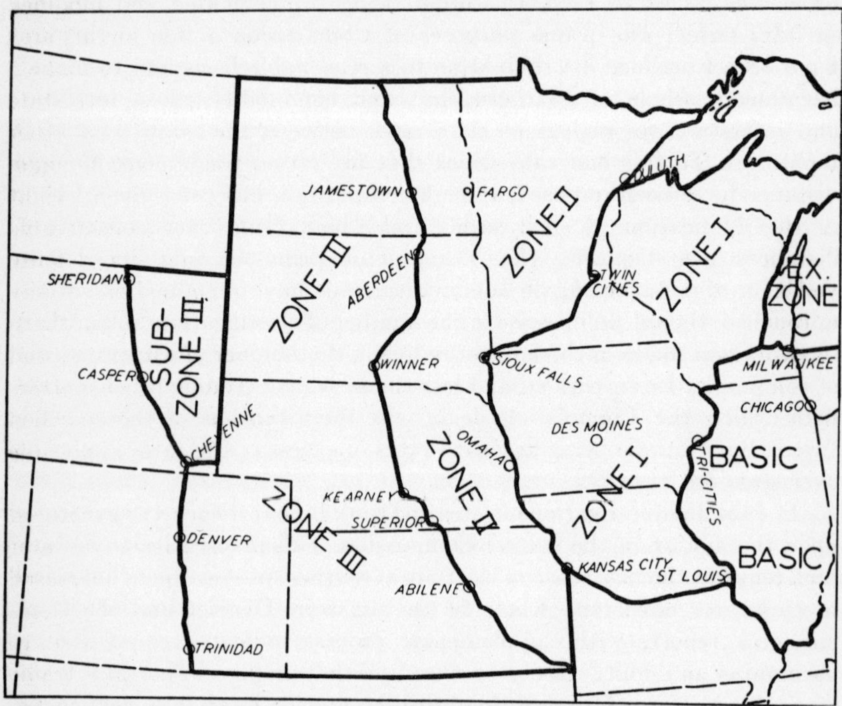

FIG. 36.—Zone boundaries as fixed to govern movements into Western Trunk Line territory.

changes often merely created other problems which gave rise to complaint.[1] Finally, in 1926, in part with a view to harmonizing the entire rate structure and in part with a view to increasing the revenues of the carriers, a general investigation was undertaken. As in the case of other

[1] Significant among the changes that compelled further action to improve rate relations in Western Trunk Line territory and between it and Central Freight Association territory were those made in accord with and consequent to the Interstate Commerce Commission's decisions in the so-called Indiana State Chamber of Commerce cases, 88 I.C.C. 709 and 728. In these cases an important modification was ordered in rates and in the principle of rate construction from Indiana to the Twin Cities and also to Kansas City and other Missouri River cities, as well as points intermediate thereto. The primary change lay in the establishment of joint through rates that were lower than combinations made upon Chicago to the Northwest and the Mississippi River to the West, this overturning a long-accepted policy.

similar general investigations, extended hearings were held and a great volume of evidence offered. In the light of all facts adduced, the Commission ordered a complete reorganization of the governing rate structure. In Western Trunk Line territory three zones were defined, these reflecting differences in transportation conditions, and mileage scales were prescribed to govern intra- and interzone movements. Specific class rates were named between key points in Western Trunk Line territory and key points in Central Freight Association, Trunk Line, and New England territories which are, in general, consonant with distance. The publication of class rates with the lower classes a percentage of first class was ordered, the same percentages governing as were fixed for Eastern territory. The scales of rates prescribed to govern movements in Zones I and II of Western Line territory were related to the rates prescribed in Eastern territory by the commission, while the Zone III scale was related both to Zone II rates and to the rates applicable in Southwestern territory. Thus a measure of unity was attained throughout an extended area. And, as in the Eastern Class Rate decision, commodity rates upon certain named items were published for limited application territorially. Other matters upon which the Commission held that the record was inadequate were left open for further consideration and later adjustment; important among these were lake-rail rates, rates between this and Southern territory, and certain barge-rail rates.

Trends in Rate Making.—Even the brief description herein given of certain of the more significant rate structures that long governed traffic movements in particular areas indicates that in their formulation definite plan played a minor rôle; rather, they were grounded upon historical developments and shaped largely by the competitive situation faced. Only one, the graded-and-maximum intrastate structure of Texas, represented an effort to accomplish a definite social end. And all but the Texas structure took form without guidance or pressure from regulatory authority. But, just as those earlier structures were the consequence of conditions governing when they took shape, so changes in conditions must operate to modify the old and even compel the acceptance of new structures.

Changes that have exerted an important influence are several. The diminution and stabilization of rail competition through corporate integration, combination, and agreement have been significant, as have been changes in the volume of water-borne tonnage and variations in market and industrial competition. Then, too, more intelligent effort on the part of individual railways to aid their own territories has been made. But no less important than these has been the purposive exercise of its present broad powers by the Interstate Commerce Commission, with a view not only to the elimination of unfair discrimination and unfair practices but also to the replacement of a hodgepodge of individual rates by rate structures that accord with sound principle and harmonize with structures that govern in adjacent areas.

That old rate structures are rapidly giving way to new is evident from the brief summary given on preceding pages of Commission investigations and orders. The old have been characterized largely by carrier self-interest and competitive necessity rather than by conformance to standards of reasonableness as developed under regulation or to the economic requirements of areas that had emerged from a period of development, to the demands of which the old schemes had been adapted. Even those structures that served sufficiently well to escape the positive condemnation of carrier and public were in need of adjustment to new conditions, while other structures were so ill-suited as to merit complete elimination. Yet, without the assistance of the federal Commission, little progress could be made: the more crying the need for change, the more certain were there to be found carrier or shipper groups unwilling to surrender some advantage enjoyed under the old régime—or the more difficult was it to secure that unity of action among railways which is essential to the elimination of unreasonable discrimination as among places, persons, and commodities. Eager though both carriers and shippers were, by and large, to modernize rate structures and to minimize discrimination, and willing though these groups have often been to cooperate under the leadership of the Interstate Commerce Commission in the accomplishment of these ends, it is true that each major rate structure has been revised in accord with Commission orders rather than upon carrier or shipper initiative or upon the basis of agreement between the two.

In these revisions that have dealt in turn with each of the principal rate structures of the United States, it appears that certain definite purposes shaped the character of Commission action. Of these purposes perhaps the most obvious has been the elimination of all undue discrimination. To this end the Commission has resorted to the prescription of mileage scales, rates being made upon a point-to-point basis or between groups of points—with these groups sufficiently small to escape the charge of undue preference. In the construction of mileage scales for application to adjacent areas, every effort has been made to relate the scales in such manner as to minimize discrimination against the area to which the higher scale applies. Departures from the long-and-short-haul principle have failed to gain approval except where such departures can be clearly justified and, to assist in minimizing discrimination as among both places and commodities, the Commission has indicated its intent to establish a large number of classes with the rate on each lower class bearing a uniform percentage relation to the first-class rate.

The establishment of a large number of classes with the percentage of first class falling as low as 13 upon the lowest class will assist, too, in the accomplishment of a second purpose, the simplification of tariffs. Thus, instead of a special commodity rate being published, it will often be possible to assign to the item that is in need of special consideration a low classification, thereby avoiding a further complication of tariffs. A third purpose of Commission action seems to be the establishment of a system of rates that is at the same time remunerative to the carrier and reasonable to the shipper. That this purpose may be accomplished with greater certainty numerous cost studies have been made, with cost judgments modified in application only in so far as reductions may be necessary to permit the railway to share tonnage with competitive agencies or as increases may be essential to provide for the carriers adequate revenues.[1]

In consequence of action already taken by the Interstate Commerce Commission and of the continuance of pressure against unsatisfactory adjustments, rate structures that have been but a conglomeration of particular charges or have outlived such justification as they once had, bid fair to be replaced within a period of years by harmonious and orderly structures suited to the needs of industry and commerce.[2] Accompanying these new structures, in part cause and in part effect, will be marked changes in economic conditions; certain sections, losing the benefit of preferential rates, may suffer a decline in activity, while others, relieved of undue burdens, may enjoy an unwonted prosperity. With these changes and as a part of the movement will come, undoubtedly, a wider acceptance and application by regulatory bodies of the cost principle as a basis of rates and a greater effort on the part of the carriers to ascertain costs: rates fixed by public authority must be set by some more demonstrable yardstick than personal judgment and it is likely that the Hoch-Smith experiences of the railways will leave them less enamored of ability as a

[1] It seems that, because of highway competition, rates upon the shorter hauls must be made below *average total cost*, with *additional cost of the specific service* as the minimum. To compensate for this failure to earn a full return upon short-haul traffic, it is probable that rates upon the longer hauls, less subject to highway inroads, will be increased. In consequence, rates are likely to advance more nearly by a steady progression, rather than the rate curve showing a tendency to "flatten out" after tonnage has moved perhaps 200–300 miles. Furthermore, it is probable that through "overhead" rates will be prescribed less often in the future and that many such rates now effective will be rescinded, the effect of such adjustments being to lessen carrier revenues upon the long-haul traffic that continues to move largely by rail.

[2] At the very time when there seems to be strong likelihood that the operation of various forces, dominantly public authority, may bring order from chaos in the field of rates, the operation of unregulated transport agencies in competition with the railways may easily destroy within a few years much of the logical organization that it has taken years to attain, and may readily make for the reappearance of gross discrimination among persons and places that regulatory bodies have struggled long and earnestly to eliminate. If with no other thought than to avoid the confusion and the discrimination that must inevitably result from unregulated competition, the public should support a reasonable yet effective program of regulation for transportation by highway, water, and air, quite as well as by rail.

basis of rates than they were in the past. Such a development, though sacrificing a degree of flexibility, will nevertheless give a permanency and stability to freight rates, as well as a scientific aspect, that has not been characteristic of American railway freight structures in the past.

Passenger Rates.—In the discussion preceding, which has dealt with rate making in practice, sole consideration has been given to freight rates. This seemingly undue emphasis may be explained by the fact that the principle governing the making of passenger rates is normally quite simple; rates tend to vary exactly with the distance and, if the distance be known and the governing rate per mile be used as a multiplier, the total charge can be readily ascertained. True, competition has functioned here as it has in the freight field but such competition, because of the peculiar character of passenger traffic, cannot be carried to the extremes of discrimination so often found in the freight service. Another important point of difference between the making of passenger rates and of freight rates appears in the extent to which the former have been determined in times past by legislative action: 2-cent, 2½-cent, and 3-cent fare laws have been enacted by the legislatures of many states. Such statutes oftentimes occasioned discrimination between intrastate and interstate movements and not infrequently threw a financial burden upon the carriers or upon other traffic. This fare-fixing movement, however, tended to subside after 1910 and, following the decision of the Supreme Court in the Wisconsin Passenger Fare case in 1922, all such legislation has become inoperative: although the rate level in the future may quite properly vary between divergent sections of the country, it is unlikely that discrimination between interstate and intrastate traffic, or among points, will have any considerable future significance with respect to passenger traffic. In short, rate making in the passenger field may be expected to be even more simple in the future than in the past, with two factors dominating: mileage and the rate per mile.

REFERENCES

Clarke, J. M.: Standards of Rate Reasonableness in Local Freight Discrimination, *Columbia University Studies*, vol. 37, No. 1.

Converse, Paul: The Problem of the Transcontinental Rate Structure, *Journal of Political Economy*, vol. 126, pp. 291–301.

Daggett, Stuart R.: *Principles of Inland Transportation*, Harper & Brothers, 1928.

Fagg, Charles J.: *The Freight Traffic Red Book*, The Traffic Publishing Company (annual).

Fink, Albert: *Railroad Transportation*, 1882.

Haney, Lewis H.: *The Business of Railway Transportation*, Ronald Press Company, 1924.

Interstate Commerce Commission: *Annual Reports; Reports.* See especially C. F. A. Class Scale Case, 45 I.C.C. 254; Proposed Increases in New England, 49 I.C.C. 421; Eastern Class Rate Investigation, 164 I.C.C. 315, 171 I.C.C. 481, and 177 I.C.C. 156; Southern Class Rate Investigation, 100 I.C.C. 513, 113 I.C.C. 200, and 128 I.C.C. 567; and numerous later findings fixing rates on particular or general movements of named commodities; Western Trunk Line Class Rates, 164 I.C.C. 1, and 173 I.C.C. 637;

Consolidated Southwestern cases, 123 I.C.C. 203; Fourth Section cases, 21 I.C.C. 329, 400; 46 I.C.C. 236; 61 I.C.C. 226, and 107 I.C.C. 421.

JACKMAN, W. T.: *Economics of Transportation*, McGraw-Hill Book Company, Inc., 1926.

JOHNSON, E. R., and G. G. HUEBNER: *Railroad Traffic and Rates*, vol. 1, D. Appleton & Company, 1911.

———, G. G. HUEBNER, and G. L. WILSON: *Principles of Transportation*, D. Appleton & Company, 1928.

JONES, ELIOT: *Principles of Railway Transportation*, The Macmillan Company, 1924.

LOCKLIN, D. P.: *Railroad Regulation since* 1920. McGraw-Hill Book Company, Inc., 1928 (Supplement 1931).

MCPHERSON, LOGAN: *Railroad Freight Rates*, Henry Holt and Company, 1909.

MILLER, S. L.: *Railway Transportation*, McGraw-Hill Book Company, Inc., 1924.

RIPLEY, W. Z.: *Railroads: Rates and Regulation*, Longmans, Green & Co., 1912.

———: *Railway Problems*, Ginn & Company, 1913.

VANDERBLUE, H. B., and K. F. BURGESS: *Railroads: Rates, Service, Management*, The Macmillan Company, 1923.

Chapter XXXII

COMPARATIVE RAILWAY CHARGES

DURING the past 100 years the steam railway has developed from a mere experiment into a transportation agency of fundamental significance, and in no country has that development been more striking than in the United States. Expanding rapidly, our railway net today comprises almost 40 per cent of the mileage of the world. Yet, since transportation agencies are not ends in themselves but instrumentalities of commerce, the comparisons of greatest value are those of service rather than of mileage. And, as the rate is the only mathematical index available of service efficiency, the rate becomes of immediate concern. How does the cost of transportation in the South compare with that in the North, in the East with that of the West? How do the rates in the coal districts of West Virginia compare with those of Illinois, upon Kansas wheat with those upon Dakota grain? Indeed, how do rates upon traffic in the United States compare with those levied upon traffic in other countries? In arriving at conclusions, the comparison of individual rates or of the totals of published rates would avail little. General conclusions so based would be hard to draw and, when drawn, would be worth little because the tonnage moving upon some rates is negligible, upon others tremendous. However deficient it may be, the only practicable basis of comparison yet proposed is that of the average cost of movement of all traffic handled by particular railways or groups of railways.

Traffic Units and Freight and Passenger Service.—In computing such an average, the first difficulty met has proved insuperable—it has been impossible to devise a common base for the two great types of traffic—for freight, upon which charges vary in general with quantity and distance, and passenger, upon which the individual charge varies with the distance factor alone. True enough, bases of equation have been devised, but the absence of agreement among these indicates the difficulty of securing a reliable consolidated figure. As a result of inability to discover a common base, therefore, service as a whole of one railway cannot be compared with service as a whole of another: such comparisons as are made must be between similar types of service rendered by the carriers or groups of carriers under consideration.

In the selection of the unit to be used in the determination of average freight charges, choice may be made from among several. Of these the train-mile is one, but variations in train length are great from day to day and from season to season upon a single line, to say nothing of the variations between plains and mountainous territory and between countries. Therefore the train-mile as well as the car-mile, objectionable because of wide variations in load from time to time and from place to place, are so open to criticism that they have been accepted by none. Indeed, the only unit which is sufficiently uniform to justify its utilization in the freight field is the *ton-mile*. By definition, the ton-mile is the movement of one ton one mile or its equivalent—as, for example, 100 pounds 20 miles. Yet it may be well to note that even ton-mile compilations may not be comparable, because, in arriving at the figures, gross tonnage, net tonnage, or net revenue tonnage may have been used. This difficulty is not experienced in the United States, however, because all American ton-mile statistics are prepared according to rules laid down by the Interstate Commerce Commission and cover, presumably, net tonnage alone, a clear differentiation between revenue and nonrevenue traffic also being made. Several methods may be followed in compiling ton-mile data, but generally it is obtained by multiplying the weight of each shipment by the number of miles it has been moved, both facts being derived from the waybill or obtained from the freight conductor's wheel report. These data are compiled in the accounting office and it is in that office that monthly aggregates are made, not only of ton-miles but also of total tons of traffic handled, classified according to commodities.

In the selection of a unit to be used for comparative purposes in the passenger field, the problem is somewhat more difficult. Although the train-mile is as faulty here as it is in connection with freight movements, the car-mile is deserving of more serious consideration. To a degree which is not true of freight, the weight of the passengers occupying a car is negligible when compared with the dead weight of the heavily built vehicle in which they are moved. Therefore, when the factor of cost is regarded, it might well seem proper to give the car-mile serious consideration. However, because of the universal significance attached to traffic units and the fact that the charge so clearly pertains to the individual movement, the *passenger-mile* has been adopted generally as the basis of comparisons in this field. This unit, like the ton-mile, may be compiled upon different bases, but figures for American roads are prepared upon the basis of what might be termed public movement, excluding movements of persons on company business. These figures, covering revenue passenger movements, are compiled by the accounting department, as are the ton-mile statistics, and usually are based upon conductors' reports submitted at the end of each run.

Computation of Unit Costs.—Once the ton-mile figures of a given division, railway, territory, or country are available, the average-cost figure to be used for comparative purposes is obtained by a simple mathematical operation—the division of the total gross revenue from freight service by the total number of ton-miles of business handled by the particular unit or area for which ton-mile costs are desired. Similarly, the average cost of passenger movement is determined by dividing passenger-miles into gross passenger revenue. The figures thus obtained show, for a given period, the average price paid by the particular public for the movement of one ton and one passenger, respectively, a distance of one mile. Conclusions based upon a comparison of these figures are given great weight by many, and railways able to show a small quotient herald the fact with pride. Such figures have been accepted, too, by the public as an infallible index of carrier efficiency. Immediately the question arises, "Are such comparisons to be accepted at their face value, or does careful analysis tend to discount obvious conclusions?"

Railway Costs and Charges.—Before entering upon such an analysis, it is desirable that the nature and elements of cost, as before mentioned, be clearly understood. Under conditions of perfect competition in any field, cost to the marginal producer—necessary profits being included—and cost to the consumer are identical. The railway industry is not one in which competition has functioned in such manner as to insure this identity of costs, however, even where the various properties are so owned as to preclude community of interest. Because of this fact, government control in one form or another is characteristic of modern railway operation, and such control tends, with few exceptions, to maintain a close relation between at least total costs and total charges, just as does competition. Within reasonable limits, therefore, it is consistent to regard any factor influencing cost as likewise affecting charges.

The cost of rendering carrier service is the resultant of many factors and considerations; and, if a specific situation be analyzed, it will be found that certain of these factors have operated to increase, and certain others to decrease, the average-cost figures—seldom will it be that all will operate favorably or unfavorably in the case of a particular road or area. To make the matter more concrete, suppose computations show that the cost of freight movement in district A averages 1 cent per ton-mile and for district B averages 2 cents. What important considerations may account for the difference?

In district A it is possible that construction was easy and inexpensive: the topography of the region is such that satisfactory grades and locations were available at slight cost in terms of labor or money. Construction in district B, on the contrary, may have been exceedingly difficult, and a reasonably efficient plant was to be had only as a result of heavy expenditures for tunneling, filling, and other similar purposes. Such a variance would, the use cost of capital being the same in both districts, burden traffic in the latter for all time with a much heavier fixed charge than must be met by traffic moving in the former; this factor alone might reasonably account for an important part of the difference between the average charges noted. Or, again, the difference in cost may reflect in part a divergence in price levels governing during the periods when the roads were largely completed, or be due to the greater expense involved in securing satisfactory locations for right of way and terminals in an older country as compared with a newer. In any case, however, the result would be the same—heavier construction cost, making for higher charges. Closely allied to original cost of plant is a second factor, maintenance cost, which may affect the two sections in such fashion as to account further for existing differences. Other considerations being the same, maintenance expenses vary with such factors as the range in temperature, the total and form of precipitation, the type of construction, and the topography of the country.

Influence of Efficiency upon Costs.—Yet another important factor in determining the total cost of movement is the degree of efficiency exhibited in the management of the plant, high efficiency here being conceived as obtaining maximum results for a given expenditure. This efficiency may evidence itself either with respect to the utilization of materials and equipment, or with respect to the proper employment of the labor force. One road, using only high-grade materials for construction and maintenance work, laying heavy rails, double-tracking at needed points, maintaining a proper relation between traffic and terminal facilities at all times, operating heavy trains of large-capacity cars, drawn by thoroughly modernized locomotives of great tractive power, may be able to reduce ton-mile costs to a figure much below the figures of another road which, because of lack of capital or the handicap of poor management, follows a policy less sound from a long-time point of view. But not only does good management prove itself worthy of its hire by securing maximum results from the physical plant; perhaps even more of good or ill for the railway, from a financial point of view, will flow from the relation established by management between the labor force and the "company." Certain roads have become conspicuous because of the splendid spirit of loyalty which permeates every class of employees, while other managements have roused a covert or open hostility that has resulted inevitably in the inefficient use of time and, often, the almost shameful waste of materials. Perhaps not even the loyalty of a shipping public is to be valued above that of the employees; without the latter the former will be lost and upon a solid foundation of employee good will the support of the public will grow.

Effect of Wage and Price Levels.—A further factor in determining the cost of operation is the wage scale. Because of the movement on the part of labor organizations toward uniformity of wages and working conditions over large areas, the wage factor is increasingly less likely to occasion variations among American railways. Between countries, however, this not only is, but probably will continue to be, important in explaining variations in cost. Yet another item involving direct expenditures which must be given clear recognition is the cost of materials and supplies. When we realize the magnitude of expenditures made in the course of one year by a single large railway for locomotives, cars, fuel, rail and tie replacements, and for other purposes incident to property maintenance and to gradual betterment, it is patent that the level of prices, just as the level of wages, is an important factor in determining costs at a particular time.

Traffic Factors.—Still another consideration determining the actual cost of transportation service per unit of traffic is the degree to which traffic is balanced. Few carriers are fortunate enough to have a tonnage so evenly balanced as to obviate the movement of large numbers of empty cars in one direction or another, perhaps even both directions during different seasons, or to have a passenger movement so evenly distributed that efficient use of such equipment may be had on both the outward and the return movement. And this should be added: it avails little from the standpoint of railway economy that the return movement of grain in the autumn balances the outward movement of machinery, building materials, and supplies in the early spring—or that those who leave a particular point at one time return after a considerable interval. Neither freight nor passenger equipment can be placed upon sidings or in the yards until crops mature or until tourists have completed their sojourn. In a new country or even in an older one where raw materials move in considerable volume, traffic is usually badly balanced and in consequence the one-way tonnage must bear a heavier cost burden. Passenger traffic of a tourist or resort type is also likely to be poorly balanced. This problem of unbalanced traffic causes railway management no little concern and many interesting and socially helpful efforts have been made to remedy the defect. Perhaps one of the most interesting of these efforts to build up a "back-haul" traffic was successfully made by the Hill lines, thus contributing significantly to the rapid development of the lumber resources of the Pacific Northwest.

Closely related, perhaps, to traffic balance as a cost factor is that of traffic density. If only a single train be operated each day over the line, expenses of considerable magnitude are necessary; these would increase little were the number of trains increased to 5 or 10, possibly even 20 per day; assuredly the cost of operating the 20 trains would be but a fraction of 20 times the cost of operating the one. Therefore, as the tonnage handled increases, the relatively constant charges can be distributed over a rapidly broadening base, with a resultant lowering of unit costs. Here again the newer country is at a disadvantage compared with the older with respect to both freight and passenger traffic, and here also is the road with well-balanced traffic in a better position than one which is not so fortunately situated: with a predominant movement in one direction, even the best of management cannot secure, when facilities are utilized to the maximum, a tonnage density comparable to that of roads with heavy two-way traffic.

Quantity of Shipment.—Quantity of shipment is another and, for the purposes of this discussion, the final factor determining actual cost figures. Goods shipped in small quantities, in less-than-carload lots, are generally handled wholly by the carrier and, billed as these small lots are to widely scattered points, they must often be shifted many times before reaching final destination. Carload shipments, handled by shipper and consignee, capable of being moved long distances without break in bulk, manifestly entail lower costs upon the railways. And further, solid through trains of some particular commodity—fruit, vegetables, live stock, grain, coal, or ore—move at a much lower car-mile and ton-mile cost than the same number of cars picked up and dropped from station to station. Therefore, a road, or group of roads, which enjoys a predominantly carload rather than less-than-carload traffic or train-load rather than single carload, is clearly in a position to render service to the public at lower cost, yet serve that public quite as well as the less fortunate carrier or group.

Nominal v. Real Costs.—Let it be assumed, then, that the varied operations of these major cost factors have given us the figures previously named—average ton-mile costs of 1 cent and 2 cents for districts A and B respectively. Without further analysis it would appear that the cost of transportation in B is double that in A, a situation which reflects credit upon the railways of the latter district and affords a great advantage to their public, *if true*. But *is* it true? Here our conclusion involves a consideration of something which goes beyond the mere mathematical accuracy of the computations that give the 1 cent and the 2 cents; there are certain considerations which may not reflect themselves directly and significantly in costs but tend, rather, to modify or vitiate conclusions resting upon a bare mathematical comparison of average-cost figures. In fact, it is entirely possible that, all elements considered, patrons of the carriers in district B have received more than double the service for the higher charge than did those in district A for the lower, rather than the higher charge being proof of lesser efficiency, an accusation of rendering a like service at greater cost.

Length of Haul.—One factor that modifies conclusions based solely upon comparative figures is a difference in length of haul. Suppose that in A the average length of haul is 200 miles, while the corresponding figure for B is but 50. In either case, there are but two terminal charges to be assessed against the movement and, though there may actually be a somewhat greater handling cost incident to the 200-mile movement, that excess cost will be but a small fraction of the total. Assuming terminal costs to be the same in both districts and movement costs per mile likewise equal, the distribution of the terminal cost over a distance of 200 miles in the one case and over 50 miles in the other would result in an average total cost per ton-mile markedly greater for B than for A. It is evident, therefore, that this consideration alone might entirely discount a wide gap between the averages to be compared.

Type of Traffic.—A second factor to be considered in evaluating mathematical comparisons is that of the relative proportion of high- and low-grade traffic. One road may move a tonnage which consists largely of high-grade manufactured goods, perishables, or raw materials of high value while another may have a tonnage made up principally of coal, ore, or other low-grade traffic. To say that the average cost of handling the former type of traffic, moving in small quantities and requiring greater handling, risk, and care, is in excess of that involved in handling the latter is but to state the obvious. Yet this consideration is often neglected in making comparisons of averages. Figures for roads handling essentially the same types of traffic in the same proportion are comparable, but great care must be exercised in comparing the figure of a given road with the figure for even that same road some years earlier because of the possibility of a fundamental change in the character of its traffic. In this variation in type of traffic from year to year lies the explanation of the fact that the average ton-mile charge often increases more sharply than rates advance and likewise declines more rapidly than rates decrease for a given road or district. With the increase in rates the movement of certain low-grade traffic may decline sharply and, with a drop in rates, such traffic will increase in quantity rapidly, high-grade traffic continuing to move in a relatively steady stream under high rates or low. Moreover, in countries in which bulky, low-grade goods are utilized locally and appear in commerce mainly in finished state, as well as in those in which such low-grade traffic moves principally by water, the average figure will be deceptively high.

Character of the Service.—A third consideration which may modify conclusions based upon mere ton-mile costs, as well as affect those costs in part, is the wide variation in the character of the service rendered. One road or group of roads may offer a speedy and frequent service, furnishing in connection with it special equipment of an expensive nature and giving unusual advantages, such as the collection and delivery of package shipments or the extension of special care and attention, while another road or group of roads may subject its patrons to the opposite of the service thus described. In the face of such unlike services, to declare that the recipients of the better treatment are the victims of an inadequate and inefficient transportation machine simply because of a somewhat greater average ton-mile cost would be a conclusion not only unwarranted but quite contrary to fact. That there is a wide divergence in the character of service between roads, between districts and, to an even greater degree, between countries, is sufficiently well known to demand that in any comparison this factor be given weight.

Purchasing Power of Money.—Yet another significant, though often neglected, modifying factor is the relative purchasing power of money in the districts or countries compared. For, after all, it is not the *absolute* amount of the charge that is significant but, rather, the relation of the charge to the value of the goods shipped. A rate upon wheat of 20 cents per bushel between two certain points at a particular time is actually less than a rate of 10 cents at another time or place, if the wheat at the one time and in the one district sells for $2 per bushel as compared with but $0.75 at the other. Between different sections of the same country at a particular time variations in the purchasing power of money will not be great but between countries the variation is often wide. Also, the variation is wide in a given country from time to time; a rate schedule increased by 75 per cent when prices have increased from 100 to 150 per cent, while *seemingly* burdening the shipper and consumer more heavily, in reality represents a lighter load than that which had been borne before with perhaps little complaint. Not even a corporation owning a plant dedicated to public use can continue to serve at old rates when the general level of prices that must be paid for labor, materials, supplies, and other essentials has advanced rapidly and far. Therefore, it is necessary to consider, in making a true and accurate comparison, not merely length of haul, type of traffic, and character of service, but also the relative purchasing power of money—in itself a difficult matter to determine.

Evaluation of Passenger-rate Comparison.—Thus far the modifying factors have been considered only with respect to the freight business. To confine their consideration thus would be improper, however, for they function in the passenger field as well, with but one exception. Because of the usual method of charging for passenger movement by the mile in contrast to the freight charge which increases with distance but not in proportion to that distance, the average length of haul in no wise vitiates comparisons. Variations in the proportion of various "grades" of traffic—first-class, second-class, "excursion," and other—will materially lessen the value of computed averages for comparative purposes, however, as will differences in purchasing power of money. Differences in the character of the service must also be "read into" any figures to be compared before conclusions are drawn, because speed of trains, frequency of service, accommodations, incidental privileges—baggage, stop-over, personal service—and type of equipment may serve to invalidate wholly a disadvantageous comparison resting solely upon average passenger-mile cost figures.

In the light of such criticism of the validity of conclusions based upon the comparisons of ton-mile and passenger-mile costs, it is natural that the question arises as to the value of comparisons, either as between two periods of time or as between two areas. In answer it may be said that, if care and discretion be exercised, such comparisons are of sufficient value to justify making them. However, conclusions must always be of a somewhat tentative character and relative in nature, rather than definite and absolute as it would seem possible on first thought to make them, based upon mathematically exact computations as they are. With this suggestion, then, certain comparisons will be undertaken—comparisons between periods in American railway history, and between American and European railway operating results.

Express Charges.—In the movement of goods two distinct types of services are offered, express and freight. Although the conduct in the United States of the former for a long period under a management distinct from that of the railways tended to give an impression of difference in kind rather than in degree, it has previously been made clear that the express service concerns itself merely with a higher type of goods traffic, or a type of goods traffic to which speed of movement is more essential than moderate charge. The express business in the United States was long characterized by high and discriminatory charges. Indeed, it was only with the exercise of regulatory power by the Interstate Commerce Commission that public interest was consulted and safeguarded. Firmly intrenched upon individual roads as the result of the famous Express Company cases,[1] and protected from the competition of other similar organizations by carefully observed agreements, the business was in a strong monopolistic position. Charges were in consequence slow to conform to the changes in the economic situation, and did so then only as the advantage of the express organizations themselves was served. As a result of regulation the rate level was distinctly lowered, though the war period necessitated an upward movement. As yet, conditions have not justified a revision downward.

In comparison with the express service of European countries, taken as a whole, the average cost here has been high. This was long due in large measure to the absence of regulatory control in the form either of governmental authority or of such competition as is furnished by the parcel-post service which has long been established abroad. However, a lower density of traffic in the United States than in the populous countries of Western Europe justifies a higher average level of charges.

American Freight Rates.—In the determination of the rate to be charged upon a freight movement, essentially the same factors are involved as in the fixation of express charges, though perhaps here both absolute and relative cost have been given more careful consideration. The movement of the average ton-mile charge of American railways during the past 60 years, as shown in Table XXXII, is distinctly interesting.

[1] 117 U. S. 1.

Table XXXII.—Freight Revenue per Ton-mile—United States*

1870	$0.01990	1912†	$0.00744
1880	0.01170	1913‡	0.00729
1887	0.01030	1914‡	0.00733
1890	0.00910	1915‡	0.00732
1892	0.00896	1916‡	0.00716
1897	0.00798	1917§	0.00773
1898	0.00753	1918§	0.00950
1899	0.00724	1919§	0.01000
1900	0.00729	1920§	0.01052
1901	0.00750	1921§	0.01275
1902	0.00757	1922§	0.01177
1903	0.00763	1923§	0.01116
1904	0.00760	1924§	0.01116
1905	0.00766	1925§	0.01097
1906	0.00748	1926§	0.01081
1907	0.00759	1927§	0.01080
1908†	0.00754	1928§	0.01081
1909†	0.00763	1929§	0.01076
1910†	0.00753	1930§	0.01063
1911†	0.00757	1931§	0.01051
		1932‖	0.01043

* Based upon the United States Census and Interstate Commerce Commission reports.
† Excluding terminal and switching companies.
‡ Including only Class I and II roads.
§ Only Class I roads.
‖ Estimated by Bureau of Railway Economics.

The decline that is evident until the effect of rate advances of the war period came into play was the result of many factors. This steady downward movement came, in part, from better balanced traffic, greater density of traffic, and an increasing proportion of goods moving in quantity lots. But one of the most significant factors in accounting for a decline in the face of higher wage scales, greater cost of materials and of new plant, was increased operating efficiency—no small tribute to those who have given their life's effort to the development of our transportation machine. For the country as a whole the average number of tons per train had risen from 175 in 1890 to 730 for 1929 and for the better roads with a relatively heavy tonnage the average had increased from about 100 in 1870 to more than 900 in 1929. And it is interesting to note that this decline in average ton-mile charges seems to be as real as the figures indicate; though the average length of haul has increased and a much larger portion of the tonnage is of low-grade character, the increased quality of the service and the decreased purchasing power of money would seem to make the ton-mile figure for 1929 in reality smaller by comparison than it appears, nominally, to be.

American and European Charges.—To make a current comparison of charges imposed for moving freight in America with charges in European countries is rather difficult because of the present disorganized state of industry and trade, and such comparisons, if made, might well be unfair to many of the countries involved. However, it is of interest and perhaps suggestive to note comparative charges in certain countries. Western European ton-mile charges exceed those of the United States by a variable margin; in France the figure is 40 per cent higher, in Germany 75 per cent higher, and in the United Kingdom 160 per cent in excess. However, such a comparison is hardly fair because of factors previously mentioned: only by analysis can relative costs be determined. In respect to cost factors, the advantage lies almost wholly with the European carriers; there traffic is much better balanced, traffic density is greater, wages are lower and material costs somewhat less than our own, though the cost of plant and the type of shipment operate to their disadvantage.

The advantage in average ton-mile rates enjoyed by American shippers is nevertheless less real than figures indicate. Though the purchasing power of money is less in the United States than abroad, several factors tend to minimize our nominal advantage. In England the railway not only carries but also collects and delivers all package freight at terminals, and throughout Europe the average length of haul is but a small fraction of that of the United States. The average class of traffic in Europe is higher, also, because much low-grade traffic abroad moves by water. When the fact is realized that average cost is not diluted there as here by the movement of an enormous tonnage of low-grade commodities—approximating two-thirds of our total, and that the typical length of haul varies from about 55 miles in England to approximately 100 miles in Germany and France as compared with an average length of haul for the United States of more than 300 miles, it is clear that the low average rates enjoyed in the United States result in considerable degree from the very nature of the American situation. Nevertheless, giving weight to all modifying factors, it appears that the American shipper enjoys more than a nominal advantage over the European, though just how great that advantage is cannot be said.

American Passenger Rates.—The passenger rate differs markedly from the freight rate in that the standard charge tends to vary directly with distance and, though perhaps recognizing variations in ability to pay as a determinant, certainly has more nearly approximated monopoly price in American practice than have freight rates. The peculiarity of passenger service as compared with freight seems to be that, until recently, competition in service in the passenger field had well-nigh supplanted competition in rates, and an examination of the average rate through a considerable period of years, together with a comparison of services offered, tends to substantiate this conclusion. The actual movement of the average charge since the close of the eighties is indicated in Table XXXIII.

TABLE XXXIII.—AVERAGE REVENUE PER PASSENGER-MILE—UNITED STATES*

1889	$0.02165	1911†	$0.01974
1890	0.02167	1912†	0.01987
1891	0.02142	1913‡	0.02008
1892	0.02126	1914‡	0.01982
1893	0.02108	1915‡	0.01985
1894	0.01986	1916	0.02045
1895	0.02040	1917	0.02103
1896	0.02019	1918	0.02453
1897	0.02022	1919	0.02557
1898	0.01973	1920§	0.02745
1899	0.01978	1921§	0.03086
1900	0.02003	1922§	0.03027
1901	0.02013	1923§	0.03018
1902	0.01986	1924§	0.02978
1903	0.02006	1925§	0.02938
1904	0.02006	1926§	0.02936
1905	0.01962	1927§	0.02896
1906	0.02003	1928§	0.02850
1907	0.02014	1929§	0.02808
1908†	0.01937	1930§	0.02717
1909†	0.01928	1931§	0.02513
1910†	0.01938	1932§‖	0.02220

* From Interstate Commerce Commission reports.
† Exclusive of switching and terminal companies.
‡ Class I and II roads only.
§ Class I roads only.
‖ Estimated by Bureau of Railway Economics.

The conspicuous feature of the table here given is the relatively slight change in the average rate per passenger-mile through a period of almost 30 years prior to 1918, despite an increased density of traffic per mile of line on the one hand and, on the other, a veritable epidemic of 2-cent fare legislation which resulted in forcing rates on both intrastate and interstate traffic to a distinctly lower level for a considerable period following 1905–1908 than had previously governed. However, the one was offset largely by improved service while the other was compensated in a considerable measure by the enactment of anti-pass legislation and the increase of traffic due to the lower rates. Increases since 1916 are due to the upward movement of rates as a result of war conditions and price inflation. In the rather sharp decline in the averages since 1929 there is unmistakable evidence of the revival of rate competition, with the attack directed toward the highway carrier.

Comparison with Foreign Charges.—The average charge per passenger-mile in the United States has long been and continues to be materially in excess of the comparable figure for European railways. The European average varies from as low as approximately 0.6 cent for Belgium and Czecho-Slovakia to as high as 1.61 cents for Italy. In Great Britain the average stands at approximately 1.5 cents, in Germany at approximately 1.2 cents, and in France at 0.75 cent. Certain significant cost factors operate to make these lower averages in Europe possible. Of these perhaps a higher density of traffic is most important, though lower wages and lower cost of materials must be taken into account, as well as the rather less expensive character of passenger equipment used by foreign railways. Then, too, the efficiency of the European railway seems to be distinctly greater in its handling of passenger traffic than of freight; there passenger revenue constitutes a considerable portion of the total, while in America passenger service is regarded often as a more or less necessary evil or as an advertising adjunct.

However, the rather marked disparity between the average fare here and abroad is far less real than nominal. In the first place, the purchasing power of money is greater abroad which greatly modifies comparisons prejudicial to American railways. But even more important, as invalidating such a conclusion, is the wide variance in type of traffic handled. In the United States but one significant type of service is rendered aside from the regular, or first-class, service, and that is a super-service—commonly termed Pullman service. In Europe, on the contrary, a classified service is offered and the bulk of travel there is third class—with a level of speed, comfort, and convenience far below that enjoyed by the typical American passenger. When it is realized that the usual American service is comparable to that enjoyed by first-class passengers in European countries, and that in Europe such service is enjoyed by very few, it argues an ignorance of facts to claim a marked cost superiority for European passenger service. So divergent are conditions between France, with her three classes of traffic and heavy suburban business, with a charge for all baggage, a tax upon all tickets, and with even an exaction for "platform" tickets, on the one side and the United States, with only standard service, a liberal baggage allowance, no railway tax on tickets, and free access to station and platform for friends and relatives, on the other, that it is actually doubtful if even the 0.75-cent average is more reasonable than 2.5 cents for the United States. To draw a definite conclusion, therefore, as to the comparative level of European and American passenger charges is even more difficult than in the case of freight; interpreted in the light of variations in type of traffic, character of service, and value of money, it appears that little or no advantage of one over the other is discernible. However, it is not an unreasonable assumption to make that, were American railway management as enterprising in the development of passenger business as of freight and somewhat less wedded to the idea of using that branch of service as an advertising medium, there might be developed a more varied service with a lower passenger-mile average, yet one yielding a greater net operating revenue than the present.

Conclusion.—In conclusion, this may fairly be said regarding the railway system of the United States: it has furnished, in the face of many obstacles and difficulties, a high-class service and has done so at reasonable rates. Its faults have grown largely out of financial management rather than plant management, out of governmental adherence to a fallacious policy of enforced competition rather than a willful desire to injure or run counter to sound public policy. It has already contributed greatly to American economic and social development and will play a vital part in future progress. When good is set off against ill, when the tremendous contribution of the railway to American life is compared with the evils and abuses which accompanied its growth, the negligible character of the latter is clearly apparent. The protests of those who discern flaws should be given heed, but the public should avoid that common error of those who give ear to protests—the tendency to see the molehill as a mountain. No people in the world owes more to the railway than the American and none other enjoys a service superior to, if the equal of, our own.

REFERENCES

Bureau of Railway Economics: *Miscellaneous Studies.*

Bureau of Railway News and Statistics: *Railway Statistics of the United States and Recent Statistics of Foreign Railways* (annual).

DAGGETT, STUART R.: *Principles of Inland Transportation,* Harper & Brothers, 1928.

DUNN, S. O.: *Government Ownership of Railways,* D. Appleton & Company, 1914.

HAINES, H. S.: *Efficient Railway Operation,* The Macmillan Company, 1919.

Interstate Commerce Commission: *Statistics of Railways in the United States.*

JOHNSON, E. R., and G. G. HUEBNER: *Railroad Traffic and Rates,* vol. 1, D. Appleton & Company, 1911.

———, and T. W. VAN METRE: *Principle of Railroad Transportation,* D. Appleton & Company, 1921.

MCPHERSON, LOGAN: *Transportation in Europe,* Henry Holt & Company, 1910.

MERRITT, A. N.: *Federal Regulation of Railway Rates,* Houghton Mifflin Company, 1907.

NOYES, WALTER, C.: *American Railroad Rates,* Little, Brown & Company, 1905.

PRATT, E. A.: *Railways and Their Rates,* John Murray, 1905.

RIPLEY, W. Z.: *Railroads: Rates and Regulation,* Longmans, Green & Co., 1912.

SAKOLSKI, A. M.: *American Railroad Economics,* The Macmillan Company, 1916.

PART V

MODERN TRANSPORT

CHAPTER XXXIII

MOTOR TRANSPORTATION: ITS DEVELOPMENT

As a background for the discussion of fundamental and significant problems that arise incident to the movement of a great and growing volume of traffic over a vast network of highways, a factual knowledge of that traffic is essential. Yet, because certain of those problems arise from the construction and maintenance of the highway itself as well as from the character of the vehicle in which traffic is moved upon it, a preliminary consideration of these two instrumentalities is essential. Since age may well give precedence, the highway will be first discussed.

THE HIGHWAY

The discovery by ancient man of the wheel and its application to primitive vehicles lies deep in antiquity. With the appearance of the wheeled cart and with its refinement in the chariot used by the Assyrians, improved highways became a necessity. Yet it is probable that, even prior to the utilization of the wheel upon vehicles, the advantage of an improved route for the speedy movement of troops had been recognized. Herodotus tells of a road built about 4000 B.C. to facilitate the movement of stone for the erection of the pyramids and Biblical history makes mention of public highways, but the first highways concerning which records are clear were those built by the Assyrians to make the more distant portions of the empire accessible from Babylon and to facilitate the flow of goods into that great center. At a later date the Greeks constructed highways but the mileage of these was comparatively small and in durability they suffered by comparison with the Roman roads. Though the Carthaginians are credited with the first paved roads, it was the Romans who adopted and developed the method, using it upon a scale quite beyond the dreams of earlier people. Or, indeed, of later—until comparatively recent times.

The Roman Roads.—The construction of highways was a vital element in Roman imperial policy: it was over these and by means of the land-locked Mediterranean that power was exercised in distant provinces and the prestige of Rome maintained. By 200 B.C. it is estimated that some 48,500 miles had been built and construction proceeded steadily as the empire was extended. These roads were built to minimize distance: bridges, retaining walls, and tunnels were utilized as needed. And, while highways of lesser consequence were built on a less pretentious scale, the major roads were so solidly constructed that sections remain intact today. Upon a sand bed layers of stone were placed to a thickness of 4 feet, the topmost layer consisting of hard materials bonded by lime mortar.[1] The maintenance of these roads was intrusted to the *curator viarum:* the superintendent of highways in Roman times was a man of high rank and in later years the office was occupied often by those of consular dignity. And upon the College of Pontiffs rested the responsibility of maintaining the bridges across the Tiber, the title of Pontifex Maximus later being assumed by the Roman emperors and, finally, by the popes. With the collapse and disintegration of the empire, however, not only did road building cease but maintenance was ignored to such degree that important highways became little more than bridle-paths. Given impetus by Charlemagne, road building enjoyed a brief renaissance, again the military purpose being dominant. Yet retrogression soon was evident and it was not until the decline of the feudal system in France that any significant progress was made.

French and English Highways.—The pioneer in the development of the present national system of highways in France was Tresageut, of the district of Limoges, whose influence was exerted late in the eighteenth century—and he it was who first proposed an effective system of maintenance. The situation in England paralleled that in France: the Roman roads fell into decay and all sense of the importance of satisfactory communication by land seemed to have been lost. In 1285 an act decreed that all bushes and trees should be cut down for a distance of 200 feet on each side of the highway—as a protection against lurking bands of robbers. Because London streets were "very foul, and full of pits and sloughs, so as to be mighty perilous and noxious," paving was begun in 1532; in 1555 provision was made for the parish roads; and in 1663 the first turnpike act was passed. Except for such turnpike development, highways continued in poor condition until MacAdam was placed in a position of authority. To him, whose name has since come to identify a type of roadway construction, and to Telford is due largely the striking progress made in highway construction after 1800 in England. Contemporaneous with this development in England and like progress in France, there was progress throughout the whole of Western Europe.

Early Highways in America.—To the Incas of Peru, seemingly, is due the honor of the first effective highways in America, the one from Quito to Cuzco being some 25 feet wide and in places paved. Yet it was long before the newcomers from Europe were to attain standards equally high. Colonies clung to the seacoast and to watercourses, overland connections between settlements being wholly by trails marked out by

[1] To construct today a highway comparable, for example, to the Appian Way would cost no less than $300,000 per mile, it has been estimated.

the Indians or by big game. The old York road between New York City and Philadelphia, laid out in 1711, was the first important highway in the colonies and it was not until 1792 that the first turnpike of broken stone was built from Philadelphia to Lancaster, Pa. Unsatisfactory as first constructed, with miscellaneous broken stones covered with earth, it was later rebuilt with a broken-stone surface. This method proved so successful that it became the model for turnpike construction. These turnpikes were privately constructed but often failed to yield a profit; they gradually came into the hands of the states and, because private capital was unwilling to venture further, highway construction and maintenance became increasingly a public function. As governmental responsibility for the construction and maintenance of highways won acceptance, the principle of forced labor—of which the privilege of "working out" the poll tax was a variant—gained recognition. Such early roads were, in general, of low grade; indeed, the only significant project credited to governmental activity until late in the nineteenth century was the Cumberland Road—and this was not carried to completion because of acceptance of the railway.

While the records of highway construction and finance do not run entirely parallel in the various states and in various sections of the country, the one common characteristic seems to have been control by local governmental units—town, township, or county—rather than by the state. In states where toll projects had reverted because of abandonment by charter companies, maintenance was undertaken locally and a semblance of a satisfactory highway provided, but in other states local finance provided little more than the minimum requisites in road and bridge for overland movement.[1] Of the accuracy of this last statement the existence in Ohio as late as 1914 of less than 200 miles of rural highways of high type surface stands as evidence, as did a total mileage in Ohio of all surfaced rural roads, including ordinary gravel, only slightly in excess of 6,000. True, prior to the appearance of the automobile in large numbers upon the highway, the inadequacies of existing provisions for overland travel were not sorely felt: it required a new means of transport, with its greater speed and lesser ability to cope with certain characteristics of the "natural highway," to give strong impetus to the demand for improvement.

Federal Aid.—It is interesting to note that the now long-defunct League of American Wheelmen, an organization of bicycle enthusiasts, is credited with pioneering the good-roads movement, their activity dating from about 1880. In 1891 New Jersey made provision for a state highway

[1] An interesting brief statement of the situation during this period of decentralized control in a New England state appears in *Report of a Survey of Transportation on the State Highway System of Connecticut*, United States Bureau of Public Roads, pp. 9–10; of Ohio in a comparable study by the same Bureau, pp. 13–15; of Iowa in *The Motor Vehicle in Iowa*, Bureau of Business Research, University of Iowa.

department and in 1892 Massachusetts took like action. In 1893 there was established in the United States Department of Agriculture a division that has become the Bureau of Public Roads. Interest in improved highways waxed steadily, with other states following New Jersey and Massachusetts in the centralization of highway control until in 1917 no state remained without such a state department. To the laggards in highway development as well as to those states that were making definite progress impetus was given in 1916 by active federal participation in highway construction under the Federal Road Act of that year. By the terms of that law the Secretary of Agriculture was permitted to contribute to the improvement of post roads, within the limits of the appropriations made by Congress from time to time, up to 50 per cent of the cost of construction; such contribution, however, was not to exceed $10,000 per mile, exclusive of major bridges as defined. As a condition to such aid the state was required to create a state highway department with adequate powers and suitably equipped to discharge the duties of such a body, specific legislative assent to the provisions of the Act being made prerequisite to participation in federal disbursements. In 1921 this earlier law was supplemented by the Federal Highway Act which, among other things, provided for the designation of 7 per cent of the then existing interstate and intercounty mileage of each state as federal-aid routes. This designation was to be by the Secretary of Agriculture in cooperation with the state highway departments, and federal aid for the future was to be restricted to these roads. Maintenance by state or federal authority was also prescribed.

Under the provisions of these and supplementary acts a national system of highways of almost 200,000 miles has been established by joint state and federal action. Upon some 110,000 miles federal funds have been expended to an amount of approximately $1,100,000,000 since 1916, federal-aid payments in 1931 closely approaching $135,000,000.[1] In addition to such expenditures, the federal government has provided some 4,650 miles of improved highways in federal areas, such as national forests and parks. But the federal-aid mileage of about 200,000 miles constitutes only a major part of the road mileage designated as state highways: this last totaled at the close of 1931 almost 329,000 miles, slightly in excess of 10 per cent of the total highway mileage of the United States in that year.

State and Local Mileage.—With the organization of state highway commissions there appeared generally a sharp differentiation between the control of the routes designated as *state* highways and the county and township, or *local*, roads. Over local roads local control persists, in

[1] *Hearings* before the committee on Interstate Commerce, United States Senate, 72d Congress, 1st session, S. 2793, pp. 207, 218. Also National Automobile Chamber of Commerce, *Facts and Figures of the Automobile Industry*, 1932, p. 44.

general, and funds for improvement are derived largely or wholly from local sources, this varying with the jurisdiction. These roads are largely unsurfaced; in too large measure they are poorly graded and inadequately maintained—if at all. In 1931 some 480,000 miles of local roads, about 18 per cent of the total, were surfaced, as against approximately 77 per cent of the state mileage. In Table XXXIV selected data relative to road mileage and expenditures upon highway improvement are given to acquaint the reader with certain basic and pertinent facts.

TABLE XXXIV.—RURAL-ROAD PROGRESS*

Year	Mileage			Finance	
	Total	Surfaced	High-type surface‡	Expenditures§	State-road bonds outstanding‖
1904	2,151,379	153,530	144	$ 79,595,418	$ 4,525,000
1909	2,199,645	190,476	725	....	20,007,500
1914	2,445,761	257,291	14,442	249,055,067	93,264,000
1921	2,941,294	387,760	35,874	994,103,567	272,205,400
1922	2,960,000	410,000	....	898,352,307	411,702,900
1923	2,995,727	439,341	54,217	938,305,299	472,868,600
1924	3,004,411	471,668	63,797	1,075,593,689	549,685,050
1925	3,006,083	521,260	76,342	1,144,415,513	700,576,150
1926	3,000,190	550,064	82,987	1,163,747,971	765,678,250
1927	3,013,584	588,721	91,935	1,283,110,631	857,315,250
1928	3,016,281	626,137	102,559	1,423,870,278	892,510,450
1929	3,024,233	662,435	112,454	1,444,668,985	1,008,856,150
1930	3,009,066	693,559	125,708	1,680,493,095	1,151,571,820
1931	3,009,066	730,000†	145,000†	1,700,000,000†	

* National Automobile Chamber of Commerce, *Facts and Figures of the Automobile Industry*, 1932, p. 42. Based upon United States Bureau of Public Roads data.

† Estimated by National Automobile Chamber of Commerce.

‡ Includes bituminous macadam by penetration and higher types.

§ Excludes after 1914 all disbursements other than upon highways.

‖ This is the total of *state* bonds only; outstanding at the end of 1914 was a total of $344,763,082 state and local bonds and at the end of 1926 a total of $2,152,016,633.

While rural-road mileage increased slightly in excess of one-third from 1904 to 1921, expenditures increased more than twelvefold; and, while during the next decade total mileage increased but slightly, expenditures were augmented by almost 70 per cent. Yet the fact that this tremendous increase in outlay within recent years has been productive of noteworthy results is evident in the approximate doubling of surfaced mileage and a fourfold increase in mileage with high-type service. To accomplish such an advance there was expended by state and local units from 1921 to 1931 for construction and maintenance, with no consideration of interest on road bonds outstanding or other like items, some $13,750,000,000—of which it is estimated that some $7,000,000,000 has been spent upon state highways. To this latter total federal aid has contributed about

15 per cent, the remaining major portion being derived from varied sources, with taxes upon the automobile owner contributing an increasing percentage year by year. Yet if the aggregate sum spent to provide ways upon which the motor vehicle may operate is desired for the period 1921–1931, there must be added to the huge total given for rural highways those outlays for city streets: it is probable that the grand total for the years indicated will exceed $20,000,000,000.[1] That a very considerable proportion of this expenditure is attributable to the motor vehicle is clear; and equally clear is it that, as improved city streets must be regarded as terminal facilities for our rural highways, so must county and local roads be considered as "feeders," vital to the adequate utilization of state routes. In short, all highway mileage, be it urban or rural, is an integral part of that extensive network of routes which the American people now have available for use by that youthful giant of the transport field, the motor vehicle.

THE VEHICLE

The automobile is a self-propelled vehicle maneuvered at will upon the highway rather than operated on a fixed track and may be powered by steam, an electric motor, or an internal-combustion engine. Therefore, just as the mechanism devised by Nicolas Cugnot[2] in 1769 represented a first step in the development of the steam locomotive, so was that contrivance itself the first automobile. Murdoch, assistant to James Watt, completed in 1784 a land carriage driven by steam and shortly thereafter Oliver Evans as well as Richard Trevithick centered attention upon this problem. In 1802 the last-named constructed a steam-propelled vehicle which he drove some 90 miles to London where it was exhibited. In the period from 1825 to 1836 a number of such vehicles were constructed and operated upon the English highways, among the leaders in this work being Walter Hancock and Guldeworthy Gurney: the former built several public coaches, the "Automaton" operating some 4,200 miles during a period of 20 weeks and carrying 12,761 passengers; the latter operated three steam coaches of his construction over a route near London, these traveling some 3,644 route miles before operations ceased. The conservatism of English public opinion, coupled with sharp opposition from railway interests, led to the passage of hampering legislation beginning in 1831, with perhaps the most restrictive of these acts being the "Red-flag Law" which required that each self-propelled vehicle be preceded by a man carrying by day a red flag and by night a red lantern. Though the

[1] The expenditure for street construction and maintenance in the year 1931, despite depleted city treasuries in that year, is estimated by the National Automobile Chamber of Commerce, in *Facts and Figures of the Automobile Industry*, 1932, at $500,000,000.

[2] See Chap. IV, Beginnings of the American Railway Net.

steam-driven car disappeared from the highways by 1836, it reappeared in the sixties, this reappearance prompting the passage of a law limiting the speed of self-propelled vehicles upon the roads to 4 miles per hour. This law remained upon the statute books until 1896. Thus, for an additional period, English highways were made safe for those ancient servants of man, the ox and the horse.

The Modern Motor Vehicle.—The first official recognition of the principle of the internal-combustion engine appears in a patent issued to an Englishman, Street, in 1794. From that date until 1867 no progress was made, but in that year a German, Otto, effected certain improvements. It was in the Otto Gas-engine Works of Cologne that Gottlieb Daimler in 1884 perfected an internal-combustion engine similar in its essential features to the modern four-cycle unit, this engine using a liquid fuel instead of manufactured or natural gas. In 1886 Daimler applied his engine to a bicycle and in 1887 he sold to a French firm, Panhard and Levassor, the French and Belgian rights, this firm building its first car in 1891. In 1894 the first of a long series of road races was held: this one, a distance of 75 miles from Paris to Rouen and return, was won by a Daimler-powered car in 5 hours, 40 minutes. In 1895 a Daimler engine won the Paris-Bordeaux race and in 1896 it was the victor in an endurance run from Paris to Marseille and return, the 1,050 miles being covered in 65 hours. In most of these early races steam and electric vehicles were also entered, the former utilizing the Serpollet principle to increase efficiency, but the internal-combustion engine was uniformly most successful. The first approach to the modern car in essential characteristics came in 1894 in a vehicle designed by Krebs, in the employ of Panhard and Levassor: it embodied the modern-type chassis, the sliding-gear transmission, clutch and brake pedals, and the foot accelerator. So rapid was development in Europe during this period that in 1900 it is estimated there were some 10,000 cars operating, half of which were in France.

Development in the United States.—Working independently but stimulated by progress abroad, American pioneers were entering the field. Among the earliest of these were Duryea, Haynes, Olds, and Winton; following them shortly came Stanley, Ford, White, Maxwell, and many others who contributed much technically as well as commercially to the use of the motor vehicle by large numbers. Road races became common and no effort was spared to increase the speed of this new instrument. In this connection it is interesting to note that in 1906 a Stanley steamer, during the course of a contest in Florida, traveled a mile at the rate of 127 miles per hour while a 200 horsepower Darracq powered by an internal-combustion engine covered 2 miles in slightly less than a minute. The rapidity with which the use of the motor car increased in the United States, once interest was stirred and production got under way, is shown in Table XXXV.

Table XXXV.—Motor Vehicles in the United States, 1895–1931*

Year	Production		Registration		Total
	Passenger cars	Motor trucks	Passenger cars	Motor trucks	
1895	4	....	4	....	4
1898	1,000	....	800	....	800
1901	7,000	....	14,800	....	14,800
1904	22,419	411†	54,590	410	55,000
1907	43,300	700	140,300	1,700	142,000
1910	181,000	6,000	458,500	10,000	468,500
1913	461,500	23,500	1,194,262	63,800	1,258,062
1916	1,525,578	92,130	3,297,996	215,000	3,512,996
1919	1,657,652	275,943	6,771,074	794,372	7,556,446
1922	2,276,251	268,971	10,862,650	1,006,082	12,238,375
1925	3,735,171	530,659	17,496,420	2,440,854	19,937,274
1928	3,814,310	544,777	21,379,125	3,113,999	24,493,124
1931	1,973,090	416,648	22,347,800	3,446,303	25,814,103

* National Automobile Chamber of Commerce, *Facts and Figures of the Automobile Industry*, 1932.
† The first year for which truck production is shown.

It is doubtful if any other industry has ever witnessed such phenomenal expansion as did this: until 1918 production increased annually without a break, the yearly increase varying from a minimum of 10 per cent to as high as 78 per cent during that period; and, despite several years since that date when production declined, the first decline in total registrations occurred in 1931. The decrease for that year was 2.8 per cent as compared with 1930, this resulting largely from a decline in the registration of passenger vehicles. The peak registration of passenger cars came in 1929 and of trucks in 1930, the figures being 23,121,589 and 3,486,019 respectively, while the peak registration for all was 26,545,281 in 1930. As measured in terms of wholesale value, the manufacture of motor vehicles became a billion-dollar industry first in 1916, and in 1929 total value reached $3,413,148,206: indeed, in 9 years since 1916 value has exceeded two billion dollars.

Of the total number of passenger cars registered in 1930, the United States Census of that year showed 18 per cent to be owned on farms; of the total registration of trucks more than 26 per cent were farm-owned in that year. The remaining vehicles registered, passenger and truck, were owned by urban residents—a total in 1930 of more than 21,500,000 units. Upon the same authority approximately 30 per cent of the farms in the United States are situated upon roads having some type of surfacing, gravel or superior; about 29 per cent are adjacent to improved dirt and sand-clay roads; and 41 per cent are served by unimproved highways.

Data on Bus and Truck.—Because of the place that the bus and the truck will occupy in the discussion of taxation and regulation, certain additional facts concerning each are pertinent. The bus is registered as a passenger vehicle, so does not appear separately in Table XXXV. *Bus Transportation* is authority for the statement that in 1932 there were 104,000 motor buses in operation in the United States, of which 47,069 were in revenue service. Of the nonrevenue vehicles 55,231 were owned by schools and 1,700 by hotels, industrial concerns, and others. It is also interesting to note that of the revenue carriers 32,213 were owned by motor-carrier groups, 11,541 by electric railways, and 1,246 by steam railways. Though upward of 2,700 of the revenue carriers in 1931 were but

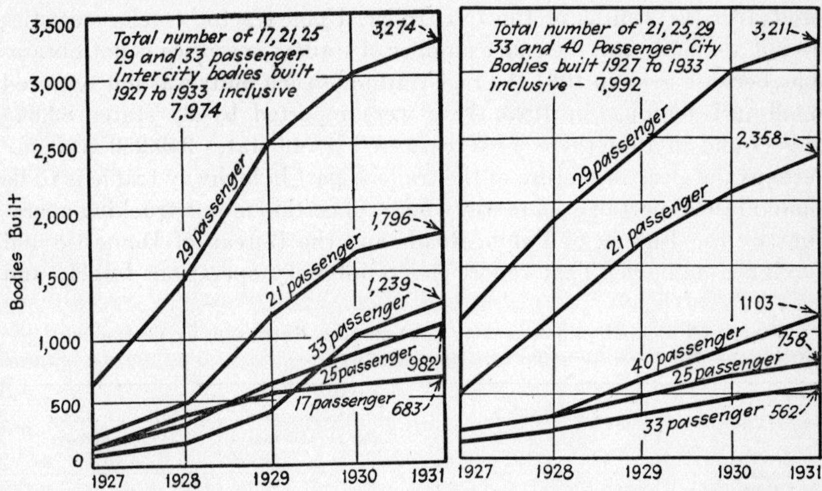

FIG. 37.—Trend in body construction of buses, 1927–1931. (*Bus Facts for* 1932.)

automobiles impressed into such service, the typical bus is a specially built unit. No data are available showing the number of units of each capacity group but the accompanying diagrams indicate that the number of certain of the larger types is growing. This increase in average size is indicated, too, by a rise in average seating capacity from 25.2 persons for all buses built in 1927 to 28.2 for all in 1931. It is not surprising, in view of this fact, that the production trend has been sharply and almost unbrokenly downward for the group with a chassis weight of 5,000 pounds or less, moderately downward for those weighing 5,100 to 7,000 pounds, and strongly upward for those with weights in excess of 7,100 pounds. With this has come a marked increase in wheel base:[1] in 1922 almost 98 per cent of production had a wheel base of less than 199 inches, while in 1930 some 58 per cent was in excess of that measurement.

[1] National Association of Motor-bus Operators, *Bus Facts for* 1930, p. 19.

Data of an exact character indicating the type of service in which trucks are engaged are not available; however, it has been estimated by the Bureau of Public Roads that some 86 per cent of these units are in the service of the owner, 9 per cent are in contract-carrier service, and 5 per cent are common carriers. An examination of truck-capacity data, 1925 to date, shows that the two popular types are the ¾-ton or less and the 1½-ton but less than 2-ton vehicles. Beginning with 1929 the latter alone has constituted more than 60 per cent of total production, displacing the 1 to 1½-ton type as leader.[1] These data also indicate a marked decline in the production of trucks with a capacity of 5 tons or greater. This apparent conflict with conditions upon the highway is explained by the rapid increase during recent years in the use of the tractor truck and its semitrailer, as well as of the full trailer. Upon tractor trucks statistics are not available and the exact number of trailers in service is not obtainable, because even in 1931 the registration of such units was not required in all jurisdictions: in 1925 there were reported by 33 states 83,625 trailers and in 1931 there were registered by 46 states 349,930 trailers.[2] Perhaps the clearest picture of the trailer's part in highway traffic is to be found in the report of a joint study made of certain motor-trucking operations by the Bureau of Public Roads and the Bureau of Domestic and Foreign Commerce. That report covers intercity operations largely and

Table XXXVI.—Rated Capacity of Vehicles Reported, by Geographic Divisions*

Geographic divisions†	Light vehicles ½ to 1¼ tons				Medium-capacity vehicles 1½ to 3 tons				Heavy vehicles 3½ tons and over			
	Trucks	Tractor trucks	Semitrailers	Trailers	Trucks	Tractor trucks	Semitrailers	Trailers	Trucks	Tractor trucks	Semitrailers	Trailers
New England	31	..	..	..	134	...	..	...	103	4	11	1
Middle Atlantic	14	..	..	..	190	...	..	8	255	86	100	54
East North Central	38	1	2	3	265	85	27	18	75	58	151	96
West North Central	39	..	..	..	260	22	9	44	32	31	80	13
South Atlantic	13	..	..	..	199	9	10	11	35	1	5	1
East South Central	19	..	1	..	58	9	3	1	26	7	11	7
West South Central	16	..	..	..	86	28	22	18	7	31	38	20
Mountain	24	..	..	1	109	5	4	11	38	...	1	3
Pacific	128	..	..	5	384	2	8	69	248	16	21	137
United States	322	1	3	9	1,685	160	83	180	819	234	418	332

* United States Department of Commerce, *Motor Truck Freight Transportation*, p. 5.

† According to the United States Bureau of the Census.

[1] National Automobile Chamber of Commerce, *Facts and Figures of the Automobile Industry*, 1932, p. 9.

[2] National Automobile Chamber of Commerce, *Facts and Figures of the Automobile Industry*, 1932, p. 37.

discloses, in addition to pertinent trailer data, that 11 per cent of the units covered were light trucks, 60 per cent were medium-duty trucks and 29 per cent heavy-duty—as against percentages found for the trucking industry at large by the General Motors Corporation of 58, 32, and 10, respectively. The rated capacity for those trucks and supplementary units for which data were obtained appear in Table XXXVI. From an examination of this table it is apparent that the heavier units are employed in the more populous sections, with the character of highway improvements also exerting a positive influence upon truck capacity: in areas where from 50 to 100 per cent of the road mileage used was of high-type surface average rated capacity in tons was 3.23 as against 2.21 where 19 per cent or less reached that standard. Yet these figures do not indicate accurately the volume of traffic moving over the highways in the trucks for which information was obtained: it is customary to load in excess of the manufacturer's rated capacity, that excess in this study averaging approximately 62, 72, 88, 94, 69, 70, 68, and 43 per cent on trucks of 1, 1½, 2, and to 5 tons rated capacity, respectively. Only trucks rated in excess of 5½ tons showed a loading below marked capacity of 7.6 per cent.

For an ordinary truck the usual load approximates half of the gross weight; for semitrailers the proportion will increase with the capacity of the trailer unit from about 65 to almost 80 per cent; and for full trailers the proportion of pay load to gross also increases with the rated capacity of the unit—from some 55 to approximately 60 per cent. While production data indicate that in 1931 only 3.1 per cent of the trucks manufactured had solid or cushion tires, the joint survey previously mentioned found almost one-fourth of the trucks and tractor trucks operating in intercity service to be so equipped and approximately one-third of the trailers[1]—a significant fact when taxation of the motor truck is considered.

TRAFFIC

The generally transitory and impermanent character of motor-vehicle operations, coupled with wide diffusion of ownership, has made it impossible to obtain complete and comprehensive data except at prohibitive cost. And, because of the highly dynamic nature of certain aspects of such operations, many of the data gathered are of historical rather than of current interest within a few years after the surveys that provide such data have been completed. Yet, if these records are an unsafe basis for present conclusions, they constitute a valuable record of the growth of highway transport. The most complete statistics upon motor-vehicle operation have been gathered by the United States Bureau of Public Roads, working in conjunction with state highway departments: typical of these surveys was that based upon observations of highway traffic

[1] United States Department of Commerce, *Motor Truck Freight Transportation*, p. 13.

in Connecticut for a year beginning in September, 1922, and another of traffic over federal-aid highways in 11 western states for the year beginning September, 1929. Surveys have also been made by many states, even in local areas such as Cook County, Ill. In addition, a great mass of information in the form of testimony and exhibits has been gathered by the Interstate Commerce Commission in the course of inquiries made by it in 1926 and 1930 in connection with Dockets 18300 and 23400. And, finally, in the hearings of Congressional committees upon proposals affecting interstate bus and truck operations may be found much of interest. From these and other sources such facts will be drawn as seem essential to a proper portrayal of highway traffic conditions.

The Individual Passenger Car.—The ordinary passenger automobile, numbering in excess of 22,000,000 and comprising units widely divergent as to weight and type, contributes approximately 90 per cent to the total of vehicle miles. The average number of persons transported per car has been shown to increase as the proportion of business traffic diminishes, with averages ascertained that vary from less than 2 to as high as 3.3; the 2.32 average found in the Western States survey is, however, probably a representative figure. If the average annual mileage of passenger cars is assumed to be even so little as 6,500, it becomes apparent that the number of passenger-miles of service rendered by the highway to the American people is enormous; indeed, the decline of some 20 billion passenger-miles in railway passenger service from 1920 to 1930 is but a small fraction of total public travel by motor vehicle. The Ohio survey showed the average length of journey of an Ohio car to be 38 miles, that of the foreign car 340; the average for business trips was 37 miles, while that of non-business (including touring) was 146. This same survey indicated a much higher average length of journey for the city-owned than the farm-owned car, a relation that the Western States study not only confirmed but supplemented by showing that the distance covered by the village-owned car was intermediate to the two others: the Western survey showed the median daily travel of the three types to be 142, 59, and 96 miles, respectively. In other sections of the country distances would perhaps be less but relative positions would doubtless be maintained. This same Western States survey indicates that, of the cars on the highway, only one-third of the city-owned traveled a trip distance of less than 100 miles and of the farm-owned only one-third of 100 miles or more. Undoubtedly the disparity between urban and rural use of highways will diminish as farm roads are improved and, with continuous improvement, the average length of journey for all will increase. In short, the use of the highway by the individually owned car for business and pleasure will impose upon that highway increasing demands; other uses that interfere with satisfactory travel conditions will be regarded with progressive disfavor by those who contribute so largely to total highway mileage.

The Bus.—The intercity transportation of persons for hire by motor-vehicle operators traversing regular routes and maintaining increasingly satisfactory schedules had an early but somewhat uncertain origin. From the rendition of such service by the light touring car during initial years to the present utilization of heavy, luxurious, and specially designed equipment is a far cry, despite the brief time elapsed; and a far cry it is, too, from the local service first rendered over a few routes to the existing national network of lines over which single companies operate across half a continent. At the close of 1931 there were engaged in intra- and interstate service between cities 21,207 and 5,558 vehicles, respectively, with all but 2,522 of the total being specially designed equipment. Over 243,118 miles of intra- and 111,627 miles of interstate routes a total of 1,344,000,000 bus-miles of service was rendered some 465,000,000 passengers, these paying $270,000,000 for transportation received.[1] In 1926 bus revenue aggregated less than one-fifth of the passenger revenues of the steam railways; in 1931, due to the continued sharp decline in rail revenues, the relation was approximately 2:1. Yet it is to the individual car, rather than the bus, that the major decline in railway travel is attributed: the proportion of loss assignable to the bus is estimated variously from 20 to 30 per cent. While bus operations tend to be coextensive with improved highways, more than 30 per cent of the total number of units engaged in intercity operations are found in the Central Atlantic states—and another 20 per cent serve the Mid-west.

The intercity bus industry is one of a few large units and many small ones. At the close of 1931 there were 24 companies with 100 buses or more each, these companies doing a large part of the aggregate business because of the strategic location of their lines and of their ability to participate in long-haul traffic; indeed, many of the lesser companies use private cars or converted equipment. Steady progress has been made in the provision of satisfactory terminal facilities in cities served, union stations being common, and arrangements by connecting lines for handling through passengers have developed rapidly. The irregularity of rates over certain of the more important routes, however, because of the irregular or "wildcat" operator or because of inability to control competition among existing lines, has been an obstacle to the establishment of satisfactory arrangements. The entire absence of federal control of interstate operations and the inadequacy of state control in many jurisdictions has been conducive to uneconomic duplication of service, to cutthroat competition, to frequent inadequate returns, and even to financial disaster. Instances are numerous of rates forced to 8 mills and as low as 5 mills per passenger-mile by excessive and often irresponsible competition over even major routes—and the writer is informed of one established line

[1] National Association of Motor Bus Operators, *Bus Facts for* 1932, pp. 5, 9.

that finally made for a brief period a rate of $1 for a distance of about 500 miles between two major Mid-western cities to drive an aggressive "wildcatter" from the field.

While intercity bus operations are dominantly common carrier in nature, there are two types of operation that are contract in character. In recent years it has been quite common for groups moving to a common destination to make the journey by chartered bus: students, convention delegates, and tourist agencies have utilized this plan most commonly, perhaps. It is no unusual occurrence for athletic teams to move wholly by bus within a radius of a day's drive and numerous instances of student groups and of delegates moving thus for upwards of a thousand miles could be given. With rates running from 30 cents a route mile for smaller buses to 50 cents for the larger which have perhaps a seating capacity of 40 persons, the economy to the individual of such travel is apparent. And, with the development of long-haul passenger traffic by highway, there has also appeared the broker in transportation. Advertising a service at rates appreciably below the standard bus fare, the broker arranges with some irregular operator, even the owner of a private car, to transport those who have purchased transportation of him at a rate which will leave to him a margin of profit. Such agencies also advertise for owners of equipment who will handle traffic secured. Such operations are wholly objectionable from the standpoint of the public, because of the typical irresponsibility of both broker and operator, as well as from the standpoint of the industry, since it makes stabilization of rates impossible and imperils reasonable profits from regular service; whether some restriction should be placed upon charter operations is problematical, but brokerage in transportation should be closely controlled.

Advantages of the Bus.—It is apparent that there must be certain advantages, inherent and perhaps other, that explain the ability of the bus to wrest from the railway a considerable volume of traffic and to develop new traffic in even greater volume. These advantages may be summarized under two heads, service and rates. The bus has a high degree of flexibility in the matter of routes and schedules; it commonly offers the prospective traveler greater convenience than the railway as to points of arrival and departure, with stations located in the business district and the possibility of receiving and discharging passengers at any point en route; the lower cost of unit operation makes possible more frequent service; well-surfaced highways offer freedom from smoke, cinders, and dust; the scenic advantages of the highway are normally greater than of the railway and it rarely traverses the poorer and industrial sections of a city; certain cross-country movements are made possible; and time in transit is even less in many cases than that of local railway passenger service. Furthermore, perhaps because of its resemblance to the individual car, many feel the "spirit of adventure" that is absent in railway travel; and, finally, novelty continues to be a factor with many.

Yet the lure of cheaper transportation draws many who might feel that, because of certain other advantages in service, the railway is preferable. While it is impossible to give a definite statement concerning the level of bus charges, testimony indicates that where the bus is in competition with the railway a materially lower rate per mile is necessary to attract and hold traffic. Rarely in such case is the rate in excess of 3 cents for the shorter hauls, with the charge diminishing until hauls of 500 miles or more are often made at 2 cents per mile. A common charge is 2.5 cents under conditions where competition is stabilized, with a reduction of 10 per cent upon round-trip tickets—though special rates are often made to proximate cities at as low as 1.5 cents per mile. Yet, as indicated before, where competition is active rates are often forced to and held at uneconomic levels. Upon runs that are essentially noncompetitive in character, however, rates run materially higher than the standard rail rate: 4 cents is not an unusual charge and even higher are found. In short, in the determination of bus charges the fundamental consideration is a level of rates that will provide traffic: the ability principle is of paramount importance.

Financial Results of Bus-line Operations.—Only scattering data are available upon the financial results of bus-transport operations, therefore positive judgments cannot be offered. In general, it may be said that the financial showing of the small operator is less satisfactory than that of the large: though the former uses less costly equipment he normally operates over routes of light traffic density and his enterprise typically lacks the expert direction of the larger units. And it is probably true that, because of inadequate depreciation and unsatisfactory accounting records, the income of the small operator is even then often overstated. Records indicate that the cost of bus operation per seat-mile is approximately 1 cent; the average number of passengers per bus as shown in the Western States survey was 10.27. If it be assumed that the 29-passenger bus was typical of operations, an average fare of 3 cents would be necessary to provide a profit. But that profits have been made by the larger companies during normal times is attested by the improvement in the status of securities issued by them. And it is attested, too, by the results of a survey made of 1930 operations: while an actual loss was shown by the smallest operator group, profits rose steadily with the extent of operations to 5.72 per cent upon the investment for the largest operator group, its buses averaging 32.5 seats each—with the rate of return diminishing for operators of smaller fleets of larger buses. That there are profits in the transportation of persons by bus is apparent but those profits seldom accrue to the small operator who often serves over marginal routes or poorer—and to the larger operator they are not assured except as the industry is stabilized and reasonable fares can be maintained.

The Motor Truck.—Until approximately 1920 the phrase, "ship by rail," was not a suggestion when addressed to the typical inland shipper; it was, rather, a statement of fact—or, perhaps, of a policy from which there was no escape. The "freighter" operated only to and from areas without rail service, for the cost in time and money of highway transport for even short distances was prohibitive as compared with rail movement: the slow-plodding team was no match for the iron horse. It was upon the basis of this essentially monopolistic position of the railway with respect to much of its traffic that regulation, in the judgment of many, rested. The motor truck had served in a limited field before the World War, yet its possibilities as a competitor of the railway were apparent to few, even of the discerning. The competitive period dates from the close of the war period; in the years that have passed since 1920 improvements in the mechanism, the construction of all-weather highways, and other factors have operated to effect changes in land transport that are little less than bewildering. Of such changes many illustrations might be given but perhaps one contrast will suffice: as recently as 1927 authority was cited by an important committee in support of the statement that need of speedy delivery or some special characteristic of the commodity explained movement by truck for distances in excess of 60 miles,[1] and in midyear, 1932, regular motor-freight service was begun over a route some 1,700 miles in length.[2] The meteoric rise of motor transport, as well as its economic and political significance, merits study.

Types of Trucks in Use.—Of the close approach to 3,500,000 trucks in service in 1931, it is known that a major portion are owner-operator (title to vehicle and load resting in the same legal person). The proportion of owner-operator trucks to the total has been shown to vary widely as between various sections of the country, surveys indicating that it falls as low as 75 per cent in certain areas and rises to more than 90 per cent in others. The most comprehensive study of motor-vehicle operations that has been made to date is the Western States survey. This showed that 85.8 per cent of the trucks upon the highway were owner-operated; of these 83.2 per cent were engaged in intra- and 2.6 per cent in interstate hauling. Contract hauling accounted for 8.7 per cent of the trucks, intra- and interstate operations contributing 5.4 and 3.3 per cent, respectively. Common-carrier trucks constituted but 5.5 per cent of the total, with the relation between intra- and interstate movements standing 4:1. Conclusions based upon studies made elsewhere would indicate that the proportion of owner-operated, contract, and common-carrier trucks to the

[1] *Report of Highway Transport Committee*, American Section, International Chamber of Commerce, 1927, p. 26.

[2] *Traffic World*, vol. 49, p. 1305.

total as here found is quite typical; though it is certain that the smaller states of the East would show a larger proportion of interstate operations to the total. Of the total traffic moved by truck, however, the distribution is quite different.[1] Owner-operated trucks are estimated to handle 50 per cent of the tonnage, of which 7.5 per cent is interstate. Contract and common-carrier trucks are judged to share upon the basis of 30 and 20 per cent of the total and, interestingly, it is estimated that one-fourth of the tonnage moved by each type is interstate. In the light of all facts available, it appears that a very large proportion of all trucks are in strictly urban or suburban service or are farm-owned; the ' truck problem" upon the highway, therefore, seems to arise from the operation in distance hauling of carriers for hire and of a limited number of owner-operator trucks.

Truck Ownership.—No study has been made upon the basis of which positive statements may be offered concerning truck ownership, yet it is a matter of common knowledge that the typical truck owner possesses but a single vehicle—and this is no less true of the contract trucker than of the owner-operator. More than one-fourth of the trucks registered are farm-owned, and here multiple ownership is infrequent; large numbers of trucks are owned by small contractors, by tradesmen, by peddlers, and others. The typical contract operation is one characterized by unit ownership, the truck being the instrumentality that provides employment for its owner. Common-carrier operations were, in the beginning, often conducted with a single truck; the consolidation of operations in the interest of greater effectiveness and the possibility of extending service as highways have been improved have tended toward fleet operation. Even yet the number of units owned by a single operator is often less than 5, though it is not unusual for 50 or more to be so owned. The great fleets, interestingly, are largely owner-operated, however; in 1931 the 10 largest of these owner-operated fleets were as follows:[2]

American Telephone and Telegraph Company	15,500
Standard Oil Company (N. J.)	12,000
Borden Company	10,000
Standard Oil Company (Ind.)	7,465
National Dairy Products	6,000
Mid-West Utilities Company	3,881
Continental Baking Company	3,500
Standard Brands, Inc.	3,275
Standard Oil Company (Calif.)	2,677
New York City, Department of Sanitation	2,587

The variety of undertakings included in this list is suggestive of the extent to which the truck has found favor with industries; indeed, to the

[1] Interstate Commerce Commission, Docket 23400, p. 275.

[2] National Automobile Chamber of Commerce, *Facts and Figures of the Automobile Industry*, 1932, p. 36.

system of commodity distribution upon which certain types of enterprise now rely the motor vehicle is vital. The Railway Express Agency, with 9,247 trucks, is the only common carrier operating a large fleet, but several contract carriers are named—among these being the United States Trucking Corporation with 860 units and the United Parcels Service with 510. Some 23,000 trucks were owned by the federal government at the close of 1931 and numerous states owned large fleets, several of these fleets containing approximately 1,000 units.

Nature of Truck Traffic.—When the truck was first employed for distance hauling, operations were limited to a relatively small number of commodities in handling which the truck had a marked advantage; prominent among these were household goods, general express, groceries, and finished products moving to jobbing or wholesaling houses. That truck operations are still confined generally to a limited field is indicated by a statement based upon extended hearings by the Interstate Commerce Commission: "Truck operators select their tonnage and take the so-called cream of the traffic, that is, high revenue-producing traffic which would move by rail at the higher rate classes."[1] Yet the expansion of truck operations into other fields, even to the movement of low-grade commodities for considerable distances, has been evident in recent years. A decade ago there was little movement of even "the cream of the traffic" for distances in excess of 60 miles; today the truck moves coal greater distances in considerable volume and competes for sand and gravel up to 40 miles upon occasion. In addition to household goods, general express, groceries, and fresh meats and produce for local distribution, the truck has become an important carrier of live stock, butter and dairy products, fruits and vegetables, cotton, automobiles, coal, cement, and other miscellaneous products for distances that are steadily increasing.[2] A railway executive in testimony before the Interstate Commerce Commission estimated that motor trucks handled in 1930 some 90 per cent of the less-than-carload freight destined to points within a radius of 50 miles of jobbing centers, about 75 per cent of that moving 50 to 100 miles, and approximately 50 per cent of that transported 100 to 150 miles. In addition to this tonnage is the movement of a large volume of traffic that has in the past been offered in carload lots to the railways. Though the limitations of space forbid extended treatment,[3] a brief statement will be made to indicate the present extent of carrier operations.

[1] *Coordination of Motor Transportation*, 72d Congress, 1st Session, Senate Document 43, p. 37.

[2] Perhaps no better concise summary of the variety and extent of such movements can be found than that given in the *Forty-fifth Annual Report of the Interstate Commerce Commission*, pp. 102–107.

[3] For a more complete statement, see Senate Document 43, cited before, pp. 44–57; or Interstate Commerce Commission, Docket 23400, pp. 283–300.

Live Stock by Truck.—Short-haul movements of live stock to market by highway antedates the motor vehicle, but such movement increased with its appearance. And, as roads have been improved and equipment suitable to the purpose developed, the volume of receipts by truck at the major markets has increased steadily and rapidly. In 1920 trucks delivered 5.21 per cent of the unloads at 16 large markets, 3,149,430 head of animals; in 1929 the truck proportion was 21.85 per cent, with the unloads totaling 13,775,905; while in 1931 to 17 markets the truck delivered 21,162,430 animals, one-third of the total unloaded and an increase of 25 per cent above the preceding year. The proportion of truck unloads to the total varies widely among markets, this variation being the consequence of several factors; among these the location of the market with respect to meat-producing areas and the type of animal butchered are significant. In 1920 Chicago received 0.3 per cent of its animals by truck and Louisville 29.5 per cent; in 1931 Chicago's percentage was 9.7 while Indianapolis received 85.8 per cent of its total by highway. In general, the proportion of hogs and calves trucked to the market is approximately double that of cattle and sheep, though both groups show a progressive increase.

With the increased capacity of equipment and the extension of hard-surfaced roads, all available facts indicate that the average load and the average length of haul have risen rapidly: from 1924 to 1929 the average length of haul into South St. Paul increased from 22 to 40.8 miles; from 1927 to 1929 the percentage of shipments moving in excess of 100 miles increased from 4.7 to 8.7; and the average length of movements into all markets in 1931 is estimated to have increased to 65 miles as compared with 60 miles in 1930. And from 1930 to 1931 the average load is estimated to have increased by almost 10 per cent—single truck shipments of hogs weighing in excess of 20,000 pounds have been delivered, this weight being materially above the carload minimum for rail shipments.

This phenomenal growth of live-stock trucking is explained largely by the greater convenience of this method and ability of the shipper to market more advantageously. Rates by truck are rarely as low as by rail; commonly they are 50 per cent in excess of the rail charge and occasionally they run almost three times as high, these differences depending upon character of highway, distance of farm from rail shipping point, quantity offered for shipment, and competition among truckers. These truckers are usually contract carriers, though occasionally a truck will be used to carry for its owner and for others in the vicinity. From these trucking operations have arisen several difficult problems, among the more important being the effect of back-haul rates upon the financial showing of regular carriers by highway and rail as well as the influence of the shipment of live stock by truck upon farmers' cooperatives. Rather than make the return movement empty, stock trucks will move feed, fertilizer, groceries, or low-grade items such as lumber and cement, at any price in excess of out-of-pocket costs. In so doing they make it impossible for regular carriers to operate at a profit; they disrupt the regular channels of trade; and, by handling the individual farmer's live stock, by filling his bins with feed, and by meeting his other needs, they destroy the economic basis for the maintenance of farmers' cooperative groups.[1] Out of such irregular operations has arisen an insistent demand for regulation in many quarters.

Fruits and Vegetables by Truck.—The zone about a city from which fresh fruits and vegetables moved by highway prior to the appearance of the motor truck was narrow; dependence was largely on the railway, with further resort to water movement where such was physically possible. With the appearance of the truck and the improvement of highways that zone has steadily widened until today movements of 200 miles rouse no comment—and "oranges have been moved from California to destinations within a distance of 1,500 miles" by highway.[2] Trucks handled 72 per cent of the fruit and vegetables received in New York City from the principal Eastern producing areas as early as 1928; in 1930 the Maryland peach crop moved almost wholly by truck, much of it to New York City; and in 1931, 25 per cent of the Carolina peaches moved by truck, many loads to northern cities. In 1931 trucks handled about 25 per cent of the Arkansas grape crop, 68 per cent of the apple crop, and 82 per cent of the peaches. One company handled four times the volume of strawberries shipped by rail from the Delmarva Peninsula to Eastern cities in 1931. Surveys conducted by the Bureau of Agricultural Economics indicate that, of farm produce shipped, trucks handled 92 per cent from Connecticut, 85 per cent from southwestern Pennsylvania, and 73 per cent from southwestern Michigan—though percentages fell as low as 7, 3, and even 2, for western Massachusetts, eastern Virginia, and a portion of West Virginia. Instances of the expanding use of the truck in this field could be multiplied indefinitely, but another aspect of truck use merits note, the movement of fresh produce from the larger markets into the smaller cities and villages. Today fruits and vegetables are distributed within a radius of 150 miles[3] by overnight truck movement, thus broadening the market for such items and improving diet in communities inadequately served under the old régime. It was estimated that, of the total receipts on the Pittsburgh and Baltimore wholesale markets in the spring of 1930, 50 and 24 per cent, respectively, were trucked out.

[1] See the testimony of William Hirth, president of the Missouri Farmers' Association, before the Committee on Interstate Commerce United States Senate, 72d Congress, 1st Session, on S. 2793, pp. 717–726.

[2] *Forty-fifth Annual Report of the Interstate Commerce Commission,* p. 106.

[3] *Hearings,* Committee on Interstate Commerce, United States Senate, previously cited, p. 162, testimony of J. W. Blood.

While a great part of this trucking of fresh fruits and vegetables is done under contract, often at rates that represent a material saving as compared with rail shipments, enough is moved by the so-called peddler-truck to give rise to a considerable disturbance of market conditions. And particularly does the market suffer when such peddler operations result in "breaking the market" for graded products with ungraded products or with culls acquired at little or no cost.[1] To such practices "complete demoralization" of the market in particular cities has been charged. And even contract trucking does not, at least under conditions now existing, make possible that marshaling of supply through diversion and reconsignment by produce houses that has tended to eliminate both glut and famine in any single market. Yet, despite these evils and the serious weakening of cooperative marketing organizations, it is certain that the speed of movement by truck, the lesser cost of distribution under certain conditions, the frequent savings in transportation charges, and the greater convenience to the grower of shipping from the field, assure the truck an important future in the movement of fresh fruits and vegetables.

Cotton by Truck.—One of the striking developments in truck transportation during the several years past has been the phenomenal increase in highway movements of cotton. As late as 1928 but 1.9 per cent of the cotton reaching Houston, Galveston, and Texas City was brought by trucks; from Aug. 1, 1931, to Feb. 5, 1932, trucks handled into Houston 47.6 per cent of the almost 2,800,000 bales delivered at the port. The records of other Texas ports are quite comparable, with cotton moving average distances of 150 to 200 miles; indeed, some of the cotton came to Texas ports by highway from Oklahoma and Arkansas, moving distances in excess of 400 miles. Into Pensacola and Mobile the Louisville and Nashville moved during the season ending Aug. 1, 1930, more than three times the volume of cotton that came by truck; during the next season truck movements were more than double those of the same railway. In Georgia practically all cotton used by local mills is transported by truck for distances up to 100 miles. And competition for cotton traffic has become no less keen in the Pacific Southwest, with truck movements reported for distances up to 250 miles. Cottonseed is trucked extensively, too.

Cotton is hauled largely by contract truckers, who solicit tonnage upon the basis of lower rates. Loads of 16 bales weighing 500 pounds each are common, with many trucks hauling 20 bales of compressed cotton; in some instances a truck-and-trailer unit has moved 40 bales. Some cotton is handled as a back-haul movement by automobile truckaway

[1] An extended discussion of this problem from the point of view of the National Potato Institute is presented in *Hearings*, Committee on Interstate Commerce, before cited, pp. 405–414, and from the point of view of the commission merchant in the same report, pp. 465–466.

units and trucks moving cotton to ports compete sharply for back-haul traffic at rates that often scarcely cover direct operating outlays. Rates have no stability, being made commonly to get the tonnage. The marked increase of cotton trucking is explained by some as the result of the presence of trucks rendered idle by reduced petroleum, forest, and other operations; also by the importance of low rates upon cotton when price is at such low levels.

Cement and Coal by Truck.—The cement industry of the country has a productive capacity greatly in excess of normal market needs. This situation has led to sharp competition but, with the organization of the industry, with the stabilization of railway rates, and with the elimination of rebating, a satisfactory basis had been attained and "cutthroat" struggles for tonnage largely eliminated. With the rapid development of truck movements of cement in recent years stability has largely disappeared, however; the spokesman of the cement industry declared, in testifying before the Senate Committee on Interstate Commerce, "In the course of five years the transportation end of the cement business has gone from certainty to chaos."[1] Though data are lacking to show for the entire country the proportion of cement hauled by truck, this same witness estimated that in 1931 between 50 and 60 per cent of all cement used moved over the highways, loadings sometimes being as great as 50,000 pounds. While the movement is largely by contract truckers, operating upon scales of rates that vary widely, the possibilities of this new method of handling the product have led certain cement plants to acquire and operate their own fleets of trucks. Though hauls are generally short, there are records of large movements for distances as great as 125 miles; and shipments have been transported by highway to points approximately 200 miles distant.

The so-called "wagon-mine" has been a factor in the coal trade since the beginning of the use of coal, and trucking merely represents an extension of the area served directly from mine mouth. But it is the magnitude of this extension that perturbs the railways and bids fair to cripple seriously or even in many communities to destroy accepted marketing machinery. The Reading system estimated the movement in its territory of anthracite coal by truck at 144,000 tons in 1929 and in 1930 at 500,000 —with distances increasing from 50 to as much as 75 and 100 miles. A great and rapidly increasing volume of coal moves into St. Louis and into Denver from mines approximately 20 miles distant; various railways report large truck movements for distances of 40 to 60 miles, with length of haul increasing steadily. This coal tonnage is handled by contract carriers, by peddlers, and by migratory operators: sometimes orders are solicited in advance, sometimes the hauler sells his load after reaching the city. The rate situation is chaotic; overloading, unsafe conditions of

[1] *Hearings* on S. 2793, previously cited, p. 665.

vehicles, and even short weighing are charged; local distributors of coal with a permanent plant are threatened with disaster. Yet the volume of coal moved by truck advances steadily, with competitive opportunities increased for the motor vehicle because railway coal rates are established for mine groups rather than particular points; thus the truck, serving near-by mines at low cost, threatens a fundamental principle in coal-tariff construction.

The Truckaway.—One of the interesting developments in highway transportation has been the appearance of a special type of vehicle for the movement by highway of motor vehicles from factory, assembly plant, or port, to destination. Using this equipment four or five cars, even six, have been hauled for distances up to 1,500 miles. Though such distances are not common, hauls of 500 miles are made regularly; most of the truckaway movements are, however, for distances less than 250 miles. This transportation is largely conducted by contractors who operate, except in occasional instances, upon the basis of a one-way load. While greater speed of delivery is asserted as compared to rail movement, the primary incentive to dealers is a saving in cost over the highways, this saving varying from as low as $5 per car to as high as $20—with $10 to $12 a rather common figure. Yet it is against these truckaway units that sharpest protest is lodged by other users of the highway because of their threat to other traffic. Already legislation has compelled the shortening of truckaway units in most areas so that three cars now constitute the typical load, four being carried occasionally. To what extent this change will affect costs and, therefore, the volume of movement is problematical.

Other Tonnage by Truck.—In view of the movement of tonnage as diverse as that already indicated, it is not surprising to learn that many other items are shipped by truck in large volume. Large quantities of fresh meats and packing-house products now move by refrigerated truck instead of refrigerator car; cream is trucked for distances up to 200 miles and butter is moving in large volume by truck for distances up to 300 miles, with regular service being maintained between points 600 miles apart. Poultry and eggs are also moving by highway in growing volume: in July, 1931, almost 60 per cent of the poultry on the Chicago market arrived by truck. A large tonnage of magazines and newspapers, even news print, is now shipped by road, with regular distribution of newspapers being made by truck for distances up to 250 miles. About 25 per cent of the paving-brick tonnage to points less than 150 miles distant moves by truck in Central territory and about 59 per cent in Southern; a great volume of petroleum products moves by highway; lumber and lumber products move in quantity to and from ports and also for considerable distances cross-country. And the movement of grain by truck into such an important terminal market as Chicago began to assume significance late in 1932. In short, there are few commodities that are not now moved by highway for increasing distances and in increasing volume; as a competitor of the railway for shipments that commonly move in carload lots, the truck has established itself in a strong position.

Length of Haul.—In the preceding sections statements have been made relative to the length of haul of particular commodities, largely by contract trucks, under conditions of irregular service. It remains to comment briefly concerning average movements as indicated by surveys and concerning the distances over which regular services are offered. The Ohio survey, made in 1925, showed an average trip mileage of 32 miles for trucks; only 19.1 per cent of the total number moved 40 miles or more, and but 4.7 per cent 100 miles or more. Five years later the Western States survey gave an average daily mileage of 103 for all trucks, while only 19.8 per cent moved less than 40 miles and 31.4 per cent moved 100 miles or more. As might be expected, the average mileage for trucks operating in another than the state of registration was shown to be much higher than for local trucks: approximately 50 per cent, in fact. And, too, the proportion of foreign trucks moving in excess of 100 miles was almost double that of local trucks moving these greater distances. Another recent study made, covering the operations of trucking concerns scattered throughout the United States and purposed by its selection of concerns to give an accurate picture of for-hire trucking, showed an average length of haul by carriers over fixed routes of 88 miles and by "anywhere-for-hire" operators of 119 miles.[1]

Overnight schedules from Chicago now call for movements of 300 miles; the 485-mile run between Los Angeles and San Francisco is made regularly, the time being 13 hours; regular movements are made between San Francisco and Portland, 727 miles, and between Portland and Salt Lake, 940 miles. Refrigerator trucks operate out of Kansas City to Tulsa, into western Kansas, to Omaha, and to Michigan points. In Oregon trucks operate over regular routes up to 450 miles, with the average length of route 70 miles. In Michigan certified operators believe that they can compete successfully with the railway up to 150 miles, although they declare they cannot beyond 200. Such successful competition and the maximum length of profitable haul there, as elsewhere, depend upon many factors: of these the more important are the character of traffic, the density of population, industrial activity, character of highway and volume of highway traffic, the nature of rail service offered, and legal burdens or restrictions imposed. But it must be realized that operations are conducted at a profit only if all costs are covered, the individual cost factor most often ignored being adequate allowances for depreciation.

Volume of Truck Traffic.—In the comments upon the movement of particular commodities by truck that precedes, statements appear concerning proportions so shipped. These statements might be supplemented

[1] *Motor Truck Freight Transportation*, pp. 17–21.

by many others: total shipments of fresh fruits and vegetables by truck for distances beyond 20 miles were estimated by the Bureau of Agricultural Economics to be 14 to 16 per cent of the total, some 150,000 to 200,000 carloads; in 1930 trucks operating in Oregon under fixed schedules and upon fixed rates transported 509,233 tons of freight, while even as early as in 1925 the Ohio survey showed that trucks were handling more than half of *all* tonnage from Columbus to selected cities for distances up to 40 miles and almost one-fourth for distances of less than 100 miles; many canneries are moving their total output by truck to centers of distribution, hauls being common for distances up to 200 miles; and great quantities of automobile tires move by highway for distances up to 800 miles. More significant than the mention of isolated cases of truck movement, however, is a statement of the proportion of the total tonnage moved by highway.

Because of the complete lack of adequate data upon which an accurate statement can be rested, since even the reports of tons carried and ton-miles of service rendered by common carriers are incomplete and undependable, no statement of proportion for the nation can be more than an intelligent estimate. Yet certain of these estimates, representing the results of careful study and analysis, are entitled to weight. For 1925 the Bureau of Public Roads estimated that ton-miles of service by truck constituted 1.96 per cent of the revenue ton-miles of the railways for that year. Upon the basis of comparable computations, the figure for 1928 was fixed at 2.1 per cent;[1] for 1929 it was put at 2.7 per cent (nonrevenue service of railways eliminated).[2] For 1929 the estimate of the Interstate Commerce Commission was much higher, however;[3] though different bases for determining a figure were suggested, the result accepted was 5.8 per cent of railway service—with the added comment that "known developments in the trucking field in the past 2 years indicate that the percentage of truck traffic is greater today than it was in 1929."[4] And the Bureau of Foreign and Domestic Commerce estimated that, for 1931, the intercity service of *for-hire* trucks only was "over 5.5 per cent of all rail revenue ton-mileage in 1931; it was 15.3 per cent of the Class I rail revenue 'tonnage carried,' and 27.5 per cent of the 'originating tonnage' in that year."[5]

Perhaps the study that offers the most complete and accurate data upon the extent of trucking and is of greatest immediate significance

[1] Bureau of Railway Economics, *An Economic Survey of Inland Waterway Transportation in the United States*, p. 28.

[2] Estimate of J. H. Parmelee in *Mechanical Engineering*, March, 1931.

[3] See Interstate Commerce Commission, *Coordination of Motor Transportation*, Docket 23400, Appendix B, pp. 400–407, for an excellent discussion of this entire problem, including methods of estimating employed.

[4] *Ibid.*, p. 403.

[5] Secretary of Commerce, *Twentieth Annual Report*, p. xiii.

because of its recency is that of the California Railroad Commission.[1] Upon the basis of comprehensive information covering 1931, that body concludes that the number of tons of freight *originated* by the various classes of trucks in that year was in excess of half of the number originated by the railways, the contributions of the two to the total being 34.74 and 65.26 per cent, respectively. To this 34.74 per cent the common carrier contributed 3.10, the contract carrier 12.42, and the owner-operator 19.22 per cent. Because conditions in various sections of the country are quite different, there is likelihood of serious error if California results are projected for an entire nation, yet there is in the data developed for California food for serious thought and in the evils shown sound cause for action.

Advantages of the Truck.—This astonishing increase in truck traffic rests upon certain definite advantages to the shipper as compared with railway service. Of these perhaps the most significant is that the truck offers a *complete service*, from door to door, and is able to give within considerable distances overnight delivery. The truck, too, will normally pick up shipments after railway freight stations have closed and can deliver before the destination station opens in the morning. The truck offers a flexible service, being more responsive to shippers' and consignees' wishes and needs; it makes possible more direct and personal contact between the shipper and the transportation agency; and the elimination of rehandling tends to minimize loss and damage on small-lot shipments. Then, too, being a smaller unit, the truck can give more frequent service. And, finally, door-to-door service without transfer and in such a unit as the modern truck minimizes or entirely eliminates packing requirements and costs; indeed, it is for this reason that certain types of shipments, notably household goods, are moved so largely by highway—with hauls in excess of 2,000 miles not infrequent. These and other advantages in service have overshadowed certain minor weaknesses, such as irregularity of schedules, irresponsibility of the truck operator, difficulty in collecting loss and damage claims, and uncertainty of rate schedules—weaknesses which, as time passes, are lessening. And other major disadvantages of truck service—lack of prestige of truck bills of lading for banking purposes, absence of certain typical rail privileges such as reconsignment and storage in transit, and inadequate protection of shipments during adverse weather—are also being minimized as the organization of the industry advances and as technical gains are made. It is largely as a consequence of steady movement of the balance of advantage in the direction of truck service that the volume of such traffic has increased so rapidly during recent years.

Yet it is only as these advantages are offered at an attractive price that the truck is enabled to increase its inroads upon railway tonnage. Because of the several types of truck operator, the wide range of conditions under which service is rendered, and uncertainty as to rates

[1] California Railroad Commission, Decision 25243, p. 25.

actually charged, comparisons of truck and rail rates are difficult.[1] In general, however, common carriers by truck tend to charge rates equal to or slightly in excess of the rail rates; where no difference in charge is made among the upper classes of freight by trucks, the truck rate will fall below the rail rate on the highest class but stand above the lowest—a rough average, perhaps. In some instances the truck rate will be as much as 50 per cent in excess of the rail charge, in others it may be fixed at even half the fourth-class rate for all classes. Contract carriers have been in the past largely free of regulatory restraints that would affect rates or scope of service; they have made changes readily and have discriminated among shippers, types of traffic, and communities. For given distances their rates are generally less than rail rates and highly unstable. They may be made on a mileage, tonnage, or hourly basis; more often they have been determined by what can be obtained. Contract hauling at rates in excess of the rail charge is generally of traffic that requires highly expeditious movement; but experience indicates that, to be remunerative, long-distance hauls must be made at approximately the rail rate. Regular contract operators in a field endeavor to maintain a rate structure that will yield a fair profit, but this has become increasingly difficult in the absence of regulation because of irresponsible or wildcat competition and of the presence in the field of operators who neither know their costs nor have the financial resources to enable them to meet current outlays without slashing rates to increase tonnage. And one of the most troublesome factors in the maintenance of rates is the struggle for a back-load; this constitutes under all conditions a serious threat to the maintenance of adequate rates and is often responsible for the breakdown of satisfactory schedules.

The owner-operator, in entering the trucking field, has by such action refused in part or in whole the services of the railway and the for-hire operator. His decision may be based upon considerations of convenience or upon the belief that the nature of his shipping is such that he can serve himself more economically than others can serve him. Because of the absence of authentic cost data covering truck operations, progress is likely to be made slowly by the owner-operator in putting a fleet of trucks upon the highway. It is probable, therefore, that the operation of a fleet in private service is an indication that the owner has found by experience he can profit therefrom under existing conditions.

Loss of Traffic by Railways.—The tremendous traffic, passenger and freight, that now moves over our highways represents three elements: business that has come into being because of the availability of the passenger vehicle and the truck; business that, except for the availability of these agencies, would have moved by rail or water as it developed;

[1] For a detailed discussion of this matter of rates, see Interstate Commerce Commission, *Coordination of Motor Transportation*, Docket 23400, pp. 302–307.

and business that has been taken from existing transportation systems. To identify and distinguish between the first two is impossible but there are reasonably accurate measures of the loss of the railway to the highway, and those who desire to speculate upon the probable development of railway traffic in the absence of motor-vehicle competition will find suggestive the statement that railway passenger traffic and railway freight traffic tended to double every 15 and 12 years, respectively, in the years prior to 1920. Instead of the normal rate of increase continuing since that year, however, there has been a significant decrease in railway passenger traffic and the trend of freight traffic has been but slightly upward.

The average level of business activity in 1921 was closely comparable to that of 1930, yet the intervening decade showed a decline in the number of revenue passengers carried by the railways of 32 per cent and a decline of 28 per cent in the number of passenger-miles of revenue service rendered. Further analysis of data available indicates that this loss occurred in coach service, with Pullman berth and seat traffic declining but little. During this same period the number of tons of freight originated increased by 23 per cent and ton-miles of revenue service by 21 per cent. Here again analysis shows interesting facts: less-than-carload tonnage has decreased sharply, this decrease being widely different in the various districts: the carriers of the Western District have suffered most and those of Southern least. And, as this type of traffic yields revenues quite out of proportion to its volume, such loss has been the more serious financially. That the loss by individual railways of passenger traffic during recent years is startling in certain instances may be shown by a few examples: in Table XXXVII appear certain pertinent data for typical railways that have suffered heavily, commutation traffic being eliminated. Striking differences, appear, too, among the various regions:

TABLE XXXVII.—PASSENGER TRAFFIC OF SELECTED RAILWAYS*

Railway	Passengers carried		Passenger-miles		Percentage decrease in passenger revenues, 1920–1929
	1920	1929	1920	1929	
New Haven	106,847,739	54,405,974	2,153,958,865	1,662,345,572	10.39
Rock Island	15,620,116	3,839,498	1,139,643,663	561,680,162	47.92
Santa Fe	15,656,333	4,253,695	2,189,000,000	1,240,000,000	40.25
Burlington	17,200,000	4,600,000	1,209,000,000	571,000,000	51.32
Kansas City Southern	2,693,688	412,655	105,907,985	39,338,853	74.54
St. Louis Southwestern	3,976,230	567,678	137,513,447	36,243,447	70.16

* *Coordination of Motor Transportation*, 72d Congress, 1st Session, Senate Document 43, pp. 10–13.

while the number of passengers carried dropped less than one-sixth in the Great Lakes and Central Eastern areas for the decade ending in 1930, the decreases in the Pocahontas and Southwestern regions were 66 and 78 per cent respectively; and, though passenger-miles diminished but 14 and 17 per cent for the first two regions named, the decline for the latter two was in excess of 50 per cent. Differences in the decline in passenger revenue are more closely comparable, ranging from 22 per cent in the Great Lakes region to 56 per cent in Southwestern territory.

Less-than-carload tonnage has failed the railways almost to the degree that passenger traffic has: in 1929 the Chicago, Burlington, and Quincy handled 60 per cent of the volume of package freight handled in 1916; from 1920 to 1929 the tonnage of small-lot shipments on the Maine Central and the St. Louis-San Francisco diminished 48 and 35 per cent, respectively; the less-than-carload movements from Denver over the Colorado and Southern to selected points dropped 70 per cent from 1920 to 1929; and the Atlantic Coast Line experienced a decline in like tonnage from 1925 to 1930 of 54 per cent. The Chicago and North Western estimated that the diversion of small-lot shipments cost it $5,237,000 annually and the Illinois Central estimated its loss at $6,855,000 yearly. And in no case have the railways been able to cut service costs in any measure comparable with declines in revenue, for either passenger or freight movements.

The Motor Vehicle Problem.—Upon the pages immediately preceding the story is told of the transformation of byways of transportation into traveled highways of commerce by the rapid development of the motor vehicle and a corresponding improvement in roads, a transformation that has occurred within a score of years and has become impressive since 1925. It is inescapable that such a change should be attended by the rise of important problems, the solution of which will offer to student and statesman a serious challenge in the future—with the likelihood that these new problems of transportation, like the old, will become more complex and difficult with time. The motor age requires the expenditure of many hundreds of millions of dollars yearly for highway construction and maintenance, while the operation of increasing millions of vehicles upon those highways in such manner as to afford pleasure, safety, and profit requires the judicious exercise of regulatory powers. And the interrelation of the highway with other forms of transport, as well as the formulation of a sound public policy with respect to transportation, will demand a clear understanding of fundamentals and the exercise of a high level of intelligence if public interest is to be well served in the long run. If the "transportation problem" has constituted a challenge in the past, it will represent a far greater challenge in the future—with less opportunity to "muddle through" and yet not do irreparable injury to society. In the following chapter brief consideration will be given to three basic problems that press for solution: certain aspects of the question of highway finance, the nature and limitations of highway regulation, and certain fundamentals of public policy.

REFERENCES

Agg, T. R., and H. S. Carter: Operating-cost Statistics of Automobiles and Trucks, *Iowa State College, Engineering Experiment Station, Bulletin* 91, 1928.

Associated Traffic Club Bulletins, vol. 1. Nos. 14–16.

Blanchard A. H., and R. L. Morrison: *Elements of Highway Engineering*, John Wiley & Sons, Inc., 1928.

Brosseau, A. J.: *Highways and the Taxpayer*, Address published by National Automobile Chamber of Commerce, 1922.

Brown, R. D.: Concrete Pavement Design Features, 1931, *Public Roads*, vol. 13, p. 47.

Bus Facts for 1932, National Association of Motor-bus Operators, Washington, D. C., 1932.

California Railroad Commission, *Decision* 25243.

Cannon, J.: Subsidized Motor-truck Competition, *The Railroad Trainman*, vol. 49, No. 11, p. 665.

Chamber of Commerce of the United States: *Relation of Highways and Motor Transport to Other Agencies*, Special Committee IV, Washington, D. C., 1923.

Corn Belt Farm Dailies, *Motor-truck Transport of Live Stock for 1931*, Chicago.

Daggett, Stuart R.: *Principles of Inland Transportation*, Harper & Brothers, 1928.

Department of Commerce: *Twentieth Annual Report.*

Edwards, Brice, and J. W. Park: The Marketing and Distribution of Fruits and Vegetables by Motor Truck, United States Department of Agriculture, *Technical Bulletin* 272, 1931.

English, W. L.: Trucks Make Alarming Freight Gains, *The Frisco Employes' Magazine*, vol. 10, No. 18, p. 6.

Facts and Figures of the Automobile Industry, National Automobile Chamber of Commerce, New York, 1932.

Flynn, Leo J.: *Coordination of Motor Transportation*, Report to Interstate Commerce Commission, published as Senate Document 43, Government Printing Office, 1932.

Hearings before the Committee on Interstate and Foreign Commerce, House of Representatives, 71st Congress, 2d Session, on H. R. 7954, *Regulation of Interstate Motor Buses on Public Highways*, Jan. 8 and 9, 1930.

Hearings before the Committee on Interstate Commerce, United States Senate, 72d Congress, 1st Session, on S. 2793, *Regulation of Motor Carrier Transportation*, Feb. 1 to Mar. 31, 1932.

Hibbs, Ben: Are the Railroads Licked? *The Country Gentleman*, vol. 102, No. 9, p. 14.

———: The Transportation Mess, *The Country Gentleman*, vol. 102, No. 8, p. 3.

Interstate Commerce Commission: *Annual Reports, Statistics of Railways in the United States. Motor-bus and Motor-truck Operation*, Docket 18300, 140 I.C.C. 685. *Coordination of Motor Transportation*, Docket 23400, 182 I.C.C. 263.

James, E. W.: *Highway Construction, Administration, and Finance.* Highway Education Board.

MacDonald, T. H.: Testimony given in *Coordination of Motor Transportation*, Docket 23400, distributed by the National Association of Motor Bus Operators, Washington, D. C., 1931.

National Association of Railroad and Public Utility Commissioners: Report of Committee on Motor-vehicle Transportation, *United States Daily*, Nov. 17, 1932, p. 1.

Report of a Survey of Transportation on the State Highway System of Connecticut, the Bureau of Public Roads, United States Department of Agriculture, and the Connecticut State Highway Department, 1926.

Report of a Survey of Transportation on the State Highway System of Ohio, the Bureau of Public Roads, United States Department of Agriculture, and the Ohio Department of Highways and Public Works, 1927.

Report of a Survey of Traffic on the Federal-aid Highway Systems of Eleven Western States, the Bureau of Public Roads, United States Department of Agriculture, and the Highway Departments of 11 states, 1930.

SANDAGE, C. H.: The Motor Vehicle in Iowa, *Iowa Studies in Business*, No. 1, Bureau of Business Research, University of Iowa, 1928.

———, and R. W. NELSON: Motor-vehicle Taxation for Highway Purposes, *Iowa Studies in Business*, No. 11, Bureau of Business Research, University of Iowa, 1932.

TRUMBOWER, HENRY R.: *Highway Transportation and Its Relation to the Railroads*, Highway Education Board, Washington, D. C., 1925.

WATERS, CHARLES A.: Beginning of Highway System in America, *United States Daily*, Nov. 25, 1932.

CHAPTER XXXIV

MOTOR TRANSPORTATION: SOME MAJOR PROBLEMS

TO THE total number of motor vehicles registered in the United States for 1931 the passenger automobile contributed more than 85 per cent. At no time has the right of this vehicle to use the highway been questioned if it conformed to certain minimum requirements imposed in the interest of public safety and if the owner had complied with particular governmental demands; of these the payment of a license charge has been most important. No noteworthy allegations have been made of the failure of this vehicle to contribute adequately to the maintenance of the highway that it uses; by some it is asserted, rather, that it has contributed disproportionately for the benefit of the commercial highway user. And at no time have fundamental powers to regulate disturbed the courts or questions of public policy seriously challenged the legislative mind. In short, then, such major problems as today give rise to controversy are concerned almost wholly with those vehicles which utilize the road for private gain. It is the carrier for hire that has been the storm center of such controversy, though the private carrier of goods becomes a party at interest increasingly, both because of alleged inadequate payments for highway use and because of his contribution to the existing maladjustment of the nation's entire transportation mechanism. Through the succeeding discussion, then, the carrier for hire will occupy a central position; the private carrier of goods will have important place only because he travels highways built and maintained by governmental units and at public cost.

HIGHWAY FINANCE

It is probable that no question affecting the motor vehicle gives rise to more heated controversy than that which centers about its payment for highway use. With increasing frequency charges of inadequate payment by certain vehicle types are made, to be answered with equal emphasis by protests against the oppressive burden of existing taxes. Fundamentally, these wide divergences in point of view are the consequence of failure to agree upon the principle in accordance with which contributions should be made to highway costs, as well as of uncertainty concerning the additional construction and maintenance costs properly attributable to heavier loads. For certainty upon the latter point dependence must be placed on further tests, carefully made by a body that is clearly impartial, while determination of the principle in accordance with which highway cost allocations shall be made among vehicle groups is a question of social policy that must await better public understanding of the problems involved.

The Old Highways.—The early colonists found available for use only Indian trails; these, as settlements were made inland from river and coast, the users casually broadened and cleared until trail became some manner of road. As areas gained population, a highway net came into being for which local governmental units slowly assumed a degree of responsibility. Communication was vital to communities and only through cooperative effort might it be provided and maintained upon an adequate basis. The most effective agency for such cooperation was township or county. Thus it became a recognized function of government to maintain passable roads, though such responsibility rested lightly upon local officials through many years. So inadequate, indeed, were the provisions made for travel in certain areas and across difficult streams that at a comparatively early date the toll project appeared: the acceptance of toll road and bridge rested upon the belief that, for a special and individual benefit conferred, a reasonable payment was due from the user. The failure of the typical toll project to yield an adequate return led gradually not only to the abandonment of those undertakings but also to the acceptance by government of greater responsibility than had formerly been assumed. The placement of such responsibility varied as among the states and changed from time to time but, characteristically, supervision and financial support were obligations of county or township, with little or no state participation prior to the renaissance of interest in the highway that followed the appearance of the motor vehicle. As a consequence of inadequate direction much of the work was inexpertly done, no systematic plan was followed, and inefficiency in the expenditure of funds was rife. Yet it is evident that decentralized control and the expenditure of an approximate $75,000,000 annually for highway construction and maintenance at the beginning of this century was providing with measurable adequacy for the current needs of the American public: mud hub-deep and villainous ruts proved no insuperable obstacle to the horse-drawn vehicle and highway surfacing even upon important routes was generally of an inexpensive character.

Financing the New Highways.—After the turn of the century, however, a phenomenally steady and rapid growth in the number of motor vehicles upon the highway occasioned a no less astonishing development of highways. In the first 25 years following 1900 the total mileage of rural highways increased approximately by half, surfaced mileage was multiplied by four, and yearly expenditures had risen to almost $1,145,000,000. Because the old highway régime merged, unperceived by many, into the new, rather than a sharp line of demarcation being drawn between, governmental units continued time-honored methods of financing not only heavier maintenance but also mounting construction costs: rural highways were improved, often to high standards, at public cost—with occasional assistance from assessments made against property adjacent to the highway. Yet, as highway costs mounted and as the public came to a realization of the pecuniary gain to the individual vehicle owner resulting from the operation of that vehicle over improved as against unimproved roads, both the necessity and the logic of a change in the highway financial plan were impressed upon the body politic. In consequence, beginning during the war period and gathering momentum steadily, there has appeared a demand that an increasing portion of highway costs be borne by the user, this demand applying no less to outlays for construction than for maintenance. The extent to which this movement has fructified is indicated by the fact that, while in 1921 motor taxes contributed but 10.8 per cent of rural highway income, in 1930 their direct contribution was 46.5 per cent—with a further credit of the major part of 17 per cent derived from the sale of bonds, which were secured largely by gasoline and other motor-vehicle taxes.

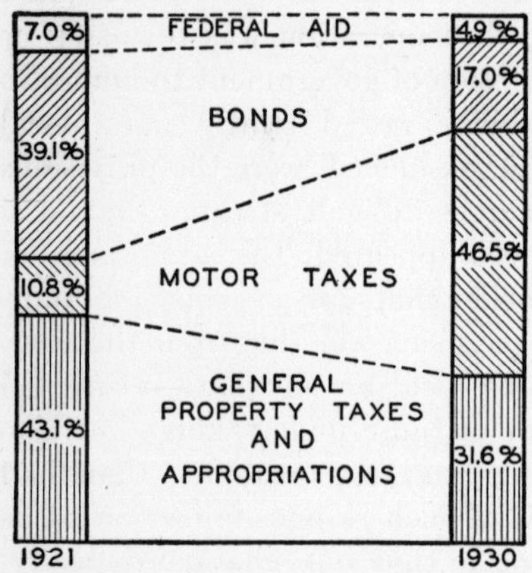

Fig. 38.—Sources of rural highway funds, 1921 and 1930. (*From National Automobile Chamber of Commerce.*)

It is with respect to the extent of this contribution that sharp controversy has arisen, with little likelihood of calm until clear and explicit adherence to some definite principle is given by the public. The principles purporting to relate special motor-vehicle taxes to highway costs may be grouped roughly under four heads: no special taxation whatsoever of the motor vehicle; highway construction costs met by general taxation, with special taxation for maintenance; all costs of improved highways assessed against the motor vehicle; and the adjustment of general taxes and motor-vehicle taxes in such manner as to place no unfair burden upon the individual motorist. While each of these principles could be discussed at length and some justification offered for all but the uncertain and opportunistic last, it must suffice to say that only the third escapes one definite major misconception: the others fail

. . . to recognize that furnishing improved highways especially adapted to use by the motor vehicle is essentially a business undertaking—a business that the government has been compelled to take over, and that should be made economically self-supporting, if it is not already so. It is doubtless true that this is a business . . . invested with a public interest to a considerable degree; in this respect it stands in much the same position as other public utilities. It can scarcely be contended, however, that providing highway facilities is of more direct concern than furnishing water, gas, or rail-transport facilities.[1]

To grant the validity of the traditional responsibility of government to maintain passable highways in no way vitiates the contention that expenditures beyond that traditional minimum represent benefits to a definite group, albeit large, with those benefits capable of exact measurement. And, as benefits may be measured, so may highway costs be apportioned with approximate equity among the users of the improved highway.

It is unfortunate that the public has lacked aggressive and discerning leadership of an impartial character in the solution of this important problem of highway finance: for a long period the only aggressive and conspicuous advocates of a definite policy were the manufacturers of motor vehicles, clearly a group with "an axe to grind." More recently, the dominant place of these proponents of *minimum* tax burdens has been challenged by another group desirous of imposing *maximum* burdens, the railways. As late as 1922 one of the leading spokesmen of the motor-vehicle manufacturers declared, "it seems that any fair plan for construction should be based upon general taxes for construction purposes"; but, since traffic "benefits first by maintenance in lowered operating costs, so traffic should be expected to meet this levy."[2] Beaten gradually from this position by logic and the force of circumstance, the manufacturing interests have more recently accepted with some measure of hopefulness the proposal of the Bureau of Public Roads that the motor-vehicle operator accept full responsibility for the so-called *state* highways. This hopefulness proceeds from the thought that, by accepting such responsibility, the operator may escape additional burdens resulting from demands for contributions to city streets and local roads. But the readiness of those concerned with the sale of additional motor-vehicle units to approve this burden upon the operator represents to the railway group, major loser from the advent of the motor vehicle, little more than one important step toward the full financial responsibility of the highway user: not only do the railways emphasize the burden imposed upon general property for local-road and city-street construction as well as maintenance, but stress the accumulated "deficits" chargeable to the motor vehicle—deficits that were great in earlier years when highway outlay

[1] SANDAGE, C. H., and R. W. NELSON, Motor-vehicle Taxation for Highway Purposes, *Iowa Studies in Business*, No. 11, Bureau of Business Research, University of Iowa, 1932, pp. 71–72.

[2] BROSSEAU, A. J., *Highways and the Taxpayer*, p. 10, an address delivered in Washington and distributed by the National Automobile Chamber of Commerce.

was large and motor-vehicle revenues relatively small, and that allegedly continue to accumulate despite license and gasoline-tax yields.[1]

Increased Costs and the Motor Vehicle.—As is characteristically true in controversial matters, a proper payment by highway users probably lies somewhere between the two extremes. To assist in determining at what point it lies between the approximate one billion dollars currently expended upon *state* highways—a sum that is now about equaled by all motor-vehicle taxes, plus receipts from bonds secured by such levies—and an outlay in excess of two billion dollars upon *all* highways, city and rural, certain facts are essential and certain applications of theory vital. In 1930 less than 20 per cent of all registered motor vehicles were owned on the farms and it has been estimated that in excess of 65 per cent of the total are city-owned. It is estimated, too, that approximately 50 per cent of all motor-vehicle mileage results from operations *within cities*. It is also important to note that the city streets constitute "terminal facilities" for the city-owned vehicles that contribute so heavily to the mileage accumulated upon rural highways.[2] Furthermore, because of the special characteristics of driving within cities, it is probable that mileage traveled within cities is responsible for the consumption of more than 50 per cent of the gasoline used by motor vehicles and, therefore, for more than 50 per cent of the gasoline-tax revenues. The justification for a considerable contribution to the $500,000,000 expended in 1930 for street construction and maintenance[3] from motor-vehicle tax revenues seems clear, therefore; and, whatever may be the explanation of meager apportionments to cities in the past from such revenues, it is unlikely that our financially hard-pressed cities will continue to accept such meager allotments without vigorous protest.

While data are not at hand to indicate the increase in the cost of street construction and maintenance since the advent of the motor vehicle and chargeable in considerable measure thereto, such facts are available for rural highways. As indicated before, the cost of rural highways to the public was in 1900 approximately $75,000,000 and in 1930 those costs approximated $1,700,000,000. In the absence of the motor vehicle, a threefold increase in the earlier figure would seem to be high for a single generation, even though that be a prosperous one, yet even a total so augmented would be but a small fraction of the expenditures in 1930. To fit our rural highways for motor-vehicle use has necessitated

[1] See an article, Who Pays for the Highways, by C. S. Duncan, in *Railway Age*, vol. 93, pp. 210–216, for a statement of this position.

[2] The Ohio survey showed that city-owned passenger cars and trucks contributed 87.6 and 84.5 per cent, respectively, of the total highway mileage, while the Western States survey showed city, village, and farm cars in the proportion of 61:20:19—with average trip-mileage per passenger car 169, 129, and 99 respectively.

[3] National Automobile Chamber of Commerce, *Facts and Figures of the Automobile Industry*, 1931, p. 44

tremendously increased outlays; since these highways confer benefits in proportion to use, it appears reasonable that costs be apportioned among the beneficiaries. Distinction between *state* and *local* highways is not one of kind; rather, it is one of definition—with volume of traffic as the common yardstick. But as "terminal facilities" the local highways have an importance much greater than is indicated by the 15 to 25 per cent which they contribute to the total volume of traffic; further, their "ready-to-serve" value to the motor vehicle is very real. Then, too, it is a recognized principle in the field of railway and utility regulation that no corporation can rightly insist that every branch line, every extension, be self-sustaining: within broad limits the undertaking must be regarded as a unit. Upon the basis both of theory and of fact, therefore, it seems that the motor vehicle must accept in large measure responsibility for *all* rural-road outlays, be those outlays for primary or secondary highways: no basis appears to exist in theory or in fact for restricting motor-vehicle taxation to that sum necessary to build and maintain *state* highways, while asking that all expenditures upon *local* highways be met from taxes levied upon already overburdened agricultural land.

Indeed, even when the motor vehicle has met through special taxes the costs of all special benefits enjoyed by it, the obligation of that type of property to society has not been absolved. From other types of personalty an exaction is made in most states to assist in defraying the general costs of government and, characteristically, the exemption of personalty in certain states is justified upon grounds of administrative expediency. The motor vehicle cannot escape listing upon the tax rolls, when registration records are available, if reasonable effort is made by assessors, and its approximate value is easily ascertained. The value of motor vehicles approximates $8,000,000,000 in the United States; from this type of property a public income should flow for varied governmental functions, just as much as from land, stocks of merchandise, locomotives and cars, and other properties now so burdened.

A Summary Statement.—To indicate with exactitude the tax burden that the motor vehicle should bear is impossible. None the less, it appears that the statement, "the motor vehicle pays its way, and handsomely," falls short of the fact. Sound public policy is unlikely to exact from this transport agency the *entire cost* of highway and street construction-maintenance, yet justice to other forms of property suggests that a much larger portion of that cost be placed upon it than has been to date. If it be urged that a greater portion of total cost cannot be borne by the motor vehicle, then careful scrutiny of highway expenditures is imperative—with a view to reducing outlay to such a point that subsidy will be unnecessary. Certainly it seems that outlays for construction may well be sharply limited for the next decade as compared with the past, the more since maintenance charges will tend to increase as highways of high-type surface age and as the mileage of local highways maintained for all-weather use increases.

Fundamentals of Tax Apportionment.—The second major problem of motor-vehicle taxation arises in the allocation of the designated total contribution upon an equitable basis among the various types of vehicle units and among the individual vehicles of each type. To the solution of this problem the ascertainment of certain engineering facts is essential, as well as the embodiment of those findings in legislation that will accomplish the desired ends. That even approximate agreement has not been attained with respect to engineering facts is apparent to the student, and the wide differences among states in the allocation of the tax burden indicate a regrettable absence of common judgment in legislative halls. Yet, so long as such sharp disagreement appears among those upon whom reliance must be placed for authoritative findings concerning the influence of weight and speed upon highway deterioration, even concerning the minimum specifications of a highway that will withstand successfully the ravages of weather, slight basis for criticism of legislative bodies exists because they fail to act in harmony. For, after all, allocation is an engineering problem and, subject to modifications necessary to make a suggested plan administratively feasible, from the engineer must come the formula in accordance with which highway costs are to be apportioned.

Motor-vehicle Charges: *The License.*—The first public burden imposed upon the operator of the motor vehicle was the license fee: in 1901 the state of New York imposed a charge for registration. This, and comparable impositions soon made by other states, was initially intended to cover only certain costs of regulation and rested upon the police power of the state. As demands for highway improvement developed, however, it appeared that an increase in the registration charge would provide an easy method of procuring funds to meet construction and maintenance costs. The license fee became, therefore, a tax: the exaction was now rested upon the taxing power of the state and, as had been the case with the fee, judicial sanction was given to it. The use of the annual registration charge soon became general; until 1919, when the gasoline tax first appeared, it was the only special tax of importance levied against the motor vehicle. Indeed, prior to 1928, the registration tax occupied first place as a source of revenue, yielding in that year to the gasoline tax. As a consequence of both increased registrations and occasional increases in the tax, receipts from registrations increased steadily until 1930 when they totaled $355,704,860.

The differences in the basis upon which this tax is fixed, not only as among the states but also as among different vehicle groups within a state, are indicative of legislative uncertainty concerning facts and disagreements as to proper public policy. At the close of 1930 the tax upon passenger cars was computed upon a single basis in 39 jurisdictions:

in 20 weight, net or gross, was used; in 13 horse power; in 3 some variation of price; and in 3 a flat rate. In 5 states horse power was combined with net or gross weight and in 5 others weight was a second factor. The most complex basis was that of North Dakota: factory price, net weight, horse power, and times registered; in other states no more than two elements entered into the determination. Weight and horse power are clearly the dominant factors, yet the levies vary widely among states using the same basis; the average charge for passenger automobiles on the basis of net weight varied in 1930 from $38.15 in Oregon to $8.93 in Nebraska and on horse power from $18.04 in New Jersey to $7.51 in Utah. Certain of these differences are explained in part by exemption of the motor vehicle from the general property tax in particular states: of these there were in 1931 no less than 16, of which Oregon and New Jersey were two. But, widely as the basis of registration fees for private passenger automobiles varies among the states, the basis of the registration charge for the passenger carrier for hire varies more widely: so widely, in fact, that a summary statement cannot well be made. It must, therefore, suffice to say that weight, net or estimated gross, and seating capacity are perhaps employed most commonly—with horse power recognized by some states. A difference is made by many states in the charge against the common carrier of persons for hire and the non-common carrier for hire, this difference invariably being in favor of the latter.

The license charge for the truck is based upon some variation of weight in practically all jurisdictions; rated capacity, gross weight, and net weight have gained recognition in that order. Other factors are horse power, value, and number of wheels together with net weight—and a flat rate is occasionally applied. A single factor is recognized generally; one of the most interesting of the dual bases is weight plus capacity. By most states the same basis is employed for owner-operated, contract, and common-carrier trucks, but it is important to note that often the *rate* applied to the base—be it capacity, gross weight, or other—is higher upon the for-hire truck than upon the owner-operated; indeed, it is quite frequently higher for the common carrier than for the non-common carrier for hire. Thus it appears that, with respect even to the license charge, statutes discriminate often against the for-hire truck in comparison with the owner-operated—with a further burden imposed upon the common carrier; yet, of the three, it is upon the common carrier that the public must rely for a regular service rendered upon terms prescribed.

The Gasoline Tax.—The registration charge is a fixed amount and is paid in a single sum. In consequence of the first fact there was no relation between payments and highway use; and, because of the second, sufficient sums to meet highway needs would be obtained with considerable difficulty from such a charge. The gasoline tax is collected in small amounts and it gives an approximate measure of highway use; to administrative merit it adds, therefore, theoretical justification. The rapid adoption of this levy after its appearance early in 1919 in Oregon was to be expected—and the more, since the need for increased funds was both great and immediate. Within 5 years 36 states had imposed such a tax, the rates varying from 1 to 4 cents per gallon, with 2 cents the more common rate; at the beginning of 1932 every state levied this tax, New York and Illinois being the last to adopt (1929), the rates varying from 1 to 7 cents. The rate most commonly charged is now 4 cents, with more states charging in excess of that figure than less. It is of interest, also, that a few states permit an additional local levy in certain areas. As a result of wider use,

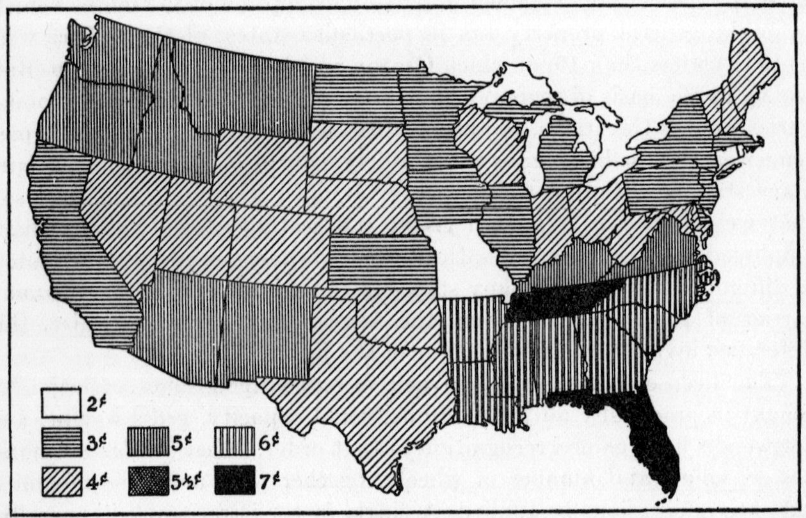

Fig. 39.—The gasoline tax in cents per gallon for the various States as of Jan. 1, 1933 (federal emergency tax of 1 cent per gallon not included). (*From Bus Facts for* 1933.)

of higher rates, of increasing mileage per car, and of a steady growth until 1931 in total registrations, the gasoline tax has proved highly productive: yielding more than a million dollars in 1919, it passed $300,000,000 in 1928, and in 1931 provided $536,397,458. Though motor-vehicle manufacturers and petroleum interests have opposed the imposition of the higher rates, fearful that sales will be diminished, there is yet no clear evidence that the tax has been pushed above the point of diminishing returns to the public treasury; doubtless such a point exists and it may appear during periods of business inactivity, but it can be ascertained with certainty under particular conditions only by experimentation—and such experimentation is difficult, with rates legislatively fixed.

Other Taxes.—The first tax imposed upon the automobile was the personal-property tax. As personalty it was subject to the rate applicable to that type of property and as such continues to be taxed in all but 16 states. These states, largely for administrative reasons, have chosen to eliminate the motor vehicle from the tax list; in general, such action has been accompanied by an increase in the registration charge. In 1930 the average registration charge in the 16 states providing exemption was $18.41, in the others $12.68, the difference between these two figures approximating roughly the average personal property tax where such is levied. The yield of this tax for 1929 was estimated by the *Oregon Voter* at $89,000,000;[1] for 1930 by the National Automobile Chamber of Commerce at $140,000,000—with no adequate basis of judging between the two. The trend of action in the future is likely to be in the direction already taken by the minority group of states; yet, as the personal property tax is displaced by increased registration charges, great care should be taken to earmark for general governmental purposes an appropriate portion of the revenues from registration. If this is not done, taxes upon other property must be increased to make good the loss, while the contribution credited to the motor-vehicle owner is correspondingly augmented. And it is this that "has generally resulted,"[2] when exemption has been accorded.

Upon the common and the private carrier for hire other special taxes have been imposed in practically all jurisdictions, primarily with a view to accomplishing a closer correlation between total payment and highway use. For carriers of passengers a gross-earnings tax is perhaps most common, with a mileage tax also used in many states; for carriers of goods the mileage basis is most frequently used, sometimes taking the form of a ton-mile tax and sometimes a straight mileage levy. A few states tax for-hire trucks upon the basis of gross earnings. The burden of these special taxes upon bus and truck varies greatly as among the states and as between the private and the public carrier. A given bus covering a certain mileage as a private carrier would pay $14.40 in registration and special taxes in Maryland, $1,000 in Utah or Minnesota; as a common carrier the charge would vary from $33 in Massachusetts to $1,000 in Utah or Minnesota and $1,007.75 in Iowa. And the comparable tax load of the private and common carrier bus as assumed above would be for California $53 and $510, respectively; for Maryland $14.40 and $513; for North Carolina $80 and $720; for West Virginia $75 and $616. In 30 jurisdictions such difference would be slight, however, or the same burden would be borne by both types.[3] That divergence in policy among the states with respect to trucks is quite as great as appears from the data offered in Table XXXVIII, in which the charges are given for an identical 3-ton truck operating in exactly the same manner in selected states. In computing payments for both bus and truck no account is taken of gasoline-tax payments. For such wide differences among states there is obviously

[1] *Oregon Voter*, vol. 59, No. 1, p. 8.

[2] SANDAGE and NELSON, *op. cit.* p. 12.

[3] *Ibid.*, pp. 54–55.

no justification; neither is there reason for such striking differences in particular states in the burden imposed upon the several types of carriers for hire. Perhaps nothing can illustrate these divergences better than the chaotic situation now existing relative to the allocation of the total vehicle-tax burden. From such a chaotic situation the allegation of subsidy easily arises.

TABLE XXXVIII.—SPECIAL TAX LEVIES UPON A GIVEN TRUCK, IDENTICAL OPERATIONS ASSUMED, AS OF APRIL, 1930*

State	Owner-operated truck	Private-carrier truck	Commercial-carrier truck
Arkansas	$125.00	$837.50	$837.50
California	43.00	43.00	750.00
Connecticut	52.50	52.50	52.50
Florida	105.00	195.00	595.00
Iowa	100.00	105.00	425.00
Maryland	11.20	11.20	260.00
Massachusetts	19.50	19.50	19.50
Missouri	30.00	30.00	30.00
Montana	37.50	43.00	43.00
North Carolina	75.00	135.00	900.00
Oklahoma	80.00	180.00	310.00
Texas	104.00	109.00	119.00
West Virginia	56.25	112.50	325.00
District of Columbia	1.00	1.00	1.00

* *Ibid.*, pp. 61–62.

Apportionment of the Tax Burden.—Annual highway costs are of two types, capital and maintenance. Capital costs arise from construction and comprise two major elements, interest upon the investment made in the highway and an adequate depreciation charge; maintenance arises from use and from weathering. To assign with measurable equity to each type of vehicle and to the individual vehicle its portion of the total outlay, it is essential that definite data be had concerning construction costs attributable to a given vehicle or group of vehicles and that the effect of the operation of such vehicle or group of vehicles upon highway-maintenance costs be known. With respect to neither of these points, because of the lack of extensive experimentation and the recency of the problem, are available data convincing. The Director of the Bureau of Public Roads declares it unwise to construct concrete highways of lesser dimensions than 7-6-7, that is, less than 6 inches thick at the center and 7 inches at the edges; to do so will result in destruction from frost and sun. Such a highway will carry safely vehicles up to 3 tons' capacity: by the addition of 0.5 inch and 1 inch, respectively, to the thickness of the minimum concrete slab, 5-ton and 7.5-ton trucks can be accommodated. Thus, by an increase of 17 per cent in materials used, which would increase construction costs much less in proportion, loads of great weight can be handled without injury to the highway—and particularly if dual axles, spaced at least 40 inches apart, are placed under the load, thereby avoiding a wheel load on pneumatic tires in excess of 9,000 pounds. Yet Mr. Clifford Older, long Chief Highway Engineer of the state of Illinois, holds that 6 inches does not represent the minimum thickness of a concrete slab that may be safely used upon northern highways: that 5 inches, even 4, would withstand frost and sun, as well as carry ordinary highway traffic. On that premise he declares that the excess construction cost necessary to care for the small number of heavy vehicles upon Illinois highways was more than $121,000,000 from 1923 to 1929, and that maintenance costs are increased because of these few vehicles by more than $9,900,000 annually. And Mr. C. F. Marvin, Jr., Mechanical Engineer, United States Bureau of Standards, holds that:[1]

> Roads designed to carry 3-ton vehicles without undue deterioration would be satisfactory for about 95 per cent of the vehicles in use today. To accommodate 4 of the remaining 5 per cent, roads of double this strength would be required, while to be correspondingly safe for the heaviest group, weighing up to 15 tons (gross) and constituting about 1 per cent of the total number of vehicles, roads from three to five times as strong would be necessary. . . . The additional costs of the stronger roads, where they are built, and any excessive maintenance costs of the lighter roads, where stronger ones are not provided, are directly chargeable to the relatively small number of heavy vehicles. In addition, these same heavy vehicles occupy more road space and require considerably wider roads, thus further increasing their share of highway costs.

For the reconstruction of bridges to carry the heavier vehicles, the Governor of Virginia announced a proposed expenditure of $10,000,000. Further, there is supporting evidence for the Older statement that a 7-6-7 concrete slab is not the minimum thickness that will withstand severe weather; and the conclusions of the Bureau of Public Roads as stated were based upon the use of dual pneumatic rear tires, which assumption is not wholly in accord with traffic facts. Though the shipment of trucks equipped with solid and cushion tires was in 1931 but 3.1 per cent of the total, a representative survey conducted in 1931 showed 23.9 per cent of the trucks and tractor trucks and 32.1 per cent of trailers so equipped.[2]

Conclusive data are lacking to support an assertion that the heavier motor vehicles upon the highway are now subsidized, though available evidence indicates that insufficient emphasis has been placed upon weight as a factor in highway costs. Before positive conclusions can be drawn regarding subsidization, even by particular states, fundamental facts must be firmly established and an analysis made of the relation of each type of vehicle to the highway. But, in the meantime, many states might well

[1] *Public Roads*, vol. 11, p. 45, A Technical Basis for Apportioning Motor-vehicle Taxes.

[2] United States Department of Commerce, *Motor Truck Freight Transportation*, p. 13.

give greater emphasis to weight in fixing the tax burden of types of vehicles—and correspondingly less to the vehicle's economic character.

A Suggested Motor-vehicle Tax Program.[1]—Any plan for the apportionment of the costs of improved highways among groups of motor-vehicle owners and, ultimately, among the individual members of each group should rest upon the basis of vehicle demand upon the highway and upon government. Such a plan should be simple in nature, equitable as among all parties, and possessed of administrative merit. For its general statement sufficient data are available; though, before any appropriate plan can be made entirely effective, certain detailed facts now lacking must be had. To meet the conditions stated the imposition of three levies is suggested: (1) a registration charge; (2) a gasoline tax; and (3) a graded ton-mile tax applicable to all vehicles, regardless of type, with a gross weight in excess of a fixed figure.

There are certain costs that attach to all motor vehicles; these costs of regulation and supervision vary somewhat among groups but remain essentially constant within the group. The registration charge should cover such costs, its burden to be determined by experience. This registration payment should cover also what might well be termed a "demand charge." This charge, in a major sense, would be analogous to that imposed upon the customer under a logical local utility rate schedule: a compensation for outlays essential to meet the peak load. It is obvious that both potential and actual demand for highway accommodation, which government will be asked to meet, increases with the number of cars in use. But the governmental burden increases not only with greater numbers: it is augmented further by the registration of units of certain types because of the additional expenditures made necessary by them. Therefore, while the "demand charge" should probably be made uniform for all units of a given type of vehicle, it might properly vary as among classes, even as among units of different sizes and perhaps speeds within a single class. The "demand charge" levied upon a light passenger car would be but a fraction of that levied upon a truck of maximum width, height, length, and weight—with the levy upon the light delivery truck but a small fraction of that imposed upon the behemoth of the highway.

For highway use by the ordinary vehicle no better measure has been offered, all facts weighed, than the gasoline tax:[2] gasoline consumption increases with the weight of the car; it increases with the speed of the vehicle when that speed becomes sufficient to increase maintenance costs greatly; it is greater upon congested city streets than upon the open road for the same distance traveled. But, because "gasoline consumption per ton-mile of use of the highway decreases as the weight of the vehicle

[1] For a more detailed discussion of this problem, see SANDAGE and NELSON, *op. cit.*, Chap. IX.

[2] HITCHCOCK, W. W., *Maintenance of Way Charges against Public Carrier Buses*, Engineering Experiment Station, Iowa State College.

increases,"[1] some further tax is essential for the vehicles of greater weight. Then, too, as weight increases beyond a certain point, additional construction costs or excess maintenance charges lie against such heavier vehicles. As a corrective for the gasoline tax and as a means of exacting a total payment more nearly in proportion to highway demands, the ton-mile tax, graduated progressively against vehicles of great weight and made effective through a hub-meter or similar device, will serve effectively.[2] For the accurate, detailed application of this tax, however, more convincing experimental data relative to the highway needs and costs arising from the operation of heavy vehicles are essential. But, in the meantime, a beginning could be made without doing violence to justice for, undoubtedly, *some* additional costs proceed from the use of the highway by great units now found upon it.

Taxes levied upon the motor vehicle beyond the three just discussed are a matter of public policy. Certainly that vehicle should contribute to general governmental costs through a personal property tax or a supplemental levy included in the registration charge but clearly distinct from it. There is no reason why those who use the highway for private gain in the movement of goods or passengers, be that movement for self or for hire, should not be compelled to pay for such privilege—and pay not only upon the basis of highway costs as usually computed but also upon the basis of the value of lands devoted to right-of-way. Neither is there good reason to exempt those who profit from the business of highway carriage from the corporate taxes upon income borne by other business enterprises. And by many a business, or occupation, tax is urged. Yet, merely because it is administratively easy to collect large sums from some type of motor-vehicle tax, proposals to divert motor-vehicle contributions to other than highway uses should be examined critically and approved only when clear justification can be shown. The formulation of a tax program, rested upon careful study and analysis, is sorely needed in the interest of all groups. Taxation, as it touches the users of highways today, is a maze of inconsistencies, contradictions, and uncertainties, to which our highest tax intelligence may to advantage be addressed without delay.

POWER TO REGULATE

During the long period that elapsed prior to the rapid extension of the railway net the wagoner and operator of the stage line occupied an important place in the world of transportation. By them was performed a vital

[1] Hitchcock, *op. cit.*, p. 32. See also data given in United States Department of Commerce, *Motor Truck Freight Transportation*, p. 52, and Decision 25243, California Railroad Commission, p. 42, for confirmation.

[2] If the graduated mileage tax for all heavier vehicles proves not feasible administratively, the alternative would seem to be an augmented "demand charge" as a part of the registration payment.

economic function and about them, together with carriers by water, developed certain common-law principles that were later to be made applicable to the railway—even before the freighter's wagon and the stagecoach had been consigned to the limbo of forgotten things. The construction of railways into those portions of the United States where economic conditions justified such construction—and, it may be added, into many where promise exceeded realization—had, before the close of the nineteenth century, almost entirely eliminated the regulation of highway carriage from public ken. But, with the rise of a new agency of transport upon the highways, this aspect of regulation reappeared and, in the years since 1900, has held an increasingly important place. Successive decisions of the courts through half a century have fixed the boundaries of the field of railway regulation in considerable detail; of major interest today is the extent to which public authority may control motor-vehicle operations without fouling constitutional guarantees to property. Decisions delimiting the field of motor-vehicle regulation have come rapidly in recent years, with certain of those already written ranking with the "landmarks" of railway regulation.

A General Statement.—The state of New York in 1901 conditioned the use of the highway by any self-propelled vehicle upon the payment of a registration fee. This requirement was challenged, but was upheld in 1903: the contention that the law was void because it applied to the owner-operator and not to the manufacturer was denied judicial recognition, the difference in the two classes being deemed sufficient to justify a difference in treatment.[1] Again, when the need for additional funds for highway construction and maintenance prompted the increase of the registration fee to the point where it became a tax, the power of the state was challenged without success: under its general police powers the state was declared to have the right to single out the automobile owner as a source of additional revenue, unreasonable discrimination not entering.[2] And, later, in another attack upon the registration charge, it received judicial sanction as a tax, not upon the vehicle but rather upon the use of the highway by the vehicle; put upon such basis constitutional requirements of equality and uniformity do not apply.[3] Then, in adjudicating an attack made upon certain restrictions imposed upon the operators of motor vehicles, it was held that the state has the power to limit and control the use of the highway to "provide for and promote the safety, peace, health, morals, and general welfare of the people,"[4] though such power must be exercised in a reasonable and equitable manner.[5]

[1] *People v. McWilliams*, 86 N.Y. Supp. 357 (1904).

[2] *Cleary v. Johnston*, 79 N. J. Law 49 (1909).

[3] *Kane v. Titus*, 81 N. J. Law 594 (1911).

[4] *Schlesinger v. City of Atlanta*, 161 Ga. 148 (1925).

[5] In *re: Opinion of the Justices*, 81 N.H. 566 (1925).

Thus, through the entire period during which government has sought in public interest to impose restrictions upon the operation of the motor vehicle, those restrictions have been persistently challenged by parties whose privileges were circumscribed. But, as a result of judicial scrutiny of legislation and of commission orders, the major points of the boundary between public and private rights seem to have been established—with many details of that boundary yet to be fixed, however. Since this body of ruling law is already voluminous, little more will be attempted here than a summary statement indicating the extent of the power of the government to regulate with respect to important matters.

Regulation under the Police Power.—Many of the essential features of an adequate plan for the regulation of motor-vehicle operation upon the highway rest upon the police power. This power has been variously defined, but perhaps the statement given by Ely is as clear and comprehensive as any that may be offered: "The police power is the power of the courts to interpret the concept property, and above all, private property; and to establish its metes and bounds."[1] Another helpful explanation of the nature of this power was made by Mr. Justice Holmes: "The police power extends to all the great public needs. It may be put forth in aid of what is sanctioned by usage or held by prevailing morality or the strong and preponderant opinion to be greatly and immediately necessary to the public welfare."[2] And, because resort to the police power as a basis for action is never denied by the courts when such action can be shown essential to the health, safety, morals, or general welfare of the body politic, it is clear that many restrictions upon the use of the motor vehicle can be rested thereupon.

Perhaps the most obvious of these restrictions is upon speed of operation. Maximum-speed laws were early passed by many states and these have been supplemented widely by municipal ordinances; these early regulations generally recognized the reasonableness of different speeds under different highway conditions, 10 miles an hour being common for congested areas and 30 miles a usual maximum upon the open road. Gradually statutory maximums for open highway operation have been increased until today, in certain jurisdictions and under certain circumstances, no maximum figure for the private automobile remains: rather, the law imposes the responsibility of "reasonable speed." Indeed, as traffic movements have speeded up during recent years, requirements of a minimum speed have sometimes been imposed, effective upon certain highways and under given conditions: this action is rested upon the fact that low speed upon a crowded highway may be quite as dangerous as high. So firmly grounded is the right to regulate speed that such regulations have rarely been challenged in the courts. In the interest of safety

[1] *Property and Contract*, vol. 1, p. 206.

[2] *Noble State Bank v. Haskell*, 219 U. S. 110 (1911).

of operation, too, the operator of the vehicle is required to use a recognized system of hand signals in some jurisdictions; in others he is compelled to come to a full stop at all railway crossings. To eliminate from the ranks of highway users certain conspicuously unfit individuals, a driver's license may be required: such licenses are commonly required of taxi, bus, and for-hire truck drivers, and are being demanded increasingly by states of the operator of the individual passenger automobile. Further requirements have to do with the use of warning signals, horn or siren; the manipulation of lights; permitting the car to stand upon the highway; the number of hours of consecutive service at the wheel, though this limitation has thus far been applied commonly to drivers of bus and truck only; and the insurance of the car for a reasonable sum against damage to persons or property through its operation.

But the police power extends beyond the operation of the vehicle to the physical character of the vehicle itself. One of the most common of the requirements having to do with the vehicle is that fixing maximum width. Though established maximums vary from 84 to 106 inches, 96 being the standard figure, the courts have upheld such divergent width limitations as they have far more divergent restrictions upon over-all length, both for a single vehicle and for vehicles operated in combination: the maximums fixed for the former vary from 28 to 40 feet, for the latter from 40 to 85 feet. The right to fix maximum height has also been recognized, maximums varying from 144 to 174 inches, and the right to limit the number of trailers drawn upon the highway is equally clear. Among other features of the car indubitably subject to regulation in the interest of safety of operation are brakes, lights, markers to indicate at night the character of the vehicle as well as its full width (applicable to truck and bus), and manner of passing other vehicles upon the highway.

In short, the scope of the police power is so broad that upon it the public may lean with great assurance in the regulation of motor vehicles. Furthermore, because it is a matter of judgment as to what is reasonable under particular conditions and the court is ever reluctant to substitute its judgment for that of the legislature, judicial interference is to be anticipated only with respect to limitations that are *clearly* unreasonable and inequitable in character. This is true, too, of the exercise of the state's powers in behalf of highway conservation.

Regulation under the Proprietary Power.—Exclusive ownership of the public highway lies in the state. From that ownership flow broad powers to fix the conditions and terms of highway use. In the interest of highway conservation vehicle weight limits may be fixed: the state may fix a maximum gross weight for any vehicle that operates upon the highway and across public bridges; it may fix the maximum wheel or axle load and prescribe the number of inches of space between axles;

and it may set the maximum net tonnage to be carried in one vehicle. Indeed, this last may be done with the express purpose of eliminating traffic from the highway.[1] Furthermore, it is clearly established that the state may make such reasonable exceptions to general weight and load requirements as it sees fit; these exceptions are made, characteristically, for the occasional movement or for local movements of agricultural products. To conserve the highway the state may impose speed limitations where necessary, these being applicable particularly to heavier vehicles and to vehicles equipped with other than pneumatic tires; in fact, the use upon the public road of other than pneumatic tires may be prohibited. Broad powers to restrict movements over particular highways to vehicles of an appropriate weight and size, temporarily or permanently, reside in the state. The right to limit the number of vehicles using a given highway, for reasons both of safety and of conservation,[2] also exists, even though the barrier be raised against an interstate operator in the enforcement of the right.

It is as proprietor of the highway, charged with the dual financial burden of construction and maintenance, that the state imposes the major taxes borne by the user. To the extent that the registration charge exceeds the cost of policing the highway and certain clerical expenses, collections therefrom constitute a payment for use. The gasoline tax clearly falls into the same category, and the ton-mile tax represents a further refinement in the attempt to exact from each group and individual within a group a proportionate part of total costs. The sole requirement with respect to taxes imposed to cover use is that they be reasonable and appropriate to their purpose[3]—with the further essential as to state levies upon interstate carriers that the law clearly assign all sums paid to highway use.[4] Indeed, the state may exempt from particular tax levies certain limited operations of a class of vehicles, if the exemption and classification be reasonable: Kansas has been upheld in such exemptions from a gross ton-mile tax,[5] the law declaring that the tax is not applicable to carriers of property or persons "who operate wholly within any city or village of this state, or private motor carriers who

[1] "It cannot be said that the state is powerless to protect its highways from being subjected to excessive burdens when other means of transportation are available. The use of highways for truck transportation has its manifest convenience, but we perceive no constitutional ground for denying to the state the right to foster a fair distribution of traffic to the end that all necessary facilities should be maintained and that the public should not be inconvenienced by inordinate uses of its highways for purposes of gain." *Sproles v. Binford*, 286 U. S. 374 (1932).

[2] *Wolverine Motor Freight Lines v. Public Utilities Commission of Ohio*, Decision 395, United States Supreme Court (Apr. 10, 1933).

[3] See *Bekins Van Lines v. Riley*, 280 U. S. 80 (1929).

[4] See *Interstate Transit, Inc., v. Lindsey*, 283 U. S. 183 (1931).

[5] *Continental Baking Company v. Woodring*, 286 U. S. 352 (1932).

operate within a radius of 25 miles beyond the corporate limits of such city, or any village, nor to the transportation of live stock and farm products to market by the owner thereof or supplies for his own use in his own motor vehicle, or to the transportation of children to and from school."[1]

Perhaps the most interesting exercise of the proprietary power yet approved by the courts is that of the regulation of the private carrier for hire, the contract truck. A series of important decisions have established beyond peradventure that a private carrier for hire may not be transformed by legislative fiat or by some strange legerdemain into a common carrier, to be regulated as such.[2] In an effort to meet certain unsatisfactory conditions existing in Texas the legislature enacted a statute that provides, among other things, that all contract carriers must secure from the state Railroad Commission a permit; that the Commission may fix maximum and/or minimum rates for the transportation of all property for hire, contract-carrier rates to be no less than those of common carriers operating over the same highways; and that permits may be refused if "the proposed operation of such contract carrier will impair the efficient public service of any authorized common carrier or common carriers then adequately serving the same territory." Such extension of public authority over the contract carrier is justified upon grounds of safety of operation upon the highway and conservation of the highway, physically and as a service agency,[3] and, because the requirements of the law appear to be consonant with the purposes indicated, the statute was upheld by the United States Supreme Court

[1] *Laws of Kansas*, 1931, Chap. 236, Sec. 2.

[2] See *Michigan Public Utilities Commission v. Duke*, 266 U. S. 570 (1925); *Frost Trucking Company v. California Railroad Commission*, 271 U. S. 583 (1926); *Smith v. Cahoon*, 283 U. S. 533 (1931). It was upon the basis of the Smith case that those engaged in the manufacture of motor vehicles were assured that "regulation, in the sense of control of contracts, rates, and practices, and the right to engage in the business, cannot be imposed upon the contract motor carrier without violating the due process clause." LARUE BROWN and S. N. SCOTT on Regulation of the Contract Motor Carrier under the Constitution, *Harvard Law Review*, vol. 144, pp. 530, 566.

[3] Sec. 22*b*, Chap. 277, *General Laws of Texas*, 1931, declares,

"The business of operating as a motor carrier of property for hire along the highways of this state is declared to be a business affected with the public interest. The rapid increase of motor-carrier traffic, and the fact that under existing law many motor trucks are not effectively regulated, have increased the dangers and hazards on public highways and make it imperative that more stringent regulation should be employed, to the end that the highways may be rendered safer for the use of the general public; that the wear of such highways may be reduced; that discrimination in rates charged may be eliminated; that congestion of traffic on the highways may be minimized, that the use of the highways for the transportation of property for hire may be restricted to the extent required by the necessity of the general public, and that the various transportation agencies of the state may be adjusted and correlated so that public highways may serve the best interest of the general public."

in a strong decision.[1] But it appears that *conservation of the highway* is the point upon which constitutionality hinged; this extension of governmental power into a field overripe for action rests fundamentally, then, upon the proprietary power of the state.

The Regulation of Common Carriage.—The scope of public authority over the common carrier of persons or of property by highway during the late medieval and early modern periods was extended to such degree as was essential to the protection of public interest. Once the regulation of railways was undertaken in the protection of that same interest, control was broadened and intensified: by 1920 state and federal statutes had made provision not only for the regulation of rates, services, and practices but had also made possible public interference at the discretion of regulatory bodies in fields normally reserved to management. When common carriage by highway again became important as a consequence of the development of the motor vehicle and a suitable highway therefor, it was but natural that the same powers exercised over common carriers by rail should be extended to common carriers by highway; in fact, many states brought the latter into the field of regulation merely by adding them to the list of those subject to laws already enacted. The obligations and restrictions imposed upon the common carrier by highway, then, have differed from those imposed upon the railway only to the degree that the nature of the two forms of transport differ; essentially the same powers have been, or may be, exerted by many commissions.

In two particulars have problems arisen. The private carrier by rail is indeed a rarity, but the private carrier by highway is common. To escape the burdens of regulation many highway carriers for hire have shifted from common carrier to private status; others have professed to do so, yet have remained common carriers in fact. That *fact*, not *profession*, determines the carrier's legal status, has been established, however.[2] Another problem arises from the mobile character of motor transport as compared with rail: to the common carrier between fixed termini has been added the common carrier without fixed termini, he who holds himself out to serve all who may apply over routes determined by traffic offered. While only the former is now regulated in many jurisdictions, the power to regulate the latter exists. Indeed, under power to require permits of private carriers, certain states have established a measure of control over the rates and rules of this type, but such control is of doubtful legal status in view of decisions cited.

The Jurisdictional Problem.—That the states would encounter difficulty in their attempts to deal with interstate operations of motor vehicles was a foregone conclusion. As a consequence of successive

[1] *Stephenson v. Binford*, 53 Sup. Ct. Rep. 181 (1932).

[2] *Haynes v. MacFarlane*, 207 Calif. 529 (1929). See also *Frost Trucking Company v. California Railroad Commission*, before cited.

challenges of state regulations certain principles have been established, however. Of these the first in point of time was that, when operating a motor vehicle in a particular state, the operator must conform to the requirements of that state, be he resident or nonresident:[1] reciprocity is a privilege that may be extended, not a right to be taken. Another group of cases has arisen from the taxation of interstate carriers by the states; by decisions in these it has been established that such carriers can be taxed so long as the tax is reasonable, as sums paid are devoted to highway use, and as the tax is upon highway use and is not a business tax.[2] The interstate common carrier may be required to secure a permit from the state,[3] but such permit may not be refused merely because the route is adequately served.[4] The use of a particular highway may be denied an interstate carrier, however, if the volume of traffic upon that highway is already so heavy as to make for unsafe or uneconomic operations.[5] The state is without power to control either rates or service upon interstate traffic but may assume full jurisdiction with respect to all intrastate operations of interstate carriers. State regulation is not infrequently evaded by routing the carrier in such way as to cross state lines, though operations remain fundamentally *and in fact* intrastate.

The jurisdictional problem is likely to be of increasing significance and difficulty as federal regulation of interstate operations develops. The sharp diversity in the character of the restrictions and requirements of the various states, the state's undoubted primary or even exclusive control of the highway as proprietor, and the inevitable conflict between state and federal authority that in the railway field eventuated in the Shreveport decision,[6] are likely to make this question of jurisdiction a veritable Pandora's box for future years.

PUBLIC POLICY

Concerning certain important proposals relative to motor-vehicle regulation there can be no serious difference of opinion; concerning others judgment varies from bitter opposition to insistent demand. Though major interest attaches to these controversial aspects, attention must be given to all. A brief presentation will first be made, then, of those

[1] See *Hendrick v. Maryland*, 235 U. S. 610 (1915), and *Kane v. New Jersey*, 242 U. S. 160 (1916). In the former case a local license was required for "foreign" cars, in the latter both a driver's license and a car license were mandatory. In each case the law was upheld.

[2] See *Clark v. Poor*, 274 U. S. 554 (1927); *Interstate Buses Corporation v. Blodgett*, 276 U. S. 245 (1928); *Sprout v. South Bend*, 277 U. S. 163 (1928); also *Bekins* and *Interstate Transit, Inc.*, citation given.

[3] *Clark v. Poor*. 274 U. S. 554 (1927).

[4] *Buck v. Kuykendall*, 267 U. S. 307 (1925), also *Bush v. Maloy*, 267 U. S. 317 (1925).

[5] *Wolverine Motor Freight Lines v. Public Utilities Commission of Ohio*, previously cited.

[6] *Houston, East and West Texas Railway Company v. United States*, 234 U. S. 342 (1913).

regulatory features upon which there is essential agreement. By and large, it may be said that legislative enactments or commission orders with a direct bearing upon safety of operation enjoy general support: though there may be differences of opinion as to the limitations that should be imposed upon the operator of the vehicle and as to vehicle specifications, none will deny that speed must be controlled, that size of vehicle must be limited, or that braking equipment must meet certain minimum requirements. Perhaps the major problem of safety regulation arises from the wide diversity among the maximums and minimums imposed by the various states. Efforts are being made by various groups, however, to attain a greater degree of uniformity among requirements: among these groups the more important are, perhaps, the railway and utility commissions through the National Association of Railroad and Public Utilities Commissioners, and the highway agencies through the American Association of State Highway Officials. Efforts are also being made to establish requirements that accord more closely with known conditions and facts than do certain of those that have lost their validity in the period since fixed. In general, the tendency is, in such change of requirements, to make limitations more narrow, yet relaxations are evident, too; particularly is this true in the matter of maximum speeds.[1] Active interest in limiting legislation has been shown not only by public groups, but also by those with a "bread-and-butter" interest; however, to the extent that legislation is unduly influenced by motor-vehicle manufacturers who fear that circumscription of operations will diminish sales or by any rival transportation agency that seeks a solution of its problem through unreasonably handicapping a competitor, such legislation is likely to prove a boomerang in the end. Limitations and

[1] Late in 1932 the Association of State Highway Officials recommended "the adoption of a uniform standard to govern gross weight, dimensions, and speed of motor vehicles operating on the highways," for the following reasons: "(*a*) To establish one of the fundamental prerequisites of highway design; (*b*) to promote efficiency in the interstate operation of the motor vehicle; (*c*) to secure safety in highway operation; (*d*) to remove from the highways undesirable equipment and operations; (*e*) to stabilize on a definite basis the many relationships between the highway and the motor vehicle." Among the specific recommendations made, based upon research and experience, were: limitation of maximum width to 96 inches, except in the case of certain equipment now in operation; limitation of height to 12 feet, 6 inches; limitation of length to 35 feet for a single vehicle and for any combination of vehicles 45 feet, over-all, except for occasional movements under permit; maximum speed for bus or truck 45 miles and for passenger automobiles such speed as "shall be consistent at all times with safety and the proper use of the roads"—with the proviso that vehicles with solid or cushion tires shall not exceed a speed of 10 miles per hour; minimum speed such that traffic shall not be impeded or blocked; and maximum wheel loads of 9,000 and 8,000 pounds for low-pressure pneumatic and all other tires, respectively. Maximum gross weights should be fixed by the several states upon the basis of bridge and culvert strength. For metropolitan areas modifications are suggested to meet the particular needs of the area. See *United States Daily*, Nov. 28, 1932, p. 1.

relaxations in policy should be made in accord with the long-time interests of the highway user and society; though, in the determination of such interests, consideration to more than load stresses and highway congestion must be given.

Few will question the fundamental soundness of the effective exercise of certain of the proprietary powers of the state, notably control over vehicle weights, restriction in the use of certain highways to particular types of vehicles, and a limited application of the taxing power to recompense the state in part for use of the highway. Further, it is unlikely that any will complain against the regulation of the common carrier when the proposition is put in the abstract. But concerning the extent and character of that regulation there will be wide differences in judgment, and this will also be true of any proposals so to burden or restrict the contract or the private carrier as to increase costs or imperil the privilege of operating at will. It is, then, with respect to taxation, to the treatment of carriers of property or persons for hire, and to appropriate action concerning certain types of private carriers of property that the broad questions of public policy arise. For an intelligent answer to those questions the first essential is the assignment of a proper place to the motor vehicle in a general transportation plan.

The Motor Vehicle and a Transportation Plan.—The American people face today, as do the people of many other lands, a novel problem: it is the formulation of a transportation plan for those agencies engaged in the inland movement of property and persons. For almost a century following the introduction of the railway, no plan was essential: the tremendous superiority of mechanical power over muscular power, in matters both of speed and of costs, relegated the use of the latter to areas lacking rail service. And for numberless centuries prior to the railway choice was limited to the type of animal to be used: for horse or ox or other draft animal attached to the wheeled cart there was no effective alternative. But today the public has available not only railways prepared to offer the finest service in their history but also the motor vehicle, capable of rendering within as yet undefined limits a speedier and more economical service than the railways can offer—to which must be added air transport and an improved, extended mileage of inland waterways. There is every evidence that volume of traffic increases steadily, yet available service has increased so much more rapidly within the past decade that there exists today a surplus of capacity to serve unparalleled in history. And, since this situation carries with it peril to all agencies in the field, the formulation of a plan and the assignment of each agency to its approximate place become imperative if public and private interests are not to be sacrificed.

State Regulation of the Common Carrier by Highway.—In a preceding section it has been indicated that state regulation of the common carrier by highway is general. This regulation is, typically, broad in scope and exacting in letter. Operation is commonly conditioned upon the issuance by the appropriate authority, railway or utility commission, of a certificate of convenience and necessity. In its judgment upon an application for such certificate the adequacy of existing service is pertinent, as is the financial stability of the applicant. Equipment must be adequate in character and in number of units; insurance in amounts prescribed by the commission must be carried to protect passengers or cargo, also to protect against public damage; and definite, dependable schedules must be maintained. Rates and service are subject to regulation; records must be kept according to a prescribed system, and such reports made as are demanded, including an annual report; schedules may be modified to serve public convenience; and provision is made for periodical inspections of equipment. Certain detailed qualifications are fixed for the drivers of common-carrier vehicles and hours of consecutive service are limited, with the prescription of a minimum rest period in each 24 hours. Certificates to operate are typically transferable only with the approval of the commission, with a certificate subject to forfeiture if any provision of the law or any proper order of the commission is violated. And finally, because of the ease of applying such a tax to carriers operating over fixed routes upon definite schedule and compelled to make detailed reports of operations and financial results, the common carrier is taxed in many states upon the basis of mileage or earnings. Since such payments, as well as practically all other requirements named, are in excess of demands commonly made of the contract carrier, it is not strange that the common carrier has tended to shift to the latter classification. And this shift has been the more marked since the line of demarcation between the two types is so dim that the major benefits of common-carrier operation can often be enjoyed unchallenged for long periods without the assumption of the responsibilities or burdens attaching thereto. Regulation of the common carrier, particularly the truck, must be at best competitively burdensome to such carrier and no more than moderately successful in serving public interest until the contract carrier is subjected to comparable restraints and responsibilities.

Evils in the Existing Situation.—The factors in the existing motor-vehicle situation that give rise to major complaint are, immediately, two: the entire lack of regulation of interstate motor-vehicle operations of every type and the freedom of the contract carrier from effective state restraint—not because of absence of desire or of legislative attempt by the states to impose such restraint in the past,[1] but because of inability to find a tenable basis for effective control until the recent approval by

[1] It was the attempt to control contract-carrier operations that gave rise to the Duke, the Frost, and the Smith cases, among others.

the United States Supreme Court of regulations prescribed by Texas.[1] Yet a third factor stands clearly in the immediate background and gives promise of greater importance, once adequate restraints are imposed upon for-hire vehicles: this factor is the owner-operator truck, now exceeding greatly in number the for-hire type and likely to become more important as effective control is extended to the contract carrier which has, during periods of cut-rate operations, been serving many enterprises more cheaply than they could serve themselves. Whether conservation of the highway, in terms of service and physical structure, can be invoked to control the owner-operator truck as it has the contract truck is yet to be determined; if not, appropriate regulation of this important element in highway traffic may be difficult to establish.

In the two extensive studies made of the motor-vehicle situation by the Interstate Commerce Commission—Dockets 18300 and 23400—with a view to recommending a course of action to Congress, in the reports of Senate and House committee hearings upon proposals to regulate interstate motor-vehicle traffic in one or another of its aspects, in investigations made by various states among which the California report is perhaps outstanding, and in other studies have been portrayed much that is objectionable in the existing motor-vehicle situation. Of the facts adduced, many are pertinent to the need of federal control, others are suggestive of ills that must be remedied largely by state action. As preliminary to the presentation of proposals for governmental action, however, it is desirable to indicate clearly the evils that have resulted from inadequate motor-vehicle regulation.

Of these evils perhaps the most significant is discrimination. A situation now exists in the motor-vehicle field comparable to that which prompted the condemnation of rail carriers by the Cullom Committee in 1886 and sped the passage of the Elkins Act in 1903 in an effort to eliminate more effectively this canker of business. After careful study the California Railroad Commission said, discussing the contract truck,[2]

> Their rates vary from day to day and are not uniform as between shippers and communities. . . . We may summarize the things that they do which regulated carriers cannot do, as follows: (*a*) discriminate between persons and places; (*b*) make rebates; (*c*) grant secret rates; (*d*) change rates at any time without notice. . . . They have disastrously affected the prosperity of regulated carriers, curtailed the ability of the latter to serve the public and, at the same time, have not prospered themselves as indicated by the continued change in truck ownership and by the lack of continuity of operation. While a few shippers were of the opinion that they benefited by these very low and noncompensatory rates they were able to secure under existing conditions, the overwhelming majority of the witnesses for industry, agriculture, and business and the shippers and receivers

[1] *Stephenson v. Binford*, 53 Sup. Ct. Rep. 181.

[2] Decision 25243, Oct. 10, 1932, pp. 9–10.

of freight . . . were emphatic in their desire to see transportation stabilized. The present condition so far as discrimination between persons and communities is concerned was likened to that prevailing on the railroads before regulatory legislation was enacted. A system of unknown transportation charges and practices is being introduced by unregulated carriers into an economic structure which has been built upon a system of known charges and practices with demoralizing results.

A representative of the cement industry, appearing before the Senate Committee on Interstate Commerce, stated,[1]

With the advent of the truck the stability of transportation costs began to cloud and as trucking of cement increased, stability diminished until it became an unknown quantity. . . . There are innumerable instances that have come to our attention where five or six different trucking concerns have quoted as many different rates. . . . In the course of five years the transportation end of the cement industry has gone from certainty to chaos.

And another witness, during the course of the same hearings, introduced three letters from the same trucking concern quoting rates of 35, 25, and 20 cents to different business houses in Washington, D.C., for the movement of identical commodities to Baltimore.[2] But multiplication of illustrations, easy to offer, is not essential: it is obvious that public interest demands corrective action upon this point.

A second important evil in the present situation is the disturbance of markets resulting from uncontrolled trucking operations. With this has come peril to marketing machinery that has evolved through a period of years and for which clear social need continues. An effective system for distributing great quantities of vegetables and fresh fruits among the important markets had been developed, whereby glut and famine were avoided: this was done by commission firms through the reconsignment of shipments upon the basis of a detailed knowledge of local situations. With tremendous quantities of such supplies now reaching the market by truck, control has become well-nigh impossible during months when weather permits truck movements; then, during the winter when the problem becomes difficult, the commission house and the railway must again assume the burden. And the situation has been made still worse in this field by the rapid increase in peddler-truck operations. The owner of such a truck buys a load of produce for a mere song, with the tune pitched low, often acquiring ungraded, substandard, or even cull items; his load is transported to some market where, at best, it serves to depress the price of inspected and graded commodities and, at worst, wholly to disorganize that market. Again quoting the California study:[3]

[1] *Hearings*, 72d Congress, 1st session, S. 2793, pp. 664–665.

[2] *Ibid.*, p. 360.

[3] *Op. cit.*, p. 10. See also pp. 28–30 for quotations from evidence.

Industry and agriculture were both said to be suffering from unsettled markets resulting in part, at least, from unsettled transportation. There was much evidence to show that heavy losses were sustained and extensive frauds perpetrated upon farmers by the wholesale entry of financially irresponsible truck operators into the transportation field.

And, did space permit, evidence could be offered to show that this disorganization of the market for fresh fruit and vegetables is paralleled in the marketing of potatoes, coal, building supplies, hay, and numberless other items. But the threat of unregulated truck competition to such marketing agencies as farmers' cooperatives merits a final note: through live-stock trucking the local live-stock shipping associations are being destroyed and, by offering to bring feeds and other supplies as a return load at a mere nominal figure, the trucker effects the collapse of other cooperative activities—with only a casual, uncertain, and irresponsible service to displace a permanent organization and plan.[1] The nation's marketing machinery may need revision in public interest, but such revision should not be in the direction of the substitution of confusion for order.

Another important weakness of unregulated competition lies in its waste and, with that waste, public inconvenience resulting from highway congestion. While state regulatory bodies have generally sought to hold duplications of highway service to a minimum in certificating common carriers by truck and bus, it has been impossible to protect certificated operators from the contract operator: in consequence, as indicated before, the common carrier often assumes burdensome responsibilities only to have his financial reward denied. This multiplication of service places vehicles upon the highway in such numbers that its use becomes hazardous for ordinary travel. But, while this multiplication of service is largely of trucks in intrastate traffic, the absence of control over interstate traffic brings duplication not only of interstate common-carrier truck services and of comparable contract-carrier operations, but also of common-carrier bus service. Such duplication of bus service may be illustrated by excerpts from the tentative report in Interstate Commerce Commission Docket 23400, which states,[2]

There are said to be about 30 interstate bus operators between Kansas City, Mo., and St. Louis, Mo.,[3] who operate whenever it is profitable for them to do so. . . . Between Boston and New York in 1929 there were 5 bus lines making 13 trips daily in each direction. In December, 1930, there were 8 lines making

[1] *Hearings*, S. 2793, *previously cited*, pp. 714–721.

[2] 72d Congress, 1st session, Senate Document 43, p. 32.

[3] To escape intrastate control, a bus will be moved for a short distance through Kansas City, Kan., or through East St. Louis. Such routing is clearly a subterfuge but serves its purpose—and well illustrates how many common-carrier lines escape *state* control and at present, therefore, all effective regulation.

21 trips daily. . . . Three railroad lines operate between St. Louis and Memphis, Tenn., a distance of 430 miles; the rail fare is $11.18. Four or five bus lines, including one operated by a railroad subsidiary, are in operation between the same points.

And in every case excessive competition has cut the rate to a figure below a reasonable basis—to as low as $2 between New York and Boston; to $4 or less between Kansas City and St. Louis; and $3.50 one way, $6 round trip, between St. Louis and Memphis. Then there is the instance already mentioned, competition over a line almost 500 miles long forcing the rate to $2 and, for a brief period, to $1. While such unregulated and cutthroat competition may be temporarily advantageous to the public, the social cost of wasteful service remains. And this is no less true of truck than of bus operations.

Other Existing Evils.—Only an extended discussion of the ills of unregulated motor vehicle operation can give a detailed statement of all that justify consideration. Brief mention of others than those discussed will be made, however, that the necessity for effective control may be made the more obvious. While financial responsibility can be required of the state-regulated common carrier, there is no compulsion upon the interstate operator or the intrastate contract operator to provide adequate protection for property or for passengers moved; in consequence, injuries and losses often occur for which no recourse exists. With the owner of the vehicle too frequently possessed of no property, without insurance, and operating the vehicle by virtue of a down payment perhaps as small as $50, recovery is obviously impossible. Then, too, the diversion of traffic from the railways because of the unreasonably low rates forced by uncontrolled highway competition will necessitate an increase in rates upon traffic that must continue to move by rail. This point is stressed by the California report, attention being called to the fundamental significance of this interrelation to the fruit-growing industry of that state,[1] and it has also been emphasized by individual shippers in the course of various hearings. A final defect in the existing situation, and one for which correction is vital if the field of motor-vehicle regulation is to be extended both extensively and intensively, is inadequate enforcement of even existing limitations and responsibilities. This situation is due primarily to an inadequate enforcement personnel: however little the prospect of a large staff of inspectors, highway police, and other officials seeking to compel observance of requirements may please a public with a revived interest in governmental economy, any program of regulation will be ineffective without such a staff. The effective control of some twenty-five million mobile units operating upon more than three million miles of highway can only be had at a price, with chaos as the alternative.

[1] *Op. cit.*, p. 11 and Appendix 7.

The Demand for Effective Regulation.—In a report issued in 1923 by Special Committee 4, Chamber of Commerce of the United States, the evils of unregulated competition were well portrayed and it was said, "Through judicious regulation, and only in this way, will it be possible to obtain efficient, economical, and adequate coordination of motor transport and electric or steam railroads. Federal regulation of interstate common carrier motor transportation has not yet been adopted, but it is believed that it is necessary."[1] At that time approximately half of the states had subjected the intrastate common carrier to regulation. In 1925 Senator Cummins of Iowa introduced into Congress the first bill proposing federal regulation of interstate motor-vehicle operations; upon it and other bills offered from time to time extended hearings have been held, but no action has resulted. Legislative inertia, opposition of certain selfish interests, unwillingness to act on the part of a few Congressmen who regard the motor vehicle as a divinely appointed scourge to be applied without restraint to the railways, and lack of legislative vision have served to block even such limited control of interstate common-carrier operations as the Interstate Commerce Commission has suggested— and this, despite the fact that with the major positive recommendation, the full regulation of interstate bus operations, the bus operators have themselves been in accord. During this period of "masterly inactivity" on the part of Congress, however, state regulation has made forward strides: in practically every jurisdiction common-carrier operations are controlled and it is probable that, with a constitutional basis found for contract-carrier regulation, state action will be had along a broad front upon that aspect of control—and with little delay if the judgments of the Michigan, North Carolina, California and other state commissions are typical. Such extension of the scope of regulation over the contract carrier will be quite as much in the interest of the regular for-hire operator as of the public: in states as diverse as Michigan and California the irregular contract carrier, particularly the "wildcat" trucker, is charged with a large measure of responsibility for inadequate returns to common carrier and legitimate contract operator. Yet only a partial solution of the problem can result from state action: comparable regulation of interstate highway operations is essential.

In summarizing the situation as it had been portrayed in the course of two broad studies made, the Interstate Commerce Commission declares relative to motor-truck regulation for which, interestingly, there has been no general shipper demand but concerning which controversy has been sharp:[2]

The immediate advantages of unrestrained competition in transportation are easy to perceive; but the more remote consequences, which may be injurious to

[1] *Relation of Highways and Motor Transport to other Transportation Agencies*, p. 37.

[2] *Coordination of Motor Transportation*, Docket 23400, pp. 382–383.

all concerned, are not so easily foreseen and recognized. This has uniformly been the experience with such competition in the public services, of which transportation is the most important.

The evidence in this investigation shows very clearly that such injurious consequences may be expected from and, to some extent, have already been produced by the unrestrained competition of motor vehicles with the railroads and with each other. Some of these consequences may thus be summarized:

1. An instability in charges for transportation affected by the competition, resulting in widespread and unjust discrimination between shippers and uncertainty as to the basis upon which business may be done.

2. The loss of much capital invested in both the railroads and the motor vehicles.

3. Radical changes in the railroad rate structure which, in the final analysis, may result in loading the traffic which is not affected by competition with the utmost charges that it is able to bear.

4. A tendency to break down wages and conditions of employment in the transportation industry.

5. Increase in the hazard of using the highways.

It is not our thought that anything should be done to suppress new means of transportation, such as those supplied by motor vehicles, which augment and improve the service furnished to the public. It is our thought that regulation should be provided which will minimize injurious consequences by restraining competition within reasonable limits, encouraging desirable coordination between the rival forms of transportation, and stabilizing rates and financial conditions.

To meet this situation the Commission suggests regulation that may take three distinct forms: appropriate adjustments of the tax burden; exercise of the police power in the interest of public safety and convenience; and regulation of rates, charges, practices, services, and other matters, as in the case of the railways.

A Program of State Action.—Because motor transportation is essentially intrastate in character, such weaknesses as appear in the existing situation must be remedied largely by state action. The first requisite to improvement is a regulatory body that is adequately financed and effectively organized—a body that is free of all extraneous influences and composed of men who possess broad social vision, who have some conception of a transportation plan. This regulatory body should be given broad powers and charged with their effective exercise. Common carriers of property and persons should be subject to thoroughgoing control as to rates, charges, practices, services, and other pertinent features; equipment should be supervised and adequate protection assured patron and public through insurance or otherwise; records should be kept and reports filed in prescribed form; discrimination should be prohibited; and, as a prerequisite to operation, a certificate of convenience and necessity should be required. Upon contract carriers should be imposed the same requirements, except that a permit be substituted for the certificate of convenience and necessity to operate over particular routes. In acting upon an application for certificate or permit the commission should consider, among other factors, (1) the need for such service; (2) the character and permanence of the proposed service; (3) the financial responsibility of the applicant; and (4) finally, but not incidentally, the effect of the proposed service upon transportation agencies already in the field and its relation to the transportation plan. Within a brief period it may appear advisable to require the same type of permit of the owner-operator as of the contract carrier, but for the present a permit should be issued to those operating trucks in the movement of their own property *in the regular course of trade*—which would not include the peddler-truck—upon application and payment of a moderate fee. Of such owner-operator regular reports should be required upon routes and tonnage. For all types of carriers the commission should have power to fix qualifications of drivers and to fix reasonable maximum hours of service; and, in conjunction with highway authorities, to control speed, weight, size, operating procedure, and such other features as may be essential to public safety upon the highway and to the physical conservation of that highway. And, finally, the commission should be charged jointly, with highway authorities and the state tax commission or commissioner, with the responsibility for advising the legislature upon, (1) the proper allocation among types of vehicles of highway costs, and (2) the character and amount of levies to be made upon commercial users of the highway to compensate for the use by them of public property for purposes of gain.

A Program of Federal Action.—To round out the program of action outlined for the states there is need of comprehensive action by Congress. Common carriers of property and persons by highway in interstate commerce should be subjected to the same character of regulation as has been suggested for common carriers operating intrastate. In the issuance of certificates of convenience and necessity, however, cooperation between federal and state authorities must be had; title to the highway rests in the state and to the state should be left final determination within all reasonable limits of the propriety of additional scheduled service over a particular route, and of the character of vehicle to be operated over state highways. Upon contract carriers operating interstate should be imposed, as in the case of like carriers operating intrastate, the same requirements that govern interstate common-carrier operations, except that again the permit be substituted for the certificate of convenience and necessity. In the issuance of such permit close cooperation with the state authorities becomes difficult because of the uncertainties of contract-carrier routes; in consequence, it must be recognized by the contract operator that his field of operations will be limited to those states with the requirements of which his equipment conforms. Such broad federal regulation of the contract carrier operating interstate will undoubtedly be challenged but, asserts the Interstate Commerce Commission in discussing this point,[1]

> It is, however, well settled that the power over commerce among the states conferred upon Congress by the Constitution is complete in itself, extends incidentally to every instrument and agent by which such commerce is carried on, may be exerted to its utmost extent over every part of such commerce, and is subject to no limitations save such as are prescribed in the Constitution; and it is sufficient for our purpose to state that the remedies we propose are, in our opinion, not only appropriate, but clearly within the constitutional power of Congress to prescribe.

And the more doubtful does it seem that the courts would deny to the federal government the right to control broadly interstate contract-carrier operations when the regulation of such operations intrastate has been approved.

The same considerations should weigh in judging applications for certificate or permit covering inter- as for intrastate operations, and a permit should be required of the owner-operated truck engaged in interstate hauling comparable to that required for intrastate operations. Of the owner-operator, too, the federal law should require the same reports as are demanded by the state. Since safety and protection of the highway are fundamentally matters of state responsibility, all interstate operators must expect to conform to the requirements of those states through which they operate; perhaps the federal Commission can assist in effecting a reasonable uniformity among the requirements of the various states but, except as state requirements are clearly unreasonable and arbitrary, final judgment upon such questions should remain with the state in which the police power is resident and ownership of the highway lies. Taxation for highway use is also a matter for state determination within broad limits, with the responsibility upon the federal Commission—after conference with appropriate state agencies—of recommending to Congress the character and amount of special taxes to be paid by those operating for gain upon the highways in interstate commerce.

Because unity of control is essential to the intelligent formulation and execution of a transportation plan, the regulation of interstate motor-vehicle operations should be vested in the Interstate Commerce Commission, such changes being made in its membership, organization, and staff as are essential to the effective performance of its full duties. Federal legislation should permit the delegation, at the discretion of the federal body, of specific matters that fall within its jurisdiction to joint boards composed of members of state regulatory bodies charged by state laws with the intrastate regulation of motor vehicle trans-

[1] Docket 23400, before cited, p. 382.

portation, right of appeal to lie to the Interstate Commerce Commission. Such coordination of state with federal control is particularly essential in this field because, while a considerable volume of traffic is interstate legally, it is in fact *local:* particularly is this true of traffic in the vicinity of many great cities located near state boundaries, and it is also true generally of interstate common- and contract-carrier truck routes that but two and rarely more than three states are concerned. Through such coordination and the delegation of initial action to joint boards the benefits of local knowledge and judgment can be gained, yet harmony of the whole maintained.

A Concluding Statement.—Against such a program as outlined, sharp protest will be voiced by motor-vehicle manufacturers, by certain trucking and shipping interests, by the professional "railroad baiter," and by those whose faith in the efficacy of unregulated competition is out of accord with the facts. Yet the only alternative to effective regulation of the motor vehicle is to release all agencies of transport from control, that all may compete upon equal terms. Such a course is, obviously, no alternative: it would be merely a long step toward catastrophe. No phase of motor-vehicle operations is now in that stage of development where the slight chill of intelligent control will cause it to wither and die; rather, every phase has made a lusty growth and, if the public and the commercial operators of motor vehicles will but learn the lesson taught by history, regulations now imposed are likely to be more equitable and more intelligent than those which undoubtedly will be imposed later when the "battle line" has been drawn between general public and commercial users of the highway—a "battle line" that is already forming. Perhaps, and this is particularly true of federal regulation with which we have had no experience, forward progress should be made surely rather than speedily; none the less, no passion for certainty should be permitted to delay action long. Our "transportation problem" is immediate, critical. Action within the limits of our knowledge, coupled with the rapid extension of those limits, *not lengthy consideration,* is desirable.

REFERENCES

Associated Traffic Club Bulletins, vol. 1, Nos. 15 and 16.

Association of Railway Executives: *Rails and Roads,* Washington, D. C., 1931.

Association of Railway Executives: *Coordination of Motor Transportation,* Docket 23400, Brief to Interstate Commerce Commission, Washington, D. C., 1931. .

BOWEN, IVAN: *Statement of the National Association of Motor-bus Operators to the Shannon Committee,* 1932.

BROSSEAU, A. J.: *Highways and the Taxpayer,* address published by the National Automobile Chamber of Commerce, 1922.

BROWN, LARUE, and STUART N. SCOTT: Regulation of the Contract Motor Carrier under the Constitution, *Harvard Law Review,* vol. 144, No. 4, p. 530.

Bus Facts for 1932: National Association of Motor-bus Operators, Washington, D. C., 1932.

California Railroad Commission, Decision 25243.

———, Decision 16176, Mimeographed decision.

Chamber of Commerce of the United States: *Relation of Highways and Motor Transport to Other Agencies*, Special Committee 4, Washington, D. C., 1923.

DAGGETT, STUART R.: *Principles of Inland Transportation*, Harper & Brothers, 1928.

DUNCAN, C. S.: Rail and Road Transport: at Home and Abroad, address before the Atlantic States Shippers Advisory Board, Rochester, N. Y., September, 1932.

———, Who Pays for the Highways? *Railway Age*, vol. 93, No. 7, p. 210.

EDWARDS, BRICE, and J. W. PARK: The Marketing and Distribution of Fruits and Vegetables by Motor Truck, United States Department of Agriculture, *Technical Bulletin* 272, 1931.

Facts and Figures of the Automobile Industry: National Automobile Chamber of Commerce, New York, 1932.

FLYNN, LEO J.: *Coordination of Motor Transportation*, report to Interstate Commerce Commission, published as Senate Document 43, Government Printing Office, 1932.

FULBRIGHT, R. C.: Where the Money for Rural Roads Comes From, *Engineering News Record*, vol. 108, No. 8, p. 284.

Hearings before the Committee on Interstate and Foreign Commerce, House of Representatives, 71st Congress, 2d Session, on H.R. 7954, *Regulation of Interstate Motor Buses on Public Highways*, Jan. 8 and 9, 1930.

Hearings before the Committee on Interstate Commerce, United States Senate, 72d Congress, 1st Session on S. 2793, *Regulation of Motor-carrier Transportation*, Feb. 1 to Mar. 31, 1932.

HIBBS, BEN: The Transportation Mess, *The Country Gentleman*, vol. 102, No. 8, August, 1932, p. 3.

Highway Services and Costs, Report 5, Commission to Investigate County and Municipal Taxation and expenditures, Trenton, New Jersey, 1931.

HUNT, FRANK R.: *The Taxation of Motor Vehicles and Its Relation to Highway Finance*, thesis prepared at Ohio State University, 1925.

International Chamber of Commerce: *Highway Transportation*, report of Highway Transport Committee, American Section, Washington, D. C., May, 1927.

Interstate Commerce Commission: *Coordination of Motor Transportation*, Docket 18300, 140 I.C.C. 685.

———: *Coordination of Motor Transportation*, Docket 23400, 182 I.C.C. 263.

———: *Annual Reports; Statistics of Railways in the United States.*

JAMES, E. W.: *Highway Construction Administration and Finance*, Highway Education Board, Washington, D. C., undated.

MACDONALD, T. H.: Testimony given in *Coordination of Motor Transportation*, Docket 23400, distributed by the National Association of Motor-bus Operators, Washington, D. C., 1931.

MARVIN, C. F., JR.: A Technical Basis for Apportioning Motor Vehicle Taxes, *Public Roads*, vol. 13, p. 41.

Ministry of Transport of Great Britain: *Report of the Conference on Rail and Road Transport*, Sir Arthur Salter, Chairman. His Majesty's Stationery Office, 1932.

National Association of Railroad and Public Utility Commissioners: Report of Committee on Motor Vehicle Transportation, *United States Daily*, November 17, 1932, p. 1.

OLDER, CLIFFORD: Testimony given before the Interstate Commerce Commission, Mar. 12, 16, and 17, 1931, in *Coordination of Motor Transportation*, Docket 23400, and reproduced by the Statistical Bureau—Western Lines.

Regulation of Truck Transport of Fruit and Produce Advocated, *United States Daily*, Dec. 1, 1932, p. 1.

SANDAGE, C. H.: The Motor Vehicle in Iowa, *Iowa Studies in Business*, No. 1, Bureau of Business Research, University of Iowa, 1928.

SANDAGE C. H., and R. W. NELSON: Motor-vehicle Taxation for Highway Purposes, *Iowa Studies in Business*, No. 11, Bureau of Business Research, University of Iowa, 1932.

WALKER, JOHN E.: *Highway Tax Costs*, National Automobile Chamber of Commerce, New York, 1931.

Western Traffic Executives' Committee: *Coordination of Motor Transportation*, Docket 23400, brief to Interstate Commerce Commission, 1931.

WETTLING, L. E.: Testimony given before the Interstate Commerce Commission, Mar. 12, 16, and 17, 1931, in *Coordination of Motor Transportation*, Docket 23400, and reproduced by the Statistical Bureau—Western Lines.

WINFREY, ROBLEY: *Automobile Operating Cost and Mileage Studies*, Iowa State College, *Engineering Experiment Station Bulletin* 106, 1931.

WOODLOCK, THOMAS F.: Fallacies in Motor Truck Cost Comparisons, *Barrons*, vol. 12, No. 32, p. 17.

Chapter XXXV

INLAND WATERWAYS: REVIVAL AND PROGRAM

HISTORY is too recent to record man's first use of lake and inland stream to facilitate the movement of himself and his possessions: from deepest antiquity man has felt the lure of the watercourse and has sensed its opportunities of escape from the heavy costs that, through long ages, rested upon overland transport. Each people developed a type of boat suited to its waters and to its economic needs; the streams became busy thoroughfares of commerce. Population clung to the water's edge, none but an essentially self-sufficing economy being feasible at any distance inland. To make streams, ill suited for transportation because of obstructions or shallows, serve him more effectively, man early expended efforts. Yet it was not sufficient to clear flowing streams for use; such activities still left rich areas unopened and valuable resources untapped. To the waterways provided by nature, then, man added those of his own making: programs of canal construction were undertaken and carried to completion that, in view of the primitive methods employed, were nothing short of stupendous. The records of the early civilizations of the Euphrates and the Nile indicate an appreciation of the important place of the canal in promoting economic well-being, and reference has been made in an earlier chapter to some 200,000 miles of canals that once served the Chinese people. But it was with the invention of the chamber lock, permitting canal traffic to overcome elevations, that the scope of usefulness of the canal was extended to meet important needs; only the problem of an adequate water supply remained.

As a consequence of the new possibilities of the canal, construction was begun in France in 1605 upon the Canal de Briare. Following the completion of this project others were undertaken, the channel now known as the Canal du Midi being 148 miles in length; it was built to accommodate 100-ton barges, overcame an elevation of 600 feet, and at one point followed a tunnel some 700 feet in length. Construction was continued in France during the eighteenth century and, during the same period, was active in Holland, Belgium, and Germany. In 1761 important English building was begun and by 1800 some 1,000 miles of artificial waterways had been made available, the Manchester Ship Canal being the only significant project undertaken since that date. Indeed, except in Germany little mileage has been added to any of the major systems of western Europe since 1800, construction being offset largely by abandonment; during the half century just past inland waterway mileage in that area has been static. In the United States interest in canal construction became active immediately following the Revolutionary War; a great number of individual projects were urged upon the public, these falling roughly into the groups distinguished in Chap. III. Though there were notable exceptions, most of the early canals were shallow, with numerous locks and frequent use of the inclined plane to overcome differences in elevation. Interest in canal construction was at its height about 1825, the date of the completion of the Erie Canal, and work was pushed rapidly upon many projects until the panic of 1837 brought activities to a halt. It was in response to public interest shown during these years that Congress assisted several undertakings with funds and others with grants of land, some 4,500,000 acres being transferred to certain states to be given in turn to private interests to encourage canal building; thus was established a precedent for federal aid to railways initiated in 1850.

But however important were artificial waterways, the rivers were far more significant to both European and American commerce in the movement of inland traffic. Of vital import to the early colonists were the short streams that flowed into the Atlantic; indispensable to the development of the territory west of the Appalachians in the years prior to 1850 were, first, the Ohio River and its numerous navigable tributaries, and, later, the entire Mississippi River system. The importance of the lower Mississippi to the people of the West as a channel of trade was increased greatly by the Louisiana Purchase: acquisition of the lower valley made it possible to move all types of produce from a great area southward to New Orleans without danger of political interference. That such movements were made in great volume, even prior to the advent of steam, in flatboat and barge with capacities ranging from 40 to 400 tons is attested by movement down the Ohio each year from 1820 to 1830 of some 3,000 flatboats alone and the arrival of almost 2,800 flatboats in New Orleans as late as 1846–1847. As early as 1820 a number of steamboats were operating upon the Western rivers, this traffic growing steadily and rapidly until interrupted by the war blockade of the early sixties: arrivals in New Orleans in 1813–1814 were 21, in 1859–1860, 3,566. The extension of the railway net, the increasing advantages offered by rail shipments from the Middle West, and the cut-throat competition that characterized transportation in the score of years following the late sixties combined to accomplish the downfall of traffic upon the Mississippi; before the close of the past century water competition throughout the inland area had been reduced to "innocuous desuetude" and the steamboat was but a picturesque memory.

Revival of Interest in Inland Waterways.—Scarcely had inland-waterway transport disappeared before a movement for revival was under way. In 1895 an International Waterways Convention was held in Cleveland, attended by some 300 delegates from all sections of the United States and Canada; 6 years later the first National Rivers and Harbors Congress was assembled in Baltimore; in 1902, by Congressional act a board of engineers within the Department of War was authorized, this board to pass judgment upon the engineering aspects of all waterway projects. In 1903, after extended discussion and a sharp political struggle, the state of New York approved a large bond issue for the modernization of the Erie Canal; the campaign in behalf of the issue was financed in a considerable measure by New York City and Buffalo interests that hoped to gain from expected increases in canal tonnage, widespread interest being commanded by the campaign throughout the entire United States. In 1906 there was held in St. Louis a convention that gave birth to the Lakes-to-Gulf Deep Waterway Association and in Washington a session of the Rivers and Harbors Congress that led to the appointment by President Roosevelt of the Inland Waterways Commission in March, 1907. This Commission, of which Senator T. E. Burton of Ohio—a political leader of high capacity and keen discrimination—was chairman, was instructed by the President to "prepare and report a comprehensive plan for the improvement and control of the river systems of the United States"; as a phase of the Rooseveltian conservation program inland-waterway utilization commanded the President's interest and support. After an examination of projects along the Atlantic coast, in the Southwest, and in the Pacific Northwest, a journey was made down the Mississippi from Keokuk to Memphis in company with President Roosevelt in early autumn: this journey provided the hopeful and the curious splendid opportunity for a tremendous demonstration, with full advantage being taken of the opportunity by waterway enthusiasts.

After its field studies and following extended hearings a report was submitted to the President early in 1908. This report was of a general character, declaring in favor of "restoring and developing such inland navigation and water transportation as upon expert examination may appear to confer a benefit commensurate with the cost, to be utilized both independently and as a necessary adjunct to rail transportation." This development should be in accordance with a definitely coordinated and continuous national plan, the Commission declared, and it was further urged that a National Waterways Commission be created to coordinate the various governmental agencies interested in waterways, continue the survey of waterways, and formulate plans for their development. In 1909 Congress provided for the creation of the National Waterways Commission, which was also headed by Senator Burton. This body offered a preliminary report to Congress in 1910, with important appendixes dealing with related conservation matters, questions of law, and European waterway experience. In 1912 a final report was filed, this document offering specific recommendations upon certain points. Three individual projects were examined by the Commission at the request of Congress: judgment was favorable to immediate action upon the Lake Erie and Ohio River Canal; further study was urged of the Lake Erie-Lake Michigan Canal; and an adverse opinion was given upon the Anacostia-Chesapeake Canal. To further the development of water traffic it was recommended that all water carriers engaged in interstate commerce which were affiliated with railways, as well as all independent water carriers operating interstate over scheduled routes, be regulated in the same manner as the railways by the Interstate Commerce Commission; that the power to order physical connections between rail and boat terminals be conferred upon the same body; and that the law permit the Commission to require of the railways rates to points of traffic interchange with water carriers that are less than the local rail rates to those points.[1] The establishment of satisfactory water terminals was urged, also any changes in existing laws that might be necessary to that end. The remainder of the report dealt with the influence of storage reservoirs and reforestation upon navigation and flood control, and with the development and control of water power as an incident to the problem in hand. Thus it appears that, while the work of the National Waterways Commission was valuable and dealt in an authoritative manner with particular problems, its report is curiously lacking in enthusiasm for the development of inland navigation without let or hindrance; in fact, the position taken by this body in its preliminary report—in which, after indicating approval of the provisions of the Act of 1909 relative to recommendations to Congress, it declared, "The Commission would advise that without a careful and unbiased examination of proposed improvements of the nature now required by statute no project should be adopted by Congress"[2]—may be assumed to be its final position.

Meanwhile many groups, some actuated by unselfish and others by selfish motives, had been active. Conventions were held in all sections of the United States; newspapers and periodicals gave extended space to the glories of inland-waterway transport in the past and to its golden future; and political leaders, quick to sense issues that have popular appeal, joined in the demands for "more water, deeper water." In the autumn of 1909 some 5,000 enthusiastic, aggressive, and determined delegates to the Deep Waterways Convention met in New Orleans—encouraged by the presence of President Taft, who had come down from St. Louis by boat with a St. Louis group—to demand of Congress im-

[1] *National Waterways Commission Report*, 62d Congress, 2d Session, Senate Documents, vol. 15, pp. 17–20.

[2] *Ibid.*, p. 78.

mediate financial aid for the construction of waterways. To make this demand effective political activity was pledged. Despite a temporary setback resulting from an adverse report by engineers upon the Lakes-to-Gulf project late in 1909 and the none-too-encouraging preliminary report of the National Waterways Commission in 1910, the momentum of the movement and the enthusiasm of its proponents made possible the authorization by Congress in 1911 of improvements upon the Ohio River at an ultimate estimated cost of $60,000,000. The demand for improved inland waterways had "caught": water traffic, moribund no less than a decade and a half previously, now lacked for its restoration only adequate channels, adequate craft, and adequate traffic—as well as, upon certain streams and during particular periods, adequate water.[1] For funds to provide the first, waterway supporters looked to the federal treasury with an assurance that time has amply justified; to obtain craft of proper design the aid of engineers was sought with satisfying results. Channels have been deepened and cleared and the mileage of waterways capable of floating the splendid new barges has steadily increased. In matters of traffic and of water supply realization has fallen somewhat short of hope but the faith of the advocate remains unshaken: so long as public funds flow freely, his hopes may yet be fulfilled and his promises of economic gain to the public be realized.

Causes of Revived Interest in Inland Waterways.—For this astonishing revival of public interest in waterways and its consequent sharp reversal in public policy, there were certain definite and fundamental causes. Of these one of the most important was the conviction that the American people were guilty of a species of economic crime in failing to utilize a natural resource: upon the inland waters had once moved a great volume of traffic and failure to continue that use appeared as improvidence to many. The speeches and the writings of those who urge rehabilitation are rich in references to the part played by waterways in the early development of important areas; the glamorous past must be made to live

[1] In the 1927 *Annual Report of the Inland Waterways Corporation*, Major General T. Q. Ashburn, chairman, said, after commenting upon the difficulties occasioned earlier in the season by floods, "During September and October, as the water receded, bars were formed in many new places, impeding the channel; the water, instead of being confined to the channel, poured through the crevasses and the result was that operations during these months were terribly handicapped."

In his discussion before a subcommittee, Committee on Appropriations, House of Representatives, early in 1931 upon the 1930 operations of the corporation, Major General Ashburn ascribed a decrease in barge-line traffic for a major part of the year to "the most extensive drought ever in the history of the Mississippi River." And in the *Annual Report of the Inland Waterways Corporation* for 1931 he declared, "Early in the year the channel and operating condition on the upper river became so acute that we were forced to notify patrons of our inability to transport freight without subjecting it to serious delay. Relief was obtained too late in the season to be beneficial and tonnage suffered materially."

again. Thus conservation and sentiment combine to give that depth of conviction and that faith to which defeat has been but a spur to effort.

A second factor that has contributed both leadership and following to the waterway movement has been antagonism toward the railway. At the time the enthusiasm for waterway development was at its height, the contest between the railways and the public had come to definite issue; those who were most vigorous in their condemnation of the railways were, in general, most active in support of waterway development. Water competition would serve as a regulator of railway rates, even as a scourge to this monster of fearful mien that had for so long "plundered the people." And many who did not challenge the fairness of existing railway rate levels welcomed lower rates upon tonnage in which they were interested; few gave thought to the possible ultimate consequences of such downward adjustments upon other rates, upon railway credit, and upon service. The upward trend of railway rates during the initial period of agitation for waterway development and a continuation of that trend during succeeding years gave support to those who insisted that water competition was essential if the "railroad monopoly" was to be controlled. It was the anti-railway aspect of the waterway movement that recommended it strongly to many political leaders during its early years and it is that same aspect that continues to serve as the basis for the support of many in positions of political consequence.

The belief that water traffic will function effectively as a regulator of railways in adjacent territory proceeds from the conviction of great numbers that water transportation is markedly cheaper than transportation by rail or highway. This conviction arises in part from analogies, in part from a knowledge of charges made over comparable routes, and in part from the unreasoned assurance that movement by water *ought* to be less costly than movement by land. Frequent statements come to the attention of the casual reader of the greater cost of moving grain a thousand miles by rail than many thousands of miles by water; of the astonishingly low cost of ore and coal movements upon the Great Lakes; and of the inability of the railways to make rates from the Mississippi Valley to Pacific coast points comparable to the rail-and-water rate via even the North Atlantic ports. The advocates of waterway rehabilitation have available cost data covering river and canal movements in European countries, cost data upon the New York Barge Canal and upon certain limited river operations in the United States, and estimated "costs" that represent the projection of known facts to the development in prospect. And is it not reasonable that the stream, awaiting its burden, will permit the movement of that burden at lesser cost than will result from handling it over a roadway that must be especially constructed for the purpose? The bounty of nature provides the roadway; it awaits only man's use. Analysis is seldom made to determine how often the roadway does await, ready for use; and seldom, too, is analysis applied to the problem of costs. The obvious convinces; to go beyond is unessential.

Another argument that had strong appeal until the past decade, even to the more thoughtful, was rested upon the need of waterways to supplement the railways. The statement of J. J. Hill, that the relation of railways and waterways "is one of harmony, of helpfulness, and of cooperation," represented an expression of possibilities. The phenomenal growth of the railway net to which the American people had become accustomed in the score of years from 1870 to 1890 did not reappear after recovery from the depression of the nineties, and the century was yet young when the railways experienced serious difficulty in moving traffic: the autumn of 1906 was marked by general congestion and consequent serious impairment of service—and during the period of the World War, as well as in several of the years immediately thereafter, the service of the railways proved grossly inadequate. Car shortages developed frequently, particularly in grain-growing and in coal-producing areas, the result, as students now realize, of the failure of the railways to utilize equipment and facilities to advantage but assumed then to be the consequence of plant inadequacy. The volume of all traffic was increasing at a steady, rapid rate; the necessity of investing billions of dollars within a relatively short period faced the railways, if they were to maintain satisfactory service. Inland waterways, if developed, would provide a means for moving millions upon millions of tons of low-grade commodities; the railways, thus relieved, would be able to devote their facilities to the handling of higher-class tonnage. From this adjustment the railways would gain both through avoidance of heavy capital expenditures necessary to handle all tonnage and through the substitution of more remunerative traffic for less. Thus, while there might be a temporary conflict of interest between rail and water carriers, the immediate gain to the public in lower rates would be matched by the ultimate advantage of the railway. Today, when it is no longer possible to summon the bogy of inadequate railway service, this supplementary function of the waterway appears frequently in the statements of waterway advocates in another form: while waterway development may for a time lessen the volume of railway traffic, it will in the long run increase it greatly because of the greater total volume of traffic that will result from the stimulation given industrial activity by low water rates.

There are numerous collateral gains also that will result, it is asserted, from deepening streams and removing obstacles to their flow to benefit navigation. Cities and industries generally draw water from the streams for their many uses. Work upon those streams will tend to provide water more nearly pure than would otherwise be available. Furthermore, to provide a regular flow of water for navigation purposes great storage reservoirs might be constructed; this regularization of flow would not only benefit the users of water but also be of immeasurable assistance in minimizing flood losses and checking soil erosion. And, finally, the possibilities of great hydroelectric development incident to the construction of dams to aid in navigation have been emphasized in connection with many projects. Not infrequently has it been declared with reference to a particular project that "the development of water power will alone justify the undertaking"; and it is interesting to note that about 40 per cent of the final report of the National Waterways Commission was devoted to problems arising from the development and sale of power, with the same subject occupying an almost proportionate place in the various appendixes. The frequent conflict between navigational and power uses of water receives infrequent attention, the supply of water being assumed to be without limit. And the strong possibilities of conflict between navigational needs and flood-control policies are also generally ignored. The less clear are the gains of a particular development, the heavier do its advocates stress these collateral advantages; in fact, the collateral gains of waterway development often overshadow in discussion the direct.

Yet another explanation of the remarkable revival of interest in the development of inland waterways and the tenacity of that interest lies in the motivating power of community and individual self-interest. When river traffic was in its prime, many cities enjoyed a prosperity and a prestige that made them preeminent in the area; with the construction of railways this preeminence passed, often, to communities that were inconsequential in "steamboatin' days." Chambers of commerce and other civic organizations are constantly alert to seize upon any proposal that may increase industrial activity or trade, likewise to champion any movement that has imaginative appeal to the local citizenry. Individuals, like organizations, are alert to grasp any opportunity for community advantage, as well as to capitalize those opportunities for personal profit. It is such a combination of community patriotism with individual self-interest that has given much of strength to the waterway movement, that has brought the movement from oblivion to the point where the federal government is committed to the expenditure of hundreds of millions of dollars upon a great number and diversity of projects. If the expenditure of tens of millions upon a certain development fails to bring the commerce of the world to the gates of the city, the cost to the local community and to the individual has been slight: membership in one or more waterway associations, attendance upon conventions, and an occasional journey to the national capital to bring pressure to bear upon Congress, represent the major outlays. And the total of these outlays is insignificant if, as a result of an improved waterway, transportation charges can be materially lowered upon an important volume of traffic. The possibilities of gain are great; the likelihood of loss, with the federal treasury meeting all costs, is negligible for the local community or the individual. It is not strange that, quite apart from all considerations of social gain resulting from waterway development, the game has been played with tremendous zest. Frankly confessing a profound interest in the transportation *charge* to the shipper and a comparable indifference to the *total*, the *social*, cost of such service, many civic groups and individuals continue an aggressive struggle. And that indifference toward social considerations has been the greater throughout the Middle West during the past decade because of the belief that, by the construction of the Panama Canal and the adjustment of tolls—as well as by the refusal of the Interstate Commerce Commission to give Fourth Section relief on tonnage from the Valley to the Pacific coast—other portions of the country have benefited at the expense of the Middle West: if now the people of the Valley can benefit at the expense of others, the balance may perhaps be restored. Efforts to secure governmental appropriations, when prompted by self-interest and characterized by social indifference, are not to be commended; yet it must not be forgotten that efforts no more worthy from a social point of view have been made with respect to matters other than waterway development. And it must be remembered, too, that there are great numbers who are convinced that both individual and social advantage will be served by waterway rehabilitation.

Though other factors have contributed to the strength of the waterway movement, perhaps none has been more important than the interest and positive support of two men so situated as to assist greatly in rousing public enthusiasm and to accomplish tangible results. The foundation of the inland-waterway movement was built during the administration of President Theodore Roosevelt: he regarded the demand for the reestablishment of river traffic, with its collateral bearing upon flood control and power, as an integral part of the great conservation program that he sponsored. To him the regulation of railways to protect water transport against the unequal battle it was fighting also had appeal. The evangelical phase of the waterway movement undoubtedly reached its high point during the closing years of the Roosevelt administration and immediately following. And the other individual who has contributed generously to the success of the movement, particularly to the realization of its hopes, has been Herbert Hoover: for 8 years as Secretary of Commerce and for 4 years as President he let pass no opportunity to lend the support of his personality and of his office to the formulation and approval of an inland-waterway plan of broad scope. The crusader and the engineer have, in turn, perhaps contributed more to the success of the movement than have economic advantage or logic.

Major Inland Waterway Projects.—At no time in our national history has interest in inland-waterway projects been wholly lacking; many canals that were dug prior to the railway era have continued to render a limited service and many of the proposals that failed to materialize survived through a century in the hopes of those whose interests were to have been served. In the heyday of railway building one of the means seriously urged for enforcing a lower railway rate level between the Middle West and the Eastern seaboard was the deepening of the Kanawha and James Rivers and the construction of a canal to connect the two. If one might paraphrase, "Projects come and projects go, while some run on forever." Yet some proposals that in one period loomed large disappeared from public notice, their places being taken by others in the public mind. Of the three proposals upon the soundness of which the National Waterways Commission was asked by Congress to pass, but one now receives consideration; yet, in the intervening years numerous others have compelled attention. Certain other proposals, such as the Illinois waterway, the improvement of particular streams, the furtherance of intracoastal projects, have persisted for a hundred years; from period to period details of the program have varied but the demand for a completed project remains. Because of the great number of individual proposals for which public support is sought, it will be necessary to confine descriptive comments to certain major ones, with occasional resort to grouping in the case of related projects. Discussion will deal first with those projects approved in the Rivers and Harbors Act of 1930, comments following upon inland waterways now completed and in service as well as upon certain proposals seeking official recognition.

Lakes-to-Gulf Waterway.—One of the desires that has survived since the early settlement of the territory about lower Lake Michigan has been for an adequate all-water route from that lake to the Mississippi and an adequate river channel to the Gulf. Agitation dates from 1812; federal aid was extended upon a minor and then upon a major scale in 1822 and later; construction was begun in 1836 and the canal was put into service in 1848. This canal, known as the Michigan and Illinois, had a minimum depth of 6 feet and was some 97 miles in length, entering the Illinois River near La Salle. The tonnage moved through the canal grew rapidly and was well maintained until the close of the century, when it declined sharply. This decline in tonnage, occurring during the period when interest in waterway development was keen, led to demands for an improved channel; Chicago interests believed, as had New York interests in the case of the Erie Canal, that enlargement was essential to rehabilitation. The first demands made were for a channel that would permit ocean vessels to ascend from the Gulf by way of the Mississippi and the Illinois Rivers and a new canal to Chicago: depths of 20 to 24 feet were suggested. Such fantastic dreams were displaced by insistence upon "Fourteen feet through the Valley," but the depth demanded was destined to suffer further revision: 14 feet was inadequate for ships and far in excess of the needs of barge traffic. When, therefore, a depth of 9 feet was adopted as standard for major federal projects, construction here proceeded upon the basis of that minimum. Much of the necessary work had been done at state expense when, in 1930, the project was assumed by the federal government and by that agency has been carried to completion. Opened for service in 1933, the new canal closely parallels the old and similar use is made of the Illinois and Mississippi Rivers to reach St. Louis, from which point the 9-foot channel continues to Baton Rouge.

Closely related to the project just discussed is the Illinois and Mississippi Canal, commonly known as the Hennepin, that was begun in 1888 and completed in 1907. This undertaking, its eastern terminus near Hennepin and its western near Rock Island, is 75 miles in length and has a minimum depth of 7 feet. It was built by the federal government to force railway rates downward between Chicago and Mississippi River towns to the West, but traffic has been negligible: during the period of its construction competition among the railways had so lowered rates that, upon its completion, "the condition it was designed to remedy no longer existed."[1] With a depth of 9 feet indicated for the waterways between which it is a link, the Hennepin Canal will doubtless, despite its record of idleness, be deepened correspondingly.

Upper Mississippi River Project.—In the years prior to the gridironing by railways of the Granger states, the upper Mississippi was a busy thoroughfare from St. Louis northward to the foot of St. Anthony's Falls. Before river traffic became negligible a 6-foot channel was approved and for a period of almost 50 years federal expenditures were made to secure and maintain that depth. Because appropriations were insufficient for the accomplishment of the difficult task, the maximum depth under normal river conditions was about 4.5 feet; during periods of low water an even lesser depth existed over certain rapids and shallows. The slope of the river is gradual from Grafton, Ill., the mouth of the Illinois River, to St. Paul: from Grafton to Keokuk the slope averages less than 0.5 foot per mile, and from Keokuk to St. Paul the slope is about 0.4 foot per mile, though long included in this stretch were the Des Moines and Le Claire Rapids with drops within a short distance of more than 22 and 21 feet respectively. The Des Moines Rapids were submerged by the pool of the Keokuk Dam in 1913, and navigation past the Le Claire Rapids has long been facilitated by lateral canals and locks. Another dam, with locks to overcome a sharp slope for a little distance, has served navigation for many years below Minneapolis.

After considerable jockeying, it was finally determined to construct a 9-foot channel from Grafton northward. Of the several proposals relative to this major undertaking, two were given careful consideration; the one called for construction of huge storage reservoirs to regulate the flow of the river in such manner as to provide the desired channel, with certain supplementary construction needed at difficult points, and the other

[1] Ashton, Bessie, *The Economic Aspects of the Illinois Waterway*, p. 29.

involved the construction of a series of dams to provide slack-water navigation for the entire distance of 653 miles. The latter plan was ap-

FIG. 40.—The present approved program of inland-waterway development, Mississippi Valley.

proved and work began in 1932 on the first of the dams that must be built.[1] It is not at all certain, however, but that in time it may be deemed

[1] To provide slack-water navigation from Grafton to Minneapolis a total of 27 dams will be required. Several of these, notably the Keokuk dam, were in service when the plan was adopted.

advisable to build the storage reservoirs to supplement the slack-water plan; if so, it is probable that the Wisconsin River and others northward will be dammed. The estimated cost of the channel planned is approximately $150,000,000. Supplementary to the improvement of the upper Mississippi is the plan to remove snags and other obstructions from the Wisconsin as far as Portage. To Portage a canal will be provided from Green Bay, on Lake Michigan; for a major portion of the distance a 6-foot depth will be provided and for the last short distance a 4-foot depth. Obviously, therefore, there is the ultimate hope of a second channel between Lake Michigan and the Mississippi River. Should storage water be impounded in the Wisconsin such a channel would become a certainty.

The Ohio Valley Projects.—It is doubtful if any stream has played a more important part in the early development of a major section of the United States than the Ohio; with numerous tributaries of comparatively easy access from the east, the area adjacent to the Ohio was developing rapidly while the lake regions remained almost a wilderness. Progress in the northern district had to await that accessibility which the Erie Canal and, later, the railways accorded. From an early time interest has been shown in an adequate channel upon the Ohio: in 1825 a stock company was chartered to build a canal around the falls at Louisville and in 1826 the federal government became a shareholder in this company, acquiring complete title in 1874. Until 1879 other work on the river was limited to snagging, removing rocks, and cutting across bars that impeded navigation with a view to maintaining a 3-foot channel; in that year Congress authorized a lock and dam just below Pittsburgh which represented the beginning of a movement toward slack-water navigation that did not reach completion until 1929. At first a 6-foot channel was planned but, as completed, a 9-foot channel has been provided for the 981 miles from Cairo Point to Pittsburgh. To obtain slack-water navigation for the Ohio a series of 50 dams have been built, all of the movable type to permit free movement to all craft during periods of high water.[1] The cost of this improvement, to the time of its opening, was $118,743,000,[2] though this figure does not include other expenditures made by the federal government upon the Ohio in years past.

Tributary to the Ohio are many important streams. These, with a flow of water that permits development and with access to territory that offers a considerable volume of traffic, have benefited from federal appropriations through an extended period. From a traffic standpoint the most important of these tributaries is the Monongahela upon which

[1] For description of the movable dam see War Department and United States Shipping Board, Transportation Series 2, *Transportation in the Mississippi and Ohio Valleys*, 1929, p. 16.

[2] United States Department of Commerce, *Commerce Yearbook*, 1930, vol. 1, p. 595.

slack-water navigation is to be provided to a point above Fairmont, W. Va., a distance of 131 miles. Traffic upon this river has been heavy and, with the provision of deeper channels, it is likely to increase: the improvements authorized will give a channel of 8 feet or more for a distance of 101.5 miles and of 7 feet for the remaining distance. Another important stream is the Kanawha, upon which a 6-foot channel has been provided; in 1930 Congress approved revisions, however, that will make available a 9-foot waterway for a distance of 90 miles. A third major tributary is the Tennessee, upon which a 9-foot channel has been authorized for a distance of 83 miles above Paducah; beyond that point a 6-foot channel is proposed to Riverton, Ala., some 143 miles farther; for the next 263 miles a 5-foot channel or deeper will be offered; and for some 163 additional miles a 3-foot depth is planned. Thus the Tennessee will reach for 652 miles into the territory to the southeast for tonnage, with the current volume of tonnage in the shallower sections surprisingly large.

Among other tributaries of the Ohio that have been developed and are producing considerable tonnage are the Cumberland, the Green and Barren, the Kentucky, and the Big Sandy: these, with developed tributaries, provide some 1,060 miles of waterways of a 6-foot depth. The Little Kanawha has a minimum depth of 4 feet for a distance of 48 miles and the Muskingum a minimum depth of 5.5 feet for 91 miles. Upon the Allegheny a 7-foot channel is to be provided for a distance of 61 miles, with a shallow channel cleared to the New York state line. In addition, improvements have been authorized upon the Youghiogheny and lesser streams, while preliminary surveys have been directed for still others. It is interesting to note that provision was made for the navigation of certain of these streams by the states in which they lie prior to 1850 or by private corporations, the federal government later taking over the state and private works for further development.

The Missouri River.—One of the most interesting of the projects that are to constitute America's inland waterways is the Missouri River. Formed by the confluence of three streams in western Montana, it flows 2,551 miles across or along seven states to the Mississippi, near St. Louis. The official "head of navigation" is Fort Benton, some 2,285 miles upstream, "although there is not a dependable depth in excess of 3 feet at low stage between Kansas City and Sioux City and 2½ feet between Sioux City and Pierre."[1] Below Kansas City the river was[2]

> . . . choked with snags, and in many places divided by permanent islands and changing sand bars into devious shallow channels. . . . Fluctuating widths ranged from 500 feet to more than a mile, and the available low-water depth at many crossings did not exceed 30 inches, yet even before any improvement the

[1] *Transportation in the Mississippi and Ohio Valleys*, p. 35.

[2] *Ibid.*, p. 36.

entire section was successfully navigated. The section from Kansas City to Sioux City was very similar to the river below Kansas City, and navigation of the low-water channels had to contend with innumerable obstructions and available depths of less than 30 inches at the crossings. Nevertheless, until construction of the railroads offered a more expeditious route to the Northwest, the river carried a large through traffic, despite the slowness and expense, and the uncertainty created by the loss of many boats and cargoes.

Because "the stream is notorious for instability of channel, shifting sand bars and shore accretions, and extensive erosion of its alluvial banks by swift, undercutting currents,"[1] it presents problems in the establishment and maintenance of a channel that are yet unsolved. Yet no effort has been spared to provide the authorized 6-foot channel for the 390 miles from the mouth to Kansas City, and work is now under way in accordance with the action of Congress in 1927 to extend that channel to Sioux City. For the latter project $27,000,000 has been appropriated to cover a portion of total costs. Beyond Sioux City, 807 miles from the Mississippi, another project calls for the removal of snags and rocks from the channel and for bank protection at strategic points to Fort Benton.

Work has been done upon two minor tributaries of the Missouri, the Osage and the Gasconade Rivers. Upon the former a 3-foot channel is planned to extend upstream for a distance of 170 miles; upon the latter, by means of snagging and regulation of channel flow, a depth of 2 feet will be provided for a distance of 62 miles. As in the case of the Ohio, preliminary surveys of other Missouri tributaries have been authorized.

The Lower Mississippi Valley Projects.—Though the importance of the lower Mississippi declined with the construction of railways, at no time did traffic virtually disappear as was the case with the upper river; a steady traffic passed Cairo Point to and from both St. Louis and Ohio River ports; between Memphis and Vicksburg the river-borne tonnage was approximately the same as between Cairo Point and Memphis; and a yet greater tonnage moved by boat between Vicksburg and New Orleans. The slope of the river is slight, averaging at low water 0.35 foot per mile from Cairo to the mouth of the Red River and but 0.01 foot per mile from that point to the Gulf. Because of the slight current, conditions are comparable to slack-water navigation; though, even were conditions otherwise, it would be impossible to construct dams to provide such navigation because of the character of the bed in the lower valley. While there is always adequate water below Cairo, if controlled, to provide a 9-foot channel, the meandering of the current is such that maintenance of an adequate depth over the sand bars that lie between deep pools is difficult; since snags were eliminated these bars "form the only serious obstacle to successful navigation, and any successful scheme of low-water improvements must provide for their removal or increase the low-water depth over

[1] *Ibid.*, p. 35.

them."[1] By necessary dredging through bars from about the mouth of the Red River to a point a short distance below Cairo a minimum channel width of 250 feet and a minimum depth of 9 feet have been maintained below Cairo for many years, "with but isolated cases of deficiency." Some bars require dredging several times during a low-water season, others but once; a reach may be badly blocked after one flood and comparatively open after another. The lower Mississippi presents problems of navigation of an unusual type for so great a stream.

Tributary to the lower river are a number of streams upon which work has been done to facilitate navigation. On the east bank is the Yazoo, with the Big Sunflower as its major tributary; upon the former it is proposed to maintain a minimum channel of 4 feet for its full length of 178 miles by clearing obstructions and upon the latter a minimum depth of 4.5 feet for a distance of 171 miles by clearing obstructions, by closure of outlets, by a single dam and lock, and by contraction works. Snagging, clearing, and dredging have been authorized also upon the Tallahatchie and Coldwater, tributary to the Yazoo, for a total distance of about 155 miles, with no minimum depth specified. To the westward of the Mississippi lie a number of streams upon which work has been and is to be done. By systematic clearing of the banks, snagging, dredging shoals, building levees, and certain other work an open channel is to be provided upon the Red River for a distance of 475 miles upstream; upon the Black and Ouachita Rivers a 6.5-foot channel is to be provided for a distance of 360 miles to Camden, Ark., by clearing, dredging, and the construction of dams, with a considerable mileage of tributaries of the Ouachita and Black cleared for navigation. The watercourse of the Arkansas is to be cleared to a point 465 miles above its mouth, to which point it has been declared navigable; the White and its several tributaries are, by means of snagging, dredging, and contraction works, to be kept open for navigation—the White for a distance of about 340 miles, the Black and Current rivers into southern Missouri. The Francis is to be kept clear of snags for a distance of 148 miles, as are its two major tributaries for short distances.

The Intracoastal System.—One of the projects that has survived in the thoughts of those interested in water transport for more than a century is that which, by a series of works, would provide for the movement of traffic along the coast by means of inland channels. This intracoastal movement would be upon rivers and inland bays in so far as possible, these being supplemented by artificial channels; as the plan was initially conceived movement was to be provided inshore from Boston to approximately Wilmington, N. C., but it has more recently been amplified to include the whole coastline from Boston to the Mexican border. And, if and as the plan develops, there will undoubtedly be a demand for a canal

[1] *Ibid.*, p. 7.

across the upper portion of the state of Florida to shorten the distance for barge and other light traffic moving between Atlantic and Gulf ports.

A ship canal across Cape Cod built by private interests was later sold to the federal government for $11,500,000, three times the maximum justifiable price set by a board of United States Army engineers. The existing Delaware and Raritan Canal is entirely inadequate to meet modern demands; a study has been authorized to determine "the most desirable route for such waterway, with a minimum depth of 25 feet and adequate width with plans, and estimate the cost of the same."[1] From the Delaware River traffic may now move through a 12-foot canal constructed by the federal government at a cost of approximately $15,000,000 into the upper reaches of Chesapeake Bay. From Norfolk, Va., to Beaufort Inlet, N. C., an inland route 198 miles long with a depth of 12 feet is practically complete, with the Dismal Swamp Canal of 9-foot depth as an alternative route to Albemarle Sound; this section, as do others to be mentioned, makes the maximum possible use of all natural waters, including canalized rivers. Work has been begun upon a 12-foot channel from Beaufort Inlet to Cape Fear, 93 miles, but progress has not been great. From Cape Fear to Charleston, 154 miles, a 12-foot project is planned. From Charleston to St. Johns River, Fla., 300 miles, a 7-foot channel is now available and for the 383 miles from St. Johns River to Miami, Fla., an 8-foot waterway is planned, with no great progress made.

While intracoastal channels along the Gulf coast have not yet made any considerable progress, a number of important projects have been authorized and some work accomplished. Plans have been made for such channels from New Orleans westward and southward to Corpus Christi and Brownsville, a 9-foot depth to be maintained throughout. From the Mississippi River, near Baton Rouge, a 9-foot channel is to be provided to the intracoastal route through Grand Lake. Eastward from New Orleans a protected course will be provided under present authorizations as far as Pensacola, Fla., with several short sections already in service at advantageous points beyond. More rapid construction and further authorization of South Atlantic and Gulf sections of the intracoastal system are probable for a period beginning in 1933, unless the inland-waterway program is hampered by the need of greater federal economy.

The New York State Barge Canals.—In 1817 the State of New York embarked upon a program of canal construction and operation that has persisted to the present day. The first two units authorized, the Erie and Champlain canals, were formally opened in 1825; so successful were they in attracting tonnage that the legislature was besieged by the people of other sections of the state who desired to share in the benefits of improved transport. As a consequence of insistent demands, further construction was authorized; though only a few minor projects were approved after

[1] Rivers and Harbors Act, 1930.

1836, several major undertakings with prior authorization were not completed until much later. The original cost of the 940.5 miles of canals that ultimately constituted the state system was approximately $23,-225,000, a comparatively modest sum. But, as with certain other instrumentalities of human devising, the burden of the state has not been in the original cost: its problem has been that of upkeep. It is true that initial outlay and current charges have been offset in part by revenues derived from tolls, yet since 1882 the state's return has been wholly of an "intangible" nature: the collection of tolls ceased at that time.

The first program of enlargement was undertaken in 1836 and completed in 1862. Included in this program were the Erie, the Oswego, and the Cayuga and Seneca canals, upon which was spent more than $35,000,-000. By this expenditure the depth was increased from 4 to 7 feet, the surface width from 40 to 70 feet, and the width at bottom from 28 to 56 feet. Upon the original canals tons carried and tolls collected tended to increase steadily until 1862; following that date tonnage continued to increase, reaching and maintaining a high level during the years from 1868 to 1880; but, because toll charges were gradually lowered, collections declined from the peak in 1862 until free use was given. After the abolition of tolls the volume of traffic declined little for another decade; then a gradual but steady shrinkage appeared that continued until the opening of the new canals in 1918. But prior to a complete revision of major channels in 1903 a second enlargement had been undertaken by the state: an extensive program of lock lengthening was begun in 1884 and continued until no further appropriations were forthcoming; and in 1895, following a popular vote, the proceeds of a $9,000,000 bond issue were spent on further enlargement work.

At this point the whole problem of future canal policy came before the people. A committee, appointed by Governor Theodore Roosevelt, recommended that an enlargement program be undertaken with respect to the Erie, Champlain, and Oswego canals, at an estimated cost of $62,000,000. After a spirited contest, the state was committed by popular vote to the construction of what have come to be known as the barge canals: the large majority in interested areas, notably New York City and Buffalo, swung the balance in the election. In 1903 bonds to the sum of $101,000,000 were issued to enlarge the three canals named, and in 1909 an additional issue of $7,000,000 was authorized to enlarge the Cayuga and Seneca canals. These sums proving inadequate, additional sums totaling $27,000,000 were approved in 1915. In 1911 a bond issue of $19,800,000 was authorized to construct canal-terminal properties. To 1929 it is estimated that the construction cost of the barge canals and terminals was approximately $176,000,000. To this large sum, to approximate total costs, must be added two major burdens: maintenance and operation, totaling approximately $39,500,000, and net capital costs of about $57,000,000. In the 3 years since 1929 total costs have increased by the sum of maintenance-operation and carrying charges, the net cost annually being typically in excess of $10,000,000. The people of New York state, therefore, seem to have invested in their present barge canals approximately $300,000,000; earlier investments may perhaps well be forgotten, since all but the barge units are now virtually unused.

The barge canals, upon which construction was completed in 1918, have a total length of 525 miles, including Seneca and Cayuga lakes. With a minimum surface width, bottom width, and depth of 123, 75, and 12 feet, respectively, and with locks that are actually about 340 by 45 feet, provision has been made for the handling of barges of unusual size and capacity for an artificial waterway. All necessary terminal facilities have been provided to handle a varied tonnage, including warehouses, grain elevators, loading machinery, and piers; indeed, to promote traffic development, facilities were provided in New York City and have there been maintained. Thus, for a period of years the state of New York has placed at the disposal of the shipping public a modern facility and, during that period, the number of tons handled has increased without break except in 1929: in 1931 the tonnage handled was more than two and a half times that of 1920. But, because of the financial burden, there has developed a demand for transfer to the federal government. This demand eventuated in a provision in the Rivers and Harbors Act of 1930 authorizing, if the state of New York shall approve, transfer of title to the federal government without cost of the Erie and Oswego sections, to be maintained and operated as navigable waterways of the United States. To this proposal strong opposition developed within a brief period; to some acceptance would mark the end of all hopes for an all-American ship canal, as well as of all hopes of reimbursement by the federal government of the state for earlier outlays if the all-American route were accepted; to others federal control represents a threat to those local interests for whose advantage the canal was built, and it is undoubtedly true that the earlier major canals contributed much to the foundation upon which the prosperity of New York state now rests, and have continued to contribute in some degree through later years.

The St. Lawrence Deep Waterway.—The most important inland waterway project now before the American people, both from the standpoint of expenditures involved and of the service that its proponents declare will be rendered the public, is the St. Lawrence Deep Waterway. From the earliest appearance of the French in Canada the St. Lawrence River was the chosen avenue of approach to the Great Lakes from that territory but this avenue was made difficult for commerce by the existence in the river of a series of difficult rapids and the barrier created by Niagara Falls. As early as 1783 canals with locks were built about two of the rapids between Lake St. Francis and Lake St. Louis and the first Welland Canal

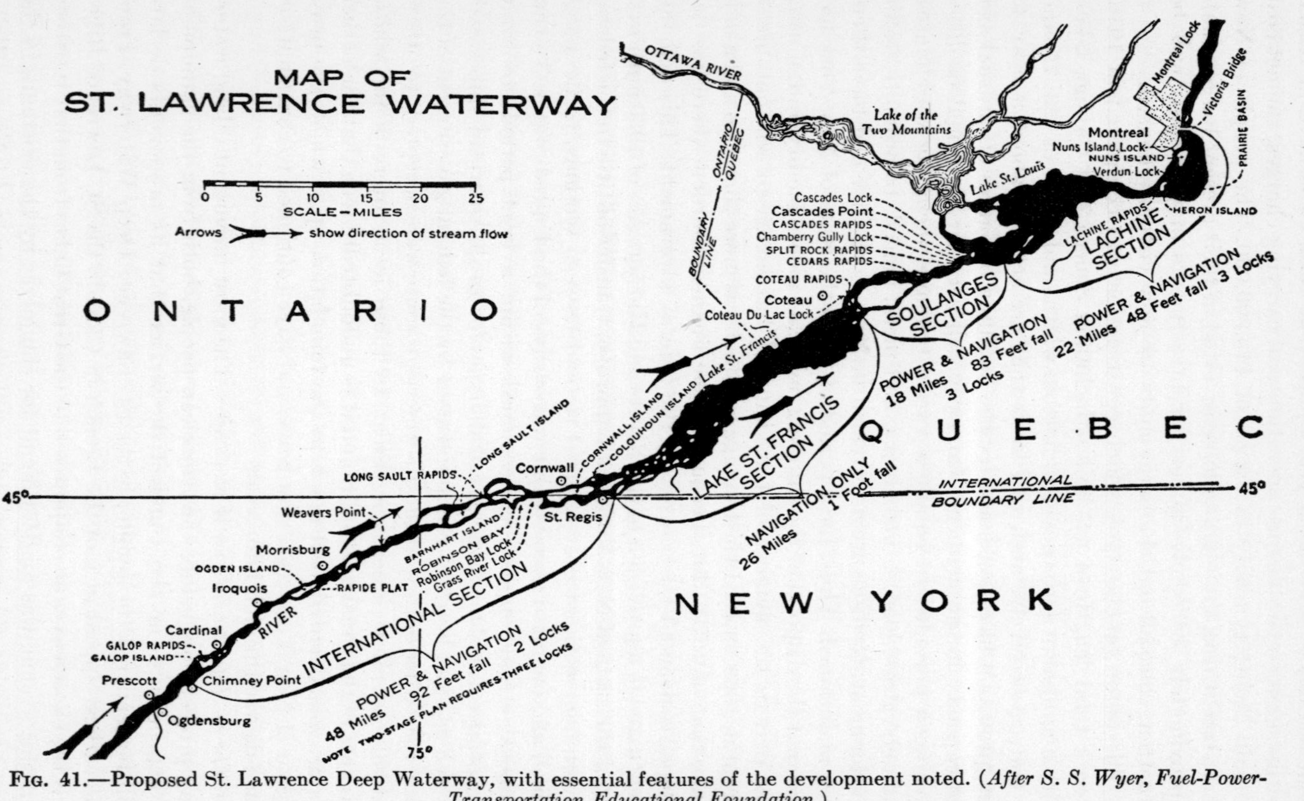

FIG. 41.—Proposed St. Lawrence Deep Waterway, with essential features of the development noted. (*After S. S. Wyer, Fuel-Power-Transportation Educational Foundation.*)

around Niagara Falls was opened to traffic in 1829. In due course canals and the necessary locks were constructed about all of the impeding rapids between Montreal and Chimney Point, beyond which navigation is clear, the canals having a minimum depth of 14 feet and the locks dimensions of approximately 270 by 45 feet. In 1887 the work on an enlarged Welland Canal was completed, the new undertaking conforming in draft and size of locks to those measurements just given for the canals above Montreal. Thus the project stood until Canada decided, shortly before the World War, to provide a ship channel between Lakes Erie and Ontario at an estimated cost of $50,000,000. In 1931 the New Welland Canal was opened; this project, with a canal depth of 27 feet and locks 820 by 80 feet (30 feet of water on the sills), was completed at a cost of $116,000,000.

The program for the enlargement of the passage from Erie to Ontario, increased shipments of American grain to Europe via Montreal because of railway congestion in the United States, together with a revival of interest in the development of water transportation and an increase in railway rates, led to action in behalf of a "shipway to the sea" immediately following the World War. In 1919 there was formed the Great Lakes-St. Lawrence Tidewater Association, the membership of which comprises states that have become convinced of the advantages of the St. Lawrence project to themselves. These states, numbering in excess of 20, have financed the activities of the Association in the intervening years in a sufficiently generous manner so that, under expert direction, the conviction has been firmly implanted in the minds of the people of a great area that economic necessity demands that the proposal be carried to completion. Upon the project there has been accumulated an astonishingly large mass of factual data, of testimony, and reports; concerning it, books have been written and endless discussion induced; and the "seaway" is commonly first-page news. In 1920 the International Joint Commission was appointed, giving a favorable report late in 1921. In 1924 the St. Lawrence Commission was appointed to study the problem for the United States, with Herbert Hoover, then Secretary of Commerce, at its head; and in the same year Canada began a study of the problem through the National Advisory Commission. By these bodies a Joint Board of Engineers was selected to examine critically the conclusions of 1921 and to answer certain questions. The Joint Board confirmed the judgment of the earlier body as to the engineering feasibility of the undertaking and estimated the cost of the project at $509,300,000 for a 25-foot channel and a full development of power resources. For the 27-foot channel, favored by the Canadians, an estimate of $536,600,000 was offered. The St. Lawrence Commission, after weighing the all-American route urged by New York interests, recommended adherence to the St. Lawrence project and stressed the importance of the completion of the undertaking to the economic well-being of a great area in both the United States and Canada.

The Advisory Commission approved the project, though within certain limitations established by the economic and financial situation of Canada: a heavy debt burden, government ownership of a great railway mileage, and doubt as to the salability of Canada's portion of developed power were among the special limitations stressed. During the administration of President Hoover further progress was made, although the treaty fixing the terms of construction failed to obtain the approval of the United States Senate in the final session of the Seventy-second Congress.

Since the avowed and primary purpose of the St. Lawrence development is to reduce transportation costs to the people of a great area, and since the only aspect of cost that can be considered justly in appraising an undertaking is *total cost*, a statement at this point of other outlays consequent upon the construction of adequate ship channels of 27-foot depth between Montreal and Lake Ontario is pertinent. If single-stage development be assumed for the improvement of the St. Lawrence, to the estimated expenditure of some $109,000,000 for navigation alone must be added $71,000,000 which represents half the sum assignable jointly to navigation and power.[1] The necessary deepening of channels between Lake Erie and Lake Superior would entail a cost of $55,000,000, the replacement of the lock in St. Mary's River $6,500,000, and compensating works in the Niagara and St. Clair rivers $3,700,000; when to these sums $1,000,000 is added to cover the cost of further work on the New Welland Canal, a total of approximately $66,000,000 is obtained.[2]

Therefore, to make the Lakes accessible for ships of 25-foot draft, an estimated expenditure of some $246,000,000 would be required. But the record of major construction projects is replete with instances of final costs that were double, even three times, the estimates prepared by expert engineering organizations, while instances are few where costs on large undertakings remained within 150 per cent of the original figure. To increase the estimated cost, then, by half would not seem unreasonable; to increase it by a third quite conservative. Thus the construction cost becomes $328,000,000. Since interest during construction is a legitimate capital charge, this sum must be increased further: the rate of interest upon government funds may be estimated at 4 per cent and the official estimate of time required to complete the project is 8 years. Assuming an average rate of expenditure, interest would aggregate 16 per cent, giving a final total cost of approximately $380,000,000. To this must be added the cost of port development; extensive dredging will be required and it will be necessary to build breakwaters as well as piers and all other terminal facilities. An estimate of the cost of such development must at best be approximate, but an examination of harbor costs and of the position of the

[1] Senate Document 183, 66th Congress, 2d Session, *The St. Lawrence Waterway Project*, p. 48.

[2] *Ibid.*, p. 28.

various points of shipment upon the Great Lakes suggests approximately $455,000,000 as a reasonable minimum.[1] If so little as 8 per cent be added to cover interest during cost of construction, a sum in excess of $490,000,000 appears, an astounding figure and yet not to be so regarded when it is realized that the opening of the St. Lawrence to ocean shipping would add almost 3,800 miles to the coastline of the United States. And if the expected volume of traffic from that opening is realized, such harbor development costs are almost certain. But, to be conservative, let the estimate of harbor costs be reduced by one-third: the total additional cost to the people of Canada and the United States—and largely to the latter—of a shipway to the sea would still seem (ignoring power costs) to be almost $710,000,000. Upon this sum annual carrying charges would be approximately $28,500,000, to which must be added certain other expenditures: outlays for maintenance of locks and channels, for maintenance of harbors, and administration. It is unlikely that these costs would be less than $7,500,000 per year. In short, the yearly burden, beyond commitments already made as illustrated by the New Welland Canal and other existing structures, resulting from the proposed development of a shipway from the Great Lakes to the sea would be in excess of $35,000,000.

Other Projects.—While innumerable other proposals to facilitate inland navigation have been made, they urge developments that are widely scattered and none has significance comparable to those which have been discussed. Funds are being expended with considerable regularity upon many streams tributary to the Atlantic and to the Gulf and for some of these streams important developments are urged; of this the effort to win support for the canalization of the Trinity River into northern Texas is illustrative. Upon the west coast the Sacramento and San Joaquin have received attention and it is probable that proposals for the development of navigation upon the Columbia and the Snake will be urged with increasing insistence. While many canals have been suggested to supplement river and open water navigation only one, in addition to

[1] Expenditures in the Chicago district might be expected, upon the basis of all facts, to exceed $75,000,000—probably by a wide margin. At Duluth-Superior, Port Arthur-Fort William, Milwaukee, Detroit, Toledo, Cleveland, and Buffalo, an average outlay of $25,000,000 would seem to be conservative. And Toronto would undoubtedly add to the investment of $40,000,000 already made in her harbor. At such points as Gary, Green Bay, Muskegon, Sandusky, Erie, Rochester, Oswego, and Hamilton, expenditures of $10,000,000 may be anticipated. Then there are perhaps 20 ports of the type of Ashland, Marquette, Racine, Port Huron, Ashtabula, Windsor, and Port Stanley where outlays would average $5,000,000. And to these must be added at least 10 lesser ports upon each of which half that sum might well be spent: among these are Manitowoc, Manistee, Fairport, Dunkirk, and Kingston. Nor will port development be restricted to the ports considered in this estimate: there are at least 35 others along the United States shore line that are of sufficient political and/or economic importance to have benefited from federal aid since 1910.

those discussed in the course of preceding pages, merits mention, and it is an old proposal revived primarily as an aid to the industries of the Beaver and Mahoning valleys that center about Youngstown. This canal would be built from the mouth of Indian Creek on Lake Erie to the Ohio at the mouth of the Beaver; it would utilize canalized rivers in so far as possible, surmounting a maximum rise of 177 feet. Its length would be slightly in excess of 100 miles, with cost estimated at more than $100,000,000. Another old project for which recent support has appeared is a connection between Lake Michigan and Lake Erie, this time by Fort Wayne, with a channel from that place to the Ohio. Recent years have been prolific with both waterway proposals and waterway accomplishments and it will be interesting to see what the next decade brings forth. Though for a time it seemed that a revived interest in governmental economy might tend to delay the completion of projects already authorized and block temporarily the approval of others, the success of waterway advocates in bringing channel development within the field of the public-works program bids fair to speed progress beyond the highest hopes of a few years ago.

(References for this chapter will be found at the close of Chap. XXXVI.)

CHAPTER XXXVI

INLAND WATERWAYS: ECONOMIC ANALYSIS

THE first appropriation of federal funds for the improvement of rivers and harbors was authorized in 1824. As the years passed and federal aid became an accepted policy, the tendency of appropriations was upward and the inevitable exploitation by individual members of Congress of opportunities afforded for local advantage became increasingly difficult to prevent. The more was this true as flood control received recognition and expenditures for navigation and flood control became more difficult of segregation. In a summary of federal outlays upon rivers and harbors for the 108 years from 1824 to 1932, it appears that a total of $1,899,901,116 was expended.[1] Of this grand total it is of interest to note that approximately $580,000,000 has been spent in the 7 fiscal years following July 1, 1925. For the completion of projects already begun or approved as of 1932 it was estimated an additional $400,000,000 would be required, yet it is probable that this sum will be exceeded by a considerable margin except as present authorizations are modified. And if the St. Lawrence project be approved, the grand total will be increased by a further sum. But, if the total outlay upon inland waterways since 1824 were to be ascertained, to the federal expenditures would have to be added hundreds of millions spent by the states during more than a century: to the state total the state of New York alone has contributed approximately $300,000,000 since the inception of the barge canals project in 1903.

Of the grand total of federal expenditures up to June 30, 1932, as shown above, however, considerable sums were spent for purposes but indirectly related to inland navigation: approximately $634,000,000 had been spent for seacoast harbors and channels; almost $205,000,000 upon lake harbors and channels; some $315,000,000 upon flood control along the Mississippi and its tributaries; and almost $48,000,000 upon the hydroelectric development at Muscle Shoals. In short, the federal outlay for *navigation purposes* for the period covered was about $456,000,000 for the Mississippi-Ohio system and about $237,000,000 for the intracoastal and other inland waterways. But it is this total that has been increased with greatest rapidity in recent years, and it will continue to mount as existing approved projects are pushed to completion. While a basis for accurate estimate is lacking, it seems probable that the additional ex-

[1] United States Army, Chief of Engineers, *Annual Report*, 1932, Pt. 1, p. 13.

penditures necessary to complete and round out our present program of inland waterway development will be sufficient to give a total outlay of not less than $1,200,000,000. This represents a considerable expenditure for what is by many regarded as an auxiliary system of transport, and unquestionably a mode of transport the benefits of which will be reaped primarily by restricted areas. The question immediately arises: is such expenditure justified? While a categorical judgment will not—and perhaps cannot—be given, certain facts will be presented with a view to assisting the reader to a more accurate evaluation of some of the major accomplishments and proposals. As a first step to this goal a brief discussion of types of waterways will be offered.

Types of Channels.—Certain streams and other channels are of such nature that, without expenditure or at slight cost, they can be navigated by craft of sufficient tonnage to justify economically their operation at that particular time and place. To routes of this character the term of *natural waterway* has been aptly applied. Perhaps one of the best illustrations of such a waterway is the Rhine, which for a long distance inland is navigable by boats of considerable draft. A channel that has loomed large in American development is the Hudson River, and used by the smaller craft of earlier days with but a minimum of preparation were the lower reaches of many other important streams tributary to the Atlantic, the Gulf, and the Pacific. And, when the inadequacy of land transport was such as to permit of the economical operation of small craft upon the upper reaches of streams that penetrated deeply into the hinterland, those streams might be regarded rightly as natural waterways; for the bateau or the steamer of small draft, competing with "freighter" or pack mule, great reaches of inland waters were navigated with but minor expenditures upon the channel. But with the coming of the railway, which provided overland movement at but a fraction of the cost in time and money that such movement had previously imposed, these smaller craft could no longer compete and many channels did not permit passage to the larger craft demanded by the change in the competitive situation. The Missouri River, for example, was no longer navigable to Fort Benton, the theoretical "head of navigation"; with lessening frequency boats reached Sioux City, Omaha, St. Joseph and Atchison, and Kansas City until at length the "Big Muddy" carried only its heavy burden of silt as it rolled toward the Mississippi. By 1900 there were few stretches of natural waterway upon our rivers except close to the sea and, because no extensive development in accordance with plan had been undertaken, the mileage of inland waterways suitable for effective navigation was small.

Yet many reaches of river once economically navigable may be made so again by the expenditure of limited sums for dredging, for construction to facilitate movement about rapids, and for other like purposes: the channel provided by nature is used as a base and upon it a serviceable waterway is builded. Of this type of waterway perhaps the most important in the United States is the lower Mississippi: federal expenditures have made possible the movement of tonnage upon that section of the river at all but exceptional periods, yet no great engineering works have been essential nor have excessive outlays been required for channel maintenance. From this situation, however, river projects advance by small degrees to the point where man contributes quite as much as does nature to the provision of a channel adequate for navigation; illustrative of this has been the development of a 9-foot channel upon the Ohio and the development of a like channel upon the upper Mississippi, work upon which is under way. And then there are those streams to which nature fails to contribute even a sufficient volume of water for navigational purposes, much less a satisfactory channel; except as sufficient diversion of water from Lake Michigan is permitted, flowage in the canalized Illinois River will be less than that demanded by a 9-foot channel, and the most puzzling feature of the proposed Trinity River development is an adequate water supply.

A third type of channel commanded a high degree of public interest in developed areas prior to the appearance of the railway and, though enthusiasm for such construction persists, interest is less active and less general. This type is the artificial waterway, or canal. As compared with the natural waterway and with the waterway that requires no major expenditure to make it serviceable, the canal labors under certain disadvantages: its banks are less stable under the wash of passing boats than those of most rivers; its course is fixed largely by the contour of the area through which it is built, populous centers being tapped largely by chance; extra widths at points along the route for passing or for terminals are to be had only at considerable additional expense; periods of high water will not permit the passage of boats of unusual draft, as will high water upon rivers; the cost of construction is materially increased by the necessity of acquiring land and the difficulties of operation are augmented by the problem of a water supply; and, finally, the outlay for excavation and for the construction of locks upon a canal capable of accommodating craft that may be operated economically remains heavy, even though powerful machinery has been substituted for the wheelbarrow and shovel, in comparison with cost of railway building. The one considerable advantage which the canal enjoys over the typical inland waterway is its relative freedom from silting, though it is necessary to dredge canals from time to time because of the wash from the banks.

Canals may be grouped, generally speaking, into two classes: those designed for craft of small draft, such as the barge, and those intended to accommodate craft that operate upon the open seas. Of the former type there are a considerable number in operation in the United States, the most important system being the New York state barge canals. It is of this type that the coastal canals will be, largely, and such is the type of waterway that now constitutes the link between the Illinois River and Lake Michigan and will constitute other links between the Great Lakes and the Ohio-Mississippi system. Of canals to accommodate larger craft there are comparatively few, either in the United States or elsewhere: the cost of construction is prohibitive except under particular circumstances and the utilization of such channels would be negligible except as peculiar advantages accrue. Such a project merits consideration, in general, under three conditions: when it is to connect adjacent navigable waters upon which a heavy traffic would move except for a barrier in the form of rapids, a narrow strip of land, or some other obstacle to continuous movement; when a comparatively short canal will make possible a great reduction in the length of voyage or permit escape from the navigation of dangerous waters; and when a short canal from open water will give an important community, located inland, free access to that water. Of each of these types illustration may be found in the United States as well as abroad: of the first the Sault Saint Marie Canal between Lakes Superior and Huron, the New Welland Canal between Lakes Erie and Ontario, and the proposed St. Lawrence Deep Waterway are conspicuous examples; of the second the Panama Canal is illustrative, with the Suez Canal a comparable work, while the Kiel Canal not only permits a saving in distance between the North and Baltic seas but also obviates the navigation of difficult waters through the Skagerrak and Kattegat; of the third the outstanding American example is the Houston Ship Canal, with the Manchester Ship Canal and channels giving access to certain important cities adjacent to the North Sea widely known. Among the obstacles to the use of ship canals except as gains loom large are the necessity of lower speed, the risk of grounding due to the narrow channel and to the difficulty of control in restricted waters, and increased insurance costs consequent upon the risk just stated. Though investment in any canal project merits close scrutiny under modern conditions, such scrutiny is particularly in point with respect to the construction of channels for the use of larger craft. It is this scrutiny that has raised, in the minds of many, points of doubt that have not yet been wholly resolved concerning the St. Lawrence proposal.

Waterways: Inherent Disadvantages.—In behalf of the development of inland waterways the one fundamental argument urged by all proponents of such a program is a lower cost of movement. This lower cost will follow, it is urged, from the fact that waterways are provided by nature and that the tractive power necessary to move a given tonnage upon the water is less than by rail or highway; in consequence, both the capital charges and operating expenses chargeable against a unit of traffic will be reduced because of water transport. And, because waterway charges are lower, the maintenance of water competition is often justified as an automatic regulator of railway rates. With respect to the assertion of lower cost, the question of fact arises: to the extent that nature *does* provide a satisfactory channel, capital costs are minimized; and, to the extent that movement by water *is* less expensive than by other agencies, operating costs are reduced. That waterway competition has tended to reduce railway rates between certain points is undoubtedly true, yet to justify the expenditure of public funds upon a waterway on this basis alone is difficult: it assumes the inability of regulatory bodies to establish a reasonable level of rates; it ignores the possible necessity of increasing railway rates elsewhere to maintain a fair return for the property as a whole; and it neglects the economic obligation to rest waterway expenditures upon the probability that the given project will render a needed transport service at an equal or lower social cost.

In stating the advantages of the railways as an explanation of the decline in waterway tonnage through a long period prior to the study made by that body, the National Waterways Commission designated those advantages as inherent or fundamental and artificial or temporary.[1] Of the former the first and most important was declared to be the wider area of distribution available to the railway because railway lines can be constructed to any portion of the country while the location of waterways is fixed within narrow limits by nature; present needs are more adequately met and adaptations to changed conditions more readily made by the railways. A second advantage of the railway lies in the fact that its terminals are generally better adapted to handling shipments than are those of water carriers, a result in part of the fact that railway terminals are built and modified to meet particular needs and in part of the fact that those terminals are more accessible to industrial and commercial organizations. A third advantage lies in the readier transfer of traffic from one railway to another than from land to water or water to land—and often from one water route to another.

In this connection may be mentioned a physical disadvantage of rivers, due to the very considerable oscillation in their levels. This fact makes it more difficult to provide convenient and adequate loading machinery and renders the receipt and shipment of freight proportionately more expensive. The variation in the Ohio River at Cincinnati is over 60 feet; that of the Mississippi at Grafton, Ill., below the mouth of the Illinois River, is 29.6 feet; at St. Louis 43.92 feet; below Cairo and the mouth of the Ohio River, 45.6 feet; between Memphis and Helena, 54.75 feet; at Vicksburg, 58.98 feet; and at New Orleans 21.02 feet.[2]

A fourth advantage of the railway, as a rule, arises from quicker delivery. This results from greater speed per hour by rail, from shorter rail

[1] *Preliminary Report of the National Waterways Commission*, 62d Congress, 2d Session, Senate Documents, vol. 15, pp. 68–70.

[2] *Ibid.*, p. 69.

distances between points,[1] and from the ability of railways to adhere more closely to schedule. And to these advantages must be added the rendition of continuous service throughout the year by railways as against the recognized seasonal character of water service over many of the more important developed and proposed projects, a condition that has the objectionable social result of duplicating transport facilities to the extent that the periods of water navigation and heavy traffic demands do not overlap.

To an evaluation of these advantages of railway as against inland water transport an examination of certain facts is essential. That the railway enjoys a wider area of distribution than the waterway without the cost in time and effort of transshipment is indubitable and certain it is, also, that the interchange of traffic among railways is more easily effected than between water and either rail or motor lines. In this latter connection it must be added, too, that the inability or inadvisability of developing all inland channels in accord with a single standard will necessitate many transfers of water-borne cargoes that would be obviated by standard gage if made by rail. Improvements in methods used to meet fluctuations in river levels will tend to lessen that obstacle to the interchange of tonnage between water and land, yet the fluctuation will remain a problem. The advantage that the railways have enjoyed and continue to enjoy generally with respect to terminal facilities need not of necessity persist indefinitely: probably no railway is more adequately equipped in this particular than are the New York state barge canals and it is likely that, as waterways are made ready for use and as traffic upon them increases in volume, municipalities and operators will make provision for the more economical and adequate handling of tonnage. The question of

[1] The distances by rail and water between certain important points in the Mississippi Valley are:

Cities	Water mileage	Rail mileage	Percentage of excess, water mileage
St. Paul—St. Louis	683	585	17
St. Louis—New Orleans	1,164	709	64
Pittsburgh—St. Louis	1,170	612	91
Pittsburgh—Memphis	1,206	773	56
Kansas City—St. Louis	407	279	46
Sioux City—St. Louis	825	479	72
Chicago—St. Louis	369	284	30

In computing rail mileages no effort was made to find the shortest distance; in each instance a commonly used route was taken, two-line hauls being used only where the one-line is obviously circuitous.

more speedy delivery is fundamentally a question of fact. Rarely will the mileage between important points by water be less than a third greater than the rail mileage, and water mileage often approximates 50 per cent in excess of rail. Further, flood and drouth will not interfere with scheduled operations of railways as they are likely to do with waterway movements, though this advantage of the land carrier has been offset at times by congestion that slowed the movement of tonnage sharply and even compelled embargoes for a period. Yet it must be admitted that improved organization and better use of facilities have enabled the railways to handle since 1922 a succession of record tonnages with remarkable freedom from congestion or car shortage.

Speed of delivery is determined to a considerable degree, however, by speed of movement between point of origin and point of destination—and here there develops a sharp difference between the apparent and the real. The long freight train thunders by at a speed of 25 to 45 miles per hour, while the tow of barges will creep quietly past: downstream a large tow will average not more than 6 miles per hour and upstream the rate will be not to exceed 3 miles per hour upon the sluggish lower Mississippi.[1] None the less, there is in the rivalry of the freight car and the barge a suggestion of the race between the tortoise and the hare. In commenting upon this relation an outstanding railway executive declared that, while he was in the service of the Baltimore and Ohio, "It was a common occurrence that a mule-drawn barge-load of coal would leave Cumberland via the canal [the Potomac and Cumberland] at the same time a carload of coal was leaving Cumberland via the railroad, both destined to Washington, distance 152 miles, and that the barge would arrive before the freight car."[2] And such conditions persisted as late as 1917, during a period of traffic congestion, the same executive declares. Because of delays in terminals through which cars must pass, because of time lost upon passing tracks between terminals, and because of other interference, it is probable that the average speed of loaded cars between points of origin and destination is not in excess of 12 miles per hour during periods of normal traffic—with the rate increasing as the volume of tonnage declines and diminishing as that volume increases. True, even this low speed in conjunction with the greater distance that shipments must move by water gives to the railway a material time advantage, yet that advantage is much less than is commonly thought to be the case.

Upon all inland waterways above 38 degrees north latitude, seasonal interruptions to navigation must be expected: while dates will vary,

[1] Ashburn, Major General T. Q., Waterway Transportation from the Viewpoint of Operation, *Transactions of the American Society of Civil Engineers*, vol. 95, p. 866.

[2] Loree, L. F., *Deep-water Navigation between Lake Erie and Tidewater*, an address before the Atlantic Deeper Waterways Association Convention, Troy, N. Y., Sept. 20, 1929, p. 13.

river and canal service is subject to intermittent or continued interruptions from early December to early March, with the hiatus progressively greater as one proceeds northward. In general, the open season will permit of the movement of much of the wheat and to that extent inland waterways will assist in meeting a peak demand; in general, however, the open season will overlap only in part the period of heavy coal movements and therefore will not preclude the need of rail facilities to handle coal in large volume. In short, then, the addition of waterways represents in part a duplication of existing facilities, in part provision of a supplementary service—with social justification differing materially in the two cases.

Waterways: Artificial Disadvantages.—In its discussion of the decline of waterway traffic in the years prior to 1910 the National Waterways Commission mentioned certain artificial disadvantages of water movement that merit a brief review if for no other reason than to indicate how far the United States has progressed in a score of years toward "equality of opportunity" for water carriers. Most important of these handicaps was said to be "the right of the railway to charge lower rates between points where their line is in competition with water routes." Inability of the Interstate Commerce Commission to deal with this situation through a long period made it possible for the railways to eliminate the water carrier from the field by abnormally low rates, after which inter- and often intrastate rates could be advanced to old levels with impunity. A second handicap arose from the power of the railways "to acquire steamboat lines or to enter into agreements with them for the purpose of stifling waterborne traffic, either by operating the steamboat lines or discontinuing their use upon competitive routes." A third disadvantage of water lines resulted from the refusal of the railways "to prorate on through routes where naturally freight would be carried part of the way by rail and part by water. In many cases the route, which apparently is the natural one, would be by water for three-fourths or more of the distance, yet the charge for the remaining railway haul is so considerable as to render carriage for the longer haul by water unprofitable." A fourth burden upon water movement has been the inadequacy of terminals upon inland routes: "On many of the waterways very little if any progress has been made during the last 50 years in furnishing modern facilities for the storage or handling of traffic," a situation sharply in contrast to that found by the Commission upon the inland waterways of Europe.

In the year in which the preliminary report, from which quotations have just been made, was published, Sec. 4 of the Interstate Commerce Act was so amended as to give the Interstate Commerce Commission full power over departures from the long-and-short-haul principle. This power has been exercised to curb unreasonable practices of the railways with respect to water traffic: its exercise, with the further aid of a provision forbidding an increase in any rail rate lowered to meet water competition except as some other justification for such increase were shown than the disappearance of water competition, has removed quite completely for inland waterways the threat of destructive rail competition. The second danger to water traffic, being stifled by the railways through the control of competing boat lines, was eliminated by the Panama Canal Act of 1912. This measure forbids ownership of or interest in water carriers by a railway with which that railway competes or may compete for traffic. Indeed, it went even further: to break port and dock monopolies railways are required to make like terms with all water lines for the interchange of traffic and the Interstate Commerce Commission is empowered to order physical connections between rail and water facilities, and is also given certain limited powers over rates on traffic moving rail-and-water.

The refusal of the railways to join with water lines in the establishment of joint rail-and-water rates continued to be an obstacle to the development of waterway tonnage until the passage of the Denison Act in 1928. Under this Act common carriers by water are authorized to apply to the Interstate Commerce Commission for a certificate of convenience and necessity, as do railways; if such certificate be granted the Commission shall

> thereupon, by order, direct all connecting common carriers and their connections to join with such water carrier in through routes and joint rates with reasonable rules, regulations, and practices . . . and . . . shall in such order, fix reasonable minimum differentials between all-rail rates and joint rates in connection with said water service.

Thus, by the exercise of mandatory powers bestowed upon the Commission in 1912 and strengthened in 1928, the common carrier by water is today in a position to share upon equitable terms in any tonnage that might advantageously move a portion of its total distance by boat. And evidence is clear that the final artificial handicap of water transport is in the process of removal: terminal facilities are being provided rapidly by cities located upon navigable channels and investments are also being made by carriers using those channels. Thus it appears that every artificial or temporary handicap under which waterways operated early in 1910 has been destroyed or effectively minimized: water traffic in the future, therefore, need face only the fundamental advantages enjoyed by land movement—with the waterway's major strength in the public mind being its asserted capacity to serve at a materially lower cost per ton-mile.

The Problem of Costs.—Before proceeding with the discussion of particular projects, it will be well to give attention to this question of the cost of traffic movement by water, for it is this question that stands at the center of the controversy between the advocates and opponents of extensive waterway development; upon a reasonable, definite answer to this question must the determination of public policy largely depend.

Because there are two quite different views of "cost of shipment by waterway," it is essential that these be stated and a judgment passed upon them. The user of waterway service is interested in what he *pays* for the movement of traffic; almost without exception in the United States cost to him is a sum merely sufficient to cover operating expenses on a waterway made available by nature or by public outlays. To society, on the other hand, it is *total cost* that is significant: the amount paid by the shipper is of concern to the public at large only as any difference between this sum and the aggregate social burden of the service rendered indicates the extent to which a limited group benefits at the expense of the body politic. Obviously, it is the *social cost* of transport, rather than the *quoted rate*, that is of concern to the student.

What are the elements that enter into the determination of the social cost of transport by water? In general, they are of the same character as those which enter into the determination of the cost of transport by rail, by highway, by air: the social cost for a given year includes interest upon the investment, depreciation upon all properties contributing to the service, adequate maintenance, movement costs, and taxes. In fixing the investment upon which interest is to be computed, the only proper procedure is to include therein all properties "used and useful" to navigation as of that year: to omit items wholly because they may have value also for other purposes, such as flood control, is no less erroneous than to include expenditures for channel maintenance during past decades or outlays for structures that have long since passed into the limbo of forgotten things. Among items "used and useful" in the case of inland waterways will be dams of various types, locks, artificial channels, levees, revetments, floating equipment, terminal facilities, and like tangible items—and these must be included at full value without regard to the incidental fact of ownership or charge therefor.

Upon every item included in the investment account adequate depreciation must be charged; except as this is done the various capital items will have to be replaced at variable intervals by the expenditure of new funds instead of being replaced by the use of reserves. Naturally, too, all maintenance costs upon physical items as different as warehouses and channels are properly chargeable against traffic, the whole of this sum in a given year as well as the annual depreciation being chargeable against the service rendered in that year. Movement costs, those arising from the operation of equipment upon the waterway and including as major items fuel and labor, as a charge against water-borne traffic are familiar to the shipper; indeed, it is this burden, supplemented by interest and depreciation on floating equipment and by maintenance of such equipment, that has too often been termed "the cost of water transportation." And, finally, the element of taxes must be included. To the extent that properties used in the rendition of water service are private, it is obvious that taxes constitute an actual element in cost. But what is a proper policy in computing the social cost of transport with respect to the capital items owned by governmental units? And this question is the more important when such a large part of the permanent investment in water transport has been made by federal, state, and local authorities. The logic of the situation suggests that, since publicly owned docks and other terminal units displace like facilities that would be furnished by private capital except for the entry of government into the field, and sometimes are so furnished, taxes upon all items "used and useful" be considered as an element in social cost. The whole of the Keokuk dam across the Mississippi is taxed by appropriate jurisdictions, yet a portion of its value is clearly assignable to navigation. Should not a tax charge be assigned to a project built at public cost in similar manner? This question, upon which there are much divergence of thought and some doubt, merits careful thought.

This distinction between the *charge* for the service and the *social cost* of that service can be further clarified, perhaps, by an actual illustration. The average rate per ton-mile paid by shippers upon the New York state barge canals in 1929 approximated 4.5 mills. In rendering this service use was made of a plant that cost the state of New York as of 1929 about $175,000,000; some $3,621,000 was expended by the state for maintenance and operation; and if no more than 3 per cent be charged for physical and functional depreciation upon the composite waterway and terminal properties, an additional charge of approximately $5,250,000 lies against the service. If interest be computed at 4 per cent, then the cost to the state of providing the waterway for 1929 was $15,871,000. Since in that year some 715,551,000 ton-miles of service were rendered, the state contributed toward each ton-mile approximately 22.2 mills. In short, while the *charge* for the service was 4.5 mills, the *social cost* of that service was 26.7 mills.[1] Of course, it is but fair to note that as service rendered by the canal increases the contribution of the state to each ton-mile will decline: capital charges will remain constant, as will depreciation, while maintenance will not increase in proportion to canal use. And this is also true of river transport for like reasons. Yet, however rapidly tonnage may mount and ton-miles of service rendered increase, a measure of "hidden cost" will remain in the case of any waterway that is operated toll-free or with tolls fixed at a point below actual cost. Instead of denying the existence of such uncompensated outlays, or ignoring them as is done by many waterway advocates, recognition of them in formulating a program of development would evidence wisdom and, in the long run, promote the legitimate development of waterways. It is unreasonable to

[1] That the *social cost* of transportation upon the barge canals may not contain any element concerning which there could be dispute, no estimated sum is included in aggregate annual costs for taxation of state-owned properties.

expect the public to accept in its reasoned moments a program that carries the threat of continued subsidies to certain interests or areas, and it is equally unfair to have projects that are justified economically imperiled by public prejudice grounded upon serious errors in past policy. Decision upon proposals to develop waterways should rest upon *facts*, weighed by an open mind—and not upon political advantage or local self-interest, too often factors.

Judgment upon a Proposed Waterway.—One group of facts upon which decision concerning a proposed waterway should depend relates to the probable cost of providing a navigable channel. These facts should be determined by competent engineers, such determination resting upon the basis of detailed surveys of the territory to be traversed by a canal or of the river to be prepared for craft of particular draft. Incidental to the examination of surface conditions borings must be made and a record of rainfall, with water levels, compiled. Then careful estimates must be made of the cost of preparing a channel and maintaining the same; or, if slack-water navigation is advantageous, the probable cost of structures must be determined. And, finally, when all appropriate costs of a feasible plan have been estimated, allowance should be made in the light of experience with similar projects for any excess of actual cost over estimated.

A second essential to a judgment upon a projected waterway is an estimate of the volume of traffic that may be expected to move by water when construction is done. Such a judgment is difficult to reach and always vulnerable to attack: to reach a conclusion so many uncertainties must be resolved in favor or against—and this makes an impartial conclusion altogether too rare. In making a study of potential traffic, each class of prospective originated tonnage must be analyzed separately. This analysis must consider the adaptability of the particular class to water movement and the importance of speed in handling that class; it must examine carefully the character of production of the areas served and the extent to which those products may move in the direction of the proposed water route; alternative routes, both actual and potential, must be scrutinized; the likelihood of a balanced traffic must be ascertained; the period of heavy tonnage movement from the area and into it must be compared with the period during which the waterway is open, if a closed season exists; methods of commodity sale, marketing arrangements, and preferences of consignors and consignees, must be given weight. And possible inbound movements must be subjected to analysis in the same manner as outbound. Effort must be made, too, to determine the possibilities of developing new "heavy industries," using low-grade raw materials and producing goods to which freight rates are highly significant —or developing such existing industries on a larger scale.

In the face of such complexities, it is not strange that estimates vary widely, when made. And the greater, too, will be the divergence as partisanship enters. Perhaps one of the most interesting contrasts in this particular is to be found in the figures of probable tonnage for the St. Lawrence project. Mr. A. H. Ritter has estimated the probable movement by water at 30,000,000 tons; the United States Department of Commerce fixed the figure at 21,800,000 to 26,500,000 tons; the United States St. Lawrence Commission suggested 21 to 25,000,000 tons; and Mr. H. G. Moulton and associates of the Brookings Institution put the total at 10,500,000. Mr. Ritter's study was made under the auspices of, and published by, the Great Lakes-St. Lawrence Tidewater Association, a promotional and propaganda organization; the estimate of the Department of Commerce was made while Herbert Hoover, an ardent advocate of waterway development in general and the St. Lawrence project specifically, was Secretary; the estimate of the St. Lawrence Commission was made with Herbert Hoover as chairman of that body; and it is charged by waterway advocates that the estimate of Mr. Moulton and associates, the only analysis that has been made by a disinterested group, reflects "his anti-waterway complex." To the extent that this challenge of Mr. Moulton's impartiality be well-founded, no impartial judgment of probable tonnage is available—yet that major lack has not been permitted to dampen the insistence of St. Lawrence Deep Waterway advocates upon immediate action. For the protection of the public treasury it is high time that knowledge displace belief as a basis of action, that traffic data displace hope.

But, assuming that traffic probabilities are such as to justify the construction of a particular project at a cost estimated by the engineers, there remain two final considerations of fundamental significance. The first of these has to do with special benefits. Can the waterway be provided and operated under a financial plan which will impose upon those who are to profit from it a major part, at least, of the costs? A system of doles to particular areas or communities is socially unsound. The second consideration has to do with the question of transport policy. Other transport agencies serve in the area for the benefit of which the proposed waterway is to be constructed. What will be the effect of such a waterway upon those agencies? If injury to them results, will that injury be minor or will it be sufficient to imperil the solvency of transport systems that are indispensable to the public? In short, does the projected waterway have a proper place in a national transportation plan, a plan under which the public as a whole is to be accorded maximum service through a period of years at minimum total cost? A problem of statesmanship arises here.

Observations Concerning the Barge Canals.—The fight for the approval of the barge-canal plan in New York was led by interested groups and was successful against the almost united opposition of those portions of the state that could hope for no direct benefit from the enlargement of the old system. For a period of 15 years the new system was in preparation; when opened, it was estimated to have a maximum capacity of 20,000,000 tons. Though the volume of tonnage moved has been disappointingly small, that volume has steadily increased since navigation began with but a single break, in 1929.[1] The striking increase in 1930 was occasioned largely by sharp upturns in the tonnage of petroleum and other oils, largely by the Standard groups in tankers, and a marked increase in the volume of wheat moved, much of which was Canadian grain moving to New York in bond for export. Increases in 1931 of the tonnage of oils, articles of iron or steel, and sugar more than offset certain important declines in products of the ground—principally sand, gravel, stone, and sulphur. In 1931 manufactured products, including oils, contributed almost half of the total; products of agriculture contributed slightly in excess of one-third; and products of forest and ground and miscellaneous contributed the remainder.

What the economic future of the barge canals may be is problematical. Yet there is little in their situation thus far to give hope that at any time in the predictable future the volume of tonnage will be such as to justify the state's expenditure. In fact, if the St. Lawrence project is carried to completion, it seems undoubted that its influence will be to lessen tonnage moving via canal to New York and tonnage moving in return. Certain it is, also, that New York state taxpayers are becoming wearied by the millstone of cost about their necks; as concrete evidence of this fact is the proposal that responsibility for operation be assumed by the federal government. Had approval of an all-American route been secured in lieu of the St. Lawrence, then the state might reasonably have expected to be reimbursed for much of its outlay. Failing that, the financial outlook is not a promising one. The barge canals are objects of pride to many and of profit to some, but the social justification of the work is clearly in doubt.

Observations: Intracoastal System.—Conceived during an era when the small craft plying in coastal trade were sorely buffeted by Atlantic storms and when overland transport moved solely by highway, the intracoastal system of canals had strong justification and wide appeal. That same system today, projected from Boston to Key West and expected

1

New York State Canals: Short Tons of Freight Moved*

Year	All canals	Erie division	Year	All canals	Erie division
1921	1,270,407	993,639	1927	2,581,892	2,047,774
1922	1,873,434	1,485,109	1928	3,089,998	2,535,684
1923	2,006,284	1,626,062	1929	2,876,160	2,422,204
1924	2,032,317	1,691,766	1930	3,605,457	3,044,271
1925	2,344,013	1,945,466	1931	3,722,012	3,277,936
1926	2,369,367	1,935,278			

* *Annual Report*, Superintendent of Public Works, state of New York.

ultimately to follow the Gulf coast to the Rio Grande, has far less to recommend it than it had a century ago.[1] Continuous navigation by boats of larger draft is rendered impossible by shallow sections and continuous navigation by barges is made difficult by stretches of open water that imperil such craft. Hauls are likely to be short and the volume of tonnage light except upon occasional sections. While it is quite probable that clear justification can be found for particular portions, it is highly questionable if an economic basis can be found for a major portion of the mileage. One of the more important proposals for which the Rivers and Harbors Act of 1930 authorized a survey, a ship canal from the Raritan River to the Delaware, seems to be of such definitely local value and interest that the justice of federal construction seems questionable; yet there are perhaps few sections of which the same comment cannot rightly be made.

Observations: Ohio River System.—Because of differences in conditions and use, the projects in this group fall under three heads. Of these the Monongahela is perhaps the outstanding instance of an inland waterway for which justification is clear. Flowing for almost its entire length through a rich coal field and a highly industrialized area, it is in a peculiarly strong position to attract tonnage; indeed, at many points coal can be loaded into barges from the mine tipple and moved directly for unloading to large steel plants and to the plants of other large users of coal. Large corporations operate their own boats and barges, many movements being little more than intraplant transportation by water. Total tonnage in a normal year approximates 25,000,000—of which approximately 99 per cent is of low grade: coal and coke are the two major items, with ores and sand and gravel also important. The average length of haul is short, not to exceed 45 miles. The total cost of this project has been less than $17,500,000, a modest sum as compared with the volume of business moved. The one transportation handicap lies in one-way loading, yet this is not a serious one in view of other advantages.

The second unit of the Ohio system is the Ohio River itself. This stream has its origin in one of the great tonnage areas of the continent, an area into which low-grade raw materials move in enormous quantity and from which a great volume of iron and steel products moves to wide markets. From the Pittsburgh district the stream passes through an industrialized section and close to rich coal areas; into this stream flow a number of smaller rivers that are capable of swelling its coal tonnage, in particular; upon its banks are located two major cities and a number of lesser importance; and, finally, it makes possible access by water to the markets of St. Louis and the whole lower Mississippi Valley. Further,

[1] Interest in these intracoastal canals received impetus during the World War as a consequence of the German submarine campaign. By using inland waters and connecting channels it was declared that danger from submarine interference could be almost wholly eliminated.

the Ohio roughly parallels an old and important route of trade. Though to a lesser degree than is true of the Monongahela, the advantages of the Ohio River are unusual. During the many years prior to the completion of slack-water navigation upon the river in 1929 tonnage was considerable, the maximum and minimum from 1895 to 1923 being approximately 14,000,000 and 5,500,000, respectively. As work progressed upon the 9-foot channel, the increase in tonnage was striking: the movement of 19,755,000 tons in 1926 was almost 2.4 times the movement of 1923. But since 1926 the growth in tonnage has been, while steady, relatively slow: the 22,337,000[1] tons of 1930 represented an increase of only 13 per cent above 1926, an average of but 3.25 per cent for each year. It appears, then, that the future is likely to bring slow increases rather than phenomenal gains. Upon this stream has been expended a large sum and upon tributaries which contribute to its tonnage considerable sums have also been spent. For the advantage which industries operating in this area have obtained in certain markets, only a minor indirect payment has been made. It will be of interest to learn the judgment of time upon this improvement.

The third portion of the Ohio system is comprised of the tributaries of the Ohio, excepting the Monongahela. To comment upon these in detail is impossible, but certain general observations may be made with regard to particular undertakings. Undoubtedly a certain minimum expenditure upon the Allegheny and the Youghiogheny is justified, yet it will require care not to carry improvements to a point where they represent a species of subventions to certain industries and small areas. The potential coal tonnage of the Kanawha perhaps justifies development of that stream, and the same justification may be urged for the Big Sandy; yet it is difficult to justify a 9-foot channel in the former and equally difficult to discover cause in tonnage data for expenditures upon other minor streams in that area. Indeed, the extension of navigable mileage to make bituminous-coal deposits more available would seem to run directly contrary to a proper public policy: of the major problems of this industry, it is certain that overdevelopment is outstanding and most difficult. But of the major tributaries of the Ohio, the development of the Tennessee on an important scale raises most serious doubts. With a channel of 4 feet normally available for a distance of some 225 miles,[2] its public service has been comparatively slight. Further, because rail distances are so much shorter from the upper Tennessee to such points as Louisville, Memphis, and New Orleans, shipment by water would appear to be uneconomical though the charge made be much less

[1] To the tonnage of the Ohio River in recent years coal and coke have contributed annually an average of some 9,500,000; sand, gravel, and stone an average of more than 9,200,000; and iron and steel about 1,500,000. In 1930 packet freight totaled 271,104 tons.

[2] *Transportation in the Mississippi and Ohio Valleys*, 1929, p. 33.

per ton-mile.[1] It will undoubtedly be feasible from an engineering standpoint to provide 9-foot and 6-foot channels upon the Tennessee River, but the wisdom of such action is open to serious challenge.

Of the total of 58,585,000 tons of freight handled on the Ohio and its tributaries in 1930, the Ohio carried 22,337,000 and the Monongahela 25,657,000. The remainder, some 10,591,000 tons, was contributed by all other units of this system. It is apparent from such data that, from an economic standpoint, the two streams named are the essential elements of this system. And there is every likelihood that they will continue to be.

Observations: The Lower Mississippi.—There are few more fascinating stories than that of transportation upon the Western rivers, with the gradual transition from canoe and "pirogue" to flatboat and keel boat and then to steamboat that steadily improved in adaptability and size until inland-waterway transport suffered definite eclipse. Because of the course of settlement, the Ohio and its tributaries had earlier significance than the Mississippi below Cairo; but, as population increased beyond the Appalachian Barrier, a cheap route to the outer world for surplus products and for items brought in for use became essential. Increasingly, therefore, the Ohio and the lower Mississippi became an important and continuous trade route. Early railways constructed were but supplementary to the rivers; with the extension of lines, however, and the establishment of advantageous routes from the Middle West to the North Atlantic ports, the lower river became of less significance to the northern valley states and its tonnage originated largely at points upon its own banks.

Yet at no time, seemingly, was there thought of permitting the Mississippi below Cairo to "revert to a state of nature": as early as 1879 the Mississippi River Commission was constituted by act of Congress and charged, among other things, with the maintenance of a navigable channel. The formation of bars at times limited the controlling depth to 4.5 feet; this, under the original plan, was to be increased to 10 feet,

[1] Distances from Chattanooga, Tenn., to important markets that can be reached both by river and rail when the Tennessee River improvement is complete are:

Cities	Water mileage	Rail mileage	Percentage of excess, water mileage
Cincinnati	928	338	175
Memphis	736	314	134
St. Louis	700	510	37
New Orleans	1,482	498	198

Thus it would appear that St. Louis is the only important center to which river transportation will give access upon a basis that is economically defensible.

but in 1896 the Commission was instructed to "maintain for low-water navigation below Cairo a channel of 250[1] feet width and 9 feet depth at all periods of the year except when stopped by ice."[2] The execution of this work has necessarily been inextricably interwoven with flood-control activities, so costs are almost impossible of accurate and complete allocation: few permanent works have been constructed below Cairo that are of value to navigation which do not also serve a function in flood control or bank protection.[3] Much of the cost of maintaining a navigable

TONNAGE UPON THE LOWER MISSISSIPPI*

Year	Cairo to Memphis	Memphis to Vicksburg	Vicksburg to New Orleans
1901	2,306,302	1,856,339	1,835,174
1906	1,719,893	2,355,901	2,554,336
1911	1,857,616	1,910,854	2,426,376
1916	1,205,667	1,809,977	2,234,238
1921	902,823	1,629,747	7,323,335
1926	1,660,188	4,792,780	11,074,488
1927	2,144,317	4,358,097	8,816,745
1928	2,531,256	4,803,840	8,654,626
1929	2,328,334	2,835,060	7,727,383
1930	2,831,347	2,377,568	9,177,705
1931	3,836,215	2,403,526	8,789,380

* *Transportation in the Mississippi and Ohio Valleys*, 1929, pp. 184–185, and United States Army, Chief of Engineers, *Annual Report*, 1932, p. 1935.

channel upon the lower river is represented by annual expenditures for dredging, that cost in the fiscal year of 1932 being $2,465,000.[4] By means of this work and other undertakings, "a navigable channel has been maintained since 1895, and a channel of project dimensions has been maintained since 1902, except" for certain brief periods over a limited number of bars.[5] Below Baton Rouge legislation requires the maintenance of a channel not less than 35 feet in depth and of varying widths, with the minimum of 300 feet between Baton Rouge and New Orleans. Thus, from Baton Rouge to the Gulf a ship channel exists.

Traffic upon the Mississippi has passed through certain cycles and figures have also varied sharply from year to year, for reasons that would appear only upon analysis of tonnage data. That the reader may follow the general course of traffic volume, the table above presents tonnages

[1] In 1928 this minimum width was increased to 300 feet.

[2] United States Army, Chief of Engineers, *Annual Report*, 1932, Pt. I, p. 1937.

[3] The Mississippi River Commission estimates the cost of permanent works built by the federal government and chargeable against the present navigation project at almost $71,000,000. Accumulated maintenance totals some $23,210,000 upon the lower river.

[4] *Ibid.*, p. 1966.

[5] *Ibid.*, pp. 1965–1966.

for the three stretches for which such data are compiled for selected years beginning with 1901, the first year for which data are available. To this tonnage a large number of products contribute appreciably; to the upbound total for each section sugar, sand and gravel, sulphur, and logs barged contributed largely; among the downbound items wheat, sand and gravel, iron and steel (as far as Vicksburg), logs, coal and coke (as far as Vicksburg), cotton (below Vicksburg), and fruits and vegetables are outstanding. Of the comparatively heavy tonnage shown below Vicksburg, however, petroleum and its products contribute approximately 80 per cent: this represents a special service of great value to a certain few large oil companies operating in that area.

With the elimination of duplications that result from counting a given ton of cargo twice if it moves through portions or all of two sections of the lower river, three times if it moves from above Memphis to any point below Vicksburg, the volume of traffic upon the Mississippi from Cairo southward is surprisingly small. And this is the more true since it is fed by the Ohio and by lesser streams,[1] since it has had the benefit for more than a decade of the services of the Inland Waterways Corporation,[2] and since New Orleans is an important port of call for ocean-going

[1] By many who expect ultimately a large interchange of traffic between the United States and the countries of Central and South America the Mississippi River and its tributaries are expected to become important channels of trade between the two. But, though the future is unpredictable, indications of such development are few at the present time.

[2] To assist in meeting the transportation needs of a nation at war, equipment serving upon the inland waterways of the United States was taken over by the Federal Railroad Administration in 1918 and operated until Mar. 1, 1920, under the immediate direction of its Division of Inland Waterways. Certain of the equipment taken over, together with that constructed prior to the date given, was then transferred to the Inland and Coastwise Waterways Service, a newly organized division of the War Department. In 1924 the Inland Waterways Corporation was created by law to continue government operations "to the point where the system can be transferred to private operation to the best advantage of the government." The authorized capitalization of the corporation was initially $5,000,000, later increased by $10,000,000, these sums coming from the federal treasury. To the corporation was transferred without cost all floating equipment and other property owned by the government and used in the rendition of service. The task of the corporation was to demonstrate the feasibility of economical inland-waterway service, the House committee declaring in 1924 that it believed "the government can and will within the next five years demonstrate not only the practicability of water transportation, but the great advantage and economy to shippers, and the profitable results that will reward private capital invested in transportation facilities on our rivers."

That this belief failed of justification is evidenced by an appeal for additional funds by the corporation in 1928. This appeal was met in the Denison Act. This Act, in addition to increasing the funds at the disposal of the corporation, has other important provisions: it gives the corporation the right to operate on any section of the Mississippi River system except the Ohio; it requires the Interstate Commerce Commission to order common carriers under its control to establish joint rates with such water lines as had been issued certificates by it to operate; and conditions are named that must be fulfilled before the corporation shall retire from service upon any stream. These conditions are that upon such stream

vessels. When one considers, however, that few important cities can utilize the river in a major way, that it flows through an agricultural rather than an industrial area, and that it does not parallel the nation's major traffic routes, the relatively light tonnage at the end of almost 30

there must be an adequate channel, adequate terminal facilities, satisfactory rail-water rates, and a willingness of private capital to establish common-carrier operations.

Until 1927 service was offered by the successive governmental agencies only upon the lower Mississippi and the Warrior Rivers; in that year service was extended to the upper Mississippi; and recent Commission decisions will permit the operation of federal barges upon the Missouri to Kansas City and upon the recently opened waterway from Grafton to Chicago, Ill. The tonnage record of the federal barge line is indicated by figures for selected years. Total gains were steady until 1928; since that year the volume of traffic has

Year	Total	Lower Mississippi	Warrior	Upper Mississippi
1920	360,719	160,702	200,017	
1924	1,071,848	849,503	222,345	
1928	1,872,597	1,435,560	317,389	119,648
1931	1,533,915	1,170,317	283,872	79,726

remained approximately constant. To the tonnage of the Warrior section in 1931 steel and sugar were major contributors; to that of the lower river sugar, wheat, and cotton; and to the upper steel, sugar, and sisal.

The reason that the Inland Waterways Corporation has loomed so large in discussions of inland water carriage lies in the fact that it has rendered a subsidized service. Not only has it paid nothing for use of the way over which it operates, a way in which heavy federal investments have been made and upon which large federal expenditures are made annually, but it has benefited in even more obvious ways. Upon properties carried upon its books at $23,354,822 no taxes have been paid: belonging to the federal government, the property of the corporation is relieved of taxation as private property in like equipment would not be. Further, a study made of the financial results of the operations of the Inland Waterways Corporation indicates that, even if adequate depreciation charges have been made, there remains from carrier revenues from June 1, 1924, to Feb. 29, 1932, only $105,000, a rather meager return upon the value of property in carrier service. While operations on the lower river have shown a continuous excess of operating revenues over expenses each year since 1924, averaging about $450,000 per year, losses have been continuous and relatively heavy on both upper river and Warrior operations. The Interstate Commerce Commission in Valuation Docket 1162 set at $6,500,000 (as of Feb. 29, 1932) the "fair commercial value" of properties used and useful on the Mississippi River that cost approximately $17,500,000 and at $500,000 the value of Warrior properties that cost almost $2,600,000. Yet these values would seem to be generous to this government enterprise, in view of its past record and its uncertain future. If provision of a free way is not a sufficient subsidy to permit of profitable operation, for how long a period should free use of government funds be accorded and benefit of exemption from taxation be enjoyed by competitors of established agencies of transport? How long must competitive agencies be handicapped and the federal treasury burdened by subsidies to the Inland Waterways Corporation, in the hope that a "successful demonstration" may succeed—or before it be abandoned? These are among the questions that relate to this "experiment" to which transportation and fiscal students are seeking an answer. Some will doubt that inland water transport is *now* socially indispensable if, even upon the lower Mississippi, it cannot stand upon its own financial bottom.

years is more understandable. Then, too, the lack of joint rates covering rail-water and rail-water-rail movements until recently has been a heavy handicap, as were certain competitive practices of the railways in the years before 1910, particularly. Yet, even under conditions as favorable as they now are to the development of tonnage, there is some doubt of a social return from the lower Mississippi comparable to its economic cost. None the less, this is undoubtedly one of the few long stretches of river in the United States that approximate *natural* waterways, and it is improbable that the policy of maintaining a navigable channel will be abandoned, regardless of the economic soundness of past or future expenditures. And, after all, much of the capital investment necessary to navigation has already been made: the problem for the future is essentially one of maintenance.

Observations: The Upper Mississippi.—The upper Mississippi was, prior to the establishment of a close network of railways in Granger territory, of great significance to a considerable area upon both its east and its west banks. Packet lines operated regularly, in later years a tremendous footage of lumber and logs was rafted down, and the "river cities" were clearly dominant in the area. With the development of the railways, however, river service diminished in importance and in time regular trips ceased. With the exhaustion of the timber resources of Wisconsin and Minnesota, an important element of tonnage disappeared. In consequence of the operation of these and other forces, the tonnage upon the river between St. Paul and the mouth of the Missouri River tended downward through the nineties and the early years of the present century until, in 1916, it dropped sharply below the million figure, averaging for the next 15 years about 750,000 tons annually. A slight upward tendency has been evident in recent years, however, due in part undoubtedly to the establishment of service by the Inland Waterways Corporation from St. Louis to Minneapolis in 1927.

As early as 1878 federal funds were appropriated with a view to providing a channel with a minimum depth of 4.5 feet from St. Paul southward. In 1907 Congress authorized a 6-foot channel with a minimum width of 300 feet in the northern section and 1,200 in the southern, such depth and width to be established by open-channel methods. Upon the various projects prior to the present that calls for a 9-foot channel, with slack-water navigation, some $47,000,000 has been spent north of the mouth of the Illinois for new work and almost $2,260,000 for maintenance. Work upon the new channel is under way, the estimated total cost being $124,000,000 for the section between the Illinois and Minneapolis. The cities upon the upper river are being solicited to construct terminals, which some have already done, and marked local interest is being evidenced. It is improbable that the development will cost less than $150,-000,000 when completed. Upon this and upon needed terminal properties the capital charge, together with a reasonable estimate for maintenance and depreciation, will be not less than $10,000,000. If grain is to move in export trade by the St. Lawrence route, it cannot move down the Mississippi; a relatively small tonnage of animals and animal products will move by water to the south; the source of supply of manufactured goods for the northern valley states is largely to the eastward; and the channels of traffic are quite definitely east-and-west through this area. On the other hand, coal should move northward from southern Illinois by barge at savings to a large area until it comes into competition with lake-cargo coal; sugar will also move northward in considerable quantity; and it is hoped by many of the upper valley manufacturers that barge transportation to ocean port will give increased opportunities in coastwise and foreign trade. Undoubtedly, too, those communities located upon the river will profit in other ways. No careful and unbiased study has been made of the probabilities of traffic development in this area, yet an annual social cost of $10,000,000 is being assumed. There are many who are doubtful of the development of tonnage to justify such an outlay, while there are others who are perturbed over the effect upon other essential elements in a regional transport system if a large water tonnage does develop. And there are few positive evidences that the lower *charge* for river movement will increase the volume of tonnage moved in the area sufficiently to provide adequately for all agencies.

Observations: The Missouri River.—To meet the needs of pioneer navigation when the Missouri River provided the only effective entrance into the West, government snagging operations were undertaken as early as 1838. The first appropriation for improvement by regulation was made by Congress in 1878 and after that year sums were provided so that, prior to 1902, some $6,971,000 had been expended for new work and maintenance. Construction has been progressing upon the 6-foot channel below Kansas City approved in 1912 and in later acts: "The entire channel is becoming fixed and there is such a marked improvement of channel depths that at ordinary stages there exists a 6-foot depth from Kansas City to the mouth," though during low-water stages "depth in partially improved sections may not exceed 3.25 feet. Dredging is required at low stages to . . . maintain the required channel depth for navigation."[1] Total cost of the completed project is estimated at $62,000,000, with annual maintenance charges of approximately $2,000,000.

Upon the lower Missouri tonnage varied widely from year to year, 1911 to 1921, but from that date it increased steadily until 1930: in that year it was more than ten times that of 1921. In 1931, however, it dropped by almost half a million tons to 1,378,000. Of this tonnage 213,000 tons were rafted and had a value of $2,284,000 and 1,145,000 tons with a value of $2,374,000 moved by vessel. From the low value per ton

[1] United States Army, *Chief of Engineers, Annual Report,* 1932, p. 1154.

and a study of available tonnage data, it seems that piles and brush for revetment work and other construction material, such as sand, gravel, and stone, have contributed chiefly to the river's increase in tonnage. In short, despite the availability of a moderately satisfactory channel, commercial use is as yet negligible. And it is difficult to discover, as in the case of the upper Mississippi, traffic that is likely to move in large volume by water in this area: manufactured goods utilize, in general, speedier agencies of transport; animals and animal products are unlikely to move by barge; and export grain is more likely to move from western Kansas and Oklahoma to Texas ports than by rail and river to New Orleans. And it would seem that grain moving eastward to the domestic markets could hardly justify the annual social cost of approximately $5,750,000 imposed by the lower Missouri improvement—this representing a minimum estimate of capital, depreciation, and maintenance charges. Furthermore, if and as the river does attract tonnage from existing agencies of transport rather than create new tonnage, the situation of those agencies is likely to become increasingly difficult: Southwestern territory, along the northern edge of which the lower Missouri flows, has long had transportation service available in excess of its needs. Nor does it seem likely that the Southwest can dispense with rail service or can gain through a service crippled by competition that is made inequitable by subsidizing one competitor.

Snagging operations by the federal government were extended to the Missouri River between Kansas City and Sioux City in 1868, systematic improvement begun under a series of acts of which the first was passed in 1882. The establishment of a 6-foot channel for the 417 miles above Kansas City will cost, it is estimated, $77,000,000 in addition to expenditures upon previous projects, though at the present time the law limits appropriations for the necessary work to $27,000,000, all of which has been authorized. To date work has been confined largely to the stretch of river below St. Joseph, this work proving successful in the stabilization of channel and banks as far as it has progressed. In behalf of this development it is urged that "the annual savings on land and property destroyed by erosion, capitalized at 4 per cent, would justify the improvement," and it is contended that it would be justified also by savings from loss and damage by flood. Further, the more common arguments are offered in support of the Sioux City-Kansas City development,[1] all centering about the lower *individual cost* of the transport service provided.

There is some doubt as to whether many millions of federal money should be spent to increase the value of property adjacent to a stream

[1] The Missouri River Navigation Association in *Railways and Waterways*, issued in June, 1931, declares on p. 22.

"We maintain that the development of the Missouri River for navigation will:

Bring an increase of population and industrial development to the whole Missouri Valley.

when its market value has been fixed with that advantage or peril in mind, and nowhere would the need of a narrow channel for navigation and of a broad channel for flood control and reduction of flood losses come into sharper conflict than on the Missouri. The Sioux City-Kansas City section of the river runs almost at right angles to the usual channels of trade and few impartial students doubt but that the annual cost of the improvement—interest, depreciation, and maintenance—will be oppressively large as compared with probable tonnage. While operations with a controlling depth of 3 feet are not proof of slight use with a greater depth, it is interesting to note that in 1931 sand and stone contributed almost 88 per cent to the total of 379,759 tons carried; it is also interesting to note that the average haul was 5½ miles. It is probable that much of the tonnage was incidental to river improvement operations, as is true of many of the rivers of the Mississippi system—and of other streams—during recent years. Before additional funds are made available for the 6-foot channel above Kansas City it is desirable, in the interest of social economy, that a careful and impartial study be made of the project, designed to distinguish between possibilities and probabilities and between public and individual responsibilities.

Observations: Lakes-to-Gulf Waterway.—This improvement, as close to the heart of the Chicago area as it is old in the history of the Middle West, has resulted from federal, state, and city cooperation: these have contributed, approximately, the Illinois River to Starved Rock, the Illinois Waterway to Lockport, and the Chicago Sanitary and Ship Canal, upon all of which a minimum channel of 9 feet is to be maintained. Upon the Sanitary Canal some $53,000,000 was expended, and the cost to the state and federal governments of the 60 miles of canal from Lockport to Starved Rock, as well as the 230 miles of river from Starved Rock to the junction of the Illinois and Mississippi rivers, will total no less than $35,000,000. If but one-third of the cost of the Sanitary Canal be charged against navigation, the cost of a 9-foot channel from Lake Michigan to the Mississippi will approximate $53,000,000. Past movements upon segments of this project give no indication of its use when completed and articulated with other channels of like depth.

Bring more tonnage to the railroads of the Missouri River Valley than the river will take from them.

Furnish more passengers to the railroads.

Increase the taxable wealth and relieve the tax burden.

Will stop declining rural population.

Help restore industrial equality.

Prevent the building of competitive rail lines.

Raise the average classification of freight handled by the railroads.

Extend the range of distribution.

Produce new tonnage for our railroads."

This waterway has the advantage of paralleling roughly an established channel of trade to the Southwest, and will provide access to Kansas City, St. Louis, and the lower valley; over it will undoubtedly move a considerable tonnage of coal, of iron and steel products, of sugar, and perhaps of manufactured goods moving into export and coastwise trade. Yet here again there is conflict between the interests of the Valley route and the St. Lawrence undertaking. And while, for example, it will lower charges on iron and steel from the Chicago area into the South where the Pittsburgh mills now dominate because of the Ohio, it will also lower the cost of delivering ore to the St. Louis steel producers—and this, in turn, will enable St. Louis to compete more effectively not only in the South and Southwest but also to the north and northwest where Chicago has dominated largely. Some reasonable hope of the Lakes-to-Gulf channel justifying itself may be held, yet there is no assurance of traffic developing to such point that annual costs of perhaps $3,500,000 for capital, depreciation, and maintenance will be balanced by an equivalent social gain.

Observations: St. Lawrence Waterway.—In the preceding chapter the character of this improvement and its annual cost were indicated. About the St. Lawrence project has arisen sharp controversy, the sharper because of positive conflict between the interests of particular groups and areas. The Trunk Line railways have, in general, opposed, while public and business interests in the "Great Lakes area"—defined as including the whole or portions of 24 states—have generally been actively favorable. The New England States, the Southern states, and the Pacific states have been indifferent, the Middle Atlantic states opposed, with the antagonism of New York City and much of New York state particularly marked. Indeed, the controversy between opposing interests has become so prominent as to obscure in the minds of many the fact that decision should be rested upon economic facts rather than upon balance of power in legislative halls. To assist the reader in evaluating an undertaking of which the United States St. Lawrence Commission has said, "the construction of the shipway from the Great Lakes to the sea is imperative both for the relief and for the future development of a vast area in the interior of the continent," a brief summary of the arguments for and against will be given, with passing comment upon such as seem to merit it. But first the reader should be reminded that this is a project to provide navigation for not to exceed 7 months of the year, upon which the legitimate annual charges will probably be not less than $35,000,000, and which plans to add to our coastline for purposes of ocean shipping some 3,774 miles and give to the population of a great area the benefits flowing from cheaper transportation costs.

The essence of the case for the St. Lawrence project is that it will provide for tonnage moving into and from a large area with a population of more than 40,000,000 people a sufficiently lower transportation charge to yield great and continuing economic benefits. At lake ports are to arrive the imports that are now received by this area through the Atlantic, Gulf, and even Pacific ports, from which they are transported to the interior by expensive and considerable rail hauls: these imports will be as diverse as asphalt and fish, as bananas and iron ores,[1] as coffee and special clays. From these lake ports are to flow into export trade grain and grain products, animal products, automobiles and parts, and a great variety of miscellaneous manufactured products. To and from these lake ports are to move heavy tonnages in coastwise and intercoastal trade, boats moving between Pacific and lake ports as well as between Gulf and Atlantic ports and the Lakes.[2] By many advocates it is declared that the seaway is needed to relieve the railways of burdensome tonnage in a heavy-traffic area and to give to the public protection against possible congestion and embargoes. Appeal has been made very skillfully to lake ports upon the basis of a greatly augmented volume of trade and it is upon the basis of asserted savings of from 8 to 11 cents per bushel upon wheat moving to Europe, with comparable savings upon other agricultural surplus, that the project has been so effectively "sold" to agricultural states in the Middle West. Furthermore, it is contended that the income from the sale of power developed as an incident to the provision of a ship channel from Montreal to Lake Ontario would be such as to "reduce the annual cost of the project to not more than $10,000,000."

Those who oppose the St. Lawrence undertaking differentiate first between *social cost* and *transportation charge*. True, some question the possibility of a lower charge, because of certain facts: unbalanced traffic;

[1] One writer declares that the St. Lawrence project is justified on the single ground that it will give the great steel mills upon and near the Great Lakes cheap access to foreign iron ores when the supply of high-grade ores in the Superior district has been exhausted, a situation that approaches. See WARNER, FAYETTE S., *Movement of Iron Ore and Coal in Relation to the St. Lawrence Waterway*, University of Pennsylvania Press.

[2] In his *Great Lakes-St. Lawrence Ship Canal*, p. 116, Mr. A. H. RITTER declares, "The important commodities which would be expected to move from the Pacific coast into the Great Lakes are lumber, canned goods, beans, dried fruits, and articles from the Orient transshipped at Pacific coast points. Cargo from the Great Lakes to Pacific ports would consist principally of iron and steel, automobiles, machinery, paper and miscellaneous manufactures. Coastwise shipments into the lakes from Gulf ports would include petroleum, gasoline, lubricating oil, sulphur, phosphate rock, rice and hardwood; while shipments from Atlantic ports would include miscellaneous manufactured goods, textiles, hardware, machinery, boots and shoes, granite, fertilizer, etc. Shipments from the Great Lakes to Atlantic and Gulf ports would include large quantities of flour and mill products, automobiles and parts, rubber goods, hides, copper, iron ore and pig iron, iron and steel manufactures, furniture, packing house products, dairy products, grain."

In this discussion of exchange between the Gulf and Great Lakes area the conflict between the expectations of the St. Lawrence route and the Lakes-to-Gulf project appear. Here mileage will be an important consideration.

uncertainty of loads; the high efficiency of cargo boats now plying the Great Lakes; increased costs of operation, occasioned by slow movement and heavier insurance for vessels of considerable draft that come above Montreal; necessity of transfer of boat operations to other waters for 5 months of the year; and greatly increased distances upon many routes. Others grant a lower charge despite these and other handicaps, yet assert that the volume of tonnage likely to develop will be so small as compared with the annual cost of the undertaking to the public that the addition of $2 to $3.50 per ton will make the social cost of the service greater than it now is—and in some cases materially greater. Because the promise of sharply lowered grain rates has been one of the principal lures of the project, this matter has received particular attention from critics. These emphasize the recent low prices of grains in the world market and call attention to the statement of students of the farm problem that the salvation of the American farmer lies in reducing production to the needs of the domestic market: without a subsidy, these students declare, few areas in the United States can compete in world markets with foreign-grown wheat—even with Canadian grain. Therefore, if intelligent farming is done, it is suggested that the wheat surplus for export will have largely disappeared before the waterway can be completed. Furthermore, that the advertised savings are excessive is indicated by the fact that the rates on wheat in recent years from the Head of the Lakes to Montreal have averaged 7.5 to 8.5 cents and from Montreal to Liverpool 4.5 to 8 cents per bushel. The maximum saving is estimated at from 3 to 4 cents, only some uncertain part of which would accrue to the American grower: the world price will itself be affected by any reduction in the cost of transportation from an important source of supply—and such a source Western Canada will remain indefinitely, without regard to the course of grain production in the United States. In fact, some suggest that our participation in this project would be rendering generous assistance to the Canadian grower to the serious disadvantage of southwestern inland areas that otherwise might compete upon relatively equal terms with Canadian grain in export trade.

The point is hotly disputed as to whether a 27-foot channel will permit the entry of any but tramp boats and second-rate line service. And facts indicate that the more modern and economical ocean craft have a draft that would prevent their entry; indeed, a channel approaching 35 feet in depth would be necessary to permit the safe entry of such boats. But perhaps it cannot be expected that a seasonal service will attract the better craft. The disadvantages of restricted channel navigation for ocean boats are emphasized as a further obstacle to participation in lake trade. "It is only the smaller tramp vessels which could operate on this route and avoid the present transfer of cargoes; but the smaller tramps are not those which can be operated most economically," declares

Professor W. T. Jackman of the University of Toronto. To which statement he adds another which emphasizes the existence of "strong forces drawing grain through the United States via New York into the international markets,"[1] among these being the abundant shipping facilities there, the utility of grain as ballast for liners, and the regularity of service.

The contention that additional facilities are needed because of the inability of the Trunk Line railways to handle traffic expeditiously at times is not supported by the facts for the past 10 years, nor does the volume of traffic upon the barge canal indicate a keen interest in cheap as against expeditious movement. Further, it is declared that the waterway cannot be regarded as a substitute for the railway in any case, in view of the fact that for some 5 months of each year the waterway is closed: to a considerable degree duplication, not substitution, results. And, granting that a market can be found for all power developed in connection with the ship channel, there is no justification for increasing power rates to meet deficits chargeable to navigation: each phase of the proposed development should be self-supporting.

Naturally, many of the arguments made against the seaway are subjected to sharp criticism and even those who have canvassed the literature thoughtfully find themselves uncertain as to a conclusion. Yet this much seems sure: the need for such a development in the fourth decade of the twentieth century is less vital than it has been asserted to be by a splendidly organized and effective association working in its behalf, though perhaps it offers more of promise for the future than many opponents appreciate. To what extent, then, is the United States justified in building for that doubtful immediate future and more doubtful distant future—the more doubtful because of our general transportation situation? It is with such questions that statesmen must deal in any attempt to solve the transportation problem of today.

Basis of River Rates.—In the discussion of transportation upon streams in the Mississippi Valley emphasis has been placed upon lower charges as one of the prime benefits to be derived by the public from considerable expenditures intended to provide navigable channels upon the nation's "natural waterways." Advocates of such projects declare that a movement charge of 2 mills represents an attainable goal upon an adequate channel, but operations seem to be more commonly at 4 mills per ton-mile or upward. Private operations, involving the movement of its own tonnage by a company, can perhaps be conducted for less than that figure and it is possible that contract operations may also cut costs below 4 mills, yet it is improbable that common-carrier service can be rendered for as little as that and all operating costs be met. Indeed, were interest and taxes upon the investment in floating and other equipment assessed

[1] JACKMAN, W. T., Canada's Weal not Fostered by the St. Lawrence Waterway Plan, *Railway Age*, vol. 92, page 601.

against the tonnage of the Inland Waterways Corporation, the 4-mill charge would be materially increased.

Curiously, for public service upon these rivers no independent basis of charge has developed; rather, a policy of making rates between river points upon the basis of 80 per cent of the rail rate has been continued. Accepted by the governmentally financed line, the adoption of this policy by independent operators has been compulsory; presumptively it represents a differential necessary to movement by the longer and slower route. And it is the greater length of the river route that explains in part the lower rate per ton-mile for water movement: the 80 per cent charge by water divided by a water mileage that commonly runs 50 per cent in excess of the rail mileage gives a deceptively low charge per ton-mile by water—one not reflected in the charge to the shipper for the whole movement. This fact must always be kept in mind in the comparison of rail and water ton-mile charges, also when allocating the costs of providing and maintaining the waterway with a view to ascertaining the total *social cost* of water transport.

The Problem of Public Policy.—It is unquestionably true that much of the success of the agitation for inland-waterway development during the past 25 years has been due to a deep-rooted public antagonism toward the railways, a survival from a period when abuses were common and regulation ineffective, and a desire to escape from the burden of a rising railway rate level. Instead of dealing directly with certain factors in the situation that have contributed to increasing rates and recognizing the inevitability of a portion of that increase, the public has sought to "force" rates down by the multiplication of agencies just as was done in early days when the effort was made to control the rates of an existing railway by promoting the construction of another. This deliberate multiplication of water routes, together with the diversion of tonnage to the highways, has been far less successful in compelling a lower schedule of railway rates than in imperiling the solvency of the rail carriers. Is social advantage to be found along that road? It is to be doubted. Therefore it appears that the individual waterway project, as well as waterways as a whole, must be considered, as suggested before, from a broad social point of view as well as from the point of view of the likelihood of tonnage that will justify all costs. Yet it seems impossible to secure, under our existing plan, thoughtful consideration of even the latter problem from public groups and legislative assemblies. Because we have functioned to such a complete degree without guide or compass in the approval of waterway projects, a definite change in policy is suggested.

There has been for a long period an increasing tendency on the part of local governmental units and of individuals to shift obligations and responsibilities to the federal government, insisting at the same time upon largess from it. The Rivers and Harbors bills have again and again been characterized as a "national scandal," with the opprobrious term of "pork barrel" commonly used in describing them. And it is a national sorrow, both morally and financially, that with astonishing frequency an active legislator has "brought home the bacon" in the form of an approved project of dubious worth. The national significance of many considerable projects is negligible and there are few important projects, the *local* significance of which is not greater than the *national:* local industries gain, local resources are developed, local trade increases, if the project is successful—with but incidental cost to the groups benefited; if the project fails to realize its goal, the local interests have but seen a hope crumble—while the federal treasury has paid for the experiment. It would be difficult to find a situation in which benefit and risk are more completely divorced.

In 1910 the National Waterways Commission, after calling attention to policies of financing waterway improvements abroad and in certain of the states, said, "The Commission finds that, in the development of waterways on a large scale, the decided tendency in other countries is toward a degree of participation by communities and localities especially benefited and is of the opinion that in order to obtain the best results this policy must ultimately be adopted in this country." How obviously true is this observation today, with expenditures for projects of varying worth totaling some $580,000,000 within the past 7 years and projects approved that call for the expenditure of perhaps as much more—and others clamoring for recognition! If the Golden River, with its bars and rapids and shoals, with its lack of water during certain seasons and its devastating floods at other times, with its fertile bottom lands and its fickle channel, is to be brought under man's yoke, none will there be to say nay to the advocates of such improvement, and none should there be—*providing that those who benefit from lower charges, from higher land values, from increased volume of business, or otherwise, meet the major portion, at least, of the costs of such improvement.*[1] With that requirement imposed, there will be fewer projects approved, perhaps, but those that receive approval will have reached the goal by appeal to the intelligence of the prospective beneficiaries rather than through appeal to hopes and resort to political machination. For all future projects a definite scale of federal participa-

[1] In its preliminary report, the National Waterways Commission gives as one of the enumerated powers of the general government under the Constitution of the Confederate States of America, drafted in 1861, this: "To regulate commerce with foreign nations, and among the several states, and with the Indian tribes; but neither this nor any other clause contained in the Constitution shall ever be construed to delegate the power to Congress to appropriate money for any internal improvement intended to facilitate commerce except for the purpose of furnishing lights, beacons, and buoys and other aids to navigation upon the coasts, and the improvement of harbors and the removing of obstructions in river navigation, in all which cases such duties shall be laid on the navigation facilitated thereby, as may be necessary to pay the costs and expenses thereof."

tion should be indicated, if federal participation on a minor scale is desired; upon existing projects, in so far as possible, tolls should be levied with a view to indemnifying the federal government for past outlays. Cooperation among communities and among states may not permit such quick realization of desires as appropriation by Congress, but it will undoubtedly result in the elimination of undeserving projects—with a great decrease in governmental costs. Or, if for administrative purposes it seems desirable to have major projects developed under federal direction and costs met by the federal treasury, it should be understood that charges will be levied against all beneficiaries through tolls or special assessments upon such basis as to liquidate the obligation. In accord with either plan suggested, internal improvements can be held within economic limits; with full assumption of costs by the federal government and complete local irresponsibility, neither standard nor guide exists. And this fact has been all too evident in the past score of years.

REFERENCES

ANDERSON, ALEX D.: *The Mississippi and its Forty-four Navigable Tributaries*, Government Printing Office, 1890.

Annals of the American Academy of Political And Social Science, vol. 135, No. 224, Great Inland Waterway Projects in the United States.

ASHBURN, T. Q., L. D. CORNISH, E. A. HADLEY and others: Relation Between Rail and Waterway Transportation, papers presented before American Society of Civil Engineers, July, 1929, *Transactions*, vol. 95, p. 861.

ASHTON, BESSIE L.: *The Economic Aspects of the Illinois Waterway*, Studies in the Social Sciences, vol. 14, No. 2, University of Illinois.

BARTLEY, GUY: *Accountant v. Engineer—Disclosed and Hidden Costs of Inland Waterways Corporation*, Inland Waterways Corporation, 1931 (mimeographed).

Bureau of Railway Economics: *Comparison of Transportation Costs by Rail and via Barge Canal*, Miscellaneous Series 36, Washington, D. C., 1925.

———: *Transportation Costs of the New York State Barge Canal*, Miscellaneous Series 40. Washington, D. C., 1926.

———: *An Economic Survey of Inland Waterway Transportation in the United States*, Special Series 56. Washington, D. C., 1930.

Chamber of Commerce of the United States: Report of Special Committee 5, *Development of Waterways and Coordination of Rail and Waterway Service*, Washington, D. C., 1923.

———: *What's Ahead for Business in Inland Water Transportation*, Proceedings of Eighteenth Annual Meeting of the United States Chamber of Commerce.

DAGGETT, STUART: *Principles of Inland Transportation*, Harper & Brothers, 1928.

FITZGERALD, JOHN M.: Do We Need More Inland Waterways? Address before Associated Traffic Clubs, St. Louis, 1929, published by Committee on Public Relations of Eastern Railroads, 1929.

Great Lakes-St. Lawrence Tidewater Association: *Transportation: A Continental System*, Washington, D. C., 1921.

———: *Railways and the Seaway*, Bulletin 46, Washington, D. C., 1929.

HANSON, CARL O.: *Federal Expenditures on Inland Waterways Since* 1910, unpublished thesis, University of Iowa, 1929.

Hearings before the Committee on Interstate and Foreign Commerce, House of Representatives, 70th Congress, 1st Session, on H.R. 10710, *Inland Waterways Corporation—Extension of Barge Line*, Mar. 27–Apr. 6, 1928.

HILL, HORACE M.: What Price Transportation? Address delivered over WCCO, Minneapolis, 1931.

Inland Navigation, printed by William Duane, Philadelphia, 1805.

Inland Waterways Corporation: *Annual Reports*, Government Printing Office.

JACKMAN, W. T.: Canada's Weal Not Fostered by St. Lawrence Waterway Plan, *Railway Age*, vol. 92, No. 15, p. 599.

LOOMIS, EDWARD E.: Railroads *v.* Waterways, *Review of Reviews*, vol. 79, pp. 79–81.

LOREE, L. F.: Deep-water Navigation Between Lake Erie and Tidewater, Address before Atlantic Deeper Waterways Association, Troy, N. Y., 1929.

MACELWEE, R. S.: *Dr. Moulton on the St. Lawrence Navigation and Power Project*, Great Lakes-St. Lawrence Tidewater Association, Washington, D. C., 1930.

Missouri River Navigation Association: *Railways and Waterways*, Kansas City, 1931.

MOULTON, HAROLD G.: *Waterways v. Railways*, Houghton Mifflin Company, 1926.

———: CHARLES S. MORGAN, and ADA L. LEE: *The St. Lawrence Navigation and Power Project*, the Brookings Institution, Washington, D. C., 1929.

NICKELL, L. P., and W. S. ABERNATHY: *Inland Waterway Freight Transportation Lines in the United States*, Domestic Commerce Series 32, Government Printing Office, 1930.

RITTER, ALFRED H.: *Transportation Economics of the Great Lakes-St. Lawrence Ship Channel*, Great Lakes-St. Lawrence Tidewater Association, Washington, D. C., 1925.

SHELTON, WILLIAM ARTHUR: *The Lakes-to-the-Gulf Deep Waterway*, University of Chicago Press, Chicago, 1912.

State of New York, Department of Public Works: *Annual Reports of the Superintendent*, J. B. Lyon Company.

Study of Transportation by Waterway as Related to Competition with Rail Carriers in Continental United States, Security Owners Association, New York, 1932.

SUMNER, JOHN D.: *New York Barge Canal Traffic*, Bureau of Business Research, University of Buffalo, 1929.

United States Army, Chief of Engineers, *Annual Reports*, Government Printing Office.

———, Corps of Engineers, and United States Shipping Board: *Transportation in the Mississippi and Ohio Valleys*, 1929, Government Printing Office, 1929.

United States Department of Commerce: *Commerce Yearbook*, vol. 1 (annual), Government Printing Office.

———: *Inland Water Transportation in the United States*, Domestic Commerce Series 119, Government Printing Office, 1923.

———: *Statistical Abstract* (annual), Government Printing Office.

United States House of Representatives, Committee on Rivers and Harbors, 69th Congress, 2d session, Document 594: *Missouri River Between Kansas City, Kan., and Pierre, S. D.*, Government Printing Office, 1926.

United States Senate, 62d Congress, 2d session, Senate Document 469: *National Waterways Commission Report*, Government Printing Office, 1912.

———, 69th Congress, 2d session, Senate Document 183: *St. Lawrence Waterway Project*, Government Printing Office, 1927.

WARNER, FAYETTE S.: *The Future Movement of Iron Ore and Coal in Relation to the St. Lawrence Waterway*, University of Pennsylvania Press, Philadelphia, 1930.

WHITFORD, NOBLE E.: *History of the Barge Canal of New York State*, J. B. Lyon Co., 1922.

WYER, SAMUEL S.: *A Study of St. Lawrence Waterway Project*, Fuel-Power-Transportation Educational Foundation, Columbus, Ohio, 1931.

———: *A Study of the Inland Waterway Situation*, Fuel-Power-Transportation Educational Foundation, Columbus, Ohio, 1931.

CHAPTER XXXVII

AIR TRANSPORTATION

MAN'S desire to navigate the air reaches far into antiquity. Doubtless that desire came forcefully to the mind of primitive man when, as he made his way slowly and with great effort through forest and across plain or as he found his forward movement blocked by stretches of water, he watched the birds wing the untrammeled space above the earth to which his feet clung. With the hunger to fly so strong, it is not strange that the power of sustained flight was attached to deity: Hermes and Mercury, messengers of the gods, were endowed with wings that they might the more promptly execute their duties, and wings sped Pegasus on his way. Again and again through the centuries man sought to emulate these mythological figures, often with tragic consequences; in the old readers the misfortunes of "Darius Green and his flying machine" were chronicled in detail and with humor. This yearning for flight, perhaps as old as man, would not down.

So far as records indicate, the first scientific approach to flight was made by the brilliant and versatile da Vinci about 1500. He concerned himself with both the helicopter, the vertical lift machine, and the ornithopter, the flapping-wing machine; though his interest centered principally in the latter type, of the former he is said to have made models that lifted themselves into the air and there remained for a brief time. The time was not ripe, however, for success: too little was known about the principles of flight and no power unit that even approached adequacy had yet been developed. For almost 300 years following the experimental work of the great Italian, little scientific thought seems to have been given the problem and no effective progress made. Indeed, the first important step made toward man's mastery of the air was in the field of the lighter-than-air craft. To the balloon in its original and its modified form, therefore, attention will first be given.

The Balloon.—The Montgolfier brothers are credited with accomplishing the first ascent of a lighter-than-air device. This ascent, from the little French village of Annonay, was made in June, 1783. A large bag was held for a time over a fire; released, the bag rose into the air and traveled a distance of 2 miles. Shortly thereafter a bag filled with hydrogen was sent up at Paris by Charles, a physicist, this bag traveling a distance of 15 miles. Within about 4 months of the first Montgolfier success, Rozier permitted himself to be carried aloft by an ascending balloon: for the first time in human history man had realized in some measure his age-old desire to navigate the air. Though experiments were being made in America at about the same time as these notable events were occurring in France, it is the French who must be credited largely with the balloon's development; under the direction of Charles the mechanism of this agency was brought almost to its present state within a brief time.

The first practical use of the balloon came early. In 1784 ascensions were made to study temperature, pressure, and humidity in the upper air. Such scientific uses continued upon an increasing scale, a balloon with instruments and two passengers in 1901 attaining a recorded altitude of 34,500 feet. Consideration was given to its military use during the French Revolution, but it seems to have been employed first by the French against the Italians in 1859 for reconnoitring. During the American Civil War some use was made of the balloon by federal forces and in 1870–1871 balloons were released from Paris, then under siege, to maintain contact with the provinces. In the World War the balloon was employed extensively: upon land it was used to assist batteries in finding the range; at sea it was towed behind ships to make easier the location of submarines. As the heavier-than-air craft developed in effectiveness, however, the utility of the balloon diminished rapidly; to it little thought is now given as an instrument of war.

The Airship.—Early in the history of the balloon Guyot suggested an egg-shaped envelope; in 1851 Henri Gifford powered an elongated balloon with a small steam engine, driving it at the rate of 4 to 5 miles per hour. In 1885 Renard and Kreb used an electric motor to drive an airship at 14 miles per hour. But it was not until 1898 that significant development in this field of striking possibilities was begun. In that year Santos Dumont, the Brazilian, evidenced an active interest in airship development, utilizing in his experiments the newly developed internal-combustion engine. He made several flights that attracted widespread attention, perhaps the most striking of these a journey of some 7 miles over Paris and about Eiffel Tower in less than a half hour. In the same year that marked Dumont's entry into the field another man began experimentation and it is he, Count F. von Zeppelin of Germany, who has contributed most to airship progress and whose name will ever be associated with its rapid advancement during the next score of years.

The first ship built under Count Zeppelin's direction was 420 feet long and 38 feet in diameter. It was supported by hydrogen confined in compartments and was powered by two 16 horse-power motors; with this ship in 1900 a speed of 20 miles per hour was made. Within a brief time the work that was being done fired public imagination in Germany and the government became interested. Work was pushed with government assistance and, during the World War, the Zeppelin became an object of great fear as a consequence of the participation of such ships in raids.

At the close of the war the peace terms imposed sharp limitations upon the operations of the Friedrichshafen plant, though large ships in the course of construction were completed for delivery to allied nations. One of these, to become known as the "Los Angeles," made the trans-Atlantic flight to the United States in 1924: a journey of about 5,000 miles was completed in 81 hours. Later, the "Graf Zeppelin" was built and driven across the Atlantic, making a journey of 6,300 miles with mail, freight, 20 passengers, and a crew of 40, in time aloft of 112 hours. Since that trip in 1928, other important flights have been made by the "Graf Zeppelin" —of these the most important being a round-the-world flight in 1929.[1] Interest in other countries has been active; both Great Britain and the United States have built large ships. The most important of the American ships was the "Akron," built for military service, with which numerous flights were made prior to its tragic end. The "Macon," a sister ship, is now in service.

The airship has been acclaimed by many as a more promising instrumentality for commercial air navigation than the heavier-than-air machine; yet, until certain difficulties have been met and weaknesses overcome, it bids fair to remain primarily a field of experimental concern. Hydrogen has lifting power materially in excess of helium and is far less expensive, yet the use of hydrogen involves great danger from fire. With the attainment of any considerable height, problems of volume and temperature of the gas arise. The free-balloon type of envelope is impossible of use and the construction of the rigid type raises questions of weight and strength, while the semi-rigid has not proved wholly successful. In still air the efficiency of the properly proportioned airship is such that its performance in terms of fuel and distance "would be almost incredible"; but, because the air is rarely still, a ship needs sufficient power to make 75 to 100 miles per hour if it is to be successful. Winds and storms impose a tremendous strain upon the structure; mooring and housing present difficulties that have not yet been solved. True, ships have been built that will approximate the speed mentioned and with a lift of more than 50 tons: ships that will carry, in addition to passengers, fuel for 50 hours in the air and a pay load of 25 tons. Yet the uncertainties of airship operation, the cost of constructing single units, and the tragic disasters that have marred the history of development, leave the airship little advanced as compared with 10 years ago. Quite possible it is that lighter-than-air craft will play a more important rôle in air transport than the heavier craft, yet progress toward realization seems slower for the former

[1] In September, 1932, this ship completed its tenth transatlantic journey, handling mail and passengers from Germany to Rio de Janeiro. The cost estimates for this journey indicate an outlay of about $3 per mile, an astonishingly low figure made possible in some part by special government assistance. The average time for the westward crossing to Brazil has been 68 hours and for the eastern 90 hours.

than for the latter. And the enormous investment in a single ship, as compared with that in one of the larger planes designed for goods or passenger movement, will also tend to discourage activity and to delay progress.

The Airplane.—While the balloon permitted man to move through the air, it did not permit him until recently to move at will; rather than lessening, it stimulated his interest in the development of a mechanism that would be wholly responsive to his wish. To the attainment of this goal Sir George Cayley was the first to contribute significantly: to him flight was purely a mechanical problem which he stated thus, "To make a surface support a given weight by the application of power to the resistance of the air." He made a number of experiments, but lacked a prime mover of sufficient power within a weight that the supporting surfaces would carry. It was this, too, that stood as one prime obstacle to Henson's success in 1843; to him are credited the tilted wing and the propeller. Toward the close of the nineteenth century the experimentation of Lilienthal (Germany), Pilcher (England), and Chanute (America) with the glider contributed significantly to the actual realization of flight. During the same period Maxim and Langley were at work upon powered units; Maxim's one attempt failed and a series of failures by Langley eliminated him from active participation. It was to be the fortune of Orville and Wilbur Wright, operators of a small bicycle and repair shop in Dayton, Ohio, to make the world's first flight and thus to realize one of man's great dreams.

The First Flight.—These brothers, whose interest was first drawn to the field by Lilienthal's death in 1896, were impressed by the lack of actual experience in the air of even such noted pilots as the German. They therefore set themselves to gain air experience as well as to gather all available facts relative to flying. After 4 years of active interest and patient effort, during which time they made innumerable glider flights, the Wrights accomplished their initial flights on Dec. 17, 1903, at Kitty Hawk, N. C. The first of these was for but 12 seconds, the plane traveling 120 feet; the fourth was for 59 seconds and 852 feet were covered in the teeth of a strong wind. So incredulous were the critical among the public that, despite the presence of witnesses, the performance was questioned; this attitude was the more pronounced because, following the tests, the plane overturned and was damaged beyond use, thus necessitating considerable delay in making corroborative tests. In 1904 a complete circle was flown in the air and in 1905 the first officially recorded flight was made at Dayton: a distance of 11.12 miles was flown in 18 minutes, 19 seconds. Despite the crude mechanism, despite an ignorance of aerodynamics that has not yet been wholly dissipated, the Wrights *flew*—and no place remained for doubt in the mind of populace or scientist. To the Wrights and to the host of others who soon became active participants must be credited a new instrumentality of transport, with its consequent economic and social gains.

A Decade of Development.—The early planes were clumsy contrivances, prone to failure and slow of speed when judged by present standards. When the first flights were made the pilot lay on the lower wing; soon thereafter a perch was fixed among the wires and struts from which it is strange early pilots were not often dislodged. Gradually the machine took on a resemblance to its present form, though at the time of the outbreak of the World War it was still "little more than a novel contraption in which daredevils risked their lives at air meets and country fairs." In fact, the only source of income for the operators of planes during this period was from these "shows": popular interest ran high and, if the plane refused to fly, it could be enclosed by canvas and admission charged to see it. Experimentation was general, a great variety of devices was tried, and definite progress made; among the changes were the adoption of the aileron, a change in the position of the propeller from the rear to the fore of the plane, and the development of the fuselage.

This initial decade was one during which individual pilots gained prominence, vying with one another for records of speed, distance, time in the air, and altitude. The early flights made by the Wrights were at approximately 37 miles per hour. This record was soon increased by the Wrights, then Farman approached 50 miles per hour, and in 1910 Curtis exceeded 50 miles. In 1913 an average of 84.5 miles per hour was made on a 930-mile flight. As the principles of flight became clear, improvement in the machine made possible steadily increasing heights: in 1908 Wilbur Wright was acclaimed "King of the Air" because of attaining a height of 187 feet—and in 1912 Garros reached 19,032. As early as 1909 the War Department of the United States purchased Wright equipment and the next year the French employed planes in their military maneuvers. Interest was shown by British and German governments, also, yet the plane was regarded merely as an observation unit. Though used in the Balkan War in 1912, it was during the World War that the plane established its practical value: during 4 short years its development was little short of phenomenal. Benefiting from the best of the world's engineering talent and financed lavishly from government treasuries, the plane made such rapid progress technically that, at the war's close, it gave promise of immediate adaptation to commercial use.

The Immediate Postwar Period.—The termination of the war found all the major powers equipped to produce planes in large numbers, possessed of a large number of trained pilots eager to capitalize their skill in the commercial field, and convinced of the military importance of maintaining during periods of peace a vigorous aviation industry. To insure continuous development, European governments granted generous subsidies to commercial aviation; as a consequence many lines were established and a superior service made available throughout the whole of Europe. The operating revenues of these lines have come largely from passenger and goods traffic, mail being of lesser importance as a source of revenue because of short distances and diverse nationalities. Operating revenues have in few instances approximated costs, however: an industry that to Americans has seemed robust would have found continuance impossible without government subventions. In the United States, on the other hand, public subsidies have been regarded with disfavor: while the importance of aviation was recognized, it was felt that the industry should essentially "stand on its own feet." Surplus stocks of war planes were sold at low figures, but these planes were ill adapted to commercial use and served to retard rather than stimulate such development. Attempts were made to establish regular service, yet these were uniformly unsuccessful because of the high unit costs of operation and lack of "air consciousness" on the part of the public. Personnel and planes in the immediate postwar period were employed largely by flying schools, traveling air circuses, air-taxi services, and individuals flying for pleasure. During these years but a single activity was begun in America that was destined to have an important bearing upon the later development of air transport: this activity was the initiation of air-mail service.

Mail had been carried by plane as early as 1911 to serve the ends of publicity, but in 1918 regular service was established by the Post Office Department between Washington and New York City and maintained for a period of 3 months. Upon the basis of the experience gained service was established a year later between Cleveland and Chicago; within a brief time the eastern terminus of the air-mail route was fixed at New York City and on Sept. 18, 1920, service was extended to San Francisco. A transcontinental air post had been brought into being and from it was destined to develop America's existing network of mail lines. But the operation of this and other lines established before the change to a contract basis presented a serious challenge to those who participated in such pioneering: all-weather flying was new, equipment was indifferently suited to the service, fields few, routes unmarked, night flying an experiment, and adequate meteorological information lacking. At first mails were moved only by daylight; later, realizing the need of overnight movement of mails, the government lighted portions of the airways to permit night flying. By 1925 the Post Office Department felt that the situation justified the transfer of air-mail operations to private hands; to that end legislation was passed under which many contract feeder lines were established and under which, by the close of 1927, private operators had taken over all government main-line routes. Inasmuch as numerous contracts for feeder-line operations were let in 1926, that may be properly regarded as the year in which commercial air transport in the United

States had its beginning. The infancy of this new enterprise has been a vigorous one.

Physical Prerequisites to Successful Air Transport.—To the successful conduct of air-transport operations there are three physical elements prerequisite; these are the airplane, the airway, and the airport. And, while each of these is fundamentally a matter of engineering concern, their bearing upon service rendered and upon the immediate promise of the industry is such that no study of the economic aspects of air transport can neglect certain facts pertaining to each element. Of the airplane as an operating unit there are three essential features; most obvious of these are the structure, which includes fuselage and wings, and the power plant. Yet of great significance to the economic success of aviation are those instruments that give to the pilot certain vital facts. Physiography will determine whether airplane, seaplane, or amphibian shall be flown, and, while experience has not yet indicated clearly the services to which biplanes and monoplanes of various types are best adapted, it is upon further experience that dependence must be placed largely for an answer to that question. The size of plane, too, that is to be used upon a particular route must be determined by knowledge gained of the route: there seem to be no serious engineering obstacles to the construction of units purposed to meet light demands or of huge units capable of transporting 100 passengers[1] or a comparably heavy cargo. But there is one point of prime economic significance that relates to size: only within narrow limits does total cost per passenger or cargo unit seem to decline as the size of the plane increases beyond a certain point. In fact, it is probable that increasing cost may be found to apply beyond a particular maximum. In consequence, since the major cost of air transport is the operating cost, the law of increasing returns in that field will be of far less importance than, for example, with the railway. With the power plant and the instruments, as such, a transportation study has no direct concern; yet, functioning in conjunction with the structure served by them, they are of vital import. The future of air transport depends upon the ability of the plane to render regular, safe, and relatively inexpensive service. Structure and power-plant failures are so few that safe flying has, by and large, been attained; mishaps and irregularities in service are today due primarily to the lack of adequate instruments upon which a pilot may call for assistance when beset by adverse weather conditions. But less progress has been made toward the reduction in flying costs than in improving instruments: operating costs per mile have not within the past 5 years been reduced to that degree which is essential if aviation is to become self-

[1] The DO-X, a European-built seaplane, has a passenger capacity of 100, with a crew of 10 persons. It is equipped with 12 motors, has a total horsepower of 6,300, and has a cruising range of 600 miles. Its length is 152 feet, its wing span 165 feet; maximum speed is 135 miles per hour, cruising speed 110 miles per hour. Its cost was approximately $500,000.

supporting. True, the evolution of a Diesel engine suitable for planes, the use of improved materials, and improvements in design give promise; more rapid materialization of that promise is needed, however. There is not the slightest reason to doubt that steady gains will be made in adapting the plane to the requisites of satisfactory service, yet only some revolutionary discovery will enable it to perform more than a supplementary and emergency service in the predictable future: while progress bids fair to be certain, because air transport has speed to sell and purchasers of speed may always be found, such progress is unlikely to be rapid.

While the plane in the air has the mobility of the ship upon open water, the regular and safe operation of plane as well as ship requires that its path be definite and safeguarded by every known device. Safe flying, even by day, must be done with reference to the availability of landing fields; night flying is highly dangerous except as a lighted course is followed. Certain routes, because of local conditions, are safer than others; particularly is this true in mountainous areas. And, with the development of the radio-range beacon which indicates at all times the location of the plane in relation to the direct course, the airway has become even less flexible. While the flying unit is owned and operated by private enterprise, all work done in fixing, marking, and maintaining airways has been at the expense of the federal government, the organization directly charged with this responsibility being the Airways Division, Aeronautics Branch, Department of Commerce. Under the direction of this organization considerable sums are spent annually, as a result of which,[1]

> At the close of the fiscal year 1932 there were in operation and under construction or installation 19,500 miles of lighted airways, 69 radio communication stations, 94 radio-range beacons, 118 radio marker beacons, and 233 teletypewriter stations on a leased-wire system comprising some 13,000 miles of circuits. The total personnel of the airways division was 2,102, of whom 897 were part-time employees serving as attendants or caretakers at intermediate fields and beacon lights.

This cooperative work on the part of the government with commercial operators of planes, together with the vital assistance given by the Weather Bureau in reporting weather conditions and probabilities, have contributed immeasurably to safety and to regularity in air-transport operations.

Quite as essential to the success of air transport as the airway is the airport: except as airports are sufficient in number, satisfactory in character, and suitable as to location, failure is sure. Early ports, even in the vicinity of large cities, were often no more than comparatively level areas occupied in turn by planes and grazing herds. As use by the former came to justify exclusive privileges, a development was begun that has flowered

[1] *Twentieth Annual Report*, Secretary of Commerce, p. 13.

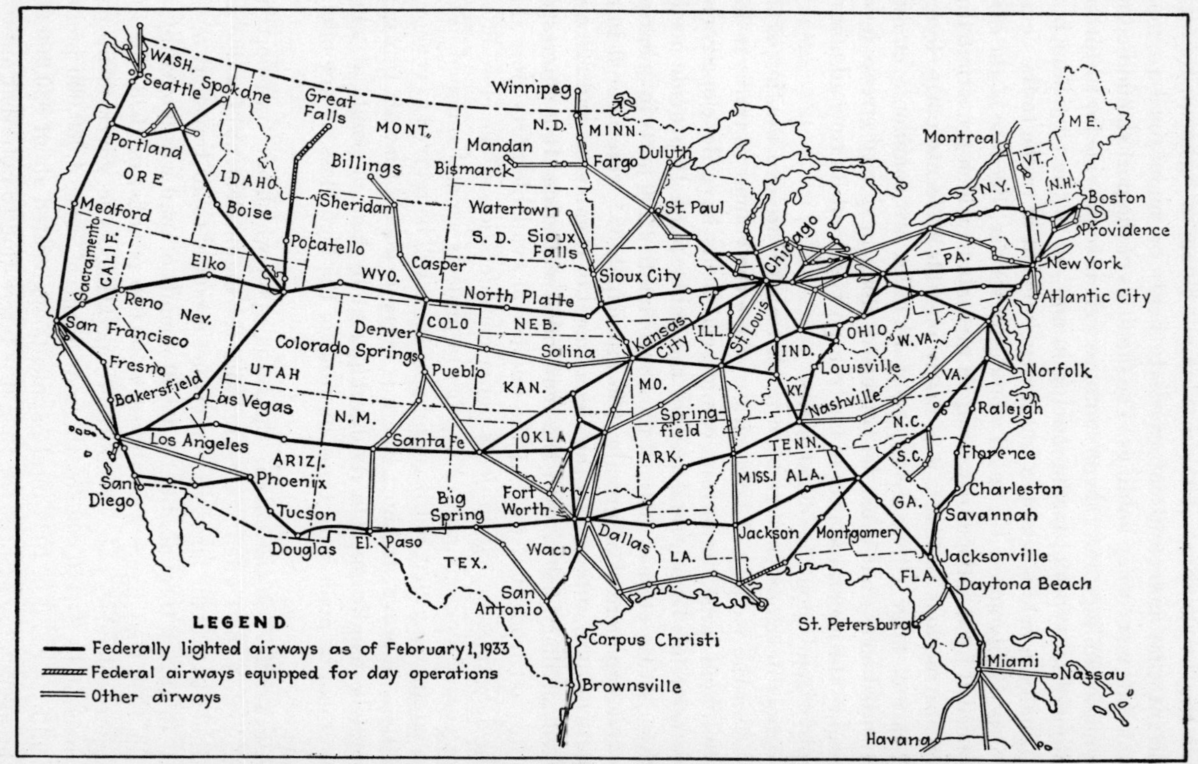

FIG. 42.—Federally equipped and other airways in the United States, Feb. 1, 1933.

in certain of the magnificent ports now serving our great centers of population. Since the port is the point at which contact is made with traffic, it is essential that a sufficient number of ports lie along any regular route to permit the development of the maximum volume of business; too, it is important that numerous intermediate fields be maintained to make possible safe emergency landings. The facilities of the port should be such as to make landings and takeoffs safe, as well as to provide for the proper handling of all types of traffic moving in and out of the particular port. And, finally, a field is adapted to the development of traffic to the degree that it is readily accessible to all who desire service. Because of the large area needed for a satisfactory field, an area about which are situated no major obstructions to flight, it is rarely possible to locate ports close to the heart of large cities: distances of 10 miles are common, yet even shorter distances that must be traversed along busy city streets lessen materially the general appeal of air transport and cut its time advantage sharply except upon the longer hauls.

Airport development has been in part at private expense, in part at public. In the vicinity of large cities, where the volume of traffic is both constant and large, important commercial fields have developed; elsewhere there has been a tendency for the public purse to provide needed facilities. At the close of 1931, of the approximate 2,100 ports in operation 673 were commercial or private, 636 municipal, 385 were lighted intermediate fields maintained by the Department of Commerce, and 300 were marked auxiliary fields, with the remainder scattering. It is interesting to note that from 1927 to 1931 the number of available ports more than doubled, with some 350 projects under consideration at the close of the latter year. Seemingly a large number of projects were abandoned in the 2 years following 1929, yet it is probable these will be revived as economic conditions improve. In short, there is every evidence that air transport will not be handicapped in its development by lack of points at which contact can be made with those desirous of the high-class service offered by planes.

Air Traffic. *Mail.*—Mail, the basis upon which air transport has developed in the United States, remains the major element of traffic and continues to provide largely the revenues essential to air-transport operations. In 1926 a total of about 810,000 pounds of mail was moved by air and in 1932 that figure was almost 7,400,000 pounds; in 1928, the first complete calendar year of contract operations, the government paid approximately $7,430,000 for the movement of some 4,060,000 pounds of mail by air and in 1932 total payments aggregated about $30,900,000. Of the aggregate payment for 1932 it is interesting to note that approximately one-fourth was made to air lines for handling foreign mail: though the volume of such matter increased little from 1928 to 1931 the compensation paid increased some thirty-five times. In the 5-year period ending

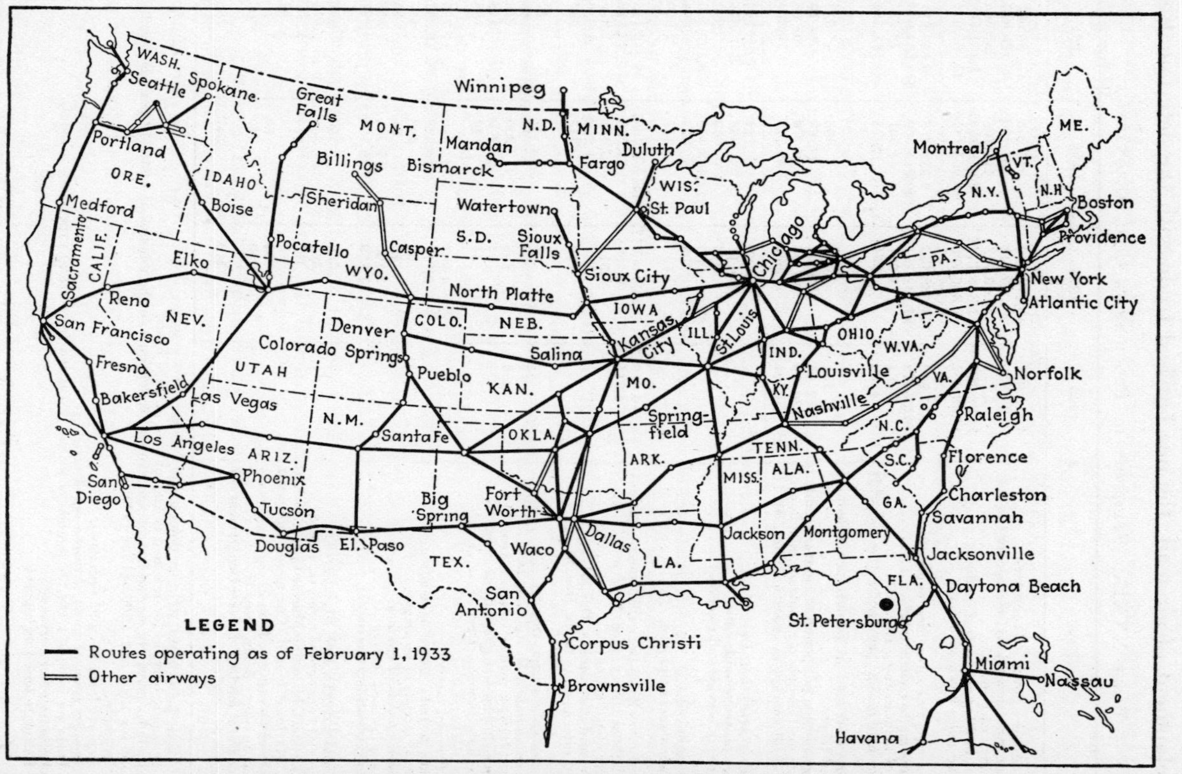

Fig. 43.—Air-mail and other routes in the United States, Feb. 1, 1933.

with 1931 the miles of airways flown in mail service increased from 8,039 to 43,735 and plane-miles from 4,200,000 to 33,100,000.[1]

Two problems have been faced by the Post Office Department in the development of air mail: the one has had to do with the determination

TABLE XXXIX.—STATISTICS OF PROGRESS IN CIVIL AERONAUTICS

Item	1926	1928	1930	1931
Airplane miles flown, all operators	4,318,087	10,673,450	36,945,203	47,385,987
Airplane miles flown daily, average for the year	11,830	29,242	101,220	129,825
Passengers carried	5,782	49,713	417,505	522,345
Express and freight carried, pounds	1,733,090	1,848,156‡	2,869,255‡	1,151,348**
Airplane miles flown with mail*	4,240,407	7,846,296	19,904,185§	29,263,042
Mail carried by contractors, pounds*	377,206	4,063,173	8,513,675	9,643,211
Mail income to contractors*	$765,549	$7,432,721	$20,015,969	$26,884,044
Miles of mail airways, Dec. 31*	8,264	14,561	41,501	43,735
Average mail income per scheduled round trip†	$590	$994	$974	$1,482
Average mail load in pounds per scheduled round trip†	182	489	608	678
Average income per pound of contract mail†	$2.03	$2.03	$1.60	$2.19
Average mail income per contract mile flown	$0.39	$0.94	$0.70	$0.68
Miles of all airways in operation, Dec. 31	8,404	16,667	49,549	50,399
Services in operation, Dec. 31	....	63	122	126
Average passenger-mile rate	....	$0.11	$0.083	$0.0674
Airplanes in service and reserve	....	325	600	590
Value	....	$7,000,000§	$11,489,450	$9,167,500
Pilots employed	....	308‖	675	690
Total personnel employed	....	1,496¶	3,475	5,650††
Airplane miles flown (miscellaneous operations)	18,746,640‡‡	60,000,000‡‡	108,269,760‡‡	94,343,115
Miles lighted airway, Dec. 31	2,041	6,988	15,258	17,512
Under construction	....	2,314	3,221	1,879
Electric and gas beacons, Dec. 31	....	1,188	1,652	1,836
Lighted intermediate fields, Dec. 31	....	210	347	385
Radio-beacon stations, Dec. 31	....	2	33	47
Radio communication stations, Dec. 31	17	29	45	56
Weather Bureau regular stations, Dec. 31	202	206	209	218
Weather Bureau airways stations, Dec. 31	12	95	279	348
Private light beacons, Dec. 31	....	54	140	188
Pilots licensed (active)	....	4,887	15,280	17,739
Students permits' issued or pending	....	9,717	18,528	16,047
Approved models of airplanes	....	96	390	456
Approved models of engines	....	13	64	75
Airplanes licensed (active)	....	3,165	7,354	7,553
Airplanes identified (active)	....	1,939	2,464	3,227
Municipal airports, Dec. 31	....	368	550	636
Private and commercial airports, Dec. 31	....	365	564	673
Navy airports, including Marine Corps, Dec. 31	....	17	14	} 90
Army, National Guard, Commerce unlighted and reserve airports, Dec. 31	....	64	60	}
Marked auxiliary fields, Dec. 31	....	340	240	300
Intermediate landing fields—Department of Commerce—lighted	....	210	347	385

* All air-mail routes, whether domestic or foreign.
† Domestic only, as foreign mail is carried on a mileage basis.
‡ Includes privately carried freight and express on schedule to the amount of 1,631,512 pounds for 1928, 1,609,436 for 1929, and 2,400,684 for 1930.
§ Estimate.
‖ Reports from 33 of 35 operators.
¶ Reports from 27 to 33 of the 35 operators.
** Does not include 1,532,156 pounds of privately carried freight and express on schedule.
†† Includes office personnel.
‡‡ Estimate based on reports.

of the postage rate, the other with the basis of payment for the movement of mail by air. When operations were wholly in the hands of the govern-

[1] Other interesting facts concerning the air-mail service will be gathered from a study of Table XXXIX, above.

ment, zone divisions were established and a charge of 8 cents per ounce was made for each zone or portion thereof that a piece of mail traversed. When contract service was established, a charge of 10 cents per ounce was made for each contract line over which a piece of air mail moved, plus 5 cents per ounce for each of the established government line zones traversed by it. To eliminate complexities and discrimination a blanket rate of 10 cents per half ounce was later established. Finally, with a view to increasing the volume of air mail and particularly of stimulating social use, a rate of 5 cents for the first ounce and 10 cents for each additional ounce was fixed in August, 1928. This rate was continued until a need for increased postal revenues in 1932 led to an increase in those rates to 8 and 13 cents, respectively. Following the application of increased rates the volume of air mail dropped rather sharply, though the continued low level of business activity has also undoubtedly been a factor in causing the decline. This indication of the inability of air mail to bear rates that will cover costs raises an important problem which is in part one of social policy, in part one of governmental economy. A cost-ascertainment study made by the Post Office Department for the fiscal year 1932 indicated that the total deficit on air-mail service, domestic and foreign, for that year was in excess of $23,845,000: the loss upon these two services was, respectively, some $17,755,000 and $6,090,000. To what extent is a service justified that pays less than 30 per cent of its total cost?

The basis of payment to air-transport lines for movement of mail has undergone many changes. Initially it was fixed in relation to postage paid on air mail moving over the route, a maximum of 80 per cent of the total air postage being allowed the contractor. Experience showed that this yielded a revenue to the carrier of about $2.50 per pound of mail carried. Because of the detailed accounting made necessary by this basis of payment a flat-rate plan was adopted with the maximum rate fixed at $3 per pound per 1,000 miles, a further payment being made of 30 cents for each additional 100 miles or fraction thereof. This change increased payments to the operators, yet also saved money for the government by the elimination of costly accounting procedure. After various adjustments of an experimental character, a general basis for future payments was outlined in the Watres Act of 1930. The significant provisions of this appear in the two sections following:

Sec. 4. The Postmaster General is authorized to award contracts for the transportation of air mail by aircraft between such points as he may designate to the lowest responsible bidder at fixed rates per mile for definite weight spaces, 1 cubic foot of space being computed as the equivalent of 9 pounds of air mail, such rates not to exceed $1.25 per mile: Provided, that where the air mail moving between designated points does not exceed 25 cubic feet, or 225 pounds, per trip, the Postmaster General may award to the lowest responsible bidder who has owned and operated an air-transportation service on a fixed daily schedule over a distance of not less than 250 miles and for a period of not less than 6 months prior to the advertisement for bids, a contract not to exceed 40 cents for a weight space of 25 cubic feet, or 225 pounds. Whenever sufficient mail is not available, first-class mail matter may be added to make up the maximum load specified in the contract.

Sec. 6. The Postmaster General may . . . upon the surrender of any air-mail contract, issue in substitution therefor a route certificate for a period of not exceeding 10 years from the date service started under such contract to any contractor or subcontractor who has satisfactorily operated an air-mail route for a period of not less than 2 years, which certificate shall provide that the holder thereof shall have the right, so long as he complies with all rules . . . issued by the Postmaster General for meeting the needs of the postal service and adjusting mail operations to the advances in the art of flying and passenger transportation, to carry air mail over the route . . . at rates of compensation to be fixed from time to time, at least annually, by the Postmaster General . . . provided, that such rates shall not exceed $1.25 per mile. Such certificate may be canceled at any time for willful neglect on the part of the holder . . . notice to be given in writing by the Postmaster General and 45 days allowed the holder in which to show cause why the certificate should not be canceled.

Under the terms of this Act the Postmaster General devised a formula in accordance with which payments for service should be made. To assist to this end, a uniform system of accounting was prescribed. Under the initial formula adopted payments varied from a minimum of 40 cents to a maximum of $1.185. Changes were made in this formula from time to time, to adapt it more closely to need and equity, the formula in effect for the 6 months ending June 30, 1932, appearing in Table XL. Under this formula payments per mile varied from a minimum of 38 cents to a maximum of 74 cents for day flying, 15 cents per mile being added for night trips. The average rate paid per mile in 1932 was 62 cents—as compared with 79 cents for the preceding year. It is interesting to note that, while the rates paid for day flying under the initial formula tended to group between 56 and 63.5 cents, those under the formula here reproduced tend to group between 39 and 43 cents.[1]

It is significant, and indicative of the government's purpose to encourage commercial operations, that the rate of pay for mail movement takes into account the number of motors of the plane, the total horse power, and the number of passengers for which the plane provides accommodations. That such fostering care will be continued for a considerable period is doubtful: the sentiment of the American public is traditionally against direct and obvious subsidies; and, furthermore, current movements toward greater economy have subjected governmental deficits

[1] For rates paid per mile of flying under the initial formula see the *Annual Report* of the Postmaster General for the fiscal year ending June 30, 1931, pp. 127–128. The rates paid under the formula given in Table XL appear in the *Annual Report* of the Postmaster General for 1932, pp. 120–122.

on air mail to close scrutiny and sharp attack. It seems probable that the Watres Act may be superseded, another method of payment being adopted that makes the service more nearly self-supporting than does the present.[1]

TABLE XL.—FORMULA EFFECTIVE JAN. 1, 1932, TO JUNE 30, 1932, FOR DETERMINING RATES OF PAY TO ROUTE CERTIFICATE HOLDERS TRANSPORTING AIR MAIL UNDER THE WATRES ACT

Class A, Cents per Mile

Base Rate	Service	Terrain	Fog	2-way radio	Night flying: 50 per cent	Night flying: 100 per cent	2 to 5 passengers	6 to 9 passengers	10 to 12 passengers	13 to 19 passengers	Single motor horse power: 325	Single motor horse power: 326 and over	Multimotor horse power: 1,000	Multimotor horse power: 1,800	Mail load
20	5	2	2	6	5	15	4.5	6	8	10	6	11	7	16	7—101 to 300 8—301 to 400 13—401 to 750 15—751 to 1,000 17—1,001 to 1,250 19—1,251 to 1,400 21—1,401 to 1,600

Class B, Cents per Mile (not over 43 cents per mile)

Base rate	Trimotor horse power: 1,000	Trimotor horse power: 1,800	9 passengers	10 to 12 passengers	2-way radio	Fog	Terrain	Mail load
20	6	10	6	8	4	2	2	3–up to 100

Passenger Service by Air.—One of the striking features of air-transport growth has been the steady and rapid increase in the volume of passenger

[1] Upon the basis of an extended study of the air-mail problem, the Committee on Post Office and Post Roads, House of Representatives, has formulated an entirely new basis of payment for service rendered. This was embodied in H. R. 14605, introduced at the 2d Session, 72d Congress. This measure would establish two groups of air-mail contractors; to the one would be paid 2 mills per pound-mile of mail carried, with a maximum of 50 cents per airplane mile; to the other the same payment per pound-mile would be made, plus an additional sum—not to exceed 25 cents per mile—based on a sliding scale. The first group would render a self-sustaining service at once and it is estimated that the second would be on a self-sustaining basis by July 1, 1939. This measure proposes an air-mail postal card, also a reduction of the air-mail letter rate to the former figure of 5 cents (see Investigation of United States Postal Air Mail Service, House Report 2087, 72d Congress, 2d Session).

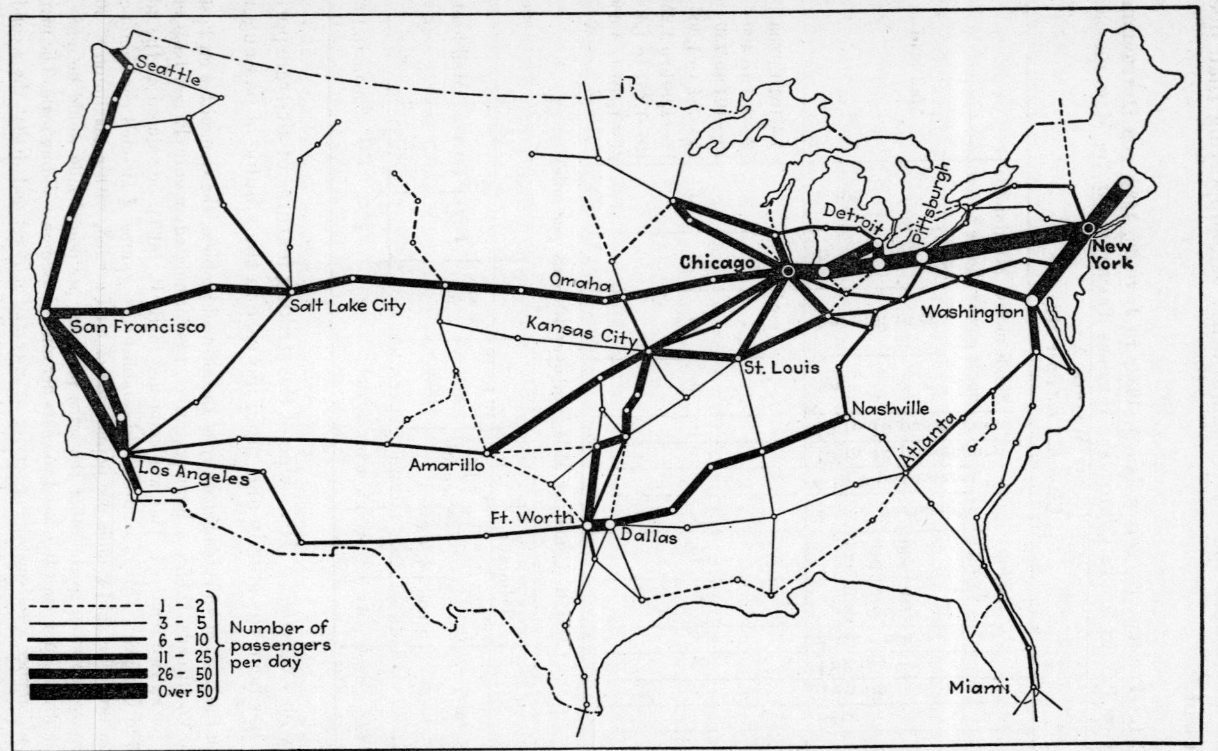

FIG. 44.—Density of air passenger traffic over regular routes, 1932. The almost 50,000,000 passenger-miles of service rendered by American air lines exceeds by half that of all other countries combined. (*Aviation.*)

traffic. In 1926, 5,782 passengers were carried over 3,715 miles of route; in 1932 scheduled air lines moved 540,681 passengers over 47,358 miles of route, performing a total service of 146,552,587 passenger-miles. Thus available data for 1932 indicate an increase in traffic volume beyond that of 1931, despite adverse business conditions. This rapid advance in volume of passenger service is due to a number of factors. The growing air-mindedness of the public is a favorable element; the steady advance of cruising speeds has increased the time advantage of air travel; steady gains in safety and in regularity of operations have made air travel more attractive; air lines are operating on more frequent and more convenient schedules, and are increasing their efforts to speed travel not only through the better coordination of air-transport schedules but through arrangements for the interchange of traffic with other agencies of transport, notably the railways; and close attention is being given to the comfort and convenience of the service offered. But perhaps a favorable rate schedule has been an even greater influence than any of those factors just indicated in stimulating air travel; rates that declined from an average of 12 cents per passenger mile in 1929 to 6.74 cents in 1931 have had a positive influence upon passenger-traffic volume. The lure of rates for air service that approximate rail plus Pullman charges between most points is undoubtedly strong.

Concerning each of the considerations that together have accounted for such a phenomenal growth in passenger travel by air many interesting facts and observations could be offered, did the space permit. Yet the limitations of space must not preclude mention of certain ones. Time has been required to accustom the public to a new mode of transportation and especially to one as foreign to common experience as is travel by air, subject as such transportation is to unusual hazards. Five years ago cruising speeds were often less than 90 miles per hour; those speeds have been increased, as a consequence of engineering advances and pressure for faster schedules, to figures commonly in excess of 140 miles and occasionally 160—with higher speeds in the immediate offing. Improved instruments and airway aids suggest a near approach to absolute "blind flying," even to the point of permitting the pilot to land safely at any modern airport "when weather conditions are such as to prevent his seeing anything outside the cockpit"; greater structural strength and more dependable power units will also tend to eliminate breaks in service because of adverse weather. Much has been done to speed the passenger to and from airports and make him more comfortable while there; experiments in sound-proofing passenger cabins have yielded tangible results; and increased stability of the planes in the air has made for increased riding comfort. In short, no opportunity to make air transport appeal to the public in such a way as to increase traffic is being overlooked. The promise is bright for the future.

Goods Traffic by Air.—In discussions of air-transport service stress is normally put upon movements of mail and of persons, with little emphasis upon movements of property. Such neglect is not justified by the facts, as an examination of pertinent data in Table XXXIX will show. There are two types of carriers of property by air: the one may well be termed the contract carrier because he handles shipments by private arrangement, either as his only work or supplementary to some other service; the other functions as a common carrier, offering to serve all. While the volume of contract traffic moved has varied rather sharply from year to year, it has shown a tendency to remain constant throughout the period: the volume of traffic in 1931—1,532,156 pounds—was but some 200,000 pounds below the figure for 1926, despite unsatisfactory business conditions. During the period 1926–1932 the volume of express handled by the lines offering a general public service has increased markedly: in the 2 years mentioned the poundage handled was 3,555 and 1,600,821, respectively. It is interesting to note that the figure for 1932 represents an increase of roughly 240 per cent over 1930, presumptively a consequence in major part of the downward revision of air-express rates by the Railway Express Agency in cooperation with the air lines over which it serves. Midyear in 1932 a number of the major air-transport companies of the United States cooperated in the formation of General Air Express[1] to function over some 17,600 miles of route, and the first announcement of this organization was that of a reduction of some 14 per cent in the air-express rates then governing, pick-up and delivery service to be performed locally by Postal Telegraph. This reduction was shortly met by the Railway Express Agency; lower express rates are now available, therefore, over practically all air lines.

The limited number of points between which express movements can be made wholly by air permits of a simple system of rate quotation. The same system is employed by both the Railway Express Agency and General Air Express: in an index table are given the numbers of the rate scales applicable to movements between named cities (see Fig. 45), and in another table appear in parallel columns under the successive rate-scale numbers the charges for shipments of various weights (see Fig. 46). Thus it appears that, in general form, tariffs governing the movement of express by air are closely comparable to those controlling movement by rail. The only differences, and these are minor, between the tariffs of the two air-express organizations are two: General Air uses in its tariff a greater number of rate scales, so the charge for a shipment of given weight is not the same for the same numbered scales of the companies; and General Air quotes rates by pounds from 1 to 200 pounds, while the

[1] The air lines which cooperate in rendering this service serve largely the Eastern, Southeastern, and Southern portions of the United States. The Railway Express Agency serves over air lines that lie largely in the Middle West and the West, though reaching New York City, also.

Railway Express Agency quotes by the half pound from 1 to 21 pounds—giving a uniform charge for each rate scale to be applied to each additional half pound beyond 21 pounds. If, because of adverse weather conditions or other obstacles, complete delivery cannot be made by air, any necessary portion of the movement is made by railway express and total charges are adjusted accordingly. One of the features of air express that is entitled to mention is the "special-delivery" service at the end of the journey; shipments are moved from airport to consignee, often, within a few minutes after the carrying plane has landed.

(Continued from Scale Chart at right)

Scale Number Between → and ↓	Abilene	Akron	Alameda	Albany	Albuquerque	Amarillo	Ann Arbor	Atlanta	Atlantic City	Austin	Bakersfield	Baltimore	Baton Rouge	Battle Creek	Bay City	Beaumont	Big Spring	Birmingham	Boston	Brownsville	Buffalo	Camden	Charleston	Charlotte	Chattanooga	Chicago	Cincinnati	Cleveland	Columbus
Dallas	2	21	33	31	12	6	22	14	31	3	28	27	10	20	23	6	5	11	33	9	25	28	24	19	14	18	17	21	19
Dayton	21	2	44	12	26	21	6	9	12	22	42	8	18	7	7	22	24	12	14	28	7	9	17	14	7	3	1	3	1
Daytona Beach	25	20	56	21	34	28	24	6	20	25	50	15	17	25	25	20	27	9	22	32	24	17	5	11	9	19	16	20	6
Denver	16	25	23	34	7	6	23	26	35	16	23	31	23	22	23	20	17	29	37	23	29	32	35	30	23	19	22	25	23
Detroit	25	3	45	11	28	22	2	18	12	26	40	9	23	2	2	31	27	19	14	33	6	10	18	18	14	5	6	3	4
Douglas	11	37	18	46	7	13	36	29	47	16	12	42	24	35	37	21	9	27	49	20	41	43	39	34	29	32	32	37	35
El Centro	20	46	11	53	16	22	45	38	50	25	5	50	34	43	46	29	18	35	51	28	50	48	48	43	38	40	41	46	43
El Paso	7	33	22	42	3	9	32	26	43	12	16	38	20	31	33	17	5	23	45	16	37	39	35	30	25	28	28	33	31
Evansville	18	7	42	17	22	17	9	6	17	19	38	13	15	8	10	19	20	9	19	26	11	14	16	11	4	4	3	7	5
Flint	25	4	45	14	30	22	x	16	15	26	44	12	23	2	2	30	27	19	19	32	x	x	x	21	14	5	7	x	7
Florence	29	12	59	13	38	33	16	11	12	30	54	7	21	15	18	25	31	13	14	37	17	9	1	10	13	19	16	13	14
Ft. Wayne	23	4	42	14	26	20	x	11	14	24	42	9	20	x	x	28	26	14	16	30	8	10	18	16	9	2	2	x	2
Ft. Worth	2	22	32	31	11	5	22	15	32	3	27	27	10	20	21	6	4	12	34	9	26	28	24	19	14	17	18	22	20
Fresno	27	48	2	53	17	23	46	45	50	31	1	50	40	44	45	36	24	42	51	38	51	48	55	50	45	41	44	48	45
Galveston	8	27	38	34	17	11	28	15	33	5	33	28	5	26	29	1	10	14	35	12	31	30	25	20	18	23	23	28	25
Glendale	23	44	6	53	13	19	44	41	50	35	4	50	36	23	41	32	20	38	51	41	47	48	51	46	41	37	40	44	42
Goodland	19	22	27	31	11	10	20	22	31	20	27	27	25	18	19	27	22	25	33	27	25	28	32	27	20	15	18	21	19
Grand Rapids	24	5	43	14	27	21	x	15	15	24	43	12	22	x	x	29	26	18	17	31	9	13	20	20	13	4	6	6	6
Greensboro	24	10	54	11	33	27	14	5	10	24	49	5	16	16	16	19	26	8	13	31	15	7	10	1	8	17	14	11	12
Greenville	20	14	51	15	30	24	18	2	14	21	46	9	12	19	19	16	23	5	16	27	19	11	12	1	4	15	11	15	14
Harrisburg	29	4	52	5	34	28	8	16	4	29	50	3	26	10	8	28	31	18	6	36	9	1	13	11	15	11	8	5	6
Hartford	35	10	50	4	40	34	13	17	3	35	50	4	27	14	14	31	37	20	1	42	9	3	14	12	19	16	13	9	11
Houston	7	27	38	33	17	11	27	14	32	4	33	27	4	26	28	1	9	14	35	11	31	29	24	19	17	22	22	27	24
Indianapolis	20	5	43	14	24	18	7	9	14	20	40	10	17	5	8	21	22	12	17	27	9	11	18	13	6	2	1	5	3
Jackson, Mich.	24	4	44	12	27	21	2	15	13	25	43	10	22	2	x	29	26	18	15	32	7	11	19	19	13	4	6	4	5

FIG. 45.—Portion of an air-express directory (General Air Express), showing scale numbers.

It seems probable that the appearance of vigorous competition for air-express traffic between many of the more important points in the United States marks the beginning of rapid development in that field. And volume is certain to increase strikingly if and as two goals are attained: rates must be within the range not only of shippers of highly perishable commodities and of emergency items but also of those who now send by railway express shipments well suited, because of value and space-weight ratio, to air movement; and service must be so organized as to provide for the expeditious handling of shipments at terminals and at points of interchange between lines. The reductions already made in rates represent a positive step in the direction of the one goal; the coordination of air and rail facilities by the Express Agency, the utilization of the Postal Telegraph delivery service by General Air, and an agreement between the two lines to interchange traffic, represent marked progress toward the other goal. But, of the two needs, that of materially reduced cost is the more important and offers the more difficult problem to air express lines.

Financial Aspects of Air Transport.—In the years prior to the World War the small number of companies engaged in airplane production built an occasional ship; manufacture was of minor proportions and financing

SECTION 3.

AIR EXPRESS PACKAGE CHARGES (IN CENTS).

POUNDS	Scale 6	Scale 7	Scale 8	Scale 9	Scale 10	Scale 11	Scale 12	Scale 13	Scale 14	Scale 15	Scale 16	Scale 17
1	100	125	125	125	125	125	125	125	125	125	125	125
1½	100	125	125	125	125	125	125	125	125	125	126	129
2	100	125	125	125	125	125	125	128	132	136	140	144
2½	104	125	125	125	125	129	134	139	144	149	154	159
3	108	125	125	126	132	138	144	150	156	162	168	174
3½	112	125	126	133	140	147	154	161	168	175	182	189
4	116	125	132	140	148	156	164	172	180	188	196	204
[illegible]	[illegible]	259	[illegible]	[illegible]	364	[illegible]	[illegible]	469	[illegible]	[illegible]	[illegible]	609
18	228	264	300	336	372	408	444	480	516	552	588	624
18½	232	269	306	343	380	417	454	491	528	565	602	639
19	236	274	312	350	388	426	464	502	540	578	616	654
19½	240	279	318	357	396	435	474	513	552	591	630	669
20	244	284	324	364	404	444	484	524	564	604	644	684
20½	248	289	330	371	412	453	494	535	576	617	658	699
21	252	294	336	378	420	462	504	546	588	630	672	714
When Weight exceeds 21 pounds the charge in cents per half pound is........	6	7	8	9	10	11	12	13	14	15	16	17

FIG. 46.—Portion of rate table (Railway Express Agency, Inc.), showing charges. Note bases of charge beyond 21 pounds.

production, as well as the irregular operations of that period, was an individual problem. At the close of the war period there were a number of producing organizations in the field but, because of the large surplus of war stocks that was dumped on the market and the tardiness of the emergence of commercial aviation, no satisfactory financial showing by manufacturers of planes, engines, or parts was possible: the major problem of the industry in the years from 1919 to 1927 was that of maintaining solvency. By 1927, however, a combination of circumstances created a situation that was as tinder awaiting the spark; transfer of air-mail operations to private lines, a growing realization by the public of the commercial possibilities of air transport, and speculative activity in the financial markets constituted the tinder—and the spark was the unparalleled up-surge of public interest that followed a series of sensational transatlantic and mainland-Hawaii flights in the spring and summer of 1927. Almost overnight public interest in aviation stocks developed, and, with continued accomplishments of a spectacular nature to feed that interest, it was soon less difficult to attract funds into patently unsound enterprises than it had been a short time previously into the soundest undertakings. Aviation flourished as the proverbial bay tree—for a time; then, when it became evident that too much money was being invested in planes and in plants to produce planes and far too little in riding in those planes or providing other traffic for them, the bubble burst. Disaster overtook the "mushroom" concerns and threatened the strongly established. Stocks that had attained high altitudes stalled, then plunged to earth or disappeared into oblivion. Production of planes in 1926 totaled 1,125 (including 171 rebuilt and reassembled), with a value of $7,449,000; in 1929 the totals were 6,482 and $46,848,000, respectively; and in 1930 the number of planes produced dropped to 3,248 and their value, excluding power plant, to $21,780,000.[1] In 1925 there were 44 establishments in the aircraft industry; in 1927 and 1929 those figures rose to 70 and 132; but in 1931 that number had dropped to 87. Strong financial support of those undertakings that gave promise for the future, extensive consolidations of surviving properties and operations, and steady growth in earnings from traffic have combined, however, to put the aircraft industry upon a relatively stable basis: except as it is again the victim of its too-enthusiastic friends or of influences not now foreseen, it should attain a sound financial position within the reasonable future: the field of aviation gives no effective promise of being a bonanza for manufacturer or operator, but it offers to both opportunities for modest gains immediately and future speculative profits.

Regulation of Air Transport.—Air operations, scheduled and otherwise, have been singularly free of regulations that affect *carrier* relations; but, because of the peculiar hazard of air transport, both the operator and the producer have been subjected to a degree of control and supervision in the interest of public safety that has few parallels. As early as 1911 Congressional action was sought; in succeeding years various states acted,

[1] Preliminary figures for 1931 give the number of powered aircraft produced in that year as 2,800. Of this number, 1,807 were for domestic civil use, 853 for military service, and 140 for export. Of those for domestic civil use 1,296 were monoplanes, 450 were biplanes, 60 were autogiros, and one was a helicopter. In addition, 225 gliders were built. For 1932 production is reported by the Aeronautics Branch at 1,396 powered units, of which 506 were monoplanes, 864 biplanes, and 26 autogiros or helicopters. The value of planes produced in 1932 is estimated at $15,287,789.25.

largely in accord with a uniform law proposed by a conference of diverse interests; and in 1926 the federal Air Commerce Act became law. The Act defines air commerce broadly, and charges the Secretary of Commerce with its promotion; among other things he is to encourage the establishment of facilities, to promote research and development work in connection with all other governmental agencies, to recommend any necessary meteorological service, to gather and disseminate information upon aeronautical development, and to determine and publish the causes of accidents in civil air operations. The same Act confers upon the Secretary of Commerce the power to regulate all interstate air operations with respect to:

1. The registration of eligible aircraft and their rating as to airworthiness.
2. The periodic examination and inspection of registered craft.
3. The periodic examination and rating of persons serving with registered craft.
4. The examination and rating of air-navigation facilities available for registered craft.
5. Establishment of air-traffic rules for the navigation, protection, and identification of aircraft, including rules as to safe altitudes of flight and rules for the prevention of collisions.
6. The issuance, termination, and suspension or revocation of such certificates as are deemed necessary to the purposes of the Act.

In addition, the Act provided among other things for the transfer of properties owned and used in connection with the government air-mail service from the Post Office Department to the jurisdiction of the Secretary of Commerce and to municipalities; for the establishment and maintenance by the Department of Commerce of civil airways; and for the appointment of an Assistant Secretary of Commerce for Aeronautics.

To assist in the performance of the functions and duties imposed, there has been organized in the Department of Commerce an Aeronautics Branch. This Branch functions through three major parts: the air-regulation service, the airways division, and the aeronautic development service. The first-named, as the title would indicate, has as its function the administration of the regulatory powers given to the Secretary of Commerce. The powers are exercised through three divisions: inspection service, licensing division, and engine-testing section. The airways division is charged with establishing and lighting airways, providing radio and other facilities to make their use more safe, and supervising the proper lighting of landing fields. Through the aeronautical development service the developmental obligations of the Department of Commerce are largely discharged. In this section are four divisions: information, research, airport, and airway-mapping. Though a detailed statement of the work of each of the minor divisions named would be both interesting and informative, it must suffice to say that the broad and varied obligations of the Aeronautics Branch have been discharged with zeal and fidelity; it is to the critical examination of types of equipment submitted for approved-type certificates, to the rigid inspection of equipment in service, and to the care exercised in licensing pilots, together with the intelligent exercise of other functions, that much of the progress of aviation in public favor is due. There is every evidence that this is one field of endeavor which has benefited equally with the public from regulation.

Though the federal Act provides for supervision only of planes moving interstate, the number of operators willing to confine themselves to a single commonwealth is negligible; furthermore, the manufacturer, producing for a national or even world market, finds an approved-type certificate requisite. Therefore, while certain states provide for inspection and for licensing planes and pilots, jurisdiction lies *in fact* almost wholly with the Secretary of Commerce, even as to intrastate operations: certain states exempt those holding federal licenses from state examination and others require that all aircraft and pilots operating intrastate shall have federal licenses. Such almost exclusive federal control of an agency of the type of the airplane is not only desirable but well-nigh requisite.

Measures have been introduced into Congress calling for the regulation of the carrier aspects of air transport. Thus far, however, action has not been favorable: by some it is felt that regulation has not been shown to be necessary, by others that the benefits of regulation would be less than its dangers to an enterprise in the formative stage. Perhaps the major obstacle, though, is legislative inertia. In any event, the likelihood of effective and detailed regulation of air carriers is not immediate. None the less, if a lesson may be learned from the experience of other enterprises that have come under public control, the establishment at a comparatively early time of reasoned control through the cooperative action of the industry and the public is more desirable from the standpoint of the long-time interests of both than a regulatory policy imposed later by an exasperated and vindictive public. And it is unlikely that "free competition" will be more effective in the field of air transport than it has been in the railway and highway fields in furthering public interest or protecting private capital.

REFERENCES

Aeronautical Chamber of Commerce, Inc.: *Proceedings of First National Air-traffic Conference*, Kansas City, Sept. 16–18, 1929.

Black, Archibald: *Transportation Aviation*, Simmons-Boardman Publishing Company, 1926.

———: *Civil Airports and Airways*, Simmons-Boardman Publishing Company, 1929.

Chamber of Commerce of the United States: *Report of Transportation and Communication Department*, 1927.

———: *Air Manual*, Washington, D. C., 1930.

Glover, Warren I.: Cost of Air-line Operation, paper read before Buffalo Aeronautic Meeting of American Society of Mechanical Engineers, June, 1932.

Haag, Frederick, Jr.: *Commodities Moved by Air Transportation*, Bureau of Foreign and Domestic Commerce, United States Department of Commerce, 1930.

National Association of Railroad and Public Utility Commissioners: *Report* at convention, Hot Springs, Ark., Nov. 15–18, 1932.

National Council on Uniform Aeronautic Regulatory Laws: Official Proceedings, *United States Daily*, vol. 5, No. 256.

PAGE, VICTOR W.: *The A B C of Aviation*, The Norman W. Henley Publishing Company, New York, 1928.

Postmaster General: *Report* (annual), Government Printing Office.

Security Owners Association: *A Study of Transportation by Airway as Related to Competition with Railway Carriers in Continental United States*, New York, 1932.

SHANNON, HOMER H.: Air Transport Builds for the Future, *Traffic World*, vol. 5, p. 23.

SMITH, WESLEY L.: *Air Transport Operation*, McGraw-Hill Book Company, Inc., 1931.

SUDBOROUGH, C. B.: The Terminals' Place in Transportation, address delivered at the opening of the Second National Airport Conference, Buffalo, 1930.

United States Daily, vol. 7.

United States Department of Commerce: *Aeronautics Trade Directory*, Government Printing Office, 1931.

———: *Air Commerce Bulletin*, vols. 1–4.

———: *Commerce Yearbook* (annual).

———: *Descriptions of Airports and Landing Fields in the United States*, Airway Bulletin 2, Government Printing Office, 1932.

———: *General Airway Information*, Airway Bulletin 1, Government Printing Office, 1932.

———: *Twentieth Annual Report*, Government Printing Office, 1932.

United States Post Office Department: *Cost-ascertainment Report* (annual). Government Printing Office.

WOOLLEY, JAMES G., and EARL W. HILL: *Airplane Transportation*, Hartwell Publishing Company, Hollywood, 1929.

CHAPTER XXXVIII

PROGRESSIVE TRANSPORT

IN CHAPTERS preceding that deal with the various agencies of transport which, separately and in conjunction, serve the American people, emphasis has been placed upon the characteristic features of the service rendered rather than upon the efforts of each of these groups to establish itself in public favor. Yet these efforts, suggestive of the future, must not be overlooked; neither should the efforts made to coordinate certain of the agencies, to the end that a more adequate and satisfactory service be rendered the public, be ignored. In this chapter, therefore, will be given a brief *résumé*, illustrative rather than exhaustive, of the efforts that are being made to win patronage by each of the major agencies previously discussed and of the extent to which coordination has progressed. In closing the chapter a statement will be offered concerning yet another agency of transport, the pipe line, that within recent years has come to loom large and to complicate certain problems of rate making and commodity use.

The Railway.—The railway, the "backbone of American transportation," offers its service through a complex agency: factors that make its service more attractive to the public are the result not only of technical progress but also of changes in policy. To understand what has been done, then, within comparatively recent years to make the railway a more formidable competitor and, by the same sign, a more effective public servant, it is essential first to note changes in a physical plant that comprises a number of diverse yet associated elements; of these the more important are the power unit, the freight car, the passenger car, the roadway, and the terminal. After these facts have been placed before the reader, consideration will be given to the service offered by these elements working in conjunction and to policies that have been adopted by management in an endeavor to promote the use of railway service by the public.

The Locomotive.—The railway locomotive assumed its general form and character many years ago and, because certain externals have changed little, there are those who ignorantly assert that the train of today is drawn by "a steam engine little different from the locomotive of thirty years ago."[1] Yet, despite the fact that change in locomotive construction is impeded by certain factors the significance of which is less in

[1] A statement credited to the chief executive of a major motor-manufacturing concern in an interview given early in 1933, as published in the *Chicago Tribune* of Jan. 15, 1933.

the motor industry, such a statement is far from the truth. Within a decade, indeed, have come such modifications and innovations that "what has been accomplished under a wide variety of operating conditions is sufficiently challenging to justify the initial assumption that any freight locomotive 10 years of age or older is obsolete."[1] Perhaps one of the most significant developments has been the general adoption of the superheater principle, with a consequent striking increase in operating efficiency and reduction in fuel consumption per thousand gross ton-miles: the average speed of freight trains was greater by one-third in 1930 than in 1920, the average number of net tons per train had increased more than 10 per cent, and fuel consumption per thousand gross tons had declined by almost 30 per cent. Contributing to these gains also are the adoption of the automatic stoker, the increase of grate area, the introduction of the feed-water heater and the thermic syphon, and marked improvement in valve-motion designs: the first two have made available much more heat; the second two have, respectively, conserved heat and increased the heat-absorbing capacity of the boiler by positive water circulation; and the last, by lengthened valve travel, has increased effective port openings, particularly at short cut-offs and high speeds—increased flow of steam makes for high sustained horse-power output while limited cut-off lessens demand on the boiler when developing maximum tractive force at low speeds and increases the speed range within which high values of tractive force may be maintained.

Steam is being used at higher pressures; 250 pounds is not uncommon and pressures of as high as 800 pounds are being used experimentally. The booster has become standard equipment for all heavy-duty locomotives, serving not only to overcome inertia in starting but also being cut in as additional power is needed while the train is in motion. Roller bearings are being applied to drivers, alloy steels find increasing use, and the locomotive bed is being cast in a single piece—all of these tending to reduce maintenance and the last serving also to preserve alignment. Larger drivers for freight locomotives, essential to the greater speed demanded of this type of equipment, have been accompanied by improved counterbalancing; the recent development of the disc wheel has made possible still further progress in this important matter. As suggested, the distinction between passenger locomotives and freight units grows less because of changes in demands: the one was once designed for maximum horse-power output to give speed, the other for maximum tractive force to drag tonnage over ruling grades; today freight trains are often operated at passenger-train speeds and heavy passenger trains make demands for high tractive capacity. In consequence, horse power is the fundamental requirement of both types, with even physical differences tending toward

[1] The Modern Locomotive—What and Why, *Railway Age*, vol. 91, p. 779.

a minimum. And, with the introduction of power lubrication, the picturesque oil-can with its long spout has become but a memory.

Interest in new sources of power has increased sharply, also, during recent years. The motor car has displaced upon many of the lighter passenger runs outmoded steam power; the Diesel-electric is the object of keen interest and careful study; and it is the purpose of the railways to add materially to electrified mileage as soon as financial conditions permit: several important projects have been approved, largely in the more populous Atlantic seaboard states, and others await only the reestablishment of satisfactory earning power. It has been carrier inability to finance purchases of modern power units, together with the large sums invested in mechanically fit units of an older type, that has delayed the substitution of new for old.

The Car.—The units in which property and passengers are moved are much simpler than the locomotive, offering therefore fewer opportunities for improvement. None the less, there have been some notable changes made in the car within recent years and this has been accompanied by a continuation of certain important tendencies that have been long evident. The trend toward larger units in freight service persists; new box cars commonly have a capacity of 100,000 pounds and the capacity of gondola equipment has increased until 140,000-pound cars have become usual in regular service. Improvement in construction has also continued: better material is being employed, particularly better steels; refinements in design and the substitution of lighter materials are making possible a further reduction of pounds of dead weight per unit of carrying capacity; and constant research is producing draft gears of a type that, in the face of the demands made by heavier loading and heavier trains, lessens injury to car and to contents. Interesting work is being done, too, in the field of special equipment. Tubular container cars are being built for the transportation of gases under high pressure; cars are being made available for the shipment in bulk of such difficult commodities as cement; and steady progress is being made in the field of mechanical refrigeration. The ice-cooled car is a source of expense and occasions loss of time; furthermore, the brine dripping from the bunkers contributes generously to the deterioration of all iron and steel items upon the roadway, including track fastenings and bridges. By mechanical refrigeration more constant temperatures, more even distribution of low temperatures, and more nearly desired temperatures can be maintained—to say nothing of such low temperatures as will permit the shipment of frozen foods for any desired distance. To meet the demand for small-shipment units, a refrigerator car is now being built that is standard in every particular except that it is one-half the size of the ordinary refrigerator unit. Certain railways are meeting this need for a smaller unit for general merchandise by the container, upon which comment is offered later.

Yet, despite recent progress in freight-carrying equipment, even greater progress has been made during recent years in passenger equipment. The contrast between the comforts offered by coach equipment built within the past 10 years and by older equipment is striking: however well maintained the latter may be the difference in comfort of seats, the contrast in lounging and lavatory facilities, and even differences in windows are indicative of the period of construction. Not only because of improved seats but also because of improved car construction easier riding is provided. One of the major improvements has been the application of roller bearings to an increasing proportion of cars entering service: with the elimination of more than 85 per cent of starting resistance, jerky starts disappear and pick-up is greatly increased. In Pullman equipment comparable, perhaps greater, progress has been made: among the more noteworthy of recent developments are the single and double bedroom, the four-position seat, the inclosed section, the provision of standing room for upper-berth passengers, and the adoption of air conditioning.

It is perhaps the application of this last principle to various types of equipment that offers greatest promise of increased comfort to the passenger. The first air-conditioned car was put in service by the Baltimore and Ohio in 1929, a day coach equipped to provide comfortable summer riding through air washing and air cooling. Its success led to the application of air conditioning to dining cars by both this railway and the Santa Fe during the following year—and the equipment in 1931 and 1932 of cars to provide constant comfort was undertaken by many railways. Because air conditioning is as yet in the experimental stage, there is no uniformity in principle or device: by some ice is used as the cooling medium; by others mechanical refrigeration is employed, all power utilized being supplied from the car axle. The future of this development, in view of the rapid progress made within so brief a period, is most promising for railway and public.

But perhaps one of the most significant developments in passenger equipment recently has been that of a light self-propelled car operating upon rubber over the rails. The prime weakness of the railway in competing with highway service has been the lack of an economical, yet wholly comfortable, unit upon the rails; though the rail motor car represents a forward step, it falls far short of the goal. This lack now seems to have been met by the development of a type of equipment of which the Budd-Micheline unit is most widely known. This car, constructed of superior stainless steel, electrically welded, and powered by a gasoline motor, seats some 40 passengers and has been built to weigh as little as 13,500 pounds—thus achieving an average dead weight per seated passenger of as little as 340 pounds, a typical figure for modern coach equipment being approximately 1,500 pounds. The pneumatic tire of a specially developed type eliminates noise and makes riding almost perfectly smooth. Experimentation has shown, too, that adhesion under normal and under abnormal conditions is greater for the rubber than for the steel wheel, so traction and braking problems seem to be eliminated as special obstacles. Operating costs, including wages, will average for this new type of unit 15 to 25 cents per mile as compared with 75 cents to $1.25 for branch-line and local main-line steam service. And, undoubtedly, this development of specially constructed equipment will stimulate interest in adapting to operation upon the rails units comparable to the highway bus; indeed, there are interesting possibilities in the development of equipment fitted to operate both upon the highway and the rails. While tardiness has been apparent until recent years in adapting rail passenger service to new conditions, railway executives now seem to be thoroughly alert to possible opportunities.

Track and Terminal.—There have been no innovations in track construction within recent years that are of note; rather, progress appears in further development along lines of effort already begun. With heavier motive power and greater speeds, as well as with increased car capacity, have come heavier rails, heavier bridges, and an improved roadbed. A few years ago 85- and 90-pound sections were standard, yet now 130-pound rail is being laid upon heavy-tonnage lines and a considerable quantity of 152-pound has been put into place. To meet the burden imposed upon the roadbed by weight and speed, it has been necessary to ballast more heavily and more generally, and to give more adequate protection to the tie, even to the rail, by improved fastenings: the tie plate and the head-free rail are finding increased use. The almost universal treatment of timbers, particularly ties, has also contributed to an improved roadway.

Because it is in terminals and in yards that major delays occur and much inconvenience develops in handling shipments, large sums have been expended by the railways within recent years to speed terminal movement. Extensive classification yards have been constructed adjacent to greater cities to assist in expediting cars: these yards, with gravity tracks and retarder systems, make it possible to handle a volume of business that otherwise would be certain to clog traffic channels during periods of heavy movement. Terminal structures have been erected to expedite the dispatch and final delivery of tonnage; among the most noteworthy of these have been the large produce terminals recently provided in certain of the larger centers.

Operating Results.—Since operating results are a consequence of management quite as much as of physical properties, it is important that mention be made of a certain few contributions of management to improved results. In 1922 there was established the first of the shippers' advisory boards that were soon to cover the entire country, boards through which the railways have succeeded in obtaining accurate estimates of probable traffic movements for a period in advance. With this information in hand, the Car Service Division of the American Railway Association has assisted in so marshaling equipment that the railways, beginning in 1923, have been able to meet the heaviest traffic demands in their history with but negligible car shortages. To this splendid result improved equipment naturally contributed, particularly improved power that has enabled the railways to move heavier trains at higher speeds than in the past. Another factor that has contributed to more effective operation is an improvement in train control resulting from signal installation: the growth of automatic-block mileage has been steady, as has been the increase in remote and centralized control installations. Increase in the number of interlocking plants has promoted efficiency of operation, too. In 1929, rendering in terms of revenue ton-miles the greatest service in their history, the railways succeeded in maintaining a car surplus of considerable magnitude throughout the year. To this result many factors, physical and managerial, have contributed. Important among these are heavier trains and higher speeds per hour, made possible by improved roadway and equipment; the more effective distribution of that equipment; a reduction to a minimum of the number of bad-order cars and locomotives; the heavier loading of cars; shipper cooperation in the release of equipment; and the more effective use of motive power through the extension of runs—with this last made possible, in turn, by improvements in both material and design of locomotives. However reluctant the railways may have been to utilize highway transport, a careful study indicates that steady advance has been made in the efficiency of the railway plant. In view of the inevitable tendency of methods to become fixed as an industry matures, and in view of the fact that the average life of railway equipment, when properly maintained, varies from perhaps 20 years for freight cars to at least 30 years for locomotives and passenger cars, it seems that the level of railway efficiency has risen rapidly during the past decade.

Railway Policy.—The physical plant of the railways has been made ready to serve; the extent to which the public uses that plant is determined by the degree to which service is adapted to needs and by the charges made for such service. Not only have the railways within recent years improved the average performance of freight trains but there has been an increasing tendency to operate certain fast freights upon regular schedule, these schedules often approaching passenger time. Night runs, with trains carrying both carload and package freight, between points upward of 200 miles apart are common and numerous runs are made regularly between points more than 350 miles distant.[1] In addition, many

[1] Perishables are moved 833 miles from New Orleans to Cincinnati in 35 hours; a full day has been cut from delivery time on movements between the eastern seaboard and points from Cleveland and Columbus, Ohio, westward. The same cut has been made from St. Louis into the South and Southwest. Between Chicago and Denver time has been

"night locals" are making shipments available for early-morning delivery at smaller stations. First morning delivery is successfully made by many carriers for distances of 300 to 400 miles and third morning delivery at destinations upwards of 1,000 miles distant. The "drag" freight, in the sense that the term was once used, has practically disappeared from the rails and the "on time" record of special freight services has become a matter of but little less pride to the railways than the maintenance of passenger schedules. This "on time" record has become, too, an important factor in freight solicitation.

While something less than might be desired has been accomplished in the reduction of running time of local passenger trains where they come into competition with the motor car and the bus, the shortening of schedules between important points where rail competition is keen has been well-nigh universal—with some of the reductions in running time marked. The establishment of 18-hour service between New York and Chicago and a comparable reduction in the running time of other trains between those points have been given wide publicity, yet even more striking gains have been made elsewhere. Perhaps the most significant reductions made have been in running schedules between Chicago and the West coast: until 1928 the time to California points had long been 68 hours and to the Pacific Northwest 72 hours, yet within 3 years reductions were accomplished in those figures approaching 20 per cent—and the faster times have been maintained since.

The last general adjustment of railway freight rates prior to the emergency increase effective early in 1932 was made in 1922 when a reduction of 10 per cent was ordered in all rates that had not been previously reduced by that or a greater percentage. True, there have been occasional orders issued by regulatory bodies reducing freight rates in a limited area or upon a limited number of commodities, yet these mandatory reductions have not been sufficient to account for more than a minor portion of the reduction in the average ton-mile charge that occurred from 1923 to 1932—1.116 cents to 1.043 cents. While hampered by heavy capital costs, by advancing wages, and by high material costs, the railways made many concessions in the postwar years to meet the needs of industry and the

lessened by 36 hours, and from Chicago to points in Kansas and Oklahoma a full day has been cut. This is a result in part of improved terminal handling, in part of speedier line service. That which in 1926 "would not have been considered possible," is in 1932 "a daily actuality" (see *Railway Age*, vol. 93, p. 828).

Perhaps the most notable single freight schedule is that of the "Blue Streak," a train operated daily by the St. Louis Southwestern between St. Louis and Shreveport, La. Leaving St. Louis at 6 P.M., it arrives at destination at 12:50 P.M., covering thus 590 miles in less than 19 hours. Few stops are made en route, but connecting rail and truck service enables the entire intervening area to benefit. A careful study of results seems to justify the unusual service given as a means of retaining and recovering tonnage (see *Railway Age*, vol. 92, p. 561).

necessities of competition—with the number and extent of those concessions increasing with the severity of competition until in particular areas rivalry of a cutthroat character has appeared, to persist for an extended period. In meeting such competition as has developed the railways have used a variety of methods; among the familiar ones have been reduction in classification, the modification of groupings, and the establishment of commodity rates; among the new methods have been the pool car,[1] the quotation of a fixed rate upon shipments made in containers, and the establishment of all-commodity rates applicable to carload movements—these rates being the same regardless of the character of the goods loaded.

Since 1920 there has been no official modification in the passenger fare of 3.6 cents per mile then fixed for standard movements. None the less, those who have noted developments in railway policy as applied to passenger traffic will find no cause for surprise in the reduction in average revenue per passenger-mile from 3.086 cents in 1921 to 2.220 cents in 1932, with 80 per cent of that decline occurring since 1927. In an effort to retain and to regain passenger traffic many experiments have been tried; among these have been the special excursion, the regular weekend rate, the "travel week" with its abnormally low rate, and the establishment in fact though not in name of class rates for one-way and round-trip movements. In this experimentation there has often been cooperation among the carriers of a considerable area and at other times the special rates have been made by a single carrier, effective only upon its lines, this latter being characteristically true of the special excursion. There has also been experimentation with a uniformly lower fare, by most railways upon a single portion—perhaps a branch—of the system but by one major property for 5 months upon a system-wide basis. The lower rate has commonly been 2 cents per mile, yet the increase in travel under the lower fare has often been inadequate to maintain passenger earnings at the level fixed by the 3.6-cent rate. One of the novel and generally successful expedients that has been employed to interest the public is the "mystery excursion," a well-planned outing at low cost. And approval has recently been given to the sale of 1,000-mile and larger coupon books by western railways at a reduction of 25 per cent from the regular 3.6-cent rate. In short, the railways are employing every allurement of service and rate to prevent further declines in passenger business, though with somewhat indifferent success: the lure of the highway and the steering-wheel proves difficult to counteract. Upon the outcome of this struggle seems to hinge the continuance of passenger service upon many railways.

[1] The pool car is one in which small-lot shipments are consolidated to move under the carload rate, when otherwise the less-than-carload rate would apply. This consolidation may be permitted to the shipper or effected by the railway.

Progress of Other Transport Agencies.—In the chapters immediately preceding a discussion of motor, air, and water transport appears that emphasizes the present capacity for public service of each of these agencies and indicates in a broad way the effort that each has made to adapt itself to public wish. Yet there remain additional facts that merit note, facts that suggest possibilities in fields in which change is likely to be more rapid than in the older and more fully developed field of railway transport.

Motor Transport.—The motor truck, in its struggle for tonnage, enjoys two major advantages that are unlikely to be taken from it. The first of these is convenience: its adaptability to the needs of shipper and consignee makes it a most effective tool. The second is low cost in certain types of service: even when the truck unquestionably pays, through various taxes, the whole of its social cost, it will serve more cheaply than the railway in the movement of certain commodities for considerable distances and of many others for shorter distances. Regulation is unlikely to lessen adaptability greatly, but heavier highway charges, regulation of hours of service, restriction of length of combined vehicles and of gross weight, and the imposition of business taxes are certain to increase costs. Such regulations will do no more, however, than restrict the field within which the truck can operate more efficiently than any rival agency.

Within its field the truck is offering a service increasingly adapted to shipping needs. Specialized services are being offered, as by refrigerator units; trucks equipped to handle perishables have made possible a wide distribution of fresh fruits, vegetables, and meats, to the advantage of both the grower and the consumer. Rapid and certain delivery has been provided; overnight service is rendered between points 300 miles or more apart, sometimes in competition with the railway, sometimes into territories otherwise lacking service. The long-distance telephone and the truck have made it possible for the merchant in small communities to carry a small stock of goods, yet meet unusual demands. In short, the truck has established during the past decade not only its utility but its indispensability in certain fields. In suitability to service it has progressed steadily, while technical advances have made for more economical operation and greater safety. In any national transportation plan the truck must occupy an important place.

Technical progress and the urge of competition have made the bus industry great within a brief period. Like the carrier of property by highway, its major advantages have been convenience and low cost. And, as with the truck, the first of these advantages is unlikely to be destroyed by any conceivable system of regulation, though the margin of advantage in cost is likely to be lessened as time passes. Because of differences in the nature of the transportation of goods and of persons, there has been a clear tendency for bus service to pass into the hands of a relatively small number of operating companies. In consequence, as compared with trucking, better management is evident, fewer abuses are apparent, and less stringent control is likely when the public takes action to bring the industry under a comprehensive regulatory plan. Such control as develops may restrict competitive operations measurably, yet the convenience of the service commends itself to the public so strongly that competition will not be eliminated. Rather, except as the railways utilize upon the rails some type of equipment comparable to the light, self-propelled unit mentioned upon a preceding page, it seems certain that the bus will be substituted widely for the passenger train, this bus being operated independently or, under wiser public policy, in conjunction with or by the railways. As a mobile, adaptable unit the outlook for the bus is most promising; and its lesser cost, as compared with the typical branch-line and local rail service, provides added social justification for increased use, as with the truck, in its appropriate field.

Air Transport.—While revolutionary changes in rail and highway transport are unlikely, there is in the field of air transport reasonable assurance that important technical progress is imminent, and a general belief that commercial possibilities have not yet been realized. It is in this field that unforeseen developments are most probable, in it that new uses are most likely to be found for the service and old uses greatly broadened. Commercial air transport in the United States has been in existence for less than a decade, it has been compelled to battle against lethargy and an absence of air-mindedness, it has suffered from speculative interest, and it has been forced to bear with other established industries the burden of a great depression; yet, despite these obstacles, its progress has been phenomenal. While no startling changes have been made in construction, progress toward more powerful and more dependable units has been continuous; and, though it has not been possible to decrease costs greatly, the air operator has increased speeds steadily—and, after all, it is reduction in time of movement rather than in transportation costs that aviation must offer the public.

The dynamic character of this industry is attested by the fact that a month rarely passes that fails to offer some gain. Cruising speeds in excess of 100 miles were regarded with surprise in 1926, yet the spring of 1933 finds planes in operation capable of cruising with a pay load of more than their own weight at speeds in excess of 165 miles per hour and with a cruising radius of 1,000 miles—these planes capable of rendering coast-to-coast service in some 16 hours, essentially an overnight service. Upon such machines no improved device is omitted that increases safety or speed. Growing interest in air transport is making it possible, even during adverse times, for a few favorably situated lines to make a satisfactory financial showing without the benefit of mail subsidies; announcements of plans looking toward lowered rates and increased speeds as a means of stimulating cargo movement are made from time to time, and it is an undoubted fact that the volume of express traffic has grown rapidly during the past year. The savings that would result from an overnight service throughout the United States for money, checks, securities, and like paper would alone be great, to say nothing of the gains upon unusual and "rush" shipments. Financial maneuvering indicates that air lines are to be consolidated into a few large groups, adequately financed and skillfully led. It is certain that, so situated, the future of air transport is bright.

Water Transport.—The place of inland water transport in a progressive system is more difficult to estimate with assurance than the place of rail, motor, or air. The glowing assurance that the construction of thousands of miles of navigable waterways is to "free great areas from economic thralldom and assure to them an unparalleled prosperity" seems entitled to little more credence than the assertion that *no* development of inland watercourses is socially justified. There is a certain anomaly in the effort to reestablish a type of transportation that disappeared even more because of its economic inadequacy in competition with a far less efficient railway service than is now rendered than because of other factors, while, at the same time, subsidies are being utilized to develop air transport, the greatest advantage of which is a speed that neither rail nor highway carrier can match. None the less, it is certain that improved channels and improved equipment will place the waterway in a stronger competitive position than it has occupied since the early sixties. Whether the volume of tonnage upon channels provided will become sufficient to justify many marginal projects is a question that time must answer: perhaps the wheels of trade can be adjusted to the greater time required for water movement because of lesser speeds, winding streams, and indirect routes for much tonnage. If so, waterway critics will be measurably confounded and those who have labored arduously for waterway development compensated in spirit.

But, whatever may be the judgment of the future upon some undertakings, it is certain that others will render an increasingly effective service. Only the exhaustion of natural resources can destroy the social value of the Monongahela, and the factors favorable to the Ohio are likely to give it an increasingly important rôle in the area through which it flows and into areas beyond. With the establishment of standard channels upon connecting streams and canals, with the construction of terminal facilities, with the slow establishment of industries upon a water as well as, or instead of, a rail basis, and with the appearance of aggressive operators upon inland waters in the event economical operation proves feasible, tonnage will undoubtedly increase and may do so in surprising measure. For certain commodities moving over particular routes water transport unquestionably offers noteworthy possibilities.

Coordinated Transport.—The coordination of transport agencies is not new: from the inception of rail transport there was coordination with important water routes and, since to many shippers the railway has never been in a position to render a *complete* transportation service, it has been necessary from the inception of that agency to supplement its performance by highway operations. With the construction of through lines, however, the relations between rail and water transport became increasingly competitive; the disappearance of many boat lines and the decline in importance of others as they came under railway control relegated water movement to the background. And, with the construction of spurs to older industries and the establishment of newer ones upon a rail basis, it became increasingly possible for the railway to provide a complete service with respect to a major portion of its tonnage. It has been with the rise of motor and air transport and the revival of waterway movement that the problem of coordination, involving as it does the assignment of an approximate place to each type of agency, has again become significant. Because the extent of coordination and the possibilities of its further development are of fundamental significance to the public, a brief discussion will be offered.

Rail-motor.—That coordination which has made greatest progress and which gives greatest promise of public benefit for the future is of the railway with the motor bus and truck. These two types of transport possess such characteristics that, when organized upon a supplementary basis, they provide maximum service at minimum cost—and, when not so organized, they tend to overlap and to occasion social waste. Coordination has been thus far a matter of little active public concern; such progress as has been made has resulted largely from railway initiative, often in the face of the opposition of a monopoly-fearing public and an antagonistic motor group.

The transportation of passengers by common carriers operating upon the highway was begun, as has been noted previously, between near-by cities by individuals alert to opportunities offered by inadequate rail facilities or through areas that were essentially suburban in character. These lines served, frequently, where interurban electric railways might have been built had not the motor vehicle forced its way to the fore. These local bus lines were often extended gradually to more distant points or other entrepreneurs, noting the success of existing lines, entered the field. The stronger competitive position of lines between major centers, as well as in some degree the desire to escape state regulation, operated to bring about a gradual consolidation of lines until, except for certain definitely local lines, service by motor bus has come into the hands of large operators. Since major highways serve between important centers of population, as do the railways, the passenger train and the bus soon came into competition and that competition has tended to increase in severity as bus service has been unified.

This development the railways first ignored but, as the volume of passenger traffic moving by rail declined, the minor portion of the loss that was moving by bus became of increasing concern. Furthermore, as the number of passengers per train diminished the margin of profit per train narrowed until, in time, many runs showed an operating loss; the bus became of interest to the railway as a possible substitute for rail service.[1] Two approaches to a coordinated service have been made, one the purchase of an interest in an established property as illustrated by Pennsylvania and Southern Pacific holdings in Greyhound subsidiaries, the other the operation of bus lines by the railway directly or through a subsidiary corporation created for the purpose. Illustrative of subsidiary operation, which is the typical method employed, are the following important units:[2]

	Buses
Boston and Maine Transportation Company	95
Boston and Maine Railroad Co.	
New England Transportation Company	638[1]
New York, New Haven and Hartford Railroad Company	
Interstate Transit Lines	188
Chicago and North Western Railway Company	
Union Pacific Railroad Company	
Missouri Pacific Transportation Company	198
Missouri Pacific Railroad Company	
Burlington Transportation Co.	38
Chicago, Burlington, and Quincy Railroad Company	

[1] Buses operated by certain other New Haven subsidiaries included in this figure.

In general, the highways over which buses controlled by or affiliated with railways operate are within the territory served by the railway, often parallel to it, with schedules so adjusted as to supplement rail operations or to take the place of trains that have been withdrawn. Occasionally a railway subsidiary will operate in the territory of a competing railway, with schedules planned in such case to obtain maximum bus traffic.

The growth in the use of the motor bus by the railways has been rapid. During the 6-month period closing June 30, 1930, some 33 Class I railways reported the operation of 3,105 buses, these covering 38,168 miles of intra- and 27,633 miles of interstate routes and earning a gross revenue of $16,182,029. These figures are in sharp contrast to those of

[1] In 1924 the Pennsylvania Railroad began the substitution of bus for unprofitable passenger-train service. By Jan. 1, 1931, some 800,000 steam train-miles per year had been eliminated, with estimated annual savings in excess of $475,000 (see *Coordination of Motor Transportation*, p. 36).

[2] *Coordination of Motor Transportation*, p. 122.

1927 when, for the entire year, Class I railways operated 745 buses over 2,856 miles of intra- and 1,050 miles of interstate routes and obtained from those operations a revenue of $6,866,475. From 1925 to 1930 the number of all railways operating buses increased from 10 to 81, while the number of buses in railway service increased from about 300 to approximately 4,000. Instances of the coordination of railway and independent bus line are not in evidence, though such coordination of semi-competitive and supplementary operations might well be arranged under a pooling agreement.

Coordination of service may take, in addition to the replacement of rail service and operations supplementary thereto, two other forms: the bus may be operated into areas not served by railways, constituting thus an extension of line, or it may be used to speed up through rail service by the elimination of local stops—the bus serving at intermediate points. Competitive operations of railway and bus occasion a duplication of terminal facilities, a duplication of terminal service, and failure to realize upon the possibilities of maximum distribution of service during the day in the area served. Coordination largely eliminates duplication, it permits spacing of service, it makes possible alternative use of rail and road in emergency or regularly, and public convenience is served at minimum cost. While coordination between railway and independent bus line is feasible, any existing legal barriers to common ownership should be removed so that unified operation may thus be attained if such be necessary in any particular situation. But, to assure adequate protection to the public, regulatory bodies should fix rates for rail and for highway movements that are appropriate to each.

Interest in truck operation by the railways rests largely upon two bases, a desire to meet more effectively competitive highway operations and the belief that the cost of local freight service can be reduced by the use of the truck. It is principally, however, to assist the railway in meeting competition that the truck is employed by them, such utilization being widespread and of a diversified character. Generally speaking, it may be said that the truck has found a place in three types of operations: it is employed in line-haul service, in terminal service, and in terminal-line-haul operations. Line-haul service, in turn, may be of different types. Trucks controlled by or operating under agreement with the railway may gather freight from off-line points, delivering it to the railway for movement to destination; and, vice versa, traffic may be turned over by the railway to trucks for movement to off-line points. Such a service is rendered, for example, by the Wilson Transportation Company, a subsidiary of the Chicago, St. Paul, Minneapolis, and Omaha Railway.

Again, the affiliated truck line may operate over highways that are essentially parallel to the railway, rendering a service that is supplementary; in this way the railway still retains control of traffic moving between points on its line that shippers prefer to send by truck because of quicker service, more satisfactory handling, or any one or more of a number of other reasons. The Wilson Transportation Company renders such a service, also, as do a great number of other railway truck lines, among which the New England Transportation Company is outstanding: this company operates daily a large fleet of trucks over approximately 1,500 miles of highway that, in general, parallel the New Haven Railroad. A third line-haul use appears in the substitution of truck for way-freight service. To points where small-lot shipments aggregating less than a carload are consigned, delivery is made by truck: traffic is moved by rail to points separated by from 15 to 50 miles and from those points consignments are handled by truck to intermediate stations—and the trucks which carry the destined shipments to such stations pick up originated shipments and deliver them to the railway for the road haul at the various distributing points. Such use of the truck is made by, among others, the New York Central, the Pennsylvania, and the St. Louis Southwestern: of these the two eastern railways utilize independent trucking concerns while the last-named operates through its subsidiary, the Southwestern Transportation Company. In addition to expediting movement, it is declared that this type of substitution results in material savings to the railway: the Pennsylvania, operating 49 routes and covering 1,770 route-miles daily, estimated annual savings at $1,335,000.[1] Thus it appears that the line-haul use of trucks by the railways yields both competitive advantage and economy. And practice indicates that such coordination of rail and truck may be had between the railway and either a subsidiary corporation or an independent trucking concern.

Perhaps the most important use of the truck by the railways, both present and future, is in the terminal zone, however. Of the terminal services rendered by the truck, store-door delivery is most significant. Through a period of many years public interest in store-door delivery grew and the demand for this "complete transportation service" became stronger. Reluctant to make a fundamental change in policy, the railways delayed action until the loss of small-lot shipments had become heavy. Yielding at length to the necessities of a changed transportation situation, the acceptance of store-door delivery by the railways has been surprisingly rapid and territorially widespread: every effort is being put forth to make it accomplish its dual purpose, the retention of all small-lot traffic remaining on the rails and the recovery of some portion of that lost. Store-door delivery, then, has been accepted as a competitive weapon, and, while employed in many areas and by many lines, it has perhaps reached its highest development in Southwestern territory where truck competition has been particularly keen. In that area, beginning Oct. 1, 1931, free pick-up and delivery service is given on all less-than-carload merchandise

[1] *Coordination of Motor Transportation*, p. 64.

moving in intra- or interstate traffic for distances up to approximately 300 miles. Upon the success of store-door delivery opinion differs in the Southwest, as elsewhere, yet the aggregate of judgments seems to be favorable; in any event, the number of communities benefiting from store-door delivery increases. But to obtain maximum results from this plan its proponents assert that it must be broadened to cover carload traffic, that the service must be rendered without regard to the distance the shipment moves, and that it be administered as a legitimate feature of transport rather than as a competitive weapon.

The trucking service is performed for some railways by a subsidiary, for others by the Railway Express Agency, but the general method is to contract with local truckers for the movement of tonnage to and from the station platform. The last has as its prime recommendations the reduction to a minimum of local opposition and freedom of the railway from direct responsibility for rendering the service; yet experience indicates that the service can be provided at lower cost by the subsidiary than by the independent operating under contract. A logical agent, at least at points where the Express Agency maintains its collection-and-delivery service, would seem to be that Agency: it possesses experience in the field, it has an organization that could be extended readily to assume the added burden, and in many places the increased cost would be comparatively small. Then, too, the Agency is a railway subsidiary and any profits made by it would be returned to them. The financial and service results under certain contracts now operative between railways and the Agency will undoubtedly be watched with great interest by rail carriers generally.

Other important terminal services are also rendered by the truck. To facilitate the handling of a considerable volume of miscellaneous small-lot shipments from a single plant, and, conversely, the delivery of such shipments thereto, it has been customary in many terminal areas to render a trap- or ferry-car service: a car would be set out at or near the plant into which package shipments, regardless of destination, might be loaded—and in such a car would be assembled shipments for delivery. This service involves considerable switching and often extensive delays; the use of the motor truck has made possible the expedited handling of such traffic. In certain cities, too, off-line stations have been established to which deliveries may be made of all lot shipments, regardless of destination, and from which lot shipments may be secured. The motor vehicle has superseded the horse-drawn truck in serving between rail platform and off-line station and has made possible extensions and improvements in this service. And, should the railway assume responsibility for carload traffic from and to off-line locations, as many railways have recently assumed it for less-than-carload, the truck could be used to reduce greatly the total time in transit; much of the time that elapses between loading and delivery to consignee, when origin or/and destination is a large terminal, is lost in getting the car through the terminal maze—and this time could be reduced by transfer from and to truck at appropriate points.

A third type of service to which the truck is important is that which combines terminal and line-haul aspects. The container, loaded by the shipper, is transferred by truck from his place of business to the rail line where it is loaded upon a specially adapted car; after this car has been moved to destination the container is delivered to the consignee by truck. Thus it appears that the truck is an important factor in the development of a service that has been accorded enthusiastic reception in areas where offered. The railways that have developed container service to the fullest extent are the Pennsylvania and the New York Central and upon both systems the increase in container shipments has been striking. While certain problems of rate making have arisen in connection with the service, particularly the adjustment of container rates to regular rates in such manner as to eliminate unreasonable discrimination, it seems certain that the use of the container will increase, both intensively and extensively. Yet a partial substitute for it is being developed in the movement of loaded truck bodies by the railways upon specially designed cars and under a flat rate. These truck bodies are the property of the trucking concern and are forwarded by rail to destination rather than being moved by highway. A variation of the truck body appears in the railwagon, a truck trailer of special construction adapted to movement upon a specialized flat car. This movement of truck body or railwagon offers perhaps the best opportunity for cooperation between railway and independent trucker, though its extensive development must await the consolidation of trucking lines, so that operations may be upon a wider territorial scale, or must follow from closer cooperation among independent lines than now exists.

Coordination between railway and motor vehicle is essential from the standpoint of satisfactory public service and, properly effected, it will provide a more economical service. Such coordination in the movement of both persons and property should be encouraged; and, if progress is unduly slow, regulatory bodies should be permitted to order at their discretion the establishment by the railways of supplementary highway service or the coordination of existing services with railway operations. With the degree of control over highway operations recommended in an earlier chapter the public need have no fear of oppression through monopoly; its concern should be with the delay in coordination, rather than with the imagined dire consequences to the public of the elimination of cutthroat competition. The motor vehicle has won an important place in a broadened railway service and is certain to occupy a position of increasing significance as its possibilities are realized and the technique of coordination is perfected.

Rail-water.—The future of inland water transport in the United States rests largely upon the extent to which it will be to the advantage of the public to route shipments by rail-and-water. This follows from the fact that so small a portion of the total productive area of the United States is served directly by waterways, as well as from the fact that many possible all-water movements are impracticable because of circuity and the resulting increase in time required for delivery. The importance to the waterway of favorable relations with rail lines is attested by the Denison Act which gives to the Interstate Commerce Commission broad powers over the establishment of through routes and joint rates for common carrier movements by rail and water. In fact, the language of the Denison Act is such that Commission action is little less than mandatory, though to it remains the right to fix the conditions under which joint rates must be established, to determine differentials between all-rail and rail-and-water rates, and to determine the division of joint rates prescribed. One of the major problems faced by the Commission in the application of this statute arises from the necessity of fixing maximum percentages that the mileage of the rail portion of proposed rail-water routes may bear to the mileage of the short all-rail route, yet not suffer disapproval because of unreasonable circuity.[1] Though the policy of the Commission has been a liberal one, seemingly, the water lines declare that the limits of permissible circuity must be extended if adequate traffic is to be available to them. The coordination of rail and inland-water facilities is now in the controversial stage.

Yet it is obvious that there are possibilities of social gain in the proper coordination of these two agencies. There are many commodities that are unlikely to move by water; there are others that might well move by water in considerable volume. The antagonism of rail and water lines arises from keen rivalry for a tonnage that is as yet, at least, inadequate

[1] "We are further of the opinion and find that . . . (*a*) no barge-rail route need be established where the shortest all-rail distance via the lines of the said rail carriers from point of origin to point of destination through the port of interchange with the barge line exceeds by more than 40 per cent the shortest all-rail distance between such points of origin and destination: (*b*) no rail-barge-rail route need be established where the shortest all-rail distance from point of origin to point of destination through the ports of interchange with the barge line exceeds by more than 33⅓ per cent the shortest all-rail distance between such points of origin and destination; (*c*) no barge-rail route need be established where the shortest all-rail distance between the inland point of origin or destination, as the case may be, and the port of interchange exceeds three-fourths of the shortest all-rail distance between point of origin and point of destination; (*d*) no rail-barge-rail route need be established where the sum of the shortest all-rail distance from the point of origin to the port of interchange where the shipment is delivered to the barge line, plus the shortest all-rail distance from the port of interchange where the shipment is relinquished by the barge line to the point of destination, exceeds two-thirds of the shortest all-rail distance between origin and destination; (*e*) no barge-rail or rail-barge-rail route need be established except over the shortest 'working' route [*i.e.*, the shortest route regularly used for the transportation of freight traffic in general] between the inland point of origin or destination, as the case may be, and the port of interchange over which the lowest corresponding rate between such points applies; and (*f*) no barge-rail or rail-barge-rail route need be established if the barge line and the interested rail carriers agree that it shall not be established." 172 I.C.C. 529.

for both. Unquestionably, as water terminals improve and shippers become habituated to rail-water movement, waterway traffic will increase. But reluctant cooperation on the part of the railways will stand as a barrier to an increase in the volume of common-carrier tonnage that lower water charges may justify—and that reluctance is understandable when coordination often reduces total railway revenue from tonnage originating upon the rails. Might not the future of coordinated rail-water service be brighter if, subject to such regulations as seem essential to the protection of public interest, rail lines were permitted to operate upon all inland waterways? By minimum rates protection could be accorded independent boat operators; yet, operating boats, the railways would be desirous of moving such tonnage by water as economy justified and service demands permitted. If an increased volume of water traffic is desired, this change in regulatory plan has much to recommend it; to regard the inland waterway as an instrument of punishment for the railways because of past or imagined present offenses must, inevitably, circumscribe its development and minimize its social benefits. Coordination offers social advantages and coordination is feasible, physically; our major need is a public policy that will more closely identify coordination and self-interest.

Air-rail.—Public interest in air transport became active with the establishment of commercial operations, beginning in 1926. Railway executives, alert to the possible coordination of air and rail facilities and determined not to be "left at the post" as most of them had been by motor-vehicle developments, showed an immediate and intelligent interest in the situation. As early as 1928 air-rail service was established between a certain few points, the first arrangement made effective being that which made possible transportation by air between Chicago and Minneapolis-St. Paul of passengers moving by rail between Eastern points and the Northwest. In 1929 numerous other coordinations were effected, the more ambitious of these providing for movement between the East and West coasts, into the West Indies, and to Mexico City. Typical of the transcontinental arrangement was a plan whereby from New York to Los Angeles the passenger would leave a Pennsylvania sleeper at Columbus, Ohio, to travel by plane during the day to Dodge City, Kan.; from there he would again travel by rail over the Santa Fe to a point in New Mexico, taking a plane the next day to complete his journey to the coast. Railways in all sections of the country became interested and an increasing number of arrangements were made to expedite the movement of passengers by combined air and rail routes; the volume of traffic upon certain air-rail routes was encouraging and efforts to coordinate were actively continued into 1931.

With the steady increase in the speed of planes the importance to air lines of railway cooperation diminished; its importance declined, too, as lighted airways made possible night flying and as air rates were brought more nearly to the level of rail and Pullman. In consequence of these facts, it seems probable that such coordination as exists in the future is more likely to be in the form of a supplementary service rendered by the railways to air lines: rail and air schedules may be so coordinated as to enable passengers to reach airports served by major air-transport systems at convenient hours, from there to speed their journey by transfer to plane. Important coordination of this type in the near future seems somewhat improbable, however.

Water-highway.—In the territory in which lies a major portion of the inland waterway mileage of the United States is also to be found a large mileage of high-type highways. Within economical trucking distance of those waterways are to be found rich agricultural areas, abundant natural resources, and a considerable population. Between highway operator and boat line there is none of the traditional rivalry that colors rail and water relations; further, rivalry for particular traffic is less keen between these two because the truck cannot move low-grade traffic for any great distance at a profit and the boat line cannot expect to attract in large volume high-value tonnage that moves economically by truck for long distances.[1] Thus there appears a sound economic basis for the coordination of barge and truck.

That such coordination has been established widely between highway and water operators appears upon inquiry.[2] Steamship lines between New York and Boston serve almost the whole of southern New England by truck connections. Joint water-and-highway movement is provided from certain North Atlantic ports through North Carolina ports to points as much as 120 miles inland; boat lines on Lake Erie offer a coordinated highway service to the inland cities of Michigan, Ohio, and western New York. A Puget Sound ferry route has arranged with trucking concerns for collection and delivery in cities reached by its boats, thus providing a complete and a highly expedited service. Further illustrations might be offered of the effective coordination of these two agencies of transport, but these given suggest the possibilities of utilizing highway carriers as feeders in the development of inland waterway traffic. Indeed, this is one of the phases of coordination that gives particular promise for the future. It is improbable that any restrictions placed upon the motor vehicle will do more than, at most, narrow the territory it can serve in conjunction with water lines, and there is no reason to believe

[1] None the less, in the 1931 *Report of the Inland Waterways Corporation* there appears on p. 7, in connection with a discussion of barge-line tonnage, the following statement, "The forceful gradual encroachment of truck transportation has become an important adverse factor."

[2] *Coordination of Motor Transportation*, pp. 61–62.

that the effectiveness of water-highway coordination in developing water traffic will be lessened by railway operation of boat lines.

The Pipe Line.—The use of pipes for the conveyance of liquids was known in antiquity: bamboo tubes, hollowed timbers, and metal pipes of lead and bronze were early put into service in various portions of the world. With the opening of rich oil fields in Pennsylvania it was natural, then, that it should occur to some that oil might be transported from well to point of use or rail shipment more economically by pipe line than by wagon. The first record of a pipe line for the movement of oil in the United States is that of a line built in western Pennsylvania in 1865, a 2-inch line some 6 miles in length; through this line oil was moved so cheaply that teamsters, deprived of employment, destroyed portions of it and its continued operation was made possible only by invoking for a time the force of the law. In 1872 the first pipe line was laid to convey natural gas, a 2-inch line bringing gas some 5 miles into Titusville, Pa. It is from these beginnings that, within a period of two generations, the great network of pipe lines now serving in the United States developed, pipe lines through which are moved in increasing volume crude oil, natural gas, and gasoline. To each of these types of lines consideration will be given in turn.

Oil Lines.—When a well is brought into production in new territory as the result of careful exploration or "wildcatting," the problem of first concern is storage. Then, with the greatest possible speed, a pipe line is laid to connect with the nearest shipping point, rail or water. Such a line for the initial well will be small, however, with its immediate excess capacity determined largely by the performance of the well and the extent of the leases held. But if, as the field develops, there is reasonable assurance of continued production upon a large scale, thought will be given to the connection of the new field with trunk pipe lines that carry oil to great refining centers and to deep-water harbors from which the crude can move by tanker to domestic refineries or into export trade. The extent to which heavy producing fields have been "tied in" is indicated by the accompanying map upon which are shown the major trunk lines now in service. But, in addition to the network of trunk lines, there is an almost equal mileage of gathering lines. These latter lines, of lesser diameter, carry the oil from the individual wells to a junction with the trunk in which it may be conveyed a short or great distance to refinery or port. In Table XLI are given the miles of each type of line, classified by diameter of pipes. Of the trunk-line total, shown for 1931, 19,000 and 11,000 miles lay in Texas and Oklahoma, respectively, these states contributing approximately 10,500 and 13,500 to the total of gathering lines, also. Other states with large trunk-line mileages are Missouri, California, Pennsylvania, Kansas, Illinois, and Ohio, while Pennsylvania, Ohio, West Virginia, and Kansas contribute largely to

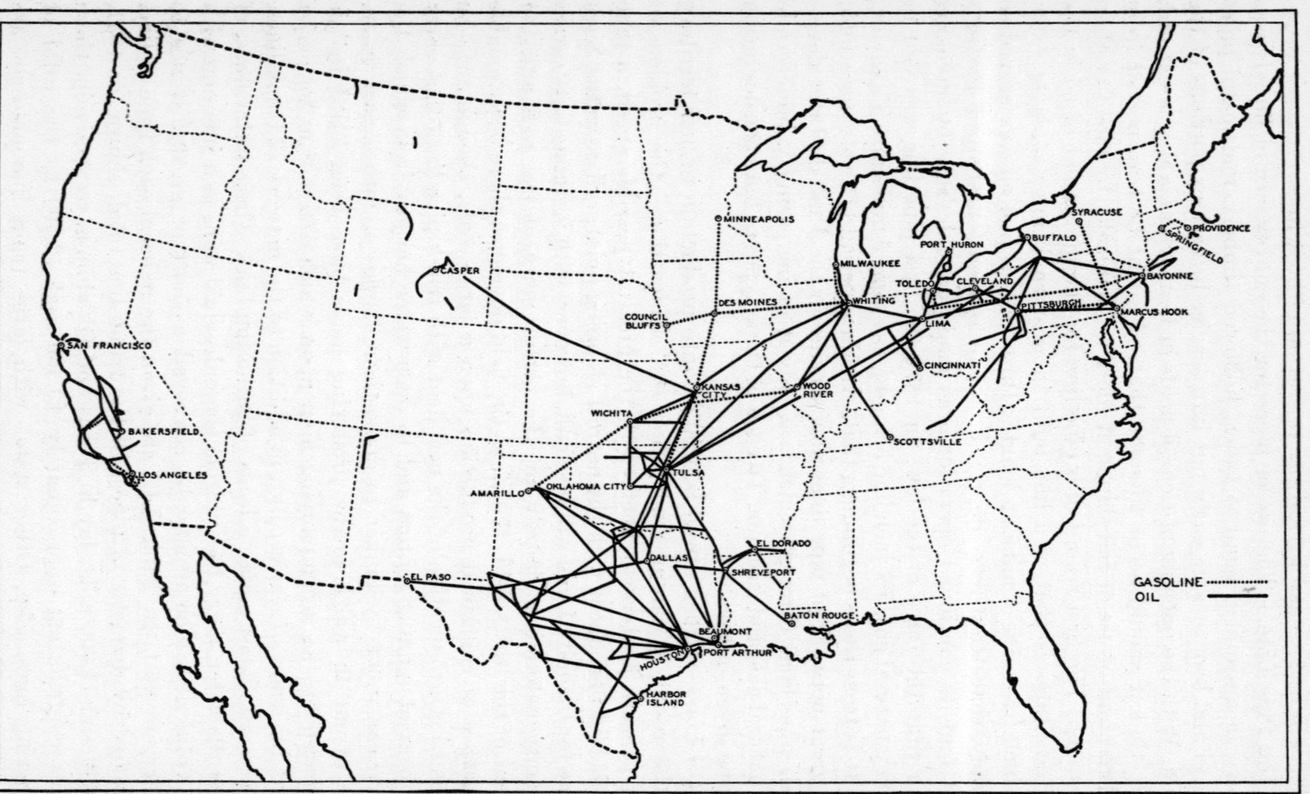

FIG. 47.—Major pipe lines in the United States used for the movement of crude petroleum and gasoline.

the mileage of gathering lines. Naturally, all states with a large mileage of gathering lines are producers, though the localization of production in Texas, Oklahoma, and California reduces the need for such lines to small proportions in relation to production. On the other hand, many states with a large trunk mileage produce little or no oil: those states merely chance to lie between producing areas and the market.

TABLE XLI.—SUMMARY OF OIL PIPE LINES SHOWING MILEAGE BY SIZES, MAY 1, 1931*

Size (inside diameter), inches	Trunk lines, miles	Gathering lines, miles	Total, miles
2	......	21,450	21,450
3	......	9,970	9,970
Below 4	3,070	......	3,070
4	4,520	11,890	16,410
6	11,140	7,360	18,500
Above 6	......	2,970	2,970
8	26,290	......	26,290
10	8,270	......	8,270
12	4,700	......	4,700
Above 12	30	......	30
Total..................	58,020	53,640	111,660

* United States Bureau of Mines, Department of Commerce.

The aggregate investment in crude-oil pipe lines is in excess of $2,000,000,000 and through these lines in 1929 moved approximately 96 per cent of the nation's total oil tonnage. Though the production of crude petroleum in the United States in 1929 was 127 per cent greater than in 1920, crude tonnage originated by the railways increased only 3 per cent during that period. Thus it appears that the dependence of the oil industry upon its specialized agency of transport becomes proportionately greater with the passage of time; that the network of trunk lines is of such nature as to justify that dependence is suggested by the map. While it would be of interest to know the capacity of existing lines in terms of maximum movement through them during a given period, that maximum depends upon too many variables—such as the viscosity of the petroleum in the line, pressure, and temperature—to make the computation possible. The capacity of existing lines in terms of storage has been estimated, however: on May 1, 1931, this capacity of trunk lines was 23,214,000 barrels—which constituted approximately 6 per cent of the petroleum stored at that time. As indicated, a number of variables affect the movement of petroleum through the lines. To increase the volume of oil moving through a given trunk, pumping stations are located at intervals of 15 to 40 miles to apply pressure; as the quality of pipe has improved with scientific progress, these pressures have been raised. During periods of low temperature flow is impeded; to overcome in part this disadvantage and to facilitate the movement of oils of high viscosity, heat is sometimes applied at pumping stations. Despite obstacles and handicaps, the movement of oil by pipe line represents the most efficient form of overland transportation, the cost being probably no more than half that of rail transport. Yet movement by oil tanker, even by barge upon satisfactory channels, is still more economical and therefore utilized by the industry as opportunity permits.

The place of the oil pipe line in transportation is fixed and certain. As soon as production becomes or gives clear promise of becoming sufficient to justify the cost of trunk-line construction, the work is undertaken. Because of the nature of the commodity transported and because of the inevitable tendency of the few dominant interests in the field to provide for themselves this specialized service, ownership of pipe lines is largely in the hands of a few companies subsidiary to the dominant corporate groups in the oil industry. At the close of 1930 almost 89,000 miles of the national total were held by 40 companies; of these the 14 largest companies operated 73,662 miles; 6 companies, each of which held in excess of 5,000 miles, contributed 45,276 to the total; and 1 company, the Prairie, owned 13,260 miles of line.[1] Should a further classification be made according to controlling interest, it would be found that the transportation of petroleum is centered largely in the hands of a few major interests. It is the control of economical transportation that contributes largely to the continued dominance by a few companies, for public weal or woe, of the petroleum industry. Though pipe lines were subjected to regulation by the Interstate Commerce Commission in 1906, the peculiar character of the business of transporting oil by pipe line is such as to preclude extensive regulatory action of a usual character. Before the public recently has been the proposal to apply the Commodities clause to the movement of petroleum; yet, before such a change in policy is made, the problems of the industry merit careful and impartial study.[2]

[1] Interstate Commerce Commission, *Statistics of Railways in the United States*, p. 150.

[2] "The pipe-line business faces problems and risks unlike those encountered in the railroad business. Railroads carry a large variety of goods, pipe lines are equipped to handle one type of commodity only. Railroads may count upon a volume of business for an indefinite period in proportion to the growth of population and its standard of living, except in so far as the railroad system fails to meet the competition of superior modes of transportation; pipe lines face a shifting and uncertain traffic which eventually is doomed to extinction.

"Unlike the railroads, pipe lines cannot generate business. They can handle only the business created by the oil producer and refiner. If the operation of a railroad results in the depletion of some of the resources upon which it depends, other resources may be developed to maintain the usefulness of the line; with the exhaustion of the sources of oil supply, no substitute traffic is possible for a pipe line. A railroad serves hundreds of thousands or millions of patrons whose needs run with the business cycle; a pipe line serves the requirements of one or, at best, several refineries, whose wants not only fluctuate with the state of general business but also vary according to the shifting conditions of the oil

It is no simple task to make certain of the adequate protection of producer and consumer, without interfering with the economical transportation of crude, the raw material of a great industry.

Gasoline Lines.—It was long regarded as impossible to transport gasoline economically by pipe line because of wastage, so by some the crude petroleum has been piped for refining to areas of major consumption and by others gasoline was moved to consuming markets by tank car from refineries located near the fields. Local distribution has been made by motor truck, with the range of the truck steadily increasing at the expense of rail movement. Within the past few years, however, the development of electric welding has made possible the production at a reasonable cost of steel tubing proof against leakage and has made possible, too, adequate welding of pipe sections in the field. This, in turn, permits the movement of gasoline by pipe line with less wastage than by tank car and at markedly less cost.[1] As a consequence, there have been constructed within recent years some 3,500 miles of line, largely of a diameter of 6 inches or greater, to transport refined gasoline, and to this must be added perhaps 500 miles of other lines used wholly or in part for the movement of natural gasoline. The construction for refined gasoline has a daily capacity of approximately 100,000 barrels, with other projects in early prospect that will double that capacity. As will be noted from an examination of the map, the termini of these lines are important consuming centers and/or points from which gasoline may be moved by tanker or barge at low rates into a wide area; thus it appears

industry. A railroad caters to every individual and every enterprise along its line; a pipe line is essential to but one business, and that a business which may change its location. A railroad is of direct utility to the general public; a pipe line has no usefulness except to the industry which it serves.

"In the development of the oil business, refining interests have supplied the initiative and capital for the construction of the pipe-line system. The reason that this course was followed is found in the desire of the refiner to reduce the risks of his enterprise. A refinery represents a large outlay; if the plant is important, millions of dollars are involved. In order to safeguard this investment, an adequate supply of crude petroleum must be assured, and the plant should have access to many sources of supply. It is also necessary to reach consuming territory with dispatch and economy, in consequence of which the plant should be located within easy reach of centers of population. To reconcile these two requirements special channels of transportation are necessary, and, except in so far as crude oil may be brought by water, the refinery needs a pipe line and ordinarily must build this line itself, since no independent agency would consider it good business to provide such facilities in view of an uncertain source of traffic at one end and a single customer at the other. The refiner has his whole manufacturing enterprise at stake, and it is he, and he alone, who is ordinarily willing to risk the effort and investment necessary to connect the sources of raw material supply with his plant." (The Economics of Pipe Lines in the Oil Industry, by Joseph E. Pogue, *Pipe-line News*, vol. 4, No. 11, p. 18.)

[1] Accurate cost estimates or statements are, naturally, difficult to obtain. It is probable, however, that pipe-line costs vary from 30 to 50 per cent of rail costs, depending upon numerous factors that influence the costs of line construction and operation.

that refiners are envisioning for the future the handling of a large tonnage of their product by the cheapest methods of transportation available to them. Indeed, one very possible result of gasoline-line construction may be a considerable contribution to the total of inland-waterway tonnage. Yet it is asserted that this more recent transport development constitutes no serious threat either to the railway or to the tank-car owners, who have in the service of the petroleum industry some 150,000 cars; while rail tonnage may decrease, it is expected that the continued growth of the industry will necessitate the utilization of the railway as well as the pipe line. The ultimate bearing of gasoline lines upon the distribution of tonnage is yet to be determined, but it is certain that these lines represent an important supplement to earlier agencies of transport.

Natural-gas Lines.—Natural gas has been conducted through pipes from areas of production to areas of important consumption for a long period; in this way it has been possible to make natural gas in certain sections of the United States a major domestic and industrial fuel. But, because of the nature of the pipe available and because the probable supply did not justify an extensive program of pipe-line construction, gas was seldom transported for more than a few hundred miles. As time passed, the production of those fields accessible to populous areas declined and the use of natural gas bade fair to come to a gradual end. Then occurred two events that completely changed the picture, the discovery of new fields of production that give promise of enormous reserves and the successful application of electric welding to steel pipe. The first justified building great trunk lines between important consuming areas and the rich new fields, most of these far removed from areas of dense population, and the second made possible the movement of gas under sufficient pressure to permit of the delivery of an adequate volume at points a thousand miles from the wells. Within an astonishingly brief period the natural-gas industry gave evidence of a vigor it had never before known: a veritable orgy of high-pressure line construction followed, not only from the new fields but also from the older Eastern production areas. By the close of 1931 there were in service some 65,000 miles of line through which natural gas was flowing to a greater or lesser number of communities in three-fourths of the states; into Chicago alone it is estimated that one pipe line from the Southwest pours the heat equivalent of 12,000 tons of coal daily.

Much of the transportation significance of this rapid construction of long-distance high-pressure gas lines lies in the effect of the availability of this new fuel upon the volume of oil and coal now moving by other agencies. The consumption of fuel oils has increased rapidly in recent years at the expense of coal; a new competitor for public favor now appears that may, because of certain inherent advantages, make heavy inroads upon the markets of both. True, certain fuel engineers declare

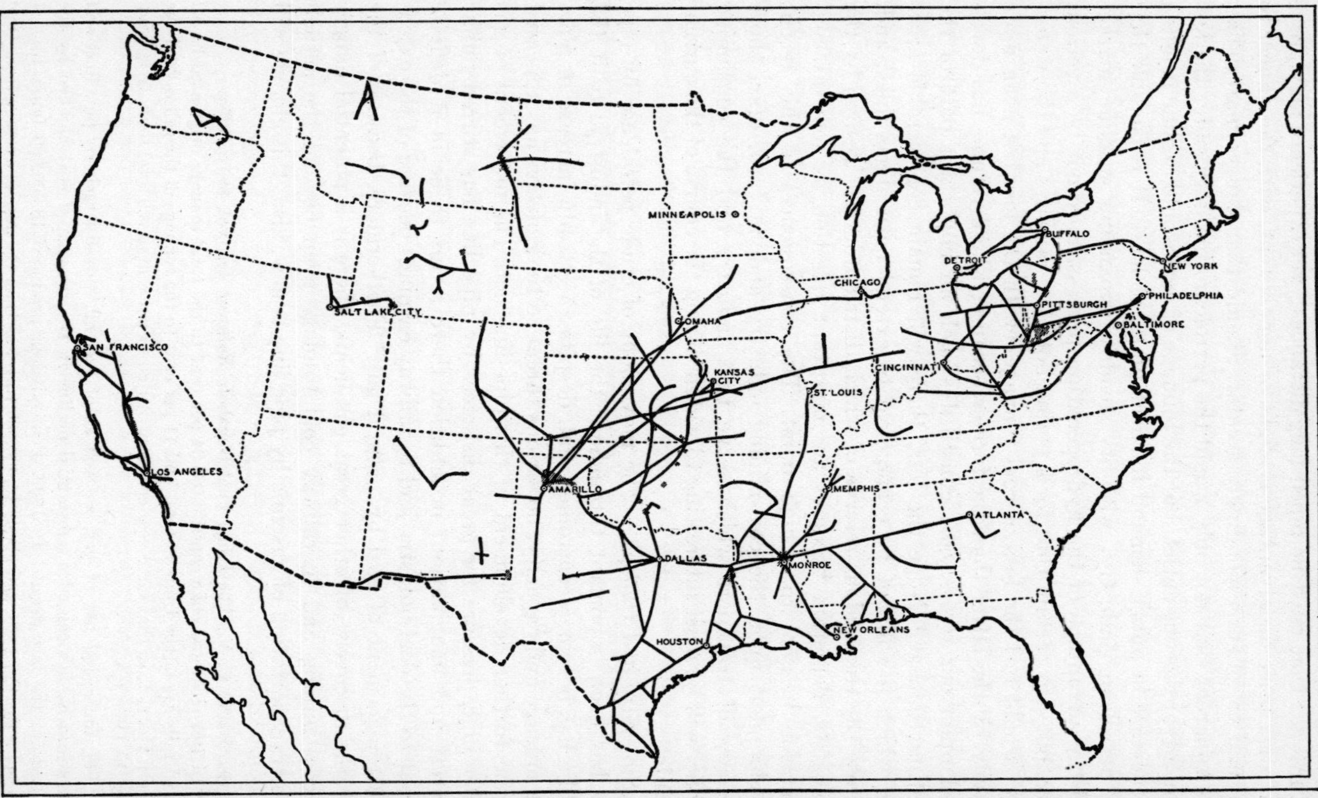

FIG. 48.—Major pipe lines in the United States used in the movement of natural gas. Important production areas shown by shading.

that for a given outlay more heat can be obtained from coal than from natural gas that must be piped long distances;[1] yet experience may prove that such price disadvantage is slight or nonexistent, with the danger to coal and to oil correspondingly greater. Should that danger materialize, it is apparent that not only would the petroleum industry suffer the loss of an advantageous outlet, but the tonnage of coal would decline pending an increase in public demand for heat units, at least. It is possible that the petroleum industry, with its steadily expanding gasoline market and the advantage of the hydrogenation process, may not be a serious loser, but it is certain that for a period both the railways and the waterways would feel the loss of coal tonnage—with the loss felt even more heavily by the latter than the former because, where volume has developed upon our rivers, coal constitutes such an important part of the existing tonnage.[2] None the less, there will remain considerable areas into which it will not be economical to extend natural-gas lines; and, despite the tremendous reserve of which distributors are assured by the geologists, depletion becomes an important question as soon as consumption mounts to a high point. The consequences of this recent development upon the coal-mining industry and, in turn, upon those agencies of transport which serve that industry and the consuming public, will be most interesting to watch during the course of the current decade.

Summary and Outlook.—The movement of crude petroleum by pipe line has been important throughout the life of the industry; to it the public has become accustomed and, despite the steady increase in pipeline mileage and capacity, no serious threat to the railways has appeared in the further development of this pipe-line net. The movement of gas under high pressure for great distances by pipe line has stirred public interest and imagination; in addition there seems to lie in it definite threat to the coal industry and to railway earnings because of the extensive replacement of coal by natural gas.[3] Furthermore, because of the possible discovery of other great gas fields, there is a potential danger to coal mining and to railway coal tonnage even beyond the actual. The transportation of gasoline by pipe line is new, also; this change will

[1] See Beck, C. V., The Piped Fuel Bugaboo, *Railway Age*, vol. 89, p. 1258.

[2] In 1929 coal and coke contributed 34 per cent to the total tonnage originated by all Class I railways of the United States and 41 per cent to the tonnage of the railways of the Eastern District. In that same year coal constituted 44 per cent of the total tonnage moving upon the Ohio River.

[3] The increasing use of gas, as well as of fuel oil, moved largely by pipe lines and tank steamers, has caused a substantial decline in the tonnage of coal handled by the railroads in the last decade. In 1930, Pennsylvania produced 18,000,000 fewer tons of anthracite than in 1920, and about 15,000,000 tons less than the annual average from 1909 to 1913, inclusive. It is estimated that in 1929 natural gas displaced about 77,500,000 tons of bituminous coal. See *Forty-fifth Annual Report of the Interstate Commerce Commission.*

doubtless influence railway revenues unfavorably, because tank-car movements of gasoline yield to the railways a considerable revenue. Yet many hold that no extensive construction of gasoline lines is likely, particularly if railway rates are adjusted more closely and without undue delay to a lower level of gasoline prices.[1]

Interesting suggestions are made, however, by those who see for pipe-line transportation a broad field of usefulness. Active experimentation is in progress upon the movement of pulverized coal by pipe line, with indications of ultimate success. Should this development justify construction of lines, it is probable that populous areas and particularly metropolitan centers would be served largely in this manner, with the railways losing a large portion of the coal tonnage now handled —unless, of course, individual carriers or groups of carriers supplemented rail by pipe-line movement. The movement of certain grains, of such a staple item as flour, and even other items by pipe line has been suggested, yet such suggestions seem to deal with fancy rather than probability. None the less, the public and other agencies of transport will do well to follow with interest and care both the intensive and extensive utilization of the pipe line in the movement of commodities.

REFERENCES

Beck, C. B.: The Piped Fuel Bugaboo, *The Railway Age*, vol. 89, No. 24, p. 1258.

Bowie, C. P.: *Transportation of Gasoline by Pipe Line*, United States Department of Commerce, Bureau of Mines, Technical paper 517.

Brown, Floyd C.: Economic Factors Confronting Natural Gas in Middle West, address delivered at Pacific Coast Gas Association Convention, *Natural Gas*, September, 1932.

Coal Men Hope Automatic Stoker Will Check Oil and Gas Sales, *The Business Week*, Feb. 25, 1931, p. 30.

Encyclopaedia Britannica, Fourteenth Edition.

Energy for Sale, *The Lamp*, October, 1931.

[1] "A study of the areas which have come to be served by gasoline lines reveals the existence there of an excessive concentration of refining capacity in respect to the requirements of near-by markets. A falling price level for gasoline coupled with a relatively rigid freight-tariff structure created economic tension requiring relief through lower transportation costs. Hence, the gasoline pipe line constituted the economic response to a lack of geographic balance, on the one hand, and a too rigid system of railroad charges, on the other. The development of the new mode of transportation, accordingly, has been stimulated by errors in plant location on the part of the refining industry and by a policy of rate making on the side of the railroad administration that failed to take into account the needs of the situation. In the light of these circumstances it may be seen that the gasoline pipe line is not a radical innovation destined to capture the bulk of the gasoline traffic of the country, but is, to a large degree at least, merely a corrective medium for an unbalanced situation; the expansion of the gasoline lines will have reached its maximum when the adjustments sought are fully brought to pass. Indeed, the opinion may be ventured that most of the needed adaptation has already been witnessed, and that much of the residual portion could be obviated by adjustments in railroad freight rates." See The Economics of Pipe Lines in the Oil Industry, by Joseph E. Pogue, *Pipe-line News*, vol. 4, No. 11, p. 18.

FLYNN, LEO J.: *Coordination of Motor Transportation*, 72d Congress, 1st Session, Senate Document 43, Report to the Interstate Commerce Commission, 1932.

House Report 2192, 72d Congress, 2d Session, *Report on Pipe Lines*, Government Printing Office, 1933.

Interstate Commerce Commission: *Annual Reports; Reports; Statistics of Railways; Statistics of Pipe Line Companies.*

Network of Fuel Pipe Lines Now Covers 162,335 Miles, *The Business Week*, July 23, 1930.

POGUE, JOSEPH E.: The Economics of Pipe Lines in the Oil Industry, *Pipe Line News*, vol. 4, No. 11, pp. 12–18.

Railway Age, vols. 80–94.

Traffic World, vols. 37–51.

United States Daily, vols. 1–7.

United States Department of Commerce, Bureau of Mines: *Oil Pipe Lines in United States Measure* 111,660 *Miles* (mimeographed copy), May, 1932.

United States Senate, 62d Congress, 2d Session, Senate Document 469: *National Waterways Commission Report*, Government Printing Office, 1912.

WALKER, PAUL A.: Pipe Line Transportation, address delivered at meeting of Associated Traffic Clubs, Tulsa, October, 1931, *Associated Traffic Club Bulletin*, vol. 1, No. 14, p. 81.

Current material upon the various problems and relations discussed in this chapter will be found in many magazines and other sources. Reference to the *Readers Guide* for the years since 1925 will be most helpful, also reference to many special index lists.

Chapter XXXIX

THE TRANSPORTATION PROBLEM

THE problem of transportation is as old as man: when the successful hunter first thought to move his prey to some crude shelter beneath the rocks, the problem of goods transport was born; and, even before that prey had been brought down by his skill, as primitive man went out to seek nuts and edible roots or to kill, the problem of the movement of persons had its beginning. As unnumbered centuries passed and the character of transportation changed, as animal power replaced human power upon land and as wind displaced muscle upon water, the transportation problem underwent change. Yet it in no wise disappeared: as recently as the opening of the nineteenth century society was compelled to endure transportation by water that was slow and uncertain and by land that was slower and rendered at high cost. It was only as man learned to utilize mechanical power upon land and upon water that rapid, certain, and cheap transportation became available. For inland movement it was soon apparent that highway and waterway were no match for the railway: within a comparatively brief time both older agencies gave ground so that for almost a century the *transportation* problem was a *railway* problem.

This "railway problem," as has been indicated in earlier chapters, has had a varied aspect. For a generation the consideration of fundamental importance was additional mileage: to make more accessible distant areas and to make available natural resources of unexcelled richness, individuals and governmental units—from township to nation—contributed generously to the end that railway mileage might be increased. Fundamental errors in public policy, the premature construction of lines, and an individualistic concept of business characteristic of a pioneer people combined with certain other factors to change, by 1870, the nature of the "railway problem": for a generation that "problem," in its public aspects, was one of subordinating the profit to the service motive. By 1910 the railways had been forced to acknowledge and had been brought to accept public regulation of a comprehensive character. But the scope of regulatory authority, extensive and intensive, became greater than the wisdom with which that authority was exercised: the "railway problem" within a single decade became a problem of educating the electorate to the fundamental mutuality of interest of railways and public and to the advantage of the intelligent, rather than punitive, regulation of an important enterprise. In 1920 a long step was made toward the substitution of constructive for restrictive control—and there was reason to hope that, through a greater public understanding of the economics of railway enterprise and a greater willingness of the railways to cooperate in the promotion of social ends, this age-old "problem" was approaching a solution. Yet within a decade the "railway problem" was to become, through the rise of important competitive agencies, but a single aspect of a more comprehensive one: it is for a solution of the "transportation problem" that the student now seeks, as he puzzles over the place in a transportation scheme of each agency that is prepared to contribute to the satisfaction of social demands. Railway, highway, waterway, airway, and pipe line stand ready to serve; to a degree perhaps never before paralleled in history a surplus of high-class service exists, to the immediate gain of the public but to the early disaster of perhaps many engaged in transportation for hire. And it is the misfortune of all interests concerned that a solution to this complex and difficult problem must be sought, and made effective, during a period when the whole economic structure is subjected to strains and stresses that have rarely been equaled.

Earlier "Solutions" Offered.—The number and variety of "solutions" offered for the American transportation problem in one or another of its aspects since 1800 are infinite, running the gamut from an early proposal to use the Bactrian camel to bridge the gap between the Missouri and Snake Rivers to a recent suggestion that transport service in a certain agricultural Mississippi Valley state would be improved if all railway mileage in the area were abandoned and sole reliance placed upon highways. Under a régime of *laissez-faire* the Windom Committee would solve the problem of the difficult period following the Civil War by the competition with existing private lines of governmentally owned and operated railways from the Middle West to the Atlantic seaboard and of a parallel water route; to meet the exigencies of the situation at the close of the World War a Plumb would have the railways, purchased by the government, operated by a board dominated by railway employees, while an Amster would have the railways of the United States unified into a single great system, privately owned and operated. Almost from the beginning of railway construction, government ownership and operation have been urged as a panacea by a greater or lesser group: urged by some because they believed that only in this way could monopoly power be shaped to public advantage, by others because of adherence to a social philosophy that demands complete public control of all productive enterprise—with the railways, acquired and operated by government, to be used as a wedge to compel the gradual socialization of other major fields of enterprise. Yet to no plan that urged sharp departure from traditional policy has serious consideration been accorded: the American people have held firmly to an economic régime in which private initiative and competitive activity have an important rôle. In consequence, as weaknesses appeared, the public chose to caulk the seams or even to man the pumps rather than to challenge the seaworthiness of the craft in which it rode—and perhaps rightly, except as it was willing to challenge many other accepted features of the existing economic and social order in the light of present-day theory and fact. The railways entered upon the period of their present difficulty organized upon a competitive basis, with the demand of the public for active competition made the more effective by a lack of solidarity among railway leaders in matters of common interest.

The "Problem" Today.—At the time of the passage in 1920 of the Transportation Act, there was little to indicate that within a brief period chaos would threaten in the field of transport, or that the financial integrity of the railways would soon be imperiled as it had not been for almost 40 years. The motor vehicle had won an important place in our economic scheme, the demand for navigable inland waterways had become emphatic, the airplane gave promise of important service, and the pipe line was a known factor; yet the threat of these services was no more than a small cloud upon the railway horizon. Within a decade, however, marked progress was to be made by all these agencies, with the progress of some almost phenomenal. In the years from 1920 to 1929 there should have been, accepting railway experience prior to 1920 as a guide, an increase in freight service rendered of approximately 75 per cent and in passenger service of 60 per cent. Instead, the increase actually experienced by the railways was 9 per cent in freight—with a decline in passenger service of 34 per cent. That industry has changed fundamentally in its character or needs, that the people are clinging more closely to particular localities, may both be rejected summarily as explanations of the failure of railway traffic to increase as in previous periods.

The explanation lies rather in the change that occurred within a single decade in the mechanism of transport, a change that falls little short of a revolution and promises to continue except as certain controls are imposed and certain artificial stimuli removed. Within that decade the number of passenger cars and trucks upon the nation's highways increased some 1.9 and 2.4 times, respectively, with mileage and service increasing more sharply. Within that decade there was a material increase in the volume of tonnage moving upon inland waterways and of domestic tonnage through the Panama Canal, of which much would have moved by rail during the preceding decade. Within this decade commercial aviation had its birth, experiencing a rapid development; and within it, too, the extension of mileage of trunk pipe lines was sufficient to absorb all but a small portion of the tremendous increase in tonnage of raw materials of the petroleum industry—though it should be noted that the increase in the tonnage of petroleum products moving by rail was marked during the decade. Because data are lacking with respect to motor transport, it is impossible to indicate with exactitude the extent to which the highway has diverted traffic from the rails, yet, in view of the comparatively small inroads made by other agencies upon the total of traffic available, it is apparent that the major diversion has been from railway to highway—with each of the other agencies contributing its minor portion to a major readjustment. But emphasizing and exaggerating a difficult transportation situation has been a business depression of unusual severity and duration: by the resultant dearth of traffic a problem that otherwise would have permitted leisurely and careful study became within a brief period a crisis demanding immediate and positive action.

The "Problem" Becomes Acute.—In an earlier chapter the downward sweep in the volume of railway traffic in the late months of 1929 was noted—with the decline unbroken until midsummer, 1932. Because the volume of traffic had been high for a period of years prior to 1930, with 1929 one of the best years financially in railway history, and because the volume of traffic did not sink to disturbingly low levels during 1930, little serious concern was then shown. This was in part because the belief was general that the duration of the depression would be brief: assurance was offered by government, by leaders of industry, and by many close students of the business cycle that "prosperity was just around the corner." But when 1931 gave clear evidence that the decline in both business activity and traffic continued unchecked, more than "watchful waiting" became necessary: diminishing revenues and inability to pare costs proportionately, coupled with the exhaustion of available reserves, were imperiling the solvency of many carriers. Meanwhile, the relative volume—if not the absolute amount—of traffic moving by highway increased; the volume of air traffic rose steadily; and the greater importance of the rate to shippers who were heavily penalized by declines in commodity prices stimulated movement by water. Though various interests identified with the railways, as diverse as organized bondholders and organized labor, had protested previously against "subsidized competition," these protests grew in volume and in emphasis as the pressure of the depression became greater. To them the public gave ear increasingly; aided by a growing resentment against certain types of operation upon the highways, restrictive legislation was passed by many state legislatures in 1931 and 1932, but the effective application of such laws had generally to await judicial scrutiny. The financial needs of the railways had become acute, and the public seemed again in the mood, as it had been in 1919, to consider thoughtfully possible solutions of the "transportation problem," as it had now become. But it was the misfortune of this period that a solution must be sought as the struggle for survival continued.

Emergency Action Taken.—With receivership in the immediate offing for many important properties that a few years before had been regarded as wholly sound, emergency action was essential if serious injury were not to be done to the railway financial structure and if public confidence were not to be sorely shaken. Such action was taken by the railways and by Congress late in 1931: the railways applied to the Interstate Commerce Commission for a 15 per cent increase in freight rates and a reduction of wages was sought, while, at the behest of President Hoover, the Reconstruction Finance Corporation was created with power to make loans to—among others—railways that were in immediate peril because of inability to meet maturities or to make interest payments. The decision of the Commission, the adjustment of wages, and the results of the rate increases granted, are indicated in a previous chapter and previously outlined, too, is the rescue work of the Reconstruction Finance Corporation. The rate increase failed by a wide margin to yield the revenues predicted by the Commission, for a variety of reasons; among these the more significant were a continued decline in the volume of traffic, the increased severity of highway and waterway competition, and Commission unwillingness to accord increases of the type demanded by the competitive situation. On the other hand, the Reconstruction Finance Corporation has extended greater aid than had been anticipated. And, in its endeavor to compel an improvement of the capital structure of one major railway through its power to deny approval of federal loans, the Commission was an important factor in furthering a revision of the bankruptcy laws as applicable to railways. Of this legislation more will be said later.

Consideration of Matters of Policy.—While emergency action was being taken, three separate movements of broad scope were initiated, each involving a critical examination of existing policies and the formulation of suggested changes. One of these movements was initiated by the United States Chamber of Commerce. By that organization a referendum was submitted to its membership late in 1932, to obtain a consensus of opinion upon 12 propositions.[1] Voting upon the proposals were business organizations of various types in each of the United States, so the judgments upon the questions submitted represent a reasonably satisfactory indication of the position of the business leaders of the country. A second movement was undertaken by parties directly

[1] The 12 propositions and the recorded vote upon each were:

1. Financial stability of railroads requires replacement of Sec. 15*a* of the Interstate Commerce Act with a provision directing the Commission, in fixing just and reasonable rates, to consider effects on traffic movement, on provision of efficient service at lowest consistent cost, and upon reasonable average return that will permit in time of general

involved. Because of the sharp conflict upon every front between railway and highway interests and because of the importance of a composition of major differences, an arrangement was made between the National Highway Users' Conference and the Association of Railway Executives for the appointment of a Joint Committee of Railroads and Highway Users.[1] This committee, after a careful canvass of the problems involved,

business activity reasonable reduction of indebtedness and accumulation of adequate reserves.

For 2184 Against 67

2. The existing Recapture clause of Sec. 15*a* should be retroactively repealed.

For 2157½ Against 95½

3. The elaborate processes of valuation should cease upon completion of the original valuation of a railroad with the Commission thereafter merely keeping itself informed as to changes in plant.

For 2225½ Against 46½

4. Regulation of railroads should be reduced to the point where it will be confined to assurance of fair rates and of public safety and will avoid interference with functions belonging to management.

For 2139 Against 83

5. Water transportation as well as highway transportation should be opened to railroads on an equal basis with water and highway carriers.

For 1953 Against 212

6. Railroads should be allowed to establish new rates quickly in order to meet competition from other forms of transportation.

For 1962½ Against 273½

7. The long-and-short-haul clause should be amended to place upon the railroads responsibility for determining whether proposed rates will be reasonably compensatory for the services performed.

For 1808 Against 406

8. Railroad management should make special efforts to accommodate rates to current economic conditions, and regulatory authorities should permit such rates to be promptly effective.

For 2105 Against 123

9. The period within which reparation claims may be filed against railroads for excessive rates and overcharges, and by railroads against shippers for undercharges, should be substantially shortened.

For 1832½ Against 415½

10. Reparation should be awarded only to persons suffering actual damage.

For 1837½ Against 412½

11. The Commission should have authority to delegate powers to individual commissioners, with right of appeal to the Commission.

For 2159½ Against 109½

12. The Commission should have authority to delegate powers in routine matters to boards of employees of the Commission, with right of appeal to the Commission.

For 2080½ Against 174½

[1] The composition of this committee was as follows: for the railways, W. W. Atterbury, president, Pennsylvania Railroad, chairman; L. W. Baldwin, president, Missouri Pacific Lines; Ralph Budd, president, Burlington Lines; George B. Elliot, president, Atlantic Coast Line Railroad; J. J. Pelley, president, New York, New Haven and Hartford; Paul Shoup, vice chairman, Southern Pacific Company. For the highway users, Alfred H. Swayne, vice-

offered its report to the public early in 1933. Many of the sections of this report were of necessity phrased in general terms to obtain agreement, and agreement was impossible upon certain points, notably the immediate regulation of commercial trucking rates; none the less, the joint consideration in committee of matters of mutual interest and the extent to which this first effort cleared the air of misunderstanding, as well as yielded results, justifies characterization of the work of the committee as important.[1]

president, General Motors Corporation, and vice-president, National Automobile Chamber of Commerce; Arthur M. Hill, president, Atlantic Greyhound Line, and president, National Association of Motor Bus Operators; R. C. Holmes, president, the Texas Company, and director, American Petroleum Institute; Robert P. Hooper, president, William E. Hooper and Sons Company, representing American Automobile Association; Clarence O. Sherrill, vice-president, the Kroger Grocery and Baking Company, representing the National Chain Stores Association; and Louis J. Taber, master of National Grange. Executive secretary William J. Cunningham, Professor of Transportation, Harvard University.

[1] The joint committee prefaced its statement of principles by the declaration that "the public is entitled to the benefit of the most economical and efficient means of transportation by any instrumentalities of transportation which may be suited to such purpose, and no legislation should be enacted which has for its purpose the stifling of any legitimate form of transportation. The supreme test must be the interest of the public. The public's right to the selection of the agency of transportation which it wants and which it finds most useful must be respected." To this is added the statement, "In principle, all those using the highways for commercial purposes in interstate and intrastate commerce should be subjected to regulation." Federal legislation is suggested subjecting common carriers of persons and/or of property to the jurisdiction of the Interstate Commerce Commission or other appropriate federal tribunal; of such carriers a certificate of convenience and necessity should be required and, in weighing the application, existing service and the effect thereon of the proposed service should be considered. Accounts should be kept in prescribed form and adequate reports made; security issues should be regulated; full common-carrier financial responsibility should be assured; qualifications and hours of service of drivers should be fixed; and a "grandfather clause" is suggested in any regulatory act. Agreement exists upon the immediate regulation of rates for the transportation of passengers, but the regulation of truck rates would be delayed by motor-vehicle interests—to follow "*if and when sufficient data have been collected to indicate the desirability of such regulation in public interest.*"

For the contract carrier of persons and/or property in interstate commerce essentially the same requirements are suggested as for the common carrier, except that for the certificate a permit is to be substituted—this permit to be granted as a privilege, under the interpretation of the railways, but as a right, all requirements having been met, under the interpretation of the highway representatives. Again, rates for the movement of persons are to be fixed—minimum rates in this instance, but concerning the prescription of rates for the movement of property by contract carrier the highway representatives insisted upon the same reservation as noted incident to common-carrier trucking rates. The principles to govern intrastate common and contract carriage of persons and/or property parallel those indicated as applicable to interstate transport.

Of private passenger vehicles and private carriers of property no federal requirements are to be made and only such state requirements imposed as attach to state registration and police regulation. To the extent, however, that the private carrier of property engages in for-hire or peddler operations and that any private carrier of persons transports passengers

The third major action taken was more comprehensive in nature than the two just mentioned: it undertook to deal with the transportation problem in its entirety. This action was initiated by numerous insurance companies with large investments in railway securities; in this enterprise the insurance group was joined, however, by others with an important financial interest in railway issues and in the future of the railway industry.[1] Yet, while this study proceeded largely from an interest in and uncertainty concerning the future status of the railways, the desire of the participating organizations was clearly that the problems of the railways be considered in relation to the transportation situation as a whole and that the findings should stress public interest and need rather than private advantage.[2] As members of the so-called National Transpor-

"on a share-expense or other irregular fare basis," a license shall be required, financial responsibility imposed, and compliance with the same safety provisions applicable to regular for-hire carriers of like type demanded.

It was agreed that "motor vehicles should pay the entire cost of the state highway system. They should also pay a part of the cost of county and/or township highways, that part to be determined by the extent to which such county and/or township highways are in general use rather than local use. Furthermore, motor vehicles should contribute to the cost of arterial routes through cities. . . . The annual cost of highways should include administration, maintenance, interest charges on highway debt, and amortization of capital expenditures." In the light of the discussion in an earlier chapter the rule for the allocation of the tax burden offered by the joint committee is interesting: "The basic cost of constructing, improving, and maintaining a given highway should be determined from a highway designed for private passenger vehicles and other vehicles commensurate therewith. All vehicles using such highways should pay their proportionate share of that total as a base tax. The additional cost of construction, improvements, and maintenance to make a road suitable for a type of vehicle requiring such additional cost should be shared by each vehicle of that type and each vehicle of greater size. Thus, each group should share in the base cost plus all increments of cost up to and including cost required by it." For all types of vehicles a gasoline tax and a registration fee are suggested: for passenger automobiles the registration fee should be graduated according to weight or horse power, for buses and other vehicles carrying passengers for hire according to mileage operated and seating capacity, and for trucks so that it will increase more than directly with weight.

Continued movement toward exclusive state control of highways is urged in the interest of simplicity of administration and economy. Railways should be required to contribute no more to the cost of eliminating any particular grade crossing than the capitalized savings in operating expenses resulting from such elimination—with only tangible savings to be reckoned. All barriers to railway operation of motor vehicles upon the public highway should be removed, the railways to be accorded the same rights as others in that field. Agreement was reached as to the maximum width and height of motor vehicles, 96 and 150 inches, respectively; weight and length the railways would leave to state regulatory bodies, while the highway users accepted the recommendations of the American Association of State Highway Officials as set forth in a previous chapter (p. 623*n*).

[1] Here were included the National Association of Mutual Savings Banks, the Investment Bankers Association of America, the Railway Business Association, and certain important endowed universities.

[2] In the instructions given the Committee, the sponsors said, "No solution, however, will be effective unless the problem of the railroads is considered as an integral part of

tation Committee were chosen five men possessed of no special knowledge of the general field of transport, yet men whose records command respect and whose fairness—as well as usual soundness—of judgment was recognized.[1] This Committee, informed by many hearings of broad scope and assisted by an independent study made by an important research organization, also issued its report early in 1933. The findings appeared as a majority and a minority report, the latter being offered by Mr. Smith. And, because of the standing of the Committee, as well as because of the fact that its study covered in an impartial way all phases of transport, the program outlined by it has been accorded thoughtful consideration by the public and by those charged with responsibility for the formulation and execution of a transportation policy.

National Transportation Committee: Majority Report.—While the text of the majority report of the National Transportation Committee is comparatively brief, considering the nature of the study, the clarity of the Committee's summary of its conclusions is such that it will serve adequately here. This summary follows:

I. The railroad system must be preserved. Changed conditions require new policies but not abandonment of railroad regulation. The development of regulation and of new methods of transport make it unnecessary for government further to create and foster competition with or among railroads as a defense against monopoly. That is an expensive and ineffective attempt to do indirectly what government has shown its ability to do directly. Regulation is sufficient. Government policies should be freed of any purpose either to favor or to handicap any form of transportation with relation to any other form. We cannot solve the problem on the theory upon which horses are handicapped in a race. In a fair field and no favor competition should be permitted to decide the result. Regu-

---

the entire transportation problem of the United States, whether by rail, highway, waterway, pipe line, or air.

"Every industry in the country is entitled to fair treatment—the railroads no less than the others. The public interest must certainly be protected, but regulation should not place the railroads at a hopeless disadvantage with competing agencies and destroy flexibility of operation and management initiative. The railroad workers are entitled to a fair wage and the greatest possible security of employment. The holders of railroad securities are entitled to a fair and stable return on the true value of their investment.

"But more important than the interests of any one group, the people of the United States are entitled to the most effective and economical form of transportation to meet their various needs, whether by land, water, or air. Each form of transportation should be unhampered to provide effectively at a reasonable cost and at a fair profit the service for which it is best fitted. No form of transportation should be favored either at the expense of another agency or at the ultimate expense of the people of the United States."

[1] The members of this Committee were Calvin Coolidge, chairman; Alfred E. Smith, ex-Governor of New York; Bernard M. Baruch, banker; Clark Howell, editor of the *Atlanta Constitution;* and Alexander Legge, president, International Harvester Company. Mr. Coolidge died before the hearings were completed, no one replacing him.

lation should not attempt to "run the business" of transportation. It should concentrate on protecting the public against discrimination and extortion and on requiring the most efficient service at the lowest competitive cost:

1. Parallel lines and systems are wasteful and unnecessary. Regional consolidations should be hastened and, where necessary, enforced, looking eventually to a single national system with regional divisions and the elimination of all excess and obsolete lines and equipment. Neither holding companies nor any other device should be permitted to hinder consolidation or evade the letter or the spirit of regulatory law.

2. Unprofitable railroad services should be replaced by cheaper alternative transport methods.

3. Railroads should be permitted to own and operate competing services, including water lines, but regulatory jurisdiction should be extended to water rates and practices in coastal, intercoastal, and lake shipping to relieve commerce of present chaotic conditions. Congress should promptly clarify its intention on the long-and-short-haul clause of the Transportation Act.

4. Government assumption of all or part of the costs of inefficient competing transport as a defense against monopoly is no longer warranted and should be abandoned. As a general principle inland waterways should bear all costs of amortization, interest, maintenance, and operation of the facilities for their navigation. If they cannot bear such charges and compete with other forms of transport, they should be abandoned. The St. Lawrence Waterway should be tested by this rule of self-support and if it fails in that test the pending treaty with Canada should not be ratified. Governmental commercial operation of the actual facilities of transportation, such as barge lines, should not be continued.

5. Automotive transportation should be put under such regulation as is necessary for public protection. It should bear its fair burden of tax, but only on a basis of compensation for public expenditure on its behalf, plus its share of the general tax load. Neither tax nor regulation should be applied for any purpose of handicapping the march of progress for the benefit of the railroads.

6. Wages and working conditions of labor in transportation are determinable by established procedure in another forum and are not within the scope of this inquiry. There should be no heavier burdens on the railroads in employing labor to operate automobiles than on their competitors. In the railroads (as in other industries) rates, capitalization, salaries, and wages must all follow changing economic conditions, but none should be sacrificed for the benefit of others.

7. Beacons, weather service, and similar auxiliaries to air traffic should be maintained at public expense, and air transport should be encouraged during its development stage, but we believe that every such service should ultimately pay its own way.

8. The committee has no recommendation to make on pipe lines.

II. The policy of trying to appraise railroad properties on some selected basis of valuation and then saying that they are entitled to earn a fair return on this appraisal should be reconsidered. Where competition with trucks and other methods exists, it will determine rates. In other cases rates must be regulated, but the basis of costs of operation under efficient management is a better general guide than any attempt to preserve capital structures regardless of economic trends. We see no reason why the rate-making rule should not say in plain English that railroads are entitled to make a reasonable profit based upon costs of efficient operation and that they are not entitled to earnings merely to preserve present structures if overcapitalized.

III. The railroads should do much that they have not done to improve their condition without any government help at all. They should promptly be freed of all unnecessary restrictions on the doing of it. It has been estimated that less than a 20 per cent increase in traffic would put most of them on an earning basis. In view of the narrowness of this margin of loss and of the very great savings possible in railroad operation, we regard their outlook as far from hopeless.

1. Railroads should adopt the competing methods of which they complain.
2. Railroads should cooperate to reduce competitive expense.
   a. Unnecessary services should be abandoned.
   b. Metropolitan terminals should be consolidated and unnecessary facilities scrapped.
   c. Circuitous haulage should be eliminated.
3. Financial management should be improved.
4. Transport methods and equipment should be brought up to date.
5. In view of what could be done by better management, the general outlook seems far from hopeless.

IV. Regulatory jurisdiction should be extended to the whole national transportation system, but applied only to the extent necessary for public protection. The existing regulatory mechanism of the Interstate Commerce Commission is inadequate and should be improved by reorganization without expansion or increased expense.

V. Emergency recommendations.

1. Corporate reorganization can and should be facilitated by revision of the bankruptcy procedure.
2. The recapture clause should be repealed retroactively.
3. The statutory rule of rate making should be revised.
4. "Adequate security" does not necessarily mean "marketable collateral."

National Transportation Committee: Minority Report.—In offering a separate report, Mr. Smith says, "While I am in substantial agreement with the greater part of the Committee's report, this supplementary memorandum states my conclusions in my own language." As an emergency measure no new rule of rate making is needed, nor will a useful purpose be served by permission to the Reconstruction Finance Corporation to make loans to railways without full collateral, he concludes. He believes that the scope of regulatory action should be restricted, rather than extended: instead of subjecting other agencies to Commission control to equalize competitive conditions, he urges the abolition of that body and "the creation in its place of a new Department of Transportation headed by one man, or a one-man bureau in the Department of Commerce determining policies with the approval of the Secretary of Commerce." He opposes all subsidies in behalf of inland-waterway development and asserts that the construction of the St. Lawrence

Waterway would be, at the present time, "a waste of public funds." Concerning the New York state barge canals, it is admitted that, "Sentiment rather than common sense makes us keep it up." The effect of competition by water, highway, pipe line, and air upon the railways is exaggerated, he believes, and he questions the contention that the railway is excessively taxed as compared with the commercial motor vehicle. Opposition is expressed to comprehensive regulation of commercial motor-vehicle operations at present: financial responsibility of operators may well be required and physical standards for vehicles fixed, but rate making should not be undertaken. The entry of the railways into the field of motor-vehicle operation is urged.

Mr. Smith expresses himself strongly in favor of a "nation-wide consolidation and reorganization of the railways to reduce costs and rates, and to write off losses. . . . The roads must reduce overhead and operating expenses. They must scrap unnecessary, competing, and weak lines. . . . They must cut out unnecessary services. They must use trucks and buses, eventually air transportation and, if necessary, waterways and pipe lines as a supplement or substitute for rails wherever these new forms of transportation are more economical." A "realistic" attitude is urged upon holders of railway securities in the inevitable scaling down of the issues of many railways: "The public will not stand for making them a preferred class of investors, who must get a hundred cents on the dollar, irrespective of the true value and condition of the business they have invested in, when values in all other fields are being readjusted and cut down." And, if consolidation and financial reorganization are not voluntarily undertaken, compulsion should be applied. In the closing paragraphs of his separate statement Mr. Smith declares forcefully:

I believe that the railroads will be unsuccessful in attempts to maintain their present physical operating and financial structure at the expense of the general public by penalizing competitors and raising competing transportation costs, inflating securities, raising rates, limiting taxation by states and municipalities through federal legislation, borrowing government money without adequate security, and other like devices.

Similarly, attempts to bring about economy largely at the expense of railroad labor will prove unsuccessful unless this is part of a logical general reorganization in the interest of the public. Undoubtedly many wasteful and unjustifiable regulations have been made governing railroad wages, hours, and conditions of labor, and others which, however, admirable in themselves, the country simply cannot afford today, but the railroads cannot expect public support in changing these regulations merely as a means of retaining and perpetuating other conditions which are equally wasteful. They cannot expect to make labor the only scapegoat.

Those who are responsible for present railroad management need not complain of radical or drastic governmental action in the near future if they are unwilling even to attempt to meet their problems in a bold, forthright way through their own initiative and cooperation. They have an unrivaled opportunity to do themselves and the country a great service. They should have the guidance and help of the national and state governments in this effort.

While there is much of truth in these final aggressive statements, they are of even greater significance, perhaps, because Mr. Smith's position is likely to be representative of that of great numbers of thinking people who have not examined critically and in their historic setting the railway aspects of the transportation problem. As evidence of this stands the bitter opposition of many major business groups to the continuance of the emergency railway rates authorized for the period of a year, as well as the demand by important interests that the level of railway charges be sharply cut to correspond with the current price level: little thought is given to, or there is conscious disregard of, the certain and immediate consequences of such major reductions upon railway solvency.

Other General Proposals.—Numerous other proposals, some of a partial character and others sufficiently comprehensive to be termed "plans," have been offered for the solution of the transportation problem. One of these plans came from the Association of Railway Executives; the proposals of this group were of a reasonable character and happily escaped the fault of heaping upon "regulation" the blame for the present status of the railways. Certain specific changes in existing regulatory acts and policies were recommended and an appropriate extension of regulation to competing agencies was urged. As an example of a plan proceeding from a specialized point of view, though none the less comprehensive in its scope, may be suggested that offered by the American Fruit and Vegetable Shippers' Association to the National Transportation Committee; among the proposals of general interest were the compulsory consolidation of railways, a revision downward of railway wage scales, resort to pooling to minimize duplication of services, the regulation of truck transportation, the elimination of subsidies to agencies competing with the railways, and a lessened tax burden upon railways.[1]

Many individuals have delivered themselves of little less than diatribes upon the evils of regulation, particularly regulation that "trenches upon the field of management," but have been strangely vague as to the specific changes that are needed in existing laws to "free the railways of this 'old man of the sea.'" Others, to a considerable degree groups, have been concerned with results rather than means: a common demand has been that the "excessive burden of existing railway rates" be lightened, yet there is a striking absence of specific proposals that—if and as made effective—would permit of such decrease in rates without precipitating bankruptcy for a major portion of the railway net. And it seems to be forgotten that the millstone of an inadequate

[1] See for complete statement *Railway Age*, vol. 93, p. 957.

service, resulting from the impoverishment of the railways, will obstruct a revival of industrial activity as effectively as a level of rates that is out of line with commodity prices. If rates are to move downward with the general price level, then they must move upward as prices advance, if justice is to be done and the financial integrity of regulated enterprise maintained. Yet this latter aspect of the adjustment of rates to prices has been curiously and persistently ignored.

Commission Recommendations.—Hardly a year has passed that the Interstate Commerce Commission has not urged upon Congress modifications in regulatory policy of both a major and minor character: in important decisions and in its annual reports these recommendations are noted.[1] Frequently, too, the Commission has admonished the carriers with respect to certain practices, certain acts of omission and of commission, and certain policies. Among the more significant recommendations made to Congress by the Commission in recent years are the repeal of Sec. 15*a* of the Interstate Commerce Act—including the Recapture clause, retroactively—and the substitution of an improved rule of rate making which will, among other things, charge the Commission with the maintenance of rates that will yield an *average* fair return through prosperous and lean years; the full regulation of interstate bus traffic; the establishment of regulatory control over railway holding companies; the authorization of changes in Commission procedure that will permit individual commissioners or employees to assume initial responsibility for specified tasks; a comprehensive investigation by Congress to determine the facts relative to the subsidization of particular agencies of transport and to suggest the steps to be taken, if such subsidization exists, to place competition upon an equitable basis; a careful consideration by Congress of the propriety of regulating the port-to-port rates of water carriers; and the requirement that the interstate operations of all motor vehicles transporting property for hire be conditioned upon the issuance of a permit and evidence of insurance appropriate to the type of carrier, common or private.

Within recent years the Commission has admonished the railways with respect to a number of matters.[2] It has condemned, among other things, the allocation of railway purchases in consideration of the favorable routing of traffic by industrial concerns, as well as excessive competitive expenditures by railways for produce terminals in certain cities. It has urged upon the railways a greater use of pooling to reduce transportation waste; the improvement of the passenger service through the

[1] For a summary of the Commission's position the student is referred to the Forty-fifth and Forty-sixth *Annual Reports*, pp. 119–123 and 100–103, respectively.

[2] See particularly the closing pages of the Fifteen per cent case, 178 I.C.C. 579; Reciprocity in Purchasing and Routing, 188 I.C.C. 417; and Practices of Carriers Affecting Operating Revenues and Expenses, 188 I.C.C. 323.

operation of lighter trains at higher speeds and of the freight service through the utilization of store-door delivery; the greater use of the container and other devices such as the railwagon; and the revision of rate structures in the light of existing competitive conditions. It has questioned the carriers concerning such a fundamental matter as the desirability of reducing the basic passenger fare per mile with a view to a possible increase in passenger earnings, and has called definitely to the attention of the railways the error of a "continual intensifying of their own competition" at a time when cooperation is essential to the maintenance of solvency. While the Commission has not been sharply critical of railway management, it has declared, "The railroads face new conditions which will compel changes in methods of operation, manner of service, and price policies, which cannot be met successfully in all respects by reliance upon methods and policies which were serviceable and became established under more nearly monopolistic conditions. The situation is one which frequently confronts private competitive industries, and they have become accustomed to such readjustments by force of necessity." In another connection the need of "drastic attention and genuinely creative enterprise" is stressed. Yet the Commission says of the railways, "there are many indications that they now realize the necessity of more or less radical readjustments and are preparing to act accordingly. We have confidence in their ability to rise to the needs of the occasion."[1]

Individual Commissioners Speak.—The recommendations of the Interstate Commerce Commission to Congress in 1919 that took form in the Esch bill were of a conservative character, builded upon experience and proceeding little beyond it. So are the more recent proposals of the Commission, despite the critical situation of the railways during the striking depression of the early thirties: condemnation of objectionable practices and policies is not aggressively sharp; optimism for the future is expressed; and no definite break with past regulatory policy is suggested. Yet particular members of the Commission, informed by their work but less bound as individuals in the expression of opinion than is a body charged with important responsibilities, have given expression to judgments that are more positive and that break more definitely with precedent than those just outlined. Mr. Joseph B. Eastman has not hesitated to emphasize the importance of managerial policies as a factor in improving the status of the railways: "There are many measures that can be taken to meet the new conditions and protect railway earnings. On the one hand are changes in railway policies and methods, and on the other, legislation. Both are important, but the changes in policies and methods are probably the more important."[2] Particularly critical

[1] See the *Forty-fifth Annual Report of the Interstate Commerce Commission*, pp. 117–118.
[2] *American Economic Review*, vol. 22, Supplement, p. 250.

of the wastes chargeable to railway competition, he declares that the present is a "peculiarly appropriate time for the railroads to abate civil strife and unite in common defense against the enemy at the gate." Recognizing that this will involve a change in policy "on the part of executives running counter to railroad traditions that are bred in the bone," Mr. Eastman adds, "but the circumstances now existing recall Benjamin Franklin's observation to the signers of the Declaration of Independence that if they did not hang together they would all hang separately." He emphasizes the necessity of a modernized service in handling less-than-carload freight, and a "considerable reconstruction of the rate structure"—this with respect to small-lot shipments, especially. Yet he warns of dangers to the independent highway operator that may proceed from railway entry into the field of motor-vehicle transport, and suggests the need of the extension of regulation along various lines. To the plaints of those who charge regulation with responsibility for the "plight of the railways" his answer is an assertion, historically grounded, that the railways have gained from it in no less measure than the public: few eliminations from existing federal regulatory legislation would be made by the railways themselves, this student of transportation believes.

One of the noteworthy plans for the coordination of all transportation facilities has been offered by Commissioner Claude R. Porter.[1] Declaring that the fundamental transportation problem is that of obtaining "the benefit of the best service possible from all of the five forms of transportation," he observes that

> The mere regulation alone of all of them will not produce the desired result. There must in some way be brought about the close and effective coordination of all of them. . . . The regulation of all kinds of transportation must be centralized so that . . . each . . . may be developed to the largest extent possible without injustice to any other kind of transportation . . . giving to the people of the country the best possible service at the lowest possible cost.

To this end Mr. Porter suggests

> . . . the creation of a new independent bureau, to be denominated a Bureau of Transportation. At the head of this Bureau I would place a director, to be known as the Director of Transportation. He should be appointed by the President and confirmed by the Senate. The tremendous importance of the duties involved in such a position demands it be occupied by a man of the highest character and ability. . . . The period of his service should be for sufficient length of time to give some degree of permanency and continuity of policy. It seems, therefore, the term of office should be at least 10 years. The salary should be fixed at a sum sufficient to secure and retain a man of high standing and ability.

[1] See the *Proceedings*, National Association of Railroad and Public Utility Commissioners, 1932.

There should be created in this Bureau three major divisions: a division of land transportation, of water transportation, and of air transportation.

The first division, that of land transportation, should be the Interstate Commerce Commission as at present constituted, with all of the duties now imposed upon it under the law. To these duties should be added that of supervising and regulating the buses and trucks engaged in interstate commerce. They should be placed, so far as practicable, under substantially the same regulation as now pertains to the railroads. The director of the Bureau should be *ex officio* chairman of the Interstate Commerce Commission, fully empowered to sit in the Commission's councils and with the same rights and duties as any other member of the Commission. . . .

The second major division of the Bureau of Transportation would have the supervision of all our water-borne carriers. I would transfer the present Shipping Board with its present personnel, and its authority and power over water-borne carriers to this Bureau of Transportation. Its jurisdiction should be extended to cover fully and completely all of our coastal water carriers and those operating on all the inland waterways of the country. It should have in the main, as to these water-borne carriers, the same power and authority over rates, equality of treatment of shippers, capitalization of companies, and establishment and abandonment of new lines, that the Interstate Commerce Commission now has over railroads. The Director of Transportation I have mentioned should be *ex officio* chairman of the Shipping Board, with the same authority that is committed to any other member of that board.

The third major division of this new Bureau of Transportation would be that in charge of air transportation. This division should be constructed by transferring to it the position of Assistant Secretary for Aeronautics and the present aeronautics branch of the Department of Commerce. They should retain all the powers now possessed by them. In addition, they should be given authority to insure the charging of reasonable rates for the carriage of both passengers and property, and also to make certain equality of treatment of all their patrons. They should be empowered to prevent all unfair methods of competition among the various operating companies or against other forms of transportation. All of the important acts of the division as above constituted should be subject to the approval of the Director of Transportation, who *ex officio* should be the head of this division as of the other two.

In this manner, by bringing these several divisions, each having supervision over its respective carriers, into one bureau under one central head, I am convinced there could be brought about a coordination of all the five present forms of transportation, which is impossible when their regulation is enforced by wholly separate and distinct bureaus of the government acting entirely independent of each other and with no knowledge or information of what the other is doing.

. . . One directing head, meeting and consulting with those in charge of each of the three divisions named, should be able and undoubtedly could bring about uniformity in the policy of regulating these five forms of transportation, and a coordination between the transportation agencies themselves, far surpassing anything that we have at the present time. He should be able to see that all are encouraged and developed and preserved in full vigor.

Proposals of Limited Scope.—Numberless suggestions of particular changes in transportation policy might be cited, and many suggestions of sufficiently broad scope to justify denomination as "plans" might be offered. Yet it is in the content, rather than the number, of suggestions that assistance is to be found; the proposals already noted seem to raise those questions of fundamental importance to which any effective solution of the "railway problem," and of the more comprehensive "transportation problem," must give regard.

Chapter XL

A NATIONAL TRANSPORTATION POLICY

IN EARLIER chapters the service contribution of each major agency of inland transport has been noted and, upon the pages just preceding, certain of the more significant proposals offered for the solution of a complex and difficult problem have been stated. The primary factual data have been presented: it remains to examine the needs of the existing situation, to the end that the basic elements of a national transportation policy may be stated. To assist in the formulation of this policy certain questions will be put and to those questions, in turn, answers will be sought. In this search consideration will be given to the proposals outlined briefly upon preceding pages and reference made to conclusions stated in earlier chapters. In so far as known facts permit, positive answers will be given; yet, so many are the unknowns and so significant are the variables that must be given weight, only omniscience would permit the statement of a program that would eliminate the "transportation problem" from the crowded *agenda* of the nation. The best that can be hoped is the formulation of a plan to meet the difficulties that now appear, and the intelligent application of that plan through legislative and administrative action. But in the formulation of any plan, clear differentiation must be made between emergency and normal needs: it is to be hoped that adjustments essential to meet conditions that obtain in 1933, at neap tide in business activity, will provide a wide margin of safety for a typical period.

Among the questions to which answers are vital in the formulation of a national transportation policy to guide legislative bodies and regulatory commissions, and to control the various agencies rendering a transport service, are:

1. To what extent is special effort to obviate railway receiverships justified and, if justified, what emergency measures should be taken to that end?

2. What important changes should be made in the Interstate Commerce Act and corresponding state statutes as they affect the railways, as well as in other legislation applicable to the railways?

3. What changes in legislative policy concerning highway, waterway, airway, and pipe-line transportation are requisite to an equitable and sound transportation plan?

4. What may management, particularly railway management, contribute to the solution of the "transportation problem" and the effective operation of a comprehensive plan?

5. In what manner is that coordination of transportation facilities which is essential to a "transportation plan" to be attained and maintained?

6. What contribution can the public, and administrative bodies regulating in behalf of that public, make to the successful operation of an effective plan?

While space forbids exhaustive treatment of the problems that arise in the formulation of answers to these fundamental questions, it is believed the conclusions stated will find a factual basis in the discussion here offered and in material presented in earlier chapters.

Appropriate Emergency Action.—It is not essential to confidence in the financial integrity of railway securities that dividends be paid upon railway stock during a prolonged depression. That interest shall be paid as due and that maturing obligations shall be met is, however, the *sine qua non* of public faith and of an even reasonable support of bond prices. Action to strengthen the railways financially was possible along any or all of several lines: government loans might be made to needy carriers, revenues might be augmented by increases in rates, expenses might be cut drastically, and railway capital structures might be readjusted to postpone maturities and lower fixed charges. Within a brief period action along each of these lines was taken. Because of the large volume of railway bonds held by savings banks, insurance companies, and other fiduciary institutions in which public interest is great, and because it was feared that the widespread collapse of railways—the bonds of many of which had but recently been regarded as sound investments—would have a disastrous psychological effect, the national administration recommended and Congress provided emergency aid for the railways through the Reconstruction Finance Corporation. Beginning its service to the railways early in 1932, this corporation made it possible for that year to end with but few receiverships precipitated, in spite of the fact that a major portion of the railways did not earn during that year their fixed charges. And that assistance continued to preserve solvency during the period following for many hard-pressed carriers.

A second emergency action, discussed previously at some length,[1] was the approval of a limited increase in rates, effective early in 1932. Though the request of the railways was granted only in part, and then subject to a rather unusual condition, the benefit resulting from the heavier charges was material during a year of abnormally light earnings. Undoubtedly rates could have been increased upon long-haul traffic

[1] See Chap. XV for a more complete discussion of this increase.

by greater amounts without causing any considerable diversion of tonnage from the railways, yet the reluctance of the Interstate Commerce Commission to increase rates when the level of commodity prices had dropped so sharply was clearly understandable. A third action taken to improve the financial showing of the railways was the negotiation of a temporary cut in railway wage rates. Railway labor agreed to accept a 10 per cent reduction for the period of 1 year, this time being later extended—as indicated in another chapter—until October, 1933. Thus, by an increase in revenue and a decrease in expenses that was the greater because of lower wage rates, Class I railways showed for 1932 a net operating income of some $334,000,000—which, it is of interest to note, was less than 27 per cent of the corresponding figure for 1929 and little more than two-thirds of the sum necessary to meet interest on funded debt.

The final action purposed to provide emergency relief to the railways came early in 1933 in the form of the passage by Congress, in response to Presidential urgency and obvious need, of a so-called Debtors' Relief Act. This Act makes possible, among other things, the reorganization of railways without the necessity of the traditional receivership and foreclosure sale. While such reorganization has been legally possible in the past, it has not been practicable: a small group of security holders could, by refusing to accept terms satisfactory to others, compel a settlement that was highly preferential or block all further action. Under the new law, briefly stated, a reorganization plan making provision for the readjustment of the capital structure of a railway may be made binding if approved by the holders of two-thirds of the amount of each class of security affected by the plan. Before such plan can be made effective, however, it must be placed before the Interstate Commerce Commission for approval, with power reserved to that body to modify the plan in the interest of equity and public advantage; in case modifications are made, the revised plan shall be resubmitted for consideration to the various classes of security owners affected. And, before the plan becomes operative, the judge under whose jurisdiction the property has been during the period of reorganization must also give his approval. Should the railway be, in the opinion of the judge, insolvent while reorganization is being attempted, then only the consent of creditor groups is essential to the proposed plan.

In accordance with the terms of this law facilitating reorganization, a convenient means is offered for the readjustment of unsatisfactory capital structures—of which, unfortunately, there are many. Had such a measure been available, it is certain that the St. Louis-San Francisco would have been able to meet the requirement of the Interstate Commerce Commission that its capital structure be improved before further loans from the Reconstruction Finance Corporation be authorized; with such a measure available there should be, even though railway earnings continue at low ebb for a period, less occasion for dependence upon the Corporation. Self-help, in the form of sharp reductions in fixed charges and the readjustment of maturities, should take the place of extended borrowings otherwise necessary. Thus, with financial assistance available in case of need and justification, with unusual opportunity to reduce excessive bond ratios and burdensome fixed charges, and with efforts continuing to safeguard net operating income as far as the volume of traffic permits, it would seem that the fundamental needs of an emergency program have been well met.

Other suggestions for emergency action have been made. By some it has been urged that collateral requirements be lightened upon loans from the Reconstruction Finance Corporation; yet to open the door to further borrowing, when the prime need for present borrowing arises from the excessive use in past financing of obligations bearing a fixed charge, does not appeal to the critical mind. By others it is suggested that the immediate and retroactive repeal of the Recapture clause—indeed, of the whole of Sec. 15*a*—is essential, yet it is difficult to grasp the emergency value of such action, particularly to the credit of most of those railways whose credit is weak. Current revenues are not lessened by a rule of rate making intended to secure to the railways a fair return upon fair value—which return it is all too obvious they cannot earn for a period, at least—nor because of the continuation upon the statute books of a provision requiring the recapture of a portion of nonexistent excess earnings. In short, it appears that there is little occasion to supplement the action already taken, except as unexpected developments occur to change the nature or intensity of emergency needs.

Needed Changes in Railway Legislation.—Legislative action to aid the railways directly may take either of two forms, the repeal or modification of existing statutes, or the enactment of additional legislation. Of action of the first type, that urged most widely is the replacement of Sec. 15*a* of the Transportation Act with another provision better calculated to accomplish the purpose of 15*a*, now so widely condemned. Among those recommending such a change is the Commission: condemnation by it of this portion of the Act assists in shifting from its shoulders some portion of the onus of the failure of the railways to earn a fair return in the years prior to 1930. And among those favorable to the change, too, are the railways: the Recapture clause has never been to their liking. To the writer the Recapture clause is a logical part of the system of rate making under the present law but if, for *administrative* reasons, the Commission favors its repeal—even retroactively, it appears that deference should be accorded its judgment; however, as indicated in an earlier chapter, it is somewhat difficult to understand how waiving obligations of tens of millions due the government under the Recapture clause from particular carriers that remain strong during adversity will benefit the weaker lines from whom little is due. But, if the Recapture clause be retained, sums due the government should be computed upon the basis of average earnings over a period of years rather than upon a single-year basis.

It is desirable that federal and state statutes permit the railways to engage directly in other forms of transportation, thus supplementing rail service. To this end the Panama Canal Act should be modified, as a minimum, in accordance with the recommendations made by the Interstate Commerce Commission for several years following its initial application. Certainly there is no reason to deny the railways the right to operate boat lines over the same routes that are covered by the rail lines if such operation has been approved, as in public interest, by the Commission. Yet it seems that it would in no wise endanger public interest to have the bar to railway operation of boat lines wholly removed, if to the Commission were given the power to fix minimum rates by water: by the exercise of this power all opportunity for the railway to destroy independent boat lines by slashing rates to an abnormally low level for a brief time would be removed. All state statutes limiting or prohibiting railway operations upon the highways should be repealed, also—and this can be done under the full plan here presented without danger to independent operators because, again, the right will lie with the state regulatory body to fix rates below which the railways cannot cut in competition with such independents. In short, the way should be cleared for railway entry into any field of transport, with that entry encouraged because unusual possibilities of effective coordination in public interest are offered by the common ownership of facilities that are essentially supplementary and complementary, rather than competitive.

Repeal of the valuation sections of the existing law has been advocated by many, by some with a view to eliminating the concept of "fair value" in the determination of a fair return, by others merely to lessen regulatory costs. While an important destruction of the railway's monopolistic power makes necessary the recognition of earning capacity as a factor in the determination of the "fair value" of railway properties, it is inconceivable that definite standards shall be abandoned: a declaration that the railways "are entitled to make a reasonable profit based upon the costs of efficient operation" is fundamentally meaningless and of no worth as a guide. The railways still occupy a semi-monopolistic, even a monopolistic, position with respect to certain traffic and will do so to an even greater degree, perhaps, when the charges of competitive agencies have been adjusted to meet *total costs*. It is the writer's firm conviction that valuation should not be abandoned, though changes in method and principle must be made as changes occur in the economic status of the property for which a value is sought.

Demands for the repeal of a large part of the existing body of law under which the railways are controlled would meet with strong opposition from railway leaders as well as from the public; for, whatever may be the evils consequent upon regulation, the evils of uncontrolled competition would be even worse. Indeed, many of the features of which critics of the railways complain so sharply now, the operation of parallel trackage, the duplication of service, the high bond ratio and heavy capitalization of many properties, are the heritage of a régime free of the "crushing burden of regulation." Any commentator who purposes to scrap regulation lacks both historical perspective and an understanding of transportation economics. Duplication of facilities, duplication of service, cutthroat competition bringing gross discrimination in its wake, and a division of responsibility for adequate service are among the evils that would soon appear under a régime of "free competition"—and these alone would occasion tremendous social waste and lead inevitably to chaos in a field where order is vital to public well-being. Regulation may adapt haltingly to changing needs, but the road to satisfactory adaptation is not by way of abolition. By and large, there appear to be few sections of existing regulatory law in need of repeal or of major change.

Furthermore, little additional legislation of a fundamental character and dealing directly with the railways seems essential. The Interstate Commerce Commission has recommended that its authority be extended to include the holding company operating in the railway field, the refrigerator-car company, and the so-called forwarding company. There seems to be no logical reason to deny this extension. In the interest of certainty, the electric railway operating in interstate traffic should be subjected to Commission control as are steam lines, the more so since freight becomes an item of increasing importance to the electric railway as passenger traffic by rail dwindles. The railways should be permitted to make lower rates for longer than for included shorter hauls to meet *active* water competition, though this privilege might better proceed from a change in Commission policy, rather than from a change in the law. By many it is urged that lower rates filed by the railways to meet competition be permitted to become effective in less than the existing 30-day period, some advocating even a single day's notice; yet, in view of the past, it would promise the shipper greater protection against discrimination if the rates of agencies competing with the railway were made subject to the 30-day requirement. Meanwhile, the policy of the Commission of permitting emergency rail rates to become effective in less than the statutory period should be continued as a temporary aid to the railways.

Thus it appears that the body of law under which the railways are now regulated is relatively sound, essentially complete. Federal action in 1887, looking toward the effective regulation of interstate operations, availed little; during the period from 1903 to 1915 a policy of restrictive control was devised and applied. In 1920, benefiting from experience and less influenced by resentment against abuses that had once inflamed the public mind, constructive legislation was enacted. It is well that such action finally came, though it is the misfortune of both the public and the railways that action of equal intelligence could not have proceeded from mutual consent half a century earlier. Had wisdom equaled the zest for battle that stirred the railways and the public during that critical period, the "railway problem" would now be far simpler.

Public Policy Relative to the Newer Agencies of Transport.—In preceding chapters the writer has stated his conviction concerning an appropriate public policy relative to highway, waterway, and air transport.[1] Of that position a brief restatement will be made, supplemented by a statement of conviction upon a certain few matters not previously discussed. There seems to be no logical basis for placing upon general property so large a portion of the costs of highway construction and maintenance, including city streets, as now rests there; a greater portion of the cost burden should rest upon the highway user. This augmented burden should be apportioned upon the basis of costs as determined by impartial and detailed studies—but enough is now known to justify an increase in the proportion of the burden borne by vehicles of maximum width, length, and weight, or which approach that maximum. Common and contract carriers of persons and/or property should be subjected to comprehensive regulation, intra- and interstate—with rates based primarily upon the *total costs* of highway operation and modified in such manner as public policy shall demand. For a time the private truck may be permitted freedom from regulation; yet, if it be found that considerations of safety or of public policy demand restrictions, those restrictions should be forthcoming without delay. Interstate operations of common-carrier and contract vehicles should be subject to the jurisdiction of the Interstate Commerce Commission and between it and state regulatory agencies close cooperation should be had.

All inland-waterway projects hereafter urged should be scrutinized with great care, final decision resting upon the ability of the particular project to "pay its way"; against all traffic upon future projects, as well as against all traffic moving upon waterways that have already been constructed at public expense, a charge should be made that covers not only the *movement* cost but also a proper share of all capital, depreciation, and maintenance costs chargeable against the particular waterway. Subsidized waterway traffic has no greater justification under an equitable transportation plan than have subsidized highway operations. Furthermore, operations upon all our inland waterways should

[1] See Chapters XXXIV, XXXVI, and XXXVII.

be subjected to regulation by the Interstate Commerce Commission no less comprehensive than that now applicable to the railways: abuses that compelled railway regulation can develop in similar manner and degree upon our waterways. And such regulation should apply to both common and contract carriers, with the private carrier remaining free of control unless and until public interest shall demand an extension of authority.

For a considerable period of time the sole advocates of the regulation of the rates of ships engaged in coastwise trade were railways that found it difficult to compete, particularly during periods of cutthroat competition among the water lines. With the increase in the number of boats plying in coastwise trade and the consequent greater difficulty of stabilizing water rates during extended periods of light traffic, even of maintaining control during months of low tonnage, strong support for the regulation of coastal shipping rates has developed among the older and established lines. Conspicuous among the opponents of such regulation today are commercial interests that seek to capitalize the breakdown of self-regulation and many of the less responsible operators. Yet the logic of the situation demands that regulation be extended at least to the prescription of minimum rates and the filing of tariffs.[1] That greater unity may be attained, it seems desirable that this phase of waterway regulation should also be placed with the Interstate Commerce Commission. And again both common and contract carriers should be subjected to control.[2]

The problem of air transport is made more difficult by the fact that present air operations might have to be curtailed sharply were existing subsidies withdrawn, yet the maintenance of extensive operations is justified by many upon two grounds. It is unquestionably an industry now in its infancy and, as such, declared to be entitled to some measure of fostering care. Furthermore, the value of a large air-trained personnel

[1] On Mar. 3, 1933, President Hoover signed a measure which represents a first step toward the effective control of coastal shipping. Under the terms of this law all common and contract carriers of property and/or persons operating in intercoastal trade through the Panama Canal must file with the United States Shipping Board and keep open for public inspection schedules of all rates, fares, and charges. To such schedules the carrier must adhere and changes must be filed 30 days in advance of effective date except as the Board may, for good cause, grant relief. Furthermore, the Board may suspend any change in schedules pending investigation as to its lawfulness. The power to fix minimum rates was voted by the Senate but opposition in the House of Representatives caused that feature to be stricken from the bill finally presented to the President. None the less, the present measure will assist greatly in eliminating such consequences of uncontrolled competition as instability of rates, discrimination, and "secret" rates.

[2] For an excellent discussion of the whole problem of the regulation of coastal shipping see Kidd, H. C., Regulation of Intercoastal Commerce, *Bureau of Business Research, Monograph 2*, University of Pittsburgh. See also *Hearings* on S. 3643, 72d Congress, 1st Session.

and a vigorous aviation industry in case of war is urged. The subsidies now enjoyed by air transport take, roughly, three forms: airways are maintained without cost to transport lines; many municipalities furnish landing fields at slight or no cost to commercial operators; and payments for air-mail movements far exceed the revenues therefrom. For the immediate future it is perhaps desirable that the first two forms of aid be accepted without serious question, yet it seems only reasonable that the air-mail service should move rapidly toward a self-supporting basis. That this is the goal of changes lately recommended in the basis of mail payment has been indicated. The approximate attainment of that goal within the reasonable future is desirable and, it is hoped, feasible.

While air transport is not an important factor as yet, quantitatively, in our transportation scheme, rapid forward strides have been made. Regulation will undoubtedly come, either to forestall abuses or to seek to eliminate them as they appear—or, perchance, after they have fastened themselves upon the industry. It would seem reasonable, then, to establish without further delay regulation of the common carrier by air: in the hands of the Interstate Commerce Commission should be placed the power to fix rates, to deal with discrimination, to require the publication of rates, to prescribe a uniform system of accounts, to control service through certificates of convenience and necessity, and to regulate security issues. If contract carriers are subjected to regulation at present, there seems to be no reason to go beyond the issuance of a permit and the prescription of the form of accounts.

The pipe line performs a highly specialized service. For the line through which natural gas is conducted to areas of large consumption there is no substitute and the problem of conservation is not significant, except as there be wastage in production or movement. It is difficult to conceive of a gas line functioning as a common or a contract carrier; yet, because the commodity moved through it displaces another that moves by rail, water, and highway, such a line has transportation significance. Upon that ground regulatory action might well be urged; furthermore, it is undoubted that the price of sale of natural gas at city gates will be fixed by public authority. If some plan can be devised whereby price regulation remains with the states, then to the Interstate Commerce Commission may well be given control over the construction and the financial policies of interstate lines: a certificate of convenience and necessity should be required, with decision rested upon a broad interpretation of public needs, and capitalization should be rigorously controlled—with detailed reports of all operations required. If, on the other hand, a federal utilities commission is created to fix the price of sale of the gas, control of construction and finance may also with propriety be vested in that body.

The gasoline pipe line transports a commodity that is marketed in the usual channels of trade. Such a line merely provides a cheaper means of movement in particular situations. But again it is difficult to conceive of such a line operating regularly as a common or contract carrier—though it is conceivable that occasional instances of contract carriage might occur.[1] For the time being it would appear to be sufficient to make a certificate of convenience and necessity, issued by the Interstate Commerce Commission upon the basis of a broad interpretation of public interest, a prerequisite to interstate construction. And it will be well, too, to exercise some measure of control over the issuance of securities and to require adequate reports upon all operations.

The pipe line for the movement of crude petroleum presents yet other problems. Not only is the service rendered a highly specialized one but the relation of the line to the refining industry is such that it tends to be merely an adjunct to an individual enterprise. As indicated in the preceding chapter, the trunk lines are controlled largely by the few great companies that dominate the oil industry—and, because of the importance of conservation in petroleum production, it is doubtful if competition should be made more active within the industry than it now is. Therefore the character of regulatory action within the field ought to be conditioned by public policy concerning the industry: if competition is to be minimized and other means employed to safeguard public interest, then interstate regulation need not go beyond control of construction and of financial policies; but if, on the other hand, a régime of competition is the purpose of governmental action, regulation of both common and contract carriers little less sweeping than that now exercised over the railways must be made effective. Such regulation would require, among other matters, the active exercise by the Interstate Commerce Commission of the rate powers it now possesses over the movement by common-carrier pipe lines of oil in interstate commerce, as well as strict policing to prevent discrimination. And, under such a régime, the principle of the Commodities clause might well be made applicable to all interstate pipe lines. Yet before such comprehensive regulation is made effective, the problems of the industry should be carefully weighed. For the time being it would seem that active exercise of authority might well be limited to the fields of construction and finance; such control will serve as a material aid to more comprehensive regulation, if it is later desired.

The Responsibilities of Management.—To an improvement of the status of the railway and to an appropriate adjustment of agencies within the field of transport, railway management can contribute greatly. The

[1] To the extent that a gasoline pipe line operates as a common carrier, its rates upon interstate movements are subject to determination by the Interstate Commerce Commission and the same prohibitions rest upon discrimination as apply to the railways.

opportunities of management lie in four directions, largely: reduction of waste; reduction of costs; increased capacity to serve and, therefore, to compete; and improvement in the railway financial structure.

Waste.—Waste in railway transport results primarily from duplications of facilities and of service and from the rendition of uneconomical services. As a consequence of enforced competition in a field where regulated monopoly should have obtained, and as a consequence of the natural individualism of pioneer enterprise, much unnecessary railway mileage was built in the developmental years—and, because of the rapid increase in the efficiency of cross-country highway transport during the past decade, large additions have been made to the mileage that may be regarded as nonessential. The same forces that have burdened the railway corporations and the public with duplicate mileage have functioned to burden them with terminal facilities far in excess of present or prospective need. Extensive duplications of service, particularly of passenger service, are also charged against the railways: of this the common illustration is the number of trains leaving a designated major city for another important point at approximately the same hour, "none of these trains being more than fractionally occupied"—with the fraction small. Duplications of service there undoubtedly are that merit positive executive action, yet it must be admitted that the common illustration cited loses value upon analysis: though duplication exists as to the two termini, the trains in question characteristically operate throughout a wide band of territory, rendering to widely scattered points an important local passenger, mail, and express service. To pool service between two important cities without imposing hardship upon a considerable intermediate area is less simple than it may appear. None the less, many opportunities for the elimination of waste through cooperative line-haul operations exist, as well as through the joint use of line mileage and terminals. For these opportunities railway management should search assiduously and, to the extent that regulatory authority will permit, pool facilities and service.[1] To a reduction of the wastes of duplication, as well as certain other needless costs, the regional consolidation of railways would contribute greatly—as would the consolidation of all the railways of continental United States into a single system.

The great opportunity to reduce waste lies, however, in the elimination of deficit operations: certain operations should be abandoned wholly and for others a service more nearly suited to need should be substituted. Numberless passenger trains, particularly on branch lines, have long failed to meet operating costs, with losses tending to increase steadily.

[1] The creation of the post of Federal Coordinator of Transportation, coupled with suspension of the application of all "antitrust" laws applicable to railway policy, has as its prime purpose the reduction of competitive wastes in the field of rail transport. For the measure to govern, see Appendix A.

Local freight service upon main lines often shows costs in excess of revenues and upon many branch lines all freight operations succeed only in increasing the deficit chargeable to passenger service. Such deficit operations upon branch and main lines should be terminated without delay; where conditions are such as to justify substitution, some lighter and less expensive type of rail operation should be continued—or the railway's responsibility to the area discharged by the operation of bus and truck. There is no doubt but that such eliminations and adjustments of service would yield savings to the railways of tens of millions of dollars annually.[1]

Yet, despite the opportunity and the pressing need for economy, it is unlikely that this drastic reorganization of service will be effected in either the immediate or the predictable future. And the onus for failure to eliminate deficit services will rest upon the public served, not upon management: one of the anomalies of a period during which revolutionary changes have occurred in the field of inland transport has been the insistence of the public upon the maintenance of a type of railway service for which it has been unwilling to pay. Few railways have shown sufficient aggressiveness in substituting a less expensive rail service for that rendered, and few have utilized the bus and the truck to full advantage; yet much of the waste for which the railways are criticized sharply has been imposed upon them by a public opinion that is even now militantly opposed to extensive abandonments of mileage or particular operations—and little less opposed when highway service is offered in place of rail.

Another type of waste to which public attention is often directed proceeds from the very nature of competition in the railway field. It is the movement of traffic by circuitous routes, rather than by direct routes. During the period of federal operation some progress was made in the elimination of this aspect of social waste, also of "cross-hauling." Yet it is obvious that, so long as the public persists in its demand for the retention of competition, the elimination—even any considerable curbing—of these practices is impossible: it is one of the many costs of competition in the railway field. And there is little to indicate the willingness of the public to accept a form of organization that removes competition; rather, the bitter attack to which the proposed merger of the Great Northern and the Northern Pacific was subjected as recently as 1930 is clearly suggestive of the determined adherence of the American people to competition as an active principle in the field of railway transport. To the public again, rather than to railway management, must be

[1] Material savings could be made by closing many small stations. These stations, spaced to meet the needs of horse-and-wagon days, are far more numerous than modern highway transport demands. Yet here again the railways face sharp opposition from the public and frequent adverse orders from commissions. It is at such points that railway truck and bus service would be of great advantage.

ascribed major responsibility for the persistence of an admitted social waste.

Unbiased and analytical studies of the railway situation characteristically recommend the consolidation of properties upon a major scale as a means of lessening waste and diminishing cost. Some believe consolidation as envisioned by the Transportation Act would be adequate; others demand no less than regional monopolies, even a single national railway corporation, privately owned and operated. Some look upon consolidation as a panacea; others—and these are undoubtedly more realistic—regard it as desirable, yet but one of the many changes essential to the rendition of maximum railway service at minimum cost. Some hold consolidation so vital that immediate compulsion is advocated; others would await the operation of economic forces, free of legal prohibitions and facilitated by Commission policy. The writer believes consolidation of railways along lines laid down by the Transportation Act would be helpful; the gains resulting from regional grouping will confer even greater benefit—if the regions are logically mapped, the railways properly articulated, and an effective organization developed. Of the soundness of a national system many will be doubtful: it is not certain an organization can be developed to assure the efficient operation of such an enormous unit, and men competent to direct so tremendous an undertaking are indeed few. Yet, as indicated upon occasion, the temper of the American people is such and their fear of monopoly so great that even the limited curtailment of competition under the existing law has met powerful opposition. Regional consolidation, much more a national railway system, is certain to face attacks so sharp that realization is improbable until the general level of economic intelligence has advanced, or until, in a moment of panic, old gods are abandoned and the counsel of desperation is accepted.

Increased Efficiency.—Opportunities exist to reduce costs in ways other than by the elimination of waste. Under conditions of normal operation railway capital costs constitute approximately 20 per cent of the total cost of service. These capital costs can be reduced in various ways. By the use of thoroughly modern equipment, by roadway construction that will permit the movement of heavier trains, by improved methods that increase the capacity of a given trackage to serve, and by the more effective use of all elements of the property, unit costs of service can be reduced. Yet is must be remembered that progress often necessitates an increase in investment—and, if serviceable property is to be retired because of obsolescence, traffic must bear a charge sufficient to cover these "costs of progress." A second means of reducing capital cost lies in the abandonment of service upon a significant fraction of the railway mileage of the United States, particularly branch mileage, and the elimination of the cost of that mileage from the investment account.

Such action constitutes, of course, a "major operation"—with the railway's *alter ego*, the public served, no less concerned and its interests no less imperiled than those of the investor. For, after all, there are certain services rendered by the railway for which there is no effective substitute; and, further, investments by individuals and corporations in property, the value of which is dependent in considerable measure upon the continuance of railway operation, is probably far in excess of the investment of the railway in the particular mileage involved. It is easy to sit in the critic's chair, far removed from the *situs* of the individual and social problems that arise from proposals to abandon railway mileage, and decree the amputation of portions of a railway property; it is easy to assert that "the railways should take positive action to prune away all dead wood." Yet to assume responsibility for particular abandonments is less pleasing and for the railway to take positive action is often impolitic in the face of strong local opposition, even impossible because of an adverse commission order. Once more the question of public policy, not profits, is basic. And it is the misfortune of the investor, as well as of shippers living upon lines of railway that enjoy an adequate traffic but must in some measure contribute to the support of deficit mileage, rather than the fault of management, that a service is demanded of the railways for which its beneficiaries are unwilling to accept full financial responsibility.

Labor.—Another opportunity for reducing costs lies in the field of labor. Under ordinary traffic conditions the railways spend some 45 cents of each dollar of revenue for labor—of which portion, contrary to common belief, but a small fraction is received by officials. A reduction of labor costs may follow from greater economy in the use of labor or from reductions in rates of pay. That railway management has economized in the use of labor will be clearly apparent to any who make a comparison over a period of years of the relation of the number of employees to the volume of traffic handled. This more economical use of labor has extended from such simple tasks as those discharged by the "section hand" to the operation of trains over the line; and, except as railway labor has been effectively organized and aggressively led, changes have been accepted by the workers without challenge. The strength of the train-service brotherhoods has been sufficient, however, to enable them within the past score of years to minimize the gains to the railway—and, in turn, to the public—of more efficient management and an improved plant. Restriction has been accomplished in part through certain working rules imposed upon the railways, in part through contriving the passage by many state legislatures of full-crew and maximum train-length laws. But outstanding in the thoughts of those who believe that management has failed the public in the matter of labor costs is, undoubtedly, the belief that railway wage rates have been permitted in recent years to advance excessively and to remain upon an inordinately high level.

Before entering upon a discussion of railway wage rates, however, it is well to emphasize the fact that railway wage rates have been increased in the face of strong railway opposition and not by railway connivance. In handling demands made by railway labor, management has long lacked freedom of action in dealing with the train-service groups and has been hedged about by legal restrictions with respect to all groups of workers since 1920: because of the public's vital interest in continuous service, tribunals have been provided by law to deal with railway-labor disputes. As a consequence of governmental interference, coupled with public sympathy with the worker as against the railway in disputes between the two, management was unable to stem the rise of wage rates in the years prior to 1929; by that year a comparatively high level had been attained in the wage rates of all workers and for certain groups the level was in excess of that of 1920. Yet if there be criticism of this situation, it lies in small measure against the railways to whom legislation and public sentiment have denied the use of coercion. And the failure of the railways to effect material reductions in rates of pay upon the basis of materially lower living costs since 1929, as demanded by many, is not a responsibility of management: negotiation was undertaken and pressure exerted, yet railway labor conceded only a temporary reduction of 10 per cent in rates of pay—and there has been no indication that the public would support positive action by the railways to force an unqualified and material reduction.

When the railways occupied a more nearly monopolistic position in the transportation field, it was possible to "pass on" through higher freight and passenger rates a considerable portion of the burden of high wage scales; today, when the railways must meet sharp competition with respect to an important volume of traffic, attempts to shift that burden to the public will accomplish only a reduction in the volume of competitive tonnage moving by rail and the imposition of an additional cost handicap in the market upon tonnage that *must* move by rail. To compete successfully with the newer agencies of transport railway rates covering certain movements, particularly short hauls, must be reduced; to such a reduction labor costs, as almost half of the total cost of service, must contribute measurably. Since the wage rates of most railway workers tend during normal periods to conform to those effective throughout industry generally, it is unreasonable to expect such rates to yield greatly; on the other hand, it is highly doubtful if the train-service groups can maintain for an extended period the preferential position now occupied. In the face of price competition that grows increasingly keen it appears that, until rival agencies are burdened with total service costs and certain other restrictions are imposed in the interest of public safety and social policy, railway workers must choose between a small volume of employment at high wage rates and a greater volume at lesser rates—which may yield a larger annual income per worker, though is not certain so to do. But there is little to indicate that railway labor has made an economic analysis of the problem with which it is faced and has recognized the necessity in self-interest of major concessions in both restrictive rules, where such exist, and rates of pay. Until this recognition comes, or until the public is ready to support a frontal attack by railway management upon railway wage scales, little change can be expected in the labor cost of transportation by rail. So, without regard to need of a reduction in labor costs and the opportunity of management to lower thereby the unit costs of handling traffic, no significant reduction in wage rates is in immediate prospect.

Competitive Policy.—An aggressive management can do much to make the railway a more effective competitor. For an extended period there was no effective alternative to shipment or travel by rail, where rail facilities were available. Methods of competition became fixed both by custom and by agreement: railway management, bound by tradition, was tardy in meeting the challenge of a new transportation era. Greater understanding of opportunities, greater aggressiveness in seizing them, have been progressively evident, yet even greater progress is essential. In preceding chapters appears discussion of the efforts of the railways to adapt service to modern conditions: store-door delivery has been made effective throughout wide areas; container service, the railwagon, the small-capacity car, and other innovations have been offered to meet the needs of certain shipments; terminal operations have been improved and speeded. The railways are being forced, also, to the reluctant realization that rate structures—the product of time and regulatory action—cannot retain their rigidity or permanence under the impact of a competition that changes constantly. In consequence of these facts the aggressive railway traffic representative finds himself equipped increasingly in his struggle for business with schedules of rates and with an available service more nearly adapted to competitive needs. That the more alert railways, those more effectively led, are utilizing advantageously these improved weapons is undoubted, though it is also undoubted that their existence is little more than suspected and their effective use understood not at all by some.

Managerial aggressiveness can make the railway a more effective competitor in other ways, also. Despite the fact that trucks and buses operate upon a highway that must be shared with many other vehicles, that they must traverse congested city streets, and that they are subject to other delays from which the railways are free, highway service often approximates and sometimes exceeds rail service in speed. Though American railways operate many fast trains, both passenger and freight, the average speed of both types of service is too low to enable the railways to capitalize upon certain advantages enjoyed by them. True, higher speeds mean higher unit costs of operation, yet speed has as definite a price in the transportation market as certainty or safety: to the salability of speed the rapid rise of air transport bears striking witness. Unless American railways emulate the example of certain foreign railways, as well as a few of the more aggressive of the American lines, an important potential asset of the railway will remain uncapitalized in the competitive struggle.

Another need of "better railroading" is an operating unit that will permit the rendition of service to the public upon what might be termed a retail instead of a wholesale basis and at a lesser cost per unit of traffic under particular conditions. This need has been largely ignored by our railways, though the rail motor car represents, as suggested before, a step in the direction of a passenger unit more nearly adapted to conditions of light traffic. But the rail motor car has not been popular with the public and it has not cut the costs of operation sufficiently to permit the rendition of the frequent service that is characteristic of highway operations. The Budd-Micheline car and others of like type that are being developed represent, however, a striking gain; it is to be hoped that management will improve upon the opportunities offered by such equipment without delay. And, by the use of the motor truck in local freight service and the further adaptation of line service to the needs of the small-lot shipper, as it has been fitted increasingly to the needs of the heavy shipper, the entire railway freight service can be speeded and made more satisfactory otherwise.

Finance.—A final and important aid that management can render the railways is to effect drastic readjustments in the capital structure of individual properties. Upon the basis of valuation principles recognized as applicable to regulated enterprise in the past the railways were in 1929 undercapitalized by a considerable sum, though that undercapitalization has lessened greatly—perhaps even disappeared—with the sharp decline in the price level since 1929. None the less, the capital structure of the railways in 1929 was not satisfactory for a regulated monopoly, much less for an enterprise subject to the vigorous competition then faced by them. The bond ratio of approximately 60 per cent was at least 10 per cent in excess of a sound figure for regulated monopoly and even greater in excess of a satisfactory figure for an industry locked in bitter competitive struggle. Action should be undertaken without delay by those responsible for the determination of railway policies to reduce the bond ratio sharply; if the volume of instruments bearing a fixed charge were reduced to one-third of the total obligations outstanding, the railway would be able to compete much more effectively—thus maintaining property values more successfully—during a period of readjustment in the transportation field and pending the establishment of comprehensive regulation according to intelligent plan.

But there is need that more be done than merely to change the status of certain groups with a financial interest in the railways from that of creditor to entrepreneur. There seems to be little justification for failure to accomplish, and many sound reasons for an adjustment to accomplish, a reduction in the rate of interest paid upon many railway issues that will continue to carry a fixed charge. These adjustments, proportioned to the change in the price level since the obligation was issued and therefore determined in each particular case by a special study, could be made effective for a limited period as an emergency aid—with future action to be determined by the movement of the general price level. In short, just as labor must contribute toward the correlation of railway rates with the general price level, so must capital make sacrifices: it is only from railways with a satisfactory volume of traffic that interest payments and dividends may come, by such railways only that great numbers can be employed and adequate wages paid.

Summary.—Upon the failures of railway management unnumbered pages have been written and countless excoriations delivered; concerning the accomplishments of railway management no fewer pages have been filled and numberless eulogies pronounced. For both attitudes there is a foundation of fact; in short, railway management has been in its accomplishments and its failures little different from management in other fields of endeavor. The mere fact that railway management has functioned in a field impressed with public interest has not given it omniscience, nor has it given to it a peculiar aspect of villainy. Considered impartially, it is surprising that management has so much to its credit, when the railway stood unchallenged in its field for almost a century. And, in view of the vulnerability of the railway to criticism because of its quasi-public nature, attacks upon managerial competence have been neither surprisingly sharp nor general. None the less, it is clear that railway management has fallen short in certain directions of what the public has a right to demand and the investor a right to expect. Upon management rests a heavy responsibility. From the proper discharge of that responsibility the public will benefit greatly through a more satisfactory railway service as well as a more effective coordination of all agencies of inland transport. For it is through the initiative of the railway, the basic agency, that the coordination essential to maximum service may be attained with greatest certainty and ease. With legal barriers removed and a leadership that is both alert to opportunity and aggressive, the railways can utilize highway and waterway transport—as well as, in certain cases, airway and pipe line—in such manner as to provide the public the most complete service possible at minimum cost.

The Coordination of Agencies of Transport.—The coordination of the various agencies of inland transport involves, in final analysis, the assignment of an approximate place or function to each agency and the performance by each of the designated tasks. Coordination does not require the entire elimination of competition between the various agencies of transport, railway and highway, railway and waterway; neither does it of necessity exclude controlled competition among the various units of a particular type. Yet, to the extent that competition remains, complete coordination has not been attained and the social wastes that follow from duplication persist. For an appropriate assignment of place in the transportation scheme, the cost of rendering particular types of service must first be determined; to that end each item of expense pertinent to the rendition of the service must be ascertained accurately. But assignment of place cannot be made solely upon the basis of mathematical computations: final judgment must be in accord with public policy, to the determination of which an interpretation of public convenience and need is essential. To the ascertainment of costs careful study, checked by experience, is essential; to such ascertainment nothing will contribute more effectively than appropriate regulatory control. And it is only by a regulatory body that public convenience and need can be interpreted, public policy formulated and made effective.

The elements that enter into the total cost of railway service are known to all; the elements of cost that are properly chargeable to highway, waterway, and air transport have been indicated. Public policy with respect to coordination is yet to be defined, yet it is elementary that social gain will proceed no more from duplication of facilities and service by competitive agencies of transport than it will from an existing duplication for which the railways are criticized sharply by many. But by whom is public policy to be defined? Upon preceding pages appears the suggestion of a member of the Interstate Commerce Commission; yet, with due regard for the importance and weight of his judgment, it would seem that the task he would impose upon the director of the Bureau of Transportation is impossible of accomplishment. Each of the major agencies of which this director would serve as chairman, *ex officio*, is entitled to a full-time, responsible head; each of these agencies will have serving upon it a group of men far more fully informed concerning the problems of that body than an itinerant chairman can possibly be and, in consequence, better fitted to formulate policies; and independent agencies, each charged with the promotion of a particular type of transport, must inevitably clash. If the director were a man of broadest training in the field of transport, of highest capacity, of exceptional diplomatic talent, and of greatest zeal, it is doubtful if he could discharge his function properly; if he is less than that, perhaps another political leader comfortably placed, the results may well be a confusion for which the public will pay dearly.

If coordination is a goal that justifies attainment, it would appear that all agencies of transportation should be made subject to the jurisdiction of one regulatory body—and that body, logically, the Interstate Commerce Commission. This Commission has a broad background of experience, a trained staff, and a prestige that will stand it in good stead during the difficult period when a working basis for comprehensive regulation and coordination is being established. To those who contend that the existing Commission is *railroad-minded*, it may be answered that long years of effective service have shown the Commission to be, to an unusual degree, *duty-minded*. There is nothing in the extensive record of the Commission to suggest bias; rather, if charged with the responsibility of regulating all agencies of inland transport to the advantage of the public, there is every reason to believe that body will discharge its responsibility with intelligence and fidelity—as conscientiously as it has, in recent years, the obligations imposed to further the development of inland-waterway traffic.

To discharge properly the duties that attach to the comprehensive regulation of inland transport the organization of the Commission may need to be changed sharply: it is conceivable that regional commissions might be set up or that state bodies—or joint state bodies—might function as agencies of original jurisdiction in all or selected types of cases, with right of appeal to the federal Commission; or within the Commission might be set up major divisions—each dealing with a single type of transport, provision being made by the Commission under recent legislation for the delegation of power to individual commissioners and to employees to hear all but major cases and to give preliminary judgments. There are few who suggest the regulation of interstate motor traffic by any agency but the Interstate Commerce Commission, when and as such regulation is established; if the administrative organization of the Commission is capable of meeting this additional burden, there is no reason to believe that the load would prove excessive if the control of air and water transport were added—the more so since the burden of air regulation will long be light and that of water regulation far less than of highway or rail. Under such a plan of centralized control the coordination which public interest demands seems far more certain than under a plan that necessitates harmonizing the policies and judgments of coordinate, independent, and perhaps contending bodies.

Some Basic Needs of Successful Regulation.—If regulation is to promote and conserve public interest through a period of years, however, appropriate legislation and a satisfactory administrative organization are not alone sufficient. Without regard to the perfection of these, desired results will not be attained except as regulation is in the hands of men who have a fundamental understanding of the problem with which they deal and a realization of the tremendously greater importance to society of long-time than of short-time advantage in the formulation and execution of regulatory policies. Commissions have been in the past niggardly, by and large, in dealing with agencies of transport subject to their control—with a heavier burden of guilt resting upon the typical state body than upon the federal. A policy that is unduly restrictive may for a time benefit the public served; but, in the end, because such a policy cripples vital agencies, the cost to the public of action that looks essentially to immediate advantage is even heavier than it is to ill-paid investors. If regulation is to succeed, and it would be difficult to estimate the social cost of its failure in terms of loss of capital and wastes resulting from duplication of facilities and services, it is essential that regulatory bodies be manned by economic statesmen rather than political opportunists: by those whose actions proceed from fact rather than from prejudice and predilection.

Yet to regulatory bodies of needed wisdom and vision is essential, in turn, an informed public opinion. For, in a democracy, it is impossible for a public body to function long upon a materially higher level of economic understanding and intelligence than that upon which public opinion stands. There is sore need of a more effective popular grasp of the fundamentals of the existing order and of basic principles that should govern in the field of transport in particular. Many of the wastes now apparent in the field of railway transport and many of the wastes consequent upon the duplication of facilities and service by competing types of transportation are chargeable directly to an almost fanatical adherence by the public to competition as a governing principle in the field. For a brief period general enthusiasm was shown for railway consolidation, as an abstract principle; great interest was evidenced in the economies that were to result from unification. Yet even the law declared that the Commission's final plan should preserve competition "as fully as possible"—and in no instance has a consolidation been proposed that bade fair to realize important savings without rousing a storm of opposition. It is undoubted that the consolidation of railways as envisioned by the Transportation Act, and far more the consolidation of the railways of the United States into regional systems or a single national unit, would make possible important economies, but it is improbable that public sentiment will support extensive unifications in the proximate future unless under the spur of indisputable emergency. An important obligation of those who realize the limited degree to which the principle of competition should operate in the field of transport is to school a public, still adhering to eighteenth century economics, to an understanding of facts; thus, and only thus, can be realized largely the convenience and the economy of a coordinated system of transport.

Since Commission policies must, from a practical point of view, reflect accurately popular beliefs and demands, it is essential that the public be brought to a realization not only of the unsoundness of competition as a governing principle in the field of transport but also of the importance of emphasis upon long-time as against short-time advantage in the formulation of policies. That the immediate gains of certain unsound regulatory policies should have strong appeal to the economic illiterate is not strange, but that support for such policies should be so common among important industrial, commercial, and agricultural groups as experience shows it to be is disturbing. If business leaders cannot think and act in terms of the morrow with respect to transportation, a problem with which they have direct contact, and concerning which the experiences of a single generation are significant, what may be expected of them when faced in broader fields with problems less tangible and less within the realm of daily experience?

There is need, too, of a more understanding and constructive public attitude with respect to such a practical problem as taxation. Discrimination in the imposition of tax burdens that results in subsidies has been discussed in earlier chapters, but brief comment must be made upon the growing tendency of the state to use the railway as a tax gatherer for the public treasury. While the tax burden upon all types of property has increased greatly during the generation past, the railway burden has grown even more rapidly than that of many other types of property. In 1900 the railways paid, with an investment in road and equipment of $10,260,000,000, a total of $48,333,273 in property taxes; in 1930, with the investment account increased to approximately $26,000,000,000, the tax burden was $353,881,476—and from 1925 to 1929, inclusive, it averaged about $388,000,000. In certain states the tax load is particularly heavy, with the only apparent remedy under our plan of government being a change in public attitude toward the use of the railway as an important collector—through the imposition of higher rates upon traffic—of funds that are to be transferred in turn to public coffers. Perhaps a realization by the public that certain types of taxes levied upon regulated enterprises, such as the railways and local utilities, tend to be shifted to the patron in whole or in major part would tend to lessen the load imposed; in any event such a realization would minimize the joy of those who believe that, by such excessive tax burdens, only the corporation is punished.

Government Ownership of Railways as a Solution.—But some, perhaps, will urge that the solution of the railway problem is vastly simpler than has been suggested: instead of the development of an informed public opinion as a foundation of regulation under appropriate laws resort need only be had to government ownership and operation. Yet it is obvious, from the experience of other peoples with that method of adapting railway service to public need, that even under conditions as they existed a score of years ago this policy gave no guarantee of more efficient service at lesser cost: the aspect of the problem changed but the problem in no wise disappeared. Today, because of the rise of new agencies of inland transport, there is greater doubt as to whether government ownership and operation represent a solution of the "transportation problem." The cry of all shipping interests is for a reduction in railway rates, made possible by drastic economies: by the elimination of duplication, by the abandonment of unprofitable service, by the utilization of improved methods, by the downward revision of wage scales, and by sharp readjustments in the capital structure. Let it be granted that the government might provide service at a lower capital cost than private enterprise, yet is there anything in the record of government to justify belief that drastic action would be taken upon any one of the other demands? Rather, it is to be feared that such wastes and excessive costs as now exist would persist, perhaps be magnified. And how long would inadequate returns from existing rates, with the consequent burden upon the federal treasury, be accepted? From this burden the logical escape of the governmentally owned railways would be an increase in rates, accompanied by rigorous control of private agencies of transport that compete with the railways—or the acceptance of either of two other alternatives, the entire elimination of private enterprise from the field of transport by the broad extension of government ownership or the restriction of private transport operations to a limited and unimportant field. Will it be in the interest of agencies now competing with the railway to assist, by blocking efforts to coordinate facilities, in precipitating governmental entry into the railway field? For rail service will be continued upon an important scale, by government, if the financial burden becomes too great for private enterprise. It is probable that motor, inland water, air, and pipe-line transport will fare more happily under a régime of comprehensive regulation calculated to secure their coordination with a privately owned railway net than under regulations designed to maintain the financial integrity of government railways afflicted with even the irreducible minimum of political domination.

The Goal of a Transportation Plan.—Frequent mention has been made upon preceding pages and in earlier chapters of the importance of the coordination of all agencies of inland transport and emphasis has been placed upon the necessity of a *plan*, under which each agency is allotted its proper place. It has been declared that, in the assignment of place, cost must be basic—with modifications made to meet such requirements as may be superior to cost, as military need or emergency use. A characteristic statement that emphasizes relative cost as a determinant is, "The public is entitled to the benefit of the most economical and efficient means of transportation by any instrumentalities of transportation that may be suited to such purpose."[1] To such a statement the acquiescence of public and railways is commonly given; yet, except as it is interpreted with a measure of understanding rarely shown, it is deceptive as but a partial statement of the truth. Far too often cost is given a particularistic interpretation and *aggregate social burden* is ignored. A more accurate statement of the principle that should govern, and one capable of complete social justification, is this: the public is entitled to the benefit of the services of each agency of transport suited to its needs *to the extent that those services, coordinated with the services of other agencies and utilized with them to maximum advantage, will provide for the complete transportation needs of the public in a satisfactory manner at minimum cost.* In short, the final test of the propriety of rendering a *particular service* by rail, by highway, by waterway, or by other means is not wholly relative cost; rather, the matter of fundamental concern is minimum cost of *all services* of a character acceptable to the public. It is in this that the significant challenge to regulatory bodies lies, to devise an appropriate *system* of transportation to which each agency contributes in an appropriate and prescribed manner.

Careful analysis will show that there is in a given area an irreducible minimum of service essential from one or another, or several, of the agencies of transport; this minimum will be determined for the area by a variety of facts as divergent as character of tonnage and topography. Beyond this irreducible minimum, service should be prescribed and rates fixed for the various agencies which are, under the plan devised, permitted to operate in the area upon such basis as will provide a fair return upon the property devoted to public use, be it railway or motor vehicle or barge or other—or combination thereof. Such a system, grounded upon study and experience, and modified from time to time as determining influences justify, will approximate as closely a solution of the transportation problem as this generation is likely to know. And the challenge to the public lies in the acceptance of an ordered transportation plan, shaped in accord with ascertained fact and sound principle, in the stead of that approach to transportation chaos which now exists because of adherence to competition as a controlling principle and because of the fatuous belief of many that from social loss can come broad individual gains.

[1] *Report of the Joint Committee of Railroads and Highway Users,* p. 7.

Appendix

EMERGENCY RAILROAD TRANSPORTATION ACT, 1933

That this Act may be cited as the "Emergency Railroad Transportation Act, 1933."

Title I—Emergency Powers

Sec. 1. As used in this title—

a. The term "Commission" means the Interstate Commerce Commission.

b. The term "Coordinator" means the Federal Coordinator of Transportation hereinafter provided for.

c. The term "committee" means any one of the regional coordinating committees hereinafter provided for.

d. The term "carrier" means any common carrier by railroad subject to the provisions of the Interstate Commerce Act, as amended, including any receiver or trustee thereof.

e. The term "subsidiary" means any company which is directly or indirectly controlled by, or affiliated with, any carrier or carriers. For the purpose of the foregoing definition a company shall be deemed to be affiliated with a carrier if so affiliated within the meaning of paragraph (8) of section 5 of the Interstate Commerce Act, as amended by this Act.

f. The term "employe" includes every person in the service of a carrier (subject to its continuing authority to supervise and direct the manner of rendition of his service) who performs any work defined as that of an employe or subordinate official in accordance with the provisions of the Railway Labor Act.

g. The term "state commission" means the commission, board, or official, by whatever name designated, exercising power to regulate the rates or service of common carriers by railroad under the laws of any state.

Sec. 2. In order to foster and protect interstate commerce in relation to railroad transportation by preventing and relieving obstructions and burdens thereon resulting from the present acute economic emergency, and in order to safeguard and maintain an adequate national system of transportation, there is hereby created the office of Federal Coordinator of Transportation, who shall be appointed by the President, by and with the advice and consent of the Senate, or be designated by the President from the membership of the Commission. If so designated, the Coordinator shall be relieved from other duties as Commissioner during his term of service to such extent as the President may direct; except that the Coordinator shall not sit as a member of the Commission in any proceedings for the review or suspension of any order issued by him as Coordinator. The Coordinator shall have such powers and duties as are hereinafter set forth and prescribed, and may, with the approval of the President, and without regard to the Civil Service laws and the Classification Act of 1923, as amended, appoint and fix the compensation of such assistants and agents in addition to the assistance provided by the Commission, as may be necessary to the performance of his duties under this Act. The office of the Coordinator shall be in Washington, D. C., and the Commission shall provide such office space, facilities, and assistance as he may request and it is able to furnish. The Coordinator shall receive such compensation as the President shall fix, except that if designated from the Commission, he shall receive no compensation in addition to that which he receives as a member of the Commission.

Sec. 3. The Coordinator shall divide the lines of the carriers into three groups, to wit, an eastern group, a southern group, and a western group, and may from time to time make such changes or subdivisions in such groups as he may deem to be necessary or desirable. At the earliest practicable date after the Coordinator shall have initially designated such groups, three regional coordinating committees shall be created, one for each group, and each committee shall consist of five regular members and two special members. The carriers in each group, acting each through its board of directors or its receiver or receivers or trustee or trustees or through an officer or officers designated for the purpose by such board, shall select the regular members of the committee representing that group, and shall prescribe the rules under which such committee shall operate; but no railroad system shall have more than one representative on any such committee. In such selection each carrier shall have a vote in proportion to its mileage lying within the group. The two special members of each committee shall be selected in such manner as the Coordinator may approve, one to represent the steam railroads within the group which had in 1932 railway operating revenues of less than $1,000,000 and the other to represent electric railways within the group not owned by a steam railroad or operated as a part of a general steam-railroad system of transportation. Each such special member shall have reasonable notice of all meetings of his committee at which any matter affecting any carrier which he represents is to be considered, and may participate in the consideration and disposition of such matter. Members of the committees may be removed from office and vacancies may be filled in like manner.

Sec. 4. The purposes of this title are (1) to encourage and promote or require action on the part of the carriers and of subsidiaries subject to the Interstate Commerce Act, as amended, which will (*a*) avoid unnecessary duplication of services and facilities of whatsoever nature and permit the joint use of terminals and trackage incident thereto or requisite to such joint use: Provided, That no routes now existing shall be eliminated except with the consent of all participating lines or upon order of the Coordinator; (*b*) control allowances, accessorial services and the charges therefor, and other practices affecting service or operation, to the end that undue impairment of net earnings may be prevented, and (*c*) avoid other wastes and preventable expense; (2) to promote financial reorganization of the carriers with due regard to legal rights, so as to reduce fixed charges to the extent required by the public interest and improve carrier credit; and (3) to provide for the immediate study of other means of improving conditions surrounding transportation in all its forms and the preparation of plans therefor.

Sec. 5. It shall be the duty of the committees on their own initiative, severally within each group and jointly where more than one group is affected, to carry out the purposes set forth in subdivision (1) of section 4, so far as such action can be voluntarily accomplished by the carriers. In such instances as the committees are unable, for any reason legal or otherwise, to carry out such purposes by such voluntary action, they shall recommend to the Coordinator that he give appropriate directions to the carriers or subsidiaries subject to the Interstate Commerce Act, as amended, by order; and the Coordinator is hereby authorized and directed to issue and enforce such orders if he finds them to be consistent with the public interest and in furtherance of the purposes of this title.

Sec. 6*a*. The Coordinator shall confer freely with the committees and give them the benefit of his advice and assistance. At his request, the committees, the carriers, the subsidiaries, and the Commission shall furnish him, or his assistants, and agents, such information and reports as he may desire in investigating any matter within the scope of his duties under this title; and the Coordinator, his assistants and agents, and the Commission.

shall at all times have access to all accounts, records, and memoranda of the carriers and subsidiaries. If, in any instance, a committee has not acted with respect to any matter which the Coordinator has brought to its attention and upon which he is of the opinion that it should have acted, under the provisions of section 5, he is hereby authorized and directed to issue and enforce such order; giving appropriate directions to the carriers and subsidiaries subject to the Interstate Commerce Act, as amended with respect to such matter, as he shall find to be consistent with the public interest.

b. In so far as may be necessary for the purposes of this title, the Commission and the members and examiners thereof shall have the same power to administer oaths and require by subpoena the attendance and testimony of witnesses and the production of books, papers, tariffs, contracts, agreements, and documents and to take testimony by deposition relating to any matter under investigation, as though such matter arose under the Interstate Commerce Act, as amended and supplemented; and any person subpoenaed to testifying in connection with any matter under investigation under this title shall have the same rights, privileges, and immunities and be subject to the same duties, liabilities, and penalties as are provided in the case of persons subpoenaed or testifying in connection with any matter under investigation under the Interstate Commerce Act, as amended.

Sec. 7*a.* A labor committee for each regional group of carriers may be selected by those railroad labor organizations which, as representatives duly designated and authorized to act in accordance with the requirements of the Railroad Labor Act, entered into the agreement of January 31, 1932, and December 21, 1932, with duly authorized representatives of the carriers, determining the wage payments of the employes of the carriers. A similar labor committee for each regional group of carriers may be selected by such other railroad labor organizations as may be duly designated and authorized to represent employes in accordance with the requirements of the Railway Labor Act. It shall be the duty of the regional coordinating committees and the Coordinator to give reasonable notice to, and to confer with, the appropriate regional labor committee or committees upon the subject matter prior to taking any action or issuing any order which will affect the interest of the employes, and to afford the said labor committee or committees reasonable opportunity to present views upon said contemplated action or order.

b. The number of employes in the service of a carrier shall not be reduced by reason of any action taken pursuant to the authority of this title below the number as shown by the payrolls of employes in service during the month of May, 1933, after deducting the number who have been removed from the payrolls after the effective date of this act by reason of death, normal retirements, or resignation, but not more in any one year than 5 per cent of said number in service during May, 1933; nor shall any employe in such service be deprived of employment such as he had during said month of May or be in a worse position with respect to his compensation for such employment, by reason of any action taken pursuant to the authority conferred by this title.

c. The Coordinator is authorized and directed to establish regional boards of adjustment whenever and wherever action taken pursuant to the authority conferred by this title creates conditions that make necessary such board of adjustment to settle controversies between carriers and employes. Carriers and their employes shall have equal representation on such boards of adjustment for settlement of such controversies, and said boards shall exercise the functions of boards of adjustment provided for by the Railway Labor Act.

d. The Coordinator is authorized and directed to provide means for determining the amount of, and to require the carriers to make just compensation for, property losses and expenses imposed upon employes by reason of transfers of work from one locality to another in carrying out the purposes of this title.

e. Carriers, whether under control of a judge, trustee, receiver, or private management, shall be required to comply with the provisions of the Railway Labor Act and with the provisions of section 77, paragraphs (*o*), (*p*), and (*q*) of the Act approved March 3, 1933, entitled "An Act to amend an act entitled An act to establish a uniform system of bankruptcy throughout the United States, approved July, 1, 1898, and acts amendatory thereof and supplementary thereto."

Sec. 8. Any order issued by the Coordinator pursuant to this title shall be made public in such reasonable manner as he may determine and shall be come effective as of such date, not less than 20 days from the date of such publication, as the Coordinator shall prescribe in the order; and such order shall remain in effect until it is vacated by him or suspended or set aside by the Commission or other lawful authority, as hereinafter provided, and such order may include provision for the creation and administration of such just pooling arrangements or for such just compensation for the use of property or for carrier services as he may deem necessary or desirable and in furtherance of the purposes of this title.

Sec. 9. Any interested party, including, among others, any carrier, subsidiary, shipper, or employe, or any group of carriers, shippers, or employes, or any state commission, or the Governor of any state, or the official representative or representatives of any political subdivision thereof, dissatisfied with any order of the Coordinator may, at any time prior to the effective date of the order, file a petition with the Commission asking that such order be reviewed and suspended pending such review, and stating fully the reasons therefor. Such petitions shall be governed by such general rules as the Commission may establish. If the Commission, upon considering such petition and any answer or answers thereto, finds reason to believe that the order may be unjust to the petitioner or inconsistent with the public interest, the Commission is hereby authorized to grant such review and, in its discretion, the Commission may suspend the order if it finds immediate enforcement thereof would result in irreparable damage to the petitioner or work grave injury to the public interest, but if the Commission suspends an order, it shall expedite the hearing and decision on that order as much as possible. Thereupon the Commission, shall, after due notice and a public hearing, review the order and take such action in accord with the purposes of this title as it finds to be just and consistent with the public interest, either confirming the order or setting it aside or reissuing it in modified form, and any order so confirmed or reissued shall thereafter remain in effect until vacated or modified by the Commission.

Sec. 10*a*. The carriers or subsidiaries subject to the Interstate Commerce Act, as amended, affected by any order of the Coordinator or Commission made pursuant to this title shall, so long as such order is in effect, be, and they are hereby, relieved from the operation of the antitrust laws, as designated in section 1 of the Act entitled "An Act to supplement existing laws against unlawful restraints and monopolies, and for other purposes," approved October 15, 1914, and of all other restraints or prohibitions by law, state or federal, other than such as are for the protection of the public health or safety, in so far as may be necessary to enable them to do anything authorized or required by such order made pursuant to this title: Provided, however, That nothing herein shall be construed to repeal, amend, suspend, or modify any of the requirements of the Railway Labor Act or the duties and obligations imposed thereunder or through contracts entered into in accordance with the provisions of said act.

b. The Coordinator shall issue no order which shall have the effect of relieving any carrier or subsidiary from the operation of the law of any state or of any order of any state commission until he has advised the state commission of said state, or the governor of said state, if there be no such commission, that such order is in contemplation, and shall afford the state commission or governor so notified reasonable opportunity to present views and information bearing upon such contemplated order, nor unless such order is necessary, in his opinion, to prevent or remove an obstruction to or a burden upon interstate commerce.

Sec. 11. Nothing in this title shall be construed to relieve any carrier from any contractual obligation which it may have assumed prior to the enactment of this Act, with regard to the location or maintenance of offices, shops, or roundhouses at any point.

Sec. 12. The willful failure or refusal of any carrier or subsidiary or of any officer or employe of any carrier or subsidiary to comply with the terms of any order of the Coordinator or of the Commission made pursuant to this title shall be a misdemeanor, and upon conviction thereof the carrier, subsidiary, or person offending shall be subject to a fine of not less than $1,000 or more than $20,000 for each offense, and each day during which such carrier, subsidiary, or person shall willfully fail or refuse to comply with the terms of such order shall constitute a separate offense. It shall be the duty of any district attorney of the United States to whom the Coordinator or the Commission may apply to institute in the proper court and to prosecute under the direction of the Attorney General of the United States all necessary proceedings for the enforcement of the provisions of this title and for the punishment of all violations thereof, and the costs and expenses of such prosecution shall be paid out of the appropriation for the expense of the courts of the United States: Provided, That nothing in this title shall be construed to require any employe or officer of any carrier to render labor or service without his consent, or to authorize the issuance of any order requiring such service, or to make illegal the failure of refusal of any employe individually, or any number of employes collectively, to render labor or services.

Sec. 13. It shall further be the duty of the Coordinator, and he is hereby authorized and directed, forthwith to investigate and consider means, not provided for in this title, of improving transportation conditions throughout the country, including cost finding in rail transportation and the ability, financial or otherwise, of the carriers to improve their properties and furnish service and charge rates which will promote the commerce and industry of the country, and including, also, the stability of railroad labor employment and other improvement of railroad labor conditions and relations, and from time to time he shall submit to the Commission such recommendations calling for further legislation to these ends as he may deem necessary or desirable in the public interest. The Commission shall promptly transmit such recommendations, together with its comments thereon, to the President and to the Congress.

Sec. 14. The expenses of the Coordinator except so far as they are borne by the Commission in accordance with the provisions of section 2, but not including the expenses of the coordinating committees, shall be allowed and paid, on the presentation of itemized vouchers therefor approved by the Coordinator, out of a fund obtained from assessments on the carriers, and said fund is hereby appropriated for the payment of such expenses. It shall be the duty of each carrier, within 30 days after the date of enactment of this Act, to pay into this fund, for the first year of the operation of this title, one and one half dollars for every mile of road operated by it on December 21, 1932, as reported to the Commission, and to pay into said fund within 30 days after the expiration of such year a proportional amount covering any period of extension of this title by proclamation of the President under section 17, and it shall be the duty of the Secretary of the Treasury to collect such assessments. Any amount remaining in the fund when this title ceases to have effect shall be returned by the Secretary of the Treasury to the carriers in proportion to their contributions. The carriers and the Pullman Company shall be permitted, anything in the Interstate Commerce Act, as amended, to the contrary notwithstanding, to provide free transportation and other carrier service to the Coordinator and his assistants and agents and to the employes of the Commission when engaged in the service of the Coordinator.

Sec. 15. The Commission shall not approve a loan to a carrier under the Reconstruction Finance Corporation Act, as amended, if it is of the opinion that such carrier is in need of financial reorganization in the public interest: Provided, however, That the term "carrier" as used in this section shall not include a receiver or trustee.

Sec. 16. Any final order made under this title shall be subject to the same right of relief in court by any party in interest as is now provided in respect to orders of the Commission made under the Interstate Commerce Act, as amended. The provisions of the Urgent

Deficiencies Appropriation Act of October 22, 1913 (38 Stat. L. 219), shall be applicable to any proceeding in court brought to suspend or set aside any order of the Coordinator of the Commission entered pursuant to the provisions of this title.

Sec. 17. This title shall cease to have effect at the end of one year after the effective date, unless extended by a proclamation of the President for one year or any part thereof, but orders of the Coordinator or of the Commission made thereunder shall continue in effect until vacated by the Commission or set aside by other lawful authority, but notwithstanding the provisions of section 10 no such order shall operate to relieve any carrier from the effect of any state law or of any order of a state commission enacted or made after this title ceases to have effect.

Title II—Amendments to Interstate Commerce Act

Sec. 201. Section 5 of the Interstate Commerce Act, as amended (U.S.C., Title 49, sec. 5) is amended by striking out paragraphs (2) and (3) and by renumbering paragraphs (4) and (5) as paragraphs (2) and (3), respectively, and by striking out the last sentence of the paragraph so renumbered as paragraph (3).

Sec. 202. Such section 5 is further amended by striking out paragraphs (6), (7), and (8), and by inserting in lieu thereof the following paragraphs:

"(4) (*a*) It shall be lawful, with the approval and authorization of the Commission, as provided in subdivision (*b*), for two or more carriers to consolidate or merge their properties, or any part thereof, into one corporation for the ownership, management, and operation of the properties theretofore in separate ownership; or for any carrier, or two or more carriers jointly to purchase, lease, or contract to operate the properties, or any part thereof, of another; or for any carrier, or two or more carriers jointly, to acquire control of another through purchase of its stock; or for a corporation which is not a carrier to acquire control of two or more carriers through ownership of their stock; or for a corporation which is not a carrier and which has control of one or more carriers to acquire control of another carrier through ownership of its stock.

"*b*. Whenever a consolidation, merger, purchase, lease, operating contract, or acquisition of control is proposed under subdivision (*a*), the carrier or carriers or corporation seeking authority therefor shall present an application to the Commission, and thereupon the Commission shall notify the Governor of each state in which any part of the properties of the carriers involved in the proposed transaction is situated, and also such carriers and the applicant or applicants, of the time and place for a public hearing. If after such hearing the Commission finds that, subject to such terms and conditions and such modifications as it shall find to be just and reasonable, the proposed consolidation, merger, purchase, lease, operating contract, or acquisition of control will be in harmony with and in furtherance of the plan for the consolidation of railway properties established pursuant to paragraph (3), and will promote the public interest, it may enter an order approving and authorizing such consolidation, merger, purchase, lease, operating contract, or acquisition of control, upon the terms and conditions and with the modifications so found to be just and reasonable.

"(5) Whenever a corporation which is not a carrier is authorized, by an order entered under paragraph (4), to acquire control of any carrier or of two or more carriers, such corporation thereafter shall, to the extent provided by the Commission, for the purposes of paragraphs (1) to (10), inclusive, of section 20 (relating to reports, accounts, and so forth, of carriers), including the penalties applicable in the case of violations of such paragraphs, be considered as a common carrier subject to the provisions of this Act, and for the purpose of paragraphs (2) to (11), inclusive, of section 20*a* (relating to issues of securities and assumptions of liability of carriers), including the penalties applicable in the case of violations of such paragraphs, be considered as a "carrier" as such term is defined in paragraph (1) of such section, and be treated as such by the Commission in the administration of the paragraphs specified. In the application of such provisions of section 20*a* in the case of any such corporation the Commission shall authorize the issue or assumption applied for only if it finds that such issue or assumption is consistent with the proper performance by each carrier which is under the control of such corporation of its service to the public as a common carrier, will not impair the ability of any such carrier to perform such service, and is otherwise compatible with the public interest.

"(6) It shall be unlawful for any person, except as provided in paragraph (4), to accomplish or effectuate, or to participate in accomplishing or effectuating, the control or management in a common interest of any two or more carriers, however such result is attained whether directly or indirectly, by use of common directors, officers, or stockholders, a holding or investment company or companies, a voting trust, or trusts, or in any other manner whatsoever. It shall be unlawful to continue to maintain control or management accomplished or effectuated after the enactment of this amendatory paragraph and in violation of its provisions. As used in this paragraph and paragraph (7), the words 'control or management' shall be construed to include the power to exercise control or management.

"(7) For the purposes of paragraphs (6) and (11), but not in any wise limiting the application thereof, any transaction shall be deemed to accomplish or effectuate the control or management in a common interest of two carriers—

"*a.* If such transaction is by a carrier, and if the effect of such transaction is to place such carrier and persons affiliated with it, taken together, in control of another carrier.

"*b.* If such transaction is by a person affiliated with a carrier, and if the effect of such transaction is to place such carrier and persons affiliated with it, taken together, in control of another carrier.

"*c.* If such transaction is by two or more persons acting together, one of whom is a carrier or is affiliated with a carrier, and if the effect of such transaction is to place such persons and carriers and persons affiliated with any one of them and persons affiliated with any such affiliated carrier, taken together, in control of another carrier.

"(8) For the purposes of paragraph (7) a person shall be held to be affiliated with a carrier if, by reason of the relationship of such person to such carrier (whether by reason of the method of, or circumstances surrounding organization or operation, or whether established through common directors, officers, or stockholders, a voting trust or trusts, a holding or investment company or companies, or any other direct or indirect means), it is reasonable to believe that the affairs of any carrier of which control may be acquired by such person will be managed in the interest of such other carrier.

"(9) For the purposes of paragraphs (6), (7), (8), and (11), wherever reference is made to control, it is immaterial whether such control is direct or indirect. As used in this paragraph and paragraphs (7), (8), and (11) the term control shall be construed to include the power to exercise control.

"(10) The Commission is hereby authorized, upon complaint or upon its own initiative without complaint, but after notice and hearing, to investigate and determine whether any person is violating the provisions of paragraph (6). If the Commission finds after such investigation that such person is violating the provisions of such paragraph, it shall by order require such person to take such action as may be necessary, in the opinion of the Commission, to prevent continuance of such violation.

"(11) For the proper protection and in furtherance of the plan for the consolidation of railway properties established pursuant to paragraph (3) and the regulation of interstate commerce in accordance therewith, the Commission is hereby authorized upon complaint or upon its own initiative without complaint, but after notice and hearing, to investigate and determine whether the holding by any person of stock or other share capital of any carrier (unless acquired with the approval of the Commission) has the effect (*a*) of subjecting such carrier to the control of another carrier or to common control with another carrier, and (*b*) of preventing or hindering the carrying out of any part of such plan or of impairing the independence, one of another, of the systems, provided for in such plan. If the Commission finds after such investigation that such holding has the effects described, it shall by order provide for restricting the exercise of the voting power of such person with respect to such stock or other share capital (by requiring the deposit thereof with a trustee, or by other appropriate means) to the extent necessary to prevent such holding from continuing to have such effects.

"(12) If in the course of any proceeding under this section before the Commission, or of any proceeding before a court in enforcement of an order entered by the Commission under this section, it appears that since the beginning of such proceeding the plan for consolidation that has been reopened under paragraph (3) for changes or modifications with respect to the allocation of the properties of any carrier involved in such proceeding, then such proceeding may be suspended.

"(13) The district courts of the United States shall have jurisdiction, upon the application of the Commission, alleging a violation of any of the provisions of this section or disobedience of any order issued by the Commission thereunder by any person, to issue such writs of injunction or other proper process, mandatory, or otherwise, as may be necessary to restrain such person from violation of such provision or to compel obedience to such order.

"(14) The Commission may from time to time, for good cause shown, make such orders, supplemental to any order made under paragraphs (1), (4), (10), or (11) as it may deem necessary or appropriate.

"(15) The carriers and any corporations affected by any order made under the foregoing provisions of this section shall be, and they are hereby, relieved from the operation of the antitrust laws as designated in section 1 of the act entitled 'An Act to supplement existing laws against unlawful restraints and monopolies, and for other purposes,' approved October 15, 1914, and of all other restraints or prohibitions by or imposed under authority of law, state or federal, in so far as may be necessary to enable them to do anything authorized or required by such order.

"(16) If any provision of the foregoing paragraphs of this section, or the applications thereof to any person or circumstances, is held invalid, the other provisions of such paragraphs, and the application of such provision to any other person or circumstances, shall not be affected thereby.

"(17) As used in paragraphs (4) to (16), inclusive, the term 'person' includes an individual, partnership, association, joint-stock company, or corporation, and the term 'carrier' means a carrier by railroad subject to this act."

Sec. 203. Such section 5 is further amended by renumbering as paragraph (18) the paragraph added by the act entitled "An act to amend section 407 of the Transportation Act of 1920," approved June 10, 1921, and by renumbering the remaining three paragraphs as paragraphs (19), (20), and (21), respectively.

Sec. 204. The provisions of the Interstate Commerce Act, as amended, and of all other applicable federal statutes, as in force prior to the enactment of this title, shall remain in force, as though this title had not been enacted, with respect to the acquisition by any carrier, prior to the enactment of this title, of the control of any other carrier or carriers.

Sec. 205. Section 15*a* of the Interstate Commerce Act, as amended (U.S.C., Title 49, sec. 15*a*), is amended to read as follows:

"Sec. 15*a*. (1) When used in this section, the term 'rates' means rates, fares, and charges, and all classifications, regulations, and practices relating thereto.

"(2) In the exercise of its power to prescribe just and reasonable rates the Commission shall give due consideration, among other factors, to the effect of rates on the movement of traffic; to the need, in the public interest, of adequate and efficient railway transportation service at the lowest cost consistent with the furnishing of such service; and to the need of revenues sufficient to enable the carriers, under honest, economical, and efficient management, to provide such service."

Sec. 206*a*. All moneys which were recoverable by and payable to the Interstate Commerce Commission, under paragraph (6) of section 15*a* of the Interstate Commerce Act, as in force prior to the enactment of this title, shall cease to be so recoverable and payable; and all proceedings pending for the recovery of any such moneys shall be terminated. The general railroad contingent fund established under such section shall be liquidated and the Secretary of the Treasury shall distribute the moneys in such fund among the carriers which have made payments under such section, so that each such carrier shall receive an amount bearing the same ratio to the total amount in such fund that the total of amounts paid under such section by such carrier bears to the total of amounts paid under such section by all carriers; except that if the total amount in such fund exceeds the total of amounts paid under such section by all carriers such excess shall be distributed among such carriers upon the basis of the average rate of earnings (as determined by the Secretary of the Treasury) on the investment of the moneys in such fund and differences in dates of payments by such carriers.

b. The income, war-profits, and excess-profits tax liabilities for any taxable period ending after February 28, 1920, of the carriers and corporations whose income, war-profits, or excess-profits tax liabilities were affected by section 15*a* of the Interstate Commerce Act, as in force prior to the enactment of this act, shall be computed as if such section had never been enacted, except that, in the case of carriers or corporations which have made payments under paragraph (6) of such section, an amount equal to such payments shall be excluded from gross income for the taxable periods with respect to which they were made. All distributions made to carriers in accordance with subdivision (*a*) of this section shall be included in the gross income of the carriers for the taxable period in which this act is enacted. The provisions of this subdivision shall not be held to affect (1) the statutes of limitations with respect to the assessment, collection, refund, or credit of income, war-profits, or excess-profits taxes, or (2) the liabilities for such taxes of any carriers or corporations if such liabilities were determined prior to the enactment of this act in accordance with section 1106 (*b*) of the Revenue Act of 1926 or section 606 of the Revenue Act of 1928, or in accordance with a final judgment of a court, an order of the Board of Tax Appeals which had become final, or an offer in compromise duly accepted in accordance with law.

Sec. 207. Paragraph (*a*) of section 19*a* of the Interstate Commerce Act, as amended (U.S.C., Title 49, sec. 19*a* (*a*)) is amended to read as follows:

"(*a*) That the Commission shall, as hereinafter provided, investigate, ascertain, and report the value of all the property owned or used by every common carrier subject to the provisions of this Act, except any street, suburban, or interurban electric railway which is not operated as a part of a general steam-railroad system of transportation; but the Commission may in its discretion investigate, ascertain, and report the value of the property owned or used by any such electric railway subject to the provisions of this Act whenever in its judgment such action is desirable in the public interest. To enable the Commission to make such investigation and report, it is authorized to employ such experts and other assistants as may be necessary. The Commission may appoint examiners who shall have power to administer oaths, examine witnesses, and take testimony. The Commission shall, subject to the exceptions hereinbefore provided for in the case of electric railways, make an inventory which shall list the property of every common carrier subject to the provisions of this act in detail, and show the value thereof as hereinafter provided, and shall classify the physical property, as nearly as practicable, in conformity with the classification of expenditures for road and equipment, as prescribed by the Interstate Commerce Commission."

Sec. 208. Paragraphs (*f*) and (*g*) of such section 19*a*, as amended (U.S.C., Title 49, sec. 19*a* (*f*), (*g*)), are amended to read as follows:

"(*f*) Upon completion of the original valuations herein provided for, the Commission shall thereafter keep itself informed of all new construction, extensions, improvements, retirements, or other changes in the condition, quantity, use, and classification of the property of all common carriers as to which original valuations have been made, and of the cost of all additions and betterments thereto and of all changes in the investment therein, and may keep itself informed of current changes in costs and values of railroad properties, in order that it may have available at all times the information deemed by it to be necessary to enable it to revise and correct its previous inventories, classifications, and values of the properties; and, when deemed necessary, may revise, correct, and supplement any of its inventories and valuations.

"(*g*) To enable the Commission to carry out the provisions of the preceding paragraph, every common carrier subject to the provisions of this Act shall make such reports and furnish such information as the Commission may require."

Sec. 209. If any provision of this Act, or the application thereof to any person or circumstances, is held invalid, the other provisions of this act or the application of such provision to any other person or circumstances shall not be affected thereby.

AUTHOR'S NOTE

In consequence of minor differences between the measures passed by House of Representatives and Senate, it was necessary that a reconciliation be effected by a conference committee. The Act as reproduced upon preceding pages represents in certain particulars, therefore, a compromise.

Immediately after the signature of the conference measure, President Roosevelt appointed, as it had been indicated previously that he would, Mr. Joseph B. Eastman to serve as Federal Coordinator. Mr. Eastman has been for a considerable period a member of the Interstate Commerce Commission. During his period of service upon that body Mr. Eastman has been critical at all times of what he has regarded as the needless wastes of competition, wastes resulting from a great variety of factors but largely from duplications of service and lack of solidarity. It is certain, therefore, that any failure of the measure to realize the high hopes of its active proponents will not be due lack of sympathetic or aggressive leadership.

None the less, there is reason to believe that the savings realized from the more effective coordination of railway facilities under the new Act will not be great. This is the more true because of the specific limitations imposed upon the carriers operating in cooperation and upon the Coordinator, the most significant of these limitations having to do with railway labor. It is undoubtedly true that the Coordinator, acting in conjunction with the Interstate Commerce Commission and the Reconstruction Finance Corporation, can be of definite assistance to the railways in effecting financial reorganizations to the end that fixed charges be reduced and carrier credit improved. Furthermore, from the Coordinator may come an effective and comprehensive plan for "improving conditions surrounding transportation in all its forms." So, considered in its entirety, the emergency features of Title I of the Act may prove of definite value; certain it is that the likelihood of harm resulting therefrom is slight.

Of the changes in permanent policy—the modification of Sec. 15*a*, the regulation of the holding company, the repeal retroactively of the Recapture Clause, and changes in the section dealing with valuation of railways—enough has been said in preceding chapters to give the reader a basis of judgment. These changes represent modifications in permanent policy, though no one of them constitutes a sharp movement to "right" or to "left"; rather, there is every indication that it is the purpose of Congress and the national Administration to continue our regulatory policy as it affects the railways essentially as it has developed in the past. Is this indicative of an ultimate purpose to extend regulation of an equally comprehensive character to competing agencies of transport? To this question time alone can give an answer. Meanwhile, developments will be watched with great interest by students in this field.

INDEX

A

Abandonment
  construction and (*see* Construction and abandonment)
  railway
    causes, 125, 220
    control of, 176
    extent, 219
    jurisdictional problem, 219
    nature
      lines, 777
      service, 775
      stations, 776*n*.
Accounting, railway, 396
  demand for regulation, 400
  diversity of systems, 401
  groupings prescribed
    general balance sheet, 403
    income, 403
    investment, 401
    operating expense, 402
    operating revenue, 401
    profit and loss, 403
  judgment upon regulation, 405
  need of adequate, 396
Accounting department, railway
  car records, 399
  divisional vs. centralized, 400
  expenditures, 397
  freight revenues, 398
  functions, 273
  organization, 273, 396
  passenger revenues, 399
Accounts, railway
  uniform system of, 140
    evaluation, 405
Acquisition of control
  legislative provision, 175
  principles governing, 201
  progress, 201
Act to Regulate Commerce, 1887, 115–119
  (*See also* Regulation, railway)
Activity, business, 1919–1932, 187–192
Acworth, W. M., 515
Adamson Act, 149
Additional cost of specific service, 519, 520
Adjustment boards, labor, 177, 212
Advisory Boards, Shippers', 216, 721
Aeronautics Branch, 714
Agriculture burdened, 193, 233, 237–240, 252
Aid, public, to railways (*see* Public aid to railways)
Air brake, development of, 111
Air conditioning, 720
Air-rail service
  earlier importance, 735
  outlook, 735, 736
Air transportation
  early interest, 693
  financial aspects, 712
  heavier-than-air craft, 696–699
  lighter-than-air craft, 693–696
  physical prerequisites, 699–702
  progress in, 726
  regulation, 713–715, 772
  statistics of operation, 704
  traffic
    goods, 710–712
    mail, 702–707
    passenger, 707–709
Airplane, the
  early experiments, 696
  first flights, 696
  post-war period, 697–699
  successful operation, 699
Airports, 700
Airship, the
  development, 694
  important voyages, 695
  problems and future, 695
Airways, 700
Akron, Canton and Youngstown Ry. Co. v. I.C.C., 226
Alabama Midland case, 118, 144
All-American route, 655, 657, 674
Alleghany Corporation, 206
American Fruit and Vegetable Shippers' Association, 759

American Railway Association, 151, 154, 155
American Railway Express Company, 162, 382
Amster, Nathan, 748
Analysis of waterway proposal, economic, 672
Annalist, The, 189, 457
Ann Arbor v. United States, 239
Application for authority, issuance of securities, 482
Ashburn, T. Q., 641*n*., 667
"Assigned cars," 215
Association of Railway Executives, 752, 759
Atchison, Topeka and Santa Fe
 beginning, 76
 completion, 98
 present system, 455
Atchison, Topeka and Santa Fe v. United States, 239
Atlanta, Birmingham and Coast, 202*n*.
Atlantic ports, rivalry of, 61, 529
Attitude, public, toward regulation, 785
Autogiro, 713*n*.
Automobile
 early steam-driven, 576
 modern, 577
 progress in United States, 577
 registrations, 1895–1931, 578
Automobiles, shipping, by truck, 593

B

Baggage allowance, 353
Balloon, the, 693
Baltimore-Atlanta rate, 535
Baltimore and Ohio system, 445
 chartered, 51
 common carrier, 52
Banker-railway relations, 448, 489
Barge canals, New York State (*see* New York State barge canals)
Baruch, Bernard M., 755*n*.
"Basing-point" rates, 532–535
Bekins Van Lines v. Riley, 619
"Belt" lines, 309, 311
Bill of lading
 information given, 316
 legal problems, 319–321
 types, 317–319
Bipartisan labor boards, 164
"Blanket" rates
 Southwestern territory, 539–542
 Transcontinental, 542
"Blue Streak," 723*n*.
Board, Railroad Labor (*see* Railroad Labor Board)
Bond interest, railway, 502
Bond ratio, 103, 681
Bonds, railway
 increased use, 103
 ratio increasing, 460
 types, 465
Book value, railway, 461
"Booster," locomotive, 718
Borrowed capital, railway
 long-term, 465
 short-term, 465
Bridges
 nature of early, 32
 toll, 33
Brown case, 116
Buck v. Kuykendall, 622
Budd-Micheline car, 720, 781
"Burden of proof" upon carriers, 144, 145
Bureau of Foreign and Domestic Commerce, 580, 595
Bureau of Public Roads, 574, 580, 581, 595, 605, 612, 613
Bureau of Transportation, proposed
 organization, 762
 scope, 763
 success, probable, 783
Burton, T. E., 639
Bus, the
 capacity, 579
 number, 579
 traffic, 583–586
 use, 579
Bus service
 advantages, 584
 competition, 583
 contract operations, 584
 extent, 583
 financial results, 585
 railway, 728–730
 types, 583, 584
Bus Transportation, 579
Bush v. Maloy, 622
Business activity, 1919–1932, 189
Business problem, railway, competition and monopoly, 438

C

Caley, George, 696
California Fruit Growers case, 239
California Railroad Commission, study of trucking, 596, 626, 627, 629
Canadian National Railways, 454
Canadian Pacific Railway, 454
Canals
  American projects, early, 28
    public aid to construction, 638
  ancient and medieval, 637
  early use of, 20
  European, 637
  movement costs, 36
Capital, inadequacy of early railway, 57
Capital value, railway
  compared with capitalization, 146–148, 461
  determination, 467–472, 769
Capitalizable items, railways, 484
Capitalization
  railway
    American and European compared, 463
    gross and net, 459
    individual properties, 462
    nature
      borrowed, 465
      owned, 464
    net, 461
    outstanding, 461
    overlapping claims, 466
    per mile of line, 462
    readjustments needed, 758, 767, 781
    regulation of (*see* Securities, regulation of)
    total, since 1890, 461
    and true worth, 466
  various conceptions of, 459
Car
  early development of, 46
  improved railway, 719–721
Car loadings, 187–192
Car records, 399
Car Service Act, Esch, 148
Car Service Division, 216, 722
Carmack Amendment, 141
Carver, Thomas N., 17
Cattle trails, western, 40
Cement by truck, 592
Cement rates uncertain, 592, 627
Central Freight Association Territory, rates in, 546
Certificate of convenience and necessity, highway, 625, 631, 632
Chamber of Commerce, United States, 751
Champlain Canal, 30
Channels, types of
  artificial, 663
  improved natural, 662
  natural, 662
Character of service, a modifying factor, 560
Charge, railway freight, determination of, 342
Charges, decline in railway, 88
  consequences, 89
  (*See also* Rates)
Charleston and Hamburg (South Carolina Railroad), 51, 59
Charter, railway
  as a contract, 266
    escape from, 266
  provisions, 265, 266
  source, 265
Chattanooga case, 118, 144
Chicago, Burlington and Quincy R.R. Co. v. Cutts, 81
Chicago, Milwaukee, St. Paul and Pacific Railroad Co., present system, 457
Chicago, North Shore and Milwaukee, securities of, 484
Chicago Tunnel railway, 315
China, canals in, 20, 637
Cincinnati Freight Bureau case, 117
Cincinnati, New Orleans and Texas Pacific Ry. Co. v. I. C. C., 117
Circuity in rail-water service, 734
Civil War and railway development, 64
Claims, freight, 321
Clark and Marshall, 261, 263
Clark v. Poor, 620
Clarke, E. E., 230
Clarke, J. M., 517
Class service, railway passenger
  general statement, 353
  in United States, 354
Classification
  express, 386
  railway freight
    committees, 335
    consolidated, 336
    designations used, 339, 346
    determinants, 337–339

Classification, railway freight, evolution, 333
items and ratings, 340
purpose, 333
regulation, 144
territories, 334
uniformity
advantages and obstacles, 343
percentages prescribed, 550
progress toward, 344
Clayton Act, 149
Cleary v. Johnston, 616
Cleveland and Powell, 56, 102, 265
Closed-pouch service, 372
"Closed" terminals, 217
Coal
and natural gas, 743, 744
by truck, 592
Coastwise shipping, regulation of, 772
Collateral trust mortgage bond, railway, 465
Columbia Transfer Company, 312
Commerce Court
established, 144
failure and abolition, 145
Commercial rivalry, a stimulus to railway building, 61
Commission, organization of, 183, 784
Commodities clause
early application, 142
nature, 140
present effectiveness, 143
Commodity rates, 339
Common and contract carriage by highway, 621
Common point territory, 539
Common stock, railway, 464
"Community of interest," 429
Commutation traffic, 307*n*.
Competition
bus, 583
railway
acceptance, 413
attempts to control
pool, 112
rate agreement, 85, 112
traffic association, 113
destructive railway, 760, 761, 762
early appearance, 83
far reaching, 414
fluctuations of rates, 84, 106
forms assumed, 418
Competition, railway, further intensification
causes, 105
consequences
discrimination, 107–109
instability of rates, 106
railway efficiency, 110
water tonnage, 109
intensity, reasons for, 419–424
need of control, 227, 424, 757, 760, 762, 775
results, 424
types
industrial, 417
market, 416
traffic, 414–416
for passenger traffic, 364–368
wasteful highway, 628
wastes of, chargeable to public, 776, 777, 785
Competitive bidding, 489
Comptroller, 396
Compulsory construction, 218
Congestion, railway traffic, 154, 187, 643, 722
Consolidated freight classification, 336
Consolidation, railway
advocated as present aid, 756, 757, 777
linear, 71
public interest and, 72
public attitude, 776
public policy modified
Act of 1920, provisions, 175
progress under Act
final plan, 196–198
modifications of final plan, 198–200
summary statement, 200
tentative plan, 194–196
savings, 777
Construction
and abandonment
control of, 176
exercise of powers, 217–221
recent railway, 219
Construction company, 101
"Constructive" freight stations, 312
Container service, 733, 761, 780
Continental Baking Co. v. Woodring, 619
Contingent fund, general, 179
Continuous operation, competition and, 420
Contract
charter as a, 266

Contract, express
new, 385
old, 384
Contract truck, regulation of the, 620, 621, 626, 631, 632, 633
"Contracting out," 211
Cook, Jay and Company, 87
Coolidge, Calvin, 755*n.*
Cooperation, railway
division of territory, 428
pooling, 426–428
rate agreements, 426
traffic associations, 113
(*See also* Unification, railway)
Cooperative freight lines, 327
Coordination
in regulation, 762, 783
of state and federal regulatory bodies, 254, 632, 784
of transport
air-rail, 735
importance, 733
rail-highway, 730–733
rail-water, 733–735
water-highway, 736
Corporation
advantages, 261
definition, 261
railway
concentration of control, 439
magnitude, 267
ownership of, 268
tendency toward large units, 438
types
private and public, 261
quasi-public, 262
regulation of, 263
Cost
aggregate social, of transportation, 788
railway road and equipment, 461
of reproduction, 470
of service, a rate principle
advantages, 521
definition, 518
difficulties, 520
evaluation, 521
types, 518–520
Cost accounting, need of, for railways, 408
Cost comparisons modified, 559–561
Costs
and charges, relation of railway, 556
economic burden of early transport costs, 20, 36
highway
city streets, 605, 606
local, 606, 607
motor-vehicle contribution, 604
principles of allocation, 604
state, 606, 607
transportation, in America prior to the railway, 20, 34–36
waterway
elements entering, 670
public policy, 690
social cost and charge, 671
Cotting case, 146
Cotton by truck, 591
Counselman case, 116
Credit, railway
appearance of problem, 125
evidences of decline, 127–129
reasons for weakness, 129–132
rehabilitation, 506–508
Crédit Mobilier, 79, 102, 477
Criticisms of regulatory policy
considered, 253–256
uninformed, 250–253
"Cross hauling," 776
Cugnot, Nicolas, 47, 576
Cullom Committee Report, 108, 115, 626
Cumberland Road, 34, 573
Cummins Amendment, 319

D

Daimler, Gottlieb, 577
Dartmouth College case, 81, 261
Daugherty Injunction, 211
Day, Clive, 14
Dayton-Goose Creek case, 223
De novo, trial of cases, 117, 142
Debenture bond, railway, 466
Debtors' Relief Act, railway reorganization under, 767
Deductions from gross income, 497
Defense, national, and transportation, 9
"Deficits," highway, 605
Deflation, railways' share in, 251–253
Delaware and Hudson, first locomotive on, 51
Delaware and Hudson Coal case, 142
Delaware and Raritan Canal, 653

Delays in enforcement of Commission orders, 116
Delivery receipt, 323
"Demand" charge, highway, 614
Demurrage, 326
  reciprocal, 326
Denison Act, 669, 734
Density of traffic, importance of, 558
Denver and Rio Grande, 99
Department of Transportation suggested, 757
Departmental organization, railway, 277, 278
Detroit, Toledo, and Ironton, 227
Development
  factors influencing railway, 63, 91, 121–123
  industrial, 92
Developmental rate, 513
Diesel engine, airplanes, 700
Directors, board of, 269
Discrimination
  highway, 626, 631
  railway
    becomes major problem, 78, 114, 137
    personal, 78, 137
    place, 118, 145
    public condemnation, 78
  (*See also* Long-and-Short-Haul clause; and Regulation, railway)
Dispatching, train, early, 55
Distances—river and rail, 666*n*., 677*n*.
Diverse routes, competition of, 415
Dividends on railway stock, 503–505
Division
  of joint rates (*see* Joint rates)
  of labor and transportation, 6
  of territory, 428
Division superintendent, railway, 276
Divisional organization, railway, 275–278
Divisions, Commission organized in, 183
Dixon, F. H., 167
Docket 18,300, 582, 626
Docket 23,400, 582, 626, 628, 630
DO-X, the, 699
Dumont, Santos, 694

E

Earning capacity, a valuation base, 467, 769
Earnings, railway
  and fair return, 251*n*.
Earnings, railway, 1921–1932, 240
East Tennessee, Virginia and Georgia Ry. Co. v. I. C. C., 118
Eastern District, defined, 281
Eastman, James B., 203, 486, 761, 762, 798
Economic conditions and rate theories, 237, 524
Efficiency, railway
  early advances, 87
  under federal operation, 161–163
  general comment, 279
  influence upon costs, 557
  passenger service, 349
  period, 1893–1919, 134
  recent gains, 777
    car, 719–721
    locomotive, 717–719
    management, 722
    progressive practice, 721
    track and terminal, 721
Electric railway competition, 363
Electric railways
  federal regulation of, suggested, 770
  jurisdiction over, 484
Electric welding, 741, 742
Elkins Act, 137–139
  (*See also* Regulation, railway)
Ely, R. T., 433, 617
End-to-end routes, competition of, 416
Engineering problems, early railway
  gage, 54
  power, 53
  roadway, 52
  train movements, 54
Equalization principle in rate making, 535–539
Equipment obligations, railway, 465
Erdman Act, 149
Erie Canal, construction of, 29
Erie-Michigan Canal, 660
Esch Car Service Act, 148
Esch-Cummins Act (*see* Transportation Act of 1920)
Esch-Townsend Bill, 139
Eurasia, trade routes of
  land, 21
  water, 22
Europe, overland trade routes of, 23
European War, influence upon railway development, 122
Evans, Oliver, 47, 49, 576

Evasion of state highway regulation, 628*n*.
"Eveners," 112, 427
Ex Parte 103, 235–237
Excessive railway rates, alleged, 252
Executive Committee, 269
Expansion, railway, 1905–1917
  actual, measured by
    capitalization, 128
    plant, 127
  need, 126
Expenditures
  accounting for railway
    divisional vs. centralized, 400
    general organization, 397
  highway, 575
  railway
    deductions from gross income, 497
    operating, 495–497
      movement since 1905, 499
  total waterway, 661
Express, air, 710–712
Express charges, American and European, 562
Express classification, railway, 386
Express contract with railways, 384–386
Express rates, railway
  block system established, 387
  block tariff, 388, 389
  directory, 387
  elements, 388
  schedule of rates, 390
Express service, railway
  development, 381–383
  future, 393
  handling of shipments, 384
  motor-truck competition, 392
  nature of traffic, 381
  organization, 383
  papers issued, 383
  regulation, demand for, 386
  versus parcel post, 391

F

Facilities, joint use of railway
  need, 432
  public regulation, 183, 790
"Fair return," railway earnings since 1920 less than, 251, 253
Fair value, railway, 461
Fares, passenger (*see* Rates, passenger)
Federal operation
  capital expenditures, 164
  costs of, 167
  efficiency measures, 161–163, 165
  judgment upon, 165–167, 168
  justification for, 156
  labor
    general policy, 166
    wages and disputes, 163
  operations, 161–163
  rates, 163
  standard contract
    provisions, 160
    reasonableness, 161
Federal Railroad Administration (*see* Federal operation)
Ferry-car, 311
Ferry charges, 35
Fifteen per Cent Emergency Rate Increase, 1932, 235–237, 249, 766
Fifteen per Cent Rate case, 1917, 145
Finance
  highway
    apportionment of taxes, 608, 612–614
    increased highway costs, 606
    motor-vehicle charges
      gasoline, 609
      license, 608
      other, 610
    payment for highways
      new, 603–606
      old, 603
    suggested tax program, 614
    tax apportionment, 608
  railway
    second period
      fraud and Granger laws, 79
      investment, total, 86
      relation to panics, 86, 87
    third period
      changes in policy, 103
      investment, 101
      overcapitalization, 101–103
Financial outlook, railway, 247
Financial results under the Transportation Act
  earnings by years, 240–243
  emergency needs, 243–245
  variations in earnings, 245–247
"Findings of fact," 117, 142
Fink, Albert, 113
Five per Cent Rate case, 1913, 145

Five per Cent Rate case, 1925, 234
Fixed charges, railway, 245, 422, 497, 758, 781
Fixity of railway capital, 420
Flood control and waterways, 643
Foreign "cars," payment for use of, 327
Foreign investment in American railways, 65, 95
Fort Benton, Montana, 650
"Four-System" Plan, 198
Fourth Section problems (*see* Long-and-Short-Haul clause)
Freight bill, 323
Freight claims division, 400
Freight handling, railway
  line, 325
  terminal, 307–313, 323–325
Freight rates, railway
  American, 562
  American and European, 563
Freight revenue accounting, 398
Freight service, railway
  demand, 126, 244, 246, 333
  importance, 321
  value of tonnage, 332
Freight shipping papers, railway, 316–319, 321–323
Freight traffic, railway
  development, 346
  increase in, 126, 244, 598
  pooling (*see* Pooling)
  volume, 188, 191, 243, 244
Frisco-Rock Island system, 453
Frost Trucking Co. v. California Railroad Commission, 620
Fruits and vegetables by truck, 590
Funding of railway indebtedness, 1920, 173

G

Gasoline tax, 609, 614
Gathering lines, oil, 737, 739
General Air Express, 710–712
General Counsel, railway, functions and staff, 273
General Order No. 27, 165
Goldstein, J. M., 293
Gooding bills, 229
"Gould" dream, 451*n.*
Government aid to railway construction (*see* Public aid to railways)
Government ownership of railways, 786
Graded and maximum rates, 523, 543–544
Grain and Grain Products within Western District, 239
Granger laws
  causes of action, 78
  nature, 79
  validity, 80–82
Granger route, 301
Granger territory, 286–288
Great Northern, 98
Gross capitalization, 459
Grouping, territorial, of railways
  major, 281
  minor, 282–290
  permanence, 290
  (*See also* under names of territories)
Growth, periods in railway, 45
Guarantee, six-months', to railways, 173
Guaranteed return, alleged, to railways, 250

H

Harbor costs, Great Lakes, 659
Harriman, E. H., 444, 450, 455, 476
Hauls, circuitous, 776
Haynes v. MacFarlane, 621
Helicopter, 713*n.*
Hendrick v. Maryland, 622
Hennepin Canal, 647
Hepburn Act, 139–143
  (*See also* Regulation, railway)
Herrick, C. A., 16
"Hidden" loss, 321
Highway, railway as an improved, 265
Highway aid, federal, 573
Highway costs, contributions to, 603–606
Highway facts, sources of, 581
Highways
  American, 572
  ancient, 571
  condition of early, 31–33
  medieval, 572
  Roman, 571
  state and local, 605, 607
Hill, James J., 98, 206, 347, 443, 448, 449, 450, 643
Hill system, 448–450
Hines, W. D., Director-General, 167, 186
Historical cost
  nature, 468
  validity, 469
  variations, 468

Hoch-Smith Resolution, 523, 524
Commission's rate policy, 237
important provisions, 238
principle controlling, 238
Resolution in action, 234, 238
Supreme Court emasculates, 239
Holding company, railway, 133
early appearance, 206
later use, 206
legislation for control of, 794–796
regulation urged, 206, 760, 770
Holmes, O. W., 617
Hoover, Herbert, 645, 673, 751
Houston, East and West Texas Railway Co. v. United States, 265
(*See also* Shreveport case)
Howell, Clark, 755*n.*
Howell-Barkley bill, 213
Hudson Bay Railway, 416
Hydroelectric development and waterways, 644, 686, 688

I

Illinois Central Coal Car Distribution case, 141, 142
Illinois Central land grant, 69
Illinois and Mississippi Canal, 647
In re: Opinion of the Justices, 616
Inbound freight house, 323
Income
non-operating
importance, 493–495
sources, 494
railway net, 497–499
Income account, railway, 1930, 404
Income bond, railway, 466
Increased rates, 1920, 230–232
Increasing returns, competition sharpened by, 421–424
Index numbers, wholesale prices, 192
Indiana State Chamber of Commerce cases, 548
Industrial competition, 417
Inland waterways, revived interest in, 639–645
Inland Waterways Commission, 639
Inland Waterways Corporation, 641
history and results, 679*n.*
Insurer, liability as, 320
Interchange, railway car, 327
Interest
and improved transportation, 10
Interest, railway bond, 502, 782
Interlocking directorates
legislative provision, 176
policy of Commission, 204
railway and supply companies, 150
railways, 429
recent data on, 204*n.*
reducing competition, 429
Intermountain territory, rates to, 545
International Joint Commission, 657
Inter-river rate, 536
Interstate Buses Corporation v. Blodgett, 622
Interstate Commerce Act (*see* Regulation, railways)
Interstate Commerce Commission, organization of, 183, 784
Interstate Commerce Commission v. Alabama Midland Ry. Co., 118
Interstate Commerce Commission v. Cincinnati, New Orleans and Pacific Ry. Co., 117
Interstate Commerce Commission v. Oregon-Washington Railroad and Navigation Co., 218
Interstate Transit, Inc., v. Lindsey, 619
Intracoastal canals
character of project, 652
evaluation, 674
historical background, 29, 652
Investment in transportation facilities
highways, 575, 576
motor vehicles, 607
railways, 461
waterways, 661
Investment accounts, 401

J

Jackman, W. T., 688
James, A. C., 450, 455
Joint Committee of Railroads and Highway Users, 752
Joint rates, division of
legislative provision, 181
operation of law, 225
Joint terminals, passenger, 306
Joint use of facilities, 183, 432, 790
Judicial review
de novo, 117
Hepburn Act, 141
Illinois Central Coal Car Distribution case, 142

Jurisdiction
  in issuance of railway securities, 483
  state and federal
    early position of courts, 81
    later policy, 115
    Shreveport decision, 180*n.*
    Transportation Act, 180

K

Kane v. New Jersey, 622
Kane v. Titus, 616
Kanawha River project, 650, 676
Kansas City, Mexico and Orient, 202*n.*, 226
Kansas City Southern, 202
"Keep everybody in business," 511–513

L

Labor, railway
  discharge of, limited, 791
  and railway rehabilitation
    adjustments of wages, 779
    regulation of, 779
    restrictions by legislation, 778
  wages and conditions of, 758
Labor Adjustment, Railroad Boards of, 177, 212
Labor legislation, railway
  Act of 1888, 149
  Adamson Act, 149
  Erdman Act, 149
  Newlands Act, 149
  Transportation Act, 177
  Watson-Parker Act, 213
Labor morale in 1920, 186
Lackawanna case, 143
La Follette, R. M., 146
Lake Erie-Ohio Canal, 660
Lakes-to-Gulf Waterway
  evaluation, 685
  history and nature, 646, 684
Land-grant railways, special governmental rates on, 70
Land grants to railways
  cessation, 71
  development of policy, 70
  extent, 71
  forfeiture, 100
  influence upon mileage, 94
  prices obtained, 94, 94*n.*
  termination, reasons for, 100
  terms of grants, 70
  in Texas, 71*n.*
Lease, means of unification, 429
Legge, Alexander, 755*n.*
Lehigh Valley case, 143
Length of haul
  a modifying factor, 559
  by truck, 594
Levels, variations in river, 665
Liability
  carrier
    beginning and termination, 320
    limitation upon, 319
    nature, 320
    problems, 319, 320, 321
    when effective, 320
  for unpaid charges, 321
License charge, automobile, 608
Live stock by truck, 589
Live stock contract, 319
"Living wage," 210, 212
Load, truck, and rated capacity, 581
Local highways defined, 574
Locomotive
  development, 47–50
  early American, 51
  importance, 47
  improvements
    early, 54
    later, 134
    recent, 717–719
  speed, 111, 718
Long-and-Short-Haul clause
  Commission policy after 1920, 645
  emasculation of original, 118
  future policy, 229
  important changes, 1910, 144
    effective regulation, 145
  minor changes, 1920, 181
  present situation, 228
  recent Commission policy, 547*n.*
Long-haul railway rates and motor-vehicle competition, 629, 631
Loree, L. F., 667
Lower Mississippi River navigation
  conditions existing, 651
  judgment, 677–681
  tributaries, 652

M

MacDonald, T. H., 612
McAdoo, William G., Director-General, 157, 186

McGraham scale, 530
Mail, air
  deficits incurred, 705
  history and growth, 702
  problems
    compensation, 705–707
    postage rate, 704
  Watres Act, 705
Mail pay, railway
  adequacy, 378
  bases, old and new, 378
  present determination, 379
  services rendered, 378
Mail service
  importance, 370
  power of government, 378
  problem arising, 378–380
  railways as factor, 370
  volume, 373
Management, responsibilities of railway
  competitive policy, 757, 758, 780
  finance, 756, 757, 758, 781
  general statement, 782
  increased efficiency, 777
  labor, 758, 778–780
  waste, 757, 758, 775–777
Manchester Ship Canal, 637
Mandatory commissions, state, 79
Mann-Elkins Act, 143–146
  (*See also* Regulation, railway)
Market competition, 416
Markets, disturbance of, 627
Marshall, John, Chief Justice, 261
Marvin, C. F., Jr., 613
Maximum Freight Rate case, 117
Maximum rates, power to fix
  denied, 117
  given, 140
Meyer, B. H., 28, 32, 35, 36, 37
Michigan Public Utilities Commission v. Duke, 620
Midwest-Gulf route, 300
Mileage
  highway, 574, 575
  individual passenger car, 582
  pipe line
    gasoline, 741
    natural gas, 742
    oil, 739
  railway
    first period
      extent of net, 58–60
      impelling forces, 61
    fourth period
      as a whole, 123
      normal growth, 123
      stagnation, 124
    relation to area and population, 291, 292
    second period
      factors in development, 63, 65–69
      increase in net, 64
    since 1920, 217–221
    third period
      causes of expansion, 94–97
      extent of growth, 93
Mileage rates, trend toward, 549–552
Minimum rates, power to fix, 180
  exercise of, 226–228
Minneapolis and St. Louis, 227
Mississippi Valley route, 299
Missouri Pacific lines, 451
Missouri River Navigation Association, 683*n*.
Missouri River project
  below Kansas City
    evaluation, 682
    nature, 650
  beyond Kansas City
    judgment, 683, 684
    problems, 651, 683
Mobile and Ohio, 448
  land grant, 69
Moffat Tunnel, 100
Money pool, 112, 426
Monongahela project, 649, 675, 727
Monopoly, railway as
  entire net, 433
  modifications of nature, 435–437
  single carrier, 433–435
    traffic analysis, 435
Montgolfier brothers, 693
Morality of stock watering, 478
Morgan group, 447
Morris, Ray, 276
Mortgage bond, railway, 465
Motor transportation, progressive, 725
Moulton, H. G., and associates, 673
Munn v. Illinois, 81, 263
Murdoch, William, 48, 576

N

National Advisory Commission, 657
National agreements abrogated, 209

National Automobile Chamber of Commerce, 611
National Highway Users' Conference, 752
National Transportation Committee, 754–759
National Waterways Commission, 639, 640, 641, 644, 665, 668, 690
Natural resources, utilization of, improved transportation and, 6
Nelson, R. W., 604
Net capitalization, 459, 461
Net income
  for division, 385
  railway
    ascertainment, 497
    disposition, 498
New England Divisions case, 225
New England territory
  defined, 282
  rates in, 546
New England Transportation Company, 731
New Haven system, 452
New York Central system, 444
New York-Chicago rate, importance of, 530
New York, Chicago and St. Louis, 202
  construction, 97
New York State barge canals
  cost of service, 671
  evaluation, 673, 758
  inception of system, 639, 653
  later developments, 654
  present status, 655
  program of enlargement, 654
  tonnage, 674
Newlands Act, 149
Newlands Committee, 230
No-par railway stock, 486
Nominal *vs.* real costs, 559
Non-transferability of railway capital, competition and, 420
Northern Pacific, 76, 98
Northern Securities case, 133, 149, 200
Northern Securities Company, 206
Northwest-Atlanta route, 298
Notes, short-term, railway, 465
No. 17,000, Rate Structure Investigation, 238

O

O'Fallon case, 147, 224
"Officer," defined, 203*n*.
Official Classification territory, 334
Off-line stations, 312, 732
Ohio highway survey, 573, 582, 595
Ohio Valley waterway projects
  evaluation, 675–677
  history and nature, 649
Older, Clifford, 613
"Open" terminals, 308, 309
Operating department, railway
  divisional and departmental, 277
  importance, 275
  line officers, 275
  staff officers, 275
Operating ratio, railway
  evaluation, 501
  importance assigned, 500
  movement, 502
  nature, 500
Operation, federal (*see* Federal operation)
Operations, improved railway, 721
Opposition, public, to railways, 76
Order bill of lading, 318, 319
Oregon trail, 40
Oregon-Washington Railroad and Navigation Company, compulsory constructions by, 218
Oregon Voter, 611
Orient Divisions case, 226
Original cost (*see* Historical cost)
Osborne case, 118
Outbound freight house, 323
Overcapitalization
  causes and conditions promoting, 101–103, 475–478
  credit factor, 129
  extent, 101
  morality, 102, 478
  need of public action, 479
  (*See also* Watered stock)
Overconstruction, relation of railway, to
  credit, 129
  panics, 86, 92
Overland transportation, early America, 27, 31–34, 38–40
Owner-operator truck, 586, 587, 609, 632, 633
Ownership
  bus, 583
  government, of railways, 786
  railway,
    concentration of, 439
Ownership groupings, railway
  appearance, 132, 442, 443

Ownership groupings
  broken, 451*n.*, 453*n.*
  gains resulting, 133
  major systems, 443–452
  methods employed, 132, 428–430
  minor systems, 452–455
  trend of movement, 442, 443

P

Pacific railways (*see* under names of individual railways)
Panama Canal Act, 148, 669
  needed modification, 769
Pangborn, J. C., 52
Panic of 1873, 87, 92
Panic of 1893, 92
Parallel building, 97
Parallel routes, competition of, 414
Parcel post service
  establishment, 374
  financial results, 377, 393
  privileges, 376
  rates, 374–376
  versus express, 391, 392
  volume, 377
Parmelee, J. H., 595
"Pass," the railway, 141, 362
Passenger-mile as traffic unit, 555
Passenger-mile costs
  American figures, 565
  comparisons modified, 561
  computation, 556
  elements determining, 556–559
  nominal versus real, 561
Passenger rates
  American, 564
  comparison with European, 565–567
  determination, 552
Passenger revenue, railway, 350
Passenger revenue accounting, 552
Passenger service, railway
  abuses, 362
  classification in, 353–355
  comparative statistics, 358
  competition as a factor, 363–368
  contrasted with freight, 348–350
  decline in volume, 368
  disadvantages, 367
  and efficiency, 359
  importance, 348
  privileges incident to, 353
  Pullman operations, 355–358
Passenger service, railway, types
  local, 350
  through, 351, 431
Passenger traffic
  development of, 360–362
  railway, future of, 368
Peddler truck, 627, 632
Peik v. North Western Ry. Co., 81, 82, 115
Pennroad Corporation, 206
Pennsylvania Federation v. Pennsylvania R.R. Co., 211
Pennsylvania Portage system, 29
Pennsylvania Railroad and the Labor Board, 211
Pennsylvania Railroad v. Labor Board, 211
Pennsylvania system, 445
People v. McWilliams, 616
Per diem, railway cars, 327
Percentage plan, railway rates, 529–532
Permit to operate, highway, 621, 625, 631, 632
Personal property tax, automobile, 607, 610, 615
Piedmont and Northern Ry. v. I.C.C., 484
Piedmont route, 298
Pipe, electric welding of, a factor in pipeline growth, 742, 743
Pipe lines (*see* Transportation, pipe line)
Plan, a transportation
  administration, 784
  allocation of place, 788
  cost as a basis
    particular, 783
    social, 783, 787
  goal, 787
Plumb, Glenn E., 748
Plumb Plan, 186
Pogue, Joseph E., 740*n.*, 745*n.*
Police power
  defined, 617
  place in highway regulation, 617
  regulation under, 617
Policy
  a national transportation
    changes in railway legislation, 768–771
    coordination of agencies, 783
    emergency action, 766–768
    extensions of regulation into new fields 771–774
    government ownership, 786
    management, contributions of, 757, 758, 761
      competitive policy, 780
      finance, 781

Policy, a national transportation, management, general statement, 782
increased efficiency, 777
labor, 778–780
waste, 775–777
plan essential, 787
public responsibility, 785
regulatory policy, 784
progressive railway
adjustments in rates, 723
increased speeds
freight, 722
passenger, 723
service, 731–733
public
air transport, 772
highway transport, 622–624, 631–634
pipe-line transport, 773
railway transport, 440, 768–771
waterway transport, 689–691, 771, 772
Pool car, 724
Pooling
difficulties, 775
early success, 427
made illegal, 116
permissive
advocated, 143
authorized, 174
effected, 205
practical obstacles, 205
types, 426
urged, 760
Population
and improved transportation, 7
westward movement of, 64, 92, 96
Porter, Claude R., 762
Ports, rivalry of Atlantic, 61, 84, 529
Post office
railway, 371
terminal, 373
Potter Law, 80
Preferred stock, railway
types and uses, 464
President, railway
responsibilities, 271
training, 270
Price relations, 1917–1932, 192–194
Prices, relative, since 1920, 253
Principles, rate
basing point, 532–535
"blanket," 539–543, 545
distance, 528–532, 546–549
equalization, 535–539
Principles, rate, graded and maximum, 543
trends, 549–552
Private car lines
advantages and objections, 328
future, 329
types, 328
Private cars, number of, 329
Problem, transportation, in 1933
background, 747–749
present situation acute
difficulties, 750
emergency action, 751
suggested policies
Joint Committee of Railroads and Highway Users, 752
National Transportation Committee
creation, 754
majority report, 755–757
minority report, 757–759
purpose, 754*n.*
other proposals, 759, 764
recommendations, Interstate Commerce Commission
individual members, 763
official, 760
United States Chamber of Commerce, 751
Profit and loss account, railway (1930), 405
Profits and improved transportation, 11
Promoter, railway, 61, 95, 97
Propriety power, a basis of highway regulation, 618–621
Public aid to railways
extent, 71, 95
justifications, 67
policy abandoned, 99, 101
results, 100
types, 68, 69, 95
Public interest, transportation burdened by, 11
Pullman service
advantages to railways, 356
contract governing, 357
determination of charge, 357
growth and future, 355, 367
surcharge, 358
Purchasing, railway, 278
Purchasing power of money, 561

Q

Quantity of shipment
classification factor, 338
cost factor, 559

R

Rail, development of the, 45, 87, 111, 134, 721
Rail-motor service
  freight
    line haul, 730
    terminal, 731–733
    terminal-line haul, 733
  importance, 733
  passenger, 728–730
    growth, 729
    ownership of buses, 729
Rail-and-water movements
  regulation of, 115
Rail-water service
  need of coordination, 733
  outlook, 734
  problems, 744
  significance of Denison Act, 734
Railroad Credit Corporation, 236, 243
Railroad Labor Act of 1926
  plan for settling disputes, 213
  success, 214
  weakness, 214
Railroad Labor Board
  provisions for, 177
  weaknesses, 212
  work of, 208–212
Railroad Labor Board v. McGuire and Robertson, 212
Railroads' War Board, 155
Railwagon, 733, 761, 780
Railway
  "burdened with public interest," 11
  business, magnitude of, 267
  construction (*see* Mileage)
  early American interest in, 50
  early conception of, 55
  growth, periods of, 45
  importance of the, 293
  mail pay (*see* Mail)
  opposition to, 56
  outlook in 1933, 243, 749–751, 755, 761
  rate theories, 509–525
  stock ownership (*see* Stock)
Railway Express Agency, Inc., 382
  air traffic, 710–712
  express operations, 382–386, 391–394
  store-door delivery, 313
  trucking operations, 732
Railway express contract, 384–386
"Railway problem," 747
  (*See also* Problem, transportation)
Railways, condition in 1920, 185–187
Rain Hill trial, 49
Rate agreements, 85
Rate making, railway, freight
  complexities, 341
  fundamental considerations, 340
  reasonable theory, 525
  (*See also* Rates; Structures; Theories)
Rate of return, railways, 1921–1932, 240
Rate relations, uniformity in, 345
Rate Structure Investigation, No. 17,000, 238
Rate structures, conclusions concerning, 549–552
Rate theories and economic conditions, 237, 524
  (*See also* Theories, rate)
Rates
  all-commodity, 724
  express (*see* Express rates)
  minimum, use of power to fix, 226–228
  parcel post (*see* Parcel post)
  passenger, 552
  railway
    adjustments following 1920, 233, 234*n.*
    alleged excessive, 237, 251, 252
    commodity, 339
    decline prior to 1870, 88
      effect upon water traffic, 89
    during federal operation, 165
    emergency increase, 1932, 766
    freight, average, 563
      (*See also* Structures, railway rate)
    highway competition a disrupting factor, 551
    inadequate, 1920, 186
    increase, 1920
      basis of determination, 230
      extent of increase, 231
      intrastate rates, 231
    lowered, 1921–1922
      cause for demand, 232
      decreases made, 233
    passenger, 552, 565
    proposed general increases, 234
    suggested emergency increase
      basis of request, 235
      nature of, approved, 236
  and surplus, provisions of Act of 1920, 178
Ratio, railway bond, 460, 781
Reading case, 143
Real estate agent, 279
Reasonable rate, theoretical basis of, 525

Rebating, railway
favors demanded by shippers, 137
forms taken, 138
magnitude, 138
Recapture clause
constitutionality, 223
needed modification, 769
operation, 223
opposition, 224, 752, 757, 760
railway indebtedness under, 222*n*., 223*n*.
retroactive repeal, 224, 760, 768, 797
statutory provisions, 179
sums paid, 222
Receipt for freight, 316
Reconsignment and title to shipment, 320
Reconstruction Finance Corporation, 243, 248, 751, 757, 766, 767, 768
loans to railways, 243*n*.
Refrigeration, improved, 719
Regulation
air transport
carrier relations, 713, 714
safety, 713–715
work of Department of Commerce, 714
highway
bases
common carriage, 621
police power, 617
proprietary power, 618–621
demand for effective, 630
early control, 615
federal, 632–634
cooperation with states, 632
general statement, 616, 771
jurisdiction, 621
objectionable conditions existing
discrimination, 626
disturbance of markets, 627
other, 629
waste, 628
state
comprehensive program, 631
existing, 624
urgency of situation, 634
needed extension of
air, 772
motor, 771
pipe line, 773
waterway, 771
railway, federal
Act to Regulate Commerce, 188
background of action, 115
Regulation railway, federal, Act to Regulate Commerce, 1887, immediate causes, 115
major provisions, 115
power denied Commission, 116–119
results, 119
demand for effective control, 136–139
Elkins Act, 1903
need of action, 137–139
provisions, 139
results, 139
Esch Car Service Act, 1916, 148
Hepburn Act, 1906
opposition to positive control, 139
provisions
powers of Commission, 140
prohibitions, 140
success of Act, 141–143
Mann-Elkins Act, 1910
background, 143
major features, 143
operation of Act, 144–146
Panama Canal Act, 1912, 148
Transportation Act, 1920
dual problem faced, 171
House and Senate bills, 171
operation, 185–247
provisions, 172–183
solutions offered, 170
worth of policy
before 1920
gains, 151
weaknesses, 151
present
considered criticisms, 253–256, 762
general worth, 255
needs, 256
public attitude important, 784–786
ungrounded charges, 250–253, 759, 770
railway, state
early
advisory control, 77, 82
mandatory
abandonment, 82
causes, 78, 79
nature, 79
validity, 80–82
further development
causes, 114
extent, 114
scope and extent, 1917, 150

Regulation waterway (*see* Waterway, regulation)
Rent and improved transportation, 10
Reorganization
 effect on capitalization, 478
 railway
  control of, 487
  costs, control of, 488
  under Debtors' Relief Act, 767
  formulation of plan, 487
  particular plans, 489*n.*
Reproduction, cost of (*see* Cost of reproduction)
Reserve fund, individual, 179
Resources, utilization of natural, 6
Retarder, car, 325
Returns, railway, since 1920, 240–243, 251*n.*
Revenues, railway
 and gasoline pipe line, 745
 non-operating, 493–495
 operating
  distribution of, 493
  movement since 1905, 499
  sources, 492
  variations among railways, 492
Revolving fund, 174
Richmond, Fredericksburg and Potomac, valuation of, 224
Right-angled routes, competition of, 415
"Rights," 477
Ringwalt, J. L., 58, 83, 88
Ripley, W. Z., 65, 96, 103, 140, 195
Ritter, A. H., 673, 686*n.*
River rates, basis of, 688
River traffic, decline in, 109, 638
Rivers, early commerce upon, 37
Rivers and Harbors Congress, 639
Roadbed, construction of early, 52
Robertson, v. Railroad Labor Board, 212
Rocket, the, 50
Roosevelt, Theodore, 139, 639, 645, 654
Routes, air
 mail and other (map), 703
 federally equipped (map), 701
Routing, control of, 182
"Rule of rate making," Congressional, 237–240

S

St. Lawrence Commission, 657, 673
St. Lawrence Deep Waterway
 adverse arguments, 686–688, 757
St. Lawrence Deep Waterway, costs
  direct, 658
  harbor, 658, 659*n.*
 effect upon grain rates, 687, 688
 history of project, 655–658
 map of rapids section, 656
 savings suggested, 686
 tonnage, probable, 673, 686
St. Lawrence-Tidewater Association, 657, 673
St. Louis and O'Fallon R.R. Co. v. United States, 147, 224, 251
Sandage, C. H., 604
Santa Fe trail, 39
Saratoga Conference, 85
"Scalping," ticket, 363
Schlesinger v. Atlanta, 616
Scope of authority, federal Commission
 Act of 1887, 115
 Hepburn Act, 1906, 140
 Mann-Elkins Act, 1910, 144
Secretary, railway, 273
Section 15a, replacement of, 761, 768, 796
Securities
 market status of railway, 505
 regulation of railway
  attitudes toward, 489
  demand for, 479
  federal
   agitation for, 480
   legislation providing
    administration, 482–489
    provisions, 176, 481
    results, 221, 489
  state, 480
 sale of, regulation of, 487
Securities Commission, Railroad
 creation, 144, 480
 findings, 146, 480
 weakness of report, 146, 481
Security issued, type of railway, 486
Service
 duplication of, 756, 757, 775
 regulation of
  legislative provisions, 182
  utilization of powers, 215–217
Sherman Anti-Trust Act, 149, 443
Shippers' Advisory Boards, 216, 721
Shopmen's Strike, 210
Shreveport case, 180, 544, 622
Signaling, primitive railway, 54
Sites, scarcity of suitable, 433

Six months' guarantee, 167, 171, 173
Slab, concrete, minimum thickness of, 613
Slack water navigation, 648, 650*n.*
Smith, Alfred E.
  member of National Transportation Committee, 755*n.*
  minority report, 757–759
Smith v. Cahoon, 620
Smyth v. Ames, 467
Social Circle case, 117, 118, 142
Social cost of water transport, 671
Social need, a basis of rate making, 522
"Solutions" of transportation problem, 748
  (*See also* Problem, transportation)
South Carolina Railroad (*see* Charleston and Hamburg)
Southeastern Express Company, 382
Southern Classification territory, 334
Southern District, defined, 281
Southern Pacific
  begun, 76
  completed, 97
  present system, 455
Southern Railway and Steamship Association, 113
Southern rate structure, 532–535, 547
Southern territory, 285
Southwestern territory, 288
Southwestern Transportation Company, 731
Speculation, a credit factor, 129
Speed
  a competitive factor, 780
  of movement, water and rail, 667
Speeds, air cruising, 709, 726
Sproles v. Binford, 619
Sprout v. South Bend, 622
Standard contract, 160
Standards, uniform highway, 623*n.*
State highways, defined, 574
State of Colorado v. United States, 219
State of Texas v. Eastern Texas Ry. Co., 219
Statistics, railway
  compilation, 406
  further development, 408
  scope, 407
  sources, 408
  uses, 406
Stephenson, George, 49
Stephenson v. Binford, 621, 626
Stock, railway
  dividends on, 503–505
Stock, railway
  no-par, 486
  ownership of
    concentration largely apparent, 456, 457
    distribution, 457
    individual properties, 457
    method of control, 429
    problem presented, 458
  types, 464
Stock dividends, railway, 485
Stockholder, function of, 269
Stockholders
  large railway, 456
  railway, number of, 267, 268, 457
Store-door delivery, 311–313, 731, 761, 780
"Stourbridge Lion," 51
Straight bill of lading, 317
Streets, costs of city, 606
Structures, railway rate
  adjustment in, 780
  rate trends, 549–552
  Southern, 532–535, 547
  Southwestern, 539–541, 543, 546
  Transcontinental, 542, 545
  Trunk Line, 529–532, 546, 547
  Western Trunk Line, 536–539, 548
  (*See also* Principles, rate)
Superheater, 718
Surcharge, Pullman, 358
Suspension of rates
  initial provisions, 143
  justification, 143
  modified in 1920, 180
  present status, 228
Switching
  "hump," 325
  reciprocal, 308

T

Taft, W. H., 640
Tariffs, railway, types and scope, 342
Tax, personal property, and motor vehicle, 611, 615
Taxation
  motor vehicle (*see* Finance, highway)
  railway, 786
Taxes, special automobile, 611
Ten per cent decrease in rates, 1921–1922, 233
Ten per Cent Rate case, 1910, 144

Tennessee River development
evaluation, 676
nature, 650
Terminals
railway
adequacy, 434
"closed," 217
cost, 305
freight
elements constituting, 308
service beyond rails, 311
unification of, 308
work performed, 309–311
future, 314
importance, 304
joint use, 183, 216, 306, 308, 431, 757
location, 304, 305, 308
a community problem, 307
passenger, 306
regulatory control, 313
unification, 308, 309
water, 665, 666, 668
Territories, rate, 527
Territory, division of, 428
Testimony, compelling, 116
Texas and Pacific
construction, 76
final land grant, 69
Texas and Pacific Ry. Co. v. I.C.C., 117
Theories, rate
need of theoretical basis, 509
public policy, 523–525
sound basis, 525
types
ability, 510–518
cost, 518–522
social need, 522
Thomson, J. E., on rate agreements, 85
Tickets, passenger
accounting, 352
classification, 352
Tires, truck, types of, 581, 613
Title to shipment, 320
Toll roads and bridges
charges, 35
construction, 33
"Tom Thumb," 51
Ton-mile as traffic unit, 555
Ton-mile costs
American figures, 563
comparisons modified, 559–561
computation, 556
elements determining, 556–559
Ton-mile costs, nominal versus real, 559
Tonnage, railway
nature and value, 332
present
Granger territory, 287
New England territory, 283
Southern territory, 286
Southwestern territory, 288
Transcontinental territory, 290
Trunk Line territory, 284
Track, construction of early, 45
Track storage, 326
Trade and transportation (*see* Transportation and trade)
Trade routes
Eurasian, 21–23
European, 23
Traffic
air passenger
charges, 709
density, by routes (map), 708
speeds, 709, 726
volume, 704
competition
diverse routes, 415
end-to-end routes, 416
parallel routes, 414
right-angled routes, 415
goods, by air
charges, 710–712
outlook, 711
system of rates, 710
volume, 704, 710
highway
bus, 583–586
gains from railway, 597–599
individual passenger car, 582
problem, 599
truck, 586–597
pool, 112, 426
railway
department, 274
development of freight, 346, 513
development of passenger, 360–362
routes, major railway
basis, 295
particular routes, 296–304
(*See also* under names of routes)
trends, 244, 246
units
freight, 555
need, 554
passenger, 555

Trailers, number of highway, 580
Trails, early American
  eastern, 27, 572
  western, 38
Train movement, early problems of, 54
Transcontinental railways
  Congressional rivalry, 74
  early proposals, 73
  later projects, 76, 97–99
  obstacles, 74
  Union Pacific-Central Pacific, 74–76
Transcontinental route, 302–304
Transcontinental territory, 289
Transfer house, freight, 324
Trans-Missouri Freight Association case, 149
Transportation
  agencies, types of, 5
  Bureau of, 762
  definition, 4
  engineering problem, 4
  importance of study of, 12
  improved, and
    distribution of wealth, 10
    division of labor, 6
    exchange, 9
    population, 7
    production and consumption, 0
    production and market centers, 7
    social progress, 8
    state, 8
    utilization of resources, 6
  need of improved, 41
  periods in development of, 16
    railway, 45
  pipe line
    future, 744
    gasoline
      advantages, 741
      capacity, 741
      mileage and location (map), 738, 741
    natural gas
      importance, 742, 744
      mileage and location (map), 742, 743
  oil
      importance, 740
      investment, 739
      mileage and location (map), 737–738
      ownership, 740
    regulation, 740, 773
  primitive
    costs, 20, 34
      socio-economic consequences, 20, 36
Transportation, primitive, nature, 17–20
  scope, 4
  and trade
    obstacles to development of, 14–16
    relation between, 14
Transportation Act of 1920, 171–247
  (*See also* Regulation, railway)
Transportation Act and "fair return," 251*n*., 254
Transportation problem, 747
  (*See also* Problem, transportation)
Treasurer, railway, 273
Trevithick, Richard, 48, 576
Trinity River, proposed development, 659, 663
Truck, the
  capacity, 580, 581
  ownership, 578, 586, 587
  registrations, 578
  traffic, 586–597
  trailers, 580
Truck service
  advantages, 596
  development, 586
  length of haul, 594
  traffic handled
    automobiles, 593
    cement, 592
    coal, 592
    cotton, 591
    fruits and vegetables, 590
    general statement, 588
    live stock, 589
    other tonnage, 593
  types of, 586
  volume, 594–596
Truckaway, the, 592
Trunk Line route, 296–298
Trunk Line territory, 283–285
Trunk lines, oil, 737, 739
Trustees of Dartmouth College v. Woodward, 261
Twin City adjustment, 537
Type of traffic, a modifying factor, 560

U

Undermaintenance during federal control, 186
Unification, railway
  factors promoting, 430
  methods employed, 428–430
Uniform classification of freight, 343–345

Uniform system, railway accounts
need, 140
progress, 141
results, 141
Union Pacific-Central Pacific, 74–76
Union Pacific system, 450
Unions, railway labor, during federal operation, 186
United States v. Abilene and Southern, 226
United States v. Akron, Canton, and Youngstown Ry. Co., 216
United States v. Chicago, North Shore and Milwaukee R.R. Co., 484
United States v. Union Pacific R.R. Co., 133
Unity of railway action, need of, 430–432
"Universal" freight stations, 308, 311
Upper Mississippi Development
evaluation, 682
history and nature, 647, 681

V

Valuation
proposal to abandon railway, 769
railway
bases recognized, 467–471, 769
importance, 466, 769
public policy, 471
statement of National Transportation Committee upon, 756
Valuation Act
administration, 147
need and importance, 146, 148
progress and results, 147, 148, 224, 248–250
provisions, 146
as amended, 797, 798
"Value of the commodity," 514
"Value of the service," 510
Vanderbilt system, 444
Van Sweringen system, 202, 206, 446
Vitiating factors in cost comparisons, 559–561
Volume of truck traffic, 594

W

Wabash, St. Louis and Pacific Ry. Co., v. Illinois, 115
Wage, a reasonable, 208, 210
Wages
and improved transportation, 11
railway
adjustments to reduce costs, 1933, 778–780
Wages, railway, decrease in 1920–1921, 209–211
high level, 1932, 214
inadequate, 1920, 186
increases
federal control, 163, 166
later, 214
in 1920, 208
temporary decrease, 1932, 215, 243, 767
War Board, Railroads', 155
Warehouseman, liability as, 320
Warner, F. S., 686
Wastes, elimination of competitive, 757, 758, 775, 790, 798
Water-highway service
opportunity, 736
present extent, 736
rivalry developing, 736*n*.
Water routes in America
natural, 25
relation to colonial development, 37
Water transport, place of, 727
"Watered stock"
conditions promoting, 476–478
meaning, 474
morality, 478
purposes, 475
tests, 474
validation alleged, 251
Waterways, American
channels, types of, 662–664
conditions justifying construction, 672
disadvantages in competition
artificial, 668
inherent, 664–668
early
initial importance, 25–27, 37, 638
traffic declines, 88, 109, 638
Inland Waterways Corporation, 679*n*.
major projects
Intracoastal, 29, 652, 674
Lakes-to-Gulf, 31, 646, 684
Lower Mississippi, 650, 677–681
Missouri, 650, 682–684
New York State barge canals, 653–655, 673–675
Ohio Valley, 649, 675–677
St. Lawrence, 655–659, 685–688
Upper Mississippi, 647–649, 681
Mississippi Valley projects (map), 648
other projects, 659
public policy concerning, 689–691
regulation of traffic upon, 772

Waterways, revival of interest
causes, 641–645
history of movement, 639–641
Watres Act, 705
Watson-Parker Act (*see* Railroad Labor Act of 1926)
Waybill, railway
functions, 321–323
types, 323
Western Classification territory, 335
Western District, defined, 281
Western Pacific, 451*n*., 454
Western Rate Advance case, 1915, 145
Western States survey, 582
Western Trunk Line class rates, 234, 235, 548
Western Trunk Line rate structures
area, 527
past, 536, 539
River Crossings, 536
present, 548
"What the traffic will bear," 515–518
Wheel, evolution and importance, 18
Whitney, Asa, 74
Wilson, Woodrow, 149, 156, 187
Wilson Transportation Company, 730, 731
Windom Committee Report, 80, 115, 748
Wisconsin Passenger Fare case, 232
Wisconsin River, 649
Wolverine Motor Freight Lines v. Public Utilities Commission of Ohio, 619, 622
Wright, Orville and Wilbur, 696

Z

Zeppelin, F. von, 694
"Zeppelin, Graf," 695
Zones
transcontinental, 545
Trunk Line, 530–532
W.T.L. class rate, 548